VISUAL BASIC® 5
SUPERBIBLE
VOLUME 2

WAITE
GROUP
PRESS ™

A Division of
Macmillan Computer
Publishing

Corte Madera, CA

Eric Winemiller
David Jung
Pierre Boutquin
John Harrington
Bill Heyman
Ryan Groom
Todd Bright
Bill Potter

PUBLISHER • Mitchell Waite
ASSOCIATE PUBLISHER • Charles Drucker

ACQUISITIONS MANAGER • Susan Walton

EDITORIAL DIRECTOR • John Crudo
PROJECT EDITOR • Laura E. Brown
DEVELOPMENTAL/TECHNICAL EDITORS • Chris Stone, Wei Li
PRODUCTION EDITORS • Kelsey McGee, Marlene Vasilieff
COPY EDITORS • Merrilee Eggleston, Debi Anker, Deirdre Greene, Michelle Goodman, Ann Longknife/Creative Solutions

MANAGING EDITOR • Brice P. Gosnell
INDEXING MANAGER • Johnna L. VanHoose
RESOURCE COORDINATORS • Deborah Frisby, Charlotte Clapp
EDITORIAL ASSISTANTS •Carmela Carvajal, Carol Ackerman, Andi Richter, Rhonda Tinch-Mize, Karen Williams

SOFTWARE SPECIALIST • Dan Scherf

DIRECTOR OF MARKETING • Kelli S. Spencer
PRODUCT MARKETING MANAGER • Wendy Gilbride
ASSOCIATE PRODUCT MARKETING MANAGER • Jennifer Pock
MARKETING COORDINATOR • Linda B. Beckwith
MARKETING ASSISTANT • Charles Kemper

PRODUCTION MANAGER • Cecile Kaufman
PRODUCTION TEAM SUPERVISORS • Brad Chinn, Andrew Stone
COVER DESIGNERS • Tim Amrhein, Regan Honda
BOOK DESIGNER • Jean Bisesi, Karen Johnston, Sandra Schroeder

PRODUCTION • Karen Johnston, Polly Lavrick, Paula Lowell, Carl Pierce, Becky Stutzman

Printed in the United States of America
98 99 • 10 9 8 7 6 5 4 3

Library of Congress Cataloging-in-Publication Data
Visual Basic 5 SuperBible / Eric Winemiller ... [etal.].
       p.   cm.
    Includes index.
    ISBN 1-57169-111-1 9vol.10. -- ISBN 1-57169-112-x (vol.2) --
ISBN 1-57169-102-2 (set)
    1. BASIC (Computer program language)   2. Microsoft Visual BASIC.
I. Winemiller, Eric, 1969-
    QA76.73.B3V567   1997
    005.13'3--dc21

97-21822
CIP

VISUAL BASIC ALPHABETICAL CONTROL TABLE

VISUAL BASIC ALPHABETICAL JUMP TABLE

VISUAL BASIC TASK JUMP TABLE

ActiveX Controls

Adding a user defined control to a project: **UserControl**, 1793-1794

Aligning to a container's edge: **Alignable**, 1815

Allowing or denying focus: **CanGetFocus**, 1816

Assign and capture an access key: **AccessKeyPress, AccessKeys**, 1814, 1813

Behave as a default or cancel button: **DefaultCancel, DisplayAsDefault**, 1817, 1409

Binding to a data source: **Bindable**, 1373

Containing other controls: **ControlContainer**, 1776

Create property pages: **Property Page Wizard**, 78, 1729, 2047

Creating an ActiveX document: **UserDocument**, 76-77, 1893-1894, 1901-1905

Edit at design time: **EditAtDesignTime**, 1818

Enumerating constants: **Enum**, 172

Fire events: **Events, RaiseEvent**, 1749, 542-543

Get remote property values: **AsyncProperty**, 1864

Host a control in a browser: **Object tag**, 1883

Making an invisible control: **InvisibleAtRuntime**, 1824

Navigate the Web: **GoBack, GoFoward, NavigateTo**, 1863, 1864

Providing a toolbox picture: **ToolboxBitmap**, 1825

Reading and writing properties: **PropertyBag, ReadProperties, WriteProperties**, 1833-1835

Clipboard

Transfer text or graphics data between windows or applications: **Clipboard** (object), 206

Find out whether the clipboard has graphics or text: **GetFormat**, 1241

Get graphics from the clipboard: **GetData**, 1240

Get text from the clipboard: **GetText**, 1242

Send graphics to the clipboard: **SetData**, 1243

Send text to the clipboard: **SetText**, 1244

Clear the contents of the clipboard: **Clear**, 1239

Communicate with DOS windows: **SendKeys**, 1187

Controls

Display an indicator of progress: **ProgressBar**, 1936

Display notebook-style tabs: **TabStrip, Tabbed Dialog**, 1945

Display an icon-filled bar: **ToolBar**, 1948

Display a hierarchical view of a set of data: **TreeView**, 1951

Store or display a collection of images: **ImageList**, 1924

Display a graphical view of data: **ListView**, 1928

Display a slider control: **Slider**, 1938

Create a status bar to display information: **StatusBar**, 1941

Associate control values with a database: **Data, DBGrid, DBCombo, DBList**, 219, 223, 228, 235

Controls (General)

Examine attributes of active control: **ActiveControl**, 673, 1814

Respond to user changes in contents: **Change**, 53, 654, 1011

Manipulate controls in a control array: **Index**, 676

Identify a particular control: **Tag**, 683

Find form that contains the control: **Parent**, 681

Label a control on a form: **Label**, 261

Create a new instance in a control array: **Load**, 150-151, 714-719

Specify 3D or "flat" look: **Appearance**, 603

Database

Use multiple databases: **WorkSpaces** (collection), **CreateWorkspace**, 1349

Perform database maintenance: **CompactDatabase**, 1547 **RepairDatabase**, 1547

Control database security: **Permissions**, 1550

Use SQL, DML, and DDL queries: **Querydef, Database** (property), 1360

Abort a transaction set: **RollbackTrans**, 1467

Commit the transaction set to the database: **CommitTrans**, 1467

Manipulate a set of records: **Recordset**, 1366-1367

Specify the source of data for a data bound control: **DataSource, DataField**, 1375-1376, 1381-1382

Debugging

Halt program execution: **Stop**, 568

Output program values for debugging: **Debug** (object), 562

Set and clear breakpoints: **Toggle Breakpoint, Clear All Breakpoints**, 562, 569

Step out of a sub or function: **Step Out**, 567

Step through code including procedures: **Step Into**, 567

Step through code without showing procedures: **Step Over**, 568

Step to the cursors location: **Step To Cursor**, 568

Set or show next statement to be executed: **Set Next Statement, Show Next Statement**, 565, 566

Show the calling order of subroutines: **Calls**, 125, 130

Use conditional compilation: **#If...#Else...#End If, #Const**, 1984, 1985

Dialog Boxes (and Related Controls)

Display a message in a box with standard icons: **MsgBox** (function and statement), 450, 455

Get text from a user by displaying a box: **InputBox**, 448

Specify choices that can be on or off: **CheckBox** (control), 200

Define a group of choices of which only one can be selected: **OptionButton** (control), 284

Create a group of related controls: **Frame** (control), 256

Label part of a dialog box: **Label**, 261

Display a button that executes a specified action: **Command button** (control), 213

Display a common dialog box: **CommonDialog**, 457

Drive, Directory, and File List Boxes

Set up boxes for working with the disk:
DriveListBox, DirListBox, FileListBox
(objects), 241, 238, 245
Set or read the current drive in a Drive list box: **Drive**, 1045
Set or read the name of the currently selected file:
FileName, 1047
Set or read the search path for a Directory or File list box:
Path, 1058
Specify what happens when the search path is changed:
PathChange, 1059
Set or read the file search pattern for a list box: **Pattern**, 1060
Specify what happens when file search pattern is changed:
PatternChange, 1062
Specify DOS attributes of files to be displayed in list: **Archive**,
Hidden, **ReadOnly**, **System**, 1044, 1048, 1063, 1067
Obtain items in a Drive, Dir, or File box's list: **List**, **ListCount**,
ListIndex, 1050, 1053-1054

Dynamic Data Exchange (DDE)

Specify type of link (hot/cold and server status):
LinkMode, 1293
Specify actions to take when a link is opened: **LinkOpen**, 1296
Get information from a linked application: **LinkRequest**, 1300
Specify item and topic to be used in a link: **LinkItem**,
LinkTopic, 1289, 1304
Send contents of a picture box to a linked application:
LinkSend, 1301
Send a command to a linked application: **LinkExecute**, 1286
Send information from a client to a server: **LinkPoke**, 1289,
1295
Deal with errors or timeouts during link: **LinkError**,
LinkTimeout, 1283, 1303
Specify what happens when a link is closed: **LinkClose**, 1282

Errors

Enable error trapping: **On Error Goto...**, 532
Disable error trapping: **On Error Goto 0**, 532
Retrieve a string expression containing a description of the
error: **Description**, 537
Associate a position within a help file with this error:
HelpContext, **HelpFile**, 538, 539
Retrieve the numeric value of an error: **Number**, 541
Retrieve the name of the object or application that generated an
error: **Source**, 543
Clear the error object after an error has been handled: **Clear**,
536, 1239
Generate a runtime error: **Raise**, 542

Focus

Specify which application gets the focus: **AppActivate**,
509, 1254
Specify which form or control gets the focus: **SetFocus**, 1265
Specify what happens when a form or control gets the focus:
GotFocus, 1262
Specify what happens when a form or control loses the focus:
LostFocus, 1264

Specify whether a control can respond to user input: **Enabled**,
1258, 1819
Control use of Tab key to move between controls:
TabIndex, **TabStop**, 1267, 1268

Fonts

Set or get name of current font: **Name**, 985
Find out what fonts are available, **FontCount**, **Fonts**, 977, 979
Set point size of font: **Size**, 987
Set typestyle: **Bold**, **Italic**, **Strikethrough**, **FontTransparent**,
Underline, 970, 981, 983, 989, 991

Forms (General)

Position form on screen: **Left**, **Top**, 769, 781
Set dimensions of form on screen: **Height**, **Width**, 766, 783
Display form title: **Caption**, 1174, 1256
Set up button to perform a specified action: **Command button**
(control), 1174, 1256
Set color and style: **BackColor**, **BorderStyle**, **ForeColor**, 605,
609, 617
Allow resizing of form: **ControlBox**, **MaxButton**, **MinButton**,
711, 719, 723
Respond to user actions: **Icon**, **MousePointer**, **Resize**,
WindowState, 729, 738
Show or hide form: **Hide**, **Show**, **Visible**, 712, 733,
1822, 1825
Load form without showing: **Load** (statement), 717
Refer to forms in code: **Name**, 671, 679-681, 985-987
Examine attributes of active form: **ActiveForm**, 675
Specify actions to take place when form is loaded: **Load**
(event), 714
Remove form: **Unload**, 737
Create an MDI main form: **New MDI Form**, 721-723
Create MDI child forms: **MDIChild**, 721
Trap keyboard input: **KeyPreview**, 1183

Graphics (Drawing)

Set Colors: **RGB**, **QBColor**, 815, 816
Specify style and width for shape boundary line: **DrawStyle**,
DrawWidth, 874, 877
Specify color and fill pattern for drawing: **FillColor**, **FillStyle**,
878, 881, 1096
Specify how drawing will interact with background:
DrawMode, 871
Draw shapes on a graphics object: **Circle**, **Line**, **PSet**, 860,
863, 869
Clear a drawing area: **Cls**, 801
Load graphics from a file: **LoadPicture**, 804
Determine graphics object initially appearing in a form:
Picture (property), 926
Determine color of a point: **Point**, 1458
Get handle to manipulate a graphics image: **Image**, 802-804
Control redrawing of graphics: **AutoRedraw**, **Paint**, 797, 806
Save graphics to a file: **SavePicture**, 818

Graphics (Setup)

Create a graphic object: **Picture** (control), 1260
Set measure to use for graphics coordinates: **ScaleMode**, 776

Numerical Expressions

Find the absolute value of a numerical
expression: **Abs**, 351
Use mathematical functions on a numerical expression: **Atn,
Cos, Exp, Log, Sin, Sqr, Tan**, 352
Change the type of a numerical expression: **CInt, CLng, CSng,
CDbl, CCur, CBool**, 387
Change the format of a numerical expression: **Fix, Hex, Int,
Oct**, 353, 392
Use a random number: **Randomize, Rnd**, 356, 357
Determine the sign of a numerical expression: **Sgn**, 358
Financial functions: **DDB, FV, IPmt, IRR, MIRR, NPer, NPV,
Pmt, PPmt, PV, Rate, SLN, SYD**, 368-379

Object-Oriented Programming

Create your own class: **ClassModule, Set** (statement), **New**
(keyword), 204, 565
Get class properties: **Property Get**, 2146
Set class properties: **Property Let**, 2148
Hide or expose data within your classes: **Private, Public**, 161
Define Initialization and Termination procedures for your
classes: **Initialize, Terminate**, 714, 735, 2145, 2150
Establish a class hierarchy: **Collection, Parent**, 207, 681
Use a custom class: **Instancing, Public**, 161, 2177

OLE

Create an embedded or linked object: **OLE** (control), **Action**,
279, 1617
Activate an object: **Action, AutoActivate**, 1617, 1620
Use the clipboard with OLE objects: **Action**, 1617
Use OLE automation: **GetObject, CreateObject**, 1677, 1679
Determine what actions an object supports: **Verb,
ObjectVerbsCount, ObjectVerbFlags, ObjectVerbs**, 643,
1662
Paste or insert an object: **Action**, 1617

Printer

Set units to be used for printing: **ScaleMode**, 776
Set page dimensions: **ScaleHeight, ScaleLeft, ScaleTop,
ScaleWidth**, 773, 775, 778, 779
Set or get current print position on page: **CurrentX, CurrentY**,
764
Draw graphics for printing: **Circle, Line, PSet**, 860, 863, 869
Determine dimensions needed to print a string: **TextHeight,
TextWidth**, 906
Print string at current position in current font: **Print**, 899,
1215
Print a Visual Basic form: **PrintForm**, 1216
Get the current page number: **Page**, 1210
Start a new page (form feed): **NewPage**, 1208
Send contents of printer object to Windows for printing:
EndDoc, 1206
Kill a current print job: **KillDoc**, 1207
Set the number of copies to be printed: **Copies**, 1203
Set the printer orientation: **Orientation**, 1209
Set the print quality: **PrintQuality**, 1218
Set the paper source and size: **PaperBin, PaperSize**, 1210,
1212

Set or get the printer port: **Port**, 1214
Set or get information on the printer device and driver:
DeviceName, DriverName, 1204
Set the printer output size: **Zoom**, 1221

Resources

Determine if your application is running on a Far East version of
Windows: **IMEStatus**, 1995
Load data from a resource file: **LoadResData**, 1997
Load a bitmap, icon, or cursor from a resource file:
LoadResPicture, 1999
Load a string from a resource file: **LoadResString**, 2000

Scroll Bars

Set up scroll bars: **Scroll bars** (control), 297
Set up scroll bars for a Text box: **ScrollBars** (property), 581,
1394, 1899
Set maximum and minimum values to be represented by a
scroll bar: **Max, Min**, 936-937
Set or return current value represented by scroll bar: **Value**,
928, 939, 1527, 1862
Specify change in scroll bar's value when user clicks on arrow:
SmallChange, 938
Specify change in scroll bar's value when user clicks on bar:
LargeChange, 935

Strings

Extract a part of a string: **Left, Mid** (function), **Right**, 330,
333, 336, 769
Work with the ASCII value of a character: **Asc, Chr**, 326, 327
Convert the case of a string: **LCase, UCase**, 329, 342
Find one string within another: **InStr**, 328
Justify a value in a string: **LSet, RSet**, 331, 337
Compare two strings: **Like, Option Compare, StrComp**, 335,
339
Deal with spaces: **LTrim, RTrim, Space, Trim**, 332, 337, 338,
341
Switch between strings and numbers: **Format, Str, Val**, 388,
394, 395
Determine the length of a string: **Len**, 331

Text

Determine dimensions needed for a text string: **TextHeight,
TextWidth**, 906
Display text string on form, picture box, or printer: **Print**, 899,
1215

Text Boxes

Set up multiline text box: **MultiLine**, 579, 949
Add scroll bars to a text box: **ScrollBars** (property), 951, 1394,
1899
Set or find out what text has been selected: **SelLength,
SelStart, SelText**, 953, 954, 956
Set or get the text inside a text box: **Text**, 957, 1386

Time and Timers

Get or set system date: **Date$** (function and statement), 404,
406

Table of Contents

Contents

CHAPTER 83 CREATING ACTIVEX CONTROLS   1811

CHAPTER 84 EXPOSING CONTROL PROPERTIES   1831

CHAPTER 85 RESPONDING TO USER ACTIONS WITH ACTIVEX CONTROLS   1847

CHAPTER 86 CREATING INTERNET-READY ACTIVEX CONTROLS   1859

PART VIII
SYSTEM INTERACTION

49

MOUSE EVENTS

Beyond the use of the keyboard, users are often dependent on the mouse device when using applications in the Windows environment. Depending on the application, the user can use the mouse to select items (such as buttons or menu options), to move objects (such as icons or the insertion point), to edit text, and to perform drawing functions.

Considered at its most basic level, the mouse can perform three basic tasks. First, moving the mouse changes the position of the mouse pointer on the screen. Second, a button on the mouse can be pressed. And finally, a pressed button on the mouse can be released.

Visual Basic provides five events to handle these three tasks; Click, DblClick, MouseDown, MouseMove, and MouseUp. The Click event is generated when the left, right, or middle (on some mice) button on the mouse has been pressed and then released. The DblClick event occurs when one of the buttons on the mouse has been pressed and then released twice in quick succession. The MouseDown event occurs when a button on the mouse is pressed. The MouseMove event is generated when the mouse is moved. Finally, the MouseUp event occurs when one of the mouse buttons is released. Each of these events is explained in detail within this chapter.

Mouse Events Summary

Table 49-1 details the five mouse-related events and their purposes. At the end of this chapter, the Mouse Events project demonstrates the use of all these events combined.

Table 49-1 Events dealing with mouse operations

Use This...	Type	To Do This...
Click	Event	React to the user clicking the left, right, or center mouse button
DblClick	Event	React to the user clicking the left, right, or center mouse button twice
MouseDown	Event	React to the user pressing any mouse button
MouseMove	Event	React to any mouse movement
MouseUp	Event	React to the user releasing any mouse button

Constant Values

It is usually best to use named constants rather than numeric values when developing software. Named constants make your code more readable and easier to maintain.

Table 49-2 lists the values of the constants relevant to this chapter, mentions their names, and briefly describes what they mean. These constants can be viewed in the VB Constants module (or, in some cases, in other object libraries) using the Object Browser. It is not necessary to explicitly add these objects to your project.

Table 49-2 Constant values for mouse events

Event	Value	VB.Constants	Meaning
MouseDown, MouseMove, MouseUp:			
Button argument	1	vbLeftButton	Left button was pressed
	2	vbRightButton	Right button was pressed
	4	vbMiddleButton	Middle button (if available on mouse) was pressed
MouseDown, MouseMove, MouseUp:			
Shift argument	1	vbShiftMask	SHIFT key was pressed during MouseDown
	2	vbCtrlMask	CONTROL key was pressed during MouseDown
	4	vbAltMask	ALT key was pressed during MouseDown

CLICK EVENT

Objects Affected   CheckBox, ComboBox, CommandButton, DBCombo, DBGrid, DBList, DirListBox, FileListBox, Form, Frame, Grid, Image, Label, ListBox, ListView, MDIForm, Menu, OLE Container, OptionButton, PictureBox, ProgessBar, PropertyPage, Slider, StatusBar, TabStrip, TextBox, Toolbar, TreeView, UserControl, UserDocument

Purpose   The Click event is called when the user presses and releases the button on the mouse. This generally selects the control or activates some action associated with it (as in a command button or menu option). Table 49-3 summarizes the arguments of the Click event.

General Syntax

```
Sub Form_Click()
Sub Name_Click([Index As Integer])
```

Table 49-3 Arguments of the Click event

Argument	Description
Form	'Form' refers to the parent form of the procedure, not the form's Name property
Name	Name property of the control
Index	Uniquely identifies an element of a control array

Example Syntax

```
Private Sub Form_Click()
    Label1.Caption = "The form has been clicked"
End Sub

Private Sub Label2_Click(Index As Integer)
    Dim Message As String
    Message = "This is index number "
    Message = Message + Format$(Index, "###")
    Message = Message + " of the Label2 control array."
    Label2(Index).Caption = Message
End Sub
```

Description

The Click event lets an application respond to a user clicking once on a control. This normally either selects something or performs an action. For instance, a user will usually click on a command button to activate whatever function is associated with the button. Clicking on a form or any control generally means the user is selecting that form or control. The user might select individual cells in a grid control, which also generates the Click event.

The Click event is defined in a sub procedure that carries the parent form's name of the control or Form, followed by an underscore and Click(). If the referenced control is part of a control array, the word "Click" is followed by an index variable within parentheses, as in the second syntax example.

The Click event triggers when a user places the mouse pointer over a form or an enabled control and then presses and releases the left or right mouse button once. If a control's Enabled property is set to False, the Click event passes through to its parent form. Depending on the control, the Click event can also be generated by certain keyboard actions, or by changing the setting of the control's Value property. Table 49-4 lists the actions in addition to a normal mouse click that may activate a Click event.

Table 49-4 Actions (in addition to a normal mouse click) that activate the Click event

With This Object...	These Actions Will Activate a Click Event...
Check Box	Pressing the SPACEBAR when the check box has the focus
	Changing the setting of the check box's Value property
Command Button	Pressing the E key when the button's Default property is True and no other button has the focus
	Pressing the Y key when the button has its Cancel property set to True
	Pressing the SPACEBAR or E key when the button has the focus
	Setting the button's Value property to True
	Pressing the button's access key
Combo Box	Pressing an ↑ or ↓ cursor key on the keyboard when the box has the focus
DBList	Pressing an ↑ or ↓ cursor key on the keyboard when the box has the focus
Directory List Box	Pressing an ↑ or ↓ cursor key on the keyboard when the box has the focus
File List Box	Pressing an ↑ or ↓ cursor key on the keyboard when the box has the focus
List Box	Pressing an ↑ or ↓ cursor key on the keyboard when the box has the focus
Form	Placing the mouse pointer on a blank area and any disabled control on the form and clicking
Option Button	Giving the focus to an option button whose Value property was previously False
	Setting the button's Value property to True

The first syntax example simply puts a message in the form's caption when the mouse is clicked on the form. The second example references an array of label controls. The Click event's code inserts the index number of the label that was clicked into the message displayed.

Event Order   With certain objects, clicking the mouse button causes more than one event to occur. On forms, file list boxes, labels, list boxes, and picture boxes, the following events in this order are activated every time the left or right mouse button is clicked once: MouseDown, MouseUp, Click. For all other eligible controls, only the Click event is activated. See the entry on DblClick for more information on the event order when the left, right, or middle mouse button is clicked more than once.

Control Array   The Index argument is only used if the related control is part of a control array. This Index specifies which element of the array is the one that activated the event. When referencing the control, the element being referenced must be specified by placing the index number between parentheses just after the control name, and before the property name (for example, Name(Index).Property).

Example   In the Mouse Events project at the end of this chapter, the two command buttons cmndClear and cmndExit use the Click event. The cmndClear_Click event will clear the canvas when the user clicks on the Clear button. The cmndExit_Click event simply ends the program when the user clicks on the Exit button.

The pictColor control array is an array of picture controls that activates the pictColor_Click event when the user clicks on any of the elements in the control array. This event changes the foreground color of the canvas.

DblClick Event

Objects Affected   ComboBox, DBCombo, DBGrid, FileListBox, Form, Frame, Grid, Image, Label, ListBox, ListView, MDIForme, OLE Container, OptionButton, PictureBox, PropertyPage, StatusBar, TextBox, Toolbar, TreeView, UserControl, UserDocument.

Purpose   The DblClick event responds to the user pressing the left, right, or middle mouse button twice in quick succession, which is known as a *double-click*. The user will usually double-click on a form or control to initiate a default action. Depending on the design of the application, a double-click on a form or control could be an alternative to clicking on an OK button or pressing Ⓔ to execute the default action. The arguments used in defining a DblClick event are summarized in Table 49-5.

General Syntax

```
Sub Form_DblClick()
Sub Name_DblClick([Index As Integer])
```

Table 49-5 Arguments of the DblClick event

Argument	Description
Form	'Form' refers to the parent form of the procedure, not the form's Name property
Name	Name property of the control
Index	Uniquely identifies an element of a control array

Example Syntax

```
Private Sub Form_DblClick()      'when the mouse button is pressed twice on the form
      ChangeColors               'calls a routine to change the form's colors
End Sub

Private Sub List1_DblClick(Index As Integer) 'automatically clicks the proper OK button
                                  'when a cmndOK_Click Index list
                                  'item is double-clicked on
End Sub
```

Description   The DblClick event is defined in a sub procedure that is named starting with the name of the control or 'Form' for the parent form, followed by an underscore and DblClick(). If the referenced control is part of a control array, the word "DblClick" is followed by an index variable within parentheses, as in the second syntax example.

The DblClick event occurs when the user presses and releases the left or right mouse button twice in quick succession. The period of time in which two clicks must occur in order to be considered a double-click is defined in the mouse settings area of the Windows Control Panel. If the mouse is clicked twice, but not in the time defined by the Control Panel, two separate Click events occur.

This event is also activated if the FileName property of a file list box is changed to a name that is the same as that of an existing DOS file.

When used with a combo box, this event is only called if the Style property is set to 1 (Simple Combo), and the double-click occurs when the mouse pointer is over one of the list items.

The first syntax example calls a routine to change the color of the form when the user double-clicks on it. (This could be used to highlight the fact that the user has selected the form.) The second sample syntax calls the Click event for the OK button whenever any list box in the control array is double-clicked. This makes double-clicking an alternative way for the user to provide the confirmation represented by the OK button.

Event Order

With certain objects, clicking the mouse button causes more than one event to occur. On forms, file list boxes, labels, list boxes, and picture boxes, the following events (in this order) are activated every time the left or right mouse button is double-clicked: MouseDown, MouseUp, Click, DblClick, MouseUp. For all other eligible controls, the event order is Click, DblClick.

If you have both Click and DblClick event procedures for a single control, the Click procedure always activates before the DblClick procedure unless you create some special trapping code. Windows automatically sends out the Click message immediately after a click to keep performance high—after all, most programs respond to many more clicks than double-clicks. If it waited to see whether the user double-clicked before sending out the first Click message, overall performance would suffer.

If you need to ensure that the Click procedure is not processed for double-clicks, follow the instructions given in the Waite Group's *Visual Basic How-To*. The basic idea is to have the Click event procedure start up a timer with the interval set to the system's double-click time. (You can obtain the system's double-click time with the API call GetDoubleClickTime.) If the DblClick event triggers before the timer goes off, it was a double-click; if the timer goes off, then it really was a click and the timer's Timer event procedure can then execute the code that would normally have been placed in the Click event.

Control Array

The Index argument is only used if the related control is part of a control array. This Index specifies which element of the array is the one that activated the event. When referencing the control, the element being referenced must be specified by placing the index number between parentheses just after the control name, and before the property name (for example, Name(Index).Property).

Example   In the Mouse Events project at the end of this chapter, the pictColor control array responds to a double-click by activating the pictColor_DblClick event. This event sets the background color of the canvas.

Comments   There is no DblClick event associated with the directory list box control. However, double-clicking on a path in the directory list box does cause the Path property of the box to change to the selected path.

MouseDown Event

Objects Affected   CheckBox, CommandButton, Data, DBCombo, DBGrid, DBList, DirListBox, FileListBox, Form, Frame, Grid, Image, Label, List, MDIForm, OLE Container, OptionButton, PictureBox, ProgressBar, PropertyPage, Slider, StatusBar, TabStrip, TextBox, Toolbar, TreeView, UserControl, UserDocument

Purpose   The MouseDown event occurs when any button—left, middle, or right—on the mouse is pressed. Unlike the Click event, the MouseDown event can be used to determine not only that a mouse button has been pushed, but which button was pushed. You can also determine whether the SHIFT, CONTROL, or ALT key was being held down when the mouse button was clicked. The arguments for the MouseDown event are summarized in Tables 49-6, 49-7, and 49-8, and explained below.

General Syntax

```
Sub Form_MouseDown(Button As Integer, Shift As Integer, X As Single, Y As Single)
Sub Name_MouseDown([Index As Integer, ]Button As Integer, Shift As Integer, X As Single, ⇐
Y As Single)
```

Table 49-6 Arguments of the MouseDown event

Argument	Description
Form	'Form' refers to the parent form of the procedure, not the form's Name property
Name	Name property of the control
Index	Uniquely identifies an element of a control array
Button	Integer variable returning number of button pressed
Shift	Integer variable returning status of SHIFT, ALT, and CONTROL keys at time of button press
X, Y	Single-precision variables returning coordinates of mouse pointer location when button was pushed

Table 49-7 Meanings of the Button values in the MouseDown event

Button	VB.Constants	Meaning
1	vbLeftButton	Left button was pressed
2	vbRightButton	Right button was pressed
4	vbMiddleButton	Middle button (if available on mouse) was pressed

Table 49-8 Meanings of the Shift values in the MouseDown event

Shift	VB.Constants	Meaning
1	vbShiftMask	[SHIFT] key was pressed during MouseDown
2	vbCtrlMask	[CONTROL] key was pressed during MouseDown
4	vbAltMask	[ALT] key was pressed during MouseDown

Example Syntax

```
Private Sub Form_MouseDown(Button As Integer, Shift As Integer, X As Single, Y As Single)
    If Button = vbLeftButton Then 'if the left button is pressed
        StartX = X                'save the current coordinates of the mouse pointer
        StartY = Y                'on the form
    End If
End Sub

Private Sub Picture_MouseDown(Index As Integer, Button As Integer, Shift As Integer, X As
Single, Y As Single)
    If Shift = vbShiftMask Then   'if the shift key is pressed
        StartX(Index) = X         'save the current coordinates of the mouse pointer
        StartY(Index) = Y         'on the picture control
    End If
End Sub
```

Description The press of a mouse button may indicate selection of an item, pressing a button control, or beginning a drag operation. (Dragging triggers its own event, as discussed in Chapter 50, "Dragging-and-Dropping.") Unlike the Click event, the MouseDown event can be used to determine not only that a mouse button has been pushed, but *which* button was pushed. You can also determine whether the [SHIFT], [CONTROL], or [ALT] key was being held down when the mouse button was clicked. This will allow for a variety of different kinds of interactions with your applications.

The MouseDown event is defined in a sub procedure that is named using the control name or 'Form' for the parent form, and variables representing the button number, shift status, and X and Y mouse position coordinates. An Index variable precedes the other variables if the sub procedure is written to handle a control array.

The MouseDown event triggers when the user presses down on any of the three buttons on the mouse. It supplies four arguments that indicate the status of the mouse at the time the event is called.

The integer variable argument Button indicates which button has been pressed. Its value is set to 1 for the left, 2 for the right, and 4 for the middle button. The Button argument will indicate the status of only one button at a time.

The integer variable argument Shift indicates the status of the (SHIFT), (ALT), and (CONTROL) keys at the time of the event. Each key is assigned a value: 1 for (SHIFT), 2 for (CONTROL), and 4 for (ALT). When any of these keys is pressed, its value is added to the Shift argument. The easiest way to test the Shift argument is with logical (bitwise) operators. Table 49-9 lists the Boolean constructions to use for checking the status of the buttons and the shift keys.

Table 49-9 How to test for Shift and Button status

When the...	This Will Return Nonzero	Constant Equivalents
(SHIFT) key is pressed	(Shift And 1)	(Shift And vbShiftMask)
(CONTROL) key is pressed	(Shift And 2)	(Shift And vbCtrlMask)
(ALT) key is pressed	(Shift And 4)	(Shift And vbAltMask)
Right button is pressed	(Button And 1)	(Button And vbLeftButton)
Left button is pressed	(Button And 2)	(Button And vbRightButton)
Center button is pressed	(Button And 4)	(Button And vbMiddleButton)

The X and Y arguments are single-precision variables that correspond to the mouse pointer's position within the related form or control at the time the event was called. Here, X is the horizontal coordinate, and Y is the vertical coordinate. These arguments use the measurement system defined for the form or control with the ScaleMode, ScaleHeight, ScaleWidth, and other Scale... properties.

When a mouse button is pressed while the mouse pointer is over a form or control, that form or control "owns" all the successive mouse events until a MouseUp event is processed, even if the mouse pointer leaves the area of the form or object. This could cause some mouse events to receive X and Y arguments that are not on the form or control.

The first sample syntax saves the current mouse pointer coordinates when the left button (button 1) is pressed. The second sample syntax uses an array of picture boxes. When the mouse is clicked with the [SHIFT] key held down on a picture, the current X and Y pointer coordinates are saved in the corresponding elements of the StartX and StartY arrays.

Control Array The Index argument is only used if the related control is part of a control array. This Index specifies which element of the array is the one that activated the event. When referencing the control, the element being referenced must be specified by placing the index number between parentheses just after the control name and before the property name (for example, Name(Index).Property).

Example In the Mouse Events project at the end of this chapter, the pictCanvas picture control initiates the pictCanvas_MouseDown event when the mouse pointer is over it and any button on the mouse is pressed. This event turns on the DrawOn flag, which tells the pictCanvas_MouseMove event to start drawing. It also saves the current coordinates of the mouse pointer for future reference.

Comments If the program is halted while inside this event, a corresponding MouseUp event may not be called when the mouse button is released. This can happen if a Stop statement is executed or a breakpoint is set inside this event.

MOUSEMOVE EVENT

Objects Affected CheckBox, CommandButton, Data, DBCombo, DBGrid, DBList, DirListBox, FileListBox, Form, Frame, Grid, Image, Label, ListBox, ListView, MDIForm, OLE Container, OptionButton, PictureBox, ProgressBar, PropertyPage, Slider, StatusBar, TabStrip, TextBox, Toolbar, TreeView, UserControl, UserDocument

Purpose The MouseMove event defines the actions to take when the user moves the mouse pointer. You can find out where the mouse pointer was when it was moved, what button (if any) was down, and whether the [SHIFT], [CONTROL], or [ALT] key was being held down. The arguments and variables for the MouseMove event are summarized in Tables 49-10, 49-11, and 49-12, and are explained below.

General Syntax

```
Sub Form_MouseMove(Button As Integer, Shift As Integer, X As Single, Y As Single)
Sub Name_MouseMove([Index As Integer, ]Button As Integer, Shift As Integer,⇐
X As Single, Y As Single)
```

Table 49-10 Arguments of the MouseMove event

Argument	Description
Form	'Form' refers to the parent form of the property
Name	Name property of the control
Index	Uniquely identifies an element of a control array
Button	Integer variable returning number of button pressed
Shift	Integer variable returning status of SHIFT, ALT, and CONTROL keys at time of button press
X, Y	Single-precision variables returning coordinates of the current mouse pointer location

Table 49-11 Meanings of the Button values in the MouseMove event

Button	VB.Constants	Meaning
1	vbLeftButton	Left button was pressed
2	vbRightButton	Right button was pressed
4	vbMiddleButton	Middle button (if available on mouse) was pressed

Table 49-12 Meanings of the Shift values in the MouseMove event

Shift	VB.Constants	Meaning
1	vbShiftMask	SHIFT key was pressed during MouseMove
2	vbCtrlMask	CONTROL key was pressed during MouseMove
4	vbAltMask	ALT key was pressed during MouseMove

Example Syntax

```
Private Sub Form_MouseMove(Button As Integer, Shift As Integer, X As Single, Y As Single)
    If Shift And vbShiftMask Then
        Line (LastX, LastY) - (X, Y)
    End If
End Sub
Private Sub Picture1_MouseMove(Index As Integer, Button As Integer, Shift As Integer, _
X As Single, Y As Single)
    If Shift And vbShiftMask Then
        Picture1(Index).Line (LastX, LastY) - (X, Y)
    End If
End Sub
```

Description

The MouseMove event is defined in a sub procedure that is named using the control name or 'Form' for the name of the parent form, and variables representing the button number, shift status, and X and Y mouse position coordinates. An index variable precedes the other variables if the sub procedure is written to handle a control array.

This event initiates when the user moves the mouse pointer. It supplies four arguments that indicate the status of the mouse at the time the event is called.

The integer argument Button indicates which button has been pressed. Its value is set to 1 for the left, 2 for the right, and 4 for the center button. The Button argument will indicate the status of only one button at a time.

The integer variable argument Shift indicates the status of the (SHIFT), (ALT), or (CONTROL) keys at the time of the event. Each key is assigned a value: 1 for (SHIFT), 2 for (CONTROL), and 4 for (ALT). When any of these keys is pressed, its value is added to the Shift argument. The easiest way to test the Shift argument is with logical (bitwise) operators. Table 49-9 in the MouseDown event entry goes into detail about handling bitwise operations.

The X and Y arguments are single-precision variables that correspond to the mouse pointer's position within the related form or control at the time the event was called. Here, X is the horizontal coordinate and Y is the vertical coordinate. These arguments use the measurement system defined for the form or control with the ScaleMode, ScaleHeight, ScaleWidth, and other Scale... properties.

When a mouse button is pressed while the mouse pointer is over a form or control, that form or control "owns" all the successive mouse events until a MouseUp event is processed, even if the mouse pointer leaves the area of the form or object. This could cause the MouseUp event to receive X and Y arguments that are not on the form or control.

The first sample syntax checks whether the (SHIFT) key is down when the mouse pointer is moved. If so, a line is drawn from the previously saved pointer position to the current pointer X,Y coordinates (that is, where the mouse was at the time the event is triggered). The second sample syntax does the same thing except that it is used with an array of picture boxes.

Control Array   The Index argument is only used if the related control is part of a control array. This Index specifies which element of the array is the one that activated the event. When referencing the control, the element being referenced must be specified by placing the index number between parentheses just after the control name and before the property name (for example, Name(Index).Property).

Example   In the Mouse Events project at the end of this chapter, the pictCanvas picture control calls the pictCanvas_MouseMove event whenever the mouse pointer is moved over its surface. If the DrawOn flag is set to True, it will then perform a drawing operation based on which button is pressed and the status of the Shift argument.

Comments   If the program is halted while inside this event, the MouseUp event may not be called when the mouse button is released. This can happen if a Stop statement is executed or a breakpoint is set inside this event.

MouseUp Event

Objects Affected CheckBox, CommandButton, Data, DBCombo, DBGrid, DBList, DirListBox, FileListBox, Form, Frame, Grid, Image, Label, ListBox, ListView, MDIForm, OLE Container, OptionButton, PictureBox, ProgressBar, PropertyPage, Slider, StatusBar, TabStrip, TextBox, Toolbar, TreeView, UserControl, UserDocument

Purpose The MouseUp event occurs when any button—left, middle, or right—on the mouse is released. You can also find out where the mouse pointer was when the button was released. You can also determine whether the (SHIFT), (CONTROL), or (ALT) key was being held down when the mouse button was released. The arguments and variables for the MouseUp event are summarized in Tables 49-13, 49-14, and 49-15 and explained below.

General Syntax

```
Sub Form_MouseUp(Button As Integer, Shift As Integer, X As Single, Y As Single)
Sub Name_MouseUp([Index As Integer, ]Button As Integer, Shift As Integer, X As Single, ⇐
Y As Single)
```

Table 49-13 Arguments of the MouseUp event

Argument	Description
Form	'Form' refers to the parent form of the procedure, not the Form's Name property
Name	Name property of the control
Index	Uniquely identifies an element of a control array
Button	Integer variable returning number of button pressed
Shift	Integer variable returning status of (SHIFT), (ALT), and (CONTROL) keys at time of button press
X, Y	Single-precision variables returning coordinates of the mouse pointer location when released

Table 49-14 Meanings of the Button values in the MouseUp event

Button	VB.Constants	Meaning
1	vbLeftButton	Left button was pressed
2	vbRightButton	Right button was pressed
4	vbMiddleButton	Middle button (if available on mouse) was pressed

Table 49-15 Meanings of the Shift values in the MouseUp event

Shift	VB.Constants	Meaning
1	vbShiftMask	SHIFT key was pressed during MouseUp
2	vbCtrlMask	CONTROL key was pressed during MouseUp
4	vbAltMask	ALT key was pressed during MouseUp

Example Syntax

```
Private Sub Form_MouseUp(Button As Integer, Shift As Integer, X As Single, Y As Single)
      If Button = vbLeftButton Then      'if the left button was released
          EndX = X                       'save the current coordinates of the mouse pointer
          EndY = Y                       'on the form
      End If
End Sub
Private Sub Picture_MouseUp(Index As Integer, Button As Integer, Shift As Integer, ⇐
X As Single, _Y As Single)
      If Button = vbRightButton Then     'if the right button was released
          PopupMenu menuPopPictureEdit   'pop up a tear-off editing menu on the picture
      End If
End Sub
```

Description

The MouseUp event is defined in a sub procedure that is named using the control name or 'Form' for the parent form, and variables representing the button number, shift status, and X and Y mouse position coordinates. An Index variable precedes the other variables if the sub procedure is written to handle a control array.

This event is initiated when the user releases any of the three buttons on the mouse. It supplies four arguments that indicate the status of the mouse at the time the event is called.

The integer variable argument Button indicates which button has been pressed. Its value is set to 1 for the left, 2 for the right, and 4 for the middle button. The Button argument will indicate the status of only one button at a time.

The integer variable argument Shift indicates the status of the SHIFT, ALT, and CONTROL keys at the time of the event. Each key is assigned a value: 1 for SHIFT, 2 for CONTROL, and 4 for ALT. When any of these keys is pressed, its value is added to the Shift argument. The easiest way to test the Shift argument is with logical (bitwise) operators. Table 49-9 in the MouseDown event entry goes into detail about handling bitwise operations.

The X and Y arguments are single-precision variables that correspond to the mouse pointer's position within the related form or control at the time the event was called. Here, X is the horizontal coordinate, and Y is the vertical coordinate. These arguments use the measurement system defined for the form or control with the ScaleMode, ScaleHeight, ScaleWidth, and other Scale... properties.

When a mouse button is pressed while the mouse pointer is over a form or control, that form or control "owns" all the successive mouse events until a MouseUp event is processed. This remains true even if the mouse pointer leaves the area of the form or object. This could cause the MouseUp event to receive X and Y arguments that are not on the form or control.

In the first sample syntax, the current mouse position in the form is saved if the left mouse button was released. The second example shows how easily you can pop up a context-sensitive tear-off menu. Many applications (including the Windows interface itself) now use the right mouse button as a "properties inspector" to bring up menus of items related to that object. The MouseUp event first checks to see whether the right mouse button was released. If so, it brings up a menu (defined with the Menu designer) related to the picture control array. Note that PopupMenu only works in Visual Basic 3.0 or later; for more information on menus, see Chapter 36, "Forms and Menus."

Control Array
The Index argument is only used if the related control is part of a control array. This Index specifies which element of the array is the one that activated the event. When referencing the control, the element being referenced must be specified by placing the index number between parentheses just after the control name, and before the property name (for example, Name(Index).Property).

Example
The pictCanvas_MouseUp event in the Mouse Events project at the end of this chapter sets the DrawOn flag to False and clears the coordinates that were saved by the pictCanvas_MouseDown event.

Comments
If the program is halted after a mouse button has been pressed, but before it has been released, this event may not be called when the mouse button is released. This can happen if a Stop statement is executed or a breakpoint is set inside the MouseDown or MouseMove event.

The Mouse Events Project

Project Overview

The Mouse Events project demonstrates the use of the five mouse-related events; Click, DblClick, MouseDown, MouseMove, and MouseUp. Each of these events is used at least once in the operation of this project. By following the examples in this project, you should be able to learn the principles behind using these events.

Assembling the Project

1. Create a new form (the Mouse form) and place on it the controls specified in Table 49-16. Note there is a group of five picture controls that share the name of "pictColor." These picture controls are part of a control array. As soon as you create a second picture control with the name of "pictColor," Visual Basic will ask whether you wish to create a control array. Click the Yes button.

Table 49-16 Property settings for the Mouse Events project

Object	Property	Setting
Form	Name	Mouse
	BackColor	Dark Gray– &H00808080&
	Border	1–Fixed Single
	Caption	"Mouse Project"
	MaxButton	False
PictureBox	Name	pictCanvas
	ScaleMode	1 - Twip
CommandButton	Name	cmndClear
	Caption	&Clear
CommandButton	Name	cmndExit
	Caption	E&xit
Label	Name	lablCurrentColor
	Alignment	2–Center
	BorderStyle	1–Fixed Single
	Caption	(bullet symbol: press ALT-0183 with NumLock set)
	Font	Symbol (Regular 18 pt.)
PictureBox	Name	pictColor
	BackColor	&H00FFFFFF& (White)
	BorderStyle	1–Fixed Single
	Index	0
PictureBox	Name	pictColor
	BackColor	&H00000000& (Black)
	BorderStyle	1–Fixed Single
	Index	1
PictureBox	Name	pictColor
	BackColor	&H000000FF& (Red)
	BorderStyle	1–Fixed Single
	Index	2

Object	Property	Setting
PictureBox	Name	pictColor
	BackColor	&H00FF0000& (Blue)
	BorderStyle	1–Fixed Single
	Index	3
PictureBox	Name	pictColor
	BackColor	&H0000FFFF& (Yellow)
	BorderStyle	1–Fixed Single
	Index	4

2. Check the appearance of your form against Figure 49-1.

3. Enter the following code in the General Declarations area of the Mouse form. These module-level variables are available to all event procedures.

```
Private DrawOn As Integer      'flags if we're in the middle of drawing something

Private StartX As Single       'remembers the original start coordinates of
Private StartY As Single       'a drawing operation

Private LastX As Single        'remembers the last used drawing coordinates
Private LastY As Single

Private SaveColor As Single     'remembers the previous color setting changed in the
                                'Click event
```

Figure 49-1   What the Mouse form should look like when complete

4. Enter the following code in the cmndClear_Click event. This code uses the Cls method to clear the pictCanvas picture control when the Clear button is clicked.

```
Private Sub cmndClear_Click ()
    pictCanvas.Cls                    'clear the canvas
End Sub
```

5. Enter the following code into the cmndExit_Click event. This event ends the program when the Exit button is clicked.

```
Private Sub cmndExit_Click ()
    End                               'end the program
End Sub
```

6. Enter the following code into the pictCanvas_MouseDown event. This event activates when the user presses down any of the buttons on the mouse while the mouse pointer is over the pictCanvas picture control. It sets the DrawOn flag to True, and saves the current mouse pointer coordinates. These coordinates are later used in the pictCanvas_MouseMove event.

```
Private Sub pictCanvas_MouseDown (Button As Integer, Shift As Integer, X As Single, ⇐
Y As Single)
    DrawOn = True                     'flag that we've started drawing
    StartX = X                        'remember our starting coordinates
    StartY = Y
End Sub
```

7. Enter the following code into the pictCanvas_MouseMove event. This event is where the fun stuff happens. When the user moves the mouse pointer across the surface of the pictCanvas picture control, this routine checks to see whether the DrawOn flag is set. If so, it then checks to see whether the left or right button is currently pressed. If the left button is pressed, it draws a line from the last known position of the mouse pointer to the current position of the mouse pointer, essentially letting the user scribble. If the right button is pressed, it draws a line from the coordinates saved by the pictCanvas_MouseDown event to the current mouse pointer coordinates. This creates a fan-like pattern. If the user is also holding the (SHIFT) key down while pressing the right mouse button, a box is drawn whose opposite corners match the coordinates saved by the pictCanvas_MouseDown event, and the current mouse pointer position. As a last step, this event saves the current mouse pointer position, so it has a reference point for the next time it is called with the left mouse button pressed.

```
Private Sub pictCanvas_MouseMove (Button As Integer, Shift As Integer, X As Single, ⇐
Y As Single)
    If DrawOn Then                                    'if we've started drawing,
        If Button And vbLeftButton Then               'left button pressed,
            pictCanvas.Line (LastX, LastY)-(X, Y) 'just let the user scribble
        ElseIf Button And vbRightButton Then          'right button makes cool
                                                      'guy designs...
            If Shift And vbShiftMask Then             'shift button draws a
                pictCanvas.Line (StartX, StartY)-(X, Y), , B    'series of boxes
            End If
```

```
        pictCanvas.Line (StartX, StartY)-(X, Y) 'this connects starting point to the
                                                'current
    End If                                      'point, making a "fan" shape
  End If
  LastX = X                                     'remember where we left off
  LastY = Y
End Sub
```

8. Enter the following code into the pictCanvas_MouseUp event. This event occurs when the user releases the mouse button. It sets the DrawOn flag to False, and zeros out the starting mouse pointer position.

```
Private Sub pictCanvas_MouseUp (Button As Integer, Shift As Integer,X As Single, ⇐
Y As Single)
    DrawOn = False                 'done drawing now!
    StartX = 0                     'reset starting coordinates
    StartY = 0
End Sub
```

9. Enter the following code into the pictColor_Click event. This event occurs when the user clicks on one of the elements of the pictColor picture control array. This event changes the foreground color of the pictCanvas picture control to the same color as the element that was clicked. The lablCurrentColor ForeColor property is also changed, so the user can see what the current color selections are. This event also happens when the user double-clicks on the element, so it saves the current ForeColor property for the pictCanvas picture control. This allows us to restore the ForeColor property to its original value if the event was actually activated by a double-click.

```
Private Sub pictColor_Click (Index As Integer)
    SaveColor = pictCanvas.ForeColor                          'remember ForeColor in case
                                                              'of double-click
    pictCanvas.ForeColor = pictColor(Index).BackColor         'reset the drawing colors
    lablCurrentColor.ForeColor = pictColor(Index).BackColor   'and give the user visual
                                                              'feedback
End Sub
```

10. Enter the following code into the pictColor_DblClick event. This event activates when the user double-clicks one of the elements of the pictColor picture control array. This event changes the background color of the pictCanvas picture control to the same color as the element that was clicked. The lablCurrentColor.BackColor property is also changed, so the user can see what the current color selections are. Because this event is triggered after the Click event, we must first restore the ForeColor property of the pictCanvas picture control to its original state.

```
Private Sub pictColor_DblClick (Index As Integer)
    pictCanvas.ForeColor = SaveColor                          'reset ForeColor changed
                                                              'during Click event
    lablCurrentColor.ForeColor = SaveColor                    'reset visual feedback...
    pictCanvas.BackColor = pictColor(Index).BackColor         'and now change the
                                                              'background color
    lablCurrentColor.BackColor = pictColor(Index).BackColor   'and the visual feedback
        End Sub
```

How It Works

The application developed in the Mouse Events project is a crude drawing program. When the program starts, the Mouse form appears with a blank canvas. The user can then use the mouse to draw on the canvas.

Pressing and holding down the left mouse button and moving the mouse while the mouse pointer is over the canvas draws a line on the canvas. The pictCanvas_MouseDown event is called first; and because there is a button pressed, it sets the DrawOn flag to True, and saves the current coordinates of the mouse pointer. Then the pictCanvas_MouseMove event is called. In this event, a line is drawn from the last known mouse pointer position to the current mouse pointer position. This causes the line to follow the mouse pointer around the canvas until the user releases the left button.

Pressing and holding down the right mouse button also draws lines on the canvas. The pictCanvas_MouseDown event is called first; and, because there is a button pressed, it sets the DrawOn flag to True, and saves the current coordinates of the mouse pointer. Then the pictCanvas_MouseMove event is called. In this event, the coordinates of the saved mouse position are used along with the coordinates of the current mouse pointer position to draw the line. This causes several lines to be drawn, all originating at the same point. This creates a fan-like pattern.

If the (SHIFT) key is held down along with the right mouse button, a box is drawn around each line generated. This creates an interesting effect, as illustrated in Figure 49-2.

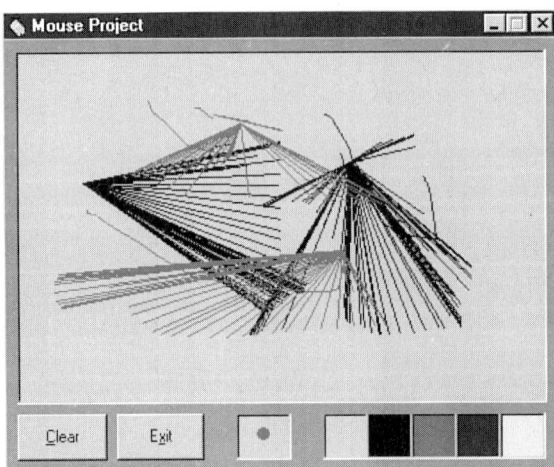

Figure 49-2 The Mouse Events project in action

When the mouse buttons are released, the pictCanvas_MouseUp event is called. This event turns the DrawOn flag off (sets it to False), and clears the saved mouse position coordinates.

The foreground color of the canvas may be changed by clicking on any of the elements of the pictColor array. This triggers the pictColor_Click event. Because a Click event is always called just prior to the DblClick event, it saves the current foreground color of the canvas before changing it. This enables the DblClick event to restore it, if need be. The pictColor_Click event then changes the foreground color of the canvas to the same color as the background of the pictColor element that was clicked. These changes are also performed on the lablCurrentColor label control. This control displays to the user which colors are currently selected.

The background color of the canvas may be changed by double-clicking on any of the elements of the pictColor array. This causes the pictColor_DblClick event to occur. The first task performed by this event is to restore the foreground color of the canvas. It then sets the background color of the canvas to the same color as the background of the pictColor element that was double-clicked. These changes are also performed on the lablCurrentColor label control. This control displays to the user which colors are currently selected

50

DRAGGING-AND-DROPPING

Drag-and-drop is a versatile Windows feature available to your Visual Basic programs. Dragging means moving a control (such as an icon or a graphic image) from one position on the screen to another. Dropping means releasing the dragged control over another control. For example, file managers often allow you to copy or move files between directories by dragging a file name or icon from one directory area to another. You drop the dragged file name or icon on another location to perform an action on it (such as Copy or Move).

To drag a control, select it by pointing at it with your mouse or other pointing device. Press the mouse button (click) on the control and—without releasing the mouse button—move the control to a new location on the screen. When you drag a control, you will see a graphic outline of the control unless you specify otherwise using the DragIcon property. Release the mouse button to drop the control at its new destination.

A drag-and-drop operation involves two controls: One acts as the source control, while the other acts as the target control. The *source control* is the one that the user clicks with the mouse. When a drag-and-drop operation ends, the control that the drag icon is over is the *target control*. If a drag-and-drop operation does not end over another control, then there is no target control. An example of a drag-and-drop operation including a source and a target is when the user clicks and drags an icon representing a file to the icon symbol of a printer to print a file. The actual printing would involve an event connected with the target. Any kind of action that follows the dropping of the source over the target is part of the target's event procedures.

Drag mode determines how a drag operation begins. There are two settings for drag mode: automatic and manual. In automatic drag mode, dragging operations begin when the user clicks the mouse. This process takes place without the use of any code. Manual drag mode prevents the starting of a drag operation with only the clicking of the mouse. The only way to begin a drag operation on a control with its drag mode set to manual is with a statement in the code of the program.

Dragging-and-Dropping Summary

Visual Basic uses several properties, events, and methods to implement dragging. A control's DragMode property indicates its drag mode setting: manual or automatic. The Drag method lets you prepare a control for dragging with a manual DragMode. Each manual drag operation begins and ends with DragMode method expressions. The DragIcon property of the control determines whether the outline of the control or another icon appears on the screen during a drag operation. The DragDrop event contains the actions that take place when a drag operation terminates over a control. The DragOver event contains the actions that take place when the user drags a control over another control.

Table 50-1 displays the Visual Basic properties, events, and methods that determine the means and results of a drag operation. Detailed descriptions follow the table.

Table 50-1 Methods, properties, and events involved in a drag operation

Use or Set This...	Type	To Do This...
Drag	Method	Begin or end manual dragging
DragDrop	Event	Initiate an action when a dragged control is dropped onto another control
DragIcon	Property	Select the icon to display when the control is part of a drag operation
DragMode	Property	Choose automatic or manual drag mode
DragOver	Event	Initiate an action when a dragged control is over a form or control

Constant Values

It is usually best to use named constants rather than numeric values when developing software. Named constants make your code more readable and easier to maintain.

Table 50-2 lists the values of the constants relevant to this chapter, mentions their names, and briefly describes what they mean. These constants can be viewed in the VB Constants module (or, in some cases, in other object libraries), using the Object Browser. It is not necessary to explicitly add these objects to your project.

Table 50-2 Methods, properties, and events involved in a drag operation

Value	VB.Constants	Description
Drag method		
0	vbCancel	Cancels a dragging operation.
1	vbBeginDrag	Begins a dragging operation.
2	vbEndDrag	Ends a dragging operation.

Value	VB.Constants	Description
DragMode property		
0	vbManual	(Default.) Drag method is required for a drag operation.
1	vbAutomatic	User pressing the mouse button over a control starts a drag operation.
DragOver event		
0	vbEnter	Control enters the space above another control.
1	vbLeave	Control exits the space above another control.
2	vbOver	Control is over the space above another control (executes once).

The following pages discuss each of the methods, events, and properties in Table 50-1 in detail. The Drag project at the end of this chapter includes step-by-step directions on how to create a Visual Basic project that uses them all.

DRAG METHOD

Objects Affected	CheckBox, ComboBox, CommandButton, Data, DBCombo, DBGrid, DBList, DirListBox, DriveListBox, FileListBox, Form, Frame, Grid, HScrollBar, Image, Label, ListView, OLE Container, OptionButton, PictureBox, ProgressBar, Slider, StatusBar, TabStrip, TextBox, Toolbar, TreeView, VScrollBar, WebBrowser
Purpose	The Drag method initiates or ends a dragging operation. With this method, you can manipulate controls on the screen when a control's DragMode property is manual. A Drag method statement typically appears in the MouseDown event of the control to be dragged. This has the effect of beginning a drag operation when the user presses the mouse button. Tables 50-3 and 50-4 summarize the arguments and possible values of the Drag method.

General Syntax

```
[form!]Name.Drag [action%]
```

Table 50-3 Arguments of the Drag method

Argument	Description
form	Name property of the parent form
Name	Name property of the control that is affected by the drag operation
action%	Value that indicates what dragging operation to take

Table 50-4 Possible values of the action% argument

action%	VB.Constants	Description
0	vbCancel	Cancels a dragging operation
1	vbBeginDrag	Begins a dragging operation
2	vbEndDrag	Ends a dragging operation

Example Syntax

```
Private Sub Picture1_MouseDown (Button As Integer, Shift As Integer, X As Single, Y As←
Single)
     Picture1.Drag                    'begins a drag operation
End Sub

Private Sub Form_DragDrop (Source As Control, X As Single, Y As Single)
     Source.Move X, Y                 'moves the picture box to the new location
End Sub
```

Description

A Drag method statement consists of three possible elements. Each Drag method expression begins with the Name property of the control being dragged. This is normally the control whose event contains the Drag method, but it can be any other control. A Drag method ends with a value that represents what type of drag operation to take.

There are three possible settings for the action% parameter: 0, 1, and 2. A value of 0 cancels a dragging operation. This prevents the triggering of any events normally associated with the ending of a drag operation, like DragDrop. Using a value of 1 begins a drag operation. Drag operations end with a value of 2. This triggers the DragDrop event of the form or control that the drag icon is over. The default for action% is 1.

The DragMode Property

The DragMode property of a control indicates whether the Drag method is necessary to initiate a drag operation. When the DragMode property of a control remains at its default value of 0 (manual), the Drag method is the only way to initiate a drag operation. If the DragMode property changes to 1 (automatic), then the Drag method is not necessary. In this case, a drag operation starts when the user presses a mouse button while the mouse pointer is over the control. With the example syntax, the Picture1 picture box's DragMode property remains at its default setting of manual. If you were to change the DragMode property to automatic and remove the Drag method statement from the MouseDown event, the example would work exactly the same.

The DragIcon Property

The DragIcon property sets the icon that appears during a drag operation to show where to move the control. This property's default setting is "none," and a gray outline of the dragged control is used instead. This outline is a guide for where the control appears when the drag operation finishes. In the example syntax, the DragIcon property is a different icon (as set at design time in the Picture1 DragIcon property) from the one displayed in the Picture1 picture box. Figures 50-1, 50-2, and 50-3 show what a drag operation looks like.

Figure 50-1 Example syntax shows original Picture1 ready to be dragged

Figure 50-2 Picture1 in the process of being dragged, showing its DragIcon

Figure 50-3 Picture1 dropped into a new location

The Move Method	The user can move a control to a new location on the screen with a Move method expression. By placing a Move method expression in the DragDrop event of the form, the control moves to the new location at the end of a drag operation. In the example syntax, the Move method places the Picture1 picture box in a new location on the screen. The X and Y values returned by the DragDrop event of the form provide the new coordinates of the Picture1 picture box. Notice that the DragDrop event has Source as Control, so the name of the control being dragged gets passed to the event handler.
The DragDrop Event	The DragDrop event contains the actions that occur when the user releases the mouse button while the drag icon is over another control or form. This event is unaffected by whether the drag operation began with a Drag method expression or mouse click. In the example syntax, releasing the mouse button over a portion of the form triggers the DragDrop event. Notice that there is no need for another Drag method statement to terminate the drag operation. The user triggers a DragDrop event by releasing the mouse button.
Example	In the Drag project at the end of this chapter, the Drag method is used several times. The Drag method initiates a dragging operation on the selected file in the fileList file list box. In the fileList_Click event, the Drag method processes when the user selects a file. The DragOver event of pictClear demonstrates the setting of action% to 0 (to cancel drag). This drag operation ends when the user clicks on the left mouse button and drags the picture from the pictIcon picture box to the pictClear picture box.

DragDrop Event

Objects Affected	CheckBox, ComboBox, CommandButton, Data, DBCombo, DBGrid, DBList, DirListBox, DriveListBox, FileListBox, Form, Frame, Grid, HScrollBar, Image, InternetExplorer, Label, ListBox, ListView, MDIForm, OLE Container, OptionButton, PictureBox, ProgressBar, PropertyPage, Slider, StatusBar, TabStrip, TextBox, Toolbar, TreeView, UserControl, UserDocument, VScrollBar, WebBrowser
Purpose	A DragDrop event contains the actions that occur at the completion of a drag-and-drop operation over another control. Drag-and-drop operations terminate with either a Drag method expression or the release of a mouse button. When the user releases the mouse button while the mouse pointer is over a control, this is known as the drop part of a drag-and-drop operation. Table 50-5 summarizes the arguments and variables of the DragDrop event.

General Syntax

```
Sub Form_DragDrop (Source As Control, X As Single, Y As Single)
Sub MDIForm_DragDrop (Source As Control, X As Single, Y As Single)
Sub Name_DragDrop ([Index As Integer,] Source As Control, X As Single, Y As Single)
```

Table 50-5 Arguments and variables of the DragDrop event

Argument	Description
Form	'Form' indicates the form.
MDIForm	'MDIForm' indicates the MDIForm.
Name	Name property of the control that the dragged control is dropped on.
Index	Identifies a control in a control array.
Source	The control that is dropped over this control.
X, Y	Current horizontal (x) and vertical (y) coordinates of the mouse pointer when mouse is released.

Example Syntax

```
Private Sub Form_Load ()
    Picture1.Picture = LoadPicture("\VB\ICONS\OFFICE\CRDFLE05.ICO")   'Rolodex w/ card
    Picture1.DragMode = 1                                            'sets automatic Drag
    Picture1.DragIcon = LoadPicture("\VB\ICONS\DRAGDROP\DRAG1PG.ICO") 'hand w/ papers
End Sub

Private Sub Picture2_DragDrop (Source As Control, X As Single, Y As Single)
    Picture2.Picture = Source.Picture       'Picture2 now has Picture1's picture
    Source.Picture = LoadPicture("")        'blank out the source picture
End Sub
```

Description   A DragDrop event triggers when the user drops a dragged control over another control or form. The X and Y coordinates define the location of the dragged control relative to the control being dragged. These coordinates measure the horizontal and vertical distance in the units defined by the container's ScaleMode property. The Source argument identifies the dragged control that caused the event. Using Source to replace the Name property of the dragged control makes the expression general, so the user can drag and drop more than one control over a control.

In the example syntax, an automatic drag operation triggers when the mouse pointer is over the Picture1 picture box (which is the source control) and the user presses the mouse button. The DragDrop event redefines the Picture property of the Picture2 picture box with the Picture property of the dragged control. Figures 50-4, 50-5, and 50-6 illustrate how the contents of the Picture1 transfer to Picture2.

Control Arrays   If the control designated in a drag-and-drop operation is a member of a control array, then Visual Basic will provide an Index property value. This Index value defines which item of the control array was dropped on the control. This is useful in situations where there is a need to have different actions for different items of the same control array.

Example   The Drag project at the end of this chapter uses the DragDrop event of the Picture1 picture box. This subroutine triggers when the user selects the file name of an icon from the list of icons (displayed in fileList) and drops it on top of the pictIcon picture box that displays the icon chosen.

Figure 50-4 Picture1 and Picture2 before the drag-and-drop operation

Figure 50-5 During the drag-and-drop (note the DragIcon)

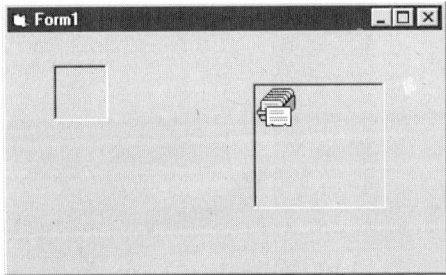

Figure 50-6 After the operation. Example syntax shows how Picture1 and Picture2's contents change during the DragDrop event

DragIcon Property

Objects Affected	CheckBox, ComboBox, CommandButton, Data, DBCombo, DBGrid, DBList, DirListBox, DriveListBox, FileListBox, Frame, Grid, HScrollBar, Image, Label, ListBox, ListView, OLE Container, OptionButton, PictureBox, ProgressBar, Slider, StatusBar, TabStrip, TextBox, Toolbar, TreeView, VScrollBar, WebBrowser
Purpose	The DragIcon property indicates what icon will be used as a pointer during a drag operation. This property is a useful way to indicate what type of drag operation is being initiated. If used with the DragOver and DragDrop events, this property can change the pointer icon during a drag operation. Table 50-6 summarizes the arguments of the DragIcon property, while Table 50-7 shows the possible settings of the DragIcon property.

General Syntax

```
[form.]DragIcon [ = icon]
[form!]Name.DragIcon [ = icon]
```

Table 50-6 Arguments of the DragIcon property

Argument	Description
form	Name property of the form
Name	Name property of the control
icon	Any valid icon file

Table 50-7 Possible settings of Icon argument of DragIcon property

Icon	Description
None	(Default) Cursor indicated by the MousePointer property, normally the outline of the control
Icon	Any function that returns a legal icon, such as the LoadPicture function

Example Syntax

```
Private Sub Form_Load ()
    Picture1.Picture = LoadPicture("\VB\ICONS\COMPUTER\TRASH01.ICO")
    Picture1.DragMode = 1                    'sets automatic Drag
    Text1.Text = "Hello World!"
    Text1.DragIcon = LoadPicture("\VB\ICONS\MAIL\MAIL01A.ICO")
    Text1.DragMode = 1                       'sets automatic Drag
End Sub

Private Sub Picture1_DragOver (Source As Control, X As Single,⇐
Y As Single, State As Integer)
    Select Case State
```

continued on next page

continued from previous page

```
            Case 0, 2
                Text1.DragIcon = Picture1.Picture
            Case 1
                Text1.DragIcon = ⇐
LoadPicture("\PROGRAM FILES\DEVSTUDIO\VB\ICONS\MAIL\MAIL01A.ICO")
    End Select
End Sub

Private Sub Picture1_DragDrop (Source As Control, X As Single, Y As Single)
    Source.Text = ""              'blanks the text
    Source.DragIcon = ⇐
LoadPicture("\PROGRAM FILES\DEVSTUDIO\VB\GRAPHICS\ICONS\MAIL\MAIL01A.ICO")
End Sub
```

Description   The DragIcon property identifies what icon to display in place of the mouse pointer during a drag operation. The Name property of the control or form identifies which control's DragIcon property to change. When no name appears, the DragIcon property of the form is changed. Note that these file locations reflect a Visual Basic 5.0 installation.

Using Icons   The DragIcon can be specified at both design time and runtime. At design time you select the DragIcon by choosing the DragIcon property in the properties box and clicking on the word (Icon) at the right-hand side of the settings bar. To set the DragIcon property at runtime, use the LoadPicture function, including the icon's file name and path.

Although the LoadPicture function is the most common way of assigning an icon, you need to distribute the icon files, along with your program to use it. A less direct but cleaner way of assigning icons is to use another control's Icon or Picture properties as a temporary storage area. For example, you might create an array of invisible image controls and store the various icons in the image controls' Picture property. You could then set the new icon with this code:

```
Private Sub Picture1_DragOver (Source As Control, X As Single, ⇐
Y As Single, State As Integer)
    Text1.DragIcon = Image1(State).Picture
End Sub
```

This not only simplifies your code, but also makes the icons a part of the executable file. You don't have to worry about the icons being separated from your application.

In the example syntax, the DragIcon property changes during the DragOver event. The Form_Load subprocedure loads the picture for Picture1 and sets the drag mode to the icon that will be used to indicate that dragging is in progress (the trash can, in this case). The DragOver event checks that the source control is no longer over the destination. Here, if the source control moves away without being dropped, DragIcon is restored to the original. In the DragDrop event, the DragIcon also changes back to the original, indicating that a drag-and-drop operation has been completed.

In the example syntax, the DragIcon changes to a trash can when it is over the Picture1 picture box. This graphically shows the user the results of completing the drag-and-drop operation. Notice that when the user drops the control, the text is erased from the Text1 text box. Figures 50-7, 50-8, 50-9, and 50-10 show what the screen looks like before, during, and after the drag-and-drop sequence.

Figure 50-7   During the Drag (note the DragIcon)

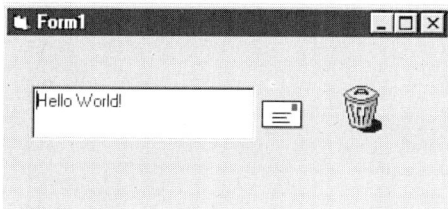

Figure 50-8   During the DragOver (note the DragIcon changes again to confirm the ability to drop)

Figure 50-9   During the DragOver (note the DragIcon changes again to confirm the ability to drop)

Figure 50-10 After the drop (note that the code clears Text1 and sets the pointer back to normal)

Example The Drag project at the end of this chapter uses the DragIcon property for the pictIcon picture box and fileList file list box. For the fileList file list box, the DragIcon specifies what icon to use when dragging the icon file to be displayed in the pictIcon picture box. In the pictIcon picture box, the DragIcon property is set at runtime to the icon displayed.

Comments Even on color displays, the icon for dragging will only be shown in monochrome.

DragMode Property

Objects Affected CheckBox, ComboBox, CommandButton, Data, DBCombo, DBGrid, DBList, DirListBox, DriveListBox, FileListBox, Frame, Grid, HScrollBar, Image, Label, ListBox, ListView, OLE Container, OptionButton, PictureBox, ProgressBar, Slider, StatusBar, TabStrip, TextBox, Toolbar, TreeView, VScrollBar, WebBrowser

Purpose The DragMode property of a control indicates whether it may be dragged in a drag operation without the use of a Drag method expression. Every control has an initial setting of manual. This indicates that the control may not normally be dragged. A drag operation may only be begun on a control with a manual setting by using the Drag method. With a control's DragMode property set to automatic, a drag operation automatically begins when the user presses and holds down a mouse button over the control. Tables 50-8 and 50-9 summarize arguments and possible settings of the DragMode property.

General Syntax

```
[form!]Name.DragMode [ = mode%]
```

Table 50-8 Arguments of the DragMode property

Argument	Description
form	Name property of the form
Name	Name property of the control
mode%	DragMode setting

Table 50-9 Possible settings of the DragMode property

mode%	VB.Constants	Description
0	vbManual	(Default) Drag method is required for a drag operation.
1	vbAutomatic	User pressing the mouse button over a control starts a drag operation.

Example Syntax

```
Private Sub Command1_Click ()
    Command1.Caption = "automatic"     'changes text on command button
    Command1.DragMode = 1              'changes DragMode to automatic
End Sub

Private Sub Form_DragDrop (Source As Control, X As Single, Y As Single)
    Source.Move X, Y                   'moves the control to the new location
    Command1.Caption = "manual"        'changes text on command button
    Command1.DragMode = 0              'changes DragMode to manual
End Sub
```

Description   The DragMode property of a control indicates whether it may be dragged in a drag operation without the use of a Drag method expression. The initial DragMode property value of any newly created control is manual (0). A value of 1 changes the DragMode property to automatic. Controls must use the Drag method unless the DragMode property is changed to automatic. While a control is being dragged, no other mouse actions (Click, DblClick, MouseDown, MouseMove, MouseUp, GotFocus) will function.

In the example syntax, both the manual and automatic DragModes are demonstrated with the Command1 command button. The command button Command1 can only be moved when it reads "automatic." When the user clicks the Command1 command button with the mouse, the DragMode property is changed to automatic. After this property changes, the automatic DragMode enables you to move the command button on the form. Notice that the control cannot be dragged when it reads "manual."

The Drag Method   While the DragMode property of a control is set to manual, the control may not normally be dragged until it is changed to automatic. If the MouseDown event of the control contains a Drag method expression, however, then this will have the same effect as changing the control's DragMode property to automatic.

Example   In the Drag project at the end of this chapter, the majority of the controls remain in manual DragMode. The pictIcon picture box can be changed from manual to automatic DragMode to demonstrate the effects of the modes on dragging icons to the pictClear icon.

DragOver Event

Objects Affected   CheckBox, ComboBox, CommandButton, Data, DBCombo, DBGrid, DBList, DirListBox, DriveListBox, FileListBox, Form, Frame, Grid, HScrollBar, Image, InternetExplorer, Label, ListBox, ListView, MDIForm, OLE Container, OptionButton, PictureBox, ProgressBar, PropertyPage, Slider, StatusBar, TabStrip, TextBox, Toolbar, TreeView, UserControl, UserDocument, VScrollBar, WebBrowser

Purpose   A DragOver event contains the actions that take place when a drag operation moves the mouse pointer over a control before the user releases the mouse button. These actions do not necessarily terminate a drag-and-drop operation, but the DragOver event can serve this purpose. Tables 50-10 and 50-11 summarize the arguments and variables of the DragOver event.

General Syntax

```
Sub Form_DragOver (Source As Control, X As Single, Y As Single, State As Integer)
Sub MDIForm_DragOver (Source As Control, X As Single, Y As Single, State As Integer)
Sub Name_DragOver ([Index As Integer,] Source As Control, X As Single, ⇐
Y As Single, _State As Integer)
```

Table 50-10 Arguments and variables of the DragOver event

Argument	Description
Form	'Form' indicates the form over which the drag-and-drop operation terminates.
MDIForm	'MDIForm' indicates the MDIForm over which the drag-and-drop operation terminates.
Name	Name property of the control over which the drag-and-drop operation terminates.
Index	Identifies a control in a control array.
Source	The dragged and dropped control.
X, Y	Current horizontal (X) and vertical (Y) coordinates of mouse pointer.
State	Whether the dragged control is entering, over, or exiting the space above another control.

Table 50-11 Arguments and variables of the DragOver event

State	VB.Constants	Description
0	vbEnter	Control enters the space above another control.
1	vbLeave	Control exits the space above another control.
2	vbOver	Control is over the space above another control (executes once).

Example Syntax

```
Const DRAG_ICO = "\PROGRAM FILES\DEVSTUDIO\VB\GRAPHICS\ICONS\DRAGDROP\DRAG1PG.ICO" ⇐
                                              'hand w/ papers
Const DROP_ICO = "\PROGRAM FILES\DEVSTUDIO\VB\GRAPHICS\ICONS\DRAGDROP\DROP1PG.ICO" ⇐
                                              'hand dropping paper

Private Sub Form_Load ()
    Picture1.Picture = ⇐LoadPicture("\PROGRAM
FILES\DEVSTUDIO\VB\GRAPHICS\ICONS\OFFICE\CRDFLEO5.ICO")        'Rolodex w/card
    Picture1.DragMode = 1                                      'sets automatic Drag
    Picture1.DragIcon = LoadPicture(DRAG_ICO)                  'sets DragIcon property
End Sub

Private Sub Picture2_DragDrop (Source As Control, X As Single, Y As Single)
    Picture2.BackColor = QBColor(15)                      'changes Background to white
    Picture2.Picture = Picture1.Picture                  'places icon in picture box
    Source.Picture = LoadPicture("")                     'blanks out source
End Sub

Private Sub Picture2_DragOver (Source As Control, X As Single, ⇐
Y As Single, State As Integer)
    Select Case State                  'checks where control is (entering, over, leaving)
        Case 0, 2                      'checks if the control is over it
            Picture2.BackColor = QBColor(7)                 'changes BackColor to gray
            Source.DragIcon = LoadPicture(DROP_ICO)         'change to dropping icon
        Case 1                         'checks if the control is no longer over it
            Picture2.BackColor = QBColor(15)                'changes BackColor to white
            Source.DragIcon = LoadPicture(DRAG_ICO)         'changes back to dragging icon
    End Select
End Sub
```

Description   A DragOver event happens when the user drags a control over another control or form. Each DragOver event uses the Name property to indicate exactly which control or form the user drags a control over. The X and Y coordinates define the location of the dragged control relative to the control's container. These coordinates measure the horizontal and vertical distance in units defined by the container's ScaleMode property. The Source argument identifies the dragged control that caused the event. Source replaces the Name property of the dragged control in expressions where more than one control can be dropped and dragged to a control.

The DragOver event for Picture2 determines what happens if another control (see Figure 50-11) is dragged over it. Here the background of Picture2 changes to gray while being dragged over (see Figure 50-12) and changes back to white as soon as the dragged control crosses back over Picture2's boundaries (see Figure 50-13). Notice how Picture2's DragOver event also changes the source control's DragIcon as further confirmation of the ability to drop.

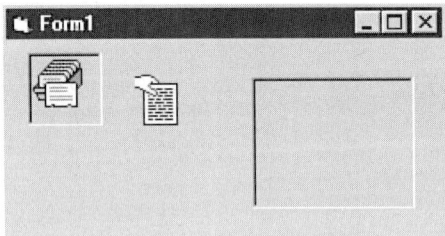

Figure 50-11   Example syntax shows drag operation before DragOver

Figure 50-12   During DragOver (note the changed icon and BackColor)

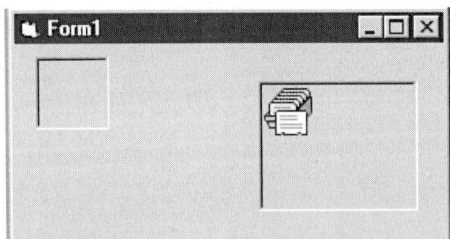

Figure 50-13   After the completed DragDrop

In the DragDrop event for Picture2 controls, what happens if the mouse button is released while another control is over the picture (that is, the other control is being "dropped on" Picture2)? When this happens, Picture2's background changes to white and the contents of Picture2 change to those of Picture1, in effect dropping a copy of Picture1 on Picture2. Notice that if the user drops the icon, the DragDrop event must have a line of code that changes the background of the Picture2 picture box to white, because the State argument is never 1 during a drop in a DragOver event—a State equal to 1 means the control is exiting, so it can't drop!

In the example syntax, the DragOver event triggers up to three separate times. The DragOver event occurs each time the control enters, is over, and exits the space above the Picture2 picture box. Notice how this one event changes the appearance of the Picture2 picture box. Figures 50-11, 50-12, and 50-13 display what the screen looks like before, during, and after a DragOver event.

The State Variable

The State variable returns the three possible ways that a control may be dragged over a control. A control's DragOver event first triggers when a control enters the space above it. When this happens, the State variable returns a value of 0. While a dragged control is over a control or form, the State variable returns the value of 2. After a dragged control leaves the space above a control or form, the DragOver event triggers one last time and gives a value of 1.

Example

In the Drag project at the end of this chapter, the DragOver event clears the icon displayed in the pictIcon picture box. When the user drags that icon over to the pictClear picture box, the State argument of the DragOver event returns the value of 0. The resulting code changes the Picture property of pictIcon to blank.

The Drag Project

Project Overview

This Drag project demonstrates dragging in Visual Basic. This example shows how to use the properties, events, and methods that directly affect dragging.

This project has one form, the formDrag form. The formDrag form's setup is broken down into three sections: assembly, source code, and how it works.

Assembling the Project

1. Make a new form (the Drag form) with the controls and properties listed in Table 50-12.

Table 50-12 Elements of the formDrag form

Control	Property	Setting
Form	BackColor	&H0000C0C0& (Light Gray)
	BorderStyle	1—Fixed Single
	Caption	"Icon View"
	Name	formDrag
	MaxButton	False
DriveListBox	Name	drivList
DirectoryListBox	Name	dirList
FileListBox	Name	fileList
	DragIcon	\PROGRAM FILES\DEVSTUDIO\VB\GRAPHICS\ICONS\COMPUTER\DISK06.ICO
	Pattern	*.ICO
	Tag	fileList
Picture	Name	pictIcon
	DragIcon	\PROGRAM FILES\DEVSTUDIO\VB\GRAPHICS\ICONS\COMPUTER\DISK06.ICO
	DragMode	0—Manual
Picture	Appearance	0-Flat
	BackColor	&H00C0C0C0& (Light Gray)
	BorderStyle	0-None
	Name	pictClear
	Picture	\PROGRAM FILES\DEVSTUDIO\VB\GRAPHICS\ICONS\COMPUTER\TRASH01.ICO
Command	Caption	&Manual
	Name	cmndMode
Command	Caption	E&xit
	Name	cmndExit

2. Size the controls as shown in Figure 50-14.

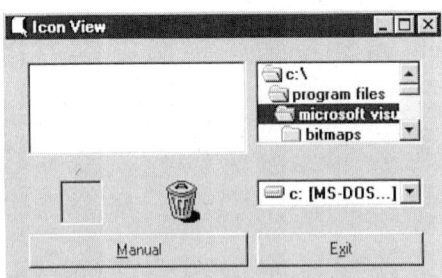

Figure 50-14 The formDrag form

3. Enter the following code in the drivList_Change event subroutine. This code triggers when the user chooses another drive in the drivList drive box. When this code changes, the path of the dirList directory list box changes to display the directories of the new drive chosen.

```
Private Sub drivList_Change ()
    dirList.Path = drivList.Drive          'change the dir list's path
End Sub
```

4. Enter the following code in the dirList_Change event subroutine. This code activates when the user selects another directory in the dirList directory list box. Another way of triggering this code is to change the drive selected in the drivList drive list box. After this happens, the contents of the fileList are modified to display the icons in the indicated directory.

```
Private Sub dirList_Change ()
    fileList.Path = dirList.Path          'change the file list's directory
    ChDir fileList.Path                   'change to that directory
    fileList.SetFocus                     'and go to the file list box
End Sub
```

5. Enter this code in the fileList_MouseDown event subroutine. This code activates when the user presses a mouse button over an icon listed in the fileList box. This routine begins a drag operation.

```
Private Sub fileList_MouseDown (Button As Integer, Shift As Integer, ⇐
X As Single, Y As Single)
    fileList.Drag vbBeginDrag              'starting to drag a file from the file list box
End Sub
```

6. Enter this code in the pictIcon_DragDrop event subroutine. This code triggers when the user releases a mouse button while the drag icon is over the Icon_Display picture box. After checking to make sure that the file dragged is from the fileList file list box, this routine displays the icon.

```
Private Sub pictIcon_DragDrop (Source As Control, X As Single, Y As Single)
    If Source.Tag = "fileList" Then        'check to make sure it's a new file being dragged
        pictIcon.Picture = LoadPicture(dirlist & "\" & Source.List(Source.ListIndex))
                                           'show the icon file now
    End If
    pictIcon.DragIcon = pictIcon.Picture   'change to the picture (for the discard drag)
End Sub
```

7. Enter this code in the pictClear_DragOver event subroutine. This code activates when the user drags the Drag icon over the pictClear. When this happens, this routine terminates the drag operation and erases the icon in pictIcon picture box.

```
Private Sub pictClear_DragOver (Source As Control, X As Single, ⇐
Y As Single, State As Integer)
    Source.Drag vbEndDrag                  'stop dragging now that we've dumped the file
    pictIcon.Picture = LoadPicture()       'blank out the picture (to simulate deletion)
End Sub
```

8. Enter this code in the cmndMode_Click event subroutine. This code triggers when the user presses the cmndMode command button. The caption on the command button alternates between manual and automatic. In this way, the caption on the command button indicates the type of drag operation that will take place.

```
Private Sub cmndMode_Click ()
    If cmndMode.Caption = "&Manual" Then      'switch modes
        cmndMode.Caption = "&Automatic"       'relabel the command button
        pictIcon.DragMode = vbAutomatic       'and switch the drag mode
    Else
        cmndMode.Caption = "&Manual"          'relabel the command button
        pictIcon.DragMode = vbManual          'and switch the drag mode
    End If
End Sub
```

9. Enter this code in the cmndExit_Click event subroutine. This code activates when the user presses the command button labeled Exit. This routine closes down the Drag project.

```
Private Sub cmndExit_Click ()
    End                         'end the program
End Sub
```

How It Works

This project shows a list of the icon files available in the selected directory. The user selects a file from this list and drags it to the pictIcon picture box. When the user releases the mouse button while the dragged icon is over the pictIcon picture box, the icon of that file displays. To erase this icon from the pictIcon picture box, the user drags it to the trash can. This erases the icon from the pictIcon picture box.

The MouseDown event of the fileList file list box contains a Drag method statement. This is necessary because the DragMode property of the fileList file list is set to manual. This shows that the only way to start a drag operation when the DragMode property is set to manual is to use the Drag method. Figure 50-15 shows what the start of a drag operation looks like.

All of the controls in the Drag project start with a default setting of manual (0). When the user presses the cmndMode command button, the pictIcon picture box's DragMode property changes. The text on the command button reflects whether the picture box's property is manual or automatic. The icon displayed in the pictIcon picture box cannot be dragged to the trash can icon when the cmndMode command button reads manual. This demonstrates that a drag operation will not work without a Drag method when a control's DragMode is set to manual.

When the user drags a file from the fileList file list box, the box's DragDrop event triggers. The code for this event changes the Picture property of the pictIcon picture box to the icon image in the file that has been dragged to it. This results in the icon from the file being displayed appearing in the picture box. Figure 50-16 shows the icon loaded into pictIcon, and how the command button changes its caption when clicked.

51

KEYBOARD INPUT

The keyboard reigns supreme as the main method for entering information into computers. Alternative input devices (like mice) are quite common, and sometimes even required, but most programs use the keyboard to do the bulk of the work. The text box control in Visual Basic can handle keyboard input in most situations, but sometimes you need more direct control over keyboard input—such as when handling special keys and key combinations. For these situations, Visual Basic provides a variety of properties, events, and statements that allow you to get down to the nitty-gritty when dealing with the keyboard.

Keyboard Shortcuts

Although using the mouse to select objects on the screen is a visually intuitive method, sometimes removing a hand from the keyboard slows the user down. The Default and Cancel properties help keep the user's hands on the keyboard by linking the (ENTER) or (ESC) key to the Click event of an existing command button. When the Default property of a command button is set to True, pressing the (ENTER) key activates that button's Click event. Similarly, setting the Cancel property of a command button to True lets the user click on the button by pressing the (ESC) key. In general, it's a good idea for your application to provide keyboard alternatives to the mouse wherever possible.

Another simple way to provide keyboard shortcuts uses the Caption property of many controls. Placing an ampersand symbol (&) in front of a character in the caption underlines the character and makes it a "speed key." For instance, setting the Caption property of a command button to "&Cash" sets the caption to <u>C</u>ash and lets you press the button with (ALT)-C.

Reading the Keyboard

A keyboard can perform only two tasks. First, it can tell a program when a key is currently pressed. Second, it can tell a program when a pressed key is released. Visual Basic has three events for handling these tasks: KeyDown, KeyPress, and KeyUp. The KeyDown event activates every time any key on the keyboard is pressed down. This includes the shift-type keys (SHIFT), (CONTROL), and (ALT). The KeyPress event activates when a key corresponding to a valid ASCII character (not a shift key) is pressed and released. The KeyUp event is the inverse of the KeyDown event. It activates when any currently pressed key, including any of the shift keys, is released.

The KeyPreview property of a form lets you determine whether the form first receives keyboard events or whether the active control does. This lets you build a form-level keyboard handling routine for such things as function key shortcuts.

Finally, Visual Basic provides the SendKeys statement. This statement is used to simulate keyboard activity. It can send keystrokes to the same program that issues the statement, or to any other Windows program that is currently running. This statement can be useful for automatic program testing or (to a limited extent) communication between programs.

Table 51-1 details these elements and their purposes.

Table 51-1 Properties, events, and statements that deal with the keyboard

Use or Set This...	Type	To Do This...
Cancel	Property	Link the (ESC) key to a command button's Click event
Caption	Property	Link an (ALT)-key combination to a control's Click event
Default	Property	Link the (ENTER) key to a command button's Click event
KeyDown	Event	Intercept a keystroke when it is pressed
KeyPress	Event	Intercept an ASCII character keystroke
KeyPreview	Property	Set whether the form or active control receives keyboard events first
KeyUp	Event	Intercept a keystroke when it is released
SendKeys	Statement	Simulate keyboard input from within the program

Constant Values It is usually best to use named constants rather than numeric values when developing software. Named constants make your code more readable and easier to maintain.

Table 51-2 lists the values of the constants relevant to this chapter, mentions their names, and briefly describes what they mean. These constants can be viewed in the VB Constants module (or, in some cases, in other object libraries) using the Object Browser. It is not necessary to explicitly add these objects to your project.

Table 51-2 Constant values for keyboard handling

Value	VB Constants	Meaning
		KeyDown and KeyUp: KeyCode values
&H1	vbKeyLButton	(uncommon)
&H2	vbKeyRButton	(uncommon)
&H3	vbKeyCancel	(uncommon)
&H4	vbKeyMButton	(uncommon)

Value	VB Constants	Meaning
&H8	vbKeyBack	B
&H9	vbKeyTab	T
&HC	vbKeyClear	L
&HD	vbKeyReturn	ENTER
&H10	vbKeyShift	SHIFT
&H11	vbKeyControl	CONTROL
&H12	vbKeyMenu	ALT
&H13	vbKeyPause	PAUSE
&H14	vbKeyCapital	CAPS LOCK
&H1B	vbKeyEscape	ESC
&H20	vbKeySpace	SPACEBAR
&H21	vbKeyPrior	PAGE UP
&H22	vbKeyNext	PAGE DOWN
&H23	vbKeyEnd	END
&H24	vbKeyHome	HOME
&H25	vbKeyLeft	Left Arrow
&H26	vbKeyUp	Up Arrow
&H27	vbKeyRight	Right Arrow
&H28	vbKeyDown	Down Arrow
&H29	vbKeySelect	(uncommon)
&H2A	vbKeyPrint	PRINT SCREEN
&H2B	vbKeyExecute	(uncommon)
&H2C	vbKeySnapshot	(uncommon)
&H2D	vbKeyInsert	INSERT
&H2E	vbKeyDelete	DELETE
&H2F	vbKeyHelp	(uncommon)
	vbKeyA through vbKeyZ are the same as their ASCII equivalents: A through Z	
	vbKey0 through vbKey9 are the same as their ASCII equivalents: 0 through 9	
&H60	vbKeyNumpad0	Numeric pad 0
&H61	vbKeyNumpad1	Numeric pad 1
&H62	vbKeyNumpad2	Numeric pad 2
&H63	vbKeyNumpad3	Numeric pad 3
&H64	vbKeyNumpad4	Numeric pad 4
&H65	vbKeyNumpad5	Numeric pad 5
&H66	vbKeyNumpad6	Numeric pad 6
&H67	vbKeyNumpad7	Numeric pad 7
&H68	vbKeyNumpad8	Numeric pad 8
&H69	vbKeyNumpad9	Numeric pad 9

continued on next page

continued from previous page

Value	VB Constants	Meaning
&H6A	vbKeyMultiply	Numeric pad *
&H6B	vbKeyAdd	Numeric pad +
&H6C	vbKeySeparator	(uncommon)
&H6D	vbKeySubtract	Numeric pad -
&H6E	vbKeyDecimal	Numeric pad .
&H6F	vbKeyDivide	Numeric pad /
&H70	vbKeyF1	1
&H71	vbKeyF2	2
&H72	vbKeyF3	3
&H73	vbKeyF4	4
&H74	vbKeyF5	5
&H75	vbKeyF6	6
&H76	vbKeyF7	7
&H77	vbKeyF8	8
&H78	vbKeyF9	9
&H79	vbKeyF10	0
&H7A	vbKeyF11	!
&H7B	vbKeyF12	@
&H7C	vbKeyF13	(uncommon)
&H7D	vbKeyF14	(uncommon)
&H7E	vbKeyF15	(uncommon)
&H7F	vbKeyF16	(uncommon)
&H90	vbKeyNumlock	NUM LOCK
&H91	n/a	S

KeyDown and KeyUp: Shift values

1	vbKeyShiftMask	SHIFT key was pressed
2	vbKeyCtrlMask	CONTROL key was pressed
4	vbKeyAltMask	ALT key was pressed

CANCEL PROPERTY

Objects Affected   CommandButton

Purpose   The Cancel property enables the ESC key to execute the Click event of a command button. Use the Cancel property when one button on the form is set up to initiate a cancel action, and you want the user to be able to use the ESC key as an alternative way to cancel an action. This property can be set at design time, and set or read at runtime. Tables 51-3 and 51-4 summarize the arguments of the Cancel property.

General Syntax

```
[form!]Name.Cancel [ = boolean%]
```

Table 51-3 Arguments of the Cancel property

Argument	Description
form	Name property of the parent form
Name	Name property of the command button
boolean%	True or False

Table 51-4 Meanings of the two possible values for the Cancel property

boolean%	Meaning
True	ESC couses Click event
False	(Default) No special handling for ESC

Example Syntax

```
Private Sub Form_Load ()
     cmndClear.Cancel = True            'Links the Clear button to the Escape key
End Sub
```

Description

Sometimes it is necessary to provide the user with a command button with which to back out of, or cancel, an operation. The Cancel property allows you to assign that cancel action to the ESC key. This property can either be set to True or False by you at design time, or by the application during runtime. Because only one button on a form may be the cancel button, setting this property to True for one button automatically sets it to False for all the other buttons on the same form.

To make a button on a form the cancel button, the Cancel, Enabled, and Visible properties must all be set to True. Also, the button's parent form must be the active form on the screen. If all these conditions are met, the cancel button's Click event will trigger when the user presses the ESC key.

Although the Click event for the cancel button executes when the user presses the ESC key, the cancel button does not receive the focus. Unless the cancel button's Click event sets the focus to another control, it stays at the control that originally had the focus when the ESC key was pressed.

In the example syntax, the Cancel property of the cmndClear control is set to True. Now if the user presses the ESC key, the effect will be the same as clicking on cmndClear, except that the focus will not shift to the button.

Example	In the Keys project at the end of this chapter, the Cancel property of the cmndClear control is set to True at design time. This setting causes the cmndClear control's Click event to occur if the user presses the ⌜ESC⌟ key.
Comments	The KeyDown, KeyPress, and KeyUp events, which are usually activated when a user presses a key on the keyboard, are bypassed when the ⌜ESC⌟ key is pressed to activate a cancel button's Click event.

CAPTION PROPERTY

Objects Affected	Button, CheckBox, Column, CommandButton, Data, DBGrid, Form, Frame, Label, MDIForm, Menu, OptionButton, PropertyPage, Tab
Purpose	The Caption property sets the text displayed in or next to a control. It also sets the text displayed on a form's title bar. Use an ampersand (&) to underline a letter in a control's caption to create an ⌜ALT⌟ key shortcut for that control. Table 51-5 summarizes the arguments of the Caption property.

General Syntax

```
[form!]Name.Caption [ = text$]
```

Table 51-5 Arguments of the Caption property

Argument	Description
form	Name property of the parent form
Name	Name of the control
text$	Text to appear in the caption

Example Syntax

```
Private Sub Command1_Click()
    If Command1.Caption = "&Blue" Then
        Command1.Caption = "&Red"
    Else
        Command1.Caption = "&Blue"
    End If
End Sub
```

Description	Most controls on a form should have a keyboard shortcut that can be used to select them. Although the mouse is an intuitive input device, it's often faster to keep your hands on the keyboard. Keyboard shortcuts make your programs easier for experienced typists to use.
	The Caption property of many controls lets you set a keyboard shortcut by simply placing an ampersand symbol (&) in front of the shortcut key letter. For instance, setting a command button's Caption property to "&Red" makes the button read <u>R</u>ed and lets the user select it directly by using ⌜ALT⌟-R. Figure 51-1 shows this example.

To include an ampersand literal within a control's caption, put two ampersands together. Figure 51-2 shows the following example:

```
Command1.Caption = "Fe&dex && UPS"
```

Some controls don't have a Caption property. For these controls, place a label next to the control and set the label's caption to include the shortcut key. Make sure the label's TabIndex is set to one less than the control's. Labels can't receive the focus, so when the user presses the shortcut key combination, the Label passes the focus to the next control in the tab order. Figure 51-3 shows how to create a label for a list box, which doesn't have a Caption property itself.

Example

The Keys project at the end of this chapter sets the command button's Caption properties to include the shortcut key combinations.

Comment

A Form's Caption property sets the text that appears in its title bar. It does not have the capacity to include a shortcut key. Placing an ampersand in the Caption does not underline the following letter; it just includes the ampersand as a literal character.

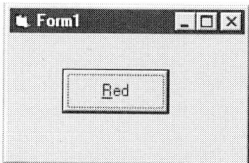

Figure 51-1   Example syntax sets the Caption to "&Red"

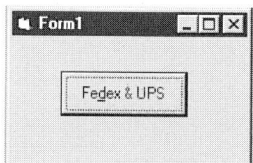

Figure 51-2   Example shows how to include
an ampersand as a literal character

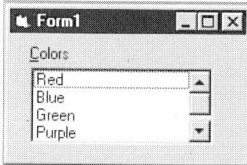

Figure 51-3   Label used to create a shortcut key for
the list box, which doesn't have any Caption property

If you need to put an ampersand in the controls which interpret ampersands in the captions as shortcut keys, you must specify two ampersands
in the string. For example, if you want a command button's caption to be
"Nuts & Bolts," you should set the caption to be "Nuts && Bolts."

DEFAULT PROPERTY

Objects Affected   CommandButton

Purpose   The Default property enables the (ENTER) key to execute the Click event of a
command button. This is used when one button on the form will initiate a
default action, and you want the user to be able to press the (ENTER) key as
an alternative way to say, "Okay, do it." This property can be set at design
time and set or read at runtime. Tables 51-6 and 51-7 summarize the
arguments of the Default property.

General Syntax

```
[form!]Name.Default [ = boolean%]
```

Table 51-6 Arguments of the Default property

Argument	Description
form	Name property of the parent form
Name	Name of the command button
boolean%	True or False

Table 51-7 Meanings of the two possible values for the Default property

boolean%	Meaning
True	(ENTER) causes Click event
False	(Default) No special handling for (ENTER)

Example Syntax

```
Private Sub Form_Load ()
    OkButton.Default = True          'links the OkButton to the Enter key
End Sub
```

Description   In most cases, a form has one command button that is used to perform the
default action for that form. The Default property allows you to assign that
default action to the (ENTER) key. This property can be set to True or False
either by you at design time or by the application during runtime. Because
only one button on a form may be the default, setting this property to True

for one button automatically sets it to False for all the other buttons on the same form.

To make a button on a form the default, the Default, Enabled, and Visible properties must all be set to True. Also, the button's parent form must be the active form on the screen. If all these conditions are met, and no other button currently has the focus, the default button's Click event will execute when the user hits the (ENTER) key.

Although the Click event for the default button executes, the focus is not shifted to the default button when the user presses the (ENTER) key. Unless the default button's Click event sets the focus to another control, it stays at the control that originally had the focus when the (ENTER) key was pressed.

The example syntax sets the Default property of the OK button to True. Pressing (ENTER) will now be equivalent to clicking on the OK button, except the focus will not shift to the button.

Example

In the Keys project at the end of this chapter, the Default property of the cmndSend control is set to True at design time. This setting causes the cmndSend control's Click event to occur if the user presses the (ENTER) key.

Comments

The KeyDown, KeyPress, and KeyUp events, which are usually activated when a user presses a key on the keyboard, are bypassed when the (ENTER) key is pressed to activate a default button's Click event.

KEYDOWN EVENT

Objects Affected

CheckBox, ComboBox, CommandButton, DBCombo, DBGrid, DBList, DirListBox, DriveListBox, FileListBox, Form, Grid, HScrollBar, ListBox, ListView, OLE Container, OptionButton, PictureBox, PropertyPage, Slider, TabStrip, TextBox, TreeView, UserControl, UserDocument, VScrollBar

Purpose

Use the KeyDown event for low-level keyboard handling. It reports the current status of the keyboard when a key is pressed and this event's control has the focus. The arguments of the KeyDown event are summarized in Tables 51-8, 51-9, and 51-10.

General Syntax

```
Sub Form_KeyDown (KeyCode As Integer, Shift As Integer)
Sub Name_KeyDown ([Index As Integer, ] KeyCode As Integer, Shift As Integer)
```

Table 51-8 Arguments of the KeyDown event

Argument	Description
Form	'Form' for the parent form
Name	Name of the control

continued on next page

continued from previous page

Argument	Description
Index	Uniquely identifies an element of a control array
KeyCode	Integer variable returning the scan code of the key pressed
Shift	Integer variable indicating the status of the CONTROL, ALT, and SHIFT keys

Table 51-9 Meanings of the KeyCode values in the KeyDown event

KeyCode	VB.Constants	Meaning
&H1	vbKeyLButton	(uncommon)
&H2	vbKeyRButton	(uncommon)
&H3	vbKeyCancel	(uncommon)
&H4	vbKeyMButton	(uncommon)
&H8	vbKeyBack	B
&H9	vbKeyTab	T
&HC	vbKeyClear	L
&HD	vbKeyReturn	ENTER
&H10	vbKeyShift	SHIFT
&H11	vbKeyControl	CONTROL
&H12	vbKeyMenu	ALT
&H13	vbKeyPause	PAUSE
&H14	vbKeyCapital	CAPS LOCK
&H1B	vbKeyEscape	ESC
&H20	vbKeySpace	SPACEBAR
&H21	vbKeyPrior	PAGE UP
&H22	vbKeyNext	PAGE DOWN
&H23	vbKeyEnd	END
&H24	vbKeyHome	HOME
&H25	vbKeyLeft	←
&H26	vbKeyUp	↑
&H27	vbKeyRight	→
&H28	vbKeyDown	↓
&H29	vbKeySelect	(uncommon)
&H2A	vbKeyPrint	PRINT SCREEN
&H2B	vbKeyExecute	(uncommon)
&H2C	vbKeySnapshot	(uncommon)
&H2D	vbKeyInsert	INSERT
&H2E	vbKeyDelete	DELETE
&H2F	vbKeyHelp	(uncommon)

KeyCode	VB.Constants	Meaning
	vbKeyA through vbKeyZ are the same as their ASCII equivalents: A through Z	
	vbKey0 through vbKey9 are the same as their ASCII equivalents: 0 through 9	
&H60	vbKeyNumpad0	Numeric pad 0
&H61	vbKeyNumpad1	Numeric pad 1
&H62	vbKeyNumpad2	Numeric pad 2
&H63	vbKeyNumpad3	Numeric pad 3
&H64	vbKeyNumpad4	Numeric pad 4
&H65	vbKeyNumpad5	Numeric pad 5
&H66	vbKeyNumpad6	Numeric pad 6
&H67	vbKeyNumpad7	Numeric pad 7
&H68	vbKeyNumpad8	Numeric pad 8
&H69	vbKeyNumpad9	Numeric pad 9
&H6A	vbKeyMultiply	Numeric pad *
&H6B	vbKeyAdd	Numeric pad +
&H6C	vbKeySeparator	(uncommon)
&H6D	vbKeySubtract	Numeric pad -
&H6E	vbKeyDecimal	Numeric pad .
&H6F	vbKeyDivide	Numeric pad /
&H70	vbKeyF1	1
&H71	vbKeyF2	2
&H72	vbKeyF3	3
&H73	vbKeyF4	4
&H74	vbKeyF5	5
&H75	vbKeyF6	6
&H76	vbKeyF7	7
&H77	vbKeyF8	8
&H78	vbKeyF9	9
&H79	vbKeyF10	0
&H7A	vbKeyF11	!
&H7B	vbKeyF12	@
&H7C	vbKeyF13	(uncommon
&H7D	vbKeyF14	(uncommon)
&H7E	vbKeyF15	(uncommon)
&H7F	vbKeyF16	(uncommon)
&H90	vbKeyNumlock	NUM LOCK
&H91	n/a	S

Table 51-10 Meanings of the Shift values in the KeyDown event

Shift	VB.Constants	Meaning
1	vbShiftMask	SHIFT key was pressed.
2	vbCtrlMask	CONTROL key was pressed.
4	vbAltMask	ALT key was pressed.

Example Syntax

```
Private Sub Form_KeyDown (KeyCode As Integer, Shift As Integer)
    Beep                        'beep any time a user tries to type on an empty form
End Sub

Private Sub Text1_KeyDown (Index As Integer, KeyCode As Integer, Shift As Integer)
    Dim AltOn As Integer
    Dim CtrlOn As Integer
    Dim ShiftOn As Integer
    If Shift And vbAltMask Then AltOn = 1       'if one of the shift keys
    If Shift And vbCtrlMask Then CtrlOn = 1     'is on, turn on its corresponding
    If Shift And vbShiftMask Then ShiftOn = 1   'check box
    Alt_Check.Value = AltOn
    Ctrl_Check.Value = CtrlOn
    Shift_Check.Value = ShiftOn
End Sub
```

Description

Each time a user presses a key on the keyboard, including the SHIFT, CONTROL, or ALT key, the KeyDown event triggers the control that currently has the focus. Forms also have a KeyDown event, but it will occur only if the form contains no active controls or if the form's KeyPreview property is set to True (-1).

This event lets the program react to the user pressing function keys 1 through 12, or any unusual key combinations such as CONTROL-SHIFT, because it processes all keys, not just character keys. This event supplies two arguments, KeyCode and Shift, that tell the program which key or keys pressed caused the event to occur.

The KeyCode argument supplies a number that uniquely identifies the key pressed. This number corresponds to the physical key on the keyboard, not the character that the key generates. For instance, if the user holds down the SHIFT key and presses A, the KeyCode argument will contain the same value as when the user presses the A key alone, even though the character generated will be different.

The Shift argument is an integer variable that indicates the status of the SHIFT, ALT, and CONTROL keys at the time the event was called. Each of the three special shift keys is assigned a value: 1 for SHIFT, 2 for CONTROL, and 4 for ALT. When any of these keys is pressed, its value is added to the Shift argument. The easiest way to test the Shift argument is with logical (bitwise) operators. Table 51-11 lists logical equations that return a nonzero value if a certain shift key is pressed.

Table 51-11 Logical equations for testing the Shift status

When the...	Will Return Nonzero	Constant
SHIFT key is pressed	(Shift and 1)	(Shift and vbShiftMask)
CONTROL key is pressed	(Shift and 2)	(Shift and vbCtrlMask)
ALT key is pressed	(Shift and 4)	(Shift and vbAltMask)

Keep in mind that this event is called when any key on the keyboard is pressed. Therefore, if the user presses any shift key combination, the event occurs for as many keys as are in the combination. For instance, if the user presses CONTROL-SHIFT-A, this event will occur three times. The first time, the KeyCode argument will be 11 (the code for the CONTROL key) and the Shift argument will be 2 (the shift code for CONTROL). The second time, KeyCode will be 10 (the code for the SHIFT key) and the Shift argument will be 3 (the shift code for CONTROL plus the shift code for SHIFT). Finally, on the third call, KeyCode will be 41 (the code for the A key) and the Shift argument will again be 3.

The first example syntax produces a beep whenever a key is pressed. The second example syntax uses the logical relationships in Table 51-11 to store the status of the ALT, CONTROL, and SHIFT keys in variables.

Control Array
The Index argument is only used if the related control is part of a control array. This Index specifies which element of the array is the one that activated the event. When referencing the control, the element being referenced must be specified by placing the index number between parentheses just after the control name and before the property name (for example, Name(Index).Property).

Example
In the Keys project at the end of this chapter, the KeyDown event is used to count the number of times a key is pressed. It is also used to set the values of the check boxes that indicate whether the ALT, CONTROL, and SHIFT keys are pressed.

Comments
Pressing and holding a key down will cause this event to be activated repeatedly until the key is released.

KEYPRESS EVENT

Objects Affected
CheckBox, ComboBox, CommandButton, DBCombo, DBGrid, DBList, DirListBox, DriveListBox, FileListBox, Form, Grid, HScrollBar, ListBox, ListView, OLE Container, OptionButton, PictureBox, PropertyPage, Slider, TabStrip, TextBox, TreeView, UserControl, UserDocument, VScrollBar

Purpose
The KeyPress event intercepts ASCII keystrokes when this event's control has the focus. This lets the program audit the user's input byte by byte. This can be useful for validating data input and alerting the user as soon as

an invalid character is entered. Table 51-12 summarizes the arguments of the KeyPress event.

General Syntax

```
Form_KeyPress(KeyAscii As Integer)
Name_KeyPress([Index As Integer], KeyAscii As Integer)
```

Table 51-12 Arguments of the KeyPress event

Argument	Description
form	'Form' for the parent form
Name	Name of the control
Index	Uniquely identifies an element of a control array
KeyAscii	An integer number representing the ASCII code of the character whose key was pressed

Example Syntax

```
Text1_KeyPress(Index As Integer, KeyAscii As Integer)
      Char = Chr(KeyAscii)            'change the code to a character
      Char = UCase(Char)             'change the character to uppercase
      KeyAscii = Asc(Char)           'replace the character code
End Sub
```

Description   The object with the focus receives this event every time the user presses a key that corresponds to a valid ASCII character. Visual Basic considers the following as valid ASCII keystrokes, as summarized in Table 51-13:

Table 51-13 Possible values for the KeyAscii argument

Valid Character	KeyAscii Code
Any printable keyboard character	ASCII code of the character
CONTROL-A through CONTROL-Z	1 through 26
ENTER and CONTROL-ENTER	13 and 10
BACKSPACE and CONTROL-BACKSPACE	8 and 127
TAB	9

Define the KeyPress event, starting with the name of the affected control and an Index variable (if using a control array). If the value of KeyAscii is modified within this event, the modification is passed on to the control. This allows you to audit the text being entered. For instance, if you only want uppercase letters to be entered in a text box, you can use the KeyPress event for that control to change each character to uppercase as it's entered. This is done in the example syntax by first getting the character code from the KeyAscii event by applying BASIC's Chr function, then using the BASIC UCase function to change the character to its uppercase equivalent. Finally, assigning the uppercase character back to the KeyAscii event changes the character just entered to uppercase (if it had been lowercase).

Note that KeyPress does not process keystrokes at as low a level as KeyDown and KeyUp. It only processes the printable characters, the control characters, and a very few special keystrokes. It does not process function keys, navigation keys, and any modifications of this with the shift modifiers. It also differentiates between upper- and lowercase printable characters. Thus KeyPress processes "a" as ASCII 97 (lowercase a); KeyDown would process this as Shift=1 and ASCII 65 (the SHIFT key, then uppercase A) in two separate triggerings of the event.

Control Array   The Index argument is used only if the related control is part of a control array. This Index specifies which element of the array is the one that activated the event. When referencing the control, the element being referenced must be specified by placing the index number between parentheses just after the control name and before the property name (for example, Name(Index).Property).

Example   In the Keys project at the end of this chapter, the KeyPress event is used to change any lowercase input to uppercase.

KEYPREVIEW PROPERTY

Objects Affected   Form, PropertyPage, UserControl, UserDocument

Purpose   Forms normally do not receive the KeyDown, KeyPress, and KeyUp events. Turning the form's KeyPreview property to True makes the form process these events before any active control on the form gets them. This lets you perform form-level keyboard processing for tasks such as function or status key checking. Tables 51-14 and 51-15 give the details for KeyPreview.

General Syntax

```
[form!]KeyPreview [ = boolean%]
```

Table 51-14 Arguments of the KeyPreview property

Argument	Description
form	Name property of the parent form
boolean%	True or False

Table 51-15 The two possible settings for KeyPreview

Value	Meaning
True	Form receives keyboard events first, then the active control.
False	(Default) Active control receives keyboard events.

Example Syntax

```
Private Sub Form_Load()
      KeyPreview = True              'set the form-level keyboard event handler to On
End Sub
```

Description   Turn the KeyPreview property to True when you want to have form-level keyboard event handling. This may be useful if you want to check for and process special keys like ① through @, ①, SHIFT, or S before they get passed to an individual control.

KeyPreview defaults to False. This means that the form doesn't receive the KeyDown, KeyUp, and KeyPress events. Setting KeyPreview to True makes the form intercept the keystrokes first. After processing the keystrokes in the form's KeyDown, KeyUp, and KeyPress events, the appropriate event in the active control then triggers, allowing for further, more specific processing at the control level.

If you want the form to capture all keystrokes and disable any control from generating the Key events, set KeyAscii to 0 in the form's KeyPress event and set KeyCode to 0 in the form's KeyDown event. This prevents the Key events from passing through to the controls.

Example   The example project at the end of the chapter uses the form's KeyPreview to check and display the status of the SHIFT, CONTROL, and ALT keys.

Comment   If there are no visible and enabled controls on a form, the form automatically receives all keyboard events, no matter what the setting of KeyPreview.

KeyUp Event

Objects Affected   CheckBox, ComboBox, CommandButton, DBCombo, DBGrid, DBList, DirListBox, DriveListBox, FileListBox, Form, Grid, HScrollBar, ListBox, ListView, OLE Container, OptionButton, PictureBox, PropertyPage, Slider, TabStrip, TextBox, TreeView, UserControl, UserDocument, VScrollBar

Purpose   The KeyUp event is used for low-level keyboard handling. It reports the current status of the keyboard when a key is released and this event's control has the focus. Tables 51-16, 51-17, and 51-18 summarize the arguments of the KeyUp event.

General Syntax

```
Sub Form_KeyUp (KeyCode As Integer, Shift As Integer)
Sub Name_KeyUp ([Index As Integer, ]KeyCode As Integer, Shift As Integer)
```

Table 51-16 Arguments of the KeyUp event

Argument	Description
Form	'Form' for the parent form
Name	Name of the control
Index	Uniquely identifies an element of a control array
KeyCode	An integer number representing the scan code of the key released
Shift	An integer number indicating the status of the CONTROL, ALT, and SHIFT keys

Table 51-17 Meanings of the KeyCode argument in KeyUp are the same as for KeyDown

KeyCode	VB.Constants	Meaning
See Table 51-9 in the KeyDown entry		

Table 51-18 Meanings of the Shift values in the KeyUp event

Shift	VB.Constants	Meaning
1	vbShiftMask	SHIFT key was pressed.
2	vbCtrlMask	CONTROL key was pressed.
4	vbAltMask	ALT key was pressed.

Example Syntax

```
Private Sub Form_KeyUp (KeyCode As Integer, Shift As Integer)
    Beep                          'beep any time a user tries to type on an empty form
End Sub

Private Sub Text1_KeyUp (KeyCode As Integer, Shift As Integer)
    Label1.Caption = Format$(KeyCode, "###")      'show last key released
End Sub
```

Description   This is the complement to the KeyDown event. Every time a user releases a pressed key on the keyboard, including the SHIFT, CONTROL, or ALT keys, the object that currently has the focus receives this event. Before this event occurs, a KeyDown event will occur at least once, with an identical KeyCode value. Where the KeyDown event may be executed several times when a user holds a key down, the KeyUp event is only executed once per keystroke, when the user releases the key. This makes this event perfect for low-level keyboard handlers when you wish to disable the automatic repetition of keys on the keyboard.

The KeyCode argument returns a number that uniquely identifies the key released. This number corresponds to the physical key on the keyboard, not the character that the key generates. For instance, if the user holds down the [SHIFT] key and then presses and releases [A], the KeyCode argument will contain the same value as when the user presses and releases the [A] key alone, even though the character generated will be different.

The Shift argument is an integer variable that indicates the status of the [SHIFT], [ALT], and [CONTROL] keys at the time the event was called. Each shift key is assigned a value: 1 for [SHIFT], 2 for [CONTROL], and 4 for [ALT]. When any of these keys is pressed, its value is added to the Shift argument. The easiest way to test the Shift argument is with logical (bitwise) operators. See Table 51-11 in the entry for KeyDown for more information on testing the value of the Shift argument.

Keep in mind that the KeyUp event is called when any key on the keyboard is released. Therefore, if the user presses and then releases any [SHIFT]-key combination, the event occurs for as many keys as are in the combination. For instance, if the user presses [CONTROL]-[SHIFT]-[A], and then releases them in reverse order, the KeyUp event will occur three times. The first time, KeyCode will be 41 (the code for the [A] key), and Shift will be 3 (the shift code for [CONTROL] plus the shift code for [SHIFT]). The second time KeyCode will be 10 (the code for the [SHIFT] key), and the Shift argument will again be 3. Finally, on the third call, the KeyCode argument will be 11 (the code for the [CONTROL] key), and the Shift argument will be 2 (the shift code for [CONTROL]).

The first example syntax simply beeps when any key is released. The second example syntax formats the KeyCode for the key just released and displays it by assigning it to the control's Caption property.

Control Array

The Index argument is only used if the related control is part of a control array. This index specifies which element of the array activated the event. When referencing the control, the element being referenced must be specified by placing the index number between parentheses just after the control name and before the property name (for example, Name(Index).Property).

Example

In the Keys project at the end of this chapter, the Key_Up event is used to count the number of times a key is released. It is also used to set the values of the check boxes that indicate whether the [ALT], [CONTROL], and [SHIFT] keys were pressed.

Comments

The only time a form receives the KeyUp event is when either its KeyPreview property is set to True or there are no visible and enabled controls on the form.

SENDKEYS STATEMENT

Purpose   The SendKeys statement allows your program to simulate keyboard input. The keystrokes created by the program go to whatever application is running in the active window. Only Windows programs can receive these characters. This statement is very useful for controlling a program that does not support DDE (Dynamic Data Exchange) and can also be used to test programs automatically with sample input. Table 51-19 summarizes the arguments of the SendKeys statement.

General Syntax

```
SendKeys Keystrokes$[, Pause%]
```

Table 51-19 Arguments of the SendKeys statement

Argument	Description
Keystrokes$	A string of keystrokes and commands that simulates keystrokes
Pause%	A True (-1) or False (0) value indicating whether to wait for the keystrokes to be processed before continuing

Example Syntax

```
Private Sub Command1_Click ()
     AppActivate "NotePad - (untitled)"          'activate notepad
     SendKeys "This is simulated keyboard input{ENTER}", True
End Sub
```

Description   The Keystrokes$ argument specifies the keyboard characters being sent and must be a string expression. When used in the Keystrokes$ argument, Visual Basic assigns special meanings to certain characters, as shown in Table 51-20.

Table 51-20 Special characters and their meanings with the SendKeys statement

Character	Meaning
%	ALT key—the string "%F" generates ALT-F; "%(ABC)" is ALT-A-ALT-B-ALT-C.
^	CONTROL key—the string "^C" generates CONTROL-C; "^(AB)" is CONTROL-A-CONTROL-B.
+	SHIFT key—the string "+D" generates SHIFT-D: "+(AB)" is SHIFT-A-SHIFT-B.
{	Beginning of a special code.
}	Ending of a special code.
~	ENTER key—same as {Enter}.
()	Parentheses group characters that are being SHIFTed, ALTed, and CTRLed.
[]	Braces cause an "Illegal function call"; use {[}and {]} if you wish to send them.

If you wish to send any of the characters that have a special meaning, you need to place braces around the character. For instance, if you wish to send the addition sign, you need to specify this string: "{+}"

Nonprintable keystrokes (such as function keys) may be sent by using one of the symbolic codes listed in Table 51-21.

Table 51-21 Nonprintable keystroke codes for the SendKeys statement

Nonprintable keystroke

{BACKSPACE}	{BKSP} (for backspace)	{BS} (for backspace)
{BREAK}	{CAPSLOCK}	{DELETE}{DEL} (for delete)
{DOWN} (down arrow)	{END}	{ENTER} or ~
{ESCAPE} or {ESC}	{HELP}	{HOME}
{INSERT}	{LEFT} (left arrow)	{NUMLOCK}
{PGDN} (page down)	{PGUP} (page up)	{PRTSC} (print screen)
{RIGHT} (right arrow)	{SCROLLOCK}	{TAB}
(UP) (up arrow)	{F1} (function key)	{F2} (function key)
{F3} (function key)	{F4} (function key)	{F5} (function key)
{F6} (function key)	{F7} (function key)	{F8} (function key)
{F9} (function key)	{F10} (function key)	{F11} (function key)
{F12} (function key)	{F13} (function key)	{F14} (function key)
{F15} (function key)	{F16} (function key)	

You can also specify that a character be repeated by placing the character and a number specifying the number of repetitions together inside braces. For instance, in the following examples, the {RIGHT} code and the character "A" are both sent 25 times:

```
SendKeys {Right 25}
SendKeys {A 25}
```

The Pause% argument is a Boolean value that specifies whether to wait for the program to process the characters. This has an effect only if the program receiving the keystrokes is not the one issuing the SendKeys statement. If the value of Pause% is True, the next statement in the sending program will not be executed until the receiving program has processed the characters. If Pause% is False, or omitted, execution continues as soon as the keystrokes are sent.

The example syntax shows one way to put specified characters into the Notepad application. Notice that the focus must first be set to the Notepad using AppActivate so that the string used with the SendKeys statement is sent there as input. See Chapter 54,"Application Focus," for more information about AppActivate.

SendKeys and Non-GUI Programs	SendKeys does not work with non-GUI (for example, DOS) programs, only Windows programs. If you try to use SendKeys to send keystrokes to the non-GUI application, you'll notice that it never receives them. That's because SendKeys doesn't send the keystrokes to the non-GUI application; it sends them to the DOS window in which the application is running.

Although this is rarely mentioned in any other books or references, you can get around some of the limitations of SendKeys not working with non-GUI applications. Set the string you'd like to send on to the Clipboard. (See Chapter 53, "Using the Clipboard," for more details on how to do this.) Set the focus to the DOS window your application is running in using AppActivate (see Chapter 54). Then use SendKeys to pull down the DOS window's control menu and use Edit Paste:

```
SendKeys "% ep"
```

This pastes the text into the DOS application. You can use this same idea to Edit Mark and Edit Copy the DOS window's screen onto the Clipboard for parsing and processing by your Visual Basic application. This lets you establish a crude two-way communication between your Windows application and the non-GUI application.

Example	In the Keys project at the end of this chapter, the cmndSend_Click event uses the SendKeys statement to send text to the Windows Notepad program. The first SendKeys statement sends an ALT-SPACE-X combination to open the Notepad's control box and maximize its window. Then the text in the text box of the Keys project form is sent to the Notepad.
Comments	If the program in the active window is the one sending the keystrokes, it will also be the one receiving the keystrokes. When this is the case, the Pause% argument has no effect. Therefore, it is generally a good idea to follow each SendKeys statement with a DoEvents() function call so the program can process the keystrokes.

The Keys Project

Project Overview

The Keys project explores the use of the properties, events, and statements covered in this chapter. Each of these is used at least once in the following project. By following the examples here, you should develop a good understanding of the subjects covered in this chapter.

Assembling the Project

1. Create a new form and place the following controls on it. Use Table 51-22 to set the properties of the form and each control.

Table 51-22 Controls and property settings for the Keys project

Object	Property	Setting
Form	BorderStyle	3—Fixed dialog
	Caption	Keys Project
	KeyPreview	True
	Name	formMain
CheckBox	Caption	&Uppercase
	Name	chekUpper
CommandButton	Caption	Send
	Default	True
	Name	cmndSend
CommandButton	Caption	Clear
	Cancel	True
	Name	cmndClear
CommandButton	Caption	E&xit
	Name	cmndExit
Label	Caption	Alt
	Name	lablAlt
	Visible	False
Label	Caption	Ctrl
	Name	lablCtrl
	Visible	False
Label	Caption	Shift
	Name	lablShift
	Visible	False
Label	BorderStyle	1—Fixed single
	Caption	Keys Pressed:
	Name	Label1
Label	BorderStyle	1—Fixed single
	Caption	Keys Released:
	Name	Label2
Label	BorderStyle	1—Fixed single
	Caption	Key Code:
	Name	Label3
Label	Alignment	1—Right justify
	BorderStyle	1—Fixed single
	Caption	
	Name	lablKeyDown

Object	Property	Setting
Label	Alignment	1–Right justify
	BorderStyle	1–Fixed single
	Caption	0
	Name	lablKeyUp
Label	Alignment	1–Right justify
	BorderStyle	1–Fixed single
	Caption	0
	Name	lablKeyCode
Text	Name	textBox
	MultiLine	True
	Text	
	ScrollBars	2–Vertical

2. Check the appearance of your form against Figure 51-4.

3. Enter the following code into the General Declarations area of formMain.

```
Const CHECKED = 1          'to read status of check box
```

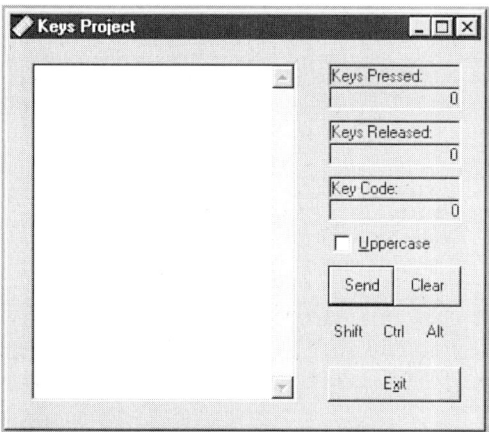

Figure 51-4 The finished Keys form

4. Enter the following code into the textBox_KeyDown event. This routine counts the number of keypresses and displays the key code of the key pressed. In addition, it displays the appropriate SHIFT, ALT, and CTRL status labels.

```
Private Sub textBox_KeyDown(KeyCode As Integer, Shift As Integer)
    Static KeysPressed As Long                'remembers how many keys pressed

    KeysPressed = KeysPressed + 1                'count total of keys pressed
    lablKeyDown.Caption = Format$(KeysPressed, "########0")    'and update the display
    lablKeyCode.Caption = Hex$(KeyCode)

    If Shift And vbShiftMask Then lablShift.Visible = True
    If Shift And vbAltMask Then lablAlt.Visible = True
    If Shift And vbCtrlMask Then lablCtrl.Visible = True
End Sub
```

5. Enter the following code into the textBox_KeyUp event. This routine counts the number of key releases. In addition, it hides the appropriate SHIFT, ALT, and CTRL status labels.

```
Private Sub textBox_KeyUp(KeyCode As Integer, Shift As Integer)
    Static KeysReleased                       'remembers number of keys released

    KeysReleased = KeysReleased + 1            'count keys released
    lablKeyUp.Caption = Format$(KeysReleased, "########0")   'and update display

    If Not (Shift And vbShiftMask) Then lablShift.Visible = False
    If Not (Shift And vbAltMask) Then lablAlt.Visible = False
    If Not (Shift And vbCtrlMask) Then lablCtrl.Visible = False
End Sub
```

6. Enter the following code into the textBox_KeyPress event. This event converts each character that is typed in the textBox text box to an uppercase character if the chekUpper check box is checked.

```
Private Sub textBox_KeyPress (KeyAscii As Integer)
    If chekUpper.Value = CHECKED Then    'if caps lock is checked,
        Char = UCase$(Chr$(KeyAscii))    '...then convert the keystroke to uppercase
        KeyAscii = Asc(Char)             '...and change it before it gets to the text box
    End If
End Sub
```

7. Enter the following code into the chekUpper_Click event. This simply sets the focus back to the text entry box.

```
Private Sub chekUpper_Click ()
    textBox.SetFocus                'back to the text box for more entry
End Sub
```

8. Enter the following code into the cmndClear_Click event. This event will clear the text to a null string.

```
Private Sub cmndClear_Click ()
    textBox.Text = ""                'blank out text box
    textBox.SetFocus                 'back to the text box for more entry
End Sub
```

9. Enter the following code into the cmndSend_Click event. This event sends text to the Notepad program. It first tries to activate the program. If the Notepad program is not currently running, an error generates, and the error-handling routine will execute it. Otherwise, an [ALT]-[SPACE]-[X] key sequence is sent to the program, thereby maximizing it. The text from textBox is then sent to the Notepad, and the program waits for the Notepad to process it.

```
Private Sub cmndSend_Click()
    On Error GoTo Load_Notepad        'can't activate? then load it
    AppActivate "Untitled - Notepad"  'activate Notepad
    On Error GoTo 0                   'successful activation
    SendKeys "%{ }x"                  'maximize Notepad
    SendKeys textBox.Text, True       'send it contents of text box
Exit Sub

Load_Notepad:                         'need to load Notepad
    Shell ("Notepad.exe")             '...load Notepad
Resume                                'go back and activate Notepad
End Sub
```

10. Enter the following code in the cmndExit_Click event. This ends the program.

```
Private Sub cmndExit_Click ()
    End                      'end the program
End Sub
```

How It Works

This project demonstrates each of the ways of handling keyboard input. Figure 51-5 shows what the project looks like when running. Note that the text varies from lowercase to uppercase, the number of keys pressed exceeds the keys released, and the [CONTROL] indicator is highlighted.

We first set some properties during the design phase that will assist us in processing the keyboard while running. We set the form's KeyPreview to True to allow us to check for the [SHIFT] key status. We also set the Send button's Default property to True and the Clear button's Cancel property to False to allow [ENTER] and [ESC] to trigger these two buttons. Finally, we set the chekUpper check box's and cmndExit's Caption properties to include a hot-key combination.

All keystrokes are first processed by the form because we set the KeyPreview property to True. The form's KeyDown and KeyUp events check on the status for the [SHIFT], [CONTROL], and [ALT] keys. They then set the Visible properties of the appropriate labels to show the Shift status to the user.

Once a keystroke gets through the form's keystroke handlers, it then is processed by textBox's KeyDown handler. This updates the lablKeyDown and lablKeyCode labels. The KeyPressed handler is next. This checks to see if Uppercase is checked, and if so, makes the text uppercase. Finally, the KeyUp handler updates lablKeyUp's display.

The Send button calls up the Notepad application and uses SendKeys to maximize Notepad (using Notepad's control box) and then "types" the text from textBox.

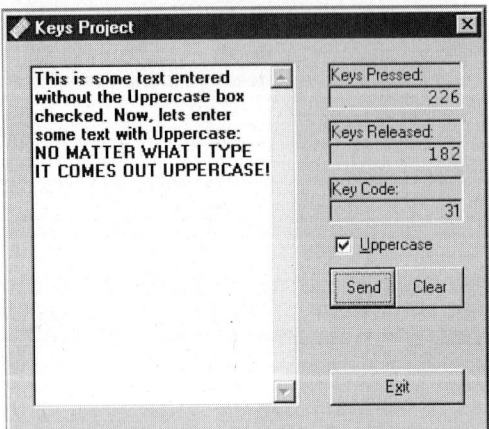

Figure 51-5 The Keys project in action

52

PRINTING

Many programs need the capability to create some sort of printed output. Because the Windows environment (rather than individual applications) handles all printer output, Visual Basic provides the predefined Printer object. This object sends printer output commands from your program to the Windows routines, which in turn send the output to the printer.

In other environments (such as QuickBASIC on DOS), the printer is usually treated as a sequential output device. Once an item is written to the printer, the print position advances and there can be no going back. With Visual Basic, however, this is not true.

You can think of the Printer object as a form that cannot be viewed until the Visual Basic program tells Windows to print it. This "form" represents one page of printed output. In most cases, until your program instructs Windows to print it, anything can be done to a page of printer output. This allows the program to move the print position anywhere on a page, regardless of where it currently resides. Although printing is one of the most challenging aspects of writing Windows programs, the Printer object makes outputting graphics and special printing effects to the printer comparatively easy.

Coordinate Systems

To control the placement of text and graphics on the printer page, the Printer object uses a coordinate system in the same manner as a form. (Coordinates for forms and controls are discussed in Chapter 36, "Forms and Menus," which makes good background reading for this chapter.) The only difference between a form's coordinate system and that of the Printer object is that the height and width of the Printer object's page is fixed as long as it represents the same model of printer.

Any point on the printer page can be referred to by specifying that point's position in the format X, Y, where X is the horizontal position, and Y is the vertical position. The coordinates of the upper-left corner of the printer page can be determined by reading the values of the Printer object's ScaleTop and ScaleLeft properties. Usually, these properties are set to 0 (meaning the upper-left corner is coordinate 0, 0). However, you are allowed to set up your own coordinate system, and in doing so to assign different values to these properties.

The coordinates for the bottom-right corner can be determined by reading the Printer object's ScaleHeight and ScaleWidth properties. These properties return the height and width of the usable page area. The ScaleMode property determines the unit of measurement that is used for the values returned by the ScaleHeight and ScaleWidth properties. It also determines the unit of measurement that is used for the coordinate system of the printer page. By default, the ScaleMode property is set to twips. A twip is equal to 1/1440 of an inch. However, the ScaleMode property can be set to several other types of measurement. Chapter 37, "The Coordinate System," covers the ScaleMode settings and measurement systems in detail.

When a method executes on the Printer object, the placement of output on the page is determined by either the coordinates specified in the method, or by the coordinates of the current print position. You can use the CurrentX and CurrentY properties of the Printer object to read or set the current print position on the page. CurrentX represents the horizontal position, while CurrentY represents the vertical position. Again, both of these properties take values that represent the unit of measurement specified by the ScaleMode property.

Methods and Properties

When creating a printed document, your application works one page at a time. All the output for a specific page is first set up with many of the same methods that work on a form, including the Circle, Line, Print, PSet, TextHeight, and TextWidth methods. (Chapter 40, "Drawing Shapes," discusses graphics methods such as Circle and Line. Chapter 45, "Fonts," discusses methods for scaling text.) These methods work exactly as they do on a form, but, for noncolor printers, any color parameters are ignored and the output is always black.

Visual Basic keeps track of the current page number via the Page property, which is specific to the Printer object. Each time a new page is generated, the value of this property is incremented. You can use this property to place page numbers on your printed output.

The NewPage method generates a new page. This method ends output to the current page and saves the page's image in memory. NewPage then increments the value of the Page property and begins a new, blank page. When your program has finished generating its printer output, it needs to send the output to the Windows printing routines. The EndDoc method sends all the printer pages that have been saved in memory to the Windows printing routines and then clears them from memory. Also, if any methods have been executed on the Printer object since the last NewPage method was executed, EndDoc automatically generates a new page. To terminate output immediately, use the KillDoc method. As your output is being sent to memory, KillDoc triggers the Printer object to cancel the current print job before it is completed.

When outputting text to the printer, you can change font styles and size with the Font... properties. These properties and their uses are covered in detail in Chapter 45.

As in previous versions, the PictureBox control can be used to display text written with the Print method. This is a handy way to do a print preview.

Through the Printer object provided by Visual Basic 5.0, you can communicate with the system printer you are currently assigned to. The DeviceName property returns the name of the printer you are currently using. This is usually the default system printer unless you decide to change it. To find out which printer driver you are using, use the DriverName property. The Port property tells you which system printer port you are currently assigned to. Using this property, you can change the port destination. The Orientation property allows you to tell the printer whether to output in landscape or portrait. The Copies property allows you specify the number of copies to be printed.

Table 52-1 details the methods and properties that affect the operation of the Printer object (although not all are discussed in this chapter).

Table 52-1 Methods and properties that affect the Printer object

Use or Set This...	Type	To Do This...
Circle	Method	Generate a circle on the current page
ColorMode	Property	Set or return the value to the Windows printer routines either output in color or monochrome, depending on the printer
Copies	Property	Set or return the number of copies to print
CurrentX	Property	Set or return the current horizontal print position
CurrentY	Property	Set or return the current vertical print position
DeviceName	Property	Return the name of the device the printer driver supports
DriverName	Property	Return the name of the printer driver
Duplex	Property	Set or return a value to determine whether output will be single-sided or double-sided
EndDoc	Method	Send generated output to the Windows printer routines
KillDoc	Method	Terminate output being sent to memory or the Windows printer routines
Line	Method	Generate a line or box on the current page
NewPage	Method	End the current page and start a new blank page
Orientation	Property	Set or return the mode in which the document will be printed, landscape or portrait
Page	Property	Return the current page number
PaperBin	Property	Set or return the current paper bin to be used
PaperSize	Property	Set or return the size of the paper for the current printer
Port	Property	Return the name of the printer port
Print	Method	Generate text output to the current page
PrintForm	Method	Send a copy of a Visual Basic form to the Windows printer routines
PrintQuality	Property	Set or return a value specifying the printer's resolution
PSet	Method	Generate a pixel on the current page
ScaleHeight	Property	Set or return the height of a page in units defined by ScaleMode
ScaleLeft	Property	Set or return the farthest left horizontal position on the printer page
ScaleMode	Property	Set or return the unit of measurement for the coordinate system
ScaleTop	Property	Set or return the top vertical position on the printer page

continued on next page

continued from previous page

Use or Set This...	Type	To Do This...
ScaleWidth	Property	Set or return the width of a page in units defined by ScaleMode
TextHeight	Method	Calculate the height of text as it would be output to the printer
TextWidth	Method	Calculate the width of text as it would be output to the printer
TrackDefault	Property	Set or return a value to determine which printer receives the output
TwipsPerPixelX	Property	Set or return the number of twips (1/1440 inch) per pixel along the x-axis
TwipsPerPixelY	Property	Set or return the number of twips (1/1440 inch) per pixel along the y-axis
Zoom	Property	Set or return the scaled percentage of the printed output

The Printers Collection

Your system can connect to more than one printer. Whether a printer is connected via a network or simply connected to LPT1 and LPT2, each printer has its own unique set of capabilities. The Printers collection is an object that contains all the printers available to the operating system. The list of printers is the same one found in the Installed Printers Listbox of the Control Panel's Printer Option. You can examine these available printers in order to specify a new default printer for your application. Each printer in the collection is indexed by a number starting with 0. The syntax for the Printers collection is

```
Printers(number%)
```

The number% represents an integer that spans the index. To find the total number of printers in the collection, use the Count property.

Table 52-2 details the properties that affect the operation of the Printer collection.

Table 52-2 Properties that affect the Printer collection

Use or Set this...	Type	To Do This...
Count	Property	Return the number of members in a collection
LBound	Property	Return the lowest consecutive number in the collection or control array
UBound	Property	Return the highest consecutive number in the collection or control array

Constant Values

It is usually best to use named constants rather than numeric values when developing software. Named constants make your code more readable and easier to maintain.

Tables 52-3 through 52-8 list the values of the constants relevant to this chapter, mention their names, and briefly describe what they mean. These constants can be viewed in the VB Constants module (or, in some cases, in other object libraries) using the Object Browser. It is not necessary to explicitly add these objects to your project.

Table 52-3 Visual Basic constants for the ColorMode property

Value	Constant Name	Meaning
1	vbPRCMMonochrome	Monochrome output
2	vbPRCMColor	Color output

Table 52-4 Visual Basic constants for the Duplex property

Value	Constant Name	Meaning
1	vbPRDPSimplex	Single-sided printing
2	vbPRDPHorizontal	Double-sided horizontal printing
3	vbPRDPVertical	Double-sided vertical printing

Table 52-5 Visual Basic constants for the Orientation property

Value	Constant Name	Meaning
1	vbPRORPortrait	Documents print across the narrow side of the paper.
2	vbPRORLandscape	Documents print across the wide side of the paper.

Table 52-6 Visual Basic constants for the PaperBin property

Value	Constant Name	Meaning
1	vbPRBNUpper	Use paper from the upper bin.
2	vbPRBNLower	Use paper from the lower bin.
3	vbPRBNMiddle	Use paper from the middle bin.
4	vbPRBNManual	Wait for manual insertion of each sheet of paper.
5	vbPRBNEnvelope	Use envelopes from the envelope feeder.
6	vbPRBNEnvManual	Use envelopes from the envelope feeder, but wait for manual insertion.
7	vbPRBNAuto	(Default) Use paper from the current default feeder.
8	vbPRBNTractor	Use paper fed from the tractor feeder.
9	vbPRBNSmallFmt	Use paper from the small paper feeder.
10	vbPRBNLargeFmt	Use paper from the large paper feeder.
11	vbPRBNLargeCapacity	Use paper from the large capacity feeder.
14	vbPRBNCassette	Use paper from the attached cassette cartridge.

Table 52-7 Visual Basic constants for the PaperSize property

Value	Constant Name	Meaning
1	vbPRPSLetter	Letter, 8.5" x 11"
2	vbPRPSLetterSmall	Letter Small, 8.5" x 11"
3	vbPRPSTabloid	Tabloid, 11" x 17"
4	vbPRPSLedger	Ledger, 17" x 11"
5	vbPRPSLegal	Legal, 8.5" x 14"
6	vbPRPSStatement	Statement, 5.5" x 8.5"
7	vbPRPSExecutive	Executive, 7.5" x 10.5"
8	vbPRPSA3	A3, 297 x 420 mm.
9	vbPRPSA4	A4, 210 x 297 mm.
10	vbPRPSA4Small	A4 Small, 210 x 297 mm.
11	vbPRPSA5	A5, 148 x 210 mm.
12	vbPRPSB4	B4, 250 x 354 mm.
13	vbPRPSB5	B5, 182 x 257 mm.
14	vbPRPSFolio	Folio, 8.5" x 13"
15	vbPRPSQuarto	Quarto, 215 x 275 mm.
16	vbPRPS10x14	10" x 14"
17	vbPRPS11x17	11" x 17"
18	vbPRPSNote	Note, 8.5" x 11"
19	vbPRPSEnv9	Envelope #9, 3.875" x 8.875"
20	vbPRPSEnv10	Envelope #10, 4.125" x 9.5"
21	vbPRPSEnv11	Envelope #11, 4.5" x 10.375"
22	vbPRPSEnv12	Envelope #12, 4.5" x 11"
23	vbPRPSEnv14	Envelope #14, 5" x 11.5" in.
24	vbPRPSCSheet	C size sheet
25	vbPRPSDSheet	D size sheet
26	vbPRPSESheet	E size sheet
27	vbPRPSEnvDL	Envelope DL, 110 x 220 mm
29	vbPRPSEnvC3	Envelope C3, 324 x 458 mm.
30	vbPRPSEnvC4	Envelope C4, 229 x 324 mm.
28	vbPRPSEnvC5	Envelope C5, 162 x 229 mm.
31	vbPRPSEnvC6	Envelope C6, 114 x 162 mm.
32	vbPRPSEnvC65	Envelope C65, 114 x 229 mm.
33	vbPRPSEnvB4	Envelope B4, 250 x 353 mm.
34	vbPRPSEnvB5	Envelope B5, 176 x 250 mm.
35	vbPRPSEnvB6	Envelope B6, 176 x 125 mm.
36	vbPRPSEnvItaly	Envelope, 110 x 230 mm.
37	vbPRPSEnvMonarch	Envelope Monarch, 3.875" x 7.5"
38	vbPRPSEnvPersonal	Envelope, 3.625" x 6.5"

Value	Constant Name	Meaning
39	vbPRPSFanfoldUS	U.S. Standard Fanfold, 14.875" x 11"
40	vbPRPSFanfoldStdGerman	German Standard Fanfold, 8.5" x 12"
41	vbPRPSFanfoldLglGerman	German Legal Fanfold, 8.5" x 13"
256	vbPRPSUser	User-defined

Table 52-8 Visual Basic constants for the PrintQuality property

Value	Constant Name	Meaning
-1	vbPRPQDraft	Draft print quality
-2	vbPRPQLow	Low print quality
-3	vbPRPQMedium	Medium print quality
-4	vbPRPQHigh	High print quality

The rest of the chapter discusses these methods and properties in detail. The Printer project at the end of the chapter demonstrates the use of each of these Visual Basic elements.

Comments

The Printer object is designed to send output to the default printer specified by Windows. Unfortunately, since there can only be one default printer at a time, the only documented way to output to multiple printers simultaneously is to directly access the Windows GDI. You can find more information on accessing the GDI directly in any competent book on programming for Windows in C or C++, such as the Waite Group's *Win32 Programming API Bible*. The Print common dialog box can return the proper handle to use in your GDI print routines. See Chapter 25, "CommonDialog Control," for more on the common dialog box.

As an alternative (if you're willing to jump into undocumented territory), you can open the system devices LPT1:, LPT2:, and LPT3: as a sequential output file, and send text to them with the Print# and Write# statements. This technique works fine, provided you understand the appropriate control codes understood by your printer. Unfortunately, you may encounter unanticipated behavior and conflict with the use of the same device by other Windows applications (through the print spool).

Not all printer drivers are alike. The effects of the properties of the Printer object vary depending on the driver supplied by your printer manufacturer. Some property settings may have little or no effect on your output, and some different settings might yield identical results. Check your printer manual to make sure you are using the correct driver.

ColorMode Property

Objects Affected   Printer

Purpose   The ColorMode property sets or returns a value that determines whether the output is to be printed in color or monochrome. This property is not available at design time. Table 52-9 shows the argument of the ColorMode property. Table 52-10 shows the constant values of some possible settings.

General Syntax

```
Printer.ColorMode [ = value%]
```

Table 52-9 Argument of the ColorMode property

Argument	Description
value%	A constant or integer specifying the print mode

Table 52-10 List of possible settings for the ColorMode property

value%	Constant Name	Meaning
1	vbPRCMMonochrome	Output will print in monochrome (usually shades of black and white).
2	vbPRCMColor	Output will print in color.

Example Syntax

```
Private Sub Command1_Click ()
    If chkPrintColor.Value = vbChecked Then 'If the checkbox is marked
        Printer.ColorMode = vbPRCMColor      'then the output will be in color
    Else   'otherwise, it will be in
        Printer.ColorMode = vbPRCMMonochrome   'black and white.
    End If
    Printer.Circle (1000,1000), 800, vbRed
        'A Red Circle with a radius of 800 twips
        'will be drawn at X coordinate 1000, and
        'Y coordinate 1000.
End Sub
```

Description   The ColorMode property reads or sets the color of your printer to print your output in either color or black and white. The default setting depends on the printer driver you are using and the current printer settings. If you are using a monochrome printer, changes to this property do not affect your output.

The example syntax first checks whether you want color printing. If the check box is marked, the ColorMode property is set to 1, vbPRCMColor; otherwise, the property is set to 2, vbPRCMMonochrome. If color printing is selected, a circle filled in with red is printed. If color printing is not selected, the circle is not filled.

Example   The example syntax uses the ColorMode property to choose between printing in color and monochrome. If your printer only prints mono-chrome, this property has no effect on your output.

COPIES PROPERTY

Objects Affected   CommandDialog, Printer

Purpose   The Copies property sets or returns the number of copies to be printed. Not available at design time. Table 52-11 describes the argument of the Copies property.

General Syntax

```
Printer.Copies [ = number%]
```

Table 52-11 Argument for the Copies property

Argument	Description
number%	Integer value specifying the number of copies to print

Example Syntax

```
Private Sub PrintMsg (msg As String, NbrCopies as Integer)
        Printer.Copies = NbrCopies
        Printer.Print msg
        Printer.EndDoc
End Sub
```

Description   Printers that have collating features can take advantage of the Copies prop-erty. This property returns the number of copies to be printed based on the user's input into the Copies box of a Print dialog box. Depending on the printer driver, you can either collate or not collate the output.

If your printer does not support collating, you should set the Copies prop-erty to 1, or an error will occur. If your printer does support collating, you need to program a loop in your code to print multiple copies of your out-put.

You might use the procedure in the example syntax to print your docu-ment. Two parameters are passed to this procedure, representing a message and the number of copies. The message to be printed is formatted by the calling routine and passed to this procedure, where it is passed to the Print method. The Copies property is set by the number of copies vari-able, NbrCopies. The EndDoc method ends the messages and sends the output to the Windows printing routines.

Example	The Copies property is not used in the Printer project at the end of this chapter. The property's value is set at 1. Looping code is used to print multiple copies of the document.
Comments	If you use the CommonDialog control and the vbPDUseDevModCopies flag is set, the Copies property always returns 1.

DeviceName Property

Objects Affected	Printer
Purpose	The DeviceName property returns the name of the device a driver supports. It is not available at design time, and is read-only at runtime.

General Syntax

```
Printer.DeviceName
```

Example Syntax

```
Private Sub Form_Click ()
    Print "The current printer is " & Printer.DeviceName & "."
End Sub
```

Description	Use the DeviceName property to read the name of the printer currently in use. The example syntax prints the name of the printer within the message on the form.
Example	The Printer project at the end of this chapter uses the DeviceName property twice. First, it's used to display the name of the printer your output will be printed on; this appears on the form that shows the status of your print job. Second, it's used with the Port property in the generic Print Setup form.

DriverName Property

Objects Affected	Printer
Purpose	The DriverName property returns the name of the driver the printer is using. This property is not available at design time, and is read-only at runtime.

General Syntax

```
Printer.DriverName
```

Example Syntax

```
Private Sub Form_Click ()
    Print "Your current printer is using the " & Printer.DriverName & " driver."
End Sub
```

Description	Every printer uses a printer driver. Many printers use the same driver even though they don't have exactly the same features. Use the DriverName property to read the name of the driver being used for printing. The example syntax prints the name of the printer driver within the message on the form.
Example	The Printer project at the end of this chapter uses the DriverName property to display the name of the printer driver your printer is using. This information appears on the frmPrintSetup form that shows the printer environment; the setting form is similar to the Print Setup dialog box in most commercial applications.

DUPLEX PROPERTY

Objects Affected   Printer

Purpose   The Duplex property sets or returns a value to determine whether printing is to occur on both sides of the page. This property is not available at design time. Table 52-12 describes the argument of the Duplex property. Table 52-13 shows constant values for some possible settings.

General Syntax

```
Printer.Duplex [ = value% ]
```

Table 52-12 Argument for the Duplex property

Argument	Description
value%	A constant or integer specifying the type of printing

Table 52-13 List of possible settings for the Duplex property

value%	VB.Constants	Meaning
1	vbPRDPSimplex	Output will print single-sided in the current orientation setting.
2	vbPRDPHorizontal	Output will print double-sided using a horizontal page turn.
3	vbPRDPVertical	Output will print double-sided using a vertical page turn.

Example Syntax

```
Private Sub Command1_Click ()
    If chkDuplex.Value = vbChecked Then      'If the Duplex Checkbox is marked,
        If optPageTurn(0).Value = True Then  'then is the Horizontal option button
                                             'marked?
            Printer.Duplex = vbPRDPHorizontal'If it is, then set the Duplex Property
                                             'to 2;
```

continued on next page

continued from previous page

```
            Else                              'otherwise,
                Printer.Duplex = vbPRDPVertical'set the Duplex property to 3.
            Else                              'If the Duplex Check box isn't marked,
                Printer.Duplex = vbPRDPSimplex 'then the Duplex property is set to 1.
        End If
        'Send two pages of messages to the printer.
        Printer.Print "This is the first line on the first page."
        Printer.Print "This is the second line."
        Printer.NewDoc       'eject the first page and start the second
        Printer.Print "This is the first line of the second page."
        Printer.Print "This is the second line."
        Printer.EndDoc       'terminate the print job
End Sub
```

Description	Not every printer can support double-sided printing. However, if your printer supports this feature, the Duplex property can be handy. This property's default value is 1, which means that your output will print on one side of the paper.
	There are two options for printing on both sides of the page. You can choose horizontal page turning, where the tops of both sides of the page are at the same end of the paper, as in a regular book. You can also choose vertical page turning, where you have to flip the page over to read what is on the other side. This type of output is most useful if you are going to read your output on a clipboard or flip-chart.
	The example syntax first determines whether the check box for Duplex printing is marked. An array control consisting of two option buttons is examined. If the option button for horizontal page turning is marked, the Duplex property is set to 2, vbPRDPHorizontal; otherwise, the property is set to 3, vbPRDPVertical. Two pages are then sent to the printer for printing.
Example	The Printer project at the end of this chapter uses the default setting of single-sided printing.

EndDoc Method

Objects Affected	Printer
Purpose	The EndDoc method ends the current document and sends output to the Windows printing routines.

General Syntax

```
Printer.EndDoc
```

Example Syntax

```
Private Sub menuFilePrintNow_Click ()
    Printer.EndDoc
End Sub
```

Description	A *document* in Visual Basic is a set of pages that have been created on the Printer object but not yet sent to the Windows print routines. Remember that in Visual Basic, printing statements do not result in immediate output to the printer but become part of the current page, which is completed by using the NewPage method. The latter method starts a new page but does not output the previous page.
	Use the EndDoc method when you've completed all of the printing for a document. It causes several things to happen. First, if any methods that output to the Printer object have been executed since the last time the NewPage method was used, EndDoc will perform all the same tasks as NewPage. This includes advancing to the next page and setting the CurrentX and CurrentY properties to 0 (top of page). It also sends all output that has been generated by the Printer object to the Windows printing routines. Windows in turn sends this output to the printer (if Print Manager, or another print spooler, is active for this printer, it will intercept the output). EndDoc also sets the value of the Page property back to 1.
	The example syntax simply executes the EndDoc method.
Example	The EndDoc method is used in two places in the Printer project at the end of this chapter. First, it is used near the end of the menuPrintGraphics_Click event. When it is used there, the graphics that have been generated are sent to the Windows printer routines. The EndDoc method in this routine sends the printer a form feed, since a NewPage method hasn't been used yet.
	Second, the menuPrintText_Click event uses the EndDoc method soon after a NewPage method executes. It sends all the text that has been generated by this event to the Windows Print Manager.
Comments	Because Visual Basic keeps all output to the Printer object in memory until the EndDoc method is used, it's a good idea to use this method in the middle of large print runs.

KILLDOC METHOD

Objects Affected	Printer
Purpose	The KillDoc method immediately ends the current print job and the printer driver resets the printer.

General Syntax

```
Printer.KillDoc
```

Example Syntax

```
Private Sub Command1_Click ()
        Printer.KillDoc
End Sub
```

Description	In many applications, when you send a document to the printer your system is locked up until the job is completed or the Print Manager has taken control of it. Using the KillDoc method, you can now cancel a print job before it starts.
	If you have Print Manager running with background printing enabled, KillDoc deletes the current print job and prevents the printer from printing anything. If the Print Manager's background printing is not enabled, some or all of the data may be sent to the printer before KillDoc takes effect. Once the printer receives the KillDoc method, it terminates the print job and resets itself.
	The example syntax sends the KillDoc method to the operating system's Print Manager and ends the print job before it can finish printing.
Example	The Printer project at the end of this chapter uses the KillDoc method to interrupt your print job when the Cancel Print button, cmdCancelPrint_Click event, is pressed.
Comments	The KillDoc method cannot be used to stop a print job that was invoked with the PrintForm method.

NewPage Method

Objects Affected	Printer
Purpose	The NewPage method ends output for the current page and sets up the next page for subsequent output.

General Syntax

```
Printer.NewPage
```

Example Syntax

```
Private Sub CheckForNewAccount (AccountName As String)
    Static oldAccount As String
    If AccountName <> oldAccount Then
        Printer.NewPage
        oldAccount = AccountName
    End If
End Sub
```

Description	The NewPage method, which has no arguments, is the Visual Basic equivalent to issuing a form feed. The current print page is saved and will be output when the program ends or the EndDoc method executes. The work area for the print page is then cleared, and the CurrentX and CurrentY properties are set to 0 to set up a new page. Executing this method also increments the Page property.
	Use this method when all printing on a page is complete. The program can then begin print operations for the next page. If the NewPage method has not been used since the last time data was output to the Printer object, executing the EndDoc method will also cause a new page operation.

The example syntax executes the NewPage event whether the routine receives an AccountName that's different than the one it last processed.

Example   The Printer project at the end of this chapter uses the NewPage method to generate a new page just after a footer has been printed for the menuPrintText_Click event. When this occurs, the current page is saved in memory, the Page property is incremented, and the page work area is cleared. The CurrentX and CurrentY properties are also set to 0.

ORIENTATION PROPERTY

Objects Affected   Printer

Purpose   The Orientation property sets or returns a value indicating whether your output will be printed in portrait or landscape mode. This property is not available at design time. Table 52-14 describes the argument of the Orientation property. Table 52-15 shows constant values for possible settings.

General Syntax

```
Printer.Orientation [ = value% ]
```

Table 52-14 Argument of the Orientation property

Argument	Description
value%	A constant or integer that determines the page orientation

Table 52-15 Settings for the Orientation property

value%	Constant	Description
1	vbPRORPortrait	Sets or returns the print orientation of the document to print across the narrow side of the paper
2	vbPRORLandscape	Sets or returns the print orientation of the document to print across the wide side of the paper

Example Syntax

```
Private Sub Option1_Click (Index as Integer)
      If Option(0).Value = True Then          'Check to see if the Portrait
                                              'Option button is marked.
              Printer.Orientation = vbPRORPortrait   'If it is, set the Orientation
                                              'property to 1, Portrait.
      Else
              Printer.Orientation = vbPRORLandscape  'otherwise, set it 2, Landscape
      End If
End Sub
```

Description	Use the Orientation property to set or return the direction of your output on the page. All printers can print in either portrait or landscape mode. This value always defaults to that of the print setup.
	The example syntax changes the orientation of your printout based on which option button is pressed.
Example	The Orientation property is used in the Printer project at the end of this chapter in a generic Print Setup form.

PAGE PROPERTY

Objects Affected	Printer
Purpose	The Page property returns the current page number. You can use this to put the proper page number on each page. Not available at design time, read-only at runtime.

General Syntax

```
Printer.Page
```

Example Syntax

```
Private Sub PrintLine (lineToPrint As String)
    Dim spaceLeft As Long
    spaceLeft = Printer.ScaleHeight - Printer.CurrentY
    If spaceLeft < 4 * Printer.TextHeight(lineToPrint) Then
        Printer.Print "Page " & Format(Printer.Page, "###")
        Printer.NewPage
    End If
    Printer.Print lineToPrint
End Sub
```

Description	Use the Page property to read the current page number that you're print-ing. You can use the returned value to print the page number on the page.
	This property starts at 1 and increments by 1 each time you issue the NewPage method. It also increments if you use the Print method to print text that would not fit on the page; Visual Basic automatically issues a NewPage before printing the text.
Example	The Printer project at the end of this chapter uses the Page property in both the PrintHeader and PrintFooter sub procedures.

PAPERBIN PROPERTY

Objects Affected	Printer
Purpose	The PaperBin property sets or returns a value indicating the paper bin the printer will use when printing. This property is not available at design time. Tables 52-16 and 52-17 summarize the arguments for the PaperBin property.

General Syntax

```
Printer.PaperBin [ = value% ]
```

Table 52-16 Argument of the PaperBin property

Argument	Description
value%	A constant or integer that determines the default paper bin

Table 52-17 value% setting for the PaperBin property

value%	VB.Constants	Description
1	vbPRBNUpper	Use paper from the upper bin
2	vbPRBNLower	Use paper from the lower bin
3	vbPRBNMiddle	Use paper from the middle bin
4	vbPRBNManual	Wait for manual insertion of each sheet of paper
5	vbPRBNEnvelope	Use envelopes from the envelope feeder
6	vbPRBNEnvManual	Use envelopes from the envelope feeder, but wait for manual insertion
7	vbPRBNAuto	(Default) Use paper from the current default bin
8	vbPRBNTractor	Use paper fed from the tractor feeder
9	vbPRBNSmallFmt	Use paper from the small paper feeder
10	vbPRBNLargeFmt	Use paper from the large paper bin
11	vbPRBNLargeCapacity	Use paper from the large capacity bin
14	vbPRBNCassette	Use paper from the attached cassette cartridge

Example Syntax

```
Private Sub cboPaperSource_Click ()
    Dim BinChoice As Index
    BinChoice = cmboPaperBin.ListIndex      'assign combo box ListIndex to a variable
    Select Case cmboPaperSource.ListIndex   'evaluate the variable
      Case 0                                'upper paper bin
        Printer.PaperBin = vbPRBNUpper      'set property to 1
      Case 1                                'manual envelope feeder
        Printer.PaperBin = vbPRBNEnvManual  'set property to 6
      Case 2                                'manual insertion
        Printer.PaperBin = vbPRBNManual     'set property to 4
      Case 3                                'lower paper bin
        Printer.PaperBin = vbPRBNLower      'set property to 2
      Case 4                                'envelope feeder
        Printer.PaperBin = vbPRBNEnvelope   'set property to 5
    End Select
End Sub
```

Description		Some printers have more than one paper feeder. Paper bins include upper and lower paper bins, envelope bins, manual paper insert slots, and even tractor feeders. The PaperBin property lets you determine which paper bin the printer uses when printing.

Not all the bin options are available on every printer. Check your printer manual to see which bins are available to you. If you attempt to use a value% that your printer does not support, you will receive a runtime error.

The example syntax checks a combo box's ListIndex value and evaluates it to determine which PaperBin constant to assign to the PaperBin property. This example assumes your system is connected to a laser printer that has several types of paper trays to choose from.

Example   The Printer project at the end of this chapter uses the PaperBin in the generic Print Setup form.

PaperSize Property

Objects Affected   Printer

Purpose   The PaperSize property sets or returns a value specifying the paper size for the current printer. This property is not available at design time. Tables 52-18 and 52-19 summarize the arguments for the PaperSize property.

General Syntax

```
Printer.PaperSize [ = value% ]
```

Table 52-18 Arguments of the PaperSize property

Argument	Constant	Description
value%	A constant or integer that specifies the paper size	
1	vbPRPSLetter	Letter, 8.5" x 11"
2	vbPRPSLetterSmall	Letter Small, 8.5" x 11"
3	vbPRPSTabloid	Tabloid, 11" x 17"
4	vbPRPSLedger	Ledger, 17" x 11"
5	vbPRPSLegal	Legal, 8.5" x 14"
6	vbPRPSStatement	Statement, 5.5" x 8.5"
7	vbPRPSExecutive	Executive, 7.5" x 10.5"
8	vbPRPSA3	A3, 297 x 420 mm.
9	vbPRPSA4	A4, 210 x 297 mm.
10	vbPRPSA4Small	A4 Small, 210 x 297 mm.

Argument	Constant	Description
11	vbPRPSA5	A5, 148 x 210 mm.
12	vbPRPSB4	B4, 250 x 354 mm.
13	vbPRPSB5	B5, 182 x 257 mm.
14	vbPRPSFolio	Folio, 8.5" x 13"
15	vbPRPSQuarto	Quarto, 215 x 275 mm.
16	vbPRPS10x14	10" x 14"
17	vbPRPS11x17	11" x 17"
18	vbPRPSNote	Note, 8.5" x 11"
19	vbPRPSEnv9	Envelope #9, 3.875" x 8.875"
20	vbPRPSEnv10	Envelope #10, 4.125" x 9.5"
21	vbPRPSEnv11	Envelope #11, 4.5" x 10.375"
22	vbPRPSEnv12	Envelope #12, 4.5" x 11"
23	vbPRPSEnv14	Envelope #14, 5" x 11.5"
24	vbPRPSCSheet	C size sheet
25	vbPRPSDSheet	D size sheet
26	vbPRPSESheet	E size sheet
27	vbPRPSEnvDL	Envelope DL, 110 x 220 mm.

Table 52-19 Settings for the PaperSize property

value%	Constant	Description
29	vbPRPSEnvC3	Envelope C3, 324 x 458 mm.
30	vbPRPSEnvC4	Envelope C4, 229 x 324 mm.
28	vbPRPSEnvC5	Envelope C5, 162 x 229 mm.
31	vbPRPSEnvC6	Envelope C6, 114 x 162 mm.
32	vbPRPSEnvC65	Envelope C65, 114 x 229 mm.
33	vbPRPSEnvB4	Envelope B4, 250 x 353 mm.
34	vbPRPSEnvB5	Envelope B5, 176 x 250 mm.
35	vbPRPSEnvB6	Envelope B6, 176 x 125 mm.
36	vbPRPSEnvItaly	Envelope, 110 x 230 mm.
37	vbPRPSEnvMonarch	Envelope Monarch, 3.875" x 7.5"
38	vbPRPSEnvPersonal	Envelope, 3.625" x 6.5"
39	vbPRPSFanfoldUS	U.S. Standard Fanfold, 14.875" x 11"
40	vbPRPSFanfoldStdGerman	German Standard Fanfold, 8.5" x 12"
41	vbPRPSFanfoldLglGerman	German Legal Fanfold, 8.5" x 13"
256	vbPRPSUser	User-defined

Example Syntax

```
Private Sub cboPaperSource_Click ()
    Dim SizeChoice As Integer
    SizeChoice = cmboPaperSize.ListIndex    'assign combo box ListIndex to a variable
    Select Case SizeChoice                  'evaluate the Paper Size combo box
        Case 0                              'letter size paper - 8.5" x 11"
            Printer.PaperSize = vbPRPSLetter  'set property to 1
        Case 1                              'legal size paper - 8.5" x 14"
            Printer.PaperSize = vbPRPSLegal   'set property to 5
        Case 2                              'A4 size paper - 210 x 297mm
            Printer.PaperSize = vbPRPSA4      'set property to 9
    End Case
End Sub
```

Description   By default, the value returned by the PaperSize property is determined by what is chosen in the Printer Setup dialog box of the Control Panel. When you change the PaperSize property, you set the paper size of the current printer. If you set the printer's Height or Width property, the PaperSize is automatically set to vbPRPSUser.

The example syntax checks a combo box's ListIndex value and evaluates it to determine which PaperSize constant is to be assigned to it.

Example   The Printer project at the end of this chapter uses the PaperSize property in the generic Print Setup form.

PORT PROPERTY

Objects Affected   Printer

Purpose   The Port property returns the name of the port to which your output will be sent.

General Syntax

```
Printer.Port
```

Example Syntax

```
Private Sub Form_Click ()
    Dim msg As String, obj as Object
    For Each obj In Printers      'iterate through each print in the object collection
        msg = msg + obj.DeviceName & " on "& obj.Port & Chr$(13) & Chr$(10)
            'Create a message
            'that names the printer and its assigned port.
    Next obj
    Msgbox msg   'display message in a popup box
End Sub
```

Description   Use the Port property to read the name of the port to which the output printer is attached. In the example syntax, the For Each statement loops through the collection of printers to find printer names and the port they are assigned to. The printers are the same as the ones you would find in the Print Setup dialog box. The result is displayed in a message box.

Example   In the Printer project at the end of this chapter, the Port property is used with the DeviceName property to choose a printer in the generic Print Setup form. You can use this technique to change from the default printer to any printer defined on your system.

PRINT METHOD

Objects Affected   Form, Picture Box, Printer

Purpose   The Print method sends text to the Printer object. Table 52-20 summarizes the arguments of the Print method.

General Syntax

```
Printer.Print [{Spc(n) | Tab(m)}][expressionlist][{ ; | , }]
```

Table 52-20 Arguments of the Print method

Argument	Description
Spc(n)	Precede expressionlist with n spaces from last print position; may be repeated.
Tab(m)	Print expressionlist at the mth column; may be repeated.
expressionlist	A list of values, string or numeric, that will be printed; may be repeated.
;	Set next print position to the next character; may be repeated.
,	Set next print position to the next column; may be repeated.

Example Syntax

```
Private Sub Command1_Click ()
    Person$ = InputBox("What is your name?")
    Printer.Print "Hello "; Person$; ", how are you?"
End Sub
```

Description   The Print method prints the text specified by the expressionlist. The expressionlist contains one or more expressions of any data type (Integer, Long, Single, Double, Currency, Date, user defined, String, or Variant). Each expression can be separated by a semicolon or a comma (if neither is used, semicolons are automatically inserted by Visual Basic). Using a semicolon to separate expressions prints each expression as if it were all one concatenated string. Using commas prints the expression that follows a comma at the next print zone. A *print zone* is every 14 columns, where a column is equal to the average width of every character in the current font and font size for the Printer object.

If a comma or semicolon trails the last expression in the list, the CurrentX and CurrentY properties remain at the point following the last character printed. However, if both are omitted from the end of the list, the CurrentX property is set to 0 and CurrentY is set to the next print line.

This is the equivalent of doing a carriage return/line feed on a traditional printer.

Each expressionlist may be preceded by the Spc(n) or Tab(m) function. The Spc(n) function inserts n spaces before the expressionlist, relative to the last print position. The Tab(m) function prints expressionlist m columns from the beginning of the line, where a column is defined as the average width of all the characters in the current font and font size. Thus, Spc(n) is a relative position on the line, and Tab(m) is an absolute position on the line.

If executing a Print method will cause the specified text to be printed below the position defined by Printer.ScaleHeight, a new page is automatically generated. However, if executing a Print method will cause the specified text to be printed beyond the position defined by Printer.ScaleWidth, no new line is generated. The text is merely truncated. Take care not to cause this method to print past position 30,000, as this will cause an overflow to occur. (Note that the exact number that causes an overflow varies depending on the font and font size you're printing with.)

The example syntax sends the literal strings "Hello" and "how are you?" to the print page. (The quote marks themselves are not sent.) Between these items, the contents of the string variable Person$ is also sent. If Person$ had been set to "Bryon," then the resulting output will look something like this:

```
Hello Bryon, how are you?
```

Notice that any spaces between strings must be included in one or the other of the strings. Semicolons rather than commas are used to separate strings, so that output is not moved to the next print zone.

Example   The Printer project at the end of this chapter uses the Print method quite often. It is most heavily used in the procedures that relate to the cmdPrint_Click event. This event occurs when the user clicks the Print command button in the Text Output frame. The PrintText procedure uses the Print method to generate a hard copy of the text in the txtTextOutput text box.

PRINTFORM METHOD

Objects Affected   Printer

Purpose   The PrintForm method sends a copy of a Visual Basic form to the Windows printing routines. This can be an easy way to take advantage of Visual Basic's form design capabilities in creating printed forms, and to format printed output so that it is identical to what is shown on the screen. Table 52-21 summarizes the argument of the PrintForm method.

General Syntax

```
[form.]PrintForm
```

Table 52-21 Argument of the PrintForm method

Argument	Description
form	Name of the form to be printed

Example Syntax

```
Private Sub Command1_Click ()
    AddressForm.PrintForm
End Sub
```

Description

This method allows you to design an output form that can be sent to the printer. The only argument used is the name of the form to be printed. If not explicitly specified, the form with the focus will be printed.

All controls on the form will also be printed, with the exception of the menu controls.

If any graphics have been added to the form, or any picture is on the form, they will only be printed if the AutoReDraw property for that form or picture was set to True (-1) at that time.

Although the form to be printed does have to be loaded into memory when this method executes, it does not need to be visible. This makes it easy to design complicated forms for printing, without having to code complex procedures in your program. You can design an output form in the same manner as a form for the screen. Picture controls can be used for letterhead and other similar features, while labels can be used for any text that will be printed on the form. The Line and Shape graphics controls make it easy to add these elements to your form. When it comes time to print the form, all the program has to do is set the caption property of any labels that represent changed data and execute the PrintForm method. Note that the PrintForm method sends the form directly to the Windows printing routines. It does not use the Printer object or the system of pages and documents used by most other printing techniques.

Although this method makes simple work out of complex form design, it only sends a bitmap of the screen to the printer. A laser printer has a far higher resolution (typically 300 or 520 dpi) than a typical screen (typically 72 or 96 dpi). This means that any diagonal or curved lines, and all text, will have visible "jaggies." For the highest quality output, you'll need to use the graphics methods and print directly to the Printer object.

The example syntax sends a copy of AddressForm to the printer.

Example   In the Printer project at the end of this chapter, the mnuForm_Click event
uses this method. This event activates when the user chooses the Print
Form option on the File menu of the Printer project. This event uses the
PrintForm method to send a copy of the current form to the printer.

PrintQuality Property

Objects Affected   Printer

Purpose   The PrintQuality property sets or returns the current resolution of the
printer. Not available at design time. Tables 52-22 and 52-23 summarize
the arguments for the PrintQuality property.

General Syntax

```
Printer.PrintQuality [ = value% ]
```

Table 52-22 Argument of the PrintQuality property

Argument	Description
value%	A constant or integer that indicates the printer resolution

Table 52-23 PrintQuality property constants

value%	VB.Constants	Description
-1	vbPRPQDraft	Draft resolution
-2	vbPRPQLow	Low resolution
-3	vbPRPQMedium	Medium resolution
-4	vbPRPQHigh	High resolution
> 0		Dots per inch (dpi) value any positive number

Example Syntax

```
Private Sub optPrintQuality_Click (Index As Integer)
    Select Case Index                        'evaluate the index
        Case 0                               'draft resolution selected
           Printer.PrintQuality = vbPRPQDraft 'set property to -1
        Case 1                               'low resolution selected
           Printer.PrintQuality = vbPRPQLow   'set property to -2
        Case 2                               'medium resolution selected
           Printer.PrintQuality = vbPRPQMedium 'set property to -3
        Case 3                               'high resolution selected
           Printer.PrintQuality = vbPRPQHigh  'set property to -4
    End Select
End Sub
```

Description   The PrintQuality property sets or returns the current printer resolution. In addition to using the negative value settings or constants defined in Table 52-23, you can use a positive number, which Visual Basic will interpret as dots per inch (dpi). For example, the values 150 or 300 would produce results similar to -2 or -4, respectively.

Many printers can change the quality of your printed output. With some printers, some or all the settings may produce the same results. You should check your printer manual to see what types of print quality it can produce.

The example syntax interprets the index of an option button array to set the PrintQuality property. This property can be set to vbPRPQDraft (-1), vbPRPQLow (-2), vbPRPQMedium (-3), or vbPRPHigh (-4).

Example   In the Printer project at the end of this chapter, the PrintQuality property is used in the generic Print Setup form. Like the example syntax, an option button index will be evaluated and the PrintQuality property will be set to the corresponding resolution.

TRACKDEFAULT PROPERTY

Objects Affected   Printer

Purpose   The TrackDefault property indicates whether the Printer object always points to the same printer if you change the default printer setting in the operating system's Control Panel. This property is not available at design time. Table 52-24 summarizes the argument of the TrackDefault property, and Table 52-25 summarizes its Boolean values.

General Syntax

```
Printer.TrackDefault [ = boolean% ]
```

Table 52-24 Argument of the TrackDefault property

Argument	Description
boolean%	Value specifying where the printer object points

Table 52-25 Boolean values for the TrackDefault property

boolean%	Description
False	Your printing destination doesn't change even though it has changed in the Control Panel.
True	(Default) Your printing destination changes when you change the default printer in the Control Panel.

Example Syntax

```
Private Sub chkTrackDefault_Click ()
    If chkTrackDefault.Value = vbChecked Then
      Printer.TrackDefault = True
    Else
      Printer.TrackDefault = False
    End If
End Sub
```

Description	The TrackDefault property can be either True or False. The default value of this property is True, which means the Printer object changes the printer it points to when you change the default printer settings in your Control Panel. When you set the property to False, the Printer object continues to point to the same printer even if you change the default printer settings in your Control Panel.
	In the example syntax, the check box value is evaluated. If the value is checked, the TrackDefault property is set to True. Otherwise, the property is set to False.
Example	The Printer project at the end of this chapter does not use the TrackDefault property. The example syntax illustrates its use in a check box object, in which you toggle the TrackDefault property to either True or False.
Comments	If you change the TrackDefault property while a print job is in progress, a NewPage statement is sent to the Printer object.

TwipsPerPixelX, TwipsPerPixelY Properties

Objects Affected	Screen, Printer
Purpose	The TwipsPerPixelX and TwipsPerPixelY return the number of twips (units of 1/1440 inch) per printer pixel.

General Syntax

```
Printer.TwipsPerPixelX
Printer.TwipsPerPixelY
```

Example Syntax

```
Private Sub Command1_Click ()
      xTwips = Printer.TwipsPerPixelX
      yTwips = Printer.TwipsPerPixelY
End Sub
```

Description	The TwipsPerPixelX and TwipsPerPixelY properties allow you to know the conversion factor between the actual printer device pixels and a standard measurement value (twips). A twip is a standard print shop unit of measure that is equal to 1/1440 inch. One point (of type) is equal to 20 twips.

ZOOM PROPERTY

Objects Affected   Printer

Purpose   The Zoom property sets or returns the percentage to which the printed output will be scaled. This property can only be manipulated at runtime. Table 52-26 summarizes the argument of the Zoom property.

General Syntax

```
Printer.Zoom [ = number!]
```

Table 52-26 Argument of the Zoom property

Argument	Description
number!	Sets or returns a user-defined percentage to scale the printed output

Example Syntax

```
Private Sub Command1_Click ()
    Printer.FontName = "Arial"      'use the Arial font
    Printer.FontSize = 24           'set the point size to 24
    Printer.Zoom = textScale.Text   'the Zoom property is set to the integer value of
                                    'the text box
    Printer.Print = "You can have"
    Printer.FontBold = True         'bold the next line of text
    Printer.Print = "different scaled"
    Printer.FontBold = False        'turn bold off
    Printer.Print = "output."
    Printer.EndDoc                  'end print job
End Sub
```

Description   Using the Zoom property to scale your output, you can get more or less material on a printed page without adjusting the point size of your font. The scaling is calculated by the number!/100.

This property default value is 0, which means the output will print at its normal size. To fit more information on a page, enter a number less than 100. To magnify your output, use a number greater than 100. In the example syntax, the output is scaled according to the value in textScale.Text.

Example   In the Printer project at the end of this chapter, the Zoom property is used to allow you to change the size of your printed output. When you're about to print, you can change the scale of your output by selecting a percentage from the combo box.

The Printer Project

Project Overview

The following project details the use of the Printer object, the Printers collection, and their related methods and properties. After you have completed this project, you should have a firm understanding of the concepts behind the Printer object and the Printers collection. By following the examples outlined in this project, you will learn how to print Visual Basic forms, output text, output graphics to the printer, and change your output destination.

Assembling the Project

1. Create a new form named frmPrint and place on it the controls specified in Table 52-27.

Table 52-27 Objects and properties for the Printer project

Object	Property	Setting
Form	Name	frmPrint
	Caption	Printer Project
Frame	Name	fraGraphics
	Caption	Graphics
Frame	Name	fraTextOutput
	Caption	&TextOutput

2. Add the objects and properties listed in Table 52-28 to fraGraphics. Be sure to create the controls on top of fraGraphics. The positioning of these controls is not critical.

Table 52-28 Objects and properties placed in fraGraphics

Object	Property	Setting
Line	Name	Line1
Shape	Name	shpRectangle
Shape	Name	shpOval
	Shape	2 - Oval
CommandButton	Name	cmdPrint
	Caption	Print
	Index	0

3. Add the objects and properties listed in Table 52-29 to fraTextOutput. Be sure to create the controls on top of fraTextOutput. The positioning of these controls is not critical.

Table 52-29 Objects and properties placed in fraTextOutput

Object	Property	Setting
TextBox	Name	txtTextOutput
	Font	Arial Regular 10 pt.
	ScrollBars	2 - Vertical
Label	Name	lblScale
	Caption	&Scale (% of Original):
ComboBox	Name	cboScale
	Style	2 - Dropdown List
CommandButton	Name	cmdPrint
	Index	1

4. Use the Menu Editor (choose the Menu Editor option from Visual Basic's Tools menu) to create a menu with the settings given in Table 52-30.

Table 52-30 Menu settings for the Printer project form

Name	Caption
mnuFile	&File
mnuPrintSetup	Print &Setup
mnuPrintForm	&Print Form
mnuFileSep1	-
mnuExit	E&xit

5. Check the appearance of your form against Figure 52-1.

6. Enter the following code into the General Declarations area of the form. These module scope constants define the printable area the output can be placed on. The values are defined in twips. There are 1440 twips per inch, so these are are 1 inch margins.

```
Private Const udcBOTTOM_MARGIN = 1440
Private Const udcTOP_MARGIN = 1440
Private Const udcLEFT_MARGIN = 1440
Private Const udcRIGHT_MARGIN = 1440
```

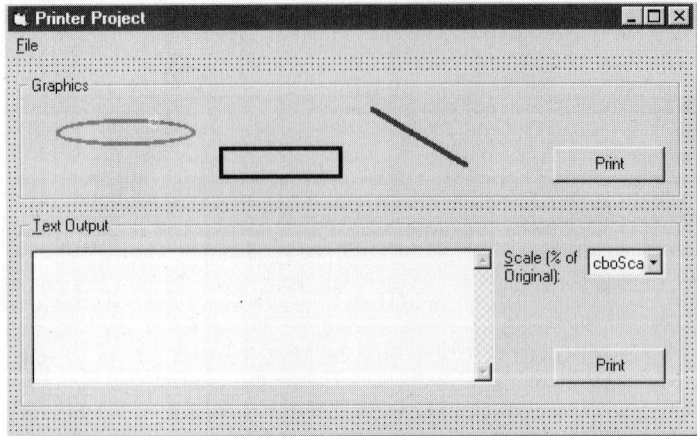

Figure 52-1 The Printer project main form during design

7. Enter the following code into the mnuPrintSetup_Click event. This event occurs when the user chooses Print Setup from the File menu.

```
Private Sub mnuPrintSetup_Click()       'load Print Setup Form
    frmPrintSetup.Show vbModal
End Sub
```

8. Enter the following code into the mnuPrintForm_Click event. This event is activated when the user chooses the Print Form option on the File menu of the Printer project. This event sends a copy of the current form to the printer.

```
Private Sub mnuPrintForm_Click()       'print the Form
    PrintForm
End Sub
```

9. Enter the following code into the Form_Load event. This event occurs when the form is loaded and adds information to the cboScale combo box.

```
Private Sub Form_Load()
    cboScale.AddItem 0
    cboScale.AddItem 50
    cboScale.AddItem 100
    cboScale.ListIndex = 0
End Sub
```

10. Enter the following code into the cmdPrint_Click event. This event occurs when one of the two Print command buttons is pressed.

```
Private Sub cmdPrint_Click(Index As Integer)
    Dim msg As String
    msg = "Printer Project"

    ' Examine the control array to see which print button was pressed
    Screen.MousePointer = vbHourglass        'hourglass, we're going to be a while
    frmPrinting.Show
```

```
        frmPrinting.Refresh
        Select Case Index
            Case 0       ' Print Graphics
                PrintBox "This text is in a box", False       'print text inside an unshaded
                                                              'box
                PrintBox "This text is in a shaded box", True 'print text inside a shaded box
                PrintLine "This test is crossed out"          'print test with line through
                                                              'the middle
                PrintCircle "This text is in a circle"        'print this text inside a circle
                Printer.EndDoc                                'end printing, send to print
                                                              'routines
            Case 1       ' Print Text
                If RTrim(txtTextOutput) = "" Then Exit Sub    'if TextBox is empty, don't
                                                              'execute routine
                ' If Scale is zero, don't change the Zoom property
                If Val(cboScale.List(cboScale.ListIndex)) <> 0 Then
                    Printer.Zoom = Val(cboScale.List(cboScale.ListIndex))
                End If
                PrintText txtTextOutput.text, msg
        End Select
        MsgBox "Done Printing"                                'inform the user printing is
                                                              'complete
        Unload frmPrinting
        Screen.MousePointer = vbDefault                       'change mouse pointer back
                                                              'to normal
    End Sub
```

11. Enter the following code into the General Declarations area of the form. This procedure is called from the cmdPrint_Click event, index equal 0 event. PrintBox prints the supplied string and then uses the Line method to draw a box around it. If the Shaded parameter is True, PrintBox shades the contents of the box. This shading is accomplished by using the PSet method to generate a dot every 50 positions horizontally and vertically. The placement and dimensions of the box are figured using the TextHeight and TextWidth methods and the CurrentX and CurrentY properties.

```
Private Sub PrintBox(msg As String, Shaded As Integer)
    Dim leftX As Long, topY As Long, rightX As Long, bottomY As Long
    Dim yPos As Long, xPos As Long
    leftX = Printer.CurrentX                               'left side of box
    topY = Printer.CurrentY                                'top of box
    rightX = Printer.CurrentY + Printer.TextWidth(msg) + 200      'a bit wider than the text
    bottomY = Printer.CurrentY + Printer.TextHeight(msg) + 200  'a bit higher than the text
    Printer.CurrentX = Printer.CurrentX + 100             'indent text in from side of box
    Printer.CurrentY = Printer.CurrentY + 100             'indent text in from top of box
    Printer.Print msg                                     'print the text
    Printer.Line (leftX, topY)-(rightX, bottomY), , B 'draw the box around the text
    If Shaded = True Then                                 'supposed to shade?
        For xPos = topY To bottomY Step 50               'go from top to bottom, every 50 dots
            For yPos = leftX To rightX Step 50           'Go from left to right, every 50 dots
                Printer.PSet (xPos, yPos)                'and make a dot.
            Next
        Next
    End If
    Printer.CurrentX = Printer.ScaleLeft                  'Go all the way back to the left
    Printer.CurrentY = bottomY + 100                      'and go down a bit from where we are.
End Sub
```

12. Enter the following code into the General Declarations area of the form. This procedure is called from the cmdPrint_Click event, index equal 0 event. PrintLine prints the supplied string and then uses the Line method to strike it out. The placement and length of the strikeout line are figured using the TextHeight and TextWidth methods and the CurrentX and CurrentY properties.

```
Private Sub PrintLine(msg As String)
    Dim yPos As Long, xStart As Long, xEnd As Long
    yPos = (Printer.TextHeight(msg) / 2) + Printer.CurrentY 'figure out center of text
    xStart = Printer.CurrentX                               'remember where text starts
    xEnd = xStart + Printer.TextWidth(msg)                  'this is where text will end
    Printer.Print msg                                       'Print the text
    Printer.Line (xStart, yPos)-(xEnd, yPos)                'and print a line through it
    Printer.CurrentX = Printer.ScaleLeft                    'all the way to the left
    Printer.CurrentY = Printer.CurrentY + 100               'and down a bit.
End Sub
```

13. Enter the following code into the General Declarations area of the form. This procedure is called from the cmdPrint_Click event, index equal 0 event. PrintCircle prints the supplied string and then uses the Circle method to draw a circle around it. The placement and radius of the circle are figured using the TextHeight and TextWidth methods and the CurrentX and CurrentY properties.

```
Private Sub PrintCircle(msg As String)
    Dim radius As Long, xPos As Long, yPos As Long

    radius = (Printer.TextWidth(msg) / 2) + 100         'radius a bit bigger than 1/2 the text
    xPos = Printer.CurrentX + radius                    'Figure out where the center of the
    yPos = Printer.CurrentY + radius                    'circle will be.
    Printer.CurrentX = Printer.CurrentX + 100           'Leave a bit of space horizontally,
    Printer.CurrentY = Printer.CurrentY + radius        'and leave enough room for the circle.
    Printer.Print msg                                   'Now print the message
    Printer.Circle (xPos, yPos), radius                 'and draw the circle around the message
    Printer.CurrentX = Printer.ScaleLeft                'back to the left side of the page.
    Printer.CurrentY = yPos + radius + 100
End Sub
```

14. Enter the following code into the General Declarations area of the form. This procedure is called from the cmdPrint_Click event, index equal 1 event. PrintText prints the supplied string. Since text in a text box is one continuous string, a Do... loop is used to process the string and word wrap when necessary using the TextHeight method, ScaleWidth property, and CurrentX property. In determining whether a new page is required, the ScaleHeight and CurrentY properties are used.

```
Private Sub PrintText (text As String, msg As String)
    ' Set up font, point size, and starting point
    Printer.FontName = "Arial"
    Printer.FontSize = 10
    Printer.CurrentX = udcLEFT_MARGIN
    Call PrintHeader(msg)                           'initialize first page
    i% = 1                                          'initialize counter
    Do Until i% > Len(text)                         'print text, word wrapping as we go
        currWord = ""                               'get next word
```

```
            Do Until i% > Len(text) Or Mid$(text, i%, 1) <= " "
                currWord = currWord & Mid$(text, i%, 1)
                i% = i% + 1
        Loop
        'Check if word will fit on this line
        If (Printer.CurrentX + Printer.TextWidth(currWord)) > Printer.ScaleWidth Then
            Printer.Print                          'send carriage return/line feed to printer
            'Check if we need to start a new page
            If Printer.CurrentY > Printer.ScaleHeight - udcBOTTOM_MARGIN Then
                Call PrintFooter
            Else
                Printer.CurrentX = udcLEFT_MARGIN
            End If
        End If
        Printer.Print currWord;                    'print this word
        'Process whitespace and any control characters
        Do Until i% > Len(text) Or Mid$(text, i%, 1) > " "
            Select Case Mid$(text, i%, 1)
                Case " "                            'space
                    Printer.Print " ";
                Case Chr$(10)                       'Line feed
                    Printer.Print                   'send carriage return/line feed to printer
                    'Check if we need to start a new page
                    If Printer.CurrentY > (Printer.ScaleHeight - udcBOTTOM_MARGIN) Then
                        Call PrintHeader(msg)
                    Else
                        Printer.CurrentX = udcLEFT_MARGIN
                    End If
                Case Chr$(9)                        'tab
                    j% = (Printer.CurrentX - udcLEFT_MARGIN) / Printer.TextWidth("0")
                    j% = j% + (10 - (j% Mod 10))
                    Printer.CurrentX = j% * Printer.TextWidth("0")
            End Select
            i% = i% + 1
        Loop
    Loop
    Printer.EndDoc
End Sub
```

15. Enter the following code into the General Declarations area of the form. This procedure is called from the PrintText procedure. It prints a header on the top line of the first page. It uses the CurrentX and ScaleWidth properties together with the TextWidth method to center the supplied string.

```
Private Sub PrintHeader(msg As String)
    'Center the header message.
    Printer.CurrentX = (Printer.ScaleWidth - Printer.TextWidth(msg)) / 2
    Printer.Print msg                              'print the message
    Printer.Print                                  'print a blank space
End Sub
```

16. Enter the following code into the General Declarations area of the form. This procedure is called from the PrintText procedure. It prints a footer on the bottom line of the page. It uses the CurrentX and ScaleLeft properties to left-justify the current date. It uses the ScaleWidth and CurrentX property together with the

TextWidth method to right-justify the page number. It also uses the NewPage method to end the current page and clear the page work area.

```
Private Sub PrintFooter()
    Dim pageNumber As String
    Printer.Print                                   'print a blank space
    Printer.CurrentX = Printer.ScaleLeft            'set left coord. to left margin
    Printer.Print Date$;                            'print the system date
    pageNumber = "Page: " + Format$(Printer.Page, "###") 'set up the page number variable
    Printer.CurrentX = Printer.ScaleWidth - Printer.TextWidth(pageNumber) 'Set left coord.
    Printer.Print pageNumber                         'to right margin minus page number
                                                     'variable width
    Printer.NewPage                                  'start a new page
End Sub
```

17. Enter the following code into the mnuExit_Click event. This simply ends the programs.

```
Private Sub mnuExit_Click ()
    End
End Sub
```

18. Create a new form named frmPrinting and place on it the controls specified in Table 52-31.

Table 52-31 Objects and properties for the Printing form

Object	Property	Setting
Form	Name	frmPrinting
	Caption	Printing...
	BorderStyle	3 - Fixed Dialog
	ControlBox	False
CommandButton	Name	cmdCancel
	Caption	Cancel
Label	Name	lblPrinterAndPort
	Caption	""
Label	Name	lblPrinting
	Caption	Printing Document on

19. Check the appearance of your form against Figure 52-2.

20. Enter the following code into the Form_Load event. The Refresh method is to immediately update the form to display your output's printer name and port. This information is found by using the DeviceName and Port properties.

```
Private Sub Form_Load ()
    Refresh
    lblPrinterAndPort = Printer.DeviceName & " on " & Printer.Port
End Sub
```

Figure 52-2
The Printing
form during
design

21. Enter the following code in the cmdCancel_Click event. This event occurs when the user chooses the Cancel button, which immediately ends the current print job. This is done by using the KillDoc method. Once the print job is terminated, the form is unloaded from memory.

```
Private Sub cmdCancel_Click ()
    Printer.KillDoc
    Unload Me
End Sub
```

22. Create a new form named frmPrintSetup and place on it the controls specified in Table 52-32.

Table 52-32 Objects and properties for the Print Setup form

Object	Property	Setting
Form	Name	frmPrintSetup
	Caption	Print Setup
	BorderStyle	3 - Fixed Dialog
	ControlBox	(0) False
Label	Name	lblPrinter
	Caption	&Printer:
ComboBox	Name	cboPrinter
	Style	2 - Dropdown List
Command Button	Name	cmdOK
	Caption	OK
Command Button	Name	cmdCancel
	Caption	Cancel
Frame	Name	fraOrientation
	Caption	Orientation
Frame	Name	fraPrintQuality
	Caption	Print Quality
Frame	Name	fraPaper
	Caption	Paper

23. Add the objects and properties listed in Table 52-33 to fraOrientation. Be sure to create the controls on top of fraOrientation. The positioning of these controls is not critical.

Table 52-33 Objects and properties placed in fraOrientation

Object	Property	Setting
OptionButton	Name	optOrientation
	Caption	Po&rtrait
	Index	0
	Value	True
OptionButton	Name	optOrientation
	Caption	&Landscape
	Index	1

24. Add the objects and properties listed in Table 52-34 to fraPrintQuality. Be sure to create the controls on top of fraPrintQuality. The positioning of these controls is not critical.

Table 52-34 Objects and properties placed in fraPrintQuality

Object	Property	Setting
Option Button	Name	optPrintQuality
	Caption	&Draft
	Index	0
	Value	(-1) True
Option Button	Name	optPrintQuality
	Caption	L&ow Resolution
	Index	1
Option Button	Name	optPrintQuality
	Caption	&Medium Resolution
	Index	2
Option Button	Name	optPrintQuality
	Caption	&High Resolution
	Index	

25. Add the objects and properties listed in Table 52-35 to fraPaper. Be sure to create the controls on top of fraPaper. The positioning of these controls is not critical.

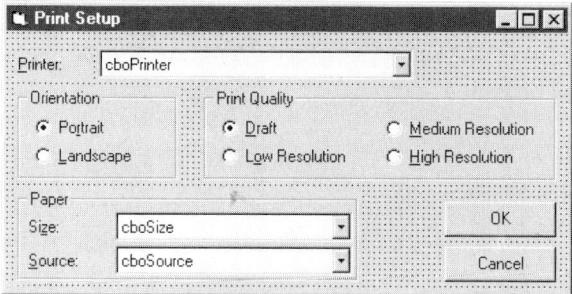

Figure 52-3 The Print Setup form during design

Table 52-35 Objects and properties placed in fraPaper

Object	Property	Setting
Label	Name	lblSize
	Caption	Si&ze:
Label	Name	lblSource
	Caption	&Source:
ComboBox	Name	cboSize
	Style	2 - Dropdown List
ComboBox	Name	cboSource
	Style	2 - Dropdown List

26. Check the appearance of your form against Figure 52-3.

27. Enter the following code into the Form_Load event. This event occurs when the form loads into memory after the user chooses Print Setup from the Print project form's File menu. First, Form_Load investigates how many printers are defined on your system. By using the DeviceName and Port properties, the combo box object, cboPrinter, is populated. Comparing the printer list, just defined, to the printer that the system is currently pointing to, by use of the DeviceName property, you establish which Printer should appear in the combo box as the default printer. The sub procedure PrinterDefinitions is called to process the printer properties and reflect them on the frmPrintSetup form.

```
Private Sub Form_Load()
    Dim Prt As String, obj As Object
    Dim indx%, x%
    Screen.MousePointer = vbHourglass
    'Check to see what printers have been assigned to operating system
    For Each obj In Printers
        cboPrinter.AddItem obj.DeviceName & " on " & obj.Port, indx%
        indx% = indx% + 1
    Next
```

continued on next page

continued from previous page

```
    'Check system for which printer is currently being used
    For x% = 0 To indx%
        If cboPrinter.List(x%) Like Printer.DeviceName & "*" Then
            cboPrinter.ListIndex = x%
            Exit For
        End If
    Next
    Call PrinterDefinitions
    Screen.MousePointer = vbDefault
End Sub
```

28. Enter the following code in the General Declarations area of the form. This procedure is called from the Form_Load and cboPrinter_Click events.
PrinterDefinitions examines the printer defined in the DeviceName property and
updates the frmPrintSetup form to reflect the operating system's printer settings.
This is done by using the Orientation, PaperSize, PrintQuality, and PaperBin
properties.

```
Private Sub PrinterDefinitions()
    'Check system printer for orientation
    If Printer.Orientation = vbPRORPortrait Then
        optOrientation(0).Value = True
    Else
        optOrientation(1).Value = True
    End If
    'Fill in combo box size with different paper sizes
    cboSize.AddItem "8.5 x 11 in.", 0
    cboSize.AddItem "8.5 x 14 in.", 1
    cboSize.AddItem "7.5 x 10.6 in.", 2
    'Check current printer settings
    If Printer.PaperSize = vbPRPSLetter Then
        cboSize.ListIndex = 0
    ElseIf Printer.PaperSize = vbPRPSLegal Then
        cboSize.ListIndex = 1
    ElseIf Printer.PaperSize = vbPRPSExecutive Then
        cboSize.ListIndex = 2
    End If
    'Check current Print Quality setting
    If Printer.PrintQuality = vbPRPQDraft Or Printer.PrintQuality = 75 Then
        optPrintQuality(0).Value = True
    ElseIf Printer.PrintQuality = vbPRPQLow Or Printer.PrintQuality = 75 Then
        optPrintQuality(1).Value = True
    ElseIf Printer.PrintQuality = vbPRPQMedium Or Printer.PrintQuality = 150 Then
        optPrintQuality(2).Value = True
    ElseIf Printer.PrintQuality = vbPRPQHigh Or Printer.PrintQuality = 300 Then
        optPrintQuality(3).Value = True
    End If
    'Fill in combo box source with paper bin options
    cboSource.AddItem "Upper Tray", 0
    cboSource.AddItem "Envelope Manual Feed", 1
    cboSource.AddItem "Manual Feed", 2
    cboSource.AddItem "Lower Tray", 3
    cboSource.AddItem "Envelope", 4
    'Check current printer settings
    If Printer.PaperBin = vbPRBNUpper Then               'upper bin
        cboSource.ListIndex = 0
```

```
    ElseIf Printer.PaperBin = vbPRBNEnvManual Then    'envelope manual insert
        cboSource.ListIndex = 1
    ElseIf Printer.PaperBin = vbPRBNManual Then       'manual insert
        cboSource.ListIndex = 2
    ElseIf Printer.PaperBin = vbPRBNLower Then        'lower bin
        cboSource.ListIndex = 3
    ElseIf Printer.PaperBin = vbPRBNEnvelope Then     'envelope
        cboSource.ListIndex = 4
    End If
End Sub
```

29. Enter the following code into the cboPrinter_Click event. This event occurs when the user clicks the Printer combo box object to change a printer. This event examines each Printer object's name and compares it to the printer name selected in the combo box object. Once a match has been found, that printer becomes the default printer by means of the Set statement. Then PrinterDefinitions is called to set the form's values to reflect the new default printer's settings.

```
Private Sub cboPrinter_Change()
    Dim ptr As Object
    'Examine each Printer object to find one connected with a similar
    'name to the one selected in the combo box and make it the default printer
    For Each ptr In Printers
        If ptr.DeviceName Like Left(cboPrinter.List(cboPrinter.ListIndex), 5) & "*" Then
            Set Printer = ptr
            Exit For
        End If
    Next
    'Get printer default information
    Call PrinterDefinitions
End Sub
```

30. Enter the following code into the cmdOK_Click event. This event occurs when the user clicks the OK command button. This event processes all the changed properties to the current printer by means of the Orientation, PaperSize, PrintQuality, and PaperBin properties.

```
Private Sub cmdOK_Click()
    Screen.MousePointer = vbHourglass
    'Determine the print layout
    If optOrientation(0).Value = True Then
        Printer.Orientation = vbPRORPortrait
    Else
        Printer.Orientation = vbPRORLandscape
    End If
    'Determine the paper size
    Select Case cboSize.ListIndex
        Case 0
            Printer.PaperSize = vbPRPSLetter
        Case 1
            Printer.PaperSize = vbPRPSLegal
        Case 2
            Printer.PaperSize = vbPRPSExecutive
    End Select
    'Determine the print quality
```

continued on next page

continued from previous page

```
    If optPrintQuality(0).Value = True Then
        Printer.PrintQuality = vbPRPQDraft
    ElseIf optPrintQuality(1).Value = True Then
        Printer.PrintQuality = vbPRPQLow
    ElseIf optPrintQuality(2).Value = True Then
        Printer.PrintQuality = vbPRPQMedium
    ElseIf optPrintQuality(3).Value = True Then
        Printer.PrintQuality = vbPRPQHigh
    End If
    'Determine which paper bin is used
    Select Case cboSource.ListIndex
        Case 0
            Printer.PaperBin = vbPRBNAuto
        Case 1
            Printer.PaperBin = vbPRBNUpper
        Case 2
            Printer.PaperBin = vbPRBNLower
    End Select
    Screen.MousePointer = vbDefault
    Unload Me
End Sub
```

31. Enter the following code into the cmdCancel_Click event. This event occurs when the user chooses the Cancel command button. The form is removed from memory and changes to any of the properties are not made.

```
Private Sub cmdCancel_Click()
    Unload Me
End Sub
```

How It Works

This example program sets up a simple graphic pattern and a simple note entry form, in which both can be printed. The form also has a menu with three choices: Print Setup, Print Form, and Exit.

You can print the form by selecting the File menu and clicking on the Print Form option. This triggers the mnuPrintForm_Click event, which uses the PrintForm method to send to the printer a copy of the form and any text that is visible in the text box.

You can look at or change any printer settings by selecting the Print Setup option from the File menu. This loads the Print Setup form, which examines your system and finds which printer you have defined. If you click on the Cancel command button, changes made on this form do not update the Printer object properties. Clicking on the OK command button triggers the cmdOK_Click event, which processes all the option button control arrays and combo boxes on this form to set the appropriate Printer object properties. The Printer object properties affected are Orientation, PaperSize, PrintQuality, and PaperBin.

Choosing either Print command button loads the frmPrinting form. This form shows the status of the print job, indicates which printer your output is going to, and allows you to terminate your print job before it finishes. The DeviceName and Port properties are used to determine your print destination. Clicking on the Cancel command button triggers the cmdCancel_Click event. This event issues a KillDoc method, which immediately terminates your print job going to the output buffer.

Choosing the Print command button in the Graphics frame triggers the cmdPrint(0)_Click event. This event calls three sub procedures that demonstrate the use of the graphics methods on the Printer object. The PrintBox procedure prints a box around the text supplied in one of its arguments by using the Line method. The dimensions and placement of the box are determined using the CurrentX and CurrentY properties along with the TextHeight and TextWidth methods. PrintBox also has the Shaded argument, which indicates whether the text inside the box is shaded. If the argument is True, the PSet method generates a dot every 50 positions inside the box.

The second procedure, PrintLine, prints its supplied text argument and then draws a line through it. The position of the line is determined by the CurrentX and CurrentY properties in conjunction with the TextHeight method. The TextWidth method calculates the length of the strikeout line.

In the third procedure, the PrintCircle method generates a circle with the supplied text argument centered within it. The placement and radius of the circle is determined using the TextHeight and TextWidth methods and the CurrentX and CurrentY properties.

Choosing the Print command button in the Text Output frame triggers the cmdPrint(1)_Click event. This event first checks the text box for any information. If it is empty, nothing is done. The event then checks the cboScale ComboBox to determine if the printout is to be scaled. Then the event calls a sub procedure, PrintText, that prints the information entered in the text box.

The PrintText procedure prints the string that was entered in the txtTextOutput text box. It uses the CurrentX and ScaleWidth properties with the TextWidth method to determine whether the string will fit on the current print line or will have to wrap to the next line. The CurrentY and ScaleHeight properties determine whether the string will fit on the current page or will have to be continued on another page.

PrintText calls two sub procedures, PrintHeader and PrintFooter. The PrintHeader procedure prints a header at the top of the page. It uses the CurrentX and ScaleWidth properties and the TextWidth method to center the supplied string. The PrintFooter procedure prints a footer at the bottom of the page. It uses the CurrentX and ScaleLeft properties to left-justify the current date. It uses the ScaleWidth and CurrentX property and the TextWidth method to right-justify the page number. It also uses the NewPage method to end the current page and clear the page work area. After both of these sub procedures end, execution returns to PrintText.

53

USING THE CLIPBOARD

All Windows programs can access an area of the environment called the Clipboard. The Clipboard is a temporary storage area for text and graphics. Your program can use it to temporarily hold data for use elsewhere in the program, or to share this data with other Windows programs.

Windows provides a program called Clipboard Viewer which allows the user to view the Clipboard area. This program only lets you view the data in the Clipboard area; it has nothing to do with the process of using the Clipboard from your application. Even though the Clipboard Viewer program is not active all the time, the Clipboard area is always accessible as long as Windows is running.

The Clipboard is the simplest way to share data between programs. It lets you exchange text and picture data on a purely manual basis, using the familiar cut-and-paste routine. The next higher level of data exchange uses DDE. This lets you automate the process of exchanging information, even to the point of having the link update in real time as the data changes in the source program. The highest level of information exchange uses OLE. This lets you embed the actual object in its native form within your application and lets you use the other application's features and functions within your Visual Basic program.

Uses of the Clipboard

The Clipboard can hold three types of items. First, it can hold text. Text is any combination of letters, numbers, or characters that can be represented by ASCII codes. Second, it can hold graphics. Windows lets the user cut and paste pictures as well as text. However, unlike the case with cutting, copying, and pasting text, each individual program must define how graphics are to be handled. Finally, the Clipboard can hold DDE messages being sent from one program to another and link information for an OLE object.

The Clipboard is a temporary storage location, and may hold only one item at a time of each of these data types. When a program copies an item to the Clipboard, it replaces any item of the same type that previously resided there. Anything on the Clipboard disappears when you exit Windows, although you can use the Clipboard program to save the Clipboard's contents to a file.

The Windows environment automatically gives the user a way to select text and send it to the Clipboard, and the Visual Basic text box inherits these automatic methods. To select text, hold down the [SHIFT] key and press one of the arrow keys. Alternately, you can click and hold the left mouse button and drag it over the text to be selected. Selected text is highlighted. Once text is selected, press the [CONTROL]-[C] key combination to copy the text to the Clipboard. Press [CONTROL]-[X] to send the text to the Clipboard and delete it from the screen. Data that is held in the Clipboard area can be retrieved by pressing the [CONTROL]-[V] key combination. Most Windows programs also give menu equivalents to these combinations, usually under the Edit menu.

All of these key combinations and their functions are handled by the Windows environment, so you don't need to program these routines into your Visual Basic application yourself. However, you may want to provide the user with alternative methods for cutting, copying, and pasting data to and from the Clipboard. Visual Basic gives you the tools you will need to clear the Clipboard, copy data or text to it, determine the type of data currently stored on it, or retrieve text or data from it.

Clipboard Summary

The Clear method is the simplest of the Clipboard methods. As you may guess by its name, it clears any data that currently resides on the Clipboard. The GetData and GetText methods (used for graphic information and for text, respectively) are used to retrieve information from the Clipboard. These methods must specify the particular type of information they are requesting. Before either method executes, you can use the GetFormat method to determine whether the desired type of information is currently held on the Clipboard. There are also two methods, SetData (for graphics) and SetText (for text), which can be used to send information to the Clipboard. Table 53-1 lists the methods that affect the Clipboard object.

Table 53-1 Methods that affect the Clipboard object

Use or Set This...	Type	To Do This...
Clear	Method	Clear the contents of the Clipboard area
GetData	Method	Retrieve graphic data from the Clipboard area
GetFormat	Method	Return True if the specified data type is stored in the Clipboard area
GetText	Method	Retrieve text from the Clipboard area
SetData	Method	Place graphic data on the Clipboard area
SetText	Method	Place text on the Clipboard area

Constant Values

It is usually best to use named constants rather than numeric values when developing software. Named constants make your code more readable and easier to maintain.

Table 53-2 lists the values of the constants relevant to this chapter, mentions their names, and briefly describes what they mean. These constants can be viewed in the VB Constants module (or, in some cases, in other object libraries), using the Object Browser. It is not necessary to explicitly add these objects to your project.

Table 53-2 Visual Basic constants for the Clipboard object

Value	Constant Name	Meaning
&HFFFFBF00	vbCFLink	Clipboard holds a DDE Link
&HFFFFBF01	vbCFRTF	Clipboard holds a Rich Text Format file
1	vbCFText	Clipboard holds text
2	vbCFBitmap	Clipboard holds a bitmap graphic
3	vbCFMetafile	Clipboard holds a Windows metafile graphic
8	vbCFDIB	Clipboard holds a device-independent bitmap graphic
9	vbCFPalette	Clipboard holds a color palette
14	vbCFEMetafile	Clipboard holds an enhanced Windows metafile graphic
15	vbCFFiles	Clipboard holds a Microsoft Windows Explorer file list

CLEAR METHOD

Objects Affected Buttons, Clipboard, ColumnHeaders, ComboBox, DataObject, DataObjectFiles, ErrObject, ListBox, ListImages, ListItems, Nodes, Panels, Tabs

Purpose The Clear method clears the contents of the Clipboard. The Clear method used on list boxes, combo boxes, and other controls is similar, but with different implications. For more on the Clear method used with list boxes and combo boxes, see Chapter 46, "List and Combo Boxes."

General Syntax

```
Clipboard.Clear
```

Example Syntax

```
Private Sub Command1_Click ()
    Clipboard.Clear
End Sub
```

Description The Clear method, which has no arguments, clears any and all text and graphics that are currently stored in the Clipboard area. After this is done, nothing can be retrieved from the Clipboard until some text or graphic information is placed on it.

The example syntax clears the Clipboard. Anything that had been stored in the Clipboard is no longer retrievable.

Example
In the Clipboard project at the end of this chapter, the command button cmndClearClipboard invokes this method to clear the Clipboard.

GetData Method

Objects Affected   Clipboard, DataObject

Purpose   Retrieves graphic information (pictures) from the Clipboard area. Table 53-3 summarizes this argument of the GetData method. Table 53-4 details possible values and their meanings.

General Syntax

```
Clipboard.GetData([format%])
```

Table 53-3 Argument of the GetData method

Argument	Description
format%	An integer expression indicating the desired data format

Table 53-4 Data formats for the GetData method

format%	Constant Name	Meaning
0 or not specified		Windows attempts to automatically use the correct format2. (default)
2	vbCFBitmap	Requesting a bitmap graphic.
3	vbCFMetafile	Requesting a metafile graphic.
8	vbCFDIB	Requesting a device-independent bitmap graphic.
14	vbCFEMetafile	Requesting an enhanced metafile graphic.

Example Syntax

```
Private Sub Command1_Click ()
    Picture1.Picture = Clipboard.GetData(vbCFBitmap)     'gets bitmap from the Clipboard
End Sub
```

Description   The GetData method copies the specified type of graphic data from the Clipboard into the specified object. The type of data requested is specified by the format% parameter. This parameter is an integer with the value of 2, 3, 8, or 14.

If the format is not specified, it will default to 0, and Windows will attempt to return the correct format.

The example syntax retrieves a bitmap graphic from the Clipboard and assigns it to the Picture property of Picture1, in essence pasting it into the picture box.

Example	In the Clipboard project at the end of this chapter, the GetData method is used in the menuEdit_Click event. This event copies any bitmap information that may be in the Clipboard to the Picture1 picture control.
Comments	If no data of the requested type is being stored on the Clipboard, nothing is returned.

GETFORMAT METHOD

Objects Affected	Clipboard, DataObject
Purpose	The GetFormat method returns an integer value (True or False) indicating whether the requested data type is stored in the Clipboard. Tables 53-5 and 53-6 summarize the arguments of the GetFormat method.

General Syntax

```
Clipboard.GetFormat(format%)
```

Table 53-5 Argument of the GetFormat method

Argument	Description
format%	An integer expression indicating the desired data format

Table 53-6 Data formats for the GetFormat method

format%	Constant Name	Meaning
&HFFFFBF00	vbCFLink	Returns True if a DDE link is stored on the Clipboard
&HFFFFBF01	vbCFRTF	Returns True if a Rich Text Format file is stored on the Clipboard
1	vbCFText	Returns True if text is stored on the Clipboard
2	vbCFBitmap	Returns True if a bitmap graphic is stored on the Clipboard
3	vbCFMetafile	Returns True if a metafile graphic is stored on the Clipboard
8	vbCFDIB	Returns True if a device-independent bitmap graphic is stored on the Clipboard
9	vbCFPalette	Returns True if a color palette is stored on the Clipboard
14	vbCFEMetafile	Returns True if an enhanced metafile graphic is stored on the Clipboard
15	vbCFFiles	Returns True if an Explorer file list is stored on the Clipboard

Example Syntax

```
Private Sub Command1_Click ()
    TextStored = GetFormat(vbCFText)        'returns True if text is stored on Clipboard
End Sub
```

Description	The GetFormat method tests the contents of the Clipboard and returns True if the requested data type is stored on it or False if not. The type of

data requested is specified by the format% parameter. This parameter is an integer and must be one of the values specified in Table 53-6.

The example syntax determines whether any text is currently residing in the Clipboard. The answer, which will be True or False, is stored in the variable TextStored.

Example   The GetFormat method is used in the menuEditBar_Click and menuEdit_Click events of the Clipboard project at the end of this chapter. The value returned by the GetFormat method is used to determine whether to copy the data from the Clipboard or to enable the correct menu commands.

GETTEXT METHOD

Objects Affected   Clipboard

Purpose   The GetText method retrieves text information from the Clipboard. Tables 53-7 and 53-8 summarize the arguments of the GetText method.

General Syntax

```
Clipboard.GetText([format%])
```

Table 53-7 Argument of the GetText method

Argument	Description
format%	An integer expression indicating the desired data format

Table 53-8 Data formats for the GetText method

format%	Constant Name	Meaning
&HFFFFBF00	vbCFLink	Requesting a DDE link
&HFFFFBF01	vbCFRTF	Requesting a Rich Text Format file
1	vbCFText	Requesting text information

Example Syntax

```
Private Sub Command1_Click ()
    Text1.Text = Clipboard.GetText(vbCFText) 'gets text from the Clipboard
End Sub
```

Description   The GetText method copies the specified type of text from the Clipboard into the specified object. The type of data requested is specified by the format% parameter. This parameter is an integer with a value of 1,

&HFFFFBF00, or &HFFFFBF01. Table 53-8 summarizes the data formats for the GetText method.

The format value vbCFLink (&HFFFFBF00) can be used to set up a Dynamic Data Exchange (DDE) link. If the format is not specified, it will default to 1 (vbCFText).

The example syntax copies any text stored on the Clipboard to the text box Text1. Assigning the text returned by the GetText method to the Text property of the text box causes the text to be displayed in the text area of the box.

Example
In the Clipboard project at the end of this chapter, the GetText method is used in the menuEdit_Click event. This event copies any text information that may be in the Clipboard to the Text1 text box control.

Comments
If the requested data type is not present on the Clipboard, a zero-length string ("") is returned.

SETDATA METHOD

Objects Affected   Clipboard, DataObject

Purpose   The SetData method places graphic information in the Clipboard object. Table 53-9 summarizes the arguments of the SetData method, and Table 53-10 gives the meanings of the format% values.

General Syntax

```
Clipboard.SetData graphic%[, format%]
```

Table 53-9 Arguments of the SetData method

Argument	Description
graphic%	An integer number that is the handle of the graphic image (Picture or Image properties)
format%	An integer expression indicating the data format of the graphic image

Table 53-10 Data formats for the SetData method

format%	Constant Name	Meaning
0, not specified		Windows will automatically determine the correct format
2	vbCFBitmap	Placing a bitmap graphic
3	vbCFMetafile	Placing a metafile graphic
8	vbCFDIB	Placing a device-independent bitmap graphic
9	vbCFPalette	Placing a color palette
14	vbCFEMetafile	Placing an enhanced metafile graphic

Example Syntax

```
Private Sub Command1_Click()
    AppActivate "CorelDRAW - UNTITLED.CDR"
    Clipboard.SetData Picture1.Picture, vbCFBitmap      'copies a bitmap to the Clipboard
    SendKeys "%ep", True                                'pastes the bitmap into Corel
    Clipboard.SetData Picture2.Picture, vbCFMetafile    'copies a metafile to the Clipboard
    SendKeys "%ep", True                                'pastes the metafile into Corel
    Clipboard.SetData Picture3.Picture, vbCFDIB         'copies a device independent bitmap
    SendKeys "%ep", True                                'pastes the dib into Corel
    Clipboard.SetData Picture4.Picture, vbCFPalette     'copies a color palette
    SendKeys "%ep", True                                'pastes the palette into Corel
    Clipboard.SetData Picture5.Picture, vbCFEMetafile   'copies an enhanced metafile to ⇐
                                                            the Clipboard.
    SendKeys "%ep", True                                'pastes the metafile into Corel
End Sub
```

Description   The SetData method is the complement to the GetData method. It copies
the specified graphic to the Clipboard in the specified format. You would
normally use the Picture or Image properties of the Picture or Image control. The type of data being sent to the Clipboard is specified by the
format% parameter. This parameter is an integer with the value of 2, 3, 8,
9, or 14. Table 53-10 details its possible values and their meanings.

If the format is not specified, it will default to 0, and Windows will
attempt to determine the proper format. If a bitmap is placed on the
Clipboard, any associated palette is automatically placed along with the
bitmap.

The example syntax gives statements showing how the four kinds of
graphics listed in Table 53-10 can be copied from a picture box to the
Clipboard.

Example   In the Clipboard project at the end of this chapter, this method is used in
the menuEdit_Click event. When this event executes, the bitmap in the
picture control Picture1 is copied to the Clipboard.

SETTEXT METHOD

Objects Affected   Clipboard

Purpose   The SetText method places text information in the Clipboard object.
Tables 53-11 and 53-12 summarize the arguments of the SetText method.

General Syntax

```
Clipboard.SetText Text$[, format%]
```

Table 53-11 Arguments of the SetText method

Argument	Description
Text$	A string expression containing the text to be sent to the Clipboard
format%	An integer expression indicating the data format of the text

Table 53-12 Data formats for the SetText method

format%	Constant	Meaning
&HFFFFBF00	vbCFLink	Sending a DDE Link
&HFFFFBF01	vbCFRTF	Sending Rich Text Format text information
1	vbCFText	Sending text information

Example Syntax

```
Private Sub menuEditCopy_Click ()
    Clipboard.SetText Text1.Text    'copies the text from the text box to the Clipboard
End Sub
```

Description   The SetText method is the compliment of the GetText method. It copies the specified text information to the Clipboard in the specified format. The type of data being sent to the Clipboard is specified by the format% parameter. This parameter is an integer with the value of 1, &HFFFFBF00, or &HFFFFBF01. Table 53-12 details its possible values and their meanings.

     The format value vbCFLink (&HFFFFBF00) can be used to set up a Dynamic Data Exchange (DDE) link.

     If the format is not specified, it will default to 1 (vbCFText) as in the example syntax, which copies the text in text box Text1 to the Clipboard.

Example   In the Clipboard project at the end of this chapter, this method is used in the menuEdit_Click event. When this event is executed, the text in the text box control Text1 is copied to the Clipboard.

The Clipboard Project

Project Overview

The project outlined on the following pages demonstrates the use of each of the elements of Visual Basic discussed in this chapter. When you have finished with this project, you should feel comfortable with the concepts behind using the Clear, GetData, GetFormat, GetText, SetData, and SetText methods. This project implements the core functions of a typical Edit menu, and you can easily adapt the techniques detailed here for use in your own programs.

Assembling the Project

1. Create a new form (the Clipboard form), and place on it the controls specified in Table 53-13. Use the Menu Editor window to create a menu structure for the project, as detailed in Table 53-14.

Table 53-13 Controls and property settings for the Clipboard project

Object	Property	Setting
Form	BorderStyle	1–Fixed Single
	Caption	Clipboard Project
PictureBox	AutoRedraw	True
	Name	Picture1
	Picture	(use any .bmp you like)
TextBox	Name	Text1
	MultiLine	True
CommandButton	Name	cmndClearClipboard
	Caption	Clear Clipboard
CommandButton	Name	cmndClearPicture
	Caption	Clear Picture
Shape	BorderColor	Palette &H00C0C0C0 (Light Gray)
	BorderWidth	7
	Name	shapPicture
	Visible	False
Shape	BorderColor	&H00C0C0C0–Light Gray
	BorderWidth	7
	Name	shapText
	Visible	False

Table 53-14 Design parameters for the menu system of the Clipboard project

Name	Caption	Property	Setting
menuFile	&File		
menuExit	E&xit		
menuBarEdit	&Edit		
menuEdit	Cu&t	Index	0
menuEdit	&Copy	Index	1
menuEdit	&Paste	Index	2

2. Check the appearance of your form against Figure 53-1. Note that the two Shape controls are exactly the same size and are in the same location as Picture1 and Text1. They are graphical controls, and will automatically place themselves behind the picture and text boxes. (See Chapter 33, "Application Appearance," for a discussion of control layering.) The BorderWidth of 7 makes their borders extend beyond the borders of the controls they're behind.

3. Enter the following code into the cmndClearClipboard_Click event. When the user clicks the cmndClearClipboard button, this event clears the Clipboard of all text and graphic information.

```
Private Sub cmndClearClipboard_Click ()
    Clipboard.Clear           'clear the Clipboard of all data
End Sub
```

4. Enter the following code in the cmndClearPicture_Click event. It queries the user to make sure it's OK to clear the picture and then does so if the user responds "Yes" to the confirmation MsgBox.

```
Private Sub cmndClearPicture_Click ()
    If MsgBox("Clear Picture?", 4) = 6 Then    'OK to clear?
        Picture1.Picture = LoadPicture()       'sure, yabetcha, zap the picture
    End If
End Sub
```

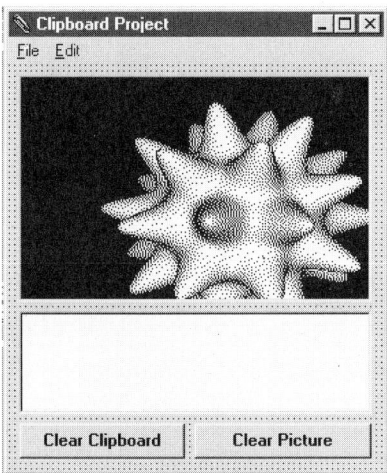

Figure 53-1 The Clipboard project during design

5. Enter the following code into the Form_Load event. This event activates the Window's Clipboard program, which displays the current contents of the Clipboard area.

```
Private Sub Form_Load ()
    On Error Resume Next        'if error occurs, it's because Clipboard isn't loaded yet
    AppActivate "Clipboard"     'try to activate Clipboard
    If Err > 0 Then A% = Shell("CLIPBRD.EXE", 1) 'if activation failed, open Clipboard
End Sub
```

6. Enter the following code in the menuBarEdit_Click event. This sets up the Edit menu properly, enabling only those commands that are applicable. It checks to see what control is active, and if it's the text box or picture box, then goes on to check if there is text selected to cut or copy, or if there is information on the Clipboard in the correct format to paste. This provides the correct visual feedback to the user by disabling commands that aren't applicable. It also makes coding in the actual edit commands easier, as no validity checking has to be done—if the command was chosen, then the target control and data must be okay.

```
Private Sub menuBarEdit_Click ()
    menuEdit(0).Enabled = False                     'Cut
    menuEdit(1).Enabled = False                     'Copy
    menuEdit(2).Enabled = False                     'Paste
    If TypeOf Screen.ActiveControl Is TextBox Then  'on the text box?
        If Text1.SelText <> "" Then                 'is there text selected?
            menuEdit(0).Enabled = True              'there is text to cut
            menuEdit(1).Enabled = True              'there is text to copy
        End If
        If Clipboard.GetFormat(vbCFText) Then       'is there text on Clipboard?
            menuEdit(2).Enabled = True              'there is text on Clipboard to paste
        End If
    ElseIf TypeOf Screen.ActiveControl Is picturebox Then 'on the picture box?
        menuEdit(0).Enabled = True                      'OK to cut picture
        menuEdit(1).Enabled = True                      'OK to copy picture
        If Clipboard.GetFormat(vbCFBitmap) Then         'is there a picture on the⇐
                                                        Clipboard?
            menuEdit(2).Enabled = True                  'there is a picture to paste
        End If
    End If
End Sub
```

7. Enter the following code in the menuEdit_Click event. These commands perform the actual edit functions of cutting, copying, and pasting. All three cases first check to see what kind of control they're on. Once that's done, each routine handles things a bit differently. The Cut routine sends the appropriate data (either text or a picture, depending on what control had the focus) to the Clipboard, then clears the data. The Copy routine does the same thing, but without clearing the data. The Paste routine checks to see if the Clipboard has the kind of data needed for the control that has the focus, and if so, copies the Clipboard data into the control.

```
Private Sub menuEdit_Click (Index As Integer)
    Select Case Index
        Case 0 '******************** Cut
            If TypeOf Screen.ActiveControl Is TextBox Then      'on text box?
                Clipboard.SetText Text1.SelText                 'copy to Clipboard
                Text1.SelText = ""                              'clear selected text
            ElseIf TypeOf Screen.ActiveControl Is picturebox Then  'on picture box?
                Clipboard.SetData Picture1.Picture, vbCFBitmap  'copy to Clipboard
                Picture1.Picture = LoadPicture("")              'clear picture
            End If
        Case 1 '******************** Copy
            If TypeOf Screen.ActiveControl Is TextBox Then      'on text box?
                Clipboard.SetText Text1.SelText                 'copy to Clipboard
            ElseIf TypeOf Screen.ActiveControl Is picturebox Then  'on picture box?
                Clipboard.SetData Picture1.Picture, vbCFBitmap  'copy to Clipboard
            End If
        Case 2 '******************** Paste
            If TypeOf Screen.ActiveControl Is TextBox Then      'on text box?
                If Clipboard.GetFormat(vbCFText) = True Then    'text to paste?
                    Text1.SelText = Clipboard.GetText(vbCFText) 'paste in text
                End If
            ElseIf TypeOf Screen.ActiveControl Is picturebox Then  'on picture box?
                If Clipboard.GetFormat(vbCFBitmap) = True Then  'picture to paste?
                    Picture1.Picture = Clipboard.GetData(vbCFBitmap) 'paste picture
                End If
            End If
    End Select
End Sub
```

8. Enter the following code in the menuExit routine. This merely ends the program.

```
Private Sub menuExit_Click ()
    End                         'end the program
End Sub
```

9. Enter the following code in the Picture1_DblClick event. This clears the picture by calling the cmndClearPicture_Click event discussed above.

```
Private Sub Picture1_DblClick ()
    cmndClearPicture_Click      'clear the picture
End Sub
```

10. Enter the following code in the appropriate GotFocus and LostFocus routines. These make the shapes that lie behind the controls visible or invisible to highlight the control that has the focus.

```
Private Sub Picture1_GotFocus ()
    shapPicture.Visible = True      'highlight the picture box to show focus
End Sub

Private Sub Picture1_LostFocus ()
    shapPicture.Visible = False     'unhighlight picture box to show loss of focus
End Sub

Private Sub Text1_GotFocus ()
    shapText.Visible = True         'highlight text box to show focus
```

continued on next page

continued from previous page

```
End Sub

Private Sub Text1_LostFocus ()
     shapText.Visible = False          'unhighlight text box to show loss of focus
End Sub
```

How It Works

This program copies graphic and text information to and from the Windows environment Clipboard. When the program begins, the Form_Load event activates the Clipboard viewing program if it is already running. If the Clipboard viewer isn't running, the Form_Load event executes it. (This program works best if the Clipboard Viewer and the Clipboard project windows are arranged so that both can be seen at the same time.)

The picture box and text box have Shape controls behind them that are made visible when the appropriate control gets the focus. This makes it obvious where the focus lies.

The command button cmndClearPicture erases the picture in the project window, as does double-clicking on the picture. Clicking the cmndClearClipboard button clears the Clipboard of all text and graphic information.

The Edit menu has the ubiquitous Cut, Copy, and Paste functions. The menuBarEdit_Click routine first sets up the menu to make sure that only the appropriate commands are enabled. For example, if there is no text selected and the text box has the focus, Cut and Copy are disabled. If there is no appropriate information on the Clipboard (either text for the text box or a bitmap for the picture box), then Paste is disabled.

Once the menu pulls down, the code to add this basic edit functionality is simple. The bulk of the code lies in checking where to cut, copy, or paste; the actual commands to perform these actions take only a couple of lines. The routine first uses the Index property of the control array to see what command was executed. Each command starts by determining what control has the focus. After each routine determines that, it performs the appropriate action, as detailed in step 7.

Figure 53-2 shows the Clipboard project in action.

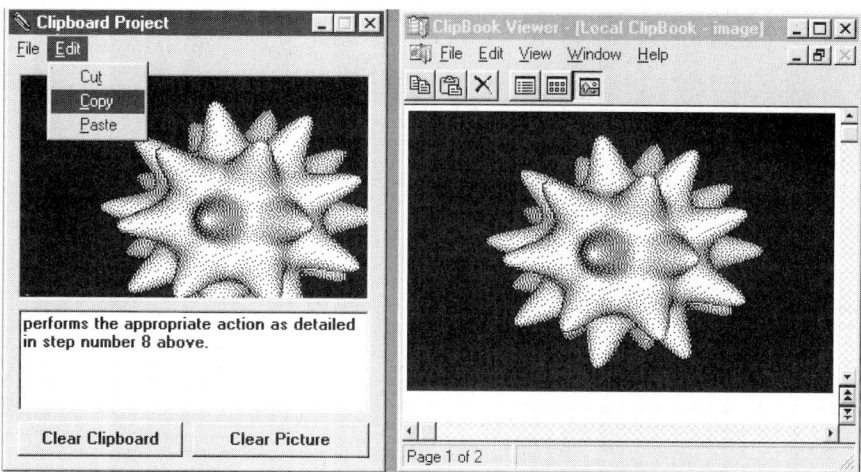

Figure 53-2   The Clipboard project in action

54

APPLICATION FOCUS

A control or form that is currently active and ready to respond to a mouse click or keypress has the application *focus*. Users should normally be able to set the focus however they wish, giving them control over the program.

Some situations, however, make it imperative that you control the focus from within your code. For example, you may wish to validate a user entry in a text box. If the entry is incorrect, your code might display a message giving the correct format and set the focus back to the text box to give the user another try. Another setting in your program might make certain options unavailable: You might have a database application that has both browse mode (for looking at records without changing them) and edit mode (for adding or updating records). A menu command might then toggle between these two modes. Browse mode would disable all the text boxes displaying database values to make sure the user couldn't inadvertently change the data; edit mode would enable these text boxes to allow editing.

This chapter covers the Visual Basic features that let you both control your application focus and respond to changes in focus.

Changing Focus

Focus can shift for a number of reasons. First, the user can establish the focus on a control using the TAB key or mouse. The user can press the TAB (or SHIFT-TAB) key until the control is graphically outlined. More commonly, the user can click on a control with the mouse to select it. If available, the user can press a speed key combination to automatically select the control, for example, by using an ALT-key combination such as ALT-C for a command button with the caption of Cash. Your code can also set focus with the SetFocus method.

Giving a control the focus triggers two events. First, the LostFocus event of the control that previously held the focus triggers. This event lets you perform any final validations before leaving the control. Your code in this event can also use the SetFocus method to selectively move the focus to any other control that's eligible. The GotFocus event of the control receiving the focus then triggers. This event lets you react appropriately to getting the focus. For instance, common programming practice highlights the contents of text boxes when they receive the focus. Note that if the LostFocus event sets the focus programmatically, focus might actually shift to a different control from the one the user selected.

Focus Summary

Several tools in Visual Basic influence the setting of the focus and its effects. The AppActivate statement gives the focus to another Windows application. A form or control within the application can be given the focus with the SetFocus method. The GotFocus event contains any actions that occur when a form or control receives the focus. Actions in the LostFocus event take place when a form or control loses the focus. A control's Enabled property indicates whether it is eligible or ineligible for receiving the focus. The Caption property of many controls lets you define an ALT-key combination to immediately set focus to that control. The TabIndex property determines the order in which the user accesses the controls on a form with the TAB key. A control's TabStop property indicates whether a control is accessible with the TAB key.

Table 54-1 displays the statements, methods, events, and properties that influence the setting and effects of focus in Visual Basic.

Table 54-1 Statement, method, properties, and events dealing with the focus

Use or Set This...	Type	To Do This...
AppActivate	Statement	Give the focus to another application
Caption	Property	Define an ALT-key combination to set focus to this control
Enabled	Property	Indicate whether a control or form can respond to events
GotFocus	Event	Initiate an action when a control or form is given the focus
LostFocus	Event	Initiate an action when a control or form gives up the focus
SetFocus	Method	Give the focus to the indicated control or form
TabIndex	Property	Set or discover a control's place in the tab order
TabStop	Property	Determine whether a control is accessible with the TAB key

The following pages discuss the statements, methods, events, and properties in Table 54-1 in detail. You'll find step-by-step directions to assemble the Focus project at the end of the chapter.

APPACTIVATE STATEMENT

Purpose   The AppActivate statement gives a particular application the focus when there are multiple Windows applications on your screen. An application keeps the focus until it is closed or another form or control receives the focus. Table 54-2 summarizes the argument of the AppActivate statement.

General Syntax

```
AppActivate titletext$[, wait]
```

Table 54-2 Arguments of AppActivate statement

Argument	Description
titletext$	The text that appears in the title bar of an application
wait	Boolean value specifying whether the calling application has the focus before activating another application

Example Syntax

```
Private Sub Command1_Click ()
On Error GoTo OpenFileMan 'file Manager not open, open it on error
    'attempts to give the focus to File Manager
    AppActivate "File Manager"
    'SendKeys maximizes File Manager
    SendKeys "%{ }{Down 4}{Enter}", -1
    'displays message with OK Button
  MsgBox "File Manager is now active"
    'sendKeys directs File Manager to close itself
    SendKeys "%{ }{Down 5}{Enter}", -1
    'sendKeys sends Enter to confirm close
    SendKeys "{Enter}", -1
Exit Sub
OpenFileMan:
    x = Shell ("C:\WINDOWS\WINFILE.EXE", 2) 'open File Manager
    DoEvents ' give file manager a chance to open
    'try activating File Manager again
    Resume
End Sub
```

Description
The AppActivate statement gives a particular application the focus when there are multiple Windows applications on your screen. This feature is useful for accessing, controlling, or obtaining information from another active Windows application from your Visual Basic program without using DDE or OLE links.

False is the default value for the wait argument. It specifies that an application is immediately activated, even though the calling application does not have the focus. When wait is set to True, the calling application waits until it has the focus, and then activates the specified application.

If the text in titletext$ does not match the called application's program name, any application whose title string begins with the titletext$ is activated. This is different from previous versions of Visual Basic, where the titletext$ had to be exact or an error would occur. If there is more than one instance of the application named by titletext$, one is arbitrarily activated.

While the host program is still in control, all the commands sent to the application with the focus must be sent using SendKeys. AppActivate does not establish a DDE connection.

In the example syntax, AppActivate works in conjunction with SendKeys to open the Windows File Manager application. Notice how the SendKeys statement is used to send the File Manager the specific keystrokes needed first to maximize, and then to close, that application. (The SendKeys statement is discussed in Chapter 51, "Keyboard Input," where you learn how to specify special keys as well as regular ASCII characters.)

Example

The Focus project at the end of this chapter uses the AppActivate statement to activate the Windows Notepad application. Once this application has the focus, a SendKeys statement sends the contents of the letter to the Notepad for viewing and editing. After sending the text, AppActivate is used once again to set the focus back to the project application.

Comments

If more than one instance of the same program is in memory, then the AppActivate statement activates one of them at random. If the program is not in memory, the AppActivate statement raises a Runtime error 5, "Invalid Procedure Call or Argument."

CAPTION PROPERTY

Objects Affected

Checkbox, Command, Data, DBGrid, Form, Frame, Label, MDI Form, Menu, Option

Purpose

The Caption property sets the text displayed in or next to a control, and provides a quick way of setting focus to that control with an ALT-key combination. Table 54-3 summarizes the arguments of the Caption property.

General Syntax

```
[form!]Name.Caption [ = text$]
```

Table 54-3 Arguments of the Caption property

Argument	Description
form	Name property of the parent form
Name	Name of the control
text$	Text to appear in the caption

Example Syntax

```
Private Sub Command1_Click()
    If Command1.Caption = "&Blue" Then
        Command1.Caption = "&Red"
    Else
```

```
        Command1.Caption = "&Blue"
    End If
End Sub
```

Description　Most controls on a form should have a keyboard shortcut that can be used to select them. Although the mouse is an intuitive input device, it's often faster to keep your hands on the keyboard. Providing keyboard shortcuts makes your programs easier for experienced typists to use.

The Caption property of many controls lets you set a keyboard shortcut that can be used by simply placing an ampersand symbol (&) in front of the shortcut key letter. For instance, setting a command button's Caption property to "&Red" makes the button read <u>R</u>ed (as illustrated in Figure 54-1) and lets the user select it directly by using ALT-R

To include an ampersand literal within a control's caption, put two ampersands together, as in the following example:

```
Command1.Caption = "Fe&dex && UPS"
```

Some controls don't have a caption property. For these controls, place a label next to the control and set the label's caption to include the shortcut key. Make sure the label's TabIndex is set to one less than the control's. Labels can't receive the focus, so when the user presses the shortcut key combination, the Label passes the focus to the next control in the tab order.

Example　The Focus project at the end of this chapter sets the Caption properties of the option buttons, labels, and command buttons to include the shortcut key combinations. Each label's TabIndex property is set to one less than the text box it labels to make sure focus automatically goes to the text box when the user presses the ALT-key combination for the label.

Comment　A Form's Caption property sets the text that appears in its Title Bar. It does not have the capacity to include a shortcut key. Placing an ampersand in the Caption does not underline the following letter; it just includes the ampersand as a literal character.

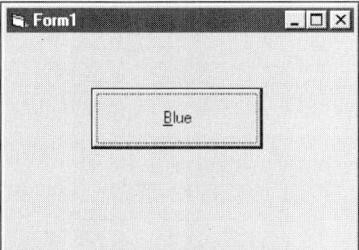

Figure 54-1　The example syntax uses accelerator keys to "click" the command button

ENABLED PROPERTY

Objects Affected	Checkbox, Combo, Command, Data, DBCombo, DBGrid, DBList, Dir, Drive, File, Form, Frame, Grid, Image, Label, List, MDI Form, Menu, OLE Container, Option, PictureBox, Remote Data, Scroll, Text, Timer, User Control
Purpose	Use the Enabled property to specify whether a control can respond to user input. Use this property to make certain controls or forms inaccessible or unchangeable while they are still visible on the screen. Read and write at both design time and runtime. Table 54-4 summarizes the arguments of the Enabled property, and Table 54-5 summarizes its Boolean values.

General Syntax

```
[form.]Enabled [= boolean%]
[form!]Name.Enabled [= boolean%]
```

Table 54-4 Arguments of the Enabled property

Argument	Description
form	Name of the form
Name	Name of the control
boolean%	True or False value

Table 54-5 Boolean values of the Enabled property

boolean%	Description
0	False—Control or form is disabled
-1	(Default) True—Control or form is enabled

Example Syntax

```
Private Sub textCityStateZip_Change
     Frame1.Enabled = False              'disables the frame
End Sub

Private Sub Drive1_Change
Dim onOff As Integer
     If Text1.Text = Password$ Then      'disables the drive box when the user has not
          Dir1.Path = Drive1.Drive       'entered the correct password in the text box
          File1.Path = Dir1.Path
     Else
          Drive1.Enabled = False
          File1.Path = Dir1.Path
          Drive1.Drive = "C:"
     End If
```

```
End Sub

Private Sub Check1_Change
    If Check1.Value = 1 Then
        onOff = True
    Else
        onOff = False
    End If
    cmndDelete.Enabled = onOff
    optnConfirm.Enabled = onOff
    menuDelete.Enabled = onOff
    pictTrashcan.Enabled = onOff
End Sub

Private Sub CommandSnooze_Click
    Timer1.Enabled = Not(Timer1.Enabled)    'toggle timer on and off
End Sub
```

Description

Use the Enabled property to specify whether a control can respond to user input. Use this property to make certain controls or forms inaccessible or unchangeable while they are still visible on the screen.

There are only two possible settings for the Enabled property: True (-1) and False (0). Using a variable makes it possible to control the Enabled property of several controls at once. With this kind of setup, entire groups of controls can be enabled and disabled by modifying only one variable as the third example above shows. This property can be changed at either design time or runtime.

The Enabled property can be used with both forms and controls. A control that has been disabled will turn gray on a color monitor (it will turn a lighter shade of gray or reverse video on monochrome). For example, the OK button on a data-entry form could be disabled until the user finishes an entry session.

A control will not recognize any input when its Enabled property is set to False. Focus may never be given to a disabled control. Mouse events (Click, DblClick, MouseDown, MouseMove, MouseUp, and GotFocus) will not affect a disabled control. No matter what place it has in a form's TabIndex order, the user will be unable to access a control using the [TAB] key.

Forms and Frames A frame is a grouping of controls within a form. Forms and frames respond to the Enabled property in the same ways. When the Enabled property of a frame or form is False, all the controls within it are also effectively disabled. Even though a control will not respond to user input or mouse events when the Enabled property of its parent form or frame is set to False, the actual value of the control's Enabled property remains unchanged. Although you can't set the focus to these controls, they are not dimmed as they would be if their individual Enabled properties were set to False. In the first example syntax, disabling the frame effectively disables all the controls it contains. Figure 54-2 shows how this might look.

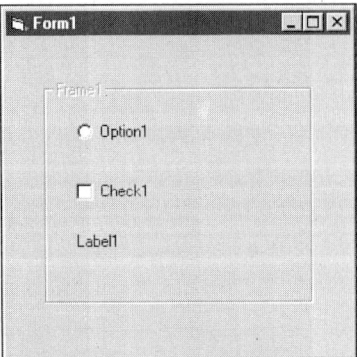

Figure 54-2 Disabling the frame effectively disables all the controls contained within it

Drive, Directory, and File Boxes

Drive, directory, and file list box controls give the user access to the files in a computer. If the Enabled property of one of these controls is False, then access to the files in the computer is restricted. The drive and directory list boxes don't change their appearance, but filenames in the file list box appear grayed. Figure 54-3 illustrates disabled drive, directory, and file list boxes. In the second sub procedure in the example syntax, a user without the password cannot access the files on other drives. When the word "Password" does not appear in the Text1 text box, the Drive1 drive box's Enabled property is changed to False.

Data, Remote Data, Option, Checkbox, Command, Picture, and Menu

Enabling and disabling the Enabled property of the data, remote data, option, checkbox, command button, picture box, or menu controls prevent the user from using these controls. This removes choices from the user if those choices are inappropriate for that particular context. Option and check boxes that do not apply to a particular situation can be disabled by changing their Enabled property to False. Command and menu controls can be turned off so that the user does not initiate inapplicable actions. The third sub procedure in the example syntax restricts the user's access to the other controls on the form, while the Check1 check box remains unmarked. Figure 54-4 shows disabled menu, data, option, checkbox, command, and picture controls.

List, Combo, and Text Boxes

Enabling and disabling the Enabled property of a list, combo, or text box prevents the user from changing the information in these controls. The text on a disabled list, combo, or text box appears gray. It is a lighter gray or reverse video on monochrome monitors.

Timer

The Enabled property of the timer control turns it on and off. This is useful for stopping previously scheduled events from taking place. In the fourth sub procedure in the example syntax, a snooze button for an alarm program postpones or terminates the upcoming alarm from sounding by changing the timer control's Enabled property to False. This change suspends the timer event's operation. Note that a timer can never receive the focus even when it's enabled because it is never visible.

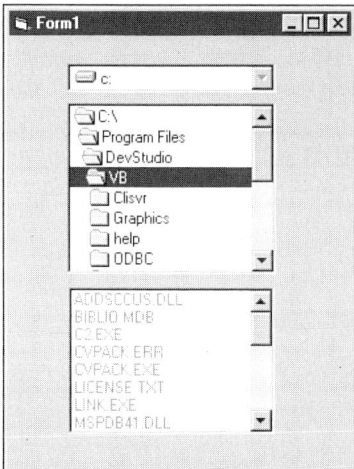

Figure 54-3 Only the file list box changes appearance when disabled; the drive and directory list boxes look the same

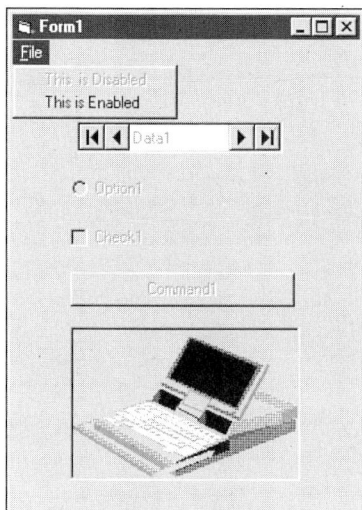

Figure 54-4 Disabled menu, data, option, check box, command, and picture controls

Example	The Focus project at the end of this chapter uses the Option_Click event to enable and disable one of the text boxes, depending on whether the user chose the Taxable or Non-Taxable option.
Comments	Notice that a control that has the Enabled property set to False cannot be accessed with either the mouse or the keyboard. If you wish to prevent TAB key access to a control, then setting the TabStop property to False will accomplish this without needing to disable the control itself. When the TabStop property of a control is set to False, the control can still be accessed or given the focus using the mouse or the SetFocus method.

LOCKED PROPERTY

Objects Affected	Column, DBCombo, DBList, Split, Text
Purpose	The Locked property specifies whether the contents of a control can be edited. A locked control can receive focus and its contents can be highlighted and scrolled, but the data cannot be changed.

General Syntax

```
name.Locked [= Boolean]
```

Table 54-6 summarizes the arguments of the Locked property.

Table 54-6 Arguments of the Locked property

Argument	Description
Name	Name property of the control with the focus
boolean%	True or False value

Example	The Focus project at the end of this chapter sets the Locked property during design time to prevent the user from changing a calculated field.
Comments	Unlike disabling a control, setting its Locked property to True does not change the color of the text.

GOTFOCUS EVENT

Objects Affected	Animation Control, Checkbox, Combo, Command, DBCombo, DBGrid, DBList, Dir, Drive, File, Form, Grid, List, ListView, Masked Edit, MSFlexGrid, OLE Container, Option, PictureBox, Property Page, RichText, Scroll, Slider, TabStrip, TreeView, Text, UpDown, User Control, User Document
Purpose	The GotFocus event specifies what actions to take when a control or form receives the focus. A control or form receives the focus either by user

action ([TAB] keypress or mouse click) or by code using the SetFocus method. Table 54-7 summarizes the arguments of the GotFocus event.

General Syntax

```
Sub Form_GotFocus ()
Sub Name_GotFocus ([Index As Integer])
```

Table 54-7 Arguments of the GotFocus event

Argument	Description
Form	'Form' for the form with the focus
Name	Name property of the control with the focus
Index	Index value of the control in a control array

Example Syntax

```
Private Sub Form_GotFocus ()
    Command2.Visible = True 'command button control made visible
    Text1.Visible = True    'text control made visible
    Picture1.Visible = True 'picture control made visible
    Option1(0).Visible = True'first option control of array made visible
    Option1(1).Visible = True'second option control of array made visible
    Command1.Enable = True   'second command button control enabled
End Sub

Private Sub Text1_GotFocus (Index As Integer)
    Text1(Index).BackColor = QBColor(15)      'highlight text box
    Select Case Index
        Case 0: lablStatusBar.Caption = "Enter the Patient's Name"
        Case 1: lablStatusBar.Caption = "Enter the Patient's Address"
        Case 2: lablStatusBar.Caption = "Enter the Patient's Status"
    End Select
End Sub
```

Description

The GotFocus event triggers when the focus shifts to a form or control. A control or form can get the focus in several ways. A user may select a new form or control with the mouse, or by moving through the controls on a form with the [TAB] key, or your code can use the SetFocus method. Begin the specification of the GotFocus event with the name of the form or control to be affected. If you are working with a control array, add an index variable in parentheses at the end of the statement.

Forms and controls can receive the focus with the SetFocus method. A form may be given the focus only when all the visible controls are disabled using the Enabled property. When a form or control receives the focus, you may use the GotFocus event to change the properties of the object with the focus. In the first example, the Enabled properties of the controls on Form1 change to True when the form receives the focus.

The first example syntax responds to a form's receiving the focus by making a variety of controls visible. This is done by setting the Visible property of each control to True (-1). Notice that two of the controls specified are part of an array of option buttons. Another common use of the GotFocus event is to display context-sensitive help messages on a status bar at the bottom of the screen as the user moves from one control or form to another. The second example syntax highlights a text box and displays a message on a status bar.

The Load, Resize, Paint, and GotFocus Events
If more than one event is attached to a particular control, the events are processed in the following order: Load, Resize, Paint, and GotFocus. This is an important point to keep in mind if any of the actions that take place in one event depend on actions in another event. For example, a data entry form for an address book would cause errors if the Load event disabled the Address1 text box and the GotFocus event tried to use it.

Control Arrays
If the control with the focus is part of a control array, then the Index argument indicates which part of the array has the focus. The index number specifies the affected part of the control array and appears in parentheses between the control's Name property and the property in the form of Control(Index%).property.

Example
The Focus project at the end of this chapter uses the GotFocus event of the text boxes to highlight the box with a different background color and then selects all the text in the box for subsequent editing.

Comments
Controls will not function with either of the Enabled and Visible properties set to False. GotFocus will not work unless they are both True. Labels and frames are not eligible to receive the focus. The User Control and User Document can receive focus only when their CanGetFocus property is True.

LostFocus Event

Objects Affected
Animation Control, Checkbox, Combo, Command, DBCombo, DBGrid, DBList, Dir, Drive, File, Form, Grid, List, ListView, Masked Edit, MSFlexGrid, OLE Container, Option, PictureBox, Property Page, RichText, Scroll, Slider, TabStrip, TreeView, Text, UpDown, User Control, User Document

Purpose
The LostFocus event specifies what actions to take when a control or form loses the focus, either because the user selected another object or the code reassigned the focus. Table 54-8 summarizes the arguments of the LostFocus event.

General Syntax

```
Sub Form_LostFocus ()
Sub Name_LostFocus ([Index As Integer])
```

Table 54-8 Arguments of the LostFocus event

Argument	Description
Form	Name property of the form losing focus
Name	Name property of the control losing focus
Index	Index value of the control in a control array

Example Syntax

```
Private Sub Text1_LostFocus ()
    Command1.ForeColor = H00FF0000&      'highlight the command button
    Command1.SetFocus                    'go to the command button
End Sub
```

Description The LostFocus event triggers when the focus changes from the current control or form to another control or form. This could occur in several ways. A user may choose another control with the use of a mouse, or by moving through the controls on a form with the [TAB] key. A SetFocus method can also give the focus to another control.

When a control loses the focus, you may want to change the properties of some other control or form. The LostFocus event can contain actions that may change the appearance of controls or forms to signify that this control has lost the focus. Certain other controls or forms may have their Enabled property changed to True or False. In the example syntax, the color of the text on the Command1 command button changes to blue when the Text1 text box loses the focus, and then focus shifts to the command button.

Control Arrays If the control with the focus is part of a control array, then the Index argument indicates which part of the array has the focus. The index number specifies the affected part of the control array and appears in parentheses between the control's Name property and the property in the form of Control(Index #).property.

Example The LostFocus event in the text box control array first removes the highlight in the box. (Each text box is highlighted by its GotFocus event.) Then it checks to see if the user is leaving the first member of the text box array, the contact name box. If so, then it performs some validity checking to make sure there is an honorific (such as Mr., Mrs., Dr.) and then sets some of the other text box's text appropriately.

Comments Because a control will not function with the Enabled and Visible properties set to False, the LostFocus event will not work until they are both True.

SetFocus Method

Objects Affected Animation Control, Checkbox, Combo, Command, DBCombo, DBGrid, DBList, Dir, Drive, File, Form, Grid, List, ListView, Masked Edit,

MSFlexGrid, OLE Container, Option, PictureBox, Property Page, RichText, Scroll, Slider, TabStrip, TreeView, Text, UpDown, User Control, User Document

Purpose   The SetFocus method gives the focus to the specified control or form. Table 54-9 summarizes the arguments for the SetFocus method.

General Syntax

```
[form.]SetFocus
[form!]Name.SetFocus
```

Table 54-9 Argument of the SetFocus method

Argument	Description
Name	Name property of form or control receiving the focus

Example Syntax

```
Private Sub CommandEdit_Click ()
    If CommandSave.Enabled = False Then      'if CommandSave button is disabled
        Text1.SetFocus              'set the focus to the Text1 box
    Else
        CommandSave.SetFocus    'set the focus to the CommandSave button
    End If
End Sub
```

Description   The SetFocus method gives a control or form the focus. The control and form arguments of a SetFocus operation must be the Name property of a form or control. Only those controls and forms with Enabled properties set to True may be given the focus. There is no difference in effect between setting the focus in the code or with user input. In the example syntax, the user could also give the focus to the Text1 text box with the mouse or by pressing the TAB key. The other way to change the focus is to activate the SetFocus method expression by pressing the CommandEdit command button.

There are several effects of changing the focus with the SetFocus method. Changing the focus to another control or form triggers the LostFocus event for the form or control that loses the focus. The GotFocus event of the form or control that receives the focus triggers when the SetFocus method gives it the focus. In the example syntax, pressing the CommandEdit command button shifts the focus to either the Text1 text box or CommandSave command button depending on whether the CommandSave button is enabled or disabled.

Example   The Focus project at the end of this chapter uses SetFocus several times. When the user selects the Taxable option, the program sets focus to the tax rate text box. If the first six text boxes are not filled in when the user clicks the send button, focus is shifted to the first empty text box. Finally, when the user clicks the Send button without having made a tax selection, the program sets focus back to the Taxable option button.

Comments | Labels, frames, and the data control are not eligible to receive the focus. Attempting to set the focus to a disabled control raises a Runtime error 5, "Invalid Procedure Call or Argument."

TabIndex Property

Objects Affected | Checkbox, Combo, Command, DBCombo, DBList, Dir, Drive, File, Frame, Grid, Label, List, OLE Container, Option, PictureBox, Scroll, Text

Purpose | The TabIndex property sets the order in which the user can access the controls on a form by pressing the TAB key. The control with the lowest TabIndex value (usually 0) is normally the control that receives the focus when the form opens. This property may be modified at either runtime or design time. The arguments of the TabIndex property are summarized in Table 54-10.

General Syntax

```
[form!]Name.TabIndex [= index%]
```

Table 54-10 Arguments of the TabIndex property

Argument	Description
form	Name property of the form
Name	Name property of the control
index%	Index value of the control in a control array

Example Syntax

```
Private Sub Command1_Click ()        'changes the tab order of the controls on the form
    Text1.TabIndex = 3               'run into a new order when the user presses Command1
    Command1.TabIndex = 0            'run in command button.
    Text2.TabIndex = 1
    Text3.TabIndex = 2
End Sub
```

Description | The TabIndex property can be changed in three possible ways. At design time you may choose to change the order of controls to meet a special need. The TabIndex property of a particular control may also be changed at runtime.

Changing the TabIndex property of a control may cause a change in that property for other controls on the form. For example, if a control with a lower TabIndex property is deleted at design time, then all the controls with higher values will have their TabIndex value reduced by 1. At runtime, altering a control's TabIndex property value to a lower value (for example, changing 2 to 0) changes the TabIndex property value of the other controls to higher values (0 becomes 1, and 1 becomes 2). Changing the TabIndex number of a control to a higher value (such as 0 to 2) reduces the value of the TabIndex property of the other controls (1 becomes 0, and 2 becomes 1).

The TabIndex property of a control can be one of a range of values equal to the number of controls on a form. The first control of a Form has a TabIndex property value of 0. By default, Visual Basic sets the value of each control in the order in which you create the controls. The first control created on a form thus has an initial TabIndex property value of 0.

The example syntax changes the TabIndex (and thus the order of access) of specified controls when the button Command1 is clicked. Note that a control with a TabIndex property of 0 is not always the first control with the focus when the form is opened.

Effects of the Visible, TabStop, and Enabled Properties	Changing the Visible, TabStop, or Enabled property of a control to False has no effect on its TabIndex property value. However, while any of these properties of a control is False, the control is inaccessible with the TAB key. In the example syntax, the Command1 command button would not receive the focus when the form loaded if any of these properties were False. The command button would retain its TabIndex property value of 0, however.
Example	The Focus project at the end of this chapter sets the TabIndex property for each of the controls on the form during the design phase. Special care is taken to make sure the labels precede each of their text boxes to allow the label's ALT-key combinations to set the focus to their associated text box.

TabStop Property

Objects Affected	Checkbox, Combo, Command, DBCombo, DBList, Dir, Drive, File, Grid, List, OLE Container, Option, PictureBox, Scroll, Text
Purpose	The TabStop property indicates whether a control is accessible with the TAB key. The TabStop property of a particular control does not affect whether a control can be selected with the mouse or accept user input from the mouse or keyboard. Table 54-11 summarizes the arguments of the TabStop property, and Table 54-12 summarizes its Boolean values.

General Syntax

```
[form!]Name.TabStop [ = boolean%]
```

Table 54-11 Arguments of the TabStop property

Argument	Description
form	Name property of the form
Name	Name of control
boolean%	Value represents whether the control is accessible or inaccessible with the TAB key

Table 54-12 Boolean values of the TabStop property

boolean%	Description
0	False—Control not accessible with the TAB key
-1	(Default) True—Control accessible with the TAB key

Example Syntax

```
Private Sub Text1.GotFocus ()
    Text2.TabStop = False    'Text2 becomes inaccessible when Text1 receives focus
    Text3.TabStop = True     'and Text3 remains accessible
End Sub
```

Description

The TabStop property of a control may be either True (-1) or False (0). All controls have this property originally set to True and are accessible with the TAB key. If the control's TabStop property is False, then it becomes inaccessible with the TAB key. In this case, the control can still be given the focus with either the SetFocus method or the mouse. This is different from setting the Enabled property to False, which makes the control completely ineligible for the focus.

In the example syntax, the TabStop property of the Text2 and Text3 text boxes changes when the Text1 text box receives the focus. The Text2 text box becomes inaccessible with the TAB key and the Text3 text boxes become accessible.

Effects of the Visible and Enabled Properties

Changing the Visible or Enabled property of a control to False has no effect on its TabStop property value. While either of these properties of a control is False, however, the control is also inaccessible with the TAB key. Even when a control's TabStop property is False, it can still receive the focus as long as the control is both Enabled and Visible. In the example syntax, both the Text2 and Text3 text boxes remain eligible for the focus by either a mouse click or by the SetFocus method.

Example

The Focus project at the end of this chapter sets the TabStop property of the members of the text box control array at design time to direct flow of the program in a natural sequence.

The Focus Project

Project Overview

The Focus project outlined in the following pages demonstrates the concept of focus in Visual Basic. This example is designed to demonstrate the properties, events, methods, and statements that directly affect focus. By following the examples of the different elements of this project, you will learn how to establish and remove focus from controls and forms.

Assembling the Project

1. Make a new form (the Focus form) with the objects and properties listed in Table 54-13.

Table 54-13 Objects and properties of the Focus form

Object	Property	Setting
Form	Name	frmBilling
	Caption	"Application Focus"
	Height	4140
	Width	6735
Frame	Name	Frame1
	Caption	"Tax Status"
	TabIndex	20
TextBox	Name	txtBilling
	BackColor	&H00C0C0C0&
	Height	285
	Index	0,1,2,3,4,5,6,7,8
	TabIndex	1,3,5,7,9,10,12,17,18
	TabStop	see text
OptionButton	Name	optNoTax
	Caption	"N&on-Taxable"
	TabIndex	15
	TabStop	0 'False
OptionButton	Name	optTax
	Caption	"&Taxable"
	TabIndex	14
	TabStop	0 'False
Label	Name	lblBilling
	AutoSize	-1 'True
	Caption	"Client &Name"
	Index	0

Object	Property	Setting
Label	Name	lblBilling
	AutoSize	-1 'True
	Caption	"&Address"
	Index	1
Label	Name	lblBilling
	AutoSize	-1 'True
	Caption	"&City, State ZIP"
	Index	2
	TabIndex	15
Label	Name	lblBilling
	AutoSize	-1 'True
	Caption	"&Hours"
	Index	3
	TabIndex	16
Label	Name	lblBilling
	AutoSize	-1 'True
	Caption	"&Rate"
	Index	4
	TabIndex	17
Label	Name	lblBilling
	AutoSize	-1 'True
	Caption	"Total"
	Index	5
	TabIndex	18
Label	Name	lblBilling
	AutoSize	-1 'True
	Caption	"&Description"
	Index	6
	TabIndex	19
Label	Name	lblBilling
	AutoSize	-1 'True
	Caption	"Tax &Pct."
	Index	7
	TabIndex	21
Label	Name	lblBilling
	AutoSize	-1 'True
	Caption	"Tax Amt."
	Index	8
	TabIndex	22

continued on next page

continued from previous page

Object	Property	Setting
CommandButton	Name	cmdBilling
	Caption	"&Send"
	Index	0
	TabIndex	11
CommandButton	Name	cmdBilling
	Caption	"E&xit"
	Index	1
	TabIndex	12

2. Size the objects on the screen, as shown in Figure 54-5.

3. Set the TabStop, Enabled, and Locked properties of the txtBilling control array according to Table 54-14.

Table 54-14 Objects and properties of the Focus form

Index	Property	Setting
0,1,2,3,4,6	Enabled	True
	Locked	False
	TabStop	True
5, 8	Enabled	True
	Locked	True
	TabStop	False
7	Enabled	False
	Locked	False
	TabStop	False

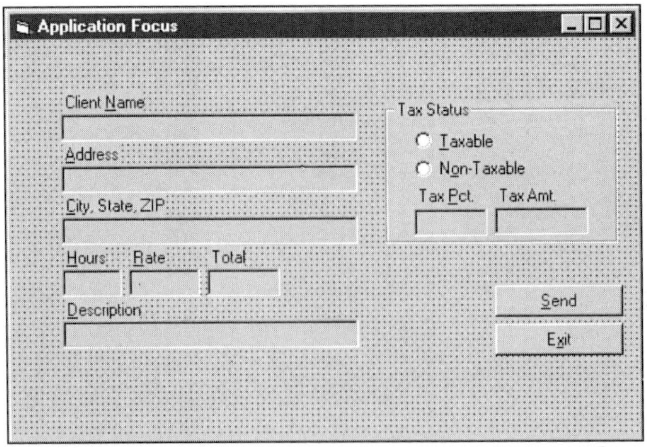

Figure 54-5   The Focus project at design time

4. Enter the following code in the cmdBilling_Click event when Index = 0. This activates Notepad, using AppActivate to set focus, and then sends the contents of the text boxes to the Notepad. After this procedure finishes sending the text, it sets focus back to the Focus project. If it fails to set the focus to the Notepad initially, the procedure attempts to open Notepad using the Shell statement using the OpenNotepad subroutine. If the procedure has already tried (and failed) to open Notepad, it gives an error message and exits. When Index = 1 it exits from the program. When Index = 1, the program ends.

```
Private Sub cmdBilling_Click(Index As Integer)
    Static Tried
    On Error GoTo OpenNotepad
    ' decide which button was pressed
    Select Case Index
        Case 0 ' Send to NotePad if all textboxes filled in
            If CheckForDone Then
                'switch focus to notepad
                AppActivate "Untitled - Notepad", Wait
                DoEvents
                On Error GoTo 0 'success! Notepad is open - disable error handler
                'send data
                'Start with "wakeup call" to NotePad
                SendKeys vbCr 'Carriage return and LineFeed
                'Give it a chance to handle the text
                DoEvents
                SendKeys "Client:" & vbCr
                DoEvents
                SendKeys txtBilling(0) & vbCr
                DoEvents
                SendKeys txtBilling(1) & vbCr
                DoEvents
                SendKeys txtBilling(2) & vbCr
                DoEvents
                SendKeys "Service: " & txtBilling(6) & vbCr
                DoEvents
                SendKeys "Hours: " & txtBilling(3) & _
                  "@ " & txtBilling(4) & vbCr
                DoEvents
                If optTax Then
                    SendKeys "Tax: " & txtBilling(8) & vbCr
                End If
                DoEvents
                SendKeys "Total: " & txtBilling(5) & vbCr
                DoEvents
                'go back to this project
                AppActivate "Application Focus"
                DoEvents
                cmdBilling(1).SetFocus
            Else
                GoTo Normal_Exit
            End If
        Case 1 ' Exit
            Unload Me
            End
    End Select
Normal_Exit:
```

continued on next page

continued from previous page

```
      Exit Sub
'need to open the notepad
OpenNotepad:
     'if we've already tried, then
     If Tried Then
          'no way
          MsgBox "Failed to open notepad"
          'bye bye
          Exit Sub
     End If
     'ok, we're trying now!
     Tried = True
     'attempt to open notepad
     X = Shell("Notepad", vbNormalFocus)
     'Yield to the operating system
     'give it time to work
     DoEvents
     'and start back where we left off (AppActivate)
     Resume
End Sub
```

5. Enter the following code in the optTax_Click event. When the user clicks in the Taxable option button, this enables the text box for the tax rate and shifts the focus there.

```
Private Sub optTax_Click()
    ' if tax
    If optTax Then
        ' enable tax rate text box
        txtBilling(7).Enabled = True
        ' set focus there
        txtBilling(7).SetFocus
    End If
End Sub
```

6. Enter the following code in the optNoTax_Click event. When the user clicks the Non-Taxable option button, this procedures clears the tax rate from txtBilling(7) and recalculates the total.

```
Private Sub optNoTax_Click()
    'if no tax then clear the tax textbox
    If optNoTax Then
        txtBilling(7) = ""
        'calculate the total
        CalcTotal
    End If
End Sub
```

7. Enter the following code in the txtBilling_GotFocus event. This highlights the text box by setting its background to white, and selects all the text in it. These are very typical actions to take when a text box is given the focus.

```
Private Sub txtBilling_GotFocus(Index As Integer)
    'Make the background color of the active
    'textbox bright white
    txtBilling(Index).BackColor = QBColor(15)
```

```
'Select all of the text in the box
txtBilling(Index).SelStart = 0
txtBilling(Index).SelLength = Len(txtBilling(Index))
End Sub
```

8. Enter the following code in the txtBilling_LostFocus event. This removes the highlight from the text box by setting its background back to gray, then recalculates the total if the change requires it.

```
Private Sub txtBilling_LostFocus(Index As Integer)
    'Make the background color of the active textbox gray
    txtBilling(Index).BackColor = QBColor(7)
    'Process data if hours or rate
    Select Case Index
        Case 3, 4, 7 'Hours, Rate, Tax Pct.
            ' these affect the total - calculate total
            CalcTotal
    End Select
End Sub
```

9. Add the following new procedure to the project. This procedure calculates the total bill.

```
Private Sub CalcTotal()
    Dim nTempVal As Currency
    'Must select either taxable or nontaxable
    If Not optTax And Not optNoTax Then Exit Sub
    'Make sure all of the calculation data is available
    If Val(txtBilling(3)) = 0 Or Val(txtBilling(4)) = 0 Or _
        (optTax = True And Val(txtBilling(7)) = 0) Then Exit Sub
    'Calculate total
    nTempVal = Val(txtBilling(3)) * Val(txtBilling(4))
    ' calculate tax and format to currency
    txtBilling(8) = Format(Str(Val(txtBilling(7)) / 100 * _
      nTempVal), "Currency")
    ' add tax, calculate total and format to currency
    txtBilling(5) = Format(nTempVal + txtBilling(8), "Currency")
End Sub
```

10. Add the following new function. This function makes sure all the text boxes are filled in before it allows data to be sent to NotePad.

```
Private Function CheckForDone()
    Dim j As Integer
    ' Assume the best
    CheckForDone = True
    ' Check for empty text box
    For j = 0 To 6
        If txtBilling(j) = "" Then
            ' is the tax info filled in?
            ' if not there is no total
            If j = 5 Then
                MsgBox "Fill in Tax Status", vbOKOnly Or _
                    vbExclamation, "Cannot send."
                ' set focus to the option button
                optTax.SetFocus
            Else
```

continued on next page

continued from previous page

```
                    ' it was filled in, something else is missing
                    MsgBox "Incomplete billing data", vbOKOnly Or _
                      vbExclamation, "Cannot send."
                    ' set focus to the empty text box
                    txtBilling(j).SetFocus
                End If
                ' set false
                CheckForDone = False
                Exit For
            End If
        Next j
    End Function
```

How It Works

This project illustrates some typical uses for the focus-setting events, methods, and statement. When it first loads, focus is initially set to txtBilling(0) because it is first in the tab order.

All the text boxes are in a control array. This makes it simple to write the code to highlight and unhighlight the boxes. Highlighting simply sets the background to white, and selects all the text in the box. Many Windows programs default to selecting the text when first entering a text box. Unhighlighting is equally simple; we just set the background back to gray. These are very typical uses for the GotFocus and LostFocus events.

Another typical use for LostFocus is for validity checking. The txtBilling_LostFocus routine checks to see if we're leaving one of the text boxes that affects the final billing amount. If so, and the CheckForDone function determines that there is data in all of the other text boxes that affect the final bill, it calls the CalcTotal procedure.

CalcTotal calculates the total, adds in the tax, if any, and displays its result in txtBilling(5). Note that this text box is locked and has its TabStop property set to False. You can click in the text box, and you can select or copy its contents, but you cannot change the contents.

Finally, the Send command button (cmdBilling(0)) activates the Notepad and sends the resultant address text to it. If it fails to activate at first, it opens the Notepad application before trying again. Once sent, focus returns to the Focus project. Figure 54-6 shows the Focus project in action.

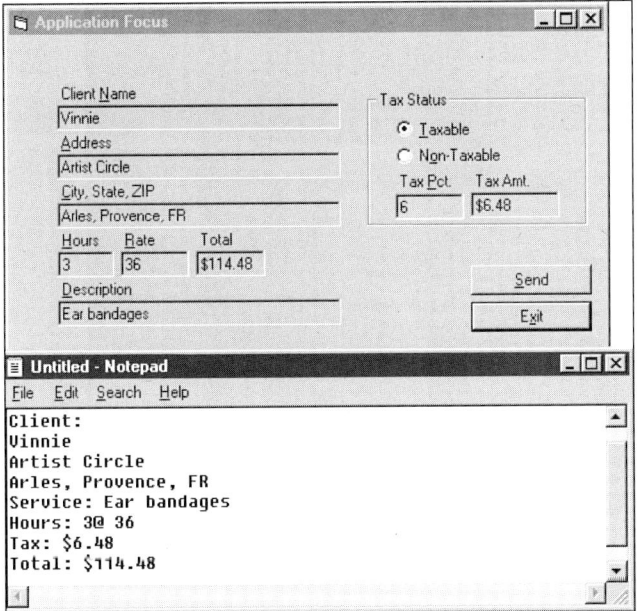

Figure 54-6   The Focus project in action

55

DDE

Dynamic Data Exchange (DDE) is a means of communication between Microsoft Windows applications. Using DDE, applications can connect to each other and exchange data. This data can either be information, which is copied from one application to another, or commands or keystrokes for the other application to process. To use DDE, both applications must support exchanging data using DDE. Check your application's documentation to see if it supports DDE.

In a DDE conversation, the application that creates the link is known as the *destination* application, and the application that responds is known as the *source* application. (These used to be referred to as *client* and *server* respectively.) Any application that supports DDE can serve as either a source or a destination. One application can serve as both a destination and a source with several other applications at the same time. Only one active DDE link should be established between a Visual Basic control or form and another application. For example, a link between a Microsoft Excel spreadsheet cell and a text control is acceptable as long as the parent form does not already have a link with the same cell. You might cause an infinite loop of updates if there were more than one link between the same two applications.

Elements of a DDE Link

A DDE conversation between two applications requires an application name, topic, and item. The *application name* is the unique name that identifies the application in Windows. Every DDE link has a *topic*, which indicates what type of data is being addressed by the link. The *item* specifically identifies the data being exchanged by the two applications. Neither the application name nor the topic may be changed once a DDE link has been established, or the DDE connection will be broken. In contrast, the item of a DDE conversation may be changed as many times as necessary.

All the applications in Windows have a name that identifies them in a DDE link. This name is normally the filename (without the extension) of the executable file used to start the program. The application name of a compiled Visual Basic program is the filename of the executable file. A Visual Basic program running within Visual Basic (for example, during design and testing) has an application name that is the project name without the .VBP extension. Table 55-1 contains the application names of some common Windows applications that support DDE.

Table 55-1 Application names of common Windows applications

Windows Application	Filename	Application Name
Microsoft Excel	EXCEL.EXE	Excel
Microsoft Word	WINWORD.EXE	WinWord
Q+E	QE.EXE	QE
Program Manager	PROGMAN.EXE	Progman
Quicken for Windows	QW.EXE	QW

A DDE link also must indicate the topic, or part of the source application, with which to establish the connection. The available topics vary from application to application, but one choice is virtually universal to all DDE supporting applications: System. With the System topic, a DDE link can obtain the other topics that the application supports as well as information about the application, such as the data formats that it supports. In Microsoft Excel, Microsoft Word, and Q+E, the path and filename of a data file may serve as a topic in a DDE link. Visual Basic applications can define the topic using the LinkTopic property.

The actual data transferred through a DDE link is called the item. In Visual Basic applications, the LinkItem property defines the item. An item in a Visual Basic application may be a text box, label, or picture on a form. When the topic of a DDE link is a spreadsheet, the item may be a cell reference such as R1C1 on an Excel spreadsheet. If a link is established with a WinWord document, the item might be a glossary name.

Types of Links

Three basic types of links may be established between two applications: automatic, manual, and notify. An *automatic* link updates the data to the other application every time the data changes. A *manual* link updates the data only when the data is specifically requested. A *notify* link notifies the other application when the data has changed, but does not send the actual data. A link, whether automatic, manual, or notify, is either a source or a destination link, depending on the direction in which the data passes.

A link may be established between a form or control in a Visual Basic application and another Windows application that supports DDE communication. The destination (initiating application) obtains information from the source (responding application).

The type of initially created source link controls when this transfer of information takes place. If this is a manual or notify link, then the transfer takes place only when requested. Data transfers in automatic source links take place every time the control or form changes.

DDE in Visual Basic

Visual Basic provides several tools that influence the operation of DDE links with other applications. Any actions tied to the opening or closing of a link appear in the LinkOpen and LinkClose events. The LinkError event provides for actions that take place when problems with links occur. A destination controls a source by sending the source's macro commands through the link with the LinkExecute method. Any actions that need to take place for your Visual Basic application to respond to link execute requests may be placed in the LinkExecute event.

Both the item and the topic of a DDE conversation may be determined with the LinkItem and LinkTopic properties. Whether a DDE link is automatic, manual, or notify may be set with the LinkMode property. When information needs to be moved from the destination to the source (opposite of the normal flow), use the LinkPoke method. Manual DDE links may transfer information manually with the LinkRequest method. Your application is notified of changes in the source data with the LinkNotify event. All the contents of a Visual Basic application's picture box may be transferred to another application with the LinkSend method. The LinkTimeout property determines how long a control will wait for a response from the other application.

Table 55-2 displays the properties, methods, and events that affect DDE communication with other Windows applications that support this protocol.

Table 55-2 Properties, methods, and events dealing with the referencing of forms and controls

Use or Set This...	Type	To Do This...
LinkClose	Event	Indicate the actions that take place when a DDE link is closed
LinkError	Event	Indicate the actions that take place when a DDE link produces an error
LinkExecute	Event	Respond to a command sent by the source
LinkExecute	Method	Send a command over the DDE link
LinkItem	Property	Indicate the item to use with a DDE link
LinkMode	Property	Determine whether a control's DDE link is off, automatic, manual, or notify
LinkNotify	Event	Indicate source data has changed
LinkOpen	Event	Indicate the actions that take place when a DDE link is opened
LinkPoke	Method	Send information from the destination to the source
LinkRequest	Method	Ask for and obtain information from another application
LinkSend	Method	Transfer contents of picture box to a connected application
LinkTimeout	Property	Determine the time that a control will wait for a response over a link
LinkTopic	Property	Indicate the topic to use with a DDE link

The following pages describe the properties, methods, and events in detail. The DDE project at the end of this section includes step-by-step instructions to assemble the project.

LinkClose Event

Objects Affected   Form, Label, MDIForm, PictureBox, TextBox

Purpose   The LinkClose event processes any actions that occur when the DDE link between a form, label, picture box, or text box and another program terminates. Changing the LinkMode property of the object to none (0) terminates a DDE link. Attempting to change the LinkTopic property of an object also closes a DDE link. The LinkClose event contains any of the actions that occur when a link terminates. Table 55-3 summarizes the arguments of the LinkClose event.

General Syntax

```
Sub Form_LinkClose()
Sub Name_LinkClose ([Index As Integer])
```

Table 55-3 Arguments of the LinkClose event

Argument	Description
Form	'Form' indicates the form
Name	Name property of control
Index	Identifies control in a control array

Example Syntax

```
Private Sub Form_LinkClose ()
    If LinkMode <> 0 Then                        'checks if LinkMode is currently at none
        LinkMode = 0                             'changes LinkMode to none
        MsgBox "DDE link closed prematurely"     'displays message on the screen
    Else If LinkMode = 0 Then                    'checks if LinkMode is currently at none
        MsgBox "DDE Link closed normally"        'displays normal termination message
    End If
End Sub
```

Description   The LinkClose event contains any actions that occur when a DDE link closes. A DDE link terminates in several ways. Any attempt to modify the topic of a link terminates the link. A form or control's link ends when its LinkMode property changes to 0. Keep each of these possible reasons in mind when setting up a LinkClose event. In the example syntax, the routine checks the current setting of the LinkMode property of the form. The code determines if the link closed with the LinkMode or another method.

The LinkMode Property	Changing the LinkMode property of an object initiates or terminates a link with another application. The LinkClose event triggers when the LinkMode property closes a link. In the example syntax, the LinkClose event checks to determine if a change to the LinkMode property terminated the link.
The LinkTopic Property	The contents of a LinkTopic are part of the unique identifying characteristics of a DDE link. The other characteristics are the application name and topic. A link's topic identifies the element of the other application being linked. Neither of these characteristics may be modified on an active link or the link will close, triggering the LinkClose event. In the example syntax, the routine checks the present setting of the LinkMode property to determine if the link was closed without a change to the LinkMode property. The abnormal message displays if the LinkClose event was triggered by an attempted change of the topic while the link was active.
Control Arrays	When there is a DDE link between a control in a control array and another application, the Index property must be provided. In this case, such a link involves a specific control in the control array and does not involve the contents or settings of the other controls in the control array. In order to access all the controls of a control array, the link must be established with the form that contains the controls.
Example	The DDE project at the end of this chapter uses the LinkClose event to notify the user of the link's changed status. The pictGraphic_LinkClose event changes lablGraphLinkStatus.Caption to read "(unlinked)."
Comments	Since the item of a DDE link is modifiable while the link is active, changes to the item do not trigger the LinkClose event.

LinkError Event

Objects Affected	Form, Label, MDIForm, PictureBox, TextBox
Purpose	The LinkError event triggers when a DDE link conversation produces an error. This error can never be caused by Visual Basic code—errors caused by code are normal trappable errors. LinkError events are only triggered as the result of problems with the connected application, the link itself, or the Windows environment. This event returns a value you can use to determine what action to take based upon the error that occurred. Tables 55-4 and 55-5 summarize the valid arguments and values of the LinkError event.

General Syntax

```
Private Sub Form_LinkError (LinkErr As Integer)
Private Sub Name_LinkError ([Index As Integer,] LinkErr As Integer)
```

Table 55-4 Valid arguments of the LinkError event

Argument	Effect
Form	'Form' indicates the form
Name	Name property of control
Index	Identifying value of the control in a control array
LinkErr	The LinkErr value returned

Table 55-5 Causes of the link error values returned in the LinkErr variable. (Missing entries were used in Visual Basic 1.0 but are now obsolete.)

Value	Problem
1	The linked application asked for data in an incompatible format
6	An application attempted a DDE operation after the source form's LinkMode was set to None
7	There are too many active DDE links established (128 max)
8	Destination control: automatic link or LinkRequest failed to update control
	Source forms: destination attempted to poke data to a control and failed
11	There is not enough memory available for a DDE link

Example Syntax

```
Private Sub TextBox_LinkError (Index As Integer, LinkErr As Integer)
    Msg$ = "Error in link. (Error #" & Str$(LinkErr) & ")"
    MsgBox Msg$
End Sub
```

Description   The LinkError event provides information about the nature of problems when they occur. The LinkError event contains actions that respond to the problem. Any actions in this event mainly serve as a warning that something is wrong. Table 55-5 lists the possible errors that can trigger this event. In the example syntax, the LinkError event informs the user about what kind of problem has occurred. Since the source application's actions (Excel in this example) cause the error, changes must be made to that application before the link may be successfully processed. Errors of this type typically require recoding in the connected application.

Control Array   When there is a DDE link between a control in a control array and another application, the Index property must be provided. In this case, such a link involves a specific control in the control array and does not involve the contents or settings of the other controls in the control array. In order to access all the controls of a control array, the link must be established with the form that contains the controls.

Example	The DDE project at the end of this chapter uses the LinkError event of three objects—the textBox, pictGraph, and formMain—to call the module-level procedure DescribeLinkError. This procedure simply produces a message indicating what kind of error occurred.
Comments	The LinkError event LinkErr values have no effect on the value of the Err variable in Err functions.

LINKEXECUTE EVENT

Objects Affected	Form, MDIForm
Purpose	The LinkExecute event contains a Visual Basic application's responses to command strings sent through a DDE link. A LinkExecute event only triggers when the form is the source of a DDE link. The destination application transmits a command through a DDE link to the source application. Forms with no code in the LinkExecute event will ignore any commands sent through the link from the destination application. Table 55-6 summarizes the arguments of the LinkExecute event, and Table 55-7 shows the values of the Cancel return value in the LinkExecute event.

General Syntax

```
Sub Form_LinkExecute (Cmdstr As String, Cancel As Integer)
```

Table 55-6 Arguments of the LinkExecute event

Argument	Effect
Form	'Form' indicates the source form
CmdStr	Contents of the command string transmitted through the link from a destination application
Cancel	Tells destination if command was accepted

Table 55-7 Values of the Cancel return value in the LinkExecute event

Cancel	Meaning
True (Default)	Set Cancel to True to show destination application that command was rejected
False	Set Cancel to False to show destination application that command was accepted

Example Syntax

```
Private Sub Form_LinkExecute (CmdStr As String, Cancel As Integer)
    Cancel = False                  'show that we've accepted command
    Select Case UCase(CmdStr)       'format text of cmdstr in all uppercase
        Case "[SETUP]"
            WindowState = 2         'maximize window
```

continued on next page

continued from previous page

```
                Cls                     'clear screen and reset coordinates
                BackColor = QBColor(1)'make the background blue
          Case "DATE"
                Print Date$,            'prints the date on the form
                Print                   'puts a space after the date
          Case "TIME"
                Print Time$,            'prints the time on the form
                Print                   'puts a space after the time
          Case "[CLOSE]"
                Hide                    'hides the current form on the screen
          Case "[SHOW]"
                Form1.Show              'displays the form on the screen
          Case Else
                Cancel = True           'command not accepted
    End Select
End Sub
```

Description

The LinkExecute event contains a library of possible commands you've created that may be sent to this form through a DDE link. There are two possible arguments for this event, CmdStr and Cancel. Any command sent through a link is stored in the text string CmdStr and may then be accessed to determine what kind of action should take place. When the command string sent does not match any of the criteria listed in a LinkExecute event, change the Cancel variable to True to indicate that the command was rejected. This informs the sending application that the command was not valid for this application. If your application recognizes and acts on CmdStr, set the Cancel variable to False to indicate the command was accepted.

In the example syntax, the LinkExecute event contains a list of commands that may be sent to its parent form. Any commands that are sent to the form through a DDE link will be checked to see if they match any of the acceptable commands. If a match is made, then the command is processed. Otherwise, the Cancel variable changes to True to inform the sending application that the command was rejected.

Example

The DDE project at the end of this chapter uses the form's LinkExecute method to allow other applications to request information or to end the program. The most important command is Update Graph, which executes a LinkSend method on pictGraph to send it to the requesting application.

Comments

The actions listed in the LinkExecute event of a form have no effect on the use of the LinkExecute method in the same form. The LinkExecute event occurs when your application is the source; your application uses the LinkExecute method when it is the destination.

LinkExecute Method

Objects Affected   Label, PictureBox, TextBox

Purpose   The LinkExecute method transmits commands to another application through a DDE link. This method permits the destination application in a

DDE link conversation to control the behavior of the source application. Commands sent with the LinkExecute method have the same effect as if the user entered them. Table 55-8 summarizes the arguments of the LinkExecute method.

General Syntax

```
[form!]Name.LinkExecute cmdstr$
```

Table 55-8 Arguments of the LinkExecute method

Argument	Effect
form	Name property of the form
Name	Name property of the text box, picture box, or label control
cmdstr$	Command string for the destination application to send to the source application to process

Example Syntax

```
Private Sub Form_Load ()
Startup:
    On Error GoTo OpenWinWord          'sets error trap to open WinWord
    Text1.LinkTimeout = -1             'turns off Timeout error
    Text1.LinkMode = 0                 'turn off any existing links
    Text1.LinkTopic = "WinWord|System" 'sets the Topic for the DDE link
    Text1.LinkMode = 2                 'opens a manual link with Winword
    Text1.LinkExecute "[FileClose 2]"  'closes the current file without saving
    Text1.LinkExecute "[FileNew 0,""Letter""]"'opens new file with Letter Template
    AppActivate "Microsoft Word - Document2" 'gives the focus to Word
    End                                'ends program

OpenWinWord:
    If Err = 282 Then                  'checks if WinWord wasn't in memory
        x = Shell("Winword.exe", 3)    'start up WinWord
        Resume Startup                 'try again
    Else
        Error Err                      'forces display of error message
    End If
End Sub
```

Description

The LinkExecute method transmits commands to another application through a DDE link. This method lets the destination application in a DDE link conversation control the behavior of the source application. Commands sent with the LinkExecute method have the same effect as if the user entered them. The cmdstr$ argument contains the command you'd like to send over the link. Example syntax contains a routine connected to the Text1 text box that sends a series of commands to Microsoft Word for Windows through a DDE link. These commands open a new file based on the Letter template. When this form opens Word for Windows, the user no longer has to press File, New, and then choose Letter from the list of templates. The program does this automatically and then exits.

The LinkTopic Property

For a LinkExecute method to be processed, a link must first be established with the other application. A control or form's LinkTopic property provides the name of the other application along with the topic, which is normally the filename. In this case the System topic is used instead of the filename, because the first command sent by the LinkExecute method closes the open file. As a result the link is maintained with WinWord without being dependent on which document is open at the time. This is a useful technique to use when dealing with multiple documents in DDE-supporting Windows applications.

The LinkTimeout Property

The LinkExecute method requires the proper setting of the LinkTimeout property of the control or form. The LinkTimeout property determines the amount of time that a control will wait for a response from the other application. When the value of the LinkTimeout property is set to -1, the control or form will wait indefinitely (actually about 1 hour and 49 minutes), or until the user presses the Y key on the keyboard or the application responds. In the example syntax, the LinkTimeout property is set to -1 to prevent any delays in execution from generating an error.

The LinkMode Property

The LinkMode property determines what type of link is to be established. Since a form may not serve as a destination in a DDE link, the LinkExecute method requires a link between a control and another application. In some cases the link may only be established with a particular type of control. For example, picture files (*.PCX, *.TIF, and so on) would only be linkable into picture boxes. Some applications may only support a manual link.

Error Trapping

The Err function, Error statement, and On Error statement are an important part of the operation of a DDE link subroutine. Through the use of the On Error statement "On Error GoTo OpenWinWord," the code provides for the possibility that WinWord is not loaded when this program runs. If WinWord is not running, an error generates and code in the OpenWinWord section is processed. This routine checks to see if WinWord is not running. If WinWord is not present, then the Shell function loads WinWord into memory. After WinWord loads, the link is established and the LinkExecute command transmits the command strings. An error message displays on the screen when an unanticipated error occurs.

Example

The DDE project at the end of this chapter uses the LinkExecute method extensively. The heaviest use occurs during the Form_Load event, when the DDE program is first setting up Excel with multiple LinkExecutes.

Comments

Notice that the commands sent in the LinkExecute method in the example are placed between square brackets, and any quotation marks placed within them are double quotation marks. This is a requirement for sending macro commands to Microsoft Word and Excel for Windows. Other applications may have different requirements, much as programs you write that accept

LinkExecute events can parse the command string for anything you choose. Consult the other application's documentation (and probably call its tech support!) for the proper formats, commands, and macros it can accept.

LinkItem Property

Objects Affected   Label, PictureBox, TextBox

Purpose   The LinkItem property refers to the data transmitted through a DDE link from the source application to the destination application. This property corresponds to the Item argument of a DDE link and may be changed without closing an active link. When a Visual Basic form is the source in a DDE link, the LinkItem property of the form contains the Name property of the control identified in the item of the DDE link. Table 55-9 summarizes the arguments of the LinkItem property.

General Syntax

[form!]Name.LinkItem [= expression$]

Table 55-9 Arguments of the LinkItem property

Argument	Description
form	Name property of the form
Name	Name property of the label, picture box, or text box
expression$	Identifies the item of a DDE link

Example Syntax

```
Private Sub Form_Load ()
Startup:
    On Error GoTo OpenQE                  'sets Error trap to OpenQE
    Text1.LinkTimeout = -1                'turns off Timeout error
    Text1.LinkMode = 0                    'deactivates any existing link
    Text1.LinkTopic = "QE|System"         'sets the Topic for DDE Link
    Text1.LinkItem = "All"                'sets the Item for DDE Link
    Text1.LinkMode = 2                    'opens a manual link with Q+E
    Text1.LinkExecute "[Open('C:\EXCEL\QE\EMP.DBF')]"'opens Data file
    Text1.LinkExecute "[Open.Index('C:\EXCEL\QE\EMPLNAME.NDX',TRUE)]"
    Text1.LinkExecute "[SAVE.QUERY.AS('C:\EXCEL\QE\EMP.QEF')]
    Text1.LinkMode = 0                    'closes link with Q+E
    Text1.LinkTopic = "QE|C:\EXCEL\QE\EMP.DBF"'changes Topic for DDE Link
    Text1.LinkItem = "C:\EXCEL\QE\EMP.QEF"   'changes Item for DDE Link
    Text1.LinkMode = 2                    'opens a manual link with Q+E
    Text1.LinkExecute "[Open('C:\EXCEL\QE\EMP.QEF')]"'opens Query file
    End                                   'ends program
OpenQE:
    If Err = 282 Then                     'checks if Q+E wasn't in memory
        x = Shell("QE.exe", 3)            'start up QE
```

continued on next page

continued from previous page

```
        Resume Startup                      'try again
    Else
        Error Err                           'forces display of error message
    End If
End Sub
```

Description

The LinkItem property refers to the data transmitted through a DDE link from the source application to the destination application. A LinkItem property's expression$ argument contains a string expression in a format acceptable to the application that is being linked with the Visual Basic application. This value must be a string expression and can contain up to 255 characters.

In the example syntax, the LinkItem of the text box Text1 is defined with two text strings. In the first link, the LinkItem is defined as All. This is a Q+E specification for DDE items that means "include the entire database file listed in the topic." In the second link, the LinkItem is defined with the path and name of the Q+E query file EMP.QEF. Notice that the query file still needs to be loaded, even though a link has been established with it.

Details of the DDE link will vary with the application being linked with. For example, links with Microsoft Excel may define the LinkItem property with the location of the cells that contain the appropriate data. In links with Q+E, the topic may be the entire database specified in the topic by defining the LinkItem property as All or the appropriate query filename. These settings are used in the following example to display the contents of the EMP.DBF file on the screen.

The LinkTopic Property

The LinkTopic property defines which items may be chosen for a DDE link. The available items also depend on which application you are linking to the Visual Basic application. When the DDE link's topic is set to System, the LinkItem may be set to any available part of the application. In the example syntax, the LinkItem is set at All when the LinkTopic property is System. After the LinkTopic is changed to C:\EXCEL\QE\EMP.DBF, the list of available items is reduced to its query files. For this reason, the newly created query file C:\EXCEL\QE\EMP.QEF is specified.

The LinkMode Property

The LinkMode property determines what type of link is to be established. Since a form may not serve as a destination in a DDE link, the LinkExecute method requires a link between a control and another application. In some cases, the link may only be established with a particular type of control. For example, picture files (*.PCX, *.TIF, and so on) are only linkable to picture boxes. Some applications may only support a manual link.

Error Trapping

The Err function, Error statement, and On Error statement are important parts of the operation of a DDE link subroutine. Through the use of the On Error statement "On Error GoTo OpenQE," the code provides for the possibility that Q+E is not loaded when this program runs. If Q+E is not running, an error generates and code in the OpenQE section opens Q+E. If Q+E is not present, then the Shell function loads Q+E into memory. After Q+E has been loaded, the link is established and the LinkExecute transmits the command strings. An error message displays on the screen when an unanticipated error occurs.

Application Items Each application has its own unique set of items and has its own way of specifying them. You'll need to refer to the other application's documentation to discover what items and formats it supports. Tables 55-10 and 55-11 show some representative applications to give you an idea of what kinds of items you'd expect to be supported. Note that each version of every program is different; newer versions of an application will likely support different (and probably more) topics.

WinWord System Items Three items may be used with the topic System in Microsoft Word for Windows: SysItems, Topics, and Formats. The SysItems item produces a list of the possible items that may be used with the System topic. The Topics item provides a list of the open documents that includes the path names. A Formats item returns a list of all the Clipboard formats supported by Word for Windows. This is very important information to keep in mind when setting up a link with WinWord. Use Table 55-10 as a reference for obtaining information about Microsoft WinWord.

Table 55-10 List of possible items for the topic System with Microsoft Word for Windows

Item	Description
SysItems	Returns a list of the available items that may be used with the System topic
Topics	Returns a list of available open documents in WinWord
Formats	Returns a list of available Clipboard formats supported by WinWord

Excel System Items Six items may be used with the topic System in Microsoft Excel for Windows: SysItems, Topics, Status, Formats, Selection, and Protocols. The SysItems item produces a list of the possible items that may be used with the System topic. The Topics item provides a list of the available topics and the path and filenames of the open spreadsheets. The Status item returns the text Ready when the Excel application is not busy with an operation of some kind. A Formats item returns a list of all the Clipboard formats supported by Excel for Windows. The Selection item indicates the reference location of the currently active cell or cells, including the name of the spreadsheet. Protocols items display the types of DDE link protocols that Excel supports, including StdFileEditing and Embedding. The items are summarized in Table 55-11.

Table 55-11 List of possible items for the topic System with Microsoft Excel for Windows

Item	Description
SysItems	Returns a list of the available items that may be used with the System topic
Topics	Returns a list of the available topics, which includes the presently open spreadsheets in Excel
Status	Returns the text Ready when Excel is not busy with an operation of some kind
Formats	Returns a list of the Clipboard formats supported by Excel
Selection	Returns the reference of the currently active cell or cells on a spreadsheet
Protocols	Returns the DDE protocols that Excel supports: StdFileEditing and Embedding

Q+E System Items

Seven items may be utilized with the topic System in Q+E for Windows. They are SysItems, Topics, Formats, Status, LogOn, LogOff, and Sources. The SysItems item produces a list of the items that may be used with the System topic. The Topics item provides a list of the available topics and the path and filenames of the open database files. The Formats item returns a list of all the Clipboard formats supported by Q+E for Windows. The Status item returns the text Ready when Q+E is not busy with an operation of some kind. Both the LogOn and LogOff items provide information about whether Q+E is presently connected to an SQL source. The Sources item returns the database formats that Q+E supports. These items are summarized in Table 55-12.

Table 55-12 List of possible items for the topic System with Q+E for Windows

Item	Description
SysItems	Returns a list of the available items that may be used with the System topic
Topics	Returns a list of the available topics, which includes the presently open files in Q+E
Formats	Returns a list of the Clipboard formats supported by Q+E
Status	Returns the text Ready when Q+E is not processing a DDE link action
LogOn	Returns if Q+E is logged into an SQL source
LogOff	Returns if Q+E is not logged into an SQL source
Sources	Returns the database formats that Q+E supports and can import

Example

The DDE project at the end of this chapter uses the LinkItem property to specify what cell in Excel the data is supposed to go in during the Form_Load event.

Comments

The example displayed in this section was written with the version of Q+E 3.0 that is shipped with Microsoft Excel and uses the EMP.DBF and EMPLNAME.NDX files that were shipped with it. This example may not work with other versions of Q+E.

LinkMode Property

Objects Affected	Form, Label, MDIForm, PictureBox, TextBox
Purpose	The LinkMode property determines the type of DDE link to establish and then creates this type of link with the application, topic, and item specified in the LinkTopic and LinkItem properties. Available at design time, read and write at runtime. Table 55-13 summarizes the arguments of the LinkMode property. Tables 55-14 and 55-15 summarize the values and effects of the LinkMode property.

General Syntax

```
[form.]LinkMode [ = mode%]
[form!]Name.LinkMode [ = mode%]
```

Table 55-13 Arguments of the LinkMode property

Argument	Description
form	Name property of the form
Name	Name property of the control
mode%	Current status of the LinkMode property

Table 55-14 Values and effects of the LinkMode property of a text box, picture box, or label

mode%	Meaning
0	(Default) No DDE link established
1	Automatic; the control is updated each time the linked data changes
2	Manual; the control is updated only when the LinkRequest method is used
3	Notify; the control is informed of changes to the linked data, but is not updated

Table 55-15 Values and effects of the LinkMode property of a form

mode%	Meaning
0	(Default) No DDE links may be established with this form
1	Source; permits controls on the form to supply data to the destination application

Example Syntax

```
Private Sub OptionUpdateStatus_Click (Index as Integer)
Startup:
    On Error GoTo OpenXL                    'sets Error trap to OpenXL
```

continued on next page

continued from previous page

```
        Picture1.LinkMode = 0              'sets Picture1's LinkMode
        Picture1.LinkTopic = "Excel|Chart1"  'sets Picture1's Topic
        Picture1.LinkMode = Index          'opens link (buttons are 1, 2, 3)
        Exit Sub                           'exits subroutine
OpenXL:
        If Err = 282 Then                  'checks if Excel wasn't running
            x = Shell("Excel.exe", 3)      'load Excel
            Resume Startup                 'try again
        Else
            Error Err                      'forces display of error
        End If
End Sub
```

Description

The LinkMode property controls whether a DDE link exists and what type of link it is, if it does exist. This property may be changed at runtime or design time. The value of the LinkMode property determines whether a form may be part of a DDE link. The LinkMode property establishes the presence or absence of an active link as well as the type of the link. When there is no link, the value is 0 (none). An active link may be either automatic (1), manual (2), or notify (3).

The example syntax demonstrates the types of LinkMode links in establishing a link to an Excel spreadsheet, which is shown and updated in the picture box. This example assumes the option button group is indexed as 1, 2, and 3 to correspond to the link modes. Note that, depending on the link status, the picture may or may not be updated automatically. For link modes 2 and 3 (manual and notify), other code in another event would have to perform a LinkRequest to update the link.

Using the LinkTopic and LinkItem Properties with Forms

The LinkMode property works with the LinkTopic and LinkItem properties of the form. With a form, the LinkTopic property determines the name for a destination application to use in order to establish a DDE link. A form's LinkItem specifies which control on the form will be connected to the destination application through a DDE link. This property contains the Name property of this indicated control. In this way, the source form has some control of the behavior of links that are established by other applications. The LinkTopic property of an active DDE link may not be changed. In contrast, the LinkItem property may be changed as many times as necessary.

Using the LinkTopic and LinkItem Properties with Controls

The LinkMode property functions with the help of the settings of the LinkTopic and LinkItem properties of the same control. With the LinkTopic property, the control, the application name, and topic (usually the filename or System) provide the information needed to establish a DDE link. A control's LinkItem property indicates which part of the source application the control will be connected to.

The LinkError Event

The LinkError event specifies what happens when a destination application initiates an action that generates an error. The LinkError event returns the error in the ErrLink variable, which may then be used to specify what the difficulty is. This is the correct method for handling errors generated by applications with their DDE LinkMode properties set to source (1).

Example   The DDE project at the end of this chapter uses LinkMode quite frequently to change modes.

LinkNotify Event

Objects Affected   Label, PictureBox, TextBox

Purpose   The LinkNotify event occurs for links set up as LinkMode 3 (notify) when the source data changes. This lets your code issue a LinkRequest to update the control. Table 55-16 summarizes the arguments of the LinkNotify event.

General Syntax

```
Sub Name_LinkNotify ([Index as Integer])
End Sub
```

Table 55-16 Arguments of the LinkNotify event

Argument	Description
Name	Name of the control
Index	Index number of the control if in a control array

Example Syntax

```
Private Sub Picture1_LinkNotify ()
    Command1.ForeColor = QBColor(1)        'highlight the "Update" button
    StatusBar.Text = "Source chart has been updated. ⇐
Press 'Update' button to see changes"
End Sub
```

Description   The LinkNotify event lets your code react to changes in the source data for controls with a LinkMode of 3 (notify). You would typically update the control immediately with LinkRequest, ignore the change, or inform the user of the change.

The example syntax takes this last strategy of informing the user of the change. It highlights the command button that contains the LinkRequest code and puts a message on a status bar informing the user of the change.

This technique is most useful for links that transfer substantial amounts of data. For instance, graphics files tend to be quite large and take an appreciable amount of time to update. Letting the user control when to update the destination control might make your application more responsive than trying to automatically update after every change.

Example   The DDE project at the end of this chapter uses the LinkNotify events of both the text box and the picture box to inform the user of the change in the links' status. Both routines update the labels immediately to the left of the controls to read "(Data Available)." The user can then select menuLink Update Links to update the links.

LinkOpen Event

Objects Affected   Form, Label, MDIForm, PictureBox, TextBox

Purpose   The LinkOpen event processes any actions that take place when a DDE link opens between a form, label, picture box, or text box and another program. A link may be opened by either a Visual Basic application or an external application. The LinkOpen event of the form triggers when another application establishes a DDE link. Tables 55-17 and 55-18 summarize the arguments and meanings of the return values for the Cancel argument of the LinkOpen event.

General Syntax

```
Private Sub Form_LinkOpen (Cancel As Integer)
Private Sub Name_LinkOpen ([Index As Integer,] Cancel As Integer)
```

Table 55-17 Arguments of the LinkOpen event

Argument	Description
form	'Form' indicates the form
Name	Name property of the control
Index	Index value of the control in a control array with which the link is established
Cancel	Return value, set to False or True to accept or refuse link

Table 55-18 Meanings of the return values for the Cancel argument in the LinkOpen event

Cancel	Meaning
False	(Default) Accept the link
True	Refuse the link

Example Syntax

```
Private Sub Command1_Click ()
    Text1.LinkTimeout = -1                    'turns off Timeout Error
    Text1.LinkMode = 0                        'deactivates any existing links
    Text1.LinkTopic = "Excel|System"    'sets Topic
    Text1.LinkMode = 2                        'opens a Manual link
    Text1.LinkExecute "[File.Close(FALSE)]"'closes presently open file in Excel
```

```
        Text1.LinkMode = 0                  'cuts the link with Excel
        End                                 'ends Program
End Sub

Private Sub Text1_LinkOpen (Cancel As Integer)
    If Text1.Text = "No" Then            'checks the contents of Text box
        Cancel = True                    'indicates that DDE link is not established
        Exit Sub                         'exits the subroutine
    Else
        x = Shell("Excel",3)             'opens Excel
        Cancel = False                   'indicates that DDE link is established
    End If
End Sub
```

Description

The LinkOpen event controls whether a link may be created between either a Visual Basic control and another application or another application and a Visual Basic form. Each LinkOpen event returns a value in the Cancel variable that accepts or refuses a DDE link. When the LinkOpen event contains no code or the Cancel variable is 0, the link is accepted. If the Cancel variable is a nonzero value, the link is not established.

In the example syntax, the LinkOpen event of the text box tests whether the Text property contains the word No. As long as the text box does not contain this word, the link is established. Notice that the expressions that are placed after the LinkMode property change are processed after the LinkOpen event executes.

The LinkMode Property

When a DDE link is created by setting the LinkMode property of a picture box, text box, or label to 1 (automatic), 2 (manual), or 3 (notify), the LinkOpen event of that control triggers. Do not place any commands that depend on the link, such as the LinkExecute, LinkRequest, and LinkPoke methods, in the LinkOpen event. The actual link is not set up until the LinkOpen event finishes processing. In cases where the Cancel variable is a nonzero value and the link is not created, any expressions that depend on the link will result in an error. This is why we place Exit Sub after the setting Cancel to True in the example syntax. The code that follows the LinkMode setting would otherwise generate an error.

Access by an External Application

If the LinkMode property of a form is 1 (source), an external application may establish a DDE link with any text box, picture box, or label on the form. Any actions in the LinkOpen event process before the link is established. The Cancel value returned by the LinkOpen event indicates whether the link is accepted or denied. If the Cancel value is 0, the link is permitted. If the Cancel value is a nonzero value, the link is denied.

Example

The DDE project at the end of this chapter uses the LinkOpen event to properly update its display. It updates the lablGraphLinkStatus caption property to "...opening link..." for the duration of the open procedure.

Comments

Any actions that depend on the link must wait until after the LinkOpen event is processed or an error will generate. This is because the link is not actually established with another application until the Cancel value is

returned at the end of the LinkOpen event. If the event contains no
actions, then the link is established normally. Otherwise, the definition of
Cancel as any nonzero value prevents the link.

LinkPoke Method

Objects Affected	Label, PictureBox, TextBox
Purpose	The LinkPoke method inserts the contents of a Visual Basic destination control into the item specified in the source application. This method temporarily reverses the flow of information. A normal link transfers data from the source to the destination when the link is automatic or the LinkRequest method is utilized. With the LinkPoke method, the destination provides information to the source. This change in the passage of data is only temporary and has no effect on the normal operation of the link either before or after the LinkPoke method. Table 55-19 summarizes the arguments of the LinkPoke method.

General Syntax

```
[form!]Name.LinkPoke
```

Table 55-19 Arguments of the LinkPoke method

Argument	Description
form	Name property of the form
Name	Name property of the control

Example Syntax

```
Private Sub Command1_Click ()
Startup:
    On Error Goto OpenXL        'sets Error trap to OpenXL
    Text1.Text = "Data Transferred"'defines Text property of Text box
    Text1.LinkTopic = "Excel|Sheet1"'defines Topic
    Text1.LinkItem = "R1C1"     'defines Item (a cell reference)
    Text1.LinkTimeout = -1      'turns off Timeout error
    Text1.LinkMode = 2          'opens a manual link
    Text1.LinkPoke              'inserts information (Text1.Text) into R1C1
    Text1.LinkMode = 0          'closes the link
    Exit Sub                    'exits the subroutine
OpenXL:
    If Err = 282 Then           'Checks if Excel wasn't in memory causing
        x = Shell("Excel.exe", 3) 'the error making it necessary to start
        Resume Startup          'Excel. Returns to the program's beginning.
    Else
        Error Err               'forces display of error message
    End If
End Sub
```

Description	A LinkPoke method transfers the contents of the control to the item in the linked application identified by the control's LinkItem property. When the specified control is a picture box, the contents of the Picture property are transferred to the item. If the control is a text box, the contents of the Text property are moved to the item. With a label box, the Caption property is transmitted to the item.

The LinkPoke method might be useful if you want to give the other application some data to work on so it could supply the result back to your application. For example, poking sales information into cells on a spreadsheet could set up the spreadsheet to calculate results such as quota attainment, variances among sales reps, and so forth. The spreadsheet would then send the results back over the link in the normal manner.

In the example syntax, the LinkPoke method places the contents of the text box Text1 into the Excel spreadsheet's R1C1 cell when the user presses the command button.

The LinkTopic Property

Each LinkPoke method requires that the LinkTopic property contain the name of the application and the topic into which the data is being inserted. The application must support DDE links. The topic is normally the name of the file. In the example syntax, the LinkTopic is defined as "Excel|Sheet1." This indicates that the data will be placed somewhere on Excel's default Sheet1.

The LinkItem Property

The LinkItem property of the control determines the exact destination of the data that the LinkPoke method inserts in the topic. A LinkItem may be changed at runtime so that each LinkPoke method can place data in a new location in the topic. Not setting the LinkItem property of the control generates an error. In the example syntax, the data is placed in the R1C1 cell of the Sheet1 spreadsheet as identified by the LinkItem property of the Text1 text box.

The LinkMode Property

A LinkPoke method will work when the LinkMode property is set to automatic (1), manual (2), or notify (3). Even though a valid link is established with the LinkMode property, the LinkPoke method will not work unless both the LinkTopic and LinkItem properties are set to valid elements of the other application that may receive the contents of the indicated control. For example, if two Visual Basic applications are linked through a picture box on the destination and a text box on the source, an error will occur.

Example

The LinkPoke method pokes data from the eight text boxes directly into the spreadsheet. Each control array's Change event triggers the LinkPoke method.

LinkRequest Method

Objects Affected   Label, PictureBox, TextBox

Purpose   The LinkRequest method updates a manual or notify link between a Visual Basic control and another application. Automatic DDE links between applications do not require this method, as this data is updated automatically. Table 55-20 summarizes the arguments of the LinkRequest method.

General Syntax

```
[form!]Name.LinkRequest
```

Table 55-20 Arguments of the LinkRequest method

Argument	Description
form	Name property of the form
Name	Name property of the control

Example Syntax

```
Private Sub Command1_Click ()
Startup:
    On Error GoTo OpenWinWord          'sets error trap to OpenWinWord
    Text1.LinkTimeout = -1             'turns off Timeout error
    Text1.LinkMode = 0                 'deactivates any existing links
    Text1.LinkTopic = "WinWord|System"'sets the Topic for the DDE link
    If Text1.Text <> "Text1" Then      'checks if Text box has default text
        Text1.LinkItem = "SysItems"    'sets the Item for the DDE link
    ElseIf Text1.LinkItem = "SysItems" Then  'checks the setting of LinkItem
        Text1.LinkItem = "Topics"        'sets the Item for the DDE link
    ElseIf Text1.LinkItem = "Topics" Then 'checks the setting of LinkItem
        Text1.LinkItem = "Formats"       'sets the Item for the DDE link
    End If
    Text1.LinkMode = 2                 'opens a manual link with Winword
    Text1.LinkRequest                  'updates the Text1 text box
    Exit Sub                           'exits sub
OpenWinWord:
    If Err = 282 Then                  'Checks if WinWord wasn't in memory causing
        x = Shell("Winword.exe", 3)    'the error making it necessary to start
        Resume Startup                 'Winword. Returns to the program's beginning.
    Else
        Error Err                      'forces display of error message
    End If
End Sub
```

Description   A LinkRequest method transfers a source item's contents to a control in a linked application. When the control is a picture box, the Picture property is updated by the item. If the control is a text box, the contents of the Text property change to match the item. With a label box, the Caption property is modified to contain the item's text.

In the example syntax, the LinkRequest method displays a list of the available items for a DDE conversation with the System topic when the user presses the Command1 command button. If the user presses the command button a second time, the LinkRequest method returns the name and path of the open documents in WinWord. When the user presses the Command1 command button a third time, the LinkRequest method returns the Clipboard formats supported by Word for Windows.

The LinkTopic Property

The LinkTopic property of a control indicates the topic to use for the DDE link. Each topic serves as a unique identifier along with the name of the application with which the link is being established. This topic may not be changed while the link is active. In the example syntax, the topic is set to System so that the different items available for that topic may be displayed in the text box with the LinkRequest method.

The LinkItem Property

The LinkItem property of the control determines exactly where the LinkRequest method obtains the data to insert into the control. A LinkItem may be changed at runtime so that each time a LinkRequest method is used, the contents of another source are inserted in the control. Not setting the LinkItem property of the control generates an error. In the example syntax, the LinkItem is changed twice, reflecting the current contents of the Text property of the Text1 text box.

The LinkMode Property

You establish a manual or notify link between a control and another application for two possible reasons. If the other application is only capable of supporting a manual DDE link, then this is the only means of establishing the link. Even if the application supports automatic linking, setting a manual or notify link makes sense if there is a lot of data transmitted. For example, extensive graphics that change constantly can take an appreciable amount of time to update. Letting the user choose when to update (or automatically updating during idle times) makes for a more responsive application than one that tries to keep current at all times.

Example

The LinkRequest method in the menuLink_Click routine updates both the text box's and the picture's links.

Comments

Use the System topic with the items listed in Tables 55-21, 55-22, and 55-23 in the LinkSend method to discover what items are available for the LinkRequest method to obtain information from.

LinkSend Method

Objects Affected   Label, PictureBox, TextBox

Purpose   The LinkSend method transfers the contents of a picture box on a form to another application. This method is only useful when the DDE link is established by another application that functions as the destination and your application is the source. This method is necessary for updating the destination application, no matter whether the link created is automatic, manual, or notify. Table 55-21 summarizes the arguments of the LinkSend method.

General Syntax

```
[form!]Name.LinkSend
```

Table 55-21 Arguments of the LinkSend method

Argument	Description
form	Name property of the form
Name	Name property of control

Example Syntax

```
Private Sub Form_LinkExecute (CmdStr As String, Cancel As Integer)
    Cancel = False                      'command was accepted
    Select Case UCase(cmdStr)           'makes all of the text of command upper case
        Case "[UPDATE]"                 'checks if command string is UPDATE
            Picture1.LinkTimeout = -1   'turns off timeout error
            Picture1.LinkSend           'updates the contents of other application
        Case Else                       'otherwise
            Cancel = True               'command was rejected
    End Select
End Sub
```

Description   The LinkSend method transfers the contents of the picture box control to the linked destination application. All links, even automatic ones, need to have LinkSend to transfer the picture box picture. Without this design, a picture box would try to update an automatic link for each and every pixel changed—a lengthy process! Visual Basic requires you to explicitly notify DDE destinations when your picture box has finished changing.

In the example syntax, the LinkSend method updates the linked application that sends the Update command through the DDE link. The item on the destination application receives the updated picture. This is an important possible use of this method that determines when a picture on another application needs updating.

The LinkExecute Event   The LinkExecute event is an excellent location for the LinkSend method to update the picture on a destination application. In the example syntax, the word UPDATE resets the contents of the picture on the destination application that sends the command. This allows the other application to indicate when the picture on it needs to be updated.

Example   The form's LinkExecute method makes a provision to LinkSend the picture.

LinkTimeout Property

Objects Affected   Label, PictureBox, TextBox

Purpose   The LinkTimeout property of a picture box, text box, or label indicates how long a Visual Basic application needs to wait for a response from another application involved in a DDE link. A control's LinkTimeout property only affects the operation of a DDE link in which the control is the destination and the other application is the source. Table 55-22 summarizes the arguments of the LinkTimeout property.

General Syntax

```
[form!]Name.LinkTimeout [ = duration%]
```

Table 55-22 Arguments of the LinkTimeout property

Argument	Description
form	Name property of the form
Name	Name property of the picture box, text box, or label control
duration%	The interval specified for the Timeout property in tenths of seconds; default 50 = 5 seconds

Example Syntax

```
Private Sub Form_Load ()
Startup:
    On Error GoTo OpenWinWord        'sets error trap to OpenWinWord
    Label1.LinkTimeout = 100         'sets Timeout interval to 100 seconds
    Label1.LinkMode = 0              'deactivates any active link
    Label1.LinkTopic = "WinWord|System"'sets the Topic for the DDE link
    Label1.LinkMode = 2              'opens a manual link with Winword
    Label1.LinkTimeout = -1          'turns off timeout interval
    Label1.LinkExecute "[FileClose 2]"'closes the current file without saving it
    Label1.LinkExecute "[FileOpen]" 'opens the File Open dialog box
    Exit Sub
OpenWinWord:
    If Err = 282 Then                  'Checks if WinWord wasn't in memory causing
        x = Shell("Winword.exe", 3) 'the error making it necessary to start
        Resume Startup                 'Winword. Returns to the program's beginning.
    Else
        Error Err                      'forces display of error message
    End If
End Sub
```

Description   The LinkTimeout property of a picture box, text box, or label sets the length of time that a link remains open without a response from the other application. The control argument of a LinkTimeout property expression contains the Name property of the control.

A control's LinkTimeout property may be adjusted to account for the time that the other application needs to process the commands sent through the link. An error generates if there is no response from the other application in the time specified by the LinkTimeout property of the control.

A control's LinkTimeout property duration% argument defines the amount of time to wait. The duration is measured in tenths of a second, so the default value of 50 represents 5 seconds. The maximum value for duration% is 65535, or about 1 hour 49 minutes. Changing the duration% variable to -1 ensures that the control will wait indefinitely for the other application to respond, or for the user to press Y. The example syntax changes the Timeout property of the label control both before and after establishing the link. First, the value is increased from 50 to 100. Next, the Timeout property is modified to -1, disabling the timeout error.

In the example syntax, the Timeout property is initially 100. This routine turns off the timeout error by changing the LinkTimeout property to -1. This prevents the display of any errors created by the opening of the FileOpen dialog box if the Visual Basic application is not closed quickly enough.

The LinkExecute Method	When the LinkExecute method sends commands through the link to the source application, the value of the Timeout property determines how long the destination application will wait for a response from the source application. In cases where the source application needs extra time to process the commands sent to it with the LinkExecute method, increase the LinkTimeout property setting to reflect this need. The example syntax completely disables the LinkTimeout property by setting it to -1. This prevents the timeout error from being generated and allows the processing of the End Statement. This is necessary because WinWord's FileOpen command displays a dialog box that normally prevents the processing of the commands that follow the LinkExecute command.
Example	The Form_Load routine sets the LinkTimeout of the picture box to a high number, just in case the picture takes a long time to evaluate.
Comments	The Timeout property of one control does not affect the Timeout property of another control.

LINKTOPIC PROPERTY

Objects Affected	Form, Label, MDIForm, PictureBox, TextBox
Purpose	The LinkTopic property defines the application name and subject that uniquely identify a DDE link between a form, picture box, text box, or label and another application. A source form's LinkTopic specifies the topic name that another application must use to create a DDE link with the form. When the control is the destination of a DDE link, the LinkTopic determines the source application and topic of the link. Since a DDE link is uniquely identified by the application name and the topic, the

LinkTopic property may not be changed on an active link. Table 55-23 summarizes the arguments of the LinkTopic property, and Tables 55-24 and 55-25 give the meanings of the link$ argument.

General Syntax

```
[form.]LinkTopic [ = link$]
[form!]Name.LinkTopic [ = link$]
```

Table 55-23 Arguments of the LinkTopic property

Argument	Description
form	Name property of the form
Name	Name property of the label, text box, or picture box
link$	Application name and topic of a DDE link

Table 55-24 Two parts of the link$ argument of the LinkTopic property for a destination control

link$	Description
Application Name	The name of the application's executable file without the EXE extension
Topic	The general location of the data in the application, like the filename

Table 55-25 Link$ argument of LinkTopic property for a source form

link$	Description
Topic	The application's project file (*.VBP without the extension) from within Visual Basic
	The application's executable file (*.EXE without the extension) when compiled

Example Syntax

```
Private Sub Command1_Click ()
Startup:
    On Error Goto OpenApp
    If Text1.Text = "Winword" Then          'checks the current contents of textbox
        Text1.LinkTopic = "Winword|System"  'changes the DDE link Topic
        App$ = "Winword.exe"                'defines App$ Text variable
    ElseIf Text1.Text = "Q+E" Then          'checks the current contents of textbox
        Text1.LinkTopic = "QE|System"       'changes the DDE link Topic
        App$ = "QE.exe"                     'defines App$ Text variable
    ElseIf Text1.Text = "Excel" Then        'checks the current contents of textbox
        Text1.LinkTopic = "Excel|System"    'changes the DDE link Topic
        App$ = "Excel.exe"                  'defines App$ Text variable
    Else
        End                                 'ends Program
    End If
```

continued on next page

continued from previous page

```
StartLink:
    Text1.LinkItem = "SysItems"        'changes the DDE link Item
    Text1.LinkMode = 2                 'establishes a link with the application
    Text1.LinkRequest                  'updates the Text1 text box
OpenApp:
    If Err = 282 Then                  'checks the err value
        x = Shell(App$, 3)             'If the application was not in memory, then
        Resume StartLink               'loads the application.
    Else
        Error Err                      'forces display of error message
    End If
End Sub
```

Description	The LinkTopic property defines the application name and subject that uniquely identify a DDE link between a form, picture box, text box, or label and another application. There are two possible definitions of the link$ string argument in a LinkTopic property expression. A form's LinkTopic property sets the application name that another application must use to establish a DDE link. The LinkTopic property of a picture box, text box, or label includes the application name and the topic. These two elements are separated from each other by a vertical line (character code 124, the pipe symbol). The LinkTopic must be a string, and there is a limit of 255 characters for the LinkTopic definition.
	In the example syntax, the LinkTopic consists of the application name followed by the topic System. This establishes a DDE link with the indicated application that is not dependent on any particular file. Additionally, the other application (WinWord, Excel, or Q+E) may be polled for the acceptable topics for a DDE link.
The LinkItem Property	The LinkItem property of the control determines the exact destination of the general information entered in the LinkTopic property. Unlike the LinkTopic property, the LinkItem property may be changed while a link is active. Some applications will allow the creation of a DDE link without a specific LinkItem. When the System topic is used, the LinkItem may be set to a variety of settings that aredependent upon the application on the other side of the link. The example syntax sets the LinkItem property to SysItems, which returns all the possible items that may be chosen with the System topic.
The LinkMode Property	A LinkTopic property will work when the LinkMode property is set to automatic (1) or manual (2). Even though the LinkMode property establishes a valid link, the link will not work unless both the LinkTopic and LinkItem properties are set to valid elements of the other application. In the example syntax, the LinkMode property is a manual link so the programmer controls when to update the information to the text box with a LinkRequest method.

The Destination Control	The LinkTopic property identifies the portion of a DDE link that may not be changed without severing the link between the control and another application. An application name is normally the filename of the executable program without the extension. The LinkTopic property of a form identifies a Visual Basic application Name property as the default setting. Each of the available topics may be obtained by setting the LinkTopic to "System" and the LinkItem to "Topics." Normally, the LinkTopic indicates the path and filename of the data file being accessed through the link.
The Source Form	A form's LinkTopic property determines the name that another application needs to establish a DDE link with this form. This is the name of the Visual Basic project (*.VBP) or executable (*.EXE) file without the extension, as summarized in Table 55-25. This property has no effect on the operation of a link in which one of the controls on the form establishes a DDE link with another application.
Example	The DDE project at the end of this chapter uses the LinkTopic quite extensively. The Form_Load, Form_Unload, and the MenuEdit_Click events all use the LinkTopic property to establish a DDE link.
Comments	Be careful that multiple DDE links between the same application do not create an infinite loop of updates. An example of this problem is if a source form is linked to another application and the text box on the same form is part of a destination link to the same application. An automatic link setup in both directions results in an infinite loop.

The DDE Project

Project Overview

The DDE project demonstrates each of the properties, methods, and events involved in setting up DDE links between applications. It does this in two distinct ways. First, it links some data entry text boxes on the main form to an Excel worksheet. It then uses Excel to chart the data and update a picture box on the form. This demonstrates a typical use for DDE as a way of setting up powerful front ends for other applications. The second demonstration of DDE is an elaboration of the Edit menu structure. You'll see how to put together a complete Edit menu that will let your users establish their own DDE links. You can cut, copy, paste, and paste link both the actual text or graphic information as well as the link information between your Visual Basic application and any other application that supports DDE.

Assembling the Project

1. Create a new form (the DDE form) and place on it the controls shown in Table 55-26.

Table 55-26 Elements of the DDE form

Object	Property	Setting
Form	BackColor	&H00C0C0C0 (Light Gray)
	BorderStyle	1—Fixed Single
	Caption	"DDE Project"
	LinkMode	1—Source
	LinkTopic	"formMain"
TextBox	MultiLine	True
	Name	textBox
PictureBox	Name	pictGraph
TextBox	Alignment	1—Right Justify
	Index	0
	MultiLine	True
	Name	textCogs
TextBox	Alignment	1—Right Justify
	Index	1
	MultiLine	True
	Name	textCogs
TextBox	Alignment	1—Right Justify
	Index	2
	MultiLine	True
	Name	textCogs
TextBox	Alignment	1—Right Justify
	Index	3
	MultiLine	True
	Name	textCogs
TextBox	Alignment	1—Right Justify
	Index	0
	MultiLine	True
	Name	textSales
TextBox	Alignment	1—Right Justify
	Index	1
	MultiLine	True
	Name	textSales
TextBox	Alignment	1—Right Justify
	Index	2
	MultiLine	True
	Name	textSales
TextBox	Alignment	1—Right Justify
	Index	3

Object	Property	Setting
	MultiLine	True
	Name	textSales
Label	Alignment	1—Right Justify
	BackColor	&H00000000 (Black)
	ForeColor	&H00FFFFFF(White)
	Index	0
	Name	lablTotal
Label	Alignment	1—Right Justify
	BackColor	&H00000000 (Black)
	ForeColor	&H00FFFFFF (White)
	Index	1
	Name	lablTotal
Label	Alignment	1—Right Justify
	BackColor	&H00000000 (Black)
	ForeColor	&H00FFFFFF (White)
	Index	2
	Name	lablTotal
Label	Alignment	1—Right Justify
	BackColor	&H00000000 (Black)
	ForeColor	&H00FFFFFF (White)
	Index	3
	Name	lablTotal
Label	Alignment	1—Right Justify
	BackStyle	0—Transparent
	Caption	"Sales"
Label	Alignment	1—Right Justify
	BackStyle	0—Transparent
	Caption	"Cost Of Goods"
Label	Alignment	1—Right Justify
	BackStyle	0—Transparent
	Caption	"Total"
Label	Alignment	1—Right Justify
	BackStyle	0—Transparent
	Caption	"Graph"
Label	Alignment	1—Right Justify
	BackStyle	0—Transparent
	Caption	"Miscellaneous Text"
Label	Alignment	1—Right Justify
	BackStyle	0—Transparent
	Name	lablGraphLinkStatus

continued on next page

continued from previous page

Object	Property	Setting
Label	Alignment	1—Right Justify
	BackStyle	0—Transparent
	FontBold	0—False
	Name	lablTextLinkStatus

Table 55-27 Menu design parameters of the DDE project

Name	Caption	Property	Setting
menuBar	&File	Index	0
menuFile	E&xit	Index	0
menuBar	&Edit	Index	1
menuEdit	Cu&t	Index	0
menuEdit	&Copy	Index	1
menuEdit	&Paste	Index	2
menuEdit	Paste &Link	Index	3
menuBar	&Link	Index	2
menuLink	&Automatic	Index	0
menuLink	&Manual	Index	1
menuLink	&Notify	Index	2
menuLink	-	Index	3
menuLink	&Update Links	Index	4

2. Size and position the controls, as shown in Figure 55-1.

3. Enter the following code in the General Declarations section. This defines the constants used in the program, and then declares a module-level variable that holds the current LinkMode status as set by the Link menu.

```
' Clipboard formats
Const CF_LINK = &HBF00
Const CF_TEXT = 1
Const CF_BITMAP = 2
Const CF_METAFILE = 3
Const CF_DIB = 8
Const CF_PALETTE = 9
' Link constants
Const NONE = 0
Const LINK_AUTOMATIC = 1
Const LINK_MANUAL = 2
Const LINK_NOTIFY = 3

' Link error
Const WRONG_FORMAT = 1
Const DDE_SOURCE_CLOSED = 6
Const TOO_MANY_LINKS = 7
Const DATA_TRANSFER_FAILED = 8
```

```
' MousePointer
Const HOURGLASS = 11
Const DEFAULT = 0

Const THISAPPNAME = "CHP25"        'used when establishing links - application name
Const TOPICNAME = "formMain"       'used when establishing links - topic name

Dim MenuLinkModeCheck As Integer   'contains current linkmode setting on the link menu
```

4. Enter the following code in the General Declarations section. This procedure describes any errors that occur during a LinkError event.

```
Private Sub describeLinkError (linkerror, where)
    Select Case linkerror          'describe the link error
      Case WRONG_FORMAT
            msg$ = "The linked application asked for data ⇐
in an incompatible format when   using the " &
where
      Case DDE_SOURCE_CLOSED
            msg$ = "An application attempted a DDE operation ⇐
after this application disabled its source abilities."
      Case TOO_MANY_LINKS
            msg$ = "Attempt to open too many DDE conversations ⇐
- 128 maximum!" Case DATA_TRANSFER_FAILED
            msg$ = "Failure to update control " & where
      Case 11
            msg$ = "Not enough remaining memory to complete DDE ⇐
link. Close applications   before trying again"
    End Select
    MsgBox msg$
End Sub
```

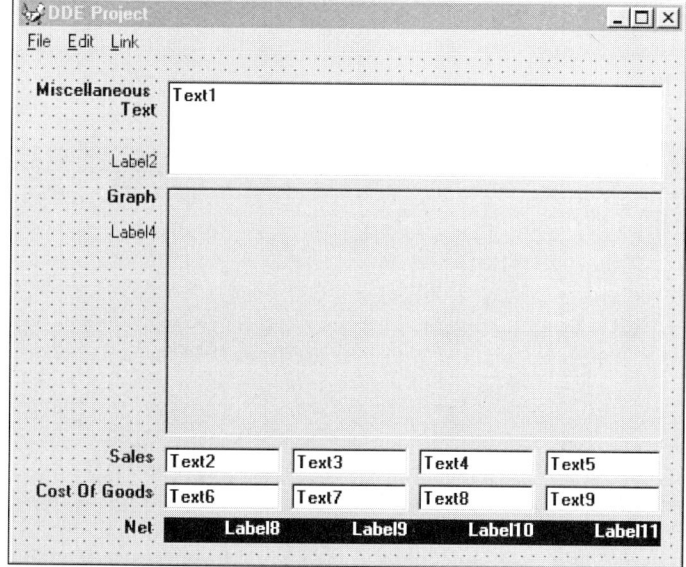

Figure 55-1 The DDE project under design

5. Enter the following code in the Form's LinkError event. This would occur only if the DDE link suffers an error that is not caused by the program itself. It calls a routine that describes the error in a message box.

```
Private Sub Form_LinkError (LinkErr As Integer)
    describeLinkError LinkErr, " the form." 'display error message
End Sub
```

6. Enter the following code in the Form_LinkExecute event. This event processes any command requests from other applications. (For example, another Visual Basic application you've written could execute a LinkExecute method over the DDE link.) It checks to see what the command is and either updates the other application's graph data, severs the graph link, or ends the program. If it doesn't recognize the command, it tells the other application by setting the Cancel return value to True.

```
Private Sub Form_LinkExecute (CmdStr As String, Cancel As Integer)
    Cancel = False                      'accept the command
    Select Case CmdStr
        Case "Update Graph"             'other app wants the graph again
            pictGraph.LinkSend          'give them the graph
        Case "Sever Graph Link"         'other app doesn't want graph at all
            pictGraph.LinkMode = NONE   'cut the link
        Case "End"                      'other app wants this program to end
            End                         'end
        Case Else
            Cancel = True               'oops! didn't recognize command
    End Select
End Sub
```

7. Enter the following code in the Form_Load event. This happens when the form first loads. It begins by setting up some of the controls' values. Notice the Tag properties for the textBox and pictGraph controls. These values hold the control's Name property for use in the Edit Cut and Edit Copy routines so the correct item can be placed in a source DDE link.

The routine then builds a simple spreadsheet model, listing four Quarters on the top and "Gross Sales," "COGS [cost of goods sold]," and "Net Sales" along the side. The interior of the spreadsheet is filled with the values of the textSales and textCogs text boxes a little later. The last row of the spreadsheet simply subtracts the cost of goods from total sales to find net sales. Note that the spreadsheet is sent to Excel as a tab and carriage-return delimited file. This is an easy way to send lots of information to the spreadsheet and is much easier and more elegant than simply using a LinkExecute command for each value and movement within the spreadsheet. (Note that this delimited format is the same as the grid control's Clip property.) After we build the string, we place it on the Clipboard.

We next execute a series of Excel macro commands with the LinkExecute method. These commands put the spreadsheet data into Excel, format the spreadsheet, and open up a new chart that graphs the data. Note that it doesn't really matter what control uses the method, as all we're doing is sending Excel the method's argument string. Unless you know Excel's macro language, you may have difficulties understanding each command. Refer to the Excel Function Reference guide for details. An easy way to create these LinkExecute arguments is to record a macro in Excel of what you want to do. When you are finished creating the macro, go to the macro sheet and copy the entire macro onto the Clipboard. Paste the macro into Visual Basic and put the LinkExecute method and a quote in front of the macro command and a quote at the end. If there are any quote characters inside the command, as in [ACTIVATE("Sheet1")], then add an extra set of quotes, as in [ACTIVATE(""Sheet1")]. This trick should work with most macro languages.

Once we've created the spreadsheet and chart, we create some dummy data in the text boxes and create the actual DDE links. Each text box is linked to the appropriate cell in Excel's spreadsheet, and the labels are linked to the SUM formula that gives the Net Sales.

If an error occurred while creating any of these links, it will trigger the error handling routine. This first checks to see if Excel didn't respond to the DDE request, thus implying that it wasn't loaded. If so, the routine checks to see if it's already tried to load Excel. If it hasn't, it loads Excel. If it has, that implies that Excel is probably busy trying to finish loading, so it just gives it some more time with the DoEvents statement.

```
Private Sub Form_Load ()
    Screen.MousePointer = HOURGLASS
    TextBox.Text = "Type some text here to link to the other app"
    menuLink_Click 0                        'set default to Automatic link
    TextBox.Tag = "textBox"                 'tags used in links
    pictGraph.Tag = "pictGraph"
    lablTextLinkStatus = "(unlinked)"

    TB = Chr$(9)                                    'tab
    CR = Chr$(13) & Chr$(10)                        'carriage return/linefeed


                            'quick little spreadsheet for excel;
                            'tab and carriage return delimited for each cell and row
    s = " " & TB & "Q1" & TB & "Q2" & TB & "Q3" & TB & "Q4" & CR
    s = s & "Gross Sales" & CR
    s = s & "COGS" & CR
    s = s & "Net Sales" & TB & "= SUM(B2 - B3)" & TB & "= SUM(C2 - C3)"
    s = s & TB & "= SUM(D2 - D3)" & TB & "= SUM(E2 - E3)"
    Clipboard.Clear
    Clipboard.SetText s                             'put spreadsheet data on clipboard

Startup:
    On Error GoTo OpenExcel                         'set trap
For i = 0 To 3
    textSales(i).LinkTopic = "Excel|Sheet1"   'blank worksheet
    textSales(i).LinkItem = "R1C1"            'arbitrary; doesn't matter what cell
    textSales(i).LinkMode = LINK_MANUAL       'set up link

    textCogs(i).LinkTopic = "Excel|Sheet1"    'blank worksheet
    textCogs(i).LinkItem = "R1C1"             'arbitrary; doesn't matter what cell
```

continued on next page

continued from previous page

```
        textCogs(i).LinkMode = LINK_MANUAL          'set up link

        lablTotal(i).LinkTopic = "Excel|Sheet1"    'blank worksheet
        lablTotal(i).LinkItem = "R1C1"             'arbitrary; doesn't
                                                   'matter what cell
        lablTotal(i).LinkMode = LINK_MANUAL        'set up link
    Next i
        textSales(0).LinkExecute "[ACTIVATE(""Sheet1"")]"        'make sure  on the worksheet
        textSales(0).LinkExecute "[SELECT(""R1C1"")]"           'make Excel select upper left
        textSales(0).LinkExecute "[PASTE]"                      'make Excel paste in clipboard
        textSales(0).LinkExecute "[SELECT(""R1C1:R4C5"")]"      'make Excel select worksheet
        textSales(0).LinkExecute "[COLUMN.WIDTH(,,,3)]"         'make Excel set column widths
        textSales(0).LinkExecute "[SELECT(""R2C2:R4C5"")]"      'make Excel select worksheet
        textSales(0).LinkExecute "[FORMAT.NUMBER(""$#,##0_);($#,##0)"")]"  'currency
        textSales(0).LinkExecute "[SELECT(""R1C1:R4C5"")]"      'make Excel select worksheet
        textSales(0).LinkExecute "[NEW(2,1)]"                   'make Excel create a new chart item
                                                   'make Excel format chart as a line chart
        textSales(0).LinkExecute "[FORMAT.MAIN(4,1,,,FALSE,FALSE,FALSE)]"
        textSales(0).LinkExecute "[LEGEND(TRUE)]" 'make Excel give it a legend
        textSales(0).LinkExecute "[SELECT(""Chart"")]"         'make Excel select entire chart
                                                   'make Excel format all text on chart as Arial 8 point
        textSales(0).LinkExecute
"[FORMAT.FONT(0,1,FALSE,""Arial"",8,FALSE,FALSE,FALSE,FALSE)]"
        For i = 0 To 3                             'iterate through all members
          textSales(i).LinkTopic = "Excel|Sheet1"    'set their link topics
          textCogs(i).LinkTopic = "Excel|Sheet1"
          lablTotal(i).LinkTopic = "Excel|Sheet1"
          textSales(i).LinkItem = "R2C" & Trim$(Str$(i + 2))     'R2C2, R2C3, R2C4, R2C5
          textCogs(i).LinkItem = "R3C" & Trim$(Str$(i + 2))      'R3C2, R3C3, R3C4, R3C5
          lablTotal(i).LinkItem = "R4C" & Trim$(Str$(i + 2))     'R4C2, R4C3, R4C4, R4C5
          textSales(i).LinkMode = LINK_MANUAL        'establish links
          textCogs(i).LinkMode = LINK_MANUAL
          lablTotal(i).LinkMode = LINK_MANUAL
          textSales(i).Text = Str$((i + 4) * 10000)   'dummy up some data
          textCogs(i).Text = Str$((i + 2) * 8345)     'more dummy data
        Next i
        pictGraph.LinkTimeout = 10000              'graphics could take a while
        pictGraph.LinkTopic = "Excel|Chart1"       'topic is the new chart
        pictGraph.LinkMode = LINK_NOTIFY           'set up notify link
        pictGraph.LinkRequest                      'immediately update the chart
        lablGraphLinkStatus = "Notify Link"        'set label correctly
        Screen.MousePointer = DEFAULT              'and we're done
    Exit Sub

OpenExcel:                                         'error trap
    If Err = 282 Then                              'if it's not loaded,
        If AlreadyStarted = False Then             'and not waiting for it to finish loading
            X = Shell("EXCEL.EXE", 2)              'then load it!
            AlreadyStarted = True                  'make sure we don't try loading again
        End If
        DoEvents                                   'give it some time to load
        Resume Startup                             'and try the link again
    Else
        Error Err                                  'whoops! something else went wrong...
    End If

End Sub
```

8. Enter the following code in the Form_Unload event. This shuts down all the links and sends a command to Excel to shut it down, too.

```
Private Sub Form_Unload (Cancel As Integer)
      For i = 0 To 3                    'iterate through each member
        textSales(i).LinkMode = NONE  'sever the links
        textCogs(i).LinkMode = NONE
        lablTotal(i).LinkMode = NONE
      Next i
      pictGraph.LinkMode = NONE           'deactivate any existing links
      pictGraph.LinkTopic = "Excel|System" 'talk to excel
      pictGraph.LinkMode = LINK_MANUAL     'set up the link
DoEvents                                   'give it some time to respond
      TextBox.LinkMode = NONE              'sever link
End Sub
```

9. Enter the following code in the General Declarations section. This code updates the labels that display the link status of the text box and picture box.

```
Private Sub labelLinkStatus ()
      Select Case pictGraph.LinkMode      'update the graph label
        Case LINK_AUTOMATIC
            lablGraphLinkStatus.Caption = "Auto Link"
        Case LINK_MANUAL
            lablGraphLinkStatus.Caption = "Manual Link"
        Case LINK_NOTIFY
            lablGraphLinkStatus.Caption = "Notify Link"
        Case Else
            lablGraphLinkStatus.Caption = "(unlinked)"
      End Select
      Select Case TextBox.LinkMode        'update the text box label
        Case LINK_AUTOMATIC
            lablTextLinkStatus.Caption = "Auto Link"
        Case LINK_MANUAL
            lablTextLinkStatus.Caption = "Manual Link"
        Case LINK_NOTIFY
            lablTextLinkStatus.Caption = "Notify Link"
        Case Else
            lablTextLinkStatus.Caption = "(unlinked)"
      End Select
End Sub
```

10. Enter the following code in the menuBar_Click event. This prepares the menus before opening them. Preparing the available menu commands like this helps the user by only displaying choices that actually apply. For example, this routine checks to see what kind of data is on the Clipboard. If the data would work with the control the user is on, it enables the Paste command. The routine systematically goes through each possibility for the four menu commands. Doing this validity checking here also makes the coding easier in the actual Edit procedures, because we can be sure that the menu choice was appropriate given the data and the active control.

```
Private Sub menuBar_Click (Index As Integer)
      Select Case Index
        Case 0 ' ------------ File
```

continued on next page

continued from previous page

```
    Case 1 ' ------------ Edit
        menuEdit(0).Enabled = False          'turn off all menu choices
        menuEdit(1).Enabled = False
        menuEdit(2).Enabled = False
        menuEdit(3).Enabled = False
        If Clipboard.GetFormat(CF_LINK) Then  'if there is link info on clipboard
          linkID = Clipboard.GetText(CF_LINK) 'find out what the link info is
          itemSeparator = InStr(linkID, "!")  'this separates topic from item
          If Left$(linkID, itemSeparator - 1) <> THISAPPNAME ⇐& "|" & TOPICNAME Then
            link = True                        'another app's link; OK for linking
          End If
        End If
        If Clipboard.GetFormat(CF_TEXT) Then Text = True      'there's text on the
                                                              'clipboard
        If Clipboard.GetFormat(CF_BITMAP) Then pict = True    'there's a bitmap on
                                                              'clipboard
        If TypeOf Screen.ActiveControl Is PictureBox Then     'are we on a picture box?
          menuEdit(0).Enabled = True          'OK to cut picture
          menuEdit(1).Enabled = True          'OK to copy picture
          If pict Then                        'if there's a picture on the clipboard
            menuEdit(2).Enabled = True        'OK to paste clipboard's picture
            If link Then                      'if the picture is linked
                menuEdit(3).Enabled = True    'OK to offer Paste Link for picture
            End If
          End If
        End If
        If TypeOf Screen.ActiveControl Is TextBox Then  'if we're on a text box,
          If Screen.ActiveControl.SelText <> "" Then    'and there is some text selected
            menuEdit(0).Enabled = True        'OK to cut text
            menuEdit(1).Enabled = True        'OK to copy text
          End If
          If Text Then                        'if there's text on the clipboard
            menuEdit(2).Enabled = True        'OK to paste text into text box
            If link And Screen.ActiveControl.Tag = "textBox" Then  'If there's a link
                                              'and we're in the top text box,
                menuEdit(3).Enabled = True    'OK to offer Paste Link for the text.
            End If
          End If
        End If
    Case 2 ' ----------- Links
  End Select
End Sub
```

11. Enter the following code in the menuEdit_Click event. This event triggers when the user selects one of the four edit commands: Cut, Copy, Paste, and Paste Link. We know that the menuBar_Click event has only enabled menu commands that are appropriate for this context—for example, if we're on the picture control and Paste Link is enabled, then there is both graphics information and link information on the Clipboard.

Text and graphics use different methods with the Clipboard, so each edit routine first checks to see what kind of control is active: text box or picture box. Each routine then performs normal Clipboard operations. The next few lines of each routine set up the link status.

Cut and Copy both set the proper link information on the Clipboard after they paste their data. The link information is the application name, the form topic, and the Name property of the control being copied. The Name property cannot be read at runtime, so we use the Tag property instead, having loaded the Tag property with the correct name during the Form_Load procedure. The link status line for Paste simply terminates any link if there was one, because a regular paste does not include the link.

The Paste Link command does include the link status. In fact, it never pastes the actual data, letting the link transfer the data instead. It parses the Clipboard's link information to get the topic name and the item and then sets up the link with whatever link mode the user chose on the Link menu.

```
Private Sub menuEdit_Click (Index As Integer)
    Select Case Index
        Case 0 '*********************************************** Cut
            If TypeOf Screen.ActiveControl Is TextBox Then        'on a text box?
                Clipboard.SetText Screen.ActiveControl.Text       'put text on clipboard
                Screen.ActiveControl.SelText = ""                 'cut out selected text
            ElseIf TypeOf Screen.ActiveControl Is PictureBox Then 'on a picture box?
                Clipboard.SetData Screen.ActiveControl.Picture    'put picture on clipboard
                Screen.ActiveControl.Picture = LoadPicture("")    'blank out picture
            End If
            itemName = Screen.ActiveControl.Tag                   'Tag has the control's
                                                                  'Name
            Clipboard.SetText THISAPPNAME & "|" & TOPICNAME & "!" & itemName, CF_LINK
        Case 1 '*********************************************** Copy
            If TypeOf Screen.ActiveControl Is TextBox Then        'on a text box?
                Clipboard.SetText Screen.ActiveControl.Text       'put text on clipboard
            ElseIf TypeOf Screen.ActiveControl Is PictureBox Then 'on a picture box?
                Clipboard.Clear                                   'get rid of any existing
                                                                  'junk on clipboard
                Clipboard.SetData Screen.ActiveControl.Picture    'put picture on clipboard
            End If
            itemName = Screen.ActiveControl.Tag                   'tag has the control's
                                                                  'Name
            Clipboard.SetText THISAPPNAME & "|" & TOPICNAME & "!" & itemName, CF_LINK
        Case 2 '*********************************************** Paste
            Screen.ActiveControl.LinkMode = NONE                  'no link status
            If TypeOf Screen.ActiveControl Is TextBox Then        'on a text box?
                Screen.ActiveControl.SelText = Clipboard.GetText() 'put text from clipboard
            ElseIf TypeOf Screen.ActiveControl Is PictureBox Then 'on a picture box?
                Screen.ActiveControl.Picture = Clipboard.GetData() 'put picture from
                                                                  'clipboard
            End If
        Case 3 '*********************************************** Paste Link
            linkID = Clipboard.GetText(CF_LINK)   'get link information from clipboard
            itemSeparator = InStr(linkID, "!")    'this separates topic name from item name
            Screen.ActiveControl.LinkMode = NONE 'turn off any existing links
            Screen.ActiveControl.LinkTopic = Left$(linkID, itemSeparator - 1)
            Screen.ActiveControl.LinkItem = Mid$(linkID, itemSeparator + 1)
            Screen.ActiveControl.LinkMode = MenuLinkModeCheck  'link mode to what's on link
                                                              'menu
    End Select
    labelLinkStatus                              'update labels with correct link status
End Sub
```

12. Enter the following code in the menuFile_Click routine. It ends the program. Note that there is only one command on the menu, so we don't even have to check to see which menu item was clicked.

```
Private Sub menuFile_Click (Index As Integer)
    End                                         'end the program
End Sub
```

13. Enter the following code in the menuLink_Click routine. This routine triggers whenever the user makes a choice on the Link menu. The first three options, Automatic, Manual, and Notify, are the three possible LinkModes to use when pasting in data. The fourth choice, Update Links, requests new information for both of the controls and then updates their link status labels.

```
Private Sub menuLink_Click (Index As Integer)
    Select Case Index
        Case 0, 1, 2    'link mode
            menuLink(0).Checked = False        'turn off all the checkmarks
            menuLink(1).Checked = False
            menuLink(2).Checked = False
            menuLink(Index).Checked = True     'check the one the user clicked
            MenuLinkModeCheck = Index + 1      'and set the correct linkmode
        Case 4          'update links
            If TextBox.LinkMode <> NONE Then   'if there is a link for text box
                TextBox.LinkRequest            'update it
            End If
            If pictGraph.LinkMode <> NONE Then 'if there is a link for picture box
                pictGraph.LinkRequest          'update it
            End If
            labelLinkStatus                    'update display of link status labels
    End Select
End Sub
```

14. Enter the following code in the pictGraph_LinkClose event. This triggers as a link is closing down; it simply updates the label caption to indicate the picture box's unlinked status.

```
Private Sub pictGraph_LinkClose ()
    lablGraphLinkStatus.Caption = "(unlinked)" 'no more link
End Sub
```

15. Enter the following code in the pictGraph_LinkError event. This triggers whenever there is an external DDE error. It calls a routine that displays an appropriate error message.

```
Private Sub pictGraph_LinkError (LinkErr As Integer)
    describeLinkError LinkErr, "picture box."  'show the error message
End Sub
```

16. Enter the following code in the pictGraph_LinkNotify event. This triggers whenever the LinkMode is set to LINK_NOTIFY (3) and the source data has changed. It changes the link status label's display to notify the user that new data is available.

```
Private Sub pictGraph_LinkNotify ()
    lablGraphLinkStatus.Caption = "(Data Available)"  'notify user new data available
End Sub
```

17. Enter the following code in the pictGraph_LinkOpen event. This triggers immediately before the link opens. (Note that the link is *not* yet open during this
event.) This updates the label to let the user know a link is taking place.
Sometimes links can take a while to complete, particularly for large graphics files.

```
Private Sub pictGraph_LinkOpen (Cancel As Integer)
    lablGraphLinkStatus.Caption = " linking "      'could take a while, eh?
End Sub
```

18. Enter the following code in the textBox_LinkError event. This triggers whenever
there is an external DDE error. It calls a routine that displays an appropriate error
message.

```
Private Sub textBox_LinkError (LinkErr As Integer)
    describeLinkError LinkErr, "text box."             'display the error message
End Sub
```

19. Enter the following code in the textBox_LinkNotify event. This triggers whenever
the LinkMode is set to LINK_NOTIFY (3) and the source data has changed. It
changes the link status label's display to notify the user that new data is available.

```
Private Sub textBox_LinkNotify ()
    lablTextLinkStatus.Caption = "(Data Available)"    'notify user new data available
End Sub
```

20. Enter the following code in the textCogs_Change event. This updates the Excel
spreadsheet whenever the text in the text box changes. After updating the display,
it requests updated totals information from Excel.

```
Private Sub textCogs_Change (Index As Integer)
    textCogs(Index).LinkPoke                 'give Excel the new data
    lablTotal(Index).LinkRequest             'and update the totals
End Sub
```

21. Enter the following code in the textCogs_GotFocus event. This selects the text in
the text box.

```
Private Sub textCogs_GotFocus (Index As Integer)
    textCogs(Index).SelLength = 100          'select all text in the box
End Sub
```

22. Enter the following code in the textSales_Change event. This triggers whenever
the text in the text box changes. It updates the Excel spreadsheet with the new
data and then requests an update for the Totals label.

```
Private Sub textSales_Change (Index As Integer)
    textSales(Index).LinkPoke                'give Excel the new data
    lablTotal(Index).LinkRequest            'and update the totals
End Sub
```

23. Enter the following code in the textSales_GotFocus event. This selects the text in the text box.

```
Private Sub textSales_GotFocus (Index As Integer)
     textSales(Index).SelLength = 100              'select all text in the box
End Sub
```

How It Works

This program does two distinct things: it serves as a front end for an Excel spreadsheet and chart, and it implements a complete DDE-enabled Edit menu. Figure 55-2 shows the DDE project in action.

The Form_Load event takes care of most of the work for the Excel front end. It creates a small spreadsheet and pastes it into Excel with a LinkExecute method, and then formats the data and creates a chart out of it. The eight text boxes all have Poke methods in their Change events to send any updated data to Excel. The picture box has a link to the Excel chart, and the Totals labels are also linked to the Excel spreadsheet. Changes to the text boxes are immediately reflected in the labels, but the picture box is set to a Notify link rather than an automatic one. Choose the Update Links command from the Link menu to update the chart after it's changed.

The menuBar_Click event determines what menu choices should be available, based on what control the user is on, data selection, and Clipboard contents. Only those choices that are applicable in this context are enabled.

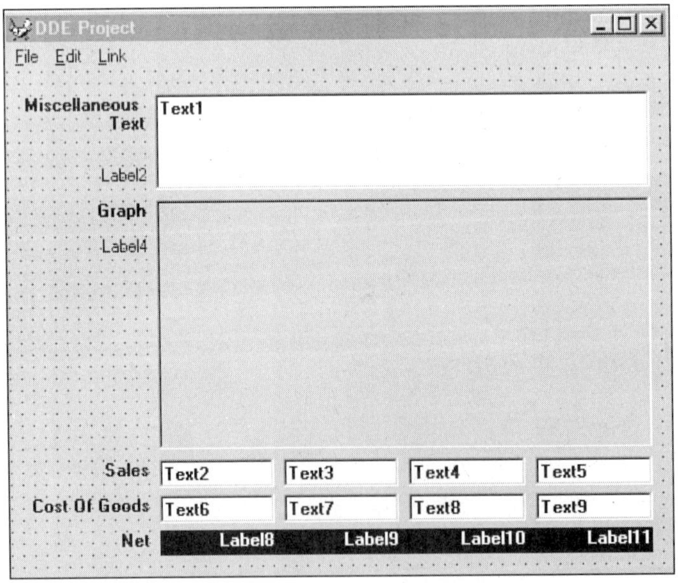

Figure 55-2   The DDE project during design

The actual editing routines—copying, cutting, pasting, and linking—are really quite simple, generally only taking up a few lines of code. Using the Clipboard is almost identical to a non-DDE routine. The DDE part simply places the correct link information on the Clipboard (for cut and copy) and puts whatever link information is on the Clipboard into the control (for paste link).

The Link menu contains the three different kinds of links and also has a command that lets you update all the links in the application. Experiment with the different kinds of linking. If you have another DDE-aware application, such as Excel, Lotus, Word, WordPerfect, AmiPro, or even Windows Write, you can see link information being updated instantly across the applications. Try setting up an automatic link with both applications visible. When you change the data in the source application, the data in the project's form updates simultaneously. You can also set up Notify links; watch the labels on the side of the text box and picture change status as the link data changes.

PART IX
DATABASE BASICS

56

DATABASE OVERVIEW AND DESIGN

Data management is one of the most important applications in Visual Basic programming. A common scenario is one in which you are asked to write a Visual Basic program that enables users to store, retrieve, and edit data being maintained in one or more files. Thanks to Visual Basic's graphical user interface and data display capabilities (including text and list boxes), it is simple to make data accessible to the user in a meaningful and easy-to-use format.

Visual Basic provides a variety of tools and approaches for data management. At the simplest level, the BASIC language itself provides the means to store and retrieve data from files. You can use the Type statement to define a data structure, then use file management commands to maintain a data file containing that type of data. This approach has the advantage of imposing little overhead on the host system, since no additional applications need to be run. But unless the data management task is very simple, the "code it yourself in BASIC" approach can easily become bogged down. After all, you must provide all the necessary facilities to enable the user to work with the data. This might include functions for editing, updating, validating, and data query. Furthermore, many real world database systems consist of several interrelated databases, and you must deal with issues of database integrity, synchronization, and transaction processing.

For significant database applications, therefore, you will want to take advantage of database functionality that already exists. Visual Basic 5.0 provides a full-fledged database engine called Jet. This engine contains virtually all the database functions many applications need. The simplest way to give your application access to the Jet database engine is through use of the data control, which is discussed in Chapter 57, "Data Control." Once you have defined a data control, you use its properties, methods, and events to manipulate the underlying database.

The Data Access Object (DAO) model consists of several object classes that are used to create and manipulate a relational database system. The DAO model is a hierarchical system with the DBEngine object as the top of a descending tree structure of interdependent object classes. All these classes have properties and methods that allow you to define and manipulate the various aspects of the native Access-type database, as well as provide substantial control over nonnative databases.

The DBEngine class actually represents the Jet 3.5 engine shipped with Visual Basic 5.0. The DBEngine (see Figure 56-1) is a container for the Workspace objects and has a set of properties and methods that control common aspects of the contained workspaces. The workspace actually represents a session within the DBEngine. Each session can contain its own set of databases, transactions, and so on. An advantage of this is that you can have two or more entirely independent transactions occur in the same database by having each transaction occur in its own workspace. The Workspace class can have multiple instances. Each instance of the Workspace class can contain a group of objects of the Database class. Each application that accesses the DBEngine gets its own default workspace (Workspaces(0)) and can instantiate subsequent objects of the Workspace class. A Workspace object can contain multiple objects of the Database class. This enables you to have several databases open at one time under one or more workspaces, as your project requirements dictate.

Database Design

A *database* is a collection of information stored in an organized way. The Access database engine translates other kinds of database formats (like dBASE or Paradox) into its own format. This means that no matter what kind of database you're accessing, you always refer to the structural elements in the same way.

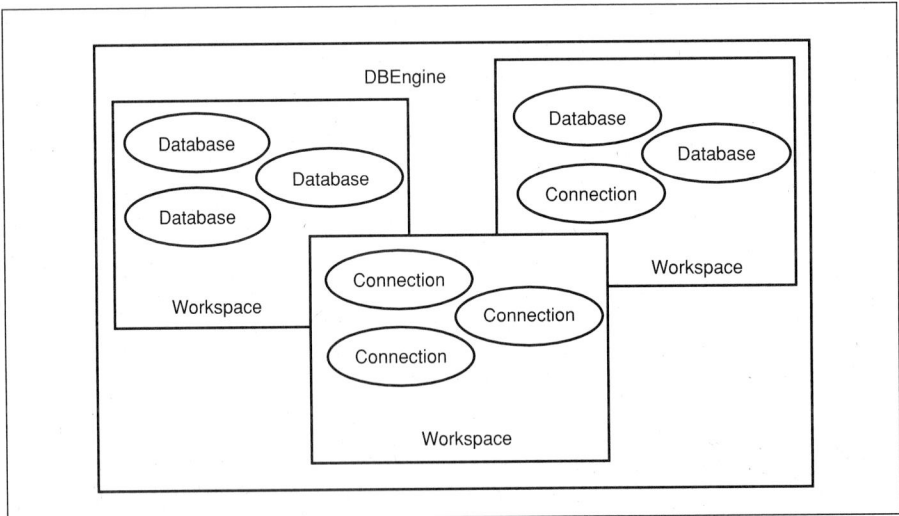

Figure 56-1 The DBEngine

A database is made up of one or more tables containing zero or more records. Each record contains one or more fields. You can think of a *table* as analogous to a spreadsheet, with a *record* being a row and a *field* being a column. The intersection of the record and field in a table is called an *item*. The record that the database is operating on is called the *current record*.

A table may be sorted, or arranged, in a particular order. For example, you may wish to see your data sorted alphabetically by the field CityName, or perhaps in descending order by ZipCode. A table may also be filtered to show just the records you need. For instance, you might want to see just the records from Wisconsin with a balance due of over $5.00. A table may have various *indexes* that let the database engine quickly find a particular record, much as the index of a book helps the reader look up topics throughout the book.

A *Recordset* is made up of a sorted, filtered subset of one or more tables. In its simplest sense, a Recordset can be a direct copy of a table. More commonly, a Recordset can be a sorted and filtered copy of the table. You can create more complex Recordsets by joining multiple tables with a variety of sorts and filters. Changes to a Recordset automatically update the underlying table; changes to the underlying table automatically update any Recordsets built with that table. The data control operates on a Recordset, not the actual table.

Relational Databases

Sometimes multiple tables can refer to related information. For instance, you might have an entry for a customer listing the name, city, and state, along with a unique identifier for each customer, called *CustID*. Each customer has a unique value stored in CustID to unambiguously identify him or her, even if multiple customers have the same name (for example, Smith). Another table might store individual transaction information on which product each customer bought, the quantity, and the date. The transaction table would also have a CustID field to identify what customer the transaction belonged to.

This kind of shared information is called a *relation*. A relational database contains multiple tables with some sort of unambiguous links between them. In the Customer table, the CustID is called the *primary key*, as it is the primary means of identifying each particular customer record. In the Transaction table, CustID is called the *foreign key*, as it refers back to another table's primary key. This lets each transaction refer unambiguously to a particular customer. The kind of relation shown in the above example is called a *one-to-many relation*. That is, one customer can have many transactions, but each transaction can only be associated with one customer. There are also *one-to-one relations* (for example, each Customer record is associated with a single Customer Credit record) and *many-to-many relations* (for example, many Transactions can refer to many Products).

The action of relating two tables together is called *making a join*. There are several types of joins, including normal joins, left outer joins, right outer joins, and inner joins. Visual Basic fully supports the relational database model. It uses SQL, or Structured Query Language, as its internal means of operation. *SQL* is a powerful database metalanguage that is at least nominally compatible between various vendors. You can use SQL statements in setting several Recordset properties. For instance, setting a data control's RecordSource property with a SQL statement can provide a sorted, filtered subset of a multiple table join for use as your Recordset. SQL also supports action queries that perform updates or deletions on a subset of your data. For instance, just one line of code can delete all records from the database that have CityName=Dallas and BalanceDue < $5.00. SQL and the concepts involved in proper database design go well beyond what we can cover in this book. See some of the database books mentioned in the BIBLIO.MDB data file that came with Visual Basic for more on SQL, proper database design, relationships, and joins. The Execute, Find, and RecordSource entries in this chapter discuss the basics of SQL.

The Jet 3.5 database engine is a relational database engine. The relational model presents the data as a collection of tables that are related to each other on the basis of a matching criteria. For example, you may have a Clients table that holds specific information such as name, type of business, credit code, YTD, QTD, and MTD purchase information, as well as other data that is common to the client. Then you might have a second Related table that contains information specific to each of the client's business sites, including the corporate offices. Furthermore, you might create tables that contain mailing, shipping, contact, and other information for each site in other tables. The process of breaking up data into related tables is called *normalization*.

Normalization is a process that endeavors to produce a stable organization of interrelated data, while minimizing structural redundancy. It is generally recognized that there are five levels of normalization, each containing a set of rules establishing the level of normalization (see Figure 56-2). As a rule, the industry standard is to achieve Third Normal Form. The three normal forms are

1. First Normal Form. To be in First Normal Form, your table must not contain any repeating groups of data. An example of a repeating group would be Home Phone, Fax Phone, Cellular Phone, and so on. It is better to put all the phone numbers into another table and link them by an ID field.

2. Second Normal Form. In addition to meeting the First Normal Form, the Second Normal Form requires that all nonkey data is functionally dependent on the entire key. This means that all nonkey fields must be uniquely dependent on the key fields.

3. Third Normal Form. With First and Second Normal Form being met, the Third Normal Form requires that the table contains no transitive dependencies. A *transitive dependency* occurs when a data field is dependent on the information in another data field that isn't part of the key. In other words, all nonkey fields must be solely dependent on the key fields.

Continuing with the Clients example, we can begin our design of a database and identify the required tables. The root table could be the Clients table, and subsidiary tables could be Sites, Contacts, and Phones. The information that each of these tables might contain is given in Table 56-1.

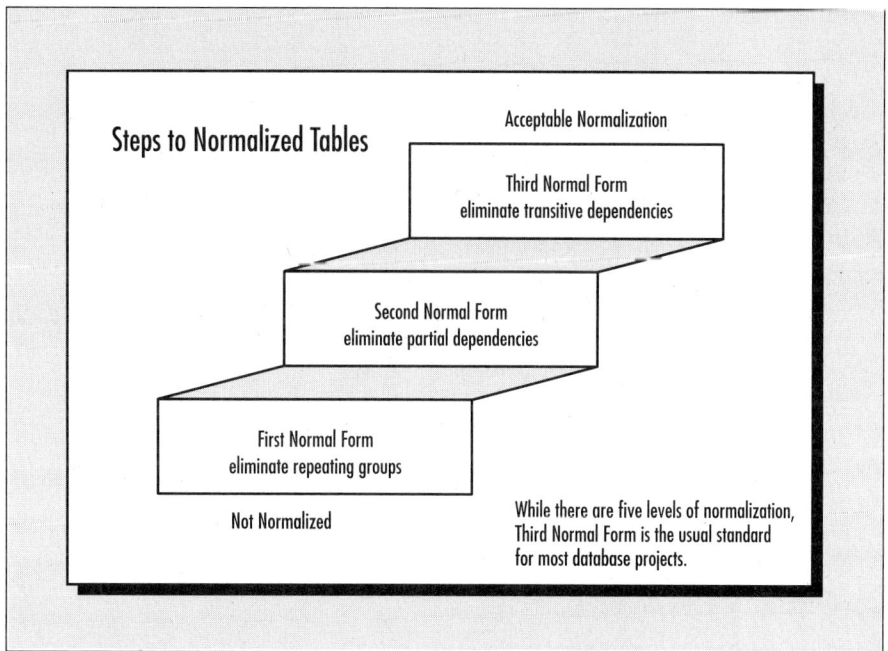

Figure 56-2 The path to normalization

Table 56-1 Client database model

Clients	Sites	Contacts	Phones
ClientID	SiteID	ContactID	PhoneID
Client name	Site name	First name	Phone type
Client type	Site type	Last name	Phone number
MTD	MTD	Middle name	Extension
QTD	QTD	Position	ContactID
YTD	YTD	SiteID	SiteID
Notes	Address1	ClientID	ClientID
	Address2	Notes	Notes
	City		
	State		
	Postal code		
	Country		
	ClientID		
	Notes		
	SuperID		

The tables laid out in Table 56-1 all meet Third Normal Form. In studying this set of tables, you can see that they all start out with an arbitrary ID field. These fields will be counters in this example, though you could adopt any arbitrary identity system. You will also notice that the ID fields show up in other tables. When they are duplicated this way they are called foreign keys. This is what forms the relationships between tables: the matching primary key of one table with the matching foreign key of another table. Let's say one of the clients in this database was a large chain store. The company has many locations throughout the country with regional distribution centers and a corporate headquarters. Your database might have to keep track of all these locations for different reasons. You might also have to maintain your different contacts at these different sites. With the above schema, you could select a retail site at Albuquerque and have at your disposal the mailing and shipping addresses, all of the contacts at that site, and the necessary phone numbers. If there are changes—for example, a contact at this Albuquerque location was transferred to another city, say Tucson—we would merely need to change the contact's SiteID and PhoneID. The main point of this design is that redundancies within an individual record are eliminated and data is easily located, given a set of matching criteria. The schema of this database has the following relationships:

- Clients: One-to-many with sites

- Clients: One-to-many with contacts

- Clients: One-to-many with phones

- Sites: One-to-many with contacts

- Sites: One-to-many with phones

- Contacts: One-to-many with phones

Data Control Versus the Data Access Objects

A Visual Basic application could include the data control controls to create a relatively powerful interface with very little code. This method is an excellent choice for the executive information type of applications that usually are referred to as Decision Support Applications. These types of applications mostly involve the retrieval of information that various levels of management need in order to make timely and informed decisions. Chapters 57; 58, "Simple Bound Controls"; 59, "DBList and DBCombo"; 60, "DBGrid Appearance"; and 61, "DBGrid Behavior," discuss the use of the data control and the data bound controls.

For the transactional type of database operations, directly programming the DBEngine through the Data Access Objects is the recommended way to proceed. Basically, transactional processing involves the repeated updating of the database by external events. A Point of Sales application is a transactional program application. While it is possible to produce transactional processing with the Data Control, you may find that the Data Access Objects will provide greater flexibility and control at the cost of a little more code writing. When using the Data Access Objects, you will not be able to use the data binding features of the data bound controls but will instead have to read from and write to the display controls using your own code logic.

Programming with the DBEngine

The DBEngine takes care of all the physical details of storing, retrieving, and updating data. It provides the Visual Basic programmer with a powerful object-oriented programmer interface with the Data Access Objects. Database programming in Visual Basic consists of a user interface, the DBEngine, and the physical database. The DBEngine lies between your program and the physical database, providing a great deal of insulation from the actual details of manipulating any particular database. The DBEngine supports several different database formats besides its native Microsoft Access format. See Table 56-2 for a list of the databases supported.

Table 56-2 Databases accessible through the DBEngine

Database Type	Database Name	Source Table Name
Microsoft Foxpro 2.0, 2.5, 2.6, 3.0, and DBC	Full path to directory with FoxPro files	.DBF filename without the extension
dBASE III, dBASE IV, and dBASE 5.0	Full path to directory with dBASE files	.DBF filename without the extension
Paradox, Versions 3x, 4x, and 5x	Full path to directory with Paradox files	.DB filename without the extension
Microsoft Access, versions 1x, 2x, and 3x	Full path to the database file	The name of the table
Open database connectivity databases	A zero-length string	The object identifier for the table
Microsoft Excel, versions 3.0, 4.0, 5.0, and 8.0	Full path to the Microsoft Excel worksheet	The name of the sheet: Sheet$Name
Lotus 1-2-3, versions WKS, WK1, WK3, and WK4	Full path to the Lotus 1-2-3 worksheet	The name of the sheet
ASCII, tabular format	Full path to the text file	Text filename without the extension
HTML, tabular data	URL of the HTML file	Either the caption, if available, if not the file-name or sequentially titled Table1, Table2, and so on
Microsoft Exchange, version 4.0	A connection string that points to the exchange mailbox	The folder name

The database is the file, or files, containing the actual data tables. If your application is using the native Microsoft Access database, then your tables will be stored in one data file with the *.MDB extension. Other formats can store their tables in several files, such as DB-III or DB-IV databases.

The user interface part of a Visual Basic application is made of standard Visual Basic forms that display data and provide the user methods for traversing and modifying the displayed data. Your code uses the DBEngine objects with their properties and methods to respond to the user's requests. The DBEngine is comprised of several dynamic link libraries that are linked to your Visual Basic program at runtime. Your application controls the DBEngine through its object classes and their associated properties and methods. Your user interface allows users to interact with the database in the manner you provide for them. Figure 56-3 illustrates the three parts of a Visual Basic database application.

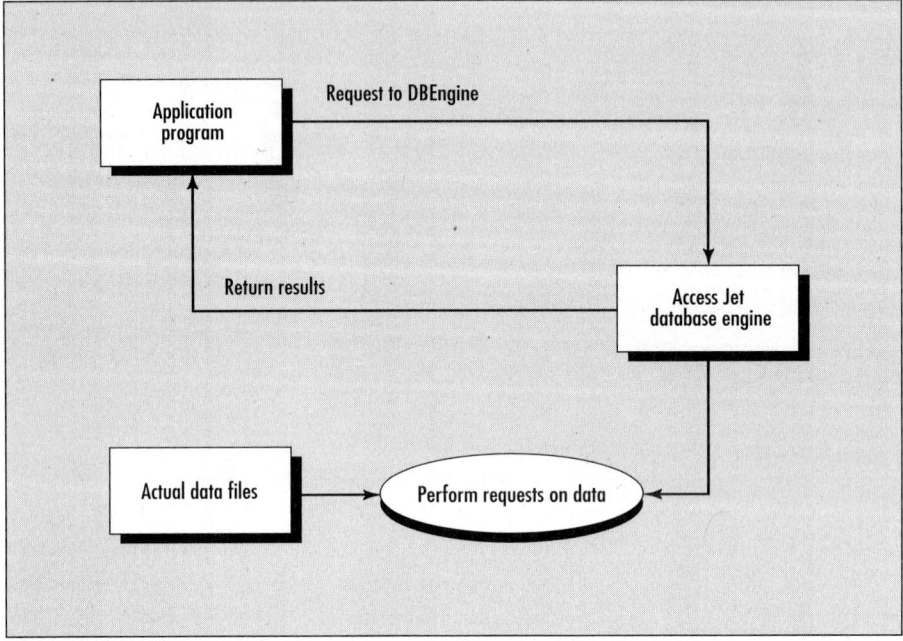

Figure 56-3 The three parts of data processing with Visual Basic

Using Workspaces

The DBEngine acts as a container for the Workspace class objects. When accessing the DBEngine, a default workspace, Workspaces(0), is automatically created. (This is actually the first member of a Workspaces collection.) You can create subsequent workspace objects and discard them when no longer needed except for the default workspace, which cannot be deleted. The Workspace object contains four collections: Databases, Users, Groups, and Properties. A Workspace object has several methods associated with it that maintain the databases within it, maintain transactions associated with those databases, and permit or deny access to those databases based on the user and group objects associated with the workspace. You can have two workspaces declared for the same database. The benefit of doing so is the ability to have different security arrangements and different transaction groups.

Opening a Database

To begin with, we must first open a database before we can start manipulating it. To open a database through the Jet database engine using the DAOs, you use the OpenDatabase method of the Workspace object. As mentioned earlier in this chapter, the Database object is contained in the Databases collection of the Workspace that you are working in. The following is an example of opening a database:

```
On Error Resume Next
'use the common dialog to get database
CommonDialog1.Action = 1
'put the full path into the Path variable
Path = CommonDialog1.FileName
'allow screen to redraw
DoEvents
'if there is an error then user cancelled
'loading the database
If Err Then
    Label2 = "OPEN DATABASE CANCELLED BY USER"
    Label2.ForeColor = vbRed
    Exit Sub
End If
'if an error occurs from this point onward
'then handle it as a bad database error
On Error GoTo BadOpen
'open the database in the default workspace non-exclusively in read/write mode
Set MyDB = Workspaces(0).OpenDatabase(Path, False, False)
```

The above code fragment illustrates how to use the common dialog control to extract a file path for use in opening a database. When designing your database, it is a good idea to provide your application a method for finding the database file. The Common Dialog control works well for this task. Also it would be a good design practice to record the last three database paths used in an APP.INI file, thus allowing the user to quickly open a database without traversing through the directories to find the last file used. Once the database variable has been set as in the above example, you can use that variable to examine or modify the records within that database.

Native, External, and ODBC Databases

The Jet 3.5 database engine provides the facilities for connecting to a variety of database types. Besides the native Access type, there are many external databases supported, such as dBASE III/IV and Paradox. Also, through Open Database Connectivity (ODBC) the Jet database engine allows you to connect to almost any data server that supports Open Database Connectivity. This includes SQL Server, Sybase, Gupta, Oracle, and several others. ODBC stands for *Open Database Connectivity,* a standard developed to allow access to any supported database engine from another application.

When using external databases in your Visual Basic application, you can create queries, forms, and reports that use the external data while the original application also uses the same data. This allows the simultaneous updating and maintenance of external databases by both the original database application and your Visual Basic application.

There are two ways to access external data:

■ Attach tables to a Jet database

■ Open tables directly

An attached table from an external database performs like a native Access table. The OpenRecordset method can be applied to this attached table, including multitable queries. A directly opened table requires that you specify the connection information with the dbname and source arguments of the OpenDatabase method each time you access the database. Attaching a table is usually faster than the directly opened table method, especially if the connection is through Open Database Connectivity.

To attach an external table to an opened Database you have to create a new TableDef object for the table using the CreateTableDef method of the Database object. You can give this table any name that is valid for a Jet 3.5 table. This is any string expression that evaluates to a set of contiguous characters. You do not have to use the name of the original table you are attaching. So if you have a FoxPro table that was named EMPLREC and you wanted to use a more definitive name, you could use the following:

```
Set MyTableDef = CurrentDatabase.CreateTableDef("Employee Records")
```

Of course, you also have to provide the connection information for the attached table so the Jet 3.5 engine can establish the link with the table. There are two methods of doing so. In the first method, you can specify the connection information in the same line that creates the TableDef:

```
Set MyTableDef = CurrentDatabase.CreateTableDef("Employee Records"), 0 _
, "EMPLREC", "FoxPro 2.5;Database=\\Foxpro\Data\empdat")
```

The other method is to use the Connect and SourceTableName properties of the TableDef object:

```
MyTableDef.Connect = "FoxPro 2.5; Database =\\FOXPRO\DATA\EMPDAT"
MyTableDef.SourceTableName ="EMPLREC"
```

The connection information in the above examples illustrates how to attach a table from a FoxPro database on a network path.

Multiple Databases

Visual Basic 5.0's DBEngine object allows multiple workspaces with multiple databases. When you open a database, you specify the workspace that contains the database.

```
Dim dbAccounts as database
Set dbAccounts = DBEngine.Workspaces(0).OpenDatabase("C:\MDBS\DBACCOUNTS.MDB")
```

The dbAccounts Database object is a part of the Workspaces(0) workspace in this declaration. The workspace can contain other databases and can be opened in the same workspace with the same syntax. All these databases will contain the same transaction and security arrangements common to the workspace. If you want to open two or more databases with their own set of transactions and security arrangements, you would do so by opening them in their own workspaces.

```
Dim db1 as database
Set db1 = DBEngine.Workspaces(1).OpenDatabase("C:\MDBS\DB1.MDB")
Dim db2 as database
Set db2 = DBEngine.Workspaces(2).OpenDatabase("D:\MDBS\DB2.MDB")
Dim db3 as database
Set db3 = DBEngine.Workspaces(3).OpenDatabase("E:\MDBS\DB3.MDB")
```

Here you have three databases open in three different workspaces. One example of such a situation occurs when you might be accessing three different databases on different servers that have entirely different security arrangements. You might also not want to tie them together in the same transaction sets. The above examples assume that the other workspaces were previously created with the CreateWorkspace method of the DBEngine object.

Opening Recordsets

A *Recordset object* is a set of rows representing data from one or more tables in your database. You can create a Recordset based on a single table quite easily:

```
'opens a table type Recordset Object
MyRS = MyDB.OpenRecordset("Sites",dbOpenTable")
```

The above example results in a Table-type Recordset object that can use indexes to rapidly search for matching criteria. Sometimes your requirements compel you to use two or more related tables combined into one Recordset. This is done with either a Dynaset-type or Snapshot-type Recordset. With these you have to provide a Select-type query that defines the tables and fields, as well as the relationship and criteria that make up the desired rows of the Recordset. A simple example of this is

```
Dim MySQL As String
Dim MyRS As Recordset

MySQL = "SELECT * FROM Clients LEFT JOIN Sites On Clients.ClientID = Sites.ClientID _
WHERE Client.TYPE = `FAST FOODS'"
Set MyRS = MyDB.OpenRecordset(MySQL, dbOpenDynaset)
```

This code returns a Recordset object of Dynaset type with rows that include all the fields from both tables related to each other and whose Client.Type=Fast Foods. This is where the Relational model shows its benefits of being able to return datasets that provide the data arranged in many different ways. In most cases, the Dynaset-type Recordset object allows adding, editing, and deleting rows. You can use the extremely flexible Find methods to locate individual rows of data. A third type of Recordset object is the Snapshot-type Recordset. It is created the same way as a Dynaset-type Recordset but uses the Snapshot parameter:

```
MySQL = "SELECT * FROM Clients LEFT JOIN Sites On Clients.ClientID = Sites.ClientID _
WHERE Client.TYPE = `FAST FOODS'"
Set MyRS = MyDB.OpenRecordset(MySQL, dbOpenSnapshot)
```

The difference with a Snapshot-type Recordset object is that it cannot be edited, it does not mirror changes in the underlying database after it is created, and all the data returned by the Recordset is loaded into the workstation's memory. The advantage of a Snapshot-type Recordset object is speed. If your Recordset fits entirely into RAM, then finds on that Recordset will be fast. With this in mind, it is best to make Snapshot-type Recordset objects with criteria that will return a relatively small number of rows.

DAO Object Summary

The following section summarizes the objects that can be found in a Jet database, together with a brief description of the relevant collections, properties, and methods. Chapters 62, "Beginning SQL"; 63, "Advanced SQL"; 64, "Adding and Editing"; 65, "Moving and Searching"; 68, "Advanced Techniques"; 69, "Maintaining Databases"; and 70, "Creating Databases," will provide a complete reference to the applicable DAO methods. More information about objects, properties, and methods is available in the Visual Basic 5.0 help system.

The *DBEngine object* is the top of the Database object hierarchy and represents the actual Jet Database Engine. The DBEngine object is used to set up Jet system parameters and the workspaces for database operations. There can be only one DBEngine object in an application. Table 56-3 summarizes the DBEngine object's collections, properties, and methods.

Table 56-3 DBEngine object's collections, properties, and methods

Name	Type	Description
BeginTrans	Method	Begins a new transaction set
CommitTrans	Method	Commits the transaction set to the database
CompactDatabase	Method	Compacts, copies, and alters the version, collating order, and encryption of database
CreateDatabase	Method	Creates a new Database object
CreateWorkspace	Method	Creates a new Workspace object
DefaultUser	Property	Sets the user name when a Workspace object is created without a specific user name
DefaultPassword	Property	Sets the password when a Workspace object is created without a specific password
DefaultType	Property	Returns or sets the type for the CreateWorkspace method
Errors	Collection	Collection of Error objects
Idle	Method	Provides processor time to the DBEngine for internal maintenance
IniPath	Property	Sets or returns the full path and filename of the DBEngine initialization file
LoginTimeout	Property	Time the DBEngine will wait before an error occurs when logging into Open Database Connectivity database
OpenConnection	Method	Opens a connection to an Open Database Connectivity datasource and returns a reference to it
OpenDatabase	Method	Opens a specified database in a session and returns a reference to it
Properties	Collection	Collection of DBEngine properties
RegisterDatabase	Method	Registers connection information for an Open Database Connectivity datasource in the ODBC.INI file
RepairDatabase	Method	Attempts to repair a corrupted database
Rollback	Method	Aborts a transaction set
SetOption	Method	Overrides values Microsoft Jet engine keys in the registry until called again or for the life of the object
SystemDB	Property	Sets or returns the full path and filename of the system MDA file
Version	Property	Version of DBEngine
Workspaces	Collection	Collection of Workspace objects

An *Error object* is populated when there is a failure in one of the Database objects. The Error object contains a description, an identification of what generated the error, and a reference to a help file that may help the user. Table 56-4 summarizes the properties of the Error object.

Table 56-4 Error object's properties

Name	Type	Description
Description	Property	Returns a description of the error
HelpContext	Property	Returns a Help Context ID
HelpFile	Property	Returns the full path to a help file
Number	Property	Returns the error number
Source	Property	Returns the name of the object or application that generated the error

A *Workspace* represents a set of Database objects that are being accessed by a particular user (or group of users). A default Workspace object, Workspaces(0), is automatically created when you first open a Database object in your application. The Workspace supports simultaneous transactions, provides the security settings for the databases it contains, and acts as a container for several open databases. The default workspace cannot be closed or removed, but is always available. Table 56-5 summarizes the Workspace object's collections, properties, and methods.

Table 56-5 Workspace object's collections, properties, and methods

Name	Type	Description
BeginTrans	Method	Begins a new transaction set
Close	Method	Closes and removes the Workspace object
Connections	Collection	Collection of Connection objects
CommitTrans	Method	Commits the transaction set to the database
CreateDatabase	Method	Creates a new Database object
CreateGroup	Method	Creates a new Group object in the workspace
CreateUser	Method	Creates a new user in the workspace
Databases	Collection	A collection of open Database objects
DefaultCursorDriver	Property	Returns or sets the type of cursor driver used for OpenConnection or OpenDatabase
Groups	Collection	Contains all stored Group objects of a workspace or user account
IsolateODBCTrans	Property	Returns or sets a Boolean of whether to have a separate Open Database Connectivity connection for each workspace
LoginTimeout	Property	The number of seconds before a login attempt fails
Name	Property	A user-defined name for a Data Access Object
OpenConnection	Method	Opens a connection to an Open Database Connectivity datasource and returns a reference to it

continued on next page

continued from previous page

Name	Type	Description
OpenDatabase	Method	Opens a specified database in a session and returns a reference to it
Properties	Collection	Collection of Workspace properties
Rollback	Method	Aborts a transaction set
Type	Property	Returns a value indicating whether this is a Jet engine or Open Database Connectivity workspace
UserName	Property	Represents the name of the owner of a Workspace object
Users	Collection	Contains all stored User objects of a workspace or group account

A *Connection object* represents a connection to an Open Database Connectivity data-source. Table 56-6 summarizes the Connection object's collections, properties, and methods.

Table 56-6 Connection object's collections, properties, and methods

Name	Type	Description
Cancel	Method	Cancels a pending asynchronous query
Close	Method	Closes the object
Connect	Property	The database source of the connection
CreateQueryDef	Method	Creates a new QueryDef in the object
Database	Property	Returns the Database object that corresponds to the connection
Execute	Method	Executes an action query
Name	Property	Used to identify the Connection object
OpenRecordset	Method	Creates a new Recordset and adds it to the Recordsets collection
QueryDefs	Collection	Contains all the QueryDef objects in a database
QueryTimeOut	Property	Returns or sets how long before a time-out error occurs
RecordsAffected	Property	Returns the number of records affected by the last execute
Recordsets	Collection	Contains all open Recordset objects in a database
StillExecuting	Property	Returns a Boolean indicating whether an asynchronous query is still executing
Transactions	Property	Boolean value indicating whether the object supports transactions
Updatable	Property	Boolean value indicating whether the object is updatable

The *Database object* can represent a Jet database, an external database, or an Open Database Connectivity connection. It contains the database's tables, relations, and stored queries. It is also used to open Recordset objects. Note that there can be more than one database in a workspace. Table 56-7 summarizes the Database object's collections, properties, and methods.

Table 56-7 Database object's collections, properties, and methods

Name	Type	Description
Close	Method	Closes the Database object
CollatingOrder	Property	Specifies the sequence of the database's sort order
Connect	Property	The source of an open database
Connection	Property	The Connection object that corresponds to the database
Containers	Collection	Contains all the Container objects that describe a database
CreateProperty	Method	Creates a user-defined property in the Database object
CreateQueryDef	Method	Creates a new QueryDef object within the database
CreateRelation	Method	Creates a new Relation object within the database
CreateTableDef	Method	Creates a new TableDef object within the database
Execute	Method	Runs an action query or executes a SQL statement on the database
MakeReplica	Method	Makes a new replica based on the current replicable database
Name	Property	Used to identify the Database object
NewPassword	Method	Changes the password for the database
OpenRecordset	Method	Creates a new Recordset object and adds it to the Recordsets collection
PopulatePartial	Method	Synchronizes changes in a partial replica with the full replica
Properties	Collection	Collection of properties
QueryDefs	Collection	Contains all the QueryDef objects in a database
QueryTimeout	Property	The time the DBEngine will wait for a query to complete on an Open Database Connectivity database
RecordsAffected	Property	Returns the number of records affected by the most recent Execute method
Recordsets	Collection	Contains all open Recordset objects in a database
Relations	Collection	Contains all the stored Relation objects of a database
Replicable	Property	Returns or sets whether this database can be replicated
ReplicaID	Property	Returns a GUID value that uniquely identifies a database replica
Synchronize	Method	Synchronizes the current replicable Database object with the current database
TableDefs	Collection	Collection of TableDef objects
Transactions	Property	Boolean value telling whether the database supports transactions
Updatable	Property	Boolean value telling whether the database is updatable
Version	Property	Returns a value indicating the version of the database
V1xNullBehavior	Property	Returns or sets a value that indicates whether zero-length strings ("") are converted to Nulls

The *TableDef object* is a stored table definition. For each table in a database, there is a corresponding TableDef in the TableDefs collection. The properties in a TableDef cannot be changed if they belong to an attached table. Table 56-8 summarizes the TableDef object's collections, properties, and methods.

Table 56-8 TableDef object's collections, properties, and methods

Name	Type	Description
Attributes	Property	A value that represents one or more characteristics of a TableDef
ConflictTable	Property	Name of a side table containing the database records that conflicted during the synchronization of two replicas
Connect	Property	The database source of the TableDef
CreateField	Method	Creates a new field object
CreateIndex	Method	Creates a new index object
CreateProperty	Method	Creates a new user-defined property
DateCreated	Property	Date that the TableDef was created
Fields	Collection	Contains all stored Field objects in a TableDef object
Indexes	Collection	Contains all stored Index objects of a TableDef object
KeepLocal	Property	Returns or sets a value that determines whether the object is to be a local (nonreplicable) object
LastUpdated	Property	Date of the last time the TableDef was modified
Name	Property	Name used in code to identify the particular object
OpenRecordset	Method	Creates a new Recordset and adds it the Recordsets collection
Properties	Collection	Collection of TableDef properties
RecordCount	Property	Number of records accessed in a TableDef object
RefreshLink	Method	Updates the connection information for an attached table
Replicable	Property	Returns or sets a value that determines if the object is local only or replicable
ReplicaFilter	Property	Returns or sets a value that indicates which records to replicate from the full replica
SourceTableName	Property	The name of the base table
Updatable	Property	Boolean value indicating whether object is updatable
ValidationRule	Property	A value that validates the data in a field as it is added or changed
ValidationText	Property	Text displayed if a field's data change is invalid

A *query* uses various specifications to extract a desired set of records from the database for processing. *QueryDefs* are a stored definition of a Query object. This object is a container for a precompiled query. The query can be modified during runtime, parameters can be set, and the query can be executed. Table 56-9 summarizes the QueryDef object's collections, properties, and methods.

Table 56-9 QueryDef object's collections, properties, and methods

Name	Type	Description
CacheSize	Property	Returns or sets number of records to cache locally from an Open Database Connectivity datasource
Cancel	Method	Cancels a pending asynchronous query
Close	Method	Closes the QueryDef object
Connect	Property	The database source of the QueryDef
CreateProperty	Method	Creates a user-defined property

Name	Type	Description
DateCreated	Property	Date that the QueryDef was created
Execute	Method	Runs an Action query
Fields	Collection	Contains all stored Field objects in a QueryDef object
KeepLocal	Property	Returns or sets a value that determines whether the object is to be a local (nonreplicable) object
LastUpdated	Property	Date that the QueryDef was last modified
LogMessages	Property	Specifies whether messages returned from Open Database Connectivity databases are recorded
MaxRecords	Property	Returns or sets the maximum number of records to be returned; 0 is no limit
Name	Property	Used to identify the QueryDef object
Parameters	Collection	A collection of elements that affect the results of a query
Prepare	Property	Returns or sets a value indicating whether the query executes directly or creates a temporary stored procedure on an Open Database Connectivity datasource
Properties	Collection	Collection of QueryDef properties
ODBCTimeOut	Property	Specifies the time the DBEngine waits before a time-out error occurs
OpenRecordset	Method	Creates a new Recordset and adds it to the Recordsets collection
RecordsAffected	Property	Returns the number of records affected by the last execute
Replicable	Property	Returns or sets a value that determines if the object is local only or replicable
ReturnsRecords	Property	Boolean value that indicates whether the query returns records
SQL	Property	The text of the stored SQL statement
StillExecuting	Property	Returns a Boolean indicating whether an asynchronous query is still executing
Type	Property	An integer that indicates the query type
Updatable	Property	Boolean value indicating whether returned Recordset is updatable

Broadly speaking, a Recordset represents the records returned by a query. It is both a view of the database and a means for editing or updating it. For example, a query that asks for all authors born before 1970 results in a Recordset representing those records in the Authors database. Depending on the type (see Table 56-10), the Recordset can be operated on in various ways, such as a batch update via a SQL update statement.

The Recordset object replaces the Table, Dynaset, and Snapshot objects of the previous version of Visual Basic. The Recordset object has three types that correspond to the Table, Dynaset, and Snapshot objects and is actually a superset of these objects.

The Table-type Recordset corresponds to a table in a native or external (ISAM) database. Table-type Recordsets cannot be opened on an ODBC-type connection or on attached tables. Table-type Recordsets give the program direct access to the underlying table, allowing direct use of the table's indexes for fast searching and navigation.

The Dynaset-type is a virtual table that is the result of a query on one or more tables, or it can be a reference to a single table which is attached or comes from an Open Database Connectivity source. It can be updatable depending on the queries' structure and relational restraints.

The Snapshot-type Recordset is a static set of records based on a query and is very similar to a Dynaset type, except that it is never updatable and does not reflect subsequent changes in the underlying database. It has very little overhead because it does not have to manage updates or database changes, and so it can be much faster to navigate and search.

Table 56-10 Recordset object's collections, properties, and methods

Name	Type	Description
AbsolutePosition	Property	Returns or sets the relative record number of a Recordset object's current record
AddNew	Method	Creates a new record for a Table-type or Dynaset-type Recordset
BatchCollisionCount	Property	Returns the number of records that failed in the last batch update
BatchCollisions	Property	Returns an array of bookmarks indicating the rows that failed in the last batch update
BatchSize	Property	Returns or sets the number of statements to send to the server in a batch
BOF	Property	Boolean value indicating the record pointer is pointing before the first record
BookMark	Property	A string value marking the place of the current record in the Recordset
BookMarkable	Property	A Boolean value indicating whether the Recordset supports bookmarks
CacheSize	Property	Returns or sets a value that represents the number of records in a Dynaset-type Recordset
CacheStart	Property	Returns or sets the starting bookmark value in a Recordset
Cancel	Method	Cancels a pending asynchronous query
CancelUpdate	Method	Cancels a pending update
Clone	Method	Creates a duplicate Recordset object
Close	Method	Closes the Recordset object
Connection	Property	The Connection object that corresponds to the database
CopyQueryDef	Method	Returns a copy of the QueryDef used to create the Recordset
DateCreated	Property	Returns the date that the underlying table was created
Delete	Method	Deletes a record from the Recordset object and underlying table
Edit	Method	Copies a record to the copy buffer for subsequent editing
EditMode	Property	Returns a value indicating the edit state for the current record
EOF	Property	Boolean value indicating whether the recordpointer is past the last record in the Recordset
Fields	Collection	Contains all stored Field objects of a Recordset
FillCache	Method	Fills all or part of a local cache for a Recordset based on an Open Database Connectivity connection
Filter	Property	Returns or sets a value that determines records included in a subsequently created Recordset
FindFirst	Method	Locates the first record in the Recordset that matches the specified criteria
FindLast	Method	Locates the last record in the Recordset that matches the specified criteria
FindNext	Method	Locates the next record in the Recordset that matches the specified criteria
FindPrevious	Method	Locates the previous record in the Recordset that matches the specified criteria
GetRows	Method	Retrieves multiple rows
Index	Property	Returns or sets the current index of a Table-type Recordset
LockEdits	Property	Returns or sets the type of locking in effect during edits
LastUpdated	Property	Returns the date that the underlying table structure was last altered
LastModified	Property	Returns a bookmark indicating the last modified record
Move	Method	Moves the recordpointer the specified number of rows (+/-)
MoveFirst	Method	Moves the recordpointer to the first record in the Recordset object

Name	Type	Description
MoveLast	Method	Moves the recordpointer to the last record in the Recordset object
MoveNext	Method	Moves the recordpointer to the next record in the Recordset object
MovePrevious	Method	Moves the recordpointer to the previous record in the Recordset object
Name	Property	A value indicating the object's name in code
NextRecordset	Method	Moves to the next Recordset when using a multipart SELECT
NoMatch	Property	Boolean value indicating whether the last Seek or Find method found a matching record
OpenRecordset	Method	Creates a new Recordset and adds it to the Recordsets collection
PercentPosition	Property	Returns or sets a value that indicates the approximate location of the record in the Recordset
Properties	Collection	Collection of properties of the Recordset object
RecordCount	Property	Returns a value indicating the relative record count of the Recordset object
RecordStatus	Property	Returns a value indicating the update status of the current record in a batch
Requery	Method	Updates the data in a Recordset object by running the underlying query again
Restartable	Property	Boolean value indicating whether the Requery method is allowed
Seek	Method	Locates a record in a Table-type Recordset that matches the specified criteria
Sort	Property	Returns or sets the sort order for records in a Recordset object
StillExecuting	Property	Returns a Boolean indicating whether an asynchronous query is still executing
Transactions	Property	Boolean value indicating whether the Recordset supports transactions
Type	Property	Returns a value indicating whether Recordset is a Table, Dynaset, or Snapshot type
Updatable	Property	Boolean value indicating whether the Recordset is updatable
Update	Method	Stores the edit buffer to the current record in the Recordset object
UpdateOptions	Property	Returns or sets a value indicating how the WHERE clause is constructed and whether to do a DELETE, then INSERT for a batch update
ValidationRule	Property	Returns or sets a value that validates edits in a Field object
ValidationText	Property	The text of the error message if the field validation rule is not met

The *Field object* represents a column of data. This column has a common data type and set of properties across all the rows of a table. The TableDef, QueryDef, Recordset, and Index object classes all contain a Fields collection. In the Recordset object, the Fields collection represents one row of data. When the recordpointer is moved to a different record, the data contained in that record is read into the Fields collection's corresponding field values. Table 56-11 summarizes the Field object's collections, properties, and methods.

Table 56-11 Field object's collections, properties, and methods

Name	Type	Description
AllowZeroLength	Property	Boolean value whether a zero-length string is an acceptable field value
AppendChunk	Method	Appends data from a string expression to a memo or OLE Field object
Attributes	Property	Returns or sets a value indicating one or more characteristics of a Field object

continued on next page

continued from previous page

Name	Type	Description
CollatingOrder	Property	Returns a value indicating the sequence of the sort order
CreateProperty	Method	Creates user-defined property in the Field object
DataUpdatable	Property	Boolean value indicating whether the Field object is updatable
DefaultValue	Property	Returns or sets the default value of a Field object
FieldSize	Property	Returns the number of bytes used in the database for a Memo or Long Binary field
ForeignName	Property	Returns or sets the name of the Field object that corresponds to a related primary field
GetChunk	Method	Returns all or part of the contents of a memo or OLE Field object
Name	Property	A string value containing the name of the field
OrdinalPosition	Property	Returns the ordinal position of a Field object in a Recordset's Fields collection
OriginalValue	Property	Returns the value of the field before the last batch update
Properties	Collection	Contains all the Field object's properties
Required	Property	Boolean indicating whether data in field is required
Size	Property	Returns or sets the size in bytes of a Field object
SourceField	Property	Returns the name of the original field supplying the data for a Field object
SourceTable	Property	Returns the name of the original table supplying the field data
Type	Property	Returns or sets a value indicating the field's data type
ValidateOnSet	Property	Boolean value indicating whether validation is immediate after the field value is changed
ValidationRule	Property	Returns or sets a value that validates edits in a Field object
ValidationText	Property	Text of the error message if field validation rule is not met
Value	Property	Returns or sets the value contained in the Field object
VisibleValue	Property	Returns a value from the database that is newer than the OriginalValue field

Index objects are stored indexes associated with TableDef objects or Table-type Recordset objects. You can specify the current index on a Table-type Recordset object by setting its Index property to the name of one of the Index objects in its Indexes collection. An *index* is an ordered list of recordpointers that facilitates quick searches for information within a database. Table 56-12 summarizes the Index object's collections, properties, and methods.

Table 56-12 Index object's collections, properties, and methods

Name	Type	Description
Clustered	Property	Boolean value indicating if the index is a clustered index
CreateField	Method	Creates a Field object for the Index object
CreateProperty	Method	Creates a user-defined property
DistinctCount	Property	Returns the number of unique values for the index
Fields	Collection	Contains all stored field objects of an Index object
Foreign	Property	Boolean value indicating whether the Index is based on a foreign key
IgnoreNull	Property	Boolean value indicating whether the index should ignore Null field values
Name	Property	String value containing the name of the index in code

Name	Type	Description
Primary	Property	Boolean value indicating whether the Index object is a primary index
Properties	Collection	Collection of an Index object's properties
Required	Property	Boolean value indicating whether the Index object requires a non-Null value
Unique	Property	Boolean value indicating whether the Index object requires unique values

The *Parameter object* is a stored query parameter that is part of a Parameters collection of a stored QueryDef object. The Parameter object allows the application program to get or set values on query parameters. Table 56-13 summarizes the Parameter object's collection and properties.

Table 56-13 Parameter object's collection and properties

Name	Type	Description
Direction	Property	Returns or sets a value indicating whether the parameter is input, output, or both
Name	Property	String value indicating the object's name in code
Properties	Collection	Collection of Parameter object's properties
Type	Property	Returns or sets the Data type of the Parameter object
Value	Property	Returns or sets the value of a Parameter object

The *User object* is part of the DBEngine's security measures. It represents an individual's access account to the workspace's objects. Each User object includes a user's name and password. Table 56-14 summarizes the User object's collections, properties, and methods.

Table 56-14 User object's collections, properties, and methods

Name	Type	Description
CreateGroup	Method	Creates a new Group object
Groups	Collection	A collection of Group objects of a user account
Name	Property	A string value indicating the name of the user
NewPassword	Method	Changes the password of an existing user account
Password	Property	Sets the password for the User object; can only be used at creation
PID	Property	Sets the Personal Identifier for the User object
Properties	Collection	A collection of User object properties

The *Group object* represents a collection of users with identical access rights. A collection of groups can be tailored to give different object access according to the permissions assigned to an object. Table 56-15 summarizes the Group object's collections, properties, and method.

Table 56-15 Group object's collections, properties, and method

Name	Type	Description
CreateUser	Method	Creates a User object and adds it to the Users collection
Name	Property	The name of the Group object
PID	Property	Sets the Personal Identifier for the Group object
Properties	Collection	A collection of the Group object's properties
Users	Collection	A collection of User objects

The *Relation object* defines the relationship between two TableDef objects based on a native and foreign field relationship. The native fields are PrimaryKey fields, and foreign fields are matching fields in the foreign table. The DBEngine enforces update and delete conditions based on the Relation object's attributes. Table 56-16 summarizes the Relation object's collections, properties, and method.

Table 56-16 Relation object's collections, properties, and method

Name	Type	Description
Attributes	Property	A Long value indicating the attributes of the Relation object
CreateField	Method	Creates a Field object and adds it to the Fields collection
Fields	Collection	A collection of Field objects
ForeignTable	Property	The name of the Foreign Table object in the relationship
Name	Property	The name of the Relation object
PartialReplica	Property	Returns or sets a value indicating whether the relation should be considered when populating a partial replica from a full replica
Properties	Collection	A collection of the Relation object's properties
Table	Property	The name of the Table object

Property objects represent both user-defined and built-in stored properties in an object's Properties collection. User-defined properties are created by appending the property to the object's Properties collection. These user-defined properties allow you to associate new properties with the data access objects you create and save these properties to the database. User-defined properties apply only to the particular object to which you append them and not to the class of the object. Table 56-17 summarizes the Property object's properties.

Table 56-17 Property object's properties

Name	Type	Description
Inherited	Property	Boolean value indicating whether underlying Property object is inherited
Name	Property	Name of Property object

Name	Type	Description
Type	Property	Data type of Property value
Value	Property	Value stored in Property object

Each Database object has a single Containers collection that enumerates all objects contained in that database. Along with the Documents collection, the *Container object's* purpose is to maintain the list of objects, along with their user permissions and ownership. Table 56-18 summarizes the Container object's collections and properties.

Table 56-18 Container object's collections and properties

Name	Type	Description
AllPermissions	Property	Returns all the permissions that apply to the current UserName
Documents	Collection	Collection of Document objects
Inherit	Property	Returns or sets whether a new Document object will inherit the default permissions
Name	Property	Name of Container object
Owner	Property	A value representing the owner of the object
Permissions	Property	Sets or returns permissions for the user or group identified in the UserName property
Properties	Collection	Collection of Container properties
UserName	Property	Sets or returns the name of a user or group of users of a workspace object

The *Document object* contains the security information of its associated objects. Table 56-19 summarizes the Document object's collection and properties.

Table 56-19 Document object's collection and properties

Name	Type	Description
AllPermissions	Property	Returns all the permissions that apply to the current UserName
Container	Property	The name of the parent container
DateCreated	Property	The date that the object was created
KeepLocal	Property	Returns or sets a value that determines whether the object will be a local (nonreplicable) object
LastUpdated	Property	The date that the object was last modified
Name	Property	Name of Document object
Owner	Property	A value specifying the owner of the object
Permissions	Property	A value specifying the security permissions for the object
Properties	Collection	Collection of Container properties
Replicable	Property	Returns or sets a value that determines if the object is local only or replicable
UserName	Property	A value specifying a user or group of users

Database Overview and Design Summary

Table 56-20 lists the methods discussed in the overview and design.

Table 56-20 Overview and design methods

Name	Type	Description
Close	Method	Closes a data access object
CreateWorkspace	Method	Creates a new Workspace object
OpenDatabase	Method	Opens a specified database in a session and returns a reference to it
OpenRecordset	Method	Creates a new Recordset and adds it to the Recordsets collection

CLOSE METHOD

Purpose   The Close method is used to close an open Data Access object. Table 56-21 summarizes the argument for the Close method.

General Syntax

```
object.close
```

Table 56-21 Argument of the Close method

Argument	Description
object	A Connection, Database, Recordset, or Workspace object

Example Syntax
```
MyRecordset.Close
MyDatabase.Close
Set MyRecordset = Nothing
Set MyDatabase = Nothing
```

Description   The Close method closes an open Data Access object and removes it from the parent object's collection. If you attempt to close the default workspace, the Close method will be ignored. In the above examples, you will notice the object variables are set to Nothing after being closed. This ensures that the memory allocated to those objects is released back to the system. Tables 56-22 and 56-23 summarize the arguments and constants for the CreateWorkspace method.

CREATEWORKSPACE METHOD

Purpose	The CreateWorkspace method of the DBEngine object is used to create additional workspaces in the particular instance of the DBEngine.

General Syntax

```
Set objectname = CreateWorkspace(name, user, password[, type])
```

Table 56-22 Arguments of the CreateWorkspace method

Argument	Description
objectname	A Workspace object
name	A string that uniquely identifies the new Workspace object
user	The owner of the new Workspace object
password	The password for the new Workspace object
type	The type of workspace

Table 56-23 Constants for the type argument of the CreateWorkspace method

Constants	Description
dbUseJet	A Workspace object that uses Jet
dbUseODBC	A Workspace object that bypasses Jet

Example Syntax

```
Dim MyWorkspace as Workspace
Dim MyUser as String
MyUser = "EISonly"
Set MyWorkspace = DBEngine.CreateWorkspace("Executive", MyUser, "InfoOnly")
DBEngine.Workspaces.Append MyWorkspace
```

Description	When using the CreateWorkspace method, you must provide the name, user, and password arguments. Creating a new workspace is fundamentally different than using the other Create*object* methods in that it does not create a persistent object. That is, the Workspace object created has a lifespan of that particular session and dies when that session of the DBEngine ends. Once you create this workspace object, you cannot change any of its properties. The main reason to create additional workspaces is to provide for different security settings and separate transaction groups from the default workspace. The workspace actually represents another session, or sequence of operations, performed by the Jet engine. You don't actually have to append it to the Workspaces collection to use it in your application. But if you intend to refer to it in an application through the

Workspaces collection, then it must be appended to the collection before you refer to it.

OpenDatabase Method

Purpose
The OpenDatabase method is used to open a database in the specified session and returns a reference to the Database object variable that represents it. Tables 56-24, 56-25, and 56-26 summarize the arguments and constants for the OpenDatabase method.

General Syntax

```
Set databaseobject = Workspace.OpenDatabase( dbname[, options[, read-only [, source]]])
```

Table 56-24 Arguments of the OpenDatabase method

Argument	Description
databaseobject	The Database object
workspace	The session in which to open the database
dbname	The full path and name of the database file or Open Database Connectivity source
options	Values to determine how the database is to be opened
read-only	True or False to open the database in read-only mode
source	A string expression with the open database connectivity connect arguments

Table 56-25 Values of the options argument in a Jet Workspace

Value	Description
True	Open the database in exclusive mode
False	Open the database in shared mode

Table 56-26 Values of the options argument in an ODBCDirect Workspace

Value	Description
dbDriverNoPrompt	The connection information is gathered from the source argument
dbDriverPrompt	The user provides the connection information
dbDriverComplete	Ask the user for connection information only if missing from the source argument
dbDriverCompleteRequired	Same as dbDriverComplete, except ask the user for only the absolutely necessary connection information

Example Syntax

```
'opening a native jet database
Dim MyDB as Database
Dim MyWS as Workspace
'get the default workspace
Set MyWS = DBEngine.Workspaces(0)
'opens  Clients' database in non-exclusive read only mode
Set MyDB = MyWS.OpenDatabase("C:\MYDIR\CLIENTS.MDB", False, True)
.....

'opening an ODBC database
Dim MyWS as Workspace
Dim MyDB as Database
Dim MyConnect as string
MyConnect = "ODBC;UID=TheBoss;PWD=UHOH;DSN=MYSERV;DATABASE=CLIENTS"
MyWS = DBEngine.Workspaces(0)
MyDB = MYWS.OpenDatabase("", False, False, MyConnect)
.....
```

Description   The OpenDatabase method opens a connection to the specified database. This database could be a native Jet/Access database, any of the installable ISAM databases, or an Open Database Connectivity database that is a registered Open Database Connectivity source. If you try to open a database that is already opened in exclusive mode, you will cause a trappable error. If it doesn't refer to a valid database or Open Database Connectivity source name, an error occurs. Also if the name portion is a zero-length string and the connect portion=ODBC, then a dialog box will be opened listing all registered Open Database Connectivity datasource names that allow the user to select the source. Once the OpenDatabase has succeeded in opening the database, it is added to the workspace's Databases collection. You use the Close method to remove it from the workspace.

OPENRECORDSET METHOD

Purpose   The OpenRecordset method creates a new Recordset object and appends it to the Recordsets collection. Table 56-27 summarizes the arguments for the OpenRecordset method. Table 56-28 summarizes the constants for specifying the type of Recordset objects being opened, Table 56-29 summarizes the options available with the OpenRecordset method, and 56-30 summarizes the constants available for the lockedits argument.

General Syntax

```
Set recordsetobject = databaseobject.OpenRecordset(source[, type[, options[, lockedits]]])
Set recordsetobject = object.Openrecordset(source[, type[, options[, lockedits]]])
```

Table 56-27 Arguments of the OpenRecordSet method

Argument	Description
recordsetobject	A Recordset object
databaseobject	An open database
object	A variable of QueryDef, Recordset, or TableDef type that references a valid object
source	A string specifying the source of the rows for the new Recordset
type	The type of the Recordset, such as Table, Dynaset, or Snapshot
options	An integer specifying the characteristics of the new Recordset object
lockedits	Locking for the new Recordset

Table 56-28 Constants for specifying the type of Recordset object opened

Constant	Description
dbOpenTable	Specifies the Recordset as Table type
dbOpenDynaset	Specifies the Recordset as Dynaset type
dbOpenSnapshot	Specifies the Recordset as Snapshot type

Table 56-29 Constants for the options argument of the OpenRecordset method

Constant	Description
dbDenyWrite	Other users can't modify or add records
dbDenyRead	Other users can't view records (valid for Table-type Recordset only)
dbReadOnly	Recordset has read-only status; other users can still edit the underlying data
dbAppendOnly	Can only append new records to the Recordset (Dynaset type only)
dbInconsistant	Inconsistent updates are allowed (Dynaset type only)
dbConsistent	Only consistent updates are allowed (Dynaset type only)
dbForwardOnly	Forward-only scrolling Snapshot type; supports only the MoveNext method
dbSeeChanges	Generates a trappable error if another user is changing data you are editing
dbSQLPassThrough	Passes the SQL to the datasource for processing
dbRunAsync	Process asynchronously; use StillExecuting property to see whether the query is completed
dbExecDirect	Does not call SQLPrepare Open Database Connectivity API function first; for Open Database Connectivity, Direct workspaces only

Table 56-30 Constants for the lockedits argument of the OpenRecordset method

Constant	Description
dbReadOnly	Cannot make changes to the Recordset
dbPessimistic	Use pessimistic locking; locks page as soon as Edit method is used

Constant	Description
dbOptimistic	Use optimistic locking; locks page as soon as Update method is used
dbOptimisticValue	Optimistic concurrency based on row values
dbOptimisticBatch	Optimistic locking; does updates in batches; ODBCDirect workspace only

Example Syntax

```
Dim MyDB as Database
Dim MyRS(2) As Recordset

Set MyDB = Workspaces(0).OpenDatabase("c:\Clients.MDB")
'Open table type Recordset object while denying others from editing the table
Set MyRS(0) = MyDB.OpenRecordset("Clients", dbOpenTable, dbDenyWrite)
'open a dynaset type Recordset object using a SQL statement
Set Myrs(1) = MyDB.OpenRecordSet("SELECT * FROM [Sites] WHERE Zip LIKE `870*'", _ ⇐
dbOpenDynaset)
'open a SnapShot type Recordset Object
Set MyRS(2) = MyDB.OPenRecordset(`SELECT * FROM [Contacts] Where ClientID = 5", _ ⇐
dbOpenSnapShot)
.....'do processing
MyRS(0).close
MyRS(1).Close
MyRS(2).Close
MyDB.Close
Set MyRS(0) = Nothing
Set MyRS(1) = Nothing
Set MyRS(2) = Nothing
Set MyDB = Nothing
```

Description

The above examples show the three different types of Recordsets being opened. If you leave out the type argument, the Recordset will default to a Table type if it can or a Dynaset type otherwise. If you are using the OpenRecordset method with a QueryDef-, Dynaset-, or Snapshot-type Recordset, you will only be able to open the Dynaset or Snapshot type. Of course, if the source is a SQL string, then the type has to be a Dynaset or Snapshot type as well. Also, if the underlying table in a TableDef object is an attached table, the Dynaset or Snapshot type is required.

If you use the dbSeeChanges option, you will get a trappable error when you attempt to update or delete a record that has been edited by someone else during the time you performed an Edit method to the Update method. For those applications using the older Dynaset, Snapshot, and Table objects, it should be noted that they are not the same as the new Recordset types bearing a similar name. In fact there are many internal differences and properties in the new types, so you really should upgrade legacy code to use the new Recordset object.

You can specify dbReadOnly in either the lockedits or options argument, but not in both. That will generate a runtime error.

57

DATA CONTROL

Many modern applications are concerned with the storage, organization, and retrieval of data. To address the needs of the software developers creating these products, Visual Basic provides a rich set of data access features. The standard data access objects were discussed in the previous chapter. Visual Basic also provides the Data control and a set of data bound controls.

Visual Basic provides many standard controls, such as text boxes and labels, that can be bound to the Data control, in addition to the DBCombo, DBGrid, and DBList. These controls are provided specifically for binding to a Data control.

This chapter will discuss the use and properties of the Data control. Chapter 58, "Simple Bound Controls," will show how to use built-in Visual Basic controls as bound controls. Chapter 59, "DBList and DBCombo," will take on the DBList and DBCombo controls, and Chapter 60, "DBGrid Appearance," and 61, "DBGrid Behavior," discuss the appearance and behavior of the DBGrid.

Why and When to Use the Data Control

The Data control is an excellent tool for rapidly developing a database information retrieval system. With very little code, you can obtain a useful view into stored information. This is practically a drop-in process in which you can place a Data control and a data bound control on a form and be able to access your database in a matter of minutes. After setting some properties, your application is ready to go. Figure 57-1 shows a simple, working browser form put together in less than five minutes.

Of course, if you want more, then you'll actually have to write some code. By adding code in the different events of the Data control and the data bound controls, you can begin to build up a very powerful data access application.

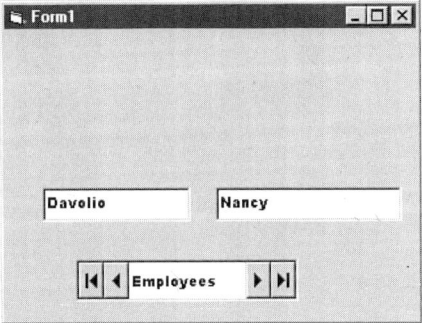

Figure 57-1   Example of a simple data browser

Data Binding

Controls that may be data bound have two standard properties determining how they will behave when bound. The *DataSource property* allows you to specify the name of the Data control to which the client control will bind. The *DataField property*, a string property of the client control, specifies which of the database field names available from the Data control the client will bind.

Once the DataSource and DataField properties are set and the Data control has been properly initialized (its properties are set to suitable values), the client control automatically displays the contents of the bound field as the Data control is used to navigate through the Recordset. You then can use appropriate editable controls, such as the text box, to change the data contained in the bound field.

Data Control Summary

Table 57-1 is a list of the methods, properties, and events of the Data control. Only methods, properties, and events specific to the Data control are detailed below. All other methods, properties, and events are covered in the chapters related to those members. For example, mouse events can be found in Chapter 49, "Mouse Events," and properties related to appearance can be found in Chapter 33, "Application Appearance."

Table 57-1 Methods, properties, and events of the Data control

Use or Set This...	Type	To Do This...
Align	Property	Set or return a value that determines how the control is placed on the form
Appearance	Property	Determine whether or not to use 3D appearance
BackColor	Property	A numeric value that determines the control's background color
BOFAction, EOFAction	Properties	Determine how the Data control reacts to EOF and BOF conditions
Caption	Property	Set or return a string representing the object's caption
Connect	Property	Set or return the type of database being used

Use or Set This...	Type	To Do This...
Database	Property	Determine the Database object underlying the Recordset
DatabaseName	Property	Set or read the name of the underlying database in a data control
Default cursor type	Property	Set or return the cursor displayed when moving the mouse over the control
DataField	Property	Set or return a value that binds the control to a field in the current record
Drag	Method	Begin, end, or cancel a drag operation of an object
DragDrop	Event	React to an object dropped on the control
DragIcon	Property	Set or return the icon to be used for drag operations
DragMode	Property	Set or return the type of drag mode available
DragOver	Event	React to an object dragged over the control
EditMode	Property	Determine the current edit state of the current record in the Recordset
Enabled	Property	Boolean value that enables or disables the control
EOFAction	Property	Determine action when the Recordset's EOF is reached
Error	Event	Read and handle external errors in the Data control
Exclusive	Property	Determine if a database is opened for single or multiple users
Font	Property	Reference the font object associated with the control
FontBold	Property	Set or return whether or not the font is bold
FontItalic	Property	Set or return whether or not the font is italic
FontName	Property	Set or return the font's name
FontSize	Property	Set or return the font's size in points
FontStrikethru	Property	Set or return whether or not the font is struck through
FontUnderline	Property	Set or return whether or not the font is underlined
ForeColor	Property	Determine the color of the text and other foreground objects
Height	Property	Set or return the height of the control
Index	Property	Reference the instance in a control array
Left	Property	Set or return the position of the left edge of the control
MouseDown	Event	Occurs when a mouse button is pressed down
MouseIcon	Property	Set or return the custom mouse picture property
MouseMove	Event	Occurs when the mousepointer is moved over the control
MousePointer	Property	Set or return the selected mousepointer
MouseUp	Event	Occurs when the mouse button is released
Move	Method	Move an object to a specified location
Name	Property	Set or return the name referenced in code of the control
Options	Property	Set or return one or more characteristics of the Recordset object
Parent	Property	Returns a reference to the control's parent
ReadOnly	Property	Determine if a Recordset is editable
Rebind	Method	Refresh and reset the properties and data in a DBGrid
Recordset	Property	The data (set of records) available to the Data control
RecordsetType	Property	Set or return the type of Recordset object of the data control
RecordSource	Property	A string used to form the data control's Recordset
Refresh	Method	Update the objects in a collection to reflect the current database

continued on next page

continued from previous page

Use or Set This...	Type	To Do This...
Reposition	Event	React to changes in the current record in the data control Recordset
Resize	Event	React to the control changing size
ShowWhatsThis	Method	Display the What's This pop-up help
Tag	Property	Set or return the tag
ToolTipText	Property	Set or return the tooltips text
Top	Property	Set or return the location of the top edge of the control
UpdateControls	Method	Refresh the data in bound control to match the values in the Recordset
UpdateRecord	Method	Write currently bound data to the database
Validate	Event	Occurs before current record changes, before an update, delete, or close operation
Visible	Property	Set or return the visible status of the control
WhatsThisHelpID	Property	The help context ID for the What's This pop-up
Width	Property	Set or return the width of the Control object
Z-order	Method	Used to change the z-order of this control in relation to its siblings

BOFAction, EOFAction Properties

Objects Affected   Data control

Purpose   The BOFAction and EOFAction properties determine the behavior of the Data control when either the EOF or BOF conditions become True. Tables 57-2 and 57-3 list the arguments of the BOFAction and EOFAction properties and their constant values.

General Syntax

```
[form!]object.BOFAction = value
[form!]object.EOFAction = value
```

Table 57-2 Arguments of the BOFAction and EOFAction properties

Argument	Description
object	The Data control's name in code
value	An intrinsic constant that determines the Data control's behavior

Table 57-3 Intrinsic constants of the BOFAction and EOFAction properties

Name	Value	Description
		For the BOFAction property, the settings are
vbBOFActionMoveFirst	0	Causes the recordpointer to move back to the first valid record
vbBOFActionBOF	1	Causes a validation event on the first record, causes a reposition to the first record, and disables the move previous button until a move off the first record occurs
		For the EOFAction property, the settings are
vbEOFActionMoveLast	0	Causes the recordpointer to move back to the last record
vbEOFActionEOF	1	Causes a validation event on the last record, causes a reposition to the last record, and disables the move next button until a move off the last record occurs
vbEOFActionAddNew	2	Moving past the last record causes an AddNew event to be triggered after a validation event has been called on the last record

Example Syntax

```
Private Sub Check1(index As Integer)
Select Case Index
      Case 1 'allow new records
            If Check1(1) Then
                  Data1.EOFAction = vbEOFActionAddNew
            Else
                  Data1.EOFAction = vbEOFActionEOF
            End If
      Case .....
End Select
End Sub
```

Description
In the Data control provided prior to Visual Basic 4.0, there were no intrinsic means for controlling the BOF and EOF conditions. Your code had to check for these conditions and act accordingly, or a trappable error would occur. In Visual Basic 4.0, this has changed dramatically. The Data control will no longer allow the user to blindly walk off the edge of the BOF/EOF cliff. The Data control will now move the recordpointer back to a valid record, or in the case of the EOFAction's being set to vbEOFActionAddNew, initiate an AddNew event when the recordpointer hits an EOF condition. In the example above, a check box control is used to control whether the EOF condition will trigger an AddNew or reposition the recordpointer back to the last record.

If you set the control to a vbEOFActionMoveFirst and/or a vbEOFActionMoveLast, the Data control will transparently move the recordpointer back to the first or last record, respectively. If you set the control to a vbEOFActionEOF and/or a vbEOFActionBOF, the Data control will trigger a validate event, then move back to the first or last record, respectively. It will also disable the MovePrevious or MoveNext button, depending on which end you are on. A subsequent move of either extreme will re-enable the button.

DATABASE PROPERTY

Objects Affected   Data control

Purpose   The Database property is a read-only property that exposes the Data controls underlying Database object. Table 57-4 lists the arguments for the Database property.

General Syntax

```
[form!]Name.Database
```

Table 57-4 Arguments of the Database property

Argument	Description
form	The Name property of the parent form
Name	The Name property of the Data control

Example Syntax

```
Dim db As Database
Set db = Data1.Database
MsgBox "There are " & db.TableDefs.Count & " tables in this database."
```

Description   The Database property exposes the Database object the Data control is using. Through the Database object, the application can access more functionality than what is available through the Data control. See Chapter 56, "Database Overview and Design," for a thorough discussion of the Database object.

DATABASENAME PROPERTY

Objects Affected   Data control

Purpose   The DatabaseName property reads or sets the name and location of the database. Setting the value in the Data control's DatabaseName property while your program is running changes the database to which the control is connected. You must use the Refresh method to reopen the control after changing databases. Table 57-5 lists the arguments of the DatabaseName property.

General Syntax

```
[form!]Name.DatabaseName = [pathname$]
```

Table 57-5 Arguments of the DatabaseName property

Argument	Description
form	The Name property of the parent form
Name	The Name property of the Data control
pathnameS	Full path and filename of the database

Example Syntax

```
Private Sub OpenNewDatabase(pathname As String)
     Label1.Caption = "Closing " & Data1.DatabaseName & " database now."
     Data1.DatabaseName = pathname
     Data1.Refresh
     Label1.Caption = "Opened " & Data1.DatabaseName & " database."
End Sub
```

Description
The DatabaseName property lets you set and retrieve the name of the database to which the Data control is connected. You may set this property at design time in the properties box DatabaseName entry for the Data control. You can supply a fully qualified network path name, such as \\Server3\data\clients.mdb, if your network supports this syntax. Changing this property at runtime implicitly closes the Data control's connection to the database. Only after the old database is closed does the control connect to the new database.

Comments
Note that the new database is not opened until you have used the Data control's Refresh method to update your Recordset and bound controls.

EDITMODE PROPERTY

Objects Affected
Data control

Purpose
The EditMode property lets you read the editing state of the current record in the Data control's Recordset. Tables 57-6 and 57-7 list the arguments of the EditMode property and their possible values.

General Syntax

```
[form!]Name.EditMode
```

Table 57-6 Arguments of the EditMode property

Argument	Description
form	The Name property of the parent form
Name	The Name property of the Data control

Table 57-7 Values of the EditMode property

Value	Constant	Meaning
0	dbEditNone	No editing operation in progress
1	dbEditInProgress	Edit methods have been invoked
2	dbEditAdd	AddNew method has been invoked

Example Syntax

```
Private Sub Data1_Validate(Action As Integer, Save As Integer)
     If Text1.DataChanged Then
          If Data1.EditMode = dbEditInProgress Then
               'we prevent the change when editing to this key field
               'rather than waiting for a data engine generated error
               MsgBox _
               "Client ID may only be set when adding a new client!"
          Text1.DataChanged = False
          End If
     End If
End Sub
```

Description   Use the Data control's EditMode property to determine the current edit status. There are three possible states: dbEditNone, dbEditInProgress, and dbEditAdd. You would typically use the EditMode property in the Validate event, as shown in the preceding example.

ERROR EVENT

Objects Affected   Data control

Purpose   The Data control's Error event lets you react to errors in reading data that are not caused by your code. It is not intended for trapping runtime errors in your code segments. Tables 57-8 and 57-9 list the arguments of the Error event and their possible values.

General Syntax

```
Private Sub Name_Error([Index As Integer,] dataerr As Integer, Response As Integer)
```

Table 57-8 Arguments of the Error event

Argument	Description
Name	The Name property of the Data control
Index	The Index property of the Data control in a control array
dataerr	The error number that has been generated
Response	The response you wish to return

Table 57-9 Values of the Error event

Value	Constant	Meaning
0	vbDataErrContinue	Continue, hiding the error message
1	vbDataErrDisplay	Display the appropriate message (default)

Example Syntax

```
Private Sub Data1_Error(dataerr As Integer, response As Integer)
    If dataerr = 3024                 'database file not found
        response = vbDataErrDisplay 'display the error message
    End If
End Sub
```

Description The Error event lets you respond to errors generated in the process of accessing or attempting to access data. Errors that are external to your code can be caused by a click on the Data control's movement buttons, the Data control automatically opening a database during the form load event, or a custom control attempting to use the Delete method. Use the Error event to handle these errors.

EXCLUSIVE PROPERTY

Objects Affected Data control

Purpose The Exclusive property reads or sets whether a database is opened for single-user or multiuser access. Read and write at both design time and runtime. Tables 57-10 and 57-11 list the arguments of the Exclusive property and their possible values.

General Syntax

```
[form!]Name.Exclusive = [boolean%]
```

Table 57-10 Arguments of the Exclusive property

Argument	Description
form	The Name property of the parent form
Name	The Name property of the Data control
boolean%	Indication of multiuser status (True or False)

Table 57-11 Values of the Exclusive property

boolean%	Meaning
True	Single-user
False	Multiuser (default)

Example Syntax

```
Private Function BeginAdminWork () As Integer
      On Error Goto iHandler
      'this routine sets the data access to exclusive for
      'the purpose of doing administrative work
      'if the change fails, the routine returns False
      Data1.Exclusive = False
      Data1.Refresh
      BeginAdminWork = True
      Exit Function

iHandler:
      BeginAdminWork = False
      Exit Function

End Function
```

Description   Use the Exclusive property to determine whether a database is open for single-user or multiuser access. *Single-user (exclusive) mode* restricts access to the database to a single concurrent user in networked settings. *Multiuser mode* lets other users on the network or multiple processes on a single machine access the database concurrently. Single-user mode is often needed for administrative functions. The previous example shows how to reset the mode to exclusive before beginning administrative procedures.

Comments   Data access tends to be somewhat faster in single-user (exclusive) mode, because there is no need to manage record locking.

OPTIONS PROPERTY

Objects Affected   Data control

Purpose   The Options property is used to set characteristics of the Data control's Recordset. This property is available to read and write at both design time and runtime. Tables 57-12 and 57-13 list the arguments of the Options property and their possible values.

General Syntax

```
[form!]Name.Options [ = Expression%]
```

Table 57-12 Arguments of the Options property

Argument	Description
form	The Name property of the parent form
Name	The Name property of the Data control
Expression%	Bitwise value indicating several settings

Table 57-13 Values of the Options property

Value	Constant	Meaning
1	dbDenyWrite	Other users may not make modifications
2	dbDenyRead	Other users may not read Recordset
4	dbReadOnly	Cannot modify existing records or add new records
8	dbAppendOnly	Can add new records but cannot make modifications
16	dbInconsistent	Does not maintain referential integrity (RI)
32	dbConsistent	Enforces referential integrity (default)
64	dbSQLPassThrough	Passes SQL string to the remote server
256	dbForwardOnly	Forward scrolling only is allowed
512	dbSeeChanges	Generates an error if others change data being edited

Example Syntax

```
Private Sub Form_Load ()
    'make the Recordset available ReadOnly and for forward scrolling only
    Data1.Options = dbReadOnly or dbForwardOnly
    Data1.Refresh
End Sub
```

Description   The Data control's Options property is used to read or set important properties of the control's underlying Recordset. Changes you make to the Options property do not go into effect until you use the Data control's Refresh method. Note that each of these option constants is available from Constants modules of the DAO library (use the Object Browser to view the available constants).

Comments   Use the OR operator to combine two or more settings for use in a single control (see the previous example).

RECORDSET PROPERTY

Objects Affected   Data control

Purpose   The Recordset property sets or returns a Recordset object defined by the Data control's RecordSource property or an existing Recordset object. Table 57-14 lists the arguments of the Recordset property.

General Syntax

```
object.Recordset [= value]
```

Table 57-14 Arguments of the Recordset property

Argument	Description
object	A reference in code to a Data control
value	A string expression that results in a reference to a Recordset object

Example Syntax

```
Dim Myamount As Currency
'places the value contained in the
'SubTotal field of the recordset
'into the MyAmount variable
MyAmount = Data1.Recordset!SubTotal
'then the sales tax is computed
'and stored in the Salestax field
Data1.Recordset.Edit
Data1.Recordset!SalesTax = Myamount * STRate
Data1.Recordset.Update
```

Description   The Data control's Recordset property is a reference to the Data control's underlying Recordset object. This Recordset object can be any of the three types defined for the Recordset object. Essentially, you can perform any of the methods and access any of the properties of the Recordset object through the Data control's Recordset property. See the reference to the Recordset object in Chapter 56 for a complete description of the Recordset object.

RecordsetType Property

Objects Affected   Data control

Purpose   The RecordsetType property sets or returns a value representing the type of Recordset object associated with the Data control. Tables 57-15 and 57-16 list the arguments of the RecordsetType property and their possible values.

General Syntax

```
object.RecordsetType [=value]
```

Table 57-15 Arguments of the RecordsetType property

Argument	Description
object	A reference in code to a Data control
value	One of three intrinsic constants in the table below

Table 57-16 Intrinsic constants of the RecordsetType property

Name	Value	Description
vbRSTyptTable	0	Table-type Recordset object
vbRSTypeDynaset	1	Dynaset-type Recordset object (default type)
vbRSTypeSnapshot	2	Snapshot-type Recordset object

Note that these constants are not interchangeable with the constants used to identify Recordset objects themselves, but are valid only for the Data control.

Example Syntax

```
'set the Recordset type
Data1.RecordsetType = vbRSTypeTable
'set the source to the required table
Data1.Recordsource = "Transactions"
'the refresh actually causes the Recordset to be populated.
Data1.Refresh
```

Description   The RecordsetType property is used to set up the type of Recordset object created when setting the Data control's RecordSource property. If the RecordsetType cannot be created with the information provided in the RecordSource property, a trappable runtime error is generated.

RECORDSOURCE PROPERTY

Objects Affected   Data control

Purpose   The RecordSource property sets or returns the underlying source of the Data control's Recordset. This source can be a table, a SQL statement, or a QueryDef object. Table 57-17 lists the arguments of the RecordSource property.

General Syntax

```
object.Recordsource [= value]
```

Table 57-17 Arguments of the RecordSource property

Argument	Description
object	The name in code that references a Data control object
value	A table name, SQL statement, or reference to a QueryDef object

Example Syntax

```
Dim DataSet(2) as Boolean

Public Property Set MyData (Index as integer, Optional Mysource as String _ ⇐
    , Optional MyQDef _ as QueryDef)
    If Index> 2 Then Exit Property
    on error goto BadSource
    'assume a valid recordsource is passed
    DataSet(Index) = True
    'set the recordsource property
    'if the MyQDef argument is missing then it
    'must be a table name or SQL statement
    If IsMissing(MyQDef) Then
        Set  Data1(Index).Recordsource = MySource
```

continued on next page

continued from previous page

```
        Else
                'if the MyQDef is not missing then set the
                'Data control with a QueryDef object
                Set Data1(Index).Recordsource = MyQDef
        End If
        'if there were no errors then refresh the Data control
        If DataSet(Index) Then Data1(Index).Refresh
        Exit Property

BadSource:
        'inform the user that there is an error
        msgbox error$
        'mark the error condition by making the DataSet variable false
        DataSet(Index) = False
        Resume Next
End Property
```

Description　　In the example above, the MyData property procedure takes a string argument to set the RecordSource property of the indexed Data control. This string argument could be either a table name or a SQL statement. The MyQDef argument takes a QueryDef object reference as an argument. This way, the Property Set argument will take either type of argument. The IsMissing() function is used to determine what type of argument is being passed. The RecordSource property can also be set at design time through the Properties window.

REPOSITION EVENT

Objects Affected　　Data control

Purpose　　The Reposition event allows the application to react when the Data control moves from one record to another. In contrast to the Validate event, the Reposition event occurs after the new record becomes current. Table 57-18 lists the argument of the Reposition event.

General Syntax

```
Private Sub Name_Reposition ()
```

Table 57-18 Argument of the Reposition event

Argument	Description
Name	The Name property of the Data control

Example Syntax

```
Private Sub Data1_Reposition()
        'We use the Reposition event to update a control whose value
        'we calculate from fields in the database
```

```
      Lab1Total.Caption = Data1.Recordset("Balance") _
            + Data1.Recordset("Interest")
End Sub
```

Description   A new record becomes current after the Data control has moved to a new valid record. This occurs after the user has pressed one of the Data control's movement buttons or his or her code has executed a move (Seek, FindFirst, FindLast, FindNext, or FindPrevious) method. The Reposition event is not suitable for validation of data, because the old record has already been written back to the database.

UPDATECONTROLS METHOD

Objects Affected   Data control

Purpose   The UpdateControls method forces a refresh of all bound controls. This resets any changed data (not yet saved) in the controls back to the original values in the database. Table 57-19 lists the arguments of the UpdateControls method.

General Syntax

```
[form!]Name.UpdateControls
```

Table 57-19 Arguments of the UpdateControls method

Argument	Description
form	The Name property of the parent form
Name	The Name property of the data control

Example Syntax

```
Private Sub ResolveValidation ()
      'this routine checks for data validation before saving and then
      'either saves the data in the bound controls or resets them to
      'their prior state
      If ValidateControls() Then
            Data1.UpdateRecord
      Else
            Data1.UpdateControls
      End If
End Sub
```

Description   UpdateControls is used primarily to restore the values of bound controls back to the underlying record. This resets them to the state they were in before the user made any changes.

UPDATERECORD METHOD

Objects Affected	Data control
Purpose	The UpdateRecord method permits the updating of a Data control bound record, without causing a validate event to be triggered. Table 57-20 lists the argument of the UpdateRecord method.

General Syntax

```
object.UpdateRecord
```

Table 57-20 Argument of the UpdateRecord method

Argument	Description
object	A reference in code to a data control object

Example Syntax

```
Public Sub RetrySave( MyData As Control) As Boolean
      On Error Goto BadRetry
      RetrySave = True
      Mydata.Update
Exit Sub

BadRetry:
      MsgBox Error$
      RetrySave = False
      Resume Next
End Sub
```

Description	In the above example, the RetrySave could be called repeatedly from the Validate event of a Data control without causing a cascading series of Validate events. The UpdateRecord method could be called from anywhere in your program to commit data, without triggering a Validate event from the Data control. Of course, your data must satisfy the validation rules established by your database or a runtime error will be generated.

VALIDATE EVENT

Objects Affected	Data control
Purpose	The Validate event is triggered in the Data control before a change in record status. Validate occurs before Delete, Update, Unload, or Close. It allows the application to maintain data integrity by verifying that suitable data has been assigned to fields before the data change is committed to the database. Tables 57-21, 57-22, and 57-23 list the arguments of the Validate event and their possible values.

General Syntax

```
Private Sub Name_Validate([Index As Integer,] action As Integer, save As Integer)
```

Table 57-21 Arguments of the Validate event

Argument	Description
Name	The Name property of the data control
Index	The Index property of the data control if it is a member of a control array
action	An integer indicating the event that triggered the Validate event
save	A Boolean indicating whether bound data has changed

Table 57-22 Values for the Validate event action parameter

Value	Constant	Meaning
0	vbDataActionCancel	Cancel the operation when the routine terminates
1	vbDataActionMoveFirst	MoveFirst method
2	vbDataActionMovePrevious	MovePrevious method
3	vbDataActionMoveNext	MoveNext method
4	vbDataActionMoveLast	MoveLast method
5	vbDataActionAddNew	AddNew method
6	vbDataActionUpdate	Update operation
7	vbDataActionDelete	Delete method
8	vbDataActionFind	One of the Find methods
9	vbDataActionBookmark	The bookmark has been set
10	vbDataActionClose	The Close method
11	vbDataActionUnload	The parent form is being unloaded

Table 57-23 Values of the Validate event save parameter

Value	Meaning
True	Bound data has been changed
False	Bound data has not been changed

Example Syntax

```
Private Sub Data1_Validate(action As Integer, save As Integer)
    'we will verify that the contents of the bound text box that
    'contains the fees charged amount is positive
    'if it is negative, reset to zero
```

continued on next page

continued from previous page

```
    If TextFees.DataChanged = True Then 'data has changed
        If Val(TextFees) < 0 Then TextFees.Text = 0
    End If
End Sub
```

Description

The Validate event is triggered with two parameters: action and save. The application can use these parameters to determine why a validation has been called for and whether the change to the database should proceed. The action value indicates the type of operation that has caused the Validate event, allowing the error-handling code in the routine to be selective in its implementation. The save parameter may be changed within the routine to abort the database changes that are about to occur.

Comments

You can also change the action parameter to modify the action taking place. In addition, note that the Validate event is triggered every time a suitable method (such as a move) is invoked. This implies that placing large or complex code in the Validate event may slow navigation of the database Recordset considerably. You can selectively reset the DataChanged property of bound controls to cancel individual fields being written to the Recordset.

58

SIMPLE BOUND CONTROLS

The Data control described in the previous chapter must be used in conjunction with a bound control. *Bound controls* are controls that are tied to a particular field in the Recordset of the Data control and allow the user to view or edit that field. Visual Basic provides a rich tool set of bound controls, and many third-party tools support binding. Binding is the act of tying the control to a database field.

Data Binding

Assuming the Data control is set up correctly, it will be very simple to bind. There are only two properties that must be set to allow the application to view and edit data in the Data control's Recordset. The first property is the DataSource property. This property tells the control which Data control it is bound to. In the design environment, Visual Basic will give a drop-down list of available Data controls. Figure 58-1 displays setting the DataSource in the design environment.

The second property that must be set is the DataField. This property tells the control which field in the Data control's Recordset it is bound to. Visual Basic provides a list of available fields if the DataSource is set, and the DatabaseName and RecordSource properties are set on the Data control. Figure 58-2 shows the list of available fields for a bound control.

Both these properties can be set at design or runtime, allowing the application to use the controls with their normal behavior and as bound controls. Table 58-1 lists the simple bound controls.

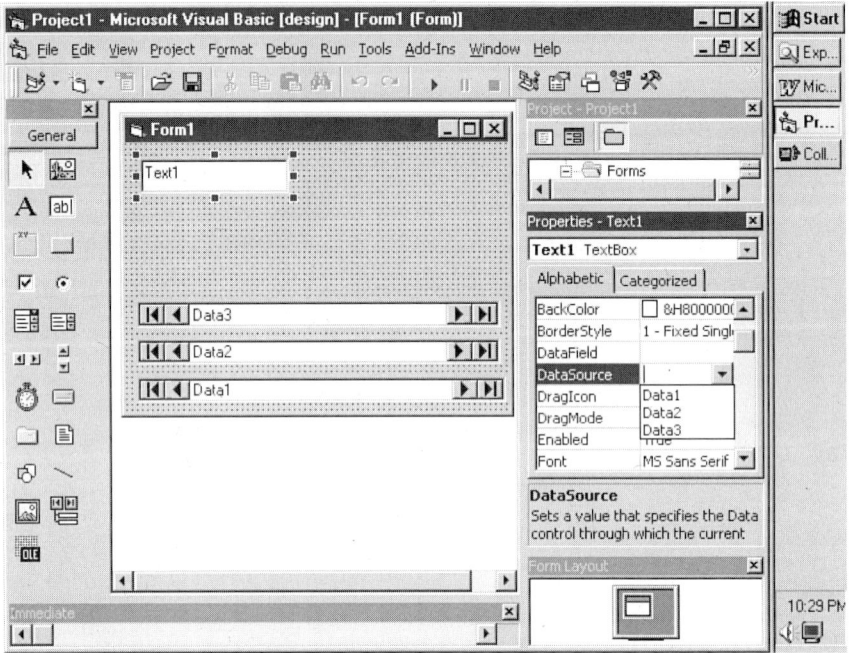

Figure 58-1 Selecting a DataSource

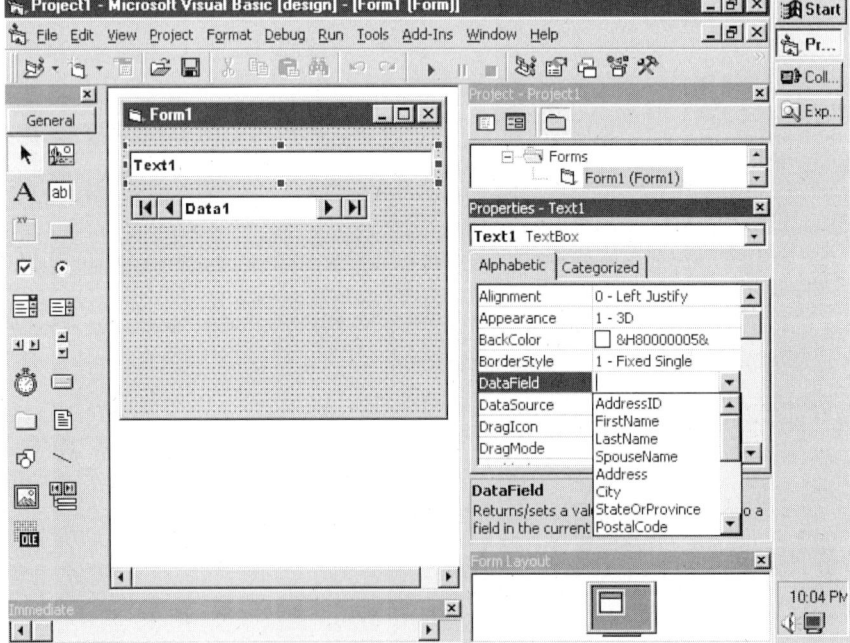

Figure 58-2 Selecting a DataField

Table 58-1 Simple bound controls

Control Name

CheckBox

ComboBox

Label

ListBox

Image

MaskedEdit

OLE

RichTextBox

TextBox

Simple Bound Controls Summary

Table 58-2 lists the properties of the simple bound controls.

Table 58-2 Simple bound control properties

Use or Set This...	Type	To Do This...
DataField	Property	Bind a control to a field of the data control's recordset
DataSource	Property	Specify the data control

DataField Property

Purpose   The DataField property specifies what field a particular control will bind to in the database. The developer sets the DataSource property to bind the control to an appropriately initialized Data control. The DataField property then specifies which field in the specified Data control's Recordset will be displayed in the bound control. This property is available to both read and write at runtime or design time.

General Syntax

```
Combo1.DataField = sFieldName$
```

Example Syntax

```
Private Sub SetDataSettings()

    Data1.Databasename = "C:\MSACCESS\CLIENT.MDB"
    Data1.RecordSource = "Customers"

    'set the list box to display the customer name data from the Data control
```

continued on next page

continued from previous page

```
    List1.DataSource = Data1
    List1.DataField = "CustomerName"

    Data1.Refresh

End Sub
```

Description   The DataField property is always used in conjunction with the DataSource
property to bind a data aware control to a Data control on a form. The
Data control must reside on the same form as the object being bound and
must be properly initialized to allow for binding. Initializing consists of
setting a valid database name and a valid recordsource for the Data control. At runtime, you may need to use the Data control's Refresh method to
establish the link to the database and activate the binding of the data
aware controls.

DATASOURCE PROPERTY

Purpose   The DataSource property specifies the Data control to which the bound
control is attached. The DataField property then specifies which field in
the specified Data control's Recordset is displayed in the bound control.
Both properties are available to both read and write at runtime or design
time.

General Syntax

```
Combo1.DataSource = Data1
```

Description   The DataSource property is always used in conjunction with the DataField
property to bind a data aware control to a Data control on a form. The
Data control must reside on the same form as the object being bound and
must be properly initialized to allow for binding. Initializing consists of
setting a valid database name and a valid recordsource for the Data control. At runtime, you may need to use the Data control's Refresh method to
establish the link to the database and activate the binding of the data
aware controls.

59

DBLIST AND DBCOMBO

In Microsoft's unending quest to allow you, the programmer, to do more with less code, Visual Basic provides the DBCombo and DBList controls. DBCombo and DBList allow the application to fill the list contents of the control from the Data control. They also enable you to bind the result of the user's selection back to a field in the database. You do this simply by setting properties in the Data control to determine what data will be available, then setting properties on the list or combo box to determine which fields will be bound.

Using the DBList and DBCombo

To use the DBList and DBCombo controls, you need two Data controls. The first Data control will be used to populate the DBList or DBCombo control with the list of selections. The second will be used exactly as the Data control was used in the previous chapter. Start by setting up the first Data control for the Recordset of selections. Now set the RowSource and ListField properties of the DBList or DBCombo control to fill them with selections. Visual Basic will assume that you want the same field as the ListField for your BoundField and will set it automatically when you choose the ListField. Often, when you are changing a foreign key in a table, the BoundField will be some sort of ID field and the ListField will be a description of the foreign key's value. In this case, you will have to change the BoundField to be the ID.

Next, set the Data control like the one used in the previous chapter. This is the table from which the DBList or DBCombo will display the selection and allow the user to change. Set the DataField and DataSource properties on the DBList or DBCombo to the field it should display.

Figure 59-1 shows a DBList control with its properties set so it gets its list from Data1. The user sees the MALL field set in the ListField property, but we only care about the BoundColumn LOCATION_CODE. The DBList is then bound to the LOCATION_CODE field from the Data2 control.

Figure 59-2 shows the same DBList in action. Joe's Auto Parts is located at the Downtown Plaza. By selecting Lakeside Mall, the LOCATION_CODE in Data2 is updated to the LOCATION_CODE associated with the NAME Lakeside Mall.

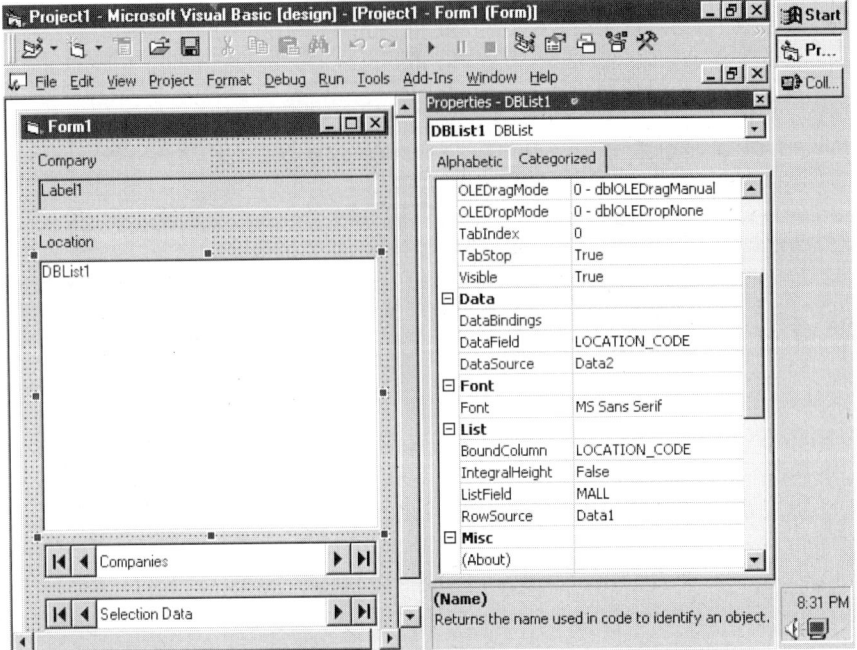

Figure 59-1   The DBList control and its properties

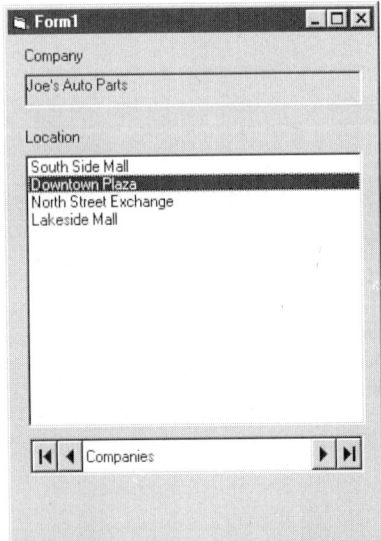

Figure 59-2   DBList in action

DBList and DBCombo Summary

Table 59-1 is a list of the methods and properties of the DBList and DBCombo controls that relate to being a bound control. All other methods, properties, and events are the equivalent of their unbound counterparts, the ListBox and ComboBox controls.

Table 59-1 Database-specific method and properties of the DBList and DBCombo controls

Use or Set This...	Type	To Do This...
BoundColumn	Property	Set or return the name of a source field in a Recordset object
BoundText	Property	Read the contents to be written to a bound field
DataField	Property	Set or return a value that binds the control to a field in the current record
DataSource	Property	Identify the Data control to be used for a bound control
ListField	Property	Determine the field in the Recordset used to fill DBCombo or DBList
MatchEntry	Property	Determine the method used to match entries in lists
Refill	Method	Refill and refresh the DBCombo or DBList
RowSource	Property	The Data control used by a DBCombo or DBList to fill its list
SelectedItem	Property	Obtain the bookmark for the currently selected row in the DBGrid
Text	Property	Set or return the selected data
VisibleCount	Property	Return the number of visible rows
VisibleItems	Property	Obtain the bookmark for each of the visible rows

BOUNDCOLUMN PROPERTY

Purpose

The BoundColumn property sets or returns the name of the Recordset field that is supplying the data to a DBList or DBCombo control. The BoundColumn property is also used to supply update data to a second Data control bound to the DBList or DBCombo control. Table 59-2 lists the arguments of the BoundColumn property.

General Syntax

```
object.BoundColumn [= value]
[value] = object.BoundColumn
```

Table 59-2 Arguments of the BoundColumn property

Argument	Description
object	The name in code of either a DBCombo or DBList control
value	A string expression that evaluates to a valid field in a Recordset

Example Syntax

```
Private Sub Option1_click(Index As Integer)
      'select Source and destination fields according
      'to option selected by user
      Select Case Index
            Case 0
                  DBCombo1.BoundColumn = SourceDC.Recordset!MyField1
                  DBCombo1.DataField = TargetDC.Recordset!MyField1
            Case 1
                  DBCombo1.BoundColumn = SourceDC.Recordset!MyField2
                  DBCombo1.DataField = TargetDC.Recordset!MyField2
            Case 2
                  DBCombo1.BoundColumn = SourceDC.Recordset!MyField3
                  DBCombo1.DataField = TargetDC.Recordset!MyField3
      End Select
      'rebuilds the control's data list
      DBCombo1.Refill
End Sub
```

Description

The BoundColumn property specifies the source field for the DBCombo or DBList control. The field selected comes from the Data control specified in the RowSource property. The BoundColumn can serve as the source of the control's list field if the ListField property of the control is not specified. The main purpose of the BoundColumn property is to provide the data related to the item selected in the list. This data is available through the BoundText property.

If the DBCombo or DBList has a second Data control specified through the DataSource property and a field specified by the DataField property, then the DataField will be updated with the BoundText provided by the BoundColumn.

BOUNDTEXT PROPERTY

Purpose

The BoundText property is used to provide access to or set the data value of the currently selected item in a DBCombo or DBList control. Table 59-3 lists the arguments of the BoundText property.

General Syntax

```
object.BoundText [= value]
```

Table 59-3 Arguments of the BoundText property

Argument	Description
object	The name in code of either a DBCombo or DBList control
value	A string expression that evaluates to a valid field in a Recordset

Example Syntax
```
Sub DBCombo_Click()
    MyItems.Close
    'SQL statement built using the BoundText property for the Criteria
    MySQL = "SELECT * FROM [Vendor Items]
    MySQL = MySQL + " WHERE [Vendor] = '" & DBCombo.BoundText & "'"
    Set MyItems = MyDB.OpenRecordset(MySQL)
    If MyItems.Recordcount < 1 Then
        MsgBox "No Items for this vendor available"
        DataState.VendorItems = False
        ReadState
    End If
End Sub
```

Description   In the above example, the BoundText property is used to provide the criteria for building a SQL statement. The DBCombo would provide the list of vendor names through the ListField property. The BoundText would contain the vendor's ID number, provided through the BoundColumn property of the DBCombo control. If the DBCombo was bound to a second Data control through the DataSource property, then the data contained in the BoundText property would be written to the DataField property, updating that field in the second Data control. If a user enters a value into the text box portion of the DBCombo or DBList and there is no match, then the BoundText property is set to Null.

DataField Property

Purpose   The DataField property specifies what field a particular control will bind to in the database. The developer sets the DataSource property to bind the control to an appropriately initialized Data control. The DataField property then specifies which field in the specified Data control's RecordSet will be displayed in the bound control. This property is available to both read and write at runtime or design time.

General Syntax

```
Combo1.DataField = sFieldName$
```

Example Syntax

```
Private Sub SetDataSettings()

    Data1.Databasename = _
        "C:\Program Files\Microsoft Office\Access\client.mdb"
    Data1.RecordSource = "Customers"

    'set the list box to display the customer name data from the Data control
    List1.DataSource = Data1
    List1.DataField = "CustomerName"

    Data1.Refresh

End Sub
```

Description
The DataField property is always used in conjunction with the DataSource property to bind a data aware control to a Data control on a form. The Data control must reside on the same form as the object being bound and must be properly initialized to allow for binding. Initializing consists of setting a valid database name and a valid recordsource for the Data control. At runtime, you may need to use the Data control's Refresh method to establish the link to the database and activate the binding of the data aware controls.

DataSource Property

Purpose
The DataSource property specifies the Data control to which the bound control is attached. The DataField property then specifies which field in the specified Data control's Recordset is displayed in the bound control. Both properties are available to both read and write at runtime or design time.

General Syntax

```
Combo1.DataSource = Data1
```

Description
The DataSource property is always used in conjunction with the DataField property to bind a data-aware control to a Data control on a form. The Data control must reside on the same form as the object being bound and must be properly initialized to allow for binding. Initializing consists of setting a valid database name and a valid recordsource for the Data control. At runtime, you may need to use the Data control's Refresh method to establish the link to the database and activate the binding of the data aware controls.

ListField Property

Purpose
The ListField property sets or returns the name of the field in a Data control's recordset used to supply the DBCombo or DBList with the display list. Table 59-4 lists the arguments of the ListField property.

General Syntax

```
object.ListField [=value]
```

Table 59-4 Arguments of the ListField property

Argument	Description
object	The name in code of either a DBCombo or DBList control
value	A string expression that evaluates to a valid field in a recordset

Example Syntax

```
Sub Combo1_Click()
    'selects a new display field based on the selection
    'made in a regular combo control.
    DBCombo1.ListField = Combo1.List(Combo1.Listindex)
    'invoking the refill method will cause the DBCombo
    'to clear and refill the display list.
    DBCombo1.Refill
End Sub
```

Description   The DBCombo and DBList controls provided with Visual Basic 5.0 offer an extremely flexible set of properties and methods. The ListField provides a displayed list while having corresponding data available from an entirely different field. If you do not specify a value for the ListField, then the display list will be populated from the BoundColumn property. In the example provided above, a standard combo box control contains a list of fields from the Data control's recordset. When the user selects a field from the standard combo box's list, then the DBCombo's ListField property is set to that field and the DBCombo's list is refilled with the available data in that field by calling the Refill method of the DBCombo.

MATCHENTRY PROPERTY

Purpose   The MatchEntry property determines how the DBCombo and DBList controls behave when matching entries in their lists with the user input received by the control. Tables 59-5 and 59-6 list the arguments of the MatchEntry property and their possible values.

General Syntax

```
object.MatchEntry [= value%]
```

Table 59-5 Arguments of the MatchEntry property

Argument	Description
object	The name in code of either a DBCombo or DBList control
value	0 or 1 to indicate the type of matching to be used

Table 59-6 Values of the MatchEntry property

Value	Constant	Meaning
0	dblBasicMatching	Simple matching (default)
1	dblExtendedMatching	Extended matching

Example Syntax

```
Private Sub SetExtendedMatching(iNewStatus)
     'goes through the form and turns on or off
     'extended matching based on a choice received from the user
     'or perhaps retrieved from an ***INI*** file
     Dim iCtl As Integer
     For iCtl = 0 To Controls.Count - 1
          If typeof Controls(iCtl) Is Combo Then
               Controls(iCtl).MatchEntry = iNewStatus
          End If
     Next iCtl
End Sub
```

Description   If simple matching is chosen, each letter entered by the user is processed separately by the control and a match is attempted for the first list entry beginning with that letter. If extended matching is chosen, consecutive letters are combined and the search is refined, based on the combination of characters entered. If vbMatchEntryExtended has been chosen, the user can press Ⓑ to reset the content of the string that the control is using for the attempted match.

REFILL METHOD

Purpose   The Refill method allows the DBList or DBCombo to be rebound to the Data control and repainted. This method is different from a standard refresh, which just causes a repaint. Table 59-7 lists the argument of the Refill method.

General Syntax

```
object.Refill
```

Table 59-7 Argument of the Refill method

Argument	Description
object	The name in code of either a DBCombo or DBList control

Example Syntax

```
Private Sub cmndRefreshList_Click()
     'this routine responds to the Click event of a button that the
     'user can press to refill the list and refresh it
     DBList1.Refill
End Sub
```

Description   The Refill method allows the application to re-establish the list of data and repaint the control. It functions in the same manner for the DBCombo and DBList controls. This method is somewhat analogous to the Rebind method for the DBGrid control.

RowSource Property

Purpose   The RowSource property specifies the Data control from which the DBCombo and DBList controls' list is filled and from which the BoundColumn property is supplied.

General Syntax

```
This Property is not available at runtime
```

Description   The RowSource property provides the DBCombo and the DBList with their source recordset. The BoundColumn, BoundText, and ListField are dependent upon this setting for their data. You must set the RowSource property at design time and cannot change it during runtime.

SelectedItem Property

Purpose   The SelectedItem property is a value containing a bookmark for the selected record (row) in the DBCombo or DBList control. Table 59-8 lists the argument of the SelectedItem property.

General Syntax

```
object.SelectedItem
```

Table 59-8 Argument of the SelectedItem property

Argument	Description
object	The name in code of either a DBCombo or DBList control

Example Syntax

```
Private Sub MoveToSelectedRecord ()
    'takes the selected record and moves to it in the Recordset
    Dim sBookmark as String
    sBookmark = DBCombo1.SelectedItem
    'move to the record chosen in the combo
    Data1.Recordset.Bookmark = sBookmark
End Sub
```

Description   When the user selects an item from the list portion of the DBCombo control, the SelectedItem property of the control takes the value of the bookmark for the record corresponding to that choice. This bookmark can then be used (as in the preceding example) to reposition the recordset to the appropriate record.

TEXT PROPERTY

Purpose   The Text property is used to read the text of the selected item in a list or combo box, or a cell entry in a grid. Additionally, the Text property can be used to set the selected item in combo boxes whose Style property is set to 0 (drop-down combo) or 1 (simple combo). Table 59-9 summarizes the arguments of the Text property when used with a list box or combo box.

General Syntax

```
[form!]Name.Text [= TextString$]
```

Table 59-9 Arguments of the Text property when used with a list box or combo box

Argument	Description
form	Name of the parent form
Name	Name of the list, combo box, or grid control
TextString$	Assigned to the edit area of the drop-down and simple combo box styles or cell of a grid

Example Syntax

```
Private Sub Command1_Click ()
    SelectedItem$ = List1.Text    'assigns the value of a list box's selected item to a
                                  'string
    Combo1.Text = "Hello"         'assigns a string to the edit area of a simple combo box
End Sub
```

Description   When used with list and combo boxes, the Text property returns a string copy of the currently selected item in the control's list. If no item has yet been selected, this property will return a Null string.

This is an alternative to using the List and ListIndex properties together. For instance, in most cases the following two lines of code are functionally equivalent:

```
A$ = List1.List(List1.ListIndex)
A$ = List1.Text
```

The only difference between these two examples occurs when the user has not yet selected an item in the list. When this is the case, the first line in the example would generate an error (because ListIndex would have a value of -1). The second line of code would not. Instead, the variable A$ would be assigned a Null value.

When used with the grid control, the Text property reads or sets the contents of the active cell. The active cell is set with the Row and Col properties.

In the example syntax, the first statement stores the text of the currently selected item for List1 in the string variable SelectedItem$. The second statement assigns the string "Hello" to the selected item in Combo1. This causes the word "Hello" to appear in the edit area of this combo box.

DROP-DOWN AND SIMPLE COMBOS

As discussed at the beginning of this chapter, the drop-down combo and simple combo box styles allow the user to edit text in the edit area of the control. Because of this, the Text property takes on a somewhat different meaning when used with these combo box styles.

When used on drop-down or simple combo boxes, the Text property is a string representation of the contents of the edit area of the control. By default, this is the selected item from the list; thus, in the default case, the Text property has the same meaning as with non-combo list boxes. However, since the user can type text into the edit area of a combo box, the Text property can sometimes contain such an input item, probably not matching any item on the list.

You can manipulate the contents of the edit area by assigning it a value, or by using it as an argument with any of Visual Basic's string functions and statements such as Left, Mid, and Right. Any operations performed on this property are reflected by the text inside the edit area.

You may assign a string to the Text property. This causes the text in the box to be replaced by the assigned string. The user can also directly edit the text represented by the Text property. Any time a combo box's Text property is modified, it causes the combo box's Change event to occur.

VISIBLECOUNT PROPERTY

Purpose

The VisibleCount property is a value containing the number of visible or partially visible rows in a DBList or DBCombo control. Table 59-10 lists the argument of the VisibleCount property.

General Syntax

```
object.VisibleCount
```

Table 59-10 Argument of the VisibleCount property

Argument	Description
object	The name in code of either a DBCombo or DBList control

Example Syntax

```
Private Sub cmdStateCount_Click()
    Dim I As Integer, Count as Integer
    'Step through the visible items and see how
    'many are located in NY
    For I = 0 To DBList1.VisibleCount - 1
        Data1.Recordset.Bookmark = DBList1.VisibleItems(I)
        if Data1.Recordset("STATE").Value = "NY" Then
            Count = Count + 1
        End If
    Next I
    Msgbox MsgBox "There are " & Count & " sites in NY"
End Sub
```

Description   The VisibleCount property returns the number of visible rows in a DBList or DBCombo. It is usually used with the VisibleItems property array.

VISIBLEITEMS PROPERTY

Purpose   The VisibleItems property is a property array containing a bookmark for the visible record (row) in the DBList or DBCombo control. Table 59-11 lists the arguments of the VisibleItems property.

General Syntax

```
object.VisibleItems(Index)
```

Table 59-11 Arguments of the VisibleItems property

Argument	Description
object	The name in code of either a DBCombo or DBList control
index	0 to VisibleCount − 1, indicating what object in the array is to be returned

Example Syntax

```
Private Sub cmdSalesTally_Click()
    Dim I As Integer, Sales as Double
    'Step through the visible items and tally the sales
    For I = 0 To DBList1.VisibleCount - 1
        Data1.Recordset.Bookmark = DBList1.VisibleItems(I)
        Sales = Sales + Data1.Recordset("SALES").Value
    Next I
    Msgbox MsgBox "There are $" & Sales & " in sales displayed."
End Sub
```

Description   The VisibleItems property can be used to access each of the rows that are visible in the DBList or DBCombo control. It is usually used in conjunction with the VisibleCount property.

60

DBGRID APPEARANCE

Perhaps the handiest bound control is the DBGrid control. It allows a user to view, edit, add, and delete a recordset with a minimum of code. The DBGrid control is incredibly easy to use. However, there is a lot to cover, so this chapter will focus on the properties that alter the DBGrid's appearance, and the next chapter will cover the behavior of the DBGrid control.

DBGrid Appearance Summary

Table 60-1 list the properties related the appearance of the DBGrid. Details of non-standard properties follow. Details on common properties can be found in Chapter 33, "Application Appearance."

Table 60-1 Appearance-related properties of the DBGrid control

Use or Set This...	Type	To Do This...
Align	Property	Set or return a value that determines how the control is placed on the form
Appearance	Property	Determine whether or not to use 3D appearance
BackColor	Property	A numeric value that determines the control's background color
BorderStyle	Property	Set or return the style of border for the object
ColumnHeaders	Property	Determine whether column headers are displayed in a grid
DefColWidth	Property	Set the default column width for the DBGrid control
Font	Property	Reference the Font object associated with the control
ForeColor	Property	Determine the color of the text and other foreground objects
HeadFont	Property	Set or read the font used for the DBGrid header
HeadLines	Property	Set the number of lines of text displayed in the DBGrid header
Height	Property	Set or return the height of the control
LeftCol	Property	Set or return the leftmost visible column
RecordSelectors	Property	Determine whether record selectors are displayed with DBGrid
RowDividerStyle	Property	Determine the style of row divider used in the DBGrid control

continued on next page

continued from previous page

Use or Set This...	Type	To Do This...
ScrollBars	Property	Set or return the scrollbars style control object
Top	Property	Set or return the location of the top edge of the control
Visible	Property	Set or return the visible status of the control
Width	Property	Set or return the width of the control object

COLUMNHEADERS PROPERTY

Purpose   The ColumnHeaders property determines whether column headers are displayed on a DBGrid control. Table 60-2 lists the arguments of the ColumnHeaders property.

General Syntax

```
object.ColumnHeaders [= boolean%]
```

Table 60-2 Arguments of the ColumnHeaders property

Argument	Description
object	The name in code of a DBGrid control
boolean%	True or False to display the column headers

Example Syntax

```
Private Sub chkColumnHeaderDisplay_Click ()
     if the box is checked, display column headers
     If chkColumnHeaderDisplay Then
          DBGrid1.ColumnHeaders = True
     Else
          DBGrid.ColumnHeaders = False
     End If
End Sub
```

Description   The value of a DBGrid's ColumnHeaders property can be set at either design or runtime to determine whether headers are displayed on the grid. The example presents a check box to the user to let him or her decide whether the column headers are displayed.

DEFCOLWIDTH PROPERTY

Purpose   The DefColWidth property is used to read or set the default column width for columns in a DBGrid control. Table 60-3 lists the arguments of the DefColWidth property.

General Syntax

```
object.DefColWidth [= value]
```

Table 60-3 Arguments of the DefColWidth property

Argument	Description
object	The name in code of a DBGrid control
value	The new default column width

Example Syntax

```
Private Sub chkSetToHeaderSize_Click ()
    'if the DefColWidth is set to 0
    'the header sizes will be used to set
    'the size of the columns
    If chkSetToHeaderSize Then DBGrid1.DefColWidth = 0
End Sub
```

Description   The DefColWidth property provides the ability to read or set a default column width for a DBGrid control. The default column width is used to set the initial width of all the columns in the grid. If the AllowColResize property is set to False, DefColWidth determines the permanent state of all column widths (unless changed in code).

Comments   If the DefColWidth property is set to 0 (it is an integer value), the initial column widths are determined by the size of the column headers and the size of the field being displayed in the column (whichever is greater).

HeadFont, HeadLines Properties

Purpose   The HeadFont property determines which font is used to display text in the DBGrid header. The HeadLines property sets or returns the number of lines used in the display of the header. Table 60-4 lists the arguments of the HeadFont and HeadLines properties.

General Syntax

```
object.HeadLines [= Value]
object.HeadFont [= FontName]
```

Table 60-4 Arguments of the HeadFont and HeadLines properties

Argument	Description
object	The name in code of a DBGrid control
value	The number of lines to be used in the header
fontname	The name of an available Font object

Example Syntax

```
Sub SetHeader (grd As Control, FontName As String, Lines as Integer)
    'this routine takes a control (a grid) and two parameters and
    'sets the appearance of the header for the grid
    grd.HeadFont = FontName
    grd.HeadLines = Lines
End Sub
```

Description   The HeadFont and HeadLines properties determine how the DBGrid control header appears to the user when the grid is displayed on a form. The previous example shows how to create a single routine that sets the appearance of the header for a grid which may be passed to the routine. You might use this technique to give all the grids in an application a uniform appearance.

Use the HeadFont property to change the appearance of text that is not part of the header.

Comments   The default HeadFont is always set to bold where available. Also, the maximum number of lines that can be set in the HeadLines property is 10 (the default is 1). A setting of 0 in the HeadLines property removes the headings from the DBGrid control.

RECORDSELECTORS PROPERTY

Purpose   The RecordSelectors property can be set at either design or runtime to determine whether record selector objects are displayed along the DBGrid control. Record selectors are used to select (highlight) entire records (rows) of the DBGrid control. Table 60-5 lists the arguments of the RecordSelectors property.

General Syntax

```
object.RecordSelectors [= boolean%]
```

Table 60-5 Arguments of the RecordSelectors property

Argument	Description
object	The name in code of a DBGrid control
boolean%	True or False to indicate the presence of record selectors

Example Syntax

```
Private Sub chkRowSelectors_Click()
    'set the visibility of row selectors
    'based on the state of the check box
    DBGrid1.RecordSelectors = chkRowSelectors
End Sub
```

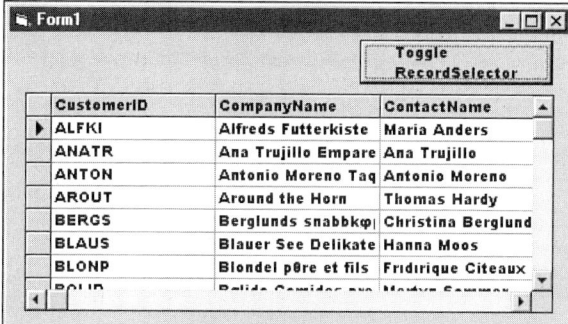

Figure 60-1   A DBGrid with record selectors

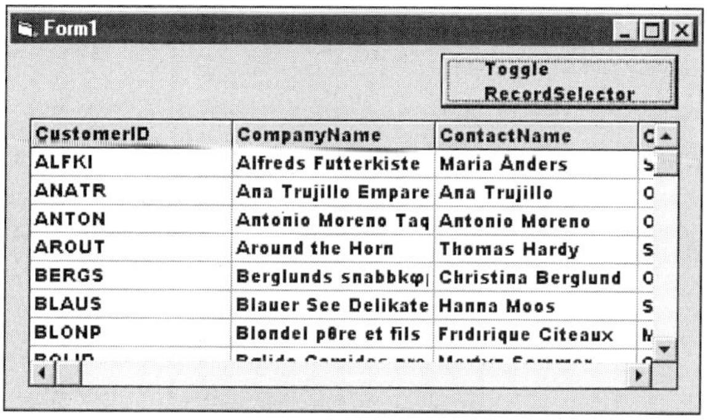

Figure 60-2   A DBGrid without record selectors

Description   If the RecordSelectors property is set to True, the record selectors are displayed along the left side of the grid. Record selectors are used to select (highlight) entire records (rows) of the DBGrid control. Figures 60-1 and 60-2 illustrate a grid with and without record selectors.

ROWDIVIDERSTYLE PROPERTY

Purpose   The RowDividerStyle property determines the appearance of the borders between the rows in the selected DBGrid control. Tables 60-6 and 60-7 list the arguments of the RowDividerStyle property and their possible values.

General Syntax

```
object.RowDividerStyle [= value]
```

Table 60-6 Arguments of the RowDividerStyle property

Argument	Description
object	The name in code of a DBGrid control
value	The integer specifying the border style

Table 60-7 Values of the RowDividerStyle property

Value	Constants	Meaning
0	dbgNoDividers	No divider
1	dbgBlackLine	Black line
2	dbgDarkGrayLine	Dark gray line (default)
3	dbgRaised	Raised
4	dbgInset	Inset
5	dbgUseForeColor	Drawn using the ForeColor property setting color
6	dbgLightGrayLine	Light gray line

Example Syntax

```
Private Sub MakeGrids3D ()
     'this gives all grids on a form raised dividers
     For j = 0 To Controls.Count - 1
          If typeof Controls(j) Is DBGrid Then
               Controls(j).RowDividerStyle = 3
          End If
     Next j
End Sub
```

Description

The RowDividerStyle property does not have any effect on dragging the border. Windows sets the colors if you set the value to raised (3) or inset (4). The value argument is an integer. The previous example shows how to set this property to the raised setting for all the grids on a specified form. This gives the grids a 3D appearance.

SCROLLBARS PROPERTY

Purpose

The ScrollBars property determines which scrollbars are visible for the DBGrid control. Tables 60-8 and 60-9 list the arguments of the ScrollBars property and their possible values.

General Syntax

```
object.ScrollBars [= value]
```

Table 60-8 Arguments of the ScrollBars property

Argument	Description
object	The name in code of a DBGrid control
value	The integer specifying the ScrollBars style

Table 60-9 Values of the ScrollBars property

Value	Constants	Meaning
0	dbgNone	No scrollbars (default)
1	dbgHorizontal	Horizontal only scrollbars
2	dbgVertical	Vertical only scrollbars
3	dbgBoth	Both scrollbars
4	dbgAutomatic	As needed scrollbars

Example Syntax

```
Private Sub AutoScrollBars(ctl as DBGrid)
      'this sets the scrollbars to automatically show if needed
      ctl.ScrollBars = 4
End Sub
```

Description   The default value is 0 and is automatic; this will show the scrollbars only if needed. All other settings force the scrollbars to always be displayed or hidden.

61

DBGRID BEHAVIOR

This chapter will cover the methods, properties, and events related to the DBGrid's behavior. The DBGrid is a powerful tool that can be used bound or unbound. Of all the controls in Visual Basic, the DBGrid fits the form of a table best. Databases are usually collections of data tables and queries (sometimes referred to as views). Both the application developer and the application user may want to inspect the contents of a view or table. Often you can do this most easily by presenting the data in a grid format. Grids are frequently used in spreadsheet applications to present financial or other numerical data. They are also a convenient means of viewing other tabular data, and are, for this reason, now commonly used in database applications. DBGrid lets you present data by populating the grid with the data records.

DBGrid Behavior Summary

Table 61-1 lists the methods, properties, and events of the DBGrid that are not related to its appearance. A detailed description of the non-standard methods, properties, and events follows.

Table 61-1 Methods, properties, and events of the DBGrid that are not directly related to appearance

Use or Set This...	Type	To Do This...
AfterColEdit	Event	Take action after column data has changed, but before it enters the data buffer
AfterColUpdate	Event	Trap changes in column values in the DBGrid
AfterDelete	Event	React to deletes in the DBGrid
AfterInsert	Event	React to inserts in the DBGrid
AfterUpdate	Event	React to changes in the DBGrid
AllowAddNew	Property	Determine if adding records to the DBGrid is allowed
AllowDelete	Property	Determine if deleting records from the DBGrid is allowed
AllowRowSizing	Property	Determine if the user can resize rows in the DBGrid
AllowSizing	Property	Determine if the user can resize columns in the DBGrid

continued on next page

continued from previous page

Use or Set This...	Type	To Do This...
AllowUpdate	Property	Determine whether updating data in the DBGrid is allowed
BeforeColEdit	Event	Take action before a user starts to edit a field in the DBGrid
BeforeColUpdate	Event	Take action before column data is changed in the DBGrid
BeforeDelete	Event	Take action before a delete from a DBGrid
BeforeInsert	Event	Take action before an insert in the DBGrid
BeforeUpdate	Event	Take action before a data update occurring in the DBGrid
Bookmark	Property	Flag a record in the Recordset for later retrieval
Change	Event	Indicate that the contents of a control have changed
Click	Event	Indicate that a mouse button is pressed over an object
ColContaining	Method	Determine the column containing a specified x coordinate
ColEdit	Event	Take action when a user edits a field
ColResize	Event	React to resizing of the columns in the DBGrid
Columns	Property	Access a collection of column objects
Container	Property	Set or return the controls container
DataMode	Property	Set or return whether the DBGrid works in bound or unbound mode
DataSource	Property	Identify the data control to be used for a bound control
DblClick	Event	Indicate that a mouse button is pressed twice rapidly over an object
DefaultValue	Property	Serves as a placeholder for a default value for a column
Drag	Method	Begin, end, or cancel a drag operation of an object
DragDrop	Event	Initiate an action when a dragged control is dropped onto another control
DragIcon	Property	Set or return the icon to be used for Drag operations
DragMode	Property	Set or return the type of drag mode available
DragOver	Event	Initiate an action when a dragged control is over a form or control
Enabled	Property	Enable or disable the control via a Boolean value
Error	Event	Read and handle external errors in the data control
GetBookmark	Method	Indicate a bookmark for a specific record in the DBGrid
GotFocus	Event	Indicate when the object receives the focus
HeadClick	Event	React to a click event on the column header of the DBGrid
Index	Property	Reference the instance in a control array
KeyDown	Event	Indicate when a key is pressed on the keyboard
KeyPress	Event	Indicate when a key is pressed on the keyboard
KeyUp	Event	Indicate when a key is released on the keyboard
LostFocus	Event	Indicate when a control loses the focus
Move	Method	Move an object to a specified location
MouseDown	Event	Indicate when a mouse button is pressed down
MouseMove	Event	Indicate when the mousepointer is moved over the control
MouseUp	Event	Indicate when the mouse button is released
Name	Property	Set or return the name referenced in code of the control
Negotiate	Property	Set or return a value that determines visibility of aligned control when toolbars are visible

Use or Set This...	Type	To Do This...
OnAddNew	Event	React to the user starting to add a new record
Rebind	Method	Refresh and reset the properties and data in a DBGrid
Refresh	Method	Update the objects in a collection to reflect the current database
RowBookmark	Method	Obtain a bookmark for a specified row (record) in the DBGrid
RowColChange	Event	React to a row or column change in a grid
RowContaining	Method	Determine the row containing a specified y coordinate
RowResize	Event	React to resizing of the rows in the DBGrid
RowTop	Method	Obtain the y coordinate at the top of a specified row
Scroll	Method	Scroll navigation about the DBGrid
SelBookmarks	Collection	Maintain a collection of bookmarks for selected records
SelChange	Event	React to changes in the item selection in a control
SelEndCol	Property	Set and retrieve the last column of a selected block of fields
SelEndRow	Property	Set and retrieve the last row of a selected block of fields
SelStartCol	Property	Set and retrieve the first column of a selected block of fields
SelStartRow	Property	Set and retrieve the first row of a selected block of fields
SetFocus	Method	Move the focus to a specified control or form
ShowWhatThis	Method	Display the help topic associated with the WhatsThisHelpID property
TabIndex	Property	Set or return the control's tab stop order
TabStop	Property	Set or return a value that determines whether control is a tab stop
Tag	Property	Identify a control or form with a unique value
ToolTipText	Property	Shows text when tool tips are activated for this control
UnboundAddData	Event	React when a user adds a row to an unbound DBGrid
UnboundDeleteRow	Event	React when a user deletes a row from an unbound DBGrid
UnboundReadData	Event	React when an unbound DBGrid needs data to display
UnboundWriteData	Event	React when an unbound DBGrid is ready to write a row of data
VisibleCols	Property	Return the number of visible columns
VisibleRows	Property	Return the number of visible rows
WhatsThisHelpID	Property	Set or return an associated Windows 95 pop-up help context
Zorder	Method	Place an object in front or back of other objects

AFTERCOLEDIT EVENT

Purpose   The AfterColEdit event notifies the application that the user has stopped editing a column in the DBGrid. Arguments for this event appear in Table 61-2.

General Syntax

```
Private Sub object_AfterColEdit([index As Integer,] colindex As Integer])
```

Table 61-2 Arguments for the AfterColEdit event

Argument	Description
object.	The name of the DBGrid in code
index	Indicates the element in an array of DBGrids
colIndex	Indicates the column being edited

Example Syntax

```
Private Sub DataGrid1_AfterColEdit (ColIndex As Integer)
     'user is done editing update visual indicator
     lblMode.Caption = "Ready"
End Select
```

Description   The AfterColEdit event is fired after the user has stopped editing the column. It differs from AfterColUpdate in that when AfterColEdit fires, the data has not moved to the grid buffer; the row still hasn't been updated.

AFTERCOLUPDATE EVENT

Purpose   The AfterColUpdate event gives the programmer the opportunity to perform needed operations immediately after an actual update event. Arguments for this event appear in Table 61-3.

General Syntax

```
Private Sub object_AfterColUpdate([index As Integer,] _
     colindex As Integer])
```

Table 61-3 Arguments for the AfterColUpdate event

Argument	Description
object	The name of the DBGrid in code
index	Indicates the element in an array of DBGrids
colIndex	Indicates the column being edited

Example Syntax

```
Private Sub DataGrid1_AfterColUpdate (ColIndex As Integer)

Select Case Colindex
            'if zip code is valid then the city
            'and state fields are automatically
            'filled in with the proper data
     Case 7 'zip code field
          ZipTable.Seek "=", Data1!ZipCode
          If Not ZipTable.Nomatch then
                Data1.Edit
                Data1.City = ZipTable.City
```

```
                    Data1.State = ZipTable.State
                    Data1.Update
              EndIf
        Case...
End Select
```

Description   The AfterColUpdate event is fired after an updated event to a cell has com-
                pleted. This event is useful for causing other events to happen as the result
                of certain types of edits. In the above example, the AfterColUpdate event is
                used to fill in the City and State fields of the current record after a user
                enters a valid Zip code.

AfterDelete, AfterInsert, AfterUpdate Events

Purpose   The AfterDelete, AfterInsert, and AfterUpdate events give you the opportu-
                nity to perform related operations immediately after the event. They do not,
                however, provide the means to cancel or otherwise recover from the event
                that triggered them. Arguments for these events appear in Table 61-4.

General Syntax

```
Sub object_AfterInsert([Index as Integer])
Sub object_AfterDelete([Index as Integer])
Sub object_AfterUpdate([Index as Integer])
```

Table 61-4 Arguments for the AfterDelete, AfterInsert, and AfterUpdate events

Argument	Meaning
object	The name of the DBGrid object in code
Index	The Index property (if the control is part of a control array)

Example Syntax

```
Private Sub DBGrid1_AfterInsert()
    Dim iCounter as Integer
    iCounter = Data1.Recordset.RecordCount
    Msgbox = "Following your insert you now have "& iCounter _
         & "records"
End Sub
```

Description   The AfterInsert, AfterDelete, and AfterUpdate events allow the application
                to easily track the addition, deletion, and updating of records using the
                DBGrid control. These events are not for validation, since they do not
                allow you to cancel the changes that are being made. However, you can
                use them to maintain counts of current records or to log which database
                user has added, deleted, or changed the records in question. The previous
                example uses the AfterInsert event to provide data for logging to a file that
                is used to track which users have made changes to the database.

Comments Data validation should be performed using the Validate event of the data control or using other events exposed by DBGrid.

ALLOWADDNEW, ALLOWDELETE, ALLOWUPDATE PROPERTIES

Purpose The AllowAddNew, AllowDelete, and AllowUpdate properties are set to True or False to indicate whether the user can add, delete, or update records in a DBGrid. They function independently of the data control's ReadOnly property. Arguments for these properties appear in Table 61-5.

General Syntax

```
object.AllowAddNew [= boolean%]
object.AllowDelete [= boolean%]
object.AllowUpdate [= boolean%]
```

Table 61-5 Arguments for the AllowAddNew, AllowDelete, and AllowUpdate properties

Argument	Description
object	The name of the DBGrid object in code
boolean%	True or False to allow add, delete, or update

Example Syntax

```
Private Sub chkAllowEditing_Click()
    'looks at the value of a check box and
    'sets the AllowUpdate property
    If chkAllowEditing then 'check the value of the check box
        DBGrid.AllowUpdate = True'if the box is checked allow editing
    Else
        DBGrid.AllowUpdate = False'if not, do not allow changes
    End If
End Sub
```

Description Corporations often need different users to have different levels of access to their data, based on security level. Individuals may be concerned about protecting their data against accidental loss. Along with the read/write restrictions available to the database itself, you can enhance the user's ability to control data access by using properties such as AllowUpdate to dictate who may change data and when.

Comments Note that AllowDelete and AllowAddNew apply to adding and deleting records, not data within records.

ALLOWROWSIZING, ALLOWSIZING PROPERTIES

Purpose The AllowRowSizing and AllowSizing properties let you control whether the user can change the size of the rows and columns in the DBGrid at runtime. Arguments for these properties appear in Table 61-6.

General Syntax

```
object.AllowRowSizing [= boolean%]
object.AllowSizing [= boolean%]
```

Table 61-6 Arguments for the AllowRowSizing and AllowSizing properties

Argument	Description
object	The name of the DBGrid object in code
boolean%	True or False to allow resizing of rows or columns

Example Syntax

```
Private Sub Form1_Load()
     'we will make the grid display only with fixed size rows
     DBGrid1.AllowUpdate = False
     DBGrid1.AllowRowSizing = False
     'however, we will allow the user to change the size of columns
     DBGrid.AllowSizing = True
End Sub
```

Description   Grids let the user customize the way in which data is presented. However, sometimes you may need to keep the grid unchanged to present data in the best possible way. You can set the AllowRowSizing property at design time or runtime to prevent the user from changing this aspect of the grid's appearance.

BeforeColEdit Event

Purpose   The BeforeColEdit event notifies the application that the user is about to start editing a column in the DBGrid. Arguments for this event appear in Table 61-7.

General Syntax

```
Private Sub object_BeforeColEdit([index As Integer,] _
     colindex As Integer, KeyAscii As Integer, Cancel As Integer)
```

Table 61-7 Arguments for the BeforeColEdit event

Argument	Description
object	The name of the DBGrid in code
index	Indicates the element in an array of DBGrids
colIndex	Indicates the column being edited
keyascii	The ASCII value of the first character typed
cancel	A place to return whether to cancel the edit

Example Syntax

```
Private Sub DataGrid1_BeforeColEdit (ColIndex As Integer _
    , KeyAscii As Integer, Cancel As Integer)
    If UserRight(ColIndex) = True Then
            'user is editing update visual indicator
            lblMode.Caption = "Editing"
    Else
            'user has no rights
            Cancel = True
    End If
End Select
```

Description   The BeforeColEdit event allows the application to respond before the user begins an update to a column. This event fires when the user presses the first key. The application can cancel the edit by setting the Cancel argument to True.

BeforeColUpdate Event

Purpose   The BeforeColUpdate event provides the programmer with the opportunity to perform operations immediately prior to the actual update event. Arguments for this event appear in Table 61-8.

General Syntax

```
Private Sub object.BeforeColUpdate([index as Integer,] _
    colindex As Integer, oldvalue As Variant, cancel As Integer)
```

Table 61-8 Arguments for the BeforeColUpdate event

Argument	Description
object	The name of the DBGrid object in code.
index	Specifies the element in an array of DBGrid objects.
colIndex	Specifies the column being updated.
oldvalue	A variant containing the column data as it was prior to the editing.
cancel	A Boolean expression that determines whether to proceed with the update.
	A setting of True causes the update to be canceled and the default setting of False allows the update to proceed.

Example Syntax

```
Private Sub DataGrid1.BeforeColUpdate (ColIndex As Integer _
    , OldValue As Variant, Cancel As Integer)
    'select validation rule according to column
    Select Case colIndex
        Case 1'SS Number
            'user defined function checks for valid SSI Number
            If not IsSSNumber(Datagrid1) Then
                MsgBox "Invalid Social Security Number"
                'prevent the update by setting Cancel to True
                Cancel = True
            End If
```

```
        Case ....
    End select
End Sub
```

Description   When you initiate an edit in a cell, the current data in that cell is moved to the copy buffer. When you have finished editing by tabbing out of the cell, pressing E, or setting focus outside the DBGrid, the BeforeColUpdate event is triggered. This event provides the programmer with the opportunity to perform any needed operations prior to actually overwriting the copy buffer with the edited data. These operations could include validation, data formatting, or user confirmation. In the example presented above, a Select Case structure is used to direct validation according to the column number being edited. It shows a call to a user-defined procedure for validation of a Social Security number if the column is 1. If the validation fails, then the user is warned that the SS number is invalid and the update is canceled. When canceled, the old data in the copy buffer is returned to the cell, and the focus is returned to the cell. If the update is not canceled, then the edited data in the cell is copied to the buffer and written to the database in the Update event.

BEFOREDELETE, BEFOREINSERT, BEFOREUPDATE EVENTS

Purpose   The BeforeDelete, BeforeInsert, and BeforeUpdate events occur before changes to the database to allow you to insert code that handles the database change. You can use these properties to validate and, if necessary, cancel the changes. Arguments for these events appear in Table 61-9.

General Syntax

```
Sub object_BeforeDelete([Index as Integer,] cancel as Integer)
Sub object_BeforeInsert([Index as Integer,] cancel as Integer)
Sub object_BeforeUpdate([Index as Integer,] cancel as Integer)
```

Table 61-9 Arguments for the BeforeDelete, BeforeInsert, and BeforeUpdate events

Argument	Description
object	The name of the DBGrid object in code
Index	The Index property of the control when it is part of a control array
Cancel	A parameter that can be set to cancel the operation

Example Syntax

```
Private Sub DBGrid_BeforeDelete(Cancel As Integer)
    'we wish to verify before deleting
    Dim iResponse As Integer
    iResponse = MsgBox("Are you sure you wish to delete?", vbYesNo)
    If iResponse = vbNo Then Cancel = True'abort the delete
End Sub
```

Description	You can use the BeforeUpdate, BeforeDelete, and BeforeInsert events to intercept the updating, deletion, or insertion of a record in the database. Canceling might be required when data validation has failed (to maintain data integrity) or to ensure that data is not accidentally changed. All of these events allow the cancel parameter to be changed to have the update to the data aborted.

COLCONTAINING, ROWCONTAINING METHODS

Purpose   The ColContaining and RowContaining methods return the column and row containing a specified x (horizontal) or y (vertical) coordinate. Arguments for these methods appear in Table 61-10.

General Syntax

```
object.ColContaining X
object.RowContaining Y
```

Table 61-10 Arguments for the ColContaining and RowContaining methods

Argument	Description
object	The name of the DBGrid object in code
X, Y	Single-precision numbers representing coordinates

Example Syntax

```
Private DBGrid1_DragDrop(Source As control, X As Single, Y As Single)
      Dim iCol As Integer
      Dim iRow As Integer
      iRow = DBGrid1.RowContaining Y 'determine the row dropped on
      iCol = DBGrid1.ColContaining X 'determine the column dropped on
      If Source Is Label Then 'verify the source type
            DBGrid1.Col = iCol
            DBGrid1.Row = iRow
            DBGrid.Text = Source.Caption 'place the caption on the grid
      End If
End Sub
```

Description   You will often want to know where the mouse is relative to the columns and rows on a grid. This information can be useful for selecting and for drag-and-drop operations. MouseDown, MouseUp, DragDrop, and various other events can provide the x and y values needed for the ColContaining and RowContaining methods to obtain column and row coordinates. The preceding example shows how to use the x and y values that are passed at the end of a drag-and-drop operation to place the caption of the drag source in the current cell of the grid. You could use DBGrid's DragOver event in conjunction with these values to highlight the current cell as an item is dragged across the grid.

ColEdit Event

Purpose The ColEdit event notifies the application that the user is editing a column in the DBGrid. Arguments for this event appear in Table 61-11.

General Syntax

```
Private Sub object_ColEdit([index As Integer,] colindex As Integer)
```

Table 61-11 Arguments for the ColEdit event

Argument	Description
object	The name of the DBGrid in code
index	Indicates the element in an array of DBGrids
collndex	Indicates the column being edited

Example Syntax

```
Private Sub DataGrid1_ColEdit (ColIndex As Integer)
    'user is editing update visual indicator
    lblMode.Caption = "Editing"
End Select
```

Description The ColEdit event allows the application to respond when the user is updating a column. This event fires when the application successfully gets past the BeforeColEdit event.

ColResize, RowResize Events

Purpose The ColResize and RowResize events are used to respond to and, if necessary, cancel the resizing of columns or rows on the DBGrid. The arguments for these events appear in Table 61-12.

General Syntax

```
Sub object_ColResize([Index As Integer,] colIndex As Integer _
    , cancel As Integer)
Sub object_RowResize([Index As Integer,] rowIndex As Integer _
    , cancel As Integer)
```

Table 61-12 Arguments for the ColResize and RowResize events

Argument	Description
object	The name of the DBGrid object in code
Index	The Index property in cases where the grid is a member of a control array
collndex, rowIndex	The Index number of the column or row being resized
cancel	An integer value that can be set to cancel the resize operation

Example Syntax

```
Private Sub DBGrid_ColResize(colIndex As Integer, Cancel As Integer)
     'we have decided to allow resizing of all rows except row 2
     If colIndex = 2 Then
          Cancel = True 'cancel the resize
     else
          'false is the default, nothing to do
     End If
End Sub
```

Description	The ColResize and RowResize events occur before the Repaint event is called after a column or row has been resized. From this event, your program code can either cancel the event by setting Cancel to True or alter the scope of the change through setting the Column.Width or Row.Height property to a specified value. If you wish for the Repaint event to occur even though you have canceled the resizing, you can call a Refresh event from this event procedure.

DataMode Property

Purpose	The DataMode property controls if the DBGrid works in bound or unbound mode. Arguments for this property appear in Table 61-13 and values in Table 61-14.

General Syntax

```
object.DataMode [= value]
```

Table 61-13 Arguments for the DataMode property

Argument	Description
object	The name of the DBGrid object in code
value	Value telling the control to work in bound or unbound mode

Table 61-14 Values for the value argument

Value	Constants	Meaning
0	dbgBound	The control is bound to a datasource.
1	dbgUnbound	The control is unbound and must be manually filled with data.

Example Syntax

```
Private Sub Unbind(ctl as Control)
     ctl.DataMode = 1
End Sub
```

Description	A DBGrid can work in two modes. It can be bound the traditional way to a Data control or you can fill it with data manually when it is in the unbound DataMode. In the unbound mode, you must use the UnboundAddData, UnboundDeleteRow, UnboundGetRelativeBookmark, UnboundReadData, and UnboundWriteData events to fill the control with the appropriate data and save it wherever you wish.

DEFAULTVALUE PROPERTY

Purpose   The DefaultValue property allows you to save or retrieve a default value for each column object. Arguments for this property appear in Table 61-15.

General Syntax

```
object.DefaultValue [= value]
```

Table 61-15 Arguments for the DefaultValue property

Argument	Description
object	A column object
value	The default value

Example Syntax

```
Private Sub SetDefaults()
    Dim i%
    For i% = 1 To DBGrid1.Columns.Count
        DBGrid1.Columns.Item(i%).DefaultValue = "0"
    Next i%
End Sub
```

Description   The DefaultValue property is typically used with the UnboundAddData event to supply columns the user did not. However, DefaultValue can also be used with a bound DBGrid and can be thought of as a Tag property for each column.

ERROR EVENT

Purpose   The data control's Error event lets you react to errors in reading data that are not caused by your code. It is not intended for trapping runtime errors in your code segments. Arguments for this event appear in Table 61-16 and values in Table 61-17.

General Syntax

```
Private Sub object_Error([Index As Integer,] dataerr As Integer _
    , Response As Integer)
```

Table 61-16 Arguments for the Error event

Argument	Description
object	The name of the DBGrid object in code
Index	The Index property of the data control in a control array
dataerr	The error number that has been generated
Response	The response you wish to return

Table 61-17 Values for the Error event

Value	Constants	Meaning
0	vbDataErrContinue	Continue hiding the error message
1	vbDataErrDisplay	(Default) Display the appropriate message

Example Syntax

```
Private Sub Data1_Error(dataerr As Integer, response As Integer)
      If dataerr = 3024'database file not found
            response = vbDataErrDisplay'display the error message
      End If
End Sub
```

Description   The Error event lets you respond to errors generated in the process of accessing or attempting to access data. Errors that are external to your code can be caused by a click on the data control's movement buttons, the data control automatically opening a database during the Form Load event, or a custom control attempting to use the Delete method. Use the Error event to handle these errors.

GetBookmark Method

Purpose   The GetBookmark method returns a string expression that represents a bookmark relative to the current row. Arguments for this method appear in Table 61-18.

General Syntax

```
bkmark = object.GetBookmark value
```

Table 61-18 Arguments for the GetBookmark method

Argument	Description
object	The name of the DBGrid object in code
bkmark	A string variable that receives the method's return value
value	A Long type numeric expression that represents the relative row position

Example Syntax

```
Private Function SampleData (Rate as Integer) As Double
     Dim accumilator As double
     Dim counter As Long
     Dim NextRow as String
     On Error Goto BadEnd
     Data1.Movefirst
     Do While Not Data1.EOF
          'loops through recordset moving
          'the number of rows specified by rate.
          counter = counter + 1
          accumilator = Data1.Recordset!Kilowatts
          NextRow DBGrid.GetBookmark Rate
          Data1.Bookmark = DNextRow
     Loop
     SampleData = Accumilator/Counter
     Exit Function
BadEnd:
End Function
```

Description   The GetBookmark method provides a way to move a specified number of rows forward or backward from the current row. The current row does not necessarily have to be visible in the Grid. The example above shows a function that moves through a recordset taking a sample every *n* number of records, where *n* is a number specified in the variable rate. It then divides the total by the number of iterations to gain an average reading. It uses the GetBookmark method to obtain a bookmark that is *n* number of rows from the current record.

HEADCLICK EVENT

Purpose   The HeadClick event allows the application to respond to the user clicking the mouse over a column header. Often this event is used to either highlight the column that has received the click or to initiate a sort of that column. Arguments for this event appear in Table 61-19.

General Syntax

```
Private Sub object_HeadClick([Index as Integer,] colIndex As Integer)
```

Table 61-19 Arguments for the HeadClick event

Argument	Description
object	The name of the DBGrid object in code
Index	The Index property if the DBGrid is part of a control array
colIndex	An integer representing the column on which the click occurred

Example Syntax

```
Private Sub DBGrid1_HeadClick(colIndex As Integer)
    'we will sort again based on a head click
    'the grid is already assigned to data1 which has
    'a sql recordsource
    Data1.RecordSource= "Select * from Customers Order By" _
        & Data1.Recordset.fields(colIndex).Name
    Data1.Refresh
    'we have not refreshed using the sort order of the clicked column
    'based on the field corresponding to column selected
End Sub
```

Description The HeadClick event occurs when a particular column header has received a click event. The application can trap the click and respond by sorting the Recordset or highlighting the column in question. The colIndex will be an integer in the range from 0 to the number of columns minus 1.

ONADDNEW EVENT

Purpose The OnAddNew event notifies the application that the user has started to add a new record. Arguments for this event appear in Table 61-20.

General Syntax

```
Private Sub object_OnAddNew([Index as Integer])
```

Table 61-20 Arguments for the OnAddNew event

Argument	Description
object	The name of the DBGrid object in code
Index	The Index property if the DBGrid is part of a control array

Example Syntax

```
Private Sub DBGrid1_OnAddNew()
    lblStatus.Caption = "Add Mode"
End Sub
```

Description The OnAddNew lets the application know the process of adding has started. The example shows an update to a status field.

REBIND METHOD

Purpose The Rebind method allows the DBGrid to be rebound to the data control. This sets its properties to those defaulted to by the underlying data control settings. The argument for this method appears in Table 61-21.

General Syntax

```
object.Rebind
```

Table 61-21 Argument for the Rebind method

Argument	Description
object	The name of the DBGrid object in code

Example Syntax

```
Private Sub cmndRefreshGrid_Click()
     'this routine responds to the Click event of a button that the
     'user can press to reset the grid to its original settings
     DBGrid1.Rebind
End Sub
```

Description As users navigate through the grid, they can resize and reposition columns and rows as they go. The original settings dictated by the data defaults are lost. The Rebind method lets the application reestablish these defaults and refresh the data in the grid. This is somewhat analogous to the Refill method for the DBList and DBCombo controls.

ROWBOOKMARK METHOD

Purpose The RowBookmark method returns a bookmark of a visible row relative to the first row of the DBGrid control. Arguments for this method appear in Table 61-22.

General Syntax

```
object.RowBookmark value
```

Table 61-22 Arguments for the RowBookmark method

Argument	Description
object	The name of the DBGrid object in code
value	An integer (0 to VisibleRows-1) indicating the desired row

Example Syntax

```
Dim iCount as integer
ReDim MyBookMarks(DBGrid.VisibleRows-1)
Data1.FindFirst MyCriteria
If not Data1.Recordset.NoMatch Then
        'sets the first element in array to
        'matching record's bookmark
        MyBookMarks(0) = Data1.Recordset.Bookmark
        'scrolls the DBGrid until first visible row
        'matches the bookmark of the matching record
        DBGrid.FirstRow = MyBookMarks(0)
        'gets the bookmarks of all the subsequently
        'visible rows in the DBGrid
        For iCount = 1 to DBGrid.VisibleRows-1
            'gets the bookmarks for all of the visible rows
            MyBookMarks(iCount) = DBGrid.RowBookmark(icount)
        Next
end if
```

Description   In the example above, the RowBookmark method is used to obtain all the visible row's bookmarks after finding a row that matches certain criteria. The RowBookmark method provides a means to programmatically select a visible row by its ordinal position from the first row. RowBookmark(0) will return the first row, and RowBookMark(2) will return the second row down from the first row if it is visible. If you attempt to get a bookmark for a row that is not visible, an invalid bookmark may be returned.

RowTop Method

Purpose   The RowTop method is used when the application requires the y (vertical) coordinate of a specified row. Arguments for this method appear in Table 61-23.

General Syntax

```
object.RowTop value
```

Table 61-23 Arguments for the RowTop method

Argument	Description
object	The name of the DBGrid object in code
value	An integer (0 to VisibleRows-1) indicating the desired row

Example Syntax

```
Private Sub FindTopOfCell (X As Single, Y As Single)
    TopOfCell = DataGrid1.RowTop DataGrid1.RowContaining(Y) _
+ Y - DataGrid1.RowHeight - /2
        'this routine gathers the information it needs from the grid to
```

```
        'calculate the top of a cell based on the top of a row
        'and the parameters passed (perhaps from a mouse click event)
End Sub
```

Description   This method returns a value based on the ScaleMode property of the container. Sometimes you want to find the coordinates of a chosen cell to perform an operation on that area of the screen (for example, a Windows Draw operation). When combined with the RowHeight, Left, and Width properties, the return value from this method can provide such a set of coordinates.

Scroll Method

Purpose   The Scroll method scrolls the DBGrid control either horizontally or vertically. This method does not support named arguments. It can perform vertical and horizontal scrolling in a single operation. Arguments for this method appear in Table 61-24.

General Syntax

```
object.Scroll colvalue, rowvalue
```

Table 61-24 Arguments for the Scroll method

Argument	Description
object	The name of the DBGrid object in code
colvalue	Specifies the desired column in the control
rowvalue	Specifies the desired row in the control

Example Syntax

```
Private StepGrid(grd As DBGrid)
    'this routine takes the current cell in a stepping motion each time
    'it is called for the grid that is passed
    grd.Scroll 1 1
End Sub
```

Description   Note that the arguments required by the Scroll method are relative positions. They are not column and row Index values in the row. Thus,

```
Name.Scroll -1 -1
```

causes the DBGrid to scroll up one row and left one column. Values that are out of the allowable range do not cause an error. The grid merely scrolls as far as possible and then stops.

SELBOOKMARKS PROPERTY AND COLLECTION

Purpose   The SelBookmarks property provides programmatic access to the
                    SelBookmarks collection of the DBGrid. The SelBookmarks collection con-
                    tains a bookmark for each row that is currently selected in the DBGrid
                    control. The argument for this property appears in Table 61-25.

General Syntax

```
object.SelBookmarks , collection=object.selBookMarks
```

Table 61-25 Argument for the SelBookmarks property

Argument	Description
object	The name of the DBGrid object in code

Example Syntax

```
Dim DeadRows as Collection
 'set deadRows to reference the SelBookmarks collection
DeadRows = DBGrid1.SelBookmarks
 'delete all the selected rows
Do while Deadrows.Count <> 0
     Data1.Recordset.Bookmark = DeadRows(0)
     Data1.Delete
Loop
```

Description   The SelBookmarks collection gives you the ability to reference selected
                    rows in a DBGrid control as a group. In the example above, the
                    SelBookmarks collection is used to delete a group of selected rows from
                    the Recordset. As a collection, you can use the methods associated with
                    collections such as Count, Append, and Remove methods. You may scroll
                    the DBGrid to selected rows by setting the FirstRow property to a book-
                    mark contained in the SelBookmarks collection. You can also select and
                    deselect rows on the DBGrid by appending and removing bookmarks to
                    and from the collection. The DBGrid will reflect these changes in selected
                    rows as you do them. To determine the number of rows selected, the
                    Count property of the collection is used.

SELENDCOL, SELENDROW, SELSTARTCOL, SELSTARTROW PROPERTIES

Purpose   The SelEndCol, SelEndRow, SelStartCol, and SelStartRow properties
                    expose the dimensions of the selected block of fields. The application can
                    change or read these properties. The arguments for these properties appear
                    in Table 61-26.

General Syntax

```
object.SelEndColumn [= value]
object.SelEndRow [= value]
object.SelStartCol [= value]
object.SelStartRow [= value]
```

Table 61-26 Arguments for the SelEndCol, SelEndRow, SelStartCol, and SelStartRow properties

Argument	Description
object	The name of the DBGrid object in code
value	The new column or row number

Example Syntax

```
Private Sub HighlightVisibleColumns()
    DBGrid1.SelStartCol = DBGrid1.LeftCol
    DBGrid1.SelEndCol = DBGrid1.LeftCol + DBGrid1.VisibleCols
End Sub
```

Description The example above highlights all the visible columns on the screen. These properties are handy for those Select All menu items.

UNBOUNDADDDATA EVENT

Purpose The UnboundAddData event notifies the application when a user has added a new record to a unbound DBGrid. The arguments for this event appear in Table 61-27.

General Syntax

```
Private Sub object_UnboundAddData([Index as Integer,] ByVal RowBuf _
    As RowBuffer, NewRowBookmark As Variant)
```

Table 61-27 Arguments for the UnboundAddData event

Argument	Description
object	The name of the DBGrid object in code
Index	The Index property if the DBGrid is part of a control array
RowBuf	The new row
NewRowBookmark	A bookmark to the row where you save the data

Example Syntax

```
Private Sub DBGrid1_UnboundAddData([Index as Integer,] _
    ByVal RowBuf As RowBuffer, NewRowBookmark As Variant)
    mLastKey& = mLastKey& + 1
    'set the bookmark to the key of the new object
```

continued on next page

continued from previous page

```
        NewRowBookmark = mLastKey&
        'add the object to my collection
        mMyCollection.Add RowBuf.Value(0, 0), CStr(mLastKey&)
End Sub
```

Description In the above event, we take the first column of the new row and stick it in a collection. The sub then returns the key to that collection as the NewRowBookmark.

UNBOUNDDELETEROW EVENT

Purpose The UnboundDeleteRow event notifies the application that the user has deleted a row in an unbound DBGrid control. The arguments for this event appear in Table 61-28.

General Syntax

```
Private Sub object_UnboundDeleteRow([Index as Integer,] _
    Bookmark As Variant)
```

Table 61-28 Arguments for the UnboundDeleteRow event

Argument	Description
object	The name of the DBGrid object in code
Index	The Index property if the DBGrid is part of a control array
Bookmark	A bookmark to the record to be deleted

Example Syntax

```
Private Sub DBGrid1_UnboundDeleteRow(Bookmark As Variant)
        mMyCollection.Remove CStr(Bookmark)
End Sub
```

Description The example above removes the record specified by the bookmark from the collection.

UNBOUNDREADDATA EVENT

Purpose The UnboundReadData event notifies the application that the DBGrid needs some data to display. Arguments for this event appear in Table 61-29.

General Syntax

```
Private Sub object_UnboundReadData([Index as Integer,] ByVal RowBuf _
As RowBuffer, StartLocation As Variant, ByVal ReadPriorRows As Boolean)
```

Table 61-29 Arguments for the UnboundReadData event

Argument	Description
object	The name of the DBGrid object in code
Index	The Index property if the DBGrid is part of a control array
RowBuf	The rows of data to be returned
StartLocation	From what bookmark does the request start; if Null, start from beginning or end
ReadPriorRows	If True, then return the records in reverse order

Example Syntax

```
Private Sub DBGrid1_UnboundReadData(ByVal RowBuf As RowBuffer, _
    StartLocation As Variant, ByVal ReadPriorRows As Boolean)
    Dim Key&, Row%, RowTally%, Step%
    Step% = IIf(ReadPriorRows, -1, 1)
    'if start is null then start from
    'beginning or end depending on direction
    If IsNull(StartLocation) Then
        If ReadPriorRows Then
            Key& = RowBuf.RowCount
        Else
            Key& = 1
        End If
    Else
        Key& = StartLocation
    End If
    For Row% = 0 To RowBuf.RowCount - 1
        'if we go past our data set then exit
        If Key& <= 0 Or Key& > mLastKey& Then
            Exit For
        End If
        'fill the buffer
        RowBuf.Value(Row%, 0) = mMyCollection.Item(CStr(Key&))
        'set the bookmark, just like in add
        RowBuf.Bookmark(Row%) = Key&
        'increment the key
        Key& = Key& + Step%
        RowTally% = RowTally% + 1
    Next Row%
    'return how many rows we read
    RowBuf.RowCount = RowTally%
End Sub
```

Description   The UnboundReadData event is called when the DBGrid wants some data
to display. It provides a RowBuffer to return the rows in and passes some
data to tell the application which rows and in what order it wants them. In
the example above, the Sub steps through the mMyCollection collection to
fill the RowBuf.

UNBOUNDWRITEDATA EVENT

Purpose   The UnboundWriteData event notifies the application when the DBGrid has an entire record to replace an existing one. Arguments for this event appear in Table 61-30.

General Syntax

```
Private Sub DBGrid1_UnboundWriteData([Index as Integer,] ByVal RowBuf _
As MSDBGrid.RowBuffer, WriteLocation As Variant)
```

Table 61-30 Arguments for the UnboundWriteData event

Argument	Description
object	The name of the DBGrid object in code
Index	The Index property if the DBGrid is part of a control array
RowBuf	The modified row
WriteLocation	The bookmark of the row to be replaced

Example Syntax

```
Private Sub DBGrid1_UnboundWriteData(ByVal RowBuf As MSDBGrid.RowBuffer _
    , WriteLocation As Variant)
    mMyCollection.Remove CStr(WriteLocation)
    mMyCollection.Add RowBuf.Value(0, 0), CStr(WriteLocation)
End Sub
```

Description   This event fires when the user replaces an existing row with new data. In the example above, the sub removes the previous entry from the collection, then adds the new value with the same key.

VISIBLECOLS PROPERTY

Purpose   The VisibleCols property provides read-only access at runtime to the number of visible columns in the DBGrid control. The argument for this property appears in Table 61-31.

General Syntax

```
object.VisibleCols
```

Table 61-31 Argument for the VisibleCols property

Argument	Description
object	The name of the DBGrid object in code

Example Syntax

```
Private Sub FindVisibleColumn(HeaderCaption$)
    Dim i%
    For i% = DBGrid1.LeftCol To DBGrid1.LeftCol + DBGrid1.VisibleCols
        If DBGrid1.Columns.Item(i%).Caption = HeaderCaption$ Then
            DBGrid1.Col = i%
            Exit For
        End If
    Next i%
    DBGrid1.SetFocusDescription
End Sub
```

Description   The example above steps through the visible columns looking for a particular column. When it finds the column it is looking for, it changes the Col property to the appropriate value and sets the focus to the DBGrid control.

VISIBLEROWS PROPERTY

Purpose   The VisibleRows property provides read-only access at runtime to the number of visible rows in the DBGrid control. The argument for this property appears in Table 61-32.

General Syntax

```
object.VisibleRows
```

Table 61-32 Argument for the VisibleRows property

Argument	Description
object	The name of the DBGrid object in code

Example Syntax

```
For I% = 0 to DBGrid1.VisibleRows - 1
    PrefetchData(DBGrid1.TopRow + I%)
Next I%
```

Description   The VisibleRows property returns the number of rows visible on the control. The example above uses the number of visible rows to call the PrefetchData Sub.

62

BEGINNING SQL

SQL is a programming language that has evolved from an earlier language called Sequel. Modern SQL has become a very powerful industry standard database programming language. Microsoft Access utilizes SQL as its standard programming language for its Jet Database engine, and it is used by Visual Basic to manipulate and modify the Jet 3.5 database. The SQL used by Access and Visual Basic is a variation on the ANSI standard, as are most other implementations. The differences between Access SQL and most other implementations are very minor and if you have any experience with MS SQL Server, Sybase, Oracle, or any of the other major relational database engines, Access SQL should have a very small to non-existent learning curve.

Access comes with a complete set of SQL functionality that includes a complete Data Definition Language (DDL) and Data Manipulation Language (DML). With Visual Basic 5.0, you will be able to create and use SQL statements within your program as well as use stored queries within the Jet database itself. You will also be able to create queries and store them in the database for use by your own programs, and by others. The queries you build, in turn, create the recordsets (filtered, sorted subsets of the database) that determine which records will be updated or otherwise processed.

The Different Types of SQL

Queries fall into two groups. These two groups are created using DDL and DML. The DDL queries define or alter the structure of the database; the DML queries act directly upon the data contained in the database. Both types have common components such as commands, clauses, operators, and aggregate functions. In MS Access, the DDL type of queries include one of three commands: CREATE, DROP, and ALTER. The DML queries include the SELECT, INSERT, UPDATE, and DELETE commands. Queries can be further classified as Join, Union, Parameter, and other types depending on their structures and uses.

The basic structure of a SQL query has three parts:

■ Parameter declaration: In the case of a Parameter query, this part is used to supply the name and type of the parameter.

■ Manipulative statement: The manipulative statement defines the action that the query is to perform upon the database.

■ Option declaration: With Owner option, gives the user owner permissions in a secure environment.

DDL Queries

DDL queries are built using a number of commands that can create, change, or remove structure elements from the database. The navigational methods provided directly by Visual Basic 4.0 also provide this functionality, but in cases where your database design includes the regular creation and destruction of temporary tables, QueryDefs that include DDL queries could prove to be much faster, and easier to maintain in this type of situation. Table 62-1 lists the commands of the DDL query.

Table 62-1 Commands of the DDL query

Command	Description
ALTER TABLE	Used to alter the structure of an existing table
CREATE TABLE	Used to create tables in an existing database
CREATE INDEX	Used to create indexes for existing tables
DROP TABLE	Used to remove a table from a database
DROP INDEX	Used to remove an index to an existing table

The DDL queries are particular to Access databases and cannot be used with external databases. DDL queries do not return any records and therefore are used only with the Execute method of a database or QueryDef object.

CREATE Queries As mentioned earlier, your application might need to create temporary tables for certain types of processing, then need to destroy them when finished. The following would create such a table:

```
SQL$ = "CREATE TABLE [Sql Books] ([Title] TEXT (255)," _
    + "[Publisher] TEXT (50),[Author] TEXT (50))"
```

This query would create a table in the specified database with the name, "Sql Books", with three text fields that have lengths of 255, 50, and 50, respectively. If you've not noticed, we are using fields that correspond to the ubiquitous BIBLIO.MDB database. As declared above, this table represents a denormalization of three existing fields in the BIBLIO.MDB database. In very large databases where the data is contained in large normalized tables, it is sometimes very useful to create a denormalized table as shown above so that the required information from these diverse tables can be quickly accessed.

ALTER Queries   Continuing with this example, we may want to add another field such as the ISBN number of the books in question. To add additional fields to an existing table, the query would look like this:

```
SQL$ = "ALTER TABLE [Sql Books] ADD COLUMN [ISBN] Text(20)"
```

The ALTER TABLE command provides the capability to alter the structure of any native Jet table. The table described so far is still lacking an index. Using the ALTER TABLE command, you can create an index on the required field that you intend to index. In the following example, a Primary key based on the "Title" field will be created.

```
SQL$ = "ALTER TABLE [Sql Books] ADD CONSTRAINT TitleIndex" _
     + " PRIMARY (Title)"
DDL in a QueryDef
```

All three of the above examples are very simple uses of the concepts they embody. Tables can be created with multiple fields, complex indexes, and relationships. Once these are created, you can populate them with data using the DML queries or the navigational methods. If, as suggested, you were to use these queries to repeatedly create temporary tables that would be destroyed after use, you would probably want to store these queries into a QueryDefs collection.

```
Dim SQL$
Dim MyWS As Workspace
Dim MyDB As Database
Dim MYQD As QueryDef
SQL$ = "CREATE TABLE [Sql Books] ([Publisher] TEXT (50), " _
     + "[Author] TEXT (50), [ISBN] TEXT (20), [Title] TEXT (255) " _
     + "CONSTRAINT TitleIndex PRIMARY)"            'Query includes
Set MyWS = WorkSpaces(0)                           'all of the above
Set MyDB = MyWS.OpenDatabase("BIBLIO.MDB")         'definitions.
Set MyQD = MyDB.CreateQueryDef("SQL BookS")        'Creates QueryDef
MyQD.SQL = SQL$                                     'named "SQL BOOKS"
```

The above code creates a QueryDef called "SQL Books" and assigns a query string that creates a table of the same name. It has all the features of the previous three DDL Query examples. Now, to create this temporary table, you just need to use the Execute method of the Database object:

```
MyDB.Execute MyQD
```

That's it! A very simple line of code creates the table, and usually does so quicker than if it were done building and executing the query entirely from Visual Basic.

DROP Queries   Continuing with the temporary tables example, let's say that your application is finished with this table and no longer needs it. The removal of this table using a DDL type of query is very simple:

```
MyDB.Execute "DROP TABLE [SQL Books]"
```

This example shows how easy it is to remove a table from the database. If the table is part of a relationship in your database, the table deletion will fail. You must first drop the relationship(s) before you can drop the table. The examples shown here are only a fraction of the DDL query capabilities. Being able to create and destroy tables through queries and through stored QueryDefs allows the development of very sophisticated applications especially in the Decision Support applications field.

DML Queries

DML queries provide the means to retrieve recordsets, update data in those recordsets, and to Add or Delete records in the underlying tables. There are a number of commands that comprise the DML queries, enumerated in Table 62-2.

Table 62-2 Commands of the DML queries

Command	Description
SELECT	Creates a recordset from one or more tables that satisfy specific criteria
INSERT	Transfers a batch of data into the database
UPDATE	Changes the data values of a particular set of records
DELETE	Deletes records from the database

SELECT Queries

The SELECT query is perhaps the most used query type of all the DML queries. Your application would use the SELECT query to create recordsets based on one or more tables that met a particular criteria. Your application can then manipulate these recordsets using the Data Access Objects properties and methods such as displaying, adding, editing, and deleting records as required. To retrieve records from a table and put them into a recordset, a SELECT query would look like this:

```
SQL$ = "SELECT * FROM [Titles] WHERE [PubID] = 3"
```

Notice the asterisk after the SELECT command. This is Access's equivalent of the ALL qualifier in ANSI standard SQL. The rest of the query is easy to understand. This query would return all the fields in the Titles table that were published by the publisher whose ID equaled 3. SELECT queries always return recordsets and, by themselves, never modify data. SELECT queries can be used in QueryDefs, as recordsource properties of data controls, and as the argument of the OpenRecordset method. The general syntax of a SELECT query has the following parts:

```
SELECT (field list) FROM (table names[IN (database name] _
[WHERE (search conditions)] [GROUP BY (field list)] _
[ORDER BY (field list)][WITH OWNERACCESS OPTION] FROM. . .IN
```

Don't let this intimidate you. A careful study of it will reveal how English-like the syntax is. The SELECT statement will always have the FROM clause indicating either the tables or the tables that will supply the records. If, in your field list, you have two fields with the same name from different tables, precede the field with the table name with the dot between them.

```
SELECT Mytable.Names, YourTable.Names FROM Mytable, YourTable...........
```

The IN part of the FROM clause is for specifying a table in another database that Access can attach to. The syntax for this would be

```
SELECT * FROM YourTable IN 'C:\MDBFILES\YOURDATA.MDB'
WHERE
```

The Where clause is used to specify the criteria for selecting the records to be included in the resulting recordset. If no Where clause is used, then all the records in the table(s) will be returned. The criteria requirements in the Where clause are very flexible:

```
....WHERE MyType = 'Credit'       'exact match.  Can also use >, >=, <, <=
....WHERE MyDate = #01/01/95#        'Exact Date match
....WHERE MYType LIKE 'J*?'`         'Pattern matching
....WHERE Mytype = 1 AND YourType = 2      'Logical operators
....WHERE MyType BETWEEN 1 and 50          'Range of values
```

You can use up to 40 expressions linked by logical operators in your Where clause. When using strings as criteria, you must wrap them in single or double quotes as in the above examples. Dates require that you wrap them in the "#" character. Pattern matching with the LIKE operator can provide a very flexible method of locating specific data. Table 62-3 illustrates the various search patterns:

Table 62-3 Pattern matching with the LIKE predicate

Symbol	Description
*	Matches any series of characters or no characters at all
?	Matches any single character
#	Matches any single digit (0-9)
[Charlist]	Matches any single character in list: [ABFG] will match A, B, F, or G
[!Charlist]	Matches any single character that is not in list: [!ABFG] will match all except A, B, F, or G
[CharRange]	Matches any single character that is within range: [A-G] will match from A to G
[!CharRange]	Matches any single character that is not within range: [B-G] will match A and all characters after G

The pattern matching summarized in Table 62-3 is an extremely flexible tool for searching data. The following examples show different ways to use them.

```
"87*"        'will find any string that begins with 87
"*87"        'will find any string that ends with 87
"87???"      'will find any 5 character string that begin with 87
871##        'will find any number from 87100 to 87199
```

continued on next page

continued from previous page

```
"SM[EIY]TH"   'Will find 'SMETH','SMITH' or 'SMYTH'
"DR[!U]G      'Will match all combinations except DRUG.
              'Matches DRAG, DREG, DRZG, etc
"P[A-C]####"  'Will match PA0000-PA9999,PB0000-PB9999,PC0000-PC9999
"P{!A-C]"'####"'Will match all but the PA through PC series: PD0000-PZ9999
```

The one caveat with the LIKE predicate is that it is much slower than most other types of searches, especially if you use the asterisk as the leading character as in the second example above. But in most cases the speed trade-off is worth the flexibility.

GROUP BY   The optional GROUP BY clause combines records with identical values in the specified field list into a single record. If you include SQL aggregate functions such as Sum or Count, then a summary value is created for each group. Null values are grouped, but no summaries are provided for null groups.

```
SELECT Sum(Transaction) as Mytotal FROM Accounts GROUP BY Type
```

This would return a set of summary records that were summarized by the value of the field Type. If one value for Type was "Credits", then MyTotal would contain a total of all Transaction values that were "Credits". If there was a Type value of "Debits", then there would also be a summary for "Debits".

HAVING   The HAVING clause would further modify the available recordsets after the GROUP BY clause using the same search criteria that would be used in a Where clause.

```
SELECT Sum(Transaction) as Mytotal FROM Accounts GROUP BY Type _
    HAVING [Trans Date] = #01/01/95#
```

This time the summaries of the Group clause will contain only records whose [Trans Date] is equal to the specified date. The HAVING clause is relevant only to the GROUP BY clause.

ORDER BY   The ORDER BY clause determines the sort order of the records returned by the query. You specify the field or fields that the recordset should be ordered by and whether the sort should be ascending or descending. The default is ascending if you do not specify it.

```
SELECT * FROM [Mytable] WHERE [Last Name] LIKE 'J*' ORDER BY [Last Name]
```

This query would return all the last names that begin with the letter *J* and sort them in ascending alphabetical order. You can specify several fields to sort by with the first field being the initial sort field.

```
SELECT * FROM [Mytable] WHERE [Last Name] LIKE 'J*' _
    ORDER BY [Last Name], [First Name]
```

The same query would now be sorted by last names, then by first names. The ORDER BY clause is usually the last statement in a query. The ORDER BY clause has a predicate that modifies even further the output of the query. The use of the Top predicate will allow you to select the top number of records you specify.

```
SELECT TOP 50 * FROM  [Mytable] WHERE [Last Name] LIKE 'J*' _
     ORDER BY [Income]
```

This will return the top 50 earners in this table ordered by the Income field. If you wanted to select by a percentage rather than a fixed number, you could modify the TOP predicate with the PERCENT keyword.

```
SELECT TOP 10 PERCENT * FROM  [Mytable] WHERE [Last Name] LIKE 'J*' _

     ORDER BY [Income]
```

Now the query will return the top 10 percent of the earners ordered by income.

INTO This clause is used to create a duplicate table in the database using an existing table as both a pattern for the fields and as a source of data. This is a variation on the SELECT query:

```
SELECT * INTO [New Table] FROM [Old Table] WHERE [Field1] > 100
```

All the records that meet this criteria will be written to the New Table table as it is created. Uses for this type of query include archival copies, backup copies, and files for export to another machine.

WITH OWNERACCESS OPTION When working in a multiuser environment that is using a secure work group, the WITH OWNERACCESS OPTION will allow a user without access permission to view the restricted data in a query without allowing actual access to the underlying tables.

DELETE Queries A DELETE query removes records from one or more tables that meet the specified criteria in a Where clause. This is very useful for batch deletions from a database. When deleting multiple tables in one query, and one of those tables contains a primary key in a relationship, the query will fail.

```
DELETE * FROM [Accounts] WHERE [Date] < #01/01/95
```

This would delete all records whose date preceded January 1, 1995. If you intend to delete an entire table including the table definitions, you would probably be better off using the DROP TABLE query.

INSERT INTO The INSERT INTO statement will add records to a table or create an append query. The following syntax will insert data from a transaction table into a general ledger table:

```
INSERT INTO [GENLED].* SELECT [TRANSACT].* FROM [TRANSACT]
```

This query would insert all the records from the Transact table into the GenLed table. This type of query is often used to transport transactional data into main data tables. If you are appending records into a table with a counter field, do not include the counter field if you want Access to maintain the counter value. If, instead, you wish to maintain the source data"s counter, then include it.

UPDATE Queries

In many circumstances you will want to do a batch update of new values for specified fields. The UPDATE query fills this need. You can specify the records to be updated using the Where clause.

```
UPDATE [INVENTORY] SET [LIST PRICE] = [LIST PRICE] * 1.05, _
[DISCOUNT PRICE] = [DISCOUNT PRICE] * 1.05 _
WHERE [VENDOR] = 'VAPOR WARE INC'
```

This query would update the list and discount prices of all items that were supplied by the specified company. The UPDATE query will not return a result set. If you need to know how many records are affected by an UPDATE query, then you should run a SELECT query with the same criteria and take a record count.

Complex Queries

The Jet 2.5 database engine is capable of complex queries such as Subqueries, Joins, Crosstabs, and Unions. These queries allow a Visual Basic application to take full advantage of modern relational database theory. The Help file and documentation supplied by Visual Basic 4.0 include several examples of these types of queries. Also, in the BIBLIO.MDB database supplied with Visual Basic, there is a list of publications that go into SQL language in a much greater depth than the scope of this book allows.

When building your queries, you should consider the following suggestions to ensure the quickest and most efficient execution of your queries

- Limit the fields returned in a SELECT query to only those you need

- Use the ORDER BY keyword on indexed fields

- Avoid using the "*" as the leading character in pattern matching criteria

- Structure your queries to return the smallest recordset possible that meets your needs

- When possible, store your queries as QueryDefs in the database

When the DBEngine builds recordsets based on queries, it uses existing indexes to order and structure the recordset. The DBEngine utilizes Rushmore technology whenever it can. How you build your table indexes can greatly affect the time it takes for the DBEngine to build the recordset depending on how well you adhere to the requirements for Rushmore. Once the Recordset is built, the table indexes are no longer relevant. The Dynaset-Type recordset uses its own internal index system for searches within the recordset.

SQL Summary

The following reference is a compendium of the most commonly used SQL components with examples of how to use them. This is not an exhaustive reference, but it will give you a good start on understanding and using these very powerful tools in your applications. Table 62-4 summarizes the SQL commands available; detailed descriptions follow.

Table 62-4 SQL commands and functions

Use This...	Type	To Do This...
ALTER TABLE	Query	Add columns to a table
Avg	Aggregate Function	Average values in a column
CONSTRAINT	Clause	Create indexes on a table
Count	Aggregate Function	Count records in a result set
CREATE	Query	Create an index or table
DELETE	Statement	Delete records from a table
DROP	Query	Delete an index or table
FROM	Clause	Specify the tables in a SELECT query
GROUP BY	Clause	Separate records in a SELECT query into groups
HAVING	Clause	Place restrictions on groups specified in the GROUP_BY clause
INSERT INTO	Statement	Append records to a table
Max	Aggregate Function	Return the maximum value for a column
Min	Aggregate Function	Return the minimum value for a column
ORDER BY	Clause	Specify an order for the results of a SELECT statement
SELECT	Statement	Query data from the database
Sum	Aggregate Function	Sum the values in a column
UPDATE	Statement	Change records

ALTER TABLE QUERY

Purpose The ALTER TABLE query is used to change the components of an existing table, such as by adding a new field. Table 62-5 lists the arguments for the ALTER TABLE query.

General Syntax

```
ALTER TABLE tablename ADD|DROP item item information
```

Table 62-5 Arguments for the ALTER TABLE query

Argument	Description
tablename	Is the unique name of the table to be altered
ADD or DROP	Action to be taken
item	Identifies what is specifically being altered
iteminformation	Required information for the specified item

Example Syntax

```
SQL$ = "ALTER TABLE [Sql Books] ADD COLUMN [ISBN] Text(20)"
SQL$ = "ALTER TABLE [Sql Books] ADD CONSTRAINT TitleIndex" _
     + " PRIMARY (Title)"
```

Continuing with the example table used in the CREATE TABLE example, we may want to add another field such as the ISBN number of the books in question. To add additional fields to an existing table, the query would look like the first example provided above. The ALTER TABLE command provides the capability to alter the structure of any native Jet table. The table described so far is still lacking an index. Using the same ALTER TABLE command, you can create an index on the required field that you intend to index. In the second example, a Primary key based on the "Title" field will be created.

AVG AGGREGATE FUNCTION

Purpose   The Avg function is used to calculate the mean of a set of values contained in a specified field. Table 62-6 lists the arguments for the Avg aggregate function.

General Syntax

```
Avg(expression) AS resultfield
```

Table 62-6 Arguments for the Avg aggregate function

Argument	Description
expression	String expression identifying the field that contains the data to be averaged
resultfield	Placeholder for the result

Example Syntax

```
Dim MySQL As String
Dim MyRS As Recordset
MySQL = "SELECT Avg(Net Due) AS [Big Average] FROM Invoices"
     + " WHERE [Net Due] > 100"
```

```
Set MyRS = MyDatabase.OpenRecordset(MySQL)
MsgBox = "The average value of Invoices over $100.00 is $" _
      & MyRS.[Big Average]
```

Description The Avg function provides the mean of the selected fields by using the sum of the values divided by the number of values. Null values are not included in the count. The Avg can be used in a query expression and in the SQL property of a QueryDef object.

CONSTRAINT CLAUSE

See also CREATE, DROP, PRIMARY KEY, UNIQUE, FOREIGN KEY

Purpose The CONSTRAINT clause allows you to create or delete indexes to a table. Table 62-7 lists the arguments for the CONSTRAINT clause.

General Syntax
```
CONSTRAINT name [PRIMARY KEY|UNIQUE|REFERENCES _
foreigntable[(foreinfield1, foreignfield2..)]
```

Table 62-7 Arguments for the CONSTRAINT clause

Argument	Description
name	String that uniquely identifies the index
foreigntable	Name of the table containing the field or fields specified by foreign field

Example Syntax
```
SQL$ = "ALTER TABLE [Sql Books] ADD CONSTRAINT TitleIndex" _
      + " PRIMARY (Title)"
```

Description Using CONSTRAINT you can create indexes as needed through the DDL queries. These indexes can be Primary, Unique, or Foreign Key indexes. With Foreign Key indexes, you are establishing relationships between two tables. You can also remove indexes using the CONSTRAINT clause.

COUNT AGGREGATE FUNCTION

Purpose The Count function is used to return the number of records in a SELECT type query. Table 62-8 lists the arguments for the Count aggregate function.

General Syntax
```
Count(expression) AS tempname
```

Table 62-8 Arguments for the Count aggregate function

Argument	Description
expression	String expression identifying the field being counted or an expression that performs a calculation using the data in a field
tempname	Designated placeholder for the count

Example Syntax

```
Dim MySQL as string
Dim MyRS as Recordset
MySQL = "SELECT COUNT(*) AS [Big Invoices] From Invoices" _
    + " WHERE [Net Due] >100"
MyRS = MYDatabase.OpenRecordset(MySQL)
MsgBox "There Are " & MyRS.[Big Invoices] & "Over $100.00"
```

Description	In the above example, Count is used to return the number of invoices over a certain amount. If you use a field name as the expression in Count, then only those records with a non-Null value will be counted. Using the asterisk instead of a field name is much faster in counting the records than by specifying the field to count.

CREATE QUERY

See also:	ALTER, CONSTRAINT, REFERENCES, WITH
Purpose	The CREATE query is used to create tables or indexes in a Jet database. Table 62-9 lists the arguments for the CREATE TABLE statement.

General Syntax

```
CREATE TABLE [table name] ([fieldname] type (size), _
[fieldname] type (size),..., _
CONSTRAINT _ indexname indextype ([fieldname],[fieldname]...));

CREATE indextype INDEX indexname ON tablename _
(fieldname WITH nulltype ,fieldname,...);
```

Table 62-9 Arguments for the CREATE TABLE statement

Argument	Description
tablename	String expression that provides a unique name for the table
fieldname	String expression that provides a unique name for the field
type	String expression that specifies the field's data type
size	Numeric value that specifies a TEXT type field's size only
CONSTRAINT	Optional keyword that specifies the table's indexes
indexname	String expression that uniquely identifies the index
indextype	String expression that specifies the index type
nulltype	Specifies whether the indexed field will allow field to be empty; the nulltype can be DISALLOW NULL or IGNORE NULL

Example Syntax

```
SQL$ = "CREATE TABLE [Sql Books] ([Title] TEXT (255)," _
     + " [Publisher] TEXT (50),[Author] TEXT (50))"
```

Description   Your application might need to create temporary tables for certain types of processing and destroy them when finished. The above example would create such a table. This query would create a table in the specified database with the name, "Sql Books", with three text fields that have lengths of 255, 50, and 50, respectively. If you hadn't noticed, we are using fields that correspond to the ubiquitous BIBLIO.MDB database sample that comes with Visual Basic. As declared above, this table represents a denormalization of three existing fields in the BIBLIO.MDB database. In very large databases where the data is contained in large normalized tables, it is sometimes very useful to create a denormalized table as shown above so that the required information from these diverse tables can be quickly accessed. Normalized tables represent data that has been separated into groups according to a set of normalization rules that are outlined in Chapter 56, "Database Overview and Design."

DELETE Statement

Purpose   The DELETE statement is used to delete records from a table. Table 62-10 lists the arguments for the DELETE statement.

General Syntax

```
DELETE [table.*] FROM tableexpression WHERE criteria
```

Table 62-10 Arguments for the DELETE statement

Argument	Description
table	Optional name of the table from which records are to be deleted
tableexpression	Name of the table or tables from which records are to be deleted
criteria	Expression that specifies which records to select for deletion

Example Syntax

```
Dim MySQL as String

MySQL ="DELETE * FROM [Accounts] WHERE [Date] < #01/01/95"
MyDatabase.Execute MySQL
```

Description   In the above sample query, all the records in the Accounts table that predated January 1, 1995 would be deleted from the table. DELETE queries are convenient and quick ways to remove records that are no longer needed. DELETE queries are action queries and do not return a recordset. Use the Execute method to run them.

DROP QUERIES

Purpose   The DROP queries are used to delete tables and indexes from the database. Table 62-11 lists the arguments for the DROP query.

General Syntax

```
DROP {TABLE tablename|INDEX indexname ON tablename}
```

Table 62-11 Argument for the DROP query

Argument	Description
tablename	Name of the table being dropped or the name of the table containing the index to be dropped

Example Syntax

```
MyDB.Execute "DROP TABLE [SQL Books]"
```

Description   Let's say that your application is finished with this table and no longer needs it. The removal of this table using a DDL type of query is very simple. The above example shows how easy it is to remove a table from the database. If the table is part of a relationship in your database, the table deletion will fail. You must first drop the relationship(s) before you can drop the table. The examples shown here are only a fraction of the DDL query capabilities. Being able to create and destroy tables through queries and through stored QueryDefs allows the development of very sophisticated applications especially in the Decision Support applications field.

FROM CLAUSE

Purpose   The FROM clause is used to specify the tables from which the records are to be selected. Table 62-12 lists the arguments for the FROM clause.

General Syntax

```
FROM tableexpression [IN externaldatabasename]
```

Table 62-12 Arguments for the FROM clause

Argument	Description
tableexpression	Identifies the table or tables from which the data is retrieved
externaldatabase	Full pathname of an external database containing

Example Syntax

```
Dim MySQL as String
Dim MyRS as Recordset
MySQL = "Select * FROM Clients WHERE Type = 'Manufacturing'"
Set MyRS = MyDatabase.Openrecordset(MySQL)
If MyRS.RecordCount> 0 Then
......

Dim MySQL as String
Dim MyRS as Recordset
MySQL = "Select * FROM Transfers IN 'C:\DATA\MYDATA.MDB' " _
     + " WHERE [Type] = 'Credits'"
Set MyRS = MyDatabase.Openrecordset(MySQL)
If MyRS.RecordCount> 0 Then
......
```

Description   The FROM clause is a required part of any SELECT query. In the first example above, the FROM clause is used in a simple SELECT query to obtain a recordset from the current database. In the second example, the SELECT query obtains its recordsource from an external database. The FROM clause can be used to specify one table or several tables that are part of a complex Join.

GROUP BY Clause

Purpose   The GROUP BY clause is used to separate selected records into specific groups. This can be used to provide reports summarizing various subsets of the data, such as total sales by product category. Table 62-13 lists the argument for the GROUP BY clause.

General Syntax

```
GROUP BY groupfieldlist
```

Table 62-13 Argument for the GROUP BY clause

Argument	Description
fieldlist	Name of the field or fields by which recordset will be grouped

Example Syntax

```
Dim MySQL as String
Dim MyRS as Recordset
MySQL = "SELECT *,Count(Postal Code] as MyCount FROM Contacts"
     + " WHERE [Postal Code] Like "87*" GROUP BY [Postal Code]"
Set MyRS = MyDatabase.OpenRecordset(MySQL)
If MySQL.RecordCount > 0 Then
MySQL.MoveFirst
Do While Not MyRS.EOF
Printer.Print "There are " & MyCount & " Contacts in the "
```

continued on next page

continued from previous page

```
& MyRS.[Postal Code]
& " Postal Code Area"
MyRS.MoveNext
Loop
End If
```

Description   The GROUP BY clause provides a method to group returned records by a given field. In the above example, the records are selected from those that start with an "87" zip code and then groups them into matching zip codes providing a count of the total records for each zip code returned. The above loop would print out each Zip code with a count of how many records are in that zip code.

HAVING CLAUSE

Purpose   The HAVING clause is used to provide selection conditions for a GROUP BY clause. Table 62-14 lists the argument for the HAVING clause.

General Syntax

```
HAVING groupcriteria
```

Table 62-14 Argument for the HAVING clause

Argument	Description
groupcriteria	Expression that determines which group records to display

Example Syntax

```
Dim MySQL as String
Dim MyRS as Recordset
MySQL = "SELECT *,Count([Postal Code])AS MyCount FROM Contacts " _
    + " WHERE [Postal Code] Like '87*'" _
    + " GROUP BY [Postal Code] HAVING Count([Postal Code]) > 50"
Set MyRS = MyDatabase.OpenRecordset(MySQL)
If MySQL.RecordCount > 0 Then
MySQL.MoveFirst
Do While Not MyRS.EOF
Printer.Print "There are " & MyCount & " Contacts in the " _
& MyRS.[Postal Code] & " Postal Code Area"
MyRS.MoveNext
Loop
End If
```

Description   The HAVING clause gives greater control over the GROUP BY clause by providing a means to specify a criteria for the GROUP BY clause. In the above example, the records are selected from those that start with an "87" Zip code and then groups them into matching Zip codes providing a count of the total records for each Zip code returned, but only if those Zip codes have a group count of greater than fifty. The above loop would print out each Zip code with a count of how many records are in that Zip code.

INSERT INTO STATEMENT

Purpose   The INSERT INTO statement is used to append new records to the end of an existing table or query. A query using the INSERT INTO statement is known as an Append Query. Table 62-15 lists the arguments for the INSERT INTO statement.

General Syntax

```
"Multiple-record append query
INSERT INTO target [IN externaldatabase] _
SELECT [source.]field1[, field2[, ...]FROM tableexpression

'Single-record append query
INSERT INTO target [(field1[, field2[, ...]])] _
VALUES (value1[, value2[, ...])
```

Table 62-15 Arguments for the INSERT INTO statement

Argument	Description
target	Name of the table or query to which to append recordsexternaldatabase. Full path of an external database to which to append.
source	Name of the table or query that supplies the records to insert.
field1, field2..	Names of the fields in a multirecord insert.
tableexpression	Name of the table or tables from which records are inserted.

Example Syntax

```
Dim MySQL as String
Dim MyRS as recordset
MySQL = "INSERT INTO GENLED.* SELECT TRANSACT.* FROM TRANSACT"
MySQL = MySQL + " WHERE Tdate = " & Date
MyDatabase.Execute MySQL
```

Description   The INSERT INTO statement appends records into a table from another table according to a SELECT subquery when doing a multirecord append as in the example above. The INSERT INTO statement can also be used to insert single records into a table. In this situation, your query would have to specify the fields and their values as part of the query.

MAX, MIN AGGREGATE FUNCTIONS

Purpose   The Max function is used to return the highest value in a given field, and the Min function is used to return the lowest value in a given field. Table 62-16 lists the arguments for the Max function.

General Syntax

```
Max|Min(expression) AS resultfield
```

Table 62-16 Arguments for the Max function

Argument	Description
expression	String expression that identifies the field that contains the data to be evaluated
resultfield	Placeholder for the result

Example Syntax

```
Dim MySQL As String
Dim MyRS As Recordset
MySQL = "SELECT Max([Net Due]) AS [Bigest Bill], Min([Net Due]) AS " _
      + "[Small Bill] FROM Invoices WHERE [Net Due] > 100 "
Set MyRS = MyDatabase.OpenRecordset(MySQL)
MsgBox = "The Range of Invoice values greater than $100 are $" _
      & MyRS.[Big Bill] & " to $" & MyRS.[Small Bill]
```

Description   The Max and Min functions provide a convenient and quick way to determine the range of values in a given set of fields. They can be used separately or in tandem as in the example above.

ORDER BY Clause

Purpose   The ORDER BY clause is used to sort the selected recordset according to a given order. Table 62-17 lists the arguments for the ORDER BY clause.

General Syntax

```
ORDER BY field1 [ASC|DESC], field1 [ASC|DESC]...
```

Table 62-17 Arguments for the ORDER BY clause

Argument	Description
field1, field2...	Names of fields
ASC|DESC	Specifies the sort as either Ascending or Descending

Example Syntax

```
Dim MySQL as String
Dim MyRS as Recordset
MySQL = "SELECT * FROM Contacts WHERE [Postal Code] Like '87*'" _
      + " Order by [Last Name]"
Set MyRS = MyDatabase.OpenRecordset(MySQL)
If MyRS.RecordCount > 0 Then
MyRS.MoveFirst
Do While Not MyRS.EOF
```

```
    Printer Print MyRS.[Last Name] & "' " & MyRS.[Last Name] & " @ " _
          & MyRS.[Postal Code]
    MyRS.MoveNext
Loop
Printer.EndDoc
EndIf
.....
```

Description   The ORDER BY clause is an optional clause unless the Top or Top n
Percent predicates are used in the query. If you omit the ORDER BY clause
in a query, then the recordset is returned unsorted. The default sort is
Ascending.

SELECT Statement

Purpose   The SELECT statement is used to retrieve records from the database and
for storing them in a Recordset object. Table 62-18 lists the arguments for
the SELECT query.

General Syntax

```
SELECT [predicate] { * | table.* | [table.]field1 _
[, [table.]field2[, ...]]} [AS alias1 [, alias2 [, ...]]] _
FROM tableexpression [, ...] [IN externaldatabase] _
[WHERE... ][GROUP BY... ][HAVING... ][ORDER BY... ] _
[WITH OWNERACCESS OPTION]
```

Table 62-18 Arguments for the SELECT query

Argument	Description
predicate	Either the All DISTINCT, DISTINCT ROW, or TOP predicates are used to restrict the records returned. * Specifies all fields in a table
table	Name of a table included in the query
field1, field2..	Names of fields to retrieve data from
alias1, alias2..	Column names to return as Field object names in the returned Recordset object
tableexpression	Name of the table or tables containing the data being retrieved

Example Syntax

```
Dim MySQL as String
Dim MyRS as Recordset
MySQL = "SELECT * FROM Clients WHERE YTD > 0 ORDER BY [Client Name]"
Set MyRS = MYDatabase.OpenRecordset(MySQL)
IF MyRS.RecordCount > 0 then
.....do something
End if
```

Description   The SELECT query is a major workhorse of relational databases. The
SELECT query searches the specified tables, and retrieves the required
information using the specified criteria to select the rows to be returned in
a recordset. There are several clauses and predicates that can be applied to

modify the results of SELECT queries. The vast majority of SQL statements are SELECT queries and can be used to join several tables together in an apparently seamless recordset for subsequent processing.

Sum Function

Purpose   The Sum function is used to return the sum of all the values in a particular field of a Recordset. Table 62-19 lists the arguments for the Sum function.

General Syntax

```
Sum(expression) AS resultfield
```

Table 62-19 Arguments for the Sum function

Argument	Description
expression	String expression identifying the field that contains the numeric data to be summed or an expression that performs a caculation using the data in that field
resultfield	Placeholder for the value returned by the function

Example Syntax

```
Dim MySQL As String
Dim MyRS As Recordset
MySQL = "SELECT Sum([Net Due]) AS [Big Sum] FROM Invoices"
MySQL = MySQL + "WHERE [Net Due] > 100"
Set MyRS = MyDatabase.OpenRecordset(MySQL)
MsgBox = "The Sum of all Invoices over $100.00 is $" & MyRS.[Big Sum]
```

Description   The Sum function will return the sum of values for a given field, or the sum of a set of calculations on that field for a given set of records. The calculations can contain the name of another field, a constant, or a function. The function cannot be another Aggregate function though.

UPDATE Statement

Purpose   UPDATE statement is used to change the value in fields of a specified table based on selection criteria.

General Syntax

```
UPDATE table SET newvalue WHERE criteria
```

Example Syntax

```
Dim MySQL As String
MySQL = "UPDATE Clients SET [YTD] = [YTD] + [MTD],[QTD] = " _
    + "[QTD] + [MTD],[MTD] = 0"
MyDatabase.Execute MySQL
```

Description   The UPDATE query is the tool to use when you need to do batch changes in a given set of records. In the above example, the UPDATE query is used to shift monthly totals at the end of the month into the yearly and quarterly fields and clear the monthly total. You can change many fields at one time using mathematical and logical functions to derive your changes. UPDATE does not return a recordset and is used with the Execute method.

PART X
DATABASE
ADVANCED

63

ADVANCED SQL

After mastering the beginning SQL syntax and techniques, it's time to move on to more advanced topics. SQL can be used to do more than return data from simple tables. This chapter will discuss the more advanced techniques for retrieving information from a database using SQL.

This chapter will also explore how to squeeze all the performance you can from the Jet database. With a little knowledge of how Jet evaluates a query, you can tune your SQL to get the best performance possible.

Complex Queries

The Jet 3.5 database engine is capable of complex queries such as subqueries, joins, crosstabs, and unions. These queries allow a Visual Basic application to take full advantage of modern relational database theory.

Joins

A *joins* is a way to create a Recordset with results from two or more tables based on the relationship between them. Table 63-1 lists the join types and their effect. Figure 63-1 shows the different results in the Recordset based on the join type.

Table 63-1 Join types and their effect

Join Type	Effect on Recordset
Inner join	Returns a record only where there are matching records in both tables
Left outer join	Returns a record for every record in the first table, with Nulls for fields in the second table when there are no matching records
Right outer join	Returns a record for every record in the second table, with Nulls for fields in the first table when there are no matching records

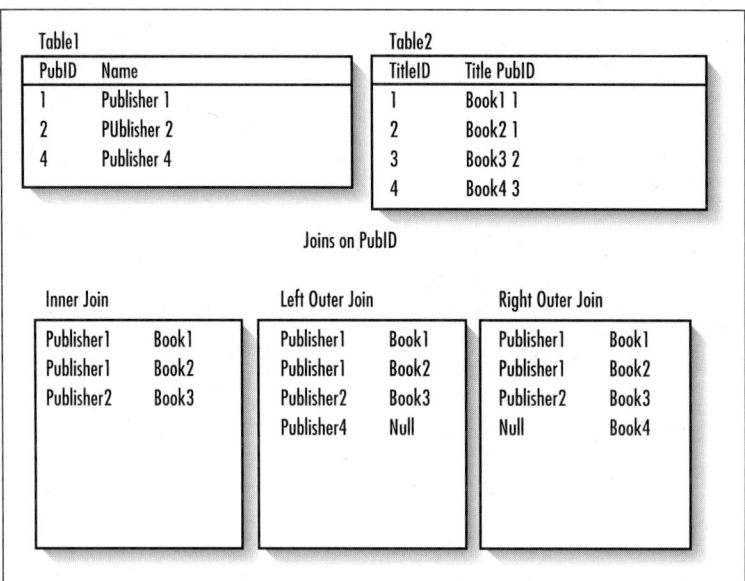

Figure 63-1 Different results based on the join type

Inner Joins

Use the INNER JOIN statement any time you want the Recordset to only have a record when there are matching records in both tables. The query below returns a list of books and their publishers. If there is no publisher listed for a book, the Recordset will not have a record for that book. Likewise, if a publisher has no books, there will not be a record in the Recordset for that publisher.

```
SELECT Name, Title
FROM Publishers INNER JOIN Titles ON Publishers.PubID = Titles.PubID
```

Outer Joins

An *outer join* allows a query to return a record for a table, even if there is no matching record in the other member of the join. The different types of outer joins determine which of the tables always has a record in the Recordset.

The LEFT OUTER JOIN statement always returns at least one record for the first table in the join. If there are no matching records in the second table, the fields from the second table will be Null. The following query returns a list of publishers and book titles. If a publisher has no books in the Titles table, they will have a record in the Recordset, but the Title field of the Recordset will be Null.

```
SELECT Name, Title
FROM Publishers LEFT OUTER JOIN Titles ON Publishers.PubID = Titles.PubID
```

The RIGHT OUTER JOIN statement ensures that there will always be a record for the second table of the join, even if there is no matching record in the first. The following query is similar to the previous one; however, this query will return all titles even if they don't have a publisher listed. If there is a publisher with no books, they will not be in the Recordset.

```
SELECT Name, Title
FROM Publishers RIGHT OUTER JOIN Titles ON Publishers.PubID = Titles.PubID
```

Nested Joins

It is possible to nest joins so that many tables can be linked together in the Recordset. The query below returns a list of authors, the books they worked on, and their publishers. It first starts by joining Authors to Title Author, then joins that set to Titles, and finally back to Publishers.

```
SELECT Author, Title, Name
FROM Publishers INNER JOIN
     (Titles INNER JOIN
          (Authors INNER JOIN [Title Author]
          ON Authors.Au_ID = [Title Author].Au_ID)
     ON Titles.ISBN = [Title Author].ISBN)
ON Publishers.PubID = Titles.PubID;
```

Subqueries

A *subquery* is a SELECT statement used as part of the WHERE clause of another SQL statement. It allows you to restrict the results of the main query based on the results of the subquery. The first type of subquery is simply a comparison between a value and a subquery that returns only one result. The query below retrieves the name of the publisher with the most expensive book. The subquery finds the maximum book price. The main query then gets the publisher of the book when the book's price matches the maximum.

```
SELECT Name
FROM Publishers AS P, Titles AS T
WHERE P.PubID = T.PubID
AND T.Price = (SELECT MAX(Price) FROM Titles)
```

A subquery can be used to compare a value against a whole set of values. The ANY, ALL, and SOME statements modify a comparison so that it applies to all the rows in the subquery. For example, the first query below doesn't make sense because there would be more than one result of the subquery:

```
'Bad query, doesn't make sense
SELECT Title
FROM Titles
WHERE Price > (SELECT Price FROM Titles WHERE PubId = 45)
```

The next query uses the ALL statement to perform the comparison between Price and all the results of the subquery. The query returns a list of the books that cost more than all the books published by PubId 45. ALL or SOME could be used to return a list of books that cost more than at least one of the books published by PubId 45. ALL and SOME are equivalent.

```
'Good query
SELECT Title
FROM Titles
WHERE Price > ALL (SELECT Price FROM Titles WHERE PubId = 45)
```

A subquery may be used to check membership or lack of membership in a group. The IN and NOT IN statements are used to check if a value is contained in the results of the subquery or not. The query below returns a list of publishers that published a book in 1994. It could just as easily return a list of publishers who did not publish a book in 1994, by changing the IN to NOT IN.

```
SELECT Name FROM Publishers
WHERE PubID IN (SELECT PubId FROM Titles WHERE [Year Published] = 1994)
```

In this case, a similar effect can be achieved with an inner join between the Publishers and Titles tables. The join, however, will return a Name for each book published in 1994, so a publisher with four books in 1994 will show up four times. The subquery provides the same effect as a DISTINCTROW statement in this case, so the Name only shows up once.

The last type of subquery is used to check whether there are results in the subquery. The EXISTS and NOT EXISTS statements evaluate True or False based on whether there are any records in the subquery. The following query inserts into the Titles table only if that title does not already exist in the table:

```
INSERT INTO Titles(Title, [Year Published], PubId,ISBN)
SELECT "Visual Basic 5.0 SuperBible", 1997,  43, "X"
FROM Publishers
WHERE PubId = 43
AND NOT EXISTS
    (SELECT Title FROM Titles WHERE Title = "Visual Basic 5.0 SuperBible")
```

Correlated Subqueries

You may also make references to the main query in a subquery, which is called a *correlated subquery*.

```
SELECT Name FROM Publishers AS P
WHERE 20 > (SELECT MIN(Price) FROM Titles WHERE P.PubID = PubID)
```

The correlated subquery in the sample above gets the minimum book price for each publisher by comparing the PubID of the aliased Publishers table in the main query with its own PubID. By aliasing the Publishers table in the main query, Jet can understand that the subquery is referring to the PubID of the Publishers table. This query returns a list of publishers whose least expensive book is under $20.

Crosstab Queries

Crosstab queries enable you to take results that you normally get using a GROUP BY and pivot them so they are easier to read. Figure 63-2 shows two queries and their results. Both return the same data, but one is a crosstab query that presents the data in an easier-to-read format.

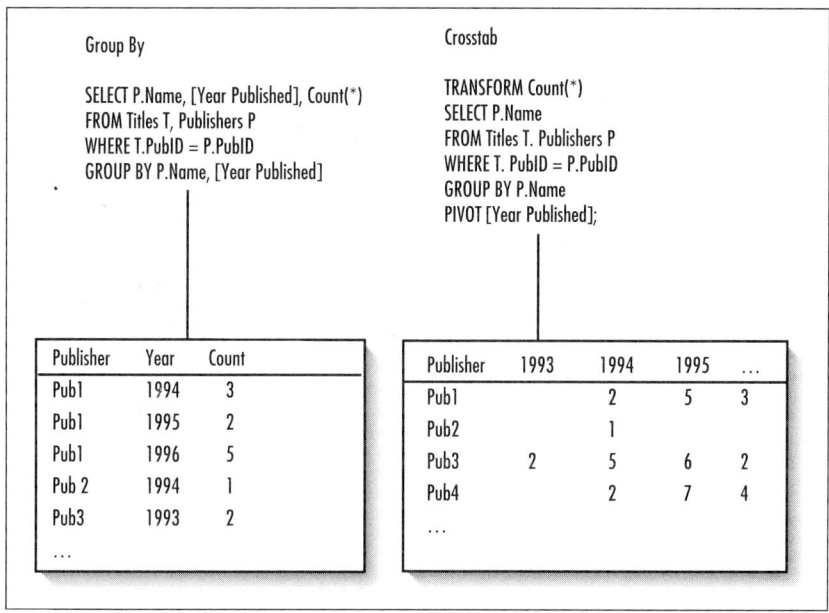

Figure 63-2 How a crosstab query differs from a GROUP BY

A crosstab query has two parts. The first part, the TRANSFORM statement, specifies what aggregate function to use when populating the fields of the Recordset. This could be any of the aggregate functions discussed in Chapter 62, "Beginning SQL," such as SUM, COUNT, or AVG. The fields in the SELECT statement are the leftmost fields of each record, with the aggregate function of the TRANSFORM statement being the rightmost fields. The second part of the crosstab query is the PIVOT statement, which specifies the column headings that will be appended to the fields in the SELECT statement. In the query below, the columns will be the name of the publisher followed by the years published, but only 1993, 1994, 1995, 1996, and 1997. This query shows a list of all publishers and a count of the number of books they published in each year between 1993 and 1997.

```
TRANSFORM Count(*)
SELECT P.Name
FROM Titles as T, Publishers as P
WHERE T.PubID = P.PubID
GROUP BY P.Name
PIVOT [Year Published] IN (1993, 1994, 1995, 1996, 1997)
```

Getting Unique Results

Sometimes when joining between tables, a query may return duplicate entries when all that's needed is just one entry. The following query is an attempt to get the names of all the authors who have published for the publisher whose PubID=3:

```
SELECT Authors.Author
FROM Authors INNER JOIN
    (Titles INNER JOIN [Title Author]
    ON Titles.ISBN = [Title Author].ISBN)
ON Authors.Au_ID = [Title Author].Au_ID
WHERE Titles.PubID=3
```

This query will return an author's name multiple times if he or she has been published by the publisher whose PubID=3 multiple times. To get each author only once, use the DISTINCTROW statement in the SELECT clause like the query below does.

```
SELECT DISTINCTROW Authors.Author
FROM Authors INNER JOIN
    (Titles INNER JOIN [Title Author]
    ON Titles.ISBN = [Title Author].ISBN)
ON Authors.Au_ID = [Title Author].Au_ID
WHERE Titles.PubID=3
```

Unions

A *union* allows a SQL query to merge the results of two or more SQL queries into one Recordset and even sort the records over the entire merged Recordset. The query below returns a list of publishers, authors, and the number of books for each. It then orders the complete list alphabetically.

```
SELECT Name AS Thing, Count(*) AS Tally
FROM Publishers INNER JOIN Titles ON Publishers.PubID = Titles.PubID
GROUP BY Name
UNION
SELECT Author AS Thing, Count(*) AS Tally
FROM Authors INNER JOIN [Title Author] ON Authors.Au_ID = [Title Author].Au_ID
GROUP BY Author
ORDER BY Thing
```

If there happens to be an author with the same name and tally as a publisher, there will only be one record for both of them. By using a UNION ALL operator instead of a UNION operator, the query would return all records, even if there are duplicates.

Often in a union, column names will not match up. In the example above, the query uses the AS statement to alias the column names so they match in both queries. This allows the ORDER BY clause to order by the Thing column. Optionally, you may specify a column number in your ORDER BY clause so that you don't have to alias the columns in the SELECT clause. The SQL query below has the same effect as the one above.

```
SELECT Name, Count(*)
FROM Publishers INNER JOIN Titles ON Publishers.PubID = Titles.PubID
GROUP BY Name
UNION
SELECT Author, Count(*)
FROM Authors INNER JOIN [Title Author] ON Authors.Au_ID = [Title Author].Au_ID
GROUP BY Author
ORDER BY 1
```

The only restriction to using the UNION operator is there must be the same number of columns in each of the queries in the union. The columns don't have to be the same data type, there just needs to be the same number of columns. If you find you have a shortfall in one of the queries, you can pad the query with Nulls to fill up the gap. The query below adds the telephone number of the publishing company. Since there is no telephone for the authors, a Null can be added to make the number of columns match.

```
SELECT Name AS Thing, Count(*) AS Tally, Telephone
FROM Publishers INNER JOIN Titles ON Publishers.PubID = Titles.PubID
GROUP BY Name, Telephone
UNION
SELECT Author AS Thing, Count(*) AS Tally, Null
FROM Authors INNER JOIN [Title Author] ON Authors.Au_ID = [Title Author].Au_ID
GROUP BY Author
ORDER BY Thing
```

Query Optimization

Performance can depend on many things: CPU, memory, bandwidth, and many other factors. However, there are few things you can keep in mind that will help no matter what platform you are running on. When building your queries, you should consider the following suggestions to ensure the quickest and most efficient execution of them:

- Limit the fields returned in a select query to only those you actually need

- Use the ORDER BY keyword on indexed fields

- Avoid using an asterisk (*) as the leading character in pattern matching criteria

- Structure your queries to return the smallest Recordset possible to meet your needs

- When possible, store your queries as QueryDefs in the database

- Use comparison operators on indexed fields

- Crosstab queries work best when column headings are specified using the IN clause

- Join on indexed fields

- The NOT IN function is very slow

When the DBEngine builds Recordsets based on queries, it uses existing indexes to order and structure the Recordset. The DBEngine utilizes Rushmore technology whenever it can. How you build your table indexes can greatly affect the time it takes for the DBEngine to build the Recordset, depending on how well you adhere to the requirements for Rushmore. Once the Recordset is built, the table indexes are no longer relevant. The Dynaset-type Recordset uses its own internal index system for searches within the Recordset.

Advanced SQL Summary

Table 63-2 lists the advanced SQL syntax, detailed descriptions follow.

Table 63-2 Advanced SQL commands and functions

Use This...	Type	To Do This...
ALL, ANY, and SOME	Statements	Modify a subquery comparison
DISTINCTROW	Function	Retrieve only unique rows
EXISTS	Function	Check for the existence of results in a subquery
IN and NOT IN	Function	Check for membership in results of a subquery or list
INNER JOIN, LEFT OUTER JOIN, and RIGHT OUTER JOIN	Statements	Specify the type of join in a SELECT statement
TRANSFORM and PIVOT	Statements	Present a more natural grouping for data
UNION	Operator	Merge two or more result sets

ALL, ANY, AND SOME STATEMENTS

Purpose The ALL, ANY, and SOME statements modify a comparison of a value against a subquery to allow the value to be compared against all values the subquery returns. Table 63-3 lists the arguments for the ALL, ANY, and SOME statements.

General Syntax

```
expression compop [ALL|ANY|SOME] (subquery)
```

Table 63-3 Arguments of the ALL, ANY, and SOME statements

Argument	Description
expression	A valid SQL expression
compop	A comparison operator like =, >, or <=
subquery	A valid SELECT statement that returns only one column

Example Syntax

```
SELECT Title
FROM Titles
WHERE Price < ALL (SELECT Price FROM Titles WHERE PubId = 45)
AND PubID = 43

SELECT Title
FROM Titles
WHERE Price < SOME (SELECT Price FROM Titles WHERE PubId = 45)
AND PubID = 43

SELECT Title
```

```
FROM Titles
WHERE Price < ANY (SELECT Price FROM Titles WHERE PubId = 45)
AND PubID = 43
```

Description   The ALL, ANY, and SOME statements allow a comparison to be performed against all members of a subquery. The first example above uses the ALL statement to return Titles from PubID=43 that cost less than all the books from PubID=45. SOME and ANY work exactly the same way, so they will return a list of books from PubID=43 that cost less than any one or more books from PubID=45. ALL requires that the comparison evaluates True against all the members of the subquery. ANY and SOME only require that the comparison evaluates True against one of the members of the subquery.

DISTINCTROW Function

Purpose   The DISTINCTROW function filters duplicate rows from a Recordset. Table 63-4 lists the arguments for the DISTINCTROW function.

General Syntax

```
SELECT DISTINCTROW field1, field2, etc.
```

Table 63-4 Argument of the DISTINCTROW function

Argument	Description
field1, field2, and so on	The remainder of a SELECT statement

Example Syntax

```
SELECT DISTINCTROW Customer.Name
FROM Customer INNER JOIN Order ON Customer.CustomerId = Order.CustomerId
WHERE Order.OrderedDate >= '11/01/96'
AND Order.OrderDate < '12/1/96'
```

Description   The query above uses the DISTINCTROW function to ensure that the customer's name will only be listed once, even if the customer placed multiple orders in the month of November. Without the DISTINCTROW function, the customer's name would be listed for each order he or she placed in November.

EXISTS Function

Purpose   The EXISTS function allows a query to check for the existence or lack of existence of results in a subquery. Table 63-5 lists the arguments of the EXISTS function.

General Syntax

```
[NOT] EXISTS (subquery)
```

Table 63-5 Argument of the EXISTS function

Argument	Description
subquery	A valid SELECT statement

Example Syntax

```
SELECT Name
FROM Customer
WHERE NOT EXISTS
      (SELECT * FROM [Customer Wish List]
      WHERE [Customer Wish List].CustomerId = Customer.CustomerId)
```

Description   The query above uses the NOT EXISTS function to look for all customers for whom the sales force hasn't collected a wish list for the next release. This query could easily be turned around by dropping the NOT to give a list of the customers who do have a wish list.

IN AND NOT IN FUNCTIONS

Purpose   The IN function checks to see if a value is a member of a subquery's results. The optional NOT checks if a value is not a member of a subquery's results. Table 63-6 lists the arguments for the IN function.

General Syntax

```
expression [NOT] IN (subquery)
```

Table 63-6 Arguments of the IN function

Argument	Description
expression	A valid SQL expression
subquery	A valid SELECT statement that returns only one column

Example Syntax

```
SELECT Name
FROM Customers
WHERE CustomerID NOT IN
      (SELECT CustomerID FROM Products
      WHERE Version = '2.0')
```

Description   The IN function evaluates to True when the value of the expression is a member of the subquery's results. The NOT IN function evaluates to True when the value is not a member of the subquery's results. The query above uses NOT IN to find all the customers who have not upgraded to version 2.0.

INNER JOIN, LEFT OUTER JOIN, AND RIGHT OUTER JOIN STATEMENTS

Purpose   The INNER JOIN, LEFT OUTER JOIN, and RIGHT OUTER JOIN statements merge data from two or more tables into one Recordset based on a relationship between the tables. Table 63-7 lists the arguments for the INNER JOIN, LEFT OUTER JOIN, and RIGHT OUTER JOIN statements.

General Syntax

```
FROM table1 INNER JOIN table2 ON table1.field1 compop table2.field2
FROM table1 LEFT OUTER JOIN table2 ON table1.field1 compop table2.field2
FROM table1 RIGHT OUTER JOIN table2 ON table1.field1 compop table2.field2
```

Table 63-7 Arguments of the INNER JOIN, LEFT OUTER JOIN, and RIGHT OUTER JOIN statements

Argument	Description
table1, table2	A SQL table
field1, field2	Fields in table1 and table2, respectively
compop	A comparison operator such as =, >, or <=

Example Syntax

```
SELECT Customer.Name, Sales.Name
FROM Customer INNER JOIN Sales ON Customer.SalesID = Sales.SalesID

SELECT Customer.Name, Sales.Name
FROM Customer LEFT OUTER JOIN Sales ON Customer.SalesID = Sales.SalesID

SELECT Customer.Name, Sales.Name
FROM Customer RIGHT OUTER JOIN Sales ON Customer.CustomerID = Sales.TopAccount
```

Description   The three different types of joins are demonstrated above. The first, an INNER JOIN, returns the list of customers and the salesperson responsible for the account. If a salesperson has not been assigned, that customer will not show up in the results.

The second type of join is a LEFT OUTER JOIN. A LEFT OUTER JOIN will return a record for the first table even if there is no matching record in the second. Thus, this query will return a list of all the customers. If the customer has not been assigned a salesperson, the Sales.Name field will be Null in the Recordset.

The last type of join is the RIGHT OUTER JOIN. A RIGHT OUTER JOIN will return a record for the second table even if there is no matching record in the first. The sample query for the RIGHT OUTER JOIN returns a list of salespeople and their top account. Salespeople with no top account will have a Null Customer.Name next to their name in the Recordset.

TRANSFORM AND PIVOT STATEMENTS

Purpose

The TRANSFORM and PIVOT statements are used to create a crosstab query that is easier to read than a standard GROUP BY. Table 63-8 lists the arguments for the TRANSFORM and PIVOT statements.

General Syntax

```
TRANSFORM aggop
select
PIVOT pivotfield [IN (value1[,value2...[, ]])]
```

Table 63-8 Arguments of the TRANSFORM and PIVOT

Argument	Description
aggop	An aggregate operator like SUM, COUNT, or AVG
select	A SELECT statement
pivotfield	The field to be used for column headings
value1, value2, and so on	Optionally specific values for the column headings

Example Syntax

```
TRANSFORM Sum(Amount)
SELECT S.Name
FROM Sales S, Invoice I
WHERE S.SalesID = I.InvoiceID
GROUP BY S.Name
PIVOT [Quarter]
```

Description

A crosstab query allows a Recordset to be reformatted in a more natural and readable way. The sample above takes the salesperson's invoices and sums them by quarter. Using a regular GROUP BY clause, there would be up to four records for each salesperson. The Recordset would be a long list of Name, Quarter, and Amount. The crosstab query above takes the Quart field and makes it a column heading. Now the Recordset looks like a list of Name, 1, 2, 3, and 4. A great way of exploring what crosstab queries can do for you is to open up Access and use the Crosstab Query Wizard to put together a few queries. Examine the SQL generated to see how it's all put together.

UNION Operator

Purpose   The UNION operator merges two or more Recordsets into one sortable Recordset. Table 63-9 lists the arguments of the UNION operator.

General Syntax

```
record1 UNION [ALL] record2[ UNION [ALL] record3[ ...]]
```

Table 63-9 Arguments of the UNION operator

Argument	Description
record1, record2, record3	Recordsets with the same number of columns

Example Syntax

```
SELECT Name, Phone
FROM Clients
UNION
SELECT Name, Phone
FROM Friends
ORDER BY Name
```

Description   The UNION operator merges two or more Recordsets into one. The resulting Recordset is sortable using an ORDER BY clause on the entire Recordset. The query above compiles a list of clients and friends to invite to a party. Since a person might be both, the optional ALL has been omitted so that they only show up once.

The only restriction on the use of the UNION operator, is that both Recordsets must have the same number of columns. If one Recordset has less columns than the other, you can pad the SELECT clause with Nulls to make up the difference.

64

ADDING AND EDITING

Before you can create those massive number crunching reports or beautiful graphs based on data from a database, you must be able to enter and update the data. Visual Basic provides the means to add, edit, and delete records from a recordset. Visual Basic also provides advanced capabilities like transactions and a way to do updates using SQL.

Adding a Record

The AddNew and Update methods allow you to add a row to the recordset. The following example shows a Sub that adds a record to the phone numbers table.

```
Public Sub AddPhone(Name$, Home$, Pager$)
Dim rs as Recordset
Set rs = db.OpenRecordset("phonenumbers")
rs.AddNew
rs("name") = Name$
rs("home") = Home$
rs("pager") = Pager$
rs.Update
rs.Close
End Sub
```

Editing a Record

The database is populated; now it's time to make some changes. To change the current record of the recordset, use the Edit method. Once you call the Edit method, each of the columns in the recordset may be set to a value. Calling the Update method then saves the changes. This example shows the use of the Edit method to update a dynaset.

```
Public Sub UpdatePhone(Name$, Home$, Pager$)
Dim SQL as String
Dim rs as Recordset
SQL = "SELECT home, pager FROM phonenumbers WHERE name = '" + Name$ +"'"
```

continued on next page

continued from previous page

```
Set rs = db.OpenRecordset(SQL, dbOpenDynaset)
Do Until rs.EOF
      rs.Edit
      rs("home") = Home$
      rs("pager") = Pager$
      rs.Update
      rs.MoveNext
Loop
rs.Close
End Sub
```

Deleting a Record

Deleting records works similarly to the Edit above. The Delete method can be used to delete the current record. The example below uses the Delete method to remove a row from a dynaset type recordset.

```
Public Sub DeletePhone(Name$)
Dim SQL as String
Dim rs as Recordset
SQL = "SELECT * FROM phonenumbers WHERE name = '" + Name$ +"'"
Set rs = db.OpenRecordset(SQL, dbOpenDynaset)
Do Until rs.EOF
      rs.Delete
      rs.MoveNext
Loop
rs.Close
End Sub
```

Executing SQL Statements

Sometimes a better way to accomplish much of what the last three sections have talked about is to use the Execute method. The Execute method allows you to apply SQL to the database instead of using the AddNew, Edit, and Delete methods. Below are the three example subs from above, rewritten to use the Execute method.

```
Public Sub AddPhone(Name$, Home$, Pager$)
Dim SQL as String
SQL = "INSERT INTO phonenumbers (name, home, pager) VALUES"
SQL = SQL + "('" + name + "'"
SQL = SQL + ",'" + home + "'"
SQL = SQL + ",'" + PAGER + "')"
db.Execute SQL
End Sub

Public Sub UpdatePhone(Name$, Home$, Pager$)
Dim SQL as String
SQL = "UPDATE phonenumbers SET home = '" + home + "'"
SQL = SQL + ", pager = '" + Pager$ + "'"
SQL = SQL + " WHERE name = '" + Name$ +"'"
db.Execute SQL
End Sub

Public Sub DeletePhone(Name$)
Dim SQL as String
```

```
SQL = "DELETE FROM phonenumbers WHERE name = '" + Name$ +"'"
db.Execute SQL
End Sub
```

Transaction Processing

In many types of database operations where records are being added, modified, or deleted, data integrity issues require that all operations be completed as a group or not done at all. An example of this would be in an accounting system where a credit must have a corresponding debit to maintain the database's integrity. If, for some reason, not all the needed debits are written, then the opposing credits should also not be written and the entire transaction should not be committed. In this situation, the debit and credit operations must be viewed as a single operation. Visual Basic's DBEngine provides this capability through transaction processing. A transaction is a set of database operations that must all be successfully committed. If one operation within the transaction fails, then all the operations fail and no updates are committed.

There is another benefit of transaction processing, and that is increased efficiency in multiple record updates. Under single updates, the DBEngine writes each update to the disk. With transactions, each update is written to a buffer that can be as large as available memory. Since these updates are written to RAM instead of directly to the disk, processing speed is dramatically increased. When your code finally calls the CommitTrans method, the buffered updates are written all at one time. Transactions affect all databases in a workspace regardless of how you declare the transaction. If you use the DatabaseObject.Transaction instead of the WorkSpaceObject.Transaction, the transaction will still be applied to the entire workspace.

```
Private Function UpdateAccounts(dbMain as Database,dbTrans as Database)

    Dim Account As Recordset
    Dim Transaction As Recordset
    Set Accounts = dbMain.OpenRecordset("Checking")
    Account.Index = "PrimaryKey"
    Set Transactions = dbTrans.OpenRecordset("Checks")
    'starts transaction for both dbMain and dbTrans
    dbMain.BeginTrans
    Transactions.MoveFirst
    'Loops through all Transactions
    Do while not Transactions.EOF
        Accounts.Seek "=", Transactions!AccountNumber
        If Not Accounts.NoMatch Then
            'post to account
            Accounts!Balance=Accounts.Balance - Transactions!Amount
            'Mark transaction as posted
            Transactions.Posted = True
        Else
            'Mark as not Posted
            Transactions.Posted = False
            'Give Reason
            Transactions.ErrText = "No Account"
        End If
        Transactions.MoveNext
    Loop
```

continued on next page

continued from previous page

```
        On Error goto BadPost           'Set up Error handler
        UpdateAccounts = True           'Mark Function as Successful.
        dbMain.CommitTrans              'Commit Transaction
        On Error goto 0.                'Turn off Error Handler
        Account.close                   'Clean up Data Objects
        Transactions.Close
        Account = Nothing
        Transactions = Nothing
Exit Function
BadPost:                                'Post Failed
        dbMain.RollBack                 'RollBack all transactions to
        UpdateAccounts = CVErr(err)     'Both Databases in the
        Resume Next                     'Workspace area. The CVErr
End Function                            'Makes the function return an error.
```

The preceding example shows a set of transactions that spans two different databases that are assumed to be opened in the same workspace. This would cause the updates to both tables to require a successful transaction set or the updates on both tables would fail. But if in the above example the dbMain database was in WorkSpaces(0) and the dbTransactions database was in WorkSpaces(1), then the posts to the Transactions table would be made immediately and not be affected at all by the Transaction Set's success or failure. In this case, you would have to provide transaction methods for the dbTransactions database as well. You may actually have a case where you want one set of updates to happen simultaneously with another set but do not want to link them into a single transaction. That is to say that one transaction's failure should not affect the other's. In this case, you would use different WorkSpaces for each database.

Adding and Editing Summary

Table 64-1 summarizes adding and editing; detailed descriptions of the methods and properties follow.

Table 64-1 Adding and editing summary

Use This...	Type	To Do This...
AddNew	Method	Add a new record to a Recordset
AppendChunk	Method	Append a value to a Memo or Long Binary field
BeginTrans, CommitTrans, RollbackTrans	Methods	Manage a transaction
Clone	Method	Create a duplicate Recordset object
Delete	Method	Delete a record from a Recordset
Edit	Method	Edit a record in a Recordset object
Execute	Method	Run an action QueryDef or SQL statement
FieldSize	Property	Get the number of bytes in a field
GetChunck	Method	Retrieve data from a OLE or Memo field
Requery	Method	Refresh a Recordset by executing the underlying query again
Update	Method	Save the contents of an edited record

ADDNEW METHOD

Purpose   The AddNew method of the Recordset object is used to add a new row (that is, an empty record) to the Recordset. Table 64-2 lists the argument for this method.

General Syntax

```
recordsetobject.AddNew
```

Table 64-2 Argument for the AddNew method

Argument	Description
recordsetobject	An open Recordset object

Example Syntax

```
Dim MyRecordset as Recordset
'open the table to update
Set MyRecordset = MyDatabase.OpenTable("Clients")
'create the new row in the edit buffer using AddNew
MyRecordset.Addnew
'Put the data into the required fields
MyRecordset!Name = Text1(0)
MyRecordSet!Type = Text1(1)
....
'store the buffer into the table
MyRecordset.Update
```

Description   The AddNew method is used to add new rows to a Recordset object. It can be used with any Table-type or Dynaset-type Recordset object where the updatable property is True and write permission is granted. The Snapshot-type Recordset object is never updatable. Once you have applied the AddNew method to a Recordset, an edit buffer is created with the empty record in it. You then enter the required data into the field objects associated with that Recordset, and finally use the Update method to actually write the new row to the database. If you are using a counter field, the counter is automatically incremented during the update.

APPENDCHUNK METHOD

Purpose   The AppendChunk method is used to append a string expression to a Memo or Long Binary field in the fields collection of a Recordset object. Table 64-3 shows the argument for this method.

General Syntax

```
recordsetobject!field.AppendChunk source
```

Table 64-3 Arguments for the AppendChunk method

Argument	Description
recordsetobject	An open Recordset object
field	A field object that is either a Memo or Long Binary
Source	The data you want to append to the field

Example Syntax

```
Const Block = 16348
Dim NumBlocks as integer
Dim TotalSize as long
Dim x as integer
Dim MyDB as Database
Dim MyRS as Recordset
Dim Fnum as Integer
Fnum = FreeFile
'Open a Bitmap file for Binary Read
Open "c:\LargeText.txt" For Binary As #Fnum
TotalSize = LOF(Fnum)
NumBlocks = TotalSize \ Block - (TotalSize Mod Block <> 0)
ReDim MyBlocks(NumBlocks +1) As String * Block
'Read it in as chunks of fixed length strings
For X = 1 to NumBlocks
      Get #Fnum, ,MyBlocks(x)
Next
Close Fnum
'open the database and get the file to append to
Set MyDB = Workspaces(0).OpenDatabase("Clients")
Set MyRS = MyDB.OpenRecordset("Company")
MyRS.FindFirst "[CompanyID] = 3"
MyRS.Edit
'Append the String chunks to the Field
For x = 1 to NumBlocks
      MyRS!CompanyFAQ.AppendChunk MyBlocks(x)
Next
'Clean up after yourself.
MyRS.Update
MyRS.Close
MyDB.Close
Set MyRS = Nothing
Set MyDB = Nothing
```

Description

In the above example, the AppendChunk method is used to read in a large text file in manageable 16K chunks and store them into a dbMemo field in an Access database one chunk at a time. The AppendChunk is used to overcome certain size limitations in Visual Basic when manipulating strings larger than 64K. Keep in mind that, when using AppendChunk, the initial AppendChunk will cause everything in the target field to be erased.

BEGINTRANS, COMMITTRANS, ROLLBACKTRANS METHODS

Purpose   The transaction methods are used to manage transaction processing within a particular Workspace object's session. Transactions are used to help ensure that changes to the database are complete in all respects before being finalized. Table 64-4 shows the argument for these methods.

General Syntax

```
workspace.BeginTrans
workspace.CommitTrans
workspace.RollbackTrans
```

Table 64-4 Argument for the BeginTrans, CommitTrans, and RollbackTrans methods

Argument	Description
workspace	A workspace object

Example Syntax

```
Private Function NewMonth() as Boolean
NewMonth = True
Dim MyWorkSpace as workspace
Dim MyDB as database
Dim MyRS as Recordset
Dim BadFlag as Boolean
Set MyWorkspace = DBEngine.Workspaces(0)
Set MyDB = MyWorkspace.OpenDatabase("Clients")
Set MyRS = MyDB. OpenRecordset("Sites")
MyRS.MoveFirst
On Error Goto BadUpdate
'Begins a new transaction set
MyWorkspace.BeginTrans
'loop though each row updating totals
Do While Not MyRS.EOF
     MyRS.Edit
     MyRS!YTD = MyRS!YTD + MYRS!MTD
     If NewQuarter() Then
          MyRS!QTR = 0
          If NewYear() Then
               MyRS!YTD = 0
          End If
     Else
          MyRS!QTR = MyRS!QTR + MyRS!MTD
     End if
     MyRS!MTD = 0
     MyRS.Update
     MyRs.MoveNext
     'exit the loop if error is encountered
     If BadFlag Then Exit Do
Loop
'if no errors then commit the transactions
If Not BadFlag then
     MyWorkspace.CommitTrans
```

continued on next page

continued from previous page

```
'if there was an error then rollback the transaction
Else
        MyWorkspace.RollBack
End If
MyRS.Close
MyDB.Close
Set MyRS = Nothing
Set MyDB = Nothing
Exit Function
BadUpdate:
BadFlag = True
NewMonth = False
Resume Next
End Function
```

Description

The BeginTrans method starts a new transaction, the CommitTrans method ends the transaction set and attempts to store the transactions to the database, and the RollBack method ends the transaction set and restores the database to its condition prior to the start of the transaction. The Transaction methods apply to all databases in a workspace. That is, if you begin a transaction in reference to a particular database's objects, the transaction set still applies to all databases in the workspace. If you are processing updates in two databases simultaneously in the same workspace, the Transaction set will apply to both of them.

Transactions are usually used to insure data integrity when you are updating data that must be completed or not done at all. In the above example, YTD, QTD, and MTD represent period totals. When the balances are being updated, all the records must be updated or all of them must be left unchanged. If there is any kind of error encountered in this example, the loop is exited and the transaction rolled back. If there is no error, then the changes are committed to the database. Once you successfully use the CommitTrans method, you can no longer undo changes made during the transaction. Transactions can be nested up to five levels deep. If you wish to have unrelated but simultaneous transactions, you will have to create and use separate workspaces for each transaction group. If you close a workspace before committing a transaction, it will be automatically rolled back.

Some external databases may not support transactional processing. This will be indicated by the Transactions property of the Database object in question. If you are using a Recordset object that contains external database objects, you can check the Recordset object's Transactions property to see if it is capable of transactions. Another benefit of transactions is that they greatly speed up iterative updates. Whenever you have a looping update, the Transaction methods will give you a substantial performance boost. When using transactions, the updates are written to a buffer in RAM until the CommitTrans is called. You should be aware that very large transactions can run out of memory, thus causing a system error.

CLONE METHOD

Purpose
The Clone method is used to create a duplicate Recordset object that refers to the original object. Table 64-5 shows the arguments for this method.

General Syntax

```
Set cloneobject = recordsetobject.Clone()
```

Table 64-5 Arguments for the Clone method

Argument	Description
recordsetobject	An open Recordset object
cloneobject	The new cloned recordset

Example Syntax

```
Dim MyDB as Database
Dim MyRS1 as Recordset
Dim MyRS2 as Recordset
Set MyDB = Workspaces(0).Opendatabase("Clients")
Set MyRS1 = MyDB.OpenRecordset("SELECT * FROM [Phones] " _
     + " WHERE [SiteID] = 15")
Set MyRS2 = MyRS1.Clone()
'find Contacts fax number
MyRS1.Findfirst "ContactID"= & Clng(Text1.Text) & "Type = 'Fax'"
If Not MyRS1.Nomatch then
     MyRS2.Bookmark = MyRS1.Bookmark
     MyRS2.FindNext "ContactID =" & Clng(Text1.Text) & "Type = 'Fax'"
     'look for duplicate fax record
     If Not MyRS2.NoMatch then
          MsgBox "Duplicate Fax Line"
     End If
End If
MyRS2.Close
MyRS1.Close
MyDB.Close
Set MyRS1 = Nothing
Set MyRS2 = Nothing
Set MyDB = Nothing
```

Description
This example opens a Recordset and makes a clone of the Recordset. It then searches for a particular contact's fax line, and, once found, uses the Clone to find any duplicate fax lines. While a rather contrived example, it does illustrate one of the uses of a cloned Recordset—that is, the searching for duplicate entries without moving the original Recordset's recordpointer. Another advantage is that you can share bookmarks between cloned Recordsets because they are interchangeable. When you create a Clone, it initially does not point to a valid row. You must either set it to the current bookmark of the original Recordset as in the example above, or do a MoveFirst/Last method to point to a valid record. The Clone operates

independently of the original Recordset, and you can perform operations with one without affecting the other. Changes to the underlying row will be reflected in both Recordsets though. If the original Recordset is based on a QueryDef object and you clone it, the QueryDef is not run again; the Clone just gets a set of duplicate row pointers. You can make subsequent clones of either Recordset object without having any effect on the other. You cannot make a Clone of a forward spooling Snapshot-type Recordset.

DELETE METHOD

Purpose
The Delete method is used to delete a record in a Dynaset or Table-type Recordset object or to delete a stored object in a collection of a parent object. Table 64-6 shows the arguments for this method.

General Syntax

```
recordsetobject.Delete
collection.Delete objectname
```

Table 64-6 Arguments for the Delete method

Argument	Description
recordsetobject	An open Recordset object
collection	A persistent collection object like a QueryDef or table
objectname	The name property of the object to delete from the collection

Example Syntax

```
MyRecordset.FindFirst "[Pub_ID] = " & MyItem&
If Not MyRecordset.Nomatch then
      Myrecordset.Delete
Else
      MsgBox "Item: " & MyItem& & " was not found"
End If

'example of deleting an index from a TableDef's Indexes collection
'Get the TableDef with the Index to delete
Set MYTableDef = MyDatabase.TableDefs(Clients")
'Use the Delete method with the TableDef's Indexes collection
MyTableDef.Indexes.Delete "SiteTypes"'Delete the Index
```

Description
In the first example, the Delete method is used to remove records from the Recordset. When used this way, it only flags the particular record for deletion and your application can no longer access the record. It is physically removed only during the DBEngine's CompactDatabase method.

In the second example, the Delete method is being used to remove an Index object from a TableDef's Indexes collection. The delete method is valid for any object's collection where the objects in that collection were originally added through program code. In other words, if you added a User Defined Property to an object's Properties collection you would be able to delete it at a later point. But you will not be able to delete a property that is actually part of the object's class description. You can delete Workspaces that have been added to the DBEngine, but you cannot delete the default Workspaces(0) workspace. Users and Groups require you to have Owner permissions to remove them.

EDIT METHOD

Purpose   The Edit method of the Recordset object is used to modify existing information in a row of data. Table 64-7 shows the argument for this method.

General Syntax

```
recordsetobject.Edit
```

Table 64-7 Argument for the Edit method

Argument	Description
recordsetobject	An open Recordset object

Example Syntax
```
Dim MyDB as Database
Dim MyRS as Recordset

Set MyDB = Workspaces(0).Opendatabase("CLIENTS.MDB")
Set MyRS = MyDB.OpenRecordset("Sites")

Do While Not MyRS.EOF
     'shows edit being used in a loop to update monthly totals
     MyRS.Edit
     MyRS!YTD = MyRS!YTD + MYRS!MTD
     If NewQuarter() Then
          MyRS!QTR = 0
          If NewYear() Then
                MyRS!YTD = 0
          End If
     Else
          MyRS!QTR = MyRS!QTR + MyRS!MTD
     End if
     MyRS!MTD = 0
     MyRS.Update
     MyRs.MoveNext
     'exit the loop if error is encountered in NewQuarter or NewYear
     If BadFlag Then Exit Do
Loop
MyRS.Close
MyDB.Close
Set MyDB = Nothing
Set MyRS = Nothing
```

Description　　　When you use the Edit method of the Recordset object, the contents of the current row are copied into an edit buffer for editing by the application. The Edit method is only valid with a Dynaset or Table-type Recordset and will not work with a Snapshot. As you make changes to the fields in the Recordset, those changes are stored in the edit buffer. When you are done with the edits, you use the Update method of the Recordset object to store those changes to the actual record. If you move the recordpointer, or close the Recordset prior to using the Update method, all your edits to that particular row will be lost without warning. If you are using pessimistic locking (Lockedits=True), then the page that the row resides on is locked until the Update method is used or the Edit is aborted. If you are using Optimistic Locking (Lockedits=False), then the page is locked only when you actually call the Update method. However, while using Optimistic locking, if the record is edited by another user between the time you call the Edit method and the Update method, a trappable error (#3197) will occur. If you are using an ODBC or an installable ISAM database, the locking is always Optimistic. Using the Edit method will also cause trappable errors if there is no current record, the Recordset or its fields are not updatable, or the page is locked by another user.

Execute Method

Purpose　　　The Execute Method of the Database object or QueryDef object is used to run an action QueryDef or a SQL statement. Table 64-8 shows the arguments for this method, and Table 64-9 shows the constants.

General Syntax

```
object.Execute source [, options]
queryDefname.Execute [options]
```

Table 64-8 Arguments for the Execute method

Argument	Description
object	A Connection or Database object
querydefname	The QueryDef object whose SQL statement is to be run
source	The SQL or QueryDef object
options	An integer indicating the data integrity characteristics

Table 64-9 The Execute method's options constants

Constant	Description
dbDenyWrite	Denies write permission to other users during the Execute
dbInconsistent	Allows inconsistent updates (Default)
dbConsistent	Requires consistent updates
dbSQLPassThrough	The SQL statement is processed by the ODBC database
dbFailOnError	Rolls back updates if an update error occurs
dbSeeChanges	Generates a trappable error if record is locked
dbRunAsync	Run asynchronously for ODBC Direct Connections and QueryDefs
dbExecDirect	Does not call SQLPrepare for ODBC Direct Connections and QueryDefs

Example Syntax

```
'example direcly using SQL statement
Dim MyDB as Database
Dim MySQL as String
MySQL = "Delete * From [Transacts] Where [Updated] = True"
Set MyDB = Workspaces(0).Opendatabase("C:\CLIENT.MDB")
'executes the Sql, but will rollback all changes if there is an error
MyDB.Execute MySQL, dbFailOnError
MyDB.Close
Set MyDB = Nothing

'Example using QueryDef object
Dim MyDB As Database
Dim MyQD as QueryDef
Set MyDB = Workspaces(0).Opendatabase("C:\CLIENT.MDB")
Set MuQD = MyDB.QueryDefs("MyQuery")
'assumes "MyQuery" query def is already created
MyQD.Execute
MyQD.close
MyDB.Close
Set MyQD = Nothing
Set MyDB = Nothing

'Example using dbRunAsync
'assuming MyQD set earlier
MyQD.Execute, dbRunAsync
Do Until MyQD.StillExecuting = False
     'DoEvents keeps UI responsive during large transactions
        DoEvents
Loop
```

Description   The preceding examples show two ways to use the Execute method. The first example uses a SQL string as the argument for the execute method. This SQL string must always result in an action type query. Also you will note that the dbFailOnError option was used with this execute. This essentially acts like a transaction set in that, if there is any error encountered during this action, all changes will be rolled back to their original state before the execute method. Table 64-9 defines the options available with their corresponding Constants.

The second example uses an existing QueryDef in the database to execute. First the reference to the QueryDef is set, then the Execute method is used with it. The QueryDef's SQL property must evaluate to an action type query, or a trappable error will occur. If your SQL statement is syntactically correct and you have all the permissions necessary to complete the query, no errors will be generated if an action on a particular row should fail. That is, if the row is on a locked page, the update to that row will not happen and you will not receive any indication that an update failed. To avoid this, it is highly recommended to use the dbFailOnError option when using the Execute method when running an update or delete query. In this case, should an update fail, a trappable error will occur and all changes made during this Execute method will be rolled back. Also, if you are going to be using the Execute method on large Recordsets or need the added speed, nest the Execute inside a Transaction set. After running the query, use the RecordsAffected property of the Database object or QueryDef object to determine how many records were affected by the Execute method.

FIELDSIZE PROPERTY

Purpose
The FieldSize property returns the number of bytes in a Memo or OLE-type field. Table 64-10 shows the arguments for this property.

General Syntax

```
recordsetobject!Fieldname.FieldSize
```

Table 64-10 Arguments for the FieldSize method

Argument	Description
recordsetobject	An open Recordset object
fieldname	The name of an OLE or Memo field in the Recordset object

Example Syntax

```
Dim MyDB as database
Dim MyRS as Recordset
Dim Fsize as Long
Set MyDB = Workspaces(0).OpenDatabase("Clients")
Set MyRS = MyDB.OpenRecordset("Sites")
MyRS.MoveFirst
If MyRS!Notes.Fieldsize > 2^15 then
      msgbox "Notes Greater than 64K"
Else
      Text1 = MyRS!Notes
End If

MyRS.Close
```

```
MyDB.Close
Set MyRS = Nothing
Set MyDB = Nothing
```

Description   The FieldSize method provides a way for your application to determine the size in bytes of an OLE or Memo field before attempting to read it into an object that might not be able to contain it. It is also used in conjunction with the GetChunk method to retrieve these fields in chunks. (See the GetChunk method earlier in this chapter for an example.) To get the size of fields other than an OLE of Memo field, use the Size property of the field.

GETCHUNK METHOD

Purpose   The GetChunk method of the Field object is used to retrieve all or part of an OLE or Memo Field object. Table 64-11 shows the arguments for this method.

General Syntax

```
stringvariable = recordsetobject!field.GetChunk(offset, numbytes)
```

Table 64-11 Arguments for the GetChunk method

Argument	Description
recordsetobject	An open Recordset object
stringvariable	A variable of string type
offset	The number of bytes to bypass before copying
numbytes	The number of bytes you want to retrieve

Example Syntax

```
Const Block = 16348
Dim NumBlocks as integer
Dim TotalSize as long
Dim x as integer
Dim MyDB as Database
Dim MyRS as Recordset
Dim Fnum as Integer
'open the database and get the file to append to
Set MyDB = Workspaces(0).OpenDatabase("Clients")
Set MyRS = MyDB.OpenRecordset("Contacts")
MyRS.FindFirst "[ContactID] = 3"
'get the size of the file
TotalSize = MyRS!Picture.FieldSize()
'how many 16k blocks are there
NumBlocks = TotalSize \ Block - (TotalSize Mod Block <> 0)
ReDim MyBlocks(NumBlocks +1) As String * Block
'Read them into the array
For X = 1 to NumBlocks
```

continued on next page

continued from previous page

```
        MyRS!Picture.GetChunk((X - 1) * Block, Block)
Next X
'get the nexrt file handle
Fnum = FreeFile
open a binary file
Open "c:\MyPICT.BMP" For Binary As #Fnum
'write the blocks to it
For X = 1 to NumBlocks
        Put #Fnum, , MyBlocks(x)
Next
Picture1.Picture = LoadPicture(C:\MYPICT.BMP")
'close up everything
Close #Fnum
MyRS.Close
MyDB.Close
Set MyRS = Nothing
Set MyDB = Nothing
```

Description   The GetChunk method provides a way for your application to access fields that exceed the 64K string limit of Visual Basic. In the above example, the GetChunk method is used to read a field that contains a bitmap. (See AppendChunk for an example that places bitmap into a field.) This bitmap is read into a string array. The string array is then read into a binary file on disk. Finally the bitmap is loaded into a Picture object using the LoadPicture method. Other uses for the GetChunk method would be to read a memo into an array and feed it to a text box a section at a time so that the 64K limit is not exceeded. The offset argument is zero based and allows you to start your reading of bytes at any point in the memo. The numbytes argument specifies the number of bytes to read in when the GetChunk method is used. If the numbytes is greater than the number of bytes left in the Field object, then the actual number of bytes remaining is returned.

REQUERY METHOD

Purpose   The Requery method is used to update the data in a Recordset object by running the underlying query again. Table 64-12 lists the argument for this method.

General Syntax

```
recordsetobject.Requery
```

Table 64-12 Argument for the Requery method

Argument	Description
recordsetobject	An open Recordset object

Example Syntax

```
MyRecordset.Requery
```

Description   The Jet database engine does not always have enough processor time to maintain dynamically created Recordsets or the underlying Table data. This can cause your Recordset to sometimes not have the most up-to-date changes in the underlying tables. The Requery method ensures that your Recordset's data is valid to be running the underlying query, again repopulating the Recordset with the latest data. The method has the same effect as that of closing the Recordset and opening it again. The Requery method only works on Dynaset or Snapshot-type Recordsets whose Restartable property is set to True. The Requery method does not work with a Table-type Recordset. After running the Requery method, it is a good practice to check to make sure that records were actually returned.

UPDATE METHOD

Purpose   The Update method of the Recordset object saves the contents of the edit buffer to the Recordset object. Table 64-13 shows the argument for this method.

General Syntax

```
recordsetobject.Update
```

Table 64-13 Argument for the Update method

Argument	Description
recordsetobject	An open Recordset object

Example Syntax

```
Dim MyDB as Database
Dim MyRS as Recordset

MyDB = Workspaces(0).OpenDatabase("Clients")
MyRS = MyDB.OpenRecordset("Select * From [Contacts] Where [ClientID] = 1"
MyRS.FindFirst "[Zip] = '87035'"
' begin the edit process for the current row
MyRS.Edit
MyRS!Type = "Management"
'update the contents of the edit buffer into the recordset
MyRS.Update
MyRS.Close
MyDB.Close
Set MyRS = Nothing
Set MyDB = Nothing
```

Description

The Update method is valid only for Recordsets of Table-type or Dynaset type. In addition, the Updatable property must be set to True. The Update method is used to complete the processes started with the AddNew or Edit methods. If you initiate an AddNew or Edit without using a subsequent Update method, your changes will be lost when you move the record-pointer, issue another AddNew or Edit, or close the Recordset. This loss of changes will occur without any warning. If, when using optimistic lock-ing, the underlying data has changed from the time you have issued the Edit method to the time you issue the Update method, a trappable error (# 3197) will occur. If this happens, it is best to read the data in again and restart your edits after reviewing the changes. When you access ODBC or installable ISAMs, you always use optimistic locking.

65

MOVING AND SEARCHING

Once you've created your database and its tables and populated it with data, you typically need a way to view and search that data. In Chapters 62, "Beginning SQL," and 63, "Advanced SQL," the Relational Model based on SQL of the DML was discussed. In this chapter, the Navigational Model will be the focus, although you will see that they are closely intertwined in the Microsoft Jet database. Most programmers who have previously worked with Xbase-type databases are familiar with the navigational models used by Microsoft FoxPro, dBase, and Paradox. The Jet's navigational model is very similar and, if you have worked with these databases before, you'll find it very easy to adapt to Jet's navigational model.

It is important, while learning to use Visual Basic 5.0's Jet database engine, to understand that Jet is not an either-or proposition with the Relational or Navigational models, but instead a blend of the techniques to gain the most benefit from the database engine. While the following discussion will concentrate on the navigational methods, you will find that they are often combined with the SQL of the relational methods.

Bookmarks

A bookmark is a marker indicating the place of a particular row in the Recordset. It is not exactly like a record number but can be used to locate a particular record very quickly. Bookmarks are system-generated strings that Jet recognizes as place markers. To use a bookmark, set a string variable to equal a Recordset object's BookMark property. Then, after you have moved around in the Recordset and need to quickly return to that row, set the Recordset object's BookMark property to equal the bookmark you previously stored.

```
Dim BkMark as String
'check if recordset is book markable
```

continued on next page

continued from previous page

```
If MyRecordset.Bookmarkable Then
      'set the bookmark
      BkMark = MyRecordset.BookMark
Else
      'set Bkmark to empty string if not bookmarkable
      BkMark = ""
End If
'do whatever processing is needed
.....
'check for valid bookmark
If Len(BkMark) > O Then
      'if valid then go to marked row
      MyRecordset.BookMark = BkMark
Else
      'if not valid then go to first row
      MyRecordset.MoveFirst
Endif
```

In this example, the procedure first checks the Recordset's Bookmarkable property. If it is True, a BookMark is stored in the BkMark variable; if it is False (not bookmarkable), an empty string is stored. After the required processing is finished, the procedure checks for a valid BookMark in the BkMark variable. If there is one, it returns to the marked row. If there is an empty string, it returns to the first record.

Filters

Once you have created a Recordset, you can further refine it by filtering the Recordset. To filter a Dynaset-type or Snapshot-type Recordset, first specify the criteria that will limit the Recordset to the rows that match your criteria. Using the Clients database, you may want to sort the Clients table for a particular client's sites.

```
Dim MyRS as Recordset      'original recordset
Dim MyFRS as Recordset     'filtered recordset
Dim MySQL as string        'SQL string
MySQL = "SELECT * FROM Clients"
MySQL = MySQL + " LEFT JOIN Sites On Clients.ClientID = Sites.ClientID"
MySQL = MySQL + " WHERE Client.TYPE = 'FAST FOODS'"
'open main recordset
'MyDB is a Database object created or opened elsewhere
Set MyRS = MyDB.OpenRecordset(MySQL, dbOpenSnapshot).
'set the filter criteria
MyRS.Filter = "Clients.[ClientID] = 1"
'open the filtered recordset
Set MyFRS = MyRS.Recordset
```

The MyFRS Recordset object now contains only rows that meet the filter specification. The filter expression can be any expression that meets the requirements of the "Where" clause of a SQL expression without the *Where* being included. It should be noted that it is much quicker to create a Recordset based on a SQL than to use the above process to create a filtered Recordset. The following produces the same effect as the preceding example:

```
Dim MyRS as Recordset      'original recordset
Dim MySQL as string        'SQL string
```

```
MySQL = "SELECT * FROM Clients"
MySQL = MySQL + " LEFT JOIN Sites On Clients.ClientID = Sites.ClientID"
MySQL = MySQL + " WHERE Client.TYPE = 'FAST FOODS'"
MySQL = MySQL + " AND Clients.[ClintsID] = 1"
'open main recordset
Set MyRS = MyDB.OpenRecordset(MySQL, dbOpenSnapshot)
```

There is only one OpenRecordset operation accomplishing the same thing as the filtered operation.

Sorting a Recordset

When you create a Recordset object as a Table type, the sort order of the Recordset is that of the order of the original entry. It is very probable that you would prefer to arrange the order of the Recordset according to the ascending or descending order of a field in that table. To order a Table-type Recordset according to a specific field, that field must be indexed. To change the sort order of a Recordset according to an indexed field, do the following:

```
MyRS.Index = 'PrimaryKey"'Sorts recordset by the PrimaryKey
MyRS.Index = 'SiteID''Sorts recordset according to SiteID index
```

When you create a Recordset object of a Dynaset-type or Snapshot-type, you must use the Order By clause in the SQL statement that creates the Recordset, or use the Sort property of an existing Recordset and create a second Recordset based on that sort order. The following code fragment shows how to use the Sort property.

```
Dim MyRS as Recordset      'original recordset
Dim MySRS as Recordset     'Sorted recordset
Dim MySQL as string        'SQL string
MySQL = "SELECT * FROM Clients"
MySQL = MySQL + " LEFT JOIN Sites On Clients.ClientID = Sites.ClientID"
MySQL = MySQL + " WHERE Client.TYPE = 'FAST FOODS'"
'open main recordset
Set MyRS = MyDB.OpenRecordset(MySQL, dbOpenSnapshot)
'set the Sort field
'Default sort order is ASC ascending, syntax follows
'sort="field1 [ASC | DESC ][, field2 [ASC | DESC ]][, ...]]]"
MyRS.Sort = "Clients.[ClientID] DESC
'open the sorted recordset
Set MySRS = MyRS.Recordset
```

As in the Filtered property, this is not the most efficient or quickest method. This second example fragment shows how to sort the Recordset while creating it.

```
Dim MyRS as Recordset'original recordset
Dim MySQL as string'SQL string
MySQL = "SELECT * FROM Clients LEFT JOIN Sites On" _
      + " Clients.ClientID = Sites.ClientID" _
      + " WHERE Client.TYPE = 'FAST FOODS' ORDER BY Clients.[ClientID]"
'open sorted recordset
Set MyRS = MyDB.OpenRecordset(MySQL, dbOpenSnapshot)
```

Chapter 62 explains the use of the Order By clause of the SQL language in more detail.

Navigating the Recordset with the Move Methods

Visual Basic 5.0 provides for methods to move around the Recordset object once you have created it. They are collectively known as the Move methods. The MoveFirst and MoveLast methods will bring you to either extreme of the Recordset. The MoveNext and MovePrevious methods will move you one row at a time in their respective directions. When using the MoveNext or MovePrevious methods, you must make provisions in your application to ensure that the user does not exceed the end of the Recordset (EOF) or beginning of the Recordset (BOF). The following code example shows a way to use these methods.

```
Private Sub Command1_Click(Index As Integer)
Select Case Index
    Case 0 'move first
        MyRS.MoveFirst
        'disable move previous because
        'there we are at the beginning
        'of recordset.
        Command1(1).Enabled = False
        'enable move next button
        Command1(2).Enabled = True
        'populate the edit display
        ReadClients                 'user defined sub
    Case 1  'move previous
        MyRS.MovePrevious
        If MyRS.BOF Then
            'oops, moved past the first row
            'so move back to valid row and
            MyRS.MoveFirst
            'disable moveprevious
            Command1(1).Enabled = False
        End If
        'enable the movenext button
        Command1(2).Enabled = True
        'populate the edit display
        ReadClients                 'user defined sub
    Case 2  'move next
        MyRS.MoveNext
        If MyRS.EOF Then
            'oops, moved past the last row
            'so move back to valid row and
            MyRS.MoveLast
            'disable the movenext button
            Command1(2).Enabled = False
        End If
            'enable the moveprevious button
            Command1(1).Enabled = True
            'populate the edit display
            ReadClients                 'user defined sub
    Case 3  'move last
        MyRS.MoveLast
        'enable the moveprevious button
        Command1(1).Enabled = True
        'disable the movenext button
        Command1(2).Enabled = False
        'populate the edit display
        ReadClients                 'user defined sub
```

Finding Particular Records with the Seek Method

If your Recordset object is a Table-type Recordset, then you must use the Seek method to search it. The Seek method uses the underlying table's current index to locate the specified criteria. While the Seek method is perhaps the fastest way to search for a particular record, it is not as flexible as the Find methods. The arguments available for the Seek method are as follows:

- = Equal to the specified key values

- >= Greater or equal to the specified key values

- > Greater than the specified key values

- <= Less than or equal to the specified key values

- < Less than the specified key values

To use the Seek method, your Recordset must first have a current index. The following is an example of the Seek method:

```
Dim MyRS as Recordset
Set MyRS = MyDatabase.OpenRecordset("Clients", dbOpenTable)
'Set the current index to the Primary Key
MyRS.Index = 'PrimaryKey"
'Have a place to return to if Seek fails
BkMark = MyRS.BookMark
'Specify the search criteria
MyRS.Seek "=", 11
 'check for match and act accordingly
If MyRS.Nomatch Then
      MsgBox = "Record Not Found"
      MyRS.BookMark = MkMark
Else
      MsgBox =  MyRS![Client Name]
End If
```

If you do not have a current index set for the Recordset when you use the Seek method, a trappable error will occur. If the current index is a multiple field index, then trailing key values can be left out and are treated as Nulls.

Finding Your Position

Visual Basic exposes several properties to help determine and control the position in the recordset. The RecordCount property returns the number of records in the recordset. The AbsolutePosition is a value that can be used to read or set the position from 0 to RecordCount −1, the recordset. A handy tool for status updates is the PercentPosition property. It can also be used to set where you are in the recordset.

Moving and Searching Summary

Table 65-1 summarizes moving and searching. Detailed descriptions of the methods and properties follow.

Table 65-1 Moving and searching summary

Use This...	Type	To Do This...
AbsolutePosition	Property	Set or check the position in the Recordset
BookMark	Property	Save a place in a Recordset
FillCache	Method	Fill the local cache for a Recordset with ODBC data
FindFirst, FindLast, FindNext, FindPrevious	Methods	Find rows in a Recordset that match given criteria
Move	Method	Navigate a Recordset in large steps
MoveFirst, MoveLast, MoveNext, MovePrevious	Methods	Navigate a Recordset
PercentPosition	Property	Set or check the position in a Recordset
RecordCount	Property	Get the number of records in a Recordset
Seek	Method	Find the row containing specific criteria in a Table-type Recordset

ABSOLUTEPOSITION PROPERTY

Purpose   The AbsolutePosition property allows the application to set or check the position in the recordset. Table 65-2 lists the arguments for the AbsolutePosition property.

General Syntax

```
recordsetobject.AbsolutePosition [= position]
```

Table 65-2 Arguments for the AbsolutePosition property

Argument	Description
recordsetobject	An open Recordset object
position	The 0 to RecordCount −1 value of where the application is in the recordset

Example Syntax
```
Sub Find2ndBest()
Dim MySQL as String
MySQL = "SELECT * FROM Clients ORDER BY Clients.[Orders]"
Set MyRS = MyDB.OpenRecordset(MySQL, dbOpenSnapshot)
MyRS.AbsolutePosition = 1
End Sub
```

Description   Sometimes there is a need to set or retrieve exactly where in the recordset the application is. The AbsolutePosition allows an application to do this. AbsolutePosition should not be used as a BookMark. It points to a position in the recordset, not a specific row. In the preceding example, AbsolutePosition is used to set a recordset to the second client with the second-highest orders (1 = 2 − 1 since AbsolutePosition goes from 0 to RecordCount −1).

BookMark Property

Purpose   The BookMark property is used to save a place in the recordset so that it may be returned to later. Arguments for the BookMark property can be found in Table 65-3.

General Syntax

```
recordsetobject.BookMark [= mark]
```

Table 65-3 Arguments for the BookMark property

Argument	Description
recordsetobject	An open Recordset object
mark	A string holding a bookmark previously retrieved

Example Syntax

```
Dim ComeBackLater as String
If MyRS.Bookmarkable = False Then
      MsgBox "Unable to return to saved position."
Else
      ComeBackLater = MyRS.BookMark
End If
'do some stuff

'now set the bookmark to return to the same place
If ComeBackLater <> "" Then MyRS.BookMark = ComeBackLater
```

Description   Often an application will want to mark a place in the recordset and return to it later. If the Bookmarkable property of the recordset is True, then you can use the BookMark property to save the current place of the recordset and then use that value to return there later.

FillCache Method

Purpose   The FillCache method is used to fill a local cache for a Recordset object that contains data from an ODBC data source. Table 65-4 shows the arguments for the FillCache method.

General Syntax

```
recordsetobject.FillCache [rows [start]]
```

Table 65-4 Arguments for the FillCache method

Argument	Description
recordsetobject	An open Recordset object
rows	The number of rows to return
start	A bookmark from which to begin filling the cache

Example Syntax

```
Dim MyDB as Database
Dim MyRS as Recordset
'Open database with attached ODBC table
Set MyDB = Workspaces(0).OpenDatabase("MYODBC.MDB")
'open a recordset on that table
Set MyRS = MyDB.OpenRecordset("BIGODBC")
'find the row to start the cache from
MyRS.FindFirst "[ACCNT]= 1001"

Do While Not MyRS.EOF

        'start the cache at the desired row
        MyRS.CacheStart = MyRS.BookMark
        'set the size of the caches in rows
        MyRS.CacheSize = 20
        'fill the cache with the rows
        MyRS.FillCache
        'loop through records in cache processing them
        For MyCount = 1 to 20
                ....'do whatever processing needed
                MyRS.MoveNext
                'if EOF then there are less than 20 records to process
                If MyRS.EOF then Exit For
        Next
        'empty the cache to clear it for more rows
        MyRS.CacheSize = 0
Loop
MyRS.Close
MyDB.Close

Set MyRS = Nothing
Set MyDB = Nothing
```

Description   When retrieving data from a remote server, performance can suffer from a variety of problems such as high network traffic, the speed of ODBC calls, Server user load, and so on. Caching improves remote server performance by allowing you to locally cache as many rows as you have allotted space for. Thus, instead of retrieving rows as you move the recordpointer, you can retrieve several at one time with a single call to the server. As you move your recordpointer, the Jet will look into the cache first for the proper rows before making a request to the server for more rows. Thus, retrieval will be from a local cache instead of from the remote server.

In the example syntax, the cache is being filled with 20 records at a time, processed, then the cache is cleared and filled with the next 20 records.

The cache could be set to any size from 5 to 1200 that gave your application the best performance boost. There are some things to consider with this method though. The most important being that the data loaded into a cache is not dynamic. It will not reflect any changes made to those rows by other users during the time it is in the cache. Also, this technique is available only to ODBC databases. If you try to use it with an installable ISAM or native table, you will generate trappable error # 3219. The FillCache method will retrieve only records not already cached. To ensure a fresh set of data, set the CacheSize to zero then back to the desired size to clear it.

FINDFIRST, FINDLAST, FINDNEXT, AND FINDPREVIOUS METHODS

Purpose   The Find methods of the Recordset object are used to find rows in a Recordset that match the criteria provided. Table 65-5 lists the arguments for the FindFirst, FindLast, FindNext, and FindPrevious methods.

General Syntax

```
recordsetobject.FindFirst|FindLast|FindNext|Findprevious criteria
```

Table 65-5 Arguments for the FindFirst, FindLast, FindNext, and FindPrevious methods

Argument	Description
recordsetobject	An open Recordset object
criteria	A string expression describing the search item

Example Syntax

```
Dim MyDB as Database
Dim MyRS as Recordset
Dim Criteria as String
Criteria = "[Name] Like 'MacBeefs*'"

Set MyDB = Workspaces(0).OpenDatabase("Clients")
Set MyRS = MyDB.OpenRecordset( _
    "Select * From [Sites] Where Zip Like '87*'")
If MyRS.Recordcount > 0 Then
    'finds the first row that matches the criteria
    MyRS.Findfirst Criteria
    Do While Not MyRS.Nomatch
        MyRS.Delete
        'finds all subsequent rows that match the criteria
        MyRS.FindNext Criteria
    Loop
Endif
MyRS.Close
MyDB.Close
Set MyRS = Nothing
Set MyDB = Nothing
```

Description	The Find methods search your Recordset for rows that match a given criteria. The criteria is the same as the Where clause of a SQL statement without the *Where*. In other words, you include the field name you wish to search and what you are searching for. You can use multiple field searches, pattern matching, the Between clause, and any other construct that you would use in the Where clause of a SQL statement. The FindFirst method will search from the beginning of the Recordset to the end for a match. The FindLast will search from the last row of the Recordset to the beginning looking for a match. The FindNext method will search from the current row to the end of the Recordset for a match. The FindPrevious method will search from the current row to the beginning of the Recordset for a match. To determine whether your Find method has found a match, check the NoMatch property of the Recordset object. If there has been a match, then the NoMatch property will be False. If there was no match, then the NoMatch property will be True. If a Find method results in a NoMatch, then the recordpointer is set to the first row.

MOVE METHOD

Purpose	The Move method of the Recordset object provides the application with the capability to navigate the Recordset in large steps. The arguments for the Move method are listed in Table 65-6.

General Syntax

```
recordsetobject.Move rows[, start]
```

Table 65-6 Arguments for the Move method

Argument	Description
recordsetobject	An open Recordset object
rows	The number of rows to move
start	An optional bookmark from which to start; default is current position

Example Syntax

```
Sub Jump(HowFar as Integer, Optional FromWhere as Variant)
if not IsMissing(FromWhere) Then
      MyRS.Move HowFar, FromWhere
else
      MyRS.Move HowFar
end if
End Sub
```

Description	The Move method allows your application to navigate the Recordset in either direction by a number of rows at a time and to optionally specify

the starting point. The sub moves the MyRS record set by the HowFar parameter. If a FromWhere parameter has been passed in, then it passes in the FromWhere as the start.

MoveFirst, MoveLast, MoveNext, and MovePrevious Methods

Purpose   The MoveFirst, MoveLast, MoveNext, and MovePrevious methods of the Recordset object provide the application with the ability to navigate the Recordset. The MoveFirst method moves to the first row of the Recordset. The MoveLast method moves to the last row of the Recordset. The MoveNext method moves to the next row of the Recordset towards the EOF. The MovePrevious moves to the next row of the Recordset towards the BOF. Table 65-7 shows the argument for the MoveFirst, MoveLast, MoveNext, and MovePrevious methods.

General Syntax

```
recordsetobject.MoveFirst|MoveLast|MoveNext|MovePrevious
```

Table 65-7 Argument for the MoveFirst, MoveLast, MoveNext, and MovePrevious methods

Argument	Description
recordsetobject	An open Recordset object

Example Syntax

```
Sub Command1_Click (Index as Integer)
'reset disabled buttons
Command1(1).Enabled = True
Command1(2).Enabled = True
Select Case Index

    Case 0      'move to first record
         MyRS.MoveFirst
         'disable the move previous button
         'because there are no previous records
         Command1(1).Enabled = False
    Case 1      'Move to previous record
         MyRs!MovePrevious
         'if past the Beginning of File then disable
         'MovePrevious button to prevent error
         'and move back to the first valid record
         If MyRS.BOF then
              MyRS.MoveFirst
              Command1(1).Enabled = False
         End If
    Case 2      'Move to Next record
         MyRS!MoveNext
         'if past the End of File then disable
         'MoveNext button and move back to
```

continued on next page

continued from previous page

```
            'the last valid record
            If MyRS.EOF then
                    MyRS.MoveLast
                    Command(2).Enabled = False
            End If
       Case 3      'Move to last record
            'disable the move next button because
            'we are already at the end with no more rows
             Command(2).Enabled = False
             MyRs!MoveLast
End Select

End Sub
```

Description The MoveFirst, MoveLast, MoveNext, and MovePrevious methods allow
your application to navigate the Recordset in either direction by one row
at a time or to go immediately to the beginning or end of the Recordset.
When using the MoveNext or MovePrevious methods, it is possible to
move into an undefined space in the Recordset, causing a trappable error.
If you observe the example above, you will see that the MoveNext/
Previous buttons are disabled whenever you are at either end of the
Recordset object's spectrum. Keep in mind that if you have issued an Edit
and then move to another record before saving your changes, you will lose
those changes.

PercentPosition Property

Purpose The PercentPosition property allows the application to set or check an
approximation of the position in the recordset. Arguments for the
PercentPosition property are listed in Table 65-8.

General Syntax

```
recordsetobject.PercentPosition [= position]
```

Table 65-8 Arguments for the PercentPosition property

Argument	Description
recordsetobject	An open Recordset object
position	The percent value of how far through the recordset the application is

Example Syntax
```
Sub AfterMove()
ProgressBar1.Value = MyRS.PercentPosition
End Sub
```

Description   A friendly application will typically let the user know just how much of a task is completed. The PercentPosition allows the application to know just how far it is through the recordset. The PercentPosition uses the RecordCount property to calculate its value; therefore, in most cases, it will not be accurate until the entire recordset has been read. This can be forced by using a MoveLast method before using the PercentPosition property.

RECORDCOUNT PROPERTY

Purpose   The RecordCount property allows the application to see how many records are in a Recordset. The argument for the RecordCount Property is shown in 65-9.

General Syntax

```
recordsetobject.RecordCount
```

Table 65-9 Argument for the RecordCount property

Argument	Description
recordsetobject	An open Recordset object

Example Syntax

```
If MsgBox("There are " & MyRS.RecordCount & " records in the table" _
    + chr$(vbKeyReturn) + "Do you wish to process now?", vbYesNo) _
    = vbYes Then
    RunReport            'a user function
End If
```

Description   The RecordCount property can be used to find the number of records in a recordset; however, this number is not accurate until the entire recordset has been read. A MoveLast method will guarantee that all records have been read and the RecordCount property has the correct value.

SEEK METHOD

Purpose   The Seek method is used in a Table-type Recordset object to find, using an Index object, the row containing the specified criteria. Arguments for the Seek method are shown in Table 65-10.

General Syntax

```
Recordsetobject.Seek comparison, key1, key2...
```

Table 65-10 Arguments for the Seek method

Argument	Description
recordsetobject	An open Recordset object
comparison	A string containing the comparison operator: <, <=, =, >=, >
key1,key2,...	Criteria that match the data type of the corresponding field

Example Syntax

```
Dim MyDB as Database
Dim MyRS as Recordset

Set MyDB = WorkSpaces(0).OpenDatabase("CLIENTS.MDB")
Set MyRS = MyDB.OpenRecordset("Contacts", dbOpenTable)

Set MyRS.Index = "ClientID"
MyRS.Seek "=", 3
If Not Nomatch Then
        MsgBox "Client Contact Found"
Else
        Msgbox "No Contacts for Client Located"
End If
.....
```

Description

The Seek method of the Recordset object works only with a Table-type Recordset that is not an attached table. You can use Seek on Table-type Recordsets that are from installable ISAM databases that you opened up directly. In addition, you can seek only on a field or fields that are indexed. It does not give you the flexibility of the Find methods such as SQL-like criteria conditions or Previous and subsequent finds on the same criteria. With these restrictions in mind, the Seek method is the fastest method of locating data in your database. The Seek method finds the first row that matches your criteria depending on the direction of the seek. If you use the =, >, or >=, the search will start at the beginning of the Recordset and search towards the end. If you use the < or <=, the search will start at the end of the Recordset and search toward the first row. If a match is found, the NoMatch prorate will be set to False. If no match is found then the NoMatch prorate will be set to True. If the index to be used is the primary key of the table, then refer to it as the 'PrimaryKey' in your Recordset's Index Property. The criteria arguments must match the data types of the index field. If the field is a numeric type, use a number as in the example syntax. If the argument is a string, use a string expression.

66

REMOTE DATA ACCESS AND DCOM

Today's applications have reached beyond the single desktop. A typical application can encompass entire networks, and some even span the Internet. The first applications that reached out from the desktop accessed remote data, through relational databases or shared files. An array of choices is available to the Visual Basic programmer who wants to connect to remote data, each with its own strengths and weaknesses. This chapter will present the choices available and hopefully help you find the strategy that is best for your application.

With the release of DCOM, Distributed Component Object Model, the application itself is no longer confined to a single machine. ActiveX servers may run on entirely different machines, completely transparent to the client application. This allows you to put the processing close to the data. If an application must sift through 50,000 rows of a table to find a simple yes or no, putting the processing on or near the server with the data can save expensive bandwidth and speed up the application.

Remote Data Access Choices

A Visual Basic programmer is presented with a myriad of data access choices. Table 66-1 summarizes the data access choices available and their features. The following sections discuss each of the choices in detail. Each section has sample code that shows the initialization, opening of a connection, retrieval of results, and shutdown to help you get an idea of the flow of the data access method.

Table 66-1 Data access options

Data Access Option	Connects To	Description
DAO (Data Access Object)	ODBC or ISAM datasources	Connects to virtually anything; query processor allows operations across data sources
RDO (Remote Data Object)	ODBC datasources	Slimmer than DAO because it has no query processor or built-in Jet support
ODBC API	ODBC datasources	Slimmest connection to ODBC datasource; no query processor; requires more care in programming
VBSQL	Microsoft SQL Server	Connects only to Microsoft SQL Server; very slim and fast; old technology

Data Access Objects

DAO has been discussed extensively in this text and is the data access option that presents the greatest flexibility. DAO can connect to ODBC and ISAM datasources. DAO has its own query processor that allows it to perform heterogeneous operations. That means an application using DAO can join between a table in an Access database, a text file, and a Microsoft SQL Server table, all in one Recordset! Any DAO Recordset can also be bound to a control. This allows quick and easy development of applications.

This flexibility is not without a cost. DAO is the slowest of the data access options and has the largest memory footprint. Some of these drawbacks may be mitigated with a new feature of DAO released with Visual Basic 5.0. DAO now allows the creation of ODBC Direct workspaces. These workspaces don't use the Jet engine for query processing, they allow the ODBC datasource to do the work. Typically, using an ODBC Direct workspace results in a significant increase in performance, but the use of heterogeneous operations is lost. However, since DAO allows the creation of ODBC Direct and Jet workspaces, you get the best of both worlds. With ODBC Direct workspaces, you get speed when you really need it; with a Jet workspace, you get access to everything.

ODBC Direct uses RDO to do its processing, so ODBC Direct is constrained by limitations as RDO. However, ODBC Direct does not get all the benefits of RDO, so if your application doesn't need the extra functionality of the Jet engine, maybe it's time to look at RDO.

The sample below uses DAO to open a connection to a remote datasource and put a small set of results in a combo box:

```
Dim conn As Connection
Dim rs As Recordset

'open the connection
On Error GoTo ConnFailed
Set conn = DBEngine.Workspaces(0).OpenConnection(" ", dbDriverNoPrompt _
    , False, "DSN=Contacts;UID=sa;PWD=;")

'send a SQL command
On Error GoTo SQLFailed
Set rs = conn.OpenRecordset("SELECT ContactId, ContactName" _
    + " FROM Contact", dbOpenDynaset)
Do Until rs.EOF
```

```
        cboSelection.AddItem rs("ContactName")
        cboSelection.ItemData(cboSelection.NewIndex) = rs("ContactId")
        rs.MoveNext
Loop

'close the resultset
rs.Close
'close the connection
conn.Close
Set rs = Nothing
Set conn = Nothing
Exit Sub

SQLFailed:
MsgBox "Query failed."
conn.Close
Set conn = Nothing
Exit Sub

ConnFailed:
MsgBox "Could not open connection."
Exit Sub
```

Remote Data Objects

RDO is a very thin (less than 250K) object layer on top of the ODBC API. This makes it very fast but still easy to use. RDO does not have its own query processor, so all work is done by the ODBC datasource. This means no heterogeneous operations. RDO cannot connect to ISAM datasources; the Access ODBC driver must be used to connect to an Access or ISAM database. This approach is slower and does not have access to all the functionality provided by using DAO to access these types of datasources.

RDO does have its own version of the data control called the remote data control, with abilities similar to the data control based on DAO. The remote data control can be used to generate applications fast without a lot of code.

RDO does require that its datasources have a 32-bit Level II-compliant driver. Since RDO is a layer on top of the ODBC API, you can often use RDO in conjunction with the ODBC API for even more flexibility and power. Mixing and matching data access methods this way is considered risky, and Microsoft warns that general protection faults and data loss may result.

RDO's object model is very similar to DAO's. It should be easy for a programmer proficient in one to learn the other and switch between the two. If you think your application needs to mix the two access options, then take a serious look at using just DAO with ODBC Direct.

The sample below performs the same function as its counterpart in the DAO section. The samples are remarkably similar, and as you can see, the object models for DAO and RDO are very close:

```
Dim conn As rdoConnection
Dim rs As rdoResultset

'open the connection
On Error GoTo ConnFailed
```

continued on next page

continued from previous page

```
Set conn = rdoEngine.rdoEnvironments(0).OpenConnection _
      ("", rdDriverNoPrompt, False, "DSN=Contacts;UID=sa;PWD=;")

'send a SQL command
On Error GoTo SQLFailed
Set rs = conn.OpenResultset("SELECT ContactId, ContactName" _
      + " FROM Contact", rdOpenKeyset, rdConcurReadOnly, rdExecDirect)
Do Until rs.EOF
      cboSelection.AddItem rs("ContactName")
      cboSelection.ItemData(cboSelection.NewIndex) = rs("ContactId")
      rs.MoveNext
Loop

'close the resultset
conn.Close
'close the connection
rs.Close
Set rs = Nothing
Set Conn =  Nothing
Exit Sub

SQLFailed:
MsgBox "Query failed."
conn.Close
Set Conn = Nothing
Exit Sub

ConnFailed:
MsgBox "Could not open connection."
Exit Sub
```

The ODBC API

For the fastest and smallest memory footprint to access multiple types of datasources, the ODBC API is the choice. However, as is typically the case, getting more speed and granular control jeopardizes complexity and ease of use. The ODBC API is not geared towards use by Visual Basic and therefore has not been made bulletproof. It is very easy to cause a general protection fault with the ODBC API, something that should be nearly impossible to do with DAO or RDO.

As with RDO, the ODBC API cannot be used to connect to an ISAPI datasource, except through the Access ODBC driver. Heterogeneous operations are not possible with the ODBC API, and even though there are fewer API functions than VBSQL, they are typically more complicated to use.

If you already have an application with working code, it may not be worth the cost to convert to RDO or DAO, but if you are starting a new application, RDO may be a better choice than the ODBC API. Typically, the object model is easier to use, and if you need one of the ODBC APIs, RDO allows you to supplement it with ODBC API calls.

The following code shows the same function again, this time with the ODBC API. As you can see, the code is quite complicated compared to the RDO, DAO, or even VBSQL versions:

```
Dim rc As Integer, henv As Long, hdbc As Long
Dim hstmt As Long
Dim StringResult As String, IntegerResult As Integer, LenRead As Long

'create the environment
rc = SQLAllocEnv(henv)

'allocate the connection
rc = SQLAllocConnect(ByVal henv, hdbc)

'open the connection
rc = SQLConnect(hdbc, "Contacts", Len("Contacts"), "sa", Len("sa"), "" _
     , 0)

If rc <> SQL_SUCCESS And rc <> SQL_SUCCESS_WITH_INFO Then
     Exit Sub
ElseIf rc = SQL_SUCCESS_WITH_INFO Then
     DescribeError henv, hdbc, 0
End If

'allocate the statement
rc = SQLAllocStmt(hdbc, hstmt)

'send the SQL command
If SQLExecDirect(hstmt, "SELECT ContactId, ContactName FROM Contact", _
     Len("SELECT ContactId, ContactName FROM Contact")) _
     = SQL_SUCCESS Then

     Do
             rc = SQLFetch(hstmt)
             If rc = SQL_SUCCESS_WITH_INFO Then
                 DescribeError henv, hdbc, hstmt
             End If
             If rc = SQL_SUCCESS Or _
                 rc = SQL_SUCCESS_WITH_INFO Then
                 StringResult = String$(1024, 0)
                 If SQLGetData(hstmt, 1, SQL_C_CHAR, StringResult _
                     , 100, LenRead) <> SQL_SUCCESS Then
                     DescribeError henv, hdbc, hstmt
                     Exit Do
                 End If
                 cboSelection.AddItem Left$(StringResult, LenRead)
                 If SQLGetData(hstmt, 2, SQL_C_USHORT, IntegerResult _
                     , 3, LenRead) <> SQL_SUCCESS Then
                     DescribeError henv, hdbc, hstmt
                     Exit Do
                 End If
                 cboSelection.ItemData(cboSelection.NewIndex) = _
                 Val(Left$(sValue, lValueLen))
             End If
     Loop While rc = SQL_SUCCESS
Else
     DescribeError henv, hdbc, hstmt
     Exit Sub
End If

'deallocate the statement
rc = SQLFreeStmt(hstmt, SQL_CLOSE)
'close the connection
```

continued on next page

continued from previous page

```
rc = SQLDisconnect(hdbc)
'deallocate the connection
rc = SQLFreeConnect(hdbc)
'deallocate the environment
rc = SQLFreeEnv(henv)
```

VBSQL

VBSQL is DB-Library. Before there was ODBC, the native library for talking to the Microsoft SQL Server or Sybase SQL Server was DB-Library. VBSQL is the implementation of DB-Library tuned for Visual Basic. It includes a custom control to handle the error callbacks and has APIs for almost all Microsoft SQL Server features, but the functions are not as complex as the ODBC API. VBSQL is more bullet resistant than the ODBC API, and it is harder to cause a protection fault through a programming error with VBSQL. However, it is still an API, which means it is easier to get in trouble with VBSQL than it is with either DAO or RDO.

VBSQL is very fast and has a small memory footprint, but only allows you to connect to Microsoft SQL Server and older versions of Sybase SQL Server. When ODBC was in its first incarnation, there was a significant performance advantage of using VBSQL. That advantage has been erased now that ODBC is also a native API for Microsoft SQL Server. VBSQL is old technology, and Microsoft now actively discourages its use. As with the ODBC API, if you have existing code, it may not be worth the cost to convert to another data access method, but if you are starting a new application, VBSQL is not recommended.

The following code shows a small example of a VBSQL application. The code begins by initializing the VBSQL environment and opening a connection. A simple select is sent through that connection, and the results are placed in a ComboBox control. The code then closes the connection and goes through itself to shut down the VBSQL environment. A typical application would only have the If… Then… Else that starts with the SqlSendCmd function in a function that performs a query. The rest of the code handles initialization and connection issues.

```
Dim Conn As Long
Dim Version as String

'initialize the VBSQL environment
'this only needs to be done once, at the beginning of the application
Version = SqlInit()
If Version = "" Then
      MsgBox "Could not initialize VBSQL."
      Exit Sub
End If

'open a connection
Conn = SqlOpenConnection("MyServer", _"sa", "", "MyMachine", "MyApp")
If Conn = 0 Then
      MsgBox "Could not open connection."
      Exit Sub
End If

'send a SQL command
```

```
If SqlSendCmd(Conn, "SELECT ContactId, ContactName FROM Contact") = _
     SUCCEED Then
     Do Until SqlNextRow(Conn) = NOMOREROWS
          cboSelection.AddItem SQLData(Conn, 2)
          cboSelection.ItemData(cboSelection.NewIndex) = _
               Val(SQLData(Conn, 1))
     Loop
Else
     MsgBox "Query failed."
     Exit Sub
End If

'close the connection
SQLClose Conn

'close down the VBSQL environment
'this only needs to be done at the end of the application
SqlExit               'closes all connections even ones we lost track of
SqlWinExit            'shuts down environment
```

VBSQL uses a custom control to return errors and messages back to the calling application as events. Those events are sampled below with a simple message box for displaying the error or message. A real error handler for VBSQL would typically be more robust and complicated than what is shown below.

```
Private Sub Vbsql1_Error(ByVal SqlConn As Long, ByVal Severity As Long _
, ByVal ErrorNum As Long, ByVal ErrorStr As String _
, ByVal OSErrorNum As Long, ByVal OSErrorStr As String, RetCode As Long)
     MsgBox ErrorNum & " " & ErrorStr
End Sub

Private Sub Vbsql1_Message(ByVal SqlConn As Long, ByVal Message As Long _
, ByVal State As Long, ByVal Severity As Long, ByVal MsgStr As String _
, ByVal ServerNameStr As String, ByVal ProcNameStr As String _
, ByVal Line As Long)
     MsgBox Message & " " & MsgStr
End Sub
```

DCOM

DCOM allows you to take your ActiveX components and fling them across a network, letting them land close to the data or processing power. To your local applications, the components appear the same as they did when they were local. To create and use DCOM components, there is nothing you as a developer must do differently. The programming model is the same.

The transparency of location allows component developers to concentrate on the component. You do not have to worry about where the component will be installed, and there are no arcane RPC APIs to learn. The only thing that has changed is the registration process. Previously, ActiveX components put some basic information about themselves in the Registry: "This is my name, this is my class ID, and this is where I am located on this machine." Now everything is the same except the Registry can hold "this is the machine where I am located" instead of "this is where I am located on this machine." This change allows a component to run on a remote machine.

Allowing remote execution of components can be a great boost in a number of situations. Processor intensive operations can be moved off slow client machines onto fast servers. Components that need to shuffle large amounts of data can run right on the server instead of moving the data back and forth across the network. Code that changes often can be kept running on one centralized site, reducing administration costs.

TERMINOLOGY CLARIFICATION

In this section, *server* refers to the computer where the ActiveX component is installed and running. A *client* is the computer that creates and controls the ActiveX component through DCOM.

DCOM Optimization Strategies

You should use the same optimization techniques for DCOM components that you would for any ActiveX component intended to run locally. Listed below are a few techniques that should be considered when designing specifically for remote execution:

- Typically, for small components, the most expensive operation is the creation of the object. One strategy suggested by Microsoft is to create an application that runs on the server and manages a pool of objects. Instead of the client machine creating the object, it requests a reference to an existing object from the already running pool manager.

- Instead of setting many properties and calling a method to perform an action based on the new property values, consider inserting many property value changes into one method call with many parameters. All the overhead involved in a remote call is performed once instead of many times.

- Consider using Microsoft Transaction Server. Transaction Server acts as a pool manager and allows components to share ODBC connections, in addition to its transaction features.

Distributing DCOM Components

Like a normal ActiveX component, a DCOM component must be registered. Visual Basic provides several tools to make this easy. At compile time, Visual Basic can create a VBR file that is used to register a component on a client machine. In Figure 66-1, checking the Remote Server Files option will generate a VBR file when you compile the application.

The Client Registration utility is used with the VBR file to register the ActiveX component. Figure 66-2 shows the command line options of the Client Registration utility. There is an option for quiet mode so this utility can be used as part of a setup application. There are 16-bit and 32-bit versions of the Client Registration utility for 16-bit and 32-bit client applications.

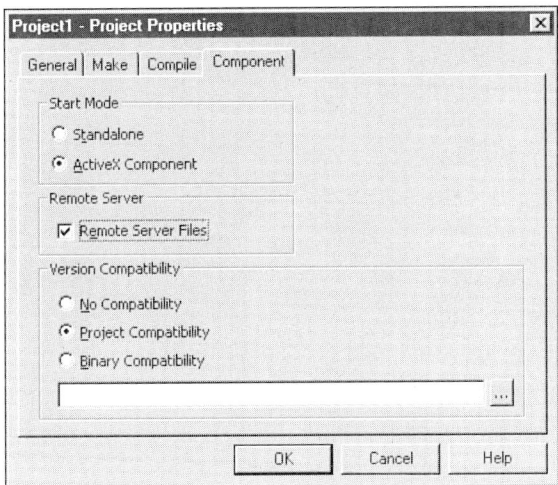

Figure 66-1   Generating a VBR file

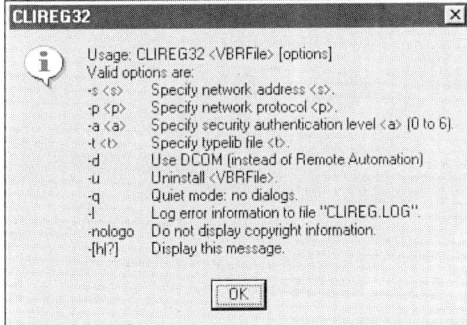

Figure 66-2   Command line parameters
for the Client Registration utility

DCOM Security

Creating distributed components without security is risky business. Imagine if your
co-workers down the hall could create objects on your machine, stealing your precious CPU time and possibly getting to data they couldn't normally access. Now
imagine that happening to a mission-critical server full of confidential data.
Thankfully, Microsoft has created a very robust and secure model for their distributed
component architecture.

If you use the SetupWizard to create a distribution disk for your DCOM component, the SetupWizard includes an application called Remote Automation Connection
Manager. This handy application allows you to configure the accessibility of an
ActiveX component. Figure 66-3 shows a screen shot of the Client Access configuration tab of Remote Automation Connection Manager.

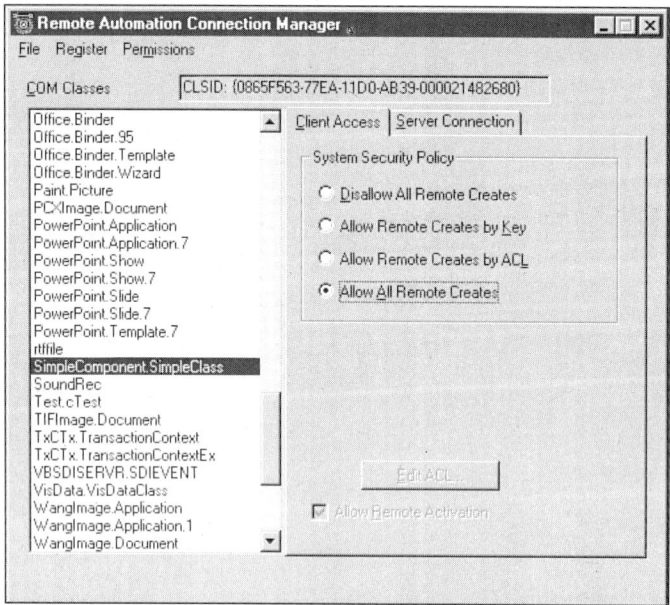

Figure 66-3 Administering DCOM security

There are four settings for Client Access to a server. The first setting is Disallow All Remote Creates, which prevents client computers from creating objects on the server. A client that attempts to create an object on the server will get an Access is Denied error. This setting in no way restricts the server's ability to create objects and pass references to them to other machines. The only restriction is on the creation of objects by other machines.

The second setting is Allow Remote Creates by Key. This setting allows the server to control which objects can be created remotely. By default, all objects cannot be created remotely. Selecting the object in the COM Classes list and checking the Allow Remote Activation check box allows client machines to create the selected objects on the server. If you allow remote creation of objects that are programmable, such as Excel, Access, or Word, the client can then use the server running programmable objects to create other objects on the server, effectively bypassing security on them. Granting remote activation status to those types of objects should be done with care.

The third setting is Allow Remote Creates by ACL. This setting gives the most granular control to the server. The server may grant access by user or group to an object. This object requires Windows NT since the users are NT accounts.

The last option, Allow All Remote Creates, allows any object to be created by a client on the server.

The DCOM Server Project

Project Overview

The DCOM server project is a simple ActiveX component to demonstrate creating a DCOM component. The component will return the time on a remote machine so that the local machine can synchronize its clock.

Assembling the Project

1. Create a new ActiveX DLL or EXE. Change the default class name from Class1 to TimeInfo. On the General tab of the Project Properties dialog, change the project name from Project1 to TimeServer. Switch to the Component tab and check the Remote Server Files option.

2. Add the following code to the TimeInfo class:

```
Public Function GetServerTime() As String
    GetServerTime = Time
End Function

Public Function GetServerDate() As String
    GetServerDate = Date
End Function
```

3. Compile the new DLL or EXE. The compiler also generates a VBR file. You will use this file to register the component on the client machine.

4. Copy the VBR file and CLIREG32.EXE from Visual Basic's CLISVR directory to the client machine. At the command line, execute the following program, in which *<SERVER>* is the name of the server machine:

```
CLIREG32 timeserver.vbr -d -l -s <SERVER>
```

5. On the client machine, create a new standard EXE. On the default form, drop a command button and place this code behind it:

```
Private Sub Command1_Click()
    Dim TimeServer As Object
    Set TimeServer = CreateObject("TimeServer.TimeInfo")
    Print TimeServer.GetServerDate() 'just to show something happened
    Print TimeServer.GetServerTime() 'just to show something happened
    Date = TimeServer.GetServerDate()
    Time = TimeServer.GetServerTime()
End Sub
```

Running the Program

When you execute the program on the client machine, it creates a new TimeServer object on the server and sets the local clock to the server's time.

How It Works

Using the VBR file, the Client Registration utility registers the TimeServer component on the client machine. When the Visual Basic application on the client uses CreateObject to create a new instance of a TimeServer.TimeInfo class, DCOM connects to the server machine and tells that machine to load and execute the component on the server. The TimeServer EXE or DLL is actually executing on the server machine, but to the Visual Basic code on the client it looks like it is running locally.

GetServerDate and GetServerTime return the date and time from the machine where the component is executing. Setting the Date and Time statements synchronizes the client's clock to the servers.

67

MICROSOFT TRANSACTION SERVER

There has been an evolution of the way multiuser transaction-based applications are developed. First came mainframes: Users with dumb terminals posted transactions directly to the database. Figure 67-1 shows the history of multiuser transaction applications.

Next came client/server. Client/server allowed users to work with intelligent machines (PCs). Work was broken down into two parts: The client PC handled the GUI, and the server handled the database. When the client needed data it requested only the data it needed, instead of directly talking to the whole database. This type of application was sometimes referred to as *two-tier architecture*, because there were two levels to the application: the GUI and the database.

Finally, we reached the state of the art today. Today's cutting edge applications are written as three-tier or n-tier applications. To break apart large, hard-to-manage applications even further, n-tier applications pull the business logic away from the database and GUI and make it another layer. Until Microsoft Transaction Server, this typically meant writing server applications or using remote procedure calls. There were no Microsoft Foundation Class Wizards to quickly whip up a framework, and to get reasonable performance the server application developer had to worry about thread and connection pooling.

Microsoft Transactions Server allows you to write simple COM objects, and it takes care of all the nasty details. To create a Transaction Server object or component you start by creating small atomic transactions and then construct larger, more complicated ones by building with these little components.

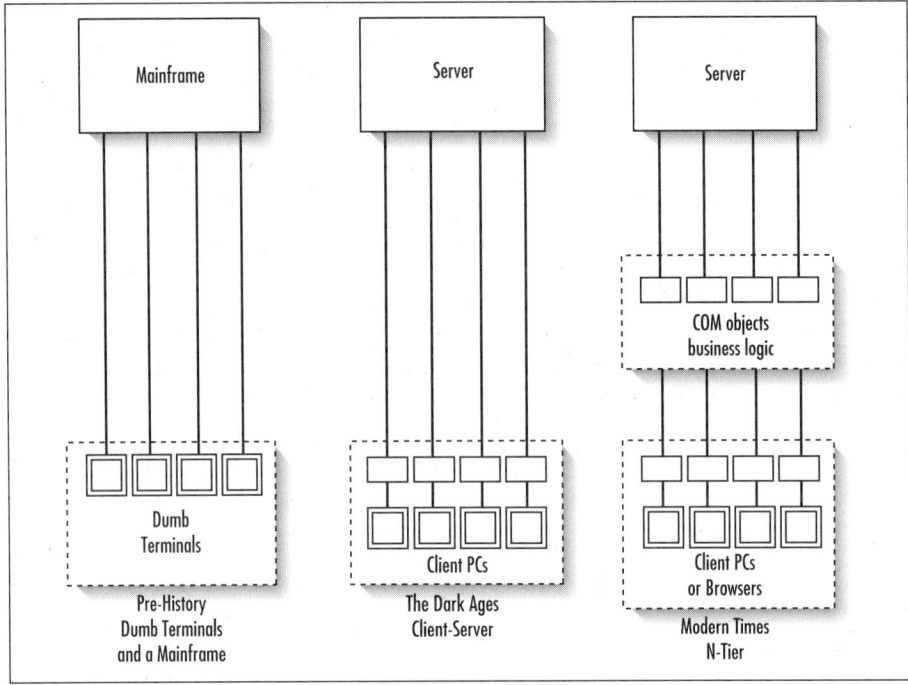

Figure 67-1 The history of multiuser transaction applications

Creating a Simple Transaction Manager Component

Transaction Manager components are ActiveX DLLs. If you have an ActiveX EXE you wish to use with Transaction Server, it must be recompiled as a DLL.

To create a simple Transaction Manager component, start a new ActiveX DLL project and change the project name to SimpleComponent on the Project Properties dialog. Change the class name of the default class to SimpleClass and leave the Instancing property on MultiUse. Add the code below for a simple method of SimpleClass:

```
Public Function GetAString() As String
    GetAString = "Hey, it worked!"
End Function
```

Compile. The simple Transaction Manager component is complete. Obviously, this object won't do much, but it demonstrates how easy it is to create a Transaction Manager component. The next section steps through installing the component so it can be called from a client application.

Installing a Component and Testing

Now that the simple component is complete, it must be installed into Transaction Manager. Transaction Manager arranges components into *packages*. Packages contain the components and the *roles* of the users who use those components. Roles will be discussed in the section titled "Securing Components," but for now, we don't need to worry about them. The first step is to create a package for the simple component. Highlight the \\Computers\My Computer\Packages Installed folder in the Transaction Server Explorer application. Select New from the File menu and choose Create an Empty Package on the first screen. On the second screen, type in a name for the new package.

Now you must add the simple component to the new package. Highlight the Components folder under the new package and select New from the File menu again. On the first screen, choose Install a new component(s). The Import component(s) that are already registered selection presents a list of objects in the registry eligible to be used with Transaction Server. Figure 67-2 shows the dialog in which you select components to add to the package. Use the Add files... button to browse for the DLL you created in the previous section and press Finish.

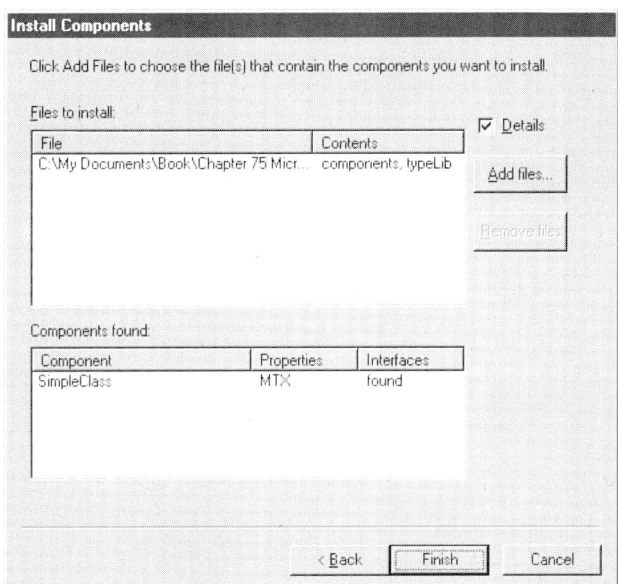

Figure 67-2 Installing a component

After installing the package and component, it's time to see if everything works. The code below creates a SimpleClass object and calls the GetAString method:

```
Private Sub Command1_Click()
    Dim Test As Object
    Set Test = CreateObject("SimpleComponent.SimpleClass")
    MsgBox Test.GetAString()
End Sub
```

Figure 67-3 shows the Transaction Server Explorer with one instance of the SimpleClass created.

Building Scalable Components

The sample above works as a Transaction Server component, but it's not very scalable. A client application can create a component and keep it active for a long time without using it very much. This ties up resources on the server that could be used for something else. Microsoft Transaction Server provides two ways of increasing the scalability of a component.

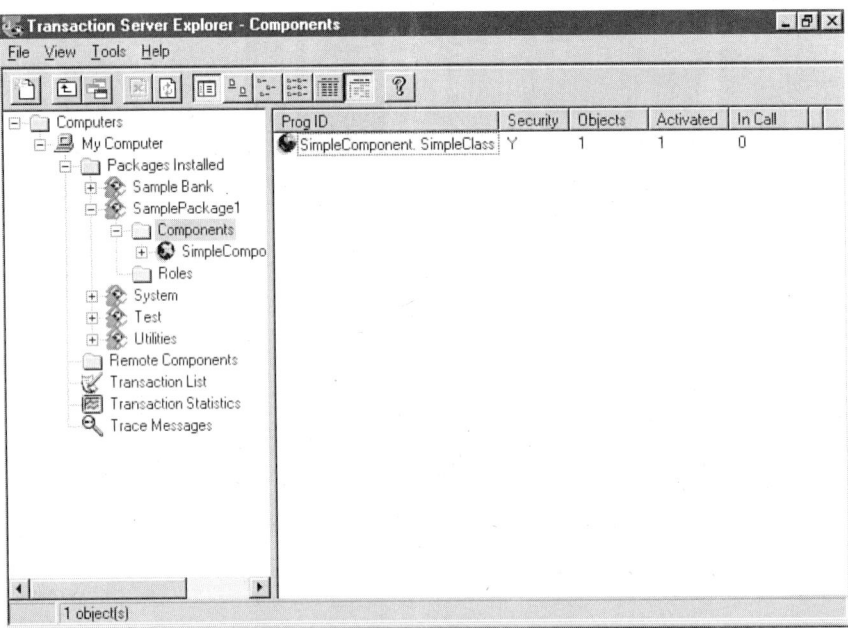

Figure 67-3   Hey, it worked!

The first helper is essentially free. If you are using ODBC or some derivative of it, RDO, or ODBC Direct Workspace, Transaction Server will automatically pool connections for the components. Components do atomic transactions. In the transaction, the component will open a connection to the ODBC datasource, manipulate data, then close the connection. A normal COM object behaving like that would be horrendously slow, but a Transaction Server component has the benefit of Transaction Server's ODBC Resource Dispenser. The ODBC Resource Dispenser manages connections so that opening a connection will give the component a connection out of a pool of connections. In the component's eyes, it has just opened a new connection, but it was really assigned an existing one.

The second helper requires a little cooperation from the component. If the component tells the server, "I have completed what I am going to do, and I don't have any state information to keep," the server knows it can reuse that component's resources. The component uses the SetComplete or SetAbort methods of the ObjectContext object to tell the server it completed or aborted. The ObjectContext is an object installed with Microsoft Transaction Server. A reference can be added to the project by selecting Transaction Context 1.0 Type Library in the References dialog available in the Project menu.

```
Public Function RemoveContact(ContactId As Long) As Long
    'get the context
    Dim Context As ObjectContext
    Set Context = GetObjectContext()
    'open the connection
    Dim conn As rdoConnection
    Set conn = rdoEngine.rdoEnvironments(0).OpenConnection _
        ("", rdDriverNoPrompt, False, "DSN=Contacts;UID=sa;PWD=;")
    'attempt the query
    conn.Execute "DELETE FROM Contact WHERE ContactId = " & ContactId
    If conn.RowsAffected <> 1 Then
        'failed to complete successfully
        Err.Raise vbObjectError, , "Record not found."
        Context.SetAbort
        Exit Function
    End If
    'completed successfully
    Context.SetComplete
    RemoveContact = True
End Function
```

The sample above removes a record from the Contact table. If the record was not found, it raises an error and aborts. If the delete is successful, the component does a SetComplete.

Using Transactions

Transaction Server transactions like DAO transactions ensure that either all changes complete or they all fail. There are several things that must be done for a Transaction Server component to use transactions. First, the component must use the SetComplete and SetAbort methods to be included in a transaction. These methods tell Transaction Server whether the component has completed successfully or not.

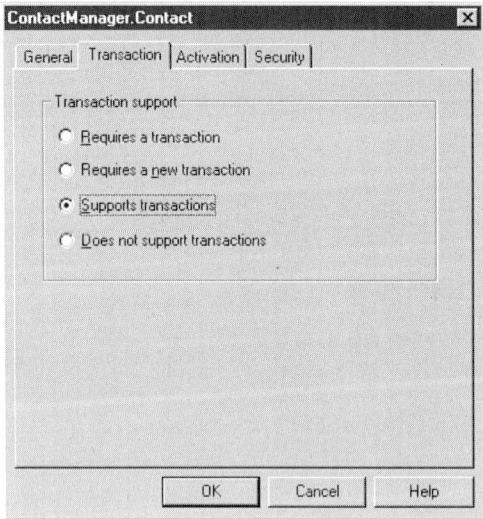

Figure 67-4 Configuring a component to use transactions

Second, the component must be configured to use transactions. In Transaction Server Explorer, examine a component's properties. The Properties dialog has a tab, shown in Figure 67-4, that allows you to configure the kind of transaction support for that component. Choosing Requires a transaction or Supports transactions will allow that component to be used in transactions with other objects. If a component's Transaction Support property is set to Requires a new transaction, a new transaction will be created for that component even if it is within another component's transaction. This is useful when one of the pieces of the transaction must go through even if the others don't. A component configured to require a new transaction is not tied to the success or failure of the transactions occurring around it.

Finally, the component that does the transaction then creates each of the transaction pieces using the CreateInstance method of its context to create other object in its context space. If any of the pieces of the transaction fail (use the SetAbort method), the whole transaction will fail when the transaction component attempts to SetComplete. The example below uses the Contact and ContactPhone components to delete a Contact from the database. If either Contact or ContactPhone calls SetAbort, an error will occur when DestroyContact attempts to SetComplete.

```
Public Function DestroyContact(ContactId As Long) As Long
    'get the context
    Dim Context As ObjectContext
    Dim oContact as Object
    Dim oPhone as Object
    Set Context = GetObjectContext()
    'create the objects in my context
```

```
        Set oPhone = Context.CreateInstance("ContactManager.Phone")
        Set oContact = Context.CreateInstance("ContactManager.Contact")
        'attempt to do the deletes
        On Error Goto DeleteFailed
        oPhone.RemovePhones ContactId
        oContact.RemoveContact ContactId
        'completed successfully
        Context.SetComplete
        DestroyContact = True
        Exit Function
DeleteFailed:
        Context.SetAbort
        Exit Function
End Function
```

The Shared Property Manager

Another resource dispenser that makes the developer's life easier is the *Shared Property Manager*. The Shared Property Manager provides a mechanism for having process-wide variables without the overhead of dealing with concurrency issues. A typical use might be a primary key generator for new table entries. In a multithreaded environment, you never know when the operating system will decide it's time to change threads. If a thread is in the middle of changing a global variable and another thread attempts to change the same global variable, the results can be disastrous. Previously, a multithreaded application needed to use a Mutex or other locking mechanism to deal with concurrency and global variables. The Shared Property Manager takes care of all the concurrency issues and in typical Microsoft developer tool fashion, all the developer has to worry about is the application-specific code.

The sample below generates lucky sweepstakes numbers. From the time Microsoft Transaction Server is started until it is stopped, repeated calls to this method will generate unique ascending values. The function begins by starting the Shared Property Group Manager:

```
Set spm = CreateObject("MTxSpm.SharedPropertyGroupManager.1")
```

If the Shared Property Group Manager has already been started, this call is ignored. Next, the function creates the property group and the NextLuckyNumber property:

```
Set spmg = spm.CreatePropertyGroup("LuckyNumbers", LockSetGet
    , Process, bexists)
Set spNextLuckyNumber = spmg.CreateProperty("NextLuckyNumber", bexists)
```

Again, if the group and property are already created, these calls are ignored. This allows the code to be simpler. You don't have to worry about checking for the existence of the group or property when writing transactions.

```
Public Function GetLuckySweepstakeNumber()
    Dim oContext As ObjectContext
    Dim spm As SharedPropertyGroupManager
    Dim spmg As SharedPropertyGroup
    Dim spNextLuckyNumber As SharedProperty
```

continued on next page

continued from previous page

```
        Dim bexists As Boolean

        Set oContext = GetObjectContext()
        'if there is an error, no lucky number
        On Error GoTo Unlucky

        'start the property group manager
        Set spm = CreateObject("MTxSpm.SharedPropertyGroupManager.1")

        'create the property group
        Set spmg = spm.CreatePropertyGroup("LuckyNumbers", LockSetGet
                , Process, bexists)

        'create the property
        Set spNextLuckyNumber = spmg.CreateProperty("NextLuckyNumber" _
                , bexists)

        'if this is the first time then set default values
        'some applications may want to start with a value
        'previously saved in a database
        If bexists = False Then
                spNextLuckyNumber.Value = 0
        End If

        'increment the value
        spNextLuckyNumber.Value = spNextLuckyNumber.Value + 1

        'SetComplete like a good transaction
        oContext.SetComplete

        'return the lucky sweepstake number
        GetLuckySweepstakeNumber = spNextLuckyNumber.Value
        Exit Function

Unlucky:
        oContext.SetAbort
        GetLuckySweepstakeNumber = 0
End Function
```

Securing Components

Microsoft Transaction Server provides a robust security mechanism that is tightly integrated with NT Security. Using Transaction Server Explorer, you create roles for packages in which security is needed. You then add NT user accounts as members of the roles. The ObjectContext provides a method IsCallerInRole. IsCallerInRole returns True if the user is a member of that role, based on his or her NT logon. The sample below builds on the sample from the Shared Property Manager section.

A function as important as dispensing lucky sweepstakes numbers shouldn't be used by just anybody. The code below is inserted immediately after the call to GetObjectContext. If security is not enabled or the user is not a Lucky Number Supervisor, the function fails and no luck number is generated. Figure 67-5 shows the runtime error generated by a user with insufficient privileges.

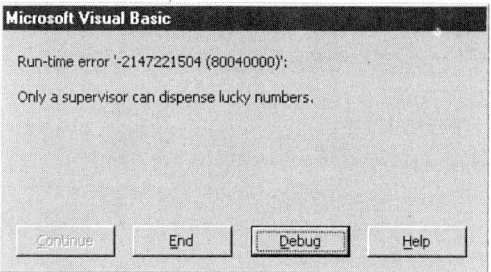

Figure 67-5 A user with no rights tries to get a lucky sweepstakes number

```
If oContext.IsSecurityEnabled() Then
     If Not oContext.IsCallerInRole("Lucky Number Supervisor") Then
          Err.Raise vbObjectError, , _
               "Only a supervisor can dispense lucky numbers."
          GoTo Unlucky
     End If
Else
     Err.Raise vbObjectError, , _
          "Security must be enabled to dispense lucky numbers."
     GoTo Unlucky
End If
```

Depending on the configuration of the component, it is possible that security may be disabled. If a component is configured to run in the creator's process and is currently doing so, the component will not have access to security information. All calls to IsCallerInRole will return True. The sample above uses IsSecurityEnabled to verify that security is active. This is recommended for components in which security is of the utmost importance. Even if the configuration is not correct, your transaction will still be secure.

Microsoft Transaction Server Summary

Table 67-1 summarizes the properties, functions, and methods of Microsoft Transaction Server. Detailed descriptions of each follow the table.

Table 67-1 Microsoft Transaction Server summary

Use This...	Type	To Do This...
Abort	Method	Abort a transaction
Commit	Method	Commit a transaction
CreateInstance	Method	Create a Microsoft Transaction Server object within a context

continued on next page

continued from previous page

Use This...	Type	To Do This...
CreateProperty and CreatePropertyByPosition	Method	Create a new shared property
CreatePropertyGroup	Method	Create a new shared property group
DisableCommit	Method	Tell Microsoft Transaction Server that updates can not currently be committed
EnableCommit	Method	Tell Microsoft Transaction Server that updates can be committed
GetObjectContext	Function	Get the associated ObjectContext
Group	Property	Get a reference to a shared property group
IsCallerInRole	Method	Check to see whether the current user is in a specified role
IsInTransaction	Method	Check to see whether the current bject is in a transaction
IsSecurityEnabled	Method	Check to see whether security is enabled for the current object
Property and PropertyByPosition	Property	Get a reference to a shared property
SafeRef	Function	Get a reference to the current object that can be passed out of context
SetAbort	Method	Abort the current transaction
SetComplete	Method	Indicate the current object has completed its work
Value	Property	Get or set the value of a shared property

ABORT METHOD

Purpose
The Abort method is used by a TransactionContext to abort the work of all objects in the current transaction. Table 67-2 shows the argument for the Abort method.

General Syntax

```
Transaction.Abort
```

Table 67-2 Argument of the Abort method

Argument	Description
Transaction	A TransactionContext object

Example Syntax

```
Sub ViewNextLuckyNumber()
    Dim objTransactionContext as Object
    Dim objLuckyNumber as Object

    Set objTransactionContext = _
        CreateObject("TxCtx.TransactionContext")

    'create the object in the transaction context
    Set objLuckyNumber = objTransactionContext.CreateInstance _
```

```
                    ("LuckyNumber.cLuckyNumber")

        'display the next lucky number
        MsgBox objLuckyNumber.GetLuckySweepstakeNumber()

        'we want to be able to give this lucky
        'number out to the next player so abort the transaction
        objTransactionContext.Abort

        Set objLuckyNumber = Nothing
        Set objTransactionContext = Nothing
End Sub
```

Description   Abort rolls back the database transactions of all objects in the transaction. The transaction is completed, and any more calls to the TransactionContext object will start a new transaction.

COMMIT METHOD

Purpose   The Commit method attempts to commit the current transaction. Table 67-3 lists the argument for the Commit method.

General Syntax

```
Transaction.Commit
```

Table 67-3 Argument of the Commit method

Argument	Description
Transaction	A TransactionContext object

Example Syntax

```
Function AssignLuckyNumber(plCustomerId as Long) as Boolean
        Dim objTransactionContext as Object
        Dim objLuckyNumber as Object
        Dim objCustomer as Object

        Set objTransactionContext = _
            CreateObject("TxCtx.TransactionContext")

        'create the two objects in the transaction context
        Set objLuckyNumber = objTransactionContext.CreateInstance _
            ("LuckyNumber.cLuckyNumber")
        Set objCustomer  = objTransactionContext.CreateInstance _
            ("Customer.cCustomer")

        'save the lucky number
        objCustomer.SaveLuckyNumber plCustomerId _
            , objLuckyNumber.GetLuckySweepstakeNumber()

        'if this errors then the transaction was aborted
```

continued on next page

continued from previous page

```
      On Error Goto FailedToAssign
      objTransactionContext.Commit
      On Error Goto 0

      'return success
      AssignLuckyNumber = True

FailedToAssign:
      Set objLuckyNumber = Nothing
      Set objCustomer = Nothing
      Set objTransactionContext = Nothing
      Exit Function
End Function
```

Description   The Commit method fails if any of the objects involved in the transaction called SetAbort or DisableCommit without later calling EnableCommit or SetComplete. The transaction is completed, and any more calls to the TransactionContext object will start a new transaction.

CREATEINSTANCE METHOD

Purpose   The CreateInstance method instantiates a Microsoft Transaction Server object that runs within the context of an ObjectContext or TransactionContext. The arguments for the CreateInstance method can be found in Table 67-4.

General Syntax

```
Set object = context.CreateInstance(ProgrammaticID)
```

Table 67-4 Arguments of the CreateInstance method

Argument	Description
object	A variable declared as type object
context	An ObjectContext orTransactionContext
ProgrammaticID	A string containing the new object's Programmatic ID

Example Syntax

```
Dim oContext As ObjectContext
Set oContext = GetObjectContext()
oContext.CreateInstance("LuckyNumber.cLuckyNumber")
```

Description   CreateInstance works like the standard CreateObject function, except that it creates the object within the same context as the context parameter. This allows the new objects SetComplete and SetAbort calls to affect the transactions of other objects within the same context.

CREATEPROPERTY AND CREATEPROPERTYBYPOSITION METHODS

Purpose   The CreateProperty and CreatePropertyByPosition methods create a new SharedProperty within a property group. If the property already exists, it returns a reference to the existing property. Arguments for the CreateProperty and CreatePropertyByPosition methods are listed in Table 67-5.

General Syntax

```
Set property = propertygroup.CreateProperty(name, exists)
Set property = propertygroup.CreatePropertyByPosition(position, exists)
```

Table 67-5 Arguments of the CreateProperty and CreatePropertyByPosition methods

Argument	Description
property	A SharedProperty object
propertygroup	A SharedPropertyGroup object
name	The name of the new property
position	The numeric position of the new property
exists	A Boolean that indicates whether the property already existed

Example Syntax

```
Dim spmg As SharedPropertyGroup
Dim spNewClient As SharedProperty
dim spNewVendor As SharedProperty
Dim bexists As Boolean
'create the property group
Set spmg = spm.CreatePropertyGroup("NewIds", LockSetGet, Process _
    , bexists)
create the properties
Set spNewClient = spmg.CreateProperty("NewClient", bexists)
Set spNewVendor = spmg.CreatePropertyByPosition(2, bexists)
```

Description   Properties created by CreateProperty can only be accessed using the Property property. Likewise, properties created by CreatePropertyByPosition can be accessed using only the PropertyByPosition property.

CREATEPROPERTYGROUP METHOD

Purpose   The CreatePropertyGroup method creates a new SharedPropertyGroup. If the group already exists, it returns a reference to the existing group. Tables 67-6, 67-7, and 67-8 list the arguments and constants for the CreatePropertyGroup method.

General Syntax

```
Set propertygroup = propertygroupmanager. _
    CreatePropertyGroup(name, isolationmode, releasemode, exists)
```

Table 67-6 Arguments of the CreatePropertyGroup method

Argument	Description
propertygroup	A SharedPropertyGroup object.
propertygroupmanager	A reference to the SharedPropertyGroupManager.
name	The name of the new group.
isolationmode	The isolation mode. If this is an existing group, the existing isolation mode is returned and nothing is changed.
releasemode	The release mode. If this is an existing group, the existing release mode is returned and nothing is changed.
exists	A Boolean that indicates whether the group already existed.

Table 67-7 Constants for specifying the isolation mode for a SharedPropertyGroup

Constant	Description
LockSetGet	Locks the property during a value all. Every get or set is atomic.
LockMethod	Locks all the properties in the group for the duration of the method. Used when there are interdependencies between properties.

Table 67-8 Constants for specifying the release mode for a SharedPropertyGroup

Constant	Description
Standard	The property group is destroyed when there are no more references.
Process	The property group is only destroyed when the creating process is destroyed.

Example Syntax

```
Dim spm As SharedPropertyGroupManager
Dim spmg As SharedPropertyGroup
Dim bexists As Boolean
'start the property group manager
Set spm = CreateObject("MTxSpm.SharedPropertyGroupManager.1")
'create the property group
Set spmg = spm.CreatePropertyGroup("ServerHits", LockSetGet _
    , Process, bexists)
```

Description   The sample above creates a property group called ServerHits. Presumably, code further on will create new properties for each server in which hits need to be tracked. Each transaction that touches the server could use the shared properties to indicate they have used the server.

DISABLECOMMIT METHOD

Purpose   The DisableCommit method allows an object to tell Transaction Server that its updates can't be committed in their current state. Table 67-9 lists the argument for the DisableCommit method.

General Syntax

```
context.DisableCommit
```

Table 67-9 Argument of the DisableCommit method

Argument	Description
context	An ObjectContext

Example Syntax

```
Public Sub SaveReportHeader(ReportItems as Long)
     'get the context
     Dim Context As ObjectContext
     Set Context = GetObjectContext()
...'do some stuff
     mReportItems = ReportItems
     Context.DisableCommit
End Sub
```

Description   The DisableCommit method allows the object to indicate it is not complete yet. The sample above calls DisableCommit because it is waiting on a number of ReportItems to be saved before it is complete.

ENABLECOMMIT METHOD

Purpose   The EnableCommit method allows an object to tell Transaction Server that its updates could be committed. Table 67-10 shows the argument for the EnableCommit method.

General Syntax

```
context.EnableCommit
```

Table 67-10 Argument of the EnableCommit method

Argument	Description
context	An ObjectContext

Example Syntax
```
Public Sub SaveReportItem()
      'get the context
      Dim Context As ObjectContext
      Set Context = GetObjectContext()
...'do some stuff
      mReportItems = ReportItems - 1
      If mReportItems = 0 Then
            Context.EnableCommit
            Context.SetComplete
      End If
End Sub
```

Description   In the sample above, EnableCommit is called to indicate that all expected ReportItems have been saved and it is OK to commit the transaction.

GetObjectContext Function

Purpose   The GetObjectContext function returns a reference to the ObjectContext associated with the current Transaction Server object. The argument for the GetObjectContext function is listed in Table 67-11.

General Syntax

```
Set context = GetObjectContext()
```

Table 67-11 Argument of the GetObjectContext function

Argument	Description
context	An ObjectContext

Example Syntax
```
Dim Context As ObjectContext
Set Context = GetObjectContext()
```

Description   The GetObjectContext function gives the Transaction Server object access to the context so it may use the various ObjectContext methods such as SetAbort and SetCommit.

Group Property

Purpose   The Group property returns a reference to an existing shared property group. Arguments for the Group property are listed in Table 67-12.

General Syntax

```
Set propertygroup = propertygroupmanager.Group(name)
```

Table 67-12 Arguments of the Group property

Argument	Description
propertygroup	A SharedPropertyGroup object
propertygroupmanager	A reference to the SharedPropertyGroupManager
name	The name of the group

Example Syntax

```
Dim spm As SharedPropertyGroupManager
Dim spg As SharedPropertyGroup
Set spm = CreateObject("MTxSpm.SharedPropertyGroupManager.1")
Set spg = spm.Group("NewIds")
```

Description   The Group property returns a reference to an existing group. It is useful if you know a group has already been created. If it is possible the group doesn't exist, then use CreatePropertyGroup instead.

IsCallerInRole Method

Purpose   The IsCallerInRole method returns a Boolean indicating whether the current user is a member of the specified role. Table 67-13 shows the arguments for the IsCallerInRole method.

General Syntax

```
context.IsCallerInRole(role)
```

Table 67-13 Arguments of the IsCallerInRole method

Argument	Description
context	An ObjectContext
role	The role name to check

Example Syntax

```
If Not oContext.IsCallerInRole("Supervisors") Then
     oContext.SetAbort
     Exit Function
End If
```

Description   The IsCallerInRole method will always return True if the object is running in a client's process. It's best to check the IsSecurityEnabled method before calling IsCallerInRole, to make sure the results are accurate.

IsInTransaction Method

Purpose   The IsInTransaction method returns a Boolean indicating whether an object is running inside a transaction. The argument for the IsInTransaction method is listed below in Table 67-14.

General Syntax

```
context.IsInTransaction()
```

Table 67-14 Argument of the IsInTransaction method

Argument	Description
context	An ObjectContext

Example Syntax

```
If Not oContext IsInTransaction() Then
     oContext.SetAbort
     Err.Raise vbObjectError, , _
          "This component must run within a transaction."
     Exit Function
End If
```

Description   The IsInTransaction method is a handy method when practicing defensive programming. If an object requires a transaction but is improperly configured in Microsoft Transaction Server Explorer, you can catch it with IsInTransaction.

IsSecurityEnabled Method

Purpose   The IsSecurityEnabled method returns a Boolean indicating if security is enabled for the current object. Table 67-15 shows the argument for the IsSecurityEnabled method.

General Syntax

```
context. IsSecurityEnabled()
```

Table 67-15 Argument of the IsSecurityEnabled method

Argument	Description
context	An ObjectContext

Example Syntax

```
If oContext.IsSecurityEnabled() Then
    If Not oContext.IsCallerInRole("Supervisors") Then
        Err.Raise vbObjectError, , "Supervisor level access required."
        oContext.SetAbort
        Exit Function
    End If
Else
    Err.Raise vbObjectError, , _
        "Security must be enabled, please reconfigure."
    oContext.SetAbort
    Exit Function
End If
```

Description   Use the IsSecurityEnabled method to determine whether calls to IsCallerInRole will return accurate results.

PROPERTY AND PROPERTYBYPOSITION PROPERTIES

Purpose   The Property and PropertyByPosition properties return a reference to existing shared properties. Arguments for the Property and PropertyByPosition properties are listed in Table 67-16.

General Syntax

```
Set sharedproperty = propertygroup.Property(name)
Set sharedproperty = propertygroup.PropertyByPosition(position)
```

Table 67-16 Arguments of the Property and PropertyByPosition properties

Argument	Description
sharedproperty	A SharedProperty object
propertygroup	A SharedPropertyGroup object
name	The name of the property
position	The numeric position of the property

Example Syntax

```
Dim spg As SharedPropertyGroup
Dim spNewAccount as SharedProperty
Dim spNewClient as SharedProperty
Set spg = spm.Group("NewIds")
Set spNewAccount = spg.Property("NewAccountId")
Set spNewClient = spg.Property(2)
```

Description   The Property and PropertyByPosition properties return a reference to an existing property. It is useful if you know a property has already been created. If it is possible the property doesn't exist, then use CreateProperty and CreatePropertyByPosition instead.

SAFEREF FUNCTION

Purpose   The SafeRef function returns a reference to the current object that is safe to pass out of the context. The argument for the SafeRef function is shown in Table 67-17.

General Syntax

```
Set object = SafeRef(Me)
```

Table 67-17 Argument of the SafeRef function

Argument	Description
object	The object to be passed out of the context

Example Syntax

```
Dim TempObject as Object
Set TempObject = SafeRef(Me)
AsynchProcessor.DoYourStuff TempObject
```

Description   The SafeRef function returns a safe reference to the current object. The sample above uses SafeRef to get a reference it can pass to AsynchProcessor. Since Microsoft Transaction Server reuses objects, passing a reference to Me may not return to the same object later.

SETABORT METHOD

Purpose   The SetAbort method allows the current object to abort the current transaction. The argument for the SetAbort method can be found in Table 67-18.

General Syntax

```
context.SetAbort
```

Table 67-18 Argument of the SetAbort method

Argument	Description
context	An ObjectContext

Example Syntax

```
If conn.RowsAffected <> 1 Then
    'failed to complete successfully
    Err.Raise vbObjectError, , "Record not found."
    Context.SetAbort
    Exit Function
End If
```

| Description | The SetAbort method cancels the current transaction and tells Transaction Server that the current object is available for reuse after returning from the current call. The sample above calls SetAbort after failing to affect only one row with its update. |

SetComplete Method

| Purpose | The SetComplete method allows the current object to indicate it has completed its work. The argument for the SetComplete method is listed in Table 67-19. |

General Syntax

```
context.SetComplete
```

Table 67-19 Argument of the SetComplete method

Argument	Description
context	An ObjectContext

Example Syntax

```
conn.Execute "DELETE FROM Contact WHERE ContactId = " & ContactId
If conn.RowsAffected <> 1 Then
     'failed to complete successfully
     Err.Raise vbObjectError, , "Record not found."
     Context.SetAbort
     Exit Function
End If
'completed successfully
Context.SetComplete
RemoveContact = True
```

| Description | The SetComplete method tells Transaction Server that the current object completed its work successfully and is available for reuse after returning from the current call. |

Value Property

| Purpose | The Value property returns or sets the value of a shared property. Table 67-20 shows the arguments for the Value property. |

General Syntax

```
sharedproperty.value[ = value]
```

Table 67-20 Arguments of the Value property

Argument	Description
sharedproperty	A SharedProperty object
value	The new value for the object

Example Syntax

```
Set spNewClient = spg.Property(2)
spNewClient.Value = spNewClient.Value + 1
GetNewClient = spNewClient.Value
```

Description   The Value property grants access to the value of the shared property. The sample above increments the new client ID, then returns the new value to the caller.

68

ADVANCED TECHNIQUES

Though it is not a full-fledged client/server database, the Jet engine does support some advanced functionality. Through the use of replication, multiple copies of the same database can be distributed just about anywhere and still keep in sync. Salespeople can take the database on the road and continue to update data. When they return to the home office, all their changes are incorporated into the company's database and they receive all other updates. If a database is getting so much traffic that performance starts to degrade, it is often possible to make a replicated copy and split the users. Jet also has support for multiple users. Several locking options ensure the integrity of your data, even when more than one user is accessing the database.

Replication

Using the Jet engine's replication, you can create an application in which multiple users who are not connected each work on a replica of the database. When the users become connected again, they can synchronize their replicas, receiving each other's updates and inserts. Salespeople can take orders without having to dial in to the network. A technician can enter service reports and in the evening when he or she comes back to the office, the changes made to the customer's profile are synchronized with the database in the office.

Jet defines two types of databases when dealing with replication. The first is a *design master*. The design master is the database that defines the structure of the replicated databases. All changes to database's objects that you wish to be replicated must be made through the design master. For example, a salesperson comes up with a better way to enter a customer's order by creating a new form in the database. All the other salespeople like it, and the company decides to add it to the replicated objects. That form must be added to the design master, removed from the salesperson's database, then all the sales databases must synchronized with the design master. The second type of database is a *replica*. A replica is a database that contains a copy of the design master's replicated objects, in addition to any locally created objects. In the preceding example above, each of the salespeople had a replica database. Their databases had copies of all the replicated objects from the design master at the head office. In addition, the salespeople could create local objects if they needed them for their own tables, forms, or other objects.

Replication Topologies

One of the first tasks in designing an application that uses replication is to determine the replication topology. A *replication topology* is the logical layout of how the databases synchronize with each other. Figure 68-1 shows a few possible topologies.

Almost any topology imaginable can be used, but it is typically best to keep the logic simple. In the *star topology*, each of the points synchronizes with the central database. For all replicas to be in sync, all but one of the points has to synchronize to the central database twice. Each of the points will synchronize their changes, but to get all the other changes the points have to wait until all the other databases are done with their own synchronization. This kind of topology is very effective for an office with employees in the field. Each of the employees synchronizes their databases with the home office database each evening when they return from calls. In the morning or at night when all the databases are available, another synchronization occurs to distribute the data that came in after the first synchronization. An organization can get away with one synchronization as long as the data collected by one field person isn't needed by another the next day. This topology is one of the easiest to set up and administer, and it should probably be considered by anyone trying to set up replication for the first time.

The *ring topology* is useful when there is no centralized database with which to synchronize. Each database is synchronized with the next database down the line. As with the star topology described above, a database may have to synchronize twice to be fully updated. Changes accumulated farther down the line must get back to databases that synchronized earlier. A useful application of this topology is a network in which replicas are created to enhance performance. The databases could be synchronized in a round-robin fashion, and each database would be almost up-to-date at any point in time.

In *fully connected topology*, each database is synchronized with all other databases in the system. As soon as a database has synchronized with another, the database is up-to-date with the second database and there is no centralized database that gets hit hard with constant updates. The problem with a fully connected topology is easy to see in Figure 68-1. Each database must connect with all the other databases to get updated. As the number of databases grows, the number of synchronizations grows exponentially. Both the ring and star topologies grow in a linear fashion and are much easier to manage when the number of databases expands beyond a handful.

The great thing about these topologies is that nothing is written in stone. If a replication topology does not meet your needs, it is relatively simple to change the way the databases are synchronized.

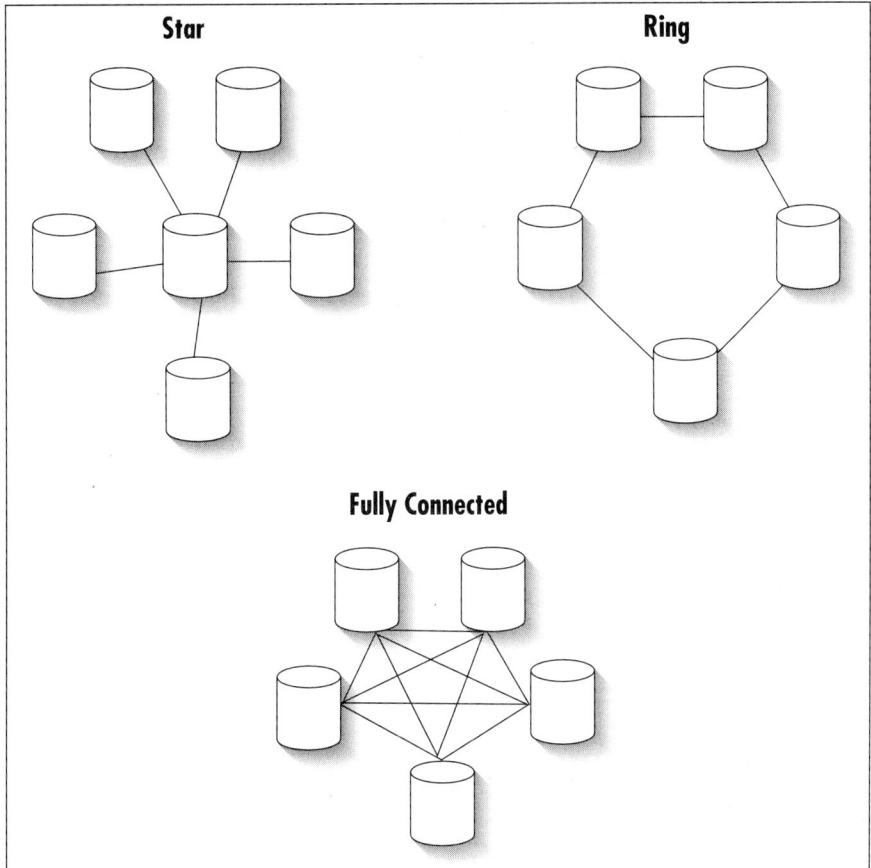

Figure 68-1   Possible replication topologies

Setting Up Replication

Microsoft Access ships with an application called Replication Manager, meant to facilitate the administration and setup of replication. This chapter will focus on the use of DAO to provide that functionality.

The first task that must be accomplished is creating the design master. To make a design master, the database must be made Replicable. The sample code below creates a new Replicable property and sets it to "T". If the Replicable property already exists, you only have to set it to "T" to make a database a design master. The database must be opened in exclusive mode to change or add the Replicable property.

```
Dim prp As Property
Set prp = db.CreateProperty("Replicable", dbText, "T")

db.Properties.Append prp
```

After making the database Replicable, all existing objects with their KeepLocal property equal to "F" become replicated objects. The sample below adds a KeepLocal property to the Customer table, so making the database Replicable will not replicate the Customer table.

```
Dim db As Database
Set db = DBEngine.OpenDatabase("test.mdb")

Dim t As TableDef
Set t = db.TableDefs("Customer")

Dim prp As Property
Set prp = t.CreateProperty("KeepLocal", dbText, "T")

t.Properties.Append prp

db.Close
```

Objects created after the database is made Replicable or objects previously kept local can be set to replicate by adding the Replicable property and setting it to "T". The sample below adds the Replicable property and sets it to "T". As with the Replicable property for the database and the KeepLocal, if the property already exists you only have to set the value to "T".

```
Dim db As Database
Set db = DBEngine.OpenDatabase("test.mdb")

Dim t As TableDef
Set t = db.TableDefs("Customer")

Dim prp As Property
Set prp = t.CreateProperty("Replicable", dbText, "T")

t.Properties.Append prp

db.Close
```

Creating a Replica

Once you have set up your design master, the hard part is done. To create a new replica, use the MakeReplica method of the Database object. New replicas may be created from the original design master or any replicas of it. The sample below creates a replica of TEST.MDB:

```
Dim db As Database
Set db = DBEngine.OpenDatabase("test.mdb")
db.MakeReplica "test replica", "replica of test"
```

To create a read-only replica, use the dbRepMakeReadOnly constant in the MakeReplica method like the following sample:

```
db.MakeReplica "test replica", "replica of test", dbRepMakeReadOnly
```

MakeReplica also supports another value in the options parameter. The dbRepMakePartial constant is discussed in the section, "Partial Replication."

There are a few things you should keep in mind when creating replicas:

■ All objects to be replicated must be unlocked before calling MakeReplica, or MakeReplica will fail.

■ Typically, a replica will be in a different location, so the paths to linked tables may have to be updated.

■ To support replication, Jet will add fields and tables to replicated databases and objects. Most will be invisible to DAO and users of Access, but they will take up space in the database and reduce the bytes available for each record in a table.

■ Replication changes the behavior of AutoNumber fields. Normal AutoNumber fields generate an ascending key. After replication is enabled, AutoNumber fields generate random numbers to help avoid key collisions when records are inserted at different sites. To completely avoid collisions, use the dbGUID data type when creating AutoNumber fields for tables meant for replication.

Synchronizing Replicas

Synchronization of the replicas is an easy process. DAO provides a method of the database object, Synchronize, that updates either one or both databases involved in the synchronization. The code sample below opens TEST.MDB and synchronizes with TEST REPLICA.MDB:

```
Dim db As Database
Set db = DBEngine.OpenDatabase("test.mdb")
db.Synchronize "test replica", dbRepImpExpChanges
db.Close
```

Synchronize first updates object changes before syncing data. This occurs even if you use dbRepExportChanges or dbRepImportChanges to specify that data should go only one way.

If both databases are full replicas, Synchronize can even work over the Internet! The sample code that follows synchronizes the same database to a replica located on an Internet server:

```
Dim db As Database
Set db = DBEngine.OpenDatabase("test.mdb")
db.Synchronize "http://www.corporate.server.com/files/Inetrep.mdb" ⇐
    , dbRepImpExpChanges + dbRepSyncInternet
db.Close
```

There are a couple of things you should keep in mind when replicating over the Internet:

■ Synchronization over the Internet does not occur the same way as synchronization between databases with a direct network connection. Essentially, all changes are bundled up in message files and transferred using FTP. This is not as fast as a direct connection, so if you have several replicas that must synchronize with a database on an Internet server, consider having one single database that synchronizes with the Internet server. All other replicas synchronize with that database instead of the Internet server.

■ There is a limit of about 64,000 replicas that may synchronize with the database on the Internet server. This may appear to be a large number, but when you start talking about Web pages that get hundreds or thousands of hits a day, it is a very small number. Jet replication is better suited for systems in which there is a limit on the number of users that may synchronize with the database.

Partial Replication

Partial replication allows you to specify a subset of data to replicate. The salespeople on the East coast may not need to know anything about the customers west of the Mississippi. By creating a partial replica, you can save space, reduce the time needed to synchronize between databases, and limit users to only the data they need.

The sample code below is a simple example of how to create a partial replica. The TEST PARTIAL REPLICA.MDB database is a partial replica of TEST.MDB. After creating the partial replica, open it. Set the ReplicaFilter property of tables you wish to replicate. The sample sets the ReplicaFilter property of the Customers table so the partial replica gets only customers with an Account Rep named Bob. The last step in creating a partial replica is to call the PopulatePartial method of the partial replica database. This method clears all the replicated tables and fills them with data from the full replica that meets the filter criteria.

```
Dim db As Database
Dim rep As Database

Set db = DBEngine.OpenDatabase("test.mdb")
db.MakeReplica "test partial replica", "replica of test", dbRepMakePartial
db.Close

Set rep = DBEngine.OpenDatabase("test partial replica", True)
rep.TableDefs("Customer").ReplicaFilter = "[Account Rep] = 'Bob'"
rep.PopulatePartial "test.mdb"
rep.Close
```

If you wish to change the ReplicaFilter property, you should follow these steps:

1. Synchronize with the full replica.
2. Make the changes to the ReplicaFilters.
3. Call the PopulatePartial method.

The sample below synchronizes with a full replica, changes the ReplicaFilter so that the partial replica will get only customer records in which the Account Rep is Janet, then calls PopulatePartial to update the partial replica. It is important to synchronize before changing a partial replica. PopulatePartial clears the replicated tables before filling them with the data that matches the filter. Synchronize generates a trappable error, and you can cancel PopulatePartial. PopulatePartial may clear data before it hits an error that you can trap. If the partial replica has not been synchronized, the data will be lost.

```
Set rep = DBEngine.OpenDatabase("test partial replica", True)
On Error Goto SynchFailure
rep.Synchronize "test.mdb", dbRepImpExpChanges
rep.TableDefs("Customer").ReplicaFilter = "[Account Rep] = 'Janet'"
rep.PopulatePartial "test.mdb"
rep.Close
Exit Sub

SynchFailure:
rep.Close
MsgBox "Failed to update partial replica."
Exit Sub
```

Partial replication is smart enough to include all the records needed to satisfy referential integrity. In the preceding example, if there was a table of account representatives and a referential integrity constraint on the Account Rep column in Customer, the record for the account representative Janet would be included in the partial replica. However, partial replication does not automatically include records in tables in which the customer is referenced. If you want to include a list of buyers for each customer, create a relation between the Buyer and Customer table and set the PartialReplica property of the relation to True.

Resolving Conflicts

Occasionally, when dealing with replicated data you may have to resolve conflicting updates. User A updates record A, and so does User B on a different replica. When the two replicas are synchronized, which one should be kept? Jet uses a rather simple way of resolving the conflict. Replicated data is stamped with a version number. Each change to the record increments this version number. When Jet comes to a record that has been updated in two replicas, it chooses the one with the highest version number. If the versions match, Jet chooses the record from the replica with the lowest ReplicaId. ReplicaId is just a GUID to uniquely identify each replica. It is an arbitrary number and has no meaning besides being a unique identifier.

Jet does provide a way to examine each of the conflicts so you can make a decision about which one to keep. Jet creates a table in the replica with the record that was not kept. The table name is in the format <table>_Conflict, with <table> being the name of the table in which the conflict occurred. This table's records can be examined and dealt with either through a manual process or a custom application.

Multiuser Databases

Jet allows multiple users to manipulate the database at one time. The simplest way to enable this is to put the database on a network server's shared drive. Users all over the network can connect to the drive and open the database. However, Jet is not a client/server database. Since the query processor resides on the client machine, any data that must be examined to evaluate a query has to be brought down to the client machine. In a client server database, only the results of the query are sent back to the client machine. All processing is done on the server. Typically, a larger set of data must be examined than what ends up in the result set, so client/server databases conserve precious network bandwidth. This does put a limit on Jet's usefulness as a shared database, but with the right design of database and application it can be surprisingly adept at the job.

Performance

One of easiest optimizations is the proper selection of indexes. A query that filters or joins on a field without an index may have to retrieve the entire table to look for the records it needs. Place indexes on fields used for filters and foreign keys. The query processor will need to retrieve only the index to look for the records it needs. The goal in designing an effective shared database is to minimize the amount of data that must be shuffled between the client and server machines.

Consider breaking the database into two parts. One part resides on the network server and contains all the tables. The second part is a database that resides on the client machines. The client machines' database contains all the static objects, like forms, queries, and code. All the tables in the client's database are links to the actual tables in the server's database. This also gives the Jet engine a local place to create temporary objects without having to worry about conflicting with other users or generating lots of network traffic.

Locking

Jet supports three levels of database locking. Table 68-1 lists the levels of locking and their effects.

Table 68-1 Locking levels

Locking Level	When Applied	Effect
Exclusive mode	OpenDatabase	Locks the entire database; only one user may access the database
Recordset locking	OpenRecordset	Locks the tables used in the Recordset; level of locking is specified by dbDenyRead, dbDenyWrite, or both
Page locking	OpenRecordset	Locks only the pages affected by the Recordset; locking strategy specified by dbPessimistic or dbOptimistic

The levels of locking in Table 68-1 are listed in descending order of concurrency. Exclusive mode obviously is the least concurrent; in it, only one user may access the database at a time. Recordset locking locks entire tables, keeping other users from either reading or writing those tables until the Recordset is closed. Page locking locks only the 2K pages in which the data resides. Other users can continue to make changes to other pages in the table.

The following sample demonstrates opening a database in exclusive mode. No other user can open the TEST.MDB until it is closed. If the database fails to open because it cannot be opened in exclusive mode or for any other reason, a trappable error occurs.

```
Set db = DBEngine.OpenDatabase("test.mdb", True)
```

The next sample opens a Recordset using Recordset locking. As with the sample above, if the OpenRecordset method fails because it failed to get the lock or any other reason, a trappable error occurs.

```
Set rs = db.OpenRecordset("Buyer", dbOpenTable, dbDenyRead + dbDenyWrite)
```

Page locking comes in two flavors, pessimistic and optimistic locking. *Pessimistic locking* locks the pages for the entire duration of the open Recordset. This is the default behavior for a Recordset. *Optimistic locking* does not lock the pages until the application attempts to save the changes. If a change has occurred since the Recordset was opened, the save fails. Optimistic locking allows the greatest concurrency, but you will have to handle potential failures during updates. With pessimistic locking you are assured that once you have a lock, the update will not fail because another user changed the data. The samples below demonstrate opening a Recordset for pessimistic, then optimistic, locking:

```
'Pessimistic locking
'OpenRecordset may fail if it can't be locked
On Error Goto CantLock
Set rs = db.OpenRecordset("select * from Buyer where CustomerId = 3", ⇐
dbOpenDynamic,, dbPessimistic)
'move around make changes
...
'update will not have to worry about other users
rs.update

'Optimistic locking
Set rs = db.OpenRecordset("select * from Buyer where CustomerId = 3", ⇐
dbOpenDynamic,, dbOptimistic)
'move around make changes
...
'update may fail if changed by other user
On Error Goto CantUpdate
rs.update
```

Advanced Topics Summary

Table 68-2 summarizes the advanced topics. Detailed descriptions follow. The summaries for the OpenRecordset and OpenDatabase methods can be found in Chapter 56, "Database Overview and Design."

Table 68-2 Advanced Topics Summary

Use This...	Type	To Do This...
KeepLocal	Property	Prevent an object from being replicated
MakeReplica	Method	Create a new replica database
PartialReplica	Property	Indicate that records in a relation should be replicated
PopulatePartial	Method	Refresh a partial replica with the full replica
Replicable	Property	Indicate that an object can be replicated
ReplicaFilter	Property	Restrict which records get replicated
Synchronize	Method	Exchange data between replicas

KEEPLOCAL PROPERTY

Purpose   The KeepLocal property indicates that the object is not available to be replicated. Table 68-3 lists the arguments for the KeepLocal property.

General Syntax

```
object.Properties("KeepLocal").Value = TorF
```

Table 68-3 Arguments of the KeepLocal property

Argument	Description
object	A database object that supports the Properties property
TorF	A string value of "T" or "F"

Example Syntax

```
Dim db As Database
Set db = DBEngine.OpenDatabase("accounts.mdb")
Dim t As TableDef
Set t = db.TableDefs("Customer")
'add the property
Dim prp As Property
Set prp = t.CreateProperty("KeepLocal", dbText, "T")
t.Properties.Append prp
'change the property
t.Properties("KeepLocal").Value = "F"
t.close
db.Close
```

Description   The KeepLocal property is used to specify whether a database object is replicated when the MakeReplica or Synchronize methods are used. A value of "T" indicates it will not replicate; a value of "F" indicates it will. All objects with either an "F" for KeepLocal (no KeepLocal property) will be replicated when the MakeReplica method is called.

MAKEREPLICA METHOD

Purpose   The MakeReplica method is used to create a new replica database. The arguments for the MakeReplica method can be found in Table 68-4. Values for the options argument are listed in Table 68-5.

General Syntax

```
database.MakeReplica name, description, options
```

Table 68-4 Arguments of the MakeReplica method

Argument	Description
database	A database object
name	The filename for the new database
description	A description for the database
options	Make partial replica and/or read-only replica

Table 68-5 Values of the options argument

Value	Description
dbRepMakePartial	Create a partial replica
dbRepMakeReadOnly	Create a read-only replica

Example Syntax

```
'creates a full replica
db.MakeReplica "NewDB", "replica db"
'creates a partial replica
db.MakeReplica "NewPartialDB", "partial replica db ", dbRepMakePartial
'creates a readonly full replica
db.MakeReplica "NewDB", "replica db", dbRepMakeReadOnly
```

Description   The MakeReplica method is used to create new replicas. It can be called from either the design master or a full replica. The dbRepMakePartial and dbRepMakeReadOnly options can be combined to create a read-only partial replica.

PARTIALREPLICA PROPERTY

Purpose   The PartialReplica property specifies that when replicating to a partial replica, records in this relation are also replicated. Arguments for the PartialReplica property are listed in Table 68-6.

General Syntax

```
relation.PartialReplica[ = boolean]
```

Table 68-6 Arguments of the PartialReplica property

Argument	Description
relation	A relation object
boolean	A Boolean specifying whether this relation replicates related records

Example Syntax

```
db.Synchronize " master.mdb", dbRepImpExpChanges
Dim rel as Relation
For Each rel In db.Relations
     If rel.Table = "Buyer" Then
            rel.PartialReplica = True
     End If
Next rel
db.PopulatePartial "master.mdb"
```

Description   In the sample above, all tables with a foreign key to Buyer would be replicated with Buyer. If the ReplicaFilter on Buyer selected only Buyers in Florida, all the Orders, Invoices, and Shipping Records for the Buyers in Florida would also be replicated.

POPULATEPARTIAL METHOD

Purpose   The PopulatePartial method gives a partial replica a way to refresh itself with a full replica. Table 68-7 lists the arguments for the PopulatePartial method.

General Syntax

```
database.PopulatePartial name
```

Table 68-7 Arguments of the PopulatePartial method

Argument	Description
database	A database object
name	The filename for a full replica database

Example Syntax

```
db.TableDefs("Buyer").ReplicaFilter = "[State] = 'FL'"
db.PopulatePartial "source.mdb"
```

Description	PopulatePartial refreshes the partial replica based on the ReplicaFilter and PartialReplica properties. It will delete data that does not fit the filters and get all data from the full replica that does fit the filters. It is important to synchronize before changing a partial replica. PopulatePartial clears the replicated tables before filling them with the data that matches the filter. Synchronize generates a trappable error, and lets you cancel PopulatePartial. PopulatePartial may clear data before it hits an error that you can trap. If the partial replica has not been synchronized, the data will be lost. Use the Synchronize method if no filters have changed.

REPLICABLE PROPERTY

Purpose	The Replicable property is used to indicate an object is allowed to be replicated. Table 68-8 lists the arguments for the Replicable property.

General Syntax

```
object.Properties("Replicable").Value = TorF
```

Table 68-8 Arguments of the Replicable property

Argument	Description
object	A database object that supports the Properties property
TorF	A string value of "T" or "F"

Example Syntax

```
Dim db As Database
Set db = DBEngine.OpenDatabase("accounts.mdb")
Dim t As TableDef
Set t = db.TableDefs("Customer")
'add the property
Dim prp As Property
Set prp = t.CreateProperty("Replicable", dbText, "T")
t.Properties.Append prp
'change the property
t.Properties("Replicable").Value = "F"
t.close
db.Close
```

Description	Use the Replicable property to indicate that an object is to be replicated.

REPLICAFILTER PROPERTY

Purpose	The ReplicaFilter property is used by a partial replica to restrict which records get replicated. Table 69-9 shows the arguments of the ReplicaFilter property.

General Syntax

```
table.ReplicaFilter[ = value]
```

Table 68-9 Arguments of the ReplicaFilter property

Argument	Description
table	A TableDef object
value	Either a True, False, or string

Example Syntax

```
db.TableDefs("Buyer").ReplicaFilter = "[State] = 'FL'"
db.TableDefs("Invoice").ReplicaFilter = True
```

Description   The ReplicaFilter property is used to filter the records copied to the partial replica. It is like a where clause without the use of subqueries and aggregate functions. The sample above restricts Buyer to records of Buyers in Florida. All records from the invoice table are replicated, and a False will not copy any records.

SYNCHRONIZE METHOD

Purpose   The Synchronize method allows the exchange of data and object changes between replicas. Table 68-10 and Table 68-11 list the arguments and options for the Synchronize method.

General Syntax

```
database.Synchronize name[, options]
```

Table 68-10 Arguments of the Synchronize method

Argument	Description
database	A database object
name	The target database filename or URL
options	Values that control the data exchange

Table 68-11 Values of the options argument

Value	Description
dbRepExportChanges	Export data only
dbRepImportChanges	Import data only
dbRepImpExpChanges	Import and export data
dbRepSyncInternet	Send the update across the Internet; name must be a URL

Example Syntax

```
db.Synchronize "localmaster.mdb", dbRepImpExpChanges
db.Synchronize "http://www.corporate.server.com/files/Inetrep.mdb" ⇐
        dbRepImpExpChanges + dbRepSyncInternet
```

Description   The Synchronize method is used to bring databases up-to-date with each other. No matter which option is specified, changes to the object will be synchronized; databases must have the same structure to be synchronized. Partial replicas can only synchronize with a full replica, not with other partial replicas. The previous sample synchronizes with a local database, then updates a database on a remote Internet server.

PART XI

DATABASE CREATION AND MAINTENANCE

69

MAINTAINING DATABASES

Over time, there are things that you need to do to a database to keep it in good working order. New users come on board and others leave, responsibility for the database changes hands, and sometimes the database just needs a little tidying up.

This chapter will discuss how to fix and maintain a Jet database. It will cover how to create and maintain users and user groups, and finally, it will discuss how to map a Jet database structure.

Periodic Maintenance and Repair

The DBEngine object offers two maintenance methods that apply to databases as a whole: CompactDatabase and RepairDatabase. Databases should be compacted periodically to ensure a high degree of performance. This is because the Jet databases do not remove discarded pages from the database until you compact it. Over a period of time, discarded pages can become a significant factor in database size and performance. Figure 69-1 shows how the CompactDatabase method works. The amount of transactions over a period of time should determine the frequency required for compacting your database.

```
DBEngine.CompactDatabase "C:\TIRED.MDB", ⇐
"C:\REFRESHED.MDB", dbLangGeneral   'Compacting Example
```

Occasionally, you will experience a database corruption when a system or application is shut down improperly or from other system problems. The best way to protect your database from such corruption is to regularly back it up. The RepairDatabase method of the DBEngine will usually recover damaged databases unless the damage is of a form that the DBEngine cannot recover, such as lost disk sectors. The RepairDatabase method will go through the entire database, ensuring that pages are properly linked, tables are validated, and indexes are validated. If the RepairDatabase

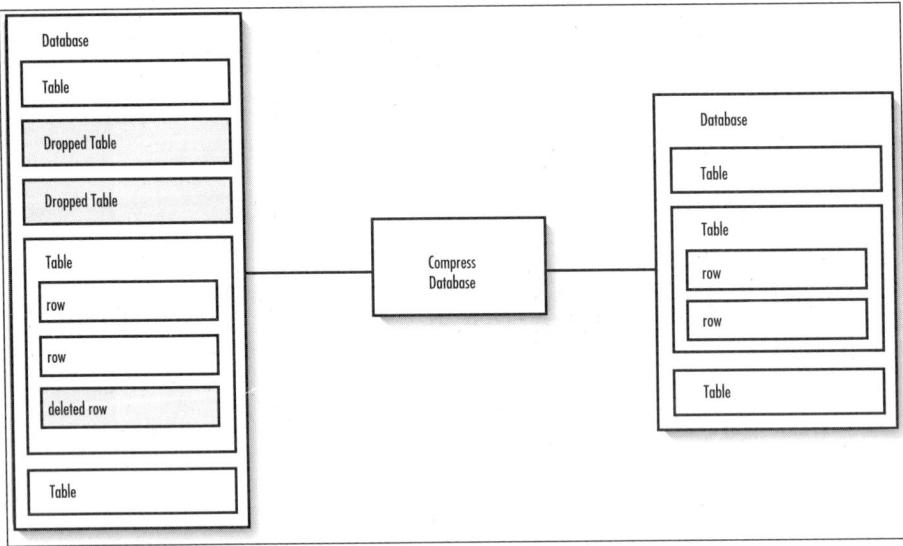

Figure 69-1   How CompactDatabase works

method cannot recover damaged pages, it will discard them and continue to repair the database. During the process of repairing the database the DBEngine invariably discards empty pages, adds new ones, and rebuilds tables and indexes. When the DBEngine is finished, it's possible that it will have created a larger database file than that with which it started. This happens for the same reason the Jet database files can grow to a size completely out of proportion to the data being entered during regular use. It is good practice to compact the database immediately after the repair or after periods of use, thus ensuring maximum efficiency.

```
DBEngine.RepairDatabase "C:\ACCOUNTS.MDB"   'Repairing a Database
```

Database Security Issues

Visual Basic 5.0 provides full programmatic control over Jet database security. Visual Basic applications can directly create passwords, set permissions, create user accounts, and create group accounts. Microsoft Access databases maintain system integrity through the SYSTEM.MDA file. Visual Basic 5.0 cannot create this file; it is created when Microsoft Access is installed on a system. Visual Basic does not require the SYSTEM.MDA file unless you want to access databases created with Microsoft Access. Because Visual Basic cannot create a SYSTEM.MDA file, it cannot create a secure database. You can modify the security settings in an existing Microsoft Access database, provided that you have Admin or Owner permission on that database. A good understanding of the Jet engine's security structure is needed to utilize Access security adequately. This structure includes Users, Groups, Containers, and Documents.

■ A *User* is an object that represents an individual with permissions for the database.

■ A *Group* is an object that represents a collection of User objects with a common set of permissions.

■ A *Container* is an object that collects information about a database and the objects contained in it.

■ A *Document* is an object that contains information on one instance of an object. This object can be a database, saved table, query, or relationship. The information that the document contains includes the object's parent container, permissions, owner, and so on. See the Visual Basic 5.0 Help file for a full list of the Document object's properties.

Users and Groups are managed by the SYSTEM.MDA file, and you are not required to open a database in order to manage them. Your application must have set the DefaultUser, DefaultPassword, and IniPath properties of the DBEngine so that the SYSTEM.MDA file can be accessed. Creating a new User object for a secured Access database is accomplished using the CreateUser method of the Workspaces object:

```
Dim MyUser As User
Dim MyWorkspace As Workspace
Set MyWorkspace = DBEngine.WorkSpaces(0)'default Workspace
'create user with provided name
Set MyUser = MyWorkspace.CreateUser("James Bond")
MyUser.PID = "007"'Add user's ID Number
MyUser.Password = "Agent"'Add user's Password
MyWorkspace.Users.Append MyUser'Append new user to Workspace Document
```

Now that this User is created, we might want to add it to a Group, or create a new Group and then add the User to it. The following code accomplishes just that.

```
Dim MyWorkspace as Workspace
Dim MyGroup As Group
Dim MyUser As User
Dim MyAdminPID As String
Set MyWorkspace = DBEngine.WorkSpaces(0)  'default Workspace
MyAdminPID = "001Boss"'new group PID
'Create new object of Group Class
Set MyGroup = MyWorkspace.CreateGroup("Administrator", MyAdminPID)
'appends new group to Workspace Document
DBEngine.MyWorkspace.Groups.Append MyGroup
'Get a user and append that user to the new group.
'Get user from workspace users collection
Set MyUser = Myworkspace.CreateUser![James Bond]
'Append to group
MyWorkspace.Groups![Administrator].Users.Append MyUser
```

After using the Append method, you may have to refresh other collections that might be affected by the new object.

Access security can be regulated at the database, table, or field object level. This security is accomplished through the granting or revoking of permissions. Permissions is a property of a data access Container or Document object. Several constants are provided to make manipulating these permissions easier. Table 69-1 illustrates those constants.

Table 69-1 Database security permissions constants

Constant	Permission Granted
dbSecNoAccess	No access to the object
dbSecFullAccess	Full access to the object
dbSecDelete	Can delete object
dbSecReadSec	Can read the object's security-related information
dbSecWriteSec	Can alter access permissions
dbSecWriteOwner	Can change the Owner property setting
dbSecCreate	Can create new documents (container object only)
dbSecReadDef	Can read the table definition, including column and index information
dbSecWriteDef	Can modify or delete the table definition including column and index information
dbSecRetrieveData	Can retrieve data from the document
dbSecInsertData	Can add records
dbSecReplaceData	Can modify records
dbSecDeleteData	Can delete records
dbSecDBAdmin	Can replicate database and change password
dbSecDBCreate	Can create new databases (valid only on the databases container object in the SYSTEM.MDA)
dbSecDBExclusive	Exclusive access
dbSecDBOpen	Can open database

As an example of how to set the security on an object, the following code will grant read and write permissions for a table object:

```
Dim MyUserName As String
Dim TableName As String
UserName = "James Bond"
TableName = "Employee Records"
Dim MyDoc As Document
'MyDB is a database declared and created or opened elsewhere
Set MyDoc = MyDB.Containers![Tables].Documents(TableName)
MyDoc.UserName = MyUserName
MyDoc.Permissions = MyDoc.Permissions Or ⇐
(dbSecRetrieveData + dbSecReplaceData +  dbSecInsertData)
```

Note that in this example the three permissions constants were added together, then ORed with Mydoc.Permissions. The Permissions property is composed of bit flags turned on by logically ORing the new constants with an existing set of permissions if you want to cumulatively add new permissions. If you just want to make a certain set of permissions available, you simply make Permissions equal to the sum of whatever permissions are desired.

Mapping an Access Database Structure

When you are faced with maintaining an existing database or creating an application front end for an existing database, it is very useful to view the underlying structure of that database. This process is known as *mapping the database*. The Data Access Objects provide you with a complete set of tools to create a definitive map of a given database. Armed with this map, you will find it much easier to write functions that manipulate the data contained in that database.

Perhaps the best approach to mapping the entire structure of a Jet 3.5 database is to walk entirely through the hierarchy of nested objects and collections by using a series of nested For Each loops. The For Each code block will easily access each element of a collection. Beginning with the Database Object, we can extract the general information of the target database:

```
Public Static Sub MapDataBase()
    Printer.FontSize = 18        'Sets up the printer for the
    Printer.FontBold = True      'first page of the Database
    Printer.CurrentX = 36        'Map printout. See the Printer
    Printer.Print "DATA BASE MAP"'Object for more information.
    Printer.CurrentX = 36
    Printer.FontSize = 12
    'Prints the Name property and Version information of the
    'MyDB database object.
    Printer.Print "Name of Database: "& MyDB.Name ⇐
    & "; Access Version: " & MyDB.Version
    Printer.CurrentX = 36.
    'Each property of the database object is printed including the
    'Connect String,'Updatable, Sort order, and the Query Time-out.
    'The database must first be open before using this procedure.
    Printer.Print "Connect String: "; MyDB.Connect
    Printer.CurrentX = 36
    Printer.Print "Transactions Supported: "; MyDB.Transactions;
    Printer.Print "; Updatable: "; MyDB.Updatable;
    Printer.Print " Sort Order: "; MyDB.CollatingOrder;
    Printer.Print "; Query Time-out: "; MyDB.QueryTimeout
End Sub
```

The above procedure will print the database object's properties to the default printer. The next level of the databases hierarchy is the TableDefs class of objects. You can access each element of the TableDefs collection conveniently, using the For Each block to step through each member of the collection.

```
Public Sub MapTableDefs()
'The For Each Block will step through each member of the 'TableDefs
'Collection. In most cases the properties of the TableDefs are strings
'that are easily printed.
    For Each MyTD In MyDB.TableDefs
        Printer.Print "NAME: ";
        Printer.FontBold = False
        Printer.Print MyTD.Name;
        Printer.Print "; Created: ";
        Printer.Print MyTD.DateCreated;
        Printer.Print "; Last Change: ";
        Printer.Print MyTD.LastUpdated
        'Boolean values, however are best used to select an appropriate
```

continued on next page

continued from previous page

```
            'string to represent their value in a more meaningful manner.
            If MyTD.Updatable = True Then
                Printer.Print "UPDATABLE.        ";
            Else
                Printer.Print "NOT UPDATABLE. ";
            End If
            Printer.Print "Attributes: "; Hex$(MyTD.Attributes) & ": ";
            'The Attributes property is represented by a bit value that
            'corresponds to an intrinsic value defined by the database object
            'constants. By using a logical AND, you can determine the
            'appropriate attributes and print a string to represent that
            'attribute.
            If (MyTD.Attributes And dbSystemObject) <> 0 Then
                Printer.Print "System Object        "
            End If
            If (MyTD.Attributes And dbAttachedTable) <> 0 Then
                Printer.Print "Attached Table       "'
            End If
            If (MyTD.Attributes And dbAttachedODBC) <> 0. Then
                Printer.Print "Attached ODBC Table"
            End If
            If (MyTD.Attributes And dbAttachExclusive) <> 0 Then'
                Printer.Print "Attached Table in Exclusive Mode"
            End If
            Printer.Print
            MapFields           'user function
            Printer.Print Chr$(13)
    Next MyTD
End Sub
```

As you can see, mapping the database is not really a difficult task. The following tables show the database objects and their mappable properties (these properties are discussed in detail in this chapter and Chapters 56, "Database Overview and Design"; 64, "Adding and Editing"; 65, "Moving and Searching"; and 70, "Creating Databases"). Using a similar approach with the For Each block you can create a complete map of the database you are working with that includes the tables, fields, indexes, relationships, and imbedded queries.

Maintaining Databases Summary

Table 69-2 lists the methods for maintaining databases. Detailed descriptions of these methods follow.

Table 69-2 Maintaining Databases Summary

Use This...	Type	To Do This...
CompactDatabase	Method	Remove deleted records and clean up database
CreateGroup	Method	Create a new Group
CreateUser	Method	Create a new User
NewPassword	Method	Change an existing password
RepairDatabase	Method	Attempt to repair a corrupt Jet database

COMPACTDATABASE METHOD

Purpose   The CompactDatabase method of the DBEngine object provides database maintenance in that it removes deleted records, reorganizes the pages, and generally cleans up the internal organization of the database. Tables 69-3, 69-4, and 69-5 list the arguments and argument values for the CompactDatabase method.

General Syntax

```
DBEngine.CompactDatabase olddatabase, newdatabase [,locale [,options]]
```

Table 69-3 Arguments of the CompactDatabase method

Argument	Description
olddatabase	The filename of the existing database to be compacted
newdatabase	Tho name of the resulting database file after the compaction
locale	The database's sort order
options	An integer that indicates one or more options

Table 69-4 Constants of the locale argument of the CompactDatabase method

Constant	Collating Order
dbLangGeneral	English, German, French, Portuguese, Italian, and modern Spanish
dbLangArabic	Arabic
dbLangChineseSimplified	Simplified Chinese
dbLangChineseTraditional	Traditional Chinese
dbLangCyrillic	Russian
dbLangCzech	Czech
dbLangDutch	Dutch
dbLangGreek	Greek
dbLangHebrew	Hebrew
dbLangHungarian	Hungarian
dbLangIcelandic	Icelandic
dbLangJapanese	Japanese
dbLangKorean	Korean
dbLangNordic	Nordic languages (Jet 1.0 only)
dbLangNorwDan	Norwegian and Danish
dbLangPolish	Polish
dbLangSlovenian	Slovenian

continued on next page

continued from previous page

Constant	Collating Order
dbLangSpanish	Traditional Spanish
dbLangSwedFin	Swedish and Finnish
dbLangThai	Thai
dbLangTurkish	Turkish

Table 69-5 Constants of the options argument of the CompactDatabase method

Constant	Description
dbEncrypt	Create an encrypted database
dbDecrypt	Create a decrypted database
dbVersion10	Create a Jet version 1.0 database (not valid for Visual Basic 4.0)
dbVersion11	Create a Jet version 1.1 database
dbVersion20	Create a Jet version 2.0 database
dbVersion30	Create a Jet version 3.0 database

Example Syntax

```
'first remove the old backup
Kill "C:\CLIENTS.BAK"
'mark the existing database as the new backup
Name "C:\CLIENTS.MDB" As "C:\CLIENTS.BAK"
'compact the old database creating a new working database
DBEngine.CompactDatabase "C:\CLIENTS.BAK", "C:\CLIENTS.MDB", dbLangGeneral
```

Description   In the above example, a pre-existing backup file is erased, and the current database is designated as the new backup by changing its file extension from .MDB to .BAK. Then the CompactDatabase method is run against the backup file, creating a new compacted copy of the database. During this process you could change the sort order, encrypt that database, or change its native format to a newer format.

The Jet database engine does not do any internal optimizing during use; thus deleted rows, modified tables, and many other operations over time leave the database in a fragmented state. The CompactDatabase method reorganizes the internal page structures, physically removes deleted rows from the database, and generally reorganizes the database into a more efficient state that is usually smaller than before the CompactDatabase was run. In order to compact a database, it must be closed and not in use by any other applications at the time. If you use the CompactDatabase to update the database's structure to the new Jet 3.5 from an older format, be advised that only the data structures are updated. Any forms or reports created with the Access product itself will not be updated. You need the latest version of Access to update those portions.

CREATEGROUP METHOD

Purpose   The CreateGroup method is used to create a new Group object for a work-space or a User object's Groups collection. Table 69-6 lists the arguments of the CreateGroup method.

General Syntax

```
Set objectname = parentobject.CreateGroup([name[,pid]])
```

Table 69-6 Arguments of the CreateGroup method

Argument	Description
objectname	The name of the Group object variable
parentobject	The name of the Parent object variable
name	The actual name of the Group object in the collection
pid	The personal identifier of the Group

Example Syntax

```
Dim MyGroup as Group
Dim MyPID as String
MyPID = "AClientsID"
'create the Group and the code reference to it
Set MyGroup = Workspaces(0).CreateGroup("SalesMgr", MyPid)
'append the new Group object to the WorkSpace's collection
DBEngine.Workspaces(0).Groups.Append MyGroup
```

Description   The Group object is used as a security measure in Jet/Access databases. Essentially, the Group object contains a collection of User objects with similar access rights. If the Group has access permissions to a particular table, then all Users in the Group have at least the same access rights. When using the CreateGroup method in the above example, the 'SalesMgr' and the PID are needed for any subsequent modifications to the Group object. For instance, in order to add or remove any User in the Users collection of the Group object, you will need to have logged onto the database as the SalesMgr User using the same PID.

CREATEUSER METHOD

Purpose   The CreateUser method creates a new User object for either the Users collection of the database or the Users collection of a Group. Arguments for the CreateUser method are listed in Table 69-7.

General Syntax

```
Set objectvariable = object.CreateUser([name [,pid [,password]]])
```

Table 69-7 Arguments of the CreateUser method

Argument	Description
objectvariable	The name of the User object reference in code
name	A string that uniquely names the User object
pid	A string that contains the PID of a user account
password	A string containing the password for the new User object

Example Syntax

```
Private MyUser as User
Private AdminPID as Sting
Private Username as String
AdminPID = "TopGun"
Username = "Uncle Bill"
'create user object
Set MyUser = Workspaces(0).CreateUser(Username, AdminPID)
MyUser.NewPassword = "BossMan"
Workspaces(0).Users.Append MyUser
```

Description   Database security in the Jet/Access database engine is maintained through Users and Groups. Users are individual access accounts that typically represent an individual's access rights. Groups are collections of User objects given similar access rights to an object on the basis of their membership in that Group. When creating a User, you first append that User to the Users collection of the Workspace object, then you can append the same User to any Group objects to which the User object will belong. The UserName and PID properties uniquely identify a User, and the Password property ensures that the individual accessing this account is indeed the correct User. When first creating this User object, you can set the password through the Password property of the object. Subsequent changes to the password must be done through the NewPassword method of the User object.

NewPassword Method

Purpose   The NewPassword method of the User object is used to change an existing password. The arguments for the NewPassword method can be found below in Table 69-8.

General Syntax

```
userobject.NewPassword oldpassword, newpassword
```

Table 69-8 Arguments of the NewPassword method

Argument	Description
userobject	An object variable of type User
oldpassword	The current password
newpassword	The new password

Example Syntax

```
Workspaces(0).Users("John Doe").NewPassword "openseseme", "abracadabra"
```

Description   The above example shows how to change a password on an existing user account. To set a new password as in this example, you must already be logged on as this user or have administrative privileges to change the password. The password can be any string of characters except CHR$(0), the Null character. The Password property is write only; you cannot read it.

REPAIRDATABASE METHOD

Purpose   The RepairDatabase method attempts to repair a corrupted native Jet database. Table 69-9 lists the arguments for the RepairDatabase method.

General Syntax

```
DBEngine.RepairDatabase dbname
```

Table 69-9 Argument of the RepairDatabase method

Argument	Description
dbname	The full path and name of the database to be repaired

Example Syntax

```
'repairing a database using DOS path and name conventions
BDEngine.RepairDatabase "C:\CLIENTS.MDB"
'Repairing a database using UNC
BDEngine.RepairDatabase "\\SERVERNAME\MYDIRECTORY\CLIENTS.MDB"
```

Description   When a Jet database becomes corrupted, this method is used to try to repair it. It is usually successful, but regular backups of your database still should be maintained. The database to repair must not be in use by the application or by any other application, otherwise a trappable error will occur. Corruption to the database can occur from power outages, faulty hardware, or improperly exiting a program without first closing the database. The RepairDatabase also validates all system tables and indexes. Any data that cannot be recovered is discarded from the database.

It is possible to have a corrupted database without the Jet recognizing that it is corrupted. If your application starts acting in an unpredictable manner, it is a good idea to do a RepairDatabase just to ensure there are no corruptions. After doing a RepairDatabase, there will probably be many discarded pages and other items that are no longer needed within the database. For this reason, it is a good idea to run a CompactDatabase method as well.

70

CREATING DATABASES

Now that you've seen the DAO class structure and surveyed its collections, properties, and methods, it's time to look at how objects are actually set up and referenced in a working database. You do this using the Data Definition Language (DDL). DDL is the part of the properties and methods involved in creating and defining the different parts of the actual database. This includes the creation of tables, fields, relationships, users, groups, and everything else that defines the database's structure.

Data Definition Language

Table 70-1 Client Database model

Clients	Sites	Contacts	Phones
ClientID	SiteID	ContactID	PhoneID
Client Name	Site Name	First Name	Phone Type
Client Type	Site Type	Last Name	Phone Number
MTD	MTD	Middle Name	Extension
QTD	QTD	Position	ContactID
YTD	YTD	SiteID	SiteID
Notes	Address1	ClientID	ClientID
	Address2	Notes	Notes
	City		
	State		
	Postal Code		
	Country		
	ClientID		
	Notes		
	SuperID		

Using the database schema above, we will create the database. Refer to Chapter 56, "Database Overview and Design," for a discussion on database design. While there are many different ways to create native Jet databases, this chapter will be concerned with creating a database using the DAO's DDL objects, properties, and methods. We start by creating the variables needed for the database structure.

```
Option Explicit

Private MyWS As Workspace              'Default WorkSpace object
Private ClientDB As Database           'Clients DataBase object

Private ClientTBD As TableDef          'Clients Tabledef object
Private ClientsIDX As Index            'Clients Indexes object
Private ClientsFLD(7) As Field         'Clients Field object array

Private SitesTBD As TableDef           'Sites TableDef Object
Private SitesIDX(1) As Index           'Sites Index object array
Private SitesFLD(11) As Field          'Sites Field object array

Private ContactsTB As TableDef         'Contacts TableDef object
Private ContactsFLD(7) As Field        'Contacts Tabledef object array
Private ContactsIDX(2) As Index        'Contacts Index object array

Private PhonesTBD As TableDef          'Phones TableDef object
Private PhonesFLD(7) As Field          'Phones Field object array
Private PhinesIDX(3) As Index          'Phones Index object array
```

The above declarations are best placed in the General Declarations section of a module. All the component objects required to create the Clients database are now in place and we can begin writing the actual procedures to create the database schema outlined earlier. We can start with a function that provides a Workspaces object and create the new Clients Database object.

```
Private Function CreateClientDB(DBPath As String) as Boolean
'DBPath is a fully qualified path for the database'
'Assume successful creation.
    CreateClientDB = True
    On Error GoTo BadClientMake
    'set default workspace and Create database object
    Set MyWS = DBEngine.Workspaces(0)
    Set ClientDB = MyWS.CreateDatabase(DBPath)
Exit Function
'If error occurs function returns false
BadClientMake:
CreateClientDB = False
Msgbox Error$
Resume Next
End Function
```

Once the above function is successfully called, the ClientDB object actually exists both within the program and on the disk drive. The next step is the creation of the tables, fields, and indexes. The tables are created using the CreateTableDef method of the Database object. The fields for the tables are created with the Createfield method of the TableDef object. Once you have set the Field object, you set the Field object's properties to the desired values. Then you append the object to the Fields collection of the TableDef. You do this for each field of the table. After you have appended all your fields, you can attach the required indexes and relationships.

```
Private Function MakeClientTable() As Boolean
    MakeClientTable = True
    On Error GoTo BadClientTBDMake
    'Create the table using CreateTableDef method
    Set ClientTBD = ClientDB.CreateTableDef("Clients")
    'Create the fields using CreateFields method
    Set ClientFLD(0) = ClientTBD.Createfield("ClientID", dbLong)
    'make it a counter field
    ClientFLD(0).Attribute = dbAutoIncrField
    'append it to the collection
    ClientTBD.Fields.Append ClientFLD(0)
    Set ClientFLD(1) = ClientTBD.Createfield("Client Name", dbText)
    'This field requires a size because it is a text field
    ClientFLD(1).Size = 128
    ClientTBD.Fields.Append ClientFLD(1)
    Set ClientFLD(2) = ClientTBD.Createfield("Client Type", dbText)
    ClientFLD(2).Size = 25
    ClientTBD.Fields.Append ClientFLD(2)
    Set ClientFLD(3) = ClientTBD.Createfield("MTD", dbCurrency)
    ClientTBD.Fields.Append ClientFLD(3)
    Set ClientFLD(4) = ClientTBD.Createfield("QTD", dbCurrency)
    ClientTBD.Fields.Append ClientFLD(4)
    Set ClientFLD(5) = ClientTBD.Createfield("YTD", dbCurrency)
    ClientTBD.Fields.Append ClientFLD(5)
    Set ClientFLD(6) = ClientTBD.Createfield("NOTES", dbMemo)
    ClientTBD.Fields.Append ClientFLD(6)
    'The only index for this table is the Primary Key field
    Set ClientIDX = ClientTBD.CreateIndex("ClientID")
    ClientIDX.Primary = True
    ClientIDX.Unique = True
    'append the new TableDef to the Database
    ClientDB.TableDefs.Append ClientTBD
Exit Function
BadClientTBDMake:
    MakeClientTable = False
    MsgBox Error$
    Exit Function
End Function
```

This function goes through the entire process of creating a TableDef, adding fields and a primary index. The ClientID field was set to a counter field by setting the field's attributes property to the dbAutoIncr constant and the data type as a Long. In fields of text type, the size of the field had to be specified by setting the Size property to the required length in characters. A more detailed description of properties associated with the Field object can be found later in this chapter under "Fields."

Making the primary key index in this example consisted of setting the ClientIDX as an object reference using the CreateIndex method of the TableDef object, using the ClientID as a field argument to the CreateIndex method. Then, by setting the Unique and Primary properties of the Index object to True, you make this Index object the primary key. Primary keys can be any field, or combination of fields that are always unique to each row of data. (That is, each key refers to one and only one data field.) If you have no field, or combination of fields, that can meet this requirement, you can use an arbitrary key such as a counter. In the examples presented here, all the primary keys are based on arbitrary keys.

The other tables of our Clients database model would be constructed in the same way with the exception that, as these are built, you would probably want to include the required Relation objects to link the tables in the manner described earlier. The following code illustrates how to do this.

```
Dim SiteREL as Relation    'dimension the Relation object
Dim TempField as Field     'and the Field object
'create one to many relationships with Client table
Set SiteREL = ClientDB.CreateRelation("ClientToSites")
SiteREL.Table = "Clients"
SiteREL.ForeignTable = "Sites"

'make the relationship a Left Outer Join with cascading deletes
SiteREL.Attributes = dbRelationLeft + dbRelationDeleteCascade
'create field object and append it to the Relation object
Set TempField = SiteREL.CreateField("ClientID")
TempField.ForeignName = "ClientID"
SiteREL.Fields.Append TempField
'append the Relation object to the database.
ClientDB.Relations.Append SiteREL
```

The above code shows the step-by-step construction of a one-to-many relationship between the Clients table and the Sites table with the Clients table being the *one* side of the relationship. The primary table is designated by the Table property of the Relation object using the primary key of that table as the foreign key in the Sites table. The foreign table is designated by the ForeignTable property of the Relation object. In this case, the primary and foreign fields have the same name. If the foreign field had a different name than the primary key field, then you would use that different name when giving the Field object's ForeignField property a value.

Creating Databases Summary

Table 70-2 shows the creating databases summary. Detailed descriptions follow.

Table 70-2 Creating Databases Summary

Use This...	Type	To Do This...
CreateDatabase	Method	Create a new Jet database
CreateField	Method	Add a new field to a TableDef, Index, or Relation object
CreateIndex	Method	Add a new index to table
CreateProperty	Method	Add a new property to a data access object
CreateQueryDef	Method	Add a new QueryDef to a database
CreateRelation	Method	Add a new Relation to a database
CreateTableDef	Method	Add a new TableDef to a database
RefreshLink	Method	Update connection information for an attached table

CREATEDATABASE METHOD

Purpose   CreateDatabase is used to create a new instance of a native Jet database. Tables 70-3, 70-4, and 70-5 list the arguments and constants for the CreateDatabase method.

General Syntax

```
database = workspace.CreateDatabase (databasename, locale [,option])
```

Table 70-3 Arguments for the CreateDatabase method

Argument	Description
database	The database object
workspace	A workspace data type that will contain the database
databasename	The name of the database being created
locale	A string expression used to specify collating order
options	An integer value that indicates one or more options

Table 70-4 Constants for specifying the collating order of a Jet database

Constant	Collating Order
dbLangGeneral	English, German, French, Portuguese, Italian, and modern Spanish
dbLangArabic	Arabic
dbLangChineseSimplified	Simplified Chinese
dbLangChineseTraditional	Traditional Chinese
dbLangCyrillic	Russian
dbLangCzech	Czech
dbLangDutch	Dutch
dbLangGreek	Greek
dbLangHebrew	Hebrew
dbLangHungarian	Hungarian
dbLangIcelandic	Icelandic
dbLangJapanese	Japanese
dbLangKorean	Korean
dbLangNordic	Nordic languages (Jet 1.0 only)
dbLangNorwDan	Norwegian and Danish
dbLangPolish	Polish
dbLangSlovenian	Slovenian
dbLangSpanish	Traditional Spanish

continued on next page

continued from previous page

Constant	Collating Order
dbLangSwedFin	Swedish and Finnish
dbLangThai	Thai
dbLangTurkish	Turkish

Table 70-5 Constants for CreateDatabase options

Constant	Description
dbEncrypt	Create an encrypted database
dbDecrypt	Create a decrypted database
dbVersion10	Create a Jet version 1.0 database (not valid for Visual Basic 4.0)
dbVersion11	Create a Jet version 1.1 database
dbVersion20	Create a Jet version 2.0 database
dbVersion30	Create a Jet version 3.0 database

Example Syntax

```
Private MyDB as Database
Private MyWS as WorkSpace
'initialize DBEngine and get default WorkSpace object
Set MyWS = DBEngine.Workspaces(0)
'create the 'Clients' database using the general language collating order
Set MyDB = MyWS.CreateDatabase(C:\MYDATA\CLIENTS.MDB",dbLangGeneral)
```

Description   The CreateDatabase method of the WorkSpaces object provides the means for creating native Jet databases. When creating these databases, you have several parameters that define different aspects of your database. First is the locale parameter, which is required. This parameter sets the sort order of the database according to different language customs. Table 70-4 shows the constants and their locales. The options part of the declaration (the constants for which are listed in Table 70-5) provides the choice to encrypt the database, and to create versions 1.0, 1.1, 2.0, or 3.0 databases. The arguments are optional and default to no encryption and Jet 3.0 if you do not specify either. The arguments are added together to make a cumulative setting.

CREATEFIELD METHOD

Purpose   The CreateField method is used by the TableDef, Index, and Relation class objects to add a Field object to their respective Fields collections. The arguments for the CreateField method can be found in Table 70-6.

General Syntax

```
Set fieldobjectname = object.CreateField([name[,type[,size]]])
```

Table 70-6 Arguments for the CreateField method

Argument	Description
fieldobjectname	A Field type object variable
object	The name of the object using the CreateField method
name	The name to be given to the field
type	A constant representing the field's data type
size	The size in characters of a String type field

Example Syntax

```
'An example of adding a field to a TableDef object.
Dim IDXfield As Field    'field object for indexes
MakeClientTable = True
'Create the table using CreateTableDef method
Set ClientTBD = ClientDB.CreateTableDef("Clients")
'Create the fields using CreateFields method
Set ClientFLD(0) = ClientTBD.CreateField("ClientID", dbLong)
'make it a counter field
ClientFLD(0).Attributes = dbAutoIncrField
'append it to the collection
ClientTBD.Fields.Append ClientFLD(0)

'An example of creating a field object for an Index object.
'Type not used for Index object
Set IDXfield = ClientIDX.CreateField("ClientID")
ClientIDX.Fields.Append IDXfield

'An example of creating a field object for a Relation Object
'Type not used for relation object
Set TempField = SiteREL.CreateField("ClientID")
'the name of the field in a foreign 'table
TempField.ForeignName = "ClientID"
SiteREL.Fields.Append TempField
```

Description   The Field object corresponds with a single column of data in a database. This column has a data type and set of properties across all rows. The TableDefs, QueryDefs, Recordset, Index, and Relation objects all have a Fields collection. When using the CreateField method, the type and size arguments are only used with the TableDef object. The three examples above illustrate the CreateField being used in three of the four object types that have this method. The Field object has several properties that can be set when being used with these objects. A listing of these properties can be found in Chapter 56. What you are actually doing when you use the CreateField method is setting a reference to a Field type object and a placeholder for that object in the parent's fields collection. After having set this reference, you can set the properties of the Field object and run any of the Field object's methods needed such as FieldSize or CreateProperty. When you have finished setting up the Field object's properties, you can then append them to the parent's Fields Collection.

CREATEINDEX METHOD

Purpose   The CreateIndex method is used to create Index objects and add them to a TableDef's Indexes Collection. Table 70-7 shows the arguments for the CreateIndex method.

General Syntax

```
Set indexobjectname = tabledefobject.CreateIndex([name])
```

Table 70-7 Arguments for the CreateIndex method

Argument	Description
indexnameobject	The name of the Index object in VB code
tabledefobject	The name of the TableDef object to which the index is being added
name	The string that gives the index a unique name in the tabldef's Index collection

Example Syntax

```
'declare index object
Dim ClintIDX as Index
Dim IDXfield as Field
'create the index reference and make a placeholder in the
' tabledef's index collection
Set ClientIDX = ClientTBD.CreateIndex("ClientID")
'set the Index object's properties to make it a unique primary key
ClientIDX.Primary = True
ClientIDX.Unique = True
'create the field object for the Index object
Set IDXfield = ClientIDX.CreateField("ClientID")
'add the field to the Index object's field collection
ClientIDX.Fields.Append IDXfield
'add the Index object to the TableDef's Indexes Collection
ClientTBD.Indexes.Append ClientIDX
```

Description   The Index object is contained in the TableDef's Indexes collection. Indexes are required for efficient database organization, searches, and establishing intertable relationships. The above example shows how to add a Primary Key index to the ClientTBD TableDef object. As created and appended, this Primary index would be an ascending sort on the ClientsID field. If a descending index was required, then the Attributes property of the Field object would have to be set to reflect this.

```
IDXfield.Attributes = IDXfield.Attributes or dbDescending
```

This line of code logically 'Ors' the existing field attributes with the dbDescending constant to set that particular flag while maintaining already existing attributes. To create a multi-field index, you would create the required Field objects, set their attributes, then append them to the Index object's Field collection. The following code illustrates this technique.

```
Dim MyFields(2) as Field
Dim MyIndex as Index

Set MyIndex = MyTableDef.CreatIndex("TripleFld")
MYindex.Primary = False
MyIndex.Unique = True
Set MyFields(0) = MyIndex.CreateField("Field1")
Set MyFields(1) = MyIndex.CreateField("Field2")
Set MyFields(2) = MyIndex.CreateField("Field3")
MyTableDef.Fields.Append MyFields(0)
MyTableDef.Fields.Append MyFields(1)
MyIndex.Fields.Append MyFields(2)
MyTableDef.Indexes.Append MyIndex
```

As shown, this code would create an index with three fields all in ascending sort, and whose combined data would make a unique index entry. All field properties need to be set prior to appending the field to the Index object, and the Index object's properties need to be set prior to being appended to the TableDef's Indexes collection

CREATEPROPERTY METHOD

Purpose   CreateProperty is used to create and append a user-defined property to a particular data access object. Arguments for the CreateProperty method are shown in Table 70-8.

General Syntax

```
Set propertyobject = parentobject.CreateProperty _
    ([Name [,type [,value [,tDDL]]]])
```

Table 70-8 Arguments for the CreateProperty method

Argument	Description
propertyobject	A variable declared as a Property object type
parentobject	A Database, Field, Index, QueryDef, or TableDef object
name	A string expression that uniquely names the new Property object
type	An integer constant that defines the data type for the Property object
value	A Variant type variable containing the initial Property value
tDDL	A Boolean value indicating whether the Property object is a DDL object

Example Index

```
Dim MyProperty as Property
Dim MyField as Field
'Create the Property object and make a place for it in the Properties
' collection of the 'Field object
Set MyProperty = MyField.CreateProperty("MaxRange")
'set the other properties of MyProperty
MyProperty.Type = dbCurrency
MyProperty.Value = 500
'save the Property Object to the Properties collection
MyField.Properties.Append MyProperty
```

Description   In the above example, a MaxRange property is added to a field object. In this instance MaxRange could indicate the maximum value range for a single transaction in this field, before triggering some sort of special verification routine. Thus you can provide your database structure with all kinds of special properties for particular applications. When you are appending a user defined property to an object, it is important to keep in mind that you are appending this property only to a particular object instance and not to that object's class.

CREATEQUERYDEF METHOD

Purpose   CreateQueryDef is used to create a new QueryDef object in the specified database. QueryDefs contain recompiled queries. Table 70-9 shows the arguments for the CreateQueryDef method.

General Syntax

```
Set querydefname = database.CreateQueryDef([name][,sqltext])
```

Table 70-9 Arguments for the CreateQueryDef method

Argument	Description
querydefname	A Visual Basic variable declared as a QueryDef
database	The database to which the QueryDef will be appended
name	The name of the new query
sqltext	A string expression that evaluates to a valid SQL string

Example Syntax

```
Dim MyDB as Database
Dim MyQueryDef as QueryDef
Dim Mysql as string
'Action QueryDef
Mysql = "INSERT INTO [HistTable] SELECT * FROM [Currenttable]" _
      + " WHERE [Trash It] = True"
Set MyDB = DBEngine.Worksaces(0).OpenDatabase("MyDatabase.MDB")
```

```
Set MyqueryDef = MyDB.CreateQueryDef("Trash_It", Mysql)
'run the query
Mydb.Execute "Trash_It"
```

Description
Being able to store precompiled queries in an Access database provides your application with a powerful method of optimizing the database for speed. When you create a query in code and then create a Recordset on the query, the Jet database engine has to interpret, then compile the query before running it. Depending on factors, this part can take significant time to complete. With stored queries, this part is done only once when it is first created. The Jet engine optimizes then compiles the query and stores it in the QueryDefs collection. In a well-designed RDBMS, these queries help to simplify and standardize database operations.

If you have several different users or applications that make the same types of searches, updates, or modifications, you can provide QueryDefs to perform these operations in which the calling applications only need to know the name of the QueryDef to accomplish their task. As the DBA improves or modifies the underlying query or schema, that improvement will be automatically available to each user of the query without having to update each calling application. In the preceding example, the query is an action query that transfers active data to an archive table. Since it is an action query, you use it with the Execute method of the Database object. It may be that you need to run a query where you need to provide some information such as a search criteria before running it. This is done with a Parameter query. With a Parameter query you provide one or more parameters to the QueryDef object's Parameters collection before running it.

```
'parameterized Select QueryDef
Mysql = "PARAMETERS [ENTER ClientID],LONG; SELECT * FROM [Sites]" _
     + " WHERE [ClientID] = [ENTER ClientID]"
Set MyDB = DBEngine.Workspaces(0).Opendatabase("Clients.MDB")
Set MyQueryDef = MyDB.CreateQueryDef("Client Sites",Mysql)
'run the Query by first setting the parameter
MyQueryDef.Parameters("ENTER ClientID") = Text1.Text
'then create a recordset based on the query
Set MyRecordset = MyQueryDef("Client Sites")
```

In this example, the parameter 'ENTER ClientID' is designated as a Long Integer data type to match the data type of the ClientID field in this table. When this query is compiled by the Jet database engine, it adds the parameter to the Parameters collection of the QueryDef object. The query is a Select-type query and returns a Recordset. To run this QueryDef, you set the value of the parameter then set a Recordset object's recordsource to the named QueryDef, in this case 'Client Sites.' Take note that the value of the Parameter will persist for the life of the application unless you change it again. This means that if you run the same QueryDef again, it will use the value previously provided.

CREATERELATION METHOD

Purpose   The CreateRelation method of the Database object creates the relationships between the database's Table objects using the primary and foreign keys of those tables. Table 70-10 lists the arguments for the CreateRelation method.

General Syntax

```
Set objectvariable = database.CreateRelation _
     ([name [,table[,foreigntable [, attributes]]]])
```

Table 70-10 Arguments for the CreateRelation method

Argument	Description
objectvariable	The Relation object's reference in code
database	The Database object to which the Relation object will be appended
name	A string that uniquely identifies this Relation object
table	A string that names the primary table in the Relation
Foreigntable	A string that names the foreign table of the Relation
attributes	A Long data type that contains the attributes flags of the Relation

Example Syntax

```
Dim SiteREL as Relation
'create Relation object
Set SiteREL = ClientDB.CreateRelation("ClientToSites")
'set the Relation's properties
'first identify the two tables in the relation
SiteREL.Table = "Clients"
SiteREL.ForeignTable = "Sites"
'make the relationship a Left Outer Join with cascading deletes
SiteREL.Attributes = dbRelationLeft + dbRelationDeleteCascade
'create a field object to append to the Relation
'object's Fields collection
Set TempField = SiteREL.CreateField("ClientID")
'name the foreign field that completes the relation
TempField.ForeignName = "ClientID"
'append the field object to the Relation Object
SiteREL.Fields.Append TempField
'then the Relation object to the Database object
ClientDB.Relations.Append SiteREL
```

Description   The above example code creates a one-to-many relation between two tables with cascading deletes. When creating a relation, you need to have a primary key or a uniquely indexed field as the basis of the left side of the relation and a corresponding foreign key in the table you want to establish the relation with. The foreign key has to be the same data type as the primary key. The field names do not have to be the same, but it makes it much easier to recognize the foreign key in a table when it has the same name as the primary key in the primary table.

The Relation object allows you to build relations based on the fields in a complex primary key. A primary key is made up of one or more fields that uniquely identify each row in a table. Each table can have only one primary key, and this primary key is always the basis of a relationship between its table and the foreign key in another table. Thus, if you had a table that had a complex primary key of three fields, your Relation object could be based on this primary key and a table that had three matching foreign fields if you wished to maintain referential integrity. If your relation in this case did not require referential integrity, then you could make a relation based on just one field of the complex primary key.

This limitation is one of the major reasons to avoid complex primary keys if you can. If you must have a complex primary key, yet need to maintain relational integrity between one of the fields and another table, you can create another Index object based on that field with the Unique property set to True and make the relationship that way. But you could end up taking a major performance hit since the Jet is being burdened with maintaining extra indexes particularly when the number of records starts to get large. If you find yourself in this situation, you may need to reconsider your overall design. You are probably not meeting the requirements of Third Normal Form in your design. It is always better to create an arbitrary primary key based on a counter or some other unique identifier that is not dependent on the value of other fields in the table. This will help insure that subsequent creation of relations is clear cut and not part of some convoluted web of fixes and patches to make unnatural relations work.

The Relation object has an Attributes property that defines the type of relationship it represents as well as the type of enforcement required. This Attributes property is a Long Integer type and the attributes are specified by turning bits on or off by logical comparisons with a set of intrinsic constants. Those constants with their descriptions are provided in Table 70-11. The join type attributes are mutually exclusive and require that you select only one. The cascading update and delete are cumulative along with one of the join attributes.

Table 70-11 Constants for the Attributes property of the Relation object

Constant	Description
dbRelationUnique	The relationship is a one-to-one relationship where there is only one matching record in either table.
dbRealtionDontEnforce	The relationship is not enforced.
dbRelationInherited	Relationship exists in a noncurrent database where the two attached tables are contained.
dbRelationUpdateCascade	Updates will cascade through related records.
dbRelationDeleteCascade	Deletions will cascade through related records.

As a final note on the Attributes property, when you set cascading updates or deletes, these actions will happen without any confirmation request by the Jet engine. In other words, if you delete a record from the primary table, all related records in the foreign table will be deleted as well—if the dbRelationsDeleteCascade attribute is set—without any warning that these deletions are pending.

CREATETABLEDEF METHOD

Purpose   The CreateTableDef method of the Database object is used to create a new TableDef object in the TableDefs collection of the Database object. The arguments for the CreateTableDef method are listed in Table 70-12.

General Syntax

```
Set objectvariable = database.CreateTableDef _
    ([name [,attributes [, source [, connect]]]])
```

Table 70-12 Arguments for the CreateTableDef method

Argument	Description
objectvariable	The name of the object reference in code
database	The Database object for which the TableDef is being created
name	A string that uniquely identifies the new TableDef object
attributes	A Long data type that indicates one or more characteristics of the TableDef object
source	The name of a table that exists in an external database and is the source table for this TableDef
connect	A string containing the connect information about the source of the external database that contains the external table that is the source for this TableDef

Example Syntax

```
Dim RELfield(3) As Field    'Field object array for relationships
    Dim IDXfield(3) As Field    'Field object array for the Indexes
    MakePhonetable = True

On Error GoTo BadPhonesTableMake
    Set PhoneTBD = ClientDB.CreateTableDef("Phones")
        'Create the fields using CreateFields method
        Set PhoneFLD(0) = PhoneTBD.CreateField("PhoneID", dbLong)
        'make it a counter field
        PhoneFLD(0).Attributes = dbAutoIncrField
        'append it to the collection
        PhoneTBD.Fields.Append PhoneFLD(0)
    ....
    ....
    Set PhoneFLD(7) = PhoneTBD.CreateField("Notes", dbMemo)
        PhoneTBD.Fields.Append PhoneFLD(7)
    'create the indexes for the TableDef object and append them
        Set PhoneIDX(0) = PhoneTBD.CreateIndex("PhoneID")
            PhoneIDX(0).Primary = True
            PhoneIDX(0).Unique = True
```

```
        Set IDXfield(0) = PhoneIDX(0).CreateField("PhoneID")
        PhoneIDX(0).Fields.Append IDXfield(0)
    PhoneTBD.Indexes.Append PhoneIDX(0)

    ....
    ....
    Set PhoneIDX(3) = PhoneTBD.CreateIndex("ContactID")
        PhoneIDX(3).Primary = False
        PhoneIDX(3).Unique = False
        Set IDXfield(3) = PhoneIDX(3).CreateField("ContactID")
        PhoneIDX(3).Fields.Append IDXfield(3)
    PhoneTBD.Indexes.Append PhoneIDX(3)
'Append new tabledef to the database
ClientDB.TableDefs.Append PhoneTBD
```

Description

The preceding example using the CreateTableDef method is meant to give you an idea of the complete process from the initial call of the method to the conclusion of the process with the TableDef object being appended to the database's TableDefs collection. The TableDef object is the stored description of a Table object. This stored description is kept in the database's TableDefs collection. The structure of this table is defined by the properties of the matching TableDef object. The TableDef object contains a collection of Fields and Indexes that make up the table's structure.

In addition, there is a collection of properties that further define the Table object or store other information about the table. You can add properties to the particular TableDef that you are working with, thus customizing the table even further. Once you have used the CreateTableDef method, you must add all the Field objects, the Index objects, and set the attributes that govern the underlying table. Also, if the table comes from an external database, you must provide the connect information and the source table name. Once this information has been provided, the TableDef is appended to the Database object's TableDefs collection and the described table will now exist in the Database. Once the TableDef is appended to the database, the properties that you can append are limited. The Attributes property of the TableDef object specifies the characteristics of the table represented by the TableDef object. The constants and their meaning are provided in Table 70-13.

Table 70-13 Constants for the TableDef object's Attributes property

Constant	Description
dbAttachExclusive	Indicates that the table is opened for exclusive use
dbAttachSavePWD	Indicates (for databases that use the Jet engine) that the user ID and password for the attached table is saved with the connection information
dbSystemObject	Indicates that the table is a system table provided by the Jet engine (read only)
dbHiddenObject	Indicates that the table is a hidden table provided by the Jet engine (read only)
dbAttachedTable	Indicates that the table is an attached table from a non-ODBC database.
dbAttachedODBC	Indicates that the table is an attached ODBC table

REFRESHLINK METHOD

Purpose
The RefreshLink method is used to update the connection information for an attached table. Table 70-14 lists the argument for the RefreshLink method.

General Syntax

```
tabledefobject.RefreshLink
```

Table 70-14 Argument for the RefreshLink method

Argument	Description
tabledefobject	A variable of TableDef type

Example Syntax

```
Dim MyDB as Database
Dim MyTable as TableDef
Dim SalesUnit as Integer
Set MyDB = Workspaces(0).OpenDatabase("C:\CLIENTS.MDB"")
Set MyTable = MyD.CreateTableDef("NEWCLIENTS", dbAttachExclusive")
MyTable.SourceName = "Clients"
SalesUnit = 1
'set the connect information
MyTable.Connect = "ODBC;UID=TheBoss;PWD=UHOH;DSN=MYSERV;DATABASE=SALES" _
    & Str(SalesUnit)
'append the table to the database
MyDB.TableDefs.Append MyTable
'user defined procedure
ProcessNewClients MyDB
'loop through the other sales units
For SalesUnit = 2 to 5
    'change the connect information to point to a
    ' different but identical database
    MyTable.Connect = _
    "ODBC;UID=TheBoss;PWD=UHOH;DSN=MYSERV;DATABASE=SALES" _
        & Str(SalesUnit)
    MyDB.TableDefs!NEWCLIENTS.RefreshLink
    ProcessNewClients MyDB
Next
```

Description
The RefreshLink method of the Database object allows you to change the connect information of a TableDef object that points to an attached table then re-establish that link using the new connect information. In the above example, it is used to cycle through different sales departments' databases updating the clients' list to the central database. When you use RefreshLink, the attached table's properties and relations are not changed. In addition, to cause all objects that refer to this TableDef to reflect the changes made to the connect information, you should also use a Refresh method against each object that refers to it.

71

USING T-SQL DEBUGGER

One of the ways to squeeze the very best performance out of a client-server application running against Microsoft SQL Server is the liberal use of stored procedures. When you create a stored procedure, SQL Server takes your Transact-SQL statements, checks the syntax, and compiles a plan to execute the stored procedure. From then on, each time the stored procedure is called, the server does not have to go through all that overhead. On very large queries in which the overhead is small compared to the execution time, it does not make much difference. However, if you have small queries that are executed many times, it can make a tremendous difference from checking the syntax and compiling each time.

Once upon a time, if something went wrong within a stored procedure, it was almost impossible to debug. Once the stored procedures were created, it was essentially a black box. You put stuff in and hoped what you were expecting came out the other end. T-SQL Debugger, included with the Enterprise Edition of Visual Basic 5.0, changes all that. Now, using T-SQL Debugger, you can step through the lines of a stored procedure almost as easily as stepping through a line of Visual Basic code. Figure 71-1 shows the T-SQL Debugger stepping through a stored procedure.

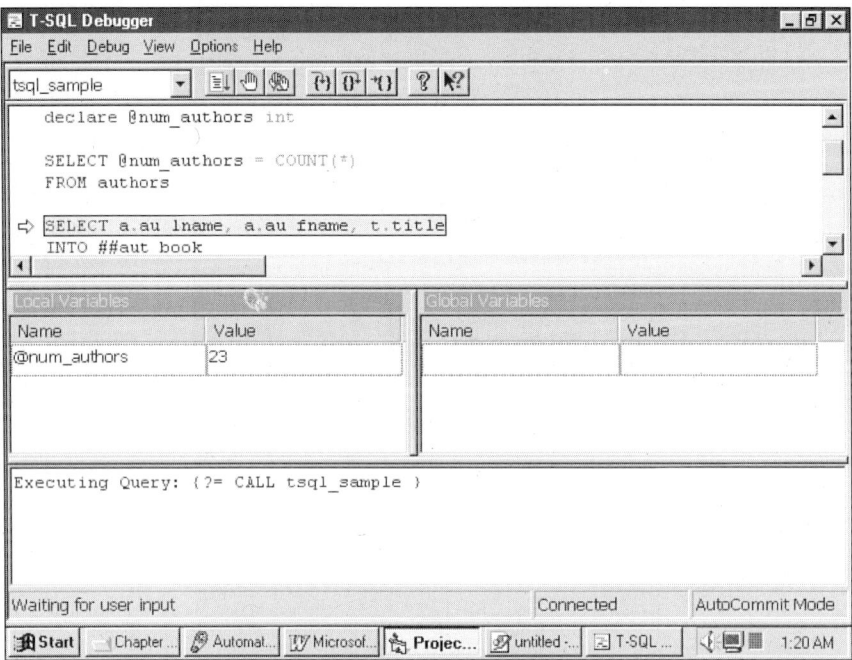

Figure 71-1   Stepping through a stored procedure

Setting Up

Before you can jump into debugging stored procedures, there are a few things you need, to prepare the client and the server. On the client side—the machine you will be debugging from—perform the following steps:

1. Choose All from the Enterprise Features option when setting up Visual Basic Enterprise Edition. This selection includes SQL Debugging, Remote Data Objects, and Connection Designer. If you didn't install this option, you can always add it using the Add/Remove function of the Visual Basic setup.

2. Using the Add-In Manager dialog, select the VB T-SQL Debugger option.

On the server side, perform the following steps:

1. Install SQL Server version 6.5 with at least Service Pack 1. The latest service pack for SQL Server is available from Microsoft's web site at http://www.microsoft.com. Service Pack 2 ships with Visual Basic 5.0 Enterprise Edition. It is located in the \Tools\Tsql\Sql65.sp2 directory on the installation CD.

2. If SQL Server is logging on with a system account, change it to a user account that has rights to start an automation server on the client machine.

3. If you are running Windows NT 4.0 on the server side, run SDI_NT4.EXE from the \Tools\Tsql\Svrsetup directory on the Visual Basic 5.0 Enterprise Edition

installation CD. This setup application will install all the components needed to run T-SQL Debugger on the server side.

4. If you are running Windows NT 3.51 on the server side, you will have to install all the components manually. First, copy the SDI.DLL from the \Tools\Tsql\Svrsetup directory on the Visual Basic 5.0 Enterprise Edition installation CD to the \binn subdirectory of SQL Server's install directory. Next, copy the AUTPRX32.DLL and the AUTMGR32.EXE from the \Tools\Tsql\Svrsetup directory to the system directory. Finally, register the components using commands similar to the ones below, depending on your install directories.

```
regsvr32 c:\mssql\binn\sdi.dll
regsvr32 c:\winnt\system32\autprx32.dll
c:\winnt\system32\autmgr32.exe /regserver
```

T-SQL Debugging Options

The T-SQL Debugging Options dialog, shown in Figure 71-2, lets you configure how the T-SQL Debugger works. You can call the T-SQL Debugging Options dialog by selecting the Tools|T-SQL Debugging Options menu. It is available after you have added the Visual Basic T-SQL Debugger through the Add-In Manager.

The first option, Automatically step into Stored Procedures through RDO connections, toggles whether or not the T-SQL Debugger activates when calling a stored procedure through RDO at runtime. Select this when you want to debug a stored procedure in the context of your running application.

The second option, Use Safe Mode (transaction rollback) for Stored Procedure calls, will rollback stored procedures debugged at design time. This allows you to debug stored procedures with your specified parameters and examine the results without making a permanent change to the database.

The last two options configure the maximum number of rows to display of any resultset in T-SQL Debugger and the maximum login time-out.

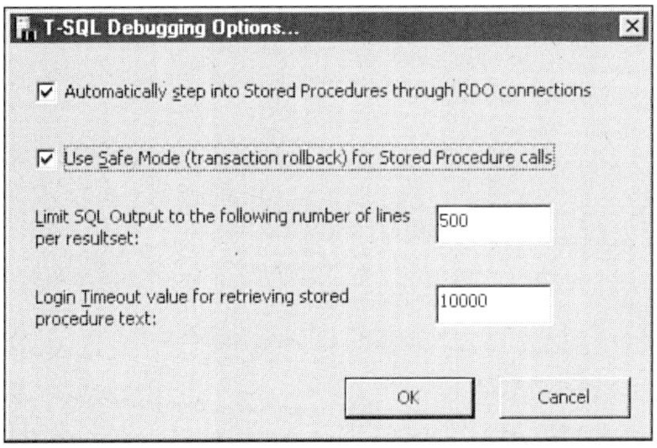

Figure 71-2 The T-SQL Debugging Options dialog

Getting There

There are three ways to use the T-SQL Debugger. First, you can use the T-SQL Debugger at design time to select a stored procedure or enter SQL to debug. You specify the parameters to simulate how the stored procedure would be called from code. The second method is for the T-SQL Debugger to be activated each time you call a stored procedure from RDO at runtime. This lets you look at debugging from within the context of your application. If you are not sure what parameters are being passed when the stored procedure is called, or you just need to debug within the surrounding code, this is the method for you. Last, Query objects that encapsulate a stored procedure in UserConnections can also be debugged.

Starting T-SQL Debugger at Design Time

At design time, you can use T-SQL Debugger to debug stored procedures and batches of SQL statements. Selecting T-SQL Debugger from the Add-Ins menu will activate the T-SQL Debugger at design time. The Visual Basic Batch T-SQL Debugger dialog is presented to collect the connection information and select what to debug. The first tab, Settings, pictured in Figure 71-3, allows you to enter the parameters that would typically be passed to the OpenConnection and OpenResultset methods for Remote Data Objects. A design time T-SQL Debugger session will behave exactly like an RDO resultset at runtime, based on your selections here. This eliminates pondering, "Did it work because I was in Microsoft SQL Enterprise Manager or because I fixed the problem?" Stored procedures and batch SQL in T-SQL Debugger should behave exactly the same as in your code.

The second tab, Stored Procedure, pictured in Figure 71-4, allows you to choose a stored procedure to debug. The Procedure Name drop-down lists all the stored procedures in the database selected on the Settings tab. You can fill in the parameters by directly editing the call in the Query field, or by selecting the parameter in the Parameters list and editing the Value field. Pressing Execute will start the debugger. The final tab on the Visual Basic Batch T-SQL Debugger dialog, Batch Query, allows you to enter a script of SQL statements to debug. Enter the script in the Batch Text field and press Execute to debug the script.

Starting T-SQL Debugger with RDO

If you have selected the Automatically step into Stored Procedures through RDO connections option on the T-SQL Debugger Options dialog, a call to OpenResultset or Execute that calls a stored procedure will start the T-SQL Debugger. In this case, no intermediary dialogs will pop up to collect information. The RDO calls have already provided it.

Starting T-SQL Debugger with UserConnections

The T-SQL Debugger can also debug the stored procedures in a UserConnection. You will have to configure the UserConnection to use the ODBC Cursor Library or the

Client-Batch cursors on the UserConnection Properties dialog. Figure 71-5 shows the UserConnection Properties dialog and the Cursor Library field.

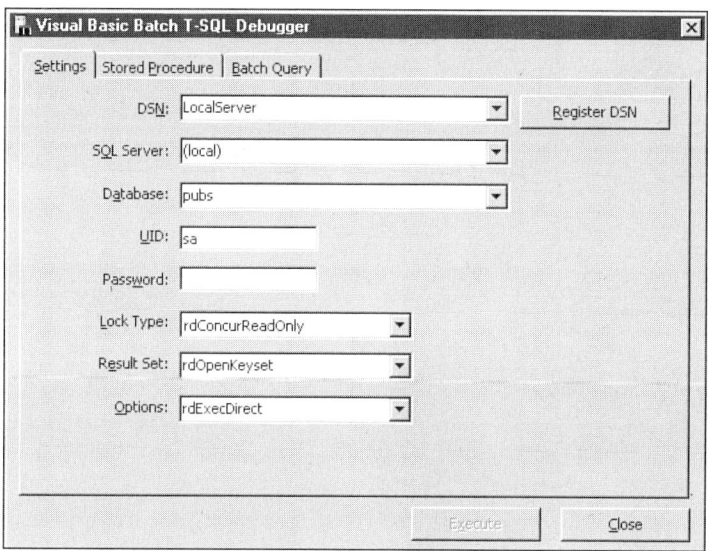

Figure 71-3   Setting options for a design time T-SQL Debugger session

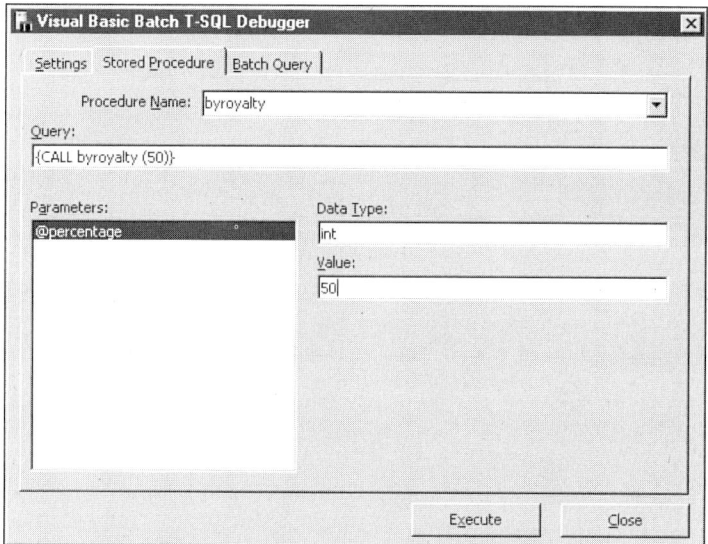

Figure 71-4   Filling in stored procedure parameters

Right-clicking and selecting the Debug Stored Procedure item from the pop-up menu will present a dialog to collect the parameters for the stored procedure. The Enter Unassigned Parameters dialog, pictured in Figure 71-6, allows you to specify the parameter values. You can either enter the values directly into the window that displays the stored procedure call, or select a parameter from the parameter list and enter its value in the Value field. After assigning the parameters and pressing OK, the T-SQL Debugger continues to the T-SQL Debugger main window.

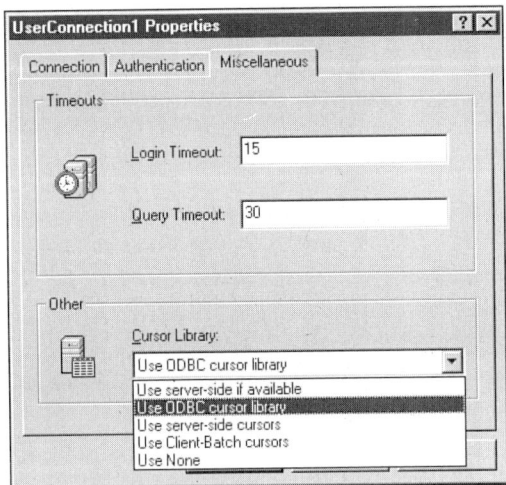

Figure 71-5   Select ODBC cursor library or Client-Batch cursors to debug a UserConnection stored procedure

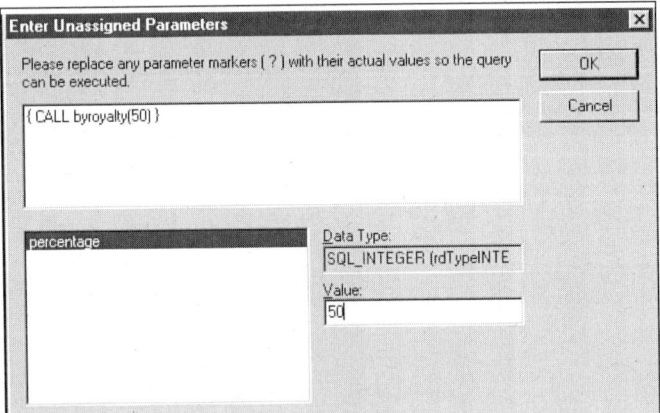

Figure 71-6   The Enter Unassigned Parameters dialog

Using T-SQL Debugger

The T-SQL Debugger has many of the debugging features a Visual Basic programmer is used to and expects. If you have done any debugging in Visual Basic, you should be very comfortable in T-SQL Debugger. Figure 71-7 shows the T-SQL Debugger at the completion of a debugging session. The top pane shows the color-coded syntax of the stored procedure. You can change the colors and font using the Options menu. The two middle panes are the watch windows. Local and global variables can be examined here. The bottom pane catches all the output from your stored procedure. If you are debugging at runtime, output also goes to the resultset.

Within T-SQL Debugger, you can step through each SQL statement, set break-points, examine resultsets, watch local and global variables, and even examine the contents of global temporary tables. The toolbar buttons differ from Visual Basic's but are the same as Visual C++. With a little help from the tooltips, it should be easy to find the function you need. Breakpoints are available from the Edit menu, and the Go, Step, and Run to Cursor functions are available from the Debug menu. Each of these functions behaves like its Visual Basic counterparts, but there are a few special functions unique to debugging stored procedures.

The Edit|Add Watch menu adds a watch to the Global Variables pane. Selecting the variable and pressing (DELETE) will remove it. Local variables are automatically added to the Local Variables pane. You can edit the value of the local variable by double-clicking the Value column in the Local Variables pane.

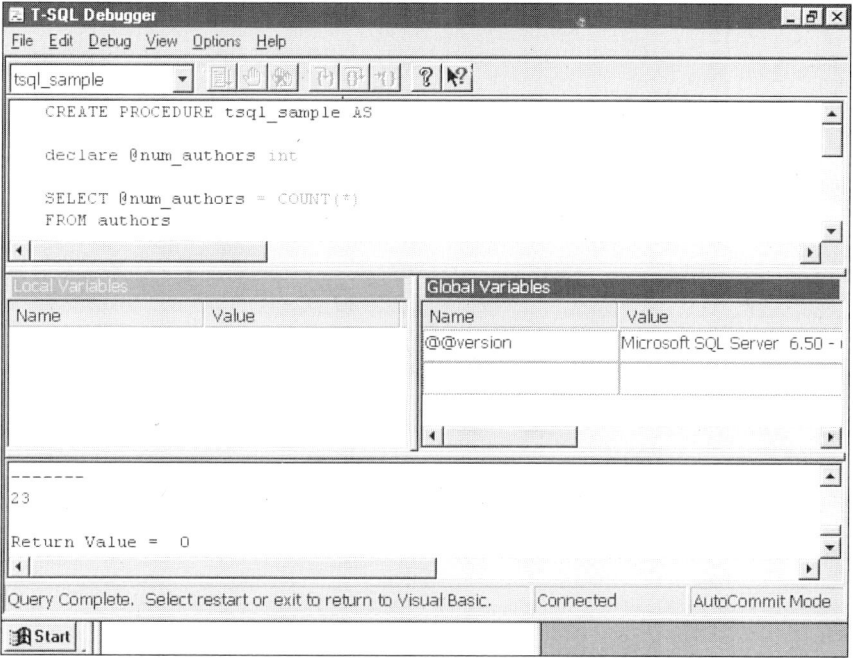

Figure 71-7 The T-SQL Debugger

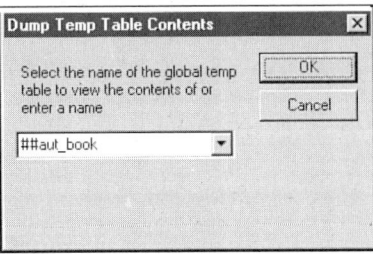

Figure 71-8   Selecting a temp
table to view

The View|Temp Table Dump menu presents the Dump Temp Table Contents dialog. This dialog, pictured in Figure 71-8, allows you to select any global temporary table and have it dump its contents to the bottom pane. This feature is extremely handy. You may want to consider changing your stored procedures to create global temporary tables during the debugging phases of your project just so you can examine them here.

You can examine the call stack through the View|Call Stack menu. This becomes handy when your stored procedures call stored procedures. You may jump back and forth between the call levels by double-clicking the list on the Call Stack window.

The T-SQL Debugger Project

Project Overview

The T-SQL Debugger exercise will step you through some of the features of the T-SQL Debugger using a stored procedure in the pubs sample database.

Assembling the Project

1. Create a stored procedure in the sample database called pubs, which is installed with SQL Server using the script below. This stored procedure does not really do anything useful, but it goes out of its way to exercise T-SQL Debugger.

```
if exists (select * from sysobjects
where id = object_id('dbo.tsql_sample') and sysstat & 0xf = 4)
drop procedure dbo.tsql_sample
GO

CREATE PROCEDURE tsql_sample AS

declare @num_authors int

SELECT @num_authors = COUNT(*)
FROM authors

SELECT a.au_lname, a.au_fname, t.title
INTO ##aut_book
FROM titles t, authors a, titleauthor ta
```

```
WHERE a.au_id = ta.au_id
AND ta.title_id = t.title_id

SELECT * FROM ##aut_book

EXEC byroyalty 50

SELECT @num_authors
GO
```

2. Create a datasource for the server on which you created the stored procedure using the ODBC settings in Control Panel. Set the Login Database Name to pubs.

3. Assuming you have configured your client and server as described in the "Setting Up" section in this chapter, open Visual Basic. You may cancel the New Project dialog; this exercise will take you through a design time debugging session, and you don't need a project for that.

4. If you have not previously added the T-SQL Debugger, use the Add-In Manager to select Visual Basic T-SQL Debugger.

5. Select the Add Ins|T-SQL Debugger menu item to activate the T-SQL Debugger. Select the new data source from the DSN drop-down. Enter an appropriate UID and Password.

6. Switch to the Stored Procedures tab. In the Procedure Name drop-down, select the tsql_sample. Press Execute to enter the T-SQL Debugger.

7. Use the Debug|Step menu to start the stored procedure. Immediately, the @num_authors variable will be added to the Local Variables pane. Step again and it is assigned a value. You can change this value by double-clicking on the Value column next to its name in the Local Variables pane.

8. Step a third time and the select statement creates a global temporary table. To examine its contents, select the View|Temp Table Dump menu and select the ##aut_book item in the drop-down. Press OK to continue. The contents of the ##aut_book temporary table are dumped to the output pane at the bottom of the T-SQL Debugger window.

9. Step twice. You will now be in the byroyalty stored procedure. Select the View|Call Stack menu item to display the Call Stack window. You can switch back and forth between viewing the two calls by double-clicking on the list.

10. Step once again from either call and you should be back in the first call with the SELECT @num_authors line highlighted. Select the Edit|Add Watch menu item and type @@version in the Variable field. Press Add Watch to continue. The @@version variable will be added to the Global Variables list.

11. Choose Debug|Go to finish up the stored procedure. All the results will be fed to the output pane. File|Exit will close the T-SQL Debugger.

How It Works

The stored procedure above, while not very useful, does demonstrate the typical insides of a stored procedure. It uses local variables, calls another stored procedure, and creates a temporary table. By stepping through the sample, just like you were stepping through lines of Visual Basic code, you can explore the features of the T-SQL Debugger.

72
VISUAL DATA MANAGER

One of the most useful add-ins for Visual Basic is the Visual Data Manager, which is a sample application and add-in for Visual Basic. Visual Data Manager and its source code are shipped with the Professional and Enterprise versions of Visual Basic. Visual Data Manager exercises almost every aspect of the DBEngine object and provides a great tool as well. If you are building an application using Data Access Objects (DAO), Visual Data Manager can be a fountain of samples and snatchable code.

Visual Data Manager as an Add-In

If you are developing an application with DAO and do not have Microsoft Access, Visual Data Manager can be used to build, alter, and populate the database. It can create tables and queries, generate data forms similar to the Data Form Wizard, administer permissions, and be used to browse and edit data.

Figure 72-1 shows the Visual Data Manager main window. The Database window shows a tree view of the objects that can be manipulated using Visual Data Manager. Expanding the entries leads to successively more detailed levels. Editable properties can be changed by double-clicking nodes in the tree.

Creating and Altering Tables

You can create database objects in code. The DBEngine object exposes everything needed to build a database from scratch. However, it is inconvenient and time-consuming to write code just to create some tables.

Once you have opened or created a new database, you can alter or add new tables using the Table Structure dialog. Right clicking on the Database Window, shown in Figure 72-1, will bring up a pop-up menu with New Table and Design options. If a table is highlighted, selecting Design will open the Table Structure dialog with the selected table's fields listed. The New Table menu will open the same dialog, shown in Figure 72-2, only it will be blank.

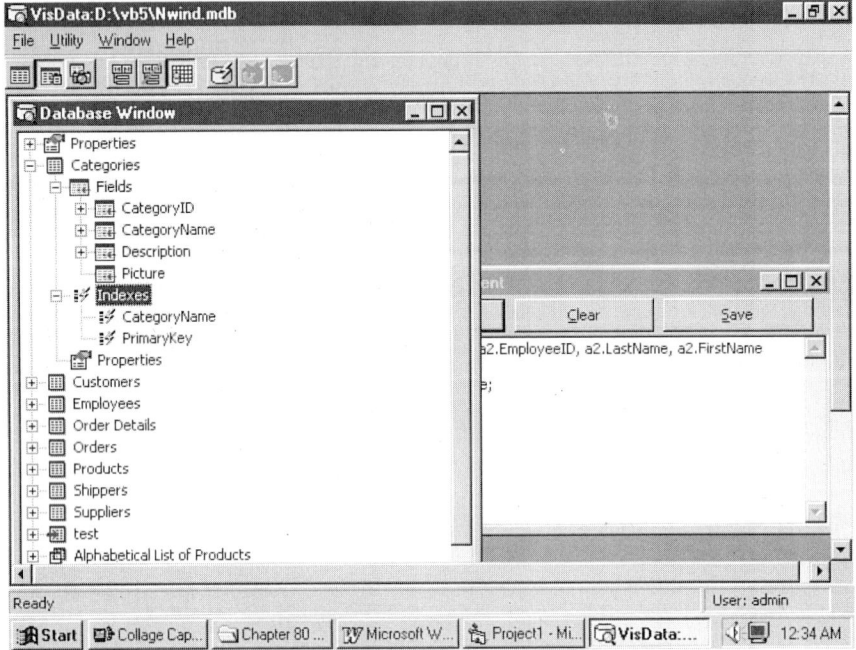

Figure 72-1 The Visual Data Manager main window

Figure 72-2 The Table Structure dialog

The Table Structure dialog lists the fields and indexes of a table. Pressing the Add Field button opens the Add Field dialog pictured in Figure 72-3. Here you can set the properties of the field, such as Type, Size, and DefaultValue. Once set, some of the field's properties cannot be changed. Unlike Microsoft Access, you cannot change a field's data type after it has been created. If you need to change one of the fixed properties, you will have to use another tool, such as Microsoft Access, or remove and then add the corrected field. The Remove Field button removes a field from the table.

The Add Index button opens the Add Index dialog, shown in Figure 72-4. Here you set the index name, choose the fields to make up the index, and set its properties. Like the Add Field function, once the index has been created, many of its properties cannot be changed in Visual Data Manager. If you need to alter an index, you will have to remove it and add the corrected one. The Remove Index button drops an index from the table.

One of the most important features of DAO is its ability to do cross-database joins. At the same time you build your database, you may want to set up the attached tables. Visual Data Manager provides a means to attach tables to the current database. The Utility|Attachments menu will open the Attachments window pictured in Figure 72-5. The list will have all the current attached tables. The ReAttach button updates connection information to the attached table. The New button opens the New Attached Table dialog, in which you can specify a new attached table.

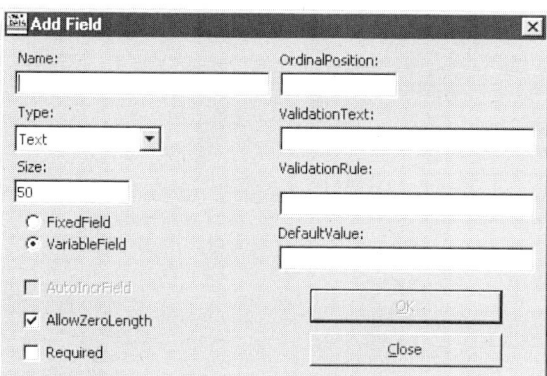

Figure 72-3   The Add Field dialog

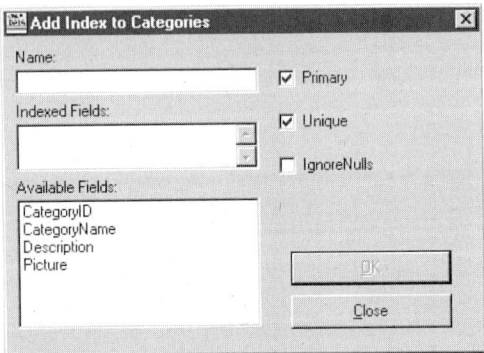

Figure 72-4 The Add Index dialog

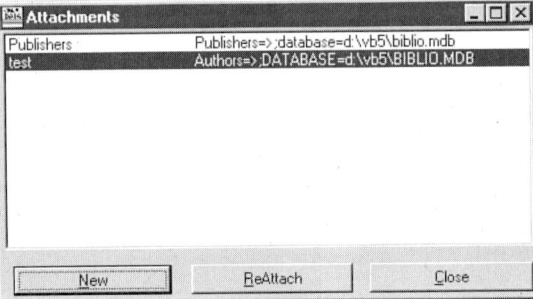

Figure 72-5 The Attachments window

Creating Queries

Another object often used in DAO projects is the query. Visual Data Manager has the facilities to create query objects. Choosing Design when right-clicking an existing query in the Database window will open the SQL Statement window shown in Figure 72-6. Unfortunately, the menu is misleading and changes in this window are not applied to the selected query object. However, the query can be edited by double-clicking on the individual properties listed in the Database window.

Visual Data Manager's facility for creating queries is the Query Builder dialog, shown in Figure 72-7. You can open the Query Builder through the Utility|Query Builder menu or by selecting the New Query item in the pop-up menu on the Database window.

Select the tables from Tables list and the Fields in the Fields to Show list. The Group By drop-down can be used to select a field from the selected tables to group by. The Order By drop-down works in a similar manner with the addition of the Asc and Desc options to sort ascending or descending.

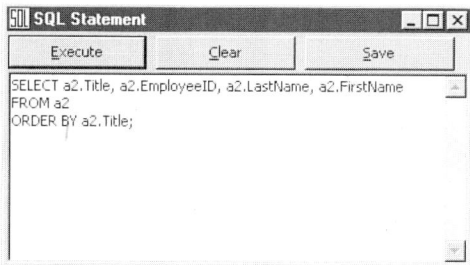

Figure 72-6   The SQL Statement window

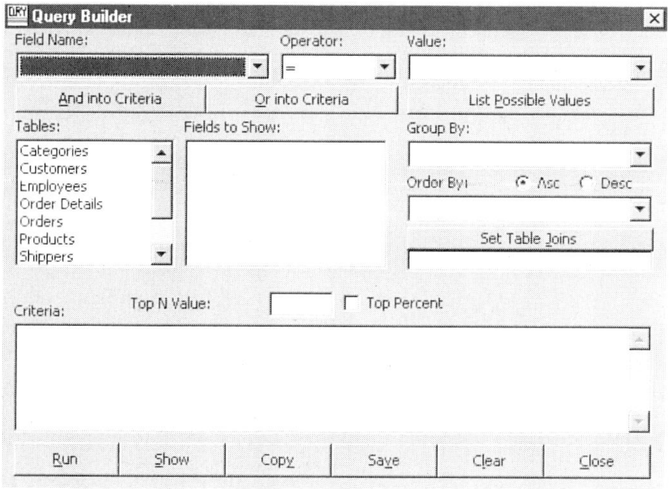

Figure 72-7   The Query Builder dialog

At the top of the dialog are fields that allow you to add filter criteria to the query. The Field Name, Operator, and Value fields specify the filter. The And into Criteria button adds the filter to the where clause with an And; the Or into Criteria adds it with an Or. You may also edit the criteria directly in the Criteria field. For particularly complicated queries, you will probably have to edit the criteria directly. For example, the Query Builder dialog does not have the ability to create a subquery without editing the criteria directly.

The Top N Value field will restrict the result set to the specified number of rows. If the Top Percent check is selected, it will restrict the result set to the specified percentage of the total records.

The Set Table Joins button opens the Join Tables dialog shown in Figure 72-8. Here you can specify the joins between the tables if you have more than one table selected. The first list shows all the tables in the query. Selecting two of these tables will show their fields in the next two lists. Select the two fields to join on and press the Add Join to Query button to join between them. The Clear All Joins button removes the previously specified joins.

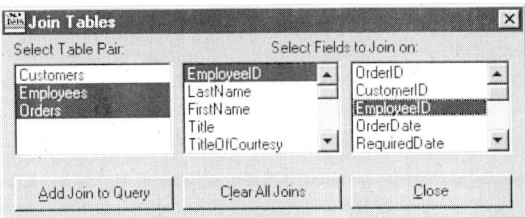

Figure 72-8   The Join Tables dialog

The Join Tables dialog does not use the join keywords, it just adds to the where clause. If you need to use the join keywords, you will have to edit the query after saving it with the Query Builder or use another tool to create the query.

Data Form Designer

If the Visual Data Manager is opened from the Add Ins menu in Visual Basic, the Data Form Designer, shown in Figure 72-9, will be available. The Data Form Designer duplicates some of the functionality available in the Data Form Wizard. You can activate the Data Form Designer from the Utility|Data Form Designer menu.

You specify the name of the form to build in the Form Name field. The RecordSource combo lists all the tables, queries, and attachments in the current database. It can also type a SQL query into the field. The Available Fields list shows all the fields returned by the query or table selected in the RecordSource combo. Use the >, >>, <<, and < buttons to add and remove the fields in the Include Fields list. The ↑ and ↓ buttons to the right of the Included Fields list change the order of the fields in that list. The Build the Form button creates the form in the current project.

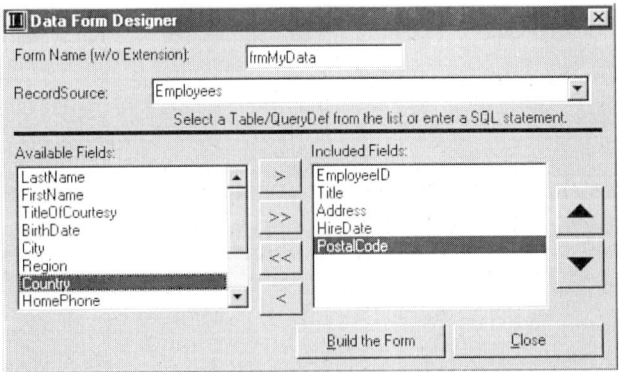

Figure 72-9   The Data Form Designer dialog

> **TIP**
> The Data Form Wizard, described in Chapter 96, is significantly faster and has a richer feature set. If it is available, you may want to use it instead of the Data Form Designer function of the Visual Data Manager.

Groups, Users, and Permissions

After building the database, it is time to create users and assign permissions. Visual Data Manager provides an easy way to create groups and users and assign permissions. The Groups/Users/Permissions dialog, shown in Figure 72-10, is opened using the Utility|Groups/Users menu.

The Groups/Users/Permissions dialog works in two modes. In Users mode, selected at the top left, the list below the User-Groups selection shows the users. Selecting a user highlights the groups in which the user is a member below. You change the user's membership by selecting and unselecting groups in the list. New and Delete buttons add and remove users from the database, and the Set/Clear Password button clears the user's password.

While in Groups mode, the top list shows the groups available. The bottom list shows the members of the group by which users are selected. Membership in the group can be altered by selecting users from the bottom list. The New and Delete buttons add and remove groups from the database.

In both modes, selecting an item in the Users/Groups list and an object in the Tables/Querys list will show the permissions in the Permissions area. Permissions can be altered by changing the selections and pressing the Assign button. To view or change the permissions for another object, change your selection in the Tables/Query list.

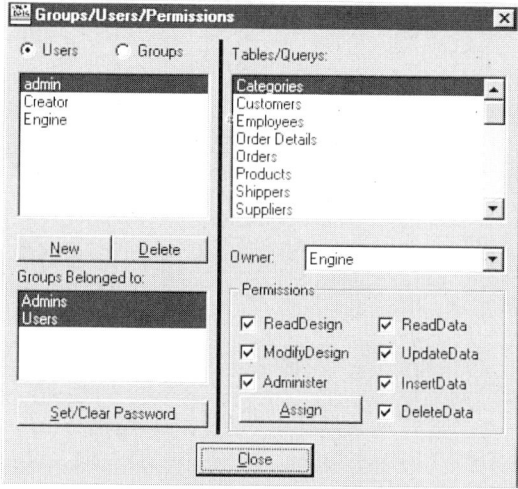

Figure 72-10   The Groups/Users/Permissions dialog

Browsing and Editing Data

Visual Data Manager provides several ways of browsing and editing data. Visual Data Manager opens result sets based on the selections on the toolbar. The first group of buttons specifies the type of Recordset: Table, Dynaset, or Snapshot. The second group of buttons specifies the style of data form to open. The first style of data form is the classic data control with bound controls data form. The second style opens a data form that does not use a data control; a scrollbar is used to navigate the results. The third style is a bound DBGrid with a data control. The data forms are opened using the Open command on the right mouse pop-up menu in the Database window, or by double-clicking the table or query.

Each of the data forms has additional functionalities like Find, Update, Delete, and Filter appropriate to the style of data form. The data forms follow the same restrictions for Recordsets as one opened through code. For example, you cannot open a query as a Table Recordset or edit Recordsets opened as a Snapshot.

Visual Data Manager as a Sample

All good programmers eventually figure out that the best kind of code is the kind they don't have to write. That is the idea behind libraries, object-oriented programming, templates, code wizards, and components. Visual Data Manager is a bounty of free code! The source code for Visual Data Manager is available in \Samples\VisData in the Visual Basic install directory or in \Vb\Samples\VisData on the Visual Basic CD if you chose not to install the samples. If you are building an application using DAO for your database access, the Visual Data Manager sample is a great place to look for samples and maybe some canned functionality. Table 72-1 shows a list of forms in the Visual Data Manager sample that can easily be incorporated into your application.

Table 72-1 Forms and their functions in the Visual Data Manager sample

Form	Function	Additional Requirements
frmAttachments	Displays a list of attached tables; allows adding	frmNewAttach
frmDataControl	Loads and displays a Recordset	
frmDataGrid	Loads and displays a Recordset in a DBGrid	
frmDynaSnap	Loads a Dynaset or Snapshot; includes search and zoom	frmFindForm and frmZoom
frmGroupUsers	Administer permissions for groups and users	frmNewPassword and frmNewUserGroup
frmQuery	A query builder	frmJoin and frmQuery; this form may not be as easy to detach from Visual Data Manager but may be a good starting point
frmSQL	Enter, execute, and save SQL statements	
frmTableObj	Loads and displays a table	frmSeek

Microsoft wrote the Visual Data Manager sample with the idea that many of its functions could be pulled into other applications. There are comments throughout the sample with instructions on how to make it work with your application. Search for the word Standalone. The comments you will find give instructions on how to make the various forms fit into your application.

Many of the forms rely on functions and global variables from the VISDATA.BAS module. You can add the module to your project or just pick and choose what you need.

73

MICROSOFT DATA TOOLS

One of the more exciting tools bundled with the Enterprise Edition of Visual Basic is Microsoft Data Tools. Microsoft Data Tools is a tool integrated into the Microsoft Developer Studio that exposes the objects in an ODBC datasource. Using Microsoft Data Tools, a developer can create database schema, specifying relationships and tables, and whip up a new query all within a graphical, easy-to-use environment. Microsoft Data Tools packages up functionality that used to require expensive CASE tools.

Getting Started

Using the Add-In Manager dialog, select the Microsoft Data Tools add-in. A new item will be added to the Add-Ins menu, labeled Visual Database Tools. Selecting the new menu item will load Microsoft Developer Studio. Visual C++, Visual InterDev, and Visual J++ users should feel right at home with this. If you have adapted to the new Visual Basic 5.0 user interface, this environment should feel familiar. Upon first entering the Microsoft Data Tools, you will be asked for a datasource. You can use Microsoft Data Tools on anything with an ODBC driver, but some functionality may be unavailable with some ODBC datasources.

Figures 73-1 and 73-2 show the selection tabs for file and machine datasources. Each tab has a New button that will use a Wizard to step you through the process of adding a new datasource. You can also add new datasources using the ODBC configuration in Control Panel. Select a datasource and press OK to start Microsoft Data Tools.

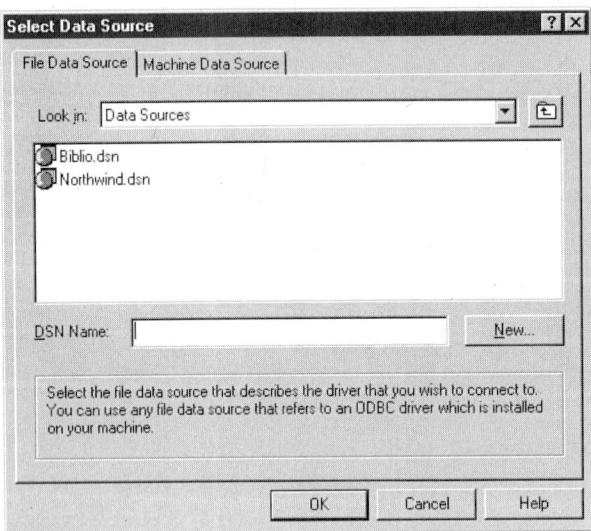

Figure 73-1   Selecting a file datasource

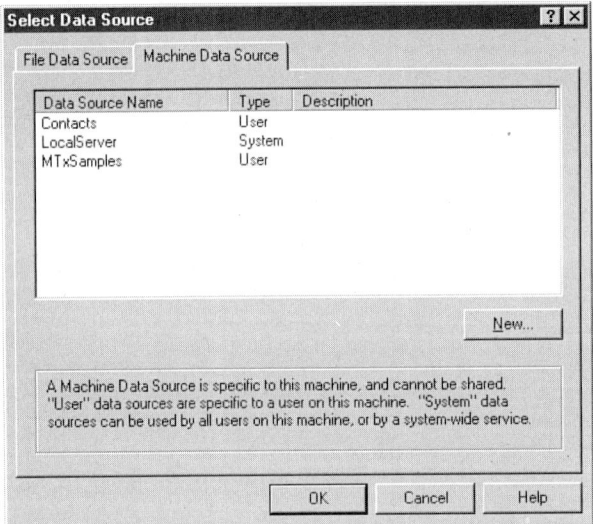

Figure 73-2   Selecting a machine datasource

Browsing and Editing Database Objects

After opening a datasource with Microsoft Data Tools, the DataView tab, shown in Figure 73-3, will be displayed shoing the objects in the datasource selected. If the window with the DataView tab is not visible, you can make it visible with the View|Workspace menu. You can add multiple datasources by selecting the Project|Add To Project|Data Connection menu. They will be added as additional entries in the DataView tab's tree view.

The DataView tab presents a hierarchical view of the objects in the selected datasources. Functions to manipulate or view the objects are available through context-sensitive right-click pop-up menus. Table 73-1 lists the objects in the DataView tab and what can be done to them. As mentioned earlier, depending on the ODBC datasource and its driver, your mileage may vary.

Table 73-1 Available objects and functions in the DataView tab

Object	Menu	To Do...
Column	Copy	Copy the entire table structure
	Properties	View the selected column's properties
Database diagrams	Open	Open the database diagram for editing or viewing
	New table	Create a new table through the diagram interface
	New diagram	Create a new database diagram
	Copy	Copy the table definition for the selected table in the database diagram
	Paste	Paste a table definition
	Delete	Delete the selected database diagram
	Rename	Rename the selected database diagram
Stored procedure	Open	Open the stored procedure definition for editing or viewing
	Run	Execute the stored procedure after collecting parameters
	Debug	Debug the stored procedure after collecting parameters
	New stored procedure	Create a new stored procedure
	Copy	Copy the stored procedure declaration
	Delete	Drop the selected stored procedure
	Rename	Rename the selected stored procedure
	Properties	View the selected stored procedure's properties
Stored procedure parameter	Properties	View the properties of the selected stored procedure parameter
Table	Open	Open to edit data or start a new query
	Design	Alter the table
	New trigger	Create a new trigger
	New table	Create a new table
	Copy	Copy the table structure; for pasting into a database diagram
	Delete	Drop the selected table
	Properties	View the selected table's properties

continued on next page

continued from previous page

Object	Menu	To Do...
Trigger	Open	Open the trigger declaration for editing or viewing
	Delete	Drop the selected trigger
	Properties	View the selected trigger's properties
View	Open	Open to edit data or start a new query
	Properties	View the selected view's properties

Database Diagrams

Possibly the most powerful feature of Microsoft Data Tools is the ability to graphically create and alter a database. The Database Diagram window, shown in Figure 73-4, displays the tables and their relationships. It also exposes objects that cannot be manipulated through the DataView tab, such as indexes, constraints, and relationships.

Functions in the Database Diagram window are available through the Database Diagram toolbar (pictured in Figure 73-5), the Edit and View menus, and the right-click pop-up menu. Table 73-2 lists the menu and button functions available in the Database Diagram window.

Figure 73-3　The DataView tab

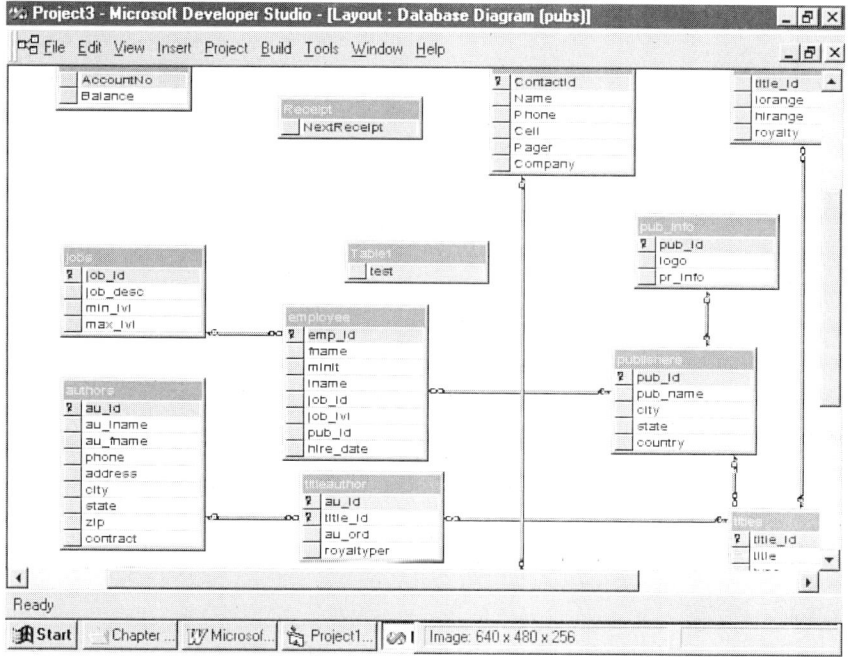

Figure 73-4   The Database Diagram window

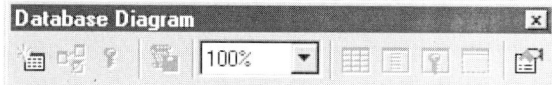

Figure 73-5   The Database Diagram toolbar

Table 73-2 Available functions in the Database Diagram window

Title	Menu	To Do...
Column names	View|Table	Display all the column names
Column properties	View|Table	Display all the columns and column properties of the selected table
Delete relationship	Edit	Deletes the currently selected relationships
Delete table from database	Edit	Drop the table from the database
Keys	View|Table	Display only the columns that are the primary key or foreign keys
Name only	View|Table	Display only the table name
New database item	Insert	Create a new database object
Properties	View	View and edit the table's properties, indexes, constraints, and relationships
Remove table from diagram	Edit	Remove the table from the diagram; does not remove it from the database
Set primary key	Edit	Sets the selected columns as the primary key for the current table

The Properties window available from the Database Diagram window's Edit menu warrants further discussion. Here you edit constraints, indexes, and relationships for the tables. Figure 73-6 shows the Table tab of the Properties window. The Table tab lets you specify constraints. A *constraint* is a filter that ensures only data meeting certain criteria is allowed as a value to a field. For example, you may have a State field in a table. A useful constraint, in the United States, would limit the field to a list of the two-character abbreviations for states. The constraint would appear similar to the following syntax:

```
State = 'FL' or State = 'GA' or State = 'PA' etc.
```

The Table tab allows you to Add and Delete constraints with the New and Delete buttons. The Check existing data on creation option will attempt to apply the constraint to the data already in the table. If some existing data does not conform, Microsoft Data Tools will not save the constraint and will give an error message. The Enable constraint for INSERT and UPDATE option checks the constraint whenever a new value is added to the table or the field is updated. Finally, the Enable constraint for replication option applies the constraint when the table is replicated.

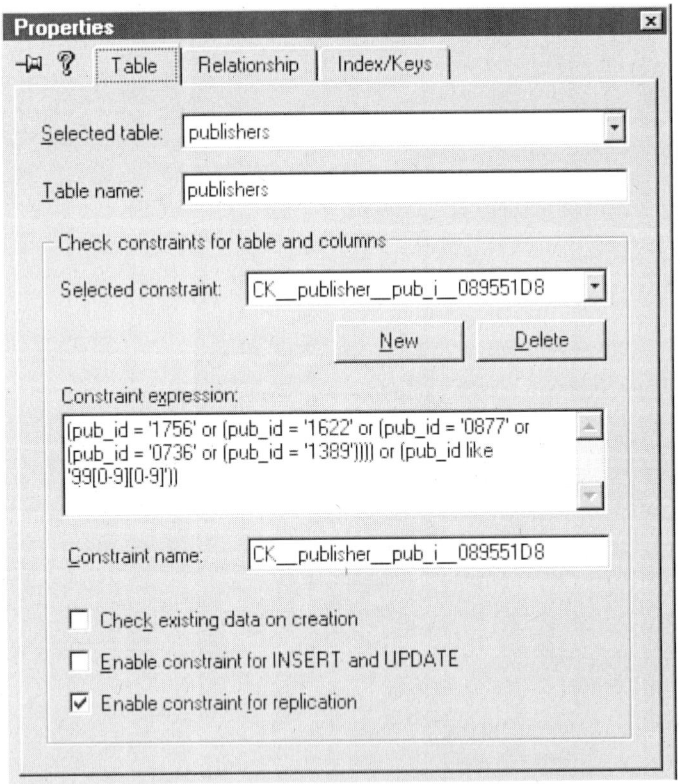

Figure 73-6 The Table tab

The Relationship tab, shown in Figure 73-7, allows you to edit relationships, or foreign keys, for the table. The Primary key table/Foreign key table grid displays and allows editing of the columns involved in the relationship. The first column shows the related table and its primary key. The second column shows the table with properties that are being examined and columns that make up the foreign key. You change the relationship by editing the grid. The Check existing data on creation option will make sure there is an entry in the related table for each reference in the current table when the relationship is saved. The Enable relationship for INSERT and UPDATE option enables the check for inserts and updates. Finally, the Enable relationship for replication option enables the check for replicated tables.

To create a relationship, select a column or group of columns in the table to reference and drag them to the referencing table. For example, suppose there were two tables in your database, Salespersons and Sales. To create a relationship between the two, highlight the SalespersonsId in the Salespersons table and drag it to the Sales table. The columns to be used in the referencing table must already exist before this will work. So, in this example, the SalespersonsId column would need to exist in the Sales table and be the correct data type.

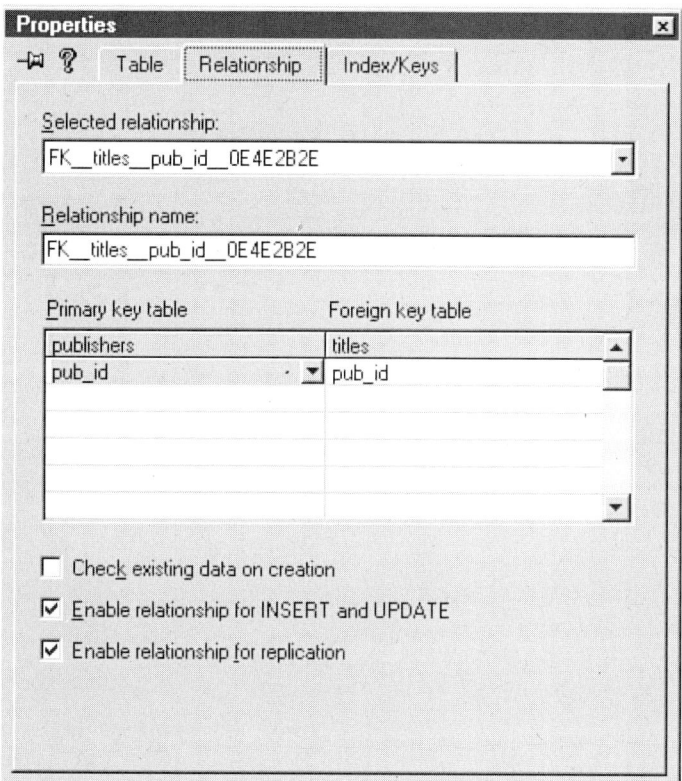

Figure 73-7 The Relationship tab

The Index/Keys tab, pictured in Figure 73-8, is where the indexes and primary key are edited. The New and Delete buttons add and delete indexes. The Delete button can also remove the primary key. You can create a primary key by highlighting the appropriate columns in the table and selecting the Edit|Set Primary Key menu. The Create UNIQUE option builds a unique constraint or index. The Ignore duplicate key option will delete entries in the table with duplicate keys. Updates and inserts that result in duplicates will be successful, but the new rows are tossed out.

Fill factor specifies how much space is used on each index page when the index is created. In SQL Server if an insert or update results in too much data on the index page, a page split occurs. This is an expensive operation. If you expect a table to handle lots of transactions in which the index will change, such as an insert or update to the key, a low fill factor may help performance. If no fill factor is specified, the default is used.

The Create as CLUSTERED option builds a clustered index. There can be only one clustered index on each table; if you set this option for more than one index, Microsoft Data Tools will notify you that another clustered index already exists. Sort data sorts the data in ascending order, and Data already sorted tells Microsoft Data Tools that the existing data is already sorted. Reorg sorted data rebuilds the clustered index.

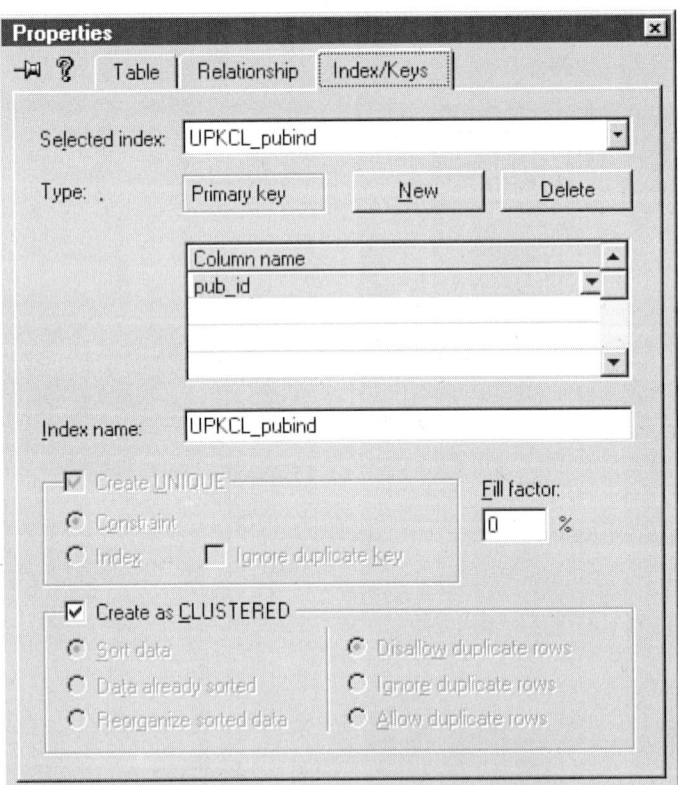

Figure 73-8   The Index/Keys tab

The remaining three options specify how the clustered index handles duplicate entries. Disallow duplicate rows will keep the index from being created if there are duplicates. It will also prevent updates or inserts that result in a duplicate row. Ignore duplicate rows will delete duplicates when the index is created. There is no control over which row might be tossed out, and it will throw out any duplicate rows created by an insert or update. Allow duplicate rows lets duplicate rows exist in the index, and accepts updates and inserts that result in duplicate rows.

The Table Design Window

The Table Design window, shown in Figure 73-9, is the place you create and alter table definitions. It can be reached by three routes: selecting Column Properties in the Database Diagram window; highlighting a table in the DataView tab and choosing Design from the pop-up menu; or adding a new table through the New Table pop-up menu or the Insert|New Database item menu.

You can alter the table definition by editing the columns in the grid. Some columns are not always editable; Microsoft Data Tools will prevent you from making changes to these. To add new columns to the table, enter the new column in a blank row and set the data type and other attributes. To delete a column, highlight the column and select the Edit|Delete menu.

The Query Builder

The Query Builder gives you a graphic way to generate SQL statements. A new query can be created by opening a table or through the Insert|New Database item menu. The Query window, shown in Figure 73-10, is divided into four panes: Diagram, Grid, SQL, and Results.

Account									
Column Name	Datatype	Length	Precision	Scale	Allow Nulls	Default Value	Identity	Identity Seed	
AccountNo	int	4	10	0	✓				
Balance	int	4	10	0	✓				

Figure 73-9   The Table Design window

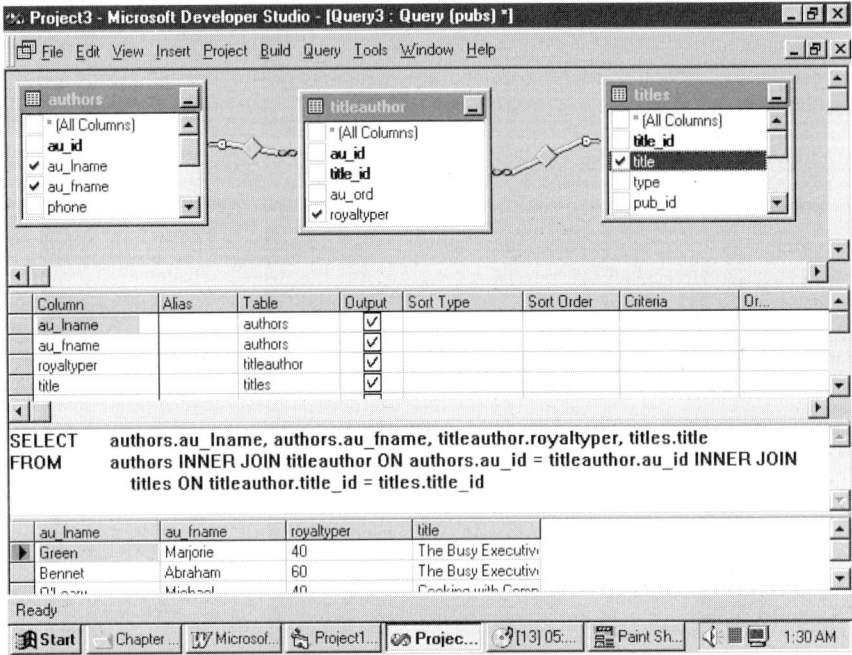

Figure 73-10   The Query window

The first pane, the Diagram, displays the query visually. You add tables to the query by dragging them from the DataView tab. Microsoft Data Tools will automatically join them by any relationships defined. You can alter the join through the Edit|Properties menu. The Properties window allows you to change the join to a right, left, or full outer join and change the comparison operator.

The second pane, the Grid, lists the columns involved in the query. Here you can specify sort order, as well as up to four ORed filter criteria. Checking the output column will add the item to the Select clause. To add more columns, for the Select clause or for a filter, use the drop-down that appears when you click on the first column, titled Column.

The third pane, the SQL, shows the assembled SQL statement. Some complicated queries cannot be shown in the Diagram pane or easily entered using the Grid pane. The SQL pane gives direct access to the SQL statement. This can be particularly handy just to generate SQL for use in your applications. You can change the type of statement through the Query|Change Type menu. This menu changes the query from a Select to an Insert, Update, or Delete and back.

The final pane displays the results. As changes are made to any of the other panes, the results are grayed out. To refresh the results, use the Tools|Run menu. The results may be edited by clicking on the field to edit and changing the value. This will only work if the database can make the change. For example, you could not update a MIN value.

PART XII

OBJECT EMBEDDING AND AUTOMATION

74

OLE OVERVIEW

An important feature of the Microsoft Windows operating system is its ability for applications to share information. Prior to Microsoft Windows, in order to share the information of one application with another, you had to save data to a file, then import the data into the target application. This technique was very time consuming and not very efficient.

As the Microsoft Windows operating system matured, so did their application. Microsoft introduced the ability of *dynamic data exchange (DDE)*. DDE is a means of communication between Microsoft Windows applications. This link acts as a conduit for the exchange of data between the connected applications. The data exchanged may either be information copied from one application to another or commands or keystrokes for the other application to process.

As with all technology, there was room for improvement. Microsoft then introduced *object linking and embedding (OLE)*. OLE gives your application the power to directly use and manipulate another Windows application's data in its native format. If the other application supports OLE automation, you may also be able to use its objects, properties, and methods just as you would a Visual Basic control. *OLE automation*, introduced in Visual Basic 3.0, is one of the most important additions to Windows and serves as the basis for creating a true object-oriented environment.

This chapter gives both an overview of the OLE container control and a thorough discussion of every property, event, and function necessary for fully implementing the linking or embedding of OLE objects in your applications.

Differences Between DDE and OLE

DDE is the basic foundation for interprocess communication among Microsoft Windows applications. In a DDE conversation, the application that creates the link is known as the *destination* application, and the application that responds is known as a *source* application. (These used to be referred to as *client* and *server*, respectively.) Any application that supports DDE can serve as either a source or a destination. One application can serve as both a destination and a source with several other applications at the same time. Only one active DDE link should be established between a Visual Basic control or form and another application. For example, a link between a Microsoft Excel spreadsheet cell and a text control is acceptable as long as the parent form does not already have a link with the same cell. You might cause an infinite loop of updates if there were more than one link between the same two applications.

Although there are many similarities between OLE and DDE (both allow you to share data and issue commands between two different applications), there are fundamental differences in how they do it and in how thoroughly the link is implemented. To discuss these differences, we must define two terms. The *originating application* is the application program that is providing services (data or functionality). The *container application* is the application that presents the information or functionality provided by the originating application. In Visual Basic programming, the container application is usually your Visual Basic program, and the originating application is usually (but not always) a non-Visual Basic application such as Microsoft Excel or Lotus 1-2-3.

When you use DDE, you are exchanging unformatted data. Your Visual Basic application needs to take the data and format it properly. For example, you might establish a link to a range of cells on a worksheet. Your application would need to process this data and place it in an appropriate Visual Basic control, like the grid control. The original spreadsheet's formatting will be unrelated to what is displayed. In most cases, you also obtain just the finished product (for example, the resultant number) rather than the underlying object (for instance, the formula that calculated the resultant number). Your application would then need to provide all necessary means for manipulating the data, such as edit boxes, a menu structure, and toolbars.

OLE, in contrast, actually transfers control back to the originating application. In our spreadsheet example, your Visual Basic application displays an image of the spreadsheet data exactly as it appears in the original spreadsheet. All formatting, grid lines, borders, coloring, and font selection remain intact.

When you edit the spreadsheet object in your Visual Basic program, you actually call up the original application and use its menus, toolbars, and other tools to do the editing. The OLE data contains the correct underlying objects (like formulas) so the information remains fully editable. Some applications also support *in-place activation*. This means that instead of the other application taking over the focus, it leaves the object embedded in your application and lets you edit the object in place. In either case, OLE lets your Visual Basic application in effect incorporate the full functionality of the embedded application. Rather than, for example, having to write a mini-spreadsheet in your accounting application, you can draw on the full capabilities of Microsoft Excel. The only drawback is that your application's users must also have access to the embedded application.

In the 32-bit world, DDE is hardly used at all. It is used in today's software world mostly in 16-bit applications that do not have OLE support. Because DDE is not used in the 32-bit development world, it is not covered in this book. For more information about DDE and Visual Basic, refer to *Visual Basic 4 OLE, Database, and Controls SuperBible* (Waite Group Press, 1995).

OLE 1.0 and OLE 2.0

Visual Basic 2.0 implemented the first version of OLE, version 1.0. This OLE specification enables an application to link and embed another application's data in its native format. It also lets the user double-click on the object to edit it. The originating application then loads the object, and the user edits the object in that application.

Visual Basic 3.0 was one of the first applications to support OLE 2.0. This advanced specification lets users link and embed objects just as in the 1.0 specification, but it also lets users edit the object totally within the container application. The originating application, rather than starting up and loading the object for editing, actually replaces the container application's menus, toolbars, and palettes with its own. It makes it look as if the container application (for instance, your Visual Basic program) is doing all the work. Figure 74-1 shows an Excel OLE object edited from within a Visual Basic program. Notice how the Excel menus and toolbar appear directly on the form. This occurs through user-interface negotiation and is part of the OLE 2.0 specifications.

OLE 2.0 also opens up the exciting capabilities of OLE automation. This lets your Visual Basic applications use another program's object just as they would a Visual Basic control. For example, you could use a commercial word processor's spell checker rather than having to either write your own or do without spell checking. OLE automation is covered in Chapter 76.

OLE 2.0-compliant applications that support in-place activation allow the object's menu system (as provided by the host) to replace the container application's menus. Visual Basic version 3.0 and earlier did not support this important feature. This means that applications written in Visual Basic 3.0 allowed you to specify in-place activation; however, it was necessary to create whatever application-specific menus you needed, and you had to create the appropriate OLE automation commands for each menu choice. Fortunately, Visual Basic 4.0 corrects this deficiency.

Visual Basic 4.0 and greater fully implement OLE 2.0 as a container application. They also implement OLE 2.0 as an originating, or host, application (which is not the

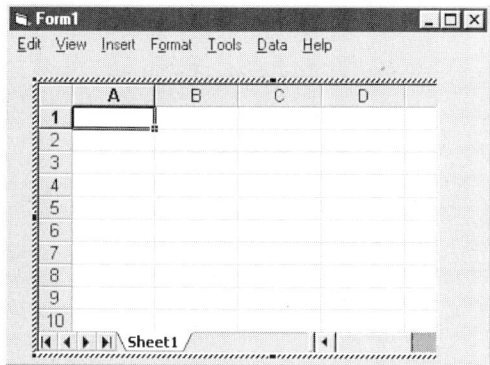

Figure 74-1   In-place activation of an Excel OLE object within a Visual Basic program

case with Visual Basic version 3.0 and before). This means that you can write Visual Basic applications that expose their own internal objects, and in addition, your application can take over another application to perform in-place editing within that application.

Linking and Embedding

Linking lets you use another application's data while leaving it available for other programs. The data remains on disk as a separate file, stored in its normal, native format. It is available for editing by the original application or any other application that can read it. The originating application can save the information to disk. The object in your Visual Basic program contains a link to the proper file (and a specific range or set of objects in that file) and an image of what the data looks like for display.

Embedding lets you completely control the data. No other application can directly access the information. The object in your Visual Basic application contains the actual data, as well as an image of what the data looks like for display. Although the Visual Basic OLE control contains the actual data, it does not automatically save it to disk. You can use the OLE control's methods and properties to save and retrieve the information. Saving embedded OLE data saves the actual data, the name of the originating application, and an image of what the data looks like. Therefore, embedding OLE objects can drastically increase the size of your applications.

User-Interface Negotiation

Almost all OLE-compliant applications will come with their own menu and toolbar systems. Visual Basic's OLE support includes *user-interface negotiation*. This means your program and the object application that is linked or embedded must negotiate for space in the object's form.

Menu and toolbar negotiation will only occur for insertable objects that support in-place activation. An MDI child's menu and toolbar that does not have an inserted object supporting in-place activation has no negotiating abilities.

Automation

Automation (originally known as OLE Automation) is a component of an OLE application that allows you to expose a set of functions other applications can use. Applications like spreadsheets and word processors have a lot of features that can be useful to other applications. Mail merge and spell checking are features built into a word processor that you might take advantage of within your application. Chapter 76, "OLE Automation," will describe this process in greater detail.

Component Object Model

In order to understand where OLE came from, where it is now, and where it is going, you need to understand a Microsoft model for building objects. This model is called the *Component Object Model*, better known by its acronym, COM. It is a general architecture that lays the foundation on which OLE version 2.0 is based. It establishes a common model for interaction among software, like applications, library modules, system software, and more. Therefore, COM can be implemented with almost any kind of software technology using the guideline layout.

There are many books on the subject of OLE, COM, and ActiveX and how they fit in with client/server development, including *Understanding ActiveX and OLE* (Microsoft Press, 1996) and *Visual Basic 5 Client/Server How-To* (Waite Group Press, 1997).

As COM became further defined, its foundation had nothing to do with the original OLE concept which was working with compound documents. The term COM refers to the technology of building interoperable components, but Microsoft felt that Object Linking and Embedding should be renamed to simply OLE with no version number attached to it.

Although COM's roots started with OLE, OLE is now merely a component of COM. This is because COM defines more than just a strategy for working with compound documents:

- It offers developers a means for developing interoperable components through an object orientation. COM-based components can be reused and safely distributed throughout the enterprise.

- It provides developers with a framework to expose software services. This allows developers to access the services of any component, no matter if it is a resource library or another application.

- COM provides language independence. Because COM defines a common interface that objects must support, you can write your COM component in any language, as long it supports the COM interface.

- Finally, it offers a safe way to deploy components across the enterprise using *versioning*. Versioning is the mechanism used to replace existing versions of software with an updated version offering new features or fixes. It also ensures that the component's new version does not break any existing application.

ActiveX

In 1996, in Microsoft's rush to establish their Internet presence, they introduced a new term to the world of developers: *ActiveX*. When the term was first introduced, it was believed to be a variation of OLE, and its technology was for the Internet and Internet-based applications. As the technology became more defined and the dust started to settle, the development world soon realized that ActiveX was not just a variation of OLE, but it was OLE itself, only redefined. ActiveX includes the OLE implementation of COM but also improves on it by extending capabilities to take advantage of the Internet. This was something OLE did not have within its model. This feat is accomplished by ActiveX controls, as well as through the support of Distributed Component Object Model, better known as DCOM.

After all the hoops and learning curves Microsoft put people through, OLE once again means Object Linking and Embedding. And it only refers to the technology of working with compound documents. A lot of earlier OLE-named technologies, such as

OLE DLLs and Servers, have been renamed to ActiveX DLLs and Servers. Do not let the names fool you into thinking their underlying technology is the same; they have been merely reclassified for clarity.

There has been a lot of commotion on the Internet newsgroups and online services like CompuServe and America Online about the definition of an OLE control versus an ActiveX control. Are they same? Are they different? The most definitive answer is that OLE controls (.OCXs) and ActiveX controls are the same thing. When the OLE control was first defined, it was based on the compound document architecture. This meant that at least 15 or more interfaces were required to be implemented into the object in order for it to be a control. In a lot of cases, this made the controls very large in file size. When these files were being distributed across an enterprise, the file size was not as much of a factor because the files were installed via the corporation's network.

Microsoft realized that this was unacceptable if OLE controls were to be used on the Internet. Even though almost every company is connected to the Internet, many are still connecting at slow connection rates (ISDN connections or less). Microsoft updated their requirements and specification for OLE controls through the OLE Control and Container Guidelines version 2.0, OLE Controls/COM Objects for the Internet, and OLE Controls 96. Under these new specifications, controls are no longer under the umbrella of OLE, but under the new standard, which requires fewer interfaces. This makes the controls smaller, allowing them to be distributed through the Internet at the slower connection speeds.

In the following chapters, you will see how OLE and ActiveX technology is used within Visual Basic.

75

OLE CONTAINER CONTROL

As mentioned in the previous chapter, OLE refers to *object linking and embedding*. OLE gives your application the power to directly use and manipulate another Windows application's data in its native format. If the other application supports *OLE automation*, you may also be able to use its objects, properties, and methods just as you would a Visual Basic control. OLE automation, introduced in Visual Basic 3.0, is one of the most important additions to Windows and serves as the basis for creating a true object-oriented environment. It is also a fundamental component of building onto COM (Component Object Model).

The OLE container control allows you to add insertable objects and call OLE servers to the visual interface of your Visual Basic applications. These objects can be either linked or embedded to your application. You would use this control rather than using OLE automation when your users' needs are viewing and manipulating an OLE server's data using the server's own visual interface.

This chapter offers both an overview of the OLE container control and a thorough discussion of every property, event, and function necessary for fully implementing linking or embedding OLE objects in your applications.

OLE Container Control Summary

Tables 75-1, 75-2, and 75-3 list the properties, methods, and events of the OLE container control.

Table 75-1 Properties of the OLE container control

Use This Property...	To Do This...
Action	Perform an action on the object (use the OLE control methods that replace these actions)
Appearance	Determine whether or not to use 3D appearance
ApplsRunning	See whether the originating application is running
AutoActivate	Determine whether the OLE container control activates by receiving focus or being double-clicked
AutoVerbMenu	Determine whether the verb menu automatically pops up
BackColor	Read or set the background color of the OLE container control
BackStyle	Determine whether the background of the OLE container control is transparent or opaque
BorderStyle	Determine the type of border for the OLE container control
Class	Set the class name of the OLE object
Container	Determine the type of container on the form
Data	Transfer data to nonautomation OLE applications
DataChanged	Read or set an indicator that data in the bound control other than the current record has been changed
DataField	Bind the OLE container control to a field in the current record
DataSource	Specify the data control through which this OLE container control is bound to a database
DataText	Transfer text to nonautomation OLE applications
DisplayType	Determine how the object displays
DragIcon	Read or set the icon displayed for drag-and-drop operations
DragMode	Determine whether automatic or manual drag is used with this OLE container control for drag-and-drop operations
Enabled	Determine whether the OLE container control is enabled
FileNumber	Set the file number to save or load an OLE object
Format	Set the format for Data and DataText transfers
ForeColor	Read or set the foreground color of the OLE container control
Height	Read or set the height of this OLE container control
HelpContextID	Associate a help context number with this OLE object
HostName	Set a user-friendly name for your object
hWnd	No longer supported for the OLE container control
Index	Work with an array of OLE container controls
Left	Read or set the position of the left edge of the OLE container control
lpOleObject	Read the memory location of the OLE object
MiscFlags	Determine access to some of the additional features of the OLE container control
MouseIcon	Set a custom mouse icon
MousePointer	Indicate the type of mouse pointer displayed when the mouse is over particular sections of an object
Name	Read or set the name used for this OLE container control in your code
Object	Access the OLE container control's object for automation
ObjectAcceptFormats	List the formats an object accepts
ObjectAcceptFormatsCount	Count the number of formats an object accepts
ObjectGetFormats	List the formats an object returns
ObjectGetFormatsCount	Count the number of formats an object returns

Use This Property...	To Do This...
ObjectVerbFlags	Determine the menu state of the object's verbs
ObjectVerbs	List the object's verbs
ObjectVerbsCount	Count the number of the object's verbs
OLEDropAllowed	Determine whether the OLE container control can be the target of OLE drag-and-drop operations
OLEType	Set or determine the type of object (link or embed)
OLETypeAllowed	Determine the types of objects allowed
Parent	Return the form on which the OLE container control is located
PasteOK	Determine whether the Clipboard can be pasted into OLE
Picture	Return the graphic displayed in the OLE container control (if one exists)
SizeMode	Set or determine how the object reacts to resize
SourceDoc	Set or determine the filename of the source document
SourceItem	Set the region or subset of data when creating an object
TabIndex	Set the tab order of this OLE container control
TabStop	Determine whether this OLE container control will be a tabstop
Tag	Store extra data related to this OLE container control
Top	Read or set the position of the top edge of this OLE container control
UpdateOptions	Set or determine how the OLE container control reacts to changes
Verb	Set or determine what action an object performs
Visible	Determine whether this OLE container control is visible
WhatThisHelpID	Set or determine an associated context number for the container for context-sensitive help
Width	Read or set the width of this OLE container control

Table 75-2 Methods of the OLE container control

Use This Method...	To Do This...
Close	Close an object and terminate its connection to the application that provided it
Copy	Copy the object in the OLE container control to the Clipboard
CreateEmbed	Create an embedded object for an OLE container control
CreateLink	Use the contents of a file as a linked object for an OLE container control
Delete	Delete an object
DoVerb	Open an object for a specified operation or the default operation if none is specified
Drag	Begin, end, or cancel a drag operation for an object
FetchVerbs	Create a current list of verbs an object supports
InsertObjDlg	Bring up the Insert Object dialog box
Move	Move the location of the OLE container control
Paste	Copy data from the Clipboard to the OLE container control
PasteSpecialDlg	Bring up the Paste Special dialog box
ReadFromFile	Load an object from a binary data file

continued on next page

continued from previous page

Use This Method...	To Do This...
Refresh	Repaint the OLE container control
SaveToFile	Save an object to a binary data file
SaveToOle1File	Save an object to a binary data file in OLE 1.0 format
SetFocus	Give focus to the OLE container control
ShowWhatsThis	Display a selected topic in a Help file using the What's This pop-up provided by Windows Help
Update	Update and display the data for an object in the OLE container control
Z-order	Place the OLE container control at the front or back of the z-order

Table 75-3 Events of the OLE container control

Use This Event...	To Do This...
Click	Respond to a mouse click on the OLE container control
DblClick	Respond to a mouse double-click on the OLE container control
DragDrop	React when an object is dragged or dropped onto the OLE container control
DragOver	Determine what happens after dragging is initiated and before a control drops onto a target
GotFocus	Take action when the OLE container control receives focus
KeyDown	Respond to the press of a key within the OLE container control
KeyPress	Respond to a keypress within the OLE control; return ANSI key code
KeyUp	Respond to the release of a key within the OLE container control
LostFocus	Take action when the OLE container control loses focus
MouseDown	Respond to the press of a mouse button within the OLE container control
MouseMove	Respond to any mouse movement
MouseUp	Respond to the release of a mouse button within the OLE container control
ObjectMove	Respond when an OLE object has been moved
Resize	Respond when the size of an OLE object has changed
Updated	React to a linked object's data changing

Using Constants

Many of the properties and events of OLE use numeric values as arguments. Using constants rather than the literal value makes your code self-documenting, more readable, and easier to debug.

Previous versions of Visual Basic came with a text file called CONSTANT.TXT that contained a lot of global constant variables defined to make coding arguments easier. Visual Basic 5.0 no longer uses this file. Instead, many of the constants and variables are now incorporated into the Visual Basic environment itself. There are two sources of constants: (1) *system-defined* constants provided by applications and controls, and (2) symbolic, or *user-defined*, constants declared using the Const statement.

System-defined constants are found in what are called *object libraries*. You can view them through the Object Browser. In previous versions of Visual Basic, user-defined constants were capitalized with an underscore instead of spaces, as in USER_DEFINED. This method is still recognized in Visual Basic 5.0, but for consistency you are encouraged to upgrade your naming standards. The new naming standards for constants are as follows: Qualify by prefix or qualify by Library Reference. Qualifying by prefix is seen in mixed-case format, with a two-character prefix indicating the object library that defines the constant. For example,

```
vbUserDefined
dbAppendOnly
xlDialogBorder
```

The vb prefix means that the constant belongs to the object library of Visual Basic or Visual Basic, Applications Edition. The db prefix represents a Data Access Object library constant. The constant prefix, xl, means the constant belongs to a Microsoft Excel object library. A constant that is qualified by Library Reference does not use a prefix by another object. When you use constants with custom controls, the syntax is

```
[libname.][modulename.]constname
```

The libname is the name of the type library that defines the constant. A *type library* is a component or file within another file that contains OLE automation standard descriptions; the modulename is the name of the module from which the type library is defined; and the constname is the name defined for the constant in the type library. For example,

```
Threed.LeftJustify
```

This means the constant "LeftJustify" is defined in the type library for the Threed (3D) control.

The following reference section describes the details of each property, method, and event particular to OLE. Properties, methods, and events that OLE controls share with other controls (such as BackColor or MouseUp) are not covered here. For example, BackColor and ForeColor properties are covered in Chapter 33, "Application Appearance," and Mouse events are covered in Chapter 49, "Mouse Events."

ACTION PROPERTY

Objects Affected CommonDlg, OLE

Purpose The Action property determines an action that the OLE control will take. It is not available at design time and will write only at runtime. Tables 75-4 and 75-5 summarize the arguments of the Action property. Table 75-5 also contains references to new OLE container control methods that you should use in place of the Action property values.

General Syntax

```
[form.]Name.Action = setting
```

Table 75-4 Arguments of the Action property

Argument	Meaning
form	Name property of the parent form
Name	Name property of the control
setting%	Value indicating what action to perform

Table 75-5 Values of the setting% argument in the OLE Action property and equivalent methods

setting%	Description	Use this OLE method instead
0	Creates an embedded object	CreateEmbed method
1	Creates a linked object from the contents of a file	CreateLink method
2	Not used	
3	Not used	
4	Copies the object to the Clipboard	Copy method
5	Copies data from the Clipboard to an OLE container control	Paste method
6	Retrieves the current data from the application	Update method
7	Opens an OLE object for an operation, such as editing	DoVerb method
8	Not used	
9	Closes an OLE object and terminates the connection	Close method
10	Deletes the specified OLE object and frees the memory	Delete method
11	Saves an OLE object to a data file	SaveToFile method
12	Loads an OLE object from a data file	ReadFromFile method
13	Not used	
14	Displays the Insert Object dialog	InsertObjDlg method
15	Displays the Paste Special dialog	PasteSpecialDlg method
16	Not used	
17	Updates the list of verbs an object supports	FetchVerbs method
18	Saves an object in the OLE1 file format	SaveToOle1File method

Example Syntax

```
Private Sub menuEditCopy_Click ()
    OLE1.Action = 4                          'copies object to Clipboard
End Sub
```

Description Use the Action property to make the OLE container control do something with the object. The example syntax shows the Action property being used to copy the OLE container control's object to the Clipboard.

There are a number of different actions that you can take. Notice that new OLE container control methods now replace the functionality of the

Action property. You should use these new methods instead of the equivalent Action property values.

Example   The Action property is not used in this chapter's project. Instead, we use the new OLE container control methods that replace the functionality of the Action property.

AppIsRunning Property

Objects Affected   OLE

Purpose   The AppIsRunning property lets you determine whether the application that created the OLE object is currently running. It is not available at design time and is read-only at runtime. Table 75-6 summarizes the arguments of the AppIsRunning property.

General Syntax

```
[form.]Name.AppIsRunning
```

Table 75-6 Arguments of the AppIsRunning property

Argument	Meaning
form	Name property of the parent form
Name	Name property of the control

Example Syntax

```
Private Sub menuEditCopy_Click ()
    If Not OLE1.AppIsRunning Then
        OLE1.DoVerb
    End If
    OLE1.Copy
End Sub
```

Description   Before you can take advantage of OLE, the originating application must be running. Use the AppIsRunning property to determine whether the application that created the OLE object is currently running. If it is not, you can start it by using the DoVerb method. AppIsRunning returns a Boolean value: True means the application is running; False means it is not. The example syntax first checks to see whether the originating application is running before copying OLE1's object to the Clipboard.

You can set the Verb property before activating an application to control how the host application activates: hidden, exposed, or in-place.

Example   The project at the end of this chapter checks the AppIsRunning property in the menuEdit_Click event and printInfo procedure before performing additional operations on the OLE object.

AUTOACTIVATE PROPERTY

Objects Affected   OLE

Purpose   Use the AutoActivate property to set how an OLE container control automatically reacts when double-clicked or given the focus. Tables 75-7 and 75-8 summarize the arguments and values of the AutoActivate property.

General Syntax

```
[form.]Name.AutoActivate [ = setting%]
```

Table 75-7 Arguments of the AutoActivate property

Argument	Meaning
form	Name property of the parent form
Name	Name property of the control
setting%	Value determines the reaction when double-clicked or given focus

Table 75-8 Meanings of the setting% argument for the AutoActivate property

setting%	VB.Constants	Description
0	vbOLEActivateManual	Not automatically activated
1	vbOLEActivateGetFocus	Automatically activated when receives focus
2	vbOLEActivateDoubleclick	Automatically activated when double-clicked (default)
3	vbOLEActivateAuto	Use the object's default method of activation; either focus or double-click

Example Syntax

```
Private Sub Check1_Click ()
    If Check1.Value = True Then
        OLE1.AutoActivate = vbOLEActivateDoubleclick
    Else
        OLE1.AutoActivate = vbOLEActivateGetFocus
    End If
End Sub
```

Description   The AutoActivate property determines how an OLE container control reacts when it receives the focus or is double-clicked. The default behavior in Visual Basic, and for most other applications, is to activate when double-clicked. Originating applications that support in-place editing might work more naturally if they are activated when the control receives the focus. It might also be appropriate to handle activation manually, and thus turn off AutoActivate. The example syntax shows how the user can control this by turning a check box on and off.

What happens when the application is activated depends on the Verb property. The default for an OLE control's Verb property is to use the originating application's default verb. This may be Edit (for spreadsheets, word processors, and related applications) or something like Play (for a multimedia application). You can also set the Verb property yourself, thereby changing the action taken when activated.

The double-click event does not get passed through to the OLE container control if AutoActivate is set to 2, vbOLEActivateDoubleclick. If you need to activate the object manually when AutoActivate is set to 0, vbOLEActivateManual, use the DoVerb method.

Example The project at the end of this chapter leaves AutoActivate set to the default setting of vbOLEActivateDoubleclick for the OLE container control.

AutoVerbMenu Property

Objects Affected OLE

Purpose Set the AutoVerbMenu property to True to automatically pop up a menu containing the object's verbs when the user clicks the object with the right mouse button. Table 75-9 lists the arguments of the AutoVerbMenu property.

General Syntax

```
[form.]Name.AutoVerbMenu [ = boolean%]
```

Table 75-9 Arguments of the AutoVerbMenu property

Argument	Meaning
form	Name property of the parent form
Name	Name property of the control
boolean%	True = pop up menu; False = do not pop up menu

Example Syntax

```
Private Sub Form_Load ()
    OLE1.AutoVerbMenu = True
End Sub
```

Description Use the AutoVerbMenu property to determine the reaction your OLE object has when clicked with the right mouse (or nondefault) button. Each OLE object has some commands (or *verbs*) that can execute on it. For example, a sound application might have Edit, Play, Record, Erase, Rewind, and Fast Forward. If AutoVerbMenu is set to True, clicking the OLE object with the right-mouse button would then bring up a menu listing each of these verbs. Visual Basic will automatically execute the appropriate action when the user clicks on one of the menu choices. In general, you should set AutoVerbMenu to True to avoid the inconvenience of constructing your own menu. The example syntax turns on AutoVerbMenu when the form loads. Figure 75-1 shows what a typical menu looks like.

Visual Basic automatically updates the AutoVerbMenu before displaying it because the verbs available may change depending on what data the object contains. If AutoVerbMenu is set to True, no Click or MouseDown events from the menu get passed through to the control.

Example   The project at the end of this chapter uses the Form_Load event to set AutoVerbMenu to True for the OLE container control.

CLASS PROPERTY

Objects Affected   OLE

Purpose   Use the Class property to determine or set the class name of an embedded OLE object. Table 75-10 lists the arguments of the Class property, and Table 75-11 lists some common class names.

General Syntax

```
[form.]Name.Class [ = className$]           'for OLE 1.0 compliant applications
[form.]Name.Class [ = "appName.objType"]    'for OLE 2.0 compliant applications
```

Table 75-10 Arguments of the Class property

Argument	Meaning
form	Name property of the parent form
Name	Name property of the control
classNameS	Class name of the object
appName	Name with which the originating application is registered
objType	Type of object the originating application supports

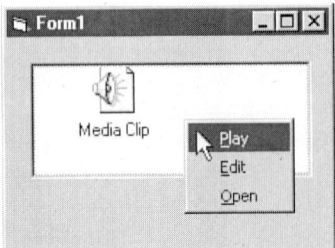

Figure 75-1   Typical menu brought up by AutoVerbMenu

Table 75-11 Common class names (OLE 1.0–compliant)

className$	Meaning
CDraw	CorelDRAW drawing
CorelChart	CorelChart chart
Equation	Microsoft Equation
ExcelChart	Microsoft Excel Chart
ExcelMacrosheet	Microsoft Excel Macro
ExcelWorksheet	Microsoft Excel Worksheet
MSDraw	Microsoft Draw drawing
MSGraph	Microsoft Graph chart
Package	Object contained by the Package applet
PBrush	Microsoft Paint Brush
PhotoPaint	Corel Paint
SoundRec	Microsoft Sound Recorder WAV file
WordArt	Microsoft Word Art
WordDocument	Microsoft Word for Windows document

Example Syntax

```
Private Sub Command1_Click
    OLE1.Class = "ExcelWorksheet"
    OLE1.SourceDoc = "C:\EXCEL\Q1TOTALS.XLS"
    OLE1.SourceItem = "R1C1:R27C14"
    OLE1.DoVerb
End Sub
```

Description

Each OLE object has a class name identifying the program that created it and, if a program can create different kinds of objects, the type of object. For example, Excel can create three different kinds of objects: worksheets, charts, and macros. Class names make it easier to identify which objects an application can or should support. The example syntax shows how to fully specify a portion of an Excel Worksheet with Class, SourceDoc, and SourceItem before activating it with the Action property.

This property is set automatically whenever you create an object at runtime or design time with the Insert Object or Paste Special dialog boxes, and at runtime when an object gets pasted from the Clipboard.

The class names illustrated in Table 75-11 are all written to the OLE 1.0 specification. OLE 2.0, with its advanced OLE automation features, has an extended naming convention:

```
className$ = "applicationName.objectType"
```

As applications are updated to the OLE 2.0 specification over the next few years, their class names will change from the existing OLE 1.0 standard.

Thus, Excel 5.0 and later versions have class names like Excel.Worksheet rather than ExcelWorksheet.

You can find out what class names are registered in your system by clicking the combo box's ellipsis (…) for the Class property in the properties box in Visual Basic. Figure 75-2 shows the ellipsis about to be clicked by the mouse, and Figure 75-3 shows what the dialog box looks like. Note that the class name is a short (sometimes cryptic) abbreviation. The Insert Object dialog brings up a more descriptive, user-friendly name. It finds these longer names in the HKEY_CLASSES_ROOT Hive in the System Registry. If you need to use these longer names in your code, you can access the System Registry with the GetProfileStringA API call. See Chapter 29, "DLLs and the Windows API," for a description of this call.

Example

In the project at the end of this chapter, the Edit Paste routine in the menuEdit_Click event sets the Class property to temp before performing a paste operation. Note that pasting into an OLE object without an existing Class property value generates an error, but the value already in the Class property is overwritten by whatever is on the Clipboard. This trick of setting the Class property to a meaningless value in the Edit Paste operation makes sure that the paste operation proceeds without error.

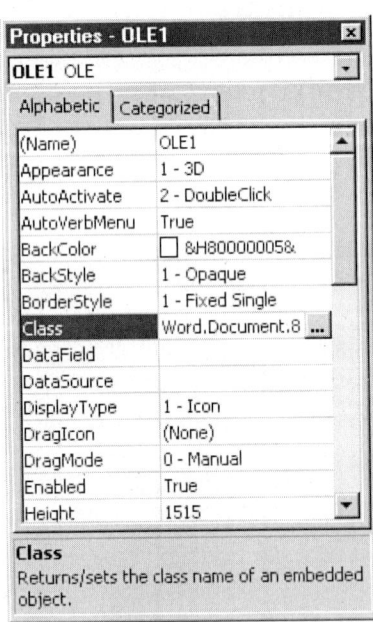

Figure 75-2   The mouse is about to click on the ellipsis to bring up the Class name...

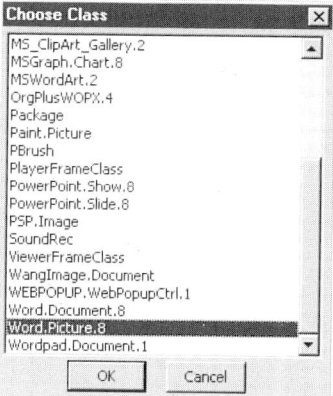

Figure 75-3 ...and here is the Class names dialog box showing all the OLE-registered applications on the system

CLOSE METHOD

Objects Affected   OLE

Purpose   Use the Close method to close an object and terminate its connection to the application that provided it. Table 75-12 summarizes the arguments of the Close method.

General Syntax

```
[form.]Name.Close
```

Table 75-12 Arguments of the Close method

Argument	Meaning
form	Name property of the parent form
Name	Name property of the control

Example Syntax

```
Private Sub Command1_Click()
    If VBVersion% < 4 Then
        OLE1.Action = 9                    'use the old Action method
    Else
        OLE1.Close                         'use the new Close method
    End If
End Sub
```

Description	The Close method closes an OLE object and cuts the connection with the originating application. It applies to embedded objects only; linked objects cannot be closed. Closing an OLE object does not automatically save any data associated with it. Therefore, you should first use the SaveToFile method to save an embedded object's data before using the Close method if you want to save any data modified by the user through the object.
Example	In the project at the end of this chapter, the Close method is used to close objects after they are used.

COPY METHOD

Objects Affected	OLE
Purpose	The Copy method lets you copy the object in the OLE container control to the Clipboard. Table 75-13 summarizes the arguments of the Copy method.

General Syntax

```
[form.]Name.Copy
```

Table 75-13 Arguments of the Copy method

Argument	Meaning
form	Name property of the parent form
Name	Name property of the control

Example Syntax

```
Private Sub Command1_Click()
    If VBVersion% < 4 Then
        OLE1.Action = 4               'use the old Action method
    Else
        OLE1.Copy                     'use the new Copy method
    End If
End Sub
```

Description	This copies the object to the Clipboard. All the data and link information associated with the object are automatically placed on the Clipboard. You can easily implement the standard Edit Cut and Edit Copy menu choices for an OLE object by using the Copy method in your OLE application. When the user selects Copy from the Edit menu, use the Copy method; when the user selects Cut from the Edit menu, use the Copy method along with the Delete method. Both linked and embedded objects may be copied.

Example   The project at the end of this chapter uses the Copy method when the user selects either the Edit Cut or Edit Copy menu choice.

CREATEEMBED METHOD

Objects Affected   OLE

Purpose   The CreateEmbed method lets you Create an embedded object for an OLE container control. Table 75-14 summarizes the arguments of the CreateEmbed method.

General Syntax

```
[form.]Name.CreateEmbed sourcedoc [, class]
```

Table 75-14 Arguments of the CreateEmbed method

Argument	Meaning
form	Name property of the parent form
Name	Name property of the control
sourcedoc	The filename that will be used as a template for the embedded object
class	The class name of the embedded object

Example Syntax

```
Private Sub Command1_Click()
    If VBVersion% < 4 Then
        OLE1.SourceDoc = "C:\MYSHEET.XLS"
        OLE1.Action = 0                          'use the old Action method
    Else
        OLE1.CreateEmbed "C:\MYSHEET.XLS"        'use the new CreateEmbed method
    End If
End Sub
```

Description   The CreateEmbed method creates an embedded object. First, set the Class property to the kind of object you'll be embedding (such as a CorelDRAW object or an Excel Worksheet). The possible values for the Class property vary with each system, depending on which applications are installed. Then, set the OLETypeAllowed property to either 1 (embedded) or 2 (either linked or embedded). Make sure that the executable file associated with the class name (for example, CORELDRW.EXE) is either currently running or in the system's path. The sourcedoc argument is required, so if you don't specify a source document, you must set the sourcedoc argument to a zero-length string ("").

CREATELINK METHOD

Objects Affected	OLE
Purpose	Use the CreateLink method to create a linked object for an OLE container control from a file. Table 75-15 summarizes the arguments of the CreateLink method.

General Syntax

```
[form.]Name.CreateLink sourcedoc [, sourceitem]
```

Table 75-15 Arguments of the CreateLink method

Argument	Meaning
form	Name property of the parent form
Name	Name property of the control
sourcedoc	The file from which the object is created
sourceitem	Particular data in the file used by the linked object

Example Syntax

```
Private Sub Command1_Click()
    If VBVersion% < 4 Then
        OLE1.SourceDoc = "C:\MYSHEET.XLS"
        OLE1.Action = 1                     'use the old Action method
    Else
        OLE1.CreateLink "C:\MYSHEET.XLS"  'use the new CreateLink method
    End If
End Sub
```

Description	The CreateLink method creates a linked OLE object from a file. First, set the OLETypeAllowed to 0 (linked) or 2 (either linked or embedded). The sourcedoc argument must be set to the full path name of the file from which the object is to be created. You may also specify sourceitem (for example, a spreadsheet range) if it is supported by the application creating the object. Make sure the executable file associated with sourcedoc is either active or in the system's path.

DATA PROPERTY

Objects Affected	OLE
Purpose	Use the Data property to transfer information to an OLE originating application that does not support OLE automation. There is no guarantee that the application will do anything with this data; most applications ignore it. Table 75-16 summarizes the arguments of the Data property.

General Syntax

```
[form.]Name.Data [ = data&]
```

Table 75-16 Arguments of the Data property

Argument	Meaning
form	Name property of the parent form
Name	Name property of the control
data&	Handle to a memory or GDI object

Example Syntax

```
Private Sub EditPicture ()
    OLE1.Format = "CF_METAFILEPICT"     'set proper format
    OLE1.Verb = vbOLEHide               'make sure the app stays hidden
    OLE1.DoVerb                         'activate the OLE app
    If OLE1.AppIsRunning Then           'If it successfully activated,
        OLE1.Data = Picture1.hDC        'give it the GDI handle
        OLE1.Update                     'and update the control's display.
    End If
End Sub
```

Description

The Data property lets you pass information back to an originating OLE application that does not support OLE automation. If the application does support automation, then using its methods and properties directly offers a much easier and more reliable solution.

You must first set the Format property to indicate the type of data contained in the memory or GDI object. You then activate the object using the Action property, and set the Data property to the handle of the object. You may then wish to use the Action property to update the OLE container control and update its display.

The example syntax passes the hDC (device context handle) of the Picture1 control to the OLE control. If the object in the OLE container control responds to the Data property, it will display the picture from Picture1.

Very few applications respond to the Data property. With the advent of OLE 2.0, the limited usability of this property will probably be even further reduced.

Example

The OLE Container Control project at the end of this chapter prints out the value of the Data property handle in the printInfo procedure. However, it does not pass data to a host with it because no standard, well-known application responds to it.

DATATEXT PROPERTY

Objects Affected	OLE
Purpose	Use the DataText property to transfer text to and from an OLE originating application that does not support OLE automation. There is no guarantee that the application will do anything with this data. Table 75-17 summarizes the arguments of the DataText property.

General Syntax

```
[form.]Name.DataText [ = data$]
```

Table 75-17 Arguments of the DataText property

Argument	Meaning
form	Name property of the parent form
Name	Name property of the control
data$	String containing the data to send to the application

Example Syntax

```
Private Sub Command1_Click ()
    OLE1.Format = "CF_TEXT"              'set the format to text
    OLE1.SizeMode = vbOLESizeAutosize    'OLE adjusts its size to fit data
    OLE1.Class = "MSGraph"               'embed an MS Graph object
    OLE1.CreateEmbed                     'create the embedded object

    data$ = Grid1.Clip                   'transfer contents of Grid into data$
    OLE1.Verb = vbOLEHide                'set up object to hide application
    OLE1.DoVerb                          'activate the object
    If OLE1.AppIsRunning Then            'If object successfully activated, then
        OLE1.DataText = data$            'paste in the string data
        OLE1.Update                      'and update the OLE control's display.
    End If
End Sub
```

Description   The DataText property lets you send and receive text information from an originating OLE application that does not support OLE automation. This property is specific to string data while the Data property can send many types of data to the originating application. In addition, the Data property only allows transfer of information to the originating application and, unlike the DataText property, it cannot be used to receive data from the originating application. If the application does support automation, then using its methods and properties directly offers a much easier, more reliable solution. The example syntax shows how to transfer text information to the OLE 1.0-compliant Graph applet that Microsoft ships with their applications.

You must first set the Format property to indicate the type of data contained in the text string. See the Format entry for more information about acceptable values. You next activate the object using the Action property and set the DataText property to the string. You may then wish to use the Action property to update the OLE container control and update its display.

Unlike the case with the Data property, many applications respond to the DataText property.

DELETE METHOD

Objects Affected   OLE

Purpose   The Delete method lets you delete an object from an OLE container control. Table 75-18 summarizes the arguments of the Delete method.

General Syntax   •

```
[form.]Name.Delete
```

Table 75-18 Arguments of the Delete method

Argument	Meaning
form	Name property of the parent form
Name	Name property of the control

Example Syntax
```
Private Sub Command1_Click()
    If VBVersion% < 4 Then
        OLE1.Action = 10            'use the old Action method
    Else
        OLE1.Delete                 'use the new Delete method
    End If
End Sub
```

Description   This deletes the object and frees the memory used for it. OLE objects are automatically deleted when a form closes or when an object is updated to a new object, but this action enables you to do so under program control as well. Any data that the user has modified with the OLE object is not automatically saved when you use the Delete method. You should use the SaveToFile method to save any relevant data before using the Delete method. The Delete method is similar to the Close method, except it does not terminate the connection to the application that provided the OLE object.

Example   The project at the end of this chapter uses the Delete method to delete an object when the Edit Cut menu choice is selected.

DISPLAYTYPE PROPERTY

Objects Affected   OLE

Purpose   Use the DisplayType property to set or determine whether an object displays as an icon or formatted data. Tables 75-19 and 75-20 summarize the arguments of the DisplayType property.

General Syntax

```
[form.]Name.DisplayType [ = setting%]
```

Table 75-19 Arguments of the DisplayType property

Argument	Meaning
form	Name property of the parent form
Name	Name property of the control
setting%	Value indicates whether an OLE container control displays data or icon

Table 75-20 Values of the setting% argument of the DisplayType property

setting%	VB.Constants	Description
0	vbOLEDisplayContent	Display actual formatted data within placeholder (default)
1	vbOLEDisplayIcon	Display icon as placeholder

Example Syntax

```
Private Sub menuEditPasteSpecial_Click ()
    OLE1.DisplayType = vbOLEDisplayIcon
    OLE1.InsertObjDlg
End Sub
```

Description   Use the DisplayType property to determine whether an object displays its contents as formatted data or as an icon placeholder. The default setting, formatted data, can sometimes significantly slow down your application if the data consists of detailed graphics. Setting the display type to an icon can improve your application's display performance by showing only an icon on your form in place of the actual OLE object data. The actual data will still appear as usual when the object is activated (by double-clicking on the icon, for example). You cannot change an object's display type once it is created.

Setting the DisplayType property before calling up the Insert Object or Paste Special dialog boxes sets the Icon check box on the dialog box appropriately. The user can change this setting before closing the dialog

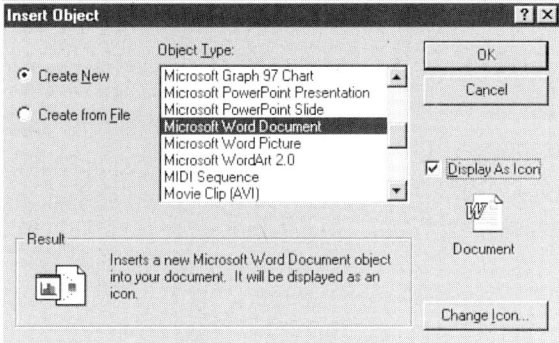

Figure 75-4   The DisplayType property sets the
default mode for the Icon check box

box, and the change is reflected in how the object is created. The example
syntax shows how to set the default value of the check box to Icon in the
Insert Object dialog box. Figure 75-4 shows the dialog box.

Example   The Form_Load event in the OLE Container Control project at the end of
this chapter sets the DisplayType property of the OLE container control to
display the actual contents.

DoVerb Method

Objects Affected   OLE

Purpose   The DoVerb method lets you open an object for a specified operation or, if
no verb is specified, for the default operation. Table 75-21 summarizes the
arguments of the DoVerb method.

General Syntax

```
[form.]Name.DoVerb [verb]
```

Table 75-21 Arguments of the DoVerb method

Argument	Meaning
form	Name property of the parent form
Name	Name property of the control
verb	The optional verb (of the object) to execute within the OLE container control

Example Syntax
```
Private Sub Command1_Click()
    If VBVersion% < 4 Then
```

continued on next page

continued from previous page

```
        OLE1.Action = 7          'use the old Action method
    Else
        OLE1.DoVerb              'use the new DoVerb method
    End If
End Sub
```

Description The DoVerb method opens an OLE object for an operation such as editing, playing a sound file, or some other operation supported by the object's application. Set the verb argument to the operation that you want to occur when the OLE object is activated. If you do not specify a verb, then the default verb is executed. There are some verbs that every application supports (such as edit), and others that are specific to each originating application. You can access these with the ObjectVerbs property; see the Verbs, ObjectVerbs, and ObjectVerbsCount properties for more details. If AutoActivate is set to 2 (Double Click), then double-clicking the OLE container control will automatically activate the object with the default verb.

Example The DoVerbs method is used in the project at the end of the chapter to activate the host object application.

FETCHVERBS METHOD

Objects Affected OLE

Purpose The FetchVerbs method lets you create a current list of verbs supported by an object. Table 75-22 summarizes the arguments of the FetchVerbs method.

General Syntax

```
[form.]Name.FetchVerbs
```

Table 75-22 Arguments of the FetchVerbs method

Argument	Meaning
form	Name property of the parent form
Name	Name property of the control

Example Syntax

```
Private Sub Command1_Click()
    If VBVersion% < 4 Then
        OLE1.Action = 17         'use the old Action method
    Else
        OLE1.FetchVerbs          'use the new FetchVerbs method
    End If
End Sub
```

Description The FetchVerbs method updates the list of verbs an object supports. This is useful if the object has changed since you last determined the verbs, for example, when the user pastes a new object into the OLE container control.

FILENUMBER PROPERTY

Objects Affected   OLE

Purpose   Use the FileNumber property to set or determine the file number used when saving or loading OLE objects to or from a disk using the Action property. The new, preferred methods for loading or saving OLE objects (ReadFromFile, SaveToFile, SaveToOle1File) do not use the FileNumber property. Table 75-23 summarizes the arguments of the FileNumber property. It is not available at design time, and will be readable and writable at runtime.

General Syntax

```
[form.]Name.FileNumber [ = number%]
```

Table 75-23 Arguments of the FileNumber property

Argument	Meaning
form	Name property of the parent form
Name	Name property of the control
number%	Valid file number as used in an Open statement

Example Syntax

```
Private Sub menuSaveObject_Click ()
    fileNum = FreeFile                           'get a file handle
    Open "SAVEFILE.OLE" For Binary As #fileNum   'open the file
    OLE1.FileNumber = fileNum                     'pass file handle to object
    OLE1.SaveToFile                               'save the file to disk
    Close #fileNum                                'close file
End Sub
```

Description   The FileNumber property lets you pass the file handle of an open binary file to the OLE object. You can then save the file (SaveToFile method) or load the file (ReadFromFile method). You may also determine the file handle that was last used with the OLE container control, although this is normally not useful information.

Reading files and writing files use almost identical code. The following example reads in a binary file. Note that the only change from the example syntax is that we use ReadFromFile. Everything else is identical.

```
Private Sub menuOpenObject_Click ()
    fileNum = FreeFile                           'get a file handle
    Open "SAVEFILE.OLE" For Binary As #fileNum   'open the file
```

continued on next page

continued from previous page

```
        OLE1.FileNumber = fileNum          'pass file handle to object
        OLE1.ReadFromFile                  'load the file to disk
        Close #fileNum                     'close file
End Sub
```

Example   The project at the end of this chapter does not set the FileNumber property directly because it is specified as an argument for both the SaveToFile and ReadFromFile methods of the OLE container control.

FORMAT PROPERTY

Objects Affected   OLE

Purpose   Use the Format property to set or determine the kind of data sent to and received from an OLE object using the Data and DataText properties. Table 75-24 summarizes the arguments of the Format property.

General Syntax

```
[form.]Name.Format [ = dataType$]
```

Table 75-24 Arguments of the Format property

Argument	Meaning
form	Name property of the parent form
Name	Name property of the control
dataType$	Type of data

Example Syntax

```
Private Sub Command1_Click ()
    OLE1.Format = "CF_TEXT"                 'set the format to text
    OLE1.SizeMode = vbOLESizeAutosize       'OLE adjusts its size to fit data
    OLE1.Class = "MSGraph"                  'embed an MS Graph object.
    OLE1.CreateEmbed                        'create the embedded object

    data$ = Grid1.Clip                      'transfer contents of Grid into data$
    OLE1.Verb = vbOLEVerbHide               'set up object to hide application
    OLE1.DoVerb                             'activate the object
    If OLE1.AppIsRunning Then               'If object successfully activated, then
        OLE1.DataText = data$               'paste in the string data
        OLE1.Update                         'and update the OLE control's display.
    End If
End Sub
```

Description   The Format property determines the kind of data sent to or received from the originating OLE application. Both the Data and the DataText properties require that you set the Format properties prior to using them. You can use the ObjectGetFormats and ObjectAcceptFormats properties to find out the acceptable formats. Note that some applications accept different formats than they provide. The example syntax sets the Format for the Graph object to CF_TEXT before passing the data to a graph.

Note that formats are actual strings, not constant values. The example syntax above shows this:

```
OLE1.Format = "CF_TEXT"    'Correct. This string looks like the constant, but
                           'the resemblance is superficial.

OLE1.Format = CF_TEXT      'Incorrect! This may look similar, but would
                           'generate an error.
```

The first example gives the value as a string and works correctly. The second example uses a numeric constant and generates an error.

Example　　　　The chapter project's printInfo procedure sets the Format before reading the value of the Data property. The printInfo routine also prints out all the available formats.

HOSTNAME PROPERTY

Objects Affected　　OLE

Purpose　　The HostName property sets the user-readable name of your OLE object. This is used by most originating applications to identify the object being edited. It can read and write at both runtime and design time. Table 75-25 summarizes the arguments of the HostName property.

General Syntax

```
[form.]Name.HostName [ = hostName$]
```

Table 75-25 Arguments of the HostName property

Argument	Meaning
form	Name property of the parent form
Name	Name property of the control
hostName$	Name that identifies the object when edited

Example Syntax

```
Private Sub Form_Load ()
    OLE1.HostName = "CorelDRAW Extrude Object"
End Sub
```

Description　　Use the HostName to give a user-friendly name to an object. This name is then used by most originating applications when editing the object. For example, assume the object contained in OLE1 in the example syntax is a CorelDRAW object. Editing this object brings up CorelDRAW, and Corel's titlebar would display something like "CorelDRAW - Editing CorelDRAW

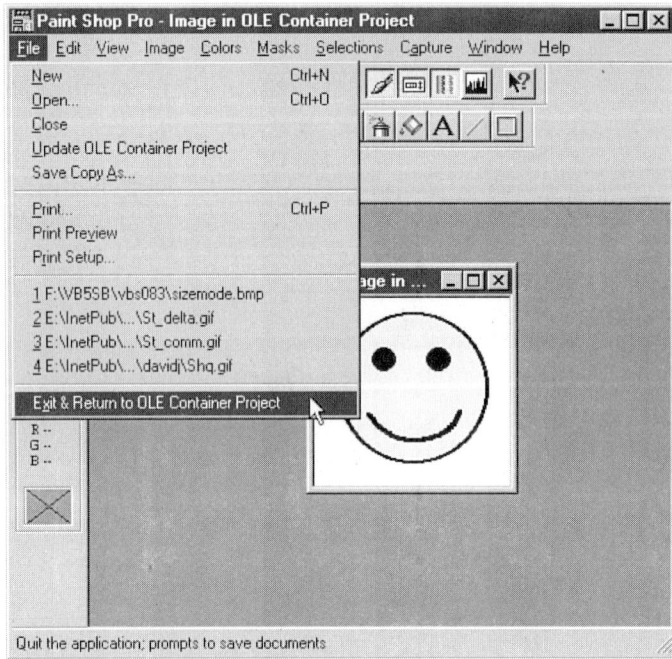

Figure 75-5   The HostName property identifies your object when edited by the originating application

Extrude Object." Most originating applications will also have an Update command on their File menu. This will sometimes indicate the name of the host object, as in "Exit and Return to CorelDRAW Extrude Object." Figure 75-5 shows this.

Not all originating applications make use of the HostName property. Setting the property will not cause an error if the originating application does not support it; the originating application simply ignores it.

Example   The HostName property for the OLE container control is initialized in this chapter project's Form_Load event.

INSERTOBJDLG METHOD

Objects Affected   OLE

Purpose   The InsertObjDlg method brings up the Insert Object dialog box. Table 75-26 summarizes the arguments of the InsertObjDlg method.

General Syntax

```
[form.]Name.InsertObjDlg
```

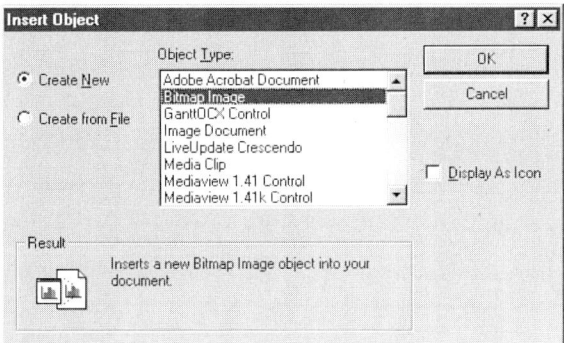

Figure 75-6   The Insert Object dialog box brought up by the InsertObjDlg method

Table 75-26 Arguments of the InsertObjDlg method

Argument	Meaning
form	Name property of the parent form
Name	Name property of the control

Example Syntax
```
Private Sub Command1_Click()
    If VBVersion% < 4 Then
        OLE1.Action = 14          'use the old Action method
    Else
        OLE1.InsertObjDlg         'use the new InsertObjDlg method
    End If
End Sub
```

Description	The InsertObjDlg method displays the Insert Object dialog box. This dialog box allows the user to create an OLE object by specifying type (linked or embedded) and the originating application. Figure 75-6 illustrates what the Insert Object dialog box looks like.
Example	The project at the end of this chapter uses the InsertObjDlg method to bring up the Insert Object dialog box.

lpOleObject Property

Objects Affected	OLE
Purpose	The lpOleObject property gives the memory address of an OLE object. You can then use this address in the OLE API calls. It is not available at design time and is read-only at runtime. Table 75-27 summarizes the arguments of the lpOleObject property.

General Syntax

```
[form.]Name.lpOleObject
```

Table 75-27 Arguments of the lpOleObject property

Argument	Meaning
form	Name property of the parent form
Name	Name property of the control

Example Syntax

```
Private Sub Command1_Click
    Dim p As Long
    p = OLE1.lpOleObject
    null = AddRef(p)            'API call using the long pointer
End Sub
```

Description	Many of the OLE 2.0 API calls require a long pointer to the memory position of the object. lpOleObject returns the pointer for use in these API calls. If there is no current object, lpOleObject returns a 0 (zero).
Example	The OLE Container Control project at the end of this chapter prints out the value of the long pointer's address in the printInfo procedure.

OBJECT PROPERTY

Objects Affected	OLE
Purpose	The Object property lets you access the underlying object in an OLE control for use in OLE automation. It is not available at design time and is read-only at runtime. OLE automation is covered in detail in Chapter 76, "OLE Automation." Table 75-28 summarizes the arguments of the Object property.

General Syntax

```
[form.]Name.Object.[property|method] [ = settings]
```

Table 75-28 Arguments of the Object property

Argument	Meaning
form	Name property of the parent form
Name	Name property of the control
property	Appropriate property of the object
method	Appropriate method of the object
settings	Appropriate arguments for the property or method

Example Syntax

```
Private Sub Command1_Click ()
    OLE1.Object.Bold = True
    OLE1.Object.Insert = "This is some text."
    OLE1.Object.SaveAs "C:\TEMP\TEST.DOC"
End Sub
```

Description   The Object property lets you manipulate the OLE container control's object with OLE automation. Contrast this technique with the CreateObject and GetObject functions: The Object property manipulates the object in an OLE container control, whereas the functions let you assign an object to an object variable, which you then manipulate. In general, if you know what type of object you will be using, it is better to use OLE automation; however, if you would like the user to be able to specify the type of object that will be used, you should use the OLE container control and the Object property to manipulate the OLE container control object.

Every originating application that supports OLE automation will have different properties and methods it makes available. Consult that application's documentation for the details and syntax of what it supports. The example syntax shows the Object property being used to issue the (hypothetical) automation commands to make the font bold, insert some text, then save the document to a file.

See "CreateObject" and "GetObject" in Chapter 76 for more details on OLE automation.

OBJECTACCEPTFORMATS PROPERTY

OBJECTACCEPTFORMATSCOUNT PROPERTY

OBJECTGETFORMATS PROPERTY

OBJECTGETFORMATSCOUNT PROPERTY

Objects Affected   OLE

Purpose   The ObjectAcceptFormats property returns the list of formats an object can accept. The ObjectGetFormats property returns the list of formats an object can provide. Both these properties return their lists as string arrays. ObjectAcceptFormatsCount and ObjectGetFormatsCount return the number of members in the appropriate array. These properties are useful for working with the Data and DataText properties for objects that do not implement OLE automation. They are not available at design time and are read-only at runtime. Table 75-29 lists the arguments of the properties.

General Syntax

```
[form.]Name.ObjectAcceptFormats(Index%)
[form.]Name.ObjectAcceptFormatsCount
[form.]Name.ObjectGetFormats(Index%)
[form.]Name.ObjectGetFormatsCount
```

Table 75-29 Arguments of the ObjectAcceptFormats, ObjectAcceptFormatsCount, ObjectAcceptGetFormats, and ObjectAcceptGetFormatsCount properties

Argument	Meaning
form	Name property of the parent form.
Name	Name property of the control.
Index%	Index to a particular member of the array. This argument is only used with the ObjectAcceptFormats and ObjectGetFormats properties.

Example Syntax

```
Private Sub Command1_Click ()
    For i = 0 To OLE1.ObjectAcceptFormatsCount - 1
        List1.AddItem OLE1.ObjectAcceptFormats(i)
    Next i
    For j = 0 to OLE1.ObjectGetFormatsCount - 1
        List2.AddItem OLE1.ObjectGetFormats(j)
    Next j
End Sub
```

Description   ObjectAcceptFormats returns the formats an object can accept; ObjectGetFormats returns the formats an object can return. These format strings are used with the Format property when you use the Data and DataText properties to transfer information. If an application is OLE automation capable, OLE automation offers an easier and more reliable method of exchanging data.

Both properties return the acceptable formats in a zero-based array. This means that the first entry is at index = 0, not index = 1. The array contains the actual strings that describe the format, and these values can be used directly in the Format property.

ObjectAcceptFormatsCount and ObjectGetFormatsCount return the total number of members in the array. This makes it simple to iterate through the arrays, as we do in the example syntax to add the formats to the list boxes. Note that, because the arrays are zero-based, the last member of the array has an index of Count -1.

The example syntax loads two list boxes with the ObjectAcceptFormats and ObjectGetFormats values. Figure 75-7 shows what this example might look like with Word 8.0.

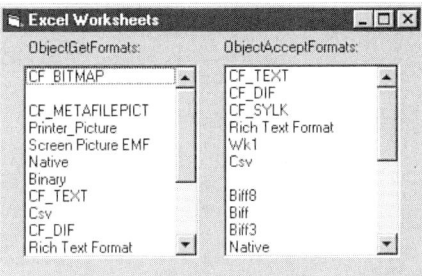

Figure 75-7 ObjectGetFormats and ObjectAcceptFormats help fill these list boxes

Example   The OLE Container Control project at the end of this chapter uses these properties in the printInfo routine. This routine iterates through each array and prints out the possible values, much like in the example syntax above.

OBJECTVERBS PROPERTY

OBJECTVERBSCOUNT PROPERTY

OBJECTVERBFLAGS PROPERTY

Objects Affected   OLE

Purpose   Each object has certain *verbs,* or actions, that apply to it. The ObjectVerbs property returns an array of applicable verbs for an object. The ObjectVerbsCount property returns the total number of verb entries in the ObjectVerbs array. The ObjectVerbFlags property returns the menu state of each item in the ObjectVerbs array. This lets you set up a menu that correctly lists each applicable verb and shows it in its proper state (checked, grayed, and so on). These properties are not available at design time and are read-only at runtime. Table 75-30 lists the arguments of the three properties, Table 75-31 lists the values that can be used with the ObjectVerbs property, and Table 75-32 lists the return values for the ObjectVerbFlags property.

General Syntax
```
[form.]Name.ObjectVerbs(Index%)
[form.]Name.ObjectVerbsCount
[form.]Name.ObjectVerbFlags(Index%)
```

Table 75-30 Arguments of the ObjectVerbs, ObjectVerbsCount, and ObjectVerbFlags properties

Argument	Meaning
form	Name property of the parent form
Name	Name property of the control
Index%	Index to a particular member of the array

Table 75-31 Values for the ObjectVerbs property

Value	VB.Constants	Description
0	vbOLEPrimary	The default action for the object. This will vary depending on the server you are using.
-1	vbOLEShow	Activates the object for editing.
-2	vbOLEOpen	Opens the object in a separate application window.
-3	vbOLEHide	Hides the server application.
-4	vbOLEInPlaceUIActivate	Prepares the object for in-place activation and shows any user interface menus and toolbars.
-5	vbOLEInPlaceActivate	Creates a window for in-place editing when the user moves application focus to the OLE container control.
-6	vbOLEDiscardUndoState	Disables the Undo feature when editing the object.

Table 75-32 The return values of the ObjectVerbFlags property

Value	Constants	Description
&H0000	n/a	The menu item should be enabled
&H0001	vbOLEFlagGrayed	The menu item should be grayed
&H0002	vbOLEFlagDisabled	The menu item should be disabled (but not grayed)
&H0008	vbOLEFlagChecked	The menu item should be checked
&H0800	vbOLEFlagSeparator	The menu item is a separator bar
&H0001	vbOLEMiscFlagMemStorage	Causes the control to use memory to store the object while it is loading
&H0002	vbOLEMiscFlagDisableInPlace	Forces the OLE container control to activate the object in its own window

Example Syntax

```
Private Sub Command1_Click ()
    OLE1.FetchVerbs                             'update the object's verbs
    For i = 0 To OLE1.ObjectVerbsCount - 1      'step through each verb
        Load menuVerbs(i)                       'create a new menu item
        flag = OLE1.ObjectVerbFlags(i)          'get the flag value
        If flag And vbOLEFlagSeparator Then
            menuVerbs(i).Caption = "-"           'separator
        Else
            menuVerbs(i).Caption = OLE1.ObjectVerbs(i)  'actual verb name
        End If
```

```
        If flag And &H0 Then menuVerbs(i).Enabled = True
        If flag And vbOLEFlagGrayed Then menuVerbs(i).Enabled = False
        If flag And vbOLEFlagDisabled Then menuVerbs(i).Tag = "disabled"
        If flag And vbOLEFlagChecked Then menuVerbs(i).Checked = True
    Next i
End Sub
```

Description   You can use the ObjectVerbFlags property to determine the correct appearance for the menu entry for each verb (checked, grayed, and so on). Each object has a number of different actions that can happen to it. For example, a sound application might be able to Play, Record, Rewind, or Reverse a sound. These verbs would then appear in the ObjectVerbs array.

However, not all verbs are applicable at any given time. For instance, if there is no sound presently loaded, then the Play, Rewind, and Reverse verbs are not applicable, but the Record verb is. The ObjectVerbFlags property for each verb lets you set its appropriate menu states. The example syntax shows how to build a menu with the appropriate entries and then set the proper display state for each menu item.

Both the ObjectVerbs and the ObjectVerbFlags arrays are zero-based. This means that the first member in the array has an index = 0, not index = 1. The last member in the arrays has an index of ObjectVerbsCount -1. The example syntax builds a menu using these arrays.

Make sure you use the FetchVerbs method before checking the ObjectVerbs or ObjectVerbFlags properties.

NOTE

In the Visual Basic Online Help and Books Online, there is a reference to the OLE Constant, vbOLEFlagEnabled. When Visual Basic 5.0 was released on March 19, 1997, this constant still did not exist. You should use the values 0 or &H0 instead.

Example   In the project at the end of this chapter, the printInfo routine uses these properties to print out the available verbs and the menu state of each for the selected OLE container control.

OLETYPE PROPERTY

Objects Affected   OLE

Purpose   Use the OLEType property to determine what kind of object (linked, embedded, or none) an OLE control contains. It is not available at design time and is read-only at runtime. Tables 75-33 and 75-34 summarize the arguments and values of the OLEType property.

General Syntax

```
[form.]Name.OLEType
```

Table 75-33 Arguments of the OLEType property

Argument	Meaning
form	Name property of the parent form
Name	Name property of the control

Table 75-34 Meanings of the values returned by the OLEType property

Value	Constants	Description
0	vbOLELinked	Object is linked
1	vbOLEEmbedded	Object is embedded
3	vbOLENone	OLE container control does not contain an object

Example Syntax

```
Private Sub Command1_Click ()
    Select Case OLE1.OLEType
        Case vbOLELinked: chekLinkStatus.Value = CHECKED
        Case vbOLEEmbedded: chekLinkStatus.Value = UNCHECKED
        Case vbOLENone: chekLinkStatus.Value = GRAYED
    End Select
End Sub
```

Description   Use the OLEType property to determine what kind of object an OLE control contains. A control may contain a linked object, an embedded object, or no object at all. The example syntax shows how to use this property to set the value of a check box control.

Linking lets you use another application's data while leaving it available for other programs. The data remains on disk as a separate file, stored in its normal, native format. It is available for editing by the original application or any other application that can read it. The originating application can save the information to disk. The object in your Visual Basic program contains a link to the proper file (and specific range or set of objects in that file) and an image of what the data looks like for display. Linked objects have an OLEType property of 0 (vbOLELinked).

Embedding lets you completely control the data. No other application can directly access the information. The object in your Visual Basic application contains the actual data as well as an image of what the data looks like for display. Although the Visual Basic OLE container control contains the actual data, it does not automatically save it to disk. You can use the OLE Action property to save and retrieve the information. Saving embedded OLE data saves the actual data, the name of the originating application, and an image of what the data looks like. Embedded objects have an

OLEType of 1 (vbOLEEmbedded). If the control does not contain an object, the OLEType property is set to 3 (vbOLENone).

Example   The OLE Container Control project at the end of this chapter uses the OLEType property in several places (such as the menuBar_Click event) to see whether there is an object embedded in the container. If the property returns 3 (vbOLENone), then no object is currently embedded.

OLETYPEALLOWED PROPERTY

Objects Affected   OLE

Purpose   Use the OLETypeAllowed property to set what kinds of objects (linked, embedded, or either) may be placed in an OLE control. It will read and write at both run and design time. Tables 75-35 and 75-36 summarize the arguments of the OLETypeAllowed property.

General Syntax

```
[form.]Name.OLETypeAllowed [ = type%]
```

Table 75-35 Arguments of the OLETypeAllowed property

Argument	Meaning
form	Name property of the parent form
Name	Name property of the control
type%	Type of object allowed (linked, embedded, or either)

Table 75-36 Meanings of the values of the OLETypeAllowed property

Value	Constants	Description
0	vbOLELinked	Can only contain a linked object
1	vbOLEEmbedded	Can only contain an embedded object
2	vbOLEEither	Can contain either a linked or an embedded object (default)

Example Syntax

```
Private Sub Command1_Click ()
    OLE1.OLETypeAllowed = vbOLELinked          'only allow linked objects
    OLE1.InsertObjDlg                          'bring up the Inert Object dialog box
End Sub
```

Description   Use the OLETypeAllowed property to set what kinds of objects (linked, embedded, or either) may be placed in an OLE container control. The example syntax sets the OLETypeAllowed property to linked before bringing up the Insert Object dialog box. This sets the default property for the Link check box in the dialog.

Linking lets you use another application's data while leaving it available for other programs. The data remains on disk as a separate file, stored in its normal, native format. It is available for editing by the original application or any other application that can read it. The originating application can save the information to disk. The object in your Visual Basic program contains a link to the proper file (and specific range or set of objects in that file), as well as an image of what the data looks like for display. Linked objects need to have an OLETypeAllowed property of 0 (vbOLELinked) or 2 (vbOLEEither).

Embedding lets you completely control the data. No other application can directly access the information. The object in your Visual Basic application contains the actual data as well as an image of what the data looks like for display. Although the Visual Basic OLE container control contains the actual data, it does not automatically save it to disk. You can use the OLE's Action property to save and retrieve the information. Saving embedded OLE data saves the actual data, the name of the originating application, and an image of what the data looks like. Embedded objects need to have an OLEType of 1 (vbOLEEmbedded) or 2 (vbOLEEither).

PASTE METHOD

Objects Affected	OLE
Purpose	The Paste method lets you copy data from the Clipboard to an OLE container control. Table 75-37 summarizes the arguments of the Paste method.

General Syntax

```
[form.]Name.Paste
```

Table 75-37 Arguments of the Paste method

Argument	Meaning
form	Name property of the parent form
Name	Name property of the control

Example Syntax

```
Private Sub Command1_Click()
    If VBVersion% < 4 Then
        OLE1.Action = 5                     'use the old Action method
    Else
```

```
      OLE1.Paste                              'use the new Paste method
   End If
End Sub
```

Description   The Paste method copies data from the Clipboard to an OLE container control. First, set the OLETypeAllowed property properly; 2 (either linked or embedded) gives you the most flexibility. Check to see whether the data on the Clipboard can be pasted with the PasteOK property (see PasteOK for details). If it can, execute the Paste method. You may then check on the success of the paste operation by checking the OLEType property to make sure it returns either linked (0) or embedded (1); if it returns none (3), the paste has failed.

In fact, you can give your user the most flexibility by displaying the Paste Special dialog box (PasteSpecialDlg method), rather than by directly using the Paste method. The dialog box lets your user specify whether he or she wants to link or embed during the paste.

Example   The project at the end of this chapter uses the Paste method when the user selects the Edit Paste menu choice.

PasteOK Property

Objects Affected   OLE

Purpose   Use the PasteOK property to determine whether the contents of the Clipboard may be pasted into the OLE container control. It is not available at design time and is read-only at runtime. Table 75-38 summarizes the arguments of the PasteOK property.

General Syntax

```
[form.]Name.PasteOK
```

Table 75-38 Arguments of the PasteOK property

Argument	Meaning
form	Name property of the parent form
Name	Name property of the control

Example Syntax

```
Private Sub menuEdit_Click ()
    menuEditPaste.Enabled = OLE1.PasteOK          'enables and disables paste command
End Sub
```

Description   Use the PasteOK property to determine whether the contents of the Clipboard may be pasted into the OLE container control. If the Clipboard contains an OLE object in the correct format, then PasteOK returns True.

If the Clipboard does not contain an OLE object, PasteOK returns False. The example syntax enables and disables an Edit Paste menu command based on the PasteOK return value.

You can paste the object with the Paste method or the PasteSpecialDlg method once you've determined that it is OK to paste. Using the Paste Special dialog box gives your users the most control, as they can choose to link or embed the object.

Example The OLE Container Control project at the end of this chapter checks the value of the PasteOK property in the menuBar_Click event. If the value is True, the routine then enables the menu controls that allow pasting (Paste and Paste Special).

PASTESPECIALDLG METHOD

Objects Affected   OLE

Purpose   Use the PasteSpecialDlg method to bring up the Paste Special dialog box. Table 75-39 summarizes the arguments of the PasteSpecialDlg method.

General Syntax

```
[form.]Name.PasteSpecialDlg
```

Table 75-39 Arguments of the PasteSpecialDlg method

Argument	Meaning
form	Name property of the parent form
Name	Name property of the control

Example Syntax

```
Private Sub Command1_Click()
    If VBVersion% < 4 Then
        OLE1.Action = 15                'use the old Action method
    Else
        OLE1.PasteSpecialDlg            'use the new PasteSpecialDlg method
    End If
End Sub
```

Description   The PasteSpecialDlg method displays the Paste Special dialog box. This dialog box allows the user to paste an object from the Clipboard into the OLE container control. The user can specify the type of object (linked or embedded) with the dialog box. Figure 75-8 illustrates what the Paste Special dialog box looks like.

Example   The project at the end of this chapter uses the PasteSpecialDlg method to bring up the Paste Special dialog box when the user selects the appropriate choice from the Edit menu.

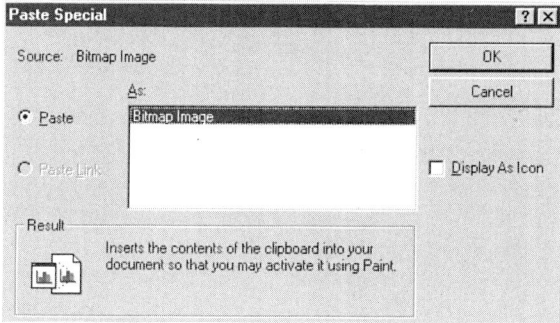

Figure 75-8 The Paste Special dialog box brought up by the PasteSpecialDlg method

READFROMFILE METHOD

Objects Affected   OLE

Purpose   Use the ReadFromFile method to load an object from a binary data file. Table 75-40 summarizes the arguments of the ReadFromFile method.

General Syntax

```
[form.]Name.ReadFromFile filenumber
```

Table 75-40 Arguments of the ReadFromFile method

Argument	Meaning
form	Name property of the parent form
Name	Name property of the control
filenumber	File number of an open binary file used when loading this object

Example Syntax

```
Private Sub Command1_Click()
    Open "MYOLEOBJ.DAT" For Binary As #1
    If VBVersion% < 4 Then
        OLE1.FileNumber = 1
        OLE1.Action = 12                    'use the old Action method
    Else
        OLE1.ReadFromFile 1                 'use the new ReadFromFile method
    End If
    Close #1
End Sub
```

Description   The ReadFromFile method loads an OLE object from a data file created using the SaveToFile method. Set the filenumber argument to the file number of the open binary file that contains the data. The file number should match the number you have used in a previous Open statement to open a file for binary input (using the For Binary clause). You should then use the Update method to synchronize the OLE container control with the originating application.

Example   The project at the end of this chapter uses the ReadFromFile method to read an object from a binary file when the File Open option is selected.

RESIZE EVENT

Objects Affected   Form, MDI Form, OLE, Picture Box

Purpose   Use the OLE container control's Resize event to react to a change in the control's size caused by new data when the SizeMode property is set to 2 (AutoSize). Table 75-41 summarizes the arguments of the Resize event.

General Syntax

```
Sub Name_Resize (HeightNew As Integer, WidthNew As Integer)
```

Table 75-41 Arguments of the Resize event

Argument	Meaning
Name	Name property of the control
HeightNew	Optimal height of the control; change this to set new height of control
WidthNew	Optimal width of the control; change this to set new width of control

Example Syntax

```
Sub OLE1_Resize (HeightNew As Integer, WidthNew As Integer)
    If HeightNew > 2000 Then
        HeightNew = 2000
    End If
    If WidthNew > 4000 Then
        WidthNew = 4000
    End If
End Sub
```

Description   You can set an OLE container control to resize itself automatically when the data it displays changes. Setting the OLE container control's SizeMode property to 2 (AutoSize) will automatically resize the control. You may then want to limit the size of the control to keep it within certain boundaries. The HeightNew and WidthNew arguments in the Resize event contain the optimal height and width (that is, how large the control would need to be in order to display the object completely). Set these arguments to a different value to force the control into a different size. The example syntax limits the OLE container control to no more than 2000 × 4000 twips.

Example	The OLE Container Control project at the end of this chapter uses the Resize event to limit the size of the document OLE container control to a maximum size equal to the graph container.

SaveToFile Method

Objects Affected	OLE
Purpose	Use the SaveToFile method to save an object to a binary data file. Table 75-42 summarizes the arguments of the SaveToFile method.

General Syntax

```
[form.]Name.SaveToFile filenumber
```

Table 75-42 Arguments of the SaveToFile method

Argument	Meaning
form	Name property of the parent form
Name	Name property of the control
filenumber	File number of an open binary file used when saving this object

Example Syntax

```
Private Sub Command1_Click()
    If VBVersion% < 4 Then
        OLE1.Action = 11                    'use the old Action method
    Else
        OLE1.SaveToFile #1                  'use the new SaveToFile method
    End If
End Sub
```

Description	The SaveToFile method saves an OLE object to a data file. Set the filenumber argument to the file number of an open binary file. If the OLEType is 0, linked, then only the link information and an image for display are saved to disk. If the OLEType is 1, embedded, then the actual data is stored along with the name of the originating application and a display image.
Example	The project at the end of this chapter uses the SaveToFile method to save an object to a binary file when the File Save option is selected.

SaveToOle1File Method

Objects Affected	OLE
Purpose	Use the SaveToOle1File method to save an object to a binary data file in OLE 1.0 format. Table 75-43 summarizes the arguments of the SaveToOle1File method.

General Syntax

```
[form.]Name.SaveToOle1File filenumber
```

Table 75-43 Arguments of the SaveToOle1File method

Argument	Meaning
form	Name property of the parent form
Name	Name property of the control
filenumber	File number of an open binary file used when saving this object

Example Syntax

```
Private Sub Command1_Click()
    If VBVersion% < 4 Then
        OLE1.Action = 18                    'use the old Action method
    Else
        OLE1.SaveToOle1File #1              'use the new SaveToOle1File method
    End If
End Sub
```

Description   The SaveToOle1File method saves an object in the older OLE 1.0 file format. OLE 2.0 is a new specification, and many applications only support OLE 1.0.

Example   The project at the end of this chapter uses the SaveToFile method rather than the SaveToOle1File method.

SIZEMODE PROPERTY

Objects Affected   OLE

Purpose   The SizeMode property determines how an object is sized within an OLE container control. Tables 75-44 and 75-45 summarize the arguments and values of the SizeMode property.

Example Syntax

```
[form.]Name.SizeMode [ = setting%]
```

Table 75-44 Arguments of the SizeMode property

Argument	Meaning
form	Name property of the parent form
Name	Name property of the control
setting%	Determines the sizing mode: clip, stretch, or AutoSize

Table 75-45 Meanings of the setting% argument in the SizeMode property

setting%	Constants	Description
0	vbOLESizeClip	Clips the object at OLE container control's boundaries (default)
1	vbOLESizeStretch	Sizes the object to exactly fill the OLE container control
2	vbOLESizeAutoSize	Resizes the OLE container control to fit the object
3	vbOLESizeZoom	Size of the object is stretched, but object is shown proportionally correct

Example Syntax

```
Private Sub List1_Click ()
    OLE1.SizeMode = List1.ListIndex
End Sub
```

Description
The SizeMode property determines how the OLE container control sizes and displays the object. The OLE container control will almost always be of a different size than the image of the object it displays. You can select whether the control will clip the object's display, size the object to fit the control, or size the control to fit the object. The example syntax sets this property with the index of a list box that has each size mode listed in the correct order.

Both the vbOLESizeClip and vbOLESizeStretch settings display the object entirely within the OLE container control's boundaries, and leave the size of the OLE container control unchanged. The vbOLESizeZoom setting stretches an object but keeps its width and height proportional. The clip setting displays the upper-left corner of the object at its actual size and clips off any part that extends past the control's border. The stretch setting resizes the object to exactly fill the OLE container control.

The vbOLESizeAutosize setting resizes the OLE container control to match the size of the object. Although you cannot regulate the size of the object, you can set the ultimate size of the OLE container control. Resizing the OLE container control generates a Resize event, and you can set the Resize event's HeightNew and WidthNew arguments to determine the control's size. This might be helpful if you want to let the control expand as much as possible, but not beyond a certain boundary on your form. If you resize the control to a smaller size than the object, then the control clips the object. Figure 75-9 shows the same information displayed in the four modes in four different OLE container controls.

Example
Try changing this property for the project at the end of this chapter to see the effect it has on the OLE container control display.

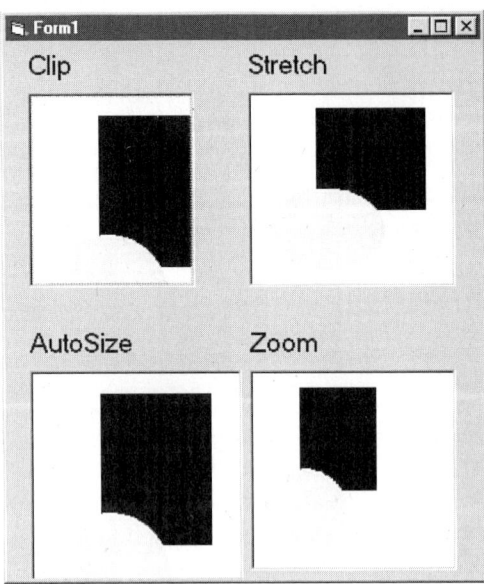

Figure 75-9   The four different OLE display modes: Clip, Stretch, AutoSize, and Zoom

SourceDoc Property

Objects Affected   OLE

Purpose   The SourceDoc property sets the filename to use when creating an object or reads the filename of an existing object. It will read and write at both design and runtime. Table 75-46 summarizes the arguments of the SourceDoc property.

General Syntax

```
[form.]Name.SourceDoc [ = document$]
```

Table 75-46 Arguments of the SourceDoc property

Argument	Meaning
form	Name property of the parent form
Name	Name property of the control
document$	Full path and filename of the document

Example Syntax

```
Private Sub Form_Load ()
    OLE1.Class = "Excel.Worksheet"
    OLE1.SourceDoc = "C:\DATA\Q1ACTUAL.XLS"
    OLE1.SourceItem = "R1C1:R587C48"
    OLE1.CreateLink
End Sub
```

Description

The SourceDoc property sets the filename to use when creating an object or reads the filename and item of an existing object. If the object being created is linked (by using the CreateLink method), then the disk file is linked to the OLE container control. If the object is embedded (using the CreateEmbed method), then the disk file is used as a template to create a new object in the OLE container control.

SourceDoc has SourceItem concatenated to it after Visual Basic creates the object. The two properties are separated by an exclamation point (!) or a backslash (\). The originating application controls whether it uses the exclamation point or the backslash. Microsoft Excel uses an exclamation and thus, after running the example syntax for the Form_Load event, SourceDoc would contain C:\DATA\Q1ACTUAL.XLS!R1C1:R587C48.

SOURCEITEM PROPERTY

Objects Affected   OLE

Purpose   Use the SourceItem property to specify exactly what data to use when creating a linked object. It will read and write at both design and runtime. Table 75-47 summarizes the arguments of the SourceItem property.

General Syntax

```
[form.]Name.SourceItem [ = item$]
```

Table 75-47 Arguments of the SourceItem property

Argument	Meaning
form	Name property of the parent form
Name	Name property of the control
item$	Specification for the particular unit of data

Example Syntax

```
Private Sub Form_Load ()
    OLE1.Class = "Excel.Worksheet"
    OLE1.SourceDoc = "C:\DATA\Q1ACTUAL.XLS"
    OLE1.SourceItem = "R1C1:R587C48"
    OLE1.CreateLink
End Sub
```

Description The SourceItem property lets you specify exactly what piece or range of data to use for a linked object. It does not apply to embedded objects. Use the SourceDoc property to specify the file in which the item resides. Visual Basic concatenates SourceItem to SourceDoc, separating the two with an exclamation point (!) or backslash (\). It then sets SourceItem to an empty string (""). For this reason, it is useless to read the SourceItem property at runtime. See the information on the SourceDoc property for more details.

The example syntax sets the SourceItem property to a subset of the Q1ACTUAL.XLS worksheet. Microsoft Excel specifies items in the familiar R1C1 row/column format, so the SourceItem here specifies everything from the upper-left corner (row 1, column 1) to the lower-right corner (row 587, column 48).

Microsoft Excel also supports named ranges, so if the worksheet had a name defined for this region, you could use that instead. For instance, R1C1:R587C48 might be defined as "MarketingExpenses." You could then set SourceItem = "MarketingExpenses." Just as constants make your Visual Basic code self-documenting and easier to debug, named ranges make spreadsheets and other documents easier to work with and change. If the spreadsheet had some rows inserted in this range, R1C1:R587C48 would become incorrect, but "MarketingExpenses" would still work.

Many originating applications let you specify some subset of data to use, but there are as many ways of specifying this as there are applications. You will need to read carefully the originating application's documentation to see how it specifies subsets of data, and to see whether it supports named ranges.

You may be able to determine how an application works with subsets even without the documentation's help by using this trick: Select the data you would like in the originating application and copy it onto the Clipboard. Then use Paste Special (set the Action property to 14) to paste it into an OLE container control in Visual Basic. Look at the Source line in the Paste Special dialog box to see whether the application uses an exclamation point (!) or backslash (\), and how it specifies the subset. Figure 75-10 shows how this looks in the property box.

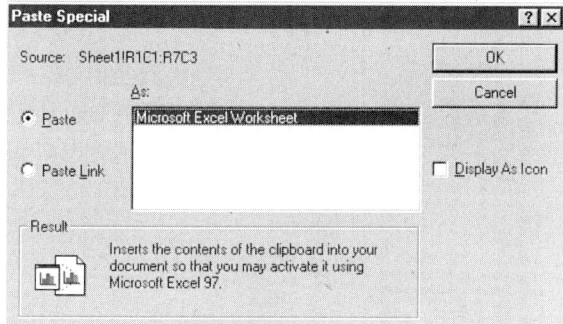

Figure 75-10 Use Paste Special to discover how an undocumented application specifies subsets

UPDATE METHOD

Objects Affected   OLE

Purpose   This method updates and displays the data for an object in the OLE container control. Table 75-48 summarizes the arguments of the Update method.

General Syntax

```
[form.]Name.Update
```

Table 75-48 Arguments of the Update method

Argument	Meaning
form	Name property of the parent form
Name	Name property of the control

Example Syntax

```
Private Sub Command1_Click()
    If VBVersion% < 4 Then
        OLE1.Action = 6                    'use the old Action method
    Else
        OLE1.Update                        'use the new Update method
    End If
End Sub
```

Description   The Update method retrieves the current data from the application that supplied the object. The example syntax displays the updated data as a picture in the OLE container control. The originating application updates the picture, and it displays in its native format.

UPDATED EVENT

Objects Affected OLE

Purpose Use the Updated event to react when an object's data changes. Tables 75-49 and 75-50 summarize the arguments of the Updated event.

General Syntax

```
Sub Name_Updated (Code As Integer)
```

Table 75-49 Arguments of the Updated event

Argument	Meaning
Name	Name property of the control
Code	Indicates what action triggered the event

Table 75-50 Meanings of the Code argument in the Updated event

setting%	Constants	Description
0	vbOLEChanged	Object's data has changed
1	vbOLESaved	Object has been saved by the originating application
2	vbOLEClosed	File containing linked object's data is closed by originating application
3	vbOLERenamed	File containing linked object's data is renamed by originating application

Example Syntax

```
Sub OLE1_Updated (Code As Integer)
    Select Case Code
        Case vbOLEChanged: NeedToSave = True
        Case vbOLESaved:   NeedToSave = False
        Case vbOLEClosed:  NeedToSave = False
        Case vbOLERenamed: NeedToSave = False
    End Select
End Sub
```

Description Use the Updated event to react to changes in an OLE container control's object. The Code argument lets you take different actions depending on what triggered the event.

The example syntax shows a typical use for this event. The Select Case statement sets the global variable NeedToSave when the control is updated. It assumes that the object needs to be saved if it has changed, and doesn't need to be saved if the user has already saved it, closed the application, or renamed it by saving under a different filename.

Example   The OLE Container Control project at the end of this chapter uses a Boolean variable to track when changes have been made to the OLE container control. The vbOLEChanged variable is flagged in the Update event, and this helps determine whether or not to enable the File Save command.

UPDATEOPTIONS PROPERTY

Objects Affected   OLE

Purpose   The UpdateOptions property sets and reads how an OLE container control is updated when the linked data changes. Tables 75-51 and 75-52 summarize the arguments of the UpdateOptions property.

General Syntax

```
[form.]Name.UpdateOptions [ = setting%]
```

Table 75-51 Arguments of the UpdateOptions property

Argument	Meaning
form	Name property of the parent form
Name	Name property of the control
setting%	Determines how the control is updated: automatic, frozen, or manual

Table 75-52 Meanings of the setting% argument of the UpdateOptions property

setting%	VB.Constants	Description
0	vbOLEAutomatic	Object updated each time link data changes (default)
1	vbOLEFrozen	Object updated when originating application saves linked data
2	vbOLEManual	Object updated only by the Action property is set to 6 (Update)

Example Syntax

```
Private Sub Check1_Click ()
    If Check1.Value = CHECKED Then
        OLE1.UpdateOptions = vbOLEAutomatic
    Else
        OLE1.UpdateOptions = vbOLEManual
    End If
End Sub
```

Description   Use the UpdateOptions property to determine how the OLE container control is updated when its linked data changes. This is only used for linked objects. An embedded object, by definition, cannot have its data changed by external applications.

This property is most useful for objects that take a long time to display or change frequently. For example, assume the object is a graph showing assembly line speed that is updated every three seconds. Setting UpdateOptions to vbOLEAutomatic would probably degrade the performance of your application as it tries to keep up with the ever-changing display. It might be wiser to set the property to vbOLEManual and have either a user action (like a mouse click) or a timer set to a longer interval update the control.

Each change in the linked data triggers an Updated event. You can then use that event with vbOLEManual to fine-tune the object's updates. You might have a static variable in the Updated event that counts a certain number of updates before it refreshes the object.

Example   All the OLE container controls in the OLE Container Control project at the end of this chapter are kept to their default value of Automatic.

VERB PROPERTY

Objects Affected   OLE

Purpose   Each object can have certain actions performed on it. The Verb property specifies what action to take. It will read and write at both design and runtime. Tables 75-53 and 75-54 summarize the arguments and settings of the Verb property.

General Syntax

```
[form.]Name.Verb [ = setting%]
```

Table 75-53 Arguments of the Verb property

Argument	Meaning
form	Name property of the parent form
Name	Name property of the control
setting%	Index number of the action to take in the ObjectVerbs list

Table 75-54 Verbs that almost all objects support

setting%	Constants	Description
0	vbOLEPrimary	Default verb for object
−1	vbOLEShow	Open object for editing (in place if supported)
−2	vbOLEOpen	Open object for editing in its own window
−3	vbOLEHide	Hide the originating application

setting%	Constants	Description
–4	vbOLEInPlaceUIActivate	Leave object open for editing with user interface elements on screen when focus leaves
–5	vbOLEInPlaceActivate	Leave object open for editing when focus leaves
–6	vbOLEDiscardUndoState	Disregard all record of changes that the object's application can undo.

Example Syntax

```
Private Sub Command1_Click ()
    OLE1.Verb = vbOLEVerbHide              'set up object to hide application
    OLE1.DoVerb                            'activate the object
    If OLE1.AppIsRunning Then              'If object successfully activated, then
        OLE1.Object.Insert "Hello"         'paste string data using automation
        OLE1.Update                        'and update the OLE control's display.
    End If
End Sub
```

Description   Each Object has a set of actions that can be performed with it. These actions are called *verbs*. Each object supports a different set of verbs, and some verbs may or may not be applicable depending on the state of the object. For example, a sound application might have Play, Rewind, and Record as verbs. If the object doesn't contain any sound, then Play and Rewind do not apply, but Record does.

Verbs can be triggered either manually or automatically. You can trigger a verb manually by using the DoVerb method. You can set an object to activate automatically and trigger the verb by setting the AutoActivate property to either vbOLEGetFocus or vbOLEDoubleClick. The verb would then trigger each time the OLE container control received the focus or the user double-clicked on it, depending on the setting you gave to the AutoActivate property. Almost all objects support the standard verbs shown in Table 75-54.

Each object has a default action that can operate on it. For instance, a sound application might define Play as its default verb. A spreadsheet might define Edit as its default verb. The default action takes place automatically if AutoActivate has been set to True. The default action can be triggered manually by executing the DoVerb method.

Almost all objects can be edited (that is, have their data altered). There are several different editing values depending on whether the object supports in-place editing and how you want it to respond. The simplest setting is –2, vbOLEOpen. This will always put the object in its own window and shift focus to the originating application, even if the object supports in-place editing. If you specify –1, vbOLEShow, the object can be edited in-place while it has the focus (assuming the object supports in-place editing). In-place editing leaves the object in the OLE container control rather than opening a separate window, and it places the originating application's user interface elements (such as floating palettes) directly in your application. It then looks as if your application is doing all the work. Figure 75-11 shows an object being edited in the originating application, and Figure 75-12 shows the same object being edited in-place.

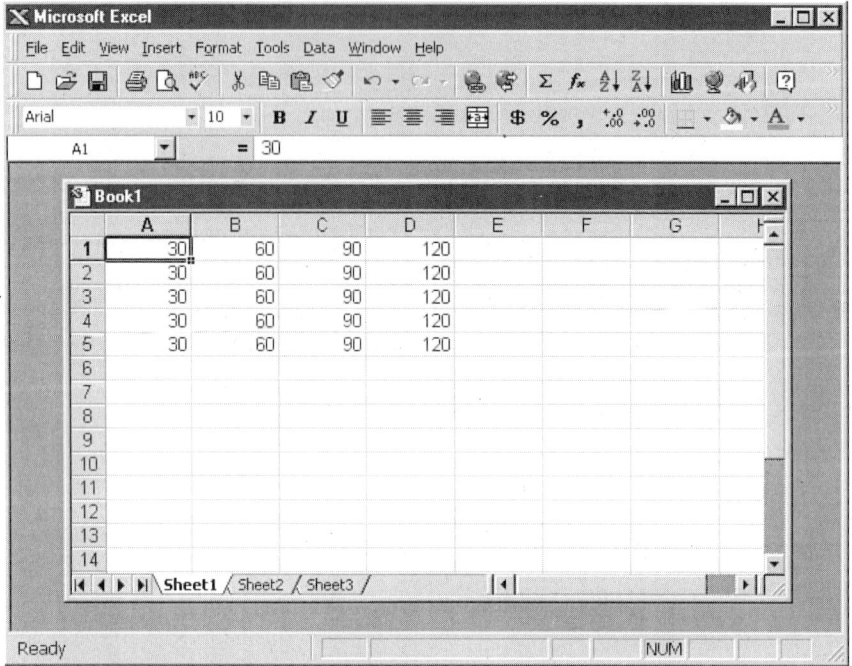

Figure 75-11   The spreadsheet can be edited in the original application or...

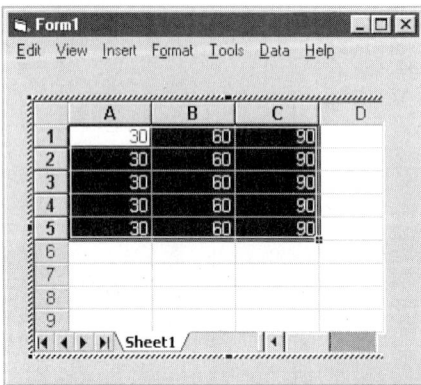

Figure 75-12   ...edited in-place with
vbOLEShow

You can also specify that the object remain active and editable even when
it loses focus by using the settings –4 and –5. Setting –5,
vbOLEInPlaceActivate, is just like –1, vbOLEShow, except that the object
is always active and will generally go into edit mode more quickly. Setting

–4, vbOLEInPlaceUIActivate, leaves the user interface elements on the screen at all times, even when the object loses focus.

Option –3, vbOLEHide, hides the originating application. This might be useful when you want to do OLE automation on an OLE control's object, as in the example syntax.

Option –6, vbOLEDiscardUndoState, causes the activated object to discard all record of changes that it could use for the Undo feature.

Many applications support more verbs than just these standard ones. You can use the ObjectVerbs list to get a complete list of supported verbs. ObjectVerbsCount gives the total number of verbs, and ObjectVerbFlags gives the status of each verb (for instance, enabled, disabled, or checked). You then specify these verbs with their index number in the ObjectVerbs array: The first verb would have a Verb property of 1, the second verb a Verb property of 2, and so on.

The standard verbs (except for 0, the default verb) listed in Table 75-54 normally do not appear in the ObjectVerbs list. Setting AutoVerbMenu to True will bring up a menu of the ObjectVerbs list when the user clicks the right-mouse button on the object.

Example
The OLE Container Control project at the end of this chapter sets the Verb property many times, and generally to -3 (vbOLEHide). The Verb property is usually set immediately before activating the OLE object. The menuDOCPop_Click event also sets the Verb property, but lets the index of the chosen menu item (as initially set by the ObjectVerb array in the menuDOC_Click event) control what verb to use.

OLE Container Control Project

Project Overview

This project can be used as a general introduction to OLE, assuming that you have the standard Paintbrush accessory that comes with Windows 3.1. We will implement a full OLE-aware Edit menu, and demonstrate both the OLE File Open and File Save techniques. This will be useful to you in any application that uses OLE.

Assembling the Project

1. Place the following controls on a form, as detailed in Table 75-55. After placing the controls on the form, use the Menu Design dialog box to create the menu structure detailed in Table 75-56. When you place the OLE container control on the form, you will see an Insert Object dialog box. Select the Create from File option button and use the file, smile.bmp, found in this chapter's folder on the CD-ROM. Figure 75-13 shows what the completed form should look like.

Figure 75-13   The completed frmMain
during the design phase

Table 75-55 Elements of frmMain

Control	Property	Value
Form	Name	frmMain
	BorderStyle	1 'Fixed Single
	Caption	"OLE Container Project"
OLE	Name	ole
	AutoVerbMenu	0 'False

Table 75-56 Menu structure for frmMain

Name	Caption	Index
mnuBar	"&File"	0
mnuFile	"&Open Object"	0
mnuFile	"&Save Object"	1
mnuFile	"-"	2
mnuFile	"E&xit"	3
mnuBar	"&Edit"	1
mnuEdit	"Cu&t"	0
mnuEdit	"&Copy"	1
mnuEdit	"&Paste"	2
mnuEdit	"-"	3
mnuEdit	"Paste &Special"	4
mnuEdit	"Insert &Object"	5

Name	Caption	Index
mnuEdit	"-"	6
mnuEdit	"&Info"	7

2. Enter the following code into the Declarations section of frmMain. This code informs Visual Basic we will be required to declare all variables, and it also declares a private variable we will use to recognize that the OLE object has been changed.

```
Option Explicit

Private oleChanged As Integer        'we will set this when we change the object
```

3. Enter the following code into the Form_Load procedure. This code initializes some of the properties of our OLE container control.

```
Private Sub Form_Load()
    Dim i As Integer

    ole.HostName = "OLE Container Project"  'set the host name
    ole.DisplayType = vbOLEDisplayContent   'and display type
    ole.AutoVerbMenu = True                 'set up automatic menus
End Sub
```

4. Enter the following code into the mnuBar_Click procedure. This code determines which of the File and Edit menus' options should be enabled, depending on whether any data in the object has been changed.

```
Private Sub mnuBar_Click(Index As Integer)
    Dim i As Integer

    Select Case Index
    Case 0                                     '*** File ***
        mnuFile(1).Enabled = False             'turn off save
        If oleChanged = True Then              'if an object has changed
            mnuFile(1).Enabled = True          'then enable File Save
        End If
    Case 1                                      '*** Edit ***
        For i = 0 To 7                          'iterate through Edit menu
                                                'commands (except separator bars)
            If (i <> 3 And i <> 6) Then
                mnuEdit(i).Enabled = False      'and turn them off
            End If
        Next i

        Dim ctlScrnControl As Control
        Set ctlScrnControl = Screen.ActiveControl  'control that has focus
        If TypeOf ctlScrnControl Is OLE Then       'if it's OLE control
            mnuEdit(5).Enabled = True              'enable Insert Object
            If ctlScrnControl.OLEType <> vbOLENone Then  'if it's got an object
                mnuEdit(0).Enabled = True          'enable Cut
                mnuEdit(1).Enabled = True          'enable Copy
                mnuEdit(7).Enabled = True          'enable Info
```

continued on next page

continued from previous page

```
            End If
            If ctlScrnControl.PasteOK Then          'if the Clipboard has a pastable
                                                     'object
                mnuEdit(2).Enabled = True            'enable Paste
                mnuEdit(4).Enabled = True            'enable Paste Special
            End If
        End If
    End Select
End Sub
```

5. Enter the following code into the mnuEdit_Click procedure. This code handles any selections from the Edit menu.

```
Private Sub mnuEdit_Click(Index As Integer)
    Dim ctlScrnControl As Control

    Set ctlScrnControl = Screen.ActiveControl        'which control is active?
    frmMain.MousePointer = Hourglass                 'show hourglass mouse cursor
    Select Case Index
    Case 0
        If Not ctlScrnControl.AppIsRunning Then      'if the app is not running
            ctlScrnControl.DoVerb vbOLEShow          'then activate it
        End If
        ctlScrnControl.Copy                          'and copy
        ctlScrnControl.Delete                        'and delete
    Case 1
        If Not ctlScrnControl.AppIsRunning Then      'if the app is not running
            ctlScrnControl.DoVerb vbOLEShow          'then activate it
        End If
        ctlScrnControl.Copy                          'and copy
    Case 2
        ctlScrnControl.Class = "temp"                'create a temp class
        ctlScrnControl.Paste                         'and paste to it
    Case 3                                           'separator bar (do nothing)
    Case 4
        ctlScrnControl.PasteSpecialDlg               'bring up the Paste Special dialog box
    Case 5
        ctlScrnControl.InsertObjDlg                  'bring up the Insert Object dialog box
    Case 6                                           'separator bar (do nothing)
    Case 7
        PrintInfo ctlScrnControl                     'print out info about object
    End Select

    If ctlScrnControl.OLEType <> vbOLENone Then      'for a linked or embedded object
        ctlScrnControl.Close                         'close the object
        ctlScrnControl.Refresh                       'and refresh the display
    End If
    frmMain.MousePointer = Default                   'return the mousepointer to normal
End Sub
```

6. Enter the following code into the mnuFile_Click procedure. This code handles any selections from the File menu.

```
Private Sub mnuFile_Click(Index As Integer)
    Dim fileNum As Integer, i As Integer

    Select Case Index
```

```
    Case 0
        fileNum = FreeFile                      'get a free file number
        Open App.Path & "\oleobj.dat" For _
            Binary As fileNum                   'load the object
        If ole.OLEType <> vbOLENone Then        'if an object exists
            ole.ReadFromFile fileNum            'read an object from a file
        End If
        oleChanged = False                      'we have just loaded the object
        Close fileNum                           'done with this file
    Case 1
        fileNum = FreeFile                      'get a free file number
        Open App.Path & "\oleobj.dat" For _
            Binary As fileNum                   'save the object
        If ole.OLEType <> vbOLENone Then        'if object exists
            ole.SaveToFile fileNum              'save an object to a file
        End If
        oleChanged = False                      'we have just saved the object
        Close fileNum                           'done with this file
    Case 2                                      'separator bar (do nothing)
    Case 3
        End                                     'exit the program
    End Select
End Sub
```

7. Enter the following code into the ole_Resize procedure. This code sets a maximum size for the OLE container control.

```
Private Sub ole_Resize(HeightNew As Single, WidthNew As Single)
    If HeightNew > 2772 Then HeightNew = 2772    'check for maximum height
    If WidthNew > 2532 Then WidthNew = 2532      'check for maximum width
End Sub
```

8. Enter the following code into the ole_Updated procedure. This code sets the oleChanged variable to True if the OLE object has been updated.

```
Private Sub ole_Updated(Code As Integer)
    If Code = 0 Then oleChanged = True          'we have updated the ole control
End Sub
```

9. Enter the following code into a new procedure called PrintInfo. This procedure prints out information about the object.

```
Private Sub PrintInfo(ctlScrnControl As Control)
    Dim i As Integer

    If Not ctlScrnControl.AppIsRunning Then              'if the app is not running
        ctlScrnControl.DoVerb vbOLEShow                  'then activate it
    End If
    frmInfo.Show                                         'bring up our information form
    frmInfo.Cls
    frmInfo.Print                                        'print out info on this form...
    frmInfo.Print "  Class:";
    frmInfo.Print Tab(20); ctlScrnControl.Class
    frmInfo.Print
    frmInfo.Print "  Accept Formats:";
    For i = 0 To ctlScrnControl.ObjectAcceptFormatsCount - 1
        frmInfo.Print Tab(20); ctlScrnControl.ObjectAcceptFormats(i)
```

continued on next page

continued from previous page

```
    Next i
    frmInfo.Print
    frmInfo.Print "  Return Formats:";
    For i = 0 To ctlScrnControl.ObjectGetFormatsCount - 1
        frmInfo.Print Tab(20); ctlScrnControl.ObjectGetFormats(i)
    Next i
    frmInfo.Print
    frmInfo.Print "  Verbs:";
    For i = 1 To ctlScrnControl.ObjectVerbsCount - 1
        frmInfo.Print Tab(20); ctlScrnControl.ObjectVerbs(i); Tab(40);
        Select Case ctlScrnControl.ObjectVerbFlags(i)
        Case vbOLEFlagChecked
            frmInfo.Print "Checked"
        Case 0
            frmInfo.Print "Enabled"
        Case vbOLEFlagGrayed
            frmInfo.Print "Grayed"
        Case vbOLEFlagSeparator
            frmInfo.Print "Separator"
        End Select
    Next i

    frmInfo.Print
    frmInfo.Print "  Long Pointer: ";
    frmInfo.Print Tab(20); Hex$(ctlScrnControl.lpOleObject)

    frmInfo.Left = frmMain.Width + frmMain.Left ' Diplay Info form next to
                                                ' the Main form

End Sub
```

10. Insert a new form to display the information printed by frmMain's Edit Info command. Table 75-57 details the components of the form. Size and position the elements as illustrated in Figure 75-14.

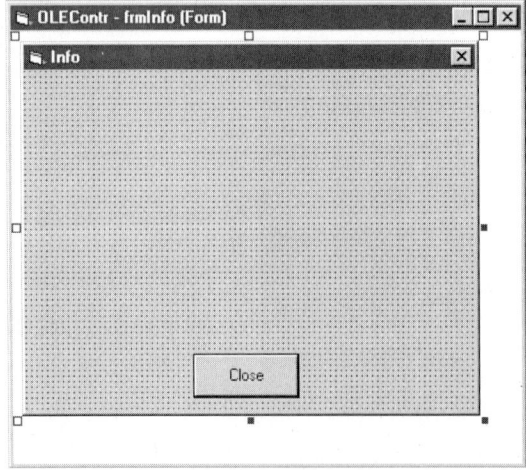

Figure 75-14   frmInfo during the design phase

Table 75-57 Elements of frmInfo

Control	Property	Value
Form	Name	frmInfo
	AutoRedraw	−1 'True
	BorderStyle	3 'Fixed Double
	Caption	"Info"
CommandButton	Name	cmdClose
	Cancel	−1 'True
	Caption	"Close"
	Default	−1 'True

11. Enter the following code into the cmdClose procedure. This hides the frmInfo form when the Close command button is clicked.

```
Private Sub cmdClose_Click()
    Me.Hide
End Sub
```

How It Works

This project is a very simple illustration of some of the OLE container control techniques you have learned in this chapter. Since the OLE container control attempts to use a Paintbrush embedded object, almost everyone should be able to activate the object, modify it, and cut or paste with the Edit menu options of this project.

When the project first opens, it displays a form with a single OLE container control on the form, which contains an embedded Paintbrush object (a smiley face). Whenever one of the menus is clicked, the active control on the screen is checked to see whether it is an OLE object. If it is, menu choices such as Cut, Copy, Paste, and Info are enabled in the Edit menu. The File menu options are enabled based on the value of the Boolean variable oleChanged. If a change has been made to the OLE object, then the Save Object option is enabled; otherwise, it is not.

Although this project is simple, it does use many of the basic tools you would use in a more complex OLE application. If you want to add some functionality to this project, try adding more OLE container controls to the form and adding code to handle each of them. Also, try embedding and linking objects other than Paintbrush objects. If you have Microsoft Word, Microsoft Excel, or other applications that support OLE, you should be able to embed or link objects from those applications. Using this project as a starting point, you are in a position to create a powerful OLE application in Visual Basic.

76

OLE AUTOMATION

Object Linking and Embedding (OLE) gives your application the power to directly use and manipulate another application's data in its native format. If the other application supports OLE automation, you may also be able to use its objects, properties, and methods just as you would a Visual Basic control. In effect, you can make the other application an integral part of your own application. OLE 2.0 was one of the most significant new features of Visual Basic 3.0, and its usefulness was maintained and enhanced in Visual Basic 4.0, and extended further in Visual Basic 5.0. OLE automation is one of the most important additions to Windows and serves as the basis for creating a true object-oriented environment.

   This chapter gives an overview of OLE automation and a thorough discussion of every property, event, and function necessary for fully implementing OLE automation in your applications.

OLE Automation versus Custom Controls

Some OLE 2.0-capable programs allow OLE automation, which exposes that application's features to your Visual Basic program as properties and methods. This means that applications that support OLE automation behave almost exactly like Visual Basic custom controls.

   The primary difference between a custom control and OLE automation lies in distribution: It is easy to distribute Visual Basic custom controls, which are designed to be distributed as part of Visual Basic programs. An application that supports OLE automation, on the other hand, is generally a full commercial application and legally cannot be distributed without the end user's purchasing that application.

   As OLE automation matures and more applications are written to support it, this situation may well change to make distribution of runtime libraries easier. For example, the Access runtime engine supplied with Visual Basic 5.0 functions in many ways like an OLE 2.0 object with full automation. Although this is a hybrid product and isn't implemented exactly like an OLE object, the ease of use and power it brings to Visual Basic gives a glimpse into what we can expect in the future.

OLE automation also differs from custom controls in that commercial applications that support OLE 2.0 tend to be large and slow to load. You'll incur performance penalties when first creating an OLE automation object (as the host application loads into memory) and will certainly sacrifice larger amounts of disk space than you would with smaller, more specialized custom controls.

Visual Basic Object Browser

Each OLE application exposes its features differently. You can explore the exposed objects of some applications using the Visual Basic Object Browser. In order to explore the exposed objects of an OLE application, you must first add a reference to that application's objects using the References choice of the Visual Basic Tools menu. Figure 76-1 shows how the References dialog box might appear. Not all applications will appear in the References dialog box. In general, applications that supply an *object library* file (file extension .OLB) which contains information about that application's exposed objects will appear in the References dialog box. To add the OLE application reference to your Visual Basic program, simply click inside the check box to the left of that application in the References dialog box. If an application does not make a list of its exposed objects available through the Object Browser, then you must refer to that application's documentation to determine the proper syntax for using its objects, properties, and methods. Many of the examples in this chapter use hypothetical sets of properties and methods from hypothetical applications.

Once you have added the reference to an OLE application, you should be able to view its objects, properties, and methods using the Visual Basic Object Browser. You can activate the Object Browser by choosing Object Browser from the View menu, by pressing [F2], or by pressing the Object Browser button on the Visual Basic toolbar.

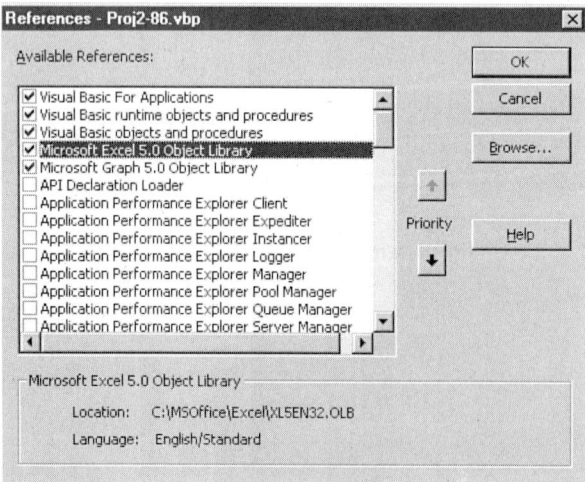

Figure 76-1 The References dialog box

Figure 76-2 shows the Object Browser listing objects exposed by the Microsoft Excel application. In the figure, the Range function's parameters are displayed in the bottom panel. The Object Browser shows you all the exposed functions, procedures, methods, properties, and constants of the OLE application.

Creating OLE Automation Objects

Applications that expose their objects for use with OLE automation are known as OLE servers. Applications that access OLE servers are known as OLE clients. You can create objects using these OLE servers and the Visual Basic Dim statement.

The Dim statement sets aside storage for an OLE automation object in much the same way that it sets aside storage for standard variable types such as Integer, Single, String, and so on. Here is the general syntax for using the Dim statement to create storage for an OLE automation object:

```
Dim myObj As server.someobject
```

In this example, *server* would be the name of the OLE application that is exposing its objects and *someobject* would be the name of the object class for which you want to create storage. For example, to create a new Excel worksheet, you would need a Dim statement similar to the following:

```
Dim myWork As Excel.Worksheet
```

You then can use the Set statement and other techniques described in the next section to make use of your newly created OLE automation object.

If you are using the Enterprise or Professional Edition of Visual Basic 5.0, you will also be able to create your own ActiveX OLE server applications that expose object classes you have created.

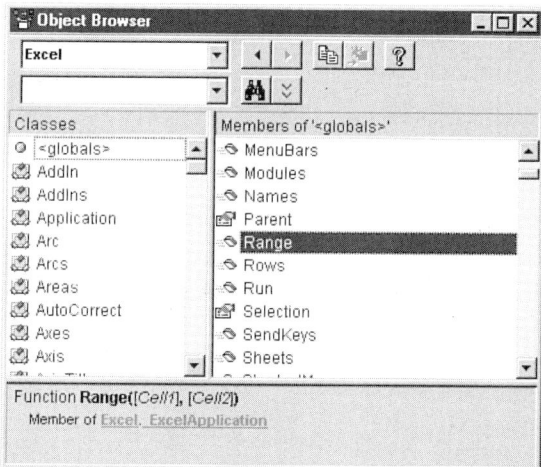

Figure 76-2   Using the Object Browser to explore the exposed objects of Microsoft Excel

Using OLE Automation Objects

Let's assume that a spreadsheet application supports OLE automation. You've embedded a spreadsheet in Ole1, and you'd like to format the data displayed in cell R4C5:

```
Private Sub Command1_Click ()
    Ole1.Object.Select "R4C5"                'select cell
    Ole1.Object.Bold True                    'turn on Bold
    Ole1.Object.Border True, 2, TOP + LEFT   'make 2 pt border on top & left
End Sub
```

This example uses the originating application (the spreadsheet) to format the information stored in the Ole1 control. See the Object property later in this chapter for more information about how to do this.

You can also use another application's properties and methods without using the OLE control. For example, let's say you want to perform a complex financial calculation that returns the number of periods for a loan. Rather than writing all the code necessary to perform the calculation, you could use the spreadsheet application's NPer function to do it for you. First, create an object that you then can manipulate by declaring a variable of type Object. Then set that object appropriately with the CreateObject function:

```
Private Function NumPeriods (rate, payment, presentValue) As Integer
    Dim sheet As Object
    Set sheet = CreateObject("SPREADSHT.WORKSHEET")
    NumPeriods = sheet.NPer(rate, payment, presentValue)
End Function
```

Unlike using the OLE control as in the first example, this example does not display the spreadsheet anywhere, and your Visual Basic application doesn't contain any embedded data. The CreateObject function is covered more thoroughly in its own entry later in this chapter.

Many applications that support OLE automation also have *collections*. A collection is an object that contains zero or more objects of a similar type. For instance, each row in a spreadsheet might be called a Row object, and the collection of all rows on the spreadsheet might be called the Rows collection. Most collections support the Count property, which gives the total number of members in the collection. This makes it easy for your application to iterate through an entire collection. This next example takes our hypothetical spreadsheet and places the value of each cell in an array by iterating through the Rows collection:

```
Private Sub GetValues (worksheetName)
    Dim sheet As Object
    Set sheet = CreateObject("SPREADSHT.WORKSHEET")
    sheet.Activate worksheetName
    rows = sheet.Rows.Count - 1
    cols = sheet.Columns.Count - 1
    ReDim Vals(rows, cols)     'Global level array
    For i = 0 To rows
        For j = 0 To cols
            Vals(i, j) = sheet.Rows(i).Cell(j).Value
        Next j
    Next i
End Function
```

You cannot assume that an application has collections, or that any collections that it does have contain numeric subscripts, or that any of its numeric subscripts are contiguous. You'll need to examine the application's documentation for the details on how to access its objects and collections.

All arguments to OLE automation objects are of the Variant data type, and all returned values are also Variants. Visual Basic will automatically convert a variable to a Variant if you attempt to assign a variable of a different data type to an OLE object argument.

OLE Automation Summary

Table 76-1 lists the properties and functions particular to OLE automation.

Table 76-1 Functions of OLE automation

Use This...	To Do This...
CreateObject	Function: Create an object for OLE automation
GetObject	Function: Load an object for OLE automation
Object	Property: Access the underlying object in an OLE control for OLE automation

CreateObject Function

Purpose The CreateObject function allows you to create an OLE object for use in OLE automation. Table 76-2 lists the argument of the CreateObject function.

General Syntax

```
CreateObject(className)
```

Table 76-2 Argument of the CreateObject function

Argument	Meaning
className	OLE 2.0-compliant class name, given as "applicationName.objectType"

Example Syntax

```
Private Sub ReverseSound (fileName as String)
    Dim soundFile As Object
    Set soundFile = CreateObject("Recorder.WAVFile")
    soundFile.Load fileName
    soundFile.Reverse
    soundFile.Save fileName
End Sub
```

Description   Use CreateObject to create an object that you manipulate using OLE automation.

To use CreateObject, you must first declare a variable of type Object. You can use Dim, ReDim, Global, or Static to declare the variable. After dimensioning the variable, use the Set keyword to assign the object returned by CreateObject to the variable:

```
Public Chart As Object
Set Chart = CreateObject("Spdsheet.Graph")
```

CreateObject will start the originating application (if it isn't already running) and create the object. The object will not display in your Visual Basic program as it would in an OLE control, and, depending on what you're doing, may not display in the originating application. For instance, if you're just going to use Word for Windows spell checker, nothing displays in either program. You'll give the spell-checking function a word, and it will return a list of suggestions for misspelled words. The data also does not reside in your Visual Basic program unless you create a storage mechanism such as an array or a data file to place it in.

Once you've created the object and put it in the object variable, you use whatever properties and methods are appropriate for that object. In the example syntax, we use three methods on a hypothetical Recorder application. We first create the object variable as described above, then we open fileName using the Recorder's Open method, use the Reverse method to reverse the sound wave, and finally use the Save method to save the file.

Example   The OLE Automation project at the end of this chapter uses OLE automation in two places: cmndGraph_Click and cmndReport_Click. The first use, in cmndGraph_Click, accesses the OLE object through the Object property; see that entry for more about how to use it. The second use, in cmndReport_Click, uses CreateObject and GetObject interchangeably. Note that the chapter project's example is specific to Word 6.0 for Windows and will not work with any other application unless you modify it.

Comment   Many applications may not support OLE at all, and those that do may not support the advanced feature of OLE automation. Applications that do support OLE automation will have different properties and methods available. You'll need to carefully check that application's documentation for the exact terminology and usage.

Even scouring the host application's documentation may leave you confused and frustrated as you attempt to control the application through OLE automation. One trick that may make it a bit easier is to record a macro in the host application to do what you want. (This trick obviously requires that the host application has a macro language! Applications that support OLE 2.0 will almost always have some sort of macro or programming language.) Edit the macro in the host application, and test it to be sure it works correctly. Once you're satisfied with the macro, copy it to your Visual Basic application and prefix each line with the object name.

For example, recording a macro in Word for Windows 6.0 lets you determine that the following line selects all the text in the document:

```
EditSelectAll
```

Once we've determined this, it's easy to create an OLE automation routine that does the same thing in Visual Basic:

```
Dim wordProc As Object
    Set wordProc = CreateObject("Word.Basic")
'
    wordProc.EditSelectAll
```

GetObject Function

Purpose   GetObject retrieves an object from a file for use in OLE automation. It is not available at design time, and is read-only at runtime. Table 76-3 summarizes the arguments of the GetObject function.

Example Syntax

```
GetObject(fileName$[, className])
```

Table 76-3 Arguments of the GetObject function

Argument	Meaning
fileNameS	Filename of the file to use, and an optional topic prefaced by an exclamation point (!)
className	OLE 2.0-compliant class name in the form "applicationName.objectType"

Example Syntax

```
Private Sub Command1_Click ()
    Dim map As Object                              'declare object variable
    Set map = GetObject("C:\MAPS\USA.CDR!Layer1")  'drawing of the US
    map.Select "Borders"                           'select named range
    map.Copy                                 'copy to Clipboard
    Picture1.Picture = Clipboard.GetData()   'paste Clipboard to picture
End Sub
```

Description   Use the GetObject function to retrieve an object for use in OLE automation. You first must declare a variable of type Object using Dim, ReDim, Global, or Static. Then, set the variable to the object returned by the GetObject function. The example syntax shows how to do this with a map of the United States. It then goes on to issue the (hypothetical) automation commands to select just the borders and copy them to the Clipboard. The contents of the Clipboard are then pasted into Picture1.

The fileName$ argument can be an empty string or a full path and filename with an optional range. If it is an empty string, the className argument is required. GetObject then returns the currently active object of the specified type. An error occurs if there is no active object of that type.

If fileName$ is a filename, GetObject starts the originating application if it is not already running and retrieves that particular file. Filenames can have an optional range argument appended to them after an exclamation point (!) for applications that support retrieving just a part of a file. For instance, many spreadsheets support retrieving either a named range of cells or a range of cells given in the familiar RC style:

```
GetObject("C:\EXCEL\BUDGETS\Q1ACTUAL.XLS!R1C1:R20C10")
```

If you do not specify className, Visual Basic automatically determines the correct application to run from the HKEY_CLASSES_ROOT key of the registry. Some applications, however, support more than one class type for an object. For instance, if the spreadsheet supports class types for the actual worksheet, embedded charts, and the toolbar, you need to specify the type in the className:

```
GetObject("C:\EXCEL\BUDGETS\Q1ACTUAL.XLS!R1C1:R20C10", "Excel.Worksheet")
```

See the entry for CreateObject for more information about OLE automation.

Example   The OLE Automation project at the end of this chapter uses CreateObject and GetObject interchangeably in the cmndReport_Click event.

OBJECT PROPERTY

Objects Affected   OLE.

Purpose   The Object property allows you to access the underlying object in an OLE control for use in OLE automation. It is not available at design time, and is read-only at runtime. Table 76-4 summarizes the arguments of the Object property.

General Syntax

```
[form!]Name.Object.[property|method] [ = settings]
```

Table 76-4 Arguments of the Object property

Argument	Meaning
form	Name property of the parent form
Name	Name property of the control
property	Appropriate property of the object
method	Appropriate method of the object
settings	Appropriate arguments for the property or method

Example Syntax

```
Private Sub Command1_Click ()
    Ole1.Object.Bold = True
    Ole1.Object.Insert = "This is some text."
    Ole1.Object.SaveAs "C:\TEMP\TEST.DOC" add a "=" sign after SaveAs just to be ⇐
    consistent
End Sub
```

Description

The Object property allows you to manipulate the OLE control's object with OLE automation. Contrast this technique with the CreateObject and GetObject functions: the Object property manipulates the object in an OLE control, whereas the functions allow you to assign an object to an object variable, which you then manipulate. If you have embedded an OLE container on your Visual Basic form, then you can use the Object property, but if you are using OLE automation and have not embedded an OLE container, you need to use the CreateObject and GetObject functions to manipulate your OLE automation object.

Every originating application that supports OLE automation makes available a different set of properties and methods. Consult the application's documentation for the details and syntax of supported properties and methods. The example syntax shows the Object property being used to issue the (hypothetical) automation commands to make the font bold, insert some text, and then save the document to a file.

Early and Late Binding

When you declare an object variable As Object, the object variable can refer to any type of object, but access to that object is *late bound*. That means that the object is bound to the OLE server when the application is run, which degrades performance. By declaring the object with a specific class ID, binding takes place when the program is compiled, which is called *early binding*. Early binding improves performance. In the example syntax below, both of the object variables are set to the same kind of object, but objXL1 is early bound and objXL2 is late bound.

```
Dim XL1 as Excel.Application ' Early bound
Dim XL2 as Object ' Late bound
Set XL1 = CreateObject("Excel.Application")
Set XL2 = CreateObject("Excel.Application")
```

Releasing Objects

Leaving object references hanging around when you no longer need them is not only impolite, it is a waste of precious system resources. You can close a program with the End statement, but there is no assurance that the objects that the program created will be cleared from memory. Use Set to release the object references, as shown below:

```
Set XL1 = Nothing
Set XL2 = Nothing
```

OLE Automation Project

This project can be used both as a general introduction to OLE no matter what applications you have on your system, and as a specific demonstration of OLE automation techniques if you have a copy of Excel 5.0, Microsoft Graph, and Word 6.0 for Windows.

We implement a full OLE-aware Edit menu, and demonstrate both OLE file open and file save techniques. This will be useful to you in any application that uses OLE.

The OLE automation techniques are, by nature, specific to individual host applications. If you don't need the required applications, you'll still find the general techniques and approaches quite useful, although you'll obviously need to change the application-specific commands.

Assembling the Project

1. Place the following controls on a form, as detailed in Table 76-5. After placing the controls on the form, use the Menu Design dialog box to create the menu structure detailed in Table 76-6. Figure 76-3 shows what the completed form should look like.

Table 76-5 Elements of formMain

Control	Property	Value
Form	Name	formMain
	BorderStyle	1 - Fixed Single
	Caption	"OLE Automation Project"
Command	Name	cmndReport
	Caption	"Create &Report"
Command	Name	cmndGraph
	Caption	"Create &Graph"
OLE	Name	ole
	AutoVerbMenu	0 - False
	BorderStyle	0 - None
	Index	0
OLE	Name	ole
	AutoVerbMenu	0 - False
	BorderStyle	1 - Fixed Single
	Index	1
OLE	Name	ole
	AutoVerbMenu	0 - False
	BorderStyle	1 - Fixed Single
	Index	2
menuBar	&File	0

Control	Property	Value
menuFile	&Open Objects	0
menuFile	&Save Objects	1
menuFile	-	2
menuFile	E&xit	3
menuBar	&Edit	1
menuEdit	Cu&t	0
menuEdit	&Copy	1
menuEdit	&Paste	2
menuEdit	-	3
menuEdit	Paste &Special	4
menuEdit	Insert &Object	5

Table 76-6 Menu structure for formMain

Name	Caption	Index
menuEdit	-	6
menuEdit	&Info	7
menuDoc	(POPUP)	
menuDOCPop	&Generate	0
menuDOCPop	&Copy	1
menuDOCPop		2

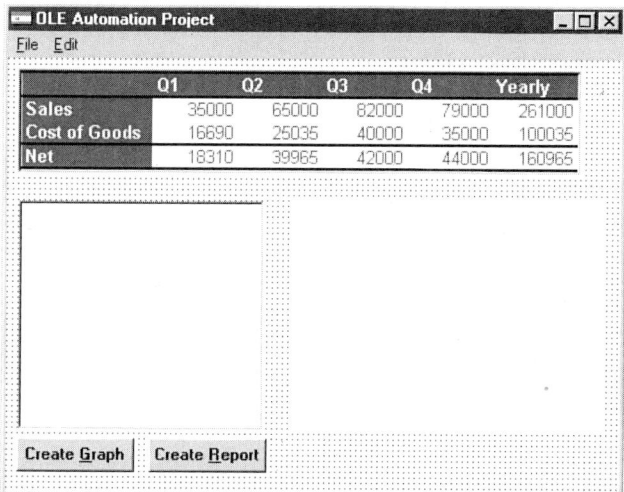

Figure 76-3   What formMain should look like at design time

2. Enter the following constant definitions into the Declarations section in the General Section of formMain.

```
Const DOC = 0
Const GRAPH = 1
Const SHEET = 2

Const DEFAULT = 0
Const HOURGLASS = 11

Dim oleChanged(3) As Integer
```

3. Enter the following code in the cmndGraph_Click event. This reads the information from the spreadsheet object and displays it as a graph object. It first accesses a range of numbers on the spreadsheet through OLE automation by way of the OLE container's Object property. Remember, we can use the Object property to manipulate this object because we have embedded an OLE container onto our form. In other cases where we have not embedded an OLE container, we can use OLE automation with the help of the CreateObject and GetObject functions. Note that the line that copies the range onto the Clipboard is specific to the spreadsheet host application—Excel 5.0 in this case. Once the data has been placed on the Clipboard, it's easy to create a new object in the graph OLE container and send text to it with the DataText property. The spreadsheet places the information on the Clipboard in the correct format: Each column is tab-delimited, each row is carriage return-delimited.

```
Private Sub cmndGraph_Click ()

 This routine relies on having Excel 5.0 or greater and MSGraph 1.0
' or greater. It will bomb unless you have both applications.
' The general techniques will work for OLE automation, but any line
' commented with ( >> ) is host-application specific

    OLE(SHEET).Verb = vbVerbHide        'keep app hidden
    OLE(SHEET).Activate 'activate host
    OLE(SHEET).Object.Range("QuarterlyFigures").Copy '>> copy to Clipboard
    AppActivate "OLE Automation Project" 'back to the project

    quarterlyFigures = Clipboard.GetText() 'contents of Clipboard

    OLE(GRAPH).Verb = vbVerbHide 'keep app hidden
    OLE(GRAPH).Format = "CF_TEXT" 'we're sending text
    OLE(GRAPH).CreateEmbed "", "MSGraph" 'embedded object
    OLE(GRAPH).Activate 'activate host
    OLE(GRAPH).DataText = quarterlyFigures 'send it the figures
    OLE(GRAPH).Update 'and update the display

End Sub
```

4. Enter the following code in the cmndReport_Click event. This analyzes the sales trends shown by the sales figures in the spreadsheet object and creates a formatted document using OLE automation. The first few lines access the spreadsheet through the OLE container's Object property with OLE automation. Once the sales figures have been obtained, the routine calculates the overall trend (down, even, or up). It then calls a subroutine that makes up a sales talk based on the results.

The next section formats the document using OLE automation. Word 6.0 for Windows does not support any OLE automation objects other than Word Basic (its macro language), so we restrict ourselves to using it exclusively. First, the routine alternates between the two methods of OLE automation, CreateObject and GetObject. Either method works well in this context, the only difference being that GetObject uses an existing document as a *template* to paste the text into, whereas CreateObject starts fresh with a new document. Once the object is created, a series of Word Basic statements are sent to the host via OLE automation. These format the document with full justification and drop caps, a job well-suited to advanced word processors and obviously easier than attempting the formatting ourselves within Visual Basic.

Finally, we issue a Word Basic command to save the object to disk. Note that the object has never been displayed anywhere, and has up to this point existed only as automation object. We set the OLE container's parameters appropriately to finally display the finished product by reading it in from the disk file.

```
Private Sub cmndReport_Click ()

'This routine relies on having Excel 5.0 or greater and Winword 6.0 or greater.
'It will bomb unless you have both applications. The general techniques will
'work for OLE automation, but any line commented with ( >> ) is host-application
'specific

        MousePointer = HOURGLASS              'going to be awhile
        ReDim q(4) As Long                    'four quarter's figures
        Dim wordProc As Object                'for word processor
        Dim avg1 As Long, avg2 As Long        'quarterly averages
        Static createOrGet As Integer         'two ways of automation

        OLE(SHEET).Verb = vbVerbHide          'keep app hidden
        For i = 1 To 4                        'for each of the 4 quarters,
            q(i) = ⇐OLE(SHEET).Object.Range("SalesFigures").Cells(1, i).Value
                                              '>> get the sales total
        Next i
        OLE(SHEET).Close         'close the host
        AppActivate "OLE Automation Project"          'the project

        avg1 = (q(1) + q(2)) / 2                      'first half of year
        avg2 = (q(3) + q(4)) / 2                      'second half of year
        textToSet = CreateSpiel(avg1, avg2)           'make up the sales talk

'You can use either CreateObject or GetObject for OLE automation.
' This block alternates between the two methods. CreateObject creates
' an automation object out of "thin air," while GetObject uses an
' existing word processor document as a "template."

        If createOrGet = False Then                   'use CreateObject?
            Set wordProc = CreateObject("Word.Basic")'create the object
            wordProc.filenew                          '>> create a new document
```

continued on next page

continued from previous page

```
                'NOTE: Word 6.0 doesn't support "getting" an object, it only
                'supports creating a WordBasic object.  Remove the comment on
                'this next line if you want to experiment with another object as
                'an OLE server
                'createOrGet = True            'flip the flag for next time

        Else
            Set wordProc = GetObject(App.Path & "\CHP76BLK.DOC")  'blank template
            createOrGet = False               'flip the flag for next time
        End If
        DoEvents                                  'give the system some time
        wordProc.FilePageSetup 0, 0, .2, .2, .2, .2, 0,  "1.6 in", "10 in"
                                                  '>> set document margins
        wordProc.Insert textToSel                 '>> sales talk
        wordProc.EditSelectAll                    '>> select entire document
        wordProc.FormatParagraph .1, .1, .1, 8, 0, 0, 3 '>> paragraph spacing
        wordProc.FormatFont 8                     '>> set font to 8 point
        wordProc.StartOfDocument                  '>> goto beginning
        wordProc.FormatDropCap 1, , 2, 1          '>> format first letter
        wordProc.ParaDown 1                       '>> goto next paragraph
        wordProc.FormatDropCap 1, , 2, 1          '>> format first letter
        wordProc.FileSaveAs App.Path & "\oledoc.dat" '>> save document
        wordProc.FileCloseAll 2                   '>> close documents

        OLE(DOC).OLETypeAllowed = vbOLEEither  'either linked or embedded
        OLE(DOC).CreateEmbed App.Path & "\oledoc.dat", "Word.Document"  'create an embedded ⇐
                                                          document

        MousePointer = DEFAULT                 'all done!

    End Sub
```

5. Type the following routine into the Declarations section. This function creates a sales talk when given two parameters. It rather simplistically calculates a trend in the two arguments (downward, even, upward) and creates the appropriate text.

```
Private Function CreateSpiel (a1 As Long, a2 As Long) As String

'create a sales talk, with different verbage dependent on last year's results
    Select Case Sgn(a2 - a1)         'down, even, or upward trend?
        Case -1
            results = "Although sales declined overall for the year, "
            results = results & "we anticipate phenomonal growth next year!"
        Case 0
            results = "Sales were relatively flat throughout the year. "
            results = results & "The strengthening economy will help us set "
            results = results & "new productivity records next year!"
        Case 1

            results = "Sales were up, up, up! We had a fantastic year, with"
            results = results & "even better prospects for next year!"
    End Select
    spiel = "Our five year goals have been met. "
    spiel = spiel & "PSA has experienced tremendous growth over the past "
    spiel = spiel & "five years, and our higher level of partnership with "
    spiel = spiel & "Puryear Enterprises sets us up for even higher levels "
    spiel = spiel & "of growth in the future!" & Chr$(13)
    spiel = spiel & "Set your sights high! The past year's sales results "
```

```
          spiel = spiel & " are quite encouraging. "
          spiel = spiel & results

          CreateSpiel = spiel

End Function
```

6. Type the following code into the Form_Load event. This routine sets some of the OLE containers' properties.

```
Private Sub Form_Load ()

    For i = DOC to SHEET                                  for each OLE container,
        OLE(i).HostName = "OLE Automation Project"     'set the host name
        OLE(i).DisplayType = vbOLEDisplayContent       'and display type
    Next i

    OLE(DOC).AutoVerbMenu = False            'does not have automatic menus
    OLE(GRAPH).AutoVerbMenu = True           'has automatic menus
    OLE(SHEET).AutoVerbMenu = True           'has automatic menus

End Sub
```

7. Type the following code into the menuBar_Click event. This event triggers when the user first pulls down a menu, and it enables the menu options appropriate to the context. The File menu checks to see if any of the containers' objects have changed, and enables the Save option if they have. The Edit menu checks to see if the focus is on an OLE container. If so, then it will enable the Cut, Copy, and Info commands if there is an object currently in the container, and will enable the Paste and Paste Special commands if there is something on the Clipboard that can be pasted.

```
Private Sub menuBar_Click (Index As Integer)

    Select Case Index
        Case 0 '*********** File
            menuFile(1).Enabled = False              'turn off save
            For i = DOC To SHEET                     'go through containers
                If oleChanged(i) = True Then         'if it has changed,
                    menuFile(1).Enabled = True 'then enable File Save
                End If
            Next i
        Case 1 '*********** Edit
            For i = 0 To 7                                'iterate through Edit
                                                         'menu commands (except
                                                         'separator bars)
                If (I <> 3 And I  <>  6) Then menuEdit(i).Enabled = False
                                                         'and turn them off
            Next i
            Dim s As Control
            Set s = Screen.ActiveControl             'control that has focus
            If TypeOf s Is OLE Then                   'if it's OLE control,
                menuEdit(5).Enabled = True           'enable Insert Object
                If s.OLEType <>  vbOLENone Then 'if it's got an object
                    menuEdit(0).Enabled = True 'enable Cut
                    menuEdit(1).Enabled = True 'enable Copy
```

continued on next page

continued from previous page

```
                            menuEdit(7).Enabled = True 'enable Info
                    End If
                    If s.PasteOK Then                   'if the Clipboard has
                                                        'a pastable object
                            menuEdit(2).Enabled = True 'enable Paste
                            menuEdit(4).Enabled = True 'enable Paste Special
                    End If
            End If
    End Select

End Sub
```

8. Type the following code into the menuDOCPop_Click routine. This event runs when the user chooses a command from the pop-up menu, which is triggered by a right mouse click on the document OLE container. The menu is built in the OLE containers' MouseDown event, and has two static menu choices, a separator bar, and then a variable number of menu commands as determined by the object's verbs. This routine first removes all the variable menu items (the verbs) to prepare the menu structure for the next time the user right-clicks the OLE container. It then calls the appropriate routine for the first two choices, and sets the appropriate verb for the variable menu items.

```
Private Sub menuDOCPop_Click (Index As Integer)

    On Error GoTo noMoreItems           'no more menu items (verbs)
    i = 3                               'custom menu items begin after
                                        'separator bar
    Do
        Unload menuDOCPop(i)            'get rid of custom menu item
        i = i + 1                       'and go to next one
    Loop

noMoreItems:                            'ok, we've zapped all the verbs!
    On Error GoTo 0

    Select Case Index                   'choose the correct menu item
        Case 0 ' ---- Generate
            cmndReport_Click            'generate the sales talk again
        Case 1 ' ---- Copy
            menuEdit_Click 1            'copy to the Clipboard
        Case 2 ' ---- Separator bar
        Case Is > 2                     'if it was a custom item (that is,
                                        'an object verb)
            OLE(DOC).DoVerb Index - 2   'perform the verb appropriately
    End Select
    Exit Sub

End Sub
```

9. Type the following code into the menuEdit_Click routine. This routine triggers when the user chooses a command from the Edit menu. Note that the menuBar_Click routine enables only commands that are appropriate for the context, so we don't have to perform any additional checks in this routine. For example, we can assume that there is acceptable data already on the Clipboard and that we're on an OLE container that can accept it if either of the Paste commands was selected. As you can see, the code to implement an OLE-aware Edit menu is not very involved.

```
Private Sub menuEdit_Click (Index As Integer)
    Dim s As Control
    Set s = Screen.ActiveControl              'control that has focus
    formMain.MousePointer = HOURGLASS         'we're going to be awhile
    Select Case Index
        Case 0 '*********** Cut
            If Not s.AppIsRunning Then        'if host app isn't running,
                s.DoVerb = vbVerbHide         'make sure it stays hidden
            End If
            s.Copy                            'copy object to Clipboard
            s.Delete                          'and get rid of it
        Case 1 '*********** Copy
            If Not s.AppIsRunning Then        'if host app isn't running,
                s.DoVerb = vbVerbHide         'make sure it stays hidden
            End If
            s.Copy                            'copy object to Clipboard
        Case 2 '*********** Paste
            s.Class = "temp"                  'If OLE container has never
                                              'been used, class needs to
                                              'be set to something (but
                                              'doesn't matter what)
            s.Paste                           'Paste the contents of
                                              'Clipboard into container.
        Case 3 '*********** (separator bar)
        Case 4 '*********** Paste Special
            s.PasteSpecialDlg                 'open Paste Special dialog
        Case 5 '*********** Insert Object
            s.InsertObjDlg                    'open Insert Object dialog
        Case 6 ' *********** Separator Bar
        Case 7 ' *********** Info
            printInfo s                       'print info about object
    End Select

    If s.OLEType  vbOLENone Then              'object in the OLE container?
        s.Close                               'close host
        s.Refresh                             'and update display
    End If
    formMain.MousePointer = DEFAULT           'all done!

End Sub
```

10. Type the following code into the menuFile_Click event. This event triggers when the user chooses a command from the File menu. The Open and Save options are very similar, differing only in what we specify for the OLE Action property. In both cases, we simply open the appropriate file as a Binary file, pass the file number to the OLE containers, and make the OLE container take the appropriate action. This allows the user to both save and open embedded OLE objects without using the host application's save or open functions.

```
Private Sub menuFile_Click (Index As Integer)

    Select Case Index
```

continued on next page

continued from previous page

```
        Case 0 ' ********** Open objects
            fileNum = FreeFile                      'get a file handle
            Open App.Path & "\oleobject.dat" For Binary As fileNum   'open
            For i = DOC To SHEET                     'iterate through containers
                If OLE(i).OLEType <> vbOLENone Then    'if it's got an object in it,
                    OLE(i).ReadFromFile fileNum  'get object from file
                End If
                oleChanged(i) = False              'disable saving
            Next i
            Close fileNum                          'close the file
        Case 1 ' ********** Save objects
            fileNum = FreeFile                     'get a file handle
            Open App.Path & "\oleobject.dat" For Binary As fileNum   'open
            For i = DOC To SHEET                     'iterate through containers
                If OLE(i).OLEType <> VbOLENone Then       'if it's got an object
                    OLE(i).SaveToFile fileNum    'save the object
                End If
                oleChanged(i) = False              'disable saving
            Next i
            Close fileNum                          'close the file
        Case 2 ' ********** (separator bar)
        Case 3                    End
    End Select

End Sub
```

11. Type the following code into the OLE_MouseDown event. This triggers whenever the user clicks on any of the OLE containers. We first filter the event to recognize only right mouse clicks on the document container (the lower-right OLE control), and check to make sure it's got an object currently in it. If so, we add whatever verbs it supports in its current state to the pop-up menu, and then display the menu.

```
Private Sub OLE_MouseDown (Index As Integer, Button As Integer, Shift As Integer, ⇐
X As _ Single, Y As Single)

    If Button = 2 And Index = DOC And OLE(DOC).OLEType <> vbOLENone Then
                                'right button, on doc, with an object in it:
        OLE(DOC).FetchVerbs       'update the available verbs
        For i = 1 To OLE(DOC).ObjectVerbsCount - 1 'iterate through each verb
            Load menuDOCPop(2 + i)                  'add a new menu item for verb
            menuDOCPop(2 + i).Caption = OLE(DOC).ObjectVerbs(i) 'and add the verb
        Next i
        PopupMenu menuDOC                          'pop up the menu
    End If

End Sub '
```

12. Type the following code into the OLE_Resize event. This event triggers whenever the OLE containers' object changes size. We first filter it to recognize only changes to the document container. If the change occurred in that container, we limit the maximum size the container can assume.

```
Private Sub OLE_Resize (Index As Integer, HeightNew As Single, WidthNew As Single)
    If Index = DOC Then                        'just for the sales talk,
```

```
          If HeightNew > 3100 Then HeightNew = 3100    'don't exceed these
          If WidthNew > 2532 Then WidthNew =  2532     'maximum dimensions
     End If

End Sub
```

13. Type the following code into the OLE_Updated event. This triggers whenever the object in the OLE container gets updated. We check to see if the kind of update is for changed data (Code = 0), and if so, flag the global tracking array so the menuFile_Click event can enable the File Save Objects command.

```
Private Sub OLE_Updated (Index As Integer, Code As Integer)

     If Code = 0 Then oleChanged(Index) = True       'if object has changed, then
                                                      'flag it to enable saving

End Sub
```

14. Type the following code into the Declarations section of formMain. This routine prints out pertinent information about the current OLE container. It displays a blank form, and prints out some of the underlying details about the object.

```
Private Sub printInfo (s As Control)

     MousePointer = HOURGLASS
     formInfo.Show                     'show info form
     formInfo!pictInfo.Cls             'wipe it clean
     If Not s.AppIsRunning Then        'If the host isn't running
         s.DoVerb vbVerbHide           'make sure it stays hidden.
     End If
     formInfo.Print
     formInfo.Print " Class:";
     formInfo.Print Tab(20); s.Class    'host class
     formInfo.Print
     formInfo.Print " Accept Formats:"; 'host accepted formats,
     For i = 0 To s.ObjectAcceptFormatsCount - 1        'iterating through each one
         formInfo.Print Tab(20); s.ObjectAcceptFormats(i)
     Next i
     formInfo.Print
     formInfo.Print " Return Formats:";      'host returned formats,
     For i = 0 To s.ObjectGetFormatsCount - 1 'iterating through each one
         formInfo.Print Tab(20); s.ObjectGetFormats(i)
     Next i
     formInfo.Print
     formInfo.Print " Verbs:";                'host verbs,
     For i = 1 To s.ObjectVerbsCount - 1       'iterating through each one
         formInfo.Print Tab(20); s.ObjectVerbs(i); Tab(40);
         Select Case s.ObjectVerbFlags(i)      'and print the menu state
             Case vbVerbFlagChecked: formInfo.Print "Checked"
             Case vbVerbFlagDisabled: formInfo.Print "Disabled"
             Case vbVerbFlagEnabled: formInfo.Print "Enabled"
             Case vbVerbFlagGrayed: formInfo.Print "Grayed"
             Case vbVerbFlagSeparator: formInfo.Print "Separator"
         End Select
     Next i

     formInfo.Print
```

continued on next page

continued from previous page

```
        formInfo.Print "  Long Pointer: ";              'memory position of object
        formInfo.Print Tab(20); Hex$(s.LpOleObject)     '(could use with API calls)

        formInfo.Print
        s.Format = "Native"
        formInfo.Print "  Data:";                       'print the GDI handle
        formInfo.Print Tab(20); Hex$(s.Data)

End Sub
Assembling the Project: formInfo
```

15. Create a new form to display the information printed by formMain's Edit Info command. Table 76-7 details the components of the form. Size and position the elements as illustrated in Figure 76-4.

Table 76-7 Elements of formInfo

Control	Property	Value
Form	BorderStyle	1 - Fixed Single
	Name	formInfo
Command	Cancel	-1 - True
	Caption	Close
	Default	-1 - True
	Name	cmndClose
PictureBox	Name	PictInfo
PictureBox	Name	PictContainer
VScrollBar	Name	Scrl

16. Type the following code into the cmndClose_Click event. This hides the form from view.

```
Private Sub cmndClose_Click ()
     Me.Hide
End Sub
```

17. Type the following code into the Form_Load event. This sets the predefined properties to the picture boxes and the vertical scrollbar.

```
Private Sub Form_Load()
    pictInfo.Left = 0
    pictInfo.Top = 0
    pictInfo.Width = pictContainer.ScaleWidth
    pictInfo.Height = 3 * pictContainer.ScaleHeight
    scrl.Min = 0
    scrl.Max = pictInfo.Height
    scrl.LargeChange = scrl.Max \ 20
    scrl.SmallChange = scrl.Max \ 100

End Sub
```

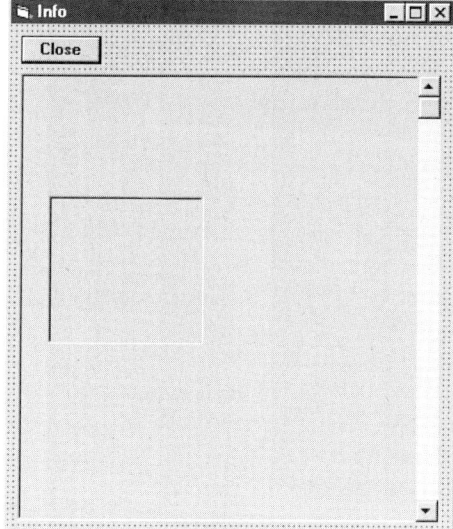

Figure 76-4 formInfo at design time

18. Type the following code into the scrl_Change event. This makes the information in the picture box scroll down every time the user clicks on the scrollbar.

```
Private Sub scrl_Change()
    pictInfo.Top = -scrl.Value
End Sub
```

How It Works

This project can be used both as a general introduction to OLE no matter what you have on your system, and as a specific demonstration of OLE automation techniques if you have a copy of Excel 5.0 and Word 6.0 for Windows.

When the project first opens, it displays an embedded Excel spreadsheet in the top container, and two empty containers on the bottom of the form. Clicking the Create Graph command button starts a routine that gets the data from the Excel spreadsheet using OLE automation, and then creates a graph using the MSGraph object that comes with Word for Windows (and other Microsoft applications). Clicking on the Create Report command button retrieves different data from the Excel spreadsheet, and then creates a formatted document using OLE automation to access the Word for Windows programming language. The formatting routine applies formatting to the document that would be difficult to achieve by just printing the words on a Visual Basic picture box control—the full justification and drop caps would require quite a bit of computation to determine the exact placement of each letter in the report. It is far simpler to use the power of Word for Windows to do the formatting.

You can also edit each of these objects by right-clicking the mouse on them and choosing either the Edit or Open command from the pop-up menu. Choosing Open will open the document in its own window, with the full power of the host application. Choosing Edit will open the document in place, allowing you to edit it without ever appearing to leave the Visual Basic project. This is the real power of OLE—it would be extraordinarily difficult to implement a full-fledged word processor, spreadsheet, or graphic application on your own, but it's very easy to do this by embedding OLE objects. Figure 76-5 shows what the project looks like after creating both the graph and the document. The document is being edited, and you can see the floating toolbars of Word for Windows.

These demonstrations require that Excel 5.0 or newer, Word for Windows 6.0 or newer, and MSGraph be available on your system, and will not work without them. This is the negative side of OLE automation: You cannot distribute a self-contained Visual Basic application, but must rely on the user's having a certain set of programs.

You'll still find this project useful even if you don't have these programs on your system. Notice that the spreadsheet still appears in the top OLE container even without Excel. Remember that OLE containers display only an image of the data unless they're active. What you're seeing is only a picture of what the spreadsheet looks like. Attempting to activate it will generate an error.

Your system will undoubtedly have at least a few OLE applications registered. At a minimum, most users will have at least Paintbrush and Sound, both of which come with Windows 3.1. You can use the Edit menu's Insert Object command to insert either a new object or retrieve an existing file. Try inserting a bitmap using the Paintbrush application. Once you've inserted the object, you can edit it (right-click to bring up the pop-up menu), cut it, copy it, or get Info on it. If you copy it to the Clipboard, you can paste it into another OLE container, or even into another application. Note that most applications will display the title we gave in the HostName property when referring to the object. You can also save the objects and open them using the File menu commands.

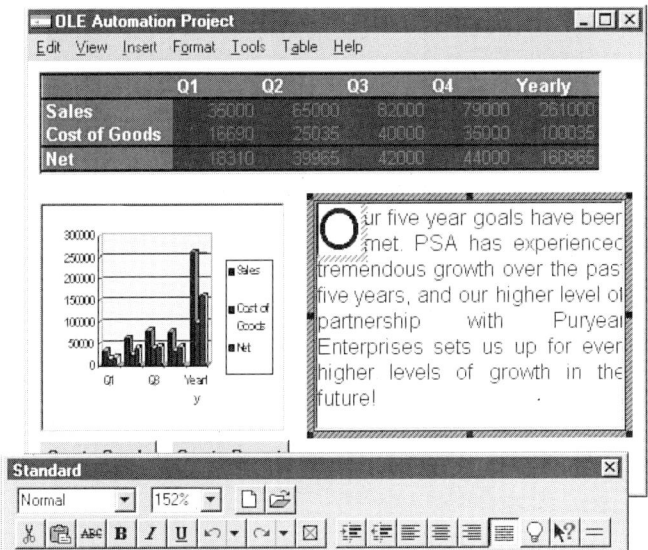

Figure 76-5 The OLE automation project in action

PART XIII
CREATING ADD-INS

77

ADD-IN OVERVIEW

An add-in is an extension of the Visual Basic 5.0 development environment that performs a specific function. For example, the Visual Data Manager add-in allows you to create, modify, and query a number of different database formats such as Access, FoxPro, and Paradox. The goal of this chapter is to give you an idea of the general purpose and functionality of each add-in.

To run an add-in from within Visual Basic, choose the add-in under the Add-Ins menu. The list of add-ins under the Add-Ins menu can be modified by using the Add-In Manager, which is also located under the Add-Ins menu. In the Add-In Manager, an add-in that is checked will be added to the list and an add-in that is not checked will not. This approach is similar to the View|Toolbars approach used in other Microsoft applications.

Visual Data Manager Add-In

Before the Visual Data Manager add-in, if you wanted to create or edit an open database connectivity (ODBC)-type database, you needed database application software such as Access or FoxPro. Of course, you could have written a Visual Basic application yourself to perform actions on multiple database types. If you are at all familiar with database programming in Visual Basic, you know that Visual Basic uses ODBC calls to access databases and their entities. This means that the same function calls are made to any ODBC-compliant database. The Visual Data Manager uses these same ODBC calls to create, edit, and query database tables. The Visual Data Manager provides you with the capability to create, edit, and query databases of any ODBC-compliant format. It also allows you to attach databases of different formats and supports in-program transactions. We will talk more about each of these capabilities in the sections that follow. For now, just think of the Visual Data Manager as a common graphical interface for performing actions on multiple database formats.

Transactions

A database transaction provides a way to release changes to a database. It is similar to the undo action in a text editor. In the text editor, if you make a change and later decide to recall the change, you hit the Undo button. A database transaction runs parallel with this arrangement except that many changes may be "rolled back" at the same time. Once a transaction is started on a database, any changes may be recalled by using a rollback operation. Likewise, any changes may be saved permanently by issuing a commit operation. For example, if an UPDATE query changes records in multiple tables and a rollback is specified, the changes will be disregarded and the tables will remain as they were before the query. But if a commit operation is specified, the table changes will be irreversible (unless you write another query to undo the changes or, for heaven's sake, do it by hand). Once a commit has been issued, even a rollback will not undo the changes. It is not necessary to use transactions, but they are the only way to undo any record changes automatically.

In Visual Data Manager, transaction operations are implemented with three buttons. When the mouse cursor is placed over each, they read "Begin transaction," "Commit current transaction," or "Rollback current transaction." These transaction buttons are the last buttons on the right of the Visual Data Manager toolbar. Keep in mind that transaction operations travel in pairs: If there is a beginning there must be an end (rollback or commit). Also keep in mind that for any task that Visual Data Manager accomplishes with its menu items and buttons, you can accomplish the same task in your Visual Basic code.

Data Form Generation

> **NOTE**
> Data forms can be created only if Visual Data Manager is run from inside Visual Basic as an add-in.

If you are familiar with data bound controls, you realize how much time and coding effort they can save. But wouldn't it be great if there was a program to draw the labels and controls, and even create the form to put them on? Well, now there is. Visual Data Manager will automatically create a Visual Basic form based on table or query results and insert it into your current Visual Basic project. It draws the data bound controls and, yes, it even labels them for you. Figure 77-1 shows a data form created with Visual Data Manager based on a table that consists of three fields: FirstName, MiddleName, and LastName.

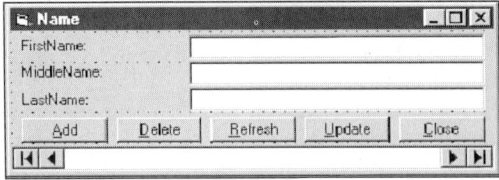

Figure 77-1 Form generated by Visual Data Manager

To create a data form automatically with Visual Data Manager, choose the Utility | Data Form Designer menu item. In the Data Form Designer window that appears, choose your record source from the Record Source combo box. This list contains existing database tables and queries. Once you have chosen your record source, field names will appear in the Available Fields list box. To include fields in your data form, use the arrow buttons. After you are satisfied with your choices, press the Build the Form button.

Query Builder

When you are working with databases, you need a way to extract a subset of information because your database may contain millions of records. Consider, for example, the Department of Motor Vehicle's (DMV's) driver database. When you go to the DMV, you are identified by your social security number (SSN). When the person at the computer types your social security number in, he or she is issuing a query to a database. The query is asking the database for a list of records that match your SSN. You hope that it will return only one record.

Writing database queries can become very complicated, even for people who know Structured Query Language (SQL). SQL is the language used to write queries. Query Builder allows you to build a query in a graphical user interface without having to learn SQL. If you have no idea what SQL can do, it will be very helpful to skim Chapters 62, "Beginning SQL," and 63, "Advanced SQL."

Query Builder can be accessed from the Utility | Query Builder menu item. To build a query in Query Builder, first choose a table name from the Tables list. Then choose a field name from the Field Name combo box. Once you have chosen your field name, you must choose an operator to compare the contents of the table field to what you enter in the Value combo box. After you fill in the Field Name, Operator, and Value boxes, choose the fields you would like displayed in your output. To view the SQL for your query, press the Show button at the bottom of the window. To run the query, press the Run button. Figure 77-2 shows a sample query created in Query Builder.

The Group By or Order By buttons may also be used to group or order your output fields, respectively.

Creating Attachments

Sometimes it is necessary to merge tables from two different databases. This is especially true for companies with existing legacy systems whose databases are used by mainframe programs. In this situation, the company has usually purchased a PC-based database solution such as Microsoft SQL Server or Sybase, but it also needs to keep its existing database intact to use with the older, mainframe software.

Visual Data Manager allows you to attach tables from other databases to your current database. Once attached, the external database table looks and acts as if it is in your current database.

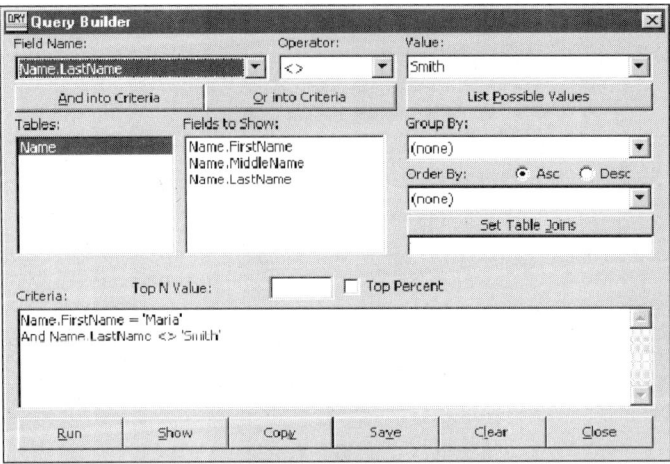

Figure 77-2 Query Builder window

To attach an external table to your database from within Visual Data Manager, select the Utility|Attachment menu item and press New in the Attachments window. In the Attachment Name field, enter a name for your attachment. This can be any alphanumeric string and can include spaces. In the Database Name field, enter the path (or path and filename) to your external database of the type you choose in Connect String. The type of database you choose in Connect String should be the same as the type of database you are going to connect to. If the information you entered in the previous fields is accurate, you will be able to choose a table to connect to in the Table to Attach combo box.

ActiveX Control Interface Wizard Add-In

When creating an ActiveX control, you will probably want to create some properties, events, and methods that are unique to your control. In the past, this had to be done by writing code for each element you wanted to add. This is where the ActiveX Control Interface Wizard makes your job easier. It allows you to create properties, events, and methods in a graphical, wizard-based environment and generates the Visual Basic code for you. You may also use this add-in to edit the existing elements that have already been configured for your control. For example, you could add another intrinsic control to your ActiveX control and use this add-in to map custom properties, events, and methods to it. The wizard windows are discussed in the following sections. These sections assume that you are running the add-in for the first time on your ActiveX control.

> **NOTE**
> For this add-in to run, you must have an ActiveX control in your current project collection.

Select a Control Window

If your project or project collection contains more than one ActiveX control, the Select a Control window, shown in Figure 77-3, will be displayed. This window allows you to choose the ActiveX control that you wish to operate on.

Select Interface Members Window

This window allows you to select properties, methods, and events that you would like to add to your control. The properties, methods, and events that you provide will define the interface to your control. Interface elements that your control will contain are listed in the Selected Names list box. As you can see in Figure 77-4, some elements are already added to the Selected Names list box. These are default elements that most ActiveX controls contain. You may choose not to include them in your control. To add or remove elements from the Selected Names list box, use the arrow buttons to the left of the list box.

Create Custom Interface Members Window

This is the window you will use to create your control's custom interface elements. To create a new interface element, press the New button and name your element in the space provided. The name that you give your interface element must be a valid variable or procedure name because any custom elements that you create will have a procedure or procedure definition by the same name in your Visual Basic program. This window is shown in Figure 77-5.

Set Mapping Window

The Set Mapping window, shown in Figure 77-6, allows you to map your ActiveX control's properties, events, and methods to constituent controls contained within your

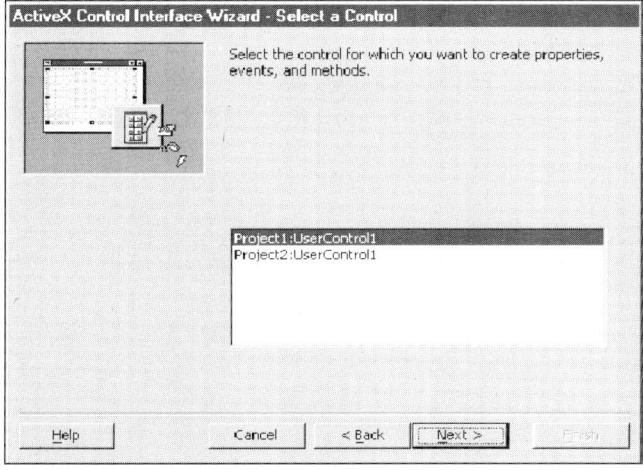

Figure 77-3　Select a Control window

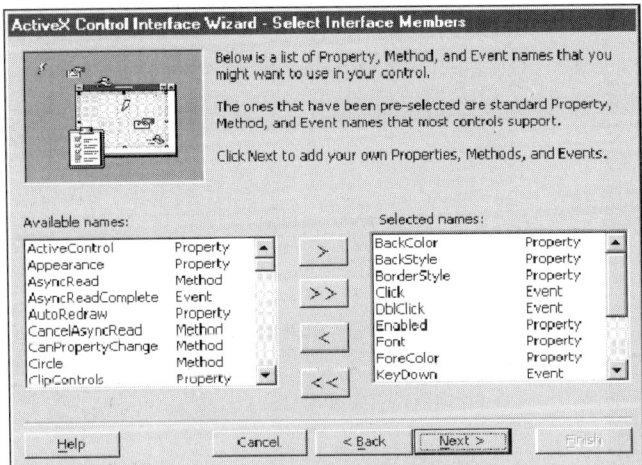

Figure 77-4   Select Interface Members window

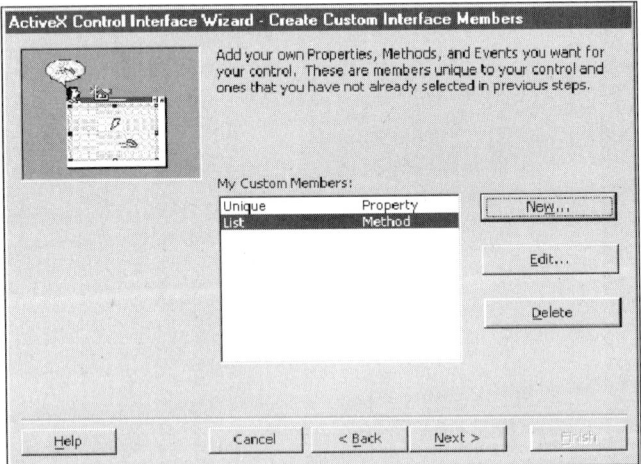

Figure 77-5   Create Custom Interface Members window

ActiveX control. To do this, choose an element from the Public Name list box, then choose a control from the Control combo box to map it to. Below the Control combo box, the Member combo box will be filled with the properties, events, or methods of the control that you choose in the Control combo. For example, if the control you choose in the Control combo is a text box control, the Member combo box will be filled with all the properties, events, or methods of a text box. The list that appears in the Member combo depends on whether you have selected a property, event, or method from the Public Name list (that is, if you select a property element from the list, the Member combo will be filled with property values).

> **NOTE**
> Any member that you do not explicitly map in this window will be mapped to its default member in your ActiveX control.

Set Attributes Window

The Set Attributes window is used to set attributes such as return values and data types of the members that were not mapped by you in the Set Mapping window. For methods, you can specify an optional argument list that will appear as the formal parameter list in your project's Visual Basic method. The format for this argument list is the same in the Arguments text box as it is in your Visual Basic code. An example argument list is Item As String, Optional Index As Variant. If you are familiar with using other ActiveX controls, you have undoubtedly noticed that some properties have different access at runtime than they do at design time. For example, a property may be read/write at design time but read-only at runtime. When a property is chosen from the Public Name list, you may choose runtime and design-time access to the property from the Run Time and Design Time combo boxes, respectively. The Set Attributes wizard window is show in Figure 77-7.

Finished! Window

On the Finished! window, check the View Summary Report box if you wish to view a list of to-do items after the add-in finishes generating its code. This window is shown in Figure 77-8.

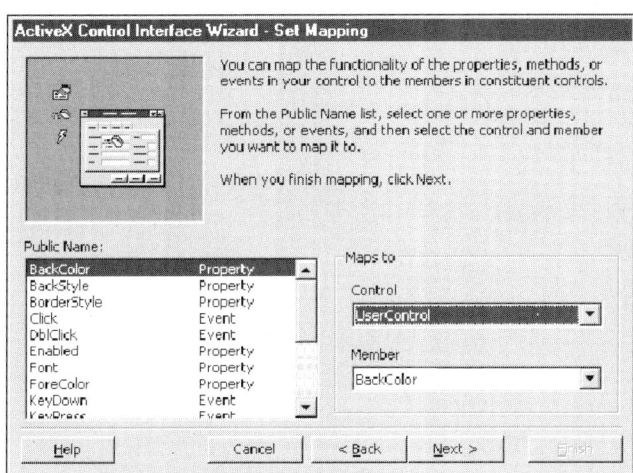

Figure 77-6   Set Mapping window

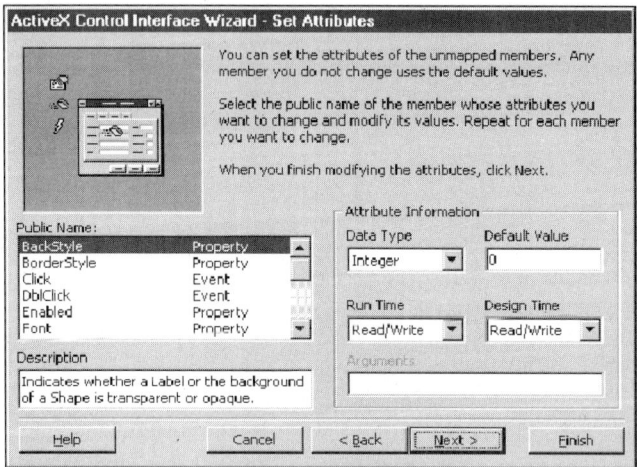

Figure 77-7   Set Attributes window

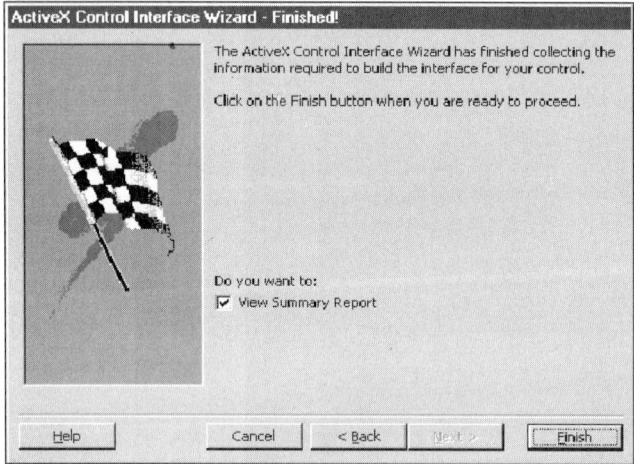

Figure 77-8   Finished! window

Report Designer Add-In

When records are added to a database, they mean nothing unless you know how to massage the data in them. In a sense, all that is in the database is data. To turn the data into usable information, you need a flexible and powerful report writer. Report Designer, shown in Figure 77-9, is a tool that is used for just such a purpose. It can be used to generate predefined reports or custom reports based on tables and fields that you choose. It also has a built-in formula editor so you can perform mathematical and other operations on your data. In the following sections, we discuss some of this

Figure 77-9   The Report Designer window

functionality in greater detail. Because report writing is a subject all its own, this is meant to be a brief overview of the functionality of Report Designer and report writing in general.

Designing Your Report Layout

The layout of your report is just as important as the data it comprises. It is what turns your data into information. Report Designer includes eight predefined reports, called *experts*, for you to choose from, or you can create your own custom report from scratch. In either case, you are not restricted from later modifying your report. When designing the layout of your report, you must first decide which tables and fields you are going to include. You want to provide the reader with enough, but not too much, information. The data you add to the report will depend on the overall information you wish to share. You must then decide whether there will be any sorting or grouping of information. This, too, can make or break the readability of your report. With Report Designer, you can have embedded groupings. For example, your data may be grouped by state and then by city within each state.

Field Types and Formulas

To create a report, you may need multiple types of fields. Some of the most frequently used types and their uses are listed in Table 77-1.

Table 77-1 Frequently used field types

Field Type	Use Field to...
Text	Place a label or caption for a data field.
Database	Hold data that is pulled from a database.
Formula	Calculate a value based on a user-defined formula.
Page Number	Number the pages of a report.

Most reports consist of these types of fields. In addition to these field types, you can change the font and even add colored borders and fills.

When creating a formula field, you can choose from three basic formula types: fields, functions, and arithmetic operators. The fields list consists of fields from the tables you have chosen to include in your report. These are usually used as the data for the other two types of formulas. The general groups of functions that you are able to choose from include mathematical, string, and date, to name a few. Most of these functions accept input, usually in the form of a database field. The arithmetic operators are something we are all familiar with. They are addition, subtraction, multiplication, division, percent, and negate. These operators can be used to perform calculations on database fields and/or constant values.

The Biblio Example Report

To give you hands-on experience in creating reports and to show you how to use a Report Designer expert, let's create our own report. We will use the BIBLIO.MDB database as the source for our data. Follow the steps listed below to create your report.

1. **Select Your Report Type.** After choosing File|New from the Report Designer menu, choose to create a standard report by pressing the Standard button on the Create New Report window. By choosing the Standard expert, your report will be formatted automatically based on the fields and groupings you choose.

2. **Choose Your Data Source.** In the Create Report Expert window, shown in Figure 77-10, press the Data File button, choose the BIBLIO.MDB database from your Visual Basic directory, and press Done. You will notice that the tables from this database are inserted into the previous window and you are moved on to the 2:Links tab.

3. **Press the Next>> Button.** On the 2:Links tab, press the Next>> button. For the purpose of this report, we will not worry about table links.

4. **Choose Your Report Fields.** On the 3:Fields tab, you will choose the table fields to put on your report. For this report, choose the following fields: Name from Publishers table, Author from Authors table, and Title from Titles table in that order, as shown in Figure 77-11. The order in which you add the fields to the Report Fields list is the order in which the fields will be placed on your report

from left to right across the page. After selecting these fields, press the Next>> button to go to the 4:Sort tab.

5. **Choose the Grouping of Your Report Data**. To make your report more readable, group your data based on publisher's name, author's name, and then titles the author has written. To do this, add the fields from step 4 from the Report Fields list to the Group Fields list in the order specified in step 5. The 4:Sort tab, shown in Figure 77-12, depicts this action.

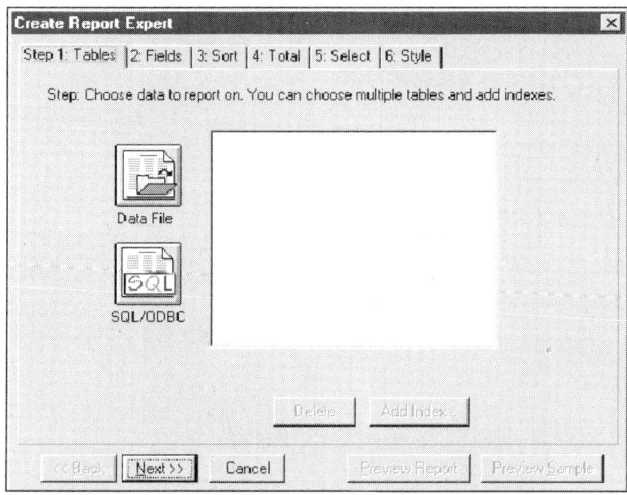

Figure 77-10   The Create Report Expert window

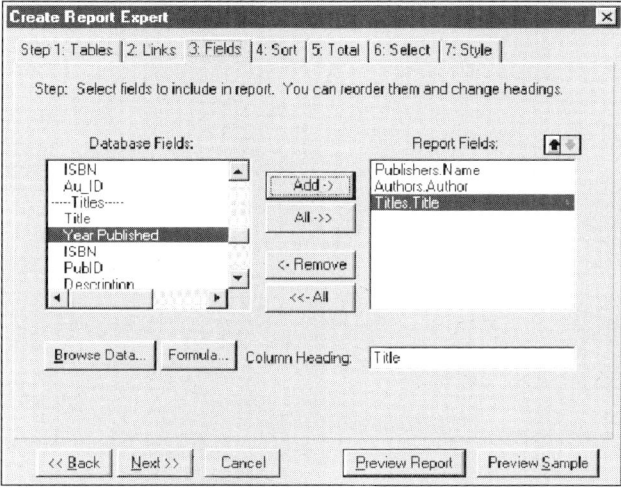

Figure 77-11   The 2:Fields tab

6. Press the Preview Report Button. Press the Preview Report button to view your report. This may take a few seconds because there are quite a few records in the Biblio database. The previewed report is shown in Figure 77-13.

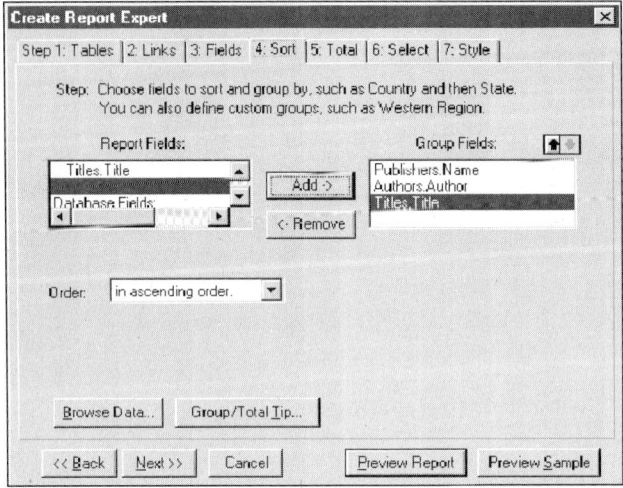

Figure 77-12   The 4:Sort tab

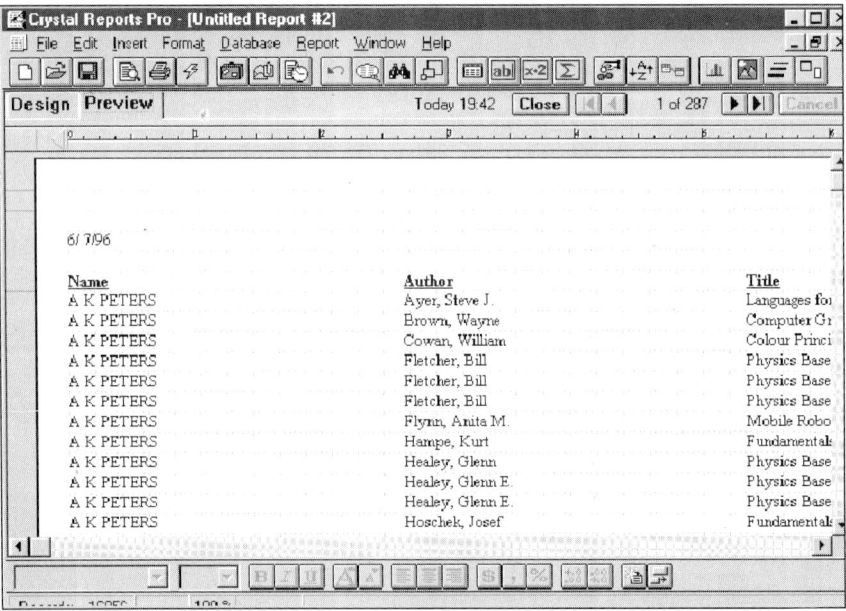

Figure 77-13   The previewed report

We leave it as an exercise to add a title and header information to your report. To modify your report in this way, choose the Design tab while previewing your report. As you will see, the changes you make while on the Design tab will be reflected when you return to the Preview tab.

ActiveX Document Migration Wizard Add-In

Sometimes it may be beneficial or even necessary to use your Visual Basic forms as documentation rather than as programming components. The ActiveX Document Migration Wizard add-in allows you to do just that. By using the wizard windows provided, you can create an ActiveX document from a Visual Basic form.

> **NOTE**
> Your original project type must be an ActiveX EXE or an ActiveX DLL.

Form Selection Window

In the Form Selection window, shown in Figure 77-14, choose which forms you wish to create ActiveX documents from. To do this, check the check box beside each form name you wish to create an ActiveX document for. The listed form names are pulled from your current project in the Visual Basic IDE.

Options Window

Use the Options window to select options for the ActiveX document(s) you are about to create. If you wish to comment out any unsupported code in your ActiveX document, check the Comment out invalid code? check box. The code that will be

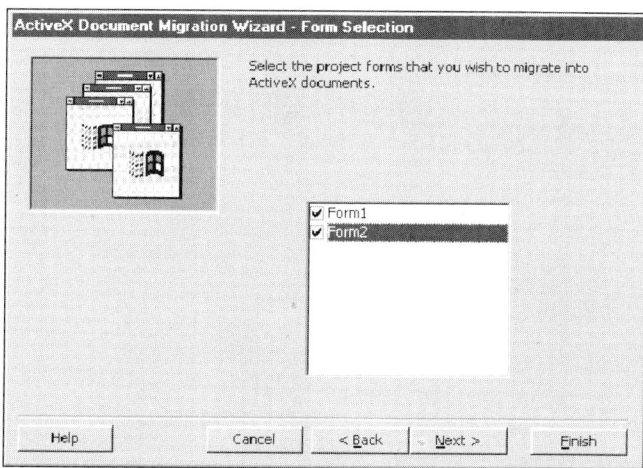

Figure 77-14   Form Selection window

commented out is any form load and form unload procedures and the End command. If you wish to remove the Visual Basic forms from your project (but not from the disk) after your ActiveX documents have been created, check the box next to Remove original forms after conversion?. This window is shown in Figure 77-15.

Finished! Window

In the Finished! window, shown in Figure 77-16, there are a couple of options. If you would like to view a to-do list of ActiveX document postcreation tasks, choose Yes. If you wish to save the settings of your current ActiveX Document Migration session, check the box next to Save current settings as default. This will save your choices in the Options window.

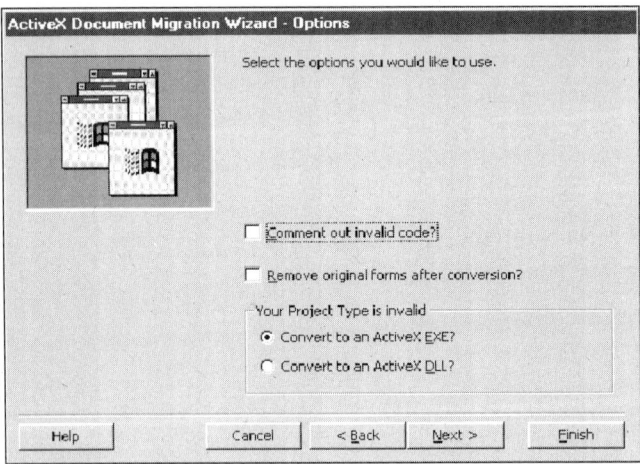

Figure 77-15 Options window

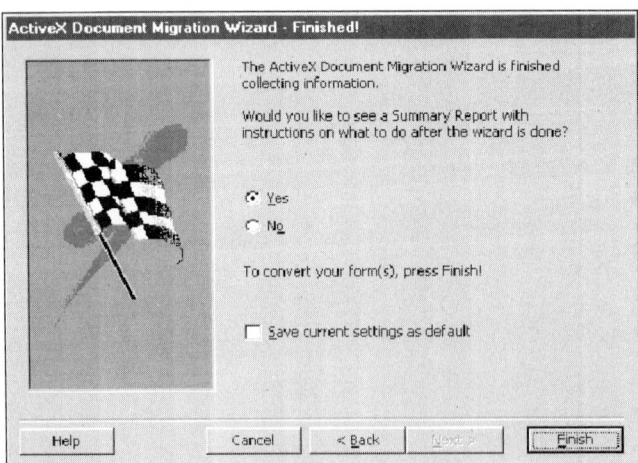

Figure 77-16 Finished! window

The Add-In Toolbar

Visual Basic 5.0 does everything it possibly can to make your life easier as a developer. Not only does it allow you to develop and use add-ins, it also makes running them simple. The Add-In Toolbar makes running add-ins easier by providing you with a button for each add-in you choose. This gives you a choice of whether you want to run the add-in from the Add-Ins menu item or from the toolbar. The Add-In Toolbar is shown in Figure 77-17 in the lower-left corner of the Visual Basic main window. As you can see, there is one toolbar button for each add-in that is included.

Customizing Your Add-In Toolbar

Like the Add-In Manager, the Add-In Toolbar allows you to add and remove items from it. This allows you to customize the toolbar to include only the add-ins you want. In the following sections, adding and removing add-ins from your toolbar are covered in greater detail.

Adding an Add-In to Your Add-In Toolbar

To add an add-in to your Add-In Toolbar, press the +/- button on the toolbar to view the Add/Remove Toolbar Items dialog box. If you do not see the add-in you are look-ing for in the Available Add-Ins list, you must insert it. To insert an add-in into the Available Add-Ins list, click the browse button and choose the EXE or DLL file that is associated with the add-in you wish to include. Once you see the add-in in the list, check the check box next to it and press OK to include it on the toolbar. As you will notice, items that are not checked in the Available Add-Ins list will not be included on the toolbar.

Removing an Add-In from Your Add-In Toolbar

To remove an item from your Add-In Toolbar, press the +/- button on the toolbar to view the Add/Remove Toolbar Items dialog box. In the Available Add-Ins list, uncheck the add-in you wish to remove from the toolbar and press OK to save your settings. If you would like to delete the add-in from the Available Add-Ins list, select the add-in from the list, then press Delete to remove the item. Press OK to save your settings.

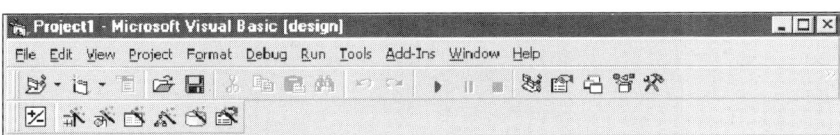

Figure 77-17   The Add-In toolbar

The API Viewer Add-In

The Windows Application Programming Interface (API) is a collection of functions that is encompassed in Windows DLL files and a myriad of constant values and data structures. It is used by programmers to access general and specific Windows functionality not encompassed in Visual Basic. For example, to read from the WIN.INI file, you call the API function GetProfileString. In Visual Basic, each API reference must have a corresponding declaration inside your program. The API Viewer is a collection of all these API references in correct Visual Basic format. It includes a complete listing of API functions, constants, and structure definitions (user-defined types). The references contained in the API Viewer can be copied to the clipboard for manual insertion into your program, or they can be automatically inserted into your program by the API Viewer.

The API Viewer Window

The API Viewer window, shown in Figure 77-18, consists of three sections: API Type, Available Items, and Selected Items. By using these three sections, you are able to obtain the Visual Basic definition of API functions, constants, and user-defined types. A brief description of each of these sections follows. (For a more detailed description on how to use the API Viewer, see "How It Works" at the end of this section.)

The API Type Section

The API Type section consists of three categories to choose from: Constants, Declares, and Types. When you choose a category, the Available Items box is filled with the references that belong to that category. Table 77-2 shows the relationship of the API reference types to their inherent Visual Basic counterparts.

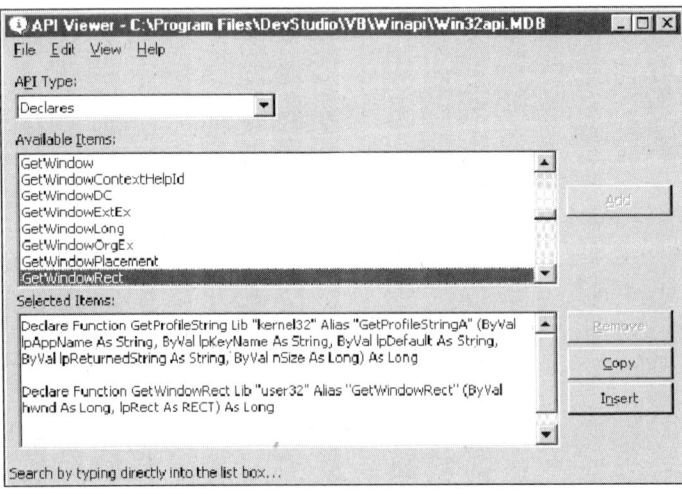

Figure 77-18   The API Viewer window

Table 77-2 API types listing

API Type	Description	VB Counterpart
Constants	Constant value definitions	Public Const var = 25
Types	Type structure definitions	Type - End Type pair
Declarations	Function and procedure definitions	No counterpart

The following sections contain brief descriptions and examples of the three API types listed.

Constants API Type

The Constants API type is used to declare a constant value inside your Visual Basic program. An example declaration from this category is

```
Public Const ABM_ACTIVATE = &H6
```

Some API functions require that you send certain values as parameters. The API constant definitions that are defined in the API Viewer apply meaningful names to these values.

Declarations API Type

API functions, as well as functions of any other DLL, require a special definition in Visual Basic called a *Declare statement*. The Declarations API type is a listing of all of the Windows API functions in Visual Basic Declare format. For example, the previously mentioned GetProfileString function would be defined as

```
Declare Function GetProfileString Lib "kernel32" Alias "GetProfileStringA" (ByVal lpAppName
As String, ByVal lpKeyName As String, ByVal lpDefault As String, ByVal lpReturnedString As
String, ByVal nSize As Long) As Long
```

A discussion of the Visual Basic Declare format and usage is presented in Chapter 29, "DLLs and the Windows API."

Types API Type

Some Windows API functions take user-defined types as parameters. For example, the API function GetWindowRect, defined as

```
Declare Function GetWindowRect Lib "user32" Alias "GetWindowRect" (ByVal hwnd As Long,
lpRect As RECT) As Long
```

accepts a user-defined RECT type as its second parameter. The RECT user-defined type is included in the Types API type category. It is defined like this:

```
Type RECT
      Left as Long
      Top as Long
            Right as Long
      Bottom as Long
End Type
```

For a discussion of passing user-defined structures to API functions, see Chapter 29.

The Available Items Section

The Available Items section holds all the available API references to choose from for the current category. To find an item in the list, use the scrollbar or type the name of the API definition. The list will jump you to the closest match each time you press a key.

The Selected Items Section

The Selected Items section lists the items you have chosen from the Available Items list for later copy to the Windows clipboard or automatic insertion into your program. This list may contain elements from any or all of the three API Types categories.

Using the API Viewer

> **NOTE**
> If you started the API Viewer from within Visual Basic 5.0, you can use the Insert button to insert your selected items automatically into your project's current form or module.

The API Viewer add-in can be started either as a standalone program from the Visual Basic folder under the Windows Start button or from within Visual Basic from the Add-Ins menu item. Once you are inside the API Viewer, you must open an API definition file. The Windows API definition file is called WIN32API.TXT and is located in the WinApi subdirectory under your Visual Basic 5.0 installation directory. The default location for the WinApi folder is

```
C:\Program Files\DevStudio\VB\WinApi.Txt
```

To open this file, select Load Text File from the File menu and browse to the appropriate directory. Once the file is loaded, the Available Items list will be filled automatically.

To choose an item from the Available Items list, use the scrollbar or type the name of the API reference you are looking for. As you type, the list will jump to the closest match. If the list stops moving as you type, either you have reached your destination or the API Viewer cannot match your keystrokes. If you do not see the API reference you are looking for, the API reference may be under a different name or you may have typed a letter in error.

When you reach your API reference, you need to add it to the Selected Items list by either double-clicking or pressing the Add button. In the Selected Items list, the items can be displayed in two ways: in full definition form or by reference name. In either case, the full definition form will always be the form that is copied into your program. To copy the selected items to the Windows clipboard, press the Copy button; to copy directly into your program, press the Insert button. (The Insert button is available only if you started API Viewer from the Add-Ins menu in Visual Basic.) The Insert button copies the API definitions to your Visual Basic project's current form or module. If the Copy button was used, you can use the traditional Windows paste methods to copy the definitions into the appropriate part of your program.

Loading the many API reference entries from the default WIN32API.TXT text file into the Available Items list usually takes a little time. To shorten the load time, convert the WIN32API.TXT file to Microsoft Access format. This can be done from within the API Viewer. To perform the conversion, open the WIN32API.TXT file in the API Viewer. Then choose Convert To Database from the File menu. You will see a File Save dialog box that has a default filename of WIN32API with MDB as the extension. You can type a different filename if you wish or accept the default. Press the Save button and the conversion is performed for you. To open the database file, choose Load Database File instead of Load Text File from the File menu.

Application Wizard Add-In

When creating a Windows application, you generally need one or more windows, menu items, and controls to put in your windows. Visual Basic makes application creation very simple and straightforward by allowing you to manipulate your forms, controls, and menus at design time instead of having to create them in your code. The Application Wizard add-in takes the creation process to a higher level in that it provides a wizard approach to creating your Windows applications. It provides you with windows that represent some of the most common application design considerations. All you have to do is tell the Application Wizard what to do. The Application Wizard's windows are discussed below.

Interface Type Window

The Interface Type window allows you to choose your application's main window type. In Figure 77-19, you will see your possible choices are SDI (single document interface), MDI (multiple document interface), and Explorer style. In SDI-style applications, each window is created on the Windows desktop. In an MDI application, all the application windows are created inside a parent window. The idea behind this type of application is that the parent (desktop) window owns all its contained windows. Most word processing programs use this approach. In these programs, each document window is contained inside the main program window. Choosing the Explorer-style main window generates a window that is similar in appearance to the Windows Explorer program.

Menus Window

The Menus window lets you pick from a list of common menu items. As you see in Figure 77-20, your choices are File, Edit, View, Window, and Help. You will not be able to choose the Window menu item if you are using the Explorer or SDI application type. Table 77-3 gives you an idea of the submenu items that fall under these choices.

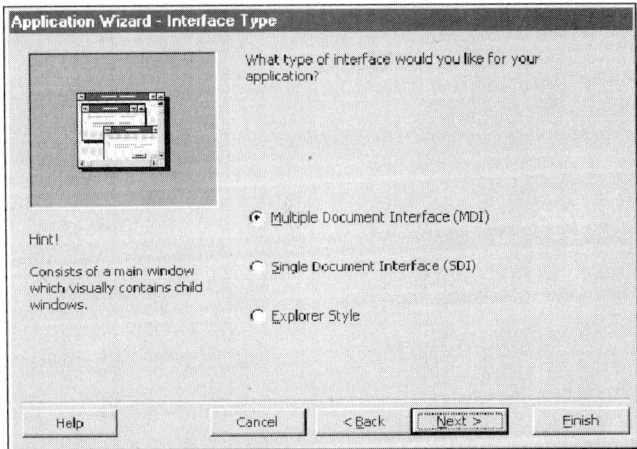

Figure 77-19 Interface Type window

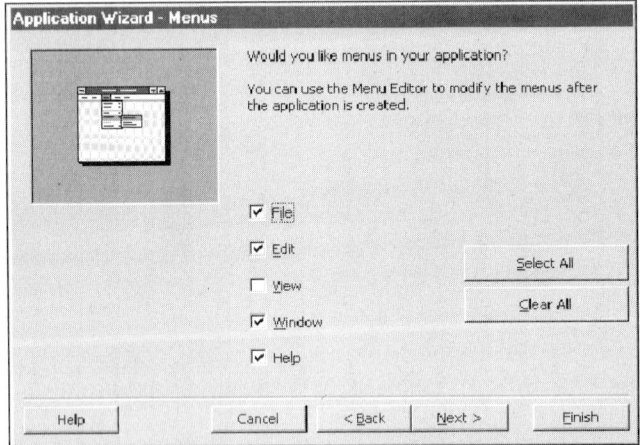

Figure 77-20 Menus window

Table 77-3 Example submenu items

Main Menu Item	Example Submenu Items
File	New, Open, Save
Edit	Undo, Cut, Copy, Paste
View	Toolbar, Status Bar, Options
Window	Cascade, Tile
Help	Contents, Search, About

Resources Window

In the next Application Wizard window, you specify a resource file if it is needed. A resource file is used by Windows applications to store strings and pictures, among other things. A common use for resource files is localization (used in international Windows programs to store program strings in multiple languages). Resource files are good for storing program data in one central area and provide a means of changing program strings without having to change any program code. Resource files can be created with a resource editor such as the one in Visual C++. For more information on creating resource files, refer to *Visual Basic Books Online*. Figure 77-21 shows this wizard window.

Internet Connectivity Window

The Internet Connectivity window, shown in Figure 77-22, allows you to include a Web browser window in your application. You can even add a default URL to your Web site. This is a nice touch to add to your application because it allows users of your application to access the World Wide Web from within your application instead of having to start a separate Web browsing program. If you wish to include a Web browser window in your application, choose the Yes option on this window.

Standard Forms Window

The Standard Forms window prompts you with choices for some common Windows application forms. Your choices and some brief descriptions are listed in Table 77-4.

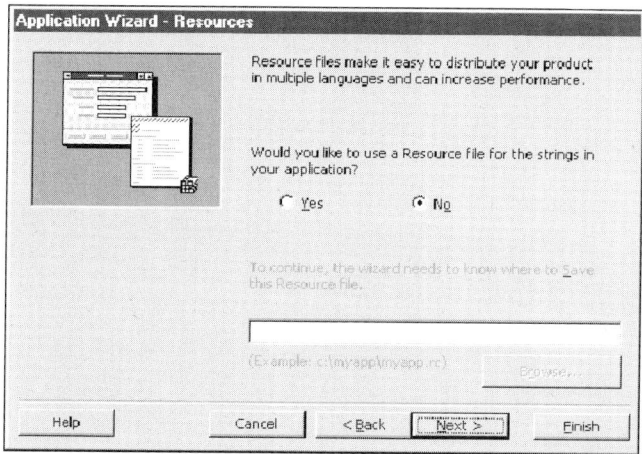

Figure 77-21   Resources window

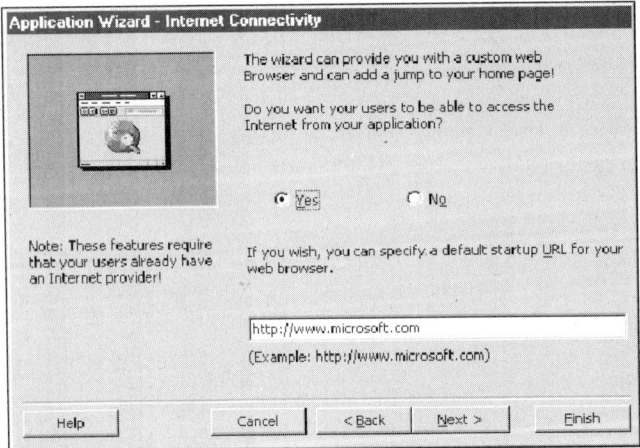

Figure 77-22   Internet Connectivity window

Table 77-4 Form type descriptions

Form Type	Description or Example
Splash screen at application startup	Picture window that is displayed while your program loads
Login dialog	To accept ID and password to allow access to your program on a per user basis
Options dialog	To allow users to change program settings
About box	Generally displayed by Help, About

In addition to these standard forms, the Form Templates button allows you to choose from the list of Visual Basic form templates. The templates that are included are Add-In, ODBC Login, and Tip of the Day. If any of these templates is chosen, a Visual Basic form for the appropriate template is inserted into your project. Figure 77-23 shows this window.

Data Access Forms Window

The Data Access Forms window, shown in Figure 77-24, allows you to specify a database for your application to connect to. The Application Wizard then uses tables and queries from this database to generate data forms into your project. In the next window, you will choose your tables and/or queries to generate data forms.

Select Tables Window

The Select Tables window is used to select the tables and/or queries to generate your data forms from. The list of tables and queries represents the tables and queries in the database you specified in the previous window. This window is displayed only if you chose to generate data forms in the Data Access Forms window. Each table or query

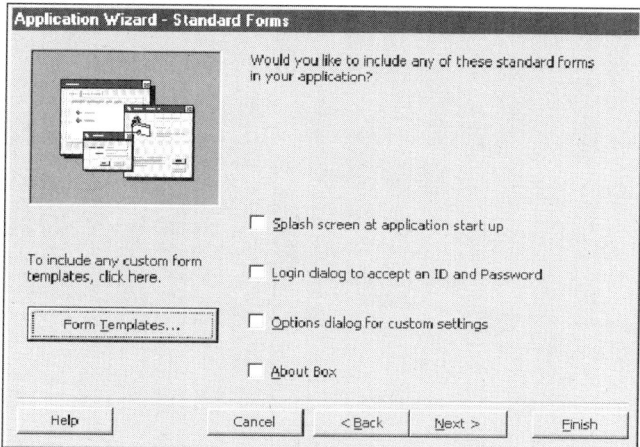

Figure 77-23   Standard Forms window

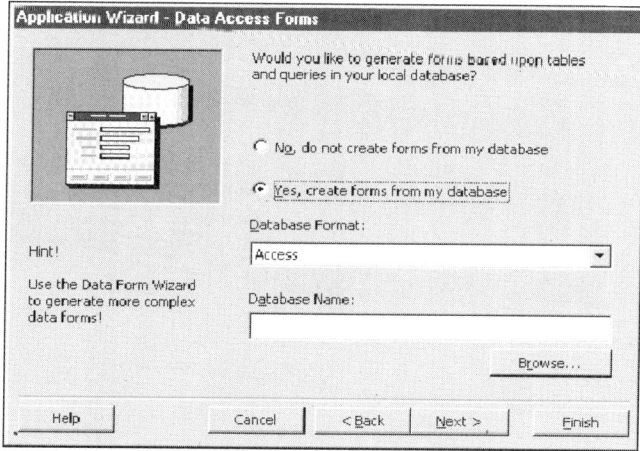

Figure 77-24   Data Access Forms window

added to the Selected list box will have its own data form generated from its fields. To add and remove tables and queries from the Selected list box, use the arrow buttons to the left of the list box. The Select Tables window is shown in Figure 77-25.

NOTE
If you need more control over data form generation, do not choose to generate data forms in the Data Access Forms window and run the Data Form Wizard after the application has been generated by the Application Wizard.

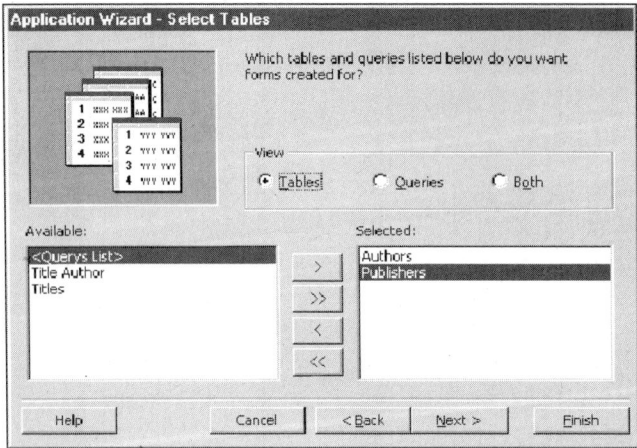

Figure 77-25　Select Tables window

Finished! Window

In the Finished! window, shown in Figure 77-26, specify your Visual Basic project name and choose whether to view the project summary report. The summary report lists to-do items that you may need or want to add to your project. That's it! To let the Application Wizard create your project, press the Finish button.

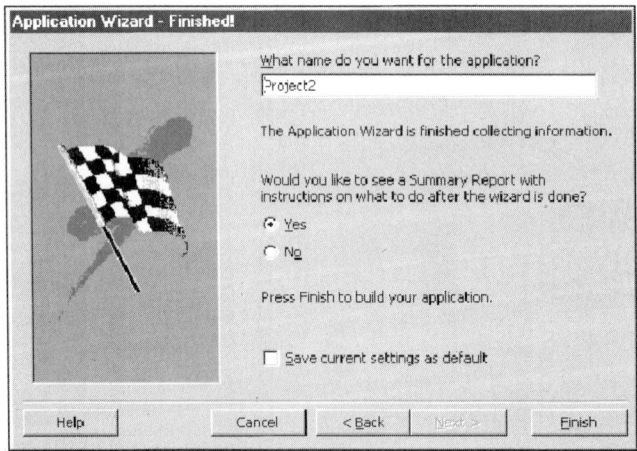

Figure 77-26　Finished! window

Class Builder Add-In

When programming in Visual Basic, you may wish to define classes to obtain layers of abstraction in your code. The Class Builder add-in provides you with a graphical interface to create and edit classes in your Visual Basic projects. This utility creates class modules and generates code for the properties, methods, and events that you define. Class Builder will also let you define collections of new or existing classes.

The Class Builder Window

The Class Builder main window is separated into two sections, shown in Figure 77-27. The left section, called the Classes section, contains a hierarchical view of the classes and collections; the right section contains tabs that list their properties, methods, or events. The properties, methods, or events that are displayed are always the elements of the current class or collection selected in the Classes section. You can view each set of elements individually by choosing the Properties, Methods, or Events tab, or you can view all the elements in the same list by choosing the All tab.

Adding Class and Collection Elements

To add a class to your existing Visual Basic project, choose the File|New|Class menu item or click the right mouse button in the Classes main window section and choose New|Class. You may also use the toolbar to create your new class. In the Class Builder window, shown in Figure 77-27, enter the class name and the class that it is based on, if necessary. If a class is based on another class, the base class will create an instance of the class that it is based on it. Take, for example, the classic definition of a Tree class that must always contain at least a root node. A class named Node could then be based on class Tree. This would mean that for every instance of class Tree that was defined,

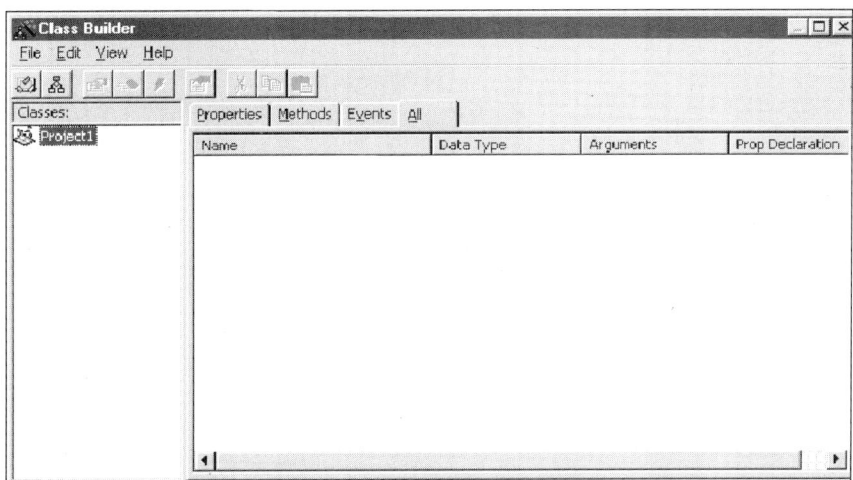

Figure 77-27   Class Builder window

class Tree would define an instance of class Node. This Node instance could be considered the root of the tree. To create a class that is not based on another class, check the Top Level check box in the Class Builder window. This will guarantee that the class will be a top-level class in your project.

When adding a new class or collection to your project, always keep in mind that the new element will be created in relation to the currently selected element in the Classes section of the main window. Therefore, if class Tree was selected when class Node was created, class Node would automatically be based on class Tree even if you didn't choose class Tree in the Based On combo box.

To add a new collection to your project, choose the File|New|Collection menu item or click the right mouse button in the Classes main window section and choose New|Collection. You may also use the toolbar to create your new collection. In the Collection Builder window, shown in Figure 77-28, enter the collection name and the collection that it is based on, if necessary.

Adding Properties, Methods, and Events

To add a property to an existing class, choose the File|New|Property menu item or click the right mouse button in the Classes section of the main window and choose New|Property. You may also click the right mouse button in the Properties list tab and choose New Property or use the toolbar. In the Property Builder window, shown in Figure 77-29, enter the property name and data type, and choose a declaration type. There is a unique distinction between the Public and Friend declaration types in that both property types are global to elements inside the project, but a Friend property is not visible outside the project it is defined in. A property defined as the Public Variable declaration type will be defined in the current class module but will not actually be a member of the class. It will be a regular project variable. If you wish the property to be

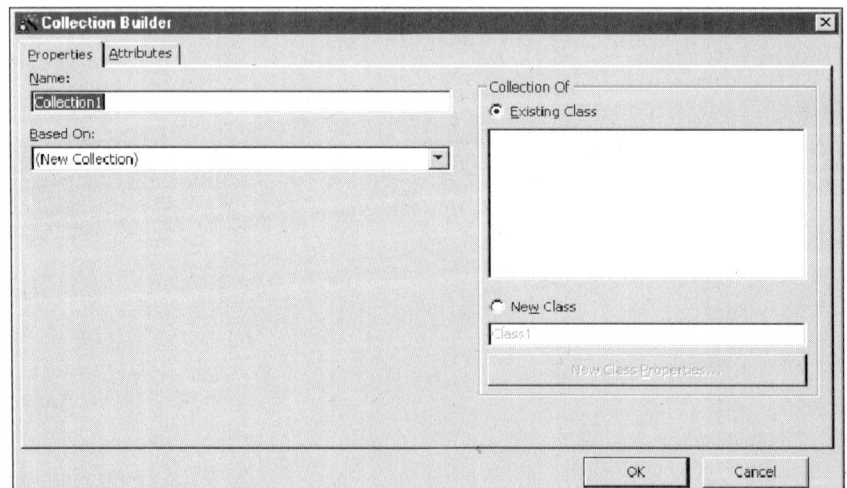

Figure 77-28   Collection Builder window

the default property of the class, check the Default Property? check box. It is not possible to declare a property as both Friend and Default. A property cannot be both friend and default because a default property needs to be able to be accessed outside of the project.

To add a method to an existing class, choose the File|New|Method menu item or click the right mouse button in the Classes section of the main window and choose New|Method. You may also click the right mouse button in the Methods list tab and choose New Method or use the toolbar. In the Method Builder window, shown in Figure 77-30, enter the name of your new method and any arguments that it may require. The arguments you enter are the arguments that will be listed in the formal parameter list in the method definition code. Also in this window, choose your method return type, if necessary. If you wish the method to be a friend method (visible only within the project), check the Declare as Friend? check box. If you wish the method to be the default method, check the Default Method? check box. A method cannot be both friend and default because a default method needs to be able to be accessed outside of the project.

To add an event to an existing class, choose the File|New|Event menu item or click the right mouse button in the Classes section of the main window and choose New|Event. You may also click the right mouse button in the Events list tab and choose New Event or use the toolbar. In the Event Builder window, shown in Figure 77-31, enter the name of your event and any arguments that it may require. Because an event procedure cannot be called directly, there are no friend or default options. In addition, event procedures cannot return a value.

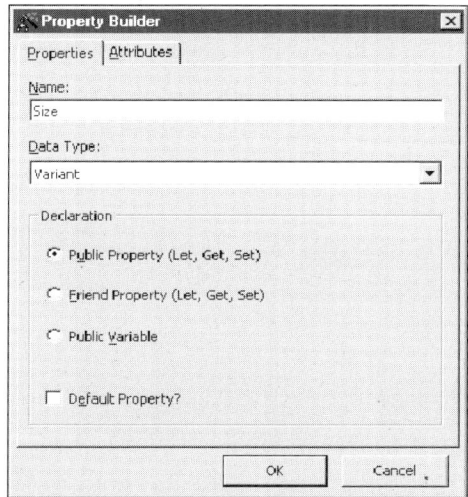

Figure 77-29   Property Builder window

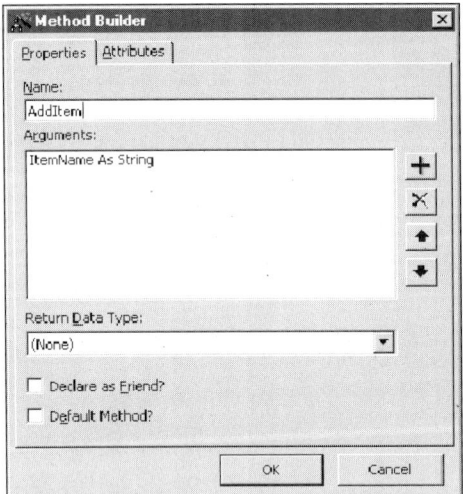

Figure 77-30 Method Builder window

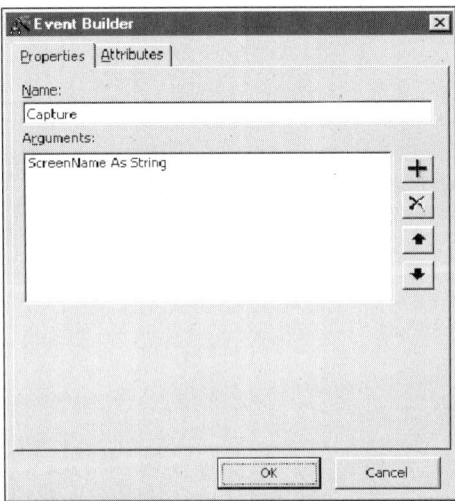

Figure 77-31 Event Builder window

Data Form Wizard Add-In

If you are familiar with data bound controls, you know how much coding and time they can save. But wouldn't it be nice if there was a program to draw the data controls and create the form for you? The Data Form Wizard add-in does just that. This add-in accomplishes the same task as the Data Form Designer menu item in the Visual Data Manager add-in but includes the wizard-style interface. In addition, the Data Form Wizard includes a master/detail form generation that represents a one-to-many relationship between the data controls it draws. Each wizard window is discussed below in the order it occurs.

Database Type Window

To generate a data form from the Data Form Wizard, you must first have an existing database of an ODBC format. In the Database Type window, choose your database format. This format generally represents the application the database was created in, for example, Microsoft Access or FoxPro 2.6.

Connection Information Window

The Connection Information window is used to specify remote database connection information. It is displayed only if the Remote (ODBC) database type was chosen from the previous window. In the ODBC Connect Data frame, enter the appropriate information to connect to your data source. In this frame, choose either a DSN (Data Source Name) or a driver. A DSN is a local or remote database connection that is set up with the 32-Bit ODBC icon in the Windows control panel. If necessary, enter a user ID (UID) and password (PWD). Whether you need to enter anything into these fields depends on the database security you have set up in your data source.

Database Window

In the Database window, choose the database you wish to use to generate your data form and choose to include tables and/or queries from the Record Sources frame. Note: You may or may not have a Record Sources frame, depending on the database type you chose in the Database Type window. Checking the Tables check box will allow you to choose from a list of tables to generate your form and checking the Queries check box will allow you to choose from a list of queries.

Form Window

In the Form window, choose your form layout. The Data Form Wizard will generate forms for three form layouts: single record, grid (datasheet), and master/detail. An example of each is shown in Figures 77-32, 77-33, and 77-34.

Record Source Window

In the Record Source window, you will choose from a list of tables and queries to generate your form. As you will see when you choose a table or query from the Record Source drop-down box, the Available Fields list box will fill with field names. If you have chosen a table as your record source, this list will include all table fields; if you have chosen a query, only the output fields of the query will be displayed. To select fields to include in your data form, use the arrow buttons between the Available Fields and Selected Fields list boxes. If you wish to order your data by a given field, choose this field from the Column to Sort By drop-down box. This field does not need to be one of your data form fields.

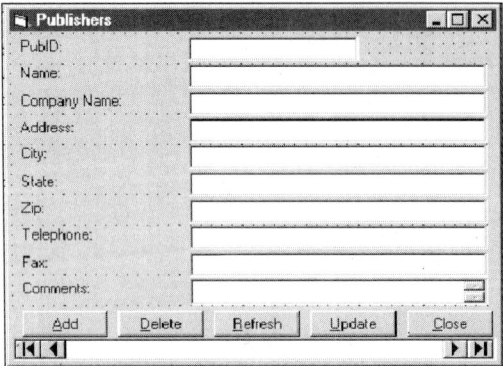

Figure 77-32   Single record layout

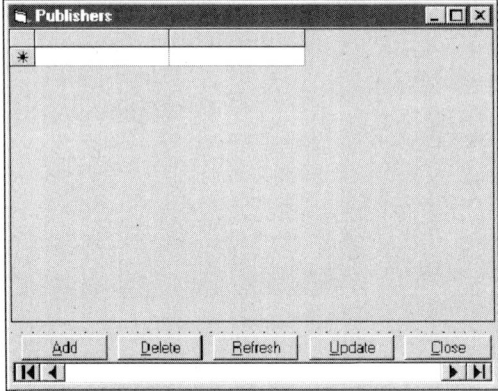

Figure 77-33   Grid layout

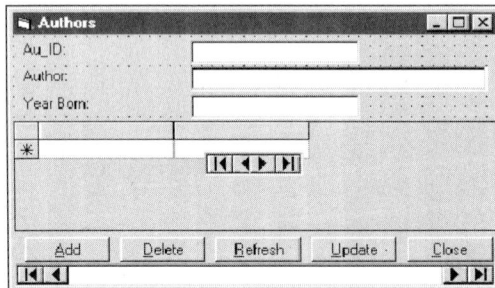

Figure 77-34   Master/detail layout

Control Selection Window

Once you have chosen the fields for the Data Form Wizard to put on your data form, use the Control Selection window to choose what database functionality you want your form to have. In the Available Controls frame, choose the functions you will want your users to perform. Uses for these control buttons are listed in Table 77-5.

Table 77-5 Button usage

Control Button	Use When You Want to Be Able To...
Add	Add new records to your database.
Delete	Delete records from your database.
Refresh	Refresh your current working record set.
Update	Make changes to your database records.
Close	Close your data form without having to use the normal window controls.

In the Finished! window, you name your form. This will be the name of the form in your Visual Basic project. If you wish to save your Data Form Wizard setting for the next time you run it, check the Save current settings check box. This will save the database and available controls that you have chosen. When you have entered your form name (or chosen to accept the default), press the Finish button to have the Data Form Wizard automatically generate your form.

Property Page Wizard Add-In

If you have used a third-party ActiveX control that has been created recently, you may have used property pages to set its properties. A *property page* is way of grouping custom control properties from the Properties design-time window in a graphical and logical manner. If you have used a property page before, you have noticed that once you exit the property page, the underlying properties in the Properties window change to match your entries. The Property Page Wizard add-in creates property pages (Visual Basic forms) for you automatically from properties that you choose. The following sections describe the windows involved in creating property pages.

> **NOTE**
> For this add-in to run, there must be existing properties in your Visual Basic project.

Select a User Control Window

If your project or project collection contains more than one ActiveX control, the Select a User Control window will be displayed, as shown in Figure 77-35. This window allows you to choose the ActiveX control that you wish to operate on.

Select the Property Pages Window

This window is used to select the property pages that you wish to include in your ActiveX control's design-time interface. It is shown in Figure 77-36. To select a property page, check the check box to the left of the property page. Only predefined property pages are listed initially. To create your own custom property page, click the Add button and enter a property page name. The name that you enter will be the name of the Visual Basic property page form that the add-in creates in your Visual Basic application.

Add Properties Window

The Add Properties window is used to select custom properties to add to your property page(s). From one of the Available Property Pages tabs, choose your property page. Properties can be added to the property page from the Available Properties list by

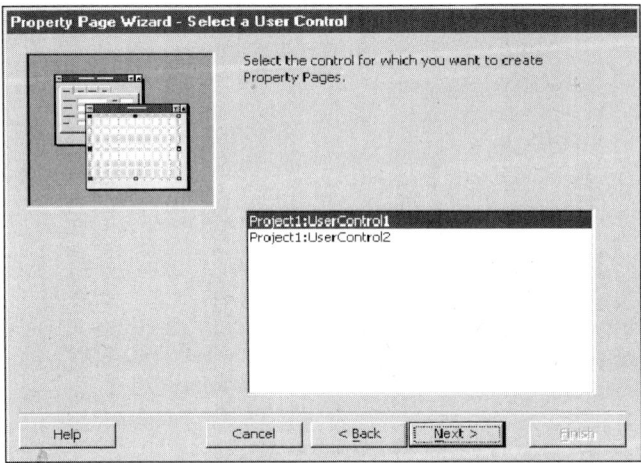

Figure 77-35   Select a User Control window

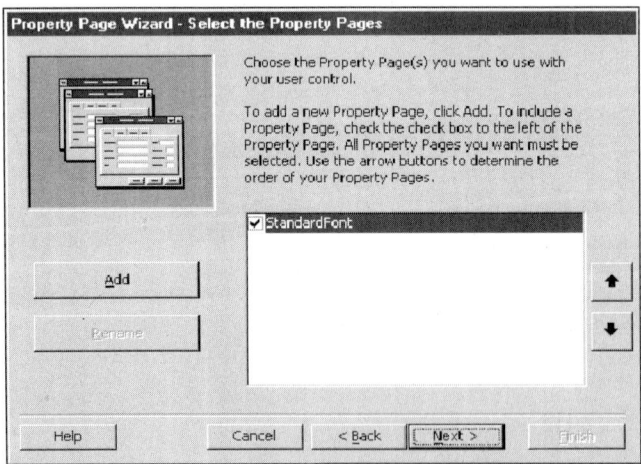

Figure 77-36   Select the Property Pages window

using the arrow buttons. The Available Properties list is filled with the control properties defined in your current ActiveX control. These properties may have been defined by you by writing the code for them or by the ActiveX Control Wizard add-in. This window is shown in Figure 77-37.

Finished! Window

If you would like to view a list of tasks to do after the wizard completes, choose Yes from the Finished! window, shown in Figure 77-38. When you are satisfied with all your selections, press Finish.

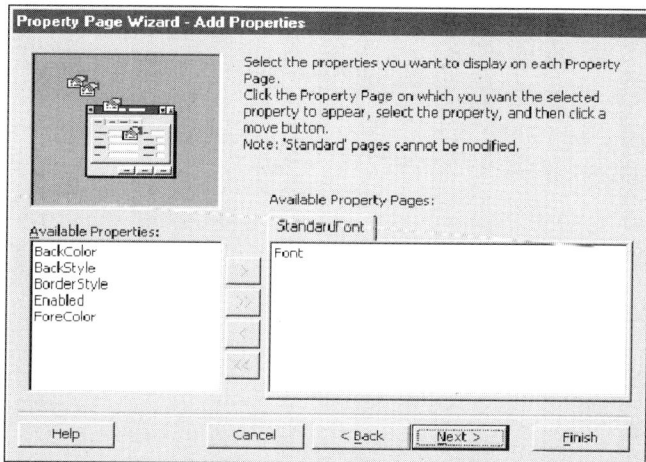

Figure 77-37   Add Properties window

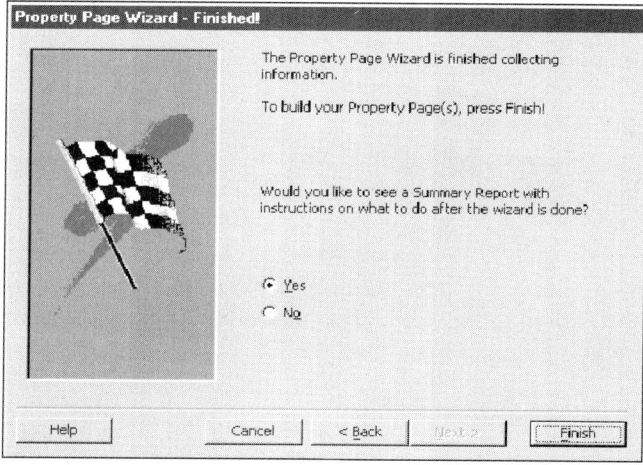

Figure 77-38   Finished! window

The Wizard Manager Add-In

The Wizard Manager add-in, shown in Figure 77-39, is a utility that is used to help you create a wizard application such as an installation or a configuration wizard. If you've ever tried to write a wizard application before, you know how much of a pain it can be, especially if you have many steps. The most efficient way to write a wizard application is to create a single form with a frame for each step, but working with more than two frames on a form at design time is confusing at best. The Wizard Manager was written to aid in the wizard application development process. By using this add-in, you can switch between steps, or frames, with the click of a button. It also gives you the capability to insert and move steps. Wizard Manager keeps track of your steps by creating and manipulating a frame control array. In the following sections, how this works is explained in more detail.

> **NOTE**
> The form you are adding steps to must be named "frmWizard" in the Properties list.

Adding a New Step to Your Wizard Application

You have two choices when adding a new step to your wizard application. You can either append the step to the end of the other steps or insert the new step ahead of an existing step. To add the new step to the end of the existing steps, press the Add Step button, positioned as the second button from the left on the Wizard Manager toolbar. If you are creating the next step in a series of steps, this is the button you will want to use. To insert a step ahead of (before) an existing one, press the Insert a Step button, positioned as the third button from the left on the Wizard Manager toolbar.

Now let's talk about how the Wizard Manager keeps track of the steps that you add. As mentioned earlier, the Wizard Manager creates an array of frame controls. This control array is nothing different than what you would create if you were creating it manually. When you add a step to your wizard, the Wizard Manager adds a new frame to the control array. If the step is being added as the last step, the new frame is added to the end of the control array and is assigned the next array index number. If the step is being inserted ahead of an existing step, the new frame is created with an array index that corresponds to its location in the step list. Because there was already a frame control at this location, the array indexes of all the steps following the new step must be increased by one. In simpler terms, the frames in the control array are always kept in the same order as the steps in your project. You can see from the steps listed in the Wizard Manager window that this ordering is preserved.

Reordering Steps in Your Wizard Application

Sometimes it may be necessary to change the ordering of one or more of the steps you have created. When reordering steps, you can move the selected step either ahead or behind in the step list. If you wish to move the selected step ahead in the list, press

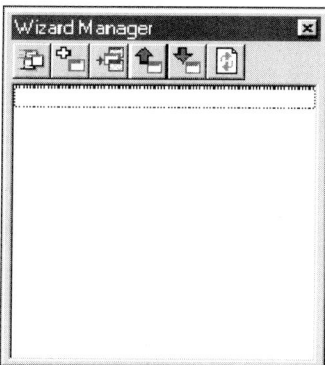

Figure 77-39 The Wizard
Manager window

the Move Step Up button, positioned as the fourth button from the left on the Wizard Manager toolbar. This actually switches the positions of the selected step and its following step in the frame control array. If you wish to move the selected step up in the step list, press the Step Down button, positioned as the fifth button from the left on the toolbar. In case you haven't guessed by now, this switches the positions of the selected step and the previous step in the frame control array.

Designing Your Steps

In addition to being able to accomplish the tasks discussed above, the Wizard Manager makes developing wizard applications easier in another way. One of the biggest hassles in creating wizards is managing all your frames in the window at the same time. To switch to a particular step with Wizard Manager, simply click on the step you wish to work with and it automatically positions all the other steps outside the design window, where they can't be seen. This is one of the nicest aspects of Wizard Manager. Also, if you wish to hide all steps, press the Move All Steps Off Screen button, positioned as the first button from the left on the toolbar. This will allow you to view the form that the frames are being placed on.

78

CREATING ADD-INS

In Visual Basic 4.0, it was possible to create add-ins using straight coding techniques. Visual Basic 5.0 has simplified add-in creation even more with the addition of an add-in project type. With the new Visual Basic Extensibility interface, you are allowed access to Visual Basic objects such as forms and controls and their underlying code. You can create add-ins to perform automatic manipulation of code objects as well as to change project properties. The Extensibility interface provides you with six basic types of manipulation objects:

- Form manipulation objects
- User interface manipulation objects
- Event response objects
- Add-in management objects
- Project and component manipulation objects
- Code manipulation objects

These manipulation objects are accessed through the Visual Basic VBE object, which is the root object of the Extensibility interface. Once you have created an instance of the VBE object in your add-in program, you automatically have access to all the underlying objects in its hierarchy. Specific coding techniques of the VBE object model are discussed in greater detail, along with the sample add-in, later in this chapter. This chapter was not written as an add-in reference, but rather as a guide to creating add-ins. Therefore, you will get the most out of this chapter if you read it from beginning to end.

Add-In Creation Issues

The safest and most obvious way to create an add-in in Visual Basic is to create a new project of type Add-In. Because an add-in is actually an ActiveX code component, you could create it by using the ActiveX EXE or ActiveX DLL project types. But it is best to use the Add-In project type and let Visual Basic generate code for the add-in template.

This way you are assured that you have all the necessary code and object definitions for a stripped-down add-in. The code that Visual Basic generates performs two actions: It adds the add-in to the Add-Ins menu item (called a command bar) and it displays a form when the add-in is run. Of course, it is not necessary to have a form-based add-in. Add-ins can run in the background, responding to Visual Basic IDE events with no user interface elements at all.

EXE Versus DLL

Because an add-in is actually an ActiveX code component, it must have a project type of ActiveX EXE or ActiveX DLL. When you create a project of type Add-In, Visual Basic defaults it to an ActiveX EXE. If you would like to change the project to an ActiveX DLL, go to the Projects tab under the Project|Project Properties menu item. For an overview on EXE and DLL ActiveX code components, refer to Chapter 76, "OLE Automation." Each project type has its advantages and disadvantages; the functionality of the add-in you are writing determines which one is best to use. In general, it is best to use the DLL (in-process) type of add-in if you need the add-in to run as fast as possible or if the add-in will access properties that are available only in Visual Basic. Most add-ins are currently built using this type. On the other hand, it is best to use the EXE (out-of-process) project type when you need to be able to run your add-in as a standalone program as well as in the Visual Basic IDE. Add-ins created as the EXE type usually have additional functionality when run within the Visual Basic IDE.

The Manipulation Objects

The manipulation objects, listed at the beginning of this chapter, are your link to the Visual Basic IDE. Many features that are available in the IDE itself can also be incorporated into your add-in code. These objects can be used to program powerful add-ins to automate common IDE tasks or to respond to IDE events such as opening code modules. What an add-in can do is limited only by your imagination and, of course, by the IDE functionality the objects will allow you to access. Keep in mind when you are accessing these objects in your code that many of the object properties are actually collections of other objects. For example, the VBControls property of the VBForm object is actually a collection of controls that are currently drawn on the form object. Also, an object or object collection may appear in multiple hierarchies.

Form Manipulation Objects

The root object of this category of manipulation objects is the VBForm object. Its object hierarchy allows you access to project forms as well as contained and selected controls within the forms. These objects can be used to perform actions on certain selected controls or all the controls on a form. For example, this object hierarchy can be used to format controls on a form, or even to create a new form. A working example of how forms can be manipulated is demonstrated in the VB Data Form Wizard add-in included with Visual Basic.

User Interface Manipulation Objects

Visual Basic includes the User Interface object hierarchy to enable you to manipulate Visual Basic windows and command bars. A command bar is a Visual Basic menu or toolbar. By using these objects, you can create a menu item or toolbar button for you to add-in. The User Interface objects also allow you to manipulate the inherent Visual Basic windows such as the Project Explorer or Properties window. You can open, close, size, and move any of these inherent Visual Basic windows, allowing you total control over how your IDE looks. You can also manipulate code windows and react to a user selecting text.

Event Response Objects

The Event Response objects are provided to give you the capability to respond to Visual Basic events. These events are generated by actions such as adding new forms and new projects. You can respond to these events to take action, such as automatically creating and formatting controls on a new form when it is created.

Add-In Management Objects

This object hierarchy is used to expose add-in properties to other add-ins. These objects can be used to perform duties such as identify other add-ins or update the collection of add-ins in the Visual Basic IDE. They are also used to connect and disconnect add-ins from the Visual Basic IDE.

Project and Component Manipulation Objects

These objects allow you to manipulate project options and components. You can use the objects in this hierarchy to perform most project-related operations that are in the Visual Basic project menus. From a project standpoint, they allow you to do things such as create new projects, remove a project from a project group, or change project properties. These objects also expose the components of a project, such as a class module or a standard module.

Code Manipulation Objects

The Code Manipulation object hierarchy allows you to access code elements from your add-in. These objects can be used to modify the code in any of your project components. For example, you could write your own wizard add-in to create the code template for a generic accounting program. By using these objects you can add, delete, search, and replace sections of code in your project components. This is the object hierarchy that the Visual Basic wizard add-ins use to generate code.

The Add-In Project

The Add-In project demonstrates some of the Visual Basic IDE features and events that are accessible through the Extensibility interface. It was written to mirror any additions and deletions from the Project Explorer. To accomplish this, the following Extensibility Interface objects and events are used:

- VBProjects collection and VBProject object
- VBComponents collection and VBComponent object
- VBComponentsEvents event
- VBProjectsEvents event
- CommandBarEvents event

The purpose and use of each of these objects and events will be discussed as we review the code sample. The steps listed below show the steps that were taken to create this project. The code for the completed program is contained in Listings 78-1, 78-2, and 78-3.

Step 1. Create a New Add-In Project Using the Add-In Project Type

By allowing Visual Basic to generate the add-in template for you, you are assured that you have an add-in that will run as is. Visual Basic generates three components for you: the main form (frmAddin), a global module (Addin), and a class module (Connect). It also performs some common duties such as adding the add-in to the Visual Basic Add-Ins menu, connecting the menu item to an event in the add-in, and displaying the form. As we continue, keep in mind that there are four procedures in the Connect class that must contain at least a comment:

- IDTExtensibility_OnConnection
- IDTExtensibility_OnDisconnection
- IDTExtensibility_OnStartupComplete
- IDTExtensibility_OnAddInsUpdate

These procedures are generated by Visual Basic when you create a new add-in project. If there is not at least a comment in each of these procedures, they will not be present in the final DLL or EXE because the compiler strips any empty procedures. The Visual Basic generated form is shown in Figure 78-1.

Step 2. Change the Default Add-In Form

The final form for the Add-In project is shown in Figure 78-2. To make the default form look like this, follow these steps:

1. Delete the Cancel button.
2. Draw an Outline control.
3. Change the caption on the OK button to read "Close."
4. Arrange the controls and resize the form.

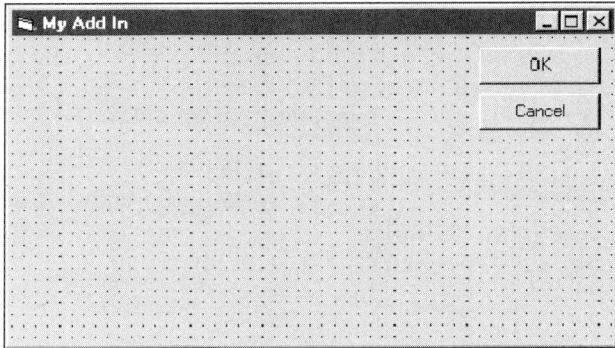

Figure 78-1   Form generated by Visual Basic

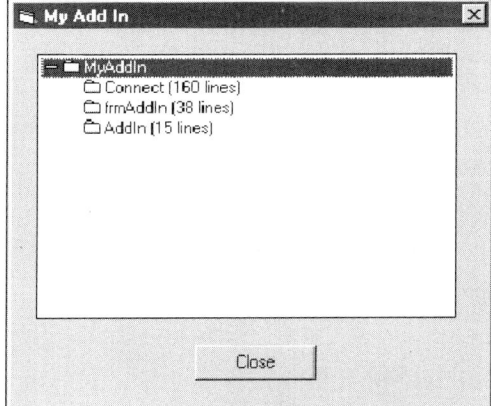

Figure 78-2   The final project form

Step 3. Add Code to Handle Events from the IDE

In the Connect class module, you must tell Visual Basic you are going to be watching for VBComponentsEvents and VBProjectsEvents. To do this, add the following lines to the General Declarations section of the class module:

```
Public WithEvents CompHandler As VBComponentsEvents     'project components event handler
Public WithEvents ProjHandler As VBProjectsEvents       'project event handler
```

The WithEvents keyword tells Visual Basic to include event procedures from the built-in VBComponentsEvents and VBProjectsEvents classes. You will use these procedures just as if you were using a button Click event.

After adding these lines, click on the Object combo box at the top left of the Connect class module code window. You should see your two event objects, called CompHandler and ProjHandler. Choose the CompHandler object. From the Declarations combo box at the top right of the code window, choose the ItemAdded procedure. Visual Basic will automatically add the procedure to the top of the code window and position your cursor in it. Your procedure should look exactly like the ItemAdded procedure below.

```
Private Sub CompHandler_ItemAdded(ByVal VBComponent As VBIDE.VBComponent)
    'When a new component is added, reload the Outline1 control.
    Call mfrmAddIn.LoadList
End Sub
```

Next, choose the ItemRemoved procedure from the Declarations combo box. Your ItemRemoved procedure should look like the one below.

```
Private Sub CompHandler_ItemRemoved(ByVal VBComponent As VBIDE.VBComponent)
    'When a component is removed, reload the Outline1 control.
    Call mfrmAddIn.LoadList
End Sub
```

The two procedures above will perform the LoadList procedure when a component is added or removed from the Project Explorer window. The LoadList procedure adds projects and their components from your project or project group to the Outline1 control.

To add event procedures for the project event handler, choose the ProjHandler object from the Object combo box and follow the same procedure you did above. Your ItemAdded and ItemRemoved procedures should look like the ones below.

```
Private Sub ProjHandler_ItemAdded(ByVal VBProject As VBIDE.VBProject)
    'When a new project is added, reload the Outline1 control.
    Call mfrmAddIn.LoadList
End Sub

Private Sub ProjHandler_ItemRemoved(ByVal VBProject As VBIDE.VBProject)
    'When a project is removed, reload the Outline1 control.
    Call mfrmAddIn.LoadList
End Sub
```

To respond to these events, you must also create instances of the event objects in your code. In the frmAddIn.Load procedure, type the following lines:

```
Set Connect.CompHandler = VBInstance.Events.VBComponentsEvents(Nothing)
Set Connect.ProjHandler = VBInstance.Events.VBProjectsEvents
```

These lines tell the Connect class to respond to these events. If you don't create an instance of the event objects, these events will not be generated in your add-in project.

Step 4. Add Code to Fill the Outline1 Control to Your frmAddIn Form

Open the code window of your form by double-clicking on it and add the LoadList procedure. The code for this procedure is listed below.

```
Sub LoadList()
    Dim proj As Object
    Dim comp As Object

    Outline1.Clear
    For Each proj In VBInstance.VBProjects
```

```
            Outline1.ListIndex = -1
            Outline1.AddItem proj.Name
            Outline1.ListIndex = Outline1.ListCount - 1
            For Each comp In proj.VBComponents
                Outline1.AddItem comp.Name & " (" & comp.CodeModule.CountOfLines & " lines)"
            Next
        Next
End Sub
```

As previously stated, the LoadList procedure fills the Outline1 control with the projects and components currently in your Project Explorer window. Letís take a look at how this procedure works.

As you can see, a For loop is nested inside another For loop. The outer For loop is the project loop, whereas the inner loop is the component loop. Below is a pseudocode version of the LoadList procedure.

```
Clear the Outline1 control
For each project in your Project Explorer window
    Add the project to the Outline1 list
    For each component in the project
        Add the component name and number of lines to the Outline1 list
    Next Component
Next Project
```

VBProjects and VBComponents are both collections. VBProjects is a collection of VBProject objects, and VBComponents is a collection of VBComponent objects. There is one VBProject object in the VBProjects collection for each project in your Project Explorer window. Likewise, there is one VBComponent object in the VBComponents collection for each component in a project. The VBComponents collection is actually a property of the VBProject object. This means that each VBProject object contains a collection of VBComponent objects. For example, you could reference a component in a project as follows:

```
VBInstance.VBProjects(1).VBComponents(1)
```

This would reference the first component of the first project in your Project Explorer window.

Step 5. Add Code to Initialize the Outline1 Control on Startup

For the Outline1 control to be filled on add-in startup, you need to perform some initialization in the Form_Load event procedure. To do this, call the LoadList procedure in your frmAddIn.Load procedure. Your code should look like the code below.

```
Private Sub Form_Load()
    'Connect the component event handler.
    Set Connect.CompHandler = VBInstance.Events.VBComponentsEvents(Nothing)
    'Connect the project event handler.
    Set Connect.ProjHandler = VBInstance.Events.VBProjectsEvents
    Call LoadList
End Sub
```

Step 6. Change Your Project Type

Because the add-in project will not need to be run as a standalone project, you need to change the project type from ActiveX EXE to ActiveX DLL. To do this, choose the Project, Properties menu item. On the General tab of the Project Properties dialog box, change the project type to ActiveX DLL. This will make it an in-process component instead of an out-of-process component.

Step 7. Add Your Add-In to the VBADDIN.INI File

For your add-in to appear in the Add-In Manager, it needs to be added to the VBADDIN.INI file. To do this, open the Visual Basic Immediate window, type AddToINI, and press ENTER. To open the Immediate window, press CTRL-G. There is no need to enter this statement each time you compile or even each time you start Windows. Your add-in will remain in the VBADDIN.INI file unless you remove it. It is worth noting here that your project name must be exactly the same as the string you pass to the AddToINI procedure. If it is not, you will not be able to run your add-in.

Step 8. Compile Your Add-In

To make your DLL file, choose File, Make MyAddin.dll from the Visual Basic IDE menu. Your component is automatically registered with Windows when you compile the project.

Step 9. Run the Add-In

To run your add-in, you must first choose it in the Visual Basic Add-In Manager. To do this, choose the Add-Ins, Add-In Manager menu item. Check the box beside the MyAddin item and click OK. Now choose My Add-In from the Add-Ins menu item. You should see a form similar to the form in Figure 78-2. Try adding or removing elements from the Project Explorer window and watch what happens. You will need to choose the add-in from the Add-Ins menu item again if you are not running your IDE in SDI mode.

Listing 78-1 Code listing for the frmAddin form

```
Public VBInstance As VBIDE.VBE
Public Connect As Connect

Option Explicit

Private Sub CancelButton_Click()
    Connect.Hide
End Sub

Private Sub Form_Load()
    'Connect the component event handler.
    Set Connect.CompHandler = VBInstance.Events.VBComponentsEvents(Nothing)
    'Connect the project event handler.
    Set Connect.ProjHandler = VBInstance.Events.VBProjectsEvents
    Call LoadList
```

```
End Sub

Sub LoadList()
    Dim proj As Object
    Dim comp As Object

    Outline1.Clear
    For Each proj In VBInstance.VBProjects
        Outline1.ListIndex = -1
        Outline1.AddItem proj.Name
        Outline1.ListIndex = Outline1.ListCount - 1
        For Each comp In proj.VBComponents
            Outline1.AddItem comp.Name & " (" & comp.CodeModule.CountOfLines & " lines)"
        Next
    Next
End Sub
```

Listing 78-2 Code listing for the Connect class

```
Option Explicit

'Tells VB to include elements of the IDTExtensibility class.
Implements IDTExtensibility

Public FormDisplayed          As Boolean
Public VBInstance             As VBIDE.VBE                  'Instance of Extensibility ⇐
                                                            Interface
Dim mcbMenuCommandBar         As Office.CommandBarControl  'The command bar (menu item)
Dim mfrmAddIn                 As New frmAddIn              'The main add-in form.
Public WithEvents MenuHandler As CommandBarEvents          'command bar event handler
Public WithEvents CompHandler As VBComponentsEvents        'project components event ⇐
                                                            handler
Public WithEvents ProjHandler As VBProjectsEvents          'project event handler


Sub Hide()
    'Hide the main form.

    On Error Resume Next

    FormDisplayed = False
    mfrmAddIn.Hide
End Sub

Sub Show()
    'Show the main form.

    On Error Resume Next

    If mfrmAddIn Is Nothing Then
        Set mfrmAddIn = New frmAddIn
    End If

    Set mfrmAddIn.VBInstance = VBInstance
    Set mfrmAddIn.Connect = Me
    FormDisplayed = True
    mfrmAddIn.Show
```

continued on next page

continued from previous page

```
End Sub

Private Sub CompHandler_ItemAdded(ByVal VBComponent As VBIDE.VBComponent)
    'When a new component is added, reload the Outline1 control.
    Call mfrmAddIn.LoadList
End Sub

Private Sub CompHandler_ItemRemoved(ByVal VBComponent As VBIDE.VBComponent)
    'When a component is removed, reload the Outline1 control.
    Call mfrmAddIn.LoadList
End Sub

Private Sub IDTExtensibility_OnConnection(ByVal VBInst As Object, ByVal ConnectMode As ⇐
vbext_ConnectMode, ByVal AddInInst As VBIDE.AddIn, custom() As Variant)
    'Adds the add-in to Visual Basic.

    On Error GoTo error_handler

    'Save the VB instance.
    Set VBInstance = VBInst

    If ConnectMode = vbext_cm_External Then
        'Used by the wizard toolbar to start this wizard.
        Me.Show
    Else
        Set mcbMenuCommandBar = AddToAddInCommandBar("My AddIn")
        'Sink the event.
        Set Me.MenuHandler = VBInst.Events.CommandBarEvents(mcbMenuCommandBar)
    End If

    If ConnectMode = vbext_cm_AfterStartup Then
        If GetSetting(App.Title, "Settings", "DisplayOnConnect", "0") = "1" Then
            'Set this to display the form on connect.
            Me.Show
        End If
    End If
    Exit Sub
error_handler:
    MsgBox Err.Description
End Sub

Private Sub IDTExtensibility_OnDisconnection(ByVal RemoveMode As vbext_DisconnectMode, ⇐
custom() As Variant)
    'Removes the add-in from Visual Basic.

    On Error Resume Next

    'delete the command bar entry
    mcbMenuCommandBar.Delete

    'shut down the Add-In
    If FormDisplayed Then
        SaveSetting App.Title, "Settings", "DisplayOnConnect", "1"
        FormDisplayed = False
    Else
        SaveSetting App.Title, "Settings", "DisplayOnConnect", "0"
    End If
```

```
      Unload mfrmAddIn
      Set mfrmAddIn = Nothing

End Sub

Private Sub IDTExtensibility_OnStartupComplete(custom() As Variant)
    'If VB has started with the add-in activated, show the main form.

    If GetSetting(App.Title, "Settings", "DisplayOnConnect", "0") = "1" Then
        'Set this to display the form on connect.
        Me.Show
    End If
End Sub

Private Sub IDTExtensibility_OnAddInsUpdate(custom() As Variant)
    'This is a required procedure for your add-in.
    'It must have at least a comment in it before you compile.
End Sub

Private Sub MenuHandler_Click(ByVal CommandBarControl As Object, handled As Boolean, ⇐
CancelDefault As Boolean)
    'This event fires when the menu is clicked in the IDE.
    Me.Show
End Sub

Function AddToAddInCommandBar(sCaption As String) As Office.CommandBarControl
    'Adds your add-in menu item under the VB Add-Ins menu (command bar).

    Dim cbMenuCommandBar As Office.CommandBarControl   'command bar object
    Dim cbMenu As Object

    On Error GoTo AddToAddInCommandBarErr

    'See if we can find the Add-Ins menu.
    Set cbMenu = VBInstance.CommandBars("Add-Ins")
    If cbMenu Is Nothing Then
        'Menu is not available so we fail.
        Exit Function
    End If

    'Add it to the command bar.
    Set cbMenuCommandBar = cbMenu.Controls.Add(1)
    'Set the caption.
    cbMenuCommandBar.Caption = sCaption

    Set AddToAddInCommandBar = cbMenuCommandBar

    Exit Function

AddToAddInCommandBarErr:

End Function


Private Sub ProjHandler_ItemAdded(ByVal VBProject As VBIDE.VBProject)
    'When a new project is added, reload the Outline1 control.

    Call mfrmAddIn.LoadList
```

continued on next page

continued from previous page

```
End Sub

Private Sub ProjHandler_ItemRemoved(ByVal VBProject As VBIDE.VBProject)
    'When a project is removed, reload the Outline1 control.

    Call mfrmAddIn.LoadList
End Sub
```

Listing 78-3 Code listing for Addin module

```
Option Explicit
Declare Function WritePrivateProfileString& Lib "Kernel32" Alias ⇐
"WritePrivateProfileStringA" (ByVal AppName$, ByVal KeyName$, ByVal keydefault$, ByVal ⇐
FileName$)

'This sub should be executed from the Immediate window
'in order to add this application to the VBADDIN.INI file.
'You must change the name in the 2nd argument to reflect
'the correct name of your project.
Sub AddToINI()
    Dim ErrCode As Long
    ErrCode = WritePrivateProfileString("Add-Ins32", "MyAddIn.Connect", "0", "vbaddin.ini")
End Sub
```

How It Works

How your add-in actually works probably seems like a mystery right now, so for purposes of discussion, let's talk a bit about the code that Visual Basic generated for you and the times at which it is called. When you choose your add-in from the Add-In Manager and select OK, Visual Basic calls your add-in's IDTExtensibility_ OnConnection procedure. This procedure contains the code to add your add-in's name under the Add-Ins menu item. You will also notice the code to register the CommandBar event with Visual Basic. This is the line that reads

```
Set Me.MenuHandler = VBInst.Events.CommandBarEvents(mcbMenuCommandBar)
```

You could also add code in this procedure to notify other add-ins that your add-in is available.

If your add-in is active (chosen in Add-In Manager) when Visual Basic is started, the IDTExtensibility_OnStartupComplete procedure is called. It is best not to put lengthy code in this or the OnConnection procedure to avoid a long wait for your add-in to start.

When you run your add-in from the Add-Ins menu, an event is generated in the add-in. This event is handled by the MenuHandler_Click procedure. As in the procedures mentioned above, it is best not to put lengthy code in this procedure to delay program startup.

When the VBADDIN.INI file is changed and saved an event also occurs in your add-in that is handled by the IDTExtensibility_OnAddInsUpdate procedure. If your add-in is dependent on another add-in, you can put code in this procedure to handle the situation in which the other add-in has been deactivated.

The IDTExtensibility_OnDisconnection procedure is called when your add-in is disconnected from the Visual Basic environment. This is analogous to the box next to your add-in being unchecked in the Add-In Manager. It is worth noting here that an add-in resides in memory until this situation occurs, even if the add-in's form is not visible. You could add code in this procedure to let other add-ins know that the add-in will no longer be available for their use.

For the sake of discussion, it wouldn't be fair if we did not say a little about the event procedures that you created. When items are added or removed from the Project Explorer window, your add-in receives events. The Project Explorer action and its event handling procedure are given in Table 78-1.

Table 78-1 Event handling procedures

Project Explorer Action	Handling Procedure Name
Project added	ProjHandler_ItemAdded
Project removed	ProjHandler_ItemRemoved
Component added	CompHandler_ItemAdded
Component removed	CompHandler_ItemRemoved

If you review the declaration of these event objects in step 3, you will notice a similarity between them and the MenuHandler event declaration. This is because all the possible events that your add-in can respond to are located in the Events property. Other event properties that your add-in can respond to are

- CommandBarEvents

- FileControlEvents

- ReferencesEvents

- SelectedVBControlsEvents

- VBControlsEvents

To respond to these events, or to user-defined events, follow the same procedure as listed in step 3.

79

RESPONDING TO USER ACTIONS WITH ADD-INS

Add-ins that respond to the actions of the user can be especially useful aids in standardizing your programs. Such an add-in can, for example, add a copyright line to the code window of every form you add to a project, or set the ForeColor and BackColor of every text box you add to a form.

IDE Events

The Visual Basic 5.0 Extensibility object exposes the IDE events in Table 79-1.

Table 79-1 Properties of the Events object

Property	Responds to
CommandBarEvents Property	Click on a Command Bar
FileControlEvents Property	After a file is added
	Before and after a filename is changed
	After a file is closed
	After a file is removed
	Before and after a file is written (saved)
	Before and after a file is loaded
ReferenceEvents Property	When a reference is added
	When a reference is removed
SelectedVBControlsEvents Property	When a new control is selected
	When a control is unselected

continued on next page

continued from previous page

Property	Responds to
VBComponentsEvents Property	When a component is activated
	When a component is added
	When a component is reloaded
	When a component is removed
	When a component is renamed
	When a component is selected
VBControlsEvents Property	When a control is added
	When a control is removed
	When a control is renamed
VBProjectsEvents Property	When a project is activated
	When a project is added
	When a project is removed
	When a project is renamed

Adding Event Handlers to the Class

Each event handler must be declared in the declarations section of the add-in's class. To use the VBControlsEvents object, declare it:

```
Public WithEvents CtlHandler As VBControlsEvents 'controls event handler
```

Simply declaring the object adds its events to the class. To use the events, connect the event handler to the current instance of the IDE in the IDTExtensibility_OnConnection event:

```
Private Sub IDTExtensibility_OnConnection(ByVal VBInst As Object, ByVal ConnectMode As
  VBIDE.vbext_ConnectMode, ByVal AddInInst As VBIDE.AddIn, custom() As Variant)
    Set gVBInstance = VBInst
    Set Me.CtlHandler = gVBInstance.Events.VBControlsEvents(Nothing, Nothing)
End Sub
```

The (Nothing, Nothing) in the assignment statement allows the add-in to respond to controls' events on any form in any loaded project. Similarly, declare and connect the VBComponents events. The declaration is:

```
Public WithEvents CmpHandler As VBComponentsEvents 'components event handler
```

and add the following declaration in the IDTExtensibility_OnConnection event:

```
Set Me.CmpHandler = gVBInstance.Events.VBComponentsEvents(Nothing)
```

Note that here there is a single (Nothing). This is because components (forms, modules, class modules, and so on) are one level higher in the hierarchy. This (Nothing) allows the add-in to respond to VBComponents events in any loaded project.

How to Crack the Hierarchy

VBOnline describes the hierarchy of the Visual Basic IDE, but leaves a lot unsaid. You can use a design-time add-in to refine your understanding of the hierarchy. The following example is a mini-project that you can use to spy on the VBE hierarchy. The project is on the CD that accompanies this book in the Hierarchy subdirectory.

1. Start a new project. Select Add-In from the New Project dialog.

2. Add the following line to the declaration section of Connect.Cls.

```
Public objA As Object, objB As Object, objC As Object
```

3. Add a breakpoint to the code in the IDTExtensibility_OnConnection event. The line you want is "Exit Sub."

4. Press CTRL-G to open the Immediate window. Type AddToIni in the Immediate window and press ENTER. This adds the project reference to the VBAddin.ini file and makes it available to the Add-In Manager.

5. Press CTRL-F5 for Start With Full Compile.

6. Open a second instance of Visual Basic 5.0.

7. On the Add-Ins|Add-In Manager menu, select MyAddIn to connect the add-in to the new project.

8. When the add-in is connected, it will stop at the breakpoint in the IDTExtensibility_OnConnection event.

9. Press CTRL-G to open the Immediate window.

10. Type the following lines into the Immediate window, pressing ENTER after each line.

```
set objA = vbinstance.addins

debug.print: for each objB in objA: debug.print objB.progid, objb.description:next
```

On the test computer, this resulted in:

```
VBSDIAddIn.Connect
DataToolsAddIn.Connect
AppWizard.Wizard
WizMan.Connect              VB Wizard Manager
ClassBuilder.Wizard         VB Class Builder Utility
AddInToolbar.Connect        VB Add-In Toolbar
ControlWiz.Wizard
DataFormWizard.Wizard
ActiveXDocumentWizard.Wizard
PropertyPageWizard.Wizard
APIDeclarationLoader.Connect
Respond.clsRespond
MyAddIn.Connect             My Add-In
```

Your own results will reflect the setups in your computer. Following are a few more examples of this technique.

COMMANDBARS COLLECTION

```
set objA = vbinstance.commandbars

debug.print: for each objB in objA: debug.print objB.name, objB.index: next
```

```
Menu Bar          1
Standard          2
Edit              3
Debug             4
Form Editor       5
Document          6
Project Window Insert           7
Toggle            8
Code Window       9
Code Window (Break)             10
Watch Window     11
Immediate Window                12
Locals Window    13
Forms             14
Controls          15
Project Window                  16
Project Window (Break)          17
Form Layout Window              18
Object Browser                  19
Toolbox           20
Toolbox Group    21
Property Browser                22
Color Palette    23
Project Window Project          24
Project Window Form Folder      25
Project Window Module/Class Folder          26
Project Window Related Documents Folder     27
Docked Window    28
Add-In Toolbar                  29
```

WINDOWS COLLECTION

```
set objA = vbinstance.windows

debug.print: for each objB in objA: debug.print objB.caption, objB.type: next
```

```
Form1             1
Project - Project1              6
Form Layout      13
                 15
Properties - Form1              7
                 14
Object Browser                  2
Watches           3
Locals            4
Immediate         5
Wizard Manager                  15
```

The next example shows the steps used on the test computer to explore more deeply into the hierarchy.

Start with:

```
set objA = vbinstance.vbprojects

debug.print: for each objb in obja: debug.print objB.name: next

Project1
```

Then, to explore into the project:

```
set objA = vbinstance.vbprojects
set objC = obja(1).vbcomponents

debug.print: for each objb in objc: debug.print objB.name: next

Form1
```

Note the use of the subscript to select the project in the example above. (Subscripts in the hierarchy are one-based.) If you add more forms, they will be listed in order. To be sure which form is which, you can add objB.Index to the Debug.Print statement.

To learn more about a form:

```
set objA = vbinstance.vbprojects
set objC = obja(1).vbcomponents(1).Properties

debug.print: for each objb in objc: debug.print objB.name: next

Name
Caption
BackColor
ForeColor
Left
Top
Width
Height
Enabled
WindowState
MousePointer
ScaleLeft
ScaleTop
ScaleWidth
ScaleHeight
ScaleMode
FontTransparent
DrawStyle
DrawWidth
FillStyle
FillColor
DrawMode
AutoRedraw
Picture
BorderStyle
Icon
LinkTopic
LinkMode
MaxButton
MinButton
```

continued on next page

continued from previous page

```
ControlBox
Visible
Tag
MDIChild
KeyPreview
ClipControls
HelpContextID
MouseIcon
NegotiateMenus
Font
Appearance
WhatsThisButton
WhatsThisHelp
ShowInTaskbar
RightToLeft
StartUpPosition
OLEDropMode
Palette
PaletteMode
Moveable
```

Again, note the use of subscripts to get to the specific project and form.

The correct syntax is not always obvious, but patience and persistence will help you beyond the sparse documentation.

Respond Project

Project Overview

The Respond project is a demonstration of how an add-in responds to user events in the IDE. Beyond the demonstration, it doesn't do anything useful. The project is also designed with no user interface to demonstrate how to create an invisible add-in.

The following pages discuss the assembly and operation of the Respond project. The first section deals with the assembly of the Respond class. Following this is a discussion that shows and briefly explains the contents of the subroutines of this project. Finally, there is a How It Works guide to the operation of the project. Read this information carefully in the process of assembling the project.

Assembling the Project

Assembling the Class

1. Start a new ActiveX DLL project.

2. Add a Basic module to the project.

3. Rename the class ClsRespond and save it as ClsRespond.Cls.

4. Add the code in Listing 79-1 to the declarations section of ClsRespond.

Listing 79-1 Declarations for ClsRespond

```
Option Explicit

Implements IDTExtensibility
Public WithEvents CmpHandler As VBComponentsEvents 'components event handler
Public WithEvents CtlHandler As VBControlsEvents 'controls event handler
Dim mcbMenuCommandBar As Office.CommandBarControl 'command bar object
```

5. Add the code in Listing 79-2 to ClsRespond.

Listing 79-2 Code for ClsRespond

```
'==================================================================
'this sub handles adding a component
'==================================================================

Private Sub CmpHandler_ItemAdded(ByVal VBComponent As VBIDE.VBComponent)
    MsgBox VBComponent.Name & " Added"
End Sub

'==================================================================
'this sub handles removing a component
'==================================================================

Private Sub CmpHandler_ItemRemoved(ByVal VBComponent As VBIDE.VBComponent)
    MsgBox VBComponent.Name & " Removed"
End Sub

'==================================================================
'this sub handles renaming a component
'==================================================================

Private Sub CmpHandler_ItemRenamed(ByVal VBComponent As ⇐
VBIDE.VBComponent, ByVal OldName As String)
    MsgBox OldName & " Renamed " & VBComponent.Name
End Sub

'==================================================================
'this sub responds when a component is selected
'==================================================================

Private Sub CmpHandler_ItemSelected(ByVal VBComponent ⇐
As VBIDE.VBComponent)
    MsgBox VBComponent.Name & " Selected"
End Sub

'==================================================================
'this sub handles adding a control
'==================================================================

Private Sub CtlHandler_ItemAdded(ByVal VBControl As VBIDE.VBControl)
    MsgBox VBControl.Properties("Name") & " added"
End Sub
```

continued on next page

continued from previous page

```
'====================================================================
'this sub handles removing a control
'====================================================================

Private Sub CtlHandler_ItemRemoved(ByVal VBControl As VBIDE.VBControl)
    MsgBox VBControl.Properties("Name") & " Removed"
End Sub

'====================================================================
'this sub handles renaming a control
'====================================================================

Private Sub CtlHandler_ItemRenamed(ByVal VBControl As VBIDE.VBControl,⇐
ByVal OldName As String, ByVal OldIndex As Long)
    MsgBox VBControl & " Renamed from " & OldName & " to " & VBControl.Properties("Name")
End Sub

Private Sub IDTExtensibility_OnAddInsUpdate(custom() As Variant)
'stub to keep the compiler from removing this empty procedure
End Sub

'====================================================================
'this sub assigns the events objects and
'tells you that the add-in is connected
'====================================================================

Private Sub IDTExtensibility_OnConnection(ByVal VBInst As Object, ⇐
ByVal ConnectMode As VBIDE.vbext_ConnectMode, ByVal AddInInst As VBIDE.AddIn, ⇐
custom() As Variant)
    Set gVBInstance = VBInst
    'components and controls event handler
    Set Me.CmpHandler = gVBInstance.Events.VBComponentsEvents(Nothing)
    Set Me.CtlHandler = _
      gVBInstance.Events.VBControlsEvents(Nothing, Nothing)
    MsgBox "Respond is now connected"
End Sub

'====================================================================
'this sub destroys the events objects and
'tells you that the add-in is disconnected
'====================================================================

Private Sub IDTExtensibility_OnDisconnection(ByVal RemoveMode As VBIDE.vbext_⇐
DisconnectMode, custom() As Variant)
    Set Me.CmpHandler = Nothing
    Set Me.CtlHandler = Nothing
    MsgBox "Respond is now disconnected"
End Sub

Private Sub IDTExtensibility_OnStartupComplete(custom() As Variant)
'stub to keep the compiler from removing this empty procedure
End Sub
```

Assembling the Basic Module

1. Add a Basic module to the project.

2. Rename the module modRespond and save it as Respond.Bas.

3. Add the code in Listing 79-3 to the module.

Listing 79-3 Code for modRespond

```
Option Explicit

'needed to pass the menu keystrokes to VB
Private Declare Sub PostMessage Lib "user32" Alias "PostMessageA" _
  (ByVal hwnd&, ByVal msg&, ByVal wp&, ByVal lp&)

'needed to pass the menu keystrokes to VB
Private Declare Sub SetFocus Lib "user32" (ByVal hwnd&)

'needed to pass the menu keystrokes to VB
Private Declare Function GetParent Lib "user32" (ByVal hwnd&) As Long

'needed to add the add-in to VBADDINS.INI
Declare Function WritePrivateProfileString& Lib "Kernel32" _
  Alias "WritePrivateProfileStringA" _
  (ByVal AppName$, ByVal KeyName$, ByVal keydefault$, ByVal FileName$)

Const WM_SYSKEYDOWN = &H104

Dim hwndMenu       As Long 'needed to pass the menu keystrokes to VB

Global gVBInstance As VBIDE.VBE        'instance of VB IDE

'=====================================================================
'this sub should be executed from the Immediate window
'in order to get this app added to the VBADDIN.INI file
'=====================================================================
Sub AddToINI()
    Dim ErrCode As Long
    ErrCode = WritePrivateProfileString("Add-Ins32", _
      "Respond.clsRespond", "0", "vbaddin.ini")
    MsgBox "Addin is now added to VBADDIN.INI file"
End Sub

'=====================================================================
'this sub handles keydown events in the IDE. It is required so
'the IDE responds to the menu
'=====================================================================

Sub HandleKeyDown(ud As Object, KeyCode As Integer, Shift As Integer)
  If Shift <> 4 Then Exit Sub 'Shift <> Alt
  If KeyCode < 65 Or KeyCode > 90 Then Exit Sub 'Keycode <> A through Z
  If gVBInstance.DisplayModel = vbext_dm_SDI Then Exit Sub

  If hwndMenu = 0 Then hwndMenu = FindHwndMenu(ud.hwnd)
  PostMessage hwndMenu, WM_SYSKEYDOWN, KeyCode, &H20000000
  KeyCode = 0
  SetFocus hwndMenu
End Sub
```

continued on next page

continued from previous page

```
'=================================================================
'this function gets the IDE window handle for the HandleKeyDown sub
'=================================================================

Function FindHwndMenu&(ByVal hwnd&)
  Dim h As Long

Loop2:
  h = GetParent(hwnd)
  If h = 0 Then FindHwndMenu = hwnd: Exit Function
  hwnd = h
  GoTo Loop2
End Function
```

Changing the Class Description

1. Press F2 to open the object browser.

2. Right-click on ClsRespond and select Properties from the pop-up menu.

3. Change the Description to Respond and click on OK. This changes the name that appears in the Add-Ins menu.

Running the Program

1. Open the Immediate window, type AddToIni, and press ENTER to add the program to the VBAddin.Ini file.

2. Open the File menu and select Make Respond.Dll to compile the new add-in.

3. Open the File menu and start a new project.

4. Select Add-Ins|Add-In Manager and add the Respond add-in to the new project.

5. Add a new form to the project, add controls to the forms, and delete or rename forms and controls. The Respond add-in takes note of all of these events and tells you about it.

How It Works

There are a couple of tricky points in this add-in. Probably the sneakiest is the fact that menu clicks and shortcuts are intercepted by the add-in and must be passed along to the Visual Basic 5.0 IDE. Two functions in the Basic module, HandleKeyDown and FindHwndMenu take care of that. HandleKeyDown uses the PostMessage API to pass the menu click along to the IDE.

The declarations in the class module convert an ordinary ActiveX DLL into an add-in, and declare the objects for two event handlers: VBComponents events and VBControls events. When the class is connected, then both event handlers are instantiated in the IDTExtensibility_OnConnection procedure, and the code in the class can respond to the events.

The event handlers in this project simply annoy you with message boxes telling you what you just did. Figure 79-1 shows Respond at work. To make the Respond do something useful, replace the message box code with your own. In the introduction to this chapter, there are a couple of suggestions for what you might have it do.

Cleaning Up

When you have finished working with an add-in like this, one that you will not use again, delete the .DLL file and run RegClean to remove all references to it from the system registry. When Visual Basic does not find the .DLL file for an add-in, it prompts you with a message box that asks permission to remove the reference from VBAddin.Ini, so you don't need to manually edit the .INI file. For the Visual Basic 5.0 release, Microsoft removed RegClean from the CD. You can find it on the Microsoft site on the World Wide Web. Search the Knowledge Base for RegClean to get the latest release.

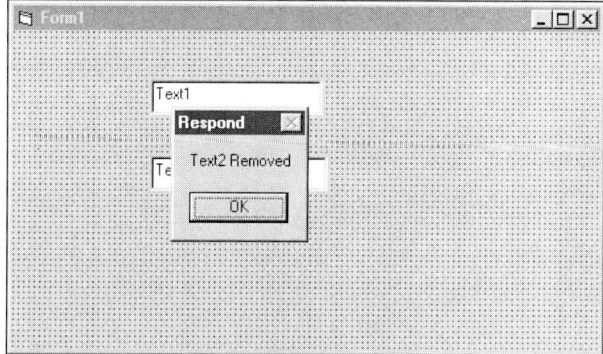

Figure 79-1 Respond at work

80

MODIFYING THE HOST'S INTERFACE

As mentioned in Chapter 78, "Creating Add-Ins," it is possible to create an add-in to customize the Visual Basic development environment. This is a powerful feature because it allows the user to manipulate the development environment to his or her satisfaction by running the add-in. For example, if there are multiple users on a single machine, an add-in could be created so that each user could have his or her own Visual Basic development environment settings. To write an add-in of this type, use the extensibility objects that provide this capability. They are CommandBars, Windows, LinkedWindows, and CodePanes. Each object is actually a collection and is described in the following sections.

The CommandBars Collection

The CommandBars extensibility collection is made available to the add-in programmer to expose a method for running the add-in. For example, the CommandBars collection could be used to add a toolbar button or menu item to the Visual Basic development environment. The CommandBars collection is a collection of CommandBar objects. Therefore, each top-level menu item and toolbar in the Visual Basic development environment is a member of the CommandBars collection. To view a list of the names of the available CommandBar objects in your development environment, create an add-in and put the following code in the IDTExtensibility_OnConnection procedure:

```
Dim i As Integer
    For i = 1 To VBInstance.CommandBars.Count
        MsgBox (VBInstance.CommandBars(i).Name)
    Next
```

When you connect the add-in via the Add-In Manager, a message box will pop up for every CommandBar object, telling you its name. These will include the names of some top-level menu items and toolbars. Some of the menu items and toolbars are not exposed through the extensibility interface to avoid changing the development environment in such a way as to limit its capabilities.

When a new add-in is generated by Visual Basic, Visual Basic adds the code to include the add-in under the Add-Ins menu item on connection. To accomplish this, the CommandBars collection is used. The following function is called by the IDTExtensibility_OnConnection method to add the add-in's name to the Add-Ins menu:

```
Function AddToAddInCommandBar(sCaption As String) As Office.CommandBarControl
    Dim cbMenuCommandBar As Office.CommandBarControl  'command bar object
    Dim cbMenu As Object

    On Error GoTo AddToAddInCommandBarErr

    'See if we can find the Add-Ins menu.
    Set cbMenu = VBInstance.CommandBars("Add-Ins")
    If cbMenu Is Nothing Then
        'The Add-Ins menu item is not available.
        Exit Function
    End If

    'Add it to the command bar.
    Set cbMenuCommandBar = cbMenu.Controls.Add(1)
    'Set the caption.
    cbMenuCommandBar.Caption = sCaption

    Set AddToAddInCommandBar = cbMenuCommandBar

    Exit Function

AddToAddInCommandBarErr:

End Function
```

The AddToAddInCommandBar function is called with the caption of the menu item passed to it. The first thing this function does is create a CommandBar object and assign it to the cbMenu object variable by issuing the following statement:

```
Set cbMenu = VBInstance.CommandBars("Add-Ins")
```

Because CommandBars is a collection of CommandBar objects and items in a collection can be referenced by name, the CommandBar object for the Add-Ins menu item is returned. In a similar fashion, this statement could be used to obtain the object reference to the standard toolbar to add a button for your add-in. It is good programming to check your return values for correctness or existence. Thus, the cbMenu variable is checked to make sure the reference to the Add-Ins menu item was returned. If it was not, no attempt is made to add the name of the add-in. However, if the reference was returned, the add-in's name is added under it. This is accomplished by accessing the CommandBar.Controls collection, as in the following statement:

```
Set cbMenuCommandBar = cbMenu.Controls.Add(1)
```

The reference to the newly created menu item is then returned to the IDTExtensibility_OnConnection procedure to have its event handler mapped to the add-in. This is an important part of adding menu items and toolbar buttons to enable your add-in, because if you do not map an event to the menu item or button, nothing will happen when the menu item or toolbar is clicked. To perform this mapping, you need to add two lines of code. The first line should be put in the Declarations section of the Connect class and should be similar to the following:

```
Public WithEvents MenuHandler As CommandBarEvents
```

The second line should be included in the IDTExtensibility_OnConnection procedure and should look like this:

```
Set Me.MenuHandler = VBInst.Events.CommandBarEvents(mcbMenuCommandBar)
```

By using these two lines of code, the Visual Basic development environment triggers an event in your add-in, which in turn shows your add-in window or simply runs code to perform some task. This code is placed in the MenuHandler_Click event procedure, which is the only event procedure included in the event.

The Windows Collection

The Windows collection is contained in the extensibility object model to allow your add-in to perform actions on windows in the Visual Basic development environment. The Windows collection should not be confused with the Windows operating system. Actions that may be performed include resizing, closing, and opening windows. The Windows collection includes permanent and temporary windows. A permanent window is a window that is a permanent part of the Visual Basic development environment, such as the Projects and Properties windows. Permanent windows are never removed from the Windows collection, even if they are closed. In effect, they are hidden from view. A temporary window is any other window, such as a code or designer window. When a temporary window is closed, it is removed from the Windows collection.

The Windows collection is a collection of Window objects, each having properties and methods that may be accessed and/or modified. Some of these properties and their definitions are included in Table 80-1.

Table 80-1 Some properties of the Window object

Caption	Action
Left	Returns/sets the horizontal position of the top-left corner.
Top	Returns/sets the vertical position of the top-left corner.
Width	Returns/sets the width of the window.
Height	Returns/sets the height of the window.
LinkedWindowFrame	Returns a reference to the window to which the current window is linked.
WindowState	Returns/sets the state of a window, such as minimized, maximized, or normal.
Type	Returns the type of window, such as Immediate, Code, Project.

There are also two methods included with the Window object. They are the SetFocus and Close methods. The SetFocus method is used to change focus to a specific window in the Windows collection. The Close method is used to close the window that currently has the focus. The rules of permanent and temporary windows apply to the Close method.

Because the LinkedWindowFrame property is closely tied to the way linked windows work, it is discussed in more detail in the section titled "The LinkedWindows Collection." As mentioned above, the Windows collection contains a Window object for each window in the Visual Basic development environment, including your open project windows. In case two or more windows are linked, there will be an entry in the Windows collection for each linked window and the linked frame window. To view a list of the windows currently in your development environment, put the following code in your IDTExtensibility_OnConnection procedure:

```
Dim i As Integer
    For i = 1 To VBInstance.Windows.Count
        MsgBox  Window.Caption =   + VBInstance.Windows(i).Caption
    Next
```

In keeping with traditional collection properties, the Count property is used to traverse through the Windows collection and display the caption of each window in the current Visual Basic development environment. Windows that do not have caption bars on them will not display a caption title in the message box output. These include any linked windows. We should also note that windows such as add-in windows and others that are not directly related to the Visual Basic development environment will not appear in the Windows collection.

The LinkedWindows Collection

Because linked windows are new to the Visual Basic development environment, we will discuss their general functionality before we get into the actual discussion of the LinkedWindows collection of objects. Windows such as Projects and Properties can be "joined" together into what seems to be one sectional window, as in Figure 80-1. When windows are joined together in the development environment, they become contained within another window, called a *linked window frame*. Windows can be added or removed from a linked window frame with the Add and Remove methods. Windows that may be linked include all windows in the Visual Basic development environment except code windows, designer windows, the Object Browser, and the Search and Replace window.

Windows contained in the linked window frame cannot have normal operations such as resizing performed on them. Therefore, a way must be provided to retrieve a reference to the frame window. This is where the Window.LinkedWindowFrame property comes into play. The LinkedWindowFrame property of the Window object returns a reference to the linked window frame if the Window object referred to is linked; otherwise, it returns nothing.

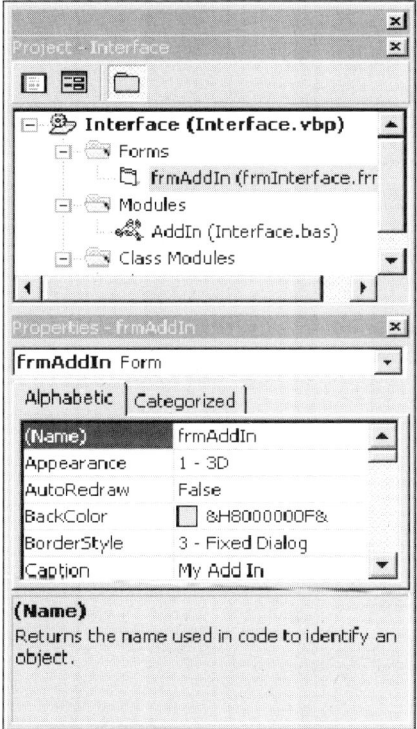

Figure 80-1   Example of a linked window frame

The Interface Example

This example is designed to show you how to manipulate windows in the Visual Basic development environment through code. On startup, this add-in fills a combo box with the captions of all the windows in the Windows collection. You may then change attributes of the window that is currently selected in the combo box, depending on what type of window you have chosen. As mentioned above, particular attributes of some window types are read-only.

As we continue this section, you are given steps to create this example add-in. The complete code listing is contained in Listings 80-1, 80-2, and 80-3, at the end of this section.

Step 1. Create the Add-In

Using the Add-In project type in Visual Basic, create a new add-in project. This will generate the necessary code for a generic add-in. For a more detailed description on creating and running an add-in, refer to Chapter 78.

Step 2. Change the Default Add-In Form

Add and remove components on the default add-in form so that the finished form looks similar to Figure 80-2.

Step 3. Add Code to Fill the Combo Box with Window Captions

To fill the Host Windows combo box, enter the following code in the frmAddin.Load procedure:

```
Private Sub Form_Load()
    Dim i As Integer

    'Fill the HostWin combo box with host window names.
    For i = 1 To VBInstance.Windows.Count
        If (Trim(VBInstance.Windows(i).Caption) <> "") Then
            HostWin.AddItem VBInstance.Windows(i).Caption
        Else
            HostWin.AddItem "<No Caption>"
        End If
        HostWin.ItemData(HostWin.ListCount - 1) = i
    Next
    HostWin.ListIndex = 0
End Sub
```

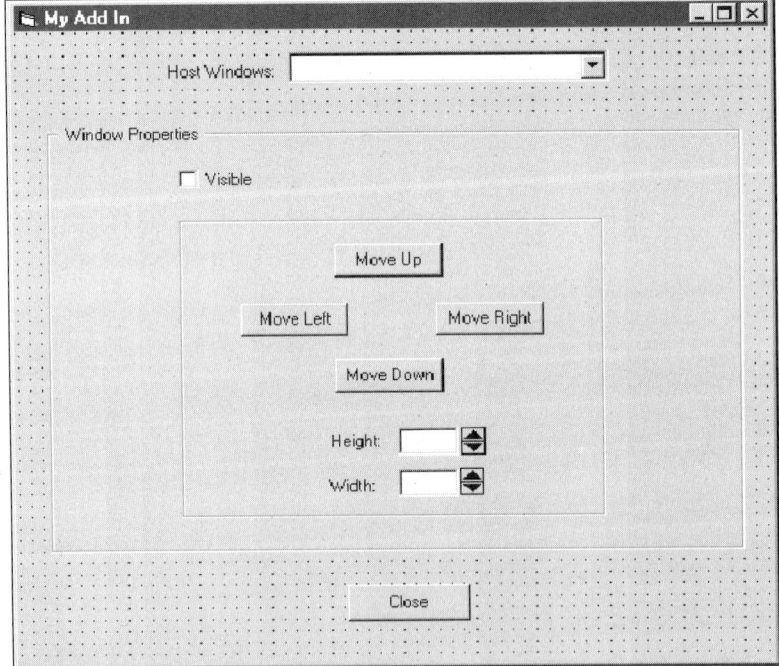

Figure 80-2 The final interface add-in form

This code loops through each element in the Windows collection, each time adding the window caption into the combo box. Windows that have no caption, such as linked window frames, will have "<No Caption>" representing them in the combo box.

Step 4. Add Code to Fill in Window Properties

When an item is chosen from the Host Windows combo box, the Width and Height text boxes need to be filled and the Visible check box must be set. To do this, add the following code to your HostWin.Click procedure:

```
Private Sub HostWin_Click()
    'Fill in host window properties.

    If VBInstance.Windows(HostWin.ItemData(HostWin.ListIndex)).Visible Then
        IsVisible.Value = 1
    Else
        IsVisible.Value = 0
    End If
    TheHeight.Text = Str(VBInstance.Windows(HostWin.ItemData(HostWin.ListIndex)).Height)
    TheWidth.Text = Str(VBInstance.Windows(HostWin.ItemData(HostWin.ListIndex)).Width)
End Sub
```

Step 5. Add Code to Respond to Changing Properties

When properties such as window position or visibility change, you must reflect these changes on the appropriate window. To accomplish this, add code under the movement buttons, the visibility check box, and the spin controls.

```
Private Sub IsVisible_Click()
    'Make the window visible or invisible.
    If (IsVisible.Value = 1) Then
        VBInstance.Windows(HostWin.ItemData(HostWin.ListIndex)).Visible = True
    Else
        VBInstance.Windows(HostWin.ItemData(HostWin.ListIndex)).Visible = False
    End If
    TheHeight.Text = Str(VBInstance.Windows(HostWin.ItemData(HostWin.ListIndex)).Height)
    TheWidth.Text = Str(VBInstance.Windows(HostWin.ItemData(HostWin.ListIndex)).Width)
End Sub

Private Sub MoveDown_Click()
    'Move the window down.
    VBInstance.Windows(HostWin.ItemData(HostWin.ListIndex)).SetFocus
    VBInstance.Windows(HostWin.ItemData(HostWin.ListIndex)).Top =
VBInstance.Windows(HostWin.ItemData(HostWin.ListIndex)).Top + 5
End Sub

Private Sub MoveLeft_Click()
    'Move the window left.
    If ((VBInstance.Windows(HostWin.ItemData(HostWin.ListIndex)).Left - 5) > 0) Then
        VBInstance.Windows(HostWin.ItemData(HostWin.ListIndex)).SetFocus
        VBInstance.Windows(HostWin.ItemData(HostWin.ListIndex)).Left =
VBInstance.Windows(HostWin.ItemData(HostWin.ListIndex)).Left - 5
    End If
```

continued on next page

continued from previous page

```
End Sub

Private Sub MoveRight_Click()
    'Move the window right.
    VBInstance.Windows(HostWin.ItemData(HostWin.ListIndex)).SetFocus
    VBInstance.Windows(HostWin.ItemData(HostWin.ListIndex)).Left =
VBInstance.Windows(HostWin.ItemData(HostWin.ListIndex)).Left + 5
End Sub

Private Sub MoveUp_Click()
    'Move the window up.
    If ((VBInstance.Windows(HostWin.ItemData(HostWin.ListIndex)).Top - 5) > 0) Then
        VBInstance.Windows(HostWin.ItemData(HostWin.ListIndex)).SetFocus
        VBInstance.Windows(HostWin.ItemData(HostWin.ListIndex)).Top =
VBInstance.Windows(HostWin.ItemData(HostWin.ListIndex)).Top - 5
    End If
End Sub

Private Sub SpinHeight_SpinDown()
    'Decrease the window's height.
    VBInstance.Windows(HostWin.ItemData(HostWin.ListIndex)).SetFocus
    TheHeight.Text = Str(Val(TheHeight.Text) - 5)
    VBInstance.Windows(HostWin.ItemData(HostWin.ListIndex)).Height = Val(TheHeight.Text)
End Sub

Private Sub SpinHeight_SpinUp()
    'Increase the window's height.
    VBInstance.Windows(HostWin.ItemData(HostWin.ListIndex)).SetFocus
    TheHeight.Text = Str(Val(TheHeight.Text) + 5)
    VBInstance.Windows(HostWin.ItemData(HostWin.ListIndex)).Height = Val(TheHeight.Text)
End Sub

Private Sub SpinWidth_SpinDown()
    'Decrease the window's width.
    TheWidth.Text = Str(Val(TheWidth) - 5)
    VBInstance.Windows(HostWin.ItemData(HostWin.ListIndex)).SetFocus
    VBInstance.Windows(HostWin.ItemData(HostWin.ListIndex)).Width = Val(TheWidth.Text)
End Sub

Private Sub SpinWidth_SpinUp()
    'Increase the window's width.
    VBInstance.Windows(HostWin.ItemData(HostWin.ListIndex)).SetFocus
    TheWidth.Text = Str(Val(TheWidth) + 5)
    VBInstance.Windows(HostWin.ItemData(HostWin.ListIndex)).Width = Val(TheWidth.Text)
End Sub
```

Now that you have added the code to give your add-in the specific behavior that you desire, it's time to run the add-in. When using the movement buttons to change the location of a window, notice that the Window object will not allow you to position a window past the edge of the screen. Also notice that before a window can be resized or moved, it must have the focus. If it does not have focus at the time the properties are set, nothing will happen.

In current form, the HostWin combo box does not refresh itself when windows are opened or closed in the development environment. We leave this as an exercise for you. Hint: Refer to the example given in Chapter 78.

Listing 80-1 Code listing for the frmAddin form

```
Public VBInstance As VBIDE.VBE
Public Connect As Connect

Option Explicit

Private Sub CloseButton_Click()
    Connect.Hide
End Sub

Private Sub Form_Load()
    Dim i As Integer

    'Fill the HostWin combo box with host window names.
    For i = 1 To VBInstance.Windows.Count
        If (Trim(VBInstance.Windows(i).Caption) <> "") Then
            HostWin.AddItem VBInstance.Windows(i).Caption
        Else
            HostWin.AddItem "<No Caption>"
        End If
        HostWin.ItemData(HostWin.ListCount - 1) = i
    Next
    HostWin.ListIndex = 0
End Sub

Private Sub HostWin_Click()
    'Fill in host window properties.

    If VBInstance.Windows(HostWin.ItemData(HostWin.ListIndex)).Visible Then
        IsVisible.Value = 1
    Else
        IsVisible.Value = 0
    End If
    TheHeight.Text = Str(VBInstance.Windows(HostWin.ItemData(HostWin.ListIndex)).Height)
    TheWidth.Text = Str(VBInstance.Windows(HostWin.ItemData(HostWin.ListIndex)).Width)
End Sub

Private Sub IsVisible_Click()
    If (IsVisible.Value = 1) Then
        VBInstance.Windows(HostWin.ItemData(HostWin.ListIndex)).Visible = True
    Else
        VBInstance.Windows(HostWin.ItemData(HostWin.ListIndex)).Visible = False
    End If
    TheHeight.Text = Str(VBInstance.Windows(HostWin.ItemData(HostWin.ListIndex)).Height)
    TheWidth.Text = Str(VBInstance.Windows(HostWin.ItemData(HostWin.ListIndex)).Width)
End Sub

Private Sub MoveDown_Click()
    VBInstance.Windows(HostWin.ItemData(HostWin.ListIndex)).SetFocus
    VBInstance.Windows(HostWin.ItemData(HostWin.ListIndex)).Top =
VBInstance.Windows(HostWin.ItemData(HostWin.ListIndex)).Top + 5
End Sub

Private Sub MoveLeft_Click()
    If ((VBInstance.Windows(HostWin.ItemData(HostWin.ListIndex)).Left - 5) > 0) Then
        VBInstance.Windows(HostWin.ItemData(HostWin.ListIndex)).SetFocus
```

continued on next page

continued from previous page

```
        VBInstance.Windows(HostWin.ItemData(HostWin.ListIndex)).Left =
VBInstance.Windows(HostWin.ItemData(HostWin.ListIndex)).Left - 5
    End If
End Sub

Private Sub MoveRight_Click()
    VBInstance.Windows(HostWin.ItemData(HostWin.ListIndex)).SetFocus
    VBInstance.Windows(HostWin.ItemData(HostWin.ListIndex)).Left =
VBInstance.Windows(HostWin.ItemData(HostWin.ListIndex)).Left + 5
End Sub

Private Sub MoveUp_Click()
    If ((VBInstance.Windows(HostWin.ItemData(HostWin.ListIndex)).Top - 5) > 0) Then
        VBInstance.Windows(HostWin.ItemData(HostWin.ListIndex)).SetFocus
        VBInstance.Windows(HostWin.ItemData(HostWin.ListIndex)).Top =
VBInstance.Windows(HostWin.ItemData(HostWin.ListIndex)).Top - 5
    End If
End Sub

Private Sub SpinButton1_SpinDown()
    VBInstance.Windows(HostWin.ItemData(HostWin.ListIndex)).SetFocus
    TheHeight.Text = Str(Val(TheHeight.Text) - 5)
    VBInstance.Windows(HostWin.ItemData(HostWin.ListIndex)).Height = Val(TheHeight.Text)
End Sub

Private Sub SpinButton1_SpinUp()
    VBInstance.Windows(HostWin.ItemData(HostWin.ListIndex)).SetFocus
    TheHeight.Text = Str(Val(TheHeight.Text) + 5)
    VBInstance.Windows(HostWin.ItemData(HostWin.ListIndex)).Height = Val(TheHeight.Text)
End Sub

Private Sub SpinButton2_SpinDown()
    TheWidth.Text = Str(Val(TheWidth) - 5)
    VBInstance.Windows(HostWin.ItemData(HostWin.ListIndex)).SetFocus
    VBInstance.Windows(HostWin.ItemData(HostWin.ListIndex)).Width = Val(TheWidth.Text)
End Sub

Private Sub SpinButton2_SpinUp()
    VBInstance.Windows(HostWin.ItemData(HostWin.ListIndex)).SetFocus
    TheWidth.Text = Str(Val(TheWidth) + 5)
    VBInstance.Windows(HostWin.ItemData(HostWin.ListIndex)).Width = Val(TheWidth.Text)
End Sub
```

Listing 80-2 Code listing for the Connect class module

```
Option Explicit

Implements IDTExtensibility

Public FormDisplayed        As Boolean
Public VBInstance           As VBIDE.VBE
Dim mcbMenuCommandBar       As Office.CommandBarControl
Dim mfrmAddIn               As New frmAddIn
Public WithEvents MenuHandler As CommandBarEvents            'command bar event handler


Sub Hide()
```

```
    On Error Resume Next

    FormDisplayed = False
    mfrmAddIn.Hide

End Sub

Sub Show()

    On Error Resume Next

    If mfrmAddIn Is Nothing Then
        Set mfrmAddIn = New frmAddIn
    End If

    Set mfrmAddIn.VBInstance = VBInstance
    Set mfrmAddIn.Connect = Me
    FormDisplayed = True
    mfrmAddIn.Show

End Sub

'-------------------------------------------------------
'this method adds the Add-In to VB
'-------------------------------------------------------
Private Sub IDTExtensibility_OnConnection(ByVal VBInst As Object, ByVal ConnectMode As ⇐
vbext_ConnectMode, ByVal AddInInst As VBIDE.AddIn, custom() As Variant)

    On Error GoTo error_handler

    'save the vb instance
    Set VBInstance = VBInst

    'this is a good place to set a breakpoint and
    'test various addin objects, properties and methods
    Debug.Print VBInst.FullName

    If ConnectMode = vbext_cm_External Then
        'Used by the wizard toolbar to start this wizard
        Me.Show
    Else
        Set mcbMenuCommandBar = AddToAddInCommandBar("Modify Interface")
        'sink the event
        Set Me.MenuHandler = VBInst.Events.CommandBarEvents(mcbMenuCommandBar)
    End If

    If ConnectMode = vbext_cm_AfterStartup Then
        If GetSetting(App.Title, "Settings", "DisplayOnConnect", "0") = "1" Then
            'set this to display the form on connect
            Me.Show
        End If
    End If

    Exit Sub

error_handler:

    MsgBox Err.Description
```

continued on next page

continued from previous page

```
End Sub

'-------------------------------------------------------
'this method removes the Add-In from VB
'-------------------------------------------------------
Private Sub IDTExtensibility_OnDisconnection(ByVal RemoveMode As vbext_DisconnectMode, ⇐
custom() As Variant)

    On Error Resume Next

    'delete the command bar entry
    mcbMenuCommandBar.Delete

    'shut down the Add-In
    If FormDisplayed Then
        SaveSetting App.Title, "Settings", "DisplayOnConnect", "1"
        FormDisplayed = False
    Else
        SaveSetting App.Title, "Settings", "DisplayOnConnect", "0"
    End If

    Unload mfrmAddIn
    Set mfrmAddIn = Nothing

End Sub

Private Sub IDTExtensibility_OnStartupComplete(custom() As Variant)
    If GetSetting(App.Title, "Settings", "DisplayOnConnect", "0") = "1" Then
        'set this to display the form on connect
        Me.Show
    End If
End Sub

Private Sub IDTExtensibility_OnAddInsUpdate(custom() As Variant)
    '
End Sub

'this event fires when the menu is clicked in the IDE
Private Sub MenuHandler_Click(ByVal CommandBarControl As Object, handled As Boolean, ⇐
CancelDefault As Boolean)
    Me.Show
End Sub

Function AddToAddInCommandBar(sCaption As String) As Office.CommandBarControl
    Dim cbMenuCommandBar As Office.CommandBarControl   'command bar object
    Dim cbMenu As Object

    On Error GoTo AddToAddInCommandBarErr

    'see if we can find the Add-Ins menu
    Set cbMenu = VBInstance.CommandBars("Add-Ins")
    If cbMenu Is Nothing Then
        'not available so we fail
        Exit Function
    End If

    'add it to the command bar
    Set cbMenuCommandBar = cbMenu.Controls.Add(1)
```

```
    'set the caption
    cbMenuCommandBar.Caption = sCaption

    Set AddToAddInCommandBar = cbMenuCommandBar

    Exit Function

AddToAddInCommandBarErr:

End Function
```

Listing 80-3 Code listing for the Add-In global module

```
Option Explicit
Declare Function WritePrivateProfileString& Lib "Kernel32" Alias
"WritePrivateProfileStringA" (ByVal AppName$, ByVal KeyName$, ByVal keydefault$, ByVal
FileName$)

Sub AddToINI()
    Dim ErrCode As Long
    ErrCode = WritePrivateProfileString("Add-Ins32", "Interface.Connect", "0", ⇐
"vbaddin.ini")
End Sub
```

81

WORKING WITH FILES

A wide variety of file-related operations occur within the Visual Basic environment. Projects are opened or closed. Forms, code modules, and class modules are created, modified, removed, saved, or saved under a new name. Controls and type libraries are added or removed. All these objects also have properties that can be modified.

The Visual Basic extensibility model contains a variety of objects and collections that allow you full programmatic access to these events and properties.

Introduction

Chapter 78, "Creating Add-Ins," explains the six extensibility groups. This chapter covers two of these: the form manipulation and the project and component manipulation objects. Table 81-1 lists the objects and collections that belong to these categories.

Table 81-1 Visual Basic extensibility collections and objects discussed in this chapter

Name	Type
ContainedVBControls	Collection
Properties	Collection
Property	Object
Reference	Object
References	Collection
SelectedVBControls	Collection
VBComponent	Object
VBComponents	Collection
VBControl	Object
VBControls	Collection
VBForm	Object
VBProject	Object
VBProjects	Collection

Extensibility Summary

ContainedVBControls Collection

Purpose	The ContainedVBControls collection replaces the ControlTemplates object in Visual Basic version 4.0. It is used to represent controls that have been placed on a form. Through this collection, you can access one or all of the controls on a form or add a new control to the form.
Properties and Methods	Tables 81-2 and 81-3 list the properties and methods that relate to the ContainedVBControls collection.

Table 81-2 Properties of the ContainedVBControls collection

Use This Property...	To Do This...
CodeModule	Modify the code associated with a component (form, class, or document)
CodePanes	Access the open code panes in the current project
Count	Determine the number of objects in the collection
LinkedWindows	Modify the docked and linked state of windows in the VB development environment
Parent	Access the control container
Properties	Access the properties displayed in the Properties window
References	Add or remove ActiveX references
VBComponents	Access, add, or remove forms, modules, or classes
VBProjects	Access specific projects in the Integrated Development Environment (IDE)
Windows	Access open windows in the IDE

Table 81-3 Methods of the ContainedVBControls collection

Use This Method...	To Do This...
Add	Add an item to the ContainedVBControls collection
Item	Retrieve an item from the ContainedVBControls collection by name or index
Remove	Remove an item from the ContainedVBControls collection

Description	If you know which specific control you wish to modify, you can access it directly using the ContainedVBControls collection. If not, you may want to use a For Each loop to cycle through each of the available controls on the active form. The related SelectedVBControls collection (described later in this chapter) has almost identical functionality, but for currently selected controls only. The items contained in the ContainedVBControls collection are VBControl objects.

PROPERTIES COLLECTION

Purpose	Use the Properties collection to access the properties of a form or control.
Properties and Method	Tables 81-4 and 81-5 list the properties and method that relate to the Properties collection.

Table 81-4 Properties of the Properties collection

Use This Property...	To Do This...
Count	Determine the number of objects in the collection
Parent	Get the parent of the Properties collection

Table 81-5 Method of the Properties collection

Use This Method...	To Do This...
Item	Retrieve an item from the Properties collection by name or index

Description	If you are developing an add-in that will modify the controls on a form in some way, then you will need to access the properties of those controls. Using the VBControl object, you can access all these properties, either to get information about the control, or to change the look or functionality of the control by setting some of the properties. The parent property of this collection can refer to a VBForm properties collection, a VBControl properties collection, or a Property properties collection.

PROPERTY OBJECT

Purpose	Use the Property object to read or set a specific property of a form or control.
Properties	Table 81-6 lists the properties that relate to the Property object.

Table 81-6 Properties of the Property object

Use This Property...	To Do This...
Collection	Get the Properties collection to which this property belongs
IndexedValue	Get or set the value for a member of a property that is in an indexed list
Name	Get the string containing the name of the property as it appears in the Property Browser
NumIndices	Get the number of indices on the property
Object	Get or set the value of a property that returns a property
Value	Get or set the value of a property that returns a value

Description   You use the Name property of the Property object to specify the property to read or set. This name is identical to the one appearing in the Visual Basic Properties window. You can read or write data to a property, assuming that it allows read-write at runtime. Some properties cannot be set at runtime. These properties are referred to as read-only properties.

REFERENCE OBJECT

Purpose   Use the Reference object to retrieve information about a type library or to add one to a project.

Properties   Table 81-7 lists the properties that relate to the Reference object.

Table 81-7 Properties of the Reference object

Use This Property...	To Do This...
BuiltIn	Determine whether the reference is a default reference that cannot be removed
Collection	Get the References collection to which this reference belongs
Description	Get the descriptive string associated with this reference
FullPath	Get the path and filename of the referenced type library
GUID	Get the class identifier of the referenced type library
IsBroken	Find out whether the Reference object points to a valid reference in the registry
Major	Get the major version number of the referenced type library
Minor	Get the minor version number of the referenced type library
Name	Get the name of the referenced type library used in code to identify the reference
Type	Find out the type of the reference (type library or project)

Description   You can use the Reference object to find out the version number of a type library, or the actual file name of the ActiveX control. A useful feature of the Reference object is the ability to determine if a reference is broken. This may happen when the reference points to a Visual Basic project without a Compatible OLE Server that has been recompiled.

REFERENCES COLLECTION

Purpose   Use the References collection to add a type library reference to a project or to find out what references a project contains.

Properties, Events, and Methods   Tables 81-8, 81-9, and 81-10 list the properties, events, and methods that relate to the References collection.

Table 81-8 Properties of the References collection

Use This Property...	To Do This...
Count	Determine the number of objects in the collection
Parent	Get the parent of the References collection

Table 81-9 Events of the References collection

Use This Event...	To Do This...
ItemAdded	Execute code after an ActiveX reference has been added to the current Visual Basic project
ItemRemoved	Execute code after an ActiveX reference has been removed from the current Visual Basic project

Table 81-10 Methods of the References collection

Use This Method...	To Do This...
AddFromFile	Delete all items from the References collection
AddFromGUID	Copy an item from the References collection
Item	Retrieve an item from the References collection by name or index
Remove	Remove an item from the References collection

Description   If you know which specific type library you wish to get information about, you can access it directly using the References collection. If not, you may want to use a For Each loop to cycle through each of the references used in the project. The items contained in the References collection are Reference objects.

SELECTEDVBCONTROLS COLLECTION

Purpose   The SelectedVBControls collection replaces the SelectedControls collection in Visual Basic version 4.0. If you need to read or modify the controls that are currently selected on the active form, use the SelectedVBControls collection.

Properties, Events, and Methods   Tables 81-11, 81-12, and 81-13 list the properties, events, and methods that relate to the SelectedVBControls collection.

Table 81-11 Properties of the SelectedVBControls collection

Use This Property...	To Do This...
CodeModule	Modify the code associated with a component (form, class, or document)
CodePanes	Access the open code panes in the current project
Count	Determine the number of objects in the collection
LinkedWindows	Modify the docked and linked state of windows in the VB development environment
Properties	Access the properties displayed in the Properties window
References	Add or remove ActiveX references
VBComponents	Access, add, or remove forms, modules, or classes
VBProjects	Access specific projects in the IDE
Windows	Access open windows in the IDE

Table 81-12 Events of the SelectedVBControls collection

Use This Event...	To Do This...
ItemAdded	Execute code after a control has been added to the current Visual Basic project
ItemRemoved	Execute code after a control has been removed from the current Visual Basic project

Table 81-13 Methods of the SelectedVBControls collection

Use This Method...	To Do This...
Clear	Delete all items from the SelectedVBControls collection
Copy	Copy an item from the SelectedVBControls collection
Item	Retrieve an item from the SelectedVBControls collection by name or index

Description If you know which specific control you wish to modify, you can access it directly using the SelectedVBControls collection. If not, you may want to use a For Each loop to cycle through each of the available controls on the active form. The related ContainedVBControls collection (described earlier in this chapter) has almost identical functionality, but it deals with all controls, not just those currently selected. The items contained in the SelectedVBControls collection are VBControl objects.

VBCOMPONENT OBJECT

Purpose The VBComponent object replaces the Component object in Visual Basic version 4.0. You use it to check what files are associated with a form, module, or class module or to save a form, module, or class module with a different filename. The Component object also allows you to determine whether a form, module, or class module is dirty (in other words, if it has been modified since it was last saved).

Properties and Methods

Tables 81-14 and 81-15 list the properties and methods that relate to the VBComponent object.

Table 81-14 Properties of the VBComponent object

Use This Property...	To Do This...
CodeModule	Modify the code associated with a component (form, class, or document)
Collection	Get the VBComponents collection this VBComponent belongs to
Description	Get the descriptive string associated with this component
Designer	Get the object that enables you to access the design characteristics of a component
DesignerWindow	Get the Window object that represents the component's designer
FileCount	Determine the number of files associated with the component
FilcNames	Determine the current path name(s) in which the component will be stored
HasOpenDesigner	Determine whether the VBComponent has an open designer
HelpContextID	Get or set the context ID for a topic in a Help file
IconState	Inspect or modify the source control icon for the current component
IsDirty	Find out whether this component was modified since the last time it was saved
Name	Get or set the name of the component
Saved	Get or set the Boolean value indicating whether the object was edited since the last time it was saved
Type	Find out what type the component is (class module, form, standard module, or document module)

Table 81-15 Methods of the VBComponent object

Use This Method...	To Do This...
Activate	Cause the currently selected component in the project window to be activated as if it were double-clicked
Export	Save the component as a separate file or files
ReadProperty	Get a string from the specified user-defined section and key in the project
Reload	Reload the component from disk, discarding any unsaved changes
SaveAs	Save the component to a specified location under a new filename
WriteProperty	Set a string in the specified user-defined section and key in the project

Description

A VBComponent object represents a single form, module, or class module in a Visual Basic project. It allows you to modify the properties of these entities. A useful feature of the VBComponent object is the ability to determine if a component is dirty. A dirty component is one that has been modified since it was last saved.

VBCOMPONENTS COLLECTION

Purpose The VBComponents collection replaces the SelectedComponents collection in Visual Basic version 4.0. You use it to access the components that are currently selected in the active project.

Properties, Events, and Methods Tables 81-16, 81-17, and 81-18 list the properties, events, and methods that relate to the VBComponents collection.

Table 81-16 Properties of the VBComponents collection

Use This Property...	To Do This...
CodeModule	Modify the code associated with a component (form, class, or document)
CodePanes	Access the open code panes in the current project
Count	Determine the number of objects in the collection
LinkedWindows	Modify the docked and linked state of windows in the VB development environment
Parent	Get the object or collection that contains the VBComponents collection
Properties	Access the properties displayed in the Properties window
References	Add or remove ActiveX references
VBComponents	Access, add, or remove forms, modules, or classes
VBProjects	Access specific projects in the IDE
Windows	Access open windows in the IDE

Table 81-17 Events of the VBComponents collection

Use This Event...	To Do This...
ItemAdded	Execute code after a control has been added to the current Visual Basic project
ItemRemoved	Execute code after a control has been removed from the current Visual Basic project

Table 81-18 Methods of the VBComponents collection

Use This Method...	To Do This...
Clear	Delete all items from the VBComponents collection
Copy	Copy an item from the VBComponents collection
Item	Retrieve an item from the VBComponents collection by name or index

Description If you know which specific component you wish to modify, you can access it directly using the VBComponents collection. If not, you may want to use a For Each loop to cycle through each of the available components in the current project. The items contained in the VBComponents collection are VBComponent objects.

VBCONTROL OBJECT

Purpose   The VBControl object replaces the ControlTemplate object in Visual Basic version 4.0. You use it to get or set the properties of an individual control.

Properties and   Method   Tables 81-19 and 81-20 list the properties and method that relate to the VBControl object.

Table 81-19 Properties of the VBControl object

Use This Property...	To Do This...
Collection	Get the collection that contains the object with which you are working
Container	Get or set the container of a control or form
ControlObject	Get a reference to the design-time IDispatch pointer (nothing if there isn't one) provided by the control
ControlType	Get the type of runtime window that a control creates
InSelection	Get or set a control's selection state
ProgID	Get the programmatic ID for the control represented by the VBControl object
Properties	Get the available properties of the control

Table 81-20 Method of the VBControl object

Use This Method...	To Do This...
ZOrder	Place a control at the front or back of the z-order within its graphical level

Description   The items contained in the VBControls collection are VBControl objects.

VBCONTROLS COLLECTION

Purpose   If you need to read or modify the controls on the active form, use the VBControls collection.

Properties, Events,   and Methods   Tables 81-21, 81-22, and 81-23 list the properties, events, and methods that relate to the VBControls collection.

Table 81-21 Properties of the VBControls collection

Use This Property...	To Do This...
Count	Determine the number of objects in the collection
Parent	Get the parent of the VBControls collection

Table 81-22 Events of the VBControls collection

Use This Event...	To Do This...
ItemAdded	Execute code after a control has been added to the current Visual Basic project
ItemRemoved	Execute code after a control has been removed from the current Visual Basic project
ItemRenamed	Execute code after a control has been renamed in the current Visual Basic project

Table 81-23 Methods of the VBControls collection

Use This Method...	To Do This...
Add	Add an item to the VBControls collection
Item	Retrieve an item from the VBControls collection by name or index
Remove	Remove an item from the VBControls collection

Description   If you know which specific control you wish to modify, you can access it directly using the VBControls collection. If not, you may want to use a For Each loop to cycle through each of the available controls on the active form. The related SelectedVBControls collection (described earlier in this chapter) has almost identical functionality, but for currently selected controls only. The items contained in the VBControls collection are VBControl objects.

VBFORM OBJECT

Purpose   The VBForm object replaces the ControlTemplate object in Visual Basic version 4.0. It provides access to the controls it contains.

Properties and Methods   Tables 81-24 and 81-25 list the properties and methods that relate to the VBForm object.

Table 81-24 Properties of the VBForm object

Use This Property...	To Do This...
CanPaste	Find out whether the Clipboard contains appropriate information, such as controls, for pasting to the form
ContainedVBControls	Access the controls on the form
Parent	Get the parent collection
SelectedVBControls	Access the currently selected controls on the form

Table 81-25 Methods of the VBForm object

Use This Method...	To Do This...
Paste	Copy controls from the Clipboard to the form
SelectAll	Select all controls on the form

Description	The VBForm object contains two collections through which you gain access to its controls: SelectedVBControls and ContainedVBControls.

VBProject Object

Purpose	The VBProject object replaces the ProjectTemplate object in Visual Basic version 4.0. The VBProject object represents a project in the IDE and allows you to access the project properties as well as the project components and references.
Properties and Methods	Tables 81-26 and 81-27 list the properties and methods that relate to the VBProject object.

Table 81-26 Properties of the VBProject object

Use This Property...	To Do This...
BuildFileName	Get the executable or DLL name that will be used when the project is built
Collection	Return the VBProjects collection that contains this project
CompatibleOLEServer	Get or set the compatible ActiveX component of this project
Description	Get or set the descriptive string associated with this project
HelpContextID	Get or set the context ID for a topic in a Help file
HelpFile	Get or set the filename for the help file associated with this project
IconState	Inspect or modify the source control icon for the current project
IsDirty	Find out whether this project was modified since the last time it was saved
Name	Get the project's name

continued on next page

continued from previous page

Use This Property...	To Do This...
Saved	Get or set a Boolean value indicating whether this project was modified since the last time it was saved
StartMode	Get or set the start mode of a project (RunMode, BreakMode or DesignMode)
Type	Get the project type (Standard .EXE, ActiveX .EXE, ActiveX .DLL, or ActiveX Control)

Table 81-27 Methods of the VBProject object

Use This Method...	To Do This...
AddToolboxProgID	Place a control or embedded component in the toolbox and add a reference to the project
MakeCompiledFile	Create the project .EXE, .DLL, or control, depending on the project type
Protection	Get the state of protection of the project
ReadProperty	Retrieve a property value
SaveAs	Save the project under a new name
WriteProperty	Save a property value

Description   The VBProject exposes the project properties. It contains a References and a VBComponents collection allowing you to inspect, modify, or add ActiveX references and components.

VBPROJECTS COLLECTION

Purpose   Through the VBProjects collection, you can access all open projects and open new or existing projects.

Properties, Events, and Methods   Tables 81-28, 81-29, and 81-30 list the properties, events, and methods that relate to the VBProjects collection.

Table 81-28 Properties of the VBProjects collection

Use This Property...	To Do This...
Count	Determine the number of objects in the collection
IconState	Inspect or modify the source control icon for the current project
Parent	Get the object or collection that contains the VBProjects collection
StartProject	Set or get the project that will start when you select Start from the Run menu or press [F5]

Table 81-29 Events of the VBProjects collection

Use This Event...	To Do This...
ItemActivated	Execute code after you switch from one project to another in the VB IDE
ItemAdded	Execute code after a project has been opened or created to the VB IDE
ItemRemoved	Execute code after a project has been closed
ItemRenamed	Execute code after a project has been renamed

Table 81-30 Methods of the VBProjects collection

Use This Method...	To Do This...
Add	Add a new, empty project to the VBProjects collection
AddFromFile	Add an existing project to the VBProjects collection
AddFromTemplate	Add a project to the VBProjects collection using an existing project as a template
FileName	Get the full path name of the project
Item	Retrieve an item from the VBProjects collection by name or Index
Remove	Remove an item from the VBProjects collection
SaveAs	Save an item from the VBProjects collection under a new name

Description The VBProjects collection is a standard collection representing all open projects in the IDE. Since Visual Basic 5.0 allows you to open several projects in the IDE, a collection is needed to keep track of all open projects.

Add-In Project

This project demonstrates how to access all open projects.

Assembling the Project

1. Create a new add-in project using the Add-In project type.

2. Add the following declaration to the General Declaration section of the frmAddIn form. You declare a constant used by the message box helper routines implemented below.

```
Const cstAppTitle = "My Add-In"
```

3. Change the caption of the OKButton to "Backup". Figure 81-1 shows what the finished form looks like.

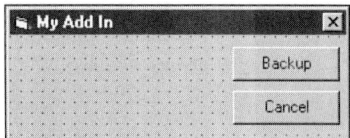

Figure 81-1 frmAddIn in
Design mode

4. Delete all code from the click event procedure of the OKButton in the frmAddIn
form and add the code below. You will ask the user permission to back up the
executable of all open projects.

```
Private Sub OKButton_Click()
    Dim vbp As VBProject
    For Each vbp In VBInstance.VBProjects
        Backup vbp.BuildFileName
    Next
End Sub
```

5. Add the following code to the frmAddin form. The Backup routine implements a
very primitive backup strategy: add a .BAK extension to the name and save the
file. The AskYN and InfoMsgBox are simple message box helper routines.

```
Private Sub Backup(strFileName As String)
    If vbYes = AskYN("Backup " & strFileName & "?") Then
        FileCopy strFileName, strFileName & ".bak"
        InfoMsgBox "Saved " & strFileName & "to " & strFileName & ".bak"
    End If
End Sub

Public Function AskYN(strQuestion As String) As Integer
    AskYN = MsgBox(strQuestion, vbYesNo + vbExclamation, cstAppTitle)
End Function

Private Sub InfoMsgBox(strMessage As String)
    MsgBox strMessage, vbOKOnly + vbInformation, cstAppTitle
End Sub
```

6. Add your add-in to the Add-In Manager. As discussed in previous chapters, this
is done by pressing CTRL-G to open the VB immediate window and typing
AddToIni in that window and pressing ENTER.

7. Make an executable by choosing File, Make MyAddIn.exe from the Visual Basic
IDE menu.

8. Close the AddIn project (save it if you have not already done so). Open another
project. Enable the add-in by choosing the Add-Ins, Add-In Manager menu item.
Check the box beside the MyAddin item and click OK. Select the Add-Ins, My
AddIn menu item. Figure 81-2 shows the project in action.

Figure 81-2 The Add-In
project in action

How It Works

When you click on the OKButton button, you cycle through the VBProjects collection
to retrieve all open projects. You use the BuildFileName property to save the executables.

PART XIV

CREATING ACTIVEX CONTROLS AND ACTIVEX DOCUMENTS

82

ACTIVEX CONTROL OVERVIEW

This section will open up the world of visual components. The next few chapters show you how to build ActiveX controls and documents. This chapter starts by taking you through the functions and features of an ActiveX control. Almost all the sections are accompanied by a minimally functional sample on the CD in the Chapter 82 directory to illustrate each feature.

Chapter 83, "Creating ActiveX Controls," next summarizes the objects discussed in this chapter and takes you through building a sample ActiveX control. From there we will be ready to tackle a few areas that deserve closer examination. Chapter 84, "Exposing Control Properties," examines the how and why on properties. Chapter 85, "Responding to User Actions with ActiveX Controls," covers user interaction. Chapter 86, "Creating Internet-Ready ActiveX Controls," tackles everybody's hot button, building controls for the Internet. Chapter 87, "ActiveX Control Distribution," shows you how to package it all up, and finally Chapter 88, "Creating ActiveX Documents," takes you back to the Internet, this time for documents.

The UserControl Object

The UserControl object is the starting point for building your ActiveX control. As a form is the visual part of an application, the UserControl is the visual part of the control. You can add a UserControl to any project just as you add a form or module. If the project is a Standard EXE project, the UserControl cannot be public, but the control can still be used on any forms within the project.

There are two ways of including an ActiveX control in a project. If the project is an ActiveX project, DLL, EXE, or Control, and the UserControl object is public, you can add the control just like adding any other control. Using the Components Dialog, select the control from the list, or if it is not already registered, browse for it. The other option is to include the CTL file and any referenced files in your project. There are advantages to each option.

The advantages to a compiled ActiveX control outside of the application are the same as when Visual Basic 1.0 shipped. If something is wrong with that small piece, it can be fixed without having to recompile the application. As long as the interface stays the same, that control can be fixed or enhanced and the application does not have to worry about it.

Including the control as part of the project can also be handy. There are no versioning issues. If the control's interface has to change for another application, no problem. It is compiled into the previous one; you will not break it. Debugging also becomes very easy with both the client and the control in one project.

The Container

The container is where the ActiveX control is used. This might be a Web browser, Visual Basic Form, Visual C++ dialog, or even another UserControl. The container is responsible for making all its children work together and for the environment for the control.

The first thing the container provides is ambient properties. You can think of ambient properties as a dress code for ActiveX controls. A well-behaved control will take cues for its appearance from the container. If you set the FontBold True for the form, any controls placed on that form should use that bold font unless overridden by their properties.

The second thing the container provides is the Extender object. This object provides properties that are kept by the container, such as Left and Top.

In both cases, not all properties are supported by all containers. Unless you are coding for a specific container and know just what properties will be there, use care when referencing Ambient and Extender objects. Make sure your control can continue without that information.

Design-Time Support

This section describes ways to make the development environment a little friendlier (and life easier) for developers who use your ActiveX control.

Providing a Toolbox Picture

The ActiveX control specification calls for a bitmap 16 pixels wide by 15 pixels high for a toolbox picture. Assign the bitmap to the UserControl object's ToolboxBitmap property. The ToolboxBitmap property will take an icon instead of a bitmap, but it will be squished to fit when displayed in a toolbox. Also note that gray will become the button face color when displayed in Visual Basic's toolbox.

Named Constants

One of the ways to make the developer's life easier is to export named constants. We have all struggled with a control that uses some obscure numeric value to set a property or perform an action. ActiveX controls built in Visual Basic can export the constants used with their properties and methods. The sample below shows a control that can draw several different borders. The public enumeration vsbBorderType exports the constants used. Now the developer using your control does not have to remember what values are available when setting the property. These values also populate the drop-down list in the properties window.

```
'named constants
Public Enum vsbBorderType
     'vsb for Visual Basic SuperBible
     'try and choose a prefix to set your constants off from other
     'objects, like vbModal, tvwChild, and vbAbortRetryIgnore
     vsbNone = 0
     vsbSingleLine = 1
     vsbButton = 2
End Enum

'Property Variables:
Dim m_BorderType As vsbBorderType

Public Property Get BorderType() As vsbBorderType
     BorderType = m_BorderType
End Property

Public Property Let BorderType(ByVal New_BorderType As vsbBorderType)
     m_BorderType = New_BorderType
     PropertyChanged "BorderType"
     Refresh
End Property

Private Sub UserControl_InitProperties()
     m_BorderType = vsbNone
End Sub

Private Sub UserControl_ReadProperties(PropBag As PropertyBag)
     m_BorderType = PropBag.ReadProperty("BorderType", vsbNone)
     Refresh
End Sub

Private Sub UserControl_WriteProperties(PropBag As PropertyBag)
     Call PropBag.WriteProperty("BorderType", m_BorderType, vsbNone)
End Sub

Private Sub UserControl_Paint()
     'draw the border based on the type
     Select Case m_BorderType
          Case vsbSingleLine
               Line (0, 0)-(ScaleWidth - 1, ScaleHeight - 1) , vb3DDKShadow, B
          Case vsbButton
               'see the sample for the focus for the
               'DrawButtonBorder code
```

continued on next page

continued from previous page

```
                DrawButtonBorder 0, 0, ScaleWidth, ScaleHeight
        Case vsbNone
                'nothing to do
    End Select
    'draw the text
    CurrentX = (ScaleWidth - TextWidth("name constants")) / 2
    CurrentY = (ScaleHeight - TextHeight("name constants")) / 2
    Print "name constants"

End Sub
```

Notice that the member variable and the public property are defined as the enumerated type. Named constants are typically prefixed by a contraction of the control name or your company name. Visual Basic is very good about figuring out which constant is appropriate if you happen to duplicate another constant name. However, it could be confusing to the developer using your control.

Basic Features

There are some basic features that most or all ActiveX controls support. The following sections review the basics needed to create a well-mannered ActiveX control.

Sizing

If your ActiveX control is composed of constituent controls, you will typically need to size them. As the ActiveX control changes size, so should the constituent controls. The UserControl object provides a Resize event just like a form. Here is where the constituent controls are also resized. The code below is a sample of the simplest case, an ActiveX control with only one constituent control, a text box.

```
Private Sub UserControl_Resize()
    Text1.Height = ScaleHeight
    Text1.Width = ScaleWidth
End Sub
```

In many cases there may be a minimum size under which the control becomes unusable. The control may want to enforce a minimum size. The sample code below enforces a minimum size when there is a picture in the constituent picture box control. Notice that a flag is set to keep the Resize event from recursing when sizing the control and the UserControl_Resize sub is called each time the Picture property is set.

```
Private mbDontRecurseSize As Boolean

Public Property Get Picture() As Picture
    Set Picture = Picture1.Picture
End Property

Public Property Set Picture(ByVal New_Picture As Picture)
    Set Picture1.Picture = New_Picture
    PropertyChanged "Picture"
    UserControl_Resize
End Property

'Load property values from storage
```

```
Private Sub UserControl_ReadProperties(PropBag As PropertyBag)
      Set Picture = PropBag.ReadProperty("Picture", Nothing)
      UserControl_Resize
End Sub

Private Sub UserControl_Resize()
      If mbDontRecurseSize = True Then
            Exit Sub
      End If
      'if there is picture enforce minimum size,
      'otherwise size to the control
      If Picture1.Picture <> 0 Then
            If Picture1.Width > ScaleWidth Or ⇐
                  Picture1.Height > ScaleHeight Then
                  mbDontRecurseSize = True            'so we don't recurse
                  Size Picture1.Width, Picture1.Height
                  mbDontRecurseSize = False
            End If
      Else
            Picture1.Height = ScaleHeight
            Picture1.Width = ScaleWidth
      End If
End Sub

'Write property values to storage
Private Sub UserControl_WriteProperties(PropBag As PropertyBag)
      Call PropBag.WriteProperty("Picture", Picture, Nothing)
End Sub
```

Drawing

There are three ways to draw an ActiveX control. First, if there are no constituent controls, the control must be drawn on the paint event using the various drawing or printing methods. Second, if the control is built using constituent controls, to allow the new control's appearance to be comprised of its various elements. Last, it can use a mixture of these methods. The constituent controls comprise some of the new controls' appearance, but additional visual pieces are done using methods during the paint event.

The UserControl object supports the same drawing methods you are used to using with Forms and PictureBoxes. A thorough discussion of drawing techniques can be found in Part V, "Graphics and Appearance."

Using Visual Basic 5 you can build transparent controls using transparent constituent controls, like Labels and Shapes. Set the UserControl's BackStyle property to transparent, and all transparent constituent controls will expose the underlying background. Any click events that hit a transparent part of the control will be passed along to the underlying window. The sample below is the code from a UserControl with one Shape control on it. The public BackStyle property has been mapped to the UserControl's BackStyle property. When the UserControl's BackStyle is set to opaque, the entire control is opaque even if the constituent controls are still transparent.

```
Option Explicit
'so the developer doesn't need to remember values
```

continued on next page

continued from previous page

```
Public Enum vsbenumTransparent
     vsbTransparent = 0
     vsbOpaque = 1
End Enum

Public Property Get BackStyle() As vsbenumTransparent
     BackStyle = UserControl.BackStyle
End Property

Public Property Let BackStyle(ByVal New_BackStyle As vsbenumTransparent)
     UserControl.BackStyle = New_BackStyle
     PropertyChanged "BackStyle"
End Property

Private Sub UserControl_ReadProperties(PropBag As PropertyBag)
     UserControl.BackStyle = PropBag.ReadProperty("BackStyle", vsbTransparent)
End Sub

Private Sub UserControl_Resize()
     Shape1.Width = Width
     Shape1.Height = Height
End Sub

Private Sub UserControl_WriteProperties(PropBag As PropertyBag)
     Call PropBag.WriteProperty("BackStyle", UserControl.BackStyle, vsbTransparent)
End Sub
```

Use care when building transparent controls; they are slower to draw than opaque controls. Visual Basic has to spend time calculating what part of the control must be drawn and what parts are transparent. The more complicated the control, the more time it takes.

Enabling and Disabling

Another of the basics is the ability to enable and disable the ActiveX control. The UserControl object has an Enabled property. This property can be mapped to the ActiveX control's public Enabled property; the sample code below does exactly that.

```
Public Property Get Enabled() As Boolean
     Enabled = UserControl.Enabled
End Property

Public Property Let Enabled(ByVal New_Enabled As Boolean)
     UserControl.Enabled() = New_Enabled
     PropertyChanged "Enabled"
End Property

Private Sub UserControl_ReadProperties(PropBag As PropertyBag)
     UserControl.Enabled = PropBag.ReadProperty("Enabled", True)
End Sub

Private Sub UserControl_WriteProperties(PropBag As PropertyBag)
     Call PropBag.WriteProperty("Enabled", UserControl.Enabled, True)
End Sub
```

However, disabling the UserControl object works just like disabling a container of controls. The user cannot interact with the child controls, but there is no visual indication of this. A better way is to pass the enabled value on to the constituent controls, too. The updated code is as follows.

```
Public Property Let Enabled(ByVal New_Enabled As Boolean)
    UserControl.Enabled = New_Enabled
    Text1.Enabled = New_Enabled
    Option1.Enabled = New_Enabled
    Option2.Enabled = New_Enabled
    PropertyChanged "Enabled"
End Property

Private Sub UserControl_ReadProperties(PropBag As PropertyBag)
    UserControl.Enabled = PropBag.ReadProperty("Enabled", True)
    Text1.Enabled = PropBag.ReadProperty("Enabled", True)
    Option1.Enabled = PropBag.ReadProperty("Enabled", True)
    Option2.Enabled = PropBag.ReadProperty("Enabled", True)
End Sub
```

Anytime the Enabled property of the UserControl is set, the Enabled property of the constituent controls is also set. Those controls give a visual indication that they are disabled so the user understands the object cannot be currently manipulated.

If the control is drawn manually, the code to draw the control will have to draw based on the Enabled property. Typically a control with the 3dD color background, like a command button, shows a disabled state by drawing the text down and to the right one pixel in the highlight color, then drawing the text again in the normal spot with the shadow color. A control with the window background color, like a text box, draws the disabled text using the shadow color. The sample code below adds Enabled property dependent drawing code to the ActiveX control. Notice that the Property Let for the Enabled property now calls Refresh. When a property that affects the control's appearance changes, you should call the Refresh method to trigger a paint event.

```
Public Property Let Enabled(ByVal New_Enabled As Boolean)
    UserControl.Enabled = New_Enabled
    Text1.Enabled = New_Enabled
    Option1.Enabled = New_Enabled
    Option2.Enabled = New_Enabled
    PropertyChanged "Enabled"
    Refresh                         'update the UI
End Property

Private Sub UserControl_Paint()
    'draw based on the state of Enabled
    'the scalemode is pixels to simplify the sample
    Cls
    If Enabled Then
        ForeColor = vbButtonText
        CurrentX = 82
        CurrentY = 1
        Print "Enabled"
    Else
        ForeColor = vb3DHighlight
        CurrentX = 83
```

continued on next page

continued from previous page

```
                CurrentY = 2
                Print "Disabled"
                ForeColor = vb3DShadow
                CurrentX = 82
                CurrentY = 1
                Print "Disabled"
        End If
End Sub
```

Focus

Most screen widgets also change their appearance based on whether they are the focus window. Some controls, such as toolbars, typically cannot get the focus and so do not need to worry about drawing based on the focus. The CanGetFocus property of the UserControl object determines if an ActiveX control can get the focus. If this property is True, the ActiveX control should visually indicate that it is the focus window.

If the ActiveX control is built using constituent controls, the constituent controls are typically responsible for drawing the focus indicators. However, if the control is drawn manually, the Paint event will have to take care of it. You should take cues from similar controls, look at the way they handle focus, and draw accordingly. The sample code below draws a control that looks like a command button. The GotFocus and LostFocus events update a member variable that tells the Paint event how to draw. The GotFocus and LostFocus events also call the Refresh method to trigger the Paint event. Based on the mbHasFocus variable, the Paint event adds the dark border and focus rectangle when painting a control with the focus. The DrawFocusRect API call is useful for drawing controls with focus and is used in the Paint event below.

```
Private Declare Function DrawFocusRect Lib "user32" ⇐
      (ByVal hdc As Long, lpRect As RECT) As Long
Private Type RECT
        Left As Long
        Top As Long
        Right As Long
        Bottom As Long
End Type
Private mbHasFocus As Boolean

Private Sub UserControl_GotFocus()
      mbHasFocus = True
      Refresh
End Sub

Private Sub UserControl_LostFocus()
      mbHasFocus = False
      Refresh
End Sub

Private Sub UserControl_Paint()
      If mbHasFocus Then
              'draw the focus rectangle
              Dim ControlRect As RECT
              ControlRect.Top = 4
              ControlRect.Left = 4
```

```
            ControlRect.Right = ScaleWidth - 4
            ControlRect.Bottom = ScaleHeight - 4
            DrawFocusRect hdc, ControlRect
            'draw the border
            Line (0, 0)-(ScaleWidth - 1, ScaleHeight - 1), vb3DDKShadow, B
            DrawButtonBorder 1, 1, ScaleWidth - 1, ScaleHeight - 1
      Else
            'draw the border
            DrawButtonBorder 0, 0, ScaleWidth, ScaleHeight
      End If
      'draw the text
      CurrentX = (ScaleWidth - TextWidth("Focus Control")) / 2
      CurrentY = (ScaleHeight - TextHeight("Focus Control")) / 2
      Print "Focus Control"
End Sub

Private Sub DrawButtonBorder(plLeft As Long, plTop As Long ⇐
      , plRight As Long, plBottom As Long)
      'draw a border that looks like a button
      'assumes pixel scale mode
      Line (plLeft, plTop)-(plRight - 1, plTop) , vb3DHighlight
      Line (plLeft, plTop)-(plLeft, plBottom - 1) , vb3DHighlight
      Line (plRight - 1, plTop)-(plRight - 1, plBottom - 1) , vb3DDKShadow
      Line (plLeft, plBottom - 1)-(plRight, plBottom - 1) , vb3DDKShadow
      Line (plRight - 2, plTop + 1)-(plRight - 2, plBottom - 2) , vb3DShadow
      Line (plLeft + 1, plBottom - 2)-(plRight - 1, plBottom - 2) , vb3DShadow
End Sub
```

Access Keys

To support quick navigation by heavy keyboard users, many ActiveX controls support access keys. There are two ways that a Visual Basic 5 ActiveX control can support access keys. First, the control can support access keys in the traditional sense; ALT + the access key will activate the control. The second option is available for controls where the CanGetFocus property is False. They can work like labels, where the access key activates the next control in the tab order.

An ActiveX control built of constituent controls will have the behavior of the constituent controls, with one small exception. If the constituent control is a control that can get the focus, such as a command button, it will respond to the access key. However, a constituent control that does not accept the focus, like a label, will not forward the focus without setting the UserControl's ForwardFocus property to true.

For ActiveX controls not built with constituent controls, the UserControl object's AccessKeys property is used to manipulate access keys. The sample code below scans the m_Caption variable each time it is set to determine the access keys. The SetAccessKey function looks for a single ampersand followed by a character to set the AccessKeys property. The Paint event uses the DrawText API to draw the caption.

DrawText knows how to format the ampersands so you do not have to worry about what is underlined or a single ampersand instead of a double. Finally, the UserControl's AccessKeyPress event raises the public Click event.

```vb
'Property Variables:
Dim m_Caption As String

'Event Declarations:
Event Click()

'API Declarations
Private Type RECT
        Left As Long
        Top As Long
        Right As Long
        Bottom As Long
End Type
Private Declare Function DrawText Lib "user32" Alias "DrawTextA" ⇐
        (ByVal hdc As Long, ByVal lpStr As String, ByVal nCount As Long ⇐
        , lpRect As RECT, ByVal wFormat As Long) As Long
Private Const DT_CENTER = &H1

Private Sub SetAccessKey()
        'search the caption for a single ampersand followed
        'by a character to make the access key(s)
        Dim lAccessStart As Long
        AccessKeys = ""
        lAccessStart = InStr(1, m_Caption, "&")
        Do Until lAccessStart >= Len(m_Caption) Or lAccessStart = 0
                If Mid$(m_Caption, lAccessStart + 1, 1) <> "&" Then
                        'single ampersand, it's an access key
                        AccessKeys = AccessKeys + Mid$(m_Caption, lAccessStart + 1, 1)
                End If
                lAccessStart = InStr(lAccessStart + 2, m_Caption, "&")
        Loop
End Sub

Private Sub UserControl_AccessKeyPress(KeyAscii As Integer)
        RaiseEvent Click
End Sub

Public Property Get Caption() As String
        Caption = m_Caption
End Property

Public Property Let Caption(ByVal New_Caption As String)
        m_Caption = New_Caption
        SetAccessKey
        PropertyChanged "Caption"
        Refresh
End Property

'Initialize Properties for User Control
Private Sub UserControl_InitProperties()
        m_Caption = Extender.Name
End Sub

Private Sub UserControl_Paint()
        Dim ControlRect As RECT
```

```
    'use the DrawText API, it takes care of all the ampersand formating
    ControlRect.Top = (ScaleHeight - TextHeight("x")) / 2
    ControlRect.Left = 0
    ControlRect.Right = ScaleWidth
    ControlRect.Bottom = ScaleHeight

    DrawText hdc, m_Caption, Len(m_Caption), ControlRect, DT_CENTER
End Sub

'Load property values from storage
Private Sub UserControl_ReadProperties(PropBag As PropertyBag)
    m_Caption = PropBag.ReadProperty("Caption", Extender.Name)
    SetAccessKey
    Refresh
End Sub

'Write property values to storage
Private Sub UserControl_WriteProperties(PropBag As PropertyBag)
    Call PropBag.WriteProperty("Caption", m_Caption, Extender.Name)
End Sub

Private Sub UserControl_Click()
    RaiseEvent Click
End Sub
```

For controls that cannot receive the focus, the ForwardFocus property of the UserControl object will activate the next control in the tab order. To change the code above to a control that forwards the focus, set the CanGetFocus property to False and the ForwardFocus property to True. Now the UserControl's AccessKeyPress event will never fire, so the code in this event can also be removed.

About Box

Most ActiveX controls have an about box. This is a dialog where copyright information, tech support numbers, and Website addresses are displayed for the developer using the control. Adding an about box to an ActiveX controls is probably the simplest of the standard features to implement.

1. Build a form for your about box.

2. Add the following code to the ActiveX control, replacing frmAbout with the name of the about box form.

```
Public Sub ShowAboutBox()
    frmAbout.Show vbModal
    Unload frmAbout
    Set frmAbout = Nothing
End Sub
```

3. Open the Procedure Attributes dialog from the Tools menu and press the Advanced >> button. This will unfold the dialog, exposing several new options.

4. In the Procedure ID: drop-down list select AboutBox. The (About) entry will now be available in the property list for instances of the ActiveX control. Selecting that item will open the about box.

Advanced Features

Now that you have the tools to put together a basic ActiveX control, it's time to look at the fancy stuff. The great part about building ActiveX controls in Visual Basic is that the fancy stuff is just as easy as the basic stuff, it's just not done as often.

Aligning

Some controls have the ability to align or snap to the edge of a form. These controls, like a picture box, are the only controls that can be placed on a MDI form. The UserControl object's Alignable property allows an ActiveX control to be aligned if the container supports it. The Align property is added to the Extender object and can be queried in the ActiveX control's code. The sample code below is from a status bar control. Based on its placement, it splits between a text pane and progress bar pane left and right or top and bottom.

```
Private Sub UserControl_Resize()
    Select Case Extender.Align
        Case vbAlignNone, vbAlignTop, vbAlignBottom
            'split right and left
            Label1.Left = 0
            Label1.Top = 0
            Label1.Width = ScaleWidth / 2
            Label1.Height = ScaleHeight
            ProgressBar1.Left = ScaleWidth / 2 + 1
            ProgressBar1.Top = 0
            ProgressBar1.Width = ScaleWidth - ProgressBar1.Left
            ProgressBar1.Height = ScaleHeight

        Case vbAlignLeft, vbAlignRight
            'split top and bottom
            Label1.Left = 0
            Label1.Top = 0
            Label1.Width = ScaleWidth
            Label1.Height = ScaleHeight / 2
            ProgressBar1.Left = 0
            ProgressBar1.Top = ScaleHeight / 2 + 1
            ProgressBar1.Width = ScaleWidth
            ProgressBar1.Height = ScaleHeight - ProgressBar1.Top
    End Select
End Sub
```

Not all changes to the Align property trigger a Resize event. A change to the opposite side, left to right or top to bottom, does not trigger the Resize event. There is also no event to tell you when the Align property's value has changed. In the sample above, those changes do not matter, but for some controls it might. One solution would be to keep a member variable with the last Align property variable. On the Paint event, check to make sure that the current Extender.Align value matches the last one. If not, resize and save the new value.

Invisible Controls

Invisible controls can be created by setting the UserControl object's InvisibleAtRuntime property to True. The control should still implement the Paint event just so it can be seen at design time. Often an invisible ActiveX control will enforce a fixed size. The sample code below enforces a fixed size and implements a simple paint so it can be seen at design time.

```
Private Sub UserControl_Paint()
    'just paint a square so I can be seen
    Line (0, 0)-(ScaleWidth - 1, ScaleHeight - 1), vb3DShadow, B
End Sub

Private Sub UserControl_Resize()
    Height = 375
    Width = 1155
End Sub
```

Before Visual Basic 5, invisible controls were often used when an object needed events. Now that ActiveX objects can have events, the need for invisible controls has been reduced. An ActiveX DLL with events is less of a drain on resources than an equivalent invisible ActiveX control. If you do not need specific features of an ActiveX control, like a built-in hWnd, you should use an ActiveX DLL with events instead.

Making a Container

Occasionally there is a need for a new container. The picture box and frame controls are examples of container controls. Other controls can be drawn on the container and grouped together. When the container control is moved, so are the children. Containers also are used to group option buttons.

Using Visual Basic, building a container is very easy. Set the ControlContainer property of the UserControl object to True to make the ActiveX control a container. This has several effects. First, the new control will now exhibit all the standard behaviors of containers. Second, the new control will now require a little more horsepower. Container controls have more overhead than a similarly functioning control that is not a container. And last, a new collection is available to the control. The ContainedControls collection gives the container access to its children. The sample below uses the ContainedControls collection to draw an edge around all the child controls.

```
Private Sub UserControl_Paint()
    Cls
    Dim oControl As Control
    'draw an outline around me
    Line (0, 0)-(ScaleWidth - Screen.TwipsPerPixelX ⇐
        , ScaleHeight - Screen.TwipsPerPixelY), vb3DShadow, B
    'draw an outline around my children
    On Error GoTo NoContainedControlsSupport:
    For Each oControl In ContainedControls
        Line (oControl.Left - Screen.TwipsPerPixelX ⇐
            , oControl.Top - Screen.TwipsPerPixelY)- ⇐
            (oControl.Left + oControl.Width , oControl.Top + oControl.Height) ⇐
```

continued on next page

continued from previous page

```
                          , vb3DShadow, B
        Next oControl
NoContainedControlsSupport:
        Exit Sub
End Sub
```

Depending on the container your control is placed on, some or all container control functionality may not be available. Visual Basic supports all the COM interfaces needed for full container support, so if the control is intended only for use with Visual Basic you are safe. Otherwise, support for containers can be done in steps. The first step allows developers to draw child controls on your control. If a container does not support ISimpleFrame, then all container control functionality is lost. The second level of support allows your control access to its children. This is enabled when the container implements the IVBGetControls interface. If this interface is not implemented by the container your control is placed on, references to the ContainedControls collection will result in an error. In the sample above, the On Error statement will trap the error if there is no support for the ContainedControls collection.

Data Bound Controls

Most of Visual Basic's built-in controls and quite a few third-party controls support data binding. If you're building the versatile super control, data binding is probably on your feature list. Once again, Microsoft has made it so easy—it almost feels like cheating.

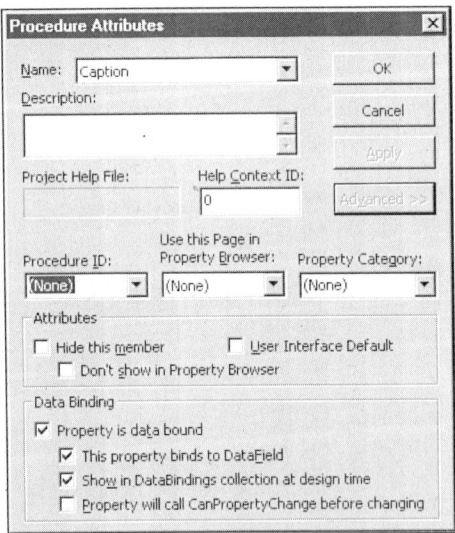

Figure 82-1   The Procedure Attributes dialog

Figure 82-1 shows the Procedure Attributes dialog. Here you set a property as bindable. Select the property in the Name drop-down list and check the "Property is data bound" check box in the Data Binding frame. The control is now a bound control, but first there are a couple of options to go through before it is usable.

The "This property binds to DataField" check box binds the selected property to the column selected in the DataField property. This should be checked for the defining property of the control, like the Text property of a text box or the Caption property of a label. This option must be checked for one property or the DataSource and DataField properties will not be available for the control.

A control with more than one bound field is supported through the next option. The "Show in DataBindings collection at design time" check box adds the selected property to the DataBindings collection. The developer using the control can then use the DataBindings dialog to assign bound fields to columns of the data source.

The last option is related to being a well-behaved bound control. The "Property will call CanPropertyChange before changing" check box indicates that before accepting a Property Let, the ActiveX control will make sure that property can change. If the control is in a Visual Basic container, CanPropertyChange will always return a True. However some other containers may produce an error if the property is set when CanPropertyChange returns False. The sample code below checks CanPropertyChange before setting the Caption property. This should be done for all properties that can be bound.

```
Public Property Let Caption(ByVal New_Caption As String)
      If CanPropertyChange("Caption") Then
            m_Caption = New_Caption
            PropertyChanged "Caption"
            Refresh
      End If
End Property
```

Editing at Design Time

Visual complicated controls are sometimes very hard to set up using the properties window of Visual Basic. Wouldn't it be great if you could edit the properties of the control exactly as you use it at runtime? An ActiveX control built in Visual Basic can do that. Imagine a text box where you can change the text property directly in the control, a spread sheet control where you can size the columns directly, or a drawing control that lets you draw the picture property right on the control!

The UserControl object's EditAtDesignTime property adds a new menu to the right mouse popup in the form design window. The Edit menu will activate the control just like the form was a document with an embedded object. Changes made in the control will be reflected in the properties window when the control is deactivated by clicking outside the control's window. The control's code will run as usual, but any attempts to raise events will be ignored.

Being the Default or Cancel Button

If you are building a control that behaves like a button, you may want it to be the default or cancel button. A typical Windows convention is for the OK button to be activated by ENTER and Cancel by ESCAPE. To enable the Default and Cancel properties set the UserControl object's DefaultCancel property to True. After that, what must be done largely depends on whether the control is built of constituent controls that support Default and Cancel or not.

If a constituent control supports Default and Cancel, set both properties to True. Changes in the control's Default and Cancel properties will be propagated automatically to the constituent control. The constituent control will also get its usual event. So, for example, to enable Default and Cancel for an ActiveX control built with the command button do the following steps.

1. Set the DefaultCancel property of the UserControl object to True.

2. Set the Default property of the command button to True.

3. Set the Cancel property of the command button to True.

4. On the Click event of the command button raise a Click event.

If the control is a user-drawn control, or none of the constituent controls support Default and Cancel, then there is a little more work. The UserControl's AccessKeyPress event will fire if ENTER is pressed and the Default property is True, or if ESCAPE is pressed and the Cancel property is True. From here, raise a Click event. Next the control should give a visual indication that it is the default button. A regular command button uses a black border to indicate it is the default button. In the sample below, a black outline is used to indicate that the control is the default. If the DisplayAsDefault property of the Ambient object is True, the outline must be drawn. Finally, since the Default property may change at any time, call Refresh from the UserControl's AmbientChanged event if the DisplayAsDefault property changes. The sample code below shows where support for Default and Cancel must be added.

```
Private Sub UserControl_AccessKeyPress(KeyAscii As Integer)
      RaiseEvent Click
End Sub

Private Sub UserControl_AmbientChanged(PropertyName As String)
      If PropertyName = "DisplayAsDefault" Then
            Refresh
      End If
End Sub

Private Sub UserControl_Paint()
      If Ambient.DisplayAsDefault Then
            'draw the border
            Line (0, 0)-(ScaleWidth - 1, ScaleHeight - 1), vbBlack, B
            'see the sample for the focus for the DrawButtonBorder code
            DrawButtonBorder 1, 1, ScaleWidth - 1, ScaleHeight - 1
      Else
            'draw the border
            DrawButtonBorder 0, 0, ScaleWidth, ScaleHeight
```

```
        End If
        'draw the text
        CurrentX = (ScaleWidth - TextWidth(m_Caption)) / 2
        CurrentY = (ScaleHeight - TextHeight(m_Caption)) / 2
        Print m_Caption
End Sub
```

Events

What would an ActiveX control be without events? The event-driven model drives Visual Basic. Below are some sample declarations for events.

```
Event Change()
Event Click()
Event KeyDown(KeyCode As Integer, Shift As Integer)
Event KeyPress(KeyAscii As Integer)
Event KeyUp(KeyCode As Integer, Shift As Integer)
```

Events can take parameters just like a sub or function call. Event declarations go in the declarations section of the control module. To raise an event you simply use the RaiseEvent keyword. Following are some examples of the RaiseEvent keyword.

```
Public Property Let Caption(ByVal New_Caption As String)
        Command1.Caption() = New_Caption
        PropertyChanged "Caption"
        RaiseEvent Change
End Property

Private Sub Command1_Click()
        RaiseEvent Click
End Sub

Private Sub Command1_KeyDown(KeyCode As Integer, Shift As Integer)
        RaiseEvent KeyDown(KeyCode, Shift)
End Sub

Private Sub Command1_KeyPress(KeyAscii As Integer)
        RaiseEvent KeyPress(KeyAscii)
End Sub

Private Sub Command1_KeyUp(KeyCode As Integer, Shift As Integer)
        RaiseEvent KeyUp(KeyCode, Shift)
End Sub
```

Most of these events are simple mappings between a constituent control and the public events. However, a new ActiveX control is not tied to the events of its constituent controls. RaiseEvent can be called from anywhere with the control's code. In the sample above, the Change event is raised within a property let. This makes a control that looks like a command button, smells like a command button, but has a Change event on the Caption change just like a label or text box.

Perhaps the easiest way to generate the code to do events is by using the ActiveX Control Interface Wizard. This Wizard, described in Chapter 99, "ActiveX Control Wizard," enables you to point and click to build mappings like the ones above between constituent controls and public events.

Methods

To add a method to a ActiveX control simply add a public Sub or Function to the control's code. Microsoft recommends that minimum support includes the Refresh method. The sample code below is all that is needed to support Refresh.

```
Public Sub Refresh()
     UserControl.Refresh
End Sub
```

Beyond Refresh, support for methods is really up to the developer. You should implement methods found in similar controls. If you are building a better widget, the better widget should at least do everything the widget does. The ActiveX Control Interface Wizard can help you find methods of constituent controls you may consider exposing. The ActiveX Control Interface Wizard is discussed in Chapter 99.

83

CREATING ACTIVEX CONTROLS

When the OLE control was renamed ActiveX, a Visual Basic programmer could finally admit to using a cool technology. The look on a nonprogrammer's face when you responded to the question, "What are you doing?" with "Creating an ActiveX control!" was a much better reaction than when you tried to explain *oh-lay* controls to them. All kidding aside, the great thing about ActiveX is not just the cool name but how Visual Basic programmers can start using this new technology quickly. For years, Visual Basic developers have used VBX and OCX controls to create applications. Now the ability to create their own controls without relying on C++ has been included in Visual Basic 5.0.

Creating an ActiveX control is basically the same as creating a standard Visual Basic program. In the next few chapters, you will learn how to leverage your existing knowledge of Visual Basic programming; by adding new ActiveX-oriented elements, you can quickly create ActiveX controls that can be used by other ActiveX-compliant development tools or shown in ActiveX-compliant Web browsers, or you can just build up your collection of reusable components.

Many of the properties, events, and methods described in this chapter are not new concepts but are slightly repackaged. Creating an ActiveX control requires the same steps as creating any other application with Visual Basic. By teaming up the new elements for building ActiveX controls with your prior knowledge of Visual Basic programming, you can be compiling new and unique controls in no time.

In the next few chapters, you will be dealing with some new Visual Basic jargon. Following is list of some of these new terms and their application in the Visual Basic lingo.

- Container. This is an object that hosts ActiveX controls. It can be a development tool such as Visual Basic, an office application such as Microsoft Word 97, or another ActiveX control that has been designed to host other controls.

- Container control. This is an ActiveX control that can host other controls.

- Constituent controls. These are controls that are used to create an ActiveX control. All the controls added to the control during the authoring of the control are constituent controls. The properties of these controls cannot be accessed unless they are exposed by the developer of the control. You will learn how to do this in a later chapter. Do not get these confused with controls that have been placed on the control at runtime.

- Authoring time. The time during which the control is being created. Some programmers use the term *design time*.

Creating ActiveX Controls Summary

Visual Basic has many new elements for creating ActiveX controls. This chapter does not discuss the new properties, events, and methods dealing with exposing the control's properties and the Internet-aware functionality, issues that are dealt with in the following chapters. Table 83-1 provides a summary of the elements discussed in this chapter. You will find that many of these new elements are very similar to items you have already learned about. This is why Visual Basic is the easiest platform to use to create ActiveX controls.

Table 83-1 Properties, methods, and events dealing with creating ActiveX controls

Use or Set This...	Type	To Do This...
AccessKeys	Property	Sets or returns the keys that will raise the AccessKeyPress event.
AccessKeyPress	Event	Occurs when a key that has been assigned to the AccessKeys property has been pressed.
ActiveControl	Property	Returns the control that is active.
Alignable	Property	Determines if the control can be aligned on a form by its container.
CanGetFocus	Property	Returns or sets if this control can receive focus.
ContainedControls	Object	The collection of controls contained on the ActiveX control.
ContainedControls	Property	Returns a collection of controls contained on the ActiveX control.
ControlContainer	Property	Returns or sets if the ActiveX control can act as a container.
DefaultCancel	Property	Determines if the ActiveX control or constituent controls can be set as a default or can be canceled.
EditAtDesignTime	Property	Determines if the control can act as it would at runtime.
Enabled	Property	Enables or disables the control and its constituent controls.
EnterFocus	Event	Occurs when the control gets focus.
EventsFrozen	Property	Returns or sets if raising of events has been disabled.
ExitFocus	Event	Occurs when the control loses focus.
ForwardFocus	Property	The control will forward focus to the next control in the tab order.
Hide	Event	Occurs when the control's Visible property is set to False.
InitProperties	Event	Raised when the control is first placed on a form.
InvisibleAtRuntime	Property	Determines if the control has a visible interface at runtime.

Use or Set This...	Type	To Do This...
ParentControls	Property	Returns a collection of the other controls within the ActiveX control's container.
Show	Event	Occurs when the Visible property of the control is set to True.
ToolboxBitmap	Property	This is the picture that is shown when the control is added to the toolbox.
UserControl	Object	The object that contains the properties, methods, and events of the ActiveX control.

ACCESSKEYS PROPERTY

Objects Affected   UserControl

Purpose   When a key that has been assigned to the AccessKeys property is pressed in conjunction with the ALT key, the AccessKeyPress event will occur.

General Syntax

```
UserControl.AccessKeys [= AccessKeyString$]
```

Table 83-2 Arguments for the AccessKeys property

Argument	Description
object	Name of the control
AccessKeyStringS	The string containing the keys to use as AccessKeys

Example Syntax

```
Private Sub Form_Load ()
      MyControl.AccessKeys="rwg" 'Set the r and w and g keys to be assigned as access keys
End Sub
```

Description   The AccessKeys property is used to assign keystrokes that will raise the AccessKeyPress event. These keystrokes do not require ALT to be pressed in conjunction with them. If the DefaultCancel property of the control is set to True and if ENTER is pressed, then the AccessKeyPress event will be raised and the KeyAscii value will be 13. Similarly, if ESC is pressed, the KeyAscii value will be 27. In the above example if R or W or G is pressed, the AccessKeyPress event will occur.

Example   S and C are assigned to this property so that when they are pressed, the appropriate button will have its Click event raised.

Comments   If the DefaultCancel property of the control is set to True, pressing ENTER will raise the AccessKeyPress event with a KeyAscii value of 13 even if the Default property of the control added to the form is set to False. This is not correct for the Cancel property. The DefaultCancel property must be set at the control's design time. When the control is added to a form, the Cancel property must be set to True in order for the pressing of ESC to raise the AccessKeyPress event.

ACCESSKEYPRESS EVENT

Objects Affected	UserControl
Purpose	The AccessKeyPress event occurs when a key has been pressed that has been assigned to the AccessKeys property. Any alphanumeric key can be assigned as an access key. If the DefaultCancel property was been set to True at the control's authoring time, then the control's Default or Cancel property can be set to True at the design time of the project so that when ENTER-ESC is pressed, the AccessKeyPress events will be raised.

General Syntax

```
Private Sub UserControl_AccessKeyPress(Keyascii As Integer)
```

Table 83-3 Arguments for the AccessKeyPress event

Arguments	Description
UserControl	Name of the user control
KeyAscii	The ASCII value of the key that was pressed

Example Syntax

```
Private Sub UserControl_AccessKeyPress(KeyAscii As Integer)
If KeyAscii=13 then
      Msgbox "You pressed the enter key."      'the enter key was pressed
End If
```

Description	The AccessKeyPress event can be used to allow a control to respond directly to input from the keyboard. This event occurs before any KeyPress or KeyDown event occurs in the ActiveX control or one of its constituent controls. This event can be used to create hot keys for the controls or to create a filter to determine what input from the keyboard the constituent controls on the ActiveX control receive.
Example	In the project at the end of this chapter, S and C are used to access the button on the ActiveX control.

ACTIVECONTROL PROPERTY

Objects Affected	Form, MDIForm, Property Page, Screen, UserControl, UserDocument
Purpose	To determine the active control.
General Syntax	

```
object.ActiveControl
```

Example Syntax

```
Private Sub Form_Load ()
    UserControl.CanGetFocus=True
End Sub
```

Description	This property can be set only at authoring time. If this property is set to True, then the control and its constituent controls can receive focus. If the control itself needs to have direct focus, all the constituent controls must have their TabStop set to False and it is the developer's job to draw the focus rectangle, if so desired. If this property is set to False, no constituent controls can receive focus.
Example	The control created in the project at the end of this chapter has the CanGetFocus property set to True so it can be used with other controls on a form and be in the tab order.

CONTAINEDCONTROLS COLLECTION

Purpose	To access the controls that have been placed on the control.
Description	This collection is similar to the Control collection on a form. For the control to contain controls, the ContainedControls property must be set to True.
Comments	Not all containers support the ContainedControls collection. The property error handling must be in place in order not to cause an error in the container.

DEFAULTCANCEL PROPERTY

Objects Affected	UserControl
Purpose	This property is used to determine if the control or its constituents can be set as a default or cancel button.

General Syntax

```
UserControl.DefaultCancel [ = boolean%]
```

Table 83-9 Arguments for the DefaultCancel property

Arguments	Description
UserControl	Name of the control
boolean%	True or False

Table 83-10 Description of the boolean% value pertaining to the DefaultCancel property

boolean%	Meaning
True	The Default and Cancel properties (also those of its constituent controls) can be set to True.
False	The Default and Cancel properties (also those of its constituent controls) can be set to False.

Description	This property can be set only at the authoring time of the control. This property is set to True if the control is going to function similarly to a button, where it needs to be set to the Default or Cancel like a button on a form. This property also needs to be set to True if one of the constituent controls needs to be set to Default or Cancel.
Example	In the project at the end of the chapter, the DefaultCancel property is set to True. The two constituent buttons on the control have the Default and Cancel properties set to allow the user to press ENTER when the input is complete or to press Cancel to clear the contents of the text boxes.

EDITATDESIGNTIME PROPERTY

Objects Affected	UserControl
Purpose	This property determines if the Edit menu appears in the content menu to have the control behave as it would during runtime.

General Syntax

```
UserControl.EditAtDesignTime [ = boolean%]
```

Table 83-11 Arguments for the EditAtDesignTime property

Arguments	Description
UserControl	Name of control
boolean%	True or False

Table 83-12 Description of the boolean% value pertaining to the EditAtDesignTime property

boolean%	Meaning
True	The control can appear as it would during runtime.
False	The control cannot appear as it would during runtime.

Description	When this property is set to True, the Edit menu appears in the context menu. When the Edit menu is selected for the selected control, it behaves as it would during runtime. No events will be raised and the Raise Method event will be ignored. This property can be set only at the control's authoring time.
Example	In the project at the end of this chapter, the control created has this property set to True.

ENABLED PROPERTY

Objects Affected	Animation control, Button object, DBCombo control, DBGrid control, DBList control, ListView control, Masked Edit control, MSChart control, MSFlexGrid control, Multimedia MCI control, Panel object, ProgressBar control, RichTextBox control, Slider control, SSTab control, StatusBar control, TabStrip control, Toolbar control, TreeView control, UpDown control
Purpose	To enable or disable a user control and all its constituent controls.
General Syntax	

```
object.Enabled [ = boolean%]
```

Table 83-13 Arguments for the Enabled property

Arguments	Description
object	Name of the object
boolean%	True or False

Table 83-14 Description of the boolean% value pertaining to the Enabled property

boolean%	Meaning
True	The control and its constituent controls are enabled.
False	The control and all its constituent controls are disabled.

Example Syntax
```
Private Sub Command1_Click ()
        MyControl.Enabled=False
End Sub
```

Description	The Enabled property works like the standard Enabled property by enabling or disabling user interaction with the control. When a control is disabled, the user can not interact with interface elements but can access underlying code. When this property is set, all the constituent controls are

also set. If the Enabled property of a control is set to True, individual constituent controls can have their Enabled property set to True or False. When the Enable property of the control is set to False, all the constituent controls are set to False and cannot be changed until the Enabled property of the control is set to True.

ENTERFOCUS EVENT

Objects Affected   UserControl, UserDocument

Purpose   This event is raised when the control gains focus.

General Syntax

```
Private Sub UserControl_EnterFocus()
```

Table 83-15 Argument for the EnterFocus event

Argument	Description
UserControl	Name of the control

Example Syntax

```
Private Sub UserControl_EnterFocus()
      Msgbox "I have been selected"
End Sub
```

Description   This event is similar to the GetFocus event of any control that can receive focus. This focus event occurs before the control or the constituent control GotEvent occurs.

EVENTSFROZEN PROPERTY

Objects Affected   UserControl

Purpose   This property determines if the events contained in a user control can be raised.

General Syntax

```
UserControl.EventsFrozen = [boolean%]
```

Table 83-16 Arguments for the EventsFrozen property

Arguments	Description
UserControl	Name of the control
boolean%	True or False

Table 83-17 Description of the boolean% value pertaining to the EventsFrozen property

boolean%	Meaning
True	The control will respond to its events.
False	The control will not respond to its events.

Example Syntax

```
Private Sub Command1_Click
        MyControls.Enabled=False        'disable user control
        MyControls.EventsFrozen=False 'disable events
End Sub
```

Description   The EventsFrozen property determines if a control can have its events raised. When a control has the Enabled property set to False, this disables only the user interface components of the control. When the EventsFrozen property is set to False, it disables all the events contained in the control. The Enabled and EventsFrozen property, when used in conjunction, truly enable and disable a control.

EXITFOCUS EVENT

Objects Affected   UserControl, UserDocument

Purpose   To determine when the control has lost focus.

General Syntax

```
Private Sub UserControl_ExitFocus ()
```

Table 83-18 Argument for the ExitFocus event

Argument	Description
UserControl	Name of the control

Example Syntax

```
Private Sub UserControl_ExitFocus ()
        'When the control loses focus set the 3 buttons to false
        command1.visible=False
        command2.visible=False
        command3.visible=False
End Sub
```

Description   The ExitFocus event is similar to the LostFocus event, which is characteristic of any control that can receive focus. This event will not occur until the control and all its constituent controls have lost focus.

| Example | The project at the end of this chapter shows how this event is used by checking to see if the user has submitted the information entered into the control before the control loses focus to the next control. |

FORWARDFOCUS PROPERTY

Objects Affected	UserControl
Purpose	This property determines whether a particular control will pass focus to the next control in the tab order

General Syntax

```
UserControl.ForwardFocus [= boolean%]
```

Table 83-19 Arguments for the ForwardFocus property

Arguments	Description
UserControl	Name of user control
boolean%	True or False

Table 83-20 Description of the boolean% value pertaining to the ForwardFocus property

boolean%	Meaning
True	The control next in the tab order will receive focus.
False	The control will gain focus and not pass it to the next control.

Description	The ForwardFocus property is used to determine when the control receives focus if it passes focus to the next control. This is set to True when you are creating a control that acts like a Label control.
Comment	The EnterFocus event will still be raised even if the ForwardFocus property is set to True.

HIDE EVENT

Objects Affected	UserControl, UserDocument
Purpose	This event occurs when the visible property of the control is set to False.
General Syntax	

```
Private Sub UserControl_Hide ()
```

Table 83-21 Argument for the Hide event

Argument	Description
UserControl	Name of control

Example Syntax

```
Private Sub UserControl_Hide ()
      'When the control is hidden set the EventsFrozen to True
       UserControl.Eventsfrozen=True
End Sub
```

Description   This event occurs when the Visible property of the control is set to False. This event does not occur when the control is hidden by an overlaying window or dragged off screen, or when the form it is on has been minimized.

INITPROPERTIES EVENT

Objects Affected   UserControl, User Document

Purpose   This event occurs when the control is first placed on a form.

General Syntax

```
Sub UserControl_InitProperties()
```

Table 83-22 Argument for the InitProperties event

Argument	Description
UserControl	Name of user control

Example Syntax

```
Sub object_InitProperties()
     BackColor=&H0  'Have the background color to Black
End Sub
```

Description   The InitProperties event is used to set the defaults of properties when a new instance of the control is created. This event occurs only when a new instance of the control is created, for example, when the developer draws the control on the form. It does not happen if the control is copied and pasted to the form while the container is in design time.

INVISIBLEATRUNTIME PROPERTY

Objects Affected   UserControl

Purpose   To determine if the control is visible at runtime.

General Syntax

```
UserControl.InvisibleAtRuntime [ = boolean%]
```

Table 83-23 Arguments for the InvisibleAtRuntime property

Arguments	Description
UserControl	Name of the control
boolean%	True or False

Table 83-24 Description of the boolean% value pertaining to the InvisibleAtRuntime property

boolean%	Meaning
True	The control is visible at runtime.
False	The control is invisible at runtime.

Description   This property determines if the control has a visible interface during runtime. If the property is set to True, the control and all its constituent controls will not be visible during runtime. If any of the visual properties (Visible, BackColor, and so forth) of the control or its constituent controls is accessed, a runtime error will occur.

PARENTCONTROLS PROPERTY

Objects Affected   UserControl

Purpose   To return a collection of controls that is hosting the control.

General Syntax

```
object.ParentsControls
```

Table 83-25 Argument for the ParentControls property

Argument	Description
UserControl	Name of the control

Example Syntax

```
Print ParentControls.Count
```

Description   This property is used to return a collection of controls containing the control on the same form as the ActiveX control. This property works the same as returning any other control collection.

SHOW EVENT

Objects Affected   UserControl, UserDocument

Purpose   This event occurs when the Visible property of the control is set to True.

General Syntax

```
Private Sub UserControl_Show ()
```

Table 83-26 Argument for the Show event

Argument	Description
UserControl	Name of the control

Example Syntax

```
Private Sub UserControl_Show ()
      'Now the control is shown change the background to black
      UserControl.Background=&H0
End Sub
```

Description   The Show event is the opposite of the Hide event. When the Visible property of the control is True, the event occurs. This event does not occur when the control is hidden by an overlaying window or dragged off screen, or if the form it is on has been minimized.

TOOLBOXBITMAP PROPERTY

Purpose   To assign a bitmap to be shown when this control is added to the toolbox.

Description   Returns or sets a bitmap that will be used as the picture control in the toolbox. The size of the bitmap while in the toolbox is 16 x 15 pixels. If the bitmap selected for this property is not of this size, it will be scaled. This property is available only at the control's authoring time.

Comments   It is not recommend to assign an icon to this property because icons do not scale well. The class name of the control will be the tooltip when the mouse is over the control.

General Syntax

```
Private Sub UserControl_ToolboxBitmap ()
```

Table 83-27 Argument for the ToolboxBitmap event

Argument	Description
UserControl	Name of the control

Example Syntax

```
Private Sub UserControl_Initialize ()
    ToolboxBitmap="c:\windows\fish.bmp"
End Sub
```

UserControl Object

Description   The UserControl contains all the properties, events, and methods of the control.

The Create ActiveX Project

Project Overview

This project is designed to leverage your knowledge of Visual Basic programming to create a simple ActiveX control. You will create an ActiveX control that writes user information to a text file. Chapter 84, "Exposing Control Properties" will allow you to expose the properties of the controls this ActiveX control will contain and add Internet function to the control.

Assembling the Project

We will assemble the project in two phases. The first will assemble the ActiveX control; the second will place the newly created control on a Visual Basic form.

1. Create a new Visual Basic 5.0 project and choose to create an ActiveX control (see Figure 83-1).

2. Assemble the object on the new form, using the properties in Table 83-28. Size the objects on the screen as shown in Figure 83-2.

Table 83-28 Properties for the elements on the form

Object	Property	Setting
UserControl1	Alignable	True
	DefaultCancel	True
Button	Name	cmdClear

Object	Property	Setting
	Cancel	True
	Caption	Clear Boxes
Button	Name	cmdSubmit
	Caption	Submit
	Default	True
Textbox	Name	txtEmail
	Text	""
TextBox	Name	txtLastName
	Text	""
TextBox	Name	txtFirstName
	Text	""
Label	Name	lbemail
	BackStyle	0 'Transparent
	Caption	Email Address
Label	Name	lbLastName
	BackStyle	0 'Transparent
	Caption	Last Name
Label	Name	lbFirstName
	BackStyle	0 'Transparent
	Caption	First Name

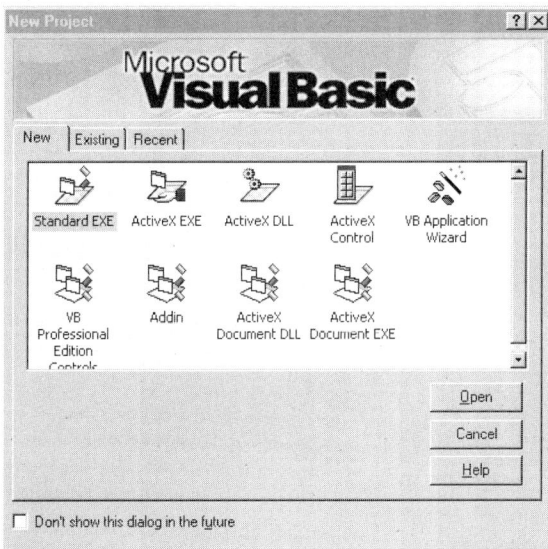

Figure 83-1   Create a new Visual Basic 5 project
and choose to create an ActiveX control

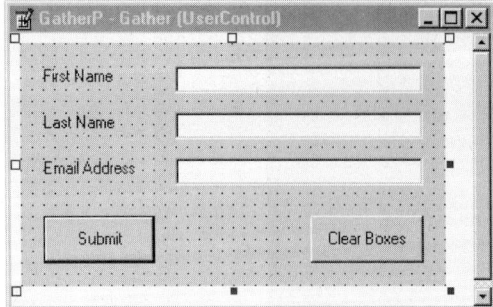

Figure 83-2 The arranged form

3. Enter the following code into the UserControl_EnterFocus event. This event code
will run when the control gains focus.

```
Private Sub UserControl_EnterFocus()
    BackColor = &HC0FFFF
End Sub
```

4. Enter the following code into the Private Sub UserControl_ExitFocus event. The
event code will run when the control loses focus.

```
Private Sub UserControl_ExitFocus()
    BackColor = &H8000000F
End Sub
```

5. Enter the following code into the Private Sub UserControl_InitProperties event.
These are the default settings when the control is placed on a new form. For the
buttons placed on this form to have their Default or Cancel property set to True,
the control's DefaultCancel property must be set to True. For the control to
receive focus, thus raising the EnterFocus and ExitFocus events, the control's
CanGetFocus property must be set to True.

```
Private Sub UserControl_InitProperties()
    DefaultCancel = True
    CanGetFocus = True
End Sub
```

6. Enter the following code into the cmdClear_Click event. When this button is
clicked or ESC is pressed, this event will clear the contents of the text controls on
the control.

```
Private Sub cmdClear_Click()
    txtFirstName.Text = ""
    txtLastName.Text = ""
    txtEmail.Text = ""
End Sub
```

7. Enter the following code into the Private Sub cmdSubmit_Click event. When this button is clicked or ENTER is pressed, this event will be raised. It places the text values from the text controls on the control, writes them to a text file, and notifies the user that the data has been submitted. Then it clears the contents of the text boxes.

```
Private Sub cmdSubmit_Click()
    Open App.Path + "\information.txt" For Append As #1
    Print #1, txtFirstName.Text, txtLastName.Text, txtEmail.Text
    Close #1
    MsgBox "The information has been submitted."
    txtFirstName.Text = ""
    txtLastName.Text = ""
    txtEmail.Text = ""
End Sub
```

8. Compile the control.

9. Create a new Standard EXE project.

10. Add the control you just compiled to the project.

11. Place the newly created control on the form. Resize the control so you can see the whole control.

How It Works

You have just created and compiled an ActiveX control that can be used in any ActiveX-compliant container. By adding this control to a project, you add its functionality to the processes already in the container.

When the control gains or receives focus, it changes color to let the user know it has entered the control. This could help if multiple groups of data that need to be entered are displayed. When you press the Submit button, the information you have entered is written to a text file. The following chapters demonstrate how the properties of the text box on the control can be exposed to the container and how to send the data contained in those text boxes to an HTTP server.

84

EXPOSING CONTROL PROPERTIES

In Chapter 83, "Creating ActiveX Controls," you created a control that at runtime allows the user to enter three pieces of information and click the Submit button, whereupon the information is saved to a text file.

However, the control you created had no way for developers using it to change the label's caption to denote the type of information they were trying to collect. Developers could not change the name of the text file or even change the background color property of the control. Developers like the ability to change every possible property and setting.

To do this, you must learn how to expose the properties of the control and its constituent controls. You can arrange things so that when a property of the control is changed, it changes the properties of various controls on the form. With the skills learned in this chapter, you will be able to create a new property that will change the font of all the label captions on the form to bold.

When you begin to expose properties, there are some new concepts to learn. These are

[a] The events that take place when a control is created or destroyed

[b] The use of PropertyBag

[c] The importance of the ReadProperties and WriteProperties events of the control

The more time you spend computing, the more you will find that many words and phrases are used to mean the same thing. For example, does your machine have a hard drive, a hard disk, or a fixed disk? We have some new terms for you, but we'll try to be consistent about using them. The first of these terms are *PropertyBag*, *ReadProperties*, and *WriteProperties*. To understand the importance of these items, you need to understand what happens when a control is displayed and hidden.

When the control is displayed so the user can see the control, it is considered to be created. Do not confuse this with the Show event or the Visible property of a user control. When a control is hidden from view, we consider it to be destroyed. A control can be destroyed when another window overlaps the control or when the form the control resides on is hidden or unloaded. In short, whenever a control is displayed, it is created. When a control is hidden or unloaded by any means, it is destroyed. In the Visual Basic manuals, this is also referred to as an *invocation of the control.*

The PropertyBag object is where the values of the properties you expose on your control are stored. These values are accessed by the ReadProperty and WriteProperty methods of PropertyBag to store and retrieve the state of the control when it is created or destroyed. The ReadProperties and WriteProperties events of the control are raised when the control is created or destroyed.

When a control is created, the ReadProperties event of the control is raised, whereupon the various properties from PropertyBag are read and applied to the exposed properties.

When the control is destroyed, the WriteProperties event of the control is raised and the various properties are written to PropertyBag. When the form that the control resides in is saved, settings in PropertyBag are written to the form definition file, designated by the extension .frm, which Visual Basic creates when a form is saved.

Exposing Control Properties Summary

This chapter discusses the objects, properties, events, and methods used to expose the properties of the control you create and their constituent controls. These are listed in Table 84-1. At the end of the chapter, there is an example that demonstrates exposing the properties of a control similar to one you built in Chapter 83.

Table 84-1 Description of elements

Use or Set This...	Type	To Do This...
PropertyBag	Object	Accesses the methods of PropertyBag.
PropertyChanged	Method	Notifies the container that the property changed.
ReadProperties	Event	Raised so the properties stored in a PropertyBag can be read.
ReadProperty	Method	Reads a property whose value is stored in PropertyBag.
WriteProperties	Event	Raised when the control has been destroyed to store its setting in a PropertyBag object.
WriteProperty	Method	Writes the value of an exposed property to a PropertyBag object.

PROPERTYBAG OBJECT

Purpose	The PropertyBag object contains the information to be saved and loaded when the ActiveX control you have built is created or destroyed. When a form is loaded, unloaded, saved, or added to a project, the container needs a method to determine the state of the ActiveX control. PropertyBag also allows developers to store the properties they have set for the various constituent controls contained in the control. The PropertyBag object has two methods that are accessed when the properties of the control are read or written. These methods are used within the ReadProperties and WriteProperties events of your ActiveX control.
Description	When you create a Visual Basic project, controls are added to forms. The properties of these controls can be changed to reflect how the developer wants the controls to look and react. The controls you build with Visual Basic must have a way to save and then load the changes made to the default settings of your controls. These settings are stored in the project's .frm files. The .frm files store the names of the controls added to the form and the settings that have been changed from the default setting. When the control is loaded, the ActiveX control raises the ReadProperties event. This event reads PropertyBag for the control and applies the settings. The same is true when the control is destroyed: The control raises the WriteProperties event and saves the values of the properties to PropertyBag.
Example	The PropertyBag object is declared and its method is used in the WriteProperties and ReadProperties events of the control in the example at the end of this chapter.

PROPERTYCHANGED METHOD

Objects Affected	UserControl, UserDocument
Purpose	This method notifies the container that the property has changed. This is used so the container can update the property windows with the new value.

General Syntax

```
object.PropertyChanged PropertyName
```

Table 84-2 Arguments for the PropertyChanged event

Argument	Description
object	Name of the object
PropertyName	The property that has changed

Example Syntax

```
Public Property Let AlarmTime(ByVal NewTime As String)
        AlarmTime = NewTime
        PropertyChanged "AlarmTime"
End Property
```

Description	When a property has been changed, the container needs to be notified to update the property window of the control and to raise the WriteProperties event if needed. If the container does not know that the property has been changed and the form is unloaded, and if no other property has been changed, the WriteProperties event will not be raised to store the new value.
Example	In the project at the end of this chapter, this method is used inside the control's BackColorT procedure to notify the container when this property has been changed.

READPROPERTIES EVENT

Objects Affected	UserControl, UserDocument
Purpose	This event occurs when a previously saved state of the control is loaded.
General Syntax	

```
Private Sub object_ReadProperties(PropBag As PropertyBag)
```

Table 84-3 Arguments for the ReadProperties event

Argument	Description
object	Name of object
PropBag	Name of the PropertyBag object

Example Syntax

```
Private Sub MyControl_ReadProperties(PropBag As PropertyBag)
        MyControl.BackColor = PropBag.ReadProperty("BackColor", &H8000000F)
        MyControl.BackStyle = PropBag.ReadProperty("BackStyle", 1)
End Sub
```

Description	This event is raised after the Initialize event occurs, thus allowing the control to load from PropertyBag and set the properties that were saved during the WriteProperties event. To set each property, you must write code in the ReadProperties event.
Example	The example at the end of this chapter demonstrates how the control loads its saved state from a PropertyBag object.
Comments	It is a good idea to write some error-trapping code in this event because the file (.frm in Visual Basic) containing the form information could have

been modified by a text editor. The error trapping will allow the container to load the control with the incorrect information and set the properties in error to their default settings. The proper information will be written during the first WriteProperties event.

READPROPERTY METHOD

Objects Affected	PropertyBag
Purpose	This method is used to read the saved state of PropertyBag.
General Syntax	

```
object.ReadProperty (PropertyName, DefaultValue) As String
```

Table 84-4 Arguments for the ReadProperty method

Argument	Description
object	Name of the object
PropertyName	Name of the property to be read
DefaultValue	The value used for the property if no value currently exists

Example Syntax
```
Private Sub MyControl_ReadProperties(PropBag As PropertyBag)
     MyControl.BackColor = PropBag.ReadProperty("BackColor", &H8000000F)
     MyControl.BackStyle = PropBag.ReadProperty("BackStyle", 1)
     m_TotalBackGround = PropBag.ReadProperty("TotalBackGround", m_def_TotalBackGround)
End Sub
```

Description	The ReadProperty method is used to read a value of a property of your control from the container form file. This allows the container to display and set the values of the control since it was last saved.
Example	In the example at the end of this chapter, the ReadProperty method is used inside the control's ReadProperties event. This method allows the control to set the properties as they were when the control was destroyed.

WRITEPROPERTIES EVENT

Objects Affected	UserControl, UserDocument
Purpose	The WriteProperties event is raised before the container destroys the instance of the control.
General Syntax	

```
Private Sub UserControl_WriteProperties (PropBag as PropertyBag)
```

Table 84-5 Arguments for the WriteProperties event

Argument	Description
UserControl	Name of the UserControl
PropBag	Name of PropertyBag

Example Syntax

```
Private Sub UserControl_WriteProperties(PropBag As PropertyBag)
     PropBag.WriteProperty("BackColor", UserControl.BackColor, &H8000000F)
     PropBag.WriteProperty("BackStyle", UserControl.BackStyle, 1)
End Sub
```

Description The WriteProperties event is raised when the container is going to destroy the control and needs to save its state. In this event, the proper code must be written to save the properties to a PropertyBag object.

WRITEPROPERTY METHOD

Objects Affected PropertyBag

Purpose Writes the value of a property to a PropertyBag object.

General Syntax

```
object.WriteProperty(DataName, Value[, DefaultValue])
```

Table 84-6 Arguments for the WriteProperty method

Argument	Description
object	Name of the object
DataName	Name of the property to be saved
Value	The value of the property to be saved
DefaultValue	The default value of the property

Example Syntax

```
Private Sub UserControl_WriteProperties(PropBag As PropertyBag)
     PropBag.WriteProperty("BackColor", UserControl.BackColor, &H8000000F)
     ProgBag.WriteProperty("BackStyle", UserControl.BackStyle, 1)
End Sub
```

Description The WriteProperty method is used to place the value of the property into PropertyBag. This setting is also the value that will be stored in the container's form definition file.

Example	In the example at the end of this chapter, the WriteProperty method of PropertyBag is used inside the WriteProperties event of the control to save the state of the control before it is destroyed.
Comments	The biggest benefit of assigning a default value is that most containers write the values that are not set to their default setting to the form definition file. This saves space and increases speed when loading the form in a project.

The Exposing Controls Project

Project Overview

By following this example, you will learn how to expose the properties for the controls you create. This includes properties of both the control and its constituent controls. The project is divided into two parts. The first part is the assembly of the project and the second is placing the assembled control on a form.

Assembling the Project

1. Open a new ActiveX control project and place in it the controls specified in Table 84-7.

Table 84-7 Property settings for the Submit control of the Exposing Control Properties project

Object	Property	Setting
UserControl	Name	ctlSubmit
	DefaultCancel	True
	EditAtDesignTime	True
CommandButton	Name	cmdCancel
	Cancel	True
	Caption	&Clear
CommandButton	Name	cmdSubmit
	Caption	&Submit
	Default	True
TextBox	Name	txtItem1
TextBox	Name	txtItem2
TextBox	Name	txtItem3
Label	Name	lblItem2
	Caption	lblItem2
Label	Name	lblItem3
	Caption	lblItem3
Label	Name	lblItem1
	Caption	lblItem1

2. Arrange the elements of the control to look like Figure 84-1.

3. Enter the following code in the General Declarations area of UserControl. The top three constants are the default values of the custom properties of the control. The bottom three variables hold the current values of the custom properties.

```
Const DefaultBackColor = 0
Const DefaultLabelBold = 0
Const DefaultDataName = "data.txt"

Dim C_BackColorT As OLE_COLOR
Dim C_LabelBold As Integer
Dim C_DataName As String
```

4. Enter the following code in the General Declarations area of UserControl. This will allow the developer who uses the control to read the setting of the Enabled property.

```
Public Property Get Enabled() As Boolean
        Enabled = UserControl.Enabled
End Property
```

5. Enter the following code in the General Declarations area of UserControl. This will create the procedure that will allow the developer to set the Enabled property of the control. When this property is set, it also sets the Enabled property for all the constituent controls on the form. The PropertyChanged method is called to notify the container that the property has changed so it can update its property window for this control.

```
Public Property Let Enabled(ByVal New_Enabled As Boolean)
    UserControl.Enabled() = New_Enabled
    PropertyChanged "Enabled"
End Property
```

6. Enter the following code in the General Declarations area of UserControl. This will allow the developer of the control to read the caption of the label named "L1Caption," which is a constituent control. Without this procedure, the developer could not read the caption.

```
Public Property Get L1Caption() As String
    L1Caption = lbItem1.Caption
End Property
```

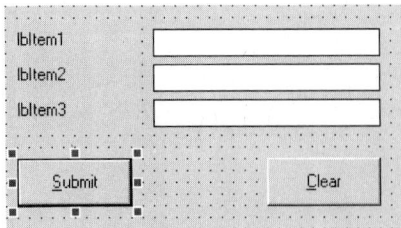

Figure 84-1 The controls on the form

7. Enter the following code in the General Declarations area of UserControl. This procedure allows the developer to set the caption of the Label control.

```
Public Property Let L1Caption(ByVal New_L1Caption As String)
    lbItem1.Caption() = New_L1Caption
    PropertyChanged "L1Caption"
End Property
```

8. Enter the following code in the General Declarations area of UserControl.

```
Public Property Get L2Caption() As String
    L2Caption = lbItem2.Caption
End Property
```

9. Enter the following code in the General Declarations area of UserControl.

```
Public Property Let L2Caption(ByVal New_L2Caption As String)
    lbItem2.Caption() = New_L2Caption
    PropertyChanged "L2Caption"
End Property
```

10. Enter the following code in the General Declarations area of UserControl. This allows the custom property called NameOfDataFile to be read. This property is used to read or write the name of the file that the output this control creates is sent when the Submit button is clicked.

```
Public Property Get NameOfDataFile() As String
    NameOfDataFile = C_DataName
End Property
```

11. Enter the code below into the General Declarations area of UserControl. The procedure works in the same way as the procedure that sets the captions of the Label controls, but sets the Text property of the control instead.

```
Public Property Get T1Text() As String
    T1Text = txtItem1.Text
End Property
```

12. Enter the code below into the General Declarations area of UserControl. The following procedure works the same way as setting the Caption property of the label does. The new value is passed to the constituent TextBox control on the control, then the container is notified of the change so it can update what is necessary.

```
Public Property Let T1Text(ByVal New_T1Text As String)
    txtItem1.Text() = New_T1Text
    PropertyChanged "T1Text"
End Property
```

13. Enter the code below into the General Declarations area of UserControl.

```
Public Property Get T2Text() As String
    T2Text = txtItem2.Text
End Property
```

14. Enter the code below into the General Declarations area of UserControl.

```
Public Property Let T2Text(ByVal New_T2Text As String)
    txtItem2.Text() = New_T2Text
    PropertyChanged "T2Text"
End Property
```

15. Enter the code below into the General Declarations area of UserControl.

```
Public Property Get T3Text() As String
    T3Text = txtItem3.Text
End Property
```

16. Enter the code below into the General Declarations area of UserControl.

```
Public Property Let T3Text(ByVal New_T3Text As String)
    txtItem3.Text() = New_T3Text
    PropertyChanged "T3Text"
End Property
```

17. Enter the code below into the General Declarations area of UserControl.

```
Public Property Get L3Caption() As String
    L3Caption = lbItem3.Caption
End Property
```

18. Enter the code below into the General Declarations area of UserControl.

```
Public Property Let L3Caption(ByVal New_L3Caption As String)
    lbItem3.Caption() = New_L3Caption
    PropertyChanged "L3Caption"
End Property
```

19. Enter the code below into the General Declarations area of UserControl. This procedure allows the developer to read the value of the BackColorT property of the control.

```
Public Property Get BackColorT() As OLE_COLOR
    BackColorT = C_BackColorT
End Property
```

20. Enter the code below into the General Declarations area of UserControl. This procedure allows the developer to write a new value to the BackColorT property. When this property is changed, the value that has been passed to it is used to set the background color of the control and its constituent Label controls. This procedure demonstrates how a value can be assigned to a custom property and used to change other controls on the form. Any sort of code can be contained in this procedure. If you want to get fancy, you might have code that determines the color and then changes the label to a complementary color.

```
Public Property Let BackColorT(ByVal New_BackColorT As OLE_COLOR)
    C_BackColorT = New_BackColorT
    BackColor = C_BackColorT
    lbItem1.BackColor = C_BackColorT
```

```
lbItem2.BackColor = C_BackColorT
lbItem3.BackColor = C_BackColorT
PropertyChanged "BackColorT"
End Property
```

21. Enter the code below into the General Declarations area of UserControl. This procedure allows the developer to set a new name for the data file to which this control will write when the Submit button is pressed.

```
Public Property Let NameOfDataFile(ByVal NewName As String)
    C_DataName = NewName
    PropertyChanged "NameOfDataFile"
End Property
```

22. Enter the code below into the General Declarations area of UserControl. The procedure allows the developer to read whether or not the constituent labels on the control have their font set to bold or not.

```
Public Property Get LabelBold() As Integer
    LabelBold = C_LabelBold
End Property
```

23. Enter the code below into the General Declarations area of UserControl. This procedure changes the constituent Label control's Font.Bold property. The procedure receives the new value, then the LabelBold property is set to a new value. This value (True or False) is then passed to the Label controls.

```
Public Property Let LabelBold(ByVal New_LabelBold As Integer)
    C_LabelBold = New_LabelBold
    lbItem1.Font.Bold = C_LabelBold
    lbItem2.Font.Bold = C_LabelBold
    lbItem3.Font.Bold = C_LabelBold
    PropertyChanged "LabelBold"
End Property
```

24. Enter the code below into the cmdCancel_Click event of the cmdCancel button. By clicking this button or pressing [ESC] (because the Cancel property is set to True), this procedure will clear the contents of the constituent TextBox controls.

```
Private Sub cmdCancel_Click()
    txtItem1.Text = ""
    txtItem2.Text = ""
    txtItem3.Text = ""
End Sub
```

25. Enter the code below into the cmdSubmit_Click event of the cmdSubmit button. When the cmdSubmit button is clicked or [ENTER] is pressed (because the Default property of the button is set to True), the following procedure will execute. The procedure will open a text file whose name is stored in the NameOfDataFile property of the control. After the procedure has written the contents (.Text) of the TextBox control, the procedure will display a message box and then clear the text from the controls.

```
Private Sub cmdSubmit_Click()
    Open NameOfDataFile For Append As #1
    Print #1, txtItem1.Text, txtItem3.Text, txtItem3.Text
    Close #1
    MsgBox "The data has been submitted."
    txtItem1.Text = ""
    txtItem2.Text = ""
    txtItem3.Text = ""
End Sub
```

26. Enter the code below into the UserControl_InitProperties event of UserControl. This is the first event the control raises when it is loaded or a new invocation is displayed. This procedure is used to assign default values to properties. After this event, the ReadProperties event is raised and any values stored in PropertyBag are overwritten.

```
Private Sub UserControl_InitProperties()
    C_BackColorT = DefaultBackColor
    C_LabelBold = DefaultLabelBold
End Sub
```

27. Enter the code below into the UserControl_ReadProperties event of UserControl. This procedure is raised after the Initialize event. This event is raised to allow the developer to read the values stored in PropertyBag and assign them to the appropriate properties of the control. Below you can see the syntax for reading a value from PropertyBag and assigning it to the appropriate property. The error trap is used in case the form definition file has been tampered with.

```
Private Sub UserControl_ReadProperties(PropBag As PropertyBag)
    On Error Resume Next
    UserControl.Enabled = PropBag.ReadProperty("Enabled", True)
    lbItem1.Caption = PropBag.ReadProperty("L1Caption", "lbItem1")
    lbItem2.Caption = PropBag.ReadProperty("L2Caption", "lbItem2")
    txtItem1.Text = PropBag.ReadProperty("T1Text", "")
    txtItem2.Text = PropBag.ReadProperty("T2Text", "")
    txtItem3.Text = PropBag.ReadProperty("T3Text", "")
    lbItem3.Caption = PropBag.ReadProperty("L3Caption", "lbItem3")
    BackColorT = PropBag.ReadProperty("BackColorT", DefaultBackColor)
    LabelBold = PropBag.ReadProperty("LabelBold", DefaultLabelBold)
    NameOfDataFile = PropBag.ReadProperty("NameOfDataFile", DefaultDataName)
    On Error Goto 0
End Sub
```

28. Enter the code below into the UserControl_WriteProperties of UserControl. The following procedure demonstrates writing the current property value of the control to a PropertyBag object. This event is raised each time the control is destroyed. Each property that is exposed must be in this event to be saved. If you are setting a property of a control at the design time of the container, and at runtime the property reverts to the default (or a strange) value, then either the property is not being set correctly during ReadProperties or it is not being included with the properties stored during the WriteProperties event.

```
Private Sub UserControl_WriteProperties(PropBag As PropertyBag)

    Call PropBag.WriteProperty("Enabled", UserControl.Enabled, True)
    Call PropBag.WriteProperty("L1Caption", lbItem1.Caption, "lbItem1")
    Call PropBag.WriteProperty("L2Caption", lbItem2.Caption, "lbItem2")
    Call PropBag.WriteProperty("T1Text", txtItem1.Text, "")
    Call PropBag.WriteProperty("T2Text", txtItem2.Text, "")
    Call PropBag.WriteProperty("T3Text", txtItem3.Text, "")
    Call PropBag.WriteProperty("L3Caption", lbItem3.Caption, "lbItem3")
    Call PropBag.WriteProperty("BackColorT", C_BackColorT, DefaultBackColor)
    Call PropBag.WriteProperty("LabelBold", C_LabelBold, DefaultLabelBold)
    Call PropBag.WriteProperty("NameOfDataFile", C_DataName, DefaultDataName)
End Sub
```

INTERLUDE

Now that you have assembled the control, take a breath of fresh air. Save the control you have just assembled and mentally prepare yourself for the second round.

Now that you have the control built, you can add it to a project form so you can set and get property settings and see how this all works.

---

29. Go to the File Menu and select Add Project. From the dialog box that appears, select to add a standard EXE. A blank form will appear on the screen.

If the windows pertaining to developing the control are not closed, UserControl will be displayed as disabled. To add the control to the new project or set the newly exposed properties, you must close all the procedure and form windows of the control. The UserControl bitmap will appear in the toolbox when the form of the Standard EXE project is selected. If you have been creative and added your own ToolBoxBitmap to this control, your own picture will appear in the toolbox instead.

30. Place the controls specified in Table 84-8 on the form of the standard EXE.

Table 84-8 Property settings for the form

Object	Property	Setting
Form	Name	frmMain
	Caption	Information Form
UserControl	ctlSubmit	ctlSubmit1
	L1Caption	Name
	L2Caption	Phone
	L3Caption	Email
Label	Name	lbTitle
	Caption	Please enter the information below:

31. Assemble the controls as in Figure 84-2.

32. Click on the control and press F4 to display the Properties window. Notice the default properties that are set. Change the exposed properties as in Figure 84-3. As you change these properties, you will notice the effect on the control. If the code entered has the wrong syntax, a runtime error will occur. If the property is not set correctly in ReadProperties and WriteProperties, then the control will misbehave.

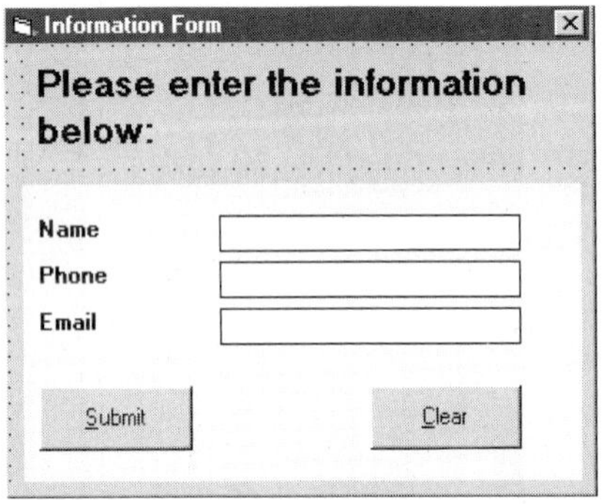

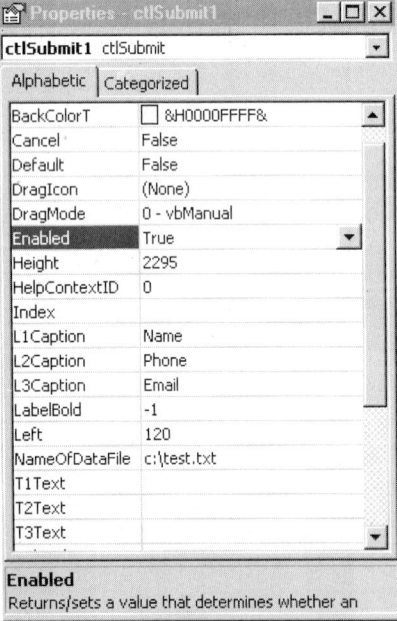

Figure 84-2   The controls on the form

Figure 84-3   The properties in the Properties window

How It Works

When the control is placed on the form, the InitProperties event will be raised and the default properties will be set using the values declared in the General Declarations module of the control. The ReadProperties event will be raised but no visible change will take effect because all the properties have not had their default properties changed.

As the properties are set by the developer, the proper Let and Get procedures will be raised. If the L1Caption property is set, the public property Let L1Captionprocedure is raised.

By setting the exposed properties in the Properties windows of the control, you will change the properties of the control visibly. When the L3Caption property is changed, the public property Let L3Caption procedure is raised. As any property is changed or read, the appropriate event is raised. A good example of how ReadProperties is used occurs when the container goes from design time to runtime. When Visual Basic enters runtime, it must create an instance of the form for the user to see. Visual Basic first saves the settings of the properties to PropertyBag. Then the form is displayed and the properties in PropertyBag are read and applied to the properties. Going from design time to runtime is one of the best ways to determine if your ReadProperties and WriteProperties events are working.

Runtime Errors

The best way to test your control before compiling it into the latest and greatest ActiveX control is to add a new project to the project group of your control. If there is a runtime error, the code windows can be edited. When a control added to a form generates a runtime error in ReadProperties or WriteProperties, then the form on which the control resides will no longer be able to be displayed.

Closing Notes

Included with Visual Basic is an add-in called the ActiveX Control Interface Wizard. This add-in will allow you to expose and create properties for your controls easily. You will see how this add-in can help you quickly expose properties and, with the added knowledge of this chapter, tweak the code the wizard creates for you in the next chapter.

85

RESPONDING TO USER ACTIONS WITH ACTIVEX CONTROLS

Most ActiveX controls must interact with the user. Some, like a status bar, just convey information, but the majority must take input from the user and give visual feedback. This chapter focuses on taking user actions and giving appropriate visual feedback for user-drawn controls. Constituent controls already handle user actions. Often all that must be done is map events from the constituent controls to public members.

The foci of this chapter are the MouseDown, MouseMove, MouseUp, KeyDown, KeyPress, and KeyUp events and how they should affect the behavior and appearance of an ActiveX control. These are the same events you have used with Visual Basic forms and controls.

This chapter will step through the process of adding responsiveness to a simple control. The control takes on the appearance and behavior of a command button. This functionality could be achieved more easily by using a command button as a constituent control. However, a command button is a common control whose responses to user actions are well known and cover all the bases needed for this discussion. One of the more important lessons when building the custom control is to leverage the user's experience with existing UI elements. If it looks like a button and smells like a button, it had better behave like a button or the user will be confused.

Mouse

A mouse's actions usually give feedback at all stages of the action. A control will visually indicate that the mouse button is down and change again when the mouse button is released. During this time, the user can typically abort the action by sliding off the control without releasing the mouse button and then releasing the mouse button when the cursor has left the area of the control. The sample code below uses information on focus from Chapter 82, "ActiveX Control Overview," to draw a control that looks like a button minus the caption. This will be the starting point for building a control that responds to user actions in a manner consistent with existing UI elements.

```vb
Private mbHasFocus As Boolean

Private Declare Function DrawFocusRect Lib "user32" ⇐
        (ByVal hdc As Long, lpRect As RECT) As Long
Private Type RECT
        Left As Long
        Top As Long
        Right As Long
        Bottom As Long
End Type

Private Sub UserControl_GotFocus()
        mbHasFocus = True
        Refresh
End Sub

Private Sub UserControl_LostFocus()
        mbHasFocus = False
        Refresh
End Sub

Private Sub UserControl_Paint()
        If mbHasFocus Then
                'draw the focus rectangle
                DrawFocus
                'draw the border
                Line (0, 0)-(ScaleWidth - 1, ScaleHeight - 1) , vb3DDKShadow, B
                DrawButtonBorder 1, 1, ScaleWidth - 1, ScaleHeight - 1
        Else
                DrawButtonBorder 0, 0, ScaleWidth, ScaleHeight
        End If
End Sub

Private Sub DrawButtonBorder(plLeft As Long, plTop As Long ⇐
        , plRight As Long, plBottom As Long)
        'draw a border that looks like a button
        'assumes pixel scale mode
        Line (plLeft, plTop)-(plRight - 1, plTop) , vb3DHighlight
        Line (plLeft, plTop)-(plLeft, plBottom - 1) , vb3DHighlight
        Line (plRight - 1, plTop)-(plRight - 1, plBottom - 1) , vb3DDKShadow
        Line (plLeft, plBottom - 1)-(plRight, plBottom - 1) , vb3DDKShadow
        Line (plRight - 2, plTop + 1)-(plRight - 2, plBottom - 2) , vb3DShadow
        Line (plLeft + 1, plBottom - 2)-(plRight - 1, plBottom - 2) , vb3DShadow
End Sub

Private Sub DrawFocus()
        'draw the focus rectangle
        'assumes pixel scale mode
```

```
        Dim ControlRect As RECT
        ControlRect.Top = 4
        ControlRect.Left = 4
        ControlRect.Right = ScaleWidth - 4
        ControlRect.Bottom = ScaleHeight - 4
        DrawFocusRect hdc, ControlRect
End Sub
```

This control looks like a button, but it does not yet respond to the user as a button does. The first thing to do is change its appearance when the user clicks on it. The sample code below shows the changes needed to make this happen. First, add a new Private Boolean member to keep track of the up or down state of the button. The MouseDown and MouseUp events of the UserControl change the mbDown member variable and call Refresh to redraw the control. The Paint event now checks the mbDown variable to see how it should draw the control. If the control is pressed, it is drawn flat like a depressed button. The control now also raises the MouseDown, MouseUp, and Click events.

```
Private mbDown As Boolean

Private Sub UserControl_MouseDown(Button As Integer, Shift As Integer ⇐
    , X As Single, Y As Single)
    If Button = vbLeftButton Then
            mbDown = True
            Refresh
    End If
    RaiseEvent MouseDown(Button, Shift, X, Y)
End Sub

Private Sub UserControl_MouseUp(Button As Integer, Shift As Integer ⇐
    , X As Single, Y As Single)
    If Button = vbLeftButton Then
            mbDown = False
            Refresh
            RaiseEvent Click
    End If
    RaiseEvent MouseUp(Button, Shift, X, Y)
End Sub

Private Sub UserControl_Paint()
    'now paint different based on being down
    If mbDown = True Then
            'draw the focus rectangle
            DrawFocus
            'draw the border
            Line (0, 0)-(ScaleWidth - 1, ScaleHeight - 1) , vb3DDKShadow, B
            Line (1, 1)-(ScaleWidth - 2, ScaleHeight - 2), vb3DShadow, B
    ElseIf mbHasFocus Then
            'draw the focus rectangle
            DrawFocus
            'draw the border
            Line (0, 0)-(ScaleWidth - 1, ScaleHeight - 1) , vb3DDKShadow, B
```

continued on next page

continued from previous page

```
            DrawButtonBorder 1, 1, ScaleWidth - 1, ScaleHeight - 1
        Else
            DrawButtonBorder 0, 0, ScaleWidth, ScaleHeight
        End If
End Sub
```

The control now responds similar to a pressed button. There is only one step left for a control responding to a user's mouse actions. The user must be able to cancel the click action when using the mouse. Many controls support the ability to cancel the click action by moving the mouse cursor off the control before releasing the mouse button. Check boxes, option buttons, and command buttons are examples of controls that you can cancel by sliding off the control. The UserControl's MouseMove event is the ticket for providing this functionality. Normally, MouseMove events occur only while the mouse is over the object. However, the UserControl object will continue to receive MouseMove events between the MouseDown and MouseUp events, even if the cursor leaves the area of the control. By checking to see if the cursor has left the area of the control in the MouseMove event, you know if the user has slid off the control.

The sample below shows the changes needed to support this functionality. A new Private Boolean keeps track of the where the cursor is, in or out. This value is set from the MouseMove event. If the cursor moves out of the control's space, the control visual pops back up. When the mouse moves back, the control is again depressed. The MouseUp event now checks the mbOut variable to see if it should fire the Click event.

```
Private mbOut As Boolean

Private Sub UserControl_MouseMove(Button As Integer, Shift As Integer ⇐
    , X As Single, Y As Single)
    If Button = vbLeftButton Then
        If X > ScaleWidth Or X < 0 Or Y > ScaleHeight Or Y < 0 Then
            'only change and refresh if needed to reduce flicker
            If Not mbOut Then
                mbOut = True
                Refresh
            End If
        Else
            'only change and refresh if needed to reduce flicker
            If mbOut Then
                mbOut = False
                Refresh
            End If
        End If
    End If
    RaiseEvent MouseMove(Button, Shift, X, Y)
End Sub

Private Sub UserControl_MouseUp(Button As Integer, Shift As Integer ⇐
    , X As Single, Y As Single)
    If Button = vbLeftButton Then
        mbDown = False
        If Not mbOut Then
            Refresh
            RaiseEvent Click
        End If
```

```
        End If
        RaiseEvent MouseUp(Button, Shift, X, Y)
End Sub

Private Sub UserControl_Paint()
        'depressed only if down and within the controls borders
        If mbDown = True And mbOut = False Then
                'draw the focus rectangle
                DrawFocus
                'draw the border
                Line (0, 0)-(ScaleWidth - 1, ScaleHeight - 1) , vb3DDKShadow, B
                Line (1, 1)-(ScaleWidth - 2, ScaleHeight - 2), vb3DShadow, B
        ElseIf mbHasFocus Then
                'draw the focus rectangle
                DrawFocus
                'draw the border
                Line (0, 0)-(ScaleWidth - 1, ScaleHeight - 1) , vb3DDKShadow, B
                DrawButtonBorder 1, 1, ScaleWidth - 1, ScaleHeight - 1
        Else
                DrawButtonBorder 0, 0, ScaleWidth, ScaleHeight
        End If
End Sub
```

This control now behaves like a command button manipulated through a user's mouse actions. However, Windows users do not live by the mouse alone.

Keyboard

Many users are strong keyboard users. Especially in heavy data-entry applications, responsiveness to keyboard control is a must. A user whose fingers leave the keyboard to use a particular control has just lost precious time and will quickly get aggravated. A mouse action typically has a parallel on the keyboard. This section will show how to respond to the user on the keyboard side like the responses in the mouse section.

The Visual Basic command button is activated by two keys: SPACE and ENTER. They each have a slightly different behavior. When building an ActiveX control, examine similar controls and respond to the same user actions. In the case of the command button, ENTER fires the Click event without visible feedback. Multiple Click events will occur as long as ENTER is held down. The SPACE key acts like a mouse press; the button flattens while the SPACE key is held; releasing the SPACE key fires the Click event and returns the button to its normal appearance.

The sample code below adds response to the user's keyboard actions. The ENTER key raises the Click event in the KeyDown; everywhere else it is ignored. The SPACE key behaves like a mouse click, first setting the mbDown variable in the KeyDown event, then raising the Click event in the KeyUp. All other keys simply pass on the event to the corresponding public events.

```
Private Sub UserControl_KeyDown(KeyCode As Integer, Shift As Integer)
        Select Case KeyCode
                Case vbKeyReturn
                        RaiseEvent Click
```

continued on next page

continued from previous page

```
                Case vbKeySpace
                    If mbDown = False Then
                        mbDown = True
                        Refresh
                    End If
                    RaiseEvent KeyDown(KeyCode, Shift)
                Case Else
                    RaiseEvent KeyDown(KeyCode, Shift)
        End Select
End Sub

Private Sub UserControl_KeyPress(KeyAscii As Integer)
    Select Case KeyAscii
            Case vbKeyReturn
                'return does not raise a KeyPress
            Case Else
                RaiseEvent KeyPress(KeyAscii)
        End Select
End Sub

Private Sub UserControl_KeyUp(KeyCode As Integer, Shift As Integer)
    Select Case KeyCode
            Case vbKeyReturn
                'return does not raise a KeyUp
            Case vbKeySpace
                mbDown = False
                Refresh
                RaiseEvent KeyUp(KeyCode, Shift)
                RaiseEvent Click
            Case Else
                RaiseEvent KeyUp(KeyCode, Shift)
        End Select
End Sub
```

ActiveX controls with a caption typically are also activated by an access key. Chapter 82 demonstrates how to implement this functionality.

Like moving the cursor off the control before releasing the mouse button, keyboard actions sometimes have a cancel option. In the case of the command button, the click can be canceled by pressing the ESC key before releasing the SPACE key. The changes below add the cancel response to the user's keyboard actions.

```
Private mbKeyDown As Boolean

Private Sub UserControl_KeyDown(KeyCode As Integer, Shift As Integer)
    Select Case KeyCode
            Case vbKeyReturn
                RaiseEvent Click
            Case vbKeySpace
                If mbDown = False Then
                    mbOut = False
                    mbDown = True
                    mbKeyDown = True
                    Refresh
                End If
```

```
                    RaiseEvent KeyDown(KeyCode, Shift)
            Case Else
                    RaiseEvent KeyDown(KeyCode, Shift)
        End Select
End Sub

Private Sub UserControl_KeyUp(KeyCode As Integer, Shift As Integer)
        Static bIgnoreNextSpaceUp As Boolean
        Select Case KeyCode
            Case vbKeyReturn
                    'return does not raise a KeyUp
            Case vbKeyEscape
                    'if depressed because of a key press
                    'then cancel the action
                    If mbKeyDown = True Then
                            mbOut = True
                            mbDown = False
                            Refresh
                            RaiseEvent KeyUp(KeyCode, Shift)
                            bIgnoreNextSpaceUp = True
                    End If
            Case vbKeySpace
                    If bIgnoreNextSpaceUp Then
                            RaiseEvent KeyUp(KeyCode, Shift)
                            bIgnoreNextSpaceUp = False
                    Else
                            mbDown = False
                            Refresh
                            RaiseEvent KeyUp(KeyCode, Shift)
                            RaiseEvent Click
                    End If
                    mbKeyDown = False
            Case Else
                    RaiseEvent KeyUp(KeyCode, Shift)
        End Select
End Sub
```

The first change is the mbKeyDown variable in the declarations section. This indicates that the control is depressed because of a key press, not a mouse action. This variable is set in the KeyDown event when the key is a SPACE. In the KeyUp event, if the key is ESC, the action is canceled. A static local variable is set telling the KeyUp event to ignore the next KeyUp from a SPACE key.

The User Actions Project

Project Overview

The User Actions project demonstrates how to respond to user actions. The completed project will allow a user to drag a circle around within a square using the mouse or keyboard. The project differs from the samples above in that it changes properties in a constituent control to provide the visual feedback to the user.

Assembling the Project

1. First, create a new Standard EXE project. This User Actions project will be a private control. It is often easier and faster to design and test a control as part of a project before wrapping it up as an OCX.

2. Next, add a UserControl with the Project|Add UserControl menu item, or by right-clicking on the project window.

3. Put a Shape control on the UserControl. Set the following properties for the UserControl and Shape.

Table 85-1 Controls for the chapter project

Object	Property	Setting
UserControl	ScaleMode	3 - Pixel
Shape	Left	0
	Top	0
	Width	25
	Height	25
	Shape	3 - Circle
	FillStyle	0 - Solid
	FillColor	ButtonFace

4. Add the following code to the declarations section of the UserControl. These are all the variables needed to keep track of the state of the control.

```
'where on the shape did I click
Dim fOffsetX As Single
Dim fOffsetY As Single
'moving with mouse
Dim mbDown As Boolean
'moving with keys
Dim mbKeyDown As Boolean
'where did the mouse drag start
Dim fStartX As Single
Dim fStartY As Single
```

5. Add the following line to the UserControl's Paint event. This gives the control a visual border so the user knows where the edge is.

```
Line (0, 0)-(ScaleWidth - 1, ScaleHeight - 1), vb3DDKShadow, B
```

6. Add the following Sub to the user control. This is the sub that will be used to move the shape around the control. It keeps the shape from leaving the visible part of the control so it cannot be lost.

```
Private Sub MoveShape(X As Single, Y As Single)
       'constrain the shape to the controls borders
```

```
        If Y < 0 Then
                Shape1.Top = 0
        ElseIf Y > ScaleHeight - Shape1.Height Then
                Shape1.Top = ScaleHeight - Shape1.Height
        Else
                Shape1.Top = Y
        End If
        If X < 0 Then
                Shape1.Left = 0
        ElseIf X > ScaleWidth - Shape1.Width Then
                Shape1.Left = ScaleWidth - Shape1.Width
        Else
                Shape1.Left = X
        End If
End Sub
```

7. The following code, when added to the UserControl, lets the mouse move the shape around the control. When the shape is being dragged, it changes color to indicate to the user that he or she is performing an action. A right-click during the drag cancels the move and returns the shape to its position before the drag started.

```
Private Sub UserControl_MouseDown(Button As Integer, Shift As Integer ⇐
    , X As Single, Y As Single)
    If Button = vbLeftButton _
            And X >= Shape1.Left And X <= Shape1.Left + Shape1.Width
            And Y >= Shape1.Top And Y <= Shape1.Top + Shape1.Height
            Then
            'if it is the left button down on the shape, set up to move
            'keep the starting position
            fStartX = Shape1.Left
            fStartY = Shape1.Top
            'where am i on the shape
            fOffsetX = X - Shape1.Left
            fOffsetY = Y - Shape1.Top
            'visible indication that the user has picked up the shape
            Shape1.FillColor = vb3DShadow
            mbDown = True
        End If
End Sub

Private Sub UserControl_MouseMove(Button As Integer, Shift As Integer ⇐
    , X As Single, Y As Single)
    If mbDown Then
            'if the button is down then move the shape
            MoveShape X - fOffsetX, Y - fOffsetY
        End If
End Sub

Private Sub UserControl_MouseUp(Button As Integer, Shift As Integer ⇐
    , X As Single, Y As Single)
    If Button = vbLeftButton Then
            'done moving
            Shape1.FillColor = vbButtonFace
            mbDown = False
    ElseIf Button = vbRightButton And mbDown Then
            'a right mouse click while we're down cancels and moves
```

continued on next page

continued from previous page

```
                    'the shape back to its position at the beginning of the drag
                    Shape1.FillColor = vbButtonFace
                    mbDown = False
                    Shape1.Left = fStartX
                    Shape1.Top = fStartY
            End If
    End Sub
```

8. Now it's time to add keyboard support. Add the following Subs to the UserControl. On the KeyUp, the directional keys move the shape. If the ESC key is pressed before the KeyUp, the move is canceled.

```
Private Sub UserControl_KeyDown(KeyCode As Integer, Shift As Integer)
    Select Case KeyCode
        Case vbKeyDown, vbKeyUp, vbKeyLeft, vbKeyRight
                'any move arrow keys then set up to move
                mbKeyDown = True
                Shape1.FillColor = vb3DShadow
                fOffsetY = 0
                fOffsetX = 0
    End Select
End Sub

Private Sub UserControl_KeyUp(KeyCode As Integer, Shift As Integer)
    If KeyCode = vbKeyEscape And mbKeyDown Then
            'if we are moving with keys then escape cancels
            mbKeyDown = False
            Shape1.FillColor = vbButtonFace
    ElseIf mbKeyDown Then
            'move the shape
            Select Case KeyCode
                Case vbKeyDown
                        MoveShape Shape1.Left, Shape1.Top + 10
                Case vbKeyUp
                        MoveShape Shape1.Left, Shape1.Top - 10
                Case vbKeyLeft
                        MoveShape Shape1.Left - 10, Shape1.Top
                Case vbKeyRight
                        MoveShape Shape1.Left + 10, Shape1.Top
            End Select
            mbKeyDown = False
            Shape1.FillColor = vbButtonFace
    End If
End Sub
```

9. Finally, it's time to test the control. Close the UserControl windows and open Form1 that was created with the new project.

10. The last control in the Toolbox should be the new control. Its tooltip should say "UserControl1". Draw one on Form1. Make it nice and large so there is plenty of room to move the circle around. Run the project using the Run | Start menu item. Use the mouse or keyboard to move the circle around the control. Figure 85-1 shows the new control in action.

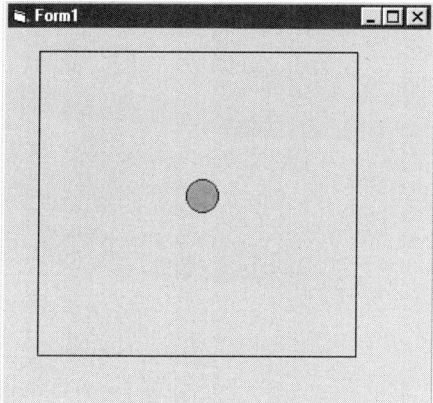

Figure 85-1 The User Actions
control in action

86

CREATING INTERNET-READY ACTIVEX CONTROLS

With the introduction of Visual Basic 5.0 Custom Control Creation Edition, followed by the full Visual Basic 5.0 package, creating Internet-ready components has never been easier. With the knowledge of control creation and the new features presented in this chapter, you can create controls that can read data from various places on the Internet and control the browser that hosts your control. The new methods shown in this chapter will enable you to control the browser to move through its history list or jump to any URL.

Hyperlink-Aware Container

The phrase *hyperlink-aware container* is used many times throughout this chapter. It refers to a container that can process commands to move or load different URLs. Microsoft Internet Explorer is the best example of a Hyperlink container. For example, with Microsoft Internet Explorer, your ActiveX control can cause the browser to move forward or backward through the history list of URLs or jump directly to a specified URL.

Creating Internet-Ready ActiveX Control Summary

The objects, properties, events, and methods pertaining to the creation of Internet-ready ActiveX controls are listed in Tables 86-1, 86-2, and 86-3. Following these tables are explanations for each element.

Table 86-1 Properties of the AsyncProperty object

Use or Set This...	Type	To Do This...
AsyncType	Property	Defines the type of data contained in the Value property of an AsyncProperty object.
PropertyName	Property	The name set by the AsyncRead method to identify an AsyncRead object.
Value	Property	The data received by the AsyncRead method.

Table 86-2 The methods of the Hyperlink object

Use or Set This...	Type	To Do This...
GoBack	Method	Instruct a hyperlink-aware container to go to the last Web page in its history list.
GoForward	Method	Instruct a hyperlink-aware container to go to the previous Web page in its history list.
NavigateTo	Method	Instruct a hyperlink-aware container to go to the URL specified.

Table 86-3 Elements concerning creating Internet-ready ActiveX controls

Use or Set This...	Type	To Do This...
AsyncProperty	Object	The object that contains the AsyncType, PropertyName, and Value properties.
AsyncRead	Method	Begin reading data from a file or URL.
AsyncReadComplete	Event	This event is raised when AsyncRead has finished downloading data into the Value property of an AsyncProperty object.
CancelAsyncRead	Method	Cancel an asynchronous read.
Hyperlink	Object	Contains the methods to instruct a hyperlink-aware container to go to a URL.
Hyperlink	Property	Returns a reference to the Hyperlink object of a UserControl.

Constant Values

It is best to use constants rather than numbers. Constants make your code easier to read. Using constants also makes it easier to remember the different settings for each item. Table 86-4 lists the constants used in this chapter.

Table 86-4 Constant values used with the AsyncProperty object

Value	VB.Constants	Meaning
0	vbAsyncTypePicture	The Value property of the AsyncProperty contains a picture.
1	vbAsyncTypeFile	The Value property of the AsyncProperty contains a file.
2	vbAsyncTypeByteArray	The Value property of the AsyncProperty contains a byte array.

AsyncType Property

Objects Affected	AsyncProperty
Purpose	Returns or sets the type of data returned by the Value property. This property is set before the AsyncRead method and is read after the AsyncReadComplete event.

General Syntax

```
object.AsyncType [ = datatype ]
```

Table 86-5 Arguments for the AsyncType property

Arguments	Description
object	Name of the object.
datatype	The type of data the Value property of the object contains.

Example Syntax

```
Private Sub UserControl_AsyncReadComplete(AsyncProp As AsyncProperty)

    If AsyncProp.AsyncType= vbAsyncTypePicture then
        Image1.Picture = AsyncProp.Value
        Image1.Refresh
    End IF

End Sub
```

Description	The AsyncProperty property of the AsyncProperty object is used to determine the type of data in the Value property of the AsyncProperty object. This property can be set only before an AsyncRead method is invoked and can be read after the AsyncReadComplete event is raised. This property will not be automatically set after the value has been written. It must be set before invoking the AsyncRead method.
Example	In the project at the end of this chapter, this property is set to vbAsyncTypePicture because the type of data being read is a picture.

PropertyName Property

Objects Affected	AsyncProperty
Purpose	To set the name of the object of the AsyncRead method or to return the name of the AsyncProperty object passed to the AsyncReadComplete event.

General Syntax

```
object.PropertyName [ = nameofproperty ]
```

Table 86-6 Arguments for the PropertyName property

Arguments	Description
object	Name of the object
NameofProperty	The value to be set or returned by the PropertyName

Example Syntax

```
Private Sub Command1_Click

    CancelAsyncRead NameofProperty

End Sub
```

Description   This property is used to identify a particular AsyncProperty object. When an AsyncRead method is active, you must know the name of the particular AsyncRead to cancel the method. Because multiple asynchronous reads can be happening at the same time, it is important to give each read in case it needs to be canceled. Also, you may write code in the AsyncReadComplete event to react to when the AsyncRead method has finished.

VALUE PROPERTY

Objects Affected   AsyncProperty

Purpose   Contains the data the AsyncRead method downloaded.

General Syntax

```
object.Value
```

Table 86-7 Argument for the Value property

Argument	Description
object	Name of the AsyncProperty object

Description   The Value property of the AsyncProperty object contains the data that the AsyncRead method initiated and passed to the AsyncReadComplete event. The type of data contained in the Value property is determined by AsyncType, which was set before the AsyncRead method.

Example   In the example at the end of this chapter, the Value property is read and then its contents are passed to the Picture property of the Image control to display the icon that was read.

GoBack Method

Objects Affected   Hyperlink

Purpose   The GoBack method is used to instruct a Hyperlink container to go to the last Web page in its history list.

General Syntax

```
object.GoBack
```

Table 86-8 Argument for the GoBack method

Argument	Description
object	The name of the Hyperlink object

Example Syntax

```
Private Sub Command_Click

    UserControl.Hyperlink.GoBack

End Sub
```

Description   GoBack is used to instruct a Hyperlink-aware container to go back to the last page in its history list.

GoForward Method

Objects Affected   Hyperlink

Purpose   This method is used to instruct a hyperlink-aware container to go to the next Web page in its history list.

General Syntax

```
object.GoForward
```

Table 86-9 Argument for the GoForward method

Argument	Description
object	Name of the Hyperlink object

Example Syntax

```
Private Sub Command_Click
    UserControl.Hyperlink.GoForward
End Sub
```

Description This method is used to instruct a hyperlink-aware container to go to the next Web page visited in its history list.

NAVIGATETO METHOD

Objects Affected Hyperlink

Purpose This method is used to instruct a Hyperlink-aware container to go to a specified URL.

General Syntax

```
object.NavigateTo URL$
```

Table 86-10 Arguments for the NavigateTo method

Arguments	Description
object	Name of the Hyperlink object
URL$	The URL to go to

Example Syntax

```
Private Sub Command_Click
    UserControl.NavigateTo."http://www.microsoft.com/vbasic"
End Sub
```

Description This method is used to instruct a hyperlink-aware container to go to the specified URL. By using this method, you can instruct the browser displaying your ActiveX control to navigate to any URL. If this control is not contained in a browser, it will launch the default browser if it is hyperlink aware. This can be useful if you want to add a button on your About screen that, when pressed, automatically launches a Web browser and opens it to your home page.

Example In the project at the end of the chapter, the NavigateTo method is used to cause the browser containing the ActiveX control to go to a URL that contains more information about the item currently displayed.

ASYNCPROPERTY OBJECT

Purpose This object contains the properties to be downloaded from a file or URL.

The cycle for this object is as follows:

[a] PropertyName is set to identify the object.

[b] AsyncType is set to identify the type of data the Value property will contain.

[c] The AsyncRead method is invoked to start retrieving the data into the Value property.

[d] When the AsyncRead method has finished, the AsyncReadComplete event is raised.

[e] An AsyncProperty object is passed to the AsyncReadComplete event.

The CancelAsyncRead method can be called to stop the AsyncRead anytime between the AsyncRead method and the AsyncRead method event. To stop the read, PropertyName must be known.

ASYNCREAD METHOD

Objects Affected   UserControl, UserDocument

Purpose   Start the reading in of data by the container from a file or URL asynchronously.

General Syntax

```
UserDocument.AsyncRead
```

Example Syntax

```
Private Sub Command1_Click ()
    UserControl.AsyncRead
End Sub
```

Description   The AsyncRead method is used to start downloading data from a file or URL. The CancelAsyncRead method can be used to interrupt this method.

ASYNCREADCOMPLETE EVENT

Objects Affected   UserControl, UserDocument

Purpose   To notify UserControl that an asynchronous read is complete and has passed an AsyncProperty object that contains the data downloaded.

General Syntax

```
UserControl.AsyncReadComplete(AsyncProperty)
```

Table 86-11 Arguments for the AsyncReadComplete event

Arguments	Descriptions
UserControl	Name of the UserControl
AsyncProperty	The name of the property being read

Example Syntax

```
Private Sub UserControl_AsyncReadComplete(AsyncProp as AsyncProperty)
    If AsyncProp.AsyncType=vbAsyncTypePicture then
    Image1.Picture = AsyncProp.Value
    Image1.Refresh
     End IF
End Sub
```

Description This event is raised when AsyncRead has finished downloading data into the Value property of an AsyncProperty object. The PropertyName of the AsyncProperty object can be used to identify which asynchronous read is complete. The data that was downloaded is contained in the Value property of the AsyncProperty object.

Example The example at the end of this chapter demonstrates how the value of the AsyncProperty object is assigned to the Picture property of an Image control when this event fires.

CancelAsyncRead Method

Objects Affected UserControl

Purpose The CancelAsyncRead method is used to cancel an asynchronous read.

General Syntax

```
object.CancelAsyncRead PropertyName
```

Table 86-12 Arguments for the CancelAsyncRead method

Arguments	Description
object	Name of UserControl
PropertyName	Name of AsyncRead

Example Syntax

```
Private Sub Form_Load
    AsyncRead "http://www.test.com/file.zip", vbAsyncTypePicture,"DownLoadPicture"
End Sub

Private Sub Command1_Click
    CancelAsyncRead "DownloadPicture"
End Sub
```

Description This method is used to cancel an asynchronous read in progress. By assigning a string to each PropertyName of the AsyncProperty object property and by using this name, you can cancel any read in progress. This is useful for large downloads that may need a time-out or to allow an impatient user to abort the download.

HYPERLINK OBJECT

Purpose	The Hyperlink object contains the methods for the UserControl to instruct the hyperlink-aware container to go to specific URLs.

HYPERLINK PROPERTY

Objects Affected	UserControl, UserDocument
Purpose	To return a reference to the Hyperlink object of a UserControl.
General Syntax	

```
object.hyperlink
```

Table 86-13 Argument for the Hyperlink property

Argument	Description
object	The name of the UserControl or UserDocument

The Creating Internet-Ready ActiveX Controls Project

Project Overview

This project will demonstrate how to build an ActiveX control that is Internet ready. The example will show how to assign values to the properties of the control that reside either on a local drive or on the Internet. The example will also demonstrate how to control the hyperlink-aware container displaying the control. After the control is built, you will used it in a Visual Basic project as well as in Microsoft Internet Explorer.

Assembling the Project: The PickPic UserControl

1. Open a new ActiveX project in Visual Basic 5. Place and assemble the elements of the control as shown in Table 86-14.

Table 86-14 List of objects and properties for PickPic UserControl

Object	Property	Setting
CommandButton	Name	cmdMore
	Caption	More Information
CommandButton	Name	cmdNext
	Caption	Next

continued on next page

continued from previous page

Object	Property	Setting
CommandButton	Name	cmdBack
	Caption	Back
Image	Name	Image1

2. Size the objects on the screen, as in Figure 86-1.

3. Enter the following code in the General Declarations procedure. These are the control-level variables needed.

```
Dim WhichPicture As Integer      'which image is currently being viewed
Dim PictureName(3) As String     'contains the name and location of the images
Dim NavTo(3) As String           'contains the location to navigate to
Dim PicPath As String            'path of the pictures
```

4. Enter the following code into the cmdBack_Click event. This code will determine if the last picture is displayed or not. If not, the procedure will instruct UserControl to get a picture.

```
Private Sub cmdBack_Click()
If WhichPicture > 0 Then
    WhichPicture = WhichPicture - 1
    AsyncRead PicPath + PictureName(WhichPicture), vbAsyncTypePicture, PictureToDisplay
End If
End Sub
```

5. Enter the following code into the cmdMore_Click event. The following event will instruct the hyperlink-aware container hosting the ActiveX control to go to the address in the NavTo variable. If this ActiveX control is in a VB project, then this procedure will launch a hyperlink-aware browser (if there is one on the system) and navigate to the specified URL.

```
Private Sub cmdMore_Click()
    Hyperlink.NavigateTo NavTo(WhichPicture - 1)
End Sub
Private Sub cmdNext_Click()
If WhichPicture < 4 Then
    AsyncRead PicPath + PictureName(WhichPicture), vbAsyncTypePicture, PictureToDisplay
    WhichPicture = WhichPicture + 1
End If
End Sub
```

6. Enter the following code in the UserControl_AsyncReadComplete event of the UserControl. The following event is raised after an AsyncRead method is complete. An AsyncProperty object is passed to the event with the data downloaded contained in the Value property of the AsyncProperty object. In the code below, the Value property is assigned to the Picture property of the Image control so it will display the new image just downloaded by the AsyncRead method.

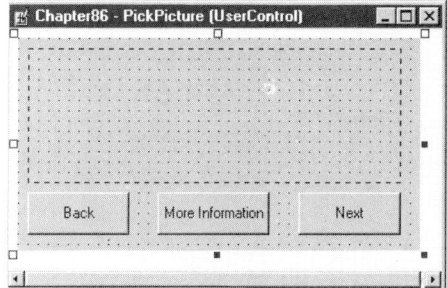

Figure 86-1 The controls on the form

```
Private Sub UserControl_AsyncReadComplete(AsyncProp As AsyncProperty)
    Image1.Picture = AsyncProp.Value
    Image1.Refresh
End Sub
```

7. Enter the following code into the UserControl_Initialize event of UserControl. The WhichPicture variable is set to 0. PicPath is set to where the pictures reside. You must change this to where you place the pictures and the source code for the control. PicPath could also be a location on an HTTP server, such as http://www.test.com/images/. This example can be quickly modified to get the pictures from an HTTP source simply by changing this variable assignment and placing the picture there. The PictureName array is assigned the name of the pictures to retrieve. The NavTo array is assigned the names of the HTML pages to be displayed when the image is clicked to give the user more information.

```
Private Sub UserControl_Initialize()
    WhichPicture = 0
    PicPath = "file:/data/Super Bible/Chapter 86/"
    PictureName(0) = "clip01.ico"
    PictureName(1) = "crdfle01.ico"
    PictureName(2) = "files01a.ico"
    PictureName(3) = "graph01.ico"
    NavTo(0) = "clip.htm"
    NavTo(1) = "card.htm"
    NavTo(2) = "files.htm"
    NavTo(3) = "graph.htm"
End Sub
```

8. Enter the following code into the General Declarations section of UserControl. The following procedure will allow the container to determine if the control is enabled or disabled.

```
Public Property Get Enabled() As Boolean
    Enabled = UserControl.Enabled
End Property
```

9. Enter the following code into the General Declarations section of UserControl. The following procedure will expose the Enabled property of the control.

```
Public Property Let Enabled(ByVal New_Enabled As Boolean)
    UserControl.Enabled() = New_Enabled
    PropertyChanged "Enabled"
End Property
```

10. Enter the following code into the General Declarations section of UserControl. This procedure will allow the container to read the control state before it is destroyed.

```
Private Sub UserControl_ReadProperties(PropBag As PropertyBag)
    UserControl.Enabled = PropBag.ReadProperty("Enabled", True)
End Sub
```

11. Enter the following code into the General Declarations section of UserControl. This procedure will allow the control to save its state before it is destroyed.

```
Private Sub UserControl_WriteProperties(PropBag As PropertyBag)
    Call PropBag.WriteProperty("Enabled", UserControl.Enabled, True)
End Sub
```

12. Four simple HTML pages must now be created. These pages need to be saved in the same location as the picture files and the source code. We will use Notepad to create these HTML pages.

13. Enter the following text in Notepad. This is the HTML page that will be displayed when the user clicks on the More Information button while the paper clip image in the picture box is being viewed. After the text is entered into Notepad, save the file as CLIP.HTM in the directory that contains the pictures and source code.

```
<html>

<head>
<title>Paper Clip</title>
</head>

<body>
<p>This is more information about the paper clip.</p>
</body>
</html>
```

14. Enter the following text in Notepad. This is the HTML page that will be displayed when the user clicks on the More Information button while the paper clip is being viewed. After the text is entered into Notepad, save it as CARD.HTM in the directory that contains the pictures and source code.

```
<html>

<head>
<title>Card FIle</title>
</head>

<p>This is more information about the card file.</p>
</body>
```

```
</html>
```

```
<html>
```

15. Enter the following text in Notepad. This is the HTML page that will be displayed when the user clicks on the More Information button while the paper clip is being viewed. After the text is entered into Notepad, save it as FILES.HTM in the directory that contains the pictures and source code.

```
<html>

<head>
<title>File Cabinet</title>
</head>

<p>This is more information about the file cabinet.</p>
</body>
</html>
```

16. Enter the following text in Notepad. This is the HTML page that will be displayed when the user clicks on the More Information button while the paper clip is being viewed. After the text is entered into Notepad, save it as GRAPH.HTM in the directory that contains the pictures and source code.

```
<html>

<head>
<title>Graph</title>
</head>

<p>This is more information about the graph.</p>
</body>
</html>
```

17. Add a new standard EXE project to the current project. Place the newly created ActiveX control on the form and position it as shown in Figure 86-2.

18. Run the project. Click on the Next button and you will see the pictures loaded in and displayed in the Image control. If you click on the More Information button and Microsoft Explorer 3.0 or greater is installed, the browser will launch and load the appropriate HTML page. Figure 86-3 shows the running application, and Figure 86-4 shows what happens when you press the More Information button.

19. Compile your UserControl in the source file directory.

20. Open an HTML editor that will allow you to place ActiveX controls on a Web page. In this example, FrontPage 97 is used. You will be able to use much the same procedure to add ActiveX controls to other editors that support them.

21. Assemble an HTML page with the ActiveX control just compiled, as shown in Figure 86-5.

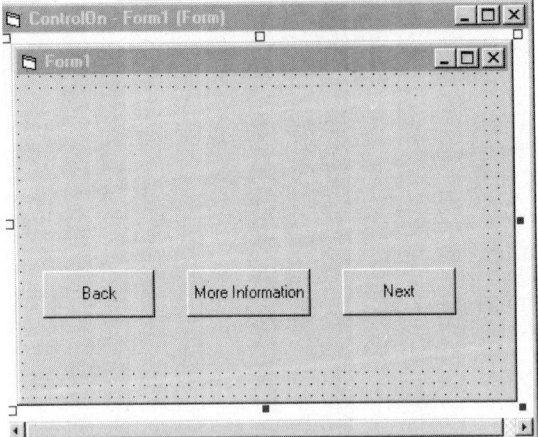

Figure 86-2 The controls on the form

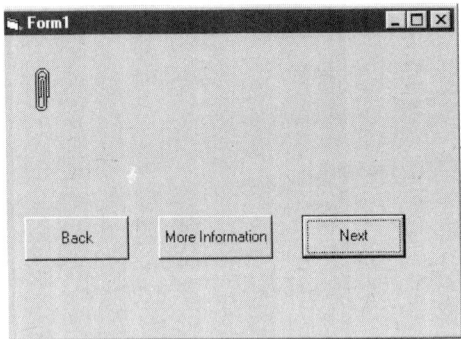

Figure 86-3 The control on a Visual
Basic form

22. Save the HTML page in the same directory as your source code.

23. Launch Internet Explorer 3.0 or greater and click on File | Open. Click on the browser button to find the HTML page you just saved.

24. When the page is loaded, click on the Next button and then the More Information button (see Figure 86-6), as you did when you added the control to a Visual Basic project. Notice the difference in execution (see Figure 86-7). The images still are displayed but a new browser window is not launched when the More Information button is pressed. After you have clicked on the More Information button, click on the Back button of Internet Explorer. You will see the HTML page with the ActiveX control.

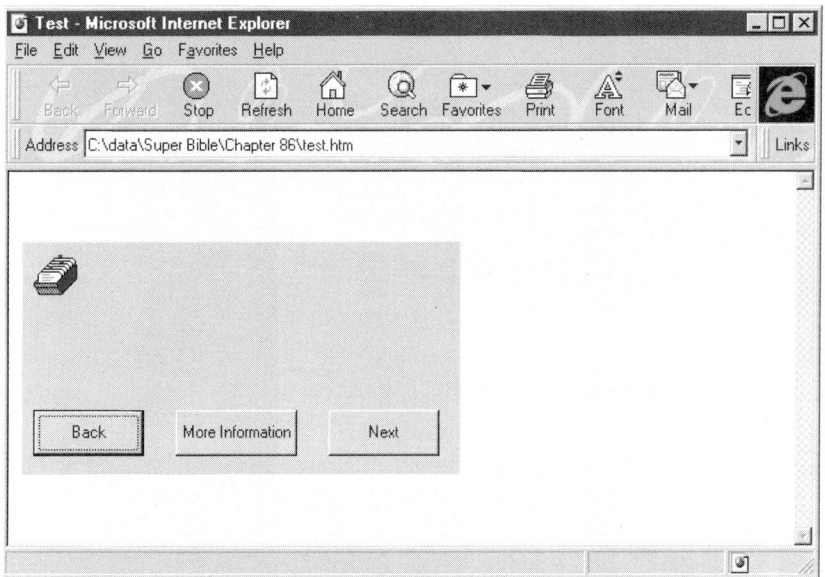

Figure 86-4 The control displayed by Internet Explorer

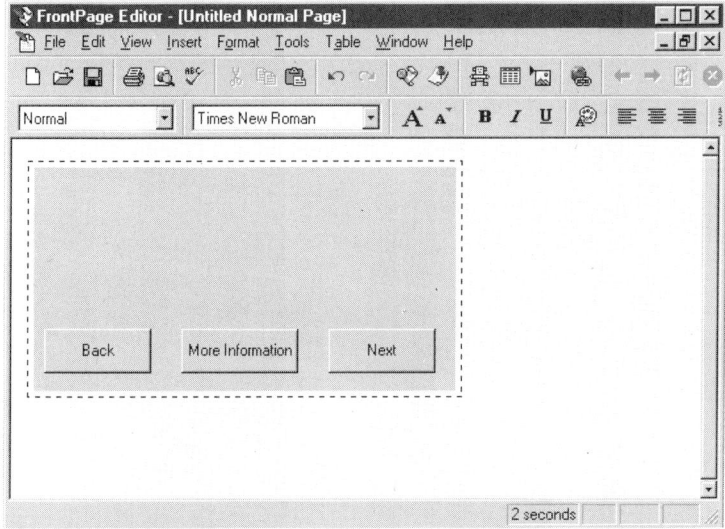

Figure 86-5 The HTML page

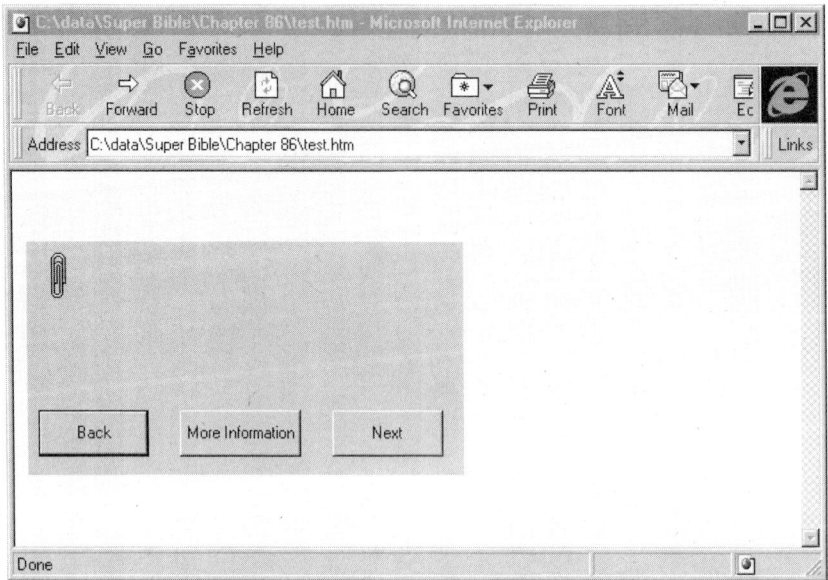

Figure 86-6　Page viewed when the Next button is clicked

Figure 86-7　Page viewed when the More Information button is clicked

How It Works

This ActiveX control is used to display different icons, which reside on the local drive or an HTTP server. For the icon to change in the Picture box, the control must get the information from a server and then set the property. It does this by using the AsyncRead method and reading the new picture value from the server.

When the More Information button is clicked, the NavigateTo method directs a container, such as Microsoft Internet Explorer, to go to the specified URL.

87

ACTIVEX CONTROL DISTRIBUTION

For the end user's system to be able to view Web pages containing your ActiveX controls, those controls must be installed on the user's system. With the Application Setup Wizard and a few utilities that come with Visual Basic 5.0, you can create the necessary files to allow Internet Explorer to download the control and install it directly to the user's system.

Before Internet Explorer 3.0, items that used the HTML Object tag needed to download a setup program, the setup program needed to be manually launched by the end user, and the browser needed to be restarted to display the Web page properly using the new plug-in. Now with Internet Explorer, you are asked only (depending on the safety level at which you have set the browser) if you want to install the new ActiveX control. If you click Yes, Internet Explorer downloads the control and installs it on your system, then displays the Web page as intended by the developer.

To have your ActiveX control download and install smoothly, you must learn how to use the Application Setup Wizard and some complementary utilities.

To distribute ActiveX controls on the Internet, you must be familiar with various tools and concepts. Each topic is summarized below. After the summary, you will run the Setup Wizard and review what it creates and how the other tools come into play.

Application Setup Wizard

The Application Setup Wizard is used to create the files necessary for distributing ActiveX controls on the Internet. It generates the CABINET file, in which the ActiveX control is contained. It also generates the HTML code to be added to a Web page for the browser to determine whether the control, or an older version of it, is already installed on the system. In the project at the end of this chapter, the Application Setup Wizard is used to create an Internet setup for the control created in Chapter 83, "Creating ActiveX Controls."

CABINET File

A CABINET file (or CAB file) contains the necessary files and information to install an ActiveX control on the end user's system. This file is created by the Application Setup Wizard. It also can be created manually by the MAKECAB.EXE utility that comes with Visual Basic 5.0. The CAB file is the actual file the Web browser downloads when it needs to download an ActiveX control currently not installed on the user's system. The Web browser extracts the files from the CAB file, then reads the .INF file the Application Setup Wizard placed in the CAB file. The .INF file informs the Web browser where to install the ActiveX control and where to find the CAB file that includes the runtime files if needed.

There are major differences in the types of files placed in CAB files. The first type is the CAB file that contains the ActiveX control; the second type is the CAB file(s) that contain the runtime files needed to use the control. The CAB file that contains the runtime files needed by the ActiveX control is called the *dependency file*. This file may contain any of the following: Visual Basic 5.0 runtime DLLs, other ActiveX controls used to create the ActiveX control, and any other supporting files needed.

License File

When creating ActiveX controls, you must determine whether the ActiveX control requires a license file to be used in design time. For a license file to be generated for a control, the Requires License option must be checked, as in Figure 87-1. The LPK_TOOL.EXE utility included on the Visual Basic 5.0 CD-ROM in the /tools/lpk_tool directory is used to create the license file. The example at the end of this chapter demonstrates how this utility is used to generate a license file and how it is added to the HTML page.

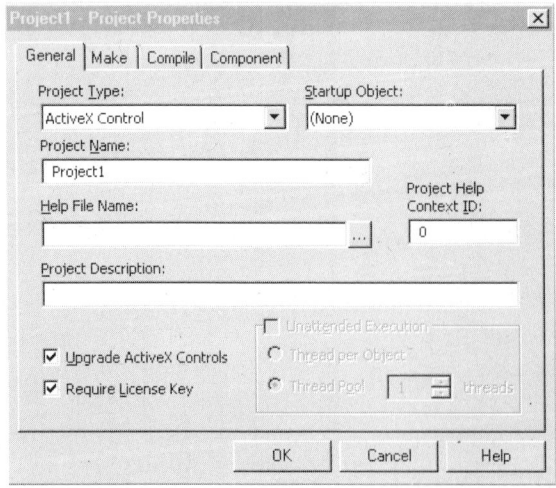

Figure 87-1   Setting to require license key

Digital Signature

The purpose of a digital signature with ActiveX controls is so that the end user, when downloading the control, can be informed before the installation of the ActiveX control where it originates.

ActiveX controls that are not digitally signed are sometimes viewed as rogue controls; most users will not download them or have their browser automatically not download them.

To sign a control digitally, a software publisher or individual software developer must obtain a digital signature. A digital signature can be obtained from a digital certificate provider. VeriSign Corporation is one of the leading providers in this area. It is located at http://www.verisign.com. For VeriSign or any another digital certificate provider to give out a digital signature, it must verify the existence of the publisher or developer. The VeriSign Web site outlines in detail how to obtain a digital signature.

The following steps demonstrate the signing of the ActiveX control created in Chapter 83. A utility that comes with the ActiveX SDK from Microsoft's Web site is used to apply the digital signature to the CAB file containing the ActiveX control. The utility is called SIGNCODE.EXE and resides in the \inetsdk\bin\i386\ folder under the installation directory of the ActiveX SDK.

As soon as the sign code utility is launched, the screen shown in Figure 87-2 will appear. This is the introduction screen to the Code Signing Wizard. Click the Next button to continue.

Three fields must be filled in. The first is the name of the EXE, OCX, or CAB file to be digitally signed. Press the Browse button and select the CAB file to be signed. If you are placing an ActiveX control on your web, the CAB file that contains the ActiveX control is the file to be signed. The second field is the name of the application to be displayed on the certificate screen. The third field is an area to add a URL a user can go to for more information about the control to be downloaded.

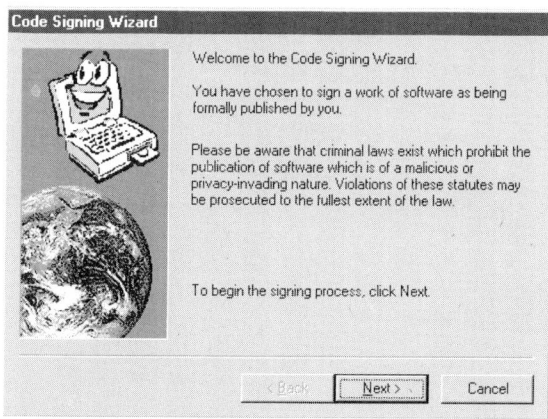

Figure 87-2   Code Signing Wizard welcome screen

As shown in Figure 87-3, the screen displays where your digital signature resides. These settings are stored at the time of receiving your digital signature.

The screen in Figure 87-4 is the final screen. Click on the Sign button and the EXE or ActiveX will be digitally signed.

Now anytime the digitally signed CAB file is download by an ActiveX-control-aware Web browser, the Authenticode certificate in Figure 87-5 will be shown before the ActiveX control is installed on the end user's system.

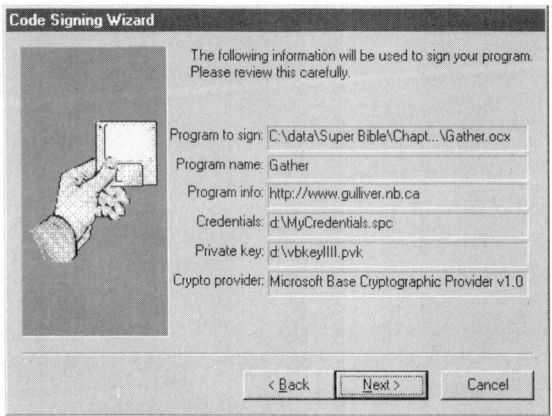

Figure 87-3 Application information screen

Figure 87-4 Finish! screen

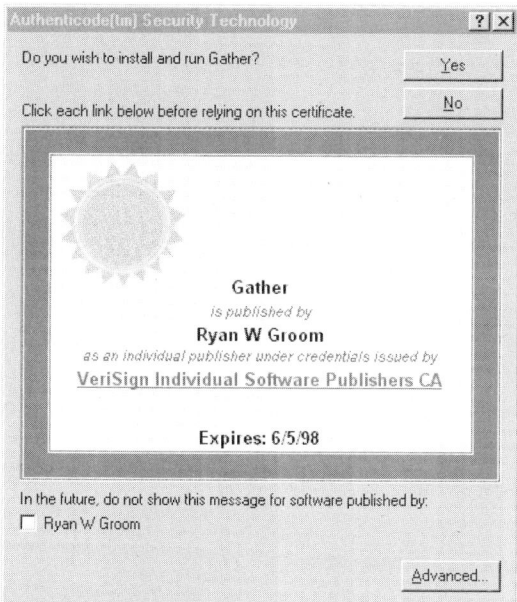

Figure 87-5   Authenticode certificate for the Gather ActiveX control

Safety

Internet Explorer 3.0 or higher has a setting that determines the safety level of a control before it is downloaded. This allows the user of Internet Explorer to determine the types of controls that will be allowed to be downloaded to the system. When the Application Setup Wizard creates the CAB file that will be used to distribute the control, an option informs the Web browser of the safety level of the contained control.

The first setting is Safe for Initialization. If this setting is checked, it informs the browser that any data that is passed to the ActiveX control cannot be used to harm the computer to which it will be installed. The control will not be able to create, change, or delete any files, including temporary ones, or change system settings.

The second setting is Safe for Scripting. When this option is set, it informs the Web browser that no matter how the control is used in the HTML page, it cannot harm the user's system.

Figure 87-6 shows the Security tab for Internet Explorer that determines what type of active content will be allowed to be viewed.

If the Safety Level button is clicked, the screen in Figure 87-7 appears. This sets the safety level of the control that can be downloaded and when the user will be prompted and warned about potentially unsafe ActiveX controls.

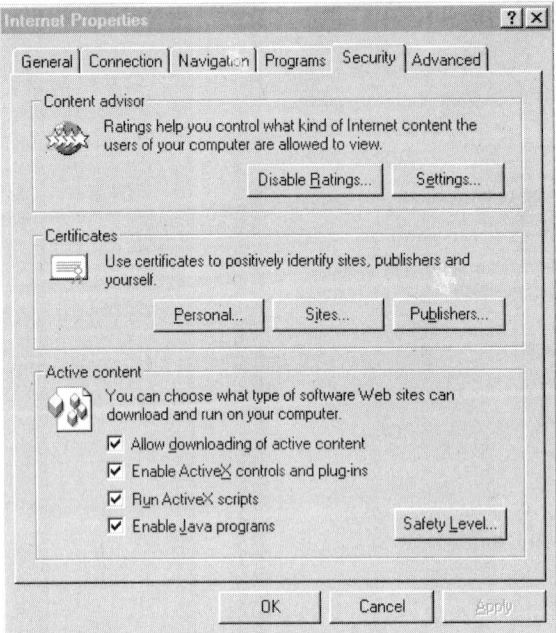

Figure 87-6 Setting for active content for Internet Explorer

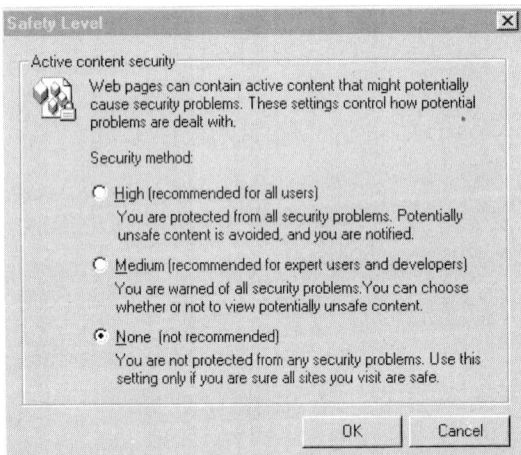

Figure 87-7 Setting for safety level of ActiveX controls download

The first setting, High, will download only controls that have their Safe for Initialization and Safe for Scripting options set. The second setting, Medium, will download controls with either Safe for Initialization or Safe for Scripting options set. The third setting, None, will download any ActiveX controls.

OBJECT TAG

Purpose   The Object tag is used when designing the HTML page that will host the ActiveX control. It is used to inform the browser that an external object will handle the visual display and the functionality of the browser window, in this case an ActiveX control.

General Syntax

```
<OBJECT ID="Mycontrol" WIDTH=305 HEIGHT=169
    CLASSID="CLSID:1234"
    CODEBASE="Gather.CAB#version=1,0,0,0">
</OBJECT>
```

Table 87-1 Arguments for the Object tag

Arguments	Description
Object ID	The name of the ActiveX control.
Width	The width of the ActiveX control displayed in the Web page.
Height	The height of the ActiveX control displayed in the Web page.
ClassID	The ID used to identify this control in the Windows 95 registry. Used to determine whether the control was previously installed.
CODEBASE	The name of the CAB file to download if the ActiveX control is not already installed on the system or is a newer version.

Example Syntax

```
<OBJECT ID="UserControl1" WIDTH=305 HEIGHT=169
    CLASSID="CLSID:85FA824D-B25E-11D0-962C-00A02421BD93"
    CODEBASE="Gather.CAB#version=1,0,0,0">
</OBJECT>
```

Description   The Object tag is used in an HTML page to instruct the browser on where to display the ActiveX control on the Web page. It is also used by the browser to determine whether the ActiveX control is installed on the system and if not, from where to download it.

The Distributing ActiveX Controls Project

Overview

This project demonstrates how to use the Application Setup Wizard to create the necessary files to distribute your ActiveX control on the Internet. The Application Setup Wizard will create the CAB and HTML files needed, and LPK_TOOL.EXE will create the license file for the ActiveX control and use the SIGNCODE.EXE utility to sign the CAB file digitally.

1. First open the ActiveX control created in Chapter 83. Go into the project properties and click the Require License Key check box. This will allow the LPK_TOOL.EXE utility to create the license file for this control.

2. Compile the control. This will create the file that the Application Setup Wizard will place in the CAB file.

3. Launch the Application Setup Wizard by selecting it from the Program Start menu, as in Figure 87-8.

4. The screen in Figure 87-9 will appear. This is the welcome screen. If you do not want the welcome screen to appear the next time the wizard is launched, click the Skip this screen in the future check box.

5. Click the Next button to proceed. The screen in Figure 87-10 will appear.

    This screen allows you to select the project for which the Application Setup Wizard will create the distribution file and by what method the project will be distributed.

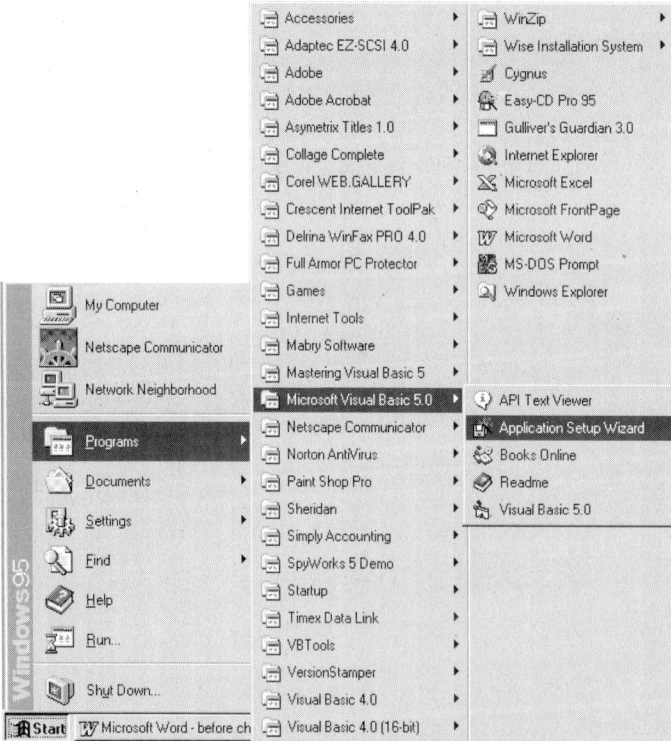

Figure 87-8   Starting the Application Setup Wizard

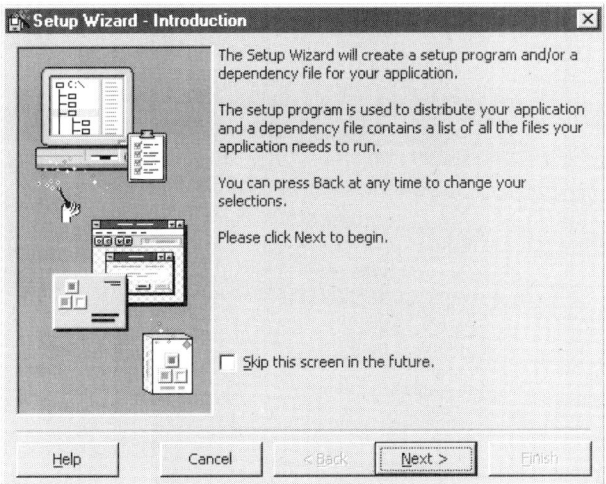

Figure 87-9   Welcome screen of the Application Setup Wizard

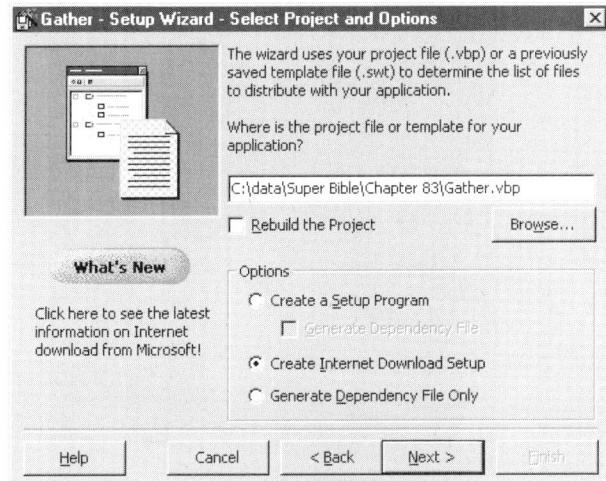

Figure 87-10   Select Project and Options screen

6. Click on the Browse button and select the sample project used in Chapter 83. Then click on the Create Internet Download Setup option. As shown in Figure 87-10, there is an option to create a CAB file for the dependencies of this project. You can rerun the Application Setup Wizard to create a CAB file for the dependency files or point the Setup Wizard to use the files from Microsoft's server. The information on where the dependency file resides is contained in an .INF file that is stored in the CAB file.

7. Click on the Next button in Figure 87-11. The screen in Figure 87-12 will appear. This screen asks where you want the Application Setup Wizard to place the files it will create. After you select the directory, click on the Next button.

8. After the Next button is clicked, the screen in Figure 87-12 will appear. This screen asks you where the runtime components reside. If you are going to have them downloaded from Microsoft's site, click on the Download from the Microsoft Web site radio button. If you want them downloaded from another site, click on the other radio button and enter the URL where they can be found.

9. Click on the Safety button as shown in Figure 87-12 to set the safety options for this control. When the Safety button is clicked, the screen in Figure 87-13 will appear. Check the safety of the controls only if you are certain of the safety level of your control.

10. Click on the OK button in Figure 87-13 and the screen in Figure 87-14 will appear. This screen is used to add any ActiveX servers that your control may use. If you click on the Add Local button, you can select the EXEs or DLLs your ActiveX control uses. When you select a file to add, the Application Setup Wizard determines whether the file can be self-registered to ensure that file is an ActiveX server.

11. Click on the Next button and the Application Setup Wizard will process what files need to be added to the CAB file. A dialog box will appear as in Figure 87-15 to ask you if the Property Page DLL needs to de distributed. If you are planning for this control to be used in design time, click the Yes button; if not, click No.

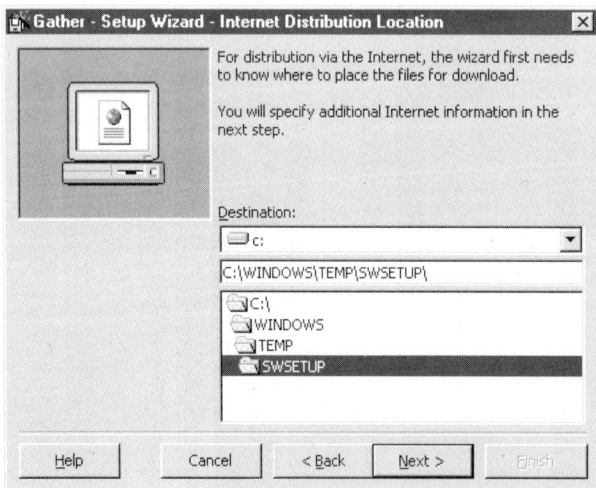

Figure 87-11 Select a folder, Internet distribution location

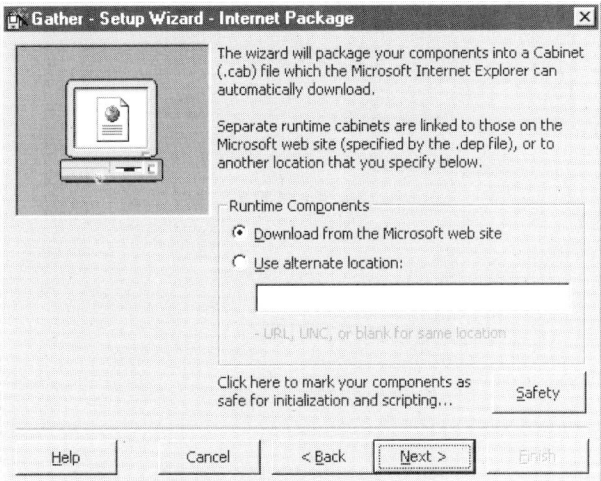

Figure 87-12   Select options screen, Internet package

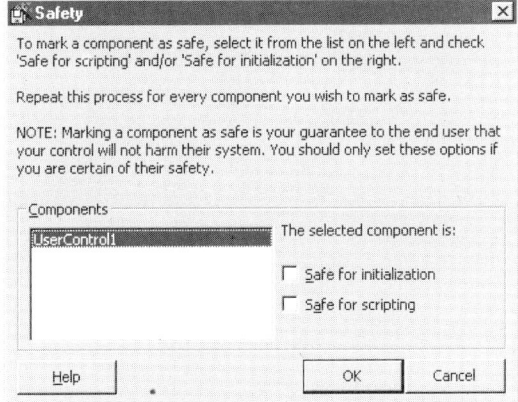

Figure 87-13   Select the safety level for this
control

12. After the Setup Wizard has determined the files needed, the screen in Figure 87-16 will appear. This screen shows a list of the files that will be included with the CAB file. If there are any files the Setup Wizard did not include, click the Add button to add additional files.

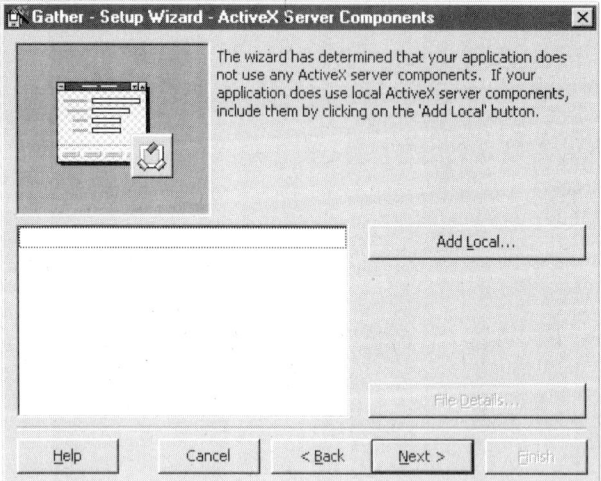

Figure 87-14 ActiveX server components

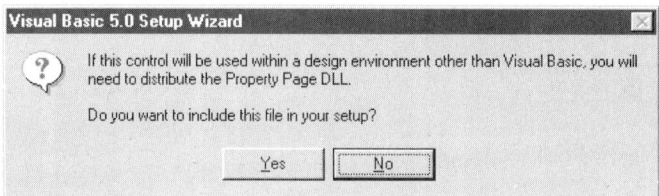

Figure 87-15 Dialog to determine distribution of the Property Page DLL

Figure 87-16 Summary of files to be included in the CAB file

13. Click the Next button. The screen shown in Figure 87-17 will appear. This screen allows you to save the current Application Setup Wizard settings by clicking the Save Template button. If you click the Save Template button, a common dialog box will appear to determine where to save the template.

14. Click on the Finish button to have the Application Setup Wizard create the CAB, HTML, and support files. After this process is completed, the screen in Figure 87-18 will appear to remind you to check the media for viruses before distribution.

15. Launch the LK_TOOL.EXE utility from the Visual Basic 5.0 CD-ROM. The screen shown in Figure 87-19 will appear.

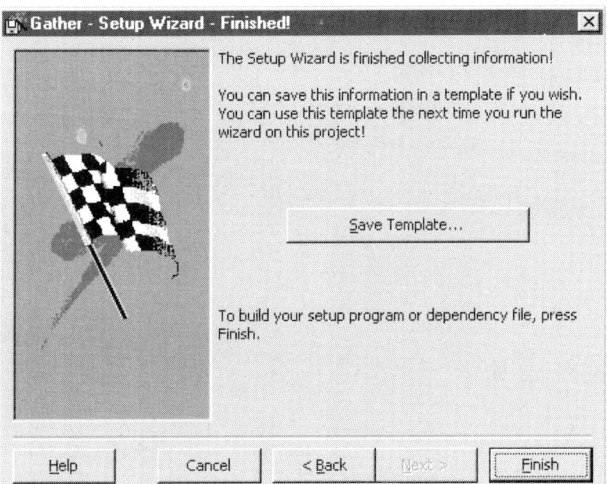

Figure 87-17   Finished! Screen

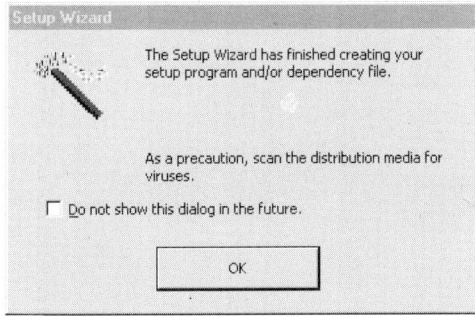

Figure 87-18   Prompt to check for viruses

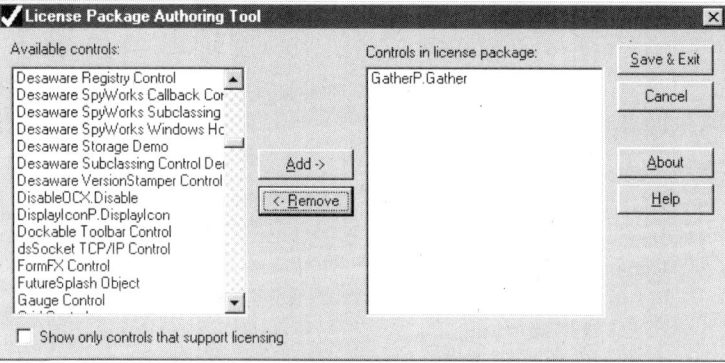

Figure 87-19 LKP_TOOL.EXE License Package Authoring Tool utility

16. In the list on the left, select the Gather ActiveX control, then click the Add button. When the control appears in the list on the right, click on the Save & Exit button. A dialog box will appear that asks where to save the license file. Select the folder in which the Application Setup Wizard created its files. After the LPK file is saved, the utility will terminate.

How It Works

The Setup Wizard creates the following files: the CAB file that contains the ActiveX control and the files that need to be installed by the Web browser, an HTML file to be added to the Web page that will host the ActiveX control, and a folder called Support. The Support folder contains the .INF file stored in the CAB file, which instructs the Web browser how and where to install the ActiveX control; a DDF file that is used if you want to use the MAKECAB.EXE utility to re-create the CAB file manually; and the ActiveX control contained in the CAB file.

If you launch Internet Explorer and open the HTML page, you will see a Web page with your control on it, as in Figure 87-20.

To simulate what would happen if a user who did not already possess your control viewed this Web page, you need to unregister the control.

To unregister the control, launch the MS-DOS prompt and change to the folder that contains the GATHER.OCX file. At the DOS prompt, type regsvr32 /u gather.ocx. This will unregister the control.

When you reload the page, Internet Explorer will act as if the control is not installed and proceed to install the ActiveX control.

When Internet Explorer downloads an HTML page to be viewed in the browser window, the following steps are taken when the HTML file contains an ActiveX control.

1. Determine whether the viewing of ActiveX controls is allowed.

2. Check the CLSID in the HTML code against the Windows registry. If there is no entry for the control, Internet Explorer proceeds to download the CAB file and license file (if applicable) as set in the CODEBASE parameter. If the entry does exist, Internet Explorer checks the version of the control against the VERSION parameter in the HTML code. If the version of the control is newer than that which resides on the Web page, the CAB file will be downloaded. If the ActiveX control is already installed and the version is current, Internet Explorer skips to step 5.

3. After the CAB file has been downloaded, Internet Explorer checks the safety level of the control and displays the digital certificate if the CAB file has been digitally signed.

4. If the safety level and the digital certificate pass the current Internet Explorer settings, the files are extracted from the CAB file and the .INF file is read to determine the setup procedure for the ActiveX control.

5. The ActiveX control is displayed in the HTML page as specified in the HEIGHT and WIDTH parameters of the ActiveX control.

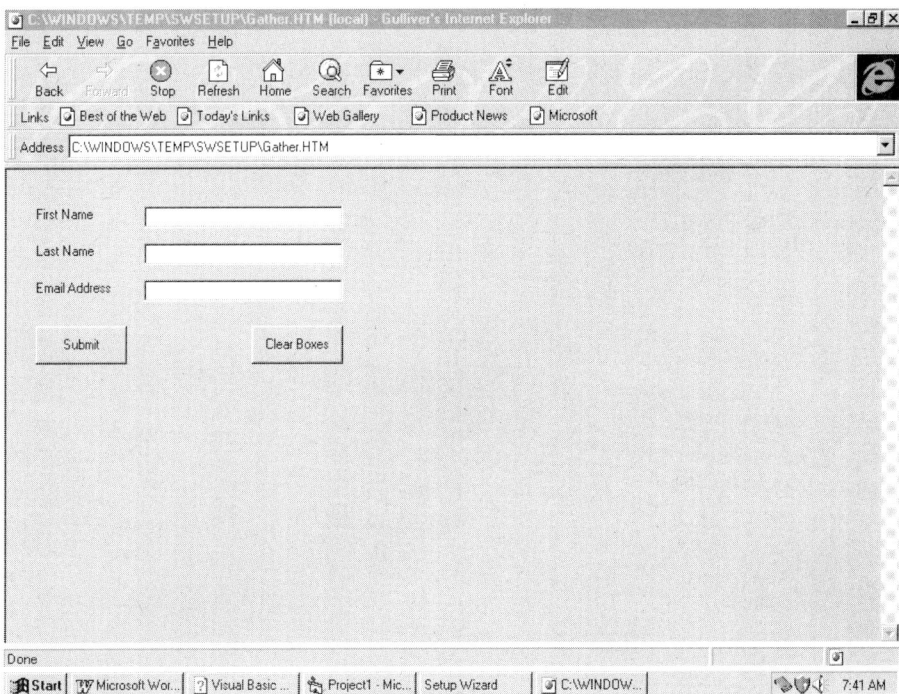

Figure 87-20   Internet Explorer displaying the Gather ActiveX control

88

CREATING ACTIVEX DOCUMENTS

Imagine all the applications you would like to create and place on a Web server: information presentation, database queries, forms to collect information...these are only a few of the many possibilities. Before Visual Basic 5.0, most of this coding had to be done in HTML and Java. Now an application can be created in the same fashion as any other Visual Basic application, compiled as an ActiveX document, placed on a Web server, and executed within a Web browser.

ActiveX documents are the result of the evolution of embedded objects. The visual display and visual editing features of ActiveX documents are richer than those available in OLE documents. When an object was embedded using OLE technology, the object needed to be activated and there was a limitation with editing the information the object contained.

With ActiveX documents, the object and data are always active and the server component can expose more properties to the container so all the data types the object contains can be edited. The ActiveX document also fills the display area of the container and exposes the toolbars and menus that can be used to edit the data. When a data file that has been created by an ActiveX server, such as Excel, is loaded by Internet Explorer, Internet Explorer reproduces the native menus and display of the original application so that the data in the file can be edited. The Office Binder that comes with Office 97 and Internet Explorer are currently the only ActiveX document containers.

Methodology of Creating ActiveX Documents

Creating ActiveX documents involves the same steps as creating ActiveX controls. The base object is a UserDocument instead of a UserControl. The properties, events, and methods are the same for both, with the addition of the elements in Table 88-1. The major difference between an ActiveX control and an ActiveX document is that an ActiveX control can used in an HTML page or any container that supports ActiveX controls, whereas an ActiveX document is a Visual Basic form that replaces the native display of the ActiveX document container.

Saving ActiveX documents creates .DOB and .DOX files. These files are similar to the .FRM and FRX files that are created when any other Visual Basic form is saved. The .DOB file contains the textual data, as does the .FRM file, and the .DOX file contains the binary data that was saved as the .FRX file. When an ActiveX document is compiled, it creates a .VBD file for each UserDocument contained in the .EXE or .DLL. The .VBD file is the actual file to which the container is pointed in order for the ActiveX document to be displayed. For example, the address http://www.test.com/docs/Test.vbd, when entered into a Web browser, will load and display the ActiveX document represented by TEST.VBD.

Showing and Hiding Forms

When displaying forms in an application created with Visual Basic 5.0, use the Show and Hide methods of the form to display and hide the form. With ActiveX documents, displaying and hiding forms is done by pointing the Web browser to different .VBD files. When the Web browser is pointed to a .VBD file, that file then loads the proper information into the Web browser.

Menus and ActiveX Documents

Unlike ActiveX controls, ActiveX documents can add menu items to Internet Explorer. By using the Menu Editor built into Visual Basic 5.0, menus can be added as easily as they are with any Visual Basic project. Not only does the ActiveX document replace the display area of Internet Explorer, it also can add menu items.

Creating ActiveX Documents Summary

Table 88-1 displays the properties, methods, and events that are unique to creating ActiveX documents.

Table 88-1 Methods, properties, and events dealing with ActiveX documents

Use or Set This...	Event	To Do This...
ContinuousScroll	Property	Determines if the ActiveX document redraws while being scrolled or when the scrolling has stopped.
HScrollSmallChange	Property	Determines the amount of movement when the horizontal scrollbar is clicked.
Icon	Property	Determines the icon viewed in the Office Binder.
MinHeight	Property	Determines the minimum height before the scrollbars are shown.
MinWidth	Property	Determines the minimum width before the scrollbars are shown.
Scroll	Event	Raised when the ActiveX document is scrolled.
ScrollBars	Property	Determines if the scrollbars are displayed when the viewable area is less than the MinHeight or MinWidth.
SetViewPort	Method	Sets the viewport area.
ViewPortTop	Property	Returns the top coordinates of the viewport.

Use or Set This...	Event	To Do This...
ViewPortLeft	Property	Returns the left coordinates of the viewport.
ViewPortWidth	Property	Returns the width of the viewport.
ViewPortHeight	Property	Returns the height of the viewport.
VScrollSmallChange	Property	Determines the distance moved when the scrollbar is clicked.

CONTINUOUSSCROLL PROPERTY

Objects Affected   UserDocument

Purpose   This property determines if the UserDocument redraws as it is scrolling or when the scrolling has stopped.

General Syntax

```
UserDocument.ContinuousScroll [ = boolean%]
```

Table 88-2 Arguments of the ContinuousScroll property

Argument	Description
UserDocument	Name of the UserDocument
boolean%	True or False

Table 88-3 Meanings of the boolean% argument in the ContinuousScroll property

boolean%	Meaning
True	The UserDocument will redraw as it is scrolled.
False	The UserDocument will redraw when the scrolling has stopped.

Example Syntax

```
Private Sub Form_Load()
    UserDocument.ContinuousScroll = True
End Sub
```

Description   The ContinuousScroll property is used to determine if the ActiveX document will redraw as it is scrolled. For ActiveX documents that rely on complex graphics, this property should probably be set to False because of the amount of processing overhead required for redrawing on the fly.

Example   In the project at the end of the chapter, the ContinuousScroll property is set to True because the visual components are simple.

HScrollSmallChange, VScrollSmallChange Properties

Objects Affected   UserDocument

Purpose   To set the amount of horizontal or vertical scrolling when the scrollbar is clicked.

General Syntax

```
UserDocument.HScrollSmallChange [ = single!]
UserDocument.VScrollSmallChange [ = single!]
```

Table 88-4 Arguments of the HScrollSmallChange and VScrollSmallChange properties

Arguments	Description
UserDocument	The name of the UserDocument
single!	The amount to move

Example Syntax

```
Private Sub Form_Load()
    UserDocument.HScrollSmallChange=1000
    UserDocument.VScrollSmallChange=2000
End Sub
```

Description   These properties are used to set the amount of scrolling that will occur when the horizontal or vertical scrollbar is clicked. Some ActiveX documents need many different scrolling requirements. This allows the developer to control the amount of movement when the horizontal or vertical scrollbar is clicked.

Example   In the project at the end of this chapter, these properties are assigned a small number so that when the scrollbars are clicked, the scrolling is very smooth and slow.

Icon Property

Objects Affected   Form, Forms Collection, MDIForm, UserDocument

Purpose   This property is used to set the icon that will appear in the left pane of the Office Binder when this ActiveX document is displayed in the Office Binder.

General Syntax

```
UserDocument.Icon=icon$
```

Table 88-5 Arguments of the Icon property

Arguments	Description
UserDocument	Name of the UserDocument
icon$	The location and name of the icon to be used

Example Syntax

```
Private Sub Form_Load()
    Icon="c:\data\blip.ico"
End Sub
```

Description   The Icon property is used to set the icon when the ActiveX document is placed in the Office Binder. This property is not used when it is displayed in Internet Explorer.

MinHeight Property

Objects Affected   UserDocument

Purpose   The MinHeight property is used to determine at what height horizontal scrollbars should appear.

General Syntax

```
UserDocument.MinHeight [ = single!]
```

Table 88-6 Arguments for the MinHeight property

Arguments	Description
UserDocument	Name of the UserDocument
single!	The value of MinHeight

Example Syntax

```
Private Sub Form_Load()
    UserDocument.MinHeight = 2000
End Sub
```

Description   The MinHeight property is used to determine when the vertical scrollbars will appear. When the height of the display area is less than the MinHeight of the ActiveX document, then the scrollbars appear. With some ActiveX documents, it may be beneficial to set the MinHeight to the height of the ActiveX control. This could be helpful when creating documents in which the layout of the form is quite static, such as in a survey input form.

Example   In the project at the end of this chapter, MinHeight is set to the height of the ActiveX document. The project is based on forms to be filled in. This setting allows the form to be larger than the display area of the container and to allow access to the hidden parts of the form by scrolling.

Comments   The scrollbars will appear only if the ScrollBars property is set to True.

MinWidth Property

Objects Affected   UserDocument

Purpose   To set the minimum width of the ActiveX document that the container can display before the horizontal scrollbars will appear.

General Syntax

```
UserDocument.MinWidth [= single!]
```

Table 88-7 Arguments for the MinWidth property

Arguments	Description
UserDocument	Name of the UserDocument
single!	The value of MinWidth

Example Syntax

```
Private Sub Form_Load()
    UserDocument.MinWidth=3000
End Sub
```

Description   This property works just like MinHeight except that it deals with the width of the ActiveX document. When the container's horizontal display area is less than the MinWidth property of the ActiveX document, then the scrollbars appear.

Example   In the project at the end of this chapter, the MinWidth property is set to the width of the ActiveX document so that when any of the ActiveX document is not displayed by the container, the scrollbars will appear.

Scroll Event

Objects Affected   ComboBox, DBGrid, DirListBox, DriveListBox, FileListBox, HScrollBar, ListBox, Slider, VScrollBar, UserDocument

Purpose   This event is raised when the scrollbar of an object has been moved.

General Syntax

```
Private Sub UserDocument_Scroll ()
```

Table 88-8 Argument for the Scroll event

Argument	Description
UserDocument	Name of the UserDocument

Example Syntax
```
Private Sub UserDocument_Scroll()
    I&=I&+1
End Sub
```

Description	This event is raised when the horizontal or vertical scrollbars are moved. This event can be used to monitor the scrolling of the ActiveX document.
Comment	The Microsoft Visual Basic Help file says not to place a Msgbox statement or function in the Scroll event.

SCROLLBARS PROPERTY

Objects Affected	DBGrid, MDIForm, Split, TextBox, UserDocument
Purpose	Determines if the scrollbars appear automatically when the height or width of the display area of the container is less than the MinHeight or MinWidth of the ActiveX document. This property is read-only at runtime.

General Syntax

```
UserDocument.ScrollBars [ = boolean%]
```

Table 88-9 Arguments for the ScrollBars property

Arguments	Description
UserDocument	Name of the UserDocument
boolean%	True or False

Table 88-10 Meaning of the boolean% argument in the ScrollBars property

boolean%	Meaning
True	The scrollbars will appear automatically when the display area of the container is less than the MinHeight or MinWidth property.
False	The scrollbars will not appear.

Example Syntax
```
Private Sub Command1_Click ()
    If UserDocument1.Scrollbars=False then
    Msgbox "The scrollbars will not be shown when needed."
    End IF
End Sub
```

Description   This property is used to determine if the scrollbars are visible when the height or width of the display area is less than the MinHeight or MinWidth of the ActiveX document. By setting this property to True, the user will be able to scroll and view the areas of the ActiveX document that are not made visible by the container.

Example   In the example at the end of this chapter, the Scrollbars property is set to True for the user to be able to view the areas not displayed by the container. Because the example document is a form, the form can be larger than the display area but still allow the user access to the complete document.

SetViewPort Method

Object Affected   UserDocument

Purpose   Sets the top and left coordinates of the ActiveX document to be displayed in the container.

General Syntax

```
UserDocumnet.SetViewPort left!, top!
```

Table 88-11 Arguments for the SetViewPort method

Arguments	Description
UserDocument	Name of the UserDocument
left	The leftmost coordinate to be displayed
top	The topmost coordinate to be displayed

Example Syntax
```
Private Sub Textbox1_GotFocus()
    UserDocument.ViewPort Textbox1.top,Textbox1.left
End Sub
```

Description   The SetViewPort method is used to set which area of the ActiveX document is displayed in the display area of the container. With this method, you can use code to move a part of an ActiveX document that is larger than the display area of the container into view.

VIEWPORTTOP, VIEWPORTLEFT, VIEWPORTHEIGHT, VIEWPORTWIDTH PROPERTIES

Objects Affected   UserDocument

Purpose   To determine the coordinates of the display area of the container.

General Syntax

```
UserDocument.ViewPortTop
UserDocument.ViewPortLeft
UserDocument.ViewPortWidth
UserDocument.ViewPortHeight
```

Table 88-12 Argument for the ViewPortTop, ViewPortLeft, ViewPortWidth, ViewPortHeight properties

Argument	Description
UserDocument	Name of the UserDocument

Example Syntax

```
Private Sub TextBox1_GotFocus()
    UserDocument.ViewPortLeft=TextBox1.Left
    UserDocument.ViewPortTop=TextBox1.Top
End Sub
```

Description   The ViewPort properties are used to position the ActiveX document in a container. This is especially useful when the display area of the container is smaller than the ActiveX document. This enables the ActiveX document to position itself within the display area of the container when needed. For a more user-friendly application, you may want to arrange the ViewPort settings so that when an item not currently in view gains focus, the document automatically moves the item into view.

Example   In the project at the end of this chapter, the ActiveX document moves items into the display area of the container as they are tabbed by changing the ViewPort coordinates.

The Creating ActiveX Document Project

Project Overview

This project demonstrates how to create a simple ActiveX document and how it interacts with Internet Explorer. The first section shows the assembly of the two forms and the addition of code. The second section demonstrates the ActiveX document running inside Internet Explorer.

Assembling the Project: Survey

1. Open Visual Basic 5.0 and start with a new ActiveX document .EXE.

2. Assemble the first UserDocument as shown in Table 88-13.

Table 88-13 Properties and controls of DocMain UserDocument

Object	Property	Setting
CommandButton	Name	cmdSurvey
	Caption	Click Me
Label	Name	lbl
	Alignment	2' Center
	Caption	"Click the following button to fill out the survey"

3. Size the object on the screen as in Figure 88-1.

4. Enter the following code in the Declarations section of the docMain UserDocument. This public variable will hold the value indicating if the survey has been filled in during the current instance of Internet Explorer.

```
Public FilledIn As Integer
```

5. Enter the following code in the cmdSurvey_Click event of the CommandButton. This code will have the Web browser jump to the UserDocument in which the survey will be taken. The FilledIn variable is first checked to make sure the survey has not been filled in during this instance of the Web browser.

```
Private Sub cmdSurvey_Click()
If FilledIn = True Then
    MsgBox "You have already filled in the survey."
Else
    MsgBox App.Path
    Hyperlink.NavigateTo "file://" + App.Path + "\docFill.vbd"
End If
End Sub
```

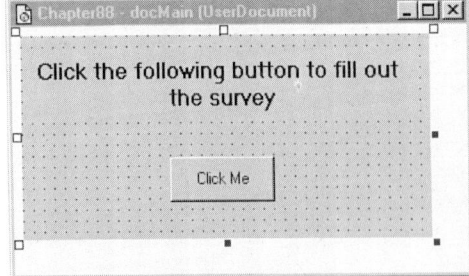

Figure 88-1 What the docMain UserDocument should look like

6. Assemble the second UserDocument as in Table 88-14.

Table 88-14 Properties and control of DocFill

Object	Property	Setting
UserDocument	Name	DocFill
CommandButton	Name	cmdClear
	Caption	Clear
CommandButton	Name	cmdComplete
	Caption	Done
TextBox	Name	txtFill
	Index	0
TextBox	Name	txtFill
	Index	1
TextBox	Name	txtFill
	Index	2
TextBox	Name	txtFill
	Index	3
Label	Name	lbFill
	Caption	Favorite Web Site
	Index	0
Label	Name	lbFill
	Caption	EMail Address
	Index	1
Label	Name	lbFill
	Caption	Age
	Index	2
Label	Name	lbFill
	Caption	Name

7. Size and place the elements on the UserDocument as shown in Figure 88-2. Set the font of each element to MS Sans Serif at 14 points.

8. Enter the following code in to the cmdClear_Click event. The code will cause any text entered in the four text boxes on the UserDocument to be cleared.

```
Private Sub cmdClear_Click()
For i% = 0 To 3
    txtFill(i).Text = ""
Next i%
End Sub
```

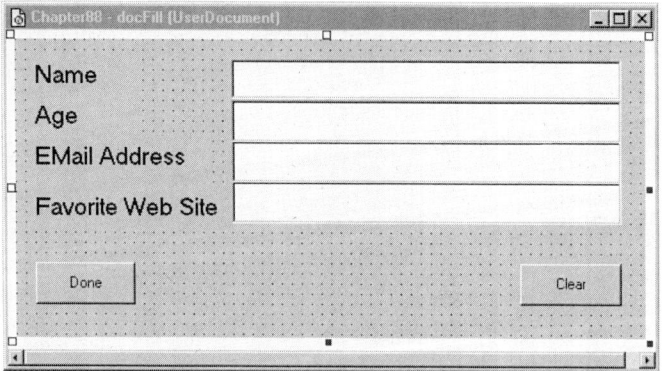

Figure 88-2   What the docFill UserDocument should look like

9. Enter the following code into the cmdComplete_Click event. This code will take the text of the text file and write it out to a text file that resides in the same directory as the UserDocument. This code also sets the public variable FilledIn to True so that the survey cannot be taken again during the current instance of the Web browser. Then it causes the Web browser to go back to the first UserDocument loaded.

```
Private Sub cmdComplete_Click()
Open "dump.txt" For Append As #1
For i% = 0 To 3
    Print #1, txtFill(i%).Text + " " + CStr(Now) + " ";
Next i%
Close #1

MsgBox "Thanks for your input."
FilledIn = True
Hyperlink.NavigateTo "file://" + App.Path + "\docMain.vbd"
End Sub
```

10. Save and compile the project.

How It Works

When an ActiveX Document is complied, two types of files are created.

The first is an .EXE file with the name of the project. The second is a .VBD file for each of the UserDocuments that made up the .EXE. To open the ActiveX document, open a .VBD file with Internet Explorer. The .VBD file is a structured storage file that Internet Explorer uses to load the proper information from the .EXE file to be displayed.

To demonstrate how this works, click on the File menu and then the Open option with Internet Explorer. When the Open dialog box appears, click on the browse button. The FileOpen dialog box will appear as shown in Figure 88-3.

Select All Files (*.*) from the Files of Type combo box. Then open the directory where the project was compiled. As shown in Figure 88-4, there is both an .EXE file with the name of project and a .VBD file for each of the UserDocuments.

Open DOCMAIN.VBD. As you can see, the HTML page is replaced with the UserDocument, as in Figure 88-5.

With the knowledge of Visual Basic programming and ActiveX document creation you have now gained, you can create applications that reside on a Web server and can be accessed by Internet Explorer. This way, when updates are made to ActiveX documents, only the .EXE and .VBD files need to be replaced.

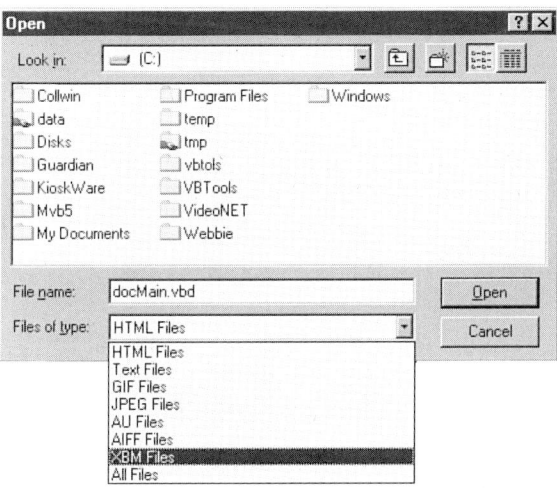

Figure 88-3   Open dialog box within Internet Explorer

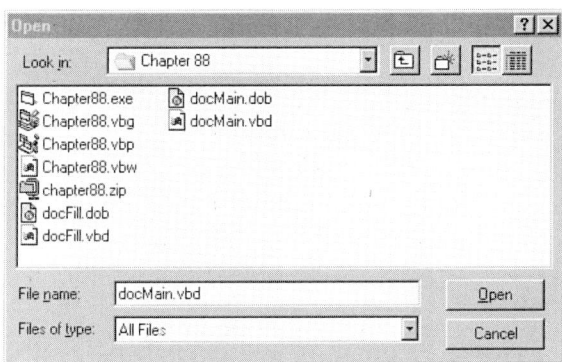

Figure 88-4   Opening a .VBD file within Internet Explorer

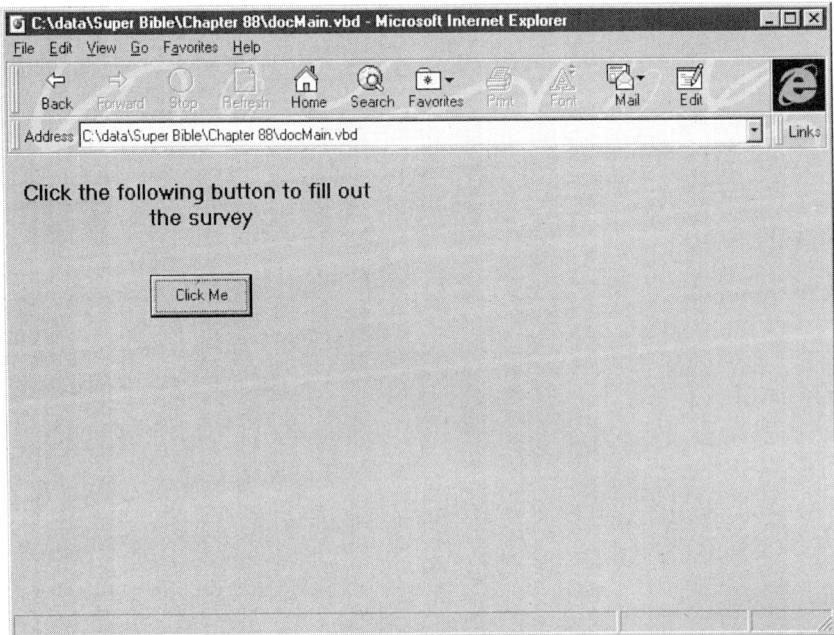

Figure 88-5 The first screen of the ActiveX document displayed with Internet Explorer

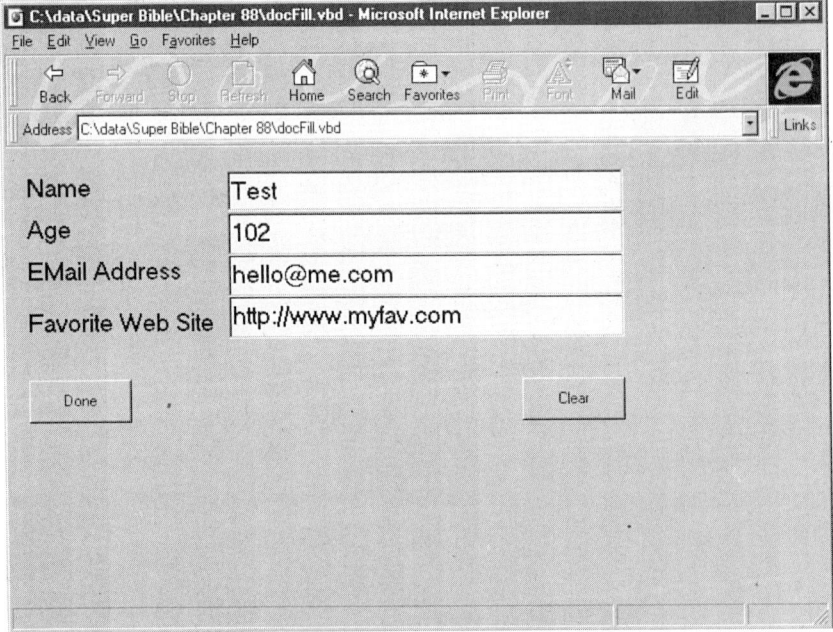

Figure 88-6 The second screen of the ActiveX document displayed with Internet Explorer

PART XV
ADVANCED TOPICS

89

USING THE COMMAND-LINE COMPILER

With the advent of graphical user interfaces (GUIs) such as Microsoft Windows, fewer programs need to use command-line switches. Their principal role has gradually been relegated to determining the desired startup mode of an application, because in a GUI other types of input are more elegantly collected via dialog or message boxes. The Windows registry editor can be started in advanced mode by using the /v command-line switch. (A word of warning: This editor is a utility designed to be used by Windows experts only, Don't experiment with it!) Other programs may have a debugging mode that can be entered by starting the application with the appropriate command-line argument.

Introduction

You can control how Visual Basic 5.0 executes with command-line switches. With these command-line switches, you can start Visual Basic and run a specified project, make an executable file or dynamic-link library, or specify a string to be passed to the Command$ function. Table 89-1 lists the Visual Basic command-line arguments. If you start VB5 with the /? command-line switch and choose Run from the startup menu as shown in Figure 89-1, the help dialog box shown in Figure 89-2 will be displayed.

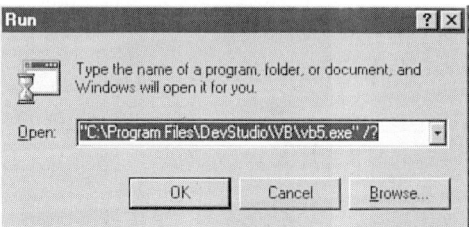

Figure 89-1 The available command-line switches are shown...

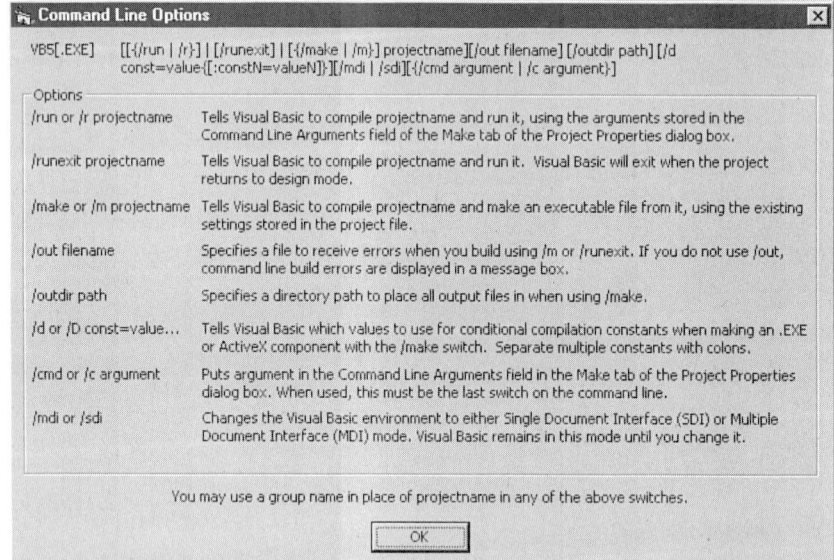

Figure 89-2 ...by starting Visual Basic with this syntax

Table 89-1 Visual Basic command-line switches

Use This Switch...	To Do This...
/cmd	Specify a command string to be passed to the Command$ function
/d	Specify conditional compilation constants
/make *MyProject*	Make the specified project into an executable
/makedll *MyProject*	Make the specified project into a dynamic link library
/mdi	Start Visual Basic in the multiple document interface mode
/out *FileName*	Output Make errors to the specified file
/run *MyProject*	Run the specified project

Use This Switch...	To Do This...
/runexit *MyProject*	Run the specified project and automatically exit
/sdi	Start Visual Basic in the single document interface mode
/?	Display a list of valid command-line switches

Command Summary

COMMAND$ FUNCTION

Purpose

The Command$ function is used to determine the command line arguments that were used when starting the application. When passing parameters to a Visual Basic application, there are three distinct ways to start the application: by selecting Run in the design environment, by using the /run or /runexit switch when starting VB5.EXE, and by running an executable program compiled with Visual Basic 5.0.

General Syntax

```
strCommandLine = Command$
```

Example Syntax

```
Private Sub Form_Load ()
    Dim strCommandLine As String

    strCommandLine = Command$

    If Len(strCommandLine) > 0 Then
        Dim lngFileNameStart As Long

        lngFileNameStart = InStr(strCommandLine, "/f")

        If lngFileNameStart > 0 Then
            Dim lngFileNameEnd As Long
            lngFileNameEnd = InStr(lngFileNameStart + 1, strCommandLine, "/") - 1
            If lngFileNameEnd = -1 Then
                lngFileNameEnd = Len(strCommandLine)
            End If

            Dim strFileName As String
strFileName = Trim$(Mid$(strCommandLine, lngFileNameStart + 2, ⇐
lngFileNameEnd - lngFileNameStart - 1))
            MsgBox strFileName
        Else
            ErrorMessage "Missing file name"
        End If
    End If

End Sub
```

Description   In the above code fragment, the command line is being parsed for a switch in the form /f *FileName*. This switch ends where the next switch starts, at the "/" character. If the filename switch is the last switch on the command line, the end is set to the length of the command line. The filename is extracted from the command line and shown in a message box.

Applications Started in the Design Environment Using the Run Command   If you want to test your application in the Visual Basic design environment, you can type your command-line options in the appropriate text box on the Make tab of the project properties dialog box. You gain access to the project properties by clicking on the last menu item in the Project menu, as shown in Figure 89-3. Figure 89-4 shows the Project Properties dialog box of the Command project.

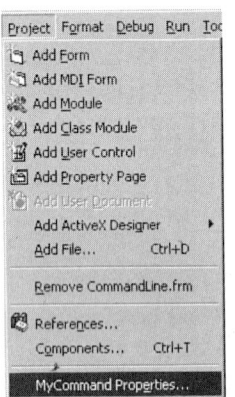

Figure 89-3   When you choose the Project Properties menu item...

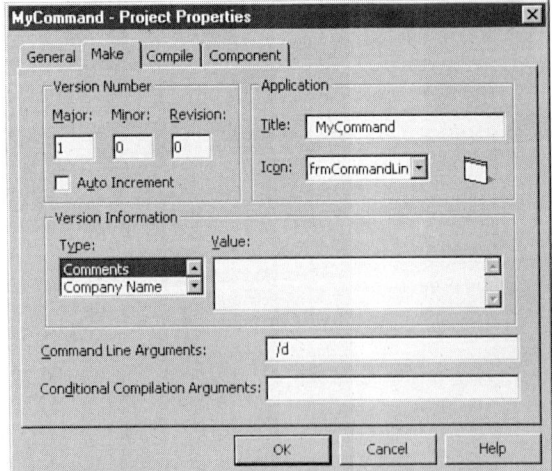

Figure 89-4   ...you get the following Project Properties dialog box

Applications in Design Environment with Command-line	If you want to test your application by starting Visual Basic with a command-line switch, use the /cmd switch as the last switch and pass the arguments, such as "C:\Program Files\DevStudio\VB\vb5.exe" /run C:\data\vb5\MyCommand.vbp /cmd /d.
Compiled Applications	If you want to test your compiled Visual Basic executable application, type the arguments after the program name in the Run dialog, for example, C:\data\vb5\MyCommand /d.
Example	In the Command project, we use the Command function to determine whether to start the application in Debugging mode. We also provide a help dialog if the application is started with a /? switch.
Comments	The /cmd switch needs to be last because everything following this switch is passed to the application. You can access what was passed via the Command$ function.

Command Project

This project demonstrates how to parse command-line parameters passed to a Visual Basic application.

Assembling the Project

1. Place the following controls on a form, as detailed in Table 89-2. Figure 89-5 shows what the completed form should look like.

Table 89-2 Elements of frmCommandLine

Control	Property	Value
Form	Name	frmCommandLine
	BorderStyle	3 - Fixed Dialog
	Caption	"Command Project"
Label	Name	lblAppMode
	Caption	"This application was started in ??? mode"
Command Button	Name	cmdClose
	Caption	"Close"

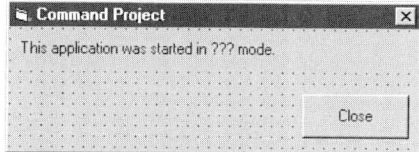

Figure 89-5   frmCommandLine in Design mode

2. Add a module called modMain, to the project and add the following code into its General section. This code informs Visual Basic that we will be required to declare all variables and defines an enumeration to be used to designate the desired application mode.

```
Option Explicit

Public Enum enmAppMode
    NormalMode = 0
    DebugMode = 1
End Enum
```

3. Enter the following code into the Declarations section of frmCommandLine. This code informs Visual Basic that we will be required to declare all variables and declares a private form variable to be used to keep track of the desired application mode.

```
Option Explicit

Private mAppMode As enmAppMode
```

4. Add the following code to the frmCommandLine form. You define a AppStartMode property that exposes the private variable mAppMode.

```
Public Property Get AppStartMode() As enmAppMode
    AppStartMode = mAppMode
End Property

Public Property Let AppStartMode(ByVal theAppMode As enmAppMode)
    mAppMode = theAppMode
End Property
```

5. Enter the following code into the Form_Load procedure of frmCommandLine. This code displays the application mode by setting the label caption.

```
Private Sub Form_Load()
Select Case AppStartMode
        Case NormalMode
            lblAppMode.Caption = "This application was started in normal mode."
        Case DebugMode
            lblAppMode.Caption = "This application was started in debugging mode."
    End Select
End Sub
```

6. Enter the following code into the cmdClose_Click procedure. This code ends the application by unloading the form.

```
Private Sub cmdClose_Click()
    Unload Me
End Sub
```

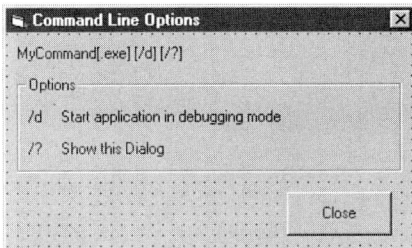

Figure 89-6 frmSwitches in Design mode

7. Insert a new form to display the command-line options available to start the application. Table 89-3 details the components of the form. When placing these components on the form, make sure you place the lblOptions labels inside the frame. Size and position the elements as illustrated in Figure 89-6.

Table 89-3 Elements of frmSwitches

Control	Property	Value
Form	Name	frmSwitches
	BorderStyle	3 - Fixed Dialog
	Caption	"Command Line Options"
Label	Name	lblSyntax
	Caption	"MyCommand[.exe] [/d] [/?]"
Command Button	Name	cmdClose
	Caption	"Close"
Frame	Name	fraOptions
	Caption	"Options"
Label	Name	lblOptions
	Index	0
	Caption	"/d Start application in debugging mode"
Label	Name	lblOptions
	Index	1
	Caption	"/? Show this Dialog"

8. Enter the following code into the cmdClose_Click procedure. This code ends the application by unloading the form.

```
Private Sub cmdClose_Click()
    Unload Me
End Sub
```

9. Enter the following mode into the modMain module. This code sets the application by unloading the form. Set the Startup Object in the Project Properties to Sub Main by choosing MyCommand Properties menu item from the Project menu as in Figure 89-7.

```
Sub Main()
    Dim strCommandLine As String

    strCommandLine = Command$

    If Len(strCommandLine) > 0 Then
        If InStr(strCommandLine, "/d") > 0 Or InStr(strCommandLine, "/D") > 0 Then
            frmCommandLine.AppStartMode = DebugMode
        Else
            frmCommandLine.AppStartMode = NormalMode
        End If

        If InStr(strCommandLine, "/?") > 0 Then
            frmSwitches.Show vbModal
        Else
            frmCommandLine.Show vbModal
        End If
    Else
        frmCommandLine.AppStartMode = NormalMode
        frmCommandLine.Show vbModal
    End If
End Sub
```

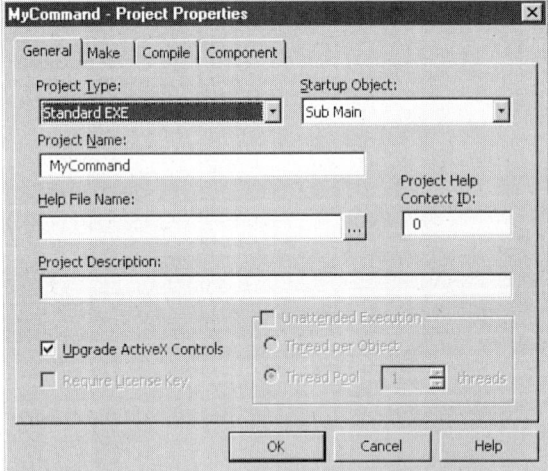

Figure 89-7 You must specify that you want to have your project start with the Main Sub in the Project Properties

How It Works

The Command$ function provides the command-line argument entered. You determine whether "/d" or "/?" was entered using InStr and act accordingly. Figure 89-8 shows the project in operation.

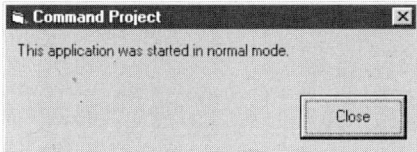

Figure 89-8   The Command project
in action

90

SDI, MDI, AND EXPLORER INTERFACE TYPES

There are three main types of Windows user interfaces: the Single-Document Interface (SDI), the Multiple-Document Interface (MDI) and the Explorer-style interface. This chapter will introduce eight common interface controls and show you how to use them in your Visual Basic applications to create such interfaces.

Introduction

In an SDI, only a single document may be open; you must close one document in order to open another. MDIs allow you to display multiple documents at the same time, with each document displayed in its own window. MDIs are discussed at length in Chapter 36, "Forms and Menus."

The Explorer-style interface is a single window containing two panes or regions, usually consisting of a tree or hierarchical view on the left and a display area on the right, as in the Microsoft Windows Explorer (See Figure 90-1). This type of interface lends itself to navigating or browsing large numbers of documents, pictures, or files.

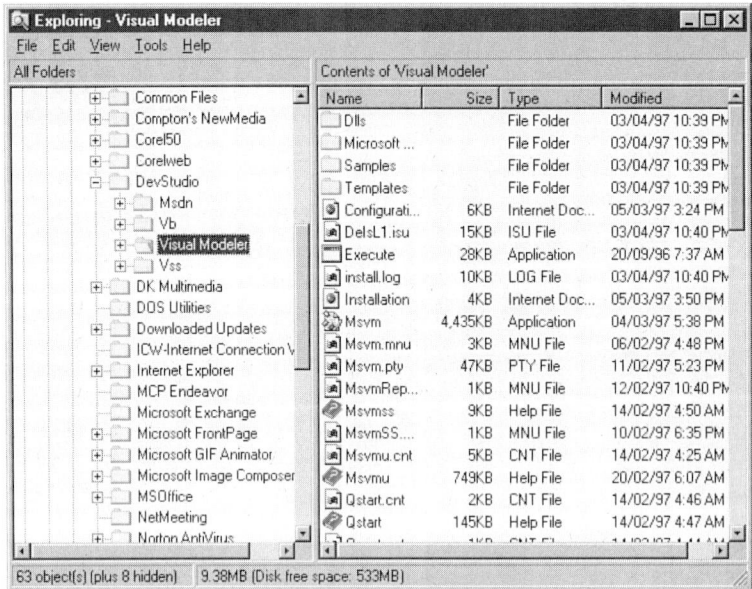

Figure 90-1   The Windows Explorer is the stereotype for Explorer-style interfaces

The Application Wizard, discussed in Chapter 94, "Application Wizard and Component Templates," provides a good way to compare the different interface types. You can use the Wizard to generate a framework for each type and view the forms and code that it generates.

The eight controls covered in this chapter are the ImageList, ListView, ProgressBar, Slider, StatusBar, TabStrip, ToolBar, and TreeView controls. If these controls are not available to you through the Visual Basic Toolbox, then you must use the Custom Controls option of the Visual Basic Tools menu to ensure that the box next to the controls you wish to use is checked. The eight controls are located in the COMCTL32.OCX file and are referred to as Microsoft Windows Common Controls 5.0.

Table 90-1 Summary of objects, collections, and common controls

Use This...	Type	To Do This...
Button	Object	Set up the buttons on a ToolBar control
Buttons	Collection	Access a collection of Button objects
ColumnHeader	Object	Set up the columns in a ListView control
ColumnHeaders	Collection	Access a collection of ColumnHeader objects
ImageList	Control	Store or display a collection of images
ListImage	Object	Store a bitmap that can be used in other controls

Use This...	Type	To Do This...
ListImages	Collection	Access a collection of ListImage objects
ListItem	Object	Set up the items in a ListView control
ListItems	Collection	Access a collection of ListItem objects
ListView	Control	Display a graphical view of a set of data
Node	Object	Set up the items in a TreeView control
Nodes	Collection	Access a collection of Node objects
Panel	Object	Set up the panels displayed in a StatusBar control
Panels	Collection	Access a collection of Panel objects
ProgressBar	Control	Display an indicator of progress toward completion
Slider	Control	Display a Slider control
StatusBar	Control	Create a status bar at the bottom of a form
Tab	Object	Set up the text and images used for the TabStrip control
Tabs	Collection	Access a collection of Tab objects
TabStrip	Control	Display notebook-style tables
ToolBar	Control	Display an icon-filled bar
TreeView	Control	Display a hierarchical view of a set of data

BUTTON OBJECT

Purpose   You can use the Button object to define an object that will be used as a button on a ToolBar control.

Properties   Table 90-2 lists the properties of the Button object.

Table 90-2 Properties of the Button object

Use This Property...	To Do This...
Caption	Read or set the caption for the button
Description	Read or set a string description for the button
Enabled	Determine if this button is enabled within the ToolBar control
Height	Read or set the vertical size of this control
Image	Associate an image with this button
Index	Create a control array
Key	Read or set a string that is used to identify this object in a collection
Left	Read or set the horizontal position of the control within the form
MixedState	Determine whether the button can appear in the indeterminate state
Style	Read or set the button style
ToolTipText	Associate ToolTip help text with this tab

continued on next page

continued from previous page

Use This Property...	To Do This...
Top	Read or set the vertical positioning of this control
Value	Read or set the state of the button object
Visible	Determine whether this button is visible on the ToolBar control
Width	Read or set the horizontal size of this control

Description	Use a Button object to read or set information about a specific button on a ToolBar control. Each button can have text (Caption property), a description (Description property), and a picture (Image property) associated with it. In addition, there are several properties such as Style and MixedState that determine how the button will appear and function on a ToolBar control.

BUTTONS COLLECTION

Purpose	You can use the Buttons collection to define a collection of objects that will be used as buttons on a ToolBar control.
Property and Methods	Tables 90-3 and 90-4 list the property and methods that relate to the Buttons collection.

Table 90-3 Property of the Buttons collection

Use This Property...	To Do This...
Count	Find out how many Button objects are in the collection

Table 90-4 Methods of the Buttons collection

Use This Method...	To Do This...
Add	Add a Button object to the collection
Clear	Clear all Button objects in the collection (remove them from the collection)
Item	Access a specific Button object in the collection
Remove	Remove a Button object from the collection

Description	The Buttons collection contains each Button object that you use for a particular ToolBar control. You can use a For Each...Next loop to process the individual Button objects within this collection.

ColumnHeader Object

Purpose   You can use the ColumnHeader object to define an object that will be used as a column header for a column in a ListView control.

Properties   Table 90-5 lists the properties of the ColumnHeader object.

Table 90-5 Properties of the ColumnHeader object

Use This Property...	To Do This...
Alignment	Read or set a value that determines the alignment of text in a ColumnHeader object
Index	Create a control array
Key	Read or set a string that is used to identify this object in a collection
Left	Read or set the horizontal position of the control within the form
SubItemIndex	Associate a subitem with this object
Tag	Store additional data about this control
Text	Read or set the text displayed for this object
Width	Read or set the horizontal size of this control

Description   The ColumnHeader object contains a heading for a column in the ListView control. ColumnHeader objects are only viewable when the ListView control is in Report view. You may add ColumnHeader objects to a ListView control at either design time or runtime. You can detect click events for the ColumnHeader object, so you may want to perform some action (such as sorting) on the items within a column when the ColumnHeader object for that column is clicked.

ColumnHeaders Collection

Purpose   You can use the ColumnHeaders collection to define a collection of objects that will be used as column headers in a ListView control.

Property and   Tables 90-6 and 90-7 list the property and methods that relate to the
Methods   ColumnHeaders collection.

Table 90-6 Property of the ColumnHeaders collection

Use This Property...	To Do This...
Count	Find out how many ColumnHeader objects are in the collection

Table 90-7 Methods of the ColumnHeaders collection

Use This Method...	To Do This...
Add	Add a ColumnHeader object to the collection
Clear	Clear all ColumnHeader objects in the collection (remove them from the collection)
Item	Access a specific ColumnHeader object in the collection
Remove	Remove a ColumnHeader object from the collection

Description	The ColumnHeaders collection contains each ColumnHeader object that you use for a particular ListView control. You can use a For Each...Next loop to process the individual ColumnHeader objects within this collection.

IMAGELIST CONTROL

Purpose	The ImageList control is used as a holder for images. This control is generally used to supply images to other controls. Each image contained by the ImageList control is a separate ListImage object.
Properties and Method	Tables 90-8 and 90-9 list the properties and method that relate to the ImageList control.

Table 90-8 Properties of the ImageList control

Use This Property...	To Do This...
BackColor	Read or set the background color of this control
ImageHeight	Read or set the height of the ListImage objects contained in the ImageList control
ImageWidth	Read or set the width of the ListImage objects contained in the ImageList control
Index	Create a control array
ListImages	Refer to the collection of ListImage objects contained by this control
MaskColor	Read or set the mask color used for the image (such as with the Overlay method)
Name	Specify the name of the control
Object	Retrieve an object reference for this control
Parent	Find the parent object of this control
Tag	Store additional data about this control

Table 90-9 Method of the ImageList control

Use This Method...	To Do This...
Overlay	Draw one image from the ListImages collection on top of another

Description The ImageList control holds multiple images that can be used with other controls, such as the ListView and TreeView controls. Each image in the ImageList control can be accessed as a ListImage object, or all the images can be accessed as a ListImages collection. The Overlay method can be used to combine two images, which may be useful for certain graphical operations.

LISTIMAGE OBJECT

Purpose Use the ListImage object to create an image that will be part of a ListImages collection. The ListImages collection can be used to provide images for a variety of the common interface controls detailed in this chapter.

Properties, Tables 90-10 and 90-11 list the properties and methods that relate to the
Methods, and ListImage object. Table 90-12 lists constant values associated with this
Constant Values object.

Table 90-10 Properties of the ListImage object

Use This Property...	To Do This...
Index	Create a control array
Key	Read or set a string that is used to identify this object in a collection
Picture	Associate an icon or bitmap with this object

Table 90-11 Methods of the ListImage object

Use This Method...	To Do This...
Draw	Draw the ListImage object in a specified device context using a specified style
ExtractIcon	Create an icon from a bitmap in a ListImage object

Table 90-12 ListImage draw constants

Constant	ComctlLib.ImageDrawConstants	Description
0	imgNormal	Draw image with no change
1	imgTransparent	Draw image transparently
2	imgSelected	Draw image selected
3	imgFocus	Draw image with focus

Description	The ListImage object is used to contain a single graphical image. The ImageList control contains a collection of ListImage objects, each of which contains a reference to a picture (generally a Windows bitmap or icon).

LISTIMAGES COLLECTION

Purpose	You can use the ListImages collection to provide a list of images to many of the common interface controls that require images.
Property and Methods	Tables 90-13 and 90-14 list the property and methods that relate to the ListImages collection.

Table 90-13 Property of the ListImages collection

Use This Property...	To Do This...
Count	Find out how many ColumnHeader objects are in the collection

Table 90-14 Methods of the ListImages collection

Use This Method...	To Do This...
Add	Add a ColumnHeader object to the collection
Clear	Clear all ColumnHeader objects in the collection (remove them from the collection)
Item	Access a specific ColumnHeader object in the collection
Remove	Remove a ColumnHeader object from the collection

Description	The ListImages collection contains a series of ListImage objects. In general, one ListImages collection is associated with each ImageList control. You can use the For Each...Next loop to process each ListImage object within the collection.

LISTITEM OBJECT

Purpose	Use the ListItem object to specify information about the items to be displayed in a ListView control.
Properties and Methods	Tables 90-15 and 90-16 list the properties and methods that relate to the ListItem object.

Table 90-15 Properties of the ListItem collection

Use This Property...	To Do This...
Ghosted	Read or set a value to enable or disable this list item
Height	Read or set the vertical size of this control
Icon	Determine the regular-sized icon image displayed for this object
Index	Create a control array
Key	Read or set a string that is used to identify this object in a collection
Left	Read or set the horizontal position of the control within the form
Selected	Determine whether a specified ListItem is selected
SmallIcon	Determine the smaller-sized icon image displayed for this object
SubItems	Associate subitems with this object
Tag	Store additional data about this control
Text	Read or set the text displayed for this object
Top	Read or set the vertical positioning of this control
Width	Read or set the horizontal size of this control

Table 90-16 Methods of the ListItem object

Use This Method...	To Do This...
CreateDragImage	Create an image to use for drag-and-drop operations
EnsureVisible	Ensure that this object is visible by scrolling and expanding the ListView control

Description	A ListItem object is an object that is part of a ListView control. A ListItem object will generally contain information about a specific picture or icon and some text. You can use the ListView control by creating a collection of ListItem objects (a ListItems collection).

LISTITEMS COLLECTION

Purpose	You can use the ListItems collection to specify a collection of ListItem objects that will be used in a ListView control.
Property and Methods	Tables 90-17 and 90-18 list the property and methods that relate to the ListItems collection.

Table 90-17 Property of the ListItems collection

Use This Property...	To Do This...
Count	Find out how many ColumnHeader objects are in the collection

Table 90-18 Methods of the ListItems collection

Use This Method...	To Do This...
Add	Add a ColumnHeader object to the collection
Clear	Clear all ColumnHeader objects in the collection (remove them from the collection)
Item	Access a specific ColumnHeader object in the collection
Remove	Remove a ColumnHeader object from the collection

Description	The ListItems collection is a collection of ListItem objects. A ListView control will generally have one ListItems collection associated with it. You can use a For Each...Next loop to process each ListItem in the collection.

LISTVIEW CONTROL

Purpose	You can use the ListView control to display a graphical view of items. You can set the properties of the ListView control to arrange the columns, column heads, icons, and text. Figure 90-2 shows a sample ListView control in operation.
Properties, Events, Methods, and Constant Values	Tables 90-19, 90-20, and 90-21 list the properties, events, and methods that relate to the ListView control. Tables 90-22 through 90-28 list constant values associated with this control.

Table 90-19 Properties of the ListView control

Use This Property...	To Do This...
Arrange	Determine the icon arrangement for either the Icon or SmallIcon view
BackColor	Read or set the background color of this object
BorderStyle	Determine the style of border that this control will have
ColumnHeaders	Access the collection of ColumnHeader objects associated with this control
Container	Read or set the container for this control within the form

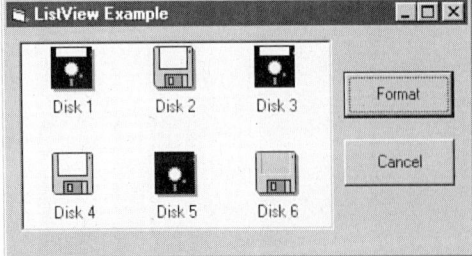

Figure 90-2 ListView control

Use This Property...	To Do This...
DragIcon	Specify the icon to use for drag-and-drop
DragMode	Set the mode to use for drag-and-drop
DropHighLight	Process drag-and-drop operations
Enabled	Determine whether this control is operational within the form
Font	Access the Font object associated with this control
ForeColor	Read or set the foreground color for this control
Height	Read or set the vertical size of this control
HelpContextID	Associate a context number that is used for context-sensitive help with this control
HideColumnHeaders	Determine whether column header objects are hidden in Report view
HideSelection	Determine whether selected list items remain highlighted when the control loses focus
hWnd	Retrieve a handle to the control's window
Icons	Determine the ImageList control used for the Icon view
Index	Create a control array
LabelEdit	Determine whether the user can edit labels of ListItem objects in the control
LabelWrap	Determine whether labels are wrapped when this control is in Icon view
Left	Read or set the horizontal position of the control within the form
ListItems	Access the collection of ListItem objects in this control
MouseIcon	Specify a custom mouse pointer
MousePointer	Specify the type of mouse pointer that will be shown within this control
MultiSelect	Determine whether and how the user can make multiple selections in the control
Name	Specify the name of the control
Object	Retrieve an object reference for this control
Parent	Find the parent object of this control
SelectedItem	Get a reference to a selected ListItem object
SmallIcons	Determine the ImageList control used for the SmallIcon view
Sorted	Determine whether the ListItem objects in the Icon and SmallIcon views are sorted
SortKey	Determine how the ListItem objects in this control are sorted
SortOrder	Determine whether the ListItem objects in this control are sorted in ascending or descending order
TabIndex	Adjust the tab order for this control
TabStop	Determine whether this control can be reached by pressing ⊤
Tag	Store additional data about this control
Top	Read or set the vertical positioning of this control
View	Read or set the appearance of ListItem objects in this control
Visible	Determine whether or not the control is visible on the form
WhatsThisHelpID	Associate a context number used for context-sensitive What's This help
Width	Read or set the horizontal size of this control

Table 90-20 Events of the ListView control

Use This Event...	To Do This...
AfterLabelEdit	Do something after the user edits the currently selected ListItem object
BeforeLabelEdit	Do something before the user edits the currently selected ListItem object
Click	Detect when this control is clicked with the mouse
ColumnClick	Detect when a ColumnHeader object in the control is clicked with the mouse
DblClick	Detect when this control is double-clicked with the mouse
DragDrop	Detect when a drag or drop has occurred
DragOver	Detect when an object is dragged over this control
GotFocus	Detect when this control receives the application focus
ItemClick	Detect when a ListView object in the control is clicked with the mouse
KeyDown	Detect when a key is pressed
KeyPress	Process a keystroke
KeyUp	Detect when a key is released
LostFocus	Detect when this control loses the application focus
MouseDown	Detect when one of the mouse buttons has been pressed
MouseMove	Process mouse movements
MouseUp	Detect when one of the mouse buttons has been released

Table 90-21 Methods of the ListView control

Use This Method...	To Do This...
Drag	Begin, end, or cancel a drag operation
FindItem	Find a specific ListItem object in the control
GetFirstVisible	Get a reference to the first ListItem object that appears in the visible control area
HitTest	Determine the ListItem object located at specified x and y coordinates
Move	Move or resize the control
Refresh	Force a repaint of the control
SetFocus	Give the application focus to this control
ShowWhatsThis	Display a specified Help topic using a What's This pop-up
StartLabelEdit	Enable a user to edit a label
ZOrder	Adjust the front-to-back ordering of this control

Table 90-22 ListView control constants

Constant	ComctlLib.ListViewConstants	Description
0	lvwIcon	(Default) Icon view
1	lvwSmallIcon	SmallIcon view
2	lvwList	List view
3	lvwReport	Report view

Table 90-23 ListView arrangement constants

Constant	ComctlLib.ListArrangeConstants	Description
0	lvwNoArrange	(Default) None
1	lvwLeft	Align along the left side of the control
2	lvwTop	Align along the top of the control
3	lvwAutoArrange	Always align to the top and left so that scrolling is avoided, if possible
4	lvwSnapToGrid	Snap to the nearest grid point

Table 90-24 ListView column alignment constants

Constant	ComctlLib.ListColumnAlignmentConstants	Description
0	lvwColumnLeft	(Default) Align text left
1	lvwColumnRight	Align text right
2	lvwColumnCenter	Center text

Table 90-25 ListView label edit constants

Constant	ComctlLib.ListLabelEditConstants	Description
0	lvwAutomatic	(Default) Automatic label editing
1	lvwManual	Manual label editing

Table 90-26 ListView sort order constants

Constant	ComctlLib.ListSortOrderConstants	Description
0	lvwAscending	(Default) Sort in ascending order
1	lvwDescending	Sort in descending order

Table 90-27 ListView find item where constants

Constant	ComctlLib.ListFindItemWhereConstants	Description
0	lvwText	(Default) Match the string with a ListItem object's Text property
1	lvwSubItem	Match the string with any string in a ListItem object's SubItem property
2	lvwTag	Match the string with any ListItem object's Tag property

Table 90-28 ListView find item how constants

Constant	ComctlLib.ListFindItemHowConstants	Description
0	lvwWholeWord	(Default) Whole word is matched
1	lvwPartial	Part of the word is matched (beginning of word)

Description   There are a variety of options available with the ListView control that allow you to customize the ListView display to meet your particular needs. You can, for example, adjust the sort order, column alignment, and size of icons used in the control. The ListItem object and ListItems collection contain information about each item displayed in the ListView control.

NODE OBJECT

Purpose   You can use the Node object to specify information about an item in a TreeView control.

Properties and Methods   Tables 90-29 and 90-30 list the properties and methods that relate to the Node object.

Table 90-29 Properties of the Node object

Use This Property...	To Do This...
Child	Obtain a reference to the first child of this node
Children	Find out how many children this node has
Enabled	Determine whether this node is enabled within the TreeView control
Expanded	Determine whether the tree under this node is expanded to reveal its child nodes
ExpandedImage	Specify an image for the node when it is expanded
FirstSibling	Obtain a reference to the first sibling of this node
FullPath	Get the full path of the currently selected node
Image	Specify an image to use for this node

Use This Property...	To Do This...
Index	Create a control array
LastSibling	Obtain a reference to the last sibling of this node
Next	Obtain a reference to the next sibling of this node
Parent	Obtain a reference to the parent of this node
Previous	Obtain a reference to the previous sibling of this node
Root	Obtain a reference to the root node in the TreeView control
Selected	Determine whether this TreeView node is selected
SelectedImage	Specify an image to use for this node when it is selected
Sorted	Read or set a value to indicate whether the child nodes of this node are sorted
Tag	Store additional data about this control
Text	Associate a text string with this node
Visible	Determine whether or not the node is visible in the TreeView control

Table 90-30 Methods of the Node object

Use This Method...	To Do This...
CreateDragImage	Create an image to use for drag-and-drop operations
EnsureVisible	Ensure that this object is visible by scrolling and expanding the ListView control

Description Each item in a TreeView control has an associated Node object that you can use to read or set information about the item. Information such as the text to be displayed and picture to use can be specified using the Text property and Image property, respectively.

NODES COLLECTION

Purpose You can use the Nodes collection to define a collection of Node objects that will be used in a TreeView control.

Property and Methods Tables 90-31 and 90-32 list the property and methods that relate to the Nodes collection.

Table 90-31 Property of the Nodes collection

Use This Property...	To Do This...
Count	Find out how many ColumnHeader objects are in the collection

Table 90-32 Methods of the Nodes collection

Use This Method...	To Do This...
Add	Add a ColumnHeader object to the collection
Clear	Clear all ColumnHeader objects in the collection (remove them from the collection)
Item	Access a specific ColumnHeader object in the collection
Remove	Remove a ColumnHeader object from the collection

Description	A Nodes collection is a collection of Node objects. You will generally have one Nodes collection associated with each TreeView control in your application. You can use a For Each...Next loop to process each Node object in the collection.

PANEL OBJECT

Purpose	You can use the Panel object to get or set information about the panels that make up a StatusBar control.
Properties and Events	Tables 90-33 and 90-34 list the properties and events that relate to the Panel object.

Table 90-33 Properties of the Panel object

Use This Property...	To Do This...
Alignment	Read or set a value indicating how text is aligned within the panel
Autosize	Determine how the size of the panel changes depending on its contents
Bevel	Determine the look of the beveled edges of the panel
Enabled	Determine whether the control can receive events
Height	Read or set the vertical size of this control
Index	Create a control array
Left	Read or set the horizontal position of the control within the form
MinWidth	Specify the minimum width allowable for the panel
Picture	Associate an image with this panel object
Style	Read or set a value indicating the style of the panel
Tag	Store additional data about this control
Text	Read or set a text string displayed in this panel
Top	Read or set the vertical positioning of this control
Visible	Determine whether this panel is visible to the user
Width	Read or set the horizontal size of this control

Table 90-34 Events of the Panel object

Use This Event...	To Do This...
PanelClick	Detect when the user has clicked a panel in a StatusBar control
PanelDblClick	Detect when the user has double-clicked a panel in a StatusBar control

Description	A Panel object is used to hold the information for a single panel in a StatusBar control. You will generally specify the text that you want to appear in a specific panel by setting the Text property of a Panel object. An optional picture can be associated with a panel by setting the Picture property.

PANELS COLLECTION

Purpose	You can use the Panels collection to define a collection of panel objects that can be used with a StatusBar control.
Property and Methods	Tables 90-35 and 90-36 list the property and methods that relate to the Panels collection.

Table 90-35 Property of the Panels collection

Use This Property...	To Do This...
Count	Find out how many ColumnHeader objects are in the collection

Table 90-36 Methods of the Panels collection

Use This Method...	To Do This...
Add	Add a ColumnHeader object to the collection
Clear	Clear all ColumnHeader objects in the collection (remove them from the collection)
Item	Access a specific ColumnHeader object in the collection
Remove	Remove a ColumnHeader object from the collection

Description	A Panels collection is a collection of Panel objects. You will generally have one Panels collection associated with each StatusBar control in your application. You can use a For Each...Next loop to process each Panel object in a collection.

PROGRESSBAR CONTROL

Purpose The progress bar is generally used to indicate progress toward the completion of some time-consuming computing task. The ProgressBar control is similar to the Gauge control that existed in previous versions of Visual Basic. The ProgressBar control is different in that it fills with rectangles rather than a solid bar. A sample ProgressBar control is shown in Figure 90-3.

Properties, Events, and Methods Tables 90-37, 90-38, and 90-39 list the properties, events, and methods that relate to the ProgressBar control.

Table 90-37 Properties of the ProgressBar control

Use This Property...	To Do This...
Align	Read or set a value that determines whether the control is attached to one of the form edges
BorderStyle	Determine the style of border that this control will have
Container	Read or set the container for this control within the form
DragIcon	Specify the icon to use for drag-and-drop
DragMode	Set the mode to use for drag-and-drop
Enabled	Determine whether the control can receive events
Height	Read or set the vertical size of this control
hWnd	Retrieve a handle to the control's window
Index	Create a control array
Left	Read or set the horizontal position of the control within the form
Max	Read or set the maximum counter value of the progress bar
Min	Read or set the minimum counter value of the progress bar
MouseIcon	Specify a custom mouse pointer
MousePointer	Specify the type of mouse pointer that will be shown within this control
Name	Specify the name of the control
Negotiate	Determine whether this control, when aligned, will be displayed when another object displays a toolbar
Object	Retrieve an object reference for this control
Parent	Find the parent object of this control
TabIndex	Adjust the tab order for this control
Tag	Store additional data about this control
Top	Read or set the vertical positioning of this control
Value	Read or set the current counter value of the progress bar
Visible	Determine whether or not the control is visible on the form
WhatsThisHelpID	Specify the ID to use for the What's This help system
Width	Read or set the horizontal size of this control

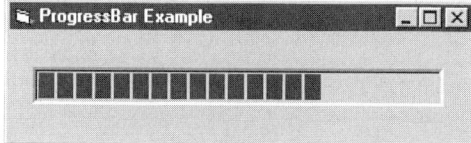

Figure 90-3   ProgressBar

Table 90-38 Events of the ProgressBar control

Use This Event...	To Do This...
Click	Detect when this control is clicked with the mouse
DragDrop	Detect when a drag or drop has occurred
DragOver	Detect when an object is dragged over this control
MouseDown	Detect when one of the mouse buttons has been pressed
MouseMove	Process mouse movements
MouseUp	Detect when one of the mouse buttons has been released

Table 90-39 Methods of the ProgressBar control

Use This Method...	To Do This...
Drag	Begin, end, or cancel a drag operation
Move	Move or resize the control
ShowWhatsThis	Display a specified Help topic using a What's This pop-up
ZOrder	Adjust the front-to-back ordering of this control

Description   The ProgressBar control shows the progress of an operation toward completion by displaying the current counter value (Value property) within the specified range (Min property and Max property). The size of the chunks used to fill the progress bar is determined automatically and is affected by the Width, Height, and BorderStyle properties.

The Align property can be used to attach the ProgressBar control to the top or bottom of the form. If the control is attached to the top or bottom of the form, it will be automatically resized when the form is resized. Table 90-40 contains the values that can be used with the ProgressBar's Align property.

Table 90-40 Values of the ProgressBar control's Align property

Value	Description
0	(Default) Location and size can be set at design time or runtime
1	Progress bar is at the top of the form, and its width is equal to the form's ScaleWidth property
2	Progress bar is at the bottom of the form, and its width is equal to the form's ScaleWidth property
3	Progress bar is at the left of the form, and its height is equal to the form's ScaleHeight property
4	Progress bar is at the right of the form, and its height is equal to the form's ScaleHeight property

SLIDER CONTROL

Purpose
You can use the Slider control to simulate a slider with optional tick marks. Figure 90-4 shows a Slider control on a form.

Properties, Events, Methods, and Constant Values
Tables 90-41, 90-42, and 90-43 list the properties, events, and methods that relate to the Slider control. Tables 90-44 and 90-45 list constant values associated with this control.

Table 90-41 Properties of the Slider control

Use This Property...	To Do This...
BorderStyle	Determine the style of border that this control will have
Container	Read or set the container for this control within the form
DragIcon	Specify the icon to use for drag-and-drop
DragMode	Set the mode to use for drag-and-drop
Enabled	Determine whether this control is operational within the form
Height	Read or set the vertical size of this control
HelpContextID	Associate a context number that is used for context-sensitive help with this control
hWnd	Retrieve a handle to the control's window
Index	Create a control array

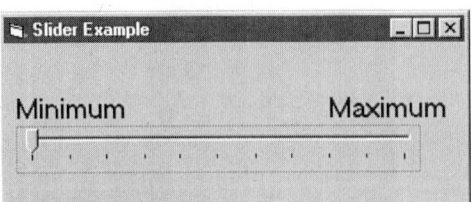

Figure 90-4 Slider control

Use This Property...	To Do This...
LargeChange	Determine the number of ticks the slider will move when the user presses PAGEUP or PAGEDOWN or clicks the mouse on either side of the current slider position
Left	Read or set the horizontal position of the control within the form
Max	Read or set the value of the last tick position
Min	Read or set the value of the first tick position
MouseIcon	Specify a custom mouse pointer
MousePointer	Specify the type of mouse pointer that will be shown within this control
Name	Specify the name of the control
Orientation	Determine whether the slider is displayed horizontally or vertically
Parent	Find the parent object of this control
SelectRange	Determine whether the slider can have a selected range
SelLength	Read or set the length of the slider's selected range
SelStart	Read or set the starting position of the slider's selected range
SmallChange	Determine the number of ticks the slider will move when the user presses ⬅ or ➡
TabIndex	Adjust the tab order for this control
TabStop	Determine whether this control can be reached by pressing T
Tag	Store additional data about this control
TickFrequency	Determine the number of tick marks displayed on the control (relative to the range)
TickStyle	Determine the positioning of the tick marks on the control
Top	Read or set the vertical positioning of this control
Value	Read or set the current value of the slider
Visible	Determine whether or not the control is visible on the form
WhatsThisHelpID	Associate a context number used for context-sensitive What's This help
Width	Read or set the horizontal size of this control

Table 90-42 Events of the Slider control

Use This Event...	To Do This...
Change	Detect when the slider has been moved
Click	Detect when this control is clicked with the mouse
DblClick	Detect when this control is double-clicked with the mouse
DragDrop	Detect when a drag or drop has occurred
DragOver	Detect when an object is dragged over this control
GotFocus	Detect when this control receives the application focus
KeyDown	Detect when a key is pressed
KeyPress	Process a keystroke
KeyUp	Detect when a key is released
LostFocus	Detect when this control loses the application focus

continued on next page

continued from previous page

Use This Event...	To Do This...
MouseDown	Detect when one of the mouse buttons has been pressed
MouseMove	Process mouse movements
MouseUp	Detect when one of the mouse buttons has been released
Scroll	Continuously manipulate other controls based on changes in the Slider control

Table 90-43 Methods of the Slider control

Use This Method...	To Do This...
ClearSel	Clear the current slider selection
Drag	Begin, end, or cancel a drag operation
GetNumTicks	Get the number of ticks in the slider range
Move	Move or resize the control
Refresh	Force a repaint of the control
SetFocus	Give the application focus to this control
ShowWhatsThis	Display a specified Help topic using a What's This pop-up
ZOrder	Adjust the front-to-back ordering of this control

Table 90-44 Orientation constants of the Slider control

Constant	ComctlLib.OrientationConstants	Description
0	sldHorizontal	Horizontal orientation
1	sldVertical	Vertical orientation

Table 90-45 Tick style constants of the Slider control

Constant	ComctlLib.TickStyleConstants	Description
0	sldBottomRight	Tick marks are positioned along the bottom or right side of the slider depending on the slider orientation
1	sldTopLeft	Tick marks are positioned along the top or left side of the slider depending on the slider orientation
2	sldBoth	Tick marks are positioned on both sides or top and bottom of the slider
3	sldNoTicks	No tick marks appear on the slider

Description	The Slider control allows the user to drag a graphical slider along a specified number of tick marks. This control is handy when a limited number of ordinal values can be selected by a user (a number from 1 to 10, for example). You specify the number of tick marks by setting the TickFrequency property, Min property, and Max property. The Min and Max properties adjust the acceptable range of values that the slider can have (via the Value property), and the TickFrequency specifies how far apart each tick mark will appear.

STATUSBAR CONTROL

Purpose	Use the StatusBar control to display information to your user (such as current application settings). Figure 90-5 shows the StatusBar control at the bottom of a form.
Properties, Events, Methods, and Constant Values	Tables 90-46, 90-47, and 90-48 list the properties, events, and methods that relate to the StatusBar control. Tables 90-49 through 90-53 list constant values associated with this control.

Table 90-46 Properties of the StatusBar control

Use This Property...	To Do This...
Align	Read or set a value that determines whether the control is attached to one of the form edges
Container	Read or set the container for this control within the form
DragIcon	Specify the icon to use for drag-and-drop
DragMode	Set the mode to use for drag-and-drop
Enabled	Determine whether this control is operational within the form
Font	Access the Font object associated with this control
Height	Read or set the vertical size of this control
hWnd	Retrieve a handle to the control's window
Index	Create a control array
Left	Read or set the horizontal position of the control within the form
MouseIcon	Specify a custom mouse pointer
MousePointer	Specify the type of mouse pointer that will be shown within this control
Name	Specify the name of the control
Negotiate	Determine whether this control, when aligned, will be displayed when another object displays a toolbar
Panels	Access the collection of Panel objects used by this control
Parent	Find the parent object of this control
SimpleText	Read or set the text of the status bar when the style of the control is simple
Style	Determine whether the status bar style is normal or simple
Tag	Store additional data about this control
Top	Read or set the vertical positioning of this control

continued on next page

continued from previous page

Use This Property...	To Do This...
Visible	Determine whether or not the control is visible on the form
WhatsThisHelpID	Associate a context number used for context-sensitive What's This help
Width	Read or set the horizontal size of this control

Table 90-47 Events of the StatusBar control

Use This Event...	To Do This...
Click	Detect when this control is clicked with the mouse
DblClick	Detect when this control is double-clicked with the mouse
DragDrop	Detect when a drag or drop has occurred
DragOver	Detect when an object is dragged over this control
MouseDown	Detect when one of the mouse buttons has been pressed
MouseMove	Process mouse movements
MouseUp	Detect when one of the mouse buttons has been released
PanelClick	Detect when one of the panels on the status bar has been clicked
PanelDblClick	Detect when one of the panels on the status bar has been double-clicked
Move	Move or resize the control
Refresh	Force a repaint of the control

Table 90-48 Methods of the StatusBar control

Use This Method...	To Do This...
ShowWhatsThis	Display a specified Help topic using a What's This pop-up
ZOrder	Adjust the front-to-back ordering of this control

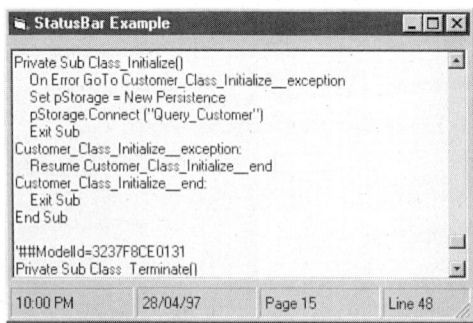

Figure 90-5   StatusBar control

Table 90-49 Style constants of the StatusBar control

Constant	ComctlLib.SbarStyleConstants	Description
0	sbrNormal	Divide the status bar into panels
1	sbrSimple	Display only one large text panel on the status bar

Table 90-50 Panel alignment constants of the StatusBar control

Constant	ComctlLib.PanelAlignmentConstants	Description
0	sbrLeft	Text to left
1	sbrCenter	Text centered
2	sbrRight	Text to right

Table 90-51 Panel autosize constants of the StatusBar control

Constant	ComctlLib.PanelAutoSizeConstants	Description
0	sbrNoAutoSize	Do not autosize panels
1	sbrSpring	Any extra space is divided among panels
2	sbrContents	Fit the panel to its contents

Table 90-52 Panel bevel constants of the StatusBar control

Constant	ComctlLib.PanelBevelConstants	Description
0	sbrNoBevel	No bevel
1	sbrInset	Bevel inset
2	sbrRaised	Bevel raised

Table 90-53 Panel style constants of the StatusBar control

Constant	ComctlLib.PanelStyleConstants	Description
0	sbrText	Display text and/or bitmap
1	sbrCaps	Display Caps Lock status
2	sbrNum	Display Number Lock status
3	sbrIns	Display Insert key status

continued on next page

continued from previous page

Constant	ComctlLib.PanelStyleConstants	Description
4	sbrScrl	Display Scroll Lock status
5	sbrTime	Display time in System format
6	sbrDate	Display date in System format

Description

The StatusBar control is useful for constantly displaying data to the user. This would be useful, for instance, for displaying the current row and column position in a word processor application. You set the Align property to determine whether the StatusBar control is attached to one of the container form's edges. If the StatusBar control is attached to the edge of a form, it will automatically be resized when the form is resized. To determine how each panel within the status bar will be sized, use the Autosize property of the appropriate Panel object. (Use the Panels property to access the collection of Panel objects associated with this control.)

TAB OBJECT

Purpose

You can use the Tab object to read or set information about a specific tab within a Tabs collection. Each tab will generally have text and an optional picture associated with it.

Properties

Table 90-54 lists the properties that relate to the Tab object.

Table 90-54 Properties of the Tab object

Use This Property...	To Do This...
Caption	Read or set the text caption of a tab
Height	Read or set the vertical size of this control
Image	Associate an image with this Tab object
Index	Create a control array
Key	Read or set a string that is used to identify this object in a collection
Left	Read or set the horizontal position of the control within the form
Selected	Determine whether a specified ListItem is selected
Tag	Store additional data about this control
ToolTipText	Associate ToolTip help text with this tab
Top	Read or set the vertical positioning of this control
Width	Read or set the horizontal size of this control

Description

Use the Tab object to specify a text caption and an optional picture (using the Text property and the Picture property, respectively) for a file folder-type tab in a TabStrip control. Each TabStrip control will generally have a Tabs collection (of Tab objects) associated with it.

TABS COLLECTION

Purpose	Use the Tabs collection to define a collection of Tab objects that will be used with a TabStrip control.
Property and Methods	Tables 90-55 and 90-56 list the property and methods that relate to the Tabs collection.

Table 90-55 Property of the Tabs collection

Use This Property...	To Do This...
Count	Find out how many ColumnHeader objects are in the collection

Table 90-56 Methods of the Tabs collection

Use This Method...	To Do This...
Add	Add a ColumnHeader object to the collection
Clear	Clear all ColumnHeader objects in the collection (remove them from the collection)
Item	Access a specific ColumnHeader object in the collection
Remove	Remove a ColumnHeader object from the collection

Description	The Tabs collection is a collection of Tab objects. You will generally maintain one Tabs collection for each TabStrip control in your application. You can access each Tab object in the collection using a For Each...Next loop.

TABSTRIP CONTROL

Purpose	You can use the TabStip control to create the effect of file folder tabs on your forms. When the user clicks each tab, you might choose to display a new set of information or controls. Figure 90-6 shows a sample TabStrip control.
Properties, Events, Methods, and Constant Values	Tables 90-57, 90-58, and 90-59 list the properties, events, and methods that relate to the TabStrip control. Tables 90-60 and 90-61 list constant values associated with this control.

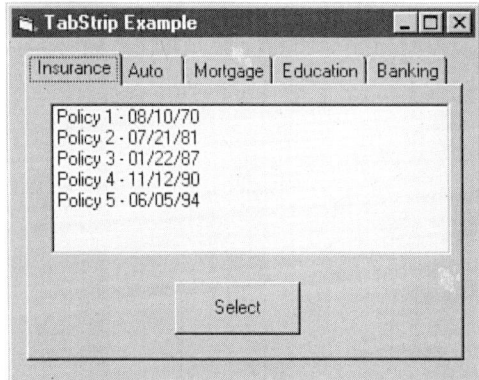

Figure 90-6 TabStrip control

Table 90-57 Properties of the TabStrip control

ClientHeight	Get the height of the display area of the TabStrip control
ClientLeft	Get the horizontal position of the display area of the TabStrip control
ClientTop	Get the vertical position of the display area of the TabStrip control
ClientWidth	Get the width of the display area of the TabStrip control
Container	Read or set the container for this control within the form
DragIcon	Specify the icon to use for drag-and-drop
DragMode	Set the mode to use for drag-and-drop
Enabled	Determine whether this control is operational within the form
Font	Access the Font object associated with this control
Height	Read or set the vertical size of this control
HelpContextID	Associate a context number that is used for context-sensitive help with this control
hWnd	Retrieve a handle to the control's window
ImageList	Read or set the ImageList control that is associated with this control
Index	Create a control array
Left	Read or set the horizontal position of the control within the form
MouseIcon	Specify a custom mouse pointer
MousePointer	Specify the type of mouse pointer that will be shown within this control
MultiRow	Determine whether this control can display more than one row of tabs
Name	Specify the name of the control
Object	Retrieve an object reference for this control
Parent	Find the parent object of this control
SelectedItem	Get a reference to a selected Tab object
ShowTips	Determine whether ToolTips are displayed for the control
Style	Determine whether tabs or buttons are displayed on the control
TabFixedHeight	Determine the fixed height of tabs if the TabWidthStyle property is set to tabFixed
TabFixedWidth	Determine the fixed width of tabs if the TabWidthStyle property is set to tabFixed

Use This Property...	To Do This...
TabIndex	Adjust the tab order for this control
Tabs	Access the collection of Tab objects used in the control
TabStop	Determine whether this control can be reached by pressing ⊤
TabWidthStyle	Determine the justification or width of all tabs in the control
Tag	Store additional data about this control
Top	Read or set the vertical positioning of this control
Visible	Determine whether or not the control is visible on the form
WhatsThisHelpID	Associate a context number used for context-sensitive What's This help
Width	Read or set the horizontal size of this control

Table 90-58 Events of the TabStrip control

Use This Event...	To Do This...
BeforeClick	Perform some actions before the click event is actually generated for this control
Click	Detect when this control is clicked with the mouse
DblClick	Detect when this control is double-clicked with the mouse
DragDrop	Detect when a drag or drop has occurred
DragOver	Detect when an object is dragged over this control
GotFocus	Detect when this control receives the application focus
KeyDown	Detect when a key is pressed
KeyPress	Process a keystroke
KeyUp	Detect when a key is released
LostFocus	Detect when this control loses the application focus
MouseDown	Detect when one of the mouse buttons has been pressed
MouseMove	Process mouse movements
MouseUp	Detect when one of the mouse buttons has been released

Table 90-59 Methods of the TabStrip control

Use This Method...	To Do This...
Drag	Begin, end, or cancel a drag operation
Move	Move or resize the control
Refresh	Force a repaint of the control
SetFocus	Give the application focus to this control
ShowWhatsThis	Display a specified Help topic using a What's This pop-up
ZOrder	Adjust the front-to-back ordering of this control

Table 90-60 Style constants of the Tab control

Constant	ComctlLib.TabStyleConstants	Description
0	tabTabs	Tabs appear as notebook tabs, and the internal area has a 3D border enclosing it
1	tabButtons	Tabs appear as push buttons, and the internal area has no border

Table 90-61 Width style constants of the TabStrip control

Constant	ComctlLib.TabWidthStyleConstants	Description
0	tabJustified	Each row of tabs spans the width of the control
1	tabNonJustified	Multiple rows of tags are jagged
2	tabFixed	The height and width of all tabs are set by the TabFixedHeight and TabFixedWidth properties

Description The TabStrip control allows you to set up tabs that resemble the tabs on file folders. Each tab has an associated Tab object that can be accessed through the Tabs collection. Use the Tabs property of the TabStrip control to get a reference to the associated Tabs collection. The TabStrip control is not a container control, so you cannot place text and controls directly on the TabStrip control and expect them to appear when a certain tab is selected. Instead, you will need to place your text and controls in separate container controls (Picture controls work well) and respond to the Click event of the TabStrip control by bringing the appropriate container control to the front (by setting the ZOrder property).

TOOLBAR CONTROL

Purpose Using the ToolBar control, you can create a toolbar for your applicaton from a set of Button objects. These button choices are generally shortcuts for often-used program operations (such as Open and Save in a word processing application). Figure 90-7 shows a sample ToolBar control.

Properties, Events, Methods, and Constant Values Tables 90-62, 90-63, and 90-64 list the properties, events, and methods that relate to the ToolBar control. Tables 90-65, 90-66, and 90-67 list constant values associated with this control.

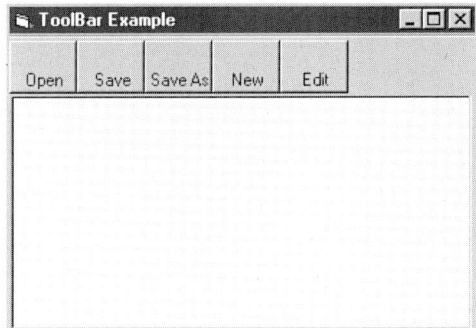

Figure 90-7   ToolBar control

Table 90-62 Properties of the ToolBar control

Use This Property...	To Do This...
Align	Read or set a value that determines whether the control is attached to one of the form edges
AllowCustomize	Determine whether the control can be customized by the end user
BackColor	Read or set the background color of the control
ButtonHeight	Determine the height of the control's buttons
Buttons	Access the collection of Button objects used in the control
ButtonWidth	Determine the width of the control's buttons
Container	Read or set the container for this control within the form
DragIcon	Specify the icon to use for drag-and-drop
DragMode	Set the mode to use for drag-and-drop
Enabled	Determine whether this control is operational within the form
Font	Access the Font object associated with this control
ForeColor	Read or set the foreground color of the control
Height	Read or set the vertical size of this control
HelpContextID	Associate a context number that is used for context-sensitive help with this control
hWnd	Retrieve a handle to the control's window
ImageList	Read or set the ImageList control that is associated with this control
Index	Create a control array
Left	Read or set the horizontal position of the control within the form
MouseIcon	Specify a custom mouse pointer
MousePointer	Specify the type of mouse pointer that will be shown within this control
Name	Specify the name of the control
Negotiate	Determine whether this control, when aligned, will be displayed when another object displays a toolbar

continued on next page

continued from previous page

Use This Property...	To Do This...
Object	Retrieve an object reference for this control
Parent	Find the parent object of this control
ShowTips	Determine whether ToolTips are displayed for the control
TabIndex	Adjust the tab order for this control
Tag	Store additional data about this control
Top	Read or set the vertical positioning of this control
Visible	Determine whether or not the control is visible on the form
WhatsThisHelpID	Associate a context number used for context-sensitive What's This help
Width	Read or set the horizontal size of this control
Wrappable	Determine whether the control buttons will automatically wrap if the window is resized

Table 90-63 Events of the ToolBar control

Use This Event...	To Do This...
ButtonClick	Detect when the user clicks a button on the control
Change	Detect when the user has customized the toolbar
Click	Detect when this control is clicked with the mouse
DblClick	Detect when this control is double-clicked with the mouse
DragDrop	Detect when a drag or drop has occurred
DragOver	Detect when an object is dragged over this control
MouseDown	Detect when one of the mouse buttons has been pressed
MouseMove	Process mouse movements
MouseUp	Detect when one of the mouse buttons has been released

Table 90-64 Methods of the ToolBar control

Use This Method...	To Do This...
Customize	Bring up the Customize ToolBar dialog box
Drag	Begin, end, or cancel a drag operation
Move	Move or resize the control
Refresh	Force a repaint of the control
RestoreToolbar	Restore the state of the toolbar from the system registry
SaveToolbar	Save the state of the toolbar to the system registry
ShowWhatsThis	Display a specified Help topic using a What's This pop-up
ZOrder	Adjust the front-to-back ordering of this control

Table 90-65 Style constants of the ToolBar control

Constant	ComctlLib.TbarStyleConstants	Description
0	tbrDefault	The button is a regular push button
1	tbrCheck	The button is a check button
2	tbrButtonGroup	The button remains pressed until another button in the group is pressed (exactly one button in the group is pressed at any time)
3	tbrCheckGroup	The button stays checked until it is pressed again, or another button in the group is pressed (at most one button is pressed)
4	tbrSeparator	The button acts as a separator with a fixed width of 8 pixels
5	tbrPlaceholder	The button is like a separator in appearance and functionality but has an adjustable width

Table 90-66 Value constants of the ToolBar control

Constant	ComctlLib.ValueConstants	Description
0	tbrUnpressed	The button is not currently pressed or checked
1	tbrPressed	The button is currently pressed or checked

Table 90-67 Mixed state constant of the ToolBar control

Constant	ComctlLib.MixedStateConstants	Description
0	tbrUnpressed	The button is not currently pressed or checked

Description   A ToolBar control can provide convenient access to a series of menu options that are used most often. Good candidates for menu options that may warrant a ToolBar button are generally Open, Save, Save As, and so on. Many times, the user has the choice of selecting from a pulldown menu (such as File|Open) or using the toolbar. Each button on the toolbar has an associated Button object, which can be used to read or set the properties for that individual button. Use the AllowCustomize property to determine whether the user will be allowed to customize the toolbar at runtime (by rearranging the button order within the toolbar, for example).

TreeView Control

Purpose   Use the TreeView control to display a hierarchical view of Node objects. Each of these Node objects consists of a label and optional bitmap. An example of a TreeView type of structure can be found in the Windows Explorer application as it displays the hierarchical view of drives and directories. Figure 90-8 shows a sample TreeView control.

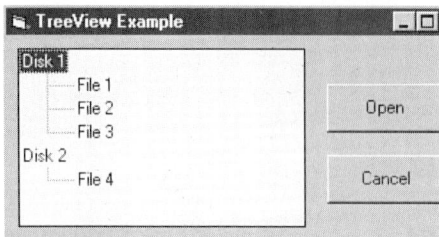

Figure 90-8 TreeView control

Properties, Events, Methods, and Constant Values Tables 90-68, 90-69, and 90-70 list the properties, events, and methods that relate to the TreeView control. Tables 90-71 through 90-74 list constant values associated with this control.

Table 90-68 Properties of the TreeView control

Use This Property...	To Do This...
BorderStyle	Determine the style of border that this control will have
Container	Read or set the container for this control within the form
DragIcon	Specify the icon to use for drag-and-drop
DragMode	Set the mode to use for drag-and-drop
DropHighlight	Determine the Node object that is highlighted with the system color
Enabled	Determine whether this control is operational within the form
Font	Access the Font object associated with this control
Height	Read or set the vertical size of this control
HelpContextID	Associate a context number that is used for context-sensitive help with this control
HideSelection	Determine whether selected nodes remain highlighted when the control loses focus
hWnd	Retrieve a handle to the control's window
ImageList	Read or set the ImageList control that is associated with this control
Indentation	Determine the amount by which each new child Node object will be indented
Index	Create a control array
LabelEdit	Determine whether the user can edit the labels of the Node objects in the control
Left	Read or set the horizontal position of the control within the form
LineStyle	Determine the style of the lines displayed between Node objects in the control
MouseIcon	Specify a custom mouse pointer
MousePointer	Specify the type of mouse pointer that will be shown within this control
Name	Specify the name of the control

Use This Property...	To Do This...
Nodes	Access the collection of Node objects used by the control
Object	Retrieve an object reference for this control
Parent	Retrieve the form on which the control is located
Parent	Find the parent object of this control
PathSeparator	Determine the delimiter string used for the path returned by the FullPath property
Scrollbars	Determine whether scrollbars are displayed in this control
SelectedItem	Get a reference to a selected Node object
Sorted	Determine whether the child nodes of each Node object are sorted alphabetically
Style	Determine the type of images, text, and lines that appear for each Node object
TabIndex	Adjust the tab order for this control
TabStop	Determine whether this control can be reached by pressing T
Tag	Store additional data about this control
Top	Read or set the vertical positioning of this control
Visible	Determine whether or not the control is visible on the form
WhatsThisHelpID	Associate a context number used for context-sensitive What's This help
Width	Read or set the horizontal size of this control

Table 90-69 Events of the TreeView control

Use This Event...	To Do This...
AfterLabelEdit	Do something after the user edits the currently selected Node object
BeforeLabelEdit	Do something before the user edits the currently selected Node object
Click	Detect when this control is clicked with the mouse
Collapse	Detect when any Node object in the control is collapsed
DblClick	Detect when this control is double-clicked with the mouse
DragDrop	Detect when a drag or drop has occurred
DragOver	Detect when an object is dragged over this control
Expand	Detect when any Node object in the control is expanded
GotFocus	Detect when this control receives the application focus
KeyDown	Detect when a key is pressed
KeyPress	Process a keystroke
KeyUp	Detect when a key is released
LostFocus	Detect when this control loses the application focus
MouseDown	Detect when one of the mouse buttons has been pressed
MouseMove	Process mouse movements
MouseUp	Detect when one of the mouse buttons has been released
NodeClick	Detect when the user clicks any of the Node objects in the control

Table 90-70 Methods of the TreeView control

Use This Method...	To Do This...
Clear	Clear all Node objects from the Nodes collection for this control
GetVisibleCount	Get the number of Node objects that fit in the display area of the control
HitTest	Determine the ListItem object located at specified x and y coordinates
Move	Move or resize the control
Refresh	Force a repaint of the control
Remove	Remove a single Node object from the Nodes collection for this control
SetFocus	Give the application focus to this control
ShowWhatsThis	Display a specified Help topic using a What's This pop-up
StartLabelEdit	Allow the user to edit the label of a Node object in the control
ZOrder	Adjust the front-to-back ordering of this control

Table 90-71 TreeView line style constants

Constant	ComctlLib.TreeLineStyleConstants	Description
0	tvwTreeLines	Show treelines
1	tvwRootLines	Show rootlines with treelines

Table 90-72 Relationship constants of the TreeView control

Constant	ComctlLib.TreeRelationshipConstants	Description
0	tvwFirst	First sibling
1	tvwLast	Last sibling
2	tvwNext	Next sibling
3	tvwPrevious	Previous sibling
4	tvwChild	Child

Table 90-73 Style constants of the TreeView control

Constant	ComctlLib.TreeStyleConstants	Description
0	tvwTextOnly	Text only
1	tvwPictureText	Picture and text
2	tvwPlusMinusText	Plus/minus and text
3	tvwPlusPictureText	Plus/minus, picture, and text
4	tvwTreelinesText	Treelines and text

Constant	ComctlLib.TreeStyleConstants	Description
5	tvwTreelinesPictureText	Treelines, picture, and text
6	tvwTreelinesPlusMinusText	Treelines, plus/minus, and text
7	tvwTreelinesPlusMinusPictureText	Treelines, plus/minus, picture, and text

Table 90-74 Label edit constants of the TreeView control

Constant	ComctlLib.LabelEditConstants	Description
0	tvwAutomatic	Label editing is automatic
1	tvwManual	Label editing must be invoked manually

Description   Use the TreeView control to display a hierarchical view of information, such as the file and directory structure displayed in the Windows Explorer. Each item of information in a TreeView control has an associated Node object that can be used to read or set information about that item (such as the text and picture associated with the item). The Sorted property determines whether the child nodes of each parent node will be sorted. The Indentation property determines the amount that the child nodes will be indented from their parent nodes when displayed, and the LineStyle property determines the type of line used to connect the nodes.

Interface Project

This project demonstrates many of the interface controls discussed in this chapter. Two controls that were excluded were the TreeView and ListView controls, but using the techniques demonstrated with the other new common interface controls, objects, and collections, you should be able to implement these on your own.

Assembling the Project

1. Place the following controls on a form, as detailed in Table 90-75. Figure 90-9 shows what the completed form should look like.

Table 90-75 Elements of frmMain ;frmMain form;Interface project

Control	Property	Value
Form	Name	frmMain
	Caption	"Interface Project"
Toolbar	Name	tlbMainBar
	(buttons as described in Table 90-76)	
RichTextBox	Name	RichTextBox1
	ScrollBars	3 - Both

continued on next page

continued from previous page

Control	Property	Value
Timer	Name	tmrStopWatch
	Interval	60000
CommonDialog	Name	CommonDialog1

Table 90-76 describes the buttons of the ToolBar control.

Table 90-76 Buttons of the ToolBar control

Property	Value
Index	1
Caption	"Font"
ToolTip Text	"Change the selected text font"
Index	2
Caption	"Style"
ToolTip Text	"Change the selected text style"
Index	3
Caption	"Size"
ToolTipText	"Change the selected text size"

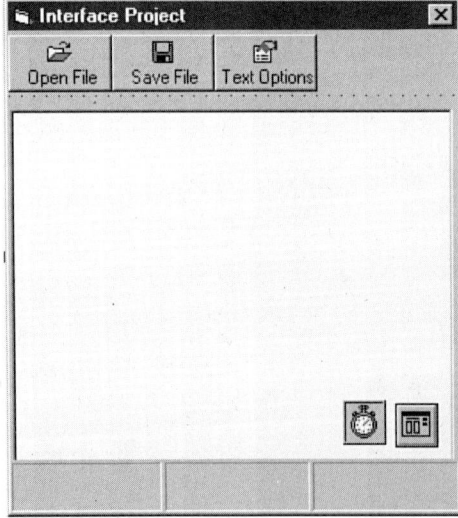

Figure 90-9   frmMain in Design mode

2. Enter the following code into the Declarations section of frmMain. This code informs Visual Basic that we will be required to declare all variables.

```
Option Explicit
```

3. Enter the following code into the Form_Load procedure. This code calls the Timer routine, which will display the current date and time in the status bar.

```
Private Sub Form_Load()
    ' Call the timer routine to print the date and time.
    Call tmrStopWatch_Timer
End Sub
```

4. Enter the following code into the tmrStopWatch_Timer procedure. This code will display the current date and time in the status bar.

```
Private Sub tmrStopWatch_Timer()
    Dim strNow As String
    Dim i As Integer

    ' Place the date in the StatusBar.
    staBottom.Panels(1).Text = Date

    ' Place the time in the StatusBar.
    strNow = Time
    i = InStr(strNow, ":")
    i = InStr(i + 1, strNow, ":")
    staBottom.Panels(2).Text = Left(strNow, i - 1)
End Sub
```

5. Enter the following code into the TlbMainBar_ButtonClick procedure. This code will open a file, save a file, or format some selected text, depending on which toolbar button was clicked.

```
Private Sub tlbMainBar_ButtonClick(ByVal Button As Button)

    ' See which Toolbar button was clicked.
    Select Case Button.Key
    Case "Open"
        ' Show the common dialog to open a file.
        CommonDialog1.ShowOpen

        ' If no file was selected, then do not process.
        If CommonDialog1.filename = "" Then Exit Sub

        ' Title the dialog.
        frmProgress.Caption = "Loading..."

        ' Bring up the form as a modal dialog.
        frmProgress.Show vbModal

        ' Load the file into the RichTextBox.
        rtfeditor.LoadFile CommonDialog1.filename

        ' Place the file name in the StatusBar.
        staBottom.Panels(3).Text = CommonDialog1.filename
```

continued on next page

continued from previous page

```
    Case "Save"
        ' Prepare to trap Cancel in Save dialog.
        CommonDialog1.CancelError = True
        On Error GoTo ButtonClick_EH

        ' Show the common dialog to save a file.
        CommonDialog1.ShowSave

        ' UnDo trap of Cancel in Save dialog.
        CommonDialog1.CancelError = False
        On Error GoTo 0

        ' If no file was selected, then do not process.
        If CommonDialog1.filename = "" Then Exit Sub

        ' Title the dialog.
        frmProgress.Caption = "Saving..."

        ' Bring up the form as a modal dialog.
        frmProgress.Show vbModal

        ' Save the text from the RichTextBox.
        rtfeditor.SaveFile CommonDialog1.filename, rtfRTF
    Case "Text"
        ' If no text is selected, then do not process.
        If rtfeditor.SelLength = 0 Then
            Beep
            MsgBox "No text selected.", vbExclamation, "Error"
        Else
            ' Otherwise, bring up the text options dialog form
            ' as a modal dialog.
            frmTextOptions.Show vbModal
        End If
    End Select
Exit Sub

ButtonClick_EH:
    If Err.Number = cdlCancel Then
        Exit Sub
    Else
        Err.Raise Err.Number
    End If
End Sub
```

6. Insert a new form to display the TabStrip control that allows the user to format the selected text in the RichTextBox control. Table 90-77 details the components of the form. When placing these components on the form, make sure you place the three option buttons in one of the PictureBox controls, the list box on another PictureBox control, and the slider and label on the third PictureBox control. Remember, the TabStrip control is not a container, so it cannot contain other controls. Instead, we use PictureBox controls as containers and bring the appropriate PictureBox to the front when a tab is clicked. Size and position the elements as illustrated in Figure 90-10.

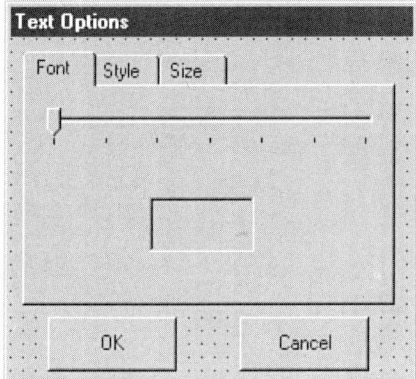

Figure 90-10   frmTextOptions in
Design mode

Table 90-77 Elements of frmTextOptions

Control	Property	Value
Form	Name	frmTextOptions
	Caption	"Text Options"
	ControlBox	False
	MaxButton	False
	MinButton	False
CommandButton	Name	cmdOk
	Caption	"OK"
CommandButton	Name	cmdCancel
	Caption	"Cancel"
Label	Name	lblSize
	Caption	""
	BorderStyle	1 - Fixed Single
ListBox	Name	List1
OptionButton	Name	optFontStyle
	Index	0
	Caption	"Normal"
OptionButton	Name	optFontStyle
	Index	1
	Caption	"Italics"
OptionButton	Name	optFontStyle
	Index	2
	Caption	"Bold"
PictureBox	Name	Picture1
	Index	0

continued on next page

continued from previous page

Control	Property	Value
PictureBox	Name	Picture1
	Index	1
PictureBox	Name	Picture1
	Index	2
Slider	Name	Slider1
	LargeChange	1
	Max	6
TabStrip	Name	TabStrip1

7. Enter the following code into the cmdOk_Click procedure. This code will set the font, style, and size of the selected text in the RichTextBox control when the user clicks the OK button.

```
Private Sub cmdOk_Click()

    ' Set the style of the selected text.
    If optFontStyle(0).Value = True Then
        frmMain.rtfeditor.SelBold = False
        frmMain.rtfeditor.SelItalic = False
    ElseIf optFontStyle(1).Value = True Then
        frmMain.rtfeditor.SelBold = False
        frmMain.rtfeditor.SelItalic = True
    ElseIf optFontStyle(2).Value = True Then
        frmMain.rtfeditor.SelBold = True
        frmMain.rtfeditor.SelItalic = False
    End If

    ' If a valid size has been selected, then set
    ' the font size of the selected text.
    If lblSize.Caption <> "" Then
        frmMain.rtfeditor.SelFontSize = Val(lblSize.Caption)
    End If

    Unload Me

End Sub
```

8. Enter the following code into the cmdCancel_Click procedure. This code will simply close (unload) the form when the user clicks Cancel. Any changes to the selected text font, style, or size will not be applied.

```
Private Sub cmdCancel_Click()

    Unload Me

End Sub
```

9. Enter the following code into the Form_Load procedure. This code will ensure that the initial tab's information is displayed first. It will also attempt to set the information for the font, style, and size based on the currently selected text.

```
Private Sub Form_Load()

    ' Make sure the initial tab's information is displayed.
    Picture1(0).ZOrder 0

    ' If a valid font size exists for the selected text then
    ' place this value in the appropriate size box.
    If frmMain!rtfEditor.SelFontSize <> Null Then
        lblSize.Caption = Format(Int(frmMain.rtfeditor.SelFontSize))
        Slider1.Value = (Int(frmMain.rtfeditor.SelFontSize) - 8) \ 2
    End If

    ' Set the correct option button depending on
    ' the style of the currently selected text.
    If frmMain.rtfEditor.SelItalic = True Then
        optFontStyle(1).Value = True
    ElseIf frmMain.rtfeditor.SelBold = True Then
        optFontStyle(2).Value = True
    Else
        optFontStyle(0).Value = True
    End If

End Sub
```

10. Enter the following code into the Slider1_Change procedure. This code will change the text in the text size label when the user moves the Slider control.

```
Private Sub Slider1_Change()

    ' When the slider is moved, adjust the size that
    ' is displayed as a label.
    lblSize.Caption = Format(8 + 2 * Slider1.Value)

End Sub
```

11. Enter the following code into the TabStrip1_Click procedure. This code will bring the appropriate set of controls and information to the front depending on which tab was clicked.

```
Private Sub TabStrip1_Click()

    ' When a tab is clicked, display the appropriate
    ' picture box of information and controls.
    Picture1(TabStrip1.SelectedItem.Index - 1).ZOrder 0

End Sub
```

12. Insert a new form to display the ProgressBar control that is displayed (only for illustration purposes) when a file is opened or saved. Table 90-78 details the components of the form. Size and position the elements as illustrated in Figure 90-11.

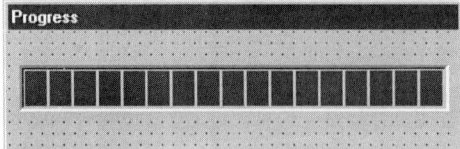

Figure 90-11   frmProgress in Design mode

Table 90-78 Elements of frmProgress

Control	Property	Value
Form	Name	frmProgress
	Caption	"Progress"
	ControlBox	False
	MaxButton	False
	MinButton	False
ProgressBar	Name	prgFeedback
	Max	300

13. Enter the following code into the Form_Activate procedure. This code will display a progress bar that does nothing except illustrate what a ProgressBar control looks like in action.

```
Private Sub Form_Activate()

Dim lngCount As Long

    ' Display a progress bar.  (NOTE: This progress
    ' bar is not actually based on the progress of the
    ' file load - it is only for demonstration.)
    For lngCount = 1 To prgFeedback.Max * 10
        prgFeedback.Value = lngCount / 10
        Me.Refresh
    Next lngCount

    Unload Me

End Sub
```

How It Works

The majority of this project is based around the frmMain form, which contains the RichTextBox control used to edit and display text. You can type your own text in the RichTextBox control, select blocks of text, and change the font, size, and style of the selected text. You can also load and save .RTF files. In essence, you have the beginnings of a functional text editor based around the RichTextBox control. Figure 90-12 shows the project in operation.

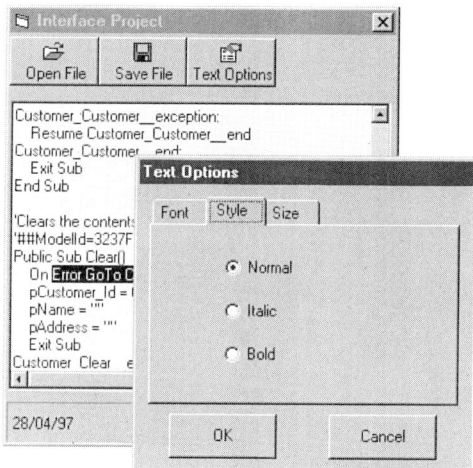

Figure 90-12 The Interface project in action

When one of the Button objects on the toolbar is clicked, we examine the key (which is a string we assigned to the button to identify it). Based on the button that was clicked, we either bring up the File Open common dialog, bring up the File Save common dialog, or bring up our own form that allows us to change the font, style, and size of any selected text. We check the SelLength property of the RichTextBox control to ensure that some text has indeed been selected. Then, we allow the user to change the font, style, or size depending on which tab of the TabStrip control the user selects.

The LoadFile and SaveFile methods of the RichTextBox control are used to load and save the text, respectively. Before loading or saving a file, we bring up a "fake" progress bar, only to demonstrate how the ProgressBar control is used. In order for this progress bar to be truly effective, we would have to be able to detect our position in either the file read or file write and set the Value property of the ProgressBar control accordingly.

Finally, we use a StatusBar control to display certain information to the user, such as the current date and time (updated by the Timer control on frmMain) and the name of the current file (if one is loaded).

If you would like to add to this project, you could start by allowing more flexibility in the formatting of the text. There are many other formatting options supplied by the RichTextBox control that you could add. Add new tabs to the TabStrip control on frmTextOptions so the user can use these new formatting functions. You could also add more buttons to the ToolBar control and write routines to implement the tools that you add.

91

APPLICATION PERFORMANCE EXPLORER

The Application Performance Explorer (APE) is a utility that is included with Visual Basic 5.0 Enterprise Edition. This utility is used to measure the performance of multi-tier client/server applications. It allows the running of "what-if" scenarios of different configuration and network loads. As with most multitier applications, there are multiple client accessing objects on the server. This utility allows the testing of multiple clients accessing the pool of objects that perform the work.

This chapter explains the use and usefulness of the APE utility, but not multitier client server application architecture. This utility was written in Visual Basic 5.0 and the source code can be analyzed to form a foundation for your own client/server applications. The source code of each component can be found on the Visual Basic 5.0 Enterprise Edition CD-ROM in the /samples/entrpris/Ape folder. The binary sections of this utility can be found in the /clisvr directory in the folder where Visual Basic was installed. It is listed as AEMANAGR.EXE.

Asynchronous or Synchronous

In the asynchronous model, the client sends a request for the work to be done to the Queue Manager. The Queue Manager then handles the instancing of the remote object and sends the data back to the Expediter, which then sends it back to the client. The notification of the return of data is usually done by a callback. This allows the client to continue execution instead of waiting for data to return. In this model, the client does not have to wait for the data to return before performing another operation. When the model is set for asynchronous, the APE main screen will appear, as in Figure 91-1.

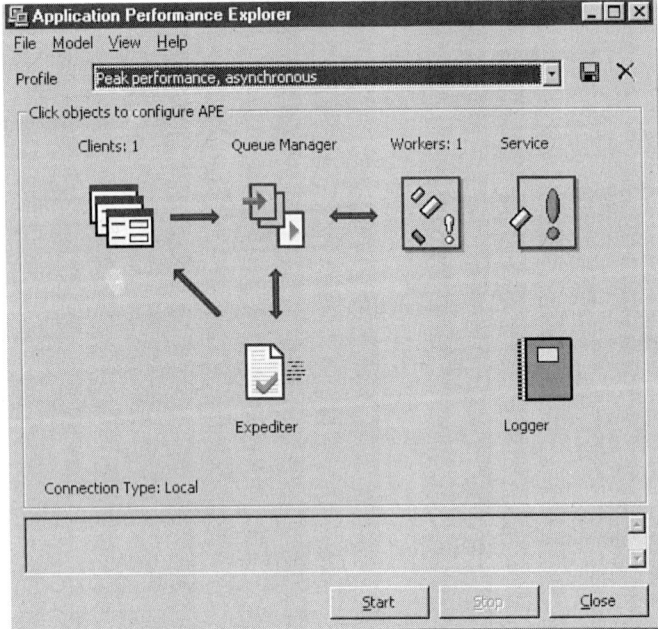

Figure 91-1   The asynchronous screen in APE

In the synchronous model, the client directly instances a remote worker object. The request is sent to the worker, and the client waits for the information to return. The Pool Manager can be used to regulate the number of instances of a class per thread that will be created before creating a new thread. The thread's usage is outlined in the Project Properties dialog box when the remote object was compiled (see Figure 91-2). When the model is set for synchronous, the APE main screen will appear, as in Figure 91-3.

Application Performance Explorer Summary

The following section explains each of the settings that can be set to run your client/server evaluation scenarios. This section explains the visual layout of APE, the tab settings, the menu options, and the configuration differences when running asynchronous or synchronous tests.

APE Screens

The main APE screen has two different layouts, one for the asynchronous model and one for the synchronous model. Each component of the layout is explained in the following section and the configuration options for each component are explained in the tab settings sections.

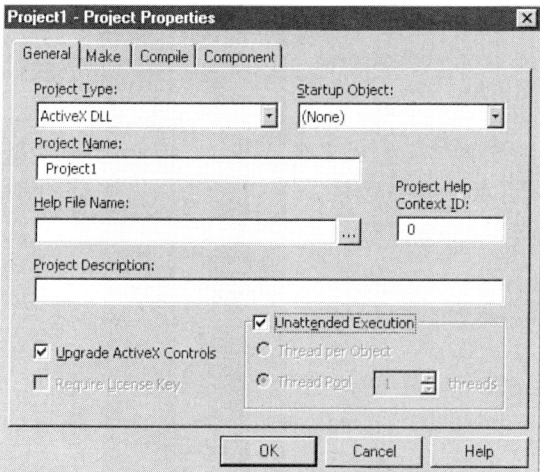

Figure 91-2 Compile options

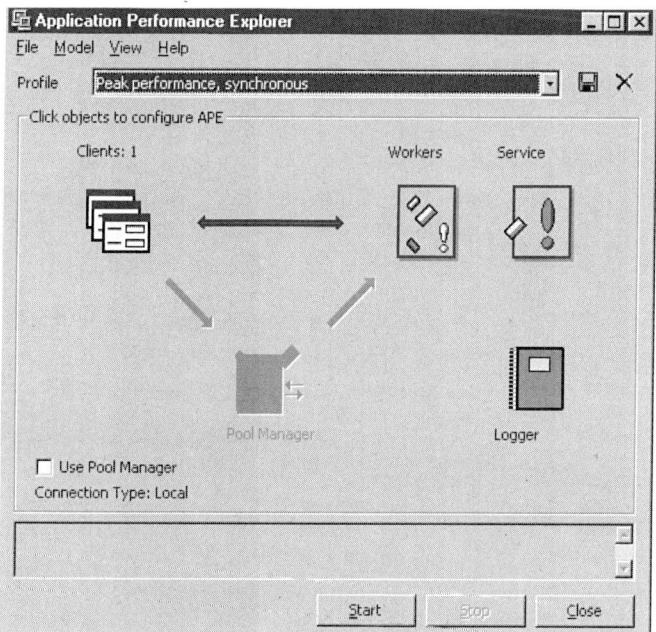

Figure 91-3 The synchronous screen in APE

Clients

This item shows the number of client processes that will be created during the test. This test, for example, could be the number of computers (or the application running on the computer) accessing the Queue Manger requesting some sort of work (calculations, information, and so forth). The item is the same for both the asynchronous and the synchronous models.

Queue Manager

The Queue Manager delegates the instancing of the workers and which worker gets what client request. The Queue Manager also returns the information returned by the worker to the Expediter to be returned to the client. This option is available only with the asynchronous model. (Note that the Queue Manager will not notify the client if all workers are busy; instead, the request will be handed off to the next available worker.)

Expediter

The Expediter returns the information that it receives via the Queue Manager from the worker to the client. The Expediter notifies the client in the form of a callback or by raising the sink event. This option is available only in the asynchronous model.

Workers

Workers are the ActiveX controls or class modules designed to work on the server as remote objects. These objects create the thread and memory space for the Service object to do the actual work. This option is used in both asynchronous and synchronous models.

Service

The Service object is the item that does the work. It can be either a database query or a business rule calculation. This item is used in both asynchronous and synchronous models.

Logger

The Logger option allows the setting of a log file to record the running of the test. This option is available in both asynchronous and synchronous models.

Pool Manager

The Pool Manger manages the threads for the remote object as outlined in the Properties dialog box shown in Figure 91-2. This option is available only in the synchronous model.

Profile Drop-Down

This drop-down shows the configurations saved for this profile.

Application Performance Explorer Option Settings

On certain tabs, the Show Form and Log check boxes appear. These settings are used in the same fashion on each tab.

Show Form

When this option is checked, a form containing statistics for the option will be shown for this configuration.

Log Settings

In the Log option, if the logging is turned on, the information pertaining to this option will be written to a log file.

Client Properties

When the Clients button is pressed, the tab in Figure 91-4 will appear. This tab allows you to determine how the client will request, what the client wants in return, and how many clients will be requesting information. This tab can also be used to configure remote clients to participate in the test.

General Tab

When the General tab is selected, as in Figure 91-4, the following options can be set:

Number of Clients Identifies the number of client processes to be created for this test.

Time Between Calls The amount of time in milliseconds the client will wait between calls to the Queue Manager or directly to a worker, depending upon the model being used.

Number of Calls Identifies the number of calls each client will make during the test.

Remote Clients This option is used to select remote clients to participate in the test. By clicking the Configure button, you can enter the names of additional clients to be used in the test. When using the Remote Client option, you must also enter the number of processes they will generate.

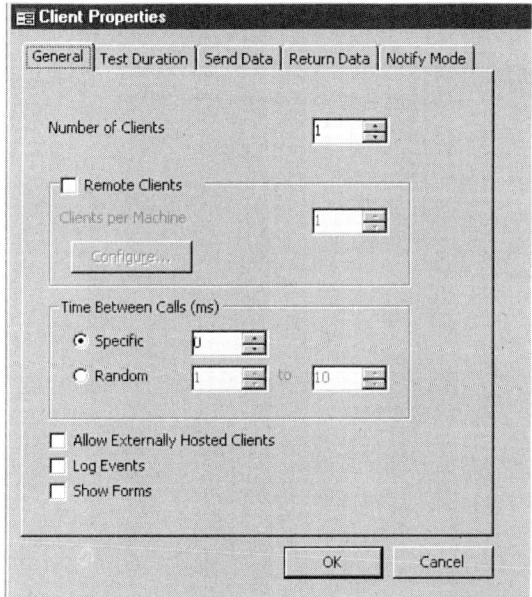

Figure 91-4 Client Properties dialog

Test Duration Tab

The Test Duration tab is used to configure the time scenario to be used in the test, as shown in Figure 91-5.

Continue Until Stopped When this option is selected, the test will continue until the Stop button is pressed.

Test Number of Calls When this option is selected, the test will end after a predefined number of calls have been performed.

Test Number of Minutes When this option is selected, the test will continue for the set number of minutes.

Send Data Tab

The Send Data tab is used to configure what type of information is passed during the test, as shown in Figure 91-6.

Pass Data to Services When this option is checked, the client will pass information to the Service object. If this setting is not checked, the following settings are not applicable. With an asynchronous model, the data is passed to the Queue Manager. With a synchronous model, the data is passed to a worker.

Dataset Type This option is used to identify the type of data to be passed during the test. We recommend that you pass variant data as opposed to collection data. The collection option is there to show how slow passing collection data really is.

Bytes per Row This option is used to determine the amount of data per row that is sent. It can be a fixed amount or a random value per call.

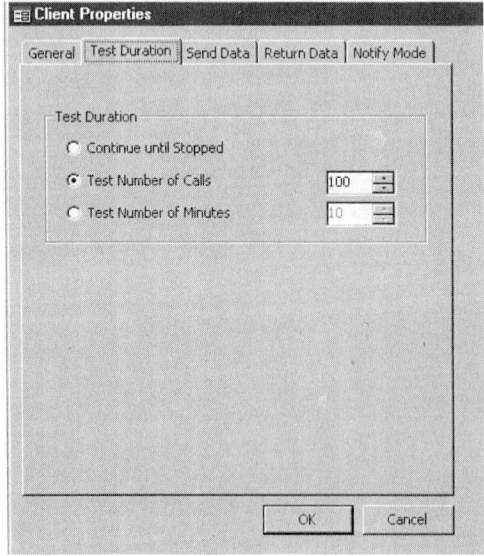

Figure 91-5   Test Duration tab

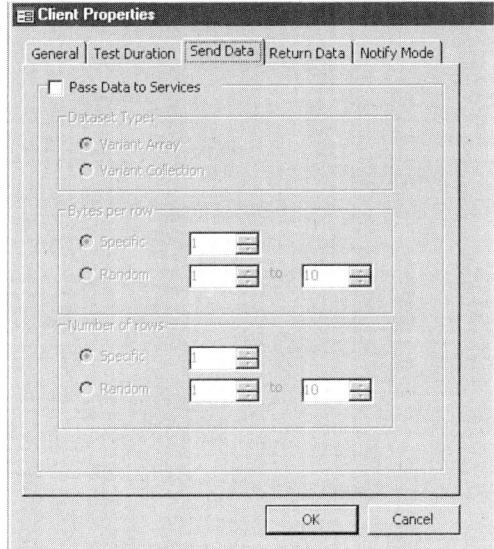

Figure 91-6 Send Data tab

Number of Rows This option is used to determine the number of rows sent. It can be a fixed number or a random value per call.

Return Data Tab

The Return Data tab is used to display the options concerning the type of information that is passed back to the client, as shown in Figure 91-7.

Return Data to Clients When this option is selected, the client will receive the information from the Service object, provided one was selected.

The Dataset Type, Bytes per row, and Number of rows options are the same as on the Send Data tab.

Notify Mode Tab

The Notify Mode tab is used to display the settings that concern how the client is notified of incoming data, as shown in Figure 91-8.

Register Callback Every Service Request When this option is selected, a callback will be generated for each call.

Register Callback Only Once When this option is selected, the client will have the Queue Manager handle the callbacks.

Return Results Using Event Sinking When this option is set, the client will wait until the information is passed back before further application execution.

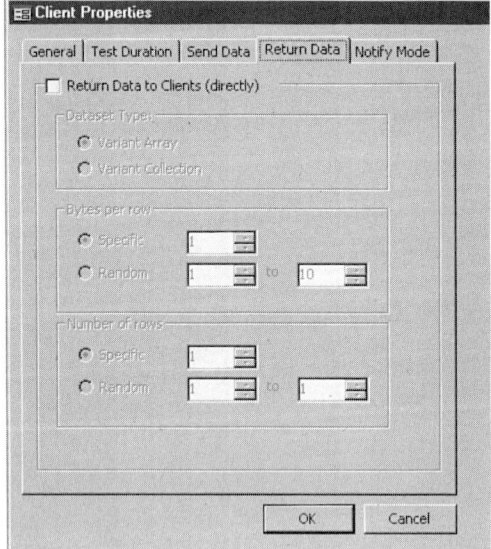

Figure 91-7   Return Data tab

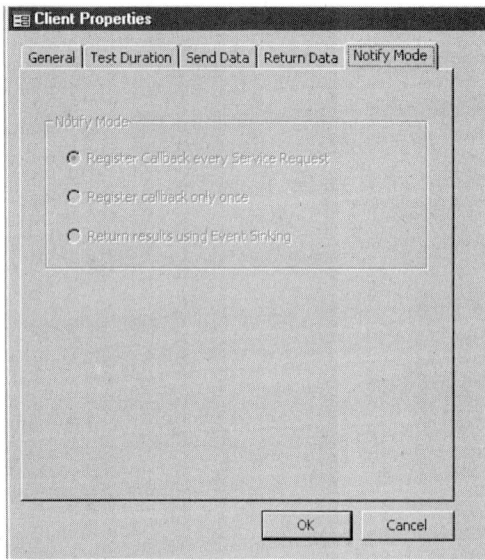

Figure 91-8   Notify Mode tab

Worker Properties

The following options are used to set the Worker option for the test. The General tab is shown in Figure 91-9.

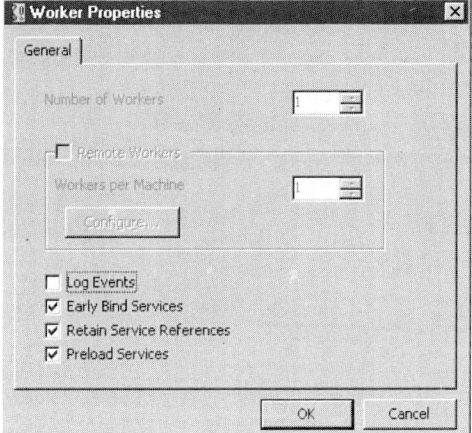

Figure 91-9   General workers options tab

Number of Workers

This option is used to set the maximum number of workers that can be executing on the remote server.

Early Bind Services

This option is used to determine the performance difference between early and late binding.

Retain Service References

When this option is checked, the worker will keep a reference to the Service object and will not have to be reinitiated each time it is used.

Preload Services

When this option is selected, the Worker object will load the Service object before running the test, so that the time needed to load the Service object will not be included in the test results.

Service Properties

These tabs are used to set the options for the Service object.

General Tab

The General tab, as shown in Figure 91-10, is used to set some general properties of the Service object.

Task Duration This option allows setting the amount of time in milliseconds each task will take. The random setting can be selected to generate a random time per call.

Task Properties This option determines whether process cycles are used and, if so, how many. The other possibility is to have the task reading and/or writing to a database.

Custom Service Tab

The Custom Service tab, as shown in Figure 91-11, is used to identify a custom service on the server.

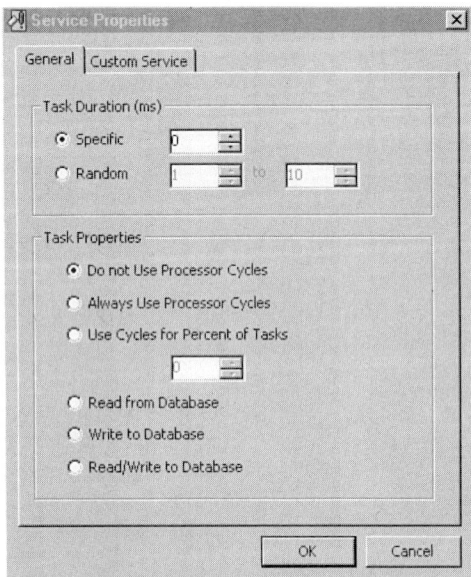

Figure 91-10 The General tab

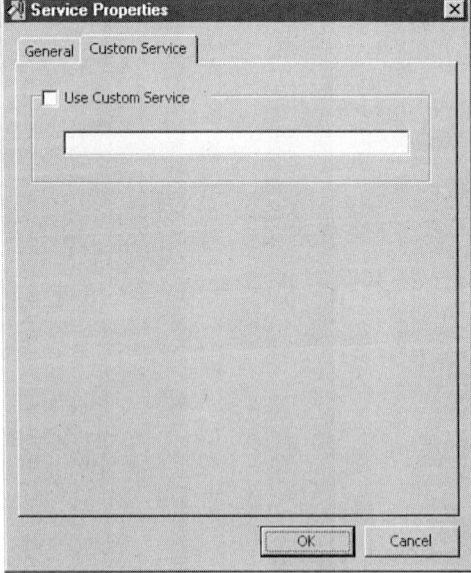

Figure 91-11 Custom Service tab

Logging Properties

If the logging option has been selected, the logging properties are enabled to be selected by the user.

General Tab

The General tab, as shown in Figure 91-12, displays the settings concerning the placement and size of the log.

Log File This option displays the name and location of the log file. When the browse button is clicked, an Open dialog box opens, requesting the name of the log file to be used. When the View button is pressed, Notepad is loaded and the log file is displayed.

Overwrite File When this option is checked, the logger will overwrite the log file each time a test is run. If the check box is clear, the logger will append the contents of each test to the same file.

Write Log File This option is used to determine when to write to the log file, either at the end of the test or when the log memory buffer reaches the specified size.

Connection Properties

This tab is displayed by selecting the View|Connection menu. The tab in Figure 91-13 will be displayed.

This tab is used to set the connection properties of the test. The type of remote communication, protocol, and authentication type can be set. These settings are used if a remote server is specified to be used during the test. Either Use Distributed COM (DCOM) or Use Remote Automation can be selected.

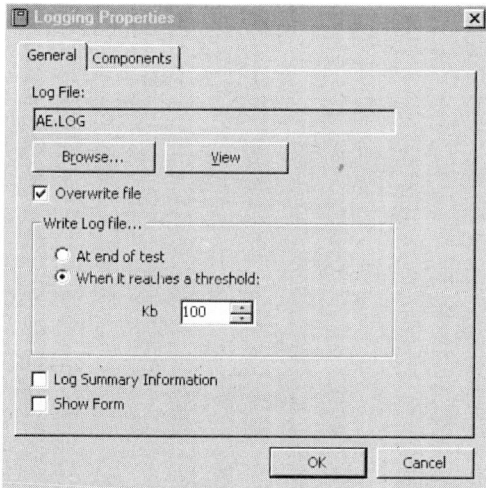

Figure 91-12   Logging Properties dialog

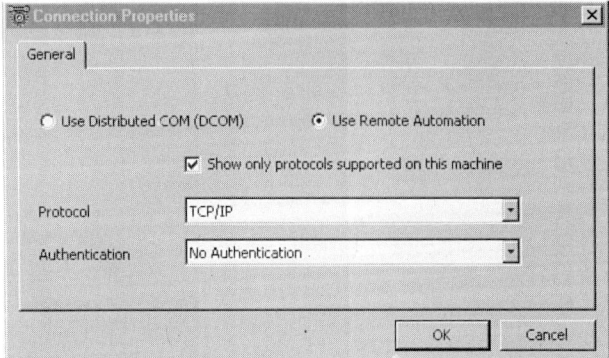

Figure 91-13   General connections settings tab

Show Only Protocols Supported on This Machine

If this option is checked, the protocol in the Protocol drop-down will list only the protocols available on the local machine. This setting does not verify which protocols are used on the server.

Protocol

This option determines which protocol the client will use to communicate with Remote Automation objects on the server.

Authentication

Determines the authentication type the client issues to the remote object before processing will begin.

Application Performance Explorer Menus

File Menu

The File menu, as shown in Figure 91-14, displays the options Set Profile Collection, Save Profile, Remove Profile, and Exit.

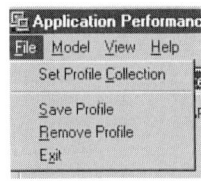

Figure 91-14
File menu

Set Profile Collection

This menu item will display an Open dialog to select the .INI file that holds the profiles.

Save Profile

This menu item will save the current configuration in the .INI file selected by the Set Profile Collection menu item. When it is selected, a prompt appears, as in Figure 91-15.

Remove Profile

This is used to remove the current configuration from the profile .INI file.

Exit

APE will close when this option is selected.

Model Menu

The Model menu, as shown in Figure 91-16, allows the user to select the asynchronous or the synchronous model.

Asynchronous

When this option is selected, the main screen of APE will display the objects that can be configured for an asynchronous test.

Synchronous

When this option is selected, the main screen of APE will display the objects that can be configured for a synchronous test.

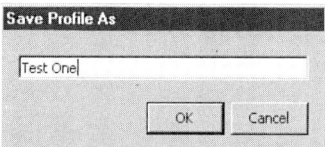

Figure 91-15   Save configuration in profile

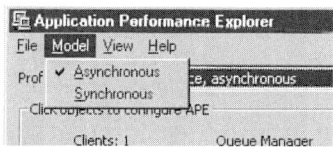

Figure 91-16   Model menu

View Menu

The View menu, as shown in Figure 91-17, displays the different tabs that can be used to set configuration options.

Properties

The Properties menu item is used to select the Property tab to be displayed.

Connection Settings

This option is used to display the tab used to select the connection settings.

Server Location

This menu item is used to display the tab used to define the server location.

Reset Objects

This menu item is used to reset the Object properties.

Help Menu

The Help menu, as shown in Figure 91-18, allows the user to access the help file or view the About screen.

Application Performance Explorer Help

This menu item displays the help file associated with APE.

About APE

This menu item displays the APE About screen.

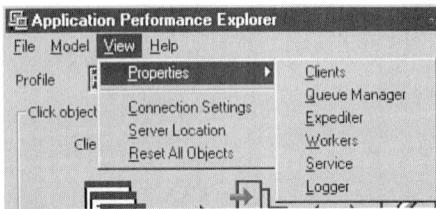

Figure 91-17   View menu

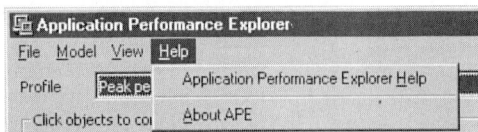

Figure 91-18   Help menu

Project: Running Application Performance Explorer

There are thousands of possible configurations to try. Almost every situation imaginable can be tested, and its performance can be measured. You can spend hours with this utility tuning and checking your remote automation or DCOM project. With APE, you don't need a room full of computer equipment to run some preliminary tests.

Project Overview

This project will measure the duration of a test with the ratio of clients to workers set at 1:1, 10:1, 10:10, and 30:10 to measure the different intervals needed to complete the test. This will demonstrate how efficient the Queue Manager is at handling multiple requests.

1. Launch the APE from the Start|Program menu, as in Figure 91-19.

2. From the profile drop-down list, select the Peak Performance, Asynchronous configuration. You will see that one client and one worker are configured.

3. Click the Start button. When the test is complete, record the results from the text box at the bottom of the screen.

4. Click on the Client button and increase the number of clients to 10.

5. Rerun the test for 10 clients and 10 workers, and then 30 clients and 10 workers. Record the results for each test.

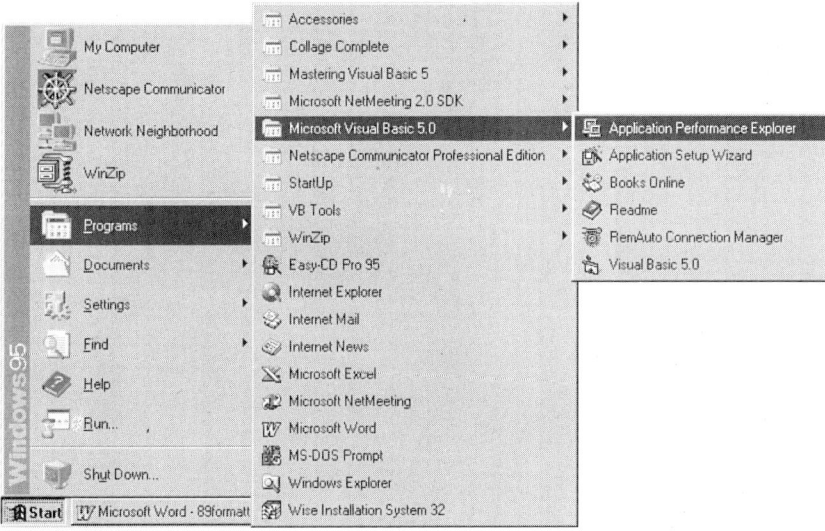

Figure 91-19   Launching APE

Table 91-1 shows the different result for each test run on a Pentium 90 with 16 MB of RAM.

Table 91-1 Result form tests run from APE

Ratio (Clients : Workers)	Total Calls per Second	Calls	Elapsed Time
1:1	100	0.396	252.5253
10:1	1000	1.883	531.0674
10:10	1000	0.49	2040.816
30:10	3000	0.575	5217.392

As the test results show, the amount of work done was the greatest with the 30:10 ratio. The Queue Manager handled the requests from the client efficiently at this saturation because the time used was only slightly greater and the number of calls per second was increased dramatically.

How It Works

The APE program loads the proper component found in the /Clisvr directory and runs the tests. These components can be replaced with other components written by a developer to test his or her own client/server applications.

92

CONDITIONAL COMPILATION

Conditional compilation is a feature that lets you use a single set of source files to compile different executable applications. Versions of Visual Basic prior to 4.0 did not support conditional compilation. In Visual Basic 4.0, Microsoft introduced the #Const and the #If...#Else...#End If set of compilation directives. These statements allow you to use a single set of source files to produce different executables based on the value of special constants called conditional compilation constants. The executables produced by conditional compilation from a single set of source files can differ from one another in a variety of ways: They can make calls to different API sets, contain special features needed in debug releases, or use different human languages.

This chapter begins by showing you how to declare compiler directive constants and use them in #If...#Else...#End If constructions. It then discusses the use of conditional compilation to develop localized applications and to build debug versions of applications. The chapter project uses conditional compilation to make API-specific Declare statements—a requirement for writing common code applications to run under Window 3.1, Windows 95, and Windows NT.

Using Conditional Compilation

The two basic considerations in using conditional compilation directives are declaring conditional compilation constants and testing conditional compilation constants in #If...#Else...#End If statements.

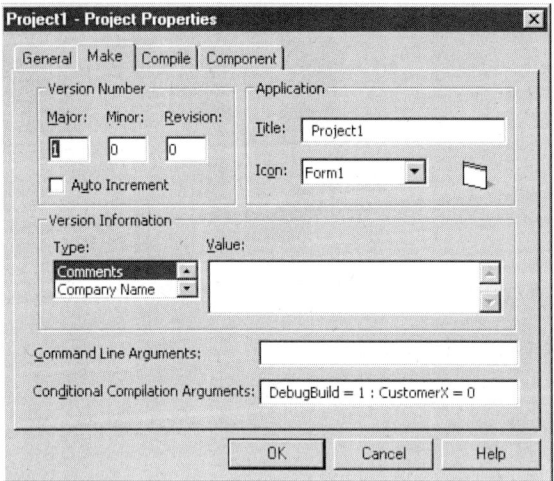

Figure 92-1 Declare conditional compilation constants in the Make section of the Project Properties dialog box

Declaring Conditional Compilation Constants

You can declare conditional compilation constants in one of three ways. You can declare them directly in your code using the #Const statement, as shown here.

```
#Const constName = 1
```

You can also declare a conditional compilation constant in the Make tab of the Project Properties dialog box, available from the Project menu. In the Conditional Compilation Arguments field of the dialog box (shown in Figure 92-1) declare the constant value in the form.

```
constantName = value[:constantName2 = value[:constantName3 = value[etc.]]]
```

And, finally, you can specify a conditional compilation constant when using the command-line compiler. Use /d switch to specify the conditional compilation constants as shown below.

```
vb.exe /make MyApplication.vbp
       /d constantName = value[:constantName2 = value[etc.]]
```

Conditional compilation constants can be used only in compiler directive statements; they can't be tested or used in other code. Conditional compilation constants declared with the #Const statement are always private to the module in which they are declared. Conditional compilation constants declared in the Project Properties dialog box and on the command line are public and can be used anywhere in your project.

Testing Conditional Compilation Constants

You test a conditional compilation constant in an #If statement just as you would a regular expression in an If statement. The difference is that the code in an #If statement is compiled only if the test returns True. If the test returns False, the compiler ignores the code and it never gets compiled into your application. Here is an example:

```
#If DebugBuild = 1 Then
    'if this is a debug build then this code gets compiled
    Global Const gcLogFile = "Debug.Log"
#End If
```

In the example, a new constant, gcLogFile, is declared to be used later when logging error conditions.

Applying Conditional Compilation

The main uses of conditional compilation are to develop international software and to create debug versions of projects. In Visual Basic 4.0, it was also used to create applications that will run in both 16-bit and 32-bit environments. There is no 16-bit Visual Basic 5.0 environment, but the built-in constants Win16 and Win32 still exist to support existing code. Win32 will always evaluate True in Visual Basic 5.0 and Win16 will always evaluate False.

International Software

In recent years, the software industry has been under great pressure to internationalize. Markets for applications are increasingly global and there is a need to support different character sets, local conventions, and culture-specific icons. Visual Basic 5.0 has two significant features for dealing with the problem of localizing international software. First, you can use resource files to allow you to isolate language and locale differences into a single location, removing them from the main body of source code (resource files are discussed in Chapter 93, "Resources and International Issues").

Second, you can use conditional compilation to include only the portions of your source code that are needed for a specific build in the executable file that you create. This eliminates the need to ship unnecessary code, minimizes executable size, and, in some cases, improves application performance. Large portions of source code that perform locale-specific functions can be eliminated from some software builds. For example, a currency exchange application might include only a specified set of currency conversion algorithms based on the specific country in which it is going to be sold.

Building Executables for Debugging

Modern software development cycles include a beta phase for most major applications. During this phase of software testing, all major features have been implemented and selected users are provided with a build of the application that has been tested internally by the software development company. Beta builds (and all earlier builds) of an application frequently include "debug code." This code is placed in the application specifically for bug tracking and reporting. Often, debug routines are used to write log files to record the state of an application as it is being used by the tester. The following example uses a conditional compilation directive in a form load event to perform debugging tasks that will be unnecessary in the release version of the software.

```
Private Sub Form_Load()

#If DebugBuild = 1 Then
    'if this EXE is going to be bug tested then compile this code
    Form1.Caption = Form1.Caption & "DEBUG"
    Open "DEBUG.TXT" For Output As #1
    Print #1, "Form1 Opened:"; Now()
    Close

#End If

End Sub
```

Once testing has concluded, debug code is no longer required. In addition to making the application larger, the debug code will tend to harm performance. When you decide that it is time to make a final release version of your software, you will want that build to be as small (code size) and efficient (execution speed) as possible. To accomplish this, you need to remove all unnecessary code. Conditional compilation directives allow you to specify portions of the code as a part of the debug build. Once you have used either a #Const declaration (for example #Const DebugBuild = 0) or the Project|Project Properties|Make dialog to set a conditional compilation constant to identify the release build, the compiler will simply ignore your debug code.

Conditional Compilation Summary

Table 92-1 lists the statements used for conditional compilation. Detailed descriptions of the two statements follow.

Table 92-1 Statements used for conditional compilation

Use This...	Type	To Do This...
#Const	Statement	Define a conditional compilation constant
#If...#Else...#End If	Statement	Direct the compiler to include or exclude code

#CONST STATEMENT

Purpose
The #Const statement is a conditional compilation directive used to define a constant for use in the #If, #Else, #End If construct to determine which version of an application will be built. These conditional compilation constants cannot be used for other purposes in code, and regular variables and constants cannot be used in conditional compilation directives. Table 92-2 explains the components of the #Const construct.

General Syntax

```
#Const ConstantName = Expression
```

Table 92-2 Arguments for the #Const statement

Argument	Description
ConstantName	The name of the conditional compilation constant
Expression	A constant or expression using operators (excluding IS) that evaluates to a constant value

Example Syntax

```
#Const DebugBuild = 1
Private Sub Form_Load()

#If DebugBuild = 1 Then
     'if this EXE is going to be bug tested then compile this code
     Form1.Caption = Form1.Caption & "DEBUG"
     Open "DEBUG.TXT" For Output As #1
     Print #1, "Form1 Opened:"; Now()
     Close

#End If

End Sub
```

Description   In the example syntax, the DebugBuild constant is explicitly declared, then tested in an #If statement. This causes the debug-specific code to be compiled.

The conditional compiler constants that are created using the #Const directive are always private. If you want your compiler directives to use public constants, use the Project Options dialog (see Figure 92-1) to set their values. An error will occur if you try to use a standard constant (declared with Const) in a conditional compiler directive. Conversely, you can't use #Const declared constants in code outside conditional compiler directives. However, you can set standard constants within conditional compilation directives to overcome this limitation.

Comments   Constants that you declare for conditional compilation, regardless of their code placement, are always evaluated at the module level.

#IF...#ELSE...#END IF STATEMENTS

Purpose   The #If...#Else...#End If construct directs the compiler to include only selected portions of code in the final executable file. Functionally, it behaves like the standard If...Then...Else statement. Note that #If...#Else...#End If can be used only for conditional compilation, and the "regular" If…Then…Else cannot be used for conditional compilation. The arguments of the #If… #Else… #End If statements are listed in Table 92-3.

General Syntax

```
#If Condition Then
'the condition has to be a conditional compilation constant
{code statements}
#Else If Condition
{code statements}
.
.
.

#Else
{code statements}
#End If
```

Table 92-3 Arguments of the #If…#Else…#End If statements

Argument	Description
Condition	An expression that tests the value of a conditional ompilation constant
{code statements}	A block of program code that is compiled if the test of the expression returns True

Example Syntax

```
#Const Win32 = 1
'The value of Win32 will now be used to determine which of the
'following declarations will be compiled.

#If Win32 = 1 Then
        Declare Function ShowWindow Lib "user32" (ByVal hWnd As Long ⇐
              , ByVal nCmdShow As Long)  As Long
#Else
        Declare Function ShowWindow Lib "User" (ByVal hWnd As Integer ⇐
              , ByVal nCmdShow As  Integer) As Integer
#End If
```

Description   The #If…#Else…#End If construct behaves almost exactly like the If…Else…End If construct. However, if you use the conditional compilation (#) statements, all expressions contained in the construct are evaluated. This means that all expressions must be valid and defined. Undefined constants evaluate to the Empty value. Because the #If…#Else…#End If construct has no single-line equivalent, no other code can appear on the same line as any of the directives.

The example syntax illustrates how you can use conditional compilation to include an appropriate Declare statement for a Windows API call in your compiled code. However, you can also use the #If…#Else…#End If construct to perform operations appropriate to debugging, to take actions necessary for localizing an international application, or for any other task that might require selective code compilation.

The Conditional Compilation Project

Project Overview

The following project uses conditional compilation to create a project that will log error messages when a conditional compilation constant is set. If the constant is not set, then the debug code is not compiled into the project.

Assembling the Project

1. Create a new Standard EXE Visual Basic project. Refer to Table 92-4 to place controls on the form and their layout. See Figure 92-2 for the controls' layout.

Table 92-4 Controls for the chapter project

Object	Property	Setting
Form	Caption	Debug Test
Command Button	Name	cmdOpen
	Caption	Open
Command Button	Name	cmdFont
	Caption	Font
Rich Text Box	Name	rtfDocument
Common Dialog	Name	cmddlg

Figure 92-2   The layout of the sample project's form

2. Open the project properties and add the following conditional complication argument to the Make tab.

```
DebugBuild = 1
```

3. Add a new module and add the following code to the module. Note that, by using a conditional compilation constant, entire subroutines and functions can be excluded from code, not just individual lines within.

```
#If DebugBuild Then
    Public Sub LogError(psFrom As String)
        Open App.Path + "\" + "DEBUG.TXT" For Append As #1
        Print #1, Now(), psFrom, Err.Number, Err.Description
        Close #1
        If Err.Number Then
            MsgBox "Error """ & Err.Description & """ written to log"
        End If
    End Sub
#End If
```

4. Open the form again and add the following code to the cmdOpen_Click event. Notice that very little of the code in the event is not debug code. You certainly do not want all the extra code to be in a shipping product.

```
Private Sub cmdOpen_Click()
    #If DebugBuild Then
        LogError "Entering cmdOpen_Click"
        On Error GoTo cmdOpenError:
    #End If

    comdlg.ShowOpen
    rtfDocument.LoadFile comdlg.filename

    #If DebugBuild Then
        On Error GoTo 0
        LogError "Exiting cmdOpen_Click"
        Exit Sub
cmdOpenError:
        LogError "cmdOpen_Click"
        Resume Next
    #End If
End Sub
```

5. Finally, add the following code to the cmdFont_Click event.

```
Private Sub cmdFont_Click()
    #If DebugBuild Then
        LogError "Entering cmdFont_Click"
        On Error GoTo cmdFontError:
    #End If

    With rtfDocument
        comdlg.FontName = .SelFontName
        comdlg.FontSize = .SelFontSize
        comdlg.FontBold = .SelBold
        comdlg.FontItalic = .SelItalic
```

```
            comdlg.FontStrikethru = .SelStrikeThru
            comdlg.FontUnderline = .SelUnderline
      End With
      comdlg.Flags = cdlCFBoth
      comdlg.ShowFont
      With rtfDocument
            .SelFontName = comdlg.FontName
            .SelFontSize = comdlg.FontSize
            .SelBold = comdlg.FontBold
            .SelItalic = comdlg.FontItalic
            .SelStrikeThru = comdlg.FontStrikethru
            .SelUnderline = comdlg.FontUnderline
      End With
      rtfDocument.SetFocus

      #If DebugBuild Then
            On Error GoTo 0
            LogError "Exiting cmdFont_Click"
            Exit Sub
cmdFontError:
            LogError "cmdFont_Click"
            Resume Next
      #End If
End Sub
```

6. The project is now ready to compile and run. You may change the debug setting in the Project Properties dialog.

How It Works

This project creates a log file when the DebugBuild constant is set. All errors, and entry and exit points of functions, are tracked so the tester can see exactly where the error occurred and what steps are necessary to re-create the error. In a typical project, this type of error handling would be used during testing to identify possible errors that were not expected by the developer. An easy way to see the logging in action is to open a document with the Open button. Highlight a section of text, but not the whole document, and change the font. Next highlight another section of text where the highlight overlaps two different fonts. Change the font again; this time an error, Invalid Use of Null, is trapped. The possibility of an error like this may not be immediately apparent to a developer building the application; however, with debug logging using conditional constants, it is easy to re-create and capture during the testing phase.

93

RESOURCES AND INTERNATIONAL ISSUES

In recent years it has become much more critical for software to be international. *International* or *locale-sensitive* software can be easily and completely modified to function in foreign languages and locales. For your application to be locale-sensitive, you need to consider foreign-language character sets, locale-specific conventions for representing dates, currencies, and locale-specific images and symbols.

The need for flexibility in localizing international software has led to increased support for *resources*. Resources permit you to isolate locale-specific elements, such as strings and pictures, so that an application can be localized without modification of source code. Although early versions of Visual Basic (releases 1, 2, and 3) did not support resource loading, Visual Basic 5.0 includes resource handling features that let the application determine the current locale (set in the user's Windows operating environment) and load resources that are appropriate to that locale.

The first half of this chapter addresses three issues related to software internationalization. First, it discusses the way the computer represents large character sets for applications intended for distribution in the Far East and in other locales that require large character sets. Second, it describes Visual Basic's locale-aware functions, which handle the way dates and currency amounts are formatted for different locales. Third, it discusses the use of resource files in Visual Basic 5.0, which make it possible to isolate locale-specific data from source code.

The second half of this chapter discusses in depth the Visual Basic functions related to internationalization and resources, then shows you how to construct this chapter's project application.

The ANSI, Unicode, and Double-Byte Character Sets

To understand the issues involved in creating international software, you need to be familiar with the way the computer stores and retrieves characters. The three major types of character sets are the single-byte character set (SBCS), the double-byte character set (DBCS), and Unicode.

Single-Byte Character Set

The native character set for all 16- and 32-bit Windows systems (except NT) is ANSI, a single-byte character set. The ANSI convention allocates a single byte (8 bits) of storage for each character. Because of the limitations on the quantity of data that can be stored in a single byte, a single-byte character set cannot have more than 256 characters. There are two common solutions to this problem: double-byte character sets (DBCS) and Unicode. Unfortunately, these two alternatives are often confused.

Double-Byte Character Set

DBCS is used by the versions of Windows distributed throughout Asia. This system for representing specialized character sets lets you use ANSI characters with values through 127, and it allows you to expand the character set by using numbers larger than 127 to indicate whether the following byte contains a character from a non-Latin character set. To parse a DBCS string, look at each byte in sequence. In a double-byte character set, characters may consist of either 1 or 2 bytes of data. If the first byte is greater than 127 (between 0x81 and 0x9F or between 0xE0 and 0xFC), treat the following byte as a member of the non-Latin character set that the first byte specifies. Otherwise, read the first byte as a standard ANSI character. Since there may be a number of lead bytes for a specific language, the first byte indicates the foreign language's character set or a subset of characters within the foreign language's character set. The second byte specifies the character within the character set specified by the first byte. This implies that the number of bytes in a DBCS character string need not be equal to the number of characters in the string (although the number of bytes is not necessarily twice the number of characters). Figure 93-1 illustrates the relationship between bytes and characters in a DBCS string.

Unicode

Although Windows NT supports ANSI strings, its native character set is Unicode. Unicode provides a consistent two-byte allocation for the storage of each character. Thus, there are 65,536 (the number of values that can be stored in two bytes) values available to assign to characters. This is enough to handle any character set. In addition to being used by NT, Unicode is used by 32-bit object linking and embedding (OLE). Unicode is a 32-bit (not 16-bit) operating system feature.

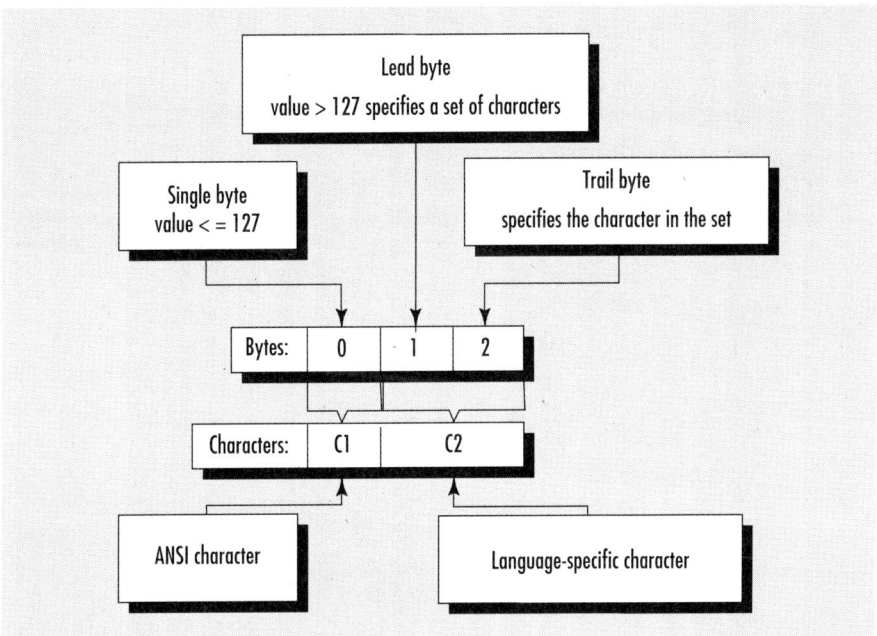

Figure 93-1 Layout of a DBCS character

Locale-Aware Functions

Although language is the most obvious concern when you are creating international software, you also have to consider the way dates and currencies are represented. For example, you cannot assume that "." is the decimal separator and "," is the thousands separator in currency amounts. In many countries, such as Russia, the role of these two symbols is reversed. In addition, while 4/10/60 is April 10, 1960 in the United States, in Britain and many other countries 4/10/60 is October 4, 1960.

Fortunately, Visual Basic provides a family of "locale-aware" functions, listed in Table 93-1, for dealing with the vagaries of international date and currency display. You can use the CDate, CCur, and Format functions to ensure that your data is correctly displayed. Be sure to use Option Compare Text to sort strings correctly in international applications. Option Compare Binary (the default setting) can produce incorrect sorts in some languages.

Table 93-1 Locale-aware functions in Visual Basic 5.0

Function	Locale Awareness
CCur	Uses the system settings from the Control Panel for currency format
CDate	Uses the system settings from the Control Panel for date format

continued on next page

continued from previous page

Function	Locale Awareness
CreateDatabase	Requires specification of a locale for determining collating order
DateValue	Interprets a string based on the Control Panel settings
Format	Uses the Control Panel settings for date/time formatting
Print	Uses the Control Panel settings for date/time printing
Write#	Writes data to a file in a fixed format so it can be read anywhere

Resource Files

Resource files are collections of resources that you can use to customize the language, as well as the look and feel, of applications. Custom resources can take the form of images (such as bitmaps and icons), strings, or even more complex objects, such as dialog boxes. You can use a resource editor to create and compile the resources into a file that you can include in the Visual Basic project. Visual Basic 5.0 includes a 32-bit resource compiler. Its name is RC.EXE and it is located in the Wizards subdirectory of the Visual Basic 5.0 install directory. The chapter project includes both an .RC and a compiled .RES file. To create resources for Visual Basic projects, you first need to collect the resources in an .RC file, then compile them into an .RES file that can be added to the Visual Basic project. Once you add the .RES file, you can compile it along with the other component forms and modules into the final .EXE file. Visual Basic allows only one .RES file per project.

When you create your resource file (using a resource editor), you assign resource IDs to the various resources included in the file. You need to keep track of these resource IDs so that you can pass them to the appropriate function when you load the resource. Since a single file can include multiple data types, you may want to establish a numbering scheme to help you manage the resources at runtime. The project for this chapter demonstrates one such numbering scheme.

Resources provide several advantages over hard coding data into your project. First, all strings, bitmaps, and other resource data can be loaded when your application needs to use them. They need not be automatically loaded when the form or module is loaded. You can localize your international application by placing language strings (or any other locale-specific data) into a resource file. You can create a single resource file, including all relevant languages. However, for larger applications, you may want to create a separate resource file for each language. Having separate files limits executable size while still providing language flexibility. If you create separate resource files, you have to make a distinct build of your application for each locale, because Visual Basic allows only one resource file per project.

"Golden Rules" for Writing International Software

Here are some basic guidelines to follow when writing an application for international markets. Be sure to plan ahead, since changes become more expensive as the software development cycle progresses.

■ Use resources, especially string tables, to keep locale-specific data out of your code

■ Design your user interface to accommodate strings (and symbols) in all applicable languages

■ Use the locale-aware functions (let the system work for you)

■ Avoid use of culture-specific metaphors and symbols (such as "?")

■ Study the issues (such as different character sets) *before you write any code*

Resources and International Issues Summary

The sections that follow discuss the Visual Basic functions that relate to international issues and resources. Table 93-2 summarizes the functions dealing with resources and international issues.

Table 93-2 Resources and international issues functions

Use This...	Type	To Do This...
IMEStatus	Function	Determine if your application is running on a Far East version of Windows
LoadResData	Function	Load a resource
LoadResPicture	Function	Load a bitmap, icon, or cursor
LoadResString	Function	Load a string resource

IMESTATUS FUNCTION

Purpose   Use the IMEStatus function to determine if your application is running on a Far East version of Windows, and if so, which Far East character set to use. It returns the Input Method Editor (IME) mode that the Windows operating environment is currently using. The IME mode tells what character set the system is using and what method the system is using to represent the characters. Tables 93-3, 93-4, and 93-5 show the values returned by IMEStatus for the Japanese and Chinese locales.

General Syntax

```
iValue% = IMEStatus()
```

Table 93-3 Japanese locale constants for the IMEStatus function

Value	VB.Constants	Meaning
0	vbIMENoOP	No IME installed
1	vbIMEOn	IME on
2	vbIMEOff	IME off
3	vbIMEDisable	IME has been disabled
4	vbIMEHiragana	Hiragana DBCS
5	vbIMEKatakanaDbl	Katakana DBCS
6	vbIMEKatakanaSng	Katakana SBCS
7	vbIMEAlphaDbl	Alphanumeric DBCS
8	vbIMEAlphaSng	Alphanumeric SBCS

Table 93-4 Chinese traditional locale constants for the IMEStatus function

Value	VB.Constants	Meaning
0	vbIMENoOP	No IME installed
1	vbIMEOn	IME on
2	vbIMEOff	IME off

Table 93-5 lists the constants' values that IMEStatus returns for the Korean locale. To interpret these values, examine the first five bits of the return value.

Table 93-5 To interpret the value returned by IMEStatus for the Korean locale, test the first five bits of the return value

Bit	Value	Meaning
0	0	No IME installed
	1	IME installed
1	0	IME disabled
	1	IME enabled
2	0	IME English mode has been set
	1	Hangeul mode has been set
3	0	Banja mode has been set (SBCS)
	1	Junja mode has been set (DBCS)
4	0	Normal mode has been set
	1	Hanja conversion mode has been set

Example Syntax

```
Private Sub ReturnStatus ()

'This subroutine returns the IME status and
'then displays the status in a message box.

'The developer of this application added an International
'option to the installation procedure.
'The value of International indicates whether the
'International option was chosen when this application
'was installed.

If IMEStatus() > 0 And Not iInternational Then
     a$ = "You are running Windows using an Input Editor. "
     b$ = "Please reinstall using the International Settings."
     Msgbox a$ & b$
End If

'The IMEStatus value can be used for conditional compilation,
'or for some other type of customization.
End Sub
```

Description   The example syntax calls IMEStatus to test whether the application is running on a Far East version of Windows. If the function is called when Windows is not running an IME, or when the current Windows system is not a Far East version, the return value is vbIMENoOP (which is 0). Your application can then load string resources and take other action appropriate to the locale. The example subprocedure displays a message box if the user of a Far East version has not selected an International Settings option during installation.

Comments   IMEStatus indicates a specific IME in the Far East versions of Windows. If it is called for other Windows versions, the function returns the Visual Basic constant value vbIMENoOP, which is 0.

LoadResData Function

Purpose   The LoadResData function loads data of any valid resource type from a resource file that's included in your Visual Basic project. Use LoadResData to load complex resource types. It can be used to load custom (non-standard) resources. LoadResData returns a byte array. Table 93-6 lists the arguments of the LoadResData function. Table 93-7 lists the values used to determine the type of resource that LoadResData loads.

General Syntax

```
bytes = LoadResData(index, format)
```

Table 93-6 Arguments of the LoadResData function

Argument	Description
bytes	A valid location (such as a variable or property) to receive the function's return byte array
index	The unique resource ID for the resource entry in the resource file
format	Value to specify the format of the data returned by the LoadResData function

Table 93-7 Resource formats (types) returned by the LoadResData function

Value	Description
1	Cursor
2	Bitmap picture
3	Icon
4	Menu
5	Dialog Box
6	String
7	Font directory
8	Font
9	Accelerator table
10	User-defined
12	Group cursor
14	Group Icon

Example Syntax

```
Private Sub FailedToOpenDataBaseError ()

'This routine generates a specific error
'(failed to open database)
'using the correct string resource for the
'current language version of the application.

'cTypeString is the constant for the string data type from LoadResData
'iCurrentLanguageMsgDB is set to the ID of
'the desired message for the current language

Dim sMessage As String
sMessage = LoadResData(iCurrentLanguageMsgDB, cTypeString)
Msgbox sMessage

End Sub
```

Description

Before you use LoadResData, you need to include a resource (.RES) file in your project. The example syntax shows code that uses a resource file to load an error message in the language appropriate to the current Windows environment. When the resource file is created, you assign appropriate IDs to the strings that you plan to load. Then, at runtime, you can use those IDs to load data as your application requires it.

LoadResData loads the actual bits in the resource. It can be used without making assumptions about the contents of the data loaded. This allows you to create custom resources that you load with this function.

Comments   Here are some important points to remember when using LoadResData:

- The resource with ID (location) zero is reserved for the application icon.

- There is a 64K limit on the size of the data loaded from the resource file.

- If you wish to display a cursor, icon, or bitmap from a resource file in your application, you should use the LoadResPicture function. The LoadResData function returns a value containing the actual bits in the resource.

LoadResPicture(index, format)

Purpose   The LoadResPicture function loads a bitmap, icon, or cursor type from a resource file included in your Visual Basic project. LoadResPicture can be useful for internationalizing software when you want to make use of locale-specific images and symbols. Versions 1, 2, and 3 of Visual Basic required that images be loaded into forms and picture boxes either at design time or using the LoadPicture function. Table 93-8 lists the arguments of the LoadResPicture function. Table 93-9 lists the Visual Basic constant values that can be passed in the function's format argument.

General Syntax

```
LoadResPicture(index, format)
```

Table 93-8 Arguments of the LoadResPicture function

Argument	Description
index	The unique resource ID (an integer) specifying the location of the picture in the resource file
format	Value to specify the type of picture returned

Table 93-9 Resource formats (types) for the LoadResPicture function

Value (format setting)	VB.Constants	Description
0	vbResBitmap	Bitmap
1	vbResIcon	Icon
2	vbResCursor	Cursor

Example Syntax

```
Private Sub formMain_Load ()

'we will load the form's picture on load
'from the resource file
'we have included with this project

'the location (resource ID) in the resource file
iMainFormPicture = 101

Me.Picture = LoadResPicture(iMainFormPicture, vbResBitmap)

End Sub
```

Description The example syntax shows how you can use the LoadResPicture function to load images from a resource file at runtime. The example loads a bitmap image into the form's Picture property. The type of image is specified by the constant value vbResBitmap. You assign the bitmap's resource ID when you create it in a resource editor.

Comments Here are some important points to remember when using LoadResPicture:

- The resource with ID (location) zero is reserved for the application icon.
- There is a 64K limit on the size of the data loaded from the resource file.

LoadResString Function

Purpose LoadResString loads a string from a resource file included in your Visual Basic project. This allows you to eliminate literal strings from your code. Loading strings from resource files improves performance (you only load strings when you actually need them) and is essential for internationalization. You can add only one .RES file to your project, so if you add a single resource file containing the language strings for all the languages you support, then you can avoid having to recompile different language versions of your application. LoadResString functions regardless of the type of string (SBCS, DBCS, or Unicode). Table 93-10 lists the arguments of the LoadResString function.

General Syntax

```
sString$ = LoadResString(index)
```

Table 93-10 Arguments of the LoadResString function

Argument	Description
sString$	The string variable into which the resource is loaded
index	The unique resource ID (an integer) specifying the location of the string in the resource file

Example Syntax

```
Private Sub FileNotFoundError ()

'this routine generates a specific error
'(file not found error)
'Using the correct string resource for the
'current language version of the application.

'note: iCurLangFileNotFound is a variable that
'indicates the resource ID of the appropriate
'message for the current language of the Windows environment.

Dim sMessage As String
sMessage = LoadResString(iCurLangFileNotFound)
Msgbox sMessage

End Sub
```

Description   The example shows how to load strings from a resource file included in your Visual Basic project. LoadResString takes as its only parameter the resource ID that you assigned to the resource when it was created in the editor. In the example, iCurLangFileNotFound indicates the ID of a specific message (the File Not Found error message) for the language of the current Windows operating environment. If you use a single resource file for multiple language builds of your application, you will need to assign resource IDs carefully to allow you to easily track resources in your code. However, you can avoid this problem by creating a single resource file for each language and then compiling your code separately with each resource file.

Comments   You should not be tempted to load multiple strings into a single resource (concatenate strings and then assign a single resource ID to the concatenation) and then parse them apart at runtime. This would destroy the value that resources provide: Parsing a composite string into individual strings would not be much better than searching for them in the body of code. Also, parsing unnecessarily slows the execution of your program.

Here are some other important points to remember when using LoadResString:

■ The resource with ID (location) zero is reserved for the application icon.

■ There is a 64K limit on the size of the data loaded from the resource file.

The Resource Project

Project Overview

The Resource project illustrates how to modify your user interface to accommodate the different locales where it may be used. In the project, you create a simple data entry form. (This form includes text boxes that could be bound to a data control or populated and saved using DAOs, which would allow the data to be entered in a database file.) The project demonstrates the use of a resource file to localize the contents of the labels and caption as well as an icon, in French, Irish, and English. It also illustrates the use of locale-aware functions to format the date and time—but you won't see the result of this unless you actually run the project in a foreign version of Windows.

Assembling the Project

1. Begin by creating the resource file using a resource editor. Create the following strings and bitmaps and assign them the IDs shown in Table 93-11. After you have created and compiled the resource file (into a .RES), include it in the Visual Basic project using the File|Add dialog.

Table 93-11 Contents of the CH93.RES resource file

ID	String or Bitmap
1	France
2	United States
3	Ireland
4	Nom (Name: French)
5	Name
6	Ainm (Name: Irish)
7	Date de naissance (Date of Birth: French)
8	Date of Birth
9	Data Breithe (Date of Birth: Irish)
10	Taille (Height: French)
11	Height
12	Airde (Height: Irish)
100	Icon of the French Flag
101	Icon of the U.S. Flag
102	Icon of the Irish Flag

2. Make a new form with the objects and properties shown in Table 93-12.

Table 93-12 Elements of the data entry form

Object	Property	Setting
Form	Name	frmDataEntry
	Appearance	vb3D
Frame	Name	fraCountry
	Caption	Country

Object	Property	Setting
Option Button	Name	optCountry
	Index	0
	Caption	France
Option Button	Name	optCountry
	Index	1
	Caption	United States
Option Button	Name	optCountry
	Index	2
	Caption	Ireland
Text Box	Name	txtHeight
	Text	""
Text Box	Name	txtDOB
	Text	""
Text Box	Name	txtName
	Text	""
Label	Name	lblHeight
	Caption	""
Label	Name	lblDOB
	Caption	""
Label	Name	lblName
	Caption	""
Image	Name	Image1

3. Enter the following code into the Declarations section of the form. These constants will be available to all the routines in the form and will provide offset values that make it easier to specify each type of resource in the resource file. (To use this technique you need to plan ahead, creating the offset scheme before you assign the resource IDs.)

```
Const CaptionOffset = 1
Const NameOffset = 4
Const DOBOffset = 7
Const HeightOffset = 10
Const IconOffset = 100
```

4. Enter the following code into the form's Load event. This code initializes the form to the default country (the United States in this example).

```
Private Sub Form_Load()

'country 1 is the default (the U.S. for this example)
optCountry(1) = True

End Sub
```

5. The following code allows the user to choose the settings for the application interface. The code changes the form icon to the current national flag and changes the text in the form labels to the appropriate language. The flag is also displayed in an image control on the form. This code also displays the date and time in the form caption using a format determined by the Windows system locale. This is accomplished using the CDate function, which is locale-sensitive. Figures 93-2 and 93-3 show the U.S. and Irish versions of the dialog.

```
Private Sub optCountry_Click(Index As Integer)

    'Set the caption to the country name and display the date using
    'the current windows environment setting.
    Me.Caption = LoadResString(Index + CaptionOffset) & " : " & CDate(Now)
    'load the flag into the icon and the image control
    Me.Icon = LoadResPicture(Index + IconOffset, vbResIcon)
    Image1.Picture = LoadResPicture(Index + IconOffset, vbResIcon)
    'load the language strings
    lblName = LoadResString(Index + NameOffset)
    lblDOB = LoadResString(Index + DOBOffset)
    lblHeight = LoadResString(Index + HeightOffset)

End Sub
```

Figure 93-2   United States display of the resource project

Figure 93-3   Ireland display of the resource project

How It Works

The Resource project illustrates how to use a resource file to localize an international application. Clearly, most commercial applications will have more extensive resource files than shown here. This project demonstrates a useful technique for organizing resource IDs.

If you refer back to Table 93-11, you will notice that the resource IDs are ordered first by control, and then by language. The constants that you declared in step 3 determine base IDs, or "offsets," for each text box. Because the user selects the language using an array of option buttons, we can use the Index property of the option button array to select the language string for each text box. The Name text box, for example, is given a base ID of 4 (NameOffset). If the user then selects option button 0 (French), the resource ID of the string will be NameOffset + 0 , which selects the string "Nom" (resource ID = 4) when we pass it to LoadResString using this statement.

```
lblName = LoadResString(Index + NameOffset)
```

An alternative scheme for larger datasets, which would not utilize the index values of control arrays, might be to organize the resource IDs first by message, and then by language. You could then select the appropriate string by adding a constant representing the base ID of the message to a constant representing the position of the specific language string within the message group. This would make it relatively easy to manage a large set of message strings in multiple languages compiled into a single resource file.

PART XVI
WIZARDS AND HELPER TOOLS

94

APPLICATION WIZARD AND COMPONENT TEMPLATES

Visual Basic 5.0 introduces an Application Wizard that allows you to generate a new application as a starting point to build further functionality. This wizard can generate a new application using one of three predefined visual interfaces: Multiple Document Interface (MDI), Single Document Interface (SDI), and Explorer style. Application Wizard should be listed under the Add-Ins menu. If not, choose Add-In Manager from the Add-Ins menu, then check the VB Application Wizard check box to make the Application Wizard appear under the Add-Ins menu.

The Application Wizard creates a new project as a starting point for further development. Templates can be used on existing projects each time a component is added and provide a starting point for forms, classes, modules, and projects. This chapter covers these time savers.

The Application Wizard

The application you generate with the Application Wizard contains a toolbar and a status bar. The status bar includes information about the status of the application and the date and time. The toolbar for SDI and MDI forms is similar to a Microsoft Office toolbar. It includes the New, Open, Save, Print, Cut, Copy, Paste, Bold, Italic, Underline, Left Justify, Center, and Right Justify buttons. Explorer-style applications have a toolbar with the Navigation Buttons, Cut, Copy, Paste, Delete, Properties, Large Icon View, Small Icon View, List View, and Details View buttons.

Once the application is created by the wizard, you can edit the code and customize its functionality to your needs. The code has comments that indicate spots where you will need to add custom code. Look for *To Do* in the comments to find these spots. Table 94-1 shows the Application Wizard steps for creating an application that does not have forms based on a local datasource, while Table 94-2 shows the steps for an application that does have forms based on a local datasource.

Table 94-1 AppWizard steps for applications without a datasource

Introduction
Interface Type
Menus
Resources
Internet Connectivity
Standard Forms
Data Access Forms
Finished!
Summary Report

Table 94-2 AppWizard steps for applications with a datasource

Introduction
Interface Type
Menus
Resources
Internet Connectivity
Standard Forms
Data Access Forms
Select Tables
Finished!
Summary Report

Component Templates

Visual Basic 5.0 facilitates component reuse through templates. When you create a new form, module, control, property page, or document, you can open an existing template in the Add Class Module dialog box. Visual Basic 5.0 comes with a variety of pre-built templates to which you may add your own. Figure 94-1 shows the Add Form dialog with the built-in form templates. Once you have added a template to your project, you can edit the code and customize its functionality to your needs.

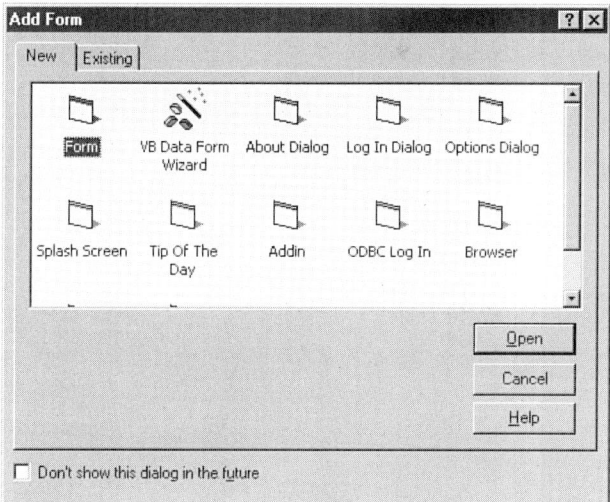

Figure 94-1   The Add Form dialog makes it easy to
select form templates or, with the other hidden tab, open
existing forms

To create your own template, save the object that you want to use as a template, then copy it to the appropriate subdirectory of the Visual Basic Template directory. For example, to create a custom MyClass class template, save your class as MyClass, then copy the MyClass.cls file to the \VB\Template\Classes directory. When you select the Add Class Module command from the Project menu, then choose the Existing tab, Visual Basic displays the MyClass template in the Add Class Module dialog box, as shown in Figure 94-2.

You can disable the display of templates for specified objects. You do so by selecting the Options command on the Tools menu and clearing the Show Templates options on the Environment tab of the Options dialog box. Figure 94-3 shows this dialog box. For example, to disable the display of class templates, clear the Class Modules option in the dialog box.

MyNotePad Project

This project demonstrates how to use the Application Wizard and templates to get a head start on an application.

Assembling the Project

1. Start a new Project and select the VB Application Wizard. Select MDI as Interface Type. Select File, Edit, Window, Help as the menus that will be available in the application. Choose not to use resource files for your strings in your application. Do not allow Internet access from this application. Include a standard About box in the application. Do not generate forms based on a local database. Name the application MyNotePad and let the Application Wizard generate the forms and modules. Figures 94-4 through 94-10 show the selections made on the screens.

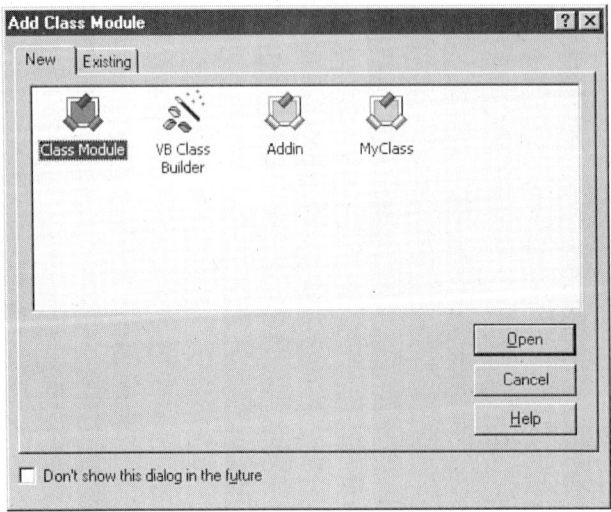

Figure 94-2 You add your own templates to the Add Class Module dialog

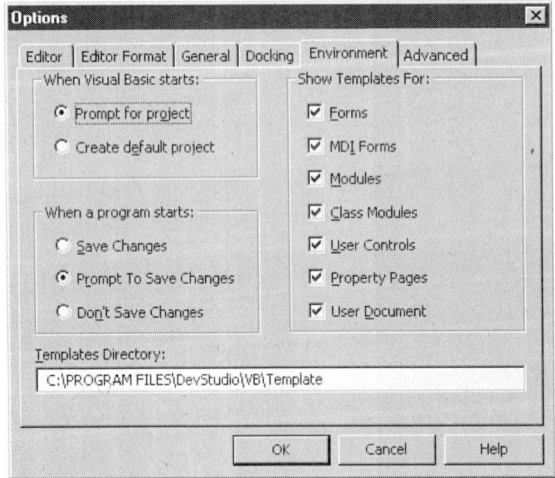

Figure 94-3 Visual Basic gives you total control over the component categories for which templates are shown

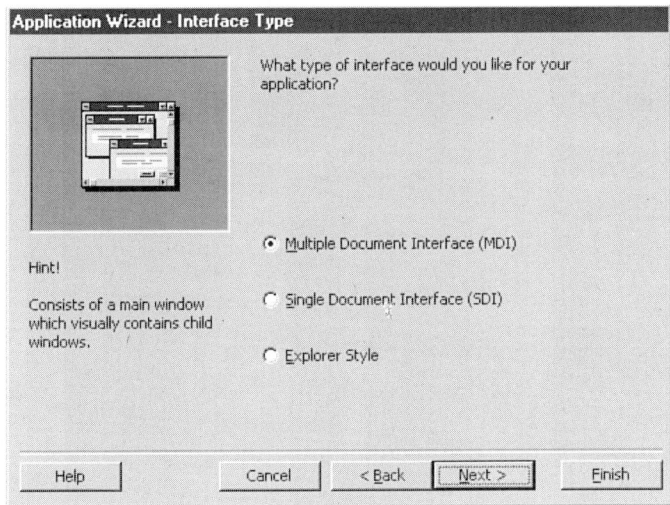

Figure 94-4 After the introductory screen in the Application Wizard, you select the interface type

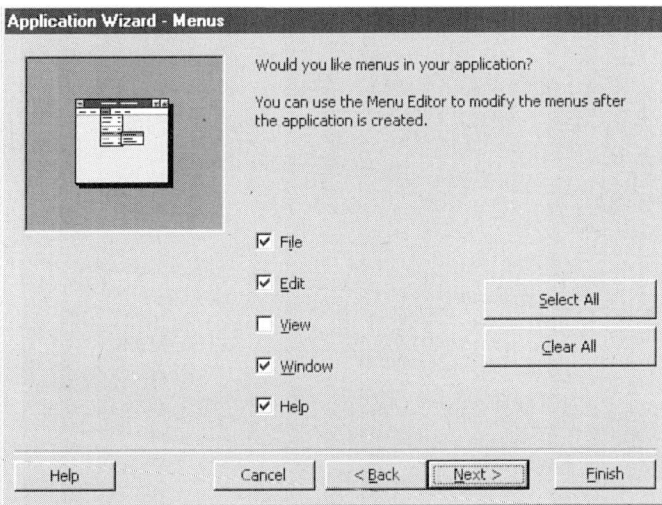

Figure 94-5 Second, you select which menus you want in your application

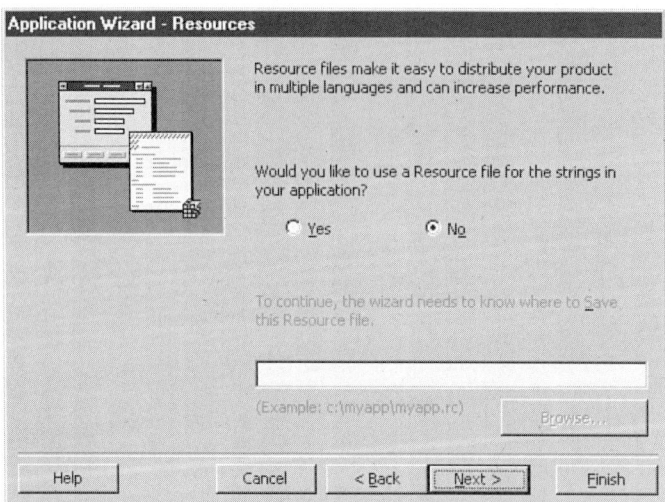

Figure 94-6   Then you must decide whether to put all strings in a resource file

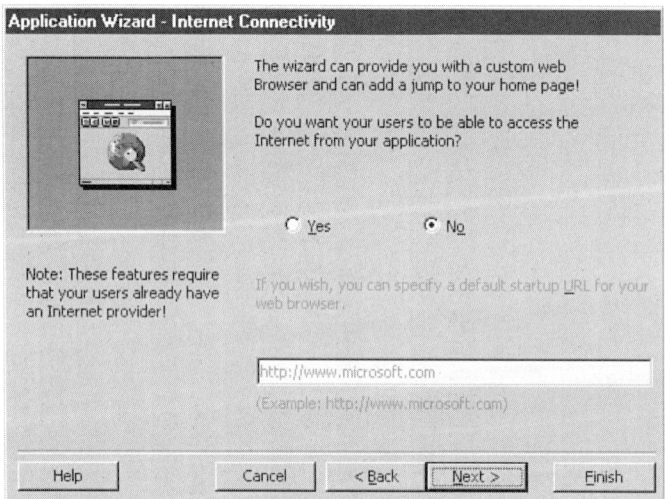

Figure 94-7   Then you are given the option to provide access to the Internet from your application

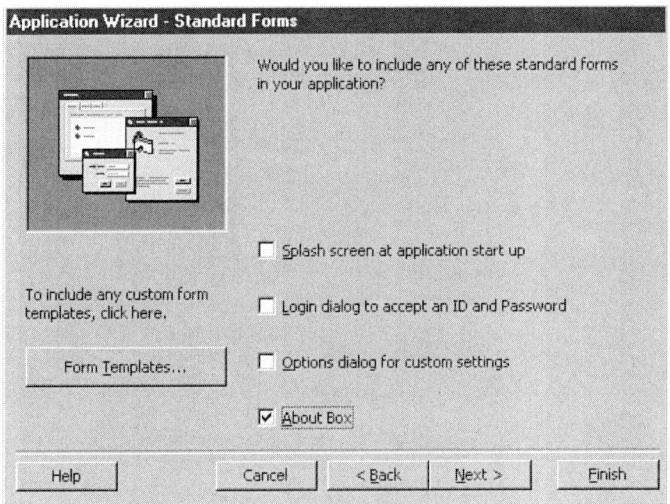

Figure 94-8 The Application Wizard allows you to include standard form templates in your application

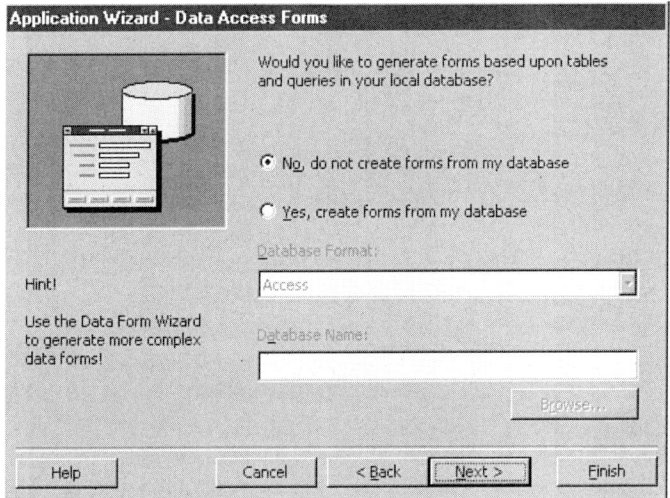

Figure 94-9 The Application Wizard can also generate forms based upon tables and queries in a database

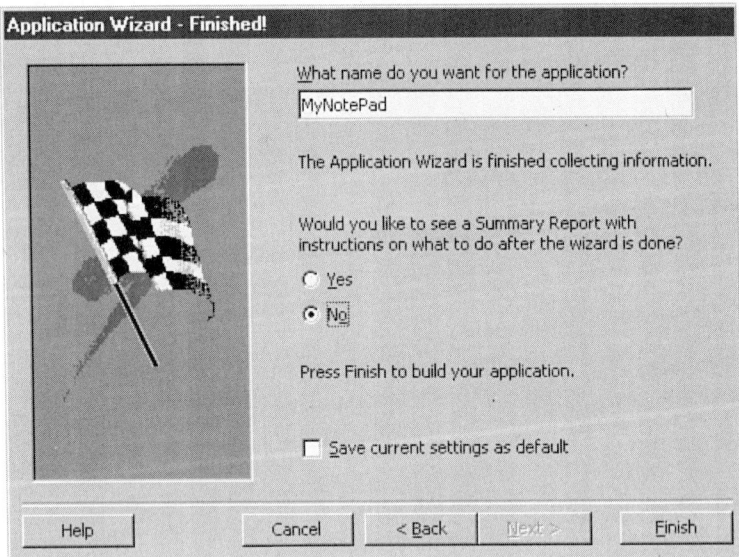

Figure 94-10   The last screen in the Application Wizard, just before the code is generated

2. Add a module to the project and add the following code into its General section. This code implements a useful message box routine and a routine to extract the filename from a full path name.

```
Option Explicit

Function getFileNameOnly(strFullPathName As String) As String
    Dim i As Integer

    For i = Len(strFullPathName) To 1 Step -1
        If Mid(strFullPathName, i, 1) = "\" Then
            Exit For
        End If
    Next

    getFileNameOnly = Right(strFullPathName, Len(strFullPathName) - i)
End Function

Public Function AskYN(strQuestion As String) As Integer
    AskYN = MsgBox(strQuestion, vbYesNo + vbExclamation, App.Title)
End Function
```

3. Add code to the Form_Load event of the About box until it matches the code below. You also need to adjust the controls on the frmAbout form to provide extra room for the lblDisclaimer caption. Figure 94-11 shows how the About box looks.

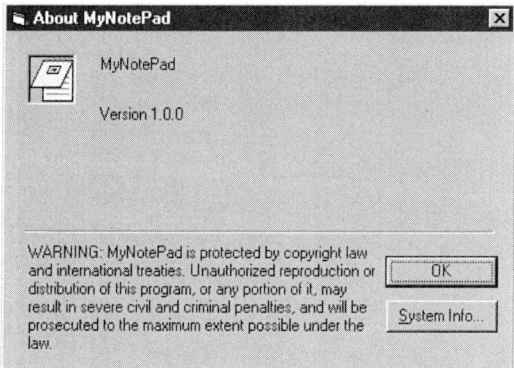

Figure 94-11 The frmAbout form

```
Private Sub Form_Load()
    lblVersion.Caption = "Version " & App.Major & "." & App.Minor & "." &        App.Revision
    lblTitle.Caption = App.Title

    '---- Added
    picIcon.Picture = fMainForm.Icon
    lblDescription.Caption = App.FileDescription
    lblDisclaimer.Caption = "WARNING: " & App.Title & " is protected by copyright
law and international treaties. "
    lblDisclaimer.Caption = lblDisclaimer.Caption & "Unauthorized reproduction or
distribution of this" & "program, or any portion of it, may result in severe civil "
& "and criminal penalties, and will be prosecuted " & "to the maximum extent possible
under the law."
    '---- End of Addition
End Sub
```

4. Add the following code to the general declarations of the frmDocument form. You declare private variables that will be exposed through properties.

```
Option Explicit

'---- Added
Private itsCurrentFileName As String

Private itsSaveFlag As Boolean
Private itsNewFlag As Boolean
'---- End of Addition
```

5. Add the rich text control (RICHTX32.OCX) in the component list obtained by selecting the Components submenu under the Project menu. Remove the text box control from frmDocument and add a rich text control instead. Table 94-3 lists the properties of the Rich Text box.

Table 94-3 Settings for frmEntry form in the MyNotepad project

Object	Property	Setting
Rich Text Box	Name	rtfText
	ScrollBars	3 - rtfBoth
	Text	""

6. Modify the Form_Resize procedure of the frmDocument by changing txtText to rtfText.

```
Private Sub Form_Resize()
    On Error Resume Next
    '---- Next Line Deleted
    'txtText.Move 100, 100, Me.ScaleWidth - 200, Me.ScaleHeight - 200
    '---- Next Line Added
    rtfText.Move 100, 100, Me.ScaleWidth - 200, Me.ScaleHeight - 200
End Sub
```

7. Add the following code to the general declarations of the frmDocument form. These read-only properties expose the private variables you defined earlier.

```
Public Property Get CurrentFileName() As String
    CurrentFileName = itsCurrentFileName
End Property

Public Property Get SaveNeeded() As Boolean
    SaveNeeded = itsSaveFlag
End Property

Public Property Get NewFile() As Boolean
    NewFile = itsNewFlag
End Property
```

8. Add the following code to the Change event of the rich text box on frmDocument form. The save flag is set if text is entered in the text box.

```
Private Sub rtfText_Change()
    If Len(rtfText.SelRTF) > 0 Then
        itsSaveFlag = True
    End If
End Sub
```

9. Add code to the general declarations of the frmMain form until it matches the code below. A few constants are defined as well as a private variable you will expose through a property.

```
Option Explicit

Private Declare Function OSWinHelp% Lib "user32" Alias "WinHelpA" (ByVal hwnd&, ByVal HelpFile$, ByVal wCommand%, dwData As Any)

'---- Added
```

```
Private Const MAX_LEN_FILENAME = 255

Private Const FILE_MRU_START = 0
Private Const FILE_MRU_END = 3

Private lngOpenDocCount As Long
'---- End of Addition
```

10. Add the following code to the general declarations of the frmMain form. The property exposes the private variable you defined earlier.

```
Public Property Get OpenDocCount() As Long
    OpenDocCount = lngOpenDocCount
End Property

Public Property Let OpenDocCount(ByVal lngCount As Long)
    lngOpenDocCount = lngCount
End Property
```

11. Add the following code to the general declarations of the frmMain form. These functions are used to update the menus.

```
Private Sub SetFileMenu(blnIsOpen As Boolean)
    mnuFileClose.Enabled = blnIsOpen
    mnuFileSave.Enabled = blnIsOpen
    mnuFileSaveAs.Enabled = blnIsOpen
    mnuFileSaveAll.Enabled = blnIsOpen
End Sub

Public Sub UpdateFileMenu()
    If OpenDocCount = 0 Then
        SetFileMenu False
    Else
        SetFileMenu True
    End If
End Sub

Public Sub SetEditMenu(blnIsOpen As Boolean)
    mnuEditCopy.Enabled = blnIsOpen
    mnuEditCut.Enabled = blnIsOpen
End Sub
```

12. Add the following code to the Form_Unload event of the frmDocument form. You save the document if needed, update the number of open documents, and update the File Menu on the frmMain form.

```
Private Sub Form_Unload(Cancel As Integer)
    SaveIfNeeded
    fMainForm.OpenDocCount = fMainForm.OpenDocCount - 1
    fMainForm.UpdateFileMenu
End Sub
```

13. Add the following code to the SelChange event of the rich text box on frmDocument form. The Edit menu and toolbar buttons on the frmMain form are updated depending on the selected text.

```
Private Sub rtfText_SelChange()
    fMainForm.tbToolBar.Buttons("Left").Value = tbrUnpressed
    fMainForm.tbToolBar.Buttons("Right").Value = tbrUnpressed
    fMainForm.tbToolBar.Buttons("Center").Value = tbrUnpressed

    fMainForm.tbToolBar.Buttons("Bold").Value = tbrUnpressed
    fMainForm.tbToolBar.Buttons("Italic").Value = tbrUnpressed
    fMainForm.tbToolBar.Buttons("Underline").Value = tbrUnpressed

    If Len(rtfText.SelRTF) > 0 Then
        fMainForm.SetEditMenu True

        If Not IsNull(rtfText.SelAlignment) Then
            Select Case rtfText.SelAlignment
            Case rtfLeft
                fMainForm.tbToolBar.Buttons("Left").Value = tbrPressed
            Case rtfRight
                fMainForm.tbToolBar.Buttons("Right").Value = tbrPressed
            Case rtfCenter
                fMainForm.tbToolBar.Buttons("Center").Value = tbrPressed
            End Select
        End If

        If Not IsNull(rtfText.SelBold) Then
            If rtfText.SelBold Then
                fMainForm.tbToolBar.Buttons("Bold").Value = tbrPressed
            End If
        End If

        If Not IsNull(rtfText.SelUnderline) Then
            If rtfText.SelUnderline Then
                fMainForm.tbToolBar.Buttons("Underline").Value = tbrPressed
            End If
        End If

        If Not IsNull(rtfText.SelItalic) Then
            If rtfText.SelItalic Then
                fMainForm.tbToolBar.Buttons("Italic").Value = tbrPressed
            End If
        End If
    Else
        fMainForm.SetEditMenu False
    End If
End Sub
```

14. Add the following code to the general declarations of the frmDocument form. These routines use the rich text properties to perform Clipboard operations or change the properties of the selected text.

```
Public Sub SetBold()
    If Len(rtfText.SelRTF) > 0 Then
        rtfText.SelBold = Not rtfText.SelBold
    End If
    rtfText_SelChange
End Sub

Public Sub SetItalic()
    If Len(rtfText.SelRTF) > 0 Then
```

```
            rtfText.SelItalic = Not rtfText.SelItalic
        End If
        rtfText_SelChange
End Sub

Public Sub SetUnderline()
    If Len(rtfText.SelRTF) > 0 Then
        rtfText.SelUnderline = Not rtfText.SelUnderline
    End If
    rtfText_SelChange
End Sub

Public Sub SetAlignment(intAlignmentMode As Integer)
    If Len(rtfText.SelRTF) > 0 Then
        rtfText.SelAlignment = intAlignmentMode
    End If
    rtfText_SelChange
End Sub

Public Sub Copy()
    If Len(rtfText.SelRTF) > 0 Then
        ' Copy the selected text onto the Clipboard.
        Clipboard.SetText rtfText.SelRTF
    End If
    rtfText_SelChange
End Sub

Public Sub Cut()
    If Len(rtfText.SelRTF) > 0 Then
        ' Copy the selected text onto the Clipboard.
        Clipboard.SetText rtfText.SelRTF
        ' Delete the selected text.
        rtfText.SelText = ""
    End If
    rtfText_SelChange
End Sub

Public Sub Paste()
    ' Place the text from the Clipboard into the Rich Text Box.
    rtfText.SelRTF = Clipboard.GetText()
    rtfText_SelChange
End Sub
```

15. Add the following code to the general declarations of the frmDocument form. These routines use the rich text box methods to save and retrieve a file.

```
Private Sub SaveIfNeeded()
    If SaveNeeded Then
        If vbYes = AskYN("Save this document?") Then
            Save
        End If
    End If
End Sub

Public Sub Init(UntitledCount As Long)
    itsCurrentFileName = "Untitled" & Trim$(UntitledCount)
    Me.Caption = itsCurrentFileName
    itsSaveFlag = False
```

continued on next page

continued from previous page

```
        itsNewFlag = True
End Sub

Public Function Retrieve(theFileName As String) As Boolean
        itsCurrentFileName = theFileName
        rtfText.LoadFile theFileName
        rtfText_SelChange

        Me.Caption = itsCurrentFileName

        itsSaveFlag = False
        itsNewFlag = False

        Retrieve = True
End Function

Public Function SaveAs(theFileName As String) As Boolean
        itsCurrentFileName = theFileName
        rtfText.SaveFile theFileName

        itsSaveFlag = False
        itsNewFlag = False

        SaveAs = True
End Function

Public Function Save() As Boolean
        Save = SaveAs(itsCurrentFileName)
End Function
```

16. Add the following code to the general declarations of the frmMain form. These routines are used to maintain the most recently used (MRU) file list. The OpenFile routine delegates the actual opening of the file to the MDI Child.

```
Private Sub OpenFile(strFullPathName As String)
        Me.MousePointer = vbHourglass

        If ActiveForm Is Nothing Then
                ' No open document
                LoadNewDoc
        Else
                If Not ActiveForm.NewFile Then
                        ' Open document is already used; open new one
                        LoadNewDoc
                End If
        End If

        If ActiveForm.Retrieve(strFullPathName) Then
                SetFileMenu True

                Me.Caption = getFileNameOnly(strFullPathName) & " - " & App.Title

                Add_MRU strFullPathName
        End If

        Me.MousePointer = vbDefault
End Sub
```

```
Private Sub Add_MRU(strFullPathName As String)
    Dim i As Integer, c As Integer

    ' Dim the work array
    ReDim FileArray(FILE_MRU_END - FILE_MRU_START + 1)

    ' Capture the open filename
    FileArray(0) = strFullPathName

    ' Capture the mnuFileMRU array elements
    For i = 0 To FILE_MRU_END - FILE_MRU_START
        If mnuFileMRU(i + FILE_MRU_START).Caption = "" Then
            Exit For
        End If
        FileArray(i + 1) = Right$(mnuFileMRU(i + FILE_MRU_START).Caption, ⇐
        Len(mnuFileMRU(i + FILE_MRU_START).Caption) - 3)
    Next i

    ' Place current file in mnuFileMRU(0)
    mnuFileMRU(FILE_MRU_START).Caption = "&1 " & FileArray(0)
    mnuFileMRU(FILE_MRU_START).Visible = True
    mnuFileBar6.Visible = True

    ' Move FileArray(1) through (FILE_MRU_END - FILE_MRU_START) to mnuFileMRU();
    ' Skip if it is the current file
    c = 1
    For i = 1 To FILE_MRU_END - FILE_MRU_START
        If FileArray(i) = "" Then
            Exit For
        End If
        If FileArray(i) <> FileArray(0) Then
            mnuFileMRU(c + FILE_MRU_START).Caption = "&" & c + 1 & " " & FileArray(i)
            mnuFileMRU(c + FILE_MRU_START).Visible = True
            c = c + 1
        End If
    Next i
End Sub

Private Sub Write_MRU()
    Dim i  As Integer, intResult As Integer
    Dim strFullPathName As String

    For i = 0 To FILE_MRU_END - FILE_MRU_START
        If Len(mnuFileMRU(i + FILE_MRU_START).Caption) > 0 Then
            SaveSetting App.Title, "MRU", "File" & Str$(i + 1), _
                Right(mnuFileMRU(i + FILE_MRU_START).Caption, ⇐
Len(mnuFileMRU(i + FILE_MRU_START).Caption) - 3)
        Else
            Exit For
        End If
    Next i
End Sub

Private Sub Get_MRU()
    Dim i  As Integer, intStrLen As Integer
    Dim strFullPathName As String

    For i = 0 To FILE_MRU_END - FILE_MRU_START
```

continued on next page

continued from previous page

```
            strFullPathName = GetSetting(App.Title, "MRU", "File" & Str$(i + 1), "None")
            If strFullPathName <> "None" Then
                mnuFileMRU(i + FILE_MRU_START).Caption = "&" & i + 1 & " " & strFullPathName
                mnuFileMRU(i + FILE_MRU_START).Visible = True
            Else
                Exit For
            End If
        Next i

        If mnuFileMRU(FILE_MRU_START).Visible = True Then
            mnuFileBar6.Visible = True
        End If
End Sub
```

17. Add code to the LoadNewDoc procedure in the frmMain form until it matches the code below. You use a property instead of a static variable to keep track of the number of open documents. This allows you to change the number of open documents when one is closed (this is done in the Form_Unload event of frmDocument).

```
Private Sub LoadNewDoc()
    '---- Deleted
    'Static lDocumentCount As Long
    'Dim frmD As frmDocument

    'lDocumentCount = lDocumentCount + 1
    'Set frmD = New frmDocument
    'frmD.Caption = "Document " & lDocumentCount
    'frmD.Show
    '---- End of Deletion
    '---- Added
    lngOpenDocCount = lngOpenDocCount + 1

    Dim frmD As frmDocument
    Set frmD = New frmDocument
    frmD.Init lngOpenDocCount
    frmD.Show

    SetFileMenu True
    '---- End of Addition
End Sub
```

18. Add code to the Form_Load event of the frmMain form until it matches the code below. You add the retrieval of the most recently used file list and the disabling of the Edit menu items that do not apply with first selecting text.

```
Private Sub MDIForm_Load()
    Me.Left = GetSetting(App.Title, "Settings", "MainLeft", 1000)
    Me.Top = GetSetting(App.Title, "Settings", "MainTop", 1000)
    Me.Width = GetSetting(App.Title, "Settings", "MainWidth", 6500)
    Me.Height = GetSetting(App.Title, "Settings", "MainHeight", 6500)
    LoadNewDoc

    '---- Added
    Get_MRU
```

```
    SetEditMenu False
    mnuEditPaste.Enabled = False
    mnuEditPasteSpecial.Enabled = False
    '---- End of Addition
End Sub
```

19. Modify the code in the tbToolBar_ButtonClick event of the About box until it matches the code below. You delegate the alignment and text property changes to the active MDI Child.

```
Case "Bold"
    'To Do
    '---- Deleted Next Line
    ' MsgBox "Bold Code goes here!"
    If Not ActiveForm Is Nothing Then
        ActiveForm.SetBold
    End If
Case "Italic"
    'To Do
    '---- Deleted Next Line
    ' MsgBox "Italic Code goes here!"
    If Not ActiveForm Is Nothing Then
        ActiveForm.SetItalic
    End If
Case "Underline"
    'To Do
    '---- Deleted Next Line
    ' MsgBox "Underline Code goes here!"
    If Not ActiveForm Is Nothing Then
        ActiveForm.SetUnderline
    End If
Case "Left"
    'To Do
    '---- Deleted Next Line
    ' MsgBox "Left Code goes here!"
    If Not ActiveForm Is Nothing Then
        ActiveForm.SetAlignment rtfLeft
    End If
Case "Center"
    'To Do
    '---- Deleted Next Line
    ' MsgBox "Center Code goes here!"
    If Not ActiveForm Is Nothing Then
        ActiveForm.SetAlignment rtfCenter
    End If
Case "Right"
    'To Do
    '---- Deleted Next Line
    ' MsgBox "Right Code goes here!"
    If Not ActiveForm Is Nothing Then
        ActiveForm.SetAlignment rtfRight
    End If
```

20. Modify the three mnuEdit handling routines in frmMain until they match the code below. As before, you delegate the actual work for the Clipboard action to the MDI Child.

```
Private Sub mnuEditCopy_Click()
    'To Do
    '---- Deleted Next Line
    ' MsgBox "Copy Code goes here!"
    If Not ActiveForm Is Nothing Then
        ActiveForm.Copy
        mnuEditPaste.Enabled = True
    End If
End Sub

Private Sub mnuEditCut_Click()
    'To Do
    '---- Deleted Next Line
    ' MsgBox "Cut Code goes here!"
    If Not ActiveForm Is Nothing Then
        ActiveForm.Cut
        mnuEditPaste.Enabled = True
    End If
End Sub

Private Sub mnuEditPaste_Click()
    'To Do
    '---- Deleted Next Line
    ' MsgBox "Paste Code goes here!"
    If Not ActiveForm Is Nothing Then
        ActiveForm.Paste
    End If
End Sub
```

21. Add code to the mnuFile handling procedures in the frmMain form until it matches the following code.

```
Private Sub MDIForm_Unload(Cancel As Integer)
    If Me.WindowState <> vbMinimized Then
        SaveSetting App.Title, "Settings", "MainLeft", Me.Left
        SaveSetting App.Title, "Settings", "MainTop", Me.Top
        SaveSetting App.Title, "Settings", "MainWidth", Me.Width
        SaveSetting App.Title, "Settings", "MainHeight", Me.Height
    End If

    '---- Added
    Write_MRU
    End
    '---- End of Addition
End Sub

Private Sub mnuFileOpen_Click()
    Dim sFile As String

    With dlgCommonDialog
        'To Do
        'set the flags and attributes of the
        'common dialog control
        '---- Deleted Next Line
        '.Filter = "All Files (*.*)|*.*"
        '---- Added Next Line
        .Filter = "Rich Text Files (*.rtf)|*.rtf" & "|All Files (*.*)|*.*"

        .ShowOpen
```

```
            If Len(.filename) = 0 Then
                Exit Sub
            End If
            sFile = .filename
        End With
        'To Do
        'process the opened file
        '---- Added
        OpenFile sFile
        '---- End Of Addition
End Sub

Private Sub mnuFileClose_Click()
        'To Do
        '---- Deleted Next Line
        ' MsgBox "Close Code goes here!"
        '---- Added Remaining Lines
        If Not ActiveForm Is Nothing Then
            Unload ActiveForm
        End If
End Sub

Private Sub mnuFileSave_Click()
        'To Do
        '---- Deleted Next Line
        ' MsgBox "Save Code goes here!"
        '---- Added Remaining Lines
        If Not ActiveForm Is Nothing Then
            Dim strFullPathName As String

            strFullPathName = ActiveForm.CurrentFileName

            If ActiveForm.NewFile Then
                mnuFileSaveAs_Click
            Else
                Me.MousePointer = vbHourglass
                If ActiveForm.SaveAs(strFullPathName) Then
                    Me.Caption = getFileNameOnly(strFullPathName) & " - " & App.Title

                    Add_MRU strFullPathName
                End If
                Me.MousePointer = vbDefault
            End If
        End If
End Sub

Private Sub mnuFileSaveAs_Click()
        'To Do
        'Setup the common dialog control
        'prior to calling ShowSave
        '---- Deleted Next Line
        'dlgCommonDialog.ShowSave
        '---- Added Remaining Lines
        If Not ActiveForm Is Nothing Then
            Dim strFullPathName As String

            With dlgCommonDialog
                .Filter = "Rich Text Files (*.rtf)|*.rtf" & "|All Files (*.*)|*.*"
                        .ShowSave
```

continued on next page

continued from previous page

```
            If Len(.filename) = 0 Then
                Exit Sub
            End If
            strFullPathName = .filename
        End With

        Me.MousePointer = vbHourglass
        If ActiveForm.SaveAs(strFullPathName) Then
            Me.Caption = getFileNameOnly(strFullPathName) & " - " & App.Title

            Add_MRU strFullPathName
        End If
        Me.MousePointer = vbDefault
    End If
End Sub

Private Sub mnuFileMRU_Click(Index As Integer)
    'To Do
    '---- Deleted Next Line
    ' MsgBox "MRU Code goes here!"
    OpenFile Right(mnuFileMRU(Index).Caption, Len(mnuFileMRU(Index) .Caption) - 3)
End Sub
```

22. Add code to the MDIForm_Unload procedure of the frmMain form until it matches the code below. Before ending the application, we write the most recently used file list to the registry.

```
Private Sub MDIForm_Unload(Cancel As Integer)
    If Me.WindowState <> vbMinimized Then
        SaveSetting App.Title, "Settings", "MainLeft", Me.Left
        SaveSetting App.Title, "Settings", "MainTop", Me.Top
        SaveSetting App.Title, "Settings", "MainWidth", Me.Width
        SaveSetting App.Title, "Settings", "MainHeight", Me.Height
    End If

    '---- Added
    Write_MRU
    End
    '---- End of Addition

End Sub
```

23. Add a new form to the project. Select the Tip Of The Day template when you are presented with the New Form dialog.

24. Add the following code to the general declarations of the frmTip form. You declare a private variable that will be exposed through a property.

```
Dim itsShowAtStartupFlag As Long
```

25. Add the following code to the general declarations of the frmTip form. The read-only property exposes the private variables you defined in the previous step.

```
Public Property Get ShowAtStartup() As Boolean
    ShowAtStartup = (itsShowAtStartupFlag = 1)
End Property
```

26. Modify the Form_Load event of the frmTip form as in the code below.

```
' See if we should be shown at startup
'---- Deleted
'ShowAtStartup = GetSetting(App.EXEName, "Options", "Show Tips at Startup", 1)
'If ShowAtStartup = 0 Then
'    Unload Me
'    Exit Sub
'End If
'---- End of Deletion
'---- Added
itsShowAtStartupFlag = GetSetting(App.EXEName, "Options", "Show Tips at Startup", 1)
If itsShowAtStartupFlag = 0 Then
    Exit Sub
End If
'---- End of Addition
```

27. Modify the Main routine in the Module1 code module so that it matches the code below.

```
Sub Main()
    Set fMainForm = New frmMain
    '---- Deleted Next Line
    fMainForm.Show
    '---- Added Remaining Lines
    Load fMainForm
    Load frmTip

    fMainForm.Show

    If frmTip.ShowAtStartup Then
        frmTip.Show vbModal
    End If
End Sub
```

How It Works

The majority of this project is based around the frmMain form, which contains the menus and the toolbar, and the frmDocument form, which contains a RichTextBox control used to edit and display text. You can type your own text in the RichTextBox control, or select, copy, cut, and paste blocks of text, or change the style and alignment of the selected text. You can also load and save .RTF files. When a menu is selected or toolbar button pressed, the action is delegated to the active child window.

You have the beginnings of a functional MDI text editor based around the RichTextBox control, complete with a tip of the day and most recently used file list. Figure 94-12 shows the project in operation.

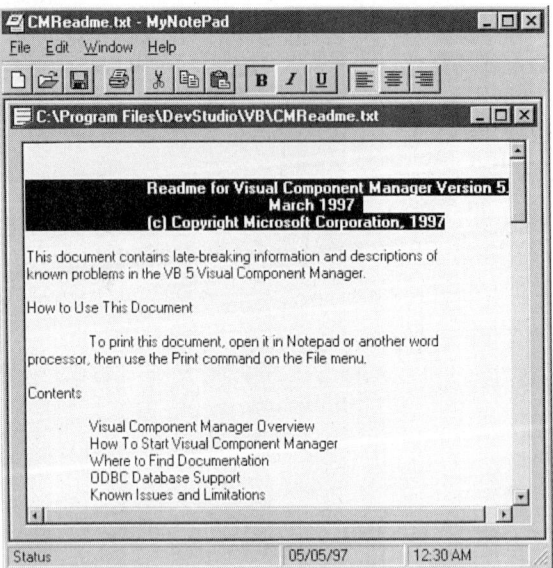

Figure 94-12 The MyNotepad project in action

95

CLASS BUILDER UTILITY

One of the best features of wizards is their ability to reduce the amount of work needed to complete a task. The Class Builder Utility is no exception. Before Visual Basic 5, creating classes and collections often involved a lot of repetitive typing. Cut-and-paste helped alleviate this, but introduced a level of danger when comments were not changed or the code was not completely adapted to its new use. Visual Basic 4 also did not allow a way to show a relation between objects. The Class Builder utility fixes all these problems.

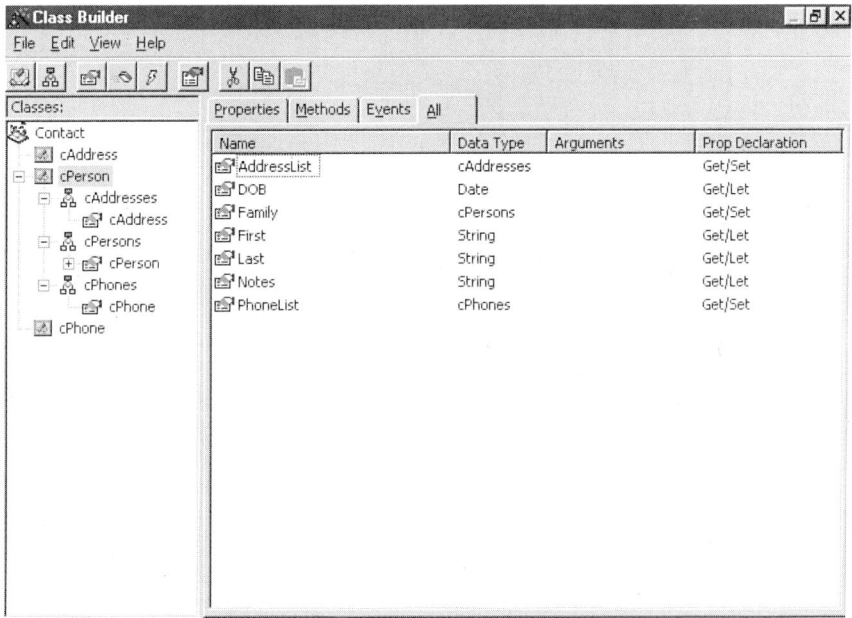

Figure 95-1 The Class Builder utility

The Class Builder utility shown in Figure 95-1 will quickly generate frameworks for classes and collections with a minimum of work. Type in the name and click a few options. Voilá! you have a new class or collection. With just a few more keystrokes and clicks you can add properties, methods, and events.

The Class Builder Utility also allows you to show hierarchical relations between your objects. By simply dragging and dropping you can move classes around the tree to show the project's object model.

Adding a Class

Adding a new class is simple with the Class Builder Utility. The Class Module Builder dialog shown in Figure 95-2 is used to create a new class. The dialog allows you to specify the name, a class to base the new class on, and the instancing.

Visual Basic's objects don't support inheritance, so often when creating a new class that builds on the functionality of another, you find yourself cutting and pasting to get the pieces you want. By selecting a class in the Based On field, the Class Builder utility will create a new class with all the properties, methods, and events of the original class. It is then very simple to use the Properties, Methods, and Events lists to delete what you don't need and add new functionality.

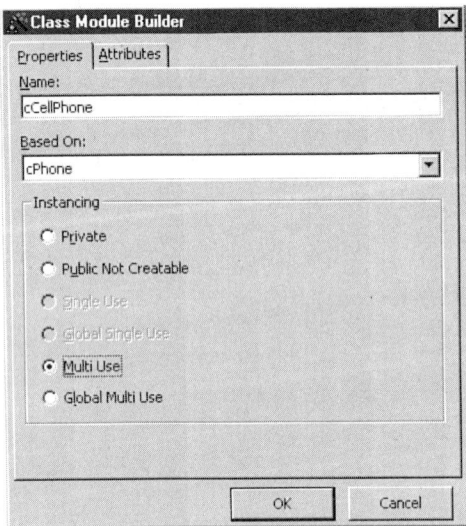

Figure 95-2 Adding a class

Adding a Collection

Creating a collection class in Visual Basic is one of those repetitive tasks that bore programmers to tears. After you have created the first few, you know the drill: Add method, Count method, Remove method, and Item method. Each collection class is almost exactly the same except for the arguments and a few lines of the Add method. Until the Class Builder utility, the only recourse was cut-and-paste. Now the Class Builder utility will do all that work for you.

The Collection Builder dialog shown in Figure 95-3 is used to create the new collection. It allows you to select an existing class to make the collection from, or choose to create a new class. If you select an existing class, the Add method will have all the properties of the existing class as arguments. If you choose to create the class there, the Add method will have no arguments except the optional key.

Like the Class Module Builder dialog described previously, the Based On field allows you to select a collection to copy all the members from.

Adding Properties, Methods, and Events

The Class Builder utility provides an easy-to use-interface to fill out your new classes and collections. Highlight the class or collection you wish to edit in the Object Model Pane and use File|New or the toolbar to add a property, method, or event. Each selection will take you to a dialog that collects information on the new member.

Figure 95-4 shows the Property Builder dialog. This dialog is used to add new properties to a class. You can specify the name, the access methodology, and whether it is the default property.

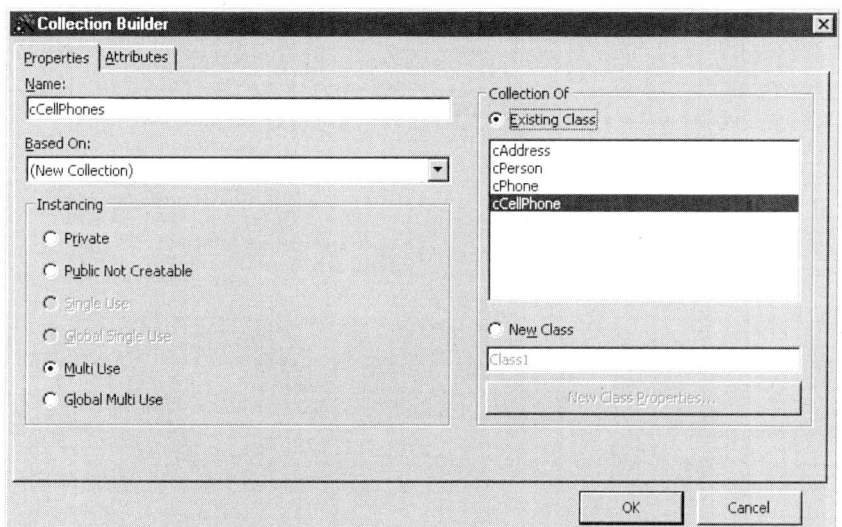

Figure 95-3 Adding a collection

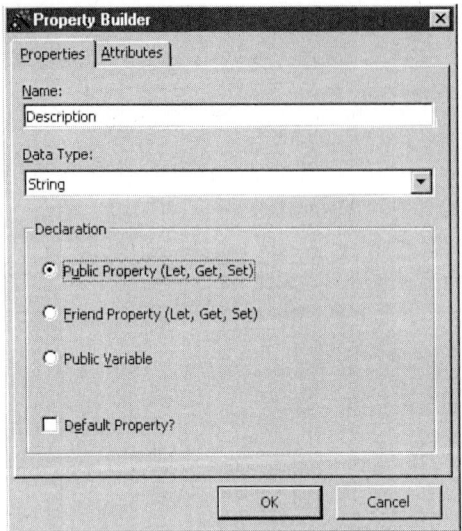

Figure 95-4 Adding a new property

The code below shows what the Class Builder utility adds to a class for the selections pictured in Figure 95-4.

```
'local variable(s) to hold property value(s)
Private mvarDescription As String 'local copy

Public Property Let Description(ByVal vData As String)
'used when assigning a value to the property, on the left side of an
'assignment.  Syntax: X.Description = 5
    mvarDescription = vData
End Property

Public Property Get Description() As String
'used when retrieving value of a property, on the right side of an
'assignment.  Syntax: Debug.Print X.Description
    Description = mvarDescription
End Property
```

Figure 95-5 shows the Method Builder dialog. This dialog allows you to specify the name, arguments, return data type, friend access, and whether it is the default method. Selecting a (None) return data type will create a sub; any other selection will create a function with a return value of the selected data type. The plus sign next to the argument list adds a new argument. It presents a dialog to collect the name and data type. The delete button removes an argument and the two arrows change the order of the arguments.

The code below shows what the Class Builder utility adds to a class for the selections pictured in Figure 95-5.

```
Public Sub Format()
End Sub
```

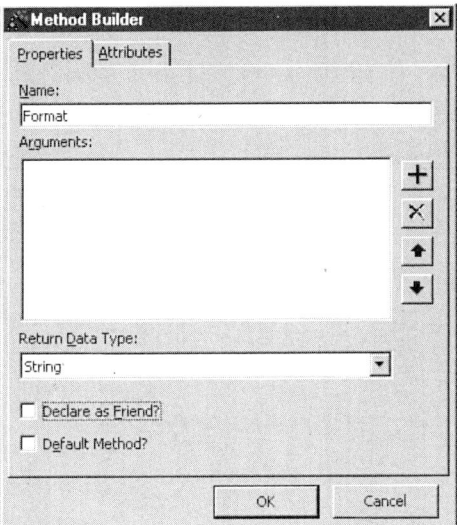

Figure 95-5 Adding a new method

Figure 95-6 shows the Event Builder dialog. It allows you to specify the name and arguments of the event. The argument list and buttons work like the argument list for the Method Builder dialog, discussed above.

The code below shows what the Class Builder utility adds to a class for the selections pictured in Figure 95-6.

```
Public Event Error(ErrorNumber As Long, ErrorDescription As String)
```

Building a Hierarchy

Visual Basic provides a very easy-to-use model for creating objects, but provides no way to show the relations between those objects. The Object Model pane is used to list the project's objects and display them in a hierarchical view to show their relations.

By selecting an object or collection and then creating a new object or collection, the Class Builder utility will add the new object as a child of the existing one and add an instance as a property of the existing object. If you have mistakenly added an object as a child of an existing object, the "This class is a Top Level Object" option on the Collection Builder and Class Module Builder dialogs will add the new object to the root. You may also use drag-and-drop to move objects around the hierarchy. Dragging an object onto another object will make it a child and create an instance as a property of the target object.

When creating a new child object, a new tab is added to the Collection Builder and Class Module Builder dialogs. Figure 95-7 shows the options on the Object Creation tab.

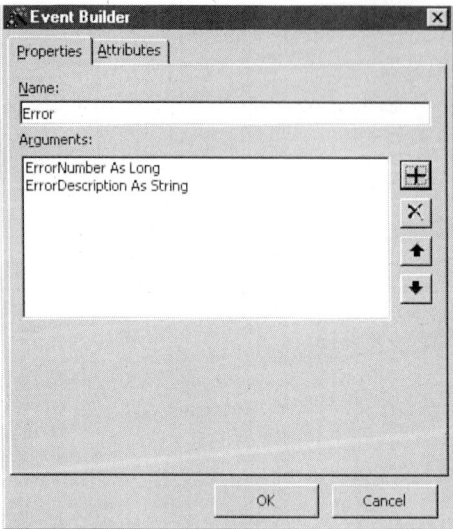

Figure 95-6 Adding a new event

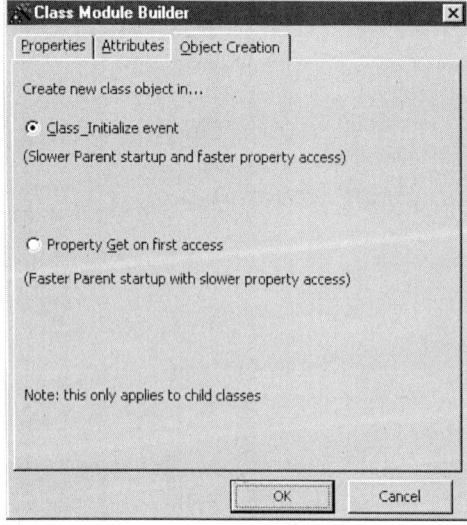

Figure 95-7 The Object Creation options

The two options are a trade-off: load time versus property access time. The Class Initialize Event option creates the child object when the parent initializes. Load time suffers, but no penalty is incurred after that. The Property Get on first access option checks to see whether the object is Nothing and creates the object if needed. The parent class will load faster, but there is a penalty each time the property is accessed.

Debug and Error Handling Options

Another tedious and repetitive task is writing the debug and error handling code. We all know we should, bulletproof code is the ultimate goal, but how many of us actually do it when faced with an impending deadline? The Class Builder utility can help make this easier. The sample below is an example of a Class Builder utility-generated class with one property, Description.

```
'local variable(s) to hold property value(s)
Private mvarDescription As String 'local copy

Public Property Let Description(ByVal vData As String)
'used when assigning a value to the property, on the left side of an
'assignment.  Syntax: X.Description = 5
    mvarDescription = vData
End Property

Public Property Get Description() As String
'used when retrieving value of a property, on the right side of an
'assignment.  Syntax: Debug.Print X.Description
    Description = mvarDescription
End Property
```

The Class Builder Options dialog, pictured in Figure 95-8, can make the Class Builder utility write the debug and error handling code for you. The first option generates a log to the Immediate window when a class is created and terminated. This can help you track down that most nefarious bug, the object leak. When your application is done running, you should have a terminate entry for every create. If you don't, something is not getting destroyed properly. This option will also add a module to your code, the modClassIDGenerator.BAS file. This module is used to generate unique identifiers for each object created.

The second option generates starter error trapping code for each call in your class. In most cases, the generated code will be all you need to point your debugging efforts to the exact spot where the problem lies. If you need to add code to handle the error, the framework is already in place. This option also adds a module to your code, the modErrorHandling.BAS file.

The code below is the same one property class as the previous code, with the addition of the Class Builder utility's debug and error trapping code. Notice the debug code in the Class Initialize and Class Terminate subs and how the Property Let and Property Get start with an On Error statement and complete with a section for error handling.

```
'set this to 0 to disable debug code in this class
#Const DebugMode = 1

#If DebugMode Then
    'local variable to hold the serialized class ID that was created
    'in Class_Initialize
    Private mlClassDebugID As Long
#End If
'local variable(s) to hold property value(s)
Private mvarDescription As String 'local copy

Public Property Let Description(ByVal vData As String)
```

continued on next page

continued from previous page

```
    On Error GoTo DescriptionLetErr
'used when assigning a value to the property, on the left side of an
'assignment.  Syntax: X.Description = 5
    mvarDescription = vData
    Exit Property
DescriptionLetErr:
    Call RaiseError(MyUnhandledError, "cPhone:Description Property Let")
End Property

Public Property Get Description() As String
    On Error GoTo DescriptionGetErr
'used when retrieving value of a property, on the right side of an
'assignment.  Syntax: Debug.Print X.Description
    Description = mvarDescription
    Exit Property
DescriptionGetErr:
    Call RaiseError(MyUnhandledError, "cPhone:Description Property Get")
End Property

Private Sub Class_Initialize()
    #If DebugMode Then
        'get the next available class ID, and print out
        'that the class was created successfully
        mlClassDebugID = GetNextClassDebugID()
        Debug.Print "'" & TypeName(Me) & "' instance " & mlClassDebugID & " created"
    #End If
End Sub

Private Sub Class_Terminate()
    'the class is being destroyed
    #If DebugMode Then
        Debug.Print "'" & TypeName(Me) & "' instance " ⇐
                & CStr(mlClassDebugID) & " is terminating"
    #End If
End Sub

#If DebugMode Then
    Public Property Get ClassDebugID()
        'if we are in debug mode, surface this property that consumers
        'can query
        ClassDebugID = mlClassDebugID
    End Property
#End If
```

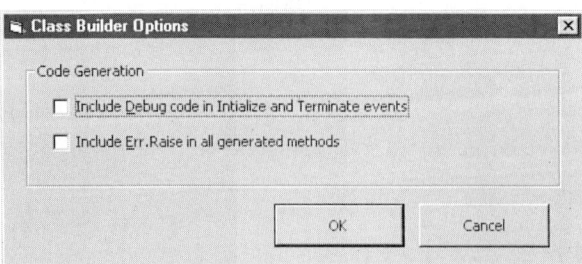

Figure 95-8   Debug and error handling options

96

DATA FORM WIZARD/DESIGNER

In Chapters 57 through 61 you saw how easy it was to use the data control to build database applications. Arrange some controls, set a few properties, write a few lines of code, and you had a fully functioning application. Well, Microsoft made it even easier than that. (Don't tell your boss about the Data Form Wizard: If this gets out, we will all be out of jobs. Quietly use it and spend the rest of your time on the schedule to surf the Internet.)

The Data Form Wizard creates three types of simple, but fully functional data forms. For most applications, they will not be everything you need in a data form, but they will certainly save a lot of time and effort.

Choosing a Datasource

The first screens of the Data Form Wizard are devoted to choosing a datasource. You may connect to either an ISAM or ODBC datasource. Figure 96-1 shows the list of available database formats.

Selecting an ISAM database type will take you to the next screen where you can specify or browse for a database file. You can also use this window to select which recordsets are available to the Data Form Wizard. The Data Form Wizard can use queries and tables to build data forms.

Choosing the Remote(ODBC) option will take you to the ODBC Connection Information window. The Connection Information window, shown in Figure 96-2, allows you to specify the standard ODBC connection information, such as datasource name, user id, and password.

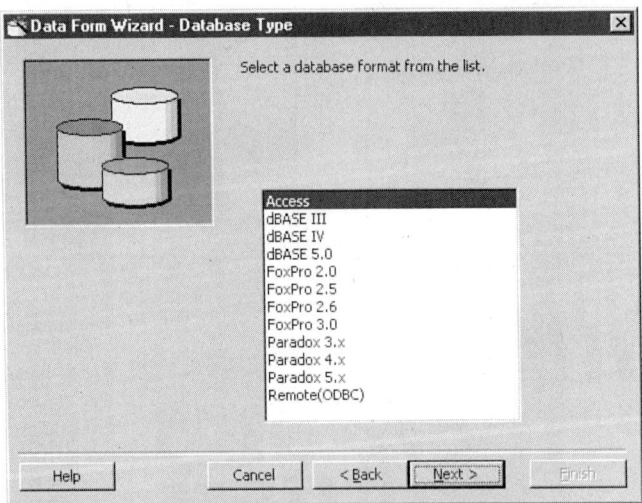

Figure 96-1 Selecting a database type

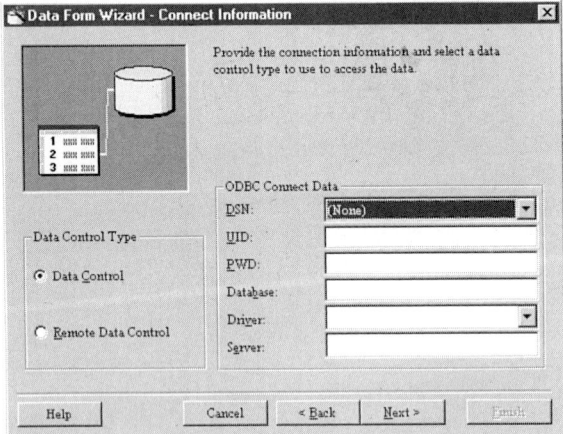

Figure 96-2 Setting up an ODBC datasource

When you connect to an ODBC datasource, you have the option of using the Remote Data control or the Data control to handle the binding. The Remote Data control uses RDO to connect to the database. The Data control uses DAO. A complete discussion of the benefits of each can be found in Chapter 66, "Remote Data Access and DCOM." Whichever you choose, the Data Form Wizard will add the appropriate references and custom controls to enable your data form.

Data Form Styles

The Data Form Wizard can create three different data forms. The single record data form displays one record at a time, using a data control to move through the recordset. The grid data form uses a DBGrid to display the entire recordset; the data control can be visible or not. The master/detail data form is a single record data form with the addition of a list. The list is used to display records where there is a one to many relationship between the master record and the details. Each of these is discussed in the following sections. Figure 96-3 shows the Data Form Wizard window where you select the data form type to create.

Single Record Data Form

The single record data form is the classic data form. It has a Data or Remote Data control that is used to move through the recordset and a bound control for each field in the recordset. You choose the recordset using the Record Source window, shown in Figure 96-4.

From here you can select a table or QueryDef in an ISAM database or a table from an ODBC database. Choose the fields you wish to see on your data form. The > and < buttons select or remove one field at a time; the >> and << buttons select all or remove all fields. Use the up and down arrow buttons to order your field selections.

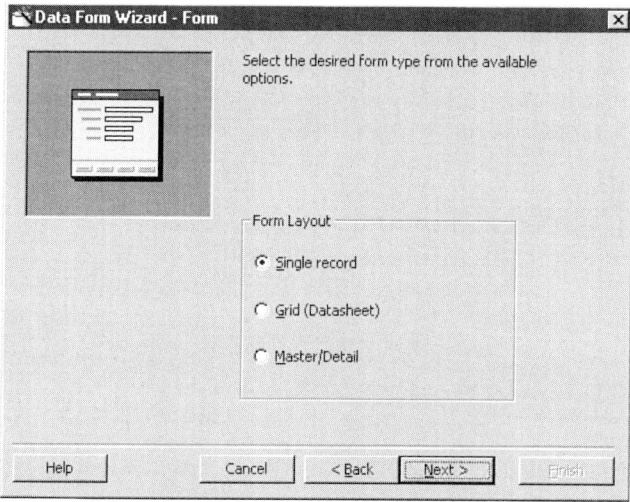

Figure 96-3 Selecting a data form style

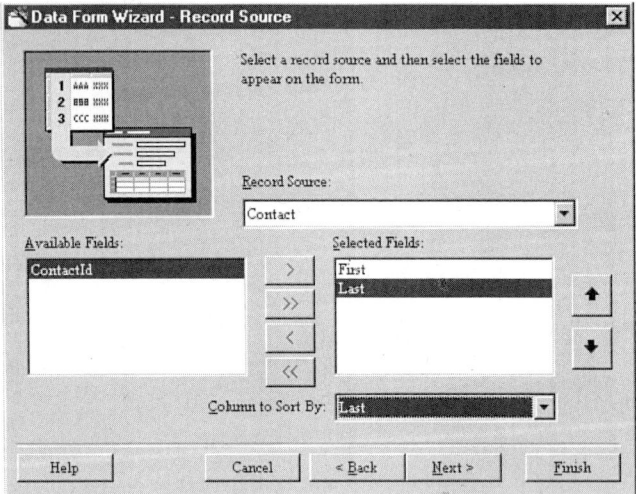

Figure 96-4   Selecting a record source for the data form

Next, using the Control Selection window pictured in Figure 96-5, you can have the Data Form Wizard also create Add, Delete, Update, Refresh, and Close buttons. Finally the Data Form Wizard will present a window where you can edit the name for the generated form.

Figure 96-6 shows a completed single record data form. It is not very pretty, but prettying up a form is probably one of the easiest tasks to do in Visual Basic. The following code was generated by the Data Form Wizard. The code works well and could be compiled to build a complete application; however, there is no error handling or

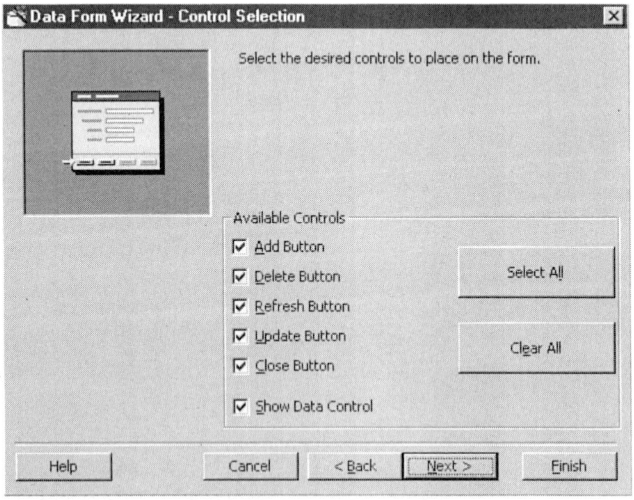

Figure 96-5   Selecting controls for the data form

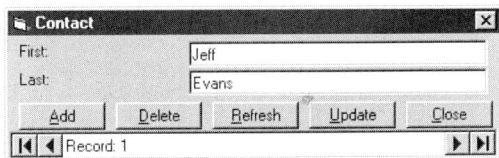

Figure 96-6 A single record data form

data validation. The Data Form Wizard has commented where you may want to expand functionality or error handling.

```
Option Explicit

Private Sub cmdAdd_Click()
  datPrimaryRS.Recordset.AddNew
End Sub

Private Sub cmdDelete_Click()
  With datPrimaryRS.Recordset
    .Delete
    .MoveNext
    If .EOF Then .MoveLast
  End With
End Sub

Private Sub cmdRefresh_Click()
  'This is only needed for multi user apps
  datPrimaryRS.Refresh
End Sub

Private Sub cmdUpdate_Click()
  datPrimaryRS.UpdateRecord
  datPrimaryRS.Recordset.Bookmark = datPrimaryRS.Recordset.LastModified
End Sub

Private Sub cmdClose_Click()
  Screen.MousePointer = vbDefault
  Unload Me
End Sub

Private Sub datPrimaryRS_Error(DataErr As Integer, Response As Integer)
  'This is where you would put error handling code
  'If you want to ignore errors, comment out the next line
  'If you want to trap them, add code here to handle them
  MsgBox "Data error event hit err:" & Error$(DataErr)
  Response = 0   'Throw away the error
End Sub

Private Sub datPrimaryRS_Reposition()
  Screen.MousePointer = vbDefault
  On Error Resume Next
  'This will display the current record position
  'for dynasets and snapshots
  datPrimaryRS.Caption = "Record: " & (datPrimaryRS.Recordset.AbsolutePosition + 1)
End Sub
```

continued on next page

continued from previous page

```
Private Sub datPrimaryRS_Validate(Action As Integer, Save As Integer)
  'This is where you put validation code
  'This event gets called when the following actions occur
  Select Case Action
    Case vbDataActionMoveFirst
    Case vbDataActionMovePrevious
    Case vbDataActionMoveNext
    Case vbDataActionMoveLast
    Case vbDataActionAddNew
    Case vbDataActionUpdate
    Case vbDataActionDelete
    Case vbDataActionFind
    Case vbDataActionBookmark
    Case vbDataActionClose
      Screen.MousePointer = vbDefault
  End Select
  Screen.MousePointer = vbHourglass
End Sub

Private Sub Form_Unload(Cancel As Integer)
  Screen.MousePointer = vbDefault
End Sub
```

Grid (Datasheet) Data Form

The grid data form is similar to the single record data form in terms of the type of recordset it can display. Instead of a Data control and a separate bound control for each field, the grid data form uses a Data control and a DBGrid control. All records are visible at once, and you do not need to use the Data control to navigate through the recordset. Figure 96-7 shows a Data Form Wizard generated grid data form.

The code generated is similar to the code generated for the single record data form; places where you may want to enhance the code are clearly commented. The application could be compiled and used. An excellent use for these Data Form Wizard

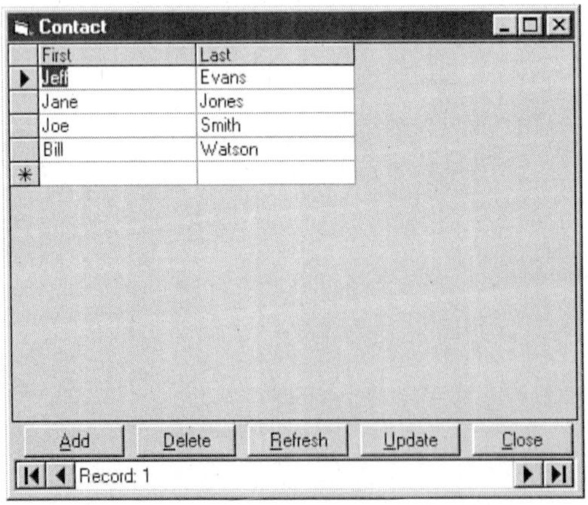

Figure 96-7   A grid data form

applications might be an in-house maintenance application, or as a temporary application to populate a database for development.

Master/Detail Data Form

The master/detail data form is the same as the single record data form with the addition a list at the bottom of the screen. Consider the database shown in Table 96-1, where you have a table of contacts and another table with a list of phone numbers for contacts. This is a simple one to many relationship. When viewing a contact, you would logically want to also view all the phone numbers where that contact could be reached. The Data Form Wizard can create a master/detail data form that does just that.

Table 96-1 Tables in contact database

Contact	Phone
ContactId	PhoneId
First	ContactId
Last	Phone
	Type

Using the Data Form Wizard to set up a master/detail data form works like the setup for a single record data form. First, you are asked to select the recordset for the master record. This is the record that will work like the single record data form. The form will have a Data control or Remote Data control and a bound control for each field selected from the recordset. The user will use the Data control or Remote Data control to move through the recordset. Next, you choose the recordset for the detail portion of the data form. In the example above, this would be the list of phone numbers, so you would select the Phone table. Finally you are asked to show the relationship between the two recordsets. Figure 96-8 shows the Record Source Relation window which indicates the relation between the two recordsets. Select the field that links the two tables.

The wizard-generated form is shown in Figure 96-9. Like the single record and grid data forms discussed earlier, the form is fully functional and can be used without additional code. Places where additional code might be wanted are commented.

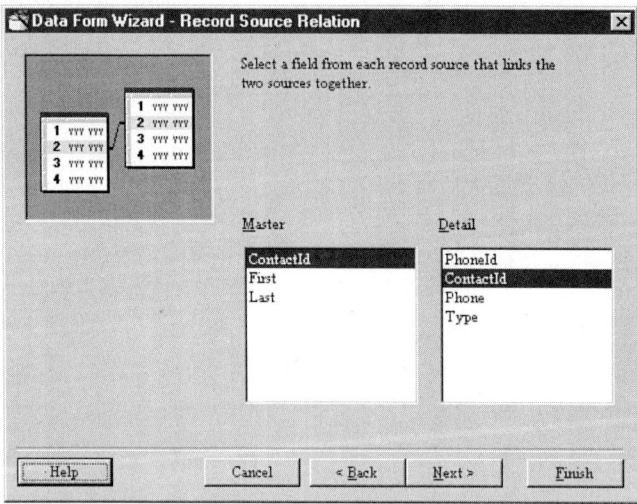

Figure 96-8 Showing the relationship between the master and detail recordsets

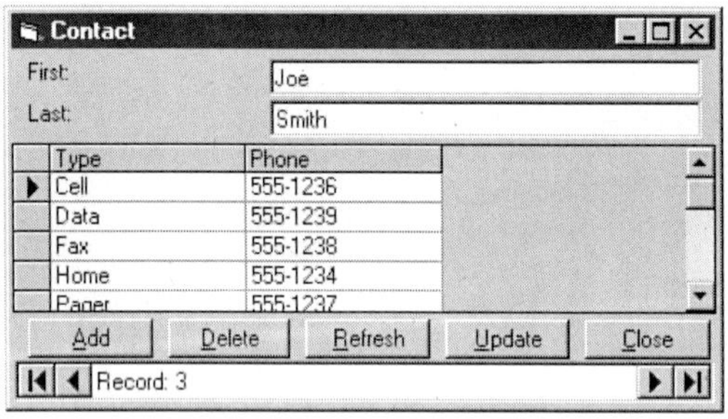

Figure 96-9 A Master/Detail data form

97

PROPERTY PAGE WIZARD

In Chapters 82 to 87 you saw how Visual Basic could be used to create ActiveX controls without having to dive into Visual C++ and MFC. In Visual C++, you use the Class Wizard to build the property dialog. It makes designing property pages fast and simple. You just draw the interface and bind class members to the controls. Well, the Visual Basic team one-upped the Visual C++ team when they created the Property Page Wizard for Visual Basic.

Almost everything about creating a property page can be done automatically or with a few clicks in the Property Page Wizard. You do not even have to draw the UI yourself. The Property Page Wizard will take care of that for you. Just tell the wizard what pages you want and assign properties to each page. It works like magic!

Adding Property Pages

To get started with the Property Page Wizard, you first select the control whose property pages you wish to change or create. Figure 97-1 shows the Select a Use Control window of the Property Page Wizard. Select the control to edit and press the Next button to continue. If the project has only one UserControl object, the Property Page Wizard will skip this window and go straight to the Property Pages window.

The Select the Property Pages window of the Property Page Wizard, shown in Figure 97-2, helps you create new property pages and arrange their order. From here you can also rename and remove property pages from your Property Page dialog.

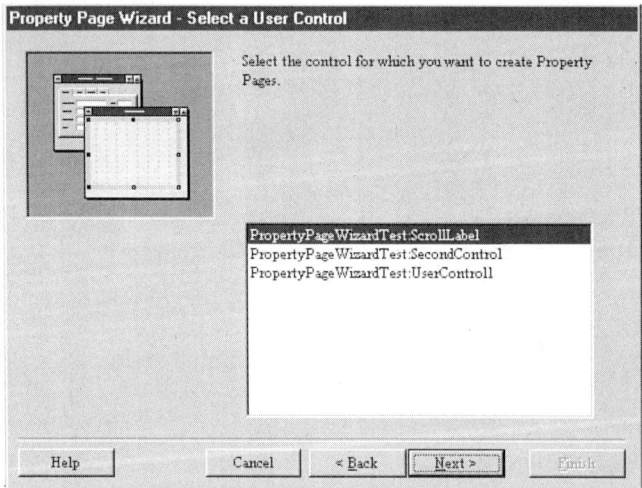

Figure 97-1   Selecting a control

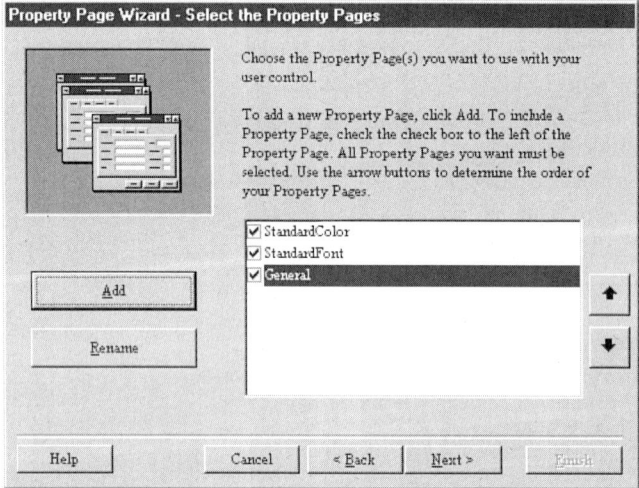

Figure 97-2   Editing the Property Page list

If you have any color, picture, or font properties, the appropriate StandardColor, StandardPicture, and StandardFont pages will already be selected. These pages take care of all your Color, Picture, and Font properties. All the appropriate properties of your control will already be assigned to these pages.

All other property pages in your project will also be available in the Property Page list; however, they will not be selected by default. If you have a project with more than one custom control, you can share pages between controls as long as the properties on the page are applied to each of the controls.

Use the Add button to insert additional property pages. Your property pages should logically group the control's properties. Most Property Page dialogs have a General tab as a catch-all for properties that do not fall into a specific category. Other possible pages might be: Appearance, Data Access, and Behavior. Each of these pages would group together properties that are similar or configure the same function.

To remove a property page from the Property Page dialog, uncheck it in the list of property pages. This will leave the code in your project, but the page will not be displayed at runtime. To completely remove it, remove the file from the project.

Use the arrow keys to the right of the list of property pages to alter the order the tabs display in the runtime dialog. Select a page and press the up or down arrow to move it.

The Rename button will present a dialog which allows you to change the name of the highlighted property page. The Property Page Wizard will change the Name of the property page in your project in addition to the Caption. If you have already saved the file, it will not change the filename.

Assigning Properties to a Page

Figure 97-3 shows the Add Properties window of the Property Page Wizard. This window has a tab for each of the pages you added in the Property Pages window and the selected standard pages. Here you assign the custom control's properties to a property page.

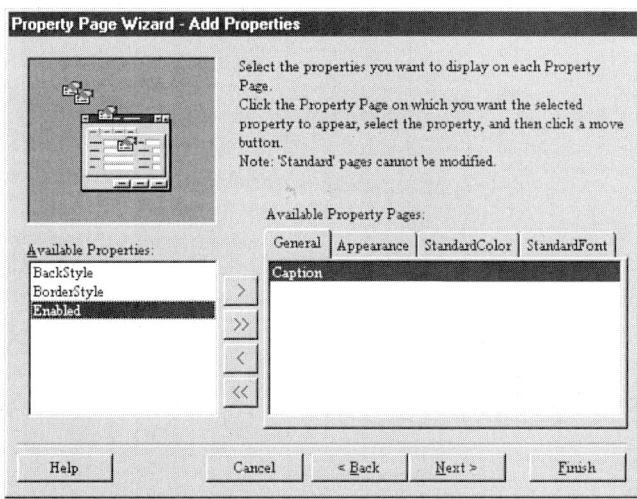

Figure 97-3   Assigning properties to a page

Use the >>, <<, >, and < buttons to move properties from an Available Property list to a property page. The >> button moves all properties left in the Available Property list to the selected property page. The << button removes all the properties on the selected property page and puts them back in the Available Property list. The > and < buttons move a single selected property to or from the selected property page. The >>, <<, >, and < buttons are not available when the standard property pages are selected. You may also drag and drop properties from the Available Property list to the pages and between the pages.

There is no way to order the properties on the page; however, it is easy to alter the layout of the generated page. It is the same as arranging controls on a form and you can do it without fear of messing up the Property Page Wizard.

Figure 97-4 shows the Property Page Wizard generated page. Below is the code for the General property page. As you can see, the code is very simple and would not be hard to write yourself, but any code that is written for you is a wonderful thing.

```
Option Explicit
Private Sub txtCaption_Change()
    Changed = True
End Sub

Private Sub chkEnabled_Click()
    Changed = True
End Sub

Private Sub PropertyPage_ApplyChanges()
    SelectedControls(0).Caption = txtCaption.Text
    SelectedControls(0).Enabled = (chkEnabled.Value = vbChecked)
End Sub

Private Sub PropertyPage_SelectionChanged()
    txtCaption.Text = SelectedControls(0).Caption
    chkEnabled.Value = (SelectedControls(0).Enabled And vbChecked)
End Sub
```

Completing the Property Page

Finally you have the option of generating a brief list of instructions. These instructions indicate that the Property Page Wizard has made changes to your project and that you can save to keep your changes or close the project to discard them. Be aware that if you choose to close your project without saving, you will also be discarding any other changes made in the rest of the project since your last save. It is a good practice to save your project before using any of the wizards. If you are unhappy with the changes they made, you can easily abandon the changes.

Figure 97-5 shows the completed Property Pages dialog. The custom and standard pages are merged into one seamless dialog without writing a line of code. A few clicks and keystrokes to name the page generates a professional looking Property Pages dialog for your ActiveX custom control.

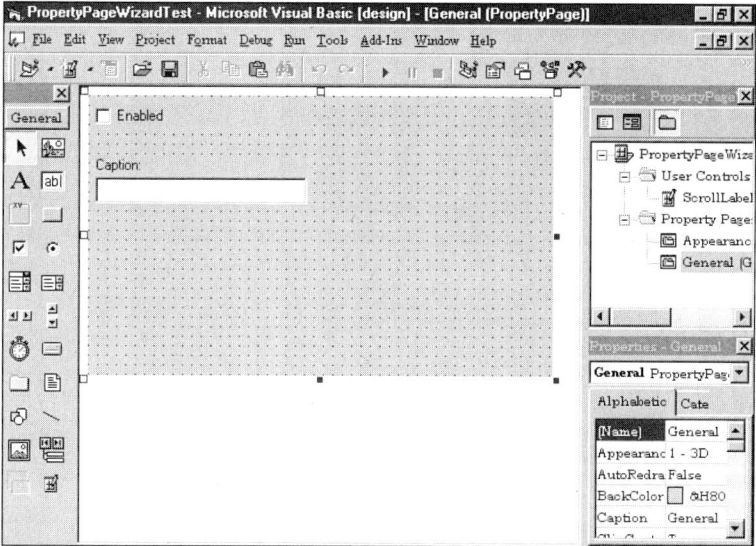

Figure 97-4   The generated property page

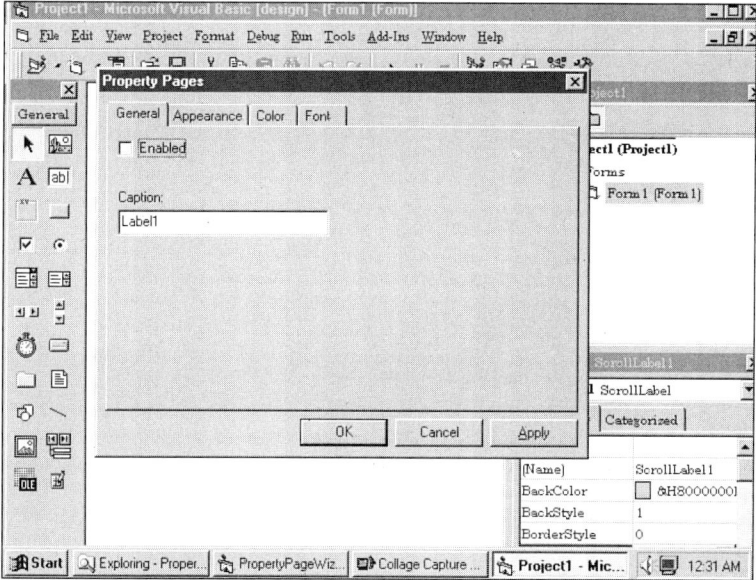

Figure 97-5   The generated property page at runtime

The Property Page Wizard Project

Project Overview

On the CD is a simple custom control to help demonstrate the use of the Property Page Wizard. This project will guide you through the process of using the Property Page Wizard to add a Property Page dialog to this control.

Assembling the Project

1. Open the ScrollLabel.VBP file.

2. If you haven't already, add the Property Page Wizard using the Add-In Manager.

3. Start the Property Page Wizard. The Property Page Wizard will display the Introduction screen; you may press Next to continue.

4. There is only one control in this project so the next screen you should see will be the Property Pages screen. The StandardColor and StandardFont pages are already in the list. Using the Add button, add two pages: first "General", then "Appearance". Now use the arrow buttons to the right of the list to move the General page to the top; follow it with the Appearance page. Your list should look like Figure 97-6. Now push the Next button to continue.

5. The next window is the Add Properties screen. The General tab should already be selected. Select the caption property in the Available Properties list and use the > button to move it over to the General tab. Repeat with the Enabled property.

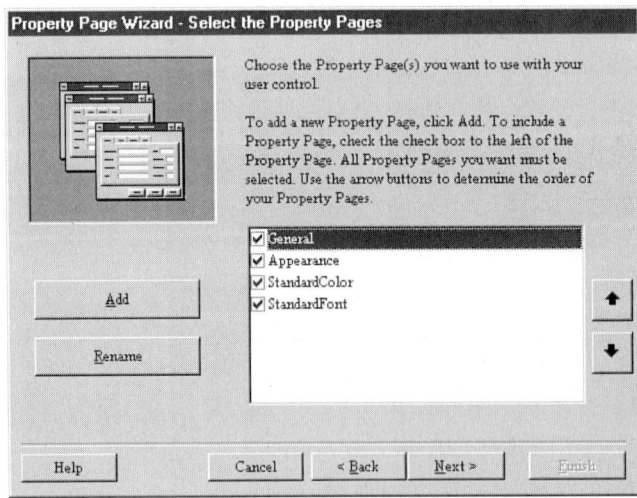

Figure 97-6　The new property pages

6. You can also drag and drop properties to the appropriate tabs, so select the BackStyle property and drag it to the Appearance tab. Drop it and the selected tab should change to Appearance with the BackStyle property in the list. Do the same to the BorderStyle property. Press the Next button to continue.

7. You now have the option of generating a few instructions to go along with the new property pages. Press Finish to continue.

8. Compile the project.

Viewing the Property Page Dialog

Start a new Visual Basic project and add the "PropertyPageWizardTest" custom control. Draw an instance of the ScrollLabel control on your default form. The left mouse button will bring up a context menu; select Properties to show the new property page.

98

ACTIVEX DOCUMENT MIGRATION WIZARD

Recently the cutting edge has moved from the desktop to the Internet. Software shops everywhere are scrambling to convert their applications to Internet applications before the competition does. Microsoft helps you keep your investment in existing code by providing the ActiveX Document Migration Wizard. The ActiveX Document Migration Wizard will take an existing form and turn it into an ActiveX document. It will not make your application into an Internet application; there is more to it than just converting your forms, but it will give you a leg up. Very simple applications may be able to recompile after the conversion to a working Internet application. However, before tackling a more complicated application, you should read Chapter 88, "Creating ActiveX Documents."

How to Use the ActiveX Document Migration Wizard

The ActiveX Document Migration Wizard will first display an introduction screen. This screen gives a brief description of the ActiveX Document Migration Wizard but provides no function; you may choose to skip this screen the next time you use the ActiveX Document Migration Wizard by checking the Skip this screen in the future option.

The next screen is the Form Selection screen, shown in Figure 98-1. All the forms in your project will be listed here. Select the forms to be converted by checking them in the list. Typically you do not want to convert all the forms in your project to ActiveX documents. Your main screen or forms that can stand alone are good candidates to be ActiveX documents. Any form that is an ActiveX document must be able to stand alone; a user can navigate to it directly using Internet Explorer or any other ActiveX document container. If it is a form that is reached by going through another form, then it is probably not a good candidate to be an ActiveX document.

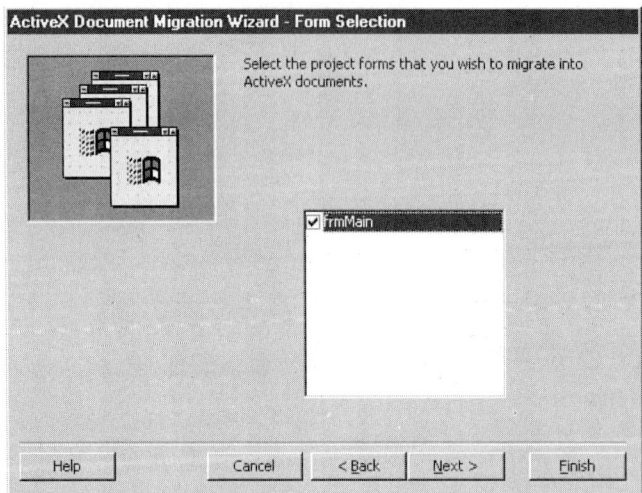

Figure 98-1   Selecting the forms

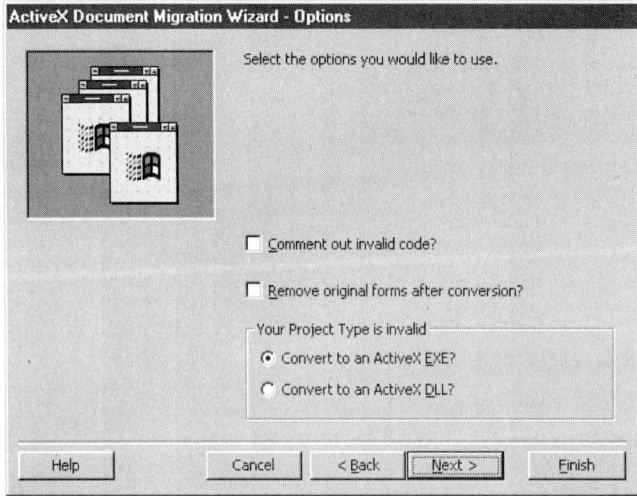

Figure 98-2   The options screen

After selecting the forms to be converted, you next specify how you want it done. Using the Options screen, shown in Figure 98-2, you can tell the ActiveX Document Migration Wizard to comment out any invalid code and remove the original forms from the project once the conversion is done. There are some statements that are invalid with ActiveX documents, including the Show, Hide, Unload, and Load methods, and the End statement. These statements will be commented out if you select that option.

If your project is not an ActiveX EXE or ActiveX DLL, you will also be prompted on how to convert the project to an ActiveX EXE or DLL.

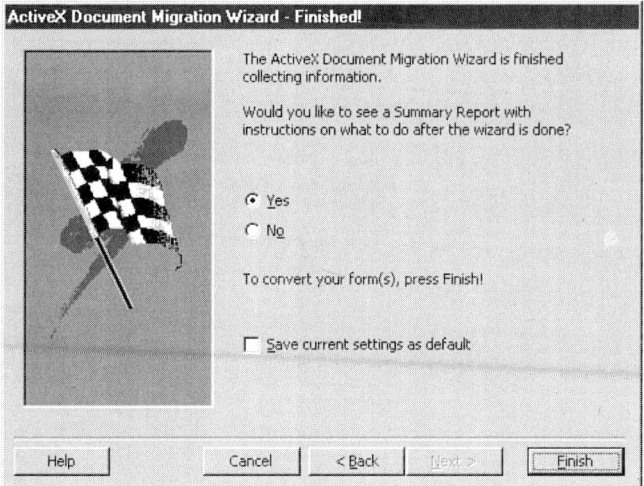

Figure 98-3   Finishing up

The final screen, shown in Figure 98-3, allows you to view a brief report on what to do next with your converted documents. You may also take the opportunity to change the default settings to your choices in this session.

At this point you have completed the wizard's conversion process. For very simple applications, it is possible that compiling now will create a working ActiveX Document. For most projects, you will have some more work ahead. See Chapter 88 for a complete discussion on creating an ActiveX document.

The ActiveX Document Migration Wizard Project

Project Overview

On the CD is a simple project to help demonstrate the use of the ActiveX Document Migration Wizard. This project will step you through the process of converting the simple project to an ActiveX document.

Assembling the Project

1. Open the DocWizardTest.VBP file.

2. If you haven't already, add the ActiveX Document Migration Wizard using the Add-In Manager.

3. Start the ActiveX Document Migration Wizard. The ActiveX Document Migration Wizard will display the Introduction screen; you may press the Next button to continue.

4. The next screen has a list of forms; this project has only one form, frmMain. Select it in the list and press the Next button to continue.

5. The next window is the Options screen. Select Comment out invalid code and Remove original forms after conversion. This form will also ask that you change the project type. The default is ActiveX EXE; that choice is just fine. Press Next to continue.

6. The last screen allows you to generate a report and save the current settings as default. Press the Finish button to convert frmMain and view the summary report.

7. The ActiveX Document Migration Wizard will pop up a message saying it found invalid code. Click OK to continue.

8. After closing the summary window, examine your new ActiveX document. Search the frmMain UserDocument file for "[AXDW]" as the message told you. It should bring you to the UserDocument_Resize sub. Remove the If WindowState <> vbMinimized Then and End If lines, so that your code looks like the code below. These are the kinds of differences you will find between forms and documents. The ActiveX Document Migration Wizard will point the way to code that may be invalid or may not make sense for an ActiveX document.

```
Private Sub UserDocument_Resize()
    RichTextBox1.Width = ScaleWidth
    If ScaleHeight - RichTextBox1.Top >= 0 Then
        RichTextBox1.Height = ScaleHeight - RichTextBox1.Top
    End If
End Sub
```

9. Compile the converted project.

Viewing the ActiveX Document

Use Internet Explorer or another ActiveX document container to open the frmMain.VBD file generated when you compiled. You should see an RTF control and Font button; they work just like the original project, but are now embedded in a browser.

99

ACTIVEX CONTROL WIZARD

Until Visual Basic 5, only the MFC gurus could build an OCX. In Chapters 82 through 87 you learned how easy it is to use Visual Basic to create powerful ActiveX controls. Now the ActiveX Control Wizard makes it even easier: It turns creating ActiveX controls into almost a point and click affair. If you plan on exposing some of the events, properties, and methods of the underlying controls, there is no code to write at all! But even if you plan on an elaborate super control, you can use the ActiveX Control Wizard to quickly build a framework for your master vision.

This chapter starts with an overview of how to use the ActiveX Control Wizard. It then follows with a project where the ActiveX Control Wizard is used to add properties and methods to an ActiveX control.

Getting Started

Using the Add-In Manager available from the Add-Ins menu, select the VB ActiveX Control Interface Wizard. Then select ActiveX Control Interface Wizard from the Add-Ins menu. The first screen you will see is the introduction. This screen gives a brief description of the ActiveX Control Wizard and some basic instructions for its use. You have the option of skipping this screen the next time you run the ActiveX Control Wizard.

If there is more than one UserControl object in the project, the next screen will be the Select a Control screen. Select the control you wish to work on and you're ready to go.

The ActiveX Control Wizard works in two steps: First you select and enter all the events, properties, and methods for the ActiveX control. Then you map those members to existing controls and specify datatypes and arguments for custom members.

Selecting Interface Members

The Select Interface Members screen of the ActiveX Control Wizard allows you to choose names of events, properties, and methods from a list accumulated from the UserControl itself and all the controls on it. If you put a PictureBox on a UserControl, it is likely that your custom control would have a Picture property, and the ActiveX Control Wizard lets you add that property with just a click. Here you would select names that you plan to map to a control later or where you just want to save some typing. You should add all the controls you will be using to build the new custom control to the UserDocument before you start the ActiveX Control Wizard. This ensures that all the names you may want will be available and can be mapped to the appropriate controls. You may always rerun the ActiveX Control Wizard later to alter your selections or add more.

Table 99-1 shows a list of the default interface members selected by the ActiveX Control Wizard. The ActiveX Control Wizard sets the appropriate types and descriptions for these interface members, but does not map them to any existing events, methods, or properties.

Table 99-1 Default Interface Members

Member	Type
BackColor	Property
BackStyle	Property
BorderStyle	Property
Click	Event
DblClick	Event
Enabled	Property
Font	Property
ForeColor	Property
KeyDown	Event
KeyPress	Event
KeyUp	Event
MouseDown	Event
MouseMove	Event
MouseUp	Event
Refresh	Method

Figure 99-1 shows the Select Interface Members screen. The Available Names list shows all the events, methods, and properties of the UserControl and all controls on it. The Selected Names list shows all the members you have already selected or the ActiveX Control Wizard has selected for you. Use the >, >>, <, and << buttons to move items from one list to another. The > button moves the selected item from the Available Names list to the Selected Names list. The >> moves all items in the Available

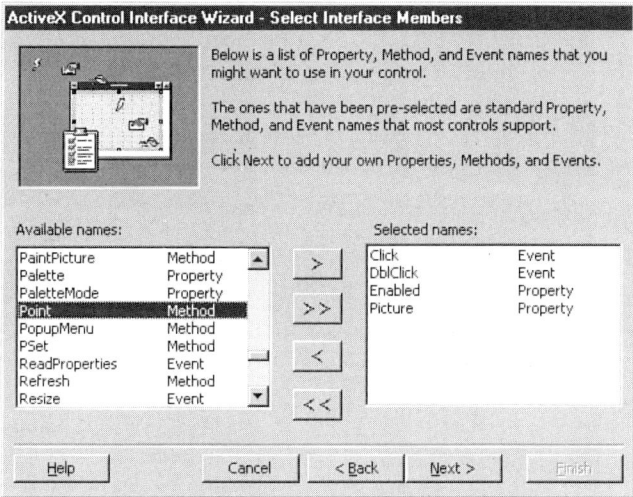

Figure 99-1   Selecting from available interface members

Names list. The < and << buttons are used to move the selected item or all items from the Selected Names list back to the Available Names list.

Adding Custom Interface Members

When you build a new ActiveX control, you probably will not be restricting yourself to the events, methods, and properties of the constituent parts. The Create Custom Interface Members screen, shown in Figure 99-2, allows you to add additional members besides the ones selected on the Select Interface Members screen.

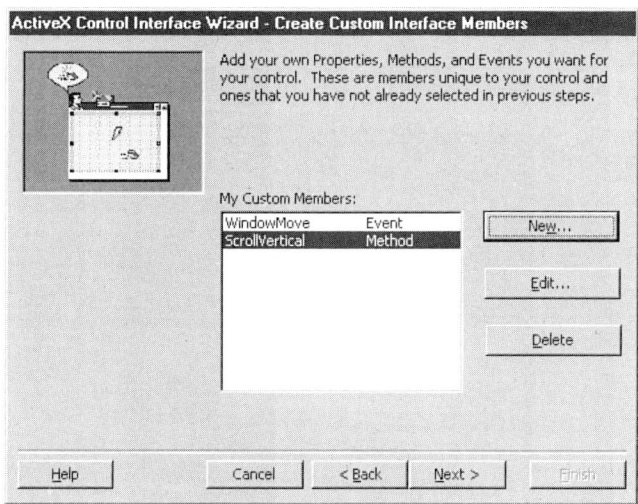

Figure 99-2   The Create Custom Interface Members screen

The Add button will take you to the dialog shown in Figure 99-3. Here you enter the name of the new member and select whether it is an event, a method, or a property. The Delete button will remove the member and the Edit button will take you to a dialog similar to the one shown in Figure 99-3 to alter your choices.

Mapping Interface Members

Now that all the members have been added, it is time to define what they are and what they do. The ActiveX Control Wizard will map the interface members of the new ActiveX control to members of its constituent controls. This is another example of how Microsoft's wizards can save lots of tedious typing. These mappings are easy to do in code; however, if you have many to do, the ActiveX Control Wizard can save you lots of time and potential mistakes.

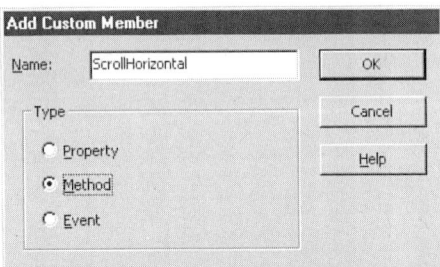

Figure 99-3   Adding a custom member

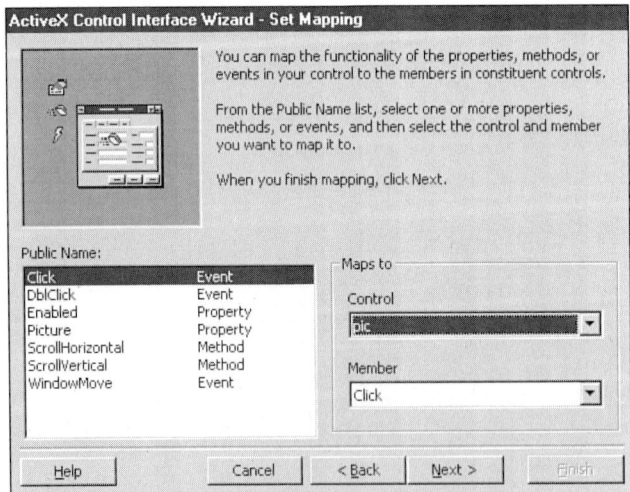

Figure 99-4   Mapping interface members to encapsulated properties and methods

Figure 99-4 shows the Set Mapping window. All the selected interface members and your custom members are shown in the Public Name list. As you select each item in the Public Name list, you can map it to one of the constituent controls' or the UserControl's members. The Control combo selects the object, and the Member combo selects the member. The Member combo will always have the appropriate type of member, so you will never have to worry about assigning a property to a method. However, it will allow you to make mappings that don't make sense, like having a Font property name that maps to a control's Picture property. If there is a matching name in the Member combo, it will be selected by default when you choose an object in the Control combo. Below is a sample of ActiveX Control Wizard generated code for event, method, and property mappings. The code was generated by mapping the Font property, Click event, and Refresh methods to the corresponding members of the UserControl. As you can see, the ActiveX Control Wizard does everything for you, including writing and reading the properties to and from the property bag.

```
'Event Declarations:
Event Click() 'MappingInfo=UserControl,UserControl,-1,Click

'Initialize Properties for User Control
Private Sub UserControl_InitProperties()
    Set Font = Ambient.Font
End Sub

'WARNING! DO NOT REMOVE OR MODIFY THE FOLLOWING COMMENTED LINES!
'MappingInfo=UserControl,UserControl,-1,Font
Public Property Get Font() As Font
    Set Font = UserControl.Font
End Property

Public Property Set Font(ByVal New_Font As Font)
    Set UserControl.Font = New_Font
    PropertyChanged "Font"
End Property

Private Sub UserControl_Click()
    RaiseEvent Click
End Sub

'Load property values from storage
Private Sub UserControl_ReadProperties(PropBag As PropertyBag)

    Set Font = PropBag.ReadProperty("Font", Ambient.Font)
End Sub

'Write property values to storage
Private Sub UserControl_WriteProperties(PropBag As PropertyBag)

    Call PropBag.WriteProperty("Font", Font, Ambient.Font)
End Sub

'WARNING! DO NOT REMOVE OR MODIFY THE FOLLOWING COMMENTED LINES!
'MappingInfo=UserControl,UserControl,-1,Refresh
Public Sub Refresh()
    UserControl.Refresh
End Sub
```

Setting Attributes

For those events, methods, and properties that aren't mapped to an existing member, the Set Properties screen allows you to set the datatype, default value, arguments, description, and whether it can be read or written at runtime and design time.

Figure 99-5 shows the Set Properties screen. The Public Name list shows all the members that have not been mapped. Selecting a member in the Public Name list will display its attributes in the Attribute Information frame to the right and the description field underneath. You can edit each of the attributes and enter a description. For methods and events, the Arguments field will also be enabled. If you wish to create a method with no return value, then choose Empty for the datatype.

The sample code below was generated by creating three custom members: a Caption property, a ScrollLines method, and a Scroll event. The ScrollLines method becomes an empty Public Sub and the Scroll event is declared but is not yet fired.

```vb
'Event Declarations:
Event Scroll()
'Default Property Values:
Const m_def_Caption = ""
'Property Variables:
Dim m_Caption As String

'Initialize Properties for User Control
Private Sub UserControl_InitProperties()
    m_Caption = m_def_Caption
End Sub

'Load property values from storage
Private Sub UserControl_ReadProperties(PropBag As PropertyBag)

    m_Caption = PropBag.ReadProperty("Caption", m_def_Caption)
End Sub

'Write property values to storage
Private Sub UserControl_WriteProperties(PropBag As PropertyBag)

    Call PropBag.WriteProperty("Caption", m_Caption, m_def_Caption)
End Sub

Public Property Get Caption() As String
    Caption = m_Caption
End Property

Public Property Let Caption(ByVal New_Caption As String)
    m_Caption = New_Caption
    PropertyChanged "Caption"
End Property

Public Sub ScrollLines(piLines As Integer)

End Sub
```

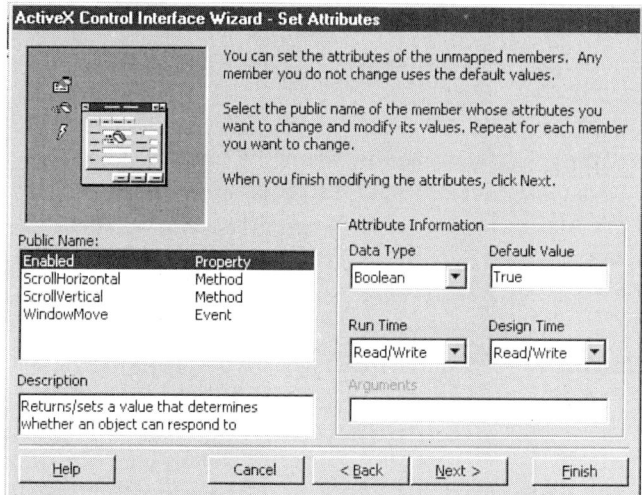

Figure 99-5 Setting member attributes

The ActiveX Control Wizard Project

Project Overview

On the CD is a starter project to help demonstrate the use of the ActiveX Control Wizard. This project will step you through using the ActiveX Control Wizard to add properties and methods to the starter project.

Assembling the Project

1. Open the Chapter99\CtlWizSampleStarter\CtlWizSample.VBP file. This project is an ActiveX control with scrollable Image; however, there is no way to set the picture or interface with it in any other way, yet.

2. If you haven't already, add the ActiveX Control Wizard using the Add-In Manager.

3. Start the ActiveX Control Wizard. The ActiveX Control Wizard will display the Introduction screen: Press the Next button to continue.

4. The next screen is the Select Interface Members screen. Press the << button to remove all the selections from the Selected Names list. Find the Picture property, Click event, DblClick event, and the Enabled property in the Available Names list and add them to the Selected Names by using the > button or double-clicking. Press the Next button to continue.

5. On the Create Custom Interface Members screen, add a new member. Use the Add button and add a WindowMove event, a ScrollHorizontal method, and a ScrollVertical method. Press the Next button to continue.

6. The next screen is the Set Mapping screen. Here you map selected interface members to members of the constituent controls. Select the Click event in the Public Names list. Assign it to the Click event of the picture control by selecting pic in the Control combo. The Click member should be selected by default. Do this again for the DblClick event and the Picture property, mapping both of them to their respective members of the picture control. Press the Next button to continue.

7. The Set Attributes screen allows you to set the datatypes and properties of members that you did not map. You should have four members left: the Enabled property, the WindowMove event, the ScrollHorizontal method, and the ScrollVertical. First, select the Enabled property. Examine the attributes: The default datatype should be Boolean and it should be Read/Write at runtime and design time. The only thing that needs to be changed is the default value. It should be True.

8. For both the ScrollVertical and ScrollHorizontal methods, change the return datatype to Empty and a parameter "piStep as Integer". This will allow an application to programmatically scroll the image.

9. Finally the WindowMove needs no work: It takes no parameters so it is just fine with the default values. Press the Finish button to continue.

10. The ActiveX Control Wizard will display a list of last minute instructions. You may want to read these.

11. Now it's time to add some code to flesh out some of our custom members. Update the Property Set Picture so that the scrollbar's properties are updated when the picture property changes.

```
Public Property Set Picture(ByVal New_Picture As Picture)
    Set pic.Picture = New_Picture
    PropertyChanged "Picture"
    'new line so that we change the scrollbars with a new picture
    UserControl_Resize
End Property
```

12. Next, in the scrollbar's Change events, add the RaiseEvent WindowMove so they look like the following code.

```
Private Sub hScroll_Change()
    pic.Left = -hScroll.Value
    RaiseEvent WindowMove
End Sub

Private Sub vScroll_Change()
    pic.Top = -vScroll.Value
    RaiseEvent WindowMove
End Sub
```

13. Finally, add the following code to the ScrollVertically and the ScrollHorizontally methods. This code takes the piStep parameter and attempts to move the view window by the number of steps the developer wants. If the number of steps would push it past the limits of the scrollbar, it moves to the limit of the scrollbar.

```
Public Sub ScrollHorizontal(piStep As Integer)
    If hScroll.Visible = False Or m_Enabled = False Then
        Exit Sub
    End If
    If piStep < 0 Then
        If hScroll.Value + piStep * hScroll.LargeChange >= hScroll.Min Then
            hScroll.Value = piStep * hScroll.LargeChange + hScroll.Value
        Else
            'too big, make it the max
            hScroll.Value = hScroll.Min
        End If
    Else
        If hScroll.Value + piStep * hScroll.LargeChange <= hScroll.Max Then
            hScroll.Value = piStep * hScroll.LargeChange + hScroll.Value
        Else
            'too big, make it the max
            hScroll.Value = hScroll.Max
        End If
    End If
End Sub

Public Sub ScrollVertical(piStep As Integer)
    If vScroll.Visible = False Or m_Enabled = False Then
        Exit Sub
    End If
    If piStep < 0 Then
        If vScroll.Value + piStep * vScroll.LargeChange >= vScroll.Min _
            Then
            vScroll.Value = piStep * vScroll.LargeChange + vScroll.Value
        Else
            'too big, make it the max
            vScroll.Value = vScroll.Min
        End If
    Else
        If vScroll.Value + piStep * vScroll.LargeChange <= vScroll.Max _
            Then
            vScroll.Value = piStep * vScroll.LargeChange + vScroll.Value
        Else
            'too big, make it the max
            vScroll.Value = vScroll.Max
        End If
    End If
End Sub
```

14. Compile the new ActiveX control.

Using the ActiveX Control

Create a new Standard EXE project in Visual Basic. Using the components menu item or by right-clicking on the Toolbox, add the CtlWizSample control to the project. The

WindowMove event will fire each time either the user or the application moves the view window. You can use the ScrollHorizontal and ScrollVertical methods to programmatically move the view window.

100

USING OFFICE IN VB

Office 97 has a robust development environment for building Visual Basic applications into Office documents. Most of the features and functions available to Visual Basic, including data access, are also available inside Office. Combined with the number-crunching power of Excel or the document formatting abilities of Word, Visual Basic for Office can be used to create very powerful applications. Office 97 and Visual Basic provide the capability to migrate an Office application to Visual Basic or share code between Office and Visual Basic.

Sharing Forms and Code Using Import and Export

An Office 97 application keeps all the code and forms within the document file, so, for instance, all code for your application in the MyBudget.XLS is in the MyBudget.XLS. This is different from VB, where each object may have one or two files for the code and possibly for the binary data. Keeping the code inside the document does make sharing the code a little troublesome. However, the Visual Basic environment in Office allows you to export and import standalone files to be used in other Office projects or Visual Basic.

The Import and Export menu items are located on the File menu in the Visual Basic environment in Office. Using import and export, classes and modules can be exchanged between Office and Visual Basic without problems. The file format is the same and, assuming that all the objects referenced are available, no code change is required. Even the code on a public object in an Office document can be exported as a class. This allows you to take all the code on Sheet1 in Excel, for example, and export it as a class to use in a VB project.

Forms exported from Office behave a little differently. A form exported from Office and opened in Visual Basic is a UserForm object in your Designers folder; it uses the Microsoft Forms Toolbox for editing the UI. To add controls to a UserForm, select an item in the Forms Toolbox and draw it on the UserForm or drag it to the UserForm from the Toolbox. A right mouse-click brings up a menu to select controls for the Forms Toolbox. There are minor variations in properties, but UserForms and their built-in controls behave similarly and can be used like regular VB forms or controls.

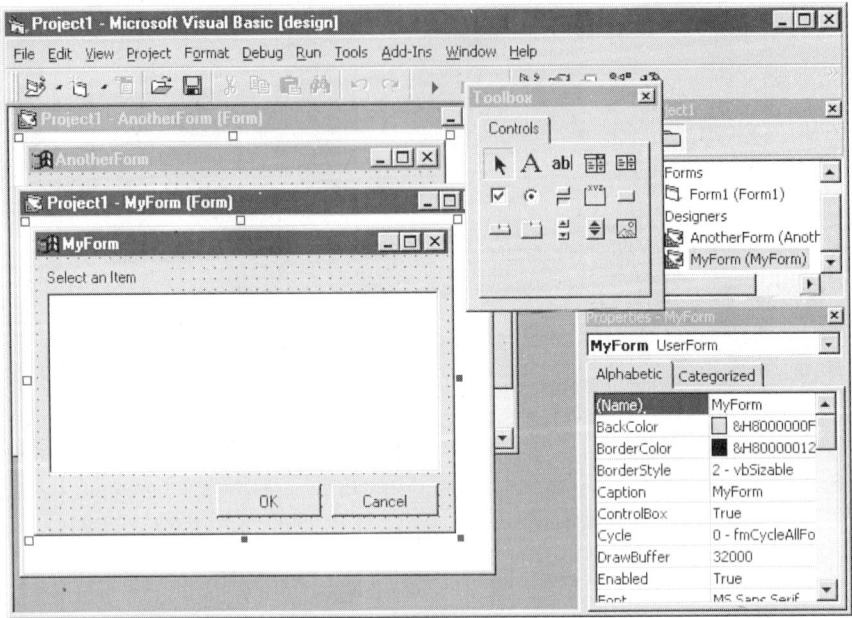

Figure 100-1 Forms created in Office in a VB project

Figure 100-1 shows forms exported from an Office project and from the Microsoft Forms Toolbox.

A regular form created in Visual Basic cannot be imported into an Office project. However, Microsoft provides a tool, Microsoft Forms 2.0, that enables you to create forms usable by Office or VB. If you intend to import a form from a VB project into an Office project, then you should create your form as a Microsoft Forms 2.0 Form. The menu item Add ActiveX Designer-Microsoft Forms 2.0 Form will add a new UserForm. A form created this way can be imported into an Office project. The default extension for a UserForm created in VB is DSR. Office 97 looks for a FRM file when importing a form, so keep that in mind when you panic: "Aaaa, I lost my file!" They are the same, no matter what the extension.

The risk of using forms or code imported from an Office application is that if the document is still in use, changes may be applied in one place and not in another. You must be careful to update both copies of the code when applying fixes or changes.

INSTALLING MICROSOFT FORMS 2.0

Microsoft Forms 2.0 is not installed when Visual Basic is installed, but it is included on the Enterprise Edition CD. It is installed with the Microsoft Visual Database Tools located in the \Tools\Datatool directory. When you have the opportunity, explore the Tools directory: There are lots of goodies here. Use the Components dialog to add the Microsoft Forms 2.0 Form designer.

Sharing Forms and Code Using OLE Automation

Perhaps the quickest and easiest way to share forms and code from an application written in VBA for Office is through OLE Automation. By leaving the code in one place, you eliminate the risk of code divergence mentioned in the section above, but there are drawbacks. First, running the code in an Office document creates an instance of that Office application and the code will run interpreted by the VBA DLL. Performance will not be able to match the performance of code compiled into your application. Second, more forethought must be put into developing the Office application. It's not a simple macro anymore: It's an integral component of your object model. For a complete discussion of OLE Automation see Chapter 76, "OLE Automation."

Forms and objects created in Office are not public, but each of the Office applications has public objects where you can add VBA code to manipulate the private objects. The sample code below opens an Excel file that contains a VBA project and calls the ShowMyForm method of the ThisWorkbook object.

```
Dim ExcelApp as Object
Set ExcelApp = GetObject("book1.xls")
ExcelApp.ShowMyForm
```

The form in this project is private, but the ThisWorkbook object is public and can do the work for you. The code below is the ShowMyForm Sub from the ThisWorkbook object.

```
Public Sub ShowMyForm()
     MyForm.Show
End Sub
```

The Office Forms Project

Project Overview

A starter project to help demonstrate the use of the Export function in the Office 97 Visual Basic Editor is on the CD-ROM. To do this project you will need Office 97.

Assembling the Project

1. Open the Chapter100\Letter Sample\Letter Sample.DOC file. This is a Word document with a form that allows you to select an address from the Address Book.MDB database in the same directory. This small Office application then puts the address in the current document at the top left of the document.

2. First, export the form. Open the Office 97 Visual Basic Editor by selecting the Tools-Macro-Visual Basic Editor menu. Highlight the frmSelectAddress form in the forms folder of the project window. Select Export from the File menu and save the file with the default name. Close Word and Open Visual Basic.

3. Within Visual Basic, create a new Standard EXE. Delete the default Form1 and Add the frmSelectAddress.FRM file you exported from Word. On the Project Properties Dialog, change the Startup Object to the frmSelectAddress form.

4. On the References dialog, add references to Microsoft DAO 3.5 Object Library and Microsoft Word 8.0 Object Library. Save the project. This is a good time to copy the Address Book.MDB to the same directory as your project (or somewhere in your path) so the application can find it.

5. At this point, if Word is already running with an open document, the form from the Letter Sample.DOC will add the selected address to the top of the document. However, it needs to work even if Word is not running.

6. To make it work when Word isn't loaded, load Word and create a new document. Add the following declaration to the frmSelectAddress form.

```
Private moWord As Object
```

7. Add the following code to create the Word.Application object and make a new document. Insert it after the Else statement.

```
Set moWord = CreateObject("word.application")
moWord.Visible = True
moWord.Activate
moWord.Documents.Add
```

8. Now add moWord. before each of the references to the Selection object so the application knows which Selection object you are referring to. The final version of the cmdOK_Click function should appear similar to the code below.

```
Private Sub cmdOK_Click()
    If listFriend.SelectedItem Is Nothing Then
        MsgBox "You must select an address or press Cancel " & _
        " to continue."
    Else
        Set moWord = CreateObject("word.application")
        moWord.Visible = True
        moWord.Activate
        moWord.Documents.Add

        Dim db As Database
        Dim rs As Recordset
        Set db = OpenDatabase("address book.mdb")
        Set rs = db.OpenRecordset( _
            "Select * from Addresses where AddressId =" _
            & Right$(listFriend.SelectedItem.Key, _
            Len(listFriend.SelectedItem.Key) - 1))
        Do Until rs.EOF
            moWord.Selection.HomeKey Unit:=wdStory
            moWord.Selection.TypeParagraph
            moWord.Selection.TypeText Text:=rs("FirstName") & " " & _
                rs("LastName")
            moWord.Selection.TypeParagraph
            moWord.Selection.TypeText Text:=CStr(rs("Address"))
            moWord.Selection.TypeParagraph
```

```
        moWord.Selection.TypeText Text:=rs("City") & ", " & _
            rs("StateOrProvince") & " " & rs("PostalCode")
        moWord.Selection.TypeParagraph
        rs.MoveNext
    Loop
    rs.Close
    db.Close
    Unload Me
    End If
End Sub
```

9. Save and run the application. Highlighting a name and pressing the OK button will open Word, create a new document, and place the select name's address at the top left of the new document.

101

THE SETUP WIZARD

Now that you have written, tested, and debugged your program, it's time to determine how to distribute it. In the old days, you could simply copy the .EXE file to the target computer and it would run flawlessly. Sadly, those days are long past. Programs written in Visual Basic 5.0 need, at the very least, MSVBVM50.DLL, which is the VB5 runtime library. Most likely, you also need several other .DLL and .OCX files to support the custom controls you have added to the program. (This is not exclusive to Visual Basic. Runtime files are a *feature* of C++ programs, as well.)

Figuring out what files to distribute and where to place them on the target computer would be a nightmare if Microsoft had not included the Setup Wizard with Visual Basic 5.0. With the Setup Wizard, basic distribution is almost trivial. This chapter explains how to use the Setup Wizard to distribute programs, ActiveX OLE servers, and ActiveX controls.

What the Setup Wizard Does

The Setup Wizard scans your project's files and determines which support files your program needs. Then it creates a setup program, compresses all of the required files, assigns them to a disk layout, and copies the entire collection of setup files to your desired distribution medium. If you have not already built the executable file for your application, the Setup Wizard will even do that for you. You can choose whether to distribute your setup via floppy disk, compact disc, or over a network.

Running the Setup Wizard

If the project you want to create a setup program for is open, close it before you run the Setup Wizard. Select the Setup Wizard from the Visual Basic 5.0 Start menu, or the Visual Basic 5.0 program group if you are using Windows NT 3.51.

Selecting the Project

After an introduction screen, the Setup Wizard starts with the Select Project and Options dialog shown in Figure 101-1. Enter the VB project file (.VBP) in the text box,

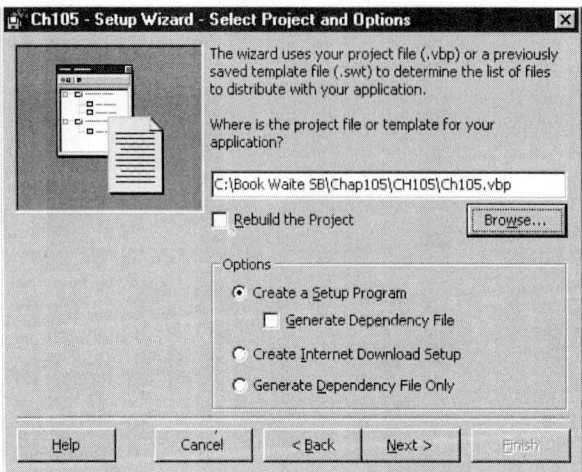

Figure 101-1 The Setup Wizard Select Project and
Options Dialog

or use the Browse button to select it. The Setup Wizard Select Project and Options dialog allows you to select the project and several important options. The options available on this dialog are listed below.

- If you select Rebuild the Project, the Setup Wizard will compile your application. Most of the time you will want to compile the application from the IDE so you can test it as an executable before you consider distributing it.

- Select Create a Setup Program if you plan to distribute your application via disk or network.

- If you are creating a setup program, you can ask the Setup Wizard to create a file that lists all of the dependencies in your program by selecting Generate Dependency File. This is a list of the files that are included in the setup.

- If you have the Professional or Enterprise Edition, you can distribute ActiveX controls, ActiveX DLL and EXE files, and ActiveX documents for use on Internet Web pages. In this case, the Setup Wizard offers you the choice of creating Internet download setups.

- By selecting Generate Dependency File Only, you can get a list of your program's dependencies. This is convenient if you are creating your own setup program, or if you are using a third-party setup utility.

Distribution Methods

When you have made your selections, click on the Next button. This opens the Distribution Method dialog box shown in Figure 101-2.

The distribution methods are outlined below.

- Floppy Disk: If you select this option, when you click on the Next button, the Setup Wizard will prompt you for the type (capacity) of the floppy disk and its drive letter on your computer. This is shown in Figure 101-3. After the Setup Wizard has compressed the distribution files, you will be told how many disks you need and will be prompted to insert the disks in their proper order. Distributing your program by floppy is slower than the other methods, but is sometimes your only choice.

- Single Directory: If you plan to distribute your program via compact disc or network, you can choose to save the files to a single directory, or as disk images. If you select Single Directory, all of the files will be copied into a single directory. When you click on the Next button, you will be prompted for the directory to use, as shown in Figure 101-4. By default, this directory is C:\WINDOWS\TEMP\ SWSETUP\. You will probably want to change the directory name. With CD-ROMs in almost all computers these days, and CD-ROM burners finally reaching affordable prices, this is a viable alternative to distribution with floppies.

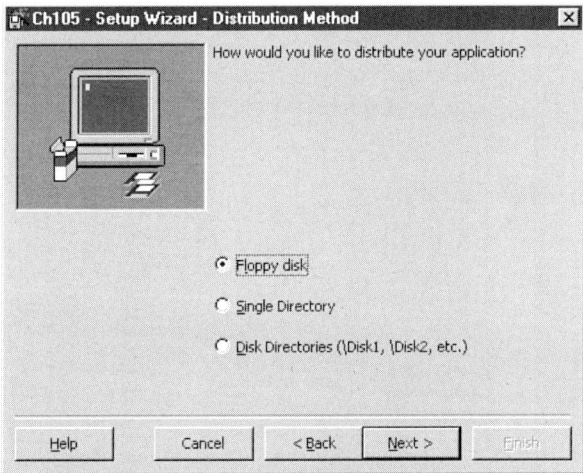

Figure 101-2   This dialog box allows you to choose how you want to distribute your setup files

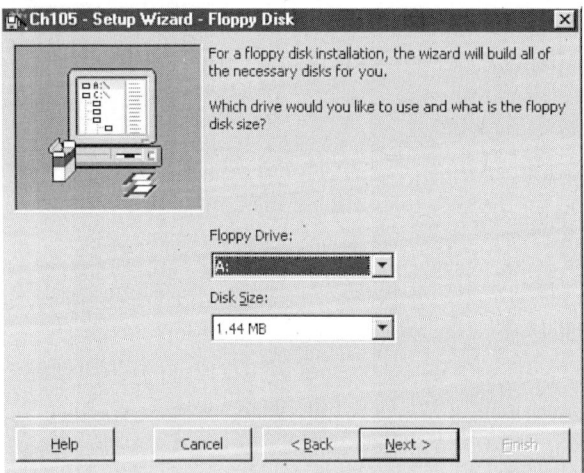

Figure 101-3   Selecting the size and drive letter for floppy disk distribution

■ Disk Directories: This option copies the files into a directory structure that resembles distribution on diskettes. The subdirectories are named Disk1, Disk2, Disk3, and so on. When you click on the Next button, you will be prompted for the directory to use, as shown in Figure 101-4. The user can install the application by opening the Disk1 directory and double-clicking the setup program. If you plan to use a disk duplicating service, this is the ideal choice. You can copy the Disk1, Disk2, and Disk3 directories to individual floppy disks for floppy disk distribution,

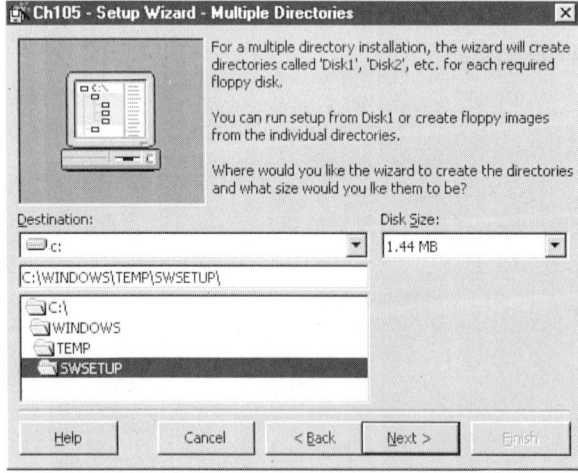

Figure 101-4   Selecting for multiple directories

and you can distribute the files via CD as well as by network. This new addition to the Setup Wizard may well be the most convenient of the choices.

Adding ActiveX Server Components

Once the distribution medium is selected and verified, the Setup Wizard offers you the chance to review the use of ActiveX server components in your application. You can select either local (on your own computer) or remote (on a network server) components if you have the Enterprise edition. The ActiveX Server Components dialog box is shown in Figure 101-5.

Confirming Dependencies

After you click on the Next button, the Setup Wizard prompts you to confirm the dependencies in your project, as shown in Figure 101-6. To avoid distributing unnecessary files, remove all of the references and components from your project before you make the final .EXE or .DLL file.

If a file is included that you don't need, you can uncheck it.

File Summary

When you click on the Next button, the Setup Wizard opens the File Summary dialog box, shown in Figure 101-7. This is a list of all of the files that will be included in your distribution set. If you uncheck a file in the list, it will not be included. Be careful; if a required file is not included, the application will not work.

Figure 101-5 Reviewing and adding ActiveX servers

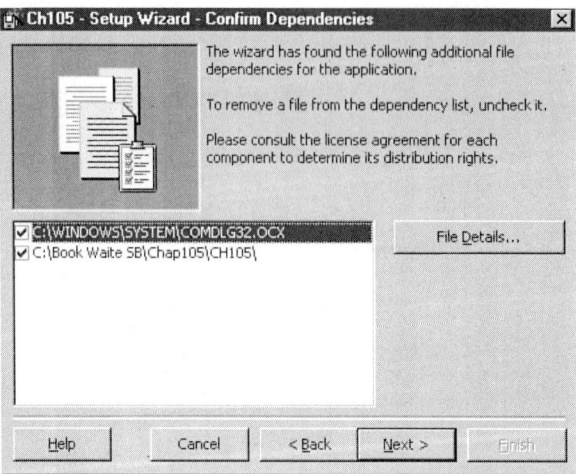

Figure 101-6   The Confirm Dependencies dialog box allows you to cancel a dependency

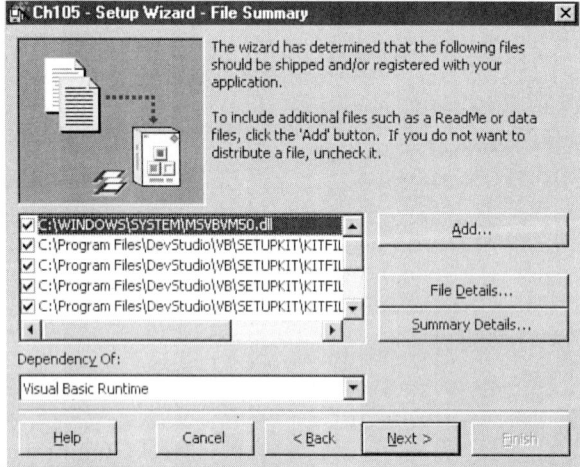

Figure 101-7   The File Summary dialog box—you can uncheck files, but be careful

If you need to include other files, for example a README.TXT file, a help file, or a database file, click on the Add button and select your file.

Finished!

After you click on the Next button, the Setup Wizard displays the Finished! dialog box, shown in Figure 101-8. If you plan to do additional setup programs for this application, click on the Save Template button. This lets you skip most of the previous steps next time.

Click on the Finished button to build the setup program. The Setup Wizard compresses all of the files. If you selected the floppy disk or disk directories as your distribution method, it also works out the placement of files on the disks. If you elected to distribute via floppy disk, the Setup Wizard will prompt you to insert the first floppy disk when it has finished its calculations. This is shown in Figure 101-9. If you elected to use either a single directory or multiple disk directories, the files will be saved on your hard disk drive.

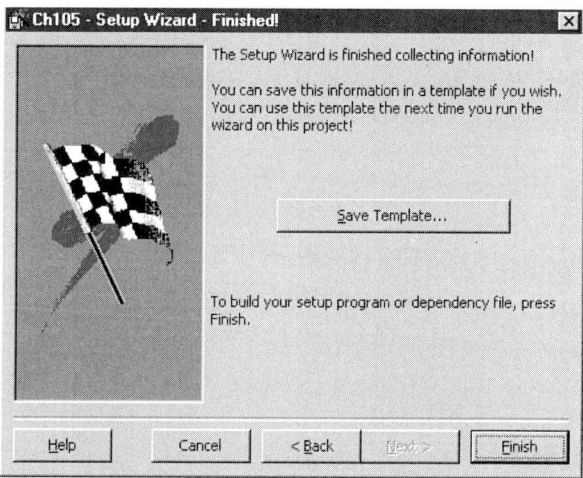

Figure 101-8   The Finished! dialog box allows you to save a setup template

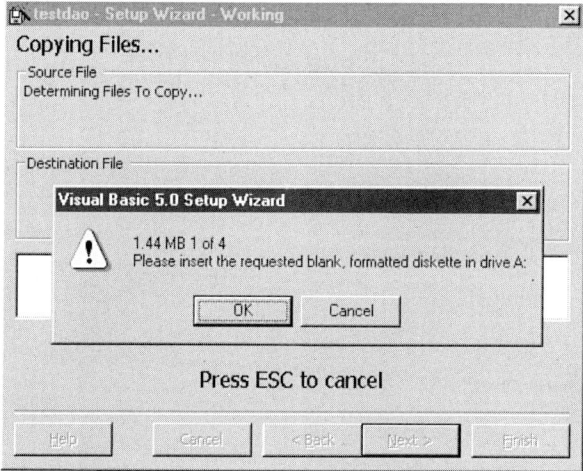

Figure 101-9   Prompting for floppy disk distribution

The Setup Wizard and Data Access

If your application uses DAO (Data Access Objects), the Setup Wizard prompts you to select the correct ISAM and workspace components. (See the chapters on data access.) The dialog box is shown in Figure 101-10.

Installable ISAM

If you are accessing an ISAM database, select the correct driver from the list box.

Workspace

The choice of Workspace is simple. If you are not using ODBC connections, select dbUseJet. If you are using ODBC connections, select dbUseODBC. You must select one of the Workspace options.

ODBC Installation

ODBC drivers are installed separately from your application, and they must be installed *before* your application is installed. Copy all of the files from your Program Files\DevStudio\VB\ODBC directory into a temporary directory on the target computer, then run the Setup.EXE program that is included with the ODBC files. It is essential to do this before you install your application; if you do not, the application will fail.

The Setup Wizard and Remote Automation

If you are building an ActiveX remote automation server (Enterprise Edition only), the Setup Wizard helps you create setup programs for both client and server in the Remote Automation or Distributed COM environment.

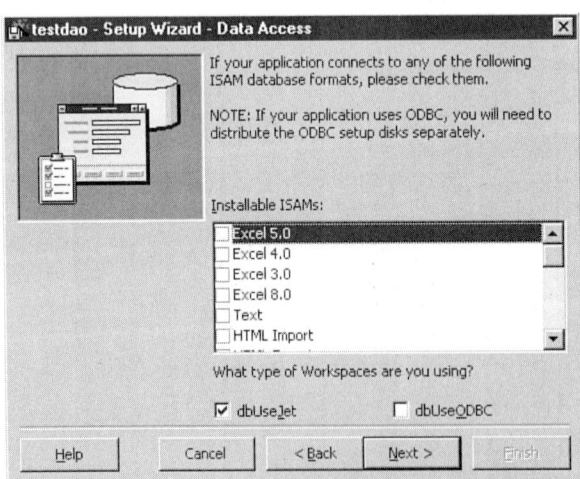

Figure 101-10 Selecting the ISAM and Workspace for data access

Before you compile the project, select the Component tab from the Project|Properties menu, and check the Remote Server option. This creates a file with a .VBR extension, which contains information the Registry needs to run an ActiveX server on the remote computer. Figure 101-11 shows the Component tab.

Figure 101-12 shows the dialog box in the Setup Wizard that allows you to create a setup program for the server.

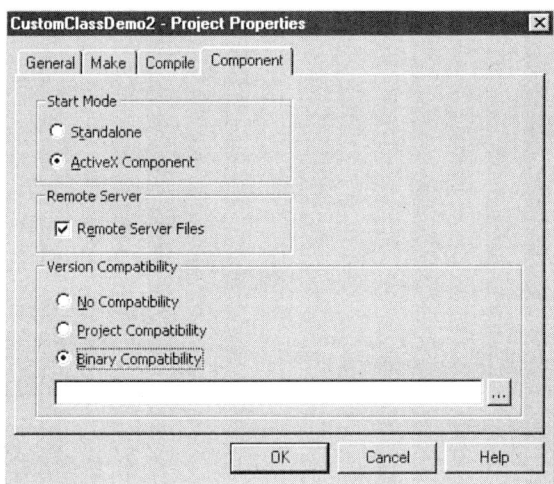

Figure 101-11 The Project Properties dialog allows you to compile an ActiveX server for remote automation

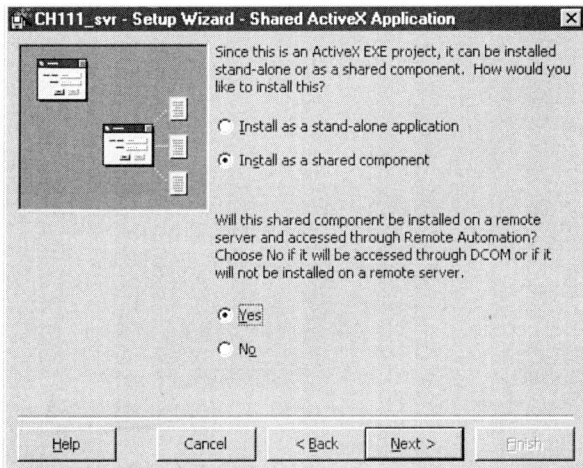

Figure 101-12 Building a server setup program

Select Install as a shared component, then Yes if you are using remote automation and No if you are using Distributed COM. The Remote Automation option adds the necessary remote automation files to the setup list. These files will be installed in the Windows/System directory of the network server. The remainder of the process is the same as the steps above.

Once the setup is built for the server, create a second distribution set for the client application. Follow the procedures for creating a standard setup program until you get to the ActiveX Components dialog box. If the .VBR file is not shown in the list box, click on the Add Remote button and select the remote ActiveX server's .VBR file. This is shown in Figure 101-13.

Adding the remote server brings up the Remote Connection Details dialog box shown in Figure 101-14. Select either the Distributed COM (DCOM) or Remote Automation option. You can also insert connection information if your project is designed for a specific system and you know the name of the network server. If you leave the Network Address text box blank, the user will be prompted for the information during installation.

The remainder of the process is the same as the steps listed above.

Figure 101-13   Adding a reference to the remote server

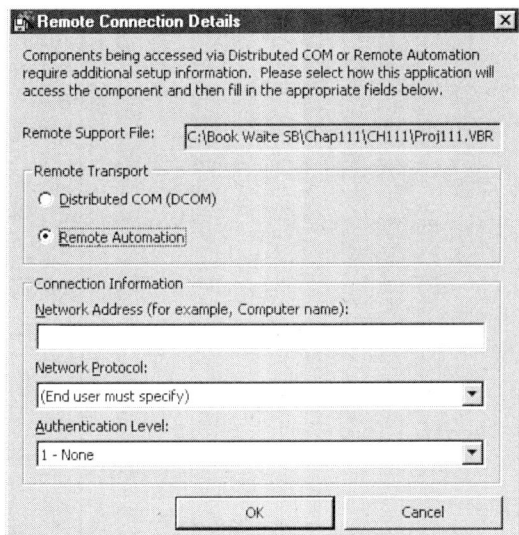

Figure 101-14   Setting the details for a remote connection

Using the Setup Wizard for Internet Applications

If you have the Professional or Enterprise edition, you can create ActiveX controls, DLLs, EXEs, and ActiveX documents that can be used on Internet Web pages. The Setup Wizard can package the components for distribution over the Internet. When a user accesses the Web, the ActiveX component is downloaded as a compressed .CAB file along with the rest of the Web page. The browser then decompresses the file, installs it on the user's computer, and registers it in the system registry.

To package a component for Internet distribution, select the Create Internet Download Setup option button, as shown in Figure 101-15. Note the What's New button that appears. Clicking on this button opens your browser and logs onto the Microsoft Web site, where you can read the latest news about Internet downloads.

The next dialog box allows you to determine the source of the runtime files the user must download. These include MSVBVM50.DLL and individual controls, DAO, and Remote Data objects. You can choose to include them in secondary .CAB files, or you can choose to have the user download them from the Microsoft Web site, which reduces the size of the files that must be stored on your own Web site. Figure 101-16 illustrates the dialog box.

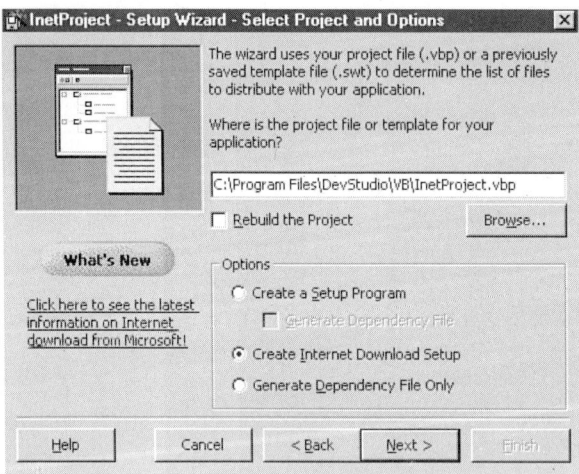

Figure 101-15 Building an Internet setup program—
the What's New button logs onto the Microsoft Internet
Web site

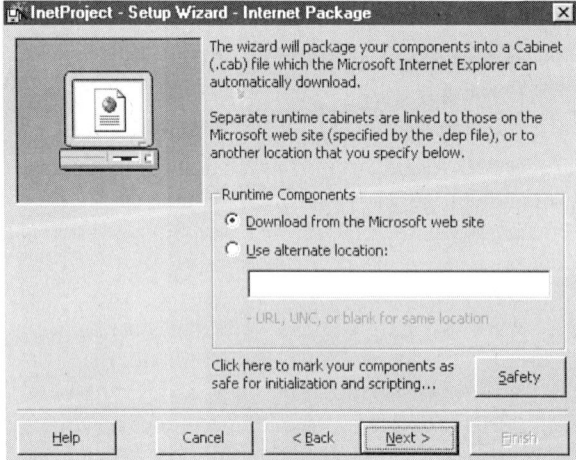

Figure 101-16 Selecting the source for runtime files

Click the Safety button to mark your components as safe for initialization and
scripting. Figure 101-17 shows the Safety dialog box. By marking your components as
safe, you are guaranteeing end users that your components will not harm their system.
See Chapter 86, "Creating Internet-Ready ActiveX Controls," for more on ActiveX
Internet components.

The remainder of the setup is straightforward. Once it is completed, the files for distribution are stored in the setup directory you specified. The illustrations in this chapter used the default directory, C:\WINDOWS\TEMP\SWSETUP\. Upload the primary .CAB file and any .VBD files to the Web site. There is also an .HTM file that contains sample HTML statements and VBScript code that you can cut and paste to your Web pages to instantiate your object.

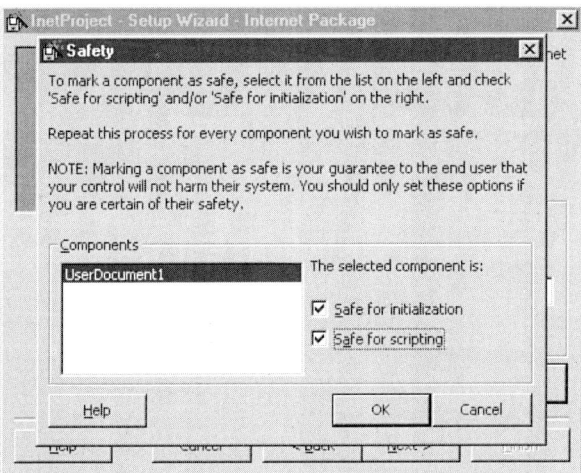

Figure 101-17 The Safety dialog box—your Internet download components should be thoroughly tested for safety before they are deployed

102

THE WIZARD MANAGER

As Visual Basic has matured, the development environment has become increasingly programmer friendly. The things that programmers must do over and over are at their fingertips. Aligning and sizing controls, spacing controls equally, and centering controls on a form can be selected from the Format menu. More complex tasks, including building the framework for an entire application, are automated as wizards and add-ins.

Still, Microsoft can't anticipate everything you might want to do, and some of the things that you do with almost every program will be unique to you. Chapter 78, "Creating Add-Ins," describes how to build an add-in to help you with some of your tasks. This chapter describes how to build a wizard to handle the more complex chores.

The Wizard Manager

A wizard is a special kind of add-in with its own peculiarities. It's possible to build a wizard piece by piece, but that path is riddled with traps. (One of them is that you can wind up with several similar, incorrect entries in your system registry.) To help avoid the risks, Visual Basic 5.0 includes a Wizard Manager utility that can take some of the pain out of wizard building.

The Wizard Manager creates a framework for your wizard but, like the other builders in Visual Basic 5.0, it leaves a lot for you to do as well. As of this writing, neither the online help nor *Books Online* provides the information you need to get the job done correctly. The following pages explain the process, and the project at the end of this chapter guides you through building a simple wizard.

The Parts of a Wizard

When you build a wizard with the Wizard Manager, the manager automatically creates the objects that you need for a wizard:

- A form named frmWizard: Do not change the name of this form; it is required.
- A form named frmConfirm.

- A standard module named WIZARD.BAS.
- A class named WIZARD.CLS.
- A resource file named WIZARD.RES.
- The source WIZARD.RC, used by the resource compiler to generate WIZARD.RES.

frmWizard

The main wizard form is exactly the same form that you see when you use one of the wizards that comes with Visual Basic. It is an SDI form that contains a control array of frames, one for each step. By default, the Wizard Manager sets you up with six steps. You can add or delete steps as required.

The familiar command buttons Help, Cancel, Back, Next, and Finish are placed along the bottom of frmWizard. These, too, are a control array.

The Frames

Each frame contains an Image control to display a picture, if desired, and a label so you can display instructions for the step. The first frame, fraStep(0), is the introduction screen. It contains a check box that allows the user to skip the introduction in the future. The next four frames are steps, and the last frame, fraStep(5), is the Finished! screen. The Finished! screen also contains a check box to allow the user to save the wizard's settings as the default settings for the wizard. There is space in the step frames, fraStep(1) through fraStep(4), to add more controls, so you can make the wizard actually do something.

frmConfirm

The confirmation form contains a label in which you can display a final message, an Image control for a picture, a check box to allow the user to elect to not see the confirmation form in the future, and a command button that closes the wizard.

WIZARD.BAS

Much of the wizard's work is done in the Basic module. The Declarations section sets up several global constants and declares the API function WritePrivateProfileString that will be used to register your wizard in the system registry. The module also contains procedures and functions that add a reference to the wizard to the VBADDIN.INI file, add the wizard to the Add-Ins menu, and access the resource file.

WIZARD.CLS

The class module contains the IDTExtensibility procedures needed to connect the wizard to the current instance of Visual Basic.

WIZARD.RES

The resource file contains the strings and images used by the wizard. You can modify the code to eliminate the need for the resource file at the cost of making your compiled wizard larger.

WIZARD.RC

The Wizard Manager provides the .RC file so you can edit and recompile the resource file to suit your needs. Chapter 93, "Resources and International Issues," discusses the use of resource files, and the project at the end of this chapter makes use of the resource file for its strings and images.

Using the Wizard Manager

The Wizard Manager adds a new window to the IDE, as shown in Figure 102-1.

If you want to work on the frame for Step 2, select it in the Wizard Manager window. To add a new step between Step 4 and the Finished! step, click on the Add Step button. Enter the step name in the dialog box that appears and click on OK. (Resist the urge to be cute. Use Step *n*, where *n* is the number of the new step.)

You can insert a step between existing steps by clicking on the Add Step Ahead button. Again, you must supply a name for the step. The toolbar buttons with the up and down arrows allow you to move up or down in the list, and the last button on the toolbar refreshes the list. To delete a step, click on it with the right mouse button and select Delete from the pop-up menu that appears.

There's a *gotcha* or two in all of this, though. The steps are a control collection of frames, with fraStep(0) being the introduction screen and the last frame being the Finished! screen. Adding a step inserts the new frame correctly in the array. What is missing is the Tag property of the new frame, which is used by the code to insert the correct caption in the step's label. You must also, of course, add the tag and caption to your new step in the resource file.

The Wizard Manager also does not add the necessary code and declarations to handle the new step. Listing 102-1 shows the Declarations section of frmWizard.

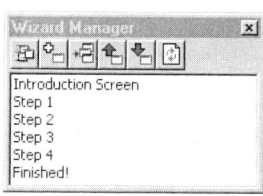

Figure 102-1   The new window

Listing 102-1 The default Declarations section from frmWizard

```
Option Explicit

Const NUM_STEPS = 7

Const RES_ERROR_MSG = 30000

'BASE VALUE FOR HELP FILE FOR THIS WIZARD:
Const HELP_BASE = 1000
Const HELP_FILE = "MYWIZARD.HLP"

Const BTN_HELP = 0
Const BTN_CANCEL = 1
Const BTN_BACK = 2
Const BTN_NEXT = 3
Const BTN_FINISH = 4

Const STEP_INTRO = 0
Const STEP_1 = 1
Const STEP_2 = 2
Const STEP_3 = 3
Const STEP_4 = 4
Const STEP_FINISH = 5

Const DIR_NONE = 0
Const DIR_BACK = 1
Const DIR_NEXT = 2

Const FRM_TITLE = "Blank Wizard"
Const INTRO_KEY = "IntroductionScreen"
Const SHOW_INTRO = "ShowIntro"
Const TOPIC_TEXT = "<TOPIC_TEXT>"

'module level vars
Dim mnCurStep          As Integer
Dim mbHelpStarted      As Boolean

Public VBInst          As VBIDE.VBE
Dim mbFinishOK         As Boolean
```

Note that the constant NUM_STEPS = 7 reflects an added step, but there are only six steps listed in the Const STEP section of the declarations. An extra step was added to the wizard before this code was copied. The declarations must be corrected for the new step to be useful. The changes are shown in the partial listing below, with the changes in bold.

```
Const STEP_INTRO = 0
Const STEP_1 = 1
Const STEP_2 = 2
Const STEP_3 = 3
Const STEP_4 = 4
Const STEP_5 = 5
Const STEP_FINISH = 6
```

Changes must also be made to the SetStep procedure on frmWizard. The default code is shown in Listing 102-2.

Listing 102-2 The default code from the SetStep procedure

```
Private Sub SetStep(nStep As Integer, nDirection As Integer)

    Select Case nStep
        Case STEP_INTRO

        Case STEP_1

        Case STEP_2

        Case STEP_3

        Case STEP_4
            mbFinishOK = False

        Case STEP_FINISH
            mbFinishOK = True

    End Select

    'move to new step
    fraStep(mnCurStep).Enabled = False
    fraStep(nStep).Left = 0
    If nStep <> mnCurStep Then
        fraStep(mnCurStep).Left = -10000
    End If
    fraStep(nStep).Enabled = True

    SetCaption nStep
    SetNavBtns nStep

End Sub
```

Note that most of the code in this procedure is empty stubs to allow you to add your own code to be executed when a step is entered. But no allowance has been made for the new step. The required changes are shown below, with the changes in bold.

```
Case STEP_4

Case STEP_5
    mbFinishOK = False

Case STEP_FINISH
    mbFinishOK = True
```

The variable mbFinishOK is used to enable and disable the Finish button. It must be set to False in the last step so that it will be disabled if the user selects the Back button from the Finished! screen.

For a final gotcha, as of this writing the frame that is added for the new step is less than the full width of the form, and the label does not show until the frame is manually made wider.

Making the Wizard Do Something

The Wizard Manager provides you with a framework. You can, if you wish, compile it and add it to the Visual Basic Add-Ins menu just as it comes out of the box. You will get a wizard named Wizard Template that provides an introduction screen, four empty steps, a Finished! screen, and a confirmation screen. You can merrily move back and forth between the steps and, finally, click on the OK button of the confirmation form, but nothing will happen in the VB project.

Remember that a wizard is an add-in. As such, it has access to all the objects exposed by the IDE. The object hierarchy begins with the Application object, now called VBE. The VBE object contains an ActiveProject object, which is itself the container of all the objects in the project. Figure 102-2 shows the hierarchy of the ActiveProject object.

Using the objects in this hierarchy, you can access and change anything in a project. You can add or modify forms, code, Basic modules, class modules, and controls. This is obvious from the actions performed by the Application Wizard and the Data Form Wizard that come with Visual Basic 5.0. The project at the end of this chapter modifies the properties of selected controls. Review the project carefully before you attempt your own wizards.

Pitfalls

When you test a wizard, be sure to use Start With Full Compile from the Start menu. Correct registration and operation are not assured if you just click on the Start icon. Another potential problem is that the wizard may be registered in the system registry several times. Close all your open programs and run RegClean to clean out the registry after running your tests.

The Color Wizard Project

The Color Wizard project takes you step-by-step through the design and use of a new wizard. The Color Wizard helps the user change the Forecolor and Backcolor properties of all the selected controls on a form.

Start the Wizard Manager

1. Start a new project and select Standard EXE.

2. Select the Add-In Manager from the Add-Ins menu and select the VB Wizard Manager.

3. Click on Yes in the Wizard Manager dialog that asks to create a new Wizard project.

4. Save the project as COLORWIZ.VBP.

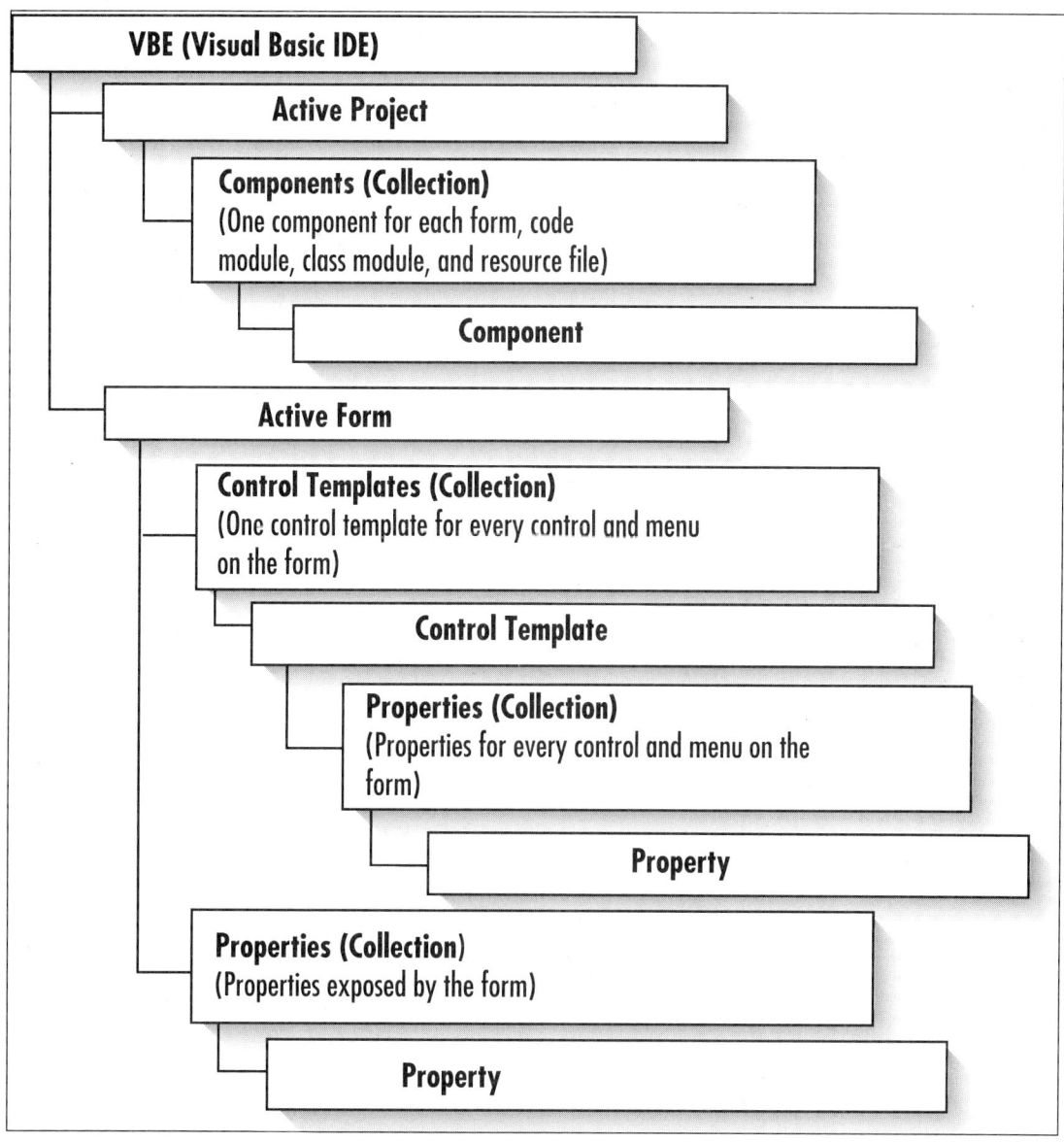

Figure 102-2 The application hierarchy

Change Some Properties

There are a number of project properties that you must change.

1. Select ColorWiz Properties from the project menu.

2. On the General tab, change Project Type to ActiveX DLL. A DLL runs more efficiently than an ActiveX EXE, and serves well for this application. Change Project Name to ColorWiz, and change Project Description to Color Wizard.

3. On the Make tab, change Application Title to ColorWiz, and change Company Name from Microsoft to VSBB. Add comments if you wish.

4. On the Compile tab, select Compile to Native Code and Optimize for Small Code.

5. Click on OK.

Change the Class Description

The Description property of the Wizard class is the name users will see when they select the Add-In Manager. By default, it is Wizard Template, which is not very descriptive.

1. Press F2 to open the object browser

2. Right-click on the Wizard class and select Properties from the pop-up menu.

3. Change Description to Color Wizard.

Work with the Resource File

The resource file, WIZARD.RES, is generic. To avoid conflict with other resource files, it needs a unique name, something other than WIZARD.RES.

1. Use NotePad or another plain Text Editor to edit the WIZARD.RC file that the Wizard Manager created. Listing 102-3 shows the edited version. You can find this file on the CD-ROM that accompanies this book as COLORWIZ.RC.

Listing 102-3 The source code for the resource file

```
STRINGTABLE DISCARDABLE
BEGIN
        //Wizard Caption
        10          "Color Wizard"
        15          "Color Wizard..."

        //Button Captions for Navigation Control:
        100         "Help"
        101         "Cancel"
        102        "< &Back"
        103         "&Next >"
        104         "&Finish"
```

```
//Intro Info:
1000      "Introduction"
1001      "The Color Wizard will help you set the fore and ⇐
          back colors of selected controls"
1002      "&Skip this screen in the future."

//Other Step Control Captions:
2000      "Step 1"
2001      "Select Fore and Back colors, then click Next. ⇐
          (Some controls do not have a ForeColor property)"

//Finish Step:
3000      "Finished!"
3001      "The Color Wizard is finished collecting information.\r\n\r\n_"
3002      "To make the color changes, press Finish!"

//Confirmation dialog
10000     "Color changes completed"
10001     "The color changes have been completed."
10002     "Don't show this dialog in the future."
10003     "OK"

//Misc strings:
20000     "(None)"

//Error messages:
30000     "Incomplete Data."
30001     "You must ... before you can continue."

END

5000    BITMAP    wizmenu.bmp
```

2. Save the file as COLORWIZ.RC.

3. Compile the new resource file. The resource compiler is RC.EXE, and can be found in the DevStudio\VB\Wizards directory. You can compile the resource file from a DOS window or from Start|Run. See Chapter 93 to refresh your memory on the resource compiler.

4. Right-click on Wizard.Res in the Project window and select Remove Wizard.Res from the pop-up menu.

5. Use Project|Add File to add the new COLORWIZ.RES file to your project.

Change the Number of Steps

This is a fairly simple wizard. It requires only four steps.

1. Right-click on Step 2 in the Wizard Manager window. Select Delete from the popup menu that appears.

2. Repeat for Steps 2, 3, and 4.

3. Open the code window for frmWizard and change the Declarations section as shown in Listing 102-4. The changes are shown in bold.

Listing 102-4 Changes to the Declarations section of frmWizard

```
Option Explicit
Const NUM_STEPS = 3
Const RES_ERROR_MSG = 30000
'BASE VALUE FOR HELP FILE FOR THIS WIZARD:
Const HELP_BASE = 1000
Const HELP_FILE = "MYWIZARD.HLP"
Const BTN_HELP = 0
Const BTN_CANCEL = 1
Const BTN_BACK = 2
Const BTN_NEXT = 3
Const BTN_FINISH = 4
Const STEP_INTRO = 0
Const STEP_1 = 1
Const STEP_FINISH = 2
Const DIR_NONE = 0
Const DIR_BACK = 1
Const DIR_NEXT = 2
Const FRM_TITLE = "Color Wizard"
Const INTRO_KEY = "IntroductionScreen"
Const SHOW_INTRO = "ShowIntro"
Const TOPIC_TEXT = "<TOPIC_TEXT>"
'module level vars
Dim mnCurStep          As Integer
Dim mbHelpStarted      As Boolean
Public VBInst          As VBIDE.VBE
Dim mbFinishOK         As Boolean
Private bChangedFore As Boolean, bChangedBack As Boolean
```

4. Change the SetStep procedure by removing the Case statements for Steps 2, 3, and 4. The corrected procedure is shown in Listing 102-5.

Listing 102-5 Changes to the SetStep procedure of frmWizard

```
Private Sub SetStep(nStep As Integer, nDirection As Integer)
    Select Case nStep
        Case STEP_INTRO

        Case STEP_1
            mbFinishOK = False

        Case STEP_FINISH
            mbFinishOK = True

    End Select

    'move to new step
    fraStep(mnCurStep).Enabled = False
    fraStep(nStep).Left = 0
    If nStep <> mnCurStep Then
        fraStep(mnCurStep).Left = -10000
    End If
    fraStep(nStep).Enabled = True

    SetCaption nStep
```

```
    SetNavBtns nStep

End Sub
```

Add a Common Dialog Control to frmWizard

1. Open the frmWizard form.
2. Click on the left-hand button of the Wizard Manager toolbar to move all the steps off the screen.
3. Place a Common Dialog control on the form. If the Common Dialog control is not visible on your toolbox, select Microsoft Common Dialog Control 5.0 from the Project|Components menu. The Common Dialog control is used to give the user access to the color dialog.
4. Name the Common Dialog control CDlg.

Add Controls to Step 1

1. Click on Step 1 in the Wizard Manager window to bring the frame for Step 1 into view on the form.
2. Add the controls in Table 102-1 to the frame. Be sure to draw each of the controls into the frame for Step 1. If you double-click on a control in the ToolBox window, the control will be placed on the form, not in the frame. Use Figure 102-3 as a guide to size and placement.

Table 102-1 New controls for Step 1

Object	Property	Setting
CommandButton	Name	cmdColor
	Caption	Set ForeColor
	Index	0
	Style	1 Graphical
	TabIndex	1
CommandButton	Name	cmdColor
	Index	0
	Style	1 Graphical
	TabIndex	3
TextBox	Name	txtColor
	Locked	-1 True
	TabStop	0 False
	Text	Text box appearance

continued on next page

continued from previous page

Object	Property	Setting
Label	Name	lblFlat
	Alignment	2 Center
	Appearance	0 Flat
	Caption	Flat Label Appearance
Label	Name	lbl3D
	Alignment	2 Center
	Appearance	1 3D
	BorderStyle	1 Fixed Single
	Caption	3D Label Appearance
Label	Name	Label2
	Caption	&BackColor
	TabIndex	2
Label	Name	Label1
	Caption	&ForeColor
	TabIndex	0

Add Code to the New Command Button

1. Add the code in Listing 102-6 to the Click event of cmdColor.

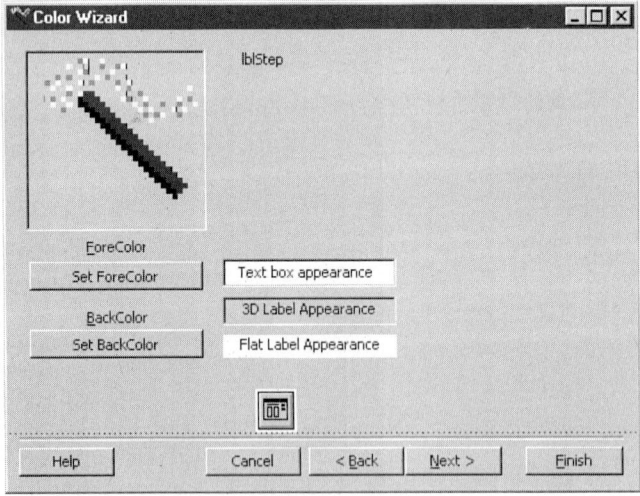

Figure 102-3   Step 1 at design time

Listing 102-6 Code for cmdColor

```
Private Sub cmdColor_Click(Index As Integer)
    Dim j As Integer
    On Error GoTo Error_Handler
    'Allow the user access to the custom color pallet
    'and make the selected color available to the program
    CDlg.Flags = cdlCCFullOpen Or cdlCCRGBInit
    'Allow cancel
    CDlg.CancelError = True
    'show the color dialog
    CDlg.ShowColor
    If Index Then 'backcolor
        bChangedBack = True
        txtColor.BackColor = CDlg.Color
        cmdColor(0).BackColor = CDlg.Color
        cmdColor(1).BackColor = CDlg.Color
        lblFlat.BackColor = CDlg.Color
        lbl3D.BackColor = CDlg.Color
        gnBackColor = CDlg.Color
    Else 'forecolor
        bChangedFore = True
        txtColor.ForeColor = CDlg.Color
        lblFlat.ForeColor = CDlg.Color
        lbl3D.ForeColor = CDlg.Color
        gnForeColor = CDlg.Color
    End If
Normal_Exit:
    Exit Sub
Error_Handler:
    If Err = cdlCancel Then GoTo Normal_Exit
    MsgBox Err & Error
    GoTo Normal_Exit
End Sub
```

2. Add code to cmdNav for the Finish button.

3. Change the code in cmdNav so clicking on Finish branches to a new procedure. Changes are shown in bold.

```
Case BTN_FINISH
        'wizard creation code goes here
        SetColors
        Unload Me

        If GetSetting(APP_CATEGORY, WIZARD_NAME, CONFIRM_KEY, ⇐
        vbNullString) = vbNullString Then
            frmConfirm.Show vbModal
        End If

    End Select
End Sub
```

4. Add the procedure in Listing 102-7 to frmWizard.

Listing 102-7 The SetColors procedure

```
Private Sub SetColors()
' sets the color of the selected controls
    'some controls don't have one or the other color property
    'ignore the error and continue
    On Error Resume Next
    'declare the object variables for early binding
    Dim vbc As VBControl
    Dim vbf As VBForm
    Dim vbcomp As VBComponent 'the forms are in the VBComponents collection
    Dim vbp As VBProject
    Dim vbprop As Property
    'reference the active project
    Set vbp = VBInst.ActiveVBProject
    'Loop through components
    For Each vbcomp In vbp.VBComponents
        If vbcomp.Type = vbext_ct_VBForm Then
            'if it is a form, activate it
            vbcomp.Activate
            'get the object that allows you to access
            'the design characteristics of a component
            Set vbf = vbcomp.Designer
            'check and modify selected controls
            'loop through the selected controls collection
            For Each vbc In vbf.SelectedVBControls
                'loop through the properties
                For Each vbprop In vbc.Properties
                    'Change command button style to graphical
                    'so backcolor shows
                    If vbc.ClassName = "CommandButton" Then _
                        If vbprop.Name = "Style" Then _
                            vbprop.Value = 1
                    'set the forecolor if it has been changed by the wizard
                    If bChangedFore Then _
                        If vbprop.Name = "ForeColor" Then _
                            vbprop.Value = gnForeColor
                    'set the backcolor if it has been changed by the wizard
                    If bChangedBack Then _
                        If vbprop.Name = "BackColor" Then _
                            vbprop.Value = gnBackColor
                Next vbprop
            Next vbc
        End If
    Next vbcomp
End Sub
```

5. Delete the Save Settings check box.

Because it is unlikely that the color settings will be the same from one project to the next, the Save Settings check box is superfluous.

6. Click on Finished! in the Wizard Manager window to bring the Finished! frame into view on frmWizard.

7. Delete chkSaveSettings from the form.

Change modWizard

1. Open the code window for modWizard.

2. Change the Declarations section as shown in Listing 102-8. Changes are in bold.

Listing 102-8 Changes to modWizard

```
Option Explicit
Global Const WIZARD_NAME = "ColorWiz"
Declare Function WritePrivateProfileString& Lib "Kernel32" ⇐
Alias "WritePrivateProfileStringA" (ByVal AppName$, ByVal KeyName$, ByVal keydefault$,⇐
ByVal FileName$)
'WinHelp Commands
Declare Function WinHelp Lib "user32" Alias "WinHelpA" ⇐
(ByVal hwnd As Long, ByVal lpHelpFile As String, ByVal wCommand As Long, ⇐
ByVal dwData As Long) As Long
Public Const HELP_QUIT = &H2              '  Terminate help
Public Const HELP_CONTENTS = &H3&        '  Display index/contents
Public Const HELP_CONTEXT = &H1          '  Display topic in ulTopic
Public Const HELP_INDEX = &H3            '  Display index
Global Const APP_CATEGORY = "Wizards"
Global Const CONFIRM_KEY = "ConfirmScreen"
Global Const DONTSHOW_CONFIRM = "DontShow"
'Global variables for ForeColor and BackColor
Global gnForeColor As Long, gnBackColor As Long
```

Test the Color Wizard

It is a good idea to test a new wizard before you compile it as a .DLL.

1. Add the Color Wizard to VBADDIN.INI.

2. Open the Immediate window by pressing CTRL-G.

3. Type AddToIni and press ENTER. This adds the Color Wizard to locate add-ins.

Test the Wizard

1. Run the wizard from the IDE by selecting Start With Full Compile from the Run menu. Do not select Start or click the Start icon on the toolbar; operation of .DLL files from within the IDE can fail if you do not use Start With Full Compile.

2. Open a second instance of Visual Basic 5.0.

3. Select Add-In Manager from the Add-Ins menu, click on Color Wizard from the list, and then click on the OK button.

4. Add several controls to the form.

5. Select the controls by holding down SHIFT and clicking on each control.

6. Open the Add-Ins menu and select Color Wizard.

7. Change the forecolor and backcolor properties with the wizard. Figure 102-4 shows the Color Wizard at work.

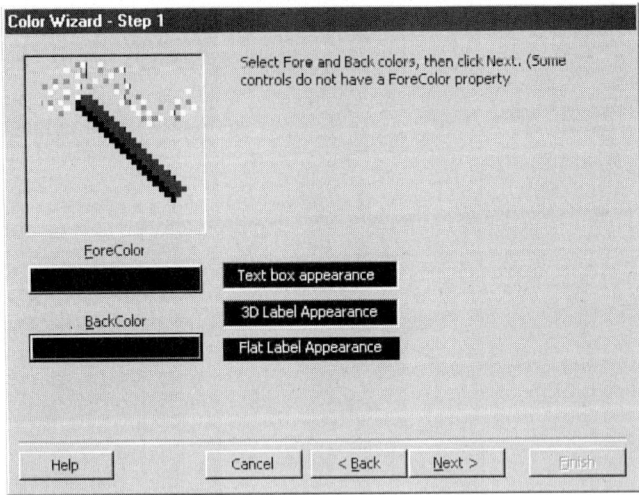

Figure 102-4   The Color Wizard at work

103

VISUAL SOURCESAFE

One of the tools included only in the Enterprise Edition of Visual Basic 5.0 is Visual SourceSafe. SourceSafe is a version-control package with a graphical user interface, making it significantly easier to use than command-line driven tools. SourceSafe also integrates nicely in the Visual Basic Integrated Development Environment (IDE). Used this way, it looks as if Visual Basic has built-in version control.

As its name implies, version-control software is used to keep track of multiple versions of computer files. These files most often consist of software artifacts (code modules, class modules, forms, and so on), but may also include analysis and design documents, test plans, user documentation, or even Web pages, spreadsheets, presentations, and so forth. There are two ways to use SourceSafe when programming in Visual Basic: as a stand-alone program or from within the Visual Basic IDE. This chapter covers the basics of version control using SourceSafe. Our coverage focuses on using SourceSafe from within the Visual Basic IDE, because this is the most natural way Visual Basic programmers use SourceSafe.

Introduction

Version control is especially indispensable when the team working on the software project is large. Without any extra effort other than the use of the version control software, team members are prevented from making changes to a file that someone else is working on and gain easy access to the latest versions of all the project files. Version control also offers advantages for a developer working alone. The ability to backtrack to any version of any file that was ever checked into version control and to get a list of the changes made to any version of any file may prove a huge time saver when tracking down errors introduced through changes.

Installing SourceSafe

Visual SourceSafe maintains the version information of the files put under its control in a proprietary database. Obviously, this database must be on a drive that is accessible to all developers working on these files. This is not an issue for a developer working alone and in such cases the SourceSafe database is often installed locally on a hard drive of his/her personal computer. When there are multiple SourceSafe users, this database is usually stored on a networked drive accessible by all the developers. To do so, the SourceSafe administrator runs the SourceSafe server installation to create the central database on the file server and performs a client installation on each user's machine.

During the installation, Visual SourceSafe asks you which type of installation (Server, Custom, or Client) you want to perform, as shown in Figure 103-1. Server installation is the method an administrator chooses to install SourceSafe on a file server that is accessible to all users. Custom installation enables you to install only the parts of SourceSafe you want and lists the hard drive space requirements for each option. Figure 103-2 shows the options you get when selecting this installation mode. The Client option does not install the SourceSafe database, it installs only the files necessary to run SourceSafe. The Client install can therefore not be used by itself and must be preceded by a server installation.

To integrate Visual SourceSafe with Visual Basic 5.0, you must first perform a Server setup of SourceSafe (either on a server or on your PC if you do not need to share the SourceSafe database with others), then perform a client setup on your PC, after you have installed Visual Basic.

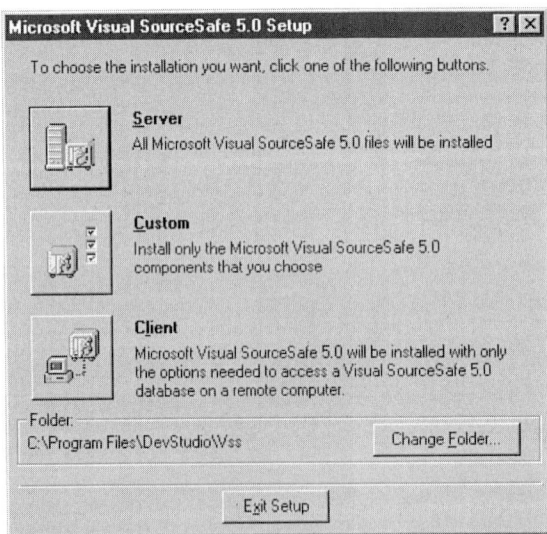

Figure 103-1 When installing Visual SourceSafe, you must choose between a Server, Custom, or Client installation

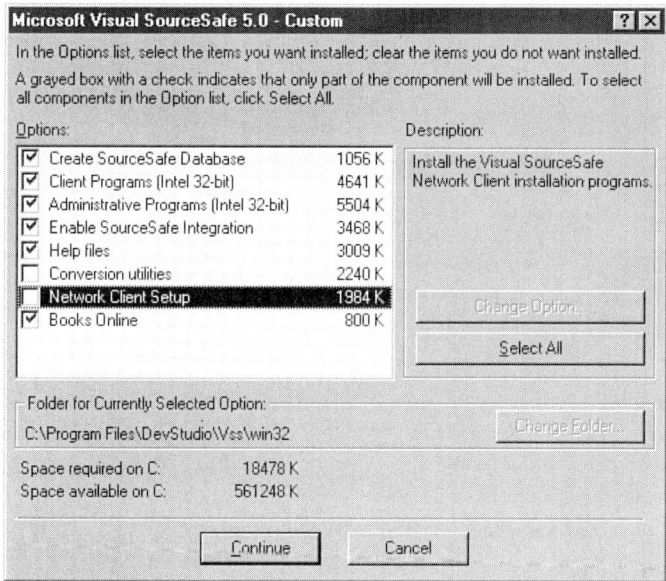

Figure 103-2 The Custom Visual SourceSafe installation allows you to select which components you want to install

Version Control Terminology

SourceSafe uses projects to group files put under its revision control. These projects are visually represented by folders in the SourceSafe Explorer, as seen in Figure 103-3. This gives you great flexibility to organize the files and allows you to avoid replication of common files by creating projects for the files that need to be shared. Often, developers create the same SourceSafe project structure as the directory structure they use to store the Visual Basic projects. The destination path where the developer stores the working copies of the files kept in SourceSafe is called the working directory. Each developer may set his own working directory for a project. For example, Paul may set his working directory for the Abracadabra project to D:\Data\VB\Abracadabra, while Janine prefers to set her working directory for the same project to F:\Work\Abracadabra.

There are three operations a developer performs on day-to-day basis when moving files from and to the SourceSafe database: getting, checking in, and checking out. Getting a file creates a read-only copy of the file stored in Visual SourceSafe in your working directory. This is done when you want to view the file or create an executable using the latest version of all files. Checking out a file creates a writable copy of the file in your working directory. Other users are prevented from checking out the same file while you have this file checked out. You typically check out a file only when you

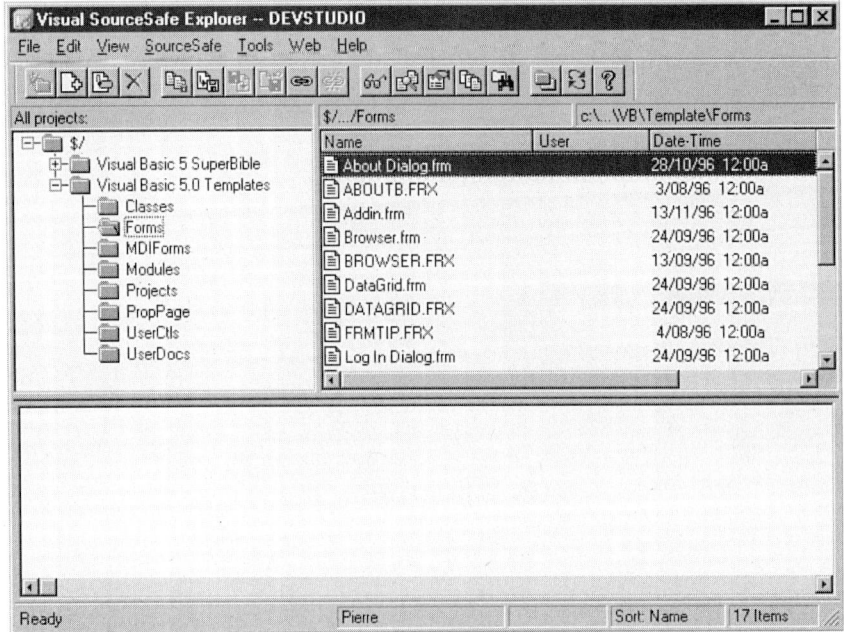

Figure 103-3   The Visual SourceSafe Explorer represents projects by folders

need to make changes to it. When you are satisfied with your changes (that is, after thorough testing), you check in the modified file. This will make the new version available to other team members and allow them to make further changes to this new version, if needed. You may also choose to undo the check out, if you did not need to make changes to the file after all. This makes the original file available for check out by others.

Integrated SourceSafe Menu Options

Figure 103-4 shows the SourceSafe menu available in Visual Basic after the SourceSafe integrated components have been installed. Table 103-1 lists the menu choices.

Table 103-1 SourceSafe menu options in the Visual Basic IDE

Use This...	To Do This...
Get Latest Version	Retrieve a read-only copy of the currently highlighted file from the SourceSafe database to your working directory
Check Out	Retrieve a writable copy of the currently highlighted file from the SourceSafe database to your working directory and disallow another check out of this file
Check In	Record in the SourceSafe database the changes to the writable copy of the currently highlighted file you checked out and make this modified file available for check out

Use This...	To Do This...
Undo Check Out	Make the file you checked out available for checking out without the changes you may have made
Show History	View the version history of the currently highlighted file
Show Differences	View what was added and deleted between versions of the currently highlighted file
SourceSafe Properties	View the properties (such as the date of check in or the comment describing the history) of the currently highlighted file
Add Files to SourceSafe	Put new files under SourceSafe's control
Share Files	Share files from other projects
Create Project from SourceSafe	Retrieve the latest version of a Visual Basic project from the SourceSafe database
Add Project to SourceSafe	Add the current Visual Basic project to the SourceSafe database
Run SourceSafe	Start SourceSafe Explorer, the stand-alone version of SourceSafe
Options	Change the degree of control over file check in and check out in the integrated environment
Refresh File Status	Update the file status indicators in the Project window

The four common file operations can also be performed by right-clicking on a file in the project. Figure 103-5 shows the menu you get by right-clicking on the frmMain form in the SourceSafe project discussed below.

Figure 103-4   The SourceSafe menu is integrated in the Visual Basic development environment

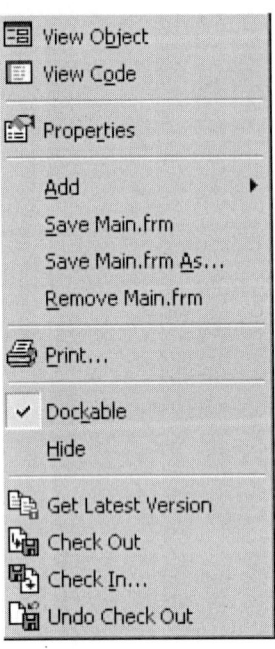

Figure 103-5   Visual SourceSafe commands are also accessible by right-clicking on a file in the Project window

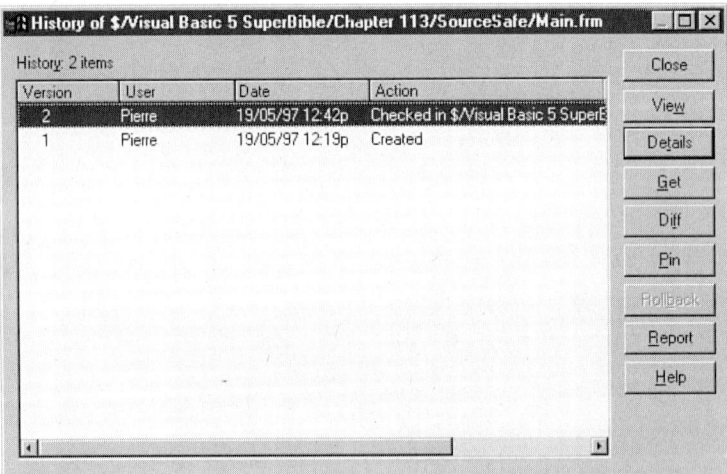

Figure 103-6   The History dialog displays the details for each version of the file

The History command is used to display the details of the different versions of the file. Figure 103-6 shows the History dialog for the frmMain form in the SourceSafe project. You can also select two versions of the file (by clicking on a first one and holding down the CTRL while clicking on the second version) and view all the differences between the two versions. The resulting display is shown in Figure 103-7. This menu option is similar to the Show Differences option available in the Tools/SourceSafe menu. The former is more flexible, since the menu option always displays the difference between the working copy and the most recent version. The properties option is mainly used to display the file comments.

The Add Files to SourceSafe command is used to put files under SourceSafe's control for the first time. This option is needed because SourceSafe requires that a file was checked out before it can be checked in. The Share option is used to share files from different projects in the current project.

Both project creation commands are typically used only once for a project. The developer who first works on a Visual Basic adds this project to SourceSafe with the Add Project to SourceSafe option. The other developers create local copies of this project with the Create Project from SourceSafe option. The Refresh File Status is used to update the symbols used in the file icons in the project window.

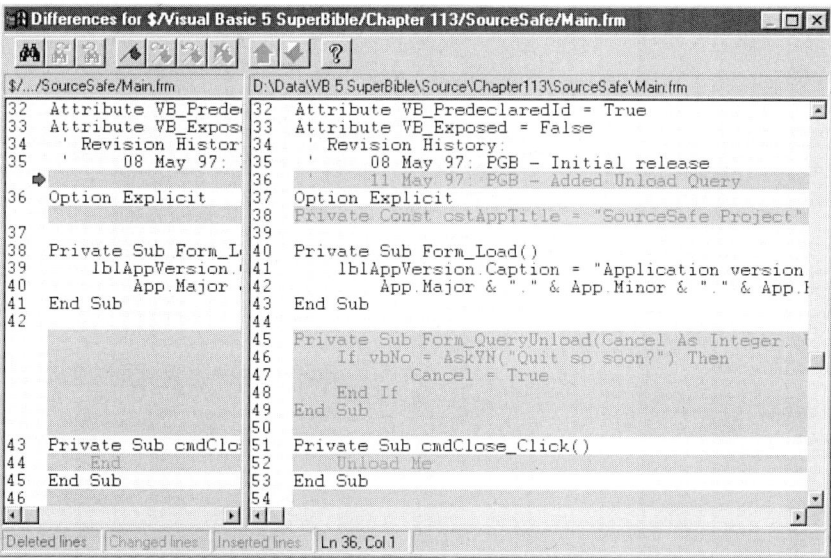

Figure 103-7   The Show Differences is a great way to visualize changes made from one release to another

SourceSafe Project

This project demonstrates how to use the integrated SourceSafe tool in Visual Basic.

Assembling the Project

1. Place the following controls on a form, as detailed in Table 103-2.

Table 103-2 Elements of frmMain

Control	Property	Value
Form	Name	frmMain
	BorderStyle	3- Fixed Dialog
	Caption	"SourceSafe Project"
Label	Name	lblAppVersion
	Caption	"Example application: version ???"
Command Button	Name	cmdClose
	Caption	"Close"

2. Size the objects on the screen as shown in Figure 103-8.

3. Go to the Form Layout Window, right-click on top of the frmMain form and select Center Screen as the startup position.

4. Enter the following code into the Form_Load procedure of frmMain. This code displays the application version by setting the label caption.

```
Private Sub Form_Load()
    lblAppVersion.Caption = "Application version " & _
        App.Major & "." & App.Minor & "." & App.Revision
End Sub
```

5. Enter the following code into the cmdClose_Click procedure. This code ends the application.

```
Private Sub cmdClose_Click()
    End
End Sub
```

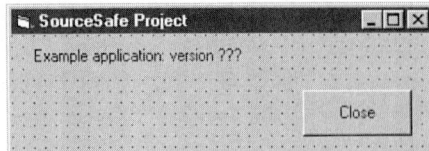

Figure 103-8   frmMain in Design mode

6. Save the project. When asked whether to create a SourceSafe project, click Yes. You will store this project in Visual Basic 5 SuperBible/Chapter 103/SourceSafe. Highlight the root project ("$/"). Type Visual Basic 5 SuperBible in the project text box and select Create. Highlight the newly created project and create a sub project named Chapter 103. Figure 103-9 shows the Add Project to SourceSafe dialog just before the creation of this project. Finally, create a sub project called SourceSafe within the Chapter 103 sub project. This is where we will store the project files. Highlight this project and click on OK. This brings up the Add Files to SourceSafe dialog box as in Figure 103-10. Type Initial Release. in the comment text box and click on OK.

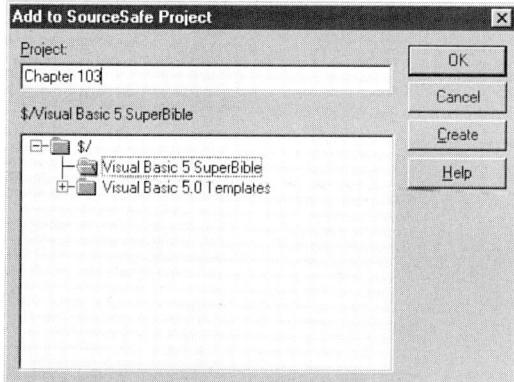

Figure 103-9 The Add Project dialog just before the project creation

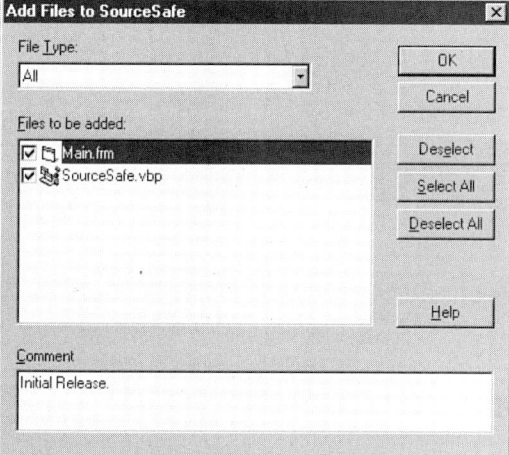

Figure 103-10 After the project has been created, you put the files under revision control

7. Now that you have put the files under revision control, you must check out files before making changes. In the project window, a lock shows that the files are read-only, as seen in Figure 103-11. Right-click on the frmMain form and select check out. A SourceSafe dialog pops up, displays successful completion of the operation, and closes itself. You now see a checkmark next to the file you just checked out, as in Figure 103-12. Also check out the project.

8. Add the following code to the general declarations section of frmMain. You simply declare a string literal used below.

```
Private Const cstAppTitle = "SourceSafe Project"
```

9. Add the following code to the Form_QueryUnload event of the frmMain form. This subroutine gives you a chance to cancel the termination of the application.

```
Private Sub Form_QueryUnload(Cancel As Integer, UnloadMode As Integer)
    If vbNo = AskYN("Quit so soon?") Then
        Cancel = True
    End If
End Sub
```

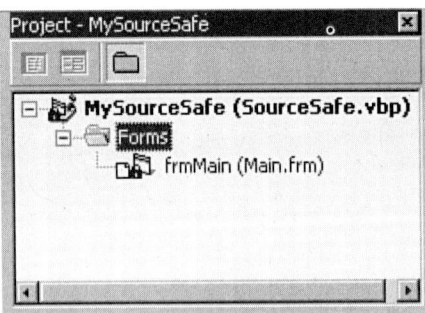

Figure 103-11 The lock icons indicate read-only files

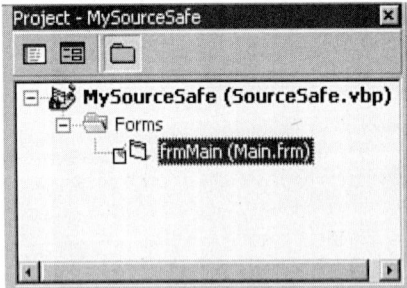

Figure 103-12 The checkmark indicates that frmMain has been checked out

10. Add the following routine to the general declaration section of frmMain. You simply put up a message box asking the question and return the answer to the caller.

```
Public Function AskYN(strQuestion As String) As Integer
    AskYN = MsgBox(strQuestion, vbYesNo + vbExclamation, cstAppTitle)
End Function
```

11. Change the code in the Click event of cmdClose as below. Instead of terminating the application, we unload the form, giving the QueryUnload routine a chance to cancel the operation.

```
Private Sub cmdClose_Click()
    Unload Me
End Sub
```

12. Right-click on the form and select Check in. Review all the changes you made by clicking on the Differences button. Close the Differences window and click on OK. Write a descriptive comment in the text box, such as "Added Unload Query." Also check in the project, as in Figure 103-13.

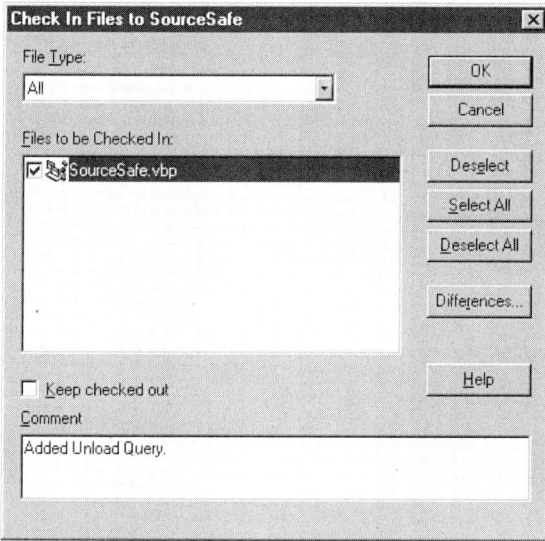

Figure 103-13 After all changes are made, files are checked in

How It Works

The SourceSafe integration into the Visual Basic IDE makes it very easy to add a project to SourceSafe and to check files in and out. This simple project does little more than display a dialog box on the screen. In a second phase, we add a dialog box to question the termination. Figure 103-14 shows the project in operation.

Figure 103-14   The SourceSafe project in action

PART XVII

NEW OBJECT-ORIENTED PROGRAMMING

104

CREATING CLASSES AND CLASS MODULES

The most exciting addition to Visual Basic 4.0 was its ability to create new objects. Visual Basic 5.0 increases the functionality of user-created objects. Although Microsoft's documentation barely hints at the power and flexibility of creating new objects, your programming skills will grow substantially if you take the time to learn about new objects. Creating and using your own objects will save you time and will help you write programs that are easier to understand and maintain.

This chapter covers the essentials of object-oriented programming and explains how to create your own classes using Visual Basic 5.0's powerful new class modules. We'll cover the basics as well as more advanced professional-level techniques, including some tricky ways of doing things that Microsoft says can't be done. Object-oriented programming makes a clear distinction between programming an object (discussed here) and using an object. Chapter 105, "Using Classes and Class Modules," explains how to use the objects we build here and includes details on making your objects into reusable OLE automation servers that can be freely distributed and used by any OLE-enabled program.

You'll notice that in this chapter and in Chapter 105, we use the word *user* to refer to someone who uses the object we're building, not someone who's using a finished program. The user may well be yourself!

Before you can understand the new terrain of object-oriented programming, it's vital to understand exactly where you are now. Visual Basic has always been a well-structured language, and its new object orientation builds on this solid foundation. Good structured programming habits are a requirement for creating your own objects, so let's begin with the foundation.

Structured Programming

Earlier versions of Visual Basic excelled at structured programming, and the newest versions uphold and even strengthen this tradition. *Structured programming* breaks large, complex problems into many smaller, simpler pieces. Each of these smaller pieces is then broken down even further, until the pieces are small enough to be expressed as keywords in the programming language.

For example, you might analyze a typical order entry system and break it down into an initialization module, a data entry module and form, a verification module, and a database update module. You've taken one large problem and turned it into four smaller problems. You now focus your attention on each of these smaller components and break them down in turn: The database update routines might logically be grouped as "look up the account number," "create a new account number," and "create a new entry record for the account." These would be the highest-level routines of the database module, and you would program them as either sub procedures or functions. Each of these high-level routines has multiple smaller steps, which could be either individual statements or another lower-level sub procedure or function. Figure 104-1 illustrates this step-by-step decomposition.

Visual Basic has many language constructs that aid in structured programming. Forms and modules serve as containers for large functional areas, and sub procedures and functions contain individual processes. Constructs such as For...Next loops and If...End If blocks let you break down sub procedures into bite-sized pieces and help make the logic flow clearly. Visual Basic code can be very clean and very well structured.

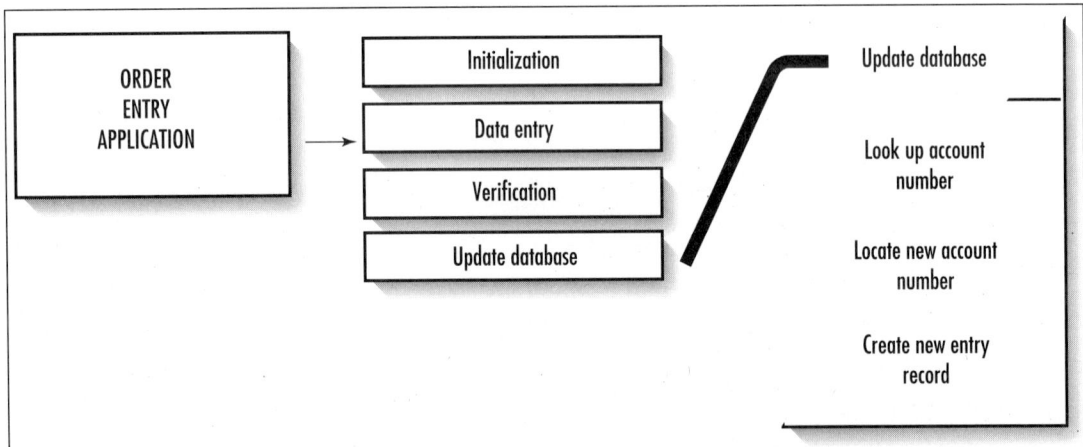

Figure 104-1   Structured programming breaks down large problems into smaller pieces

The whole idea behind decomposing a large problem into smaller pieces is to make it simpler to work with. You'll find that the fewer interactions between components, the easier your program is to understand. The concept of *information hiding* means that you want each routine to know as little as possible about the information in other routines. For example, the create a new account number routine in the database module shouldn't need to know anything at all about the inner workings of the display of the account address routine in the data input form.

Structured programmers refer to this as creating *black box* routines. It's possible to be mystified by *how* the routine does what it does; you just need to understand what it does and how to control it. (Indeed, this is the normal state of affairs for maintenance programmers!) The black box might have a red button and a green light; pressing the red button turns on the green light. You need not understand how the button works or how the light works; as long as you know that pressing the button lights the light, you can use the black box.

Similarly, the create a new account number function accepts a single parameter called customer ID and always returns a value that is the account number. You don't need to know the convolutions necessary to retrieve that account number, just as long as you know that the function retrieves it.

As you create a program using structured techniques, you'll eventually need to get inside the black box and program it. The black box paradigm continues to help you here: You don't need to know anything at all about the rest of the world (Is it after 4:00 p.m. Friday? Does the user have sufficient security privileges to edit this information?), you just need to know that your routine accepts the customer ID and returns the account number. This vastly simplifies the programming process. It also makes it easier to divide responsibility for a program among several programmers.

You maintain a high level of information hiding primarily through tight scoping. *Scope* refers to how many routines can see a variable. Scoping means letting as few routines as possible have access to variables. You accomplish this by declaring most of your variables as private in the routine that uses them, using private module-level variables as sparingly as possible, and minimizing or eliminating public global variables. Scoping tightly is probably the single easiest technique for reducing the number of bugs in your program, yet it is also the one most commonly neglected in magazines, books, and even Microsoft's own sample programs.

Keep these ideas of information hiding, tight scoping, and black box routines in your mind as you read about creating and programming your own objects. Objects are the ultimate black box, and object-oriented programming flows very naturally from structured programming techniques.

Object-Oriented Programming

Object-oriented programming lets you solve your programming challenges from a higher, more abstract level than does structured programming. It generally uses structured programming techniques once it gets down to the individual routine level, but starts by analyzing the large problem differently.

Structured analysis usually emphasizes process: What am I doing? Its solutions tend to be expressed by verbs: Our order entry application needs to *initialize, enter, verify,* and *update*.

Object-oriented analysis emphasizes real-world and abstract objects: What am I working on? Its solutions tend to be expressed by nouns: Our order entry application has a *user interface, accounts, business rules*, and a *permanent database*. This emphasis on objects and the information inherent in the objects, rather than on process, creates a more solid foundation for future program growth and maintenance. Data definitions (information) are much more stable than the shifting sands of process-oriented business rules, corporate guidelines, consumer desires, and hot programming trends.

Objects usually have three different aspects. They have certain characteristics (or *properties*), they can have certain processes (or *methods*), and they might be able to trigger other processes (or *events*). This should sound familiar, because Visual Basic has always been object based. All Visual Basic's user interface components are objects, and most possess all three of these aspects. For example, a command button has a Caption property, a Move method, and a Click event. Figure 104-2 shows what the problem posed in the structured programming example would look like if analyzed using object-oriented methods.

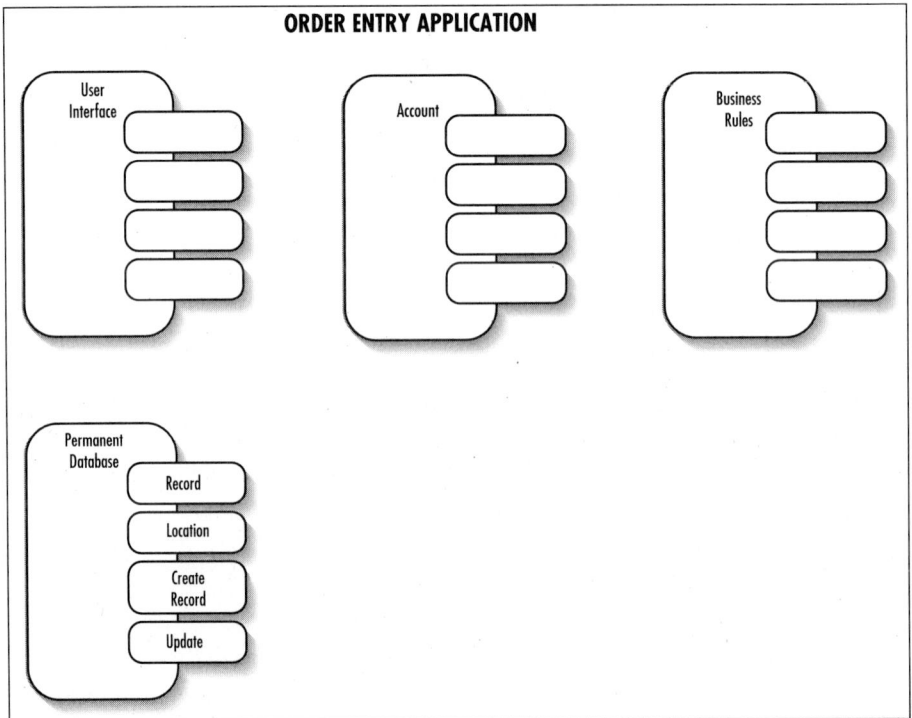

Figure 104-2 Object-oriented programming breaks down large entities into smaller entities that possess certain characteristics, can perform specified actions, and can trigger other actions

Objects are created from classes. Think of a *class* as a blank template or as a potential—but not-yet-created—object. A class contains all the information necessary to create an actual object, but it *isn't* the object. You build an object from a class by *instantiating* it. For example, if the class object is a command button, it's automatically instantiated when the form that it's on first appears. Each form can have many command buttons, and a single program can have many forms. Each of the command buttons is created from the same template built into Visual Basic—the CommandButton class—yet each command button is individual and can have unique property values and event definitions.

In Visual Basic 5.0, you can define your own classes with custom properties, methods, and events. You might define an account class that has an AccountNumber property, a CreateAccount method, and a BeforeDelete event. This type of object orientation can dramatically simplify the analysis and design of larger programs. Visual Basic has enough object orientation to be truly helpful, without the steep learning curve and overly complex class structures of some other, earlier object-oriented languages.

Building New Classes with Visual Basic

Visual Basic's object implementation is disarmingly simple. The new *class module* object lets you build custom classes. The class module looks almost the same as a regular code module, and you can do most of the same things with it. Any procedure or variable that you declare public becomes part of the *public interface* that defines how other programs and external procedures work with the new class—the outside of the black box. You'll continue to use Visual Basic's powerful structured programming elements, such as forms, modules, and all the familiar statements, keywords, and functions to build the inner workings of your object class—the inside of the black box.

Programs often need several classes. An accounting application might have an Account class, a BusinessRule class, and a Database class. These multiple classes may be related to each other, or they may be independent. See the "Class Hierarchies" section for details on how to manage multiple classes. Each class needs its own class module.

Visual Basic Learning Edition lets you create your own custom classes and use them directly in an application. This lets you take full advantage of the power inherent in object-oriented analysis and programming. You'll always include the class modules in the .VBP file of each project that uses them. This book refers to these kinds of projects, where you include the class directly in the project that uses them, as a *regular application*.

Visual Basic Professional and Enterprise Editions let you take one additional step: You can compile your classes into ActiveX .EXE or ActiveX .DLL files. Any OLE automation client (which includes most large, modern programs, including Visual Basic) can then use the objects. This is an extremely powerful capability. You can distribute a single .EXE or .DLL file that includes dozens of class modules, standard modules, and forms. Users of a variety of languages can then use whatever parts of your OLE automation server they need. Users will notice very little difference between an OLE automation server created with Visual Basic and one created in another language such as C++. Building the "inside" of the black box is almost the same no matter which edition of Visual Basic you have.

How to Build a Simple Class

Let's start by building a simple class. This class will emulate some aspects of a pile of paper—a type of data structure programmers refer to as a *stack*. You can add a new item to the top of the stack, and you can remove the top item in the stack. This is called pushing something onto the stack and popping something off. (Chapter 16, "Objects and Collections," discusses this example from a different perspective in the section describing the Collection object.)

First, pull down Visual Basic's Project menu and choose the Add Class Module menu command. VB opens the Add Class Module dialog box, which lets you select an existing class module or, with the Professional or Enterprise Editions, select the Class Builder Utility or create a new VB add-in. The Add Class Module dialog box is shown in Figure 104-3.

Double-click on the Class Module icon. This adds a class to your project. Next, type these lines into the class module's code window:

```
Dim MyStack_m As New Collection

Public Sub Push(newItem As Variant)
    On Error Resume Next
    If MyStack_m.Count > 0 Then
        MyStack_m.Add Item:=newItem, Before:=1
    Else
        MyStack_m.Add Item:=newItem
    End If
End Sub

Public Sub Pop()
    On Error Resume Next
    MyStack_m.Remove 1
End Sub

Public Property Get Value() As Variant
    On Error Resume Next
    Value = MyStack_m.Item(1)
End Property
```

Press F4 and use the Properties window to set the class name to Stack, as shown in Figure 104-4. Congratulations, you've just created your first class!

The Stack class has two methods, Push and Pop, and one property called Value. The Push method puts a new item on top of the stack. It first checks to see items are already on the stack by checking the collection's Count property. If Count is greater than 0, then items are already in the collection. It then uses the collection's Add method to add the new item to the stack by inserting it before the item in the first position.

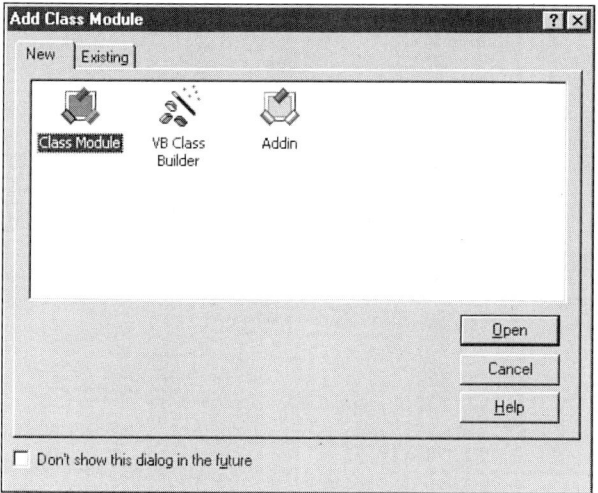

Figure 104-3 The Add Class Module dialog box

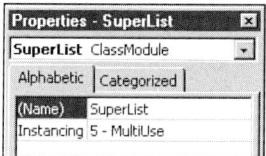

Figure 104-4 The Properties window

Visual Basic supports named arguments. *Named arguments* let you pass a value into an argument of a method, function, or procedure by specifying the name of the argument, rather than relying on the position of the argument in the argument list of the method, procedure, or function. The := symbol is the assignment operator for a named argument, so Item:=newItem, Before:=1 translates into "Assign newItem to the Item parameter, and 1 to the Before parameter."

The Collection object will automatically move all existing items down the stack because we used the Before parameter. The new item is now the first item in the collection, and it is on top of the stack. The Pop method is even easier: It just removes whatever was in the first position. The Collection object will automatically move everything up one position. The Value property is equally easy; it returns the actual item stored in the first position. Press F2 to display the Object Browser dialog box, then choose Stack in the Project combo box, as shown in Figure 104-5. It displays your custom class's properties and methods just as it would for any object.

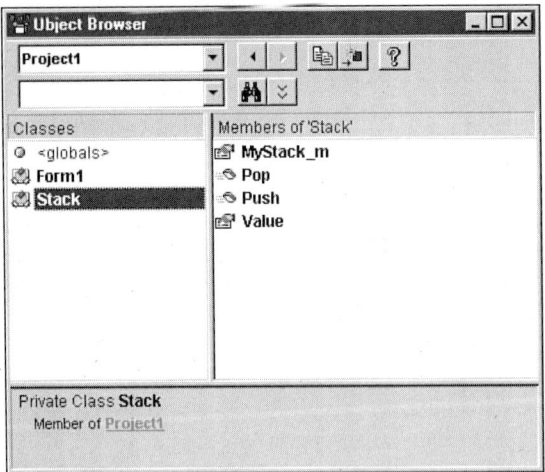

Figure 104-5   The Object Browser

Now let's use this new class. Add a command button to a blank form. Type the following lines into the form's code window:

```
Private TheFormStack As New Stack

Private Sub Form_Click()
    Dim msg As String
    msg = InputBox("Type a message to push onto the stack")
    TheFormStack.Push msg
End Sub

Private Sub Command1_Click()
    Debug.Print TheFormStack.Value
    TheFormStack.Pop
End Sub
```

This simple program uses the Stack class we just built. The module-level variable TheFormStack is declared as private, so the stack is available to any procedure within the form, but not available outside of the form. The New keyword tells Visual Basic to create a new object from the Stack class, as opposed to creating a variable that would refer to an already existing stack. Clicking anywhere on the form triggers the Form_Click event, which brings up an input box into which you can type a message. The message is then pushed onto the top of the stack. Click the form a couple of times to push some messages onto the stack. Clicking the command button triggers the Command1_Click event, which displays the message that's on top of the stack, and then pops the value off of the stack.

As you can see, there's not much to using a custom class—it's just like using any of Visual Basic's built-in objects. Classes are easy to use. Many programming problems are easier to analyze and solve using the power and flexibility of classes instead of standard modules. You'll be well rewarded for the time you invest in learning how to think through problems from an object-oriented perspective.

Step-by-Step: Building Complex Classes

Most real programs are a bit more involved than the previous example. You'll find object-oriented analysis and programming most useful on larger projects. This section covers a number of tricks and techniques for bringing out the full power of custom classes. It takes you step-by-step through the process of creating a complete class structure.

Step 1: Design the Class Interface

The first step in building a new class structure is to define the public interface for each class. The public interface is how other programmers (or you, if you'll be using the class as well as building it) will interact with the class. Don't confuse a class interface with a user interface: A class interface defines the properties, methods, and events that a programmer uses, whereas a user interface consists of the visible elements of the program. Some classes do expose user interface elements, but many do not.

A class interface should closely mimic the objects it represents. Take some time to analyze the real world object that you're attempting to model. What data, information, or characteristics does it have? Can the user both read and write the information, or are some things read-only and others write-only? These become properties, and will usually make up the bulk of most class definitions. What kinds of things will the object need to do, or create, or have done to it? These are the class methods. What kinds of events might need to be responded to by other procedures elsewhere in the program? Finally, does this class logically belong as an individual member of another class or does it contain other objects? This defines a class hierarchy, which is covered in the "Class Hierarchies" section later in this chapter. Spend some time thinking through the interface, and work away from the computer until you feel you've got a good idea of the object's definition.

Pay attention to how you will program the classes (inside the black box) as well as how the user will manipulate the objects (outside the black box). You may wish to use the Object Browser to review existing objects, such as the DBEngine object included with Visual Basic, for good ideas on how to define a public interface. Note some of the naming conventions and try to emulate them. Your object will be easier to use if it has a familiar look and feel to its interface.

As you design your object, pay close attention to the techniques of information hiding and tight scoping discussed in the "Structured Programming" section earlier in this chapter. You have little control over the number of object instances that are created from your classes, and you must be especially careful to minimize interactions between instances. Be brutal with your code to make the scoping as tight and as small as possible. If you're in the habit of using lots of global variables, you will have problems debugging your object applications. When in doubt, keep things private to an individual procedure.

Step 2: Add Class Modules

The next step is simple: Create a new class module for each class you'll be defining. Pull down the Project menu in the Visual Basic design environment and choose the Add Class Module menu command. This inserts a new class module into your project. Give the new class a name.

Step 3: Define Each Property

Next, define each property with a Property Get, Let, or Set statement. These procedures should appear in the class module of the class they belong to. Use a Property Get statement to define a property that the user can read, a Property Let statement for a property that the user can write to with a variable, and a Property Set statement for a property the user can write to with an object reference. Most properties are read/write, so you'll often use a Property Let/Set or Let/Get pair. Notice that all procedures that define the public interface should start with the Public keyword.

The following example properties might belong to a Hotel class that models a hotel. Hotels are complex, and we'll explore only a few possible properties that a real Hotel class might contain. Our hypothetical hotel has a collection of rooms, modeled in a separate Room class not shown here. The properties of the Room class are Occupied (whether the room is occupied or not), Available (whether it's available for rental), Wing (what wing of the hotel it's in), and MaintenanceStartDate (when maintenance for that room is scheduled to begin). The Hotel class also uses an instance of an Employee class, which models the hotel's employees. The examples below don't manipulate the instance of the Employee class, they just set it, return it, and store it.

The Hotel class properties are Season (reads or sets the season, such as spring, fall, winter, holiday, and summer), Manager (reads or sets the manager of the hotel), Rates (sets the rates to charge for each class of rooms in each season), VacancyRate (returns the percentage of rooms that are vacant), and WingMaintenance (reads or sets the maintenance date for an entire wing's rooms).

First, we define how we're going to store all the data for the class, as shown here:

```
'note that we use the _m convention to indicate a module level variable
Private Rooms_m As New Collection        'stores references for each room in hotel
Private Rates_m As Variant               'holds rate structure, as defined by a
                                         '(separate) module
Private Season_m As String               'holds the name of the current season
Private Manager_m As Employee            'holds reference to the hotel's manager
Private WingMaintenanceDate_m(1 To 4) As Variant   'holds dates of scheduled maintenance
                                                   'for each wing
```

You'll commonly store a class's data internally as module-level variables, arrays, and collections. We store the rooms in a collection. This makes it easy to go through all the rooms in the hotel, as we do in the following property examples, or access any individual room, as the method code samples show in the next step. The rates are stored in a variant, which lets us store and manipulate any arbitrarily complex data structure—it could be a simple constant or a multidimensional set of arrays. Variants are quite flexible. The wing maintenance dates are stored in a normal array. We specify the Variant data type (rather than the Date data type), because we need to distinguish between a scheduled date and no maintenance scheduled. The Variant data type can hold a date if maintenance is scheduled, or it can have the value Empty if no maintenance is scheduled. The WingMaintenanceDate property explains this in more detail. The season is stored in a simple string variable, and the manager is stored in an object variable.

Next, let's define the Season property. This is a simple read/write property that stores a piece of data. This is the easiest kind of property procedure to write. We define two procedures with the same name (Season) and the same data types (String). The first procedure allows the user to write to the property, and the second procedure returns the value of the property.

```
 'simple read-write property
Public Property Let Season(newSeason As String)
    Season_m = newSeason
End Property

Public Property Get Season() As String
    Season = Season_m
End Property
```

The property pair for setting and returning the manager is just as easy. The only difference is that instead of a Property Let statement, you use a Property Set statement, because Manager is an object variable rather than a standard data type:

```
 'simple read-write property for an object reference
Public Property Set Manager(newManager As Employee)
    Set Manager_m = newManager
End Property

Public Property Get Manager() As Employee
    Set Manager = Manager_m
End Property
```

The next property accepts a variant rate structure. We don't delve into what the rate structure is in our example, but it could be a constant value (all rooms rent for the same price), a three-dimensional array (one dimension specifies room type, another the current season, and the third the actual rate), or perhaps even a reference to a Rate object that has its own properties and methods. The only thing our property procedure has to do is accept the new rate structure and store it.

```
 'write-only property
Public Property Let Rates(newRates As Variant)
    'accept a new rate structure
    Rates_m = newRates
End Property
```

The VacancyRate property is read-only. It's actually a derived property calculated from information contained within the Hotel class. Read-only properties often provide high-level summary information like this. The procedure goes through the entire collection of rooms and determines what percentage is vacant.

```
'read-only property
Public Property Get VacancyRate() As Single
    'go through each room and count the number of vacant rooms
```

continued on next page

continued from previous page

```
    Dim room As Variant, occupiedCnt As Integer
    For Each room In Rooms_m
        If room.Occupied = True Then
            occupiedCnt = occupiedCnt + 1
        End If
    Next room
    VacancyRate = (Rooms_m.Count - occupiedCnt) / Rooms_m.Count
End Property
```

The last set of property procedures is more complex. We need to set and read a property that determines when a wing's rooms are scheduled for maintenance. Setting a maintenance date, however, must trigger some other actions. We need to set the room's individual maintenance date and prevent the room from being reserved if the date of maintenance is within a week of the current date. We also need a way to clear a maintenance date if the hotel manager's plans change.

A Variant data type makes it simple to distinguish between a scheduled date and no scheduled date: Variants can have the value Empty, which is different from 0 or "" or #1/1/00#. Our property will accept an actual date to schedule maintenance and a data value of Empty to clear any maintenance. We also specify what wing we want to read or set. Notice how the pair of property procedures' parameter data types match up, even though we're specifying multiple parameters: the Property Let statement specifies (Integer, Variant) and the Property Get statement specifies (Integer) As Variant.

The procedure first sets the wing maintenance date in the tracking array. It then goes through each room in the hotel. If the room is in the given wing, we test the startDate parameter. The IsEmpty function returns True if the value of the variant is Empty; if so, we clear out the room's maintenance date and make the room available for reservations. The IsDate function returns True if the variant contains something that can be evaluated as a date. If startDate holds a date, we then set the room's maintenance date and make it unavailable for reservations if the maintenance date is scheduled for sometime within the next week. The Property Get procedure is much simpler. It simply returns the value of the appropriate slot in the WingMaintenanceDate_m array.

```
'more complex read-write property
Public Property Let WingMaintenanceDate(wingNumber As Integer, startDate As Variant)
    'set the wing maintenance date in the tracking array
    WingMaintenanceDate_m(wingNumber) = startDate
    'go through all rooms and set the maintenance date
    Dim room As Variant
    For Each room In Rooms_m
        If room.Wing = wingNumber Then
            'if the startDate is empty, it means cancel out any scheduled maintenance
            If IsEmpty(startDate) = True Then
                room.MaintenanceStartDate = Empty
                room.Available = True
            'if the startDate is really a date, then set the room's maintenance date
            ElseIf IsDate(startDate) = True Then
                room.MaintenanceStartDate = startDate
                'if the date is within a week, block out room availability
                If DateDiff("d", Now, startDate) <= 7 Then
                    room.Available = False
                End If
```

```
            End If
        End If
    Next room
End Property

Public Property Get WingMaintenanceDate(wingNumber As Integer) As Variant
    'return the scheduled date of wing maintenance
    WingMaintenanceDate = WingMaintenanceDate_m(wingNumber)
End Property
```

Although Chapter 105 goes into detail about how to use the custom classes you create, you might find it helpful to see how these procedures look from the "outside" perspective of a programmer using the Hotel class. Here are some examples:

```
Private maui As Hotel
set maui = New Hotel
'set the season to summer
maui.Season = "Summer"

'set a front end control's value to the hotel's season
Label1.Caption = maui.Season

'set the hotel's manager
Dim mgr As New Employee
Set maui.Manager = mgr

'use the reference to the hotel manager
maui.Manager.Salary = 80000
maui.Manager.Name = "Michael Baker"

'tell the hotel what the current rate schedule is
maui.Rates = Array(105.50, 110, 155.75, 85)

'schedule maintenance in wing 3 starting July 4th
maui.WingMaintenanceDate(3) = #07/04/96#

'if there's any maintenance scheduled, call the routine to schedule maintenance
Dim wingNum As Integer
For wingNum = 1 To 4
    If Not IsEmpty(maui.WingMaintenanceDate(wingNum)) Then
        ScheduleMaintenance maui.WingMaintenanceDate(wingNum)
    End If
Next wingNum

'cancel the maintenance scheduled for wing 2
maui.WingMaintenanceDate(2) = Empty
```

You can use a shortcut method for defining properties: Just declare a module-level variable as public rather than private. This makes the variable "visible" to any other procedure, which makes the variable behave very much like a property. This is much quicker than having to define a property procedure for each property. Note, however, that there are three distinct disadvantages to this method. First, you cannot do any processing whatsoever when you set or return the variable, which means that, for example, a room could have a negative maintenance date. Second, the user will always be able to both read and write the variable, which is not always desirable. Third, by exposing the variable itself, you limit the ways in which you can store the data internally within the class—the internal implementation becomes the public representation. A property procedure insulates the public interface from any changes that are internal to the class module.

You will probably make the most use of this shortcut during prototyping and initial testing. It's very simple to declare a variable as public, and this saves time as you begin to write the class. You can later hide the variable by scoping it as private, and build property procedures to control access to the variable. Be wary of any remaining public variables as you bring your class to completion. A public variable is just another word for a global variable, and the bugs they tend to create aren't worth the time they save. It's unlikely that you'll have more than a handful of properties that require no validation or checking when they're written; if you do, you should question what will happen if the user writes incorrect or inconsistent values to the properties. Insulate values properly with a property procedure to create the tightest, most maintainable code.

Step 4: Define Each Method

Now define each of the methods. We'll implement most methods as sub procedures, although a function works better for methods that return a value.

Let's continue using the Hotel class from Step 3 as our example. First, we'll write methods to create new rooms (CreateRoom) and manipulate individual rooms (Rooms). We'll also define a method to show a list of all unoccupied rooms, and another method to print out a maintenance list.

The first method creates new rooms. See the section on class hierarchies later in this chapter for more details about how objects can be contained within other objects and for more examples on the techniques for doing this. This method is simple: It takes a pair of parameters for the room number and wing number of the room, creates a new room object, and then adds it to the Rooms collection.

```
Public Sub CreateRoom(roomNumber As Integer, wingNumber As Integer)
    'create a new room object
    Dim thisRoom As New Room
    thisRoom.Wing = wingNumber
    'add it to the collection
    Rooms_m.Add item:=thisRoom, key:="Room Number " & CStr(roomNumber)
End Sub
```

The next procedure returns a reference for any given room. It takes the room number as a parameter and returns a reference to the appropriate room.

```
Public Function Rooms(roomNumber As Integer) As Room
    Set Rooms = Rooms_m("Room Number " & CStr(roomNumber))
End Function
```

The next method achieves its flexibility through the magic of variants. It returns a list of all available rooms and accepts arguments that tell it whether to look at all rooms in the hotel or only rooms in a particular wing, and what the maintenance start date is. We make it easier to use this method by making the parameters optional. If the user doesn't specify a particular parameter, we set that parameter to a default value using the IsMissing function. It builds the array by walking through each room in the Rooms_m collection, seeing whether it fits the parameters, and then places the room number into the array if it does. The last line of the procedure makes the array the value of the function, which converts a normal integer array into a variant array of integers.

```
Public Function AvailableRooms(Optional wingNumber, Optional startDate) As Variant

    'set defaults for missing parameters
    If IsMissing(wingNumber) Then wingNumber = Empty   'default is all rooms
    If IsMissing(startDate) Then startDate = Now       'default is today

    'go through each room and put the room number into an array if it's available
    Dim available() As Integer, room As Variant, roomCnt As Integer
    For Each room In Rooms_m
        'if it's available now, no maintenance is scheduled, and room is the one we're⇐
            interested in
        If (room.Available = True) And (room.MaintenanceDate > startDate + 7) ⇐
            And ((IsEmpty(wingNumber) = True) Or (room.Wing = wingNumber)) Then
            'yes, room is available
            roomCnt = roomCnt + 1
            ReDim Preserve available(1 To roomCnt)
            available(roomCnt) = room.Number
        End If
    Next room

    'place the available array as the return value; the integer array gets transformed ⇐
        into a variant array of integers
    AvailableRooms = available

End Function
```

The final method takes a variant array of room numbers and prints a list of the rooms along with some other data. The method goes through each entry in the array to obtain the room number. It calls the Rooms method to get a reference to the actual room (the Me keyword is optional, but makes it explicitly clear that the Rooms method is part of this class). Once the method has gotten the reference to the room, it uses the room's properties to determine what to print on each line.

```
Public Sub PrintRoomData(printRooms As Variant)
    'print header information
    Printer.Print "Room #"; Tab(10); "Status"; Tab(20); "Occupied"; Tab(30); "Maintenance⇐
Date"
    'go through each room in the array and print out information
    Dim roomNbr As Variant, room As Room
    For Each roomNbr In printRooms
        Set room = Me.Rooms(roomNbr)
        Printer.Print room.Number;
        If room.Available = True Then Printer.Print Tab(10);"Available";
        If room.Occupied = True Then Printer.Print Tab(20); "***";
        If IsDate(room.MaintenanceDate) = True Then
            Printer.Print Tab(30); Format(room.MaintenanceDate, "mmm d, yy");
        End If
        Printer.Print
    Next roomNbr
End Sub
```

Here is some sample code demonstrating what these methods look like to a programmer using the class:

```
'assume that fiji is the instance of the hotel object we're using

'first, define some rooms giving the room number and wing number
fiji.CreateRoom 100, 1
fiji.CreateRoom 101, 1
fiji.CreateRoom 200, 1
fiji.CreateRoom 205, 1
fiji.CreateRoom 110, 2
fiji.CreateRoom 111, 2
fiji.CreateRoom 210, 2

'populate a list box with all available room numbers in the entire hotel
Dim roomNbr As Variant
For Each roomNbr In fiji.AvailableRooms()
    List1.AddItem "Room #" & CStr(roomNbr)
Next roomNbr

'print a list of all available rooms in wing 2
fiji.PrintRoomData fiji.AvailableRooms(wingNumber:=2)

'clear the maintenance date from all available rooms that had a maintenance date of
'August 24, 1996
Dim roomNbr As Variant
For Each roomNbr In fiji.AvailableRooms(startDate:=#8/24/96#)
    fiji.Rooms(roomNbr).MaintenanceDate = Empty
Next roomNbr
```

Step 5: Define Each Event (Optional)

In Visual Basic 4.0, Microsoft implemented class modules with no support for creating custom events. Fortunately, this omission was corrected in Visual Basic 5.0.

An event is simply a procedure that your class triggers when "something" happens inside the class. The something is up to you to define. A property may have exceeded a certain value or the user may have invoked a method that the class can respond to in a number of different ways. The challenge is that, although you define something that triggers the procedure, the *user* must specify the code that's inside the procedure!

Think of a typical Visual Basic object, such as a command button. A command button has a number of different events that allow it to respond to user actions such as clicking it or dragging it. If you place a command button on a form and immediately run the program without defining anything for the command button's Click event, then clicking the command button will make it visually "click" down (a built-in behavior of the class) but it won't do anything else.

The Click event starts as an empty procedure stub:

```
Private Sub Command1_Click()

End Sub
```

It does something only when the user writes code inside the procedure stub:

```
Private Sub Command1_Click()
    Beep
```

```
    Form1.BackColor = QBColor(3)
End Sub
```

To see how to add an event, let's continue using the Hotel class and add a custom event to it. We'd like to define an event that triggers when a room is made unavailable. This would allow a program to override other functions that are trying to block out a room when a customer might be standing at the reservations desk asking for the same room. This event will trigger immediately before the room is blocked. The user's program can elect to do nothing, in which case the room will be made unavailable, or the user can cancel the block. This procedure will be defined in the Rooms class, because it applies to each room in the hotel.

```
'this declaration is in the Room class s Declarations section
Public Event BeforeBlock(ByVal RoomNumber As Integer, Cancel As Boolean)
Private Available_m As Boolean

'this procedure is in the Room class.

'You'd probably also want to define a Property Get as well
Public Property Let Available(newSetting As Integer)
    'if making a room available, just set it
    If newSetting = True Then
        Available_m = True
    Else
        'Other things might want to prevent blocking out the room.
        Dim Cancel As Boolean
        Cancel = False
        RaiseEvent Room_BeforeBlock Me.Number, Cancel
        If Cancel = True Then
        'user cancelled request
            Exit Property
        End If
    End If
    'the user didn't cancel the request
    Available_m = False
End Property
```

Our example creates an event called BeforeBlock. Use whatever naming standard you like except that the name cannot have underscores in it. Our class is now an *event source*. Note that all you must do to create an event is to declare it in the Declarations section in each class module.

```
Public Event BeforeBlock(ByVal RoomNumber As Integer, Cancel As Boolean)
```

To use the event, the user changes the declaration of the Hotel object, as shown below:

```
'declare this in the Declaration section
Private WithEvents maui As Hotel
```

The variable maui is just like any other object variable, except that the variable can also be used to handle the object's events. As soon as you declare the variable as a WithEvents variable, the object appears in the left-hand drop-down of the code module. If you select the object, its events appear in the right-hand drop-down. The RaiseEvent statement in the class module triggers the new event.

```
Private Sub maui_Room_BeforeBlock(ByVal RoomNumber As Integer, Cancel As Boolean)

End Sub
```

As you can see, it doesn't do anything! If the user chooses not to define how to respond to this event, then execution falls right through this procedure and back to the If Cancel = True statement in the Room class's Available property procedure. Notice that we pass the Cancel argument by reference (Visual Basic's default) so the user of the EventClass class can change it and pass those changes back to the Room class. For example, the user program might pop up a dialog box asking if the block should be allowed or not. If the block is to be canceled, the user program sets the Cancel argument to True.

```
Private Sub maui_Room_BeforeBlock(ByVal RoomNumber As Integer, Cancel As Boolean)
    Dim Response as integer
    Response = MsgBox ("Scheduled fr Blocking. Make available?', vbYesNo, "Warning")
    If Response = vbYes Then Cancel = True
End Sub
```

At this point, even though the event is part of the program, nothing can happen until an object is actually assigned to the object variable. You might assign the object in Form_Load:

```
Private Sub Form_Load
    Set maui = New Hotel
End Sub
```

There are some restrictions to using WithEvents variables. They are outlined in the following list.

1. A WithEvents variable must be early bound. You cannot assign it As Object.

2. You cannot declare a WithEvents variable as New. The event source object must be explicitly declared, as shown in the previous code.

3. You cannot declare WithEvents variables in a standard Basic module. They can be declared in class modules and form modules. (Note that the online help states—incorrectly—that WithEvents variables may be declared only in class modules.)

4. You cannot create arrays of WithEvents variables.

Step 6: Write Initialization and Termination Procedures

You might need to initialize some variables or internal data structures when your custom class is first instantiated, or you might wish to perform some cleanup when the instance goes out of existence. Visual Basic provides two built-in events, Class_Initialize and Class_Terminate, to handle these chores. (Note that these are built in to the class module and have nothing to do with the custom events discussed in Step 5.)

The Initialize event triggers when a class object is first instantiated. This is the perfect place to set default values for properties and to initialize any internal variables or data. This initialization event triggers for each object that is instantiated from the class definition, not just the first object. The values of any module-level variables for the class are independent for each object, so setting a freshly instantiated object's properties won't affect any objects of the same class that already exist.

The Terminate event triggers immediately before a class object goes out of existence, as it would if the user set the object to Nothing or allowed the object variable referencing the class object to go out of scope. You should clear out any internal object references by setting internal objects to Nothing before the class terminates.

Step 7: Write Support Procedures and Create Dialog Boxes

If you're writing a regular application, then you'll probably already have either Sub Main or a form's Load event designated as a startup procedure. You won't need to do anything special just because you're using classes, and you won't necessarily need to add another module to your project.

If you're writing a self-contained object application that will be compiled into an ActiveX .EXE or ActiveX .DLL, as Chapter 105 describes, then you'll need to insert a standard module into your project. This module must contain at least a blank Sub Main procedure. This procedure will run the first time any of the object application's classes are used. It runs just once, so it's a good place to put any initialization procedures that apply to the object application as a whole rather than to an individual class.

You'll need to put some types of code, such as DLL declarations, in a standard module rather than a class module. You might also want to put some utility functions and sub procedures that your classes use in a standard module.

Some classes might need to display a custom dialog box to perform an action. If you're writing a regular application, in which the class modules are in the same project as the rest of the application, then handling forms is completely transparent—there really is no difference at all in calling a form from a class module. Object applications are a little different, however. You can create a custom form (say, for a dialog box that one of your classes needs to display) and include it in your project. You can call this form from any class within the project, just as you would with standard code. The difference is that these forms are "invisible" to code outside the project. That means that if a user has instantiated some of your custom classes in his or her program, the code can't work directly with the form. You'll need to provide a public interface to the form through your classes. For example, your class might have a FormShow method to show the form and a FormValue property to read what the user inputs. You let the user control your class, and your class controls access to the form.

One thing that Microsoft says can't be done is to integrate a form contained in an object application into a regular application. You can easily call up a modal dialog box, as just discussed, but you'll find it frustrating to try tighter integration, such as creating an MID child form from an object application or providing a small set of user interface controls to display on a regular application's form. Adventurous programmers writing object applications might want to try the following technique to perform the impossible. Note that Microsoft doesn't document this technique, so test carefully to make sure it doesn't blow your applications to shreds.

Include a form in your object application. Place a PictureBox control on the form and put your controls in the picture box. Write whatever user interface code you need to handle the controls' events. Write a Property procedure for one of your public classes that accepts an Integer parameter. The user will pass the window handle (hWnd property) of a form or picture box to this property. The property then uses the Windows API function SetParent to tell your picture box that it's actually a child of the user's window. The code should look something like this:

```
'this is in your class
Public Property Let HostHandle(hWnd As Integer)
'set the parent for our internal control container to an external parent window
    dim oldHandle As Integer
    oldHandle = SetParent(formObjectApp.Picture1.hWnd, hWnd)
End Property

'the user would set it like this...
magicInterface.HostHandle = Me.pictContainer.hWnd
```

Your controls will appear in the designated window as if by magic. All user interaction will correctly trigger the events contained in your object application's form. Your public classes can provide appropriate properties to retrieve and provide information to the user's application.

Step 8: Provide Error Handling

Your objects may generate errors for any number of reasons. Your user may send an illegal parameter, for example. It is even remotely possible that you have a coding error! If you do not include error-handling methods in your code, then the user's program will "handle" the error, but the results will be unsatisfactory because the code will have no idea what the error is.

There are two ways to handle errors in classes. The first is to always return an error value, which is how Windows API calls work. The user must then use inline error handling. The preferred method is to *raise an error* the same way that Visual Basic does, with an error number and an error string. This allows the user to use inline error handling (On Error Resume Next) or to write error-handling routines (On Error GoTo,) in the familiar Visual Basic Style. (See Chapter 30, "Error Handling," for error-handling techniques.)

Use the Raise method of the Err object to raise errors that your user's code can trap. The error will be raised in the procedure that called your class, which should handle it. The following list contains guidelines for raising errors.

1. The error number is generated by adding your internal error number to a Visual Basic intrinsic constant, vbObjectError.

2. The internal error number must be in the range of 512 to 65536. Numbers below 512 are reserved by Microsoft.

3. When calling Err.Raise, supply an error number and a descriptive text string.

4. If you are distributing the component, document your errors in a help file.

The following code modifies the Property Let procedure of the WingMaintenanceDate property in the Hotel class to protect against improper dates. The internal error number was selected arbitrarily for this example. In practice, you must assure that your internal error numbers do not conflict with those used by other objects your program uses.

```
Public Property Let WingMaintenanceDate(wingNumber As Integer, startDate As Variant)
    'set the wing maintenance date in the tracking array
    If startDate <> Empty And startDate < Date Then
        Err.Raise vbObjectError + 800, "Maintenance date: " & startDate & _
            " is earlier than today."
        Exit Property
    End If
    WingMaintenanceDate_m(wingNumber) = startDate
    'go through all rooms and set the maintenance date
    Dim room As Variant
    For Each room In Rooms_m
        If room.Wing = wingNumber Then
            'if the startDate is empty, it means cancel out any scheduled maintenance
            If IsEmpty(startDate) = True Then
                room.MaintenanceStartDate = Empty
                room.Available = True
            'if the startDate is really a date, then set the room's maintenance date
            ElseIf IsDate(startDate) = True Then
                room.MaintenanceStartDate = startDate
                'if the date is within a week, block out room availability
                If DateDiff("d", Now, startDate) <= 7 Then
                    room.Available = False
                End If
            End If
        End If
    Next room
End Property

Public Property Get WingMaintenanceDate(wingNumber As Integer) As Variant
    'return the scheduled date of wing maintenance
    WingMaintenanceDate = WingMaintenanceDate_m(wingNumber)
End Property
```

Step 9: Debug

Microsoft hasn't figured out how to make Visual Basic read your mind yet, so you'll undoubtedly have some debugging to do. Debugging class objects in a regular application is the same as debugging standard code. You can set breakpoints, single-step through code, and add watch expressions just as you normally would.

Debugging object applications is a bit trickier. You'll need to run one instance of Visual Basic with the object application and another instance in a test application that controls and uses the objects. Chapter 105 goes into more detail on how to do this.

Class Hierarchies

Most applications use several classes. Large, complex, real-world systems are typically made up of several related objects. For example, a hotel is made up of rooms. Each room contains furniture. The hotel also has employees. Each employee has a supervisor (who is also an employee) and might have other employees as subordinates. These types of relationships, called *class hierarchies*, are often best expressed by a diagram. See Figure 104-6 for how you might diagram this example.

Most complex class structures start with a single class that forms the root of the hierarchy. This class is visible and creatable outside of the project so that a controlling application can instantiate a member of this root class. Our example shows the Hotel class as the root. If this were a chain of hotels, then Hotel would be a subsidiary member of a larger object, such as Corporate Division. See Chapter 105 for a more detailed explanation of how to make a class visible and creatable.

Classes subsidiary to another class are called *child classes*. Classes that have subsidiary classes contained within them are called *parent classes*. Our hotel example shows that the Hotel class is the parent of both Room and Employee classes; Room and Employee classes are children of the Hotel class. Furniture is a child of the Room class.

Parent-child relationships among classes are typically *one to many*, where one parent object can contain any number of child objects. For example, a hotel can contain a variable number of rooms and it can have a variable number of employees. The easiest way of dealing with this type of relationship is with Visual Basic's new Collection object. A *collection* is an ordered set of objects, and the Collection object has several methods that make it simple to add, delete, or find individual members of the collection. You'll generally find that a collection is easier to use than an object array.

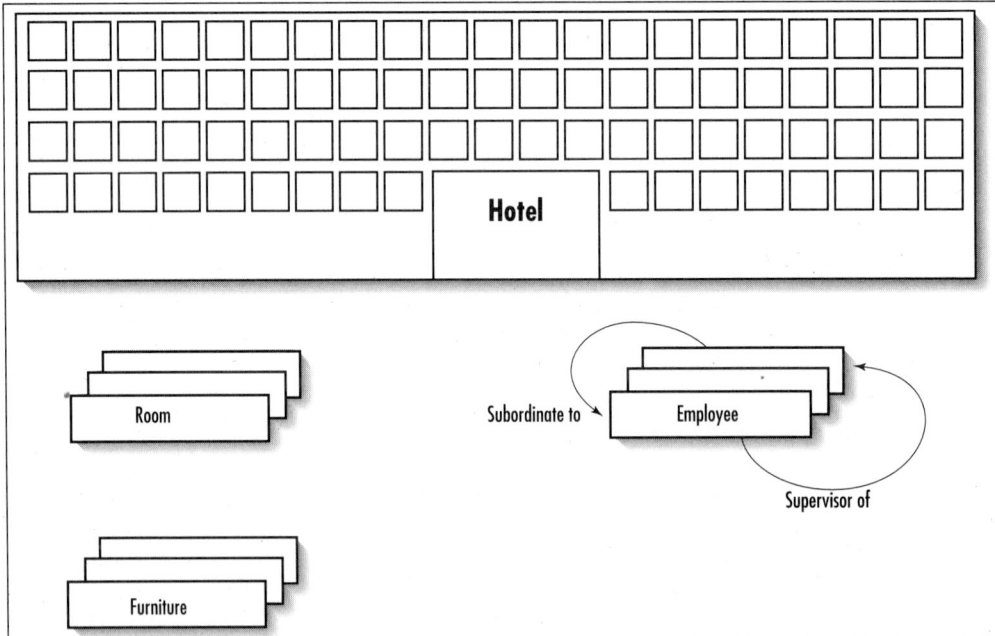

Figure 104-6　Complex objects are often arranged in a class hierarchy

You'll typically want to implement the creation and deletion of child objects as methods of the parent class. For example, the Hotel class might have CreateRoom and DeleteRoom methods. Make the child class visible but not creatable outside of the project. This means that once the parent class has instantiated a child object with the Create… method, the controlling application can use the child object. It can't, however, use the New keyword to create a new child object. This lets you control the children rather than letting them run wild, as they would if you let users create children at will. Chapter 26, "File System," goes into more detail about the issues of visibility and creatability.

You can expose the items in the parent's collection so that the user can manipulate any of the children. Note that you shouldn't expose the collection itself, because the user could really mess things up by using the collection's Add method to add anything he or she wants to the collection.

If your class hierarchy is deep, you'll find that it's particularly helpful to give each class in your hierarchy a Parent property. Set this property to reference the instance that's creating the child. This makes it easy to traverse the object tree from top to bottom (through each object's collection of children) and from bottom to top (through each object's parent).

The next code example is a variation on the CreateRoom method discussed in Step 4 of the step-by-step examples. It creates a new room, sets the Number property, and then sets the room's Parent property to CreateRoom before adding the room to the collection. The Rooms method exposes individual rooms from the collection.

```
'parent class can create a new child object, add it to a collection, and expose⇐
    collection items
Private Rooms_m As New Collection

Public Sub CreateRoom(roomNumber As String)
    On Error Resume Next
    Dim newRoom As New Room
    newRoom.RoomNumber = roomNumber
    Set newRoom.Parent = Me
    Rooms_m.Add(item:=newRoom, key:=roomNumber)
End Sub

Public Function Rooms(roomNumber As String) As Room
    Set Rooms = Rooms_m.Item(roomNumber)
End Function
```

The controlling application would then instantiate each room using the Hotel class's CreateRoom method and could access any room with the Hotel object's Rooms method. This example instantiates a hotel at the module level with the Private Hotel_m As New Hotel statement and sets minimum and maximum values for the room numbers. The MakeHotel routine creates each room in the hotel. The BookRoom function accepts the name of a client and a date to book the room until and returns the room number of the assigned room. It searches through each room in the hotel, looking for the first available room. Once the available room is found, BookRoom sets some of the room's properties and returns the number of the room it found.

```
'this shows how a controlling application would create and use rooms in the hotel

Private Hotel_m As New Hotel
Private Const MINROOM = 100, MAXROOM = 239

Sub MakeHotel()
    Dim roomNum As Integer
    For roomNum = MINROOM To MAXROOM
    Hotel_m.CreateRoom CStr(roomNum)
    Next roomNum
End Sub

Function BookRoom(clientName As String, bookUntil As Date) As String
    Dim roomNumber As Integer, room As Room
    roomNumber = MINROOM
    Do
        If Hotel_m.Rooms(CStr(roomNumber)) = "" Then
            Set room = Hotel_m.Rooms(CStr(roomNumber))
        End If
        roomNumber = roomNumber + 1
    Until (roomNumber > MAXROOM) Or (Not(room Is Nothing))
    If Not(room Is Nothing) Then
        'room is available, so book it
        room.Occupant = clientName
        room.StartTime = Now
        room.EndTime = bookUntil
        BookRoom = room.RoomNumber
    End If
End Function
```

Some relationships are more difficult to model. Our example includes a class called Employee, but almost all employees have a supervisor who's also an employee, and some employees have other employees as subordinates. Visual Basic's object variables and collections make this surprisingly easy to model.

First, write a method that lets the parent object create an employee, much as we did with the CreateRoom method. This method should add the employee to the parent's collection of employees.

Next, add two properties to the employee class. The first is Supervisor, which will hold a reference to the employee's supervisor. The other is Subordinates, which will hold references to the employee's subordinates. Remember that creating references to other objects takes very little memory (only 4 bytes), so don't be concerned if you need to reference even very large objects.

You'll also need to provide a way to manage the subordinates. The best way is to write methods to do this, which insulates your class from mistakes the user might make. You could take a shortcut and expose the entire Subordinates collection, but this is somewhat risky: The user could put a reference to anything in the collection, which might throw your program logic off. Here's an example of creating multiple object references for our employee class. It shows insulating routines for adding and removing employees from the collection and another way of exposing a collection's contents without exposing the collection itself.

The first set of declarations and property procedures should seem familiar to you by now. We declare a module-level variable to hold the reference to the supervisor and declare a new module-level collection to store the subordinates. The Property Set and Property Get procedures provide access to the Supervisor object.

```
'these all appear in the Employee class (we assume the Hotel class already has a⇐
 CreateEmployee method)

Dim Supervisor_m As Employee
Dim Subordinates_m() New Collection

'provides read/write access to this employee's supervisor
Public Property Set Supervisor(newSupervisor As Employee)
    Set Supervisor_m = newSupervisor
End Property
Public Property Get Supervisor() As Employee
    Set Supervisor = Supervisor_m
End Property
```

These next two methods let a user add and remove subordinates from the collection. The Collection object is extremely convenient for this: Its Add and Remove methods let us take care of all the details with just a single line of code.

```
'these let the user add and remove subordinates; it assumes the Employee class has a Name⇐
 property
Public Sub AddSubordinate(newSubordinate As Employee)
    On Error Resume Next
    Subordinates_m.Add item:=newSubordinate, key:=newSubordinate.Name
End Sub
Public Sub RemoveSubordinate(newSubordinate As Employee)
    On Error Resume Next
    Subordinates_m.Remove newSubordinate.Name
End Sub
```

This last example shows a very convenient way of exposing the members of the Subordinates collection as a Variant array. We first declare the local dummy() variant array, and then place a reference to each subordinate into the array. Assigning the dummy() array as the value of the property allows us to expose the structure of the collection without exposing the collection itself.

```
'This is another way of exposing a collection's items without exposing the collection⇐
 itself.
'The return value is a variant array, so it can be used in a
' For Each...  In thisEmployee.Subordinates style of construction

Public Property Get Subordinates() As Variant
    Dim dummy() As Variant, subCount As Integer, sub As Variant
    For Each sub In Subordinates_m
        subCount = subCount + 1
        Redim Preserve dummy(subCount)
        Set dummy(subCount) = sub
    Next sub
    Subordinates = dummy
End Property
```

Code that uses the Subordinates property looks very natural, because it can refer to both an individual member in the array or to the entire array in a For Each… construction.

```
'access a single subordinate
Dim secretary As Employee
Set secretary = maui.Manager.Subordinates(1)

'access all subordinates
Dim headGardener As Employee, gardeners As Variant
Set headGardener = fiji.Maintenance.Groundskeepers.HeadGardener
For Each gardener In headGardener.Subordinates
    gardener.PayRate = gardener.PayRate * 1.3
Next gardener
```

Forms as Custom Classes

Visual Basic 5.0 lets you add custom properties and methods to regular forms. Forms are very much like a class module with a visual interface. Visual Basic is now much more object oriented in its treatment of forms and the data contained in a form, and you may wish to change your programming style somewhat to take advantage of this greater object orientation.

Older versions of Visual Basic scoped all procedures and variables in a form as private to that form. You could not run a form's procedures or access its data from any procedure outside the form except through a series of kludges. The form itself, along with its controls, was public to the entire application, so you could access a control's properties and methods from anywhere in the application. The typical workaround for triggering code in the form was to write an event procedure for a control and then trigger the event procedure. For example, you could write a procedure in a label's Change event. Any procedure in the project could then set the label's caption and trigger the change event. A typical kludge for getting data back out of a form was to use a control's Tag property, which could contain up to about 32K of text.

The ability to write public methods and properties does away with these kludges. You should now write your code exactly as you would for any class: Define the public interface and write the public routines. Keep everything else private to the form. You can pass extremely complex data structures to and from a form, which makes it much more desirable to treat the form as a full object, complete with its own data.

You can directly access a form's methods and properties in the project that contains them. If you're designing an object application, you'll need to design an intermediary class, as discussed in Step 7 of the "Step-by-Step: Building Complex Classes" section.

Summary of Creating Custom Classes

Table 104-1 summarizes the events and statements needed to build custom classes. The properties of class modules are covered in Chapter 105.

Table 104-1 Declarations and events dealing with classes

Use or Set This...	Type	To Do This...
Initialize	Event	React to when a class object is first instantiated.
Property Get	Declaration	Define a class property that returns a value or object reference.
Property Let	Declaration	Define a class property that accepts a value.
Property Set	Declaration	Define a class property that accepts an object reference.
Terminate	Event	React to when a class object is about to cease existing.

INITIALIZE EVENT

Objects Affected	Form Object, Forms Collection, MDIForm Object, PropertyPage Object, UserControl Object, UserDocument Object
Purpose	Use the Initialize event to set defaults for class properties or to create internal data structures when the class is first instantiated. Table 104-2 summarizes the arguments of the Initialize event.

General Syntax

```
[Public|Private] Sub name_Initialize()
```

Table 104-2 Arguments of the Initialize event

Argument	Description
Public	Procedure is available to all other procedures (can use with Initialize, but not recommended).
Private	Procedure is available only to procedures in this module (default scoping).
name	Class for a class module, Form for a form, MDIForm for an MDI form.

Example Syntax

```
Private Sub Class_Initialize()
    Me.Rate = 75
    Me.Occupant = ""
End Sub
```

Description	An object doesn't exist until code first refers to it. The usual way for code to create a new object is to declare the object with the New keyword:

```
Dim bedroom As New Room
bedroom.Carpet = False
```

The code refers to the new object for the first time in the second line, where the room's Carpet property is set to False. This is the line that first instantiates the room object. The Room class's Initialize event will trigger immediately before this line executes.

The Initialize event is the correct place to set initial default values for an object, to initialize any other data structures, or to run any internal housekeeping functions.

Note that the Initialize event defaults to private, as all event procedures do. It is possible to change the private scoping to public, but this doesn't make much sense.

Forms and MDI forms have an Initialize event as well as a Load event. The Initialize event triggers before the Load event and is particularly handy when you take a more object-oriented view of forms. You can manipulate custom properties and methods in a Form object without loading the form. In this case, the Form_Initialize event will trigger when you begin to manipulate the form's custom properties or methods. The Form_Load event will trigger when you refer to Visual Basic's built-in properties or methods, such as reading or setting a control's property. Think of the Initialize event as initializing the form object and the Load event as initializing the form's user interface.

PROPERTY GET DECLARATION

Purpose The Property Get statement declares the name and parameters for a procedure block that returns a property value or object. It is often paired with either a Property Let or a Property Set statement. Table 104-3 gives the meaning of the parameters for the Property Get statement.

General Syntax

```
[Public|Private][Static] Property Get propertyName [argument list][As type]
```

Table 104-3 Arguments of the Property Get statement

Argument	Description
Public	Property is available to all other procedures.
Private	Property is available only to procedures in this module.
Static	All local variables retain their value between calls.
propertyName	Name of the property.
argument list	List of parameters passed to the procedure.
As type	Declares the type of the data returned by the property.

Example Syntax
```
Public Property Get Color() As Long
Color = QBColor(2)
End Property
```

Description   Custom classes (as well as forms, which are a variety of a custom class) may possess certain characteristics, or *properties*. The Property Get procedure block returns a value for a property. propertyName should adhere to standard variable naming conventions. Code that calls the property uses this name as a qualifier to the object name that the property belongs to. For example:

```
Dim masterBedroom As Room
Set masterBedroom = House.Rooms(3)
Picture1.BackColor = masterBedroom.Color
```

The Property Get procedure can return almost any data type, including all standard variable types, user types, variants, and object references. It cannot return fixed-length strings, nor can it return arrays of any type. It is simple to get around the restriction of not returning arrays: Return a variant containing an array instead. Variant arrays are extraordinarily powerful and convenient. This next example shows how simple it is to convert a regular array into a variant array. (The "Class Hierarchies" section earlier in this chapter has an example that converts items in a collection into a variant array.)

```
'this converts a normal array into a variant array so it can be passed back from ⇐
  Property Get
Private Positions_m(10) As Single        'this is a module-level normal array

Public Property Get Positions() As Variant
        Positions = Positions_m
End Property

'code calling this property can use it just like a regular array
Dim docImage As FaxPicture
Set docImage = DBLayer_m.FetchImage()
pictDisplay.Width = docImage.Positions(0)
pictDisplay.Height = docImage.Positions(1)

'code can also treat it much as it would a collection, using the For... Each construct
Dim pos As Variant
For Each pos In docImage.Positions
        Debug.Print pos
Next pos
```

The ability to return object references is also very powerful. You can return any of the built-in objects, such as ListBox, Font, or Form. Professional Edition users can return any of the Add-in Manager or DBEngine objects, such as RecordSet. This makes it very easy to associate an object's data (as contained by the RecordSet) with its methods and other properties (as written by you in the custom class). You can also return a reference to an OLE automation object. This makes it easy to build even very complex class hierarchies, with objects contained within other objects.

Although you normally won't need parameters in your property statements, you may include them if you find it necessary. They follow the same rules as parameters in regular Sub and Function declarations, except that you cannot use optional arguments or parameter arrays. Note that Sub and Function procedures do allow optional arguments, so class methods don't have the same restriction on optional parameters as class properties do.

Property Get used alone creates a read-only property. The Property Get procedure block is often paired with Property Let or Property Set to create a read/write property. If you do use pairs of property procedures, then both procedures must have the same name. You must use the same data type returned by Property Get as the last parameter (and often the only parameter) specified in the Property Set or Property Let declaration. If you've used parameters in the Property Get declaration, then Property Set or Let must include these same parameters.

Property Get defaults to being public in scope. You will be able to maintain your code more easily if you explicitly use the Public keyword in the Property Get declaration, because this makes your intent obvious. Language defaults have a tendency to change from version to version, and explicitly declaring the procedure as public will help prevent future incompatibilities.

You can use the Exit Property statement as many times as you wish inside the procedure block. This causes code execution to exit the block immediately, just as it would with Exit Sub or Exit Function. The procedure block must end with an End Property statement.

Property Let, Property Set Declarations

Purpose   Property Let and Property Set declare the name and parameters for a procedure block that assigns a value or object to a property. They are often paired with a Property Get statement. Table 104-4 gives the meaning of the parameters for the Property Let and Set statements.

General Syntax

```
[Public|Private][Static] Property Let propertyName([argument list])
[Public|Private][Static] Property Set propertyName([argument list])
```

Table 104-4 Arguments of the Property Let and Set statements

Argument	Description
Public	Property is available to all other procedures.
Private	Property is available only to procedures in this module.
Static	All local variables retain their value between calls.
propertyName	Name of the property.
argument list	List of parameters passed to the procedure.

Example Syntax

```
Public Property Let Color(newColor As Long)
Color_m = newColor
End Property

Public Property Set Font(newFont As Font)
Set Font_m = newFont
End Property
```

Description

Custom classes (as well as forms, which are a variety of a custom class) can possess *properties*. Use the Property Let procedure block to assign a value to a property. Use the Property Set procedure block to assign an object reference to a property. The propertyName must follow normal variable naming conventions. Code that calls the property uses this name as a qualifier to the object name that the property belongs to. For example:

```
Dim masterBedroom As Room
Set masterBedroom = House.Rooms(3)
masterBedroom.Color = QBColor(1)

Dim bed As New Furniture
bed.Alignment = hsHorizontal
bed.Softness = 0.2
Set masterBedroom.SleepingSurface = bed
```

The Property Let procedure accepts almost any data type, including all standard variable types, user types, and variants. See the discussion in "Property Get" for restrictions and workarounds on accepting arrays. The Property Set procedure accepts object references.

You will often use module-level variables in the class module to hold property values. The Property Let and Set procedure blocks serve as an insulating wrapper around the variables to help control access to these variables. Whereas Property Get often returns the value of this variable without much processing, Property Set and Let commonly perform data validation on the incoming values. For example:

```
Dim Color_m As Long 'module level, holds color of this instance
Dim Sleep_m As Furniture 'module level, holds sleeping surface for this instance

Public Property Let Color(newColor As Long)
Select Case newColor
   Case QBColor(0), QBColor(1), QBColor(2), QBColor(3) 'color is OK, so set it
     Color_m = newColor
   Case Else 'color isn't in the approved list, so forget about it
End Select
End Property

Public Property Set SleepingSurface(newSurface As Furniture)
If (newSurface.Alignment = hsHorizontal) Then
    If (newSurface.Softness > 0.1) And (newSurface.Softness < 0.4) Then
       'looks like a bed to me!
       Set Sleep_m = newSurface
    End If
End If
End Property
```

The ability to accept object references is very powerful. You can accept any of the built-in objects, such as ListBox, Font, or Form. Professional Edition users can accept any of the Project or DBEngine objects, such as RecordSet. This makes it very easy to associate an object's data (as contained by the RecordSet) with its methods and other properties (as written by you in the custom class). You can also accept a reference to any OLE automation object. This makes it easy to build even very complex class hierarchies, with objects contained within other objects. The preceding example shows this, with the Property Set SleepingSurface accepting a custom class called Furniture.

You'll normally just use one parameter in Property Set or Let, which is the value that will be assigned to the property. You may include other parameters before the one that assigns the value if you find it necessary. They follow the same rules as parameters in regular Sub and Function declarations, except that you cannot use optional arguments or parameter arrays. Note that Sub and Function procedures do allow optional arguments, so class methods don't have the same restriction as class properties.

Property Set or Let used alone creates a write-only property. The Property Let or Set procedure block is often paired with Property Get to create a read/write property. If you do use pairs of property procedures, then both procedures must have the same name. You must use the same data type returned by Property Get as the last parameter (and often the only parameter) specified in the Property Set or Property Let declaration. If you've used parameters in the Property Get declaration, then the Property Set or Let must also include these same parameters.

Property Set and Let default to being public in scope. You will be able to maintain your code more easily if you explicitly use the Public keyword in the Property declaration, because this makes your intent obvious. Language defaults have a tendency to change from version to version, and explicitly declaring the procedure as public will help prevent future incompatibilities.

You can use the Exit Property statement as many times as you wish inside the procedure block. This causes code execution to exit the block immediately, just as it would with Exit Sub or Exit Function. The procedure block must end with an End Property statement.

TERMINATE EVENT

Objects Affected	Form Object, Forms Collection, MDIForm Object, PropertyPage Object, UserControl Object, UserDocument Object
Purpose	Use the Terminate event to perform any clean-up actions when an object instance is about to go out of existence. Table 104-5 summarizes the arguments of the Terminate event.

General Syntax

```
[Public|Private] Sub name_Terminate()
```

Table 104-5 Arguments of the Terminate event

Argument	Description
Public	Procedure is available to all other procedures (can use with Terminate, but not recommended).
Private	Procedure is available only to procedures in this module (default scoping).
name	Class for a class module, Form for a form, MDIForm for an MDI form.

Example Syntax

```
Private Sub Class_Terminate()
Me.Recordset.Close
Set Me.Recordset = Nothing
Set Me.Contact = Nothing
End Sub
```

Description

An object goes out of existence when you explicitly set it to Nothing or when you allow all object variables that reference it to go out of scope. Visual Basic will normally handle all memory cleanup for you, but it's good programming practice to set all internal object references explicitly to Nothing when you no longer need them; for example, in the Class Terminate event. Some other situations require you to take action during the Terminate event. For example, the Jet Database engine will leave a connection to MS SQL Server open if you set a RecordSet object to Nothing without also explicitly closing the RecordSet. You can place code in the Terminate event to make sure the RecordSet is properly closed.

Note that the Terminate event defaults to private, as all event procedures do. It is possible to change the private scoping to public, but this doesn't make much sense.

Forms and MDIForms have a Terminate event as well as an Unload event. The Terminate event triggers after the Unload event, and is particularly handy when you take a more object-oriented view of forms. You can manipulate custom properties and methods in a form object without ever having triggered the Form_Load event. Think of the Terminate event as cleaning up for the form object and the Unload event as cleaning up the form's user interface.

The Superlist Class Project

This project shows how to build your own custom class. It demonstrates how to use each of the reference entries covered in this chapter and shows a number of professional-level techniques that you can adapt as you create large complex objects. The project in Chapter 105, goes into detail on how to use the classes built here.

Have you ever wanted a list box to display multiple columns? Many applications would benefit from a simple list box with two or three columns of data rather than just one. Visual Basic's list box doesn't support multiple columns with its built-in properties. (The list box does support snaking columns, which is not the same and is not nearly as useful. See Chapter 18, "String Manipulation," for details on the list box's Columns property.) Visual Basic does have the Grid control, but this is often overkill for a simple two-column list. This project gives a regular list box full support for multiple columns.

We take a regular list box and turn it into a "superlist" that's capable of more grid-oriented behavior, such as multiple columns and access to any individual column item in a row. The advantage of this approach is twofold. First, using Visual Basic's built-in list box as a base class means we don't have to write any code that duplicates what the list box already does, such as scrolling the list or retaining the data we give it. Second, subclassing the list box gives us exact control over how we want these new properties to act.

Project Overview

Visual Basic's list box class uses the standard list box that the Windows API provides. Visual Basic exposes most of the capabilities of the standard Windows list box, but omits a few. One of the glaring omissions is the ability to set tab stops. This means that the Visual Basic programmer is restricted to displaying data in a list box in only one column.

Experienced Visual Basic programmers have used the Windows API function SendMessage function to overcome this limitation. It's easy to include the SendMessage function in a program to set list box tab stops, and this is one of the most requested techniques on CompuServe's MSBASIC forum and the Internet's Visual Basic Usenet newsgroups. There's clearly a demand for this functionality!

There are a couple of problems with using the SendMessage API. First, it's easy to forget exactly how to call it and what constants and parameters are needed to set the tab stops. It's also easy to forget exactly how to convert the dialog box units the Windows API uses as its measurement scheme into something more understandable, such as inches. Finally, the SendMessage API requires that the strings displayed by the list box have a tab character (Chr$(9)) embedded between columns. This takes a bit of code to get your information into the right format, and then you have to strip the tab characters back out if you want to read the data. Third, there's no support for the concept of a "cell" at a row and column intersection. Updating a list box can be difficult without support for this concept.

This project uses three classes to overcome these difficulties. The SuperList class is the root of the class hierarchy. It provides access to two child classes, the Row and Column classes. The ideas are pretty simple. The Row class provides access to a row's data, both as an array and as individual cells. The Column class provides access to the size of each column to give the user an easy way to set column widths.

Assembling the Project: SuperList Class

1. Professional and Enterprise users, start a new ActiveX EXE project. Learning Edition users, start a new Standard EXE project.

2. Use the Project menu to add a new class module to your project. Set the properties for the class module as shown in Table 104-6. Note that the Instancing property is not available (and not needed) if you are using the Learning Edition.

Table 104-6 Properties for the ClassModule object of the SuperList class

Property	Value
Instancing	5-MultiUse
Name	SuperList

3. Add the following code to the module's Declarations section. Option Explicit forces you to declare all variables. This is a key technique for avoiding bugs, and most professionals use it all the time without even thinking about it. The three variables declared as private store the class's data. Each variable uses the naming convention of appending _m to the end of the variable name to indicate that it is module level in scope.

```
Option Explicit

Private MyListBox_m As Object
Private Columns_m As New Collection
Private Row_m As New Row
Private Const ILLEGAL_NUM_COLUMNS = 512 ' offset for error number
```

4. Add the following two properties. These are simple read/write properties that allow the user to set and retrieve a reference to the list box that we are subclassing. The whole project is based on using Visual Basic's built-in list boxes, and these are the routines that tell the SuperList object what list box to use.

```
Public Property Get Box() As Object
    'returns the list box that's bound into the superlist
    Set Box = MyListBox_m
End Property

Public Property Set Box(newBox As Object)
    'sets the list box to bind to the superlist
    On Error Resume Next
    Set MyListBox_m = newBox
End Property
```

5. These two properties return a reference to the Row and Column objects. Notice the two very different implementations. The Rows property accepts the row number as a parameter and returns a single row item. The Columns property doesn't accept any parameters and returns a variant array. The user of the SuperList class

won't know the difference between these two internal implementations; they look very similar from the outside. For example, to work with the second row, the user would write mySuperList.Rows(2), and to work with the fourth column, the user would write mySuperList.Columns(4). The technique used in the Rows property simulates a collection, even though only one Row object exists. The technique shown by the Columns property is quite handy for exposing the contents of a collection without exposing the collection itself.

```
Public Property Get Rows(rowNum As Integer) As Row
    'returns a row reference to the desired row
    Row_m.CurrentRow = rowNum
    Set Rows = Row_m
End Property

Public Property Get Columns() As Variant
    'returns all columns as a variant array
    Dim temp() As Variant, colNum As Integer, col As Column
    For Each col In Columns_m
        colNum = colNum + 1
        ReDim Preserve temp(1 To colNum)
        Set temp(colNum) = col
    Next col
    Columns = temp
End Property
```

6. These two property procedures expose the ColumnsCount property. Setting ColumnsCount erases tab stops that are already set and creates the number of columns given by the numColumns parameter. Setting the module-level Columns_m collection to Nothing removes the contents of the collection, terminating all the existing column objects the collection contained. The procedure then creates as many new column objects as specified in numColumns. Note the technique for creating multiple column instances: Use Dim outside of the loop to create an object variable for the column, and use Set with the New keyword to create new instances inside the loop. The procedure sets the new column's Parent property to point to this instance of the SuperList class before adding the new column to the collection. The Parent property makes code easier to write when we get to the Column class. The routine finishes by calling the UpdateColumns method to refresh the display. The Me keyword isn't required, but it makes it explicitly clear that we're calling a method of the same object that this routine is in. The Get part of this property pair is simple: It returns the number of columns, which is simply the number of entries in the Columns_m collection.

```
Public Property Let ColumnsCount(numColumns As Integer)
    'sets the number of columns in the SuperList
    If numColumns < 1 Or numColumns > 20 Then
        ' invalid number -- raise an error
        Err.Raise vbObjectError + ILLEGAL_NUM_COLUMNS, _
            "Illegal number of columns: " & numColumns
        Exit Property
    End If
    Dim newColumn As Column, colNum As Integer
```

```
    Set Columns_m = Nothing
    For colNum = 1 To numColumns
        Set newColumn = New Column
        Set newColumn.Parent = Me
        Columns_m.Add Item:=newColumn
    Next colNum
    Me.UpdateColumns
End Property

Public Property Get ColumnsCount() As Integer
    'returns the number of columns
    ColumnsCount = Columns_m.Count
End Property
```

7. This method updates the list box's display to show the current tab stops. It first goes through each column and retrieves the column's left-hand coordinate and converts the coordinate from inches into the dialog units used by the Windows API. The method then calls the windows SendMessage API function. This API function literally "tells" the list box to set tab stops, which is a typically object-oriented way of thinking of things. The LB_SETTABSTOPS message expects to be told the number of tab stops to set and a pointer to the array that holds the tab stops. The number of tab stops can be determined with UBound(tabStops). Visual Basic always passes arrays by reference, so (tabStops(1)) is essentially a pointer to the array. The two conditional compilation blocks starting with #If Win32 allow this code to work equally well in both 16- and 32-bit environments. The first block takes care of the difference in parameter types in the SendMessage declaration, as set in the CH104MOD.BAS module. The second block accounts for the differences in constant declarations between the two platforms.

```
Public Sub UpdateColumns()
    'set the tab stops in the list box
    Dim tabNum As Integer, col As Column
    Dim tabStops() As Long
    ReDim tabStops(1 To Me.ColumnsCount)
    Const UNITCONVERSION = 40 ' converts inches to the API
                              'dialog-units (approximately!)

    'go through each column and determine where the tab stop is
    For Each col In Columns_m
        tabNum = tabNum + 1
        tabStops(tabNum) = col.Left * UNITCONVERSION
    Next col

    'this calls the windows API to set the list box's tab stops
    Dim result As Integer
    Const LB_SETTABSTOPS = &H192
    On Error Resume Next
    result = SendMessage(Me.Box.hWnd, LB_SETTABSTOPS, _
    UBound(tabStops), tabStops(1))
    Me.Box.Refresh
End Sub
```

8. These two routines take care of initialization and termination of the class.

```
Private Sub Class_Initialize()
    Set Row_m.Parent = Me
    Me.ColumnsCount = 1
End Sub

Private Sub Class_Terminate()
    Set Row_m = Nothing
    Set Columns_m = Nothing
    Set MyListBox_m = Nothing
End Sub
```

Assembling the Project: Row Class

1. Use the Insert menu to add a new class module to your project. Set the properties for the class module as shown in Table 104-7. Note that the Instancing property is not available (and not needed) if you are using the Learning Edition.

Table 104-7 Properties for the ClassModule object of the Row class

Property	Value
Instancing	5-MultiUse
Name	Row

2. Add the following code to the module's Declarations section. We've declared the Parent variable as public, which effectively makes it into a property of the class without explicitly using a property procedure block. This is a handy shortcut that saves development time if the property is read/write and doesn't require any processing.

```
Option Explicit

Public Parent As SuperList
Private RowNum_m As Integer
Private Const BAD_COLUMN_NUMBER = 513
```

3. The CurrentRow property sets and retrieves the item in the list box to which the Row object points. There are several references to properties of the list box, and Set list = Me.Parent.Box shortens and speeds up these references a bit. See Chapter 3, "The VB Programming Environment," if you need more details about object references like this. The first If... clause checks to see whether the desired row is already in the list box. If it is, it just sets the property. If it isn't, the ElseIf... clause will add enough blank rows to the end of the list box before setting the property.

```
Public Property Let CurrentRow(newRowNum As Integer)
    'sets the current row; will add rows to the list box if there aren't enough
```

```
    'this just shortens up the references in the If... Then block
    Dim list As Object
    Set list = Me.Parent.Box
    'if the desired row already exists, just set the row
    If newRowNum >= 0 And newRowNum <= list.ListCount Then
        RowNum_m = newRowNum
    'if the desired row is more than what exists, create some more rows in the listbox
    ElseIf newRowNum > list.ListCount Then
        Dim newRow As Integer
        For newRow = list.ListCount To newRowNum - 1
            list.AddItem ""
        Next newRow
        RowNum_m = newRowNum
    End If

End Property

Public Property Get CurrentRow() As Integer
    'Returns the number of the current row
    CurrentRow = RowNum_m
End Property
```

4. Here are the core routines that convert the list box's internal representation (tab-delimited strings) to the more direct array representation. The newValues parameter is a variant array, which gets around the property procedure's inability to deal with regular arrays. The For…Each loop goes through each value in the array and builds a tab-delimited string from it. Note that the use of For…Each is an easier and more elegant way of going through each array element than the traditional For…Next loop with an explicit index variable. If there are no errors in the conversion, we replace the current row's entry with the new one. The Visual Basic list box doesn't have a replace or edit method, so we need to delete the current row and then add the new one back in the original place.

The Get half of this pair does just the opposite. It first retrieves the data from the list box and it then parses the list box's string looking for tab characters. Once it has put all the individual column information into a temporary array, it assigns the array as the return value of the function. Once again, using a variant array like this overcomes the Property procedure's inability to deal with regular arrays.

```
Public Property Let ValuesArray(newValues As Variant)
    'add data to the indicated row; data is in a variant array, with each column ⇐
     as an array position
    On Error Resume Next

    'make a tab-delimited string from the data
    Dim colValue As Variant, tabString As String
    For Each colValue In newValues
        tabString = tabString & colValue & vbTab
    Next colValue

    If Err.Number = 0 Then
        'now add the row's data; we need to delete the existing row, and then
        'add in the new row, because there is no "replace" method for a list box
        Dim currentListIndex As Integer
```

continued on next page

continued from previous page

```
            currentListIndex = Me.Parent.Box.ListIndex
            Me.Parent.Box.RemoveItem Me.CurrentRow
            Me.Parent.Box.AddItem tabString, Me.CurrentRow
            Me.Parent.Box.ListIndex = currentListIndex
        End If
End Property

Public Property Get ValuesArray() As Variant
    'retrieve a row's data as an array. Each row is stored in the list box ⇐
     as a tab-delimited string
    On Error Resume Next
    ReDim columnData(1 To Me.Parent.ColumnsCount)

    Dim colNum As Integer, tabPosition As Integer, oldTabPosition ⇐
As Integer, _      rowContents As String
    rowContents = Me.Parent.Box.list(Me.CurrentRow) & vbTab
    Do
        'look for a tab character starting at the last tabPosition
        tabPosition = InStr(oldTabPosition + 1, rowContents, vbTab)
        'if we found a tab, add the data to the columns array
        If tabPosition > 0 Then
            colNum = colNum + 1
            columnData(colNum) = Mid$(rowContents, oldTabPosition + 1, _
            (tabPosition - 1   - oldTabPosition))
            oldTabPosition = tabPosition
        End If
    'loop until there are no more tabs, we've reached the last tab, ⇐
     or we've gotten all the column data
    Loop Until (tabPosition = 0) Or (tabPosition >= Len(rowContents)) Or  _
    (colNum = Me.Parent.ColumnsCount)

    'this returns the data as a variant array
    ValuesArray = columnData
End Property
```

5. These two procedures enable the user to set or retrieve an individual cell's value. They're both short and elegant because the ValuesArray property does all the hard work. The way these are implemented makes it easy to reference any cell. For example, to set Row 17, Column 3, the user would write mySuperList.Rows(17).Values(3) = 'hello'. This makes it very convenient to get to any portion of the data contained in the list box.

```
Public Property Get Values(colNum As Integer) As String
    'return value of the individual column
    If colNum < 1 Or colNum > Me.Parent.ColumnsCount Then Exit Property
    Values = Trim$(Me.ValuesArray(colNum))
End Property

Public Property Let Values(colNum As Integer, newValue As String)
    'add data to the indicated column in the row
    If colNum < 1 Or colNum > Me.Parent.ColumnsCount Then
        ' invalid column number -- raise error
        Err.Raise vbObjectError + BAD_COLUMN_NUMBER, _
            "Illegal column number: " & colNum
        Exit Property
    End If
```

```
      Dim colData As Variant
      colData = Me.ValuesArray
      colData(colNum) = newValue
      Me.ValuesArray = colData
End Property
```

Assembling the Project: Column Class

1. Use the Insert menu to add a new class module to your project. Set the properties for the class module as shown in Table 104-8. Note that the Instancing property is not available (and not needed) if you are using the Learning Edition.

Table 104-8 Properties for the ClassModule object of the Row class

Property	Value
Instancing	5-MultiUse
Name	Column

2. Add the following code to the module's Declarations section.

```
Option Explicit

Public Parent As SuperList
Private Width_m As Single
Private Const ILLEGAL_WIDTH = 514
```

3. The Width property sets the width of each column in inches. Notice how Property Let calls the SuperList class's UpdateColumns method after updating the width. The Column class's Parent property makes it simple to travel up the class hierarchy.

```
Public Property Get Width() As Single
    Width = Width_m
End Property

Public Property Let Width(newWidth As Single)
'set width of column
    If newWidth >= 0 Then
        Width_m = newWidth
        Me.Parent.UpdateColumns
    Else
    ' raise an error
        Err.Raise vbObjectError + ILLEGAL_WIDTH, _
          "Illegal column width: " & newWidth
    End If
End Property
```

4. The Left property is a read-only property that's calculated on the fly. It returns the left-hand coordinate of this particular column, which is the sum of the widths of all columns to the left of this column. Notice two interesting techniques here.

First, the For…Each loop uses the SuperList's Columns property to return a reference to all the columns. This makes it look as if the Columns property were returning a collection (which is how you typically use a For…Each loop), but in reality it's a variant array. You probably wouldn't guess this unless you looked at the internal implementation of the Columns property in the SuperList class. This is one of the advantages of object-oriented programming: It encourages a high degree of independence between how you expose the public interface and how you implement it internally. The second interesting technique is the comparison If col Is Me. You'll find the If…Is… construction very helpful as you use objects.

```
Public Property Get Left() As Single
    'return left coordinate of column
    Dim col As Variant, totalLeft As Single
    For Each col In Me.Parent.Columns
        totalLeft = totalLeft + col.Width
        If col Is Me Then
            Left = totalLeft
            Exit Property
        End If
    Next col
End Property
```

5. This initializes the class to have a default column width of half an inch.

```
Private Sub Class_Initialize()
    Width_m = 0.5 'default column width of 1/2 an inch
End Sub
```

Assembling the Project: Standard Module and Project Settings

1. Insert a standard code module (not a class module) into the project. We need this for two reasons: First, we have to declare a DLL, and these declarations can't be made in a class module. Second, Professional and Enterprise Edition users need to add a Sub Main in a standard module to their project for it to compile correctly.

2. Place the following code in the code module's Declarations section. The Declare statement declares the Windows API SendMessage function.

```
Option Explicit

    Declare Function SendMessage Lib "user32" Alias "SendMessageA" _
    (ByVal hwnd As Long, ByVal wMsg As Long, ByVal wParam As Long, _
    lParam As Any) As Long
#End If
```

3. Professional and Enterprise Edition users should type in the following code after the Declare statement. It seems ridiculous to have a procedure that doesn't do anything, but Visual Basic requires all projects to have either a startup form or a Sub Main procedure. Professional and Enterprise Edition users compile this project into a standalone object application in Chapter 105 so you need this.

Standard Edition users add the classes to a regular project that already has a start-up form or an existing Sub Main and should not add this procedure.

```
Sub Main()
End Sub
```

4. Professional and Enterprise Edition users should use the Project Properties/General dialog box to set the startup procedure to Sub Main and set the Component/StartMode to ActiveX Component. Chapter 105 gives more details about this step.

Running the Project

There's not much to running the project—press F5 to run it and nothing happens! Objects are pretty boring unless you use them. Chapter 105 examines this project from the outside perspective of a user, and things become much more interesting.

105

USING CLASSES AND CLASS MODULES

Creating a class is only half the job; you also need to use it. This chapter provides details on using custom classes that you design or you obtain from others. It also covers how custom classes you design will look to users and how to create professional object applications. There is sure to be a tidal wave of new freeware, shareware, and commercial custom object applications in the next few years. The techniques you'll learn in this chapter will help ensure that you successfully ride this wave.

The introduction to Chapter 104, "Creating Classes and Class Modules" mentions that objects and custom classes have two very different aspects. The first is the *inside* of the object, which determines how the object does its job. Chapter 104 discusses how to build the insides of custom classes. The second aspect is the *outside* of the object, which is how the object is used. This chapter covers the outside. We refer to a programmer who uses a custom class as a *user* of the class. If you design classes that you use in your own programs, you may work on both aspects of the same class.

You'll find many similarities between using custom classes and using OLE automation servers. There's good reason for this: Custom classes *are* OLE automation servers. In fact, Visual Basic Professional and Enterprise Editions can create object applications that any program that functions as an OLE controller can use. That means the objects you build in Visual Basic can be used within Visual Basic and also in major programs such as Microsoft's Access, Excel, Project, PowerPoint, and Word; Lotus's 1-2-3, AmiPro, and Freelance; Corel's WordPerfect and Quattro Pro; and many others. OLE automation is one of the hot trends in the programming community, and more and more programs are adding this capacity.

Differences Between Standard, Professional, and Enterprise Editions

Visual Basic Standard, Professional, and Enterprise Editions can create custom classes. These classes can be used in any Visual Basic program simply by including the class module in the project, just as you would include a standard module or form.

Visual Basic Professional and Enterprise Editions can take one additional and vitally important step. They can create an ActiveX EXE program called an *object application* that is a standalone set of objects. You can use this object application just as you would use a commercial object's type library, such as the DAO object that comes with Visual Basic. The Professional and Enterprise Editions also can create ActiveX DLLs, which provide the same functionality with the added benefits of speed and in-process operation.

The project that uses the object doesn't need to include the individual class modules. Rather, it adds a single reference to the EXE or DLL file using the Project|References menu command, thus exposing all the public classes of the object application. This is a much more compact and maintainable strategy, and it is a major reason for using the Visual Basic Professional or Enterprise Edition.

Other programs can't use a native Visual Basic class module, but they can use an ActiveX EXE or DLL created with the Professional or Enterprise Edition. You can quickly build and debug objects using Visual Basic, even if your intended target language is something entirely different. Object applications written with Visual Basic run efficiently, and you can keep their source code in Visual Basic. If you find that an object you've written requires higher performance, you can treat the Visual Basic code as a prototype and rewrite the object in a language such as C++. The great advantage of this technique is that you can very quickly prototype objects in Visual Basic to get target programs into production as fast as possible and fine-tune performance later. You won't need to change the client program at all if you've carefully defined the object's public interface.

If you're working on a large client/server project, you will want the Visual Basic Enterprise Edition. This offers a number of features specifically geared for client/server work. One of the key benefits of the Enterprise Edition is its ability to create *remote automation servers*. A remote server runs on one computer on the network, and any client on any other computer can instantiate an object from that remote server. This is very powerful and is a critical technique for implementing three-tier client/server systems. You will typically encapsulate the business rules of an organization in automation servers and interpose these between the user interface and the back-end data. All the techniques and principles discussed in this chapter and in Chapter 104 apply to creating remote servers, although this book does not delve into the many details peculiar to remote servers.

If you're a professional programmer working in a mixed programming environment or on a programming team, Professional Edition is a must. You need the capacity to build object applications.

The choice is not as clear if you program exclusively in Visual Basic and work by yourself. Object applications are easier to use but harder to program and debug. You need to be more careful with the interface, and you may have to resort to some of the advanced tricks and techniques discussed in Chapter 104. It's easier to build and debug custom classes if you include the classes directly in the project, in which case the Standard Edition is perfectly adequate.

Using a Class Module

You can use custom classes by including the class module directly in the project. This makes it easy to debug the class. You can set watch variables and breakpoints just as you would with a standard module or form, and you can single-step code that calls an object's properties or methods directly into the class module.

Professional or Enterprise Edition users who are planning to create an object application will find it easiest to start with the class modules integrated directly into the target application's project. This cuts your debugging and development time. You can later follow the procedures given below for debugging the classes as a separate object application.

Use Visual Basic's Project|Add File command to add an existing class module, just as you would add a standard form or module. Use the Project|Add Class Module menu command to add a new class module to an existing project, as detailed in Chapter 104.

Using an Object Application

All Visual Basic editions can use an object application EXE or DLL file, even though only the Professional or Enterprise Editions can *create* them. You'll need to add a reference to the object application to your project before you can use any of its classes. Use the Project|References menu command to bring up the References dialog box shown in Figure 105-1. If your object application doesn't appear in the list yet, click the browse button and use the File Open common dialog box to navigate to the correct directory. Choose Executable Files from the List Files of Type combo box and select the correct EXE or DLL file. This will add the object name and description to the References dialog box. Click the object name to select it and click OK to add the reference to your project.

This process of adding a reference is no different than with any other OLE automation server. Again, an object application EXE or DLL created with Visual Basic *is* an OLE automation server, and almost all the techniques will be the same.

Once a reference to an object has been added to your project, you don't have to change the reference even if you later update the EXE or DLL file. This is a very powerful encapsulation technique that will prove invaluable for professional programming teams. The team that's maintaining the object application can update it at will without breaking any projects that rely on the object—assuming it does a good job of maintaining backward compatibility! Visual Basic 5.0 helps keep the public interface compatible by checking the existing EXE or DLL copy of the object application against the current revision that's about to be compiled. If there are differences in the public interface that would cause an incompatibility, such as a change in a property's parameters or return type, Visual Basic will inform you. To enable this automatic version checking, check Project Compatibility on the Component tab of the Project|Properties dialog box (see Figure 105-2) in the project that creates the object. Note that this checks only for compatibility in the public interface, not program logic. If you change a property or method so that it does something different, you'll create a bug that Visual Basic can't flag for you. When you have completed the design and debugging phases of your project, change your selection to Binary Compatibility.

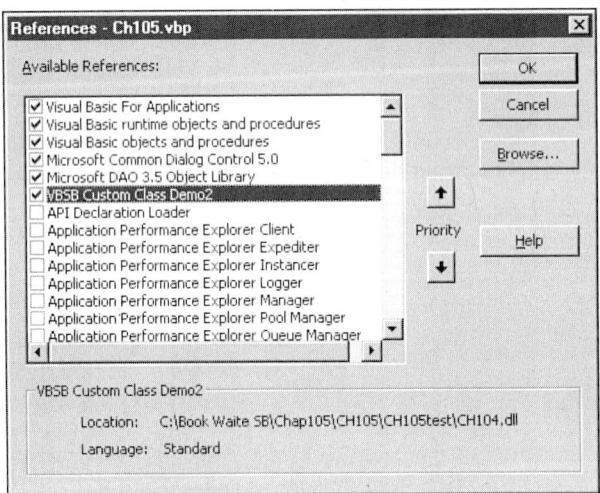

Figure 105-1 The References dialog box

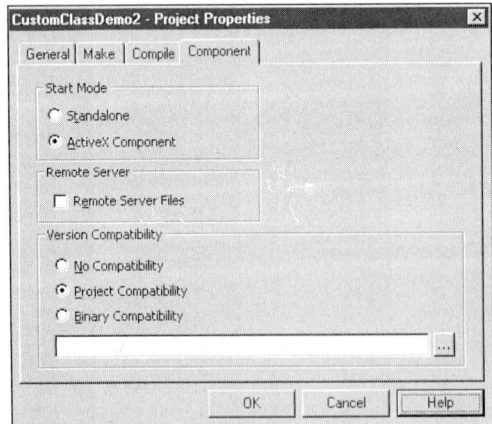

Figure 105-2 The Properties window

Debugging an Object Application

As you develop an object application, you'll reach a point when the classes are stable enough to test as a separate object application, but not so stable as to warrant compiling the EXE or DLL after each change. Follow these steps to take the classes out of the target application, put them into their own project, and set them up for simultaneous debugging. (Note: This applies only to Professional or Enterprise Edition users. You cannot create an object application in Standard Edition.)

1. Right-click on each of the class modules in the Project Explorer window and select the Remove option from the popup menu that appears. If there are any supporting standard modules or forms, do the same with them. Open a second instance of Visual Basic. Select ActiveX EXE or ActiveX DLL from the New Project dialog box. This second instance is a new project waiting for the class modules. Use the Project|Add File menu command to add each of the class modules (and any supporting standard modules or forms) to the second project.

2. Use the Project|Properties menu command and fill in at least the Project Name and Application Description fields on the General tab for the new project. The Project Name should be short, and it appears on the left side of the dot when you specify the class name in the CreateObject function. (You generally don't need to use it if you use your object solely within Visual Basic.) The Application Description is what appears in the References dialog box. Make sure the Startup object is set to Sub Main or None, depending on your application. If the object is an ActiveX EXE, select the Component tab and set the StartMode to Object Application.

3. Now run your new object application in the second instance of Visual Basic. If all goes well, it should run and continue running. If it is an ActiveX EXE and it runs for only a second and then stops, make sure you've set StartMode to Object Application. If it gives you any error messages, make sure you've included all the necessary files from the first project. You may have left out a few constants, or you might have used a global variable in the class modules that is no longer visible because it's visible only in the first project—yet another reason to banish global variables from your programs!

4. After you have the object application successfully running in its own instance, go back to the first instance with the remains of your project. Use the Project|References menu command to bring up the References dialog box. You should see the object application in the list. Check the reference entry to add it to your project. If you don't see the reference to your object application, go back to the object application's instance and check that you've properly filled in the Application Description and Project Name fields and that the object application runs and remains running while you're adding the reference. Also make sure that at least one of your class modules has the Instancing property set to MultiUse.

You should be able to run the first project now. It will use the temporary reference entry to the object application running in the other instance. If you stop the object application from running, you will need to rereference it in the original project.

You can control Visual Basic's behavior when it encounters an error in the object application. If you've set the Break in Class Module check box on the General tab in the Tools|Options dialog box of the object program, then Visual Basic will place the focus on the instance with the object application and it will break on the offending line in that instance. If not, then Visual Basic will leave the focus on your original project and will break on the line that made the call to the offending object application procedure.

Out-of-Process Servers and In-Process Servers

Visual Basic 5.0 can compile *in-process* automation servers with a .DLL extension and *out-of-process* automation servers with an .EXE extension. In-process servers offer far higher performance than out-of-process servers, although at the expense of a bit of flexibility.

Out-of-Process Servers (.EXE)

When Visual Basic makes a call to an out-of-process server, it has to make a number of memory translations to pass information to and receive information from the server, a process called *marshalling*. Marshalling takes time, and the performance hit can be quite noticeable if you're passing a lot of data or are making lots of calls to the server. If you know you will be compiling an out-of-process server, be sure to keep the performance degradation imposed by marshalling foremost in your mind as you design the server's interface. For example, the following code will run very slowly with an out-of-process server:

```
Dim idx As Integer
For idx = 0 To 1000
    myOutOfProcServer.DoSomething idx
Next idx
```

You can speed this up by building the array first, then passing the complete data structure in just once:

```
Dim idx As Integer, tempArray(0 To 1000) As Integer
For idx = 0 To 1000
    tempArray(idx) = idx
Next idx
myOutOfProcServer.DoSomething tempArray()
```

Always think in terms of passing the minimum amount of data possible the least number of times. You will never get truly speedy performance from an out-of-process server that requires a lot of marshalling.

As long as you design your server interface with this in mind, out-of-process servers can be quite useful and still give excellent performance. Once the code is running within the server, it's just as fast as any other Visual Basic code.

If you are creating a standalone application but want to share some of its objects, methods, and events with other programs—as Excel does—then an out-of-process server is your only choice. If you need your component to process requests as an independent thread that notifies the client of the completion of its task by raising an event or using an asynchronous callback, you need an out-of-process server. This allows the client to respond to the user instead of waiting for a task to be completed. Finally, if you plan to use the component as a remote automation server with the Enterprise Edition, an out-of-process server is a must.

Out-of-process servers give you the most flexibility and are the easiest to use. It's very simple to create and compile an out-of-process server: Either choose ActiveX EXE from the New Project dialog box or change the Project Type in the Project|Properties dialog.

In-Process Servers (.DLL)

When you create an in-process server, Visual Basic loads the server into the same address space as the program that instantiates the server. No marshalling takes place, and performance is substantially faster—basically as fast as including the class modules directly in the project that instantiates the server. Although the performance benefits might tempt you to create in-process servers always, they have a few restrictions that out-of-process servers don't.

First, some commands work differently or are not allowed in in-process servers. For example, the Command$ function will always return an empty string, even if legitimate entries were on the command line. You'll need to have the main application pass these as property settings to the in-process server. You also cannot use the End statement in the in-process server. The server will stop running when all references to it in the main application have been set to Nothing. Note that the in-process server's Terminate event does not trigger when it stops running. DDE doesn't work at all within in-process servers. DoEvents can give unpredictable results if used in an in-process server. Use the Sleep API call instead:

```
' Declare this in a Basic module
Declare Sub Sleep Lib "kernel32" Alias "Sleep" (ByVal dwMilliseconds As Long)

' Use this in your .DLL class instead of DoEvents
Call Sleep (250) ' set time accordingly
```

Second, some of the global objects Visual Basic provides behave differently. The App object represents the in-process OLE Server DLL, not the main program, and the OLE properties such as OLERequestPendingMsgText are not available and will result in a runtime error if used. The Screen.ActiveControl and Screen.ActiveForm properties will return Null if the currently active control or form isn't owned by the in-process server. The Screen.Mousepointer property, the Printer object, and the Forms collection are all local to the server rather than being global for the entire application.

Additionally, you must be careful of how you handle object references. In-process servers can't have an End statement, and the only way they'll terminate is when all references to them have been set to Nothing. You will have problems if you have any circular references to the server's objects (that is, if one object refers to a second object, which in turn refers back to the first object). You will also experience problems if you set any public object references declared in the in-process server's standard modules to objects supplied by that server. Finally, you can't pass references to collection objects; you must wrap the collection inside another class module as demonstrated in Chapter 104.

If your server passes all the preceding restrictions, then you should seriously consider compiling it as an in-process server to gain greater performance. The process for doing this is almost identical to that of compiling a normal, out-of-process, ActiveX EXE server.

You cannot debug an in-process server in a true in-process mode: The way you debug any server is to run a second instance of Visual Basic, and it's impossible for this second instance to be truly "in-process."

You'll find that most of your servers work well as an in-process DLL and the performance gains are quite significant. The chapter project lets you experiment with both in-process and out-of-process implementations, and you can visibly see the difference in speed.

Property Considerations for All Servers

Some considerations are important for all servers, in-process or out-of-process.

1. Be sure to give the project a unique name: The name appears in the Object Browser, the name is given to the component in the Windows registry, and the name of the type library contains descriptions of the objects and interfaces in your component.

2. Enter a project description, a brief string that users see when setting a reference to your client.

3. Set the startup object. If there is no code that must be executed when the component is initialized, select None. If initialization must be done, select Sub Main, add a Basic module to the project, and put the initialization code in Sub Main. Keep it to a minimum to avoid possible time-outs. *Never* use a form as the startup object for a server.

4. If a code component has no user interface, you can set the Unattended Execution property. In an ActiveX DLL project, the DLL is made thread-safe. In an ActiveX EXE project, the component can be multithreaded. (Components that contain UserDocuments, UserControls, and forms cannot be marked for Unattended Execution.)

5. If you have a help file for your component, enter the help file name. You can provide context-sensitive help for your object if you add a help context ID to the project and the help file.

6. If the project is a standalone EXE that also provides objects to other programs, you can compile it as both standalone and an ActiveX EXE so you can debug both startup modes. The option is on the Components tab.

7. Also on the Components tab are the version compatibility options. Select Project Compatibility while you are testing and Binary Compatibility for the distribution version.

8. You will find another important set of properties on the Make tab. Enter major, minor, and revision numbers and select Auto Increment before you produce a distribution version of your code component. Incrementing the version numbers is critical to assure that programs compiled with the older versions continue to work with the new version.

9. Finally, if you have the Enterprise Edition, you can build a remote server by selecting Remote Server Files on the Component tab. This will generate the support files necessary for the component to operate remotely.

Threads

Thirty-two-bit operating systems such as Windows 95 and Windows NT support multithreaded applications that can do several things at the same time within a single program. For example, it's possible to build an application that can simultaneously recalculate a complex formula, reindex a large document, query a database, and still remain responsive to the user. Each of these tasks is a *thread* of operation independent of the others, even though all tasks are within the same program. The threads operate parallel to each other to accomplish several things at once. The CPU, of course, can't actually *do* everything at once and gives each thread just a portion of its total capacity, but the application gives the illusion of juggling all the balls while responding to the user's mouse movements and keyboard input.

Visual Basic 5.0 supports threads in ActiveX servers. VB uses what Microsoft calls *apartment model threading*. The objects created in each thread "live" in their own apartments (a block of memory in the process space of the component) blissfully unaware of objects in other apartments. Each apartment has its own copy of global data, which means that you cannot use global data as a means of communicating between threads. See Figure 105-3 for a graphical representation of apartment model threading.

Differences Between In-Process and Out-of-Process Components

Multithreaded in-process components (DLL files) have no threads of their own. The threads that define the apartments belong to the client. On the other hand, out-of-process components can have a thread pool with a fixed number of threads or a separate thread for each object that the client creates. One characteristic they both share is that multithreaded components may not have any visible interface.

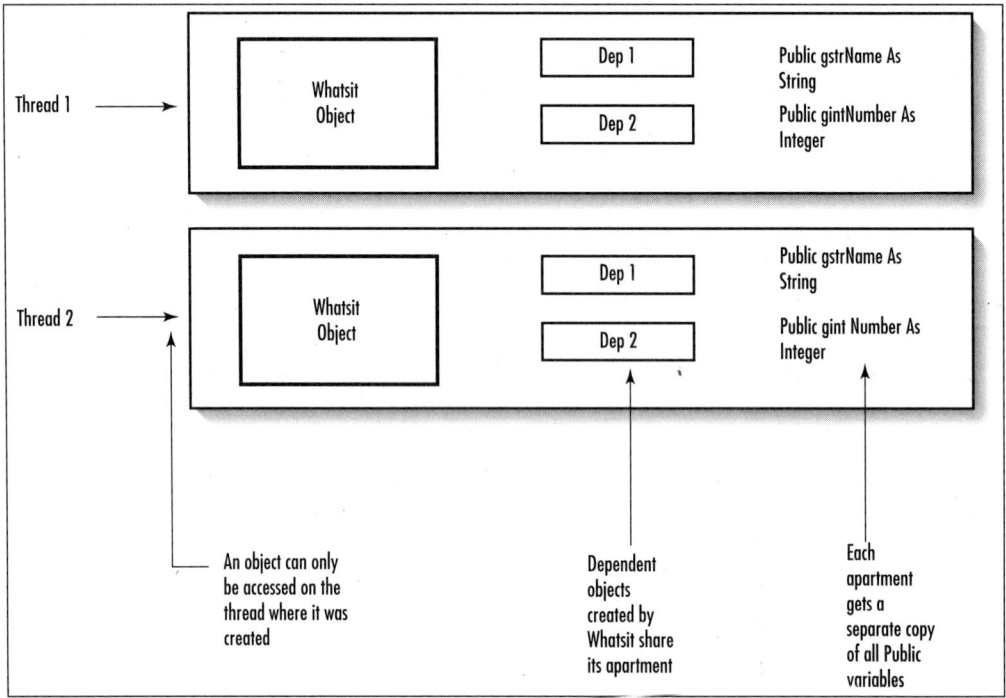

Figure 105-3   The apartment model

Considerations for Out-of-Process Components

To create a multithreaded ActiveX EXE, select the Unattended Execution check box on the general tab in the Project|Properties menu. Then select the thread assignment model. Table 105-1 describes how to select the thread assignment model.

Table 105-1 Properties dealing with a class's external characteristics

Thread Assignment Model...	Does This...
One thread of execution	Select Thread Pool with one thread.
Thread Pool with round-robin thread assignment	Select Thread Pool and specify the number of allowable threads.
Every externally created object in its own thread	Select Thread per object.

One Thread of Execution

This is the default mode. Its main purpose is to allow you to recompile Visual Basic 4.0 OLE servers without having to modify them.

Thread Pool with Round-Robin Thread Assignment

As each object is created, Visual Basic assigns it to the next thread in the pool until it reaches the end of the pool. Then it starts over again with the first thread. As a result, you cannot predict which objects will be on the same thread and which will share global data. If there is more than one client, objects created by different clients may share global data and objects created by the same client may not.

Additionally, calls to properties and methods on the same thread are serialized, which means that one call may block another. The advantage is that it puts a limit on the total number of threads, which is an important advantage.

Thread per Object

Each object is created in its own thread. When the client releases its last reference to objects on that thread, the thread is destroyed. This sounds simple, but it is fraught with danger if you are not careful.

If an object creates its own dependent objects whose references are passed to the client, the thread is not destroyed until the last dependent object is released (set to nothing). Be careful to release all the dependent objects when you are finished with the primary object. Unused threads seriously degrade system performance.

The disadvantage of the thread per object model is that it offers no control over the number of threads. Too many active threads (those executing code) will degrade performance even more quickly than unused threads.

Considerations for In-Process Components

To make an ActiveX DLL multithreaded, check the Unattended Execution check box on the General tab in the Project|Properties menu. No Thread Assignment Model options are provided because in-process components can use only threads on which their clients create objects and call methods. All the objects created in a single thread are created in the same apartment. Calls to objects or methods in an apartment are serialized; a call is never interrupted by a call from another thread.

Instancing

By including a class module directly in a project, you avoid any issues of *instancing* (that is, whether your project can create a new instance of an object and use its methods).

An object application poses more possibilities. You can set the class module's Instancing property to determine whether a controlling application can directly create a new instance of an object using the New keyword and whether an object's methods are available to the application. If a class is not creatable, then it must be created in the object application itself. This behavior is highly desirable if you've created a class hierarchy as described in Chapter 104. The parent class will have a method that creates a new child object and passes back a reference to the child. This gives you maximum control over the creation of child classes. Table 105-2 lists the possible settings.

Table 105-2 Instancing

Setting	Effect
Private	Can be created and used only within the component.
PublicNotCreatable	Must be created within the component, but it is then accessible to the client application.
MultiUse	Allows other applications to create objects from the class. Can supply multiple objects.
GlobalMultiUse	Similar to MultiUse, except that properties and methods can be invoked like global functions. If an instance of the object does not exist, it will be created automatically.
SingleUse	Other applications can create objects from the class, but each object creates a new instance of the component. (Not allowed for DLLs.)
Global SingleUse	Similar to SingleUse, except that properties and methods can be invoked like global functions. If an instance of the object does not exist, it will be created automatically.

Custom Classes and the Object Browser

Visual Basic's Object Browser dialog box shows the properties and methods of your custom classes and an object application, just as it would for any other object. Because you've joined the ranks of object creators rather than object consumers, you've got one additional feature available to you. You can define help text that displays along with the property or method in the Object Browser dialog box. This makes it easier for a user to figure out how to use your snazzy new object.

To create this text, go to the instance of Visual Basic in which your object application project is open. In design mode, start the Class Builder utility from the Add-Ins menu. (If the Class Builder doesn't show up in your Add-Ins menu, use the Add-Ins Manager and select it.) The Class Builder is shown in Figure 105-4.

Select one of the classes in your project from the Classes list, select the All tab in the right-hand pane, and then select one of the properties, methods, or events that appears. Now select Properties from the Edit menu and click on the Attributes tab.

Fill out the Description text box. This description will appear immediately below the line in the Object Browser that gives the name and parameters of the property. You can also fill in an appropriate help context ID (in the Help Context ID text box) if you've written a help file for your object application. This will make the help system jump directly to that subject when a user gets help in the Object Browser. Figure 105-5 illustrates this with the ColumnsCount property of SuperList.

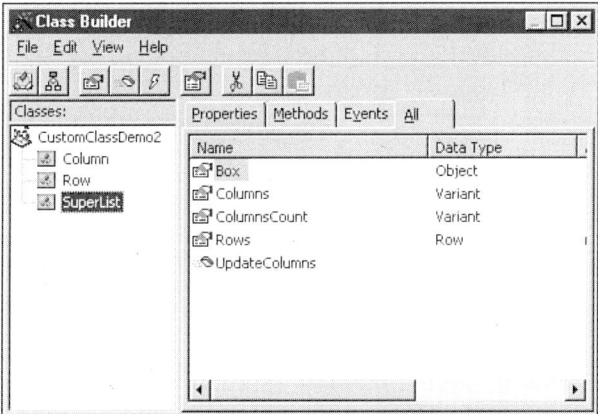

Figure 105-4   The Visual Basic 5.0 Class Builder
utility

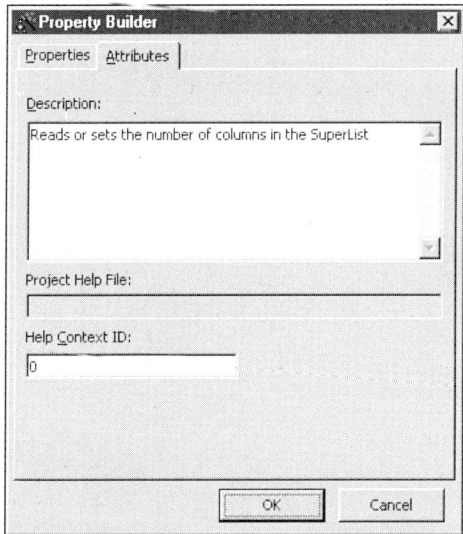

Figure 105-5   Adding a description to
the ColumnsCount property

Instantiating and Using Objects

Just including a class module or a reference to an object application doesn't do much.
You'll need to *instantiate* an object to use it. A class is like a blank template that defines
a potential object that has not yet been created. When you instantiate an object, Visual

Basic uses the class template and builds an object that has the same initial characteristics of all other objects built from the same class, yet is totally independent. You can set each object's properties without interacting with any other similar objects.

Use the New keyword to instantiate a new object from a class template. You can use the New keyword when you declare an object variable or when you assign a new instance of the object to a variable using the Set statement. Use the name of the class as the object type. See Step 7 of the "Assembling the Project: SuperList Class" section in Chapter 104 for an example of when to use the Set statement instead of the Dim…New declaration.

```
'use the new keyword in a declaration...
Dim employeePhoto As New Photograph
employeePhoto.Zoom 22
employeePhoto.ID = employeeID

'...or in a set statement
Dim employeePhoto As Photograph
Set employeePhoto = New Photograph
employeePhoto.Zoom 22
employeePhoto.ID = employeeID
```

Using the Set statement without the New keyword to set one object variable to equal another does *not* instantiate another copy of the object. In this case, both object variables point to the same object. See Chapter 16, "Objects and Collections," for a discussion of object variables.

Once an object is instantiated, it remains in existence until all object variables that reference it go out of scope or until the user explicitly sets the object variables that reference it to Nothing. You'll need to use either a Static object variable or a module- or global-level object variable if you want your objects to exist for longer than the duration of the procedure in which they're used.

Using Custom Classes Summary

Table 105-3 summarizes the properties that affect how custom classes are created and how they respond to a controlling application.

Table 105-3 Properties dealing with a class's external characteristics

Use or Set This Property...	To Do This...
Instancing	Determine whether an external application can create and manipulate an instance of this object.
OLERequestPendingMsgText	Return or set the message that displays when a server is processing.
OLERequestPendingMsgTitle	Return or set the caption of the dialog box when a server is processing.
OLERequestPendingTimeout	Return or set the time until a dialog box appears when a server is processing.
OLEServerBusyMsgText	Return or set the message that displays when a server doesn't respond.
OLEServerBusyMsgTitle	Return or set the caption of the dialog box when a server doesn't respond.
OLEServerBusyRaiseError	Return or set whether a dialog box appears when a server doesn't respond.
OLEServerBusyTimeout	Return or set the time until a dialog box appears when a server doesn't respond.

INSTANCING PROPERTY

Objects Affected   Class Module

Purpose   The Instancing property determines whether a controlling application can directly create an object and, if so, how the object is instantiated. If Instancing is set to 1 - Private, a controlling application cannot directly create the object, nor can it use the objects properties and methods. If Instancing is set to 2 - PublicNotCreatable, a controlling application cannot create an object of this class but it can access its properties, methods, and events once the parent class has created it. If Instancing is set to 3-SingleUse or 4 - GlobalSingleUse, a controlling application can directly instantiate new objects with the New keyword. Each object has its own copy of the class code. If Instancing is set to 5 - Multiuse or 6 - GlobalMultiUse, all instances share the same code space as a single executable.

Description   This property affects only classes in an object application, so Standard Edition users can ignore it. If you've included a class directly in a project, it will always be creatable. If the class is a member of an object application, however, you may wish to restrict the ability of the controlling application to create the object.

Many object applications will have a class hierarchy in which some objects contain other subsidiary objects. See "Class Hierarchies" in Chapter 104 for a full discussion of this. If your object application does have a class hierarchy, you'll generally want to restrict the creation of objects so that you can correctly maintain the hierarchy. In this case, set the root object's Instancing property to either SingleUse or MultiUse (the default value) and set the Instancing property of all other classes in the hierarchy to Private or PublicNotCreatable. Each class that contains other objects should have a method that creates the child object and passes a reference back to the child. This example shows a typical way of doing this:

```
'in module declarations
Private Kids As New Collection

Public Function CreateChild() As ChildClass
Dim newKid As New ChildClass
Set newKid.Parent = Me
    Set newKid.ID = CStr(Now)
Kids.Add item:=newKid, key:=newKid.ID
Set CreateChild = newKid
End Function
```

The danger of letting users create objects in their applications is that you can't make sure that the objects they create are properly positioned in the object hierarchy. If a class's Instancing property allows external creation, then the user can create a new child with the New keyword directly in the code. To what parent does this child belong? It belongs to no parent and it doesn't have a place in your carefully thought-out hierarchy. This is a problem even if you expose a property called Parent, as we do in this example. If the classes store child objects inside collections, as is common, then a child created in a controlling application never gets added to an object application's internal collections.

There are some benefits to leaving the Instancing property as MultiUse, because that gives the user more flexibility. You can design your classes so that the user maintains the hierarchy and the collections that store the child objects. The more work your classes do, the easier the user's life becomes but the more restrictive you have to be. Carefully weigh the pros and cons of class creatability while you design your class hierarchy.

If you do opt for allowing the user to instantiate the class externally, MultiUse will generally be more efficient than SingleUse. MultiUse allows a single copy of the class to instantiate as many child objects as desired. This makes sense for most classes, particularly deep in the hierarchy where there could be hundreds or thousands of instances.

Some conditions may call for setting the Instancing property to SingleUse. What will happen if you've written a class that can be called by several different programs that are all running at the same time?

In a preemptive multitasking environment such as Windows 95 or Windows NT, several client applications might make requests to your ActiveX EXE OLE server before the server finishes processing the first request. Visual Basic 5.0 Standard Edition is single-threaded, which means a single program can't do more than one task at a time. If you've implemented your object server as MultiUse, then there is only a single executable for the server no matter how many instances of the server the user programs have instantiated. The client requests get queued and processed in the order received. This won't cause any problems, but it might cause a bottleneck if some of the requests require lengthy processing. For example, some client/server query requests can take several seconds to return a set of records. A delay like this could halt the processing of several other programs while they wait for your OLE server to process their requests.

Setting the Instancing property to SingleUse is the answer to this potential bottleneck. Each time an object is instantiated from the server class, it runs as its own separate executable program. Although Visual Basic is still running your server class as a single thread, the operating system will preemptively multitask each of the separately instantiated server executables.

You would typically implement a SingleUse class as the root of your class hierarchy, or at least fairly high in the hierarchy. It's not too much overhead to have a handful of server executables running, but it would be inefficient to have hundreds of them running, as would happen if you did this for a commonly used class deep in the hierarchy. Also note that you may compile an out-of-process EXE file only if a class is SingleUse. You may not have SingleUse classes in an in-process DLL server because DLLs always run in the same application space as the program that instantiates them.

OLEREQUESTPENDINGMSGTEXT PROPERTY

OLEREQUESTPENDINGMSGTITLE PROPERTY

OLEREQUESTPENDINGTIMEOUT PROPERTY

Objects Affected   App

Purpose   The OLERequestPendingMsgTitle and OLERequestPendingMsgText properties determine what the dialog box text and caption are when an OLE server displays the request pending dialog box. The OLERequestPendingTimeout property determines how long an OLE request will run before user actions such as keyboard activity or mouse movement will trigger a request pending message. Table 105-4 lists the arguments of the OLERequest... properties.

General Syntax

```
App.OLERequestPendingMsgText  [ = newText]
App.OLERequestPendingMsgTitle [ = newTitle]
App.OLERequestPendingTimeout  [ = numMilliseconds]
```

Table 105-4 Arguments of the OLERequest... properties

Argument	Description
App	The global App object
newText	Text to display in the alternate dialog box, or "" for the default dialog box
newTitle	Caption to display in the alternate dialog box's title bar
numMilliseconds	Number of milliseconds to wait before displaying dialog box

Example Syntax

```
Private Sub Main()
    App.OLERequestPendingMsgText = "Server is not responding."
    App.OLERequestPendingMsgTitle = "Problem..."
    App.OLERequestPendingTimeout = 50000
End Sub
```

Description   Visual Basic will display a default dialog box when keyboard or mouse input is received while an OLE automation server is processing a request.

The default dialog box has a Switch To command button and works well for automation servers that have a visible user interface. You may have designed an automation server without any user interface at all, in which case the default dialog box is inappropriate. Setting the OLERequestPendingMsgText property to something other than an empty string will display a simple message box with just an OK button and the message you specify. You can modify the caption that displays in the dialog with the OLERequestPendingMsgTitle property.

The OLERequestPendingTimeout property determines the amount of time that elapses between receiving user input and displaying the dialog box. It defaults to 5 seconds, which should be adequate for most normal servers. If you have a very lengthy process, you may wish to set this property higher. Its values are in milliseconds, so a setting of 10000 means 10 seconds.

These properties are global to an entire application and will apply for all OLE automation servers.

OLEServerBusyMsgText Property

OLEServerBusyMsgTitle Property

OLEServerBusyRaiseError Property

OLEServerBusyTimeout Property

Objects Affected   App

Purpose   The OLEServerBusyMsgTitle and OLEServerBusyMsgText properties determine what the dialog box text and caption are when an OLE server displays the server busy dialog box. The OLEServerBusyTimeout property determines how long an OLE request will be retried before displaying the dialog box or raising an error. The OLEServerBusyRaiseError property determines whether the dialog box is displayed at all, or whether an error should be generated instead. Table 105-5 lists the arguments of the OLEServerBusy... properties.

General Syntax

```
App.OLEServerBusyMsgText   [ = newText]
App.OLEServerBusyMsgTitle  [ = newTitle]
App.OLEServerBusyTimeout   [ = numMilliseconds]
App.OLEServerBusyRaiseError [ = newSetting]
```

Table 105-5 Arguments of the OLEServerBusy... properties

Argument	Description
App	The global App object
newText	Text to display in the alternate dialog box, or "" for the default dialog box
newTitle	Caption to display in the alternate dialog box's title bar
numMilliseconds	Number of milliseconds to wait before displaying dialog box
newSetting	False (default) to display dialog box; True to raise an error and not display dialog box

Example Syntax

```
Private Sub Main()
    App.OLERequestPendingMsgText = "Server is not responding."
    App.OLERequestPendingMsgTitle = "Problem..."
    App.OLERequestPendingTimeout = 50000
End Sub
```

Description

OLE servers take a small amount of time to accept requests. This time is usually just a few milliseconds, but servers that can take requests from many different client programs can sometimes get bogged down servicing the pending requests. This applies to servers running in 32-bit environments, especially for remote servers compiled with the Enterprise Edition that may be servicing hundreds of users on a network.

Visual Basic will retry an automation request for the number of milliseconds set by the OLEServerBusyTimeout property, which defaults to 10000 milliseconds, equivalent to 10 seconds. If it does not get a response from the server in that length of time, it will either display a dialog box or raise an error, depending on the OLERaiseError property.

If the OLEServerBusyMsgText property is left at the default of an empty string, then the default Server Busy dialog box displays, which may be inappropriate for some servers. It has a Switch To command button that makes sense for automation servers with a visible interface, but isn't correct for servers without a visible interface. Setting the OLEServerBusyMsgText to something other than an empty string will display your custom message in a simple message box with OK and Cancel buttons. You can also set the caption for the dialog box with the OLEServerBusyMsgTitle property. If the user presses OK, the server is retried again; if the user presses Cancel, an error is raised in your application.

You can bypass the dialog box entirely by setting the OLERaiseError property to True. This will raise an error immediately rather than display the dialog box. You can then either display a custom dialog box of your own design or take some other automatic action.

These properties are global for the entire application and affect all automation servers.

The Using Custom Classes Project

Project Overview

This project shows how to use custom classes. It uses the object built in the Chapter 104 project, so you may wish to review that project before continuing. Chapter 104's object is called SuperList, and it gives a regular list box the ability to display multiple columns, giving access to any individual column item in a row. We'll use this capability to design a very simple name and phone number card file. The names and phone numbers will be displayed in a multicolumn list box.

This project is broken up into three phases. First, we include SuperList directly in a project as individual class modules. This is how Standard Edition users will most commonly use classes. This is also how Professional Edition users will normally begin development of classes that will later be built into an object application. Second, we will explore how to set up SuperList in a second instance of Visual Basic and debug it as an object application. Standard Edition users can skip over this part, but Professional and Enterprise Edition users should go through this in detail—this is the trickiest part of building object applications. Professional and Enterprise Edition users will finish this step by creating both an out-of-process EXE server and an in-process DLL server. The third step removes the class modules from the original project and substitutes a single reference to the object application EXE or DLL. Standard Edition users can continue from here because we've included the EXE and DLL for you on the projects disk. Professional and Enterprise Edition users should use the EXE and DLL they built in the second step.

Step 1: Build the Controlling Project

1. Add the following controls to a blank form and set the properties as shown in Table 105-6. The Common Dialog control will probably already be in your Tools palette. If it isn't, you'll need to add it. Use the Project|Components menu command to bring up the Components dialog box. Click the entry for the Microsoft Common Dialog Control to add the Common Dialog OCX control to your palette. Now you can select the Common Dialog control and draw it on your form. See Chapter 24, "Dialog Boxes," for more information about this wonderful time-saving control.

Table 105-6 Object and property settings for the project form

Object	Property	Setting
Form	Appearance	vb3D
	BorderStyle	3 - Fixed Double
	Caption	Chapter 105 - Using Custom Classes

Object	Property	Setting
CommonDialog	Name	cdlg
Command	Caption	&New
	Name	cmndNew
Command	Caption	&Open
	Name	cmndOpen
Command	Caption	&Save
	Name	cmndSave
Command	Caption	E&xit
	Name	cmndExit
Label	Caption	&Last Name
Label	Caption	&First Name
Label	Caption	&Phone
ListBox	Name	List1
TextBox	Index	1
	Left	180
	Name	textEntry
TextBox	Index	2
	Left	1680
	Name	textEntry
TextBox	Index	3
	Left	3300
	Name	textEntry

2. Size and position the controls as shown in Figure 105-6.

3. Add the classes and modules of the SuperList object to the project. Use the Project|Add File command to add CH104SLST.CLS, CH104ROW.CLS, CH104COL.CLS, and CH104MOD.BAS.

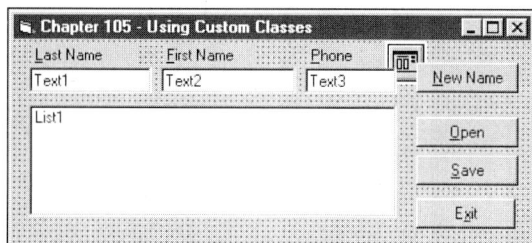

Figure 105-6   Form1 at design time

4. Place the following declarations in the form's General Declarations section. Note that we scope the PhoneList_m object variable as module-level. This makes sense because many routines in the form refer to it, so scoping it privately in an individual procedure wouldn't work, and there isn't any need to expose it outside of the form as public. Declaring it at the module level also keeps the instance of the SuperList available for the life of the form. Declaring an object variable like this doesn't instantiate an object, it merely creates a place in memory to store a reference to an object. Using the New keyword would instantiate the object and place the reference into the memory location. See the Form_Load event for the line that has the New keyword in it.

```
Option Explicit
Private PhoneList_m As SuperList
```

5. Enter this code into the cmndExit's Click event. Ending a program with the End keyword will automatically close all instances of all objects, so the SuperList object application gets terminated at this point as well.

```
Private Sub cmndExit_Click()
    End
End Sub
```

6. Enter this code into the cmndNew_Click event. This creates a blank record on which to add a new entry. It first checks to see how many entries have been made, and it then calls a method in the SuperList to add the row. See Chapter 104 for more details on what each property and method of the SuperList does. The SuperList's Rows method will add more rows to the list if it's called with an index greater than the number of entries in the list. That is the case here: We're calling the Rows method with an index of one more than the highest entry in the list. The ValuesArray property accepts an array of values to place in the row. We're creating a blank entry, so we add three zero-length strings.

```
Private Sub cmndNew_Click()
    'create a blank record
    Dim highestEntry As Integer
    highestEntry = List1.ListCount - 1
    PhoneList_m.Rows(highestEntry + 1).ValuesArray = Array("", "", "")
    List1.ListIndex = highestEntry + 1
    textEntry(1).SetFocus
End Sub
```

7. Enter this code into the cmndOpen_Click event. It opens a data file and reads the names and phone numbers from the file into the list. The bulk of this routine is the overhead associated with getting a file name and opening the file. We make our life much easier by using the Common Dialog control to retrieve the name of the file the user wants to open. The Common Dialog control saves a great deal of time: We don't need to create and debug a separate form, and we can use 5 lines of code rather than the 40 or so we would use if we were to do it ourselves. This is a great example of the power of object-oriented programming. Custom OCX controls, such as the Common Dialog control, are based on OLE automation and work very much like the custom classes you create with Visual Basic. See Chapter 24 for more information about the Common Dialog control.

The routine first sets a few properties of the Common Dialog control, such as what file name to display initially and what file filters to use. We tell the control to trigger an error if the user clicks Cancel (cdlg.CancelError = True) and then show the File Open common dialog. Visual Basic shows the common dialog modally, so program execution stops until the user closes the box. If the user doesn't click Cancel, we proceed into the If... block. The routine first opens the file and then reads each line. We again make use of the SuperList's Row class's ValuesArray property to set the values for an entire row at a time. Notice how the SuperList has put an entirely different face on Visual Basic's list box control: There is no AddItem method being invoked and there's no string manipulation to separate the items with tab characters; we're not even aware that we're working with a list box.

```
Private Sub cmndOpen_Click()
    'open a names data file
    cdlg.Filter = "Names data files|*.nms"
    cdlg.FileName = "CH105DATA.NMS"
    cdlg.CancelError = True
    On Error Resume Next
    cdlg.ShowOpen
    If Err.Number = 0 Then
        'user gave a file name, so open up file
        Dim fileNum As Integer
        fileNum = FreeFile
        Open cdlg.FileName For Input As #fileNum
        Dim entryNum As Integer, firstName As String, _
          lastName As String, phone As String
        'read all entries in the file and place in the superlist
        Do Until EOF(1)
            Input #fileNum, firstName, lastName, phone
            PhoneList_m.Rows(entryNum).ValuesArray = _
              Array(firstName, lastName, phone)
            entryNum = entryNum + 1
        Loop
        Close #fileNum
    End If
    List1.ListIndex = 0
    List1.SetFocus
End Sub
```

8. Type this entry into the cmndSave_Click event. It saves the contents of the list into a data file. This routine is almost an exact duplication of the cmndOpen event. The difference is that we use the ValuesArray property to retrieve values rather than set them. The ValuesArray property returns a Variant array, which explains how we can refer to entries(1) and so forth even though we used Dim entries As Variant.

```
Private Sub cmndSave_Click()
    'save a names data file
```

continued on next page

continued from previous page

```
'open a names data file
cdlg.Filter = "Names data files|*.nms"
cdlg.FileName = "CH105DATA.NMS"
cdlg.CancelError = True
On Error Resume Next
cdlg.ShowSave
If Err.Number = 0 Then
    'user gave a file name, so open up file
    Dim fileNum As Integer
    fileNum = FreeFile
    Open cdlg.FileName For Output As #fileNum
    Dim entryNum As Integer, entries As Variant
    'read all entries in the superlist and save to the file
    For entryNum = 0 To PhoneList_m.Box.ListCount - 1
        entries = PhoneList_m.Rows(entryNum).ValuesArray
        Write #fileNum, entries(1), entries(2), entries(3)
    Next entryNum
    Close #fileNum
End If

End Sub
```

9. Type this entry into the Form_Load event. This initializes the application as well as the SuperList. Recall that we declared the PhoneList_m object variable in the form's General Declarations section. That declaration created an empty object variable, but did not instantiate a SuperList object. The PhoneList_m object variable doesn't reference anything until we actually instantiate an object for it. The Set PhoneList_m = New SuperList in the Form_Load event instantiates a new SuperList object, and now PhoneList_m points to it. The next line gives the new SuperList a reference to the list box that it's subclassing.

The next three lines set up the columns in the SuperList. We need three columns (Last Name, First Name, and Phone), and the ColumnsCount property creates these three columns. The Columns property returns a Column object, and we use the Column object's Width property to set the width (in inches) of each column. Notice how we're navigating the SuperList's object hierarchy, starting with the root SuperList object, proceeding to the child Column object, and finally referring to the child object's property. This is exactly the same as using Visual Basic's built-in objects (Form1.Command1.Caption) or another OLE automation server, such as the DBEngine object (DBEngine.Workspaces(0).Databases(3).QueryTimeout).

The last set of lines sets the application's behavior for server problems. We set alternate messages and captions for the Request Pending and Server Busy dialog boxes and set the respective time-outs to 30 seconds. We also set the Server Busy dialog box to come up, rather than raising an error.

```
Private Sub Form_Load()
    Set PhoneList_m = New SuperList
    Set PhoneList_m.Box = List1
    PhoneList_m.ColumnsCount = 3
    PhoneList_m.Columns(1).Width = 1.65
    PhoneList_m.Columns(2).Width = 1.8
```

```
    textEntry(1).Text = ""
    textEntry(2).Text = ""
    textEntry(3).Text = ""
    App.OLERequestPendingMsgTitle = "Server Problem"
    App.OLERequestPendingMsgText = "Server is processing request"
    App.OLERequestPendingTimeout = 30000
    App.OLEServerBusyMsgTitle = "Server Problem"
    App.OLEServerBusyMsgText = "Server is busy"
    App.OLEServerBusyTimeout = 30000
    App.OLEServerBusyRaiseError = False
End Sub
```

10. Enter this code into the list box's Click event. It displays the SuperList's contents in the three text boxes so that the user can edit the contents of the current row. We first declare an object variable of type Row and set it to equal the currently selected item in the list box. Notice how natural it is to declare an object variable of a custom type; it's exactly the same as declaring a variable as one of Visual Basic's built-in data types or built-in objects. Also note that declaring an object variable like this does not instantiate a new object; it only creates a memory location to store a reference to an object. The Set statement places a reference to the actual Row object into this memory location. The SuperList creates and manages the Row object; we only get a reference to an already existing object. See Chapter 104 for details about the internal mechanisms the SuperList class uses to manage its Row object and how SuperList emulates a collection of multiple rows even though only one Row object exists. The next three lines show how easy the SuperList makes it to get individual values for an individual cell. This is why object-oriented programming is so powerful: Programming an object may be hard, but using an object is easy!

```
Private Sub List1_Click()
    'display the currently selected items in the text boxes
    Dim thisRow As Row
    Set thisRow = PhoneList_m.Rows(List1.ListIndex)
    textEntry(1).Text = thisRow.Values(1)
    textEntry(2).Text = thisRow.Values(2)
    textEntry(3).Text = thisRow.Values(3)
End Sub
```

11. Enter this code into the textEntry_LostFocus event. This updates the contents of an individual cell in the SuperList. The procedure uses the Values property again, just as the List1_Click event did. This time we're writing to the property rather than reading it.

```
Private Sub textEntry_LostFocus(Index As Integer)
    'update the superlist
    PhoneList_m.Rows(List1.ListIndex).Values(Index) = _
      textEntry(Index).Text
End Sub
```

12. Enter this code into the textEntry_GotFocus event. This highlights the contents of a text box when it receives the focus. See Chapter 11, "Structural Elements," for more details on the SelStart and SelLength properties.

```
Private Sub textEntry_GotFocus(Index As Integer)
    'select all the text in the text box
    textEntry(Index).SelStart = 0
    textEntry(Index).SelLength = 999
End Sub
```

13. Run the program. Operation should be fairly obvious. Press the Open command button to open a data file; one comes with the projects CD that you can use right away. Press the New command button to add a new entry. The list is updated as soon as you press Tab to leave the entry text boxes. Scrolling up and down the list immediately updates the text boxes; you can edit any entry at will. Press Save to save the updated list and Exit to end the program. Figure 105-7 shows the project in action.

Next, stop the program and start it up again in single-step mode by pressing F8. Trace the program's operation line by line, pressing 8 to step into a line and F8 to step through an entire procedure. You'll be especially interested in the lines that refer to the SuperList object. The very first line of the program, the Set PhoneList_m = New SuperList that appears in the Form_Load event, sets off a flurry of activity in the SuperList as it creates a new SuperList object and initializes its child objects. Trace the program in single-step mode until you feel comfortable with how it controls the custom classes and how the custom classes interact with their controller.

Step 2: Debug the Object Application (Professional and Enterprise Editions Only)

1. Select each class and use the Project|Remove File command to remove everything but Form1, the controlling application. Open a second instance of Visual Basic and open the project from Chapter 104. This project consists of the three custom classes and a supporting module. Open the Tools|Options dialog box and verify that the entries correspond to Figure 105-8. Use the Project|Options menu to change the Project Type to ActiveX EXE, then press F5 to start the object application.

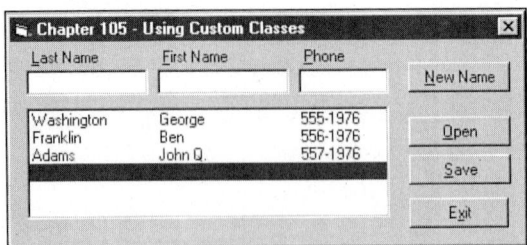

Figure 105-7   The SuperList in action

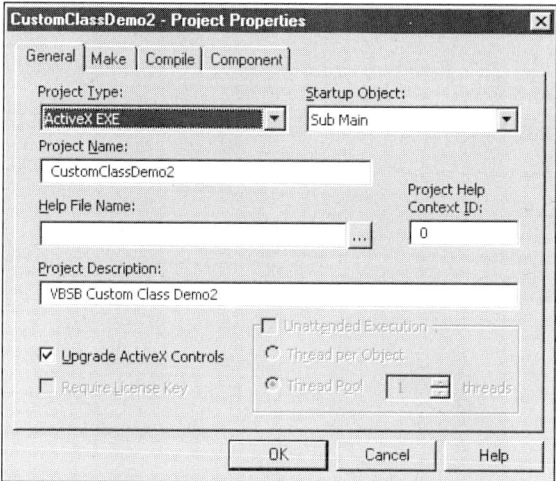

Figure 105-8 Using the Project|Properties dialog to change the SuperList project to compile an ActiveX EXE

2. Go back to the first instance of Visual Basic to the controlling application project. Use the Project|References menu command to display the References dialog box. You should see an entry in the box for the object application running in the other instance of Visual Basic.

3. Run the controlling application. It should work exactly as it did before. Stop it and single-step through the program. Notice that as you single-step through it, pressing F8 does not single-step through the object application. This is in direct contrast to single-stepping through the program when the class modules were included directly in the controlling project. This is why you should normally create classes and do most of the debugging with them actually included in the project; it's *much* easier than doing the initial work as a separate object application.

4. Try setting breakpoints in the object application's code to get used to going automatically from one instance of Visual Basic to another. Also try creating a few bugs in the object application's class modules so that you can experiment with the two settings of Break in Class Module in the Tools|Options dialog box.

5. Once you feel comfortable running an object application debugging environment, compile an EXE for it. Go to the instance of Visual Basic that contains the object application and choose the File|Make EXE File menu command. Compile the EXE just as you would any other program; there is no difference whatsoever.

6. Return to the Project|Properties menu and change the Project Type to ActiveX DLL. Change the project description by adding DLL to the end of the exiting description. Compile the in-process DLL as well.

Step 3: Run the Controlling Project with an Object Application (Standard Edition users can rejoin the project at this point.)

1. If you haven't already done so, remove the class modules and standard module from the controlling application by right-clicking on each of them in the Project Explorer window and using the Remove File command. This will leave just the Form1 file. If you try running the program, you'll get a rather cryptic error message, "User-defined type not defined." This translates into "You forgot to reference the custom objects."

2. Use the Project|References menu command to add a reference to the custom object application EXE file. If VSB Custom Class Demo2 does not appear in the Available References list box, use the References Browse button to select the CH104.EXE file. This adds the correct reference to your project so that you can instantiate and use the custom classes.

3. Run the project. You should note no difference between running the project with a reference to an object application, as we're doing now, and running it with the class modules directly in the project, as we did in Step 1, other than an obvious slowness when scrolling through the list and especially when initially opening the list.

4. Stop the project, and run it again in single-step mode. You'll note that it steps over procedures that call the SuperList object rather than single-stepping into them as it did in Step 1.

5. Use the Project|References menu command to remove the reference to the EXE file and add a reference to the DLL file. You've now substituted an in-process server for the out-of-process server.

6. Run the project again. You should notice a significant increase in speed compared to the out-of-process server, especially when initially loading the names list.

NOTE

The final steps will make permanent references in the system registry. If you want to delete them, run REGEDIT.EXE and use the Edit|Search menu command to find VSB. Select the key in the left-hand panel and use Edit|Delete to remove the key. (As always, back up the registry before making any changes.) Figure 105-9 shows the Registry entry.

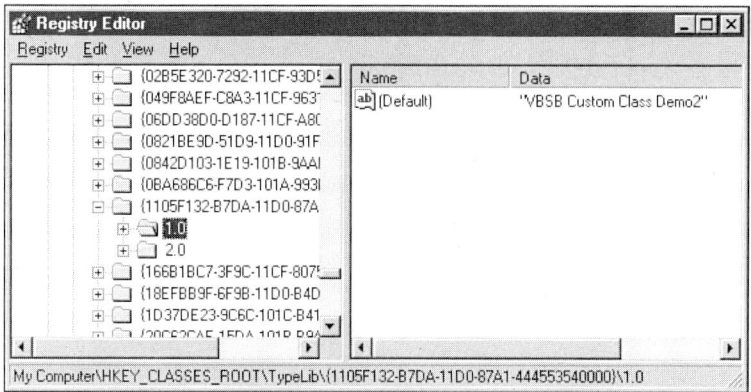

Figure 105-9   The new object servers are now in the system registry

INDEX

Symbols

& (ampersand)
> keyboard shortcuts, 1169
> literal, 1175

= (equal sign), assignment operator, 173-174, 2125

! (exclamation point)
> bang operator, 189-190
> exclamation operator, 668

. (period), dot operator, 189, 668

_ (underscore), referencing events, 190, 668

3D, Appearance property, 603-604

A

Abort method, 1516-1517
About box, ActiveX controls, 1803
Abs function, 351
absolute values, 351
AbsolutePosition property, 1486
abstraction, 131
Access
> controls, ContainedControls collection, 1817
> database design, 1326
> database permissions, 1550
> DDL queries, 1424-1426
>> *commands, 1423*
> files
>> *locking/unlocking, 499-501*
>> *networked environments, 492-493*
> OLEobjects, 1640-1641
> project
>> *Add-In project, 1787, 1789*
>> *VBProject object, 1785-1786*
>> *VBProjects collection, 1786-1787*
> remote, 1495-1506
>> *DAO, 1496-1497*
>> *DCOM, 1501-1504*
>> *ODBC API, 1498-1500*
>> *RDO, 1497-1498*
>> *VBSQL, 1500-1501*
>> *see also DCOM server project*
> tables, MDB extension, 1331

access keys, ActiveX controls, 1801, 1803

accessing forms/controls
> ActiveControl property, 673-674
> ActiveForm property, 675-676
> Index property, 676-679

AccessKeyPress event, 1814
> raising, 1813

AccessKeys property, 1813

Action property, OLE container control, 1617, 1619

Action% argument values, 1150

actions, *see* events

activating applications, 509-510

active objects, 672

ActiveControl property, 673-674, 1814-1815

ActiveForm property, 675-676

ActiveX, 5, 1611-1612
> Add-In project type, 1735
> APE workers, 1968
> controls, 18, 93-101
>> *about box, 1803*
>> *access keys, 1801, 1803*
>> *accessing, 1817*
>> *adding/removing, 94-96*
>> *adding to projects, 1075, 1793*
>> *aligning, 1804, 1815-1816*
>> *ambient properties, 1794*
>> *authoring time, 1812*
>> *collections (returning), 1824-1825*
>> *Components dialog box, 95-96*
>> *components, 23-24*
>> *container, 1794*
>> *containers, 1811*
>> *creating, 76, 1826-1829, 2059-2064*
>> *creating container, 1805-1806*
>> *data bound, 100, 1806-1807*
>> *default/cancel button, 1808-1809, 1817-1818*
>> *distributing, 100-101, 1877-1883*
>> *drawing, 1797-1798*
>> *editing at design time, 1807, 1818-1819*
>> *enabling/disabling, 1798-1800, 1819-1820*
>> *events, 1809, 1820-1821*
>> *exposing properties, 1831-1832*
>> *Extender object, 1794*

E

G

M

macros, Excel, DDE example, 1313
maintenance, database, 1547-1548
    compacting, 1547, 1553-1554
    mapping, 1551-1552
    recovery, 1547, 1557-1558
Make Project dialog box, 39-44
Make tab
    conditional compilation constants, 1982
    Project Properties dialog box, 66-67
MakeReplica method, 1539
manipulation objects, 1736
    add-in management, 1737
    code, 1737
    component, 1737
    event response, 1737
    form, 1736
    project, 1737
    user interface, 1737
manual links, 1280
    LinkMode property, 1288
many-to-many relations, 1327
mapping databases, 1551-1552
marshalling, 2168
master/detail data forms, 2045-2046
MatchEntry property, 1383-1385
Math project, 361-363, 365
mathematical functions
    Abs, 351
    Fix, 353-354
    Int, 355
    list of, 351
    logarithms, 349
        Exp function, 349, 353
        Log function, 349, 356
    random numbers, 350
        Rnd, 350, 357-358
    Sgn, 358-359
    Sqr, 359-360
    trigonometric, 347-349
        Atn, 348, 352
        Cos, 348-349, 352-353
        Sin, 348, 359
        Tan, 347-348, 360-361
    see also financial functions; Math project
Max property, 936-937
Max/Min functions, 1439-1440
MaxButton property, 719-720

Maximize/minimize buttons, forms, 698
    placement, 719-725
MaxLength property, 578-579
MDI (Multiple Document Interface), 699,
    1919-1921
    Button object, 1921
    Buttons collection, 1922
    ColumnHeader object, 1923
    ColumnHeaders collection, 1923
    forms, 699
        arranging, 708-709
        defining, 721-723
        displaying, 700
        hiding/showing children, 710
        initializing, 714
        resizing, 729, 731
        see also Forms project
    ImageList control, 1924
    ListImage object, 1925
    ListImages collection, 1926
    ListItem object, 1926
    ListItems collection, 1927
    ListView control, 1928-1932
    menus, 704-705
        displaying, 704
    Node object, 1932
    Nodes collection, 1933
    Panel object, 1934
    Panels collection, 1935
    ProgressBar control, 1936
    Slider control, 1938
    StatusBar control, 1941-1944
    Tab object, 1944
    Tabs collection, 1945
    TabStrip control, 1945, 1948
    ToolBar control, 1948-1951
    TreeView control, 1951-1963
MDI child property, 721-723
MDIForm object, 269-272
    events, 270-271
        Initialize, 714
        Load, 714-717
        QueryUnload, 728-729
        Resize, 729-731
        Terminate, 735-736
        Unload, 736-737
    methods, 271
        Arrange, 708-709
        Hide, 712-713

LIMITED WARRANTY

The following warranties shall be effective for 90 days from the date of purchase: (i) The Waite Group, Inc. warrants the enclosed disk to be free of defects in materials and workmanship under normal use; and (ii) The Waite Group, Inc. warrants that the programs, unless modified by the purchaser, will substantially perform the functions described in the documentation provided by The Waite Group, Inc. when operated on the designated hardware and operating system. The Waite Group, Inc. does not warrant that the programs will meet purchaser's requirements or that operation of a program will be uninterrupted or error-free. The program warranty does not cover any program that has been altered or changed in any way by anyone other than The Waite Group, Inc. The Waite Group, Inc. is not responsible for problems caused by changes in the operating characteristics of computer hardware or computer operating systems that are made after the release of the programs, nor for problems in the interaction of the programs with each other or other software.

THESE WARRANTIES ARE EXCLUSIVE AND IN LIEU OF ALL OTHER WARRANTIES OF MERCHANTABILITY OR FITNESS FOR A PARTICULAR PURPOSE OR OF ANY OTHER WARRANTY, WHETHER EXPRESS OR IMPLIED.

EXCLUSIVE REMEDY

The Waite Group, Inc. will replace any defective disk without charge if the defective disk is returned to The Waite Group, Inc. within 90 days from date of purchase.

This is Purchaser's sole and exclusive remedy for any breach of warranty or claim for contract, tort, or damages.

LIMITATION OF LIABILITY

THE WAITE GROUP, INC. AND THE AUTHORS OF THE PROGRAMS SHALL NOT IN ANY CASE BE LIABLE FOR SPECIAL, INCIDENTAL, CONSEQUENTIAL, INDIRECT, OR OTHER SIMILAR DAMAGES ARISING FROM ANY BREACH OF THESE WARRANTIES EVEN IF THE WAITE GROUP, INC. OR ITS AGENT HAS BEEN ADVISED OF THE POSSIBILITY OF SUCH DAMAGES.

THE LIABILITY FOR DAMAGES OF THE WAITE GROUP, INC. AND THE AUTHORS OF THE PROGRAMS UNDER THIS AGREEMENT SHALL IN NO EVENT EXCEED THE PURCHASE PRICE PAID.

COMPLETE AGREEMENT

This Agreement constitutes the complete agreement between The Waite Group, Inc. and the authors of the programs, and you, the purchaser.

Some states do not allow the exclusion or limitation of implied warranties or liability for incidental or consequential damages, so the above exclusions or limitations may not apply to you. This limited warranty gives you specific legal rights; you may have others, which vary from state to state.

Message from the
Publisher

WELCOME TO OUR NERVOUS SYSTEM

Some people say that the World Wide Web is a graphical extension of the information superhighway, just a network of humans and machines sending each other long lists of the equivalent of digital junk mail.

I think it is much more than that. To me, the Web is nothing less than the nervous system of the entire planet—not just a collection of computer brains connected together, but more like a billion silicon neurons entangled and recirculating electro-chemical signals of information and data, each contributing to the birth of another CPU and another Web site.

Think of each person's hard disk connected at once to every other hard disk on earth, driven by human navigators searching like Columbus for the New World. Seen this way the Web is more of a super entity, a growing, living thing, controlled by the universal human will to expand, to be more. Yet, unlike a purposeful business plan with rigid rules, the Web expands in a nonlinear, unpredictable, creative way that echoes natural evolution.

We created our Web site not just to extend the reach of our computer book products but to be part of this synaptic neural network, to experience, like a nerve in the body, the flow of ideas and then to pass those ideas up the food chain of the mind. Your mind. Even more, we wanted to pump some of our own creative juices into this rich wine of technology.

TASTE OUR DIGITAL WINE

And so we ask you to taste our wine by visiting the body of our business. Begin by understanding the metaphor we have created for our Web site—a universal learning center, situated in outer space in the form of a space station. A place where you can journey to study any topic from the convenience of your own screen. Right now we are focusing on computer topics, but the stars are the limit on the Web.

If you are interested in discussing this Web site or finding out more about the Waite Group, please send me email with your comments, and I will be happy to respond. Being a programmer myself, I love to talk about technology and find out what our readers are looking for.

Sincerely,

Mitchell Waite

Mitchell Waite, C.E.O. and Publisher

200 Tamal Plaza
Corte Madera, CA 94925
415-924-2575
415-924-2576 fax

Website:
http://www.waite.com/waite

CREATING THE HIGHEST QUALITY COMPUTER BOOKS IN THE INDUSTRY

Waite Group Press

Come Visit

WAITE.COM

Waite Group Press
World Wide Web Site

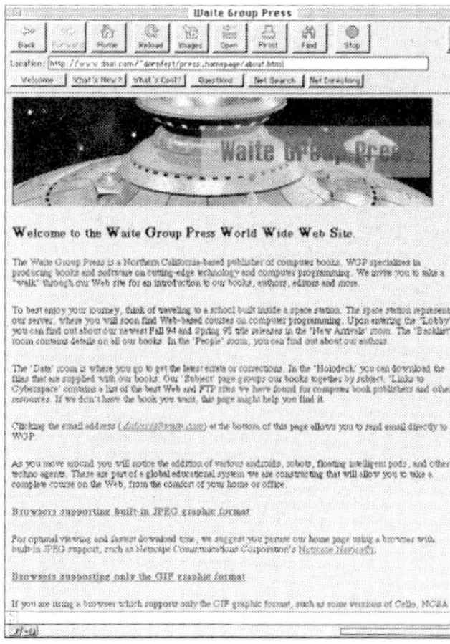

Now find all the latest information on Waite Group books at our new Web site, **http://www.waite.com/waite.** You'll find an online catalog where you can examine and order any title, review upcoming books, and send email to our authors and editors. Our FTP site has all you need to update your book: the latest program listings, errata sheets, most recent versions of Fractint, POV Ray, Polyray, DMorph, and all the programs featured in our books. So download, talk to us, ask questions, on **http://www.waite.com/waite.**

The New Arrivals Room has all our new books listed by month. Just click for a description, Index, Table of Contents, and links to authors.

The Backlist Room has all our books listed alphabetically.

The People Room is where you'll interact with Waite Group employees.

Links to Cyberspace get you in touch with other computer book publishers and other interesting Web sites.

About WGP · New Arrivals · Backlist Room · People Room

FTP · Order · Subject Room · Links to Cyberspace

The FTP site contains all program listings, errata sheets, etc.

The Order Room is where you can order any of our books online.

The Subject Room contains typical book pages that show description, Index, Table of Contents, and links to authors.

MACMILLAN COMPUTER PUBLISHING USA

A VIACOM COMPANY

Technical ---- Support:

If you cannot get the CD/Disk to install properly, or you need assistance with a particular situation in the book, please feel free to check out the Knowledge Base on our Web site at **http://www.superlibrary.com/general/support**. We have answers to our most Frequently Asked Questions listed there. If you do not find your specific question answered, please contact Macmillan Technical Support at **(317) 581-3833**. We can also be reached by email at **support@mcp.com**.

SATISFACTION REPORT CARD

Please fill out this card if you wish to know of future updates to
Visual Basic 5 SuperBible, **or to receive our catalog.**

First Name: _____   **Last Name:** _____

Street Address: _____

City: _____   **State:** _____   **Zip:** _____

Email Address _____

Daytime Telephone: (   ) _____

Date product was acquired: Month _____ **Day** _____ **Year** _____   **Your Occupation:** _____

Overall, how would you rate *Visual Basic 5 SuperBible*?

☐ Excellent   ☐ Very Good   ☐ Good
☐ Fair   ☐ Below Average   ☐ Poor

What did you like MOST about this book? _____
_____
_____

What did you like LEAST about this book? _____
_____
_____

Please describe any problems you may have encountered with installing or using the disk: _____
_____

How did you use this book (problem-solver, tutorial, reference...)?
_____

What is your level of computer expertise?
☐ New   ☐ Dabbler   ☐ Hacker
☐ Power User   ☐ Programmer   ☐ Experienced Professional

What computer languages are you familiar with? _____
_____

Please describe your computer hardware:

Computer _____   Hard disk _____
5.25" disk drives _____   3.5" disk drives _____
Video card _____   Monitor _____
Printer _____   Peripherals _____
Sound Board _____   CD-ROM _____

Where did you buy this book?

☐ Bookstore (name): _____
☐ Discount store (name): _____
☐ Computer store (name): _____
☐ Catalog (name): _____
☐ Direct from WGP   ☐ Other _____

What price did you pay for this book? _____

What influenced your purchase of this book?
☐ Recommendation   ☐ Advertisement
☐ Magazine review   ☐ Store display
☐ Mailing   ☐ Book's format
☐ Reputation of Waite Group Press   ☐ Other

How many computer books do you buy each year? _____

How many other Waite Group books do you own? _____

What is your favorite Waite Group book? _____
_____

Is there any program or subject you would like to see Waite Group Press cover in a similar approach? _____
_____

Additional comments? _____
_____
_____

Please send to: **Waite Group Press**
200 Tamal Plaza
Corte Madera, CA 94925

☐ **Check here for a free Waite Group catalog**

END-USER LICENSE AGREEMENT FOR MICROSOFT SOFTWARE
ActiveX Control Pad, Microsoft Visual Basic, Control Creation Edition

IMPORTANT—READ CAREFULLY: This Microsoft End-User License Agreement ("EULA") is a legal agreement between you (either an individual or a single entity) and Microsoft Corporation for the Microsoft software product identified above, which includes computer software and may include associated media, printed materials, and "online" or electronic documentation ("SOFTWARE PRODUCT"). By installing, copying, or otherwise using the SOFTWARE PRODUCT, you agree to be bound by the terms of this EULA. If you do not agree to the terms of this EULA, do not install or use the SOFTWARE PRODUCT; you may, however, return it to your place of purchase for a full refund.

SOFTWARE PRODUCT LICENSE

The SOFTWARE PRODUCT is protected by copyright laws and international copyright treaties, as well as other intellectual property laws and treaties. The SOFTWARE PRODUCT is licensed, not sold.

1. GRANT OF LICENSE. This EULA grants you the following rights:
    a. Software Product. Microsoft grants to you as an individual, a personal, nonexclusive license to make and use copies of the SOFTWARE for the sole purposes of designing, developing, and testing your software product(s) that are designed to operate in conjunction with any Microsoft operating system product. You may install copies of the SOFTWARE on an unlimited number of computers provided that you are the only individual using the SOFTWARE. If you are an entity, Microsoft grants you the right to designate one individual within your organization to have the right to use the SOFTWARE in the manner provided above.
    b. Electronic Documents. Solely with respect to electronic documents included with the SOFTWARE, you may make an unlimited number of copies (either in hardcopy or electronic form), provided that such copies shall be used only for internal purposes and are not republished or distributed to any third party.
    c. Storage/Network Use. You may also store or install a copy of the SOFTWARE PRODUCT on a storage device, such as a network server, used only to install or run the SOFTWARE PRODUCT on your other computers over an internal network; however, you must acquire and dedicate a license for each separate computer on which the SOFTWARE PRODUCT is installed or run from the storage device. A license for the SOFTWARE PRODUCT may not be shared or used concurrently on different computers.
    d. Redistributable Components.
        (i) Sample Code. In addition to the rights granted in Section 1, Microsoft grants you the right to use and modify the source code version of those portions of the SOFTWARE designated as "Sample Code" ("SAMPLE CODE") for the sole purposes of designing, developing, and testing your software product(s), and to reproduce and distribute the SAMPLE CODE, along with any modifications thereof, only in object code form provided that you comply with Section d(iii), below.
        (ii) Redistributable Components. In addition to the rights granted in Section 1, Microsoft grants you a nonexclusive royalty-free right to reproduce and distribute the object code version of any portion of the SOFTWARE listed in the SOFTWARE file REDIST.TXT ("REDISTRIBUTABLE SOFTWARE"), provided you comply with Section d(iii), below.
        (iii) Redistribution Requirements. If you redistribute the SAMPLE CODE or REDISTRIBUTABLE SOFTWARE (collectively, "REDISTRIBUTABLES"), you agree to: (A) distribute the REDISTRIBUTABLES in object code only in conjunction with and as a part of a software application product developed by you that adds significant and primary functionality to the SOFTWARE and that is developed to operate on the Windows or Windows NT environment ("Application"); (B) not use Microsoft's name, logo, or trademarks to market your software application product; (C) include a valid copyright notice on your software product; (D) indemnify, hold harmless, and defend Microsoft from

and against any claims or lawsuits, including attorney's fees, that arise or result from the use or distribution of your software application product; (E) not permit further distribution of the REDISTRIBUTABLES by your end user. The following exceptions apply to subsection (iii)(E), above: (1) you may permit further redistribution of the REDISTRIBUTABLES by your distributors to your end-user customers if your distributors only distribute the REDISTRIBUTABLES in conjunction with, and as part of, your Application and you and your distributors comply with all other terms of this EULA; and (2) you may permit your end users to reproduce and distribute the object code version of the files designated by ".ocx" file extensions ("Controls") only in conjunction with and as a part of an Application and/or Web page that adds significant and primary functionality to the Controls, and such end user complies with all other terms of this EULA. NOTE: The rights granted in the foregoing subsection (2) DO NOT APPLY to those files identified in the SOFTWARE as Dbgrid.ocx and Graph32.ocx.

2. DESCRIPTION OF OTHER RIGHTS AND LIMITATIONS.

    a. Not for Resale Software. If the SOFTWARE PRODUCT is labeled "Not for Resale" or "NFR," then, notwithstanding other sections of this EULA, you may not resell, or otherwise transfer for value, the SOFTWARE PRODUCT.

    b. Limitations on Reverse Engineering, Decompilation, and Disassembly. You may not reverse engineer, decompile, or disassemble the SOFTWARE PRODUCT, except and only to the extent that such activity is expressly permitted by applicable law notwithstanding this limitation.

    c. Separation of Components. The SOFTWARE PRODUCT is licensed as a single product. Its component parts may not be separated for use on more than one computer.

    d. Rental. You may not rent, lease, or lend the SOFTWARE PRODUCT.

    e. Support Services. Microsoft may provide you with support services related to the SOFTWARE PRODUCT ("Support Services"). Use of Support Services is governed by the Microsoft policies and programs described in the user manual, in "online" documentation, and/or in other Microsoft-provided materials. Any supplemental software code provided to you as part of the Support Services shall be considered part of the SOFTWARE PRODUCT and subject to the terms and conditions of this EULA. With respect to technical information you provide to Microsoft as part of the Support Services, Microsoft may use such information for its business purposes, including for product support and development. Microsoft will not utilize such technical information in a form that personally identifies you.

    f. Software Transfer. You may permanently transfer all of your rights under this EULA, provided you retain no copies, you transfer all of the SOFTWARE PRODUCT (including all component parts, the media and printed materials, any upgrades, this EULA, and, if applicable, the Certificate of Authenticity), and the recipient agrees to the terms of this EULA. If the SOFTWARE PRODUCT is an upgrade, any transfer must include all prior versions of the SOFTWARE PRODUCT.

    g. Termination. Without prejudice to any other rights, Microsoft may terminate this EULA if you fail to comply with the terms and conditions of this EULA. In such event, you must destroy all copies of the SOFTWARE PRODUCT and all of its component parts.

3. UPGRADES. If the SOFTWARE PRODUCT is labeled as an upgrade, you must be properly licensed to use a product identified by Microsoft as being eligible for the upgrade in order to use the SOFTWARE PRODUCT. A SOFTWARE PRODUCT labeled as an upgrade replaces and/or supplements the product that formed the basis for your eligibility for the upgrade. You may use the resulting upgraded product only in accordance with the terms of this EULA. If the SOFTWARE PRODUCT is an upgrade of a component of a package of software programs that you licensed as a single product, the SOFTWARE PRODUCT may be used and transferred only as part of that single product package and may not be separated for use on more than one computer.

4. COPYRIGHT. All title and copyrights in and to the SOFTWARE PRODUCT (including but not limited to any images, photographs, animations, video, audio, music, text, and "applets" incorporated into the SOFTWARE PRODUCT), the accompanying printed materials, and any copies of the SOFTWARE PRODUCT are owned by Microsoft or its suppliers. The SOFTWARE PRODUCT is protected by copyright laws and international treaty provisions. Therefore, you must treat the SOFTWARE PRODUCT like any other

copyrighted material except that you may install the SOFTWARE PRODUCT on a single computer provided you keep the original solely for backup or archival purposes. You may not copy the printed materials accompanying the SOFTWARE PRODUCT.

5. DUAL-MEDIA SOFTWARE. You may receive the SOFTWARE PRODUCT in more than one medium. Regardless of the type or size of medium you receive, you may use only one medium that is appropriate for your single computer. You may not use or install the other medium on another computer. You may not loan, rent, lease, or otherwise transfer the other medium to another user, except as part of the permanent transfer (as provided above) of the SOFTWARE PRODUCT.

6. U.S. GOVERNMENT RESTRICTED RIGHTS. The SOFTWARE PRODUCT and documentation are provided with RESTRICTED RIGHTS. Use, duplication, or disclosure by the Government is subject to restrictions as set forth in subparagraph (c)(1)(ii) of the Rights in Technical Data and Computer Software clause at DFARS 252.227-7013 or subparagraphs (c)(1) and (2) of the Commercial Computer Software-Restricted Rights at 48 CFR 52.227-19, as applicable. Manufacturer is Microsoft Corporation/One Microsoft Way/Redmond, WA 98052-6399.

7. EXPORT RESTRICTIONS. You agree that neither you nor your customers intend to or will, directly or indirectly, export or transmit (i) the SOFTWARE or related documentation and technical data or (ii) your software product as described in Section 1(b) of this License (or any part thereof), or process, or service that is the direct product of the SOFTWARE, to any country to which such export or transmission is restricted by any applicable U.S. regulation or statute, without the prior written consent, if required, of the Bureau of Export Administration of the U.S. Department of Commerce, or such other governmental entity as may have jurisdiction over such export or transmission.

MISCELLANEOUS

If you acquired this product in the United States, this EULA is governed by the laws of the State of Washington. If you acquired this product in Canada, this EULA is governed by the laws of the Province of Ontario, Canada. Each of the parties hereto irrevocably attorns to the jurisdiction of the courts of the Province of Ontario and further agrees to commence any litigation which may arise hereunder in the courts located in the Judicial District of York, Province of Ontario. If this product was acquired outside the United States, then local law may apply.

Should you have any questions concerning this EULA, or if you desire to contact Microsoft for any reason, please contact the Microsoft subsidiary serving your country, or write: Microsoft Sales Information Center/One Microsoft Way/Redmond, WA 98052-6399.

LIMITED WARRANTY

NO WARRANTIES. Microsoft expressly disclaims any warranty for the SOFTWARE PRODUCT. The SOFTWARE PRODUCT and any related documentation is provided "as is" without warranty of any kind, either express or implied, including, without limitation, the implied warranties or merchantability, fitness for a particular purpose, or noninfringement. The entire risk arising out of use or performance of the SOFTWARE PRODUCT remains with you.

NO LIABILITY FOR DAMAGES. In no event shall Microsoft or its suppliers be liable for any damages whatsoever (including, without limitation, damages for loss of business profits,business interruption, loss of business information, or any other pecuniary loss) arising out of the use of or inability to use this Microsoft product, even if Microsoft has been advised of the possibility of such damages. Because some states/jurisdictions do not allow the exclusion or limitation of liability for consequential or incidental damages, the above limitation may not apply to you.

BEFORE OPENING THE CD-ROM PACKAGE ON THE FACING PAGE, CAREFULLY READ THE LICENSE AGREEMENT.

By opening this package you agree to abide by the license agreement found in the back of this book. If you do not agree with it, promptly return the unopened disk package (including the related book) to the place you obtained them for a refund. By opening this package, you are bound by the following agreement:

You may not copy or redistribute the entire CD-ROM as a whole. Copying and redistribution of individual software programs on the CD-ROM is governed by the terms set by individual copyright holders. The installer and code from the author is copyrighted by the publisher and the author. Individual programs and other items on the CD-ROM are copyrighted by their various authors or other copyright holders.

Microsoft® Visual Basic® Control Creation Edition and ActiveX® Control Pad were reproduced by Macmillan Computer Publishing (MCP) under a special arrangement with Microsoft Corporation. For this reason, MCP is responsible for the product warranty and for support. If your disc is defective, please return it to MCP, which will arrange for its replacement. PLEASE DO NOT RETURN IT TO MICROSOFT CORPORATION. Any product support will be provided, if at all, by MCP. PLEASE DO NOT CONTACT MICROSOFT CORPORATION FOR PRODUCT SUPPORT. End users of these Microsoft programs shall not be considered "registered owners" of Microsoft products and therefore shall not be eligible for upgrades, promotions or other benefits available to "registered owners" of Microsoft products. This software is sold as is without warranty of any kind, either expressed or implied, including but not limited to the implied warranty of merchantability and fitness for a particular purpose. Neither the publisher nor its dealers or distributors assumes any liability for any alleged or actual damages arising from the use of this program. (Some states do not allow for the exclusion of implied warranties, so the exclusion may not apply to you.)

This CD-ROM uses long and mixed case file names requiring the use of a protected mode CD-ROM driver.